*Less managing. More teaching.*

 **INSTRUCTORS...**

Would you like your **students** to show up for class **more prepared**?
*(Let's face it, class is much more fun if everyone is engaged and prepared...)*

Want an **easy way to assign** homework online and track student **progress**?
*(Less time grading means more time teaching...)*

Want an **instant view** of student or class performance relative to learning objectives? *(No more wondering if students understand...)*

Need to **collect data and generate reports** required for administration or accreditation? *(Say goodbye to manually tracking student learning outcomes...)*

Want to **record and post your lectures** for students to view online?

 **With McGraw-Hill's *Connect® Plus Accounting*,**

**INSTRUCTORS GET:**

- Simple **assignment management**, allowing you to spend more time teaching.
- **Auto-graded** assignments, quizzes, and tests.
- **Detailed Visual Reporting** where student and section results can be viewed and analyzed.
- Sophisticated **online testing** capability.
- A **filtering and reporting** function that allows you to easily assign and report on materials that are correlated to accreditation standards, learning outcomes, and Bloom's taxonomy.
- An easy-to-use **lecture capture** tool.
- The option to **upload course documents** for student access.

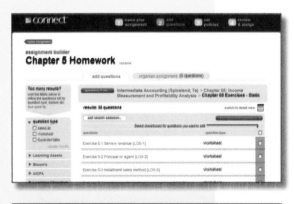

Want an online, **searchable version** of your textbook?

Wish your textbook could be **available online** while you're doing your assignments?

## *Connect® Plus Accounting* eBook

If you choose to use *Connect® Plus Accounting*, you have an affordable and searchable online version of your book integrated with your other online tools.

### *Connect® Plus Accounting* eBook offers features like:

- Topic search
- Direct links from assignments
- Adjustable text size
- Jump to page number
- Print by section

Want to get more **value** from your textbook purchase?

Think learning accounting should be a bit more **interesting**?

## Check out the STUDENT RESOURCES section under the *Connect®* Library tab.

Here you'll find a wealth of resources designed to help you achieve your goals in the course. You'll find things like **quizzes, PowerPoints, and Internet activities** to help you study. Every student has different needs, so explore the STUDENT RESOURCES to find the materials best suited to you.

# Intermediate Accounting

Volume I

# Intermediate Accounting

## SEVENTH EDITION

**J. DAVID SPICELAND**
*University of Memphis*

**JAMES F. SEPE**
*Santa Clara University*

**MARK W. NELSON**
*Cornell University*

McGraw-Hill
Irwin

# McGraw-Hill
# Irwin

INTERMEDIATE ACCOUNTING: VOLUME 1

Published by McGraw-Hill/Irwin, a business unit of The McGraw-Hill Companies, Inc., 1221 Avenue of the Americas, New York, NY, 10020. Copyright © 2013, 2011, 2009, 2007, 2004, 2001, 1998 by The McGraw-Hill Companies, Inc. All rights reserved. Printed in the United States of America. No part of this publication may be reproduced or distributed in any form or by any means, or stored in a database or retrieval system, without the prior written consent of The McGraw-Hill Companies, Inc., including, but not limited to, in any network or other electronic storage or transmission, or broadcast for distance learning.

Some ancillaries, including electronic and print components, may not be available to customers outside the United States.

This book is printed on acid-free paper.

3 4 5 6 7 8 9 0 DOW/DOW 1 0 9 8 7 6 5 4 3 2

ISBN 978-0-07-802532-7 (combined edition)
MHID 0-07-802532-X (combined edition)
ISBN 978-0-07-744649-9 (volume 1)
MHID 0-07-744649-6 (volume 1)
ISBN 978-0-07-744648-2 (volume 2)
MHID 0-07-744648-8 (volume 2)

Vice president and editor-in-chief: *Brent Gordon*
Publisher: *Tim Vertovec*
Executive editor: *Stewart Mattson*
Director of development: *Ann Torbert*
Development editor: *Rebecca Mann*
Marketing director: *Brad Parkins*
Senior marketing manager: *Kathleen Klehr*
Vice president of editing, design, and production: *Sesha Bolisetty*
Lead project manager: *Pat Frederickson*
Senior buyer: *Michael R. McCormick*
Designer: *Laurie Entringer*
Senior photo research coordinator: *Jeremy Cheshareck*
Photo researcher: *Editorial Image, LLC*
Media project manager: *Rachel Townsend*
Cover designer: *Laurie Entringer*
Cover photo credit: © *Ian McKinnell Getty Images*
Typeface: *10.5/12 Times Lt Std-Roman*
Compositor: *Laserwords Private Limited*
Printer: *R. R. Donnelley*

**Library of Congress Cataloging-in-Publication Data**

Spiceland, J. David, 1949–
    Intermediate accounting/J. David Spiceland, James F. Sepe, Mark W. Nelson.—7th ed.
        p. cm.
    Includes index.
    ISBN 978-0-07-802532-7 (combined edition: alk. paper)
    ISBN 0-07-802532-X (combined edition: alk. paper)
    ISBN 978-0-07-744649-9 (volume 1: alk. paper)
    ISBN 0-07-744649-6 (volume 1: alk. paper)
    ISBN 978-0-07-744648-2 (volume 2: alk. paper)
    ISBN 0-07-744648-8 (volume 2: alk. paper)
    1. Accounting. I. Sepe, James F. II. Nelson, Mark (Mark W.) III. Title.
HF5636.S773 2013
657'.044—dc23
                                                                2011052284

# About the Authors

## DAVID SPICELAND

David Spiceland is professor of accounting at the University of Memphis, where he teaches intermediate accounting and other financial accounting courses at the undergraduate and master's levels. He received his BS degree in finance from the University of Tennessee, his MBA from Southern Illinois University, and his PhD in accounting from the University of Arkansas.

Professor Spiceland's primary research interests are in earnings management and educational research. He has published articles in a variety of journals including *The Accounting Review, Accounting and Business Research, Journal of Financial Research,* and *Journal of Accounting Education.* David has received university and college awards and recognition for his teaching, research, and technological innovations in the classroom.

## JIM SEPE

Jim Sepe is an associate professor of accounting at Santa Clara University where he teaches primarily intermediate accounting in both the undergraduate and graduate programs. He previously taught at California Poly State University–San Luis Obispo and the University of Washington and has visited at Stanford University and the Rome campus of Loyola University of Chicago.

Professor Sepe received his BS from Santa Clara University, MBA from the University of California–Berkeley, and PhD from the University of Washington. His research interests concern financial reporting issues and the use of financial information by capital markets. He has published articles in *The Accounting Review,* the *Journal of Business Finance and Accounting, Financial Management,* the *Journal of Forensic Accounting,* the *Journal of Applied Business Research,* and the *Journal of Accounting Education.* He is a past recipient of the American Accounting Association's Competitive Manuscript Award and has served as a member of the editorial board of *The Accounting Review.*

Jim has received numerous awards for his teaching excellence and innovations in the classroom, including Santa Clara University's Brutocao Award for Excellence in Curriculum Innovation.

## MARK NELSON

Mark Nelson is the Eleanora and George Landew Professor of Accounting at Cornell University's Johnson Graduate School of Management, where he teaches intermediate accounting at the MBA level. He received his BBA degree from Iowa State University and his MA and PhD degrees from Ohio State University. Professor Nelson has won teaching awards at Ohio State and Cornell, including three of the Johnson School's Apple Award for Teaching Excellence.

Professor Nelson's research is focused on decision making in financial accounting and auditing. His research has been published in *The Accounting Review,* the *Journal of Accounting Research, Contemporary Accounting Research, Accounting Organizations and Society, Auditing: A Journal of Practice and Theory,* and several other journals. He has won the American Accounting Association's Notable Contribution to Accounting Literature Award, and also the AAA's Wildman Medal for work judged to make the most significant contribution to the advancement of the public practice of accountancy. He has served three times as an editor or associate editor of *The Accounting Review,* and serves on the editorial boards of several journals. Professor Nelson also served for four years on the FASB's Financial Accounting Standards Advisory Council.

# Building Success

> "SSN do a marvelous job of explaining the conceptual underpinnings of the accounting standards before describing the details of the rules. In sum, this is an excellent textbook that should be strongly considered for any intermediate accounting course."
>
> —Albert Nagy,
> *John Carroll University*

As your students embark on their professional careers, they will be challenged to think critically and make good decisions. This new edition of *Intermediate Accounting* has been designed to ensure that your students' careers are built upon a solid conceptual foundation.

*Intermediate Accounting* is the work not just of its talented authors, but of the more than 600 faculty reviewers who shared their insights, experience, and opinions with us. Our reviewers helped us to build *Intermediate Accounting* into the very best learning system available.

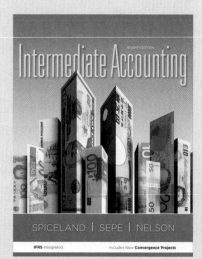

Our development process began in the spring of 2010, when we received the first of what would become more than 140 in-depth reviews of *Intermediate Accounting*. A blend of Spiceland users and non-users, these reviewers explained how they use textbooks in their teaching, and many answered detailed questions about every one of Spiceland's 21 chapters. And the work of improving *Intermediate Accounting* is ongoing—even now, we're scheduling new symposia and reviewers' conferences to collect even more opinions from faculty.

*Intermediate Accounting* was designed from the start to be not simply a textbook, but a complete learning system, encompassing the textbook, key ancillaries, and online cotent, all of which are written by authors Spiceland, Sepe, and Nelson.

> "SSN should be students' bible for intermediate accounting classes. The text will definitely improve tremendously the scholarship of teaching and learning in intermediate accounting courses."
>
> —Akinloye Akindayomi,
> *University of Massachusetts-Dartmouth*

# in Intermediate Accounting

The *Intermediate Accounting* learning system is built around five key attributes:

① **Clarity:** Reviewers, instructors, and students all have hailed *Intermediate Accounting*'s ability to explain both simple and complex topics in language that is clear and approachable. Its highly acclaimed conversational writing style establishes a friendly dialogue between the text and each individual student. So readable is Spiceland that we've even received letters from students who bought the book themselves—despite their instructors using competing books in the course!

② **A Decision-Making Perspective:** Recent events have focused public attention on the key role of accounting in providing information useful to decision makers. The CPA exam, too, is redirecting its focus to emphasize the professional skills needed to critically evaluate accounting method alternatives. *Intermediate Accounting* provides a decision maker's perspective to emphasize the professional judgment and critical thinking skills required of accountants today.

③ **Flexible Technology:** Today's accounting students have come of age in a digital world, and Spiceland's Learning System reflects that trend through its comprehensive technology package. The seventh edition of Spiceland's Learning System features: McGraw-Hill *Connect Accounting*, LearnSmart self-study technology, Self-Quiz and Study, Guided Examples, and Tegrity Campus. See pages xiv, xv and xviii for more details!

④ **Consistent Quality:** The *Intermediate Accounting* author team ensures seamless compatibility throughout the Spiceland learning package by writing every major supplement themselves: Study Guide, Instructor's Resource Manual, Solutions Manual, Testbank, and website content are all created by authors Spiceland, Sepe, and Nelson. The end-of-chapter material, too, is written by the author team and tested in their classrooms before being included in *Intermediate Accounting*

⑤ **A Commitment to Currency:** Few disciplines see the rapid change that accounting experiences, and the Spiceland team is committed to keeping your course up to date. The seventh edition fully integrates the latest FASB standards, including ASU No. 2011-05: Comprehensive Income (Topic 220): Presentation of Comprensive Income; ASU No. 2011-04: Fair Value Measurement (Topic 820): Amendments to Achieve Common Fair Value Measurement and Disclosure Requirements in U.S. GAAP and IFRS; and ASU No. 2011-08: Intangibles-Goodwill and Other (Topic 350): Testing for Goodwill Impairment. What's more, the authors have added supplements addressing the joint FASB/IASB projects on revenue recognition, leases and financial instruments.

"SSN is a student-friendly book that presents a good balance between theoretical concepts and practical application in an easy-to-read text. It contains currency in theory, good illustrations, and excellent end-of-chapter materials."

—Kathy Terrell,
*University of Central Oklahoma*

"An excellent textbook that covers accounting procedures thoroughly from a real-world perspective. It is very current and is accompanied by a great variety of learning aids to help students succeed."

—Kathy Hsiao Yu Hsu,
*University of Louisiana–Lafayette*

"Overall, I find the Spiceland end-of-chapter material far superior to that in Kieso in terms of quantity, especially as it relates to the diversity of the problem material."

—Chula King,
*University of West Florida*

# What Stands Out in the Seventh Edition?

> "Provides up to date material on many topics, for example IFRS. Students will find it easy to follow and to find examples in working homework."
>
> —Terry G. Elliott,
> *Morehead State University*

Financial accounting is undergoing a period of unprecedented change. The FASB and IASB have been working together to issue converged accounting standards that will dramatically change key reporting areas, and more generally have sought to converge accounting standards over time. However, the convergence process is proceeding slowly, and it is not clear when, if ever, IFRS will be fully incorporated into U.S. GAAP. So, while there currently is considerable overlap between U.S. GAAP and IFRS, and that overlap is increasing as convergence continues, important differences between U.S. GAAP and IFRS will remain for the foreseeable future.

To help instructors deal with this very challenging environment, the Spiceland team is committed to providing **current, comprehensive** and **clear** coverage of intermediate accounting. The seventh edition reflects this commitment with the following innovations:

**1** Enhanced coverage is provided of U.S. and international standard setting and the **convergence process,** including coverage of the SEC's "condorsement" proposal and alternative approaches to convergence.

**2** Increased coverage of the key differences between U.S. GAAP and International Financial Reporting Standards in *IFRS boxes* within the flow of each chapter, along with enhanced end-of-chapter assignment material to test student understanding of those differences. The Spiceland approach allows instructors to integrate coverage of IFRS (or skip that coverage) in the flow of covering related U.S. GAAP, minimizing redundancy and maximizing flexibility for the instructor and coverage of the key differences that are tested on the CPA exam.

**3** New, comprehensive **Where We're Headed Chapter Supplements** immediately following Chapters 5, 12 and 15 cover the three joint FASB/IASB projects on revenue recognition, financial instruments and leases. Based on the current status of these projects as the text went to press, each supplement provides a thorough treatment of the relevant proposed *Accounting Standards Update* and is supported by end-of-chapter questions, exercises and problems to encourage students to gauge and reinforce their understanding of concepts. The test bank also includes new test questions to evaluate students' mastery of the new ASUs. These Supplements are augmented with online updates to reflect any changes in these projects going forward. The desirability of providing the new ASUs as Chapter Supplements in addition to retaining extensive coverage of existing GAAP relates to the abnormally long implementation periods for the new guidance. Even after the new Accounting

Revising a book as successful as *Intermediate Accounting* takes careful consideration and a strong vision of what a textbook should be. New features aren't piled on for their own sake; the Spiceland team only implements changes that constitute real improvements that have been identified through extensive research with users. The result is a book that never loses its original strengths as it gains in usefulness and flexibility with each revision.

Standard Updates are issued, previous U.S. GAAP will be relevant until the new ASUs become effective, and students taking the CPA or CMA exams will be responsible for the previous U.S. GAAP until six months after that effective date. Conversely, prior to the effective date of the new Accounting Standard Updates it is useful for soon-to-be graduates to have an understanding of the new guidance on the horizon.

A new section of **IFRS CPA exam multiple choice questions** is included in most chapter's assignment material. The questions are added as a distinct section of the CPA and CMA exam questions provided in previous editions.

A new **Comprehensive Air France–KLM Case,** with questions appearing as a Broaden Your Perspective case, is included with most of the text's chapters, allowing instructors to discuss IFRS and U.S. GAAP differences in the context of a single IFRS-based financial reporting setting. For instructors who prefer to cover IFRS in a more concentrated fashion, the Air France–KLM Case questions are repeated in Appendix C but divided into six broad topical classifications to permit coverage in logical groupings.

Text material has been enhanced to reflect **changes in current GAAP,** such as revisions to the conceptual framework, reporting of other comprehensive income, recognizing revenue on multiple-element arrangements, accounting for transfers of receivables as sales v. secured borrowings, impairments of debt and equity investments, and when to test for goodwill impairment.

New **Guided Examples** in *Connect Accounting* provide a narrated, animated, step-by-step walk-through of select exercises similar to those assigned. These short presentations provide reinforcement when students need it most.

What hasn't changed for the Seventh Edition? The Spiceland text will not waiver in its commitment to making the complex seem simple and to providing rigorous coverage in a clear, approachable fashion. The conversational writing style is maintained, as is the **authors' personal preparation of all supporting materials** (e.g., test bank, instructors resource manual, student study guide), so that the instructor can be confident that the same commitment to excellence is reflected consistently between the text and supporting materials.

What stands out in the Seventh Edition is what makes the Spiceland text outstanding – no other text is as current, comprehensive, and clear—the "3 C's" of intermediate accounting.

**AIRFRANCE**

"This puts a hands on approach to IFRS and engages the students in a manner where they care to learn—a real-world example."

—Bradley Lail,
*North Carolina State University*

"Very well written in a streamlined 21 chapter approach with IFRS incorporated throughout and excellent end of chapter materials."

—Michael Slaubaugh,
*Indiana University/Purdue University*

# What Keeps SPICELAND Users Coming Back?

## Where We're Headed

These boxes describe the potential financial reporting effects of many of the FASB and IASB joint projects intended to further align U.S. GAAP and IFRS, as well as other projects the Boards are pursuing separately. Where We're Headed boxes allow instructors to deal with ongoing projects to the extent they desire.

## Financial Reporting Cases

Each chapter opens with a Financial Reporting Case that places the student in the role of the decision maker, engaging the student in an interesting situation related to the accounting issues to come. Then, the cases pose questions of the student in the role of decision maker. Marginal notations throughout the chapter point out locations where each question is addressed. The case questions are answered at the end of the chapter.

## Decision Makers' Perspective

These sections appear throughout the text to illustrate how accounting information is put to work in today's firms. With the CPA exam placing greater focus on application of skills in realistic work settings, these discussions help your students gain an edge that will remain with them as they enter the workplace.

### Where **We're Headed**

● LO4–10

The FASB and IASB are working together on a standard that would have a dramatic impact on the format of financial statements.

Demonstrating the cohesiveness among the financial statements is a key objective of the

The FASB and IASB are working together on a project, Financial Statement Presentation, to establish a common standard for presenting information in the financial statements, including classifying and displaying line items and aggregating line items into subtotals and totals. This standard would have a dramatic impact on the format of financial statements. An important part of the proposal involves the organization of elements of the balance sheet (statement of financial position), statement of comprehensive income (including the in   classifications.

   The income s   cash flows are sh   SCF would retai   (and balance she   financing activiti

> "Where We're Headed" boxes allows the students to be updated with the most current accounting changes without inundating them with needless technical specifications. A perfect balance!"
>
> —Cheryl Bartlett, *Indiana University—South Bend*

### Financial Reporting Case Solution

1. **How would you explain restructuring costs to Becky? Are restructuring costs something Becky should worry about?** *(p. 179)*   Restructuring costs include employee severance and termination benefits plus other costs associated with the shutdown or relocation of facilities or downsizing of operations. Restructuring costs are not necessarily bad. In fact, the objective is to make operations more efficient. The costs are incurred now in hopes of better earnings later.

2. **Explain to Becky what is meant by discontinued operations and describe to her how that item**   tion occurs wh   effect of disco   operations. If   income effect   nent from the

> "The case at the beginning of each chapter is very captivating. After I read the case, I wanted to get paper and pencil and answer the questions."
>
> —Carol Shaver, *Louisiana Tech University*

### Decision Makers' Perspective

Cash often is referred to as a *nonearning* asset because it earns no interest. For this reason, managers invest idle cash in either cash equivalents or short-term investments, both of which provide a return. Management's goal is to hold the minimum amount of cash necessary to conduct normal business operations, meet its obligations, and take advantage of opportunities. Too much cash reduces profits through lost returns, while too little cash increases risk. This trade-off between risk and return is a   decision makers). Whether the choice ma   by investors and creditors (external decisi

   A company must have cash available f   previous section as well as for planned dis   and financing cash flows. However, becau   amounts, a company needs an additional   gency. The size of the cushion depends o

> "This is an excellent feature of the book. It is so important to know why and how information is used and not just memorizing the "right" answers."
>
> —Jeff Mankin, *Lipscomb University*

In talking to so many intermediate accounting faculty, we heard more than how to improve the book—there was much, much more that both users and nonusers insisted we keep exactly as it was. Here are some of the features that have made Spiceland such a phenomenal success in its previous editions.

## Additional Consideration

We discuss in significant depth in Chapter 7 the problem of accounting for bad debts. However, bad debts related to receivables on sales accounted for using the installment method create a unique problem. A company uses the installment method because it can't reliably estimate bad debts. Therefore, the company doesn't explicitly recognize bad debts or create an allowance for uncollectible accounts in the installment method. Rather, bad debts are dealt with implicitly by deferring gross profit until cash is collected. If the cash never is collected, the related deferred gross profit never gets included in net income. To illustrate, assume that in the example described in Illustration 5–7, the Belmont Corporation collected the first payment but the customer was unable to make the remaining payments. Typically, the seller would repossess the item sold and make the following journal entry:

Repossessed inventory............
Deferred gross profit..............
    Installment receivable.........

This entry removes the receiv
the repossessed land in an inver

> "This is a good technique that I actually use in my class and it's good to see it in a book!"
>
> —Ramesh Narasimhan, *Montclair State University*

## Ethical Dilemma

The Precision Parts Corporation manufactures automobile parts. The company has reported a profit every year since the company's inception in 1980. Management prides itself on this accomplishment and believes one important contributing factor is the company's incentive plan that rewards top management a bonus equal to a percentage of operating income *if the operating income goal for the year is achieved*. However, 2013 has been a tough year, an
are bleak.

Tony Smith, the company's ch
December sales by an amount s
year and earn bonuses for all top
of parts to be shipped on Janua
know we can get that order read
production line overtime. We ca
shipment. I see nothing wrong v
have been manufactured and w

> "Having ethical dilemma boxes in every chapter is much more significant than having a separate chapter devoted to ethics. Students can relate to the importance of being ethical in every aspect of business dealings."
>
> —Gloria Worthy, *Southwest Tennessee Community College*

### Broaden Your Perspective

Apply your critical-thinking ability to the knowledge you've gained. These cases will provide you an opportunity to develop your research, analysis, judgment, and communication skills. You also will work with other students, integrate what you've learned, apply it in real world situations, and consider its global and ethical ramifications. This practice will broaden your knowledge and further develop your decision-making abilities.

**Real World Case 12–1**
Intel's investments
● LO12–3

The following disclosure note appeared in the July 2, 2011 quarterly financial statement of the Intel Corporation.
Note 7: **Available-for-Sale Investments (partial)**
Table 1: Availabl

> "I think students would benefit tremendously from the cases."
>
> —Joyce Njoroge, *Drake University*

## Additional Consideration Boxes

These are "on the spot" considerations of important, but incidental or infrequent aspects of the primary topics to which they relate. Their parenthetical nature, highlighted by enclosure in Additional Consideration boxes, helps maintain an appropriate level of rigor of topic coverage without sacrificing clarity of explanation.

## Ethical Dilemmas

Because ethical ramifications of business decisions impact so many individuals as well as the core of our economy, Ethical Dilemmas are incorporated within the context of accounting issues as they are discussed. These features lend themselves very well to impromptu class discussions and debates.

## Broaden Your Perspective Cases

Finish each chapter with these powerful and effective cases, a great way to reinforce and expand concepts learned in the chapter.

## Star Problems

In each chapter, particularly challenging problems, designated by a ☆, require students to combine multiple concepts or require significant use of judgment.

# Market-Leading Technology

Connect
Learn
Succeed™

## McGraw-Hill *Connect Accounting*®

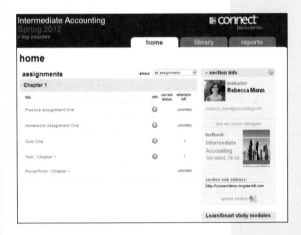

### Less Managing. More Teaching. Greater Learning.

McGraw-Hill *Connect Accounting* is an online assignment and assessment solution that connects students with the tools and resources they'll need to achieve success.

McGraw-Hill *Connect Accounting* helps prepare students for their future by enabling faster learning, more efficient studying, and higher retention of knowledge.

### McGraw-Hill *Connect Accounting* Features

*Connect Accounting* offers a variety of powerful tools and features to make managing assignments easier, so faculty can spend more time teaching. With *Connect Accounting*, students can engage with their coursework anytime and anywhere, making the learning process more accessible and efficient.

### Simple Assignment Management and Auto Grading

With *Connect Accounting*, creating assignments is easier than ever, so you can spend more time teaching and less time managing. The assignment management function enables you to:

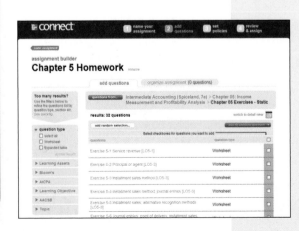

- Create and deliver assignments easily with selectable end-of-chapter assignments and test bank items.

- Streamline lesson planning, student progress reporting, and assignment grading to make classroom management more efficient than ever.

- Go paperless with the eBook and online submission and grading of student assignments.

- Have assignments scored automatically, giving students immediate feedback on their work and side-by-side comparisons with correct answers.

- Access and review each response; manually change grades or leave comments for students to review.

- Reinforce classroom concepts with practice tests and instant quizzes.

## Instructor Library

The *Connect Accounting* Instructor Library is your repository for additional resources to improve student engagement in and out of class. You can select and use any asset that enhances your lecture. The *Connect Accounting* Instructor Library includes access to the eBook version of the text, PowerPoint files, Solutions Manual, Instructor Resource Manual, and Test Bank. The *Connect Accounting* Instructor Library also allows you to upload your own files. Your students can access these through the student library.

## Student Library

The *Connect Accounting* Student Library is the place for students to access additional resources. The Student Library:

- Offers students quick access to lectures, practice materials, eBooks, and more.

- Gives students access to LearnSmart described on page xvi.

- Provides instant practice material and study questions, easily accessible on the go.

- Gives students access to the Self-Quiz and Study resource described on page xvi.

## McGraw-Hill *Connect Plus Accounting*

McGraw-Hill reinvents the textbook learning experience for the modern student with *Connect Plus Accounting*. A seamless integration of an eBook and *Connect Accounting*, *Connect Plus Accounting* provides all of the *Connect Accounting* features plus the following:

- An integrated eBook, allowing for anytime, anywhere access to the textbook.

- Dynamic links between the problems or questions you assign to your students and the location in the eBook where that problem or question is covered.

- A powerful search function to pinpoint and connect key concepts in a snap.

For more information about *Connect Plus Accounting*, go to **www.mcgrawhillconnect.com**, or contact your local McGraw-Hill sales representative.

# How Does Spiceland Help My Students

**LearnSmart**

> "In my first semester of assigning LearnSmart, the improvement in my students' performance was easy to see. Plus, they really liked using it."
>
> —Wayne Thomas,
> *University of Oklahoma*

## Diagnostic and Adaptive Learning of Concepts: LearnSmart

Students want to make the best use of their study time. The amazing Learn-Smart adaptive self-study technology within *Connect Accounting* provides students with a seamless combination of practice, assessment, and remediation for every concept in the textbook. LearnSmart's intelligent software adapts to every student response and automatically delivers concepts that advance the student's understanding while reducing time devoted to the concepts already mastered. The result for every student is the fastest path to mastery of the chapter concepts. LearnSmart:

- Applies an intelligent concept engine to identify the relationships between concepts and to serve new concepts to each student only when he or she is ready.

- Adapts automatically to each student, so students spend less time on the topics they understand and practice more those they have yet to master.

- Provides continual reinforcement and remediation, but gives only as much guidance as students need.

- Integrates diagnostics as part of the learning experience.

- Enables you to assess which concepts students have efficiently learned on their own, thus freeing class time for more applications and discussion.

## Self-Quiz and Study

Self-Quiz and Study (SQS) resource in *Connect Accounting* connects each student to the learning resources needed for success in the course. For each chapter, students:

- Take a practice test to initiate the Self-Quiz and Study.

- Immediately upon completing the practice test, see how their performance compares to chapter learning objectives or content by sections within chapters.

- Receive a Self-Quiz and Study resource that recommends specific readings from the text, supplemental study material, and practice work that will improve their understanding and mastery of each learning objective.

## Student Progress Tracking

*Connect Accounting* keeps instructors informed about how each student, section, and class is performing, allowing for more productive use of lecture and office hours. The progress-tracking function enables you to:

- View scored work immediately and track individual or group performance with assignment and grade reports.

- Access an instant view of student or class performance relative to learning objectives.

# Improve Their Performance?

## Online Learning Center (OLC)

**www.mhhe.com/spiceland7e**

Today's students are every bit as comfortable using a web browser as they are reading a printed book. That's why we offer an Online Learning Center (OLC) that follows *Intermediate Accounting* chapter by chapter. It doesn't require any building or maintenance on your part, and is ready to go the moment you and your students type in the URL.

As your students study, they can refer to the OLC website for such benefits as:

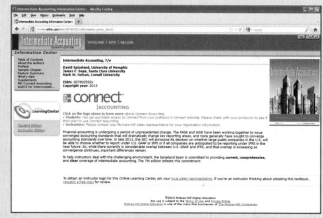

Self-grading quizzes

Electronic flash cards

Audio narrated PowerPoints

Alternate exercises and problems

Check figures

Practice exams

FASB pronouncements, summaries and updates

Text updates

A secured Instructor Resource Center stores your essential course materials to save you prep time before class. The Instructor's Resource Manual, Solutions Manual, Power-Point, and sample syllabi are now just a couple of clicks away. You will also find useful packaging information and transition notes.

## CPA Simulations

Kaplan CPA Exam Simulations allow students to practice intermediate accounting concepts in a web-based environment similar to that used in the actual CPA exam. There will be no hesitation or confusion when your students sit for the real exam: they'll know exactly what they need to do.

### CPA and CMA Review Questions

CPA Exam Questions

● LO5–1

The following questions are adapted from a variety of sources inclu... Review Course and those developed by the AICPA Board of Exam... preparing for the CPA examination. Determine the response that be...

1. On October 1, 2013, Acme Fuel Co. sold 100,000 gallons of he... thousand gallons we... delivered on December 15, 2013, and the...

> "*Intermediate Accounting* is current, complete, well written, and highly detailed. It belongs in the library of anyone who is preparing for the CPA exam."
>
> —Barbara K. Parks, American *Intercontinental University—Online*

## CPA and CMA Review Questions

A CPA and CMA Review Questions section includes multiple choice questions adapted from a variety of sources including questions developed by the AICPA Board of Examiners and those used in the Kaplan CPA Review Course to prepare for the CPA examination and focus on the key topics within each chapter, permitting quick and efficient reinforcement of those topics as well as conveying a sense of the way the topics are covered in the CPA exam. New with this edition is a special section of multiple choice questions dealing with coverage of IFRS. The CMA questions are adapted from questions that previously appeared on Certified Management Accountant (CMA) exams.

# More Market-Leading Digital Solutions

The **Best** of
**Both Worlds**

## CourseSmart

CourseSmart is a new way to find and buy eTextbooks. At CouseSmart you can can save up to 45 percent off the cost of a printed textbook, reduce your impact on the environment, and gain access to powerful Web tools for learning. You can **search**, **highlight**, **take notes**, and **share** with friends, as well as print the pages you need. Try a chapter to see if it's right for you. Visit www.CourseSmart.com and search by title, author, or ISBN.

## McGraw-Hill Higher Education and Blackboard® have teamed up. What does this mean for you?

1. **Your life, simplified.** Now you and your students can access McGraw-Hill Connect® and McGraw-Hill Create™ right from within your Blackboard course—all with one single sign-on. Say goodbye to the days of logging in to multiple applications.

2. **Deep integration of content and tools.** Not only do you get single sign-on with Connect and Create, you also get deep integration of McGraw-Hill content and content engines right in Blackboard. Whether you're choosing a book for your course or building Connect assignments, all the tools you need are right where you want them—inside of Blackboard.

3. **Seamless Gradebooks.** Are you tired of keeping multiple gradebooks and manually synchronizing grades into Blackboard? We thought so. When a student completes an integrated Connect assignment, the grade for that assignment automatically (and instantly) feeds your Blackboard grade center.

4. **A solution for everyone.** Whether your institution is already using Blackboard or you just want to try Blackboard on your own, we have a solution for you. McGraw-Hill and Blackboard can now offer you easy access to industry leading technology and content, whether your campus hosts it, or we do. Be sure to ask your local McGraw-Hill representative for details.

## Tegrity Campus: Lectures 24/7

Tegrity Campus is a service that makes class time available 24/7 by automatically capturing every lecture in a searchable format for students to review when they study and complete assignments. With a simple one-click start-and-stop process, you capture all computer screens and corresponding audio. Students can replay any part of any class with easy-to-use browser-based viewing on a PC or Mac.

Educators know that the more students can see, hear, and experience class resources, the better they learn. In fact, studies prove it. With Tegrity Campus, students quickly recall key moments by using Tegrity Campus's unique search feature. This search helps students efficiently find what they need, when they need it, across an entire semester of class recordings. Help turn all your students' study time into learning moments immediately supported by your lecture.

To learn more about Tegrity watch a 2-minute Flash demo at: http://tegritycampus.mhhe.com.

From innovative self-guided assessment and guidance to complete online course solutions, McGraw-Hill/Irwin lets you take full advantage of everything the digital age has to offer.

# ALEKS®

## ALEKS Accounting Cycle

ALEKS Accounting Cycle is a web-based program that provides targeted coverage of prerequisite and introductory material necessary for student success in Intermediate Accounting. ALEKS uses artificial intelligence and adaptive questioning to assess precisely a student's preparedness and deliver personalized instruction on the exact topics the student is **most ready to learn**. Through comprehensive explanations, practice, and immediate feedback, ALEKS enables students to quickly fill individual knowledge gaps in order to build a strong foundation of critical accounting skills.

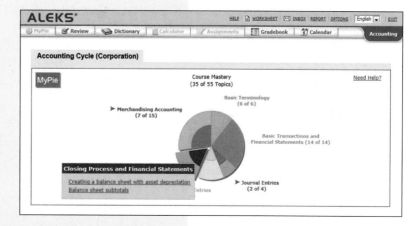

Use ALEKS Accounting Cycle during the first six weeks of the term to see improved student confidence and performance, as well as fewer drops.

### ALEKS Accounting Cycle Features:

- **Artificial Intelligence:** Targets Gaps in Prerequisite Knowledge
- **Individualized Learning and Assessment:** Ensure Student Preparedness
- **Open-Response Environment:** Avoids Multiple-Choice and Ensures Mastery
- **Dynamic, Automated Reports:** Easily Identify Struggling Students

For more information, please visit:
www.aleks.com/highered/business.

Read ALEKS Success Stories:
www.aleks.com/highered/business/success_stories.

## McGraw-Hill Customer Experience Group Contact Information

At McGraw-Hill, we understand that getting the most from new technology can be challenging. That's why our services don't stop after you purchase our products. You can e-mail our Product Specialists 24 hours a day to get product-training online. Or you can search our knowledge bank of Frequently Asked Questions on our support website. For Customer Support, call 800-331-5094, e-mail hmsupport@mcgraw-hill.com, or visit www.mhhe.com/support. One of our Technical Support Analysts will be able to assist you in a timely fashion.

ALEKS is a registered trademark of ALEKS Corporation.

# A Great Learning System Doesn't Stop with the Book

## Instructor Supplements

### Assurance of Learning Ready

Many educational institutions today are focused on the notion of *assurance of learning,* an important element of some accreditation standards. *Intermediate Accounting* is designed specifically to support your assurance of learning initiatives with a simple, yet powerful solution.

Each test bank question for *Intermediate Accounting* maps to a specific chapter learning objective listed in the text. You can use our test bank software, EZ Test Online, or *Connect Accounting* to easily query for learning objectives that directly relate to the learning objectives for your course. You can then use the reporting features of EZ Test to aggregate student results in similar fashion, making the collection and presentation of assurance of learning data simple and easy.

### AACSB Statement

The McGraw-Hill Companies is a proud corporate member of AACSB International. Understanding the importance and value of AACSB accreditation, *McGraw-Hill's Accounting series* recognizes the curricula guidelines detailed in the AACSB standards for business accreditation by connecting selected questions in the text and the test bank to the six general knowledge and skill guidelines in the AACSB standards.

The statements contained in *Intermediate Accounting* are provided only as a guide for the users of this textbook. The AACSB leaves content coverage and assessment within the purview of individual schools, the mission of the school, and the faculty. While *Intermediate Accounting* and the teaching package make no claim of any specific AACSB qualification or evaluation, we have within *Intermediate Accounting* labeled selected questions according to the six general knowledge and skills areas.

### Instructor's Resource Manual

This manual provides for each chapter: (a) a chapter overview; (b) a comprehensive lecture outline; (c) extensive teaching transparency masters that can be modified to suit an instructor's particular needs or preferences; (d) a variety of suggested class activities (real world, ethics, Dell, professional development activities including

> "Very readable, impressive web-based supplements, excellent topic coverage."
>
> —Karen Foust, *Tulane University*

research, analysis, communication and judgment, and others); and (e) an assignment chart indicating topic, learning objective, and estimated completion time for every question, exercise, problem, and case.

### Solutions Manual

The Solutions Manual includes detailed solutions for every question, exercise, problem, and case in the text.

### Instructor's CD-ROM

*ISBN-13: 9780077446413 (ISBN-10: 0077446410)*
This all-in-one resource contains the Instructor's Resource Manual, Solutions Manual, Testbank Word files, Computerized Testbank, and PowerPoint® slides.

### Testbank

The **Testbank** is a key component of our Learning System. For the seventh edition, an extensive review process was undertaken to ensure the most complete, accurate, rigorous, and flexible Testbank available. Greater variety was added at each level of rigor. It has been revised for all changes and additions to the text. In addition, new materials on the proposed Accounting Standard Updates on revenue recognition, financial instruments and leases in the Where We're Headed chapter supplements in Chapters 5, 12, and 15 were added to the Testbank, Instructor Resource Manual, Online Quizzes, and the Study Guide.

### Audio PowerPoint Slides

The Audio PowerPoint slides are created by Jon Booker and Charles Caldwell of Tennessee Technological University, Susan Galbreath of David Lipscomb University, and Cynthia J. Rooney, University of New Mexico, Los Alamos. The slides include an accompanying audio lecture with notes and are available on the Online Learning Center (OLC).

## Online Learning Center (OLC): www.mhhe.com/spiceland7e

Intermediate Accounting authors Spiceland, Sepe, and Nelson know from their years of teaching experience what separates a great textbook from a merely adequate one. Every component of the learning package must be imbued with the same style and approach, and that's why the *Intermediate Accounting* authors write every major ancillary themselves, whether printed or online. It's one more thing that sets *Intermediate Accounting* far above the competition.

# Student Supplements

## Study Guide

*Volume 1: ISBN-13: 9780077446437 (ISBN-10: 0077446437)*
*Volume 2: ISBN-13: 9780077446444 (ISBN-10: 0077446445)*
The Study Guide, written by the text authors, provides chapter summaries, detailed illustrations, and a wide variety of self-study questions, exercises, and multiple-choice problems (with solutions).

## Working Papers

*ISBN-13: 9780077446451 (ISBN-10: 0077446453)*
Working Papers provide students with formatted templates to aid them in doing homework assignments.

## Excel Templates e**X**cel

Selected end-of-chapter exercises and problems, marked in the text with an icon, can be solved using these Microsoft Excel templates, located on the OLC.

## Understanding Corporate Annual Reports

Seventh Edition, by William R. Pasewark

*ISBN-13: 9780073526935 (ISBN-10: 0073526932)*
This project provides students with instruction for obtaining an annual report from a publicly traded corporation and for making an industry or competitor comparison.

> "This is a well-written text, with good integration. It has a full range of computerized and other support materials; and the authors personally write and check the practice questions, examples, and text items."
>
> —Elaine Henry, *University of Miami*

## Alternate Exercises and Problems

This online manual includes additional exercises and problems for each chapter in the text. Available on the OLC.

## Problem Sets

*ISBN-13: 9780077328771 (ISBN-10: 0077328779)*
Grady Wholesale Practice Set: Review of the Accounting Cycle

> "The quality of the material presented is second to none. Chapters can be re-arranged as we constantly improve our accounting curriculum. Most important, students will read this book! The end-of-chapter material is outstanding."
>
> —Barbara Reider, *University of Montana*

# What's New in the Seventh Edition?

## Chapter 1

**ENVIRONMENT AND THEORETICAL STRUCTURE OF FINANCIAL ACCOUNTING**

- Re-organized parts of the chapter to highlight factors affecting the quality of financial reporting and recent changes in the conceptual framework included in *SFAC No. 8*.
- Enhanced discussion of FASB and IASB standard setting process, and compared and contrasted their organizations.
- Discussed the convergence process and alternative approaches to achieving convergence, including the SEC's "condorsement" approach.
- Expanded discussion of measurement attributes, particularly fair value.

## Chapter 2

**REVIEW OF THE ACCOUNTING PROCESS**

- Enhanced the section on preparing the financial statements by adding a subsection on the now required statement of comprehensive income.

## Chapter 3

**THE BALANCE SHEET AND FINANCIAL DISCLOSURES**

- Revised the Where We're Headed box to reflect changes in the FASB and IASB tentative decisions regarding their joint project on Financial Statement Presentation.
- Added an Air France case related to the presentation of the balance sheet under IFRS.

## Chapter 4

**THE INCOME STATEMENT, COMPREHENSIVE INCOME, AND THE STATEMENT OF CASH FLOWS**

- Revised the discussion of what constitutes a discontinued operation to reflect the new FASB Accounting Standards Update.
- Revised the section on accounting changes to be more concise, avoiding any unnecessary duplication of coverage with subsequent chapters.

- Revised the discussion of comprehensive income to reflect the new FASB Accounting Standards Update on Comprehensive Income (Topic 220): Presentation of Comprehensive Income.
- Revised the Where We're Headed box to reflect changes in the FASB and IASB tentative decisions regarding their joint project on Financial Statement Presentation.
- Added an Air France case related to the presentation of the income statement and statement of cash flows under IFRS.

## Chapter 5

**INCOME MEASUREMENT AND PROFITABILITY ANALYSIS**

- Added discussion of distinguishing between revenue recognition arrangements when the seller is a principal or an agent.
- Enhanced the discussion of multiple-element arrangements, including recent changes in standards affecting arrangements involving hardware and software.
- Added chapter supplement comprehensively discussing the joint FASB/FASB revenue recognition project, including key parts of the proposed ASU. (The supplement included 11 illustrations and is accompanied by a concept review exercise and end-of-chapter material including six questions, six brief exercises, eight exercises, and four problems.)
- Added an Air France case related to accounting for revenue under IFRS.

## Chapter 6

**TIME VALUE OF MONEY CONCEPTS**

- Added a Where We're Headed box to describe the proposed revenue recognition Accounting Standards Update requirement to reflect the time value of money when valuing prepayments.

## Chapter 7

**CASH AND RECEIVABLES**

- Added discussion of accounting for transfers of receivables as sales v. loans, and used Lehman's Repo 105 transactions to discuss relevant criteria and recent changes in GAAP.

- Significantly rewrote Appendix 7b on accounting for impairment of receivables and troubled debt restructurings, including enhanced discussion of differences between U.S. GAAP and IFRS.
- Added an Air France case related to accounting for bank overdrafts and receivables.

## Chapter 8

**INVENTORIES: MEASUREMENT**

- Added an Air France case related to the measurement of inventories under IFRS.

## Chapter 9

**INVENTORIES: ADDITIONAL ISSUES**

- Added an Air France case related to the lower-of-cost-or market-rule for valuing inventories under IFRS.

## Chapter 10

**PROPERTY, PLANT, AND EQUIPMENT AND INTANGIBLE ASSETS: ACQUISITION AND DISPOSITION**

- Added an IFRS box that describes and illustrates the differences between U.S. GAAP and IFRS in accounting for government grants.
- Added a Where We're Headed box that describes the requirement to capitalize as an intangible asset the incremental costs of obtaining and fulfilling a long-term contract according to the proposed revenue recognition Accounting Standards Update.
- Added an Air France case related to accounting for the acquisition and disposition of property, plant, and equipment and intangible assets under IFRS.

## Chapter 11

**PROPERTY, PLANT, AND EQUIPMENT AND INTANGIBLE ASSETS: UTILIZATION AND IMPAIRMENT**

- Added a section on when to test for impairment of goodwill to reflect the new FASB Accounting Standards Update on Intangibles (Topic 350): Testing for Goodwill Impairment.
- Enhanced the IFRS boxes on depreciation and biological assets.

We received an incredible amount of feedback prior to writing the seventh edition of *Intermediate Accounting*. The following list of changes and improvements is a testament to our users and their commitment to making *Intermediate Accounting* the best book of its kind.

- Added a Where We're Headed box that discusses the measurement of impairment of capitalized incremental costs of obtaining and fulfilling a long-term contract according to the proposed revenue recognition Accounting Standards Update.
- Added an Air France case related to accounting for the utilization and impairment of property, plant, and equipment and intangible assets under IFRS.

## Chapter 12
### INVESTMENTS

- Enhanced the discussion of fair value disclosures, including updates to reflect new standards.
- Enhanced the discussion of differences between IFRS and U.S. GAAP for equity method investments.
- Significantly rewrote Appendix 12B on accounting for impairment of debt and equity investments, including enhanced discussion of differences between U.S. GAAP and IFRS to reflect new standards.
- Added chapter supplement comprehensively discussing the joint FASB/FASB financial instruments project, including key parts of the proposed ASU. (The supplement included five illustrations and is accompanied by a concept review exercise and end-of-chapter material including five questions, four brief exercises, two exercises, and one problem)
- Added an Air France case related to accounting for investments under IFRS.

## Chapter 13
### CURRENT LIABILITIES AND CONTINGENCIES

- Enhanced the discussion of asserted and unasserted legal claims.
- Enhanced the discussion of differences between U.S. GAAP and IFRS.
- Added an Air France case related to accounting for current liabilities and contingencies under IFRS.

## Chapter 14
### BONDS AND LONG-TERM NOTES

- Added discussion of the potential effect of the FASB/IASB joint Financial Instruments project on the accounting and disclosure requirements for long-term debt.
- Added an Air France case related to accounting for bonds and long-term notes under IFRS.

## Chapter 15
### LEASES

- Enhanced the discussion of rent abatements or rent holidays.
- Added an in-depth chapter supplement discussing the joint FASB/FASB lease accounting project, comparing key parts of the new ASU with current GAAP. (The supplement includes fifteen illustrations and is accompanied by new end-of-chapter material including twelve questions, sixteen brief exercises, sixteen exercises, and six problems.)
- Added an Air France case related to accounting for leases under IFRS.

## Chapter 16
### ACCOUNTING FOR INCOME TAXES

- Enhanced the discussion of the Coping with Uncertainty section.
- Added an Air France case related to accounting for income taxes under IFRS.

## Chapter 17
### PENSIONS AND OTHER POSTRETIREMENT BENEFIT PLANS

- Revised and updated each of the integrated IFRS boxes to reflect the new IASB amendment to its postemployment benefit standard, IAS No. 19. Revised all related end-of-chapter assignment materials.
- Modified the discussion of comprehensive income to reflect the new FASB Accounting Standards Update on Comprehensive Income (Topic 220): Presentation of Comprehensive Income.

- Added an in-depth Where We're Headed section discussing the new IASB amendment to its postemployment benefit standard, IAS No. 19, including illustrations. The discussion includes the potential impact of the international guidance and the future of U.S. GAAP.
- Added an Air France case related to accounting for postretirement benefit plans under IFRS.

## Chapter 18
### SHAREHOLDERS' EQUITY

- Revised the discussion of comprehensive income to reflect the new FASB Accounting Standards Update on Comprehensive Income (Topic 220): Presentation of Comprehensive Income.
- Modified the Where We're Headed section to reflect changes in the FASB and IASB tentative decisions regarding their joint project on Financial Statement Presentation.
- Added an Air France case related to accounting for shareholders' equity under IFRS.

## Chapter 19
### SHARE-BASED COMPENSATION AND EARNINGS PER SHARE

- Added an Air France case related to accounting for share-based compensation and earnings per share under IFRS.

## Chapter 21
### STATEMENT OF CASH FLOWS REVISITED

- Revised the Where We're Headed section to reflect changes in the FASB and IASB tentative decisions regarding their joint project on Financial Statement Presentation.
- Added an Air France case related to reporting a statement of cash flows under IFRS.
- Added a discussion of the theoretically correct method of reporting cash flows from bonds issued at a discount or premium that's often not used in practice.

# Acknowledgments

## Seventh Edition Reviewers

**Patricia Abels,** *University of Findlay*

**John Abernathy,** *Oklahoma State University–Stillwater*

**Dawn Addington,** *Central New Mexico Community College*

**Noel Addy,** *Mississippi State University*

**Peter Aghimien,** *Indiana University–South Bend*

**John Ahern,** *Depaul University*

**John G. Ahmad,** *Nova Cc Annandale*

**Akinloye Akindayomi,** *University of Massachusettes-Dartmouth*

**Matt Anderson,** *Michigan State University–East Lansing*

**Charles P. Baril,** *James Madison University*

**Cheryl Bartlett,** *Central New Mexico Community College*

**Homer Bates,** *University of North Florida*

**Ira Bates,** *Florida A & M University*

**Sheila Bedford,** *American University*

**Yoel Beniluz,** *Rutgers University–New Brunswick*

**Scott Boylan,** *Washington & Lee University*

**Brian Bratten,** *University of Kentucky–Lexington*

**John Brozovsky,** *Virginia Tech*

**Phillip Buchanan,** *George Mason University*

**Mary Calegari,** *San Jose State University*

**Ronald L. Campbell,** *North Carolina A & T University*

**Charles Carslaw,** *University of Nevada-Reno*

**Joan Cezair,** *Fayetteville State University*

**Chiaho Chang,** *Montclair State University*

**Lynette Chapman-Vasill,** *Texas A & M University*

**Linda G. Chase,** *Baldwin–Wallace College*

**Nancy Christie,** *Virginia Tech*

**Stan Chu,** *Borough of Manhattan Community College*

**Kwang Chung,** *Pace University Nyc*

**Christie Comunale,** *Long Island University–Cw Post*

**Elizabeth C. Conner,** *University of Colorado-Denver*

**John Dallmus,** *Arizona State University–West*

**Johnny Deng,** *California State University Sacramento*

**Emily Drogt,** *Grand Valley State University*

**Jan Duffy,** *Iowa State University*

**Tim Eaton,** *University of Miami Ohio*

**Dennis Elam,** *Texas A & M University*

**Ed Etter,** *Eastern Michigan University*

**Anita Feller,** *University of Illinois–Champaign*

**Mark Felton,** *University of Saint Thomas*

**Gary Freeman,** *Northeastern State University*

**Clyde Galbraith,** *West Chester University of Pa*

**John Giles,** *Nc State University-Raleigh*

**Kathrine Glass,** *Indiana University–Bloomington*

**Robert T. Gregrich,** *Brevard Community College*

**Amy Haas,** *Kingsborough Community College*

**Abo-El-Yazeed T. Habib,** *Minnesota State University–Mankato*

**John Hathorn,** *Metropolitan State College of Denver*

**Frank Heflin** *Florida State University*

**John Hoffer** *Stark State College of Tech*

**Travis Holt** *University of Tennessee–Chattanooga*

**Donald Hoppa** *Roosevelt University–Schaumburg*

**Tom Hrubec** *Franklin University*

**Kathy Hsiao Yu Hsu** *University of Louisiana–Lafayette*

**Mark Jackson** *University of Nevada–Reno*

**Ching-Lih Jan** *California State University–East Bay*

**Randy Johnston** *University of Colorado–Boulder*

**Christopher Jones** *California State University–Northridge*

**Jessica Jones** *Chandler-Gilbert Community College*

**Celina Jozsi** *University of South Florida–Tampa*

**Beth Kane** *Columbia College–Columbia*

**Shannon Knight** *Texas A & M University*

**Adam Koch** *University of Virginia*

**John Krahel** *Rutgers University–Newark*

**Jerry G. Kreuze** *Western Michigan University–Kalamazoo*

**Lisa Kutcher** *Colorado State University*

**Brad Lail** *Nc State University–Raleigh*

**Sheldon Langsam** *Western Mich University–Kalamazoo*

As you know if you've read this far, *Intermediate Accounting* would not be what it is without the passionate feedback of our colleagues. Through your time and effort, we were able to create a learning system that truly responds to the needs of the market, and for that, we sincerely thank each of you.

**Howard Lawrence** *University of Mississippi*

**Janice Lawrence** *University of Nebraska–Lincoln*

**Gerald P. Lehman** *Madison Area Technical College–Truax*

**Wei Li** *Kent State University–Kent*

**Terry Lindenberg** *University of Maryland–University College*

**Henock Louis** *Penn State University–University Park*

**Steven Lustgarten** *Bernard M. Baruch College*

**Victoria Mahan** *Clark State Community College*

**Bob Maust** *West Virginia University–Morgantown*

**Katie Maxwell** *University of Arizona*

**Alan Mayer-Sommer** *Georgetown University*

**John Mills** *University of Nevada-Reno*

**Gary Mingle** *Golden Gate University*

**Tommy Moores** *University of Nevada–Las Vegas*

**John Murphy** *Iowa State University*

**Ramesh Narasimhan** *Montclair State University*

**Sia Nassiripour** *William Paterson University*

**Siva Nathan** *Georgia State University*

**Linda Nichols** *Texas Tech University*

**Sewon O** *Texas Southern University*

**Emeka Ofobike** *University of Akron*

**Stevan Olson** *Missouri State University*

**William Padley** *Madison Area Technical College–Truax*

**Hong Pak** *California State Polytechnic University–Pomona*

**Moses Pava** *Yeshiva University*

**Alee Phillips** *University of Kansas–Lawrence*

**Byron Pike** *Minnesota State University–Mankato*

**Kevin Poirier** *Johnson & Wales University*

**Atul Rai** *Wichita State University*

**Philip M Reckers** *Arizona State University–Tempe*

**Barbara Reider** *University of Montana*

**Eric Rothenburg** *Kingsborough Community College*

**Anwar Salimi** *California State Polytechnic University–Pomona*

**Timothy Sigler** *Stark State College of Tech*

**Kathleen Simons** *Bryant University*

**Craig Sisneros** *Wichita State University*

**Kevin Smith** *Utah Valley University–Orem*

**Sheldon R. Smith** *Utah Valley University–Orem*

**Victor Stanton** *University of Calif–Berkeley*

**Dan Stubbs** *Rutgers University–New Brunswick*

**Pamela S. Stuerke** *University of Missouri–St Louis*

**Domenic Tavella** *Pittsburgh Technical Institute*

**Kathy Terrell** *University of Central Oklahoma*

**Paula B. Thomas** *Middle Tennessee State University*

**Samuel Tiras** *Louisiana State University–Baton Rouge*

**Ingrid Ulstad** *University of Wisconsin–Eau Claire*

**Rishma Vedd** *California State University–Northridge*

**Marcia Veit** *University of Central Florida*

**Bruce Wampler** *University of Tennessee–Chattanooga*

**Isabel Wang** *Michigan State University–East Lansing*

**Kun Wang** *Texas Southern University*

**Nancy Wilburn** *Northern Arizona*

**Mike Wilson** *Metropolitan State University*

**Jennifer Winchel** *University of South Carolina*

**Joni J. Young** *University of New Mexico–Albuquerque*

## Sixth Edition Reviewers

The Spiceland team also extends sincere thanks to the reviewers of our previous edition, without whose input we could not have made *Intermediate Accounting* the extraordinary success it has been.

**Peter Aghimien,** *Indiana University–South Bend*

**Pervaiz Alam,** *Kent State University*

**Dave Alldredge,** *Salt Lake Community College*

**Matthew J. Anderson,** *Michigan State University–East Lansing*

**Marie Archambault,** *Marshall University*

**Debbie Archambeault,** *University of Tennessee–Chattanooga*

**Paul Ashcroft,** *Missouri State University*

**Florence Atiase,** *University of Texas–Austin*

**Steven Balsam,** *Temple University*

**James Bannister,** *University of Hartford*

**Charles P. Baril,** *James Madison University*

**Cheryl Bartlett,** *Central New Mexico Community College*

**Homer Bates,** *University of North Florida*

**Ira Bates,** *Florida A & M University*

**Deborah F. Beard,** *Southeast Missouri State University*

**Yoel Beniluz,** *Rutgers University–New Brunswick*

**Rick Berschback,** *Walsh College*

**Mark Bezik,** *Idaho State University*

**Bruce Branson,** *NC State University–Raleigh*

**Phil Buchanan,** *George Mason University*

**Jay Buchanon,** *Burlington Community College*

**Charles A. Carslaw,** *University of Nevada–Reno*

**Dennis Chambers,** *Kennesaw State University*

**Kimberly Charland,** *Kansas State University*

**Linda Chase,** *Baldwin-Wallace College*

**Agnes Cheng,** *Louisiana State University–Baton Rouge*

**Cal Christian,** *East Carolina University*

**Stan Chu,** *Borough of Manhattan Community College*

**Karen Collins,** *Lehigh University*

**Elizabeth Conner,** *University of Colorado–Denver*

**Teresa Conover,** *University of North Texas*

**Paul Copley,** *James Madison University*

**John Dallmus,** *Arizona State University–West*

**Li Dang,** *California Polytechnic State University*

**Charles Davis,** *California State University–Sacramento*

**Denise de la Rosa,** *Grand Valley State University*

**Keren Deal,** *Auburn University–Montgomery*

**Robert Depasquale,** *Saint Vincent College*

**Patricia Derrick,** *Salisbury University*

**Robert Derstine,** *Villanova University*

**Doug DeVidal,** *University of Texas–Austin*

**Victoria Dickinson,** *University of Florida–Gainesville*

**Jan Duffy,** *Iowa State University*

**Barbara Durham,** *University of Central Florida*

**Terry G. Elliott,** *Morehead State University*

**James Emig,** *Villanova University*

**Denise English,** *Boise State University*

**Kathryn Epps,** *Kennesaw State University*

**Ed Etter,** *Eastern Michigan University*

**Larry Farmer,** *Middle Tennessee State University*

**Anita Feller,** *University of Illinois–Champaign*

**Pat Fort,** *University of Alaska–Anchorage*

**Karen Foust,** *Tulane University*

**Gail Fraser,** *Kean University*

**Ann Gabriel,** *Ohio University–Athens*

**Clyde Galbraith,** *West Chester University of PA*

**Aloke Ghosh,** *Bernard M. Baruch College*

**Daniel Gibbons,** *Columbia College–Christian County*

**John Giles,** *NC State University–Raleigh*

**Lisa Gillespie,** *Loyola University–Chicago*

**Dan Givoly,** *Penn State University–University Park*

**Ronald Gray,** *University of West Florida*

**Daryl Max Guffey,** *Clemson University*

**Ronald Halsac,** *Community College of Allegheny County*

**Coby Harmon,** *University of California–Santa Barbara*

**Carolyn Hartwell,** *Wright State University–Dayton*

**Daniel He,** *Monmouth University*

**John Hoffer,** *Stark State College of Technology*

**Harry Howe,** *State University College–Geneseo*

**Kathy Hsiao Yu Hsu,** *University of Louisiana–Lafayette*

**Patricia Hughes,** *University of Pittsburgh*

**Evelyn Hwang,** *Eastern Michigan University*

**Raghavan J. Iyengar,** *North Carolina Central University*

**Christopher Jones,** *California State University–Northridge*

**Lisa Koonce,** *University of Texas–Austin*

**Jerry Kreuze,** *Western Michigan University–Kalamazoo*

**Timothy Krumwiede,** *Bryant University*

**Steven Lafave,** *Augsburg College*

**Sheldon Langsam,** *Western Michigan University–Kalamazoo*

**Doug Laufer,** *Metro State College of Denver*

**Janice Lawrence,** *University of Nebraska–Lincoln*

Charles Leflar, *University of Arkansas–Fayetteville*

Tim Lindquist, *University of Northern Iowa*

Joseph Lipari, *Montclair State University*

Danny Litt, *University of California–Los Angeles*

Chao-Shin Liu, *University of Notre Dame*

Heidemarie Lundblad, *California State University–Northridge*

Susan A. Lynn, *University of Baltimore*

Jeff Mankin, *Lipscomb University*

Josephine Mathias, *Mercer County Community College*

Florence McGovern, *Bergen Community College*

Tammy Metzke, *Milwaukee Area Technical College*

John Mills, *University of Nevada–Reno*

Birendra Mishra, *University of California–Riverside*

Richard Monbrod, *DeVry University–Chicago*

Louella Moore, *Arkansas State University–State University*

Tommy Moores, *University of Nevada–Las Vegas*

Lisa Murawa, *Mott Community College*

Brian Nagle, *Duquesne University*

Albert Nagy, *John Carroll University*

Ramesh Narasimhan, *Montclair State University*

Siva Nathan, *Georgia State University*

Linda Nichols, *Texas Tech University*

Michelle Nickla, *Ivy Tech Community College of Indiana*

Sewon O, *Texas Southern University*

Emeke Ofobike, *University of Akron*

Lori Olsen, *North Dakota State University–Fargo*

Don Pagach, *NC State University–Raleigh*

Hong S. Pak, *California State Polytechnic University–Pomona*

Susan Pallas, *Southeast Community College*

Patricia Parker, *Columbus State Community College*

Simon Pearlman, *California State University–Long Beach*

Ray Pfeiffer, *University of Massachusetts–Amherst*

Catherine Plante, *University of New Hampshire*

John Plouffe, *California State University–Los Angeles*

Grace Pownall, *Emory University*

Dale Prondzinski, *Davenport University*

Monsur Rahman, *Indiana University of PA–Indiana*

Kenneth C. Rakow, *Louisiana State University–Baton Rouge*

Barbara Reider, *University of Montana*

Raymond Reisig, *Pace University*

Jeri Ricketts, *University of Cincinnati*

Carol Rogers, *Central New Mexico Community College*

Eric Rothenburg, *Kingsborough Community College*

Huldah A. Ryan, *Iona College–New Rochelle*

Maria Sanchez, *Rider University*

Lisa Sandifer, *Delta State University*

Alexander Sannella, *Rutgers University–Newark*

William Schwartz, *University of Arizona*

Michael Serif, *Dowling College*

Kathy Sevigny, *Bridgewater State College*

Andreas Simon, *California Polytechnic State University*

Kathleen Simons, *Bryant University*

Debra Sinclair, *Georgia Southern University*

Mike Slaubaugh, *Indiana University/Purdue University–Ft. Wayne*

Cynthia Sneed, *Jacksonville State University*

Nancy Snow, *University of Toledo*

Victor Stanton, *University of California–Berkeley*

Lorraine Stern, *York College*

Benjamin Tai, *California State University–Fresno*

Pavani Tallapally, *Slippery Rock University of PA*

Karen Teitel, *College of the Holy Cross*

Forrest Thompson, *Florida A & M University*

Samuel Tiras, *Louisiana State University–Baton Rouge*

Terry Tranter, *University of Minnesota–Minneapolis*

Mike Vasilou, *Devry University–Chicago*

Marcia Veit, *University of Central Florida*

Kenton Walker, *University of Wyoming–Laramie*

Bruce Wampler, *Louisiana State University–Shreveport*

Jane Wells, *University of Kentucky–Lexington*

Michael Yampuler, *University of Houston*

Linda Zucca, *Kent State University*

# We Are Grateful

We would like to acknowledge Ilene Persoff, CW Post Campus/Long Island University, and Lisa Gillespie, Loyola University, for their detailed accuracy check of the Testbank. Special thanks are also due to Beth Kane, Columbia College, for her contributions to the accuracy and quality of the PowerPoints. Bill Padley of Madison Area Technical College contributed greatly to the production of the Working Papers. In addition, we thank Jon A. Booker and Charles W. Caldwell of Tennessee Technological University, Cynthia J. Rooney of University of New Mexico, and Susan C. Galbreath of David Lipscomb University for crafting the PowerPoint Slides; and Jack E. Terry, ComSource Associates, for developing the Excel Templates. Anita Feller of the University of Illinois-Champaign, Lawrence Tomassini of the Ohio State University, Andreas Simon of California Polytechnic State University, Barbara Muller of Arizona State University, Mark McCarthy of East Carolina University as well as the team of experts who contributed new content and accuracy checks of Connect, LearnSmart and Self-Quiz and Study products. We greatly appreciate everyone's hard work on these products!

Ilene Persoff, CW Post Campus/Long Island University, and Mark McCarthy, East Carolina University, made significant contributions to the accuracy of the text, end-of-chapter material, and solutions manual.

We were saddened to learn of the death of Anita Feller while we were preparing this edition. Anita was a long-time supporter and contributor to the project. She will be greatly missed.

We are most grateful for the talented assistance and support from the many people at McGraw-Hill/Irwin. We would particularly like to thank Brent Gordon, editor in chief; Tim Vertovec, publisher; Stewart Mattson, executive editor; Dana Woo, senior sponsoring editor; Rebecca Mann, developmental editor; Kathleen Klehr, senior marketing manager; Pat Frederickson, lead project manager; Michael McCormick, buyer; Laurie Entringer, designer; Jeremy Cheshareck, senior photo research coordinator; and Rachel Townsend, media project manager.

Finally, we extend our thanks to Kaplan CPA Review for their assistance developing simulations for our inclusion in the end-of-chapter material, as well as Dell and Air France–KLM for allowing us to use their Annual Reports throughout the text. We also acknowledge permission from the AICPA to adapt material from the Uniform CPA Examination, the IMA for permission to adapt material from the CMA Examination, and Dow Jones & Co., Inc., for permission to excerpt material from The Wall Street Journal.

*David Spiceland*    *Jim Sepe*    *Mark Nelson*

# Contents in Brief

# Contents

# 1 | The Role of Accounting as an Information System

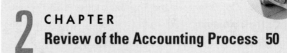

# 3 CHAPTER
## The Balance Sheet and Financial Disclosures 112

# 4 CHAPTER
## The Income Statement, Comprehensive Income, and the Statement of Cash Flows 170

# 5 CHAPTER
## Income Measurement and Profitability Analysis 230

# 2 | Economic Resources

## 11 CHAPTER
## Property, Plant, and Equipment and Intangible Assets: Utilization and Impairment  588

# 3 | Financial Instruments and Liabilities

## 12 CHAPTER
## Investments  652

# Intermediate Accounting

# 1

# Environment and Theoretical Structure of Financial Accounting

**OVERVIEW** ——————

The primary function of financial accounting is to provide useful financial information to users who are external to the business enterprise, particularly investors and creditors. These users make critical resource allocation decisions that affect the global economy. The primary means of conveying financial information to external users is through financial statements and related notes.

In this chapter you explore important topics, such as the reason why financial accounting is useful, the process by which accounting standards are produced, and the conceptual framework that underlies financial accounting. The perspective you gain in this chapter serves as a foundation for a more detailed study of financial statements, the way the statement elements are measured, and the concepts underlying these measurements and related disclosures.

**LEARNING OBJECTIVES** ——————

**After studying this chapter, you should be able to:**

- **LO1–1** Describe the function and primary focus of financial accounting. (*p. 4*)
- **LO1–2** Explain the difference between cash and accrual accounting. (*p. 6*)
- **LO1–3** Define generally accepted accounting principles (GAAP) and discuss the historical development of accounting standards, including convergence between U.S. and international standards. (*p. 8*)
- **LO1–4** Explain why the establishment of accounting standards is characterized as a political process. (*p. 13*)
- **LO1–5** Explain factors that encourage high-quality financial reporting. (*p. 15*)
- **LO1–6** Explain the purpose of the conceptual framework. (*p. 19*)
- **LO1–7** Identify the objective and qualitative characteristics of financial reporting information, and the elements of financial statements. (*p. 21*)
- **LO1–8** Describe the four basic assumptions underlying GAAP. (*p. 25*)
- **LO1–9** Describe the recognition, measurement and disclosure concepts that guide accounting practice. (*p. 27*)
- **LO1–10** Contrast a revenue/expense approach and an asset/liability approach to accounting standard setting. (*p. 33*)
- **LO1–11** Discuss the primary differences between U.S. GAAP and IFRS with respect to the development of accounting standards and the conceptual framework underlying accounting standards. (*pp. 15* and *21*)

## FINANCIAL REPORTING CASE

### Misguided Marketing Major

During a class break in your investments class, a marketing major tells the following story to you and some friends:

The chief financial officer (CFO) of a large company is interviewing three candidates for the top accounting position with his firm. He asks each the same question:

| | |
|---|---|
| *CFO:* | What is two plus two? |
| *First candidate:* | Four. |
| *CFO:* | What is two plus two? |
| *Second candidate:* | Four. |
| *CFO:* | What is two plus two? |
| *Third candidate:* | What would you like it to be? |
| *CFO:* | You're hired. |

After you take some good-natured ribbing from the non-accounting majors, your friend says, "Seriously, though, there must be ways the accounting profession prevents that kind of behavior. Aren't there some laws, or rules, or something? Is accounting based on some sort of theory, or is it just arbitrary?"

By the time you finish this chapter, you should be able to respond appropriately to the questions posed in this case. Compare your response to the solution provided at the end of the chapter.

— QUESTIONS

1. What should you tell your friend about the presence of accounting standards in the United States and the rest of the world? Who has the authority for standard setting? Who has the responsibility? (*p. 8*)

2. What is the economic and political environment in which standard setting occurs? (*p. 13*)

3. What is the relationship among management, auditors, investors, and creditors that tends to preclude the "What would you like it to be?" attitude? (*p. 15*)

4. In general, what is the conceptual framework that underlies accounting principles? (*p. 19*)

# FINANCIAL ACCOUNTING ENVIRONMENT

PART **A**

In 1984 an undergraduate student at the University of Texas used $1,000 of his own funds to found a company called PC's Limited. The student's vision was to capitalize on the emerging personal computer (PC) business by selling directly to customers rather than through traditional retail outlets. The customer's PC would not be manufactured until it was ordered. This just-in-time (JIT) approach to production combined with the direct sales model would allow the company to better understand customer needs and more efficiently provide the most effective computing solutions.

In 1985, the first full year of company operations, the student's family contributed $300,000 in expansion capital, and revenue topped $73 million.[1] These were the humble beginnings for a visionary student named Michael Dell and a company eventually renamed **Dell Inc.** that has become the world's largest PC manufacturer. Company profits for the year ended January 28, 2011, exceeded $2.6 billion and revenue topped $61 billion.

Many factors have contributed to the success of Dell Inc. The company's founder was visionary in terms of his approach to marketing and production. Importantly, too, the ability to raise external capital from investors and creditors at various times in the company's history was critical to its growth. Funding began with Michael Dell's initial $1,000 outlay and his family's $300,000 investment. In 1988, an initial public offering of the company's stock provided $30 million in equity financing.

> "Michael S. Dell built the multibillion-dollar company that bears his name not by inventing new products or services, but by constantly looking for ways to sell technology 'better, faster, cheaper,' as the company's mantra goes."[2]

Investors and creditors use many different kinds of information before supplying capital to business enterprises like Dell. The information is used to assess the future risk and return of their potential investments in the enterprise.[3] For example, information about the enterprise's products and its management is of vital importance to this assessment. In addition, various kinds of financial information are extremely important to investors and creditors.

● **LO1–1**

The primary focus of *financial accounting* is on the information needs of investors and creditors.

Think of accounting as a special "language" used to communicate financial information about a business to those who wish to use the information to make decisions. **Financial accounting**, in particular, is chiefly concerned with providing relevant financial information to various *external* users.[4] The chart in Illustration 1–1 lists a number of financial information supplier groups as well as several external user groups. Of these groups, the primary focus of financial accounting is on the financial information provided by *profit-oriented companies to their present and potential investors and creditors.* The reason for this focus is discussed in a later section of this chapter. One external user group, often referred to as *financial intermediaries,* includes financial analysts, stockbrokers, mutual fund managers, and credit rating organizations. These users provide advice to investors and creditors and/or make investment-credit decisions on their behalf.

**Illustration 1–1**

Financial Information Providers and External User Groups

| PROVIDERS OF FINANCIAL INFORMATION | EXTERNAL USER GROUPS |
|---|---|
| • Profit-oriented companies | • Investors |
| | • Creditors (banks, bondholders, other lenders) |
| | • Employees |
| | • Labor unions |
| • Not-for-profit entities (e.g., government entities, charitable organizations, schools) | • Customers |
| | • Suppliers |
| | • Government regulatory agencies (e.g., Internal Revenue Service, Securities and Exchange Commission) |
| • Households | • Financial intermediaries (e.g., financial analysts, stockbrokers, mutual fund managers, credit-rating organizations) |

---

[1] "Dell, Inc.—Company History," **www.fundinguniverse.com**.

[2] Elizabeth Schwinn. "A Focus on Efficiency," *The Chronicle of Philanthropy* (April 6, 2006).

[3] Risk refers to the variability of possible outcomes from an investment. Return is the amount received over and above the investment and usually is expressed as a percentage.

[4] In contrast, managerial accounting deals with the concepts and methods used to provide information to an organization's *internal* users, that is, its managers. You study managerial accounting elsewhere in your curriculum.

The primary means of conveying financial information to investors, creditors, and other external users is through financial statements and related disclosure notes. The financial statements most frequently provided are (1) the balance sheet, also called the statement of financial position, (2) the income statement, also called the statement of operations, (3) the statement of cash flows, and (4) the statement of shareholders' equity. Also, starting in 2012, companies must either provide a statement of other comprehensive income immediately following the income statement, or present a combined statement of comprehensive income that includes the information normally contained in both the income statement and the statement of other comprehensive income.[5] As you progress through this text, you will review and expand your knowledge of the information in these financial statements, the way the elements in these statements are measured, and the concepts underlying these measurements and related disclosures. We use the term financial reporting to refer to the process of providing this information to external users. Keep in mind, though, that external users receive important financial information in a variety of other formats as well, including news releases and management forecasts, prospectuses, and reports filed with regulatory agencies.

**Dell Inc.**'s 2011 financial statements and related disclosure notes are provided in Appendix B located at the back of the text. You also can locate the 2011 statements and notes online at **www.dell.com**. To provide context for our discussions throughout the text, we occasionally refer to these statements and notes. Also, as new topics are introduced in later chapters, you might want to refer to the information to see how Dell reported the items being discussed.

# The Economic Environment and Financial Reporting

In the United States, we have a highly developed free-enterprise economy with the majority of productive resources privately owned rather than government owned. For the economy to operate efficiently, these resources should be allocated to private enterprises that will use them best to provide the goods and services desired by society and not to enterprises that will waste them. The mechanisms that foster this efficient allocation of resources are the capital markets. We can think of the capital markets simply as a composite of all investors and creditors.

> The *capital markets* provide a mechanism to help our economy allocate resources efficiently.

Businesses go to the capital markets to get the cash necessary for them to function. The three primary forms of business organization are the sole proprietorship, the partnership, and the corporation. In the United States, sole proprietorships and partnerships outnumber corporations. However, the dominant form of business organization, in terms of the ownership of productive resources, is the corporation. Investors provide resources, usually cash, to a corporation in exchange for an ownership interest, that is, shares of stock. Creditors lend cash to the corporation, either by making individual loans or by purchasing publicly traded debt such as bonds.

> *Corporations* acquire capital from investors in exchange for ownership interest and from creditors by borrowing.

Stocks and bonds usually are traded on organized security markets such as the New York Stock Exchange and the NASDAQ. New cash is provided by initial market transactions in which the corporation sells shares of stock or bonds to individuals or other entities that want to invest in it. Subsequent transfers of these stocks and bonds between investors and creditors are referred to as secondary market transactions. Corporations receive no new cash from secondary market transactions. Nevertheless, secondary market transactions are extremely important to the efficient allocation of resources in our economy. These transactions help establish market prices for additional shares and for bonds that corporations may wish to issue in the future to acquire additional capital. Also, many shareholders and bondholders might be unwilling to initially provide resources to corporations if there were no available mechanism for the future sale of their stocks and bonds to others.

> *Initial market* transactions involve issuance of stocks and bonds by the corporation.

> *Secondary market* transactions involve the transfer of stocks and bonds between individuals and institutions.

What information do investors and creditors need when determining which companies will receive capital? We explore that question next.

---

[5]FASB ASC 220: Comprehensive Income (originally "Presentation of Comprehensive Income," *Accounting Standards Update No. 2011–05* (Norwalk, CT: FASB, June 2011)).

## The Investment-Credit Decision—A Cash Flow Perspective

While the decisions made by investors and by creditors are somewhat different, they are similar in at least one important way. Investors and creditors are willing to provide capital to a corporation (buy stocks or bonds) only if they expect to receive more cash in return at some time in the future. A corporation's shareholders will receive cash from their investment through the ultimate sale of the ownership shares of stock. In addition, many corporations distribute cash to their shareholders in the form of periodic dividends. For example, if an investor provides a company with $10,000 cash by purchasing stock at the end of 2012, receives $400 in dividends from the company during 2013, and sells the ownership interest (shares) at the end of 2013 for $10,600, the investment would have generated a rate of return of 10% for 2013, calculated as follows:

$$\frac{\$400 \text{ dividends} + \$600 \text{ share price appreciation}}{\$10,000 \text{ initial investment}} = 10\%$$

All else equal, investors and creditors would like to invest in stocks or bonds that provide the highest expected rate of return. However, there are many factors to consider before making an investment decision. For example, the *uncertainty,* or *risk,* of that expected return also is important. To illustrate, consider the following two investment options:

1. Invest $10,000 in a savings account insured by the U.S. government that will generate a 5% rate of return.
2. Invest $10,000 in a profit-oriented company.

While the rate of return from option 1 is known with virtual certainty, the return from option 2 is uncertain. The amount and timing of the cash to be received in the future from option 2 are unknown. The company in option 2 will be able to provide investors with a return only if it can generate a profit. That is, it must be able to use the resources provided by investors and creditors to generate cash receipts from selling a product or service that exceed the cash disbursements necessary to provide that product or service. Therefore, potential investors require information about the company that will help them estimate the potential for future profits, as well as the return they can expect on their investment and the risk that is associated with it. If the potential return is high enough, investors will prefer to invest in the profit-oriented company, even if that return has more risk associated with it.

In summary, the primary objective of financial accounting is to provide investors and creditors with information that will help them make investment and credit decisions. More specifically, the information should help investors and creditors evaluate the *amounts, timing,* and *uncertainty* of the enterprise's future cash receipts and disbursements. The better this information is, the more efficient will be investor and creditor resource allocation decisions. But financial accounting doesn't only benefit companies and their investors and creditors. By providing key elements of the information set used by capital market participants, financial accounting plays a vital role by providing information that helps direct society's resources to the companies that utilize those resources most effectively.

## Cash versus Accrual Accounting

● LO1–2

Even though predicting future cash flows is the primary goal of many users of financial reporting, the model best able to achieve that goal is the accrual accounting model. A competing model is cash basis accounting. Each model produces a periodic measure of performance that could be used by investors and creditors for predicting future cash flows.

**CASH BASIS ACCOUNTING.**   Cash basis accounting produces a measure called net operating cash flow. This measure is the difference between cash receipts and cash payments from transactions related to providing goods and services to customers during a reporting period.

Over the life of a company, net operating cash flow definitely is the variable of concern. However, over short periods of time, operating cash flows may not be indicative of the company's long-run cash-generating ability. Sometimes a company pays or receives cash in one period that relates to performance in multiple periods. For example, in one period a company receives cash that relates to prior period sales, or makes advance payments for costs related to future periods. Therefore, net operating cash flow may not be a good predictor of long-run cash-generating ability.

To see this more clearly, consider Carter Company's net operating cash flows during its first three years of operations, shown in Illustration 1–2. Over this three-year period Carter generated a positive net operating cash flow of $60,000. At the end of the three-year period, Carter has no outstanding debts. Because total sales and cash receipts over the three-year period were each $300,000, nothing is owed to Carter by customers. Also, there are no uncompleted transactions at the end of the three-year period. In that sense, we can view this three-year period as a micro version of the entire life of a company.

| | Year 1 | Year 2 | Year 3 | Total |
|---|---|---|---|---|
| Sales (on credit) | $100,000 | $100,000 | $100,000 | $300,000 |
| **Net Operating Cash Flows** | | | | |
| Cash receipts from customers | $ 50,000 | $125,000 | $125,000 | $300,000 |
| Cash disbursements: | | | | |
| Prepayment of three years' rent | (60,000) | –0– | –0– | (60,000) |
| Salaries to employees | (50,000) | (50,000) | (50,000) | (150,000) |
| Utilities | (5,000) | (15,000) | (10,000) | (30,000) |
| Net operating cash flow | $ (65,000) | $ 60,000 | $ 65,000 | $ 60,000 |

**Illustration 1–2**

Cash Basis Accounting

At the beginning of the first year, Carter prepaid $60,000 for three years' rent on the facilities. The company also incurred utility costs of $10,000 per year over the period. However, during the first year only $5,000 actually was paid, with the remainder being paid the second year. Employee salary costs of $50,000 were paid in full each year.

Is net operating cash flow for year 1 (negative $65,000) an accurate indicator of future cash-generating ability?[6] Clearly not, given that the next two years show positive net cash flows. Is the three-year pattern of net operating cash flows indicative of the company's year-by-year performance? No, because the years in which Carter paid for rent and utilities are not the same as the years in which Carter actually consumed those resources. Similarly, the amounts collected from customers are not the same as the amount of sales each period.

> Over short periods of time, operating cash flow may not be an accurate predictor of future operating cash flows.

**ACCRUAL ACCOUNTING.**    If we measure Carter's activities by the accrual accounting model, we get a more accurate prediction of future operating cash flows and a more reasonable portrayal of the periodic operating performance of the company. The accrual accounting model doesn't focus only on cash flows. Instead, it also reflects other resources provided and consumed by operations during a period. The accrual accounting model's measure of resources provided by business operations is called *revenues,* and the measure of resources sacrificed to earn revenues is called *expenses.* The difference between revenues and expenses is *net income,* or net loss if expenses are greater than revenues.[7]

Illustration 1–3 shows how we would measure revenues and expenses in this very simple situation.

Revenue for year 1 is the $100,000 sales. Given that sales eventually are collected in cash, the year 1 revenue of $100,000 is a better measure of the inflow of resources from company operations than is the $50,000 cash collected from customers. Also, net income of $20,000 for year 1 appears to be a reasonable predictor of the company's cash-generating ability, as total net operating cash flow for the three-year period is a positive $60,000. Comparing the three-year pattern of net operating cash flows in Illustration 1–2 to the three-year

> *Net income* is the difference between *revenues* and *expenses.*

> Net income is considered a better indicator of future operating cash flows than is current net operating cash flow.

---

[6]A negative cash flow is possible only if invested capital (i.e., owners contributed cash to the company in exchange for ownership interest) is sufficient to cover the cash deficiency. Otherwise, the company would have to either raise additional external funds or go bankrupt.

[7]Net income also includes gains and losses, which are discussed later in the chapter.

| CARTER COMPANY Income Statements | | | | |
|---|---|---|---|---|
| | Year 1 | Year 2 | Year 3 | Total |
| Revenues | $100,000 | $100,000 | $100,000 | $300,000 |
| Expenses: | | | | |
| Rent | 20,000 | 20,000 | 20,000 | 60,000 |
| Salaries | 50,000 | 50,000 | 50,000 | 150,000 |
| Utilities | 10,000 | 10,000 | 10,000 | 30,000 |
| Total expenses | 80,000 | 80,000 | 80,000 | 240,000 |
| Net Income | $ 20,000 | $ 20,000 | $ 20,000 | $ 60,000 |

pattern of net income in Illustration 1–3, the net income pattern is more representative of Carter Company's steady operating performance over the three-year period.[8]

While this example is somewhat simplistic, it allows us to see the motivation for using the accrual accounting model. Accrual income attempts to measure the resource inflows and outflows generated by operations during the reporting period, which may not correspond to cash inflows and outflows. Does this mean that information about cash flows from operating activities is not useful? No. Indeed, one of the basic financial statements—the statement of cash flows—reports information about cash flows from operating, investing and financing activities, and provides important information to investors and creditors.[9] The key point is that focusing on accrual accounting as well as cash flows provides a more complete view of a company and its operations.

# The Development of Financial Accounting and Reporting Standards

● LO1–3

Accrual accounting is the financial reporting model used by the majority of profit-oriented companies and by many not-for-profit companies. The fact that companies use the same model is important to investors and creditors, allowing them to *compare* financial information among companies. To facilitate these comparisons, financial accounting employs a body of standards known as generally accepted accounting principles, often abbreviated as GAAP (and pronounced *gap*). GAAP is a dynamic set of both broad and specific guidelines that companies should follow when measuring and reporting the information in their financial statements and related notes. The more important broad principles underlying GAAP are discussed in a subsequent section of this chapter and revisited throughout the text in the context of accounting applications for which they provide conceptual support. Specific standards, such as how to measure and report a lease transaction, receive more focused attention in subsequent chapters.

## Historical Perspective and Standards

Pressures on the accounting profession to establish uniform accounting standards began to surface after the stock market crash of 1929. Some felt that insufficient and misleading financial statement information led to inflated stock prices and that this contributed to the stock market crash and the subsequent depression.

The 1933 Securities Act and the 1934 Securities Exchange Act were designed to restore investor confidence. The 1933 Act sets forth accounting and disclosure requirements for

---

[8]Empirical evidence that accrual accounting provides a better measure of short-term performance than cash flows is provided by Patricia DeChow, "Accounting Earnings and Cash Flows as Measures of Firm Performance: The Role of Accrual Accounting," *Journal of Accounting and Economics* 18 (1994), pp. 3–42.

[9]The statement of cash flows is discussed in detail in Chapters 4 and 21.

initial offerings of securities (stocks and bonds). The 1934 Act applies to secondary market transactions and mandates reporting requirements for companies whose securities are publicly traded on either organized stock exchanges or in over-the-counter markets.[10] The 1934 Act also created the **Securities and Exchange Commission (SEC)**.

In the 1934 Act, Congress gave the SEC the authority to set accounting and reporting standards for companies whose securities are publicly traded. However, the SEC, a government appointed body, has *delegated* the task of setting accounting standards to the private sector. It is important to understand that the power still lies with the SEC. If the SEC does not agree with a particular standard issued by the private sector, it can force a change in the standard. In fact, it has done so in the past.[11]

> The *Securities and Exchange Commission (SEC)* was created by Congress with the 1934 Securities Exchange Act.
>
> The SEC has the authority to set accounting standards for companies, but has delegated the task to the private sector.

**EARLY U. S. STANDARD SETTING.**    The first private sector body to assume the task of setting accounting standards was the **Committee on Accounting Procedure (CAP)**. The CAP was a committee of the **American Institute of Accountants (AIA)**. The AIA, which was renamed the **American Institute of Certified Public Accountants (AICPA)** in 1957, is the national professional organization for certified professional public accountants. From 1938 to 1959, the CAP issued 51 *Accounting Research Bulletins (ARBs)* which dealt with specific accounting and reporting problems. No theoretical framework for financial accounting was established. This piecemeal approach of dealing with individual issues without a framework led to criticism.

In 1959 the **Accounting Principles Board (APB)** replaced the CAP. The APB operated from 1959 through 1973 and issued 31 *Accounting Principles Board Opinions (APBOs)*, various *Interpretations,* and four *Statements.* The *Opinions* also dealt with specific accounting and reporting problems. Many *ARBs* and *APBOs* have not been superseded and still represent authoritative GAAP.

> The *Accounting Principles Board (APB)* followed the CAP.

The APB suffered from a variety of problems. It was never able to establish a conceptual framework for financial accounting and reporting that was broadly accepted. Also, members served on the APB on a voluntary, part-time basis, so the APB was not able to act quickly enough to keep up with financial reporting issues as they developed. Perhaps the most important flaw of the APB was a perceived lack of independence. Because the APB was composed almost entirely of certified public accountants and supported by the AICPA, critics charged that the clients of the represented public accounting firms exerted self-interested pressure on the board and inappropriately influenced decisions. A related complaint was that other interest groups lacked an ability to provide input to the standard-setting process.

**THE FASB.**    Criticism of the APB led to the creation in 1973 of the **Financial Accounting Standards Board (FASB)** and its supporting structure. There are seven full-time members of the FASB.[12] FASB members represent various constituencies concerned with accounting standards, and have included representatives from the auditing profession, profit-oriented companies, accounting educators, financial analysts, and government. The FASB is supported by its parent organization, the **Financial Accounting Foundation (FAF)**, which is responsible for selecting the members of the FASB and its Financial Accounting Standards Advisory Council (FASAC), ensuring adequate funding of FASB activities and exercising general oversight of the FASB's activities.[13] The FASB is, therefore,

> The *FASB* was established to set U.S. accounting standards.

---

[10]Reporting requirements for SEC registrants include Form 10-K, the annual report form, and Form 10-Q, the report that must be filed for the first three quarters of each fiscal year.

[11]The SEC issues *Financial Reporting Releases (FRRs),* which regulate what information companies must report to it. The SEC also issues *Staff Accounting Bulletins* that provide the SEC's interpretation of standards previously issued by the private sector. To learn more about the SEC, consult its Internet site at **www.sec.gov.**

[12]The FASB reduced its membership from seven to five members in 2008, but returned to seven members in 2011.

[13]The FAF's primary sources of funding are fees assessed against issuers of securities under the *Public Company Accounting Reform and Investor Protection Act of 2002,* commonly referred to as the *Sarbanes-Oxley Act.* The FAF is governed by trustees, the majority of whom are appointed from the membership of eight sponsoring organizations. These organizations represent important constituencies involved with the financial reporting process. For example, one of the founding organizations is the Association of Investment Management and Research (formerly known as the Financial Analysts Federation) which represents financial information users, and another is the Financial Executives International which represents financial information preparers. The FAF also raises funds to support the activities of the Government Accounting Standards Board (GASB).

an independent, private sector body whose members represent a broad constituency of interest groups.[14]

The *Emerging Issues Task Force (EITF)* identifies financial reporting issues and attempts to resolve them without involving the FASB.

In 1984, the FASB's Emerging Issues Task Force (EITF) was formed to improve financial reporting by resolving narrowly defined financial accounting issues within the framework of existing GAAP. The EITF primarily addresses implementation issues, thereby speeding up the standard setting process and allowing the FASB to focus on pervasive long-term problems. EITF rulings are ratified by the FASB and are considered part of GAAP.

Illustration 1–4 summarizes this discussion on accounting standards. The graphic shows the hierarchy of accounting standard setting in order of authority.

**Illustration 1–4**
Accounting Standard Setting

HIERARCHY OF STANDARD-SETTING AUTHORITY

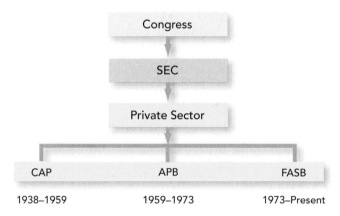

**CODIFICATION.**    Present-day GAAP includes a huge amount of guidance. The FASB has developed a conceptual framework (discussed in Part B of this chapter) that is not authoritative GAAP but provides an underlying structure for the development of accounting standards. The FASB also has issued over 160 specific accounting standards, called *Statements of Financial Accounting Standards (SFASs)*, as well as numerous FASB *Interpretations, Staff Positions, Technical Bulletins* and *EITF Issue Consensuses*.[16] The SEC also has issued various important pronouncements. Until 2009, determining the appropriate accounting treatment for a particular event or transaction might require an accountant to research several of these sources.

> The Codification does not change GAAP; instead it reorganizes the thousands of U.S. GAAP pronouncements into roughly 90 accounting topics, and displays all topics using a consistent structure.[15]

The *FASB Accounting Standards Codification* is now the only source of authoritative U.S. GAAP, other than rules and interpretive releases of the SEC.

To simplify the task of researching an accounting topic, in 2009 the FASB implemented its *FASB Accounting Standards Codification*. The Codification integrates and topically organizes all relevant accounting pronouncements comprising GAAP in a searchable, online database. It represents the single source of authoritative nongovernmental U.S. GAAP, and also includes portions of SEC accounting guidance that are relevant to financial reports filed with the SEC. When the FASB issues a new standard, it is called an Accounting Standards Update (ASU) and becomes authoritative when it is entered into the Codification. The Codification is organized into nine main topics and approximately 90 subtopics. The main topics and related numbering system are presented in Illustration 1–5.[17] The Codification can be located at **www.fasb.org**.

---

[14]The major responsibility of the FASAC is to advise the FASB on the priorities of its projects, including the suitability of new projects that might be added to its agenda. FASAC includes approximately 35 representatives from auditing firms, private companies, various user groups, and academia.

[15]"FASB Accounting Standards Codification™ Expected to Officially Launch on July 1, 2009," *FASB News Release* (Norwalk, Conn.: FASB, December 4, 2008).

[16]For more information, go to the FASB's Internet site at **www.fasb.org**.

[17]FASB ASC 105–10: Generally Accepted Accounting Principles—Overall (previously "The FASB Accounting Standards Codification™ and the Hierarchy of Generally Accepted Accounting Principles—a replacement of FASB Statement No. 162," *Statement of Financial Accounting Standards No. 168* (Norwalk, Conn.: FASB: 2009)).

**Illustration 1–5**
FASB Accounting Standards Codification Topics

| FASB Accounting Standards Codification Topics | |
| --- | --- |
| **Topic** | **Numbered** |
| General Principles | 100–199 |
| Presentation | 200–299 |
| Assets | 300–399 |
| Liabilities | 400–499 |
| Equity | 500–599 |
| Revenues | 600–699 |
| Expenses | 700–799 |
| Broad Transactions | 800–899 |
| Industry | 900–999 |

Throughout the text, we use the Accounting Standards Codification System (ASC) in footnotes when referencing generally accepted accounting principles (FASB ASC followed by the appropriate number). Each footnote also includes a reference to the original accounting standard that is codified in ASC. Your instructor may assign end-of-chapter exercises and cases that ask you to research the FASB's Accounting Standards Codification.

# Additional Consideration

Accounting standards and the standard-setting process discussed above relate to profit-oriented organizations and nongovernmental not-for-profit entities. In 1984, the Government Accounting Standards Board (GASB) was created to develop accounting standards for governmental units such as states and cities. The FAF oversees and funds the GASB, and the Governmental Accounting Standards Advisory Council (GASAC) provides input to it.

**INTERNATIONAL STANDARD SETTING.**    Most industrialized countries have organizations responsible for determining accounting and reporting standards. In some countries, the United Kingdom, for instance, the responsible organization is a private sector body similar to the FASB in the United States. In other countries, such as France, the organization is a governmental body.

Accounting standards prescribed by these various groups are not the same. Standards differ from country to country for many reasons, including different legal systems, levels of inflation, culture, degrees of sophistication and use of capital markets, use of financial reports by taxing authorities or government planners, and political and economic ties with other countries. These differences can cause problems for multinational corporations. A company doing business in more than one country may find it difficult to comply with more than one set of accounting standards if there are important differences among the sets. These differences also cause problems for investors who must struggle to compare companies whose financial statements are prepared under different standards. It has been argued that different national accounting standards impair the ability of companies to raise capital in international markets.

In response to this problem, the International Accounting Standards Committee (IASC) was formed in 1973 to develop global accounting standards. The IASC reorganized itself in 2001 and created a new standard-setting body called the International Accounting Standards Board (IASB). The IASB's main objective is to develop a single set of high-quality, understandable, and enforceable global accounting standards to help participants in the world's capital markets and other users make economic decisions.[18]

As shown in Illustration 1–6, the way international standard setting is structured is similar in many respects to the way standard setting is structured in the U.S.

The *International Accounting Standards Board (IASB)* is dedicated to developing a single set of global accounting standards.

---
[18]www.iasb.org.

**Illustration 1–6**

Comparison of Organizations of U.S. and International Standard Setters

|  | **U.S. GAAP** | **IFRS** |
|---|---|---|
| **Regulatory oversight provided by:** | Securities Exchange Commission (SEC) | International Organization of Securities Commissions (IOSCO)* |
| **Foundation providing oversight, appointing members, raising funds:** | Financial Accounting Foundation (FAF): 20 trustees | International Accounting Standards Committee Foundation (IASCF): 22 trustees |
| **Standard-setting board:** | Financial Accounting Standards Board (FASB): 7 full-time members | International Accounting Standards Board (IASB): 14 members (12 full-time; 2 part-time) |
| **Advisory council providing input on agenda and projects:** | Financial Accounting Standards Advisory Council (FASAC): 30–40 members | Standards Advisory Council (SAC): 30–40 members |
| **Group to deal with emerging issues:** | Emerging Issues Task Force (EITF): 15 members | International Financial Reporting Interpretations Committee (IFRIC): 14 members |

*Each country's security regulator has authority. IOSCO includes representatives from numerous regulators, including the SEC, to facilitate coordination among those organizations and encourage effective capital markets.

*International Financial Reporting Standards are gaining support around the globe.*

The IASC issued 41 International Accounting Standards (IASs), and the IASB endorsed these standards when it was formed in 2001. Since then, the IASB has revised many IASs and has issued new standards of its own, called **International Financial Reporting Standards (IFRSs)**. More and more countries are basing their national accounting standards on IFRS. By late 2011, over 115 jurisdictions, including Hong Kong, Egypt, Australia, and the countries in the European Union (EU), require or permit the use of IFRS or a local variant of IFRS.[19]

## EFFORTS TO CONVERGE U.S. AND INTERNATIONAL STANDARDS

Should the U.S. also adopt IFRS? Many argue that a single set of global standards will improve comparability of financial reporting and facilitate access to capital. However, others argue that U.S. standards should remain customized to fit the stringent legal and regulatory requirements of the U.S. business environment. There also is concern that differences in implementation and enforcement from country to country will make accounting under IFRS appear more uniform and comparable than actually is the case. Another argument is that competition between alternative standard-setting regimes is healthy and can lead to improved standards.[20]

Regardless, the FASB and IASB have been working for many years to converge to one global set of accounting standards. Here are some important steps along the path to convergence:

- **September 2002:** The FASB and IASB sign the Norwalk Agreement, pledging to remove existing differences between their standards and to coordinate their future standard-setting agendas so that major issues are worked on together.

- **December 2007:** The SEC signaled its view that IFRS are of high quality by eliminating the requirement for foreign companies that issue stock in the United States to include in their financial statements a reconciliation of IFRS to U.S. GAAP. As a consequence, those companies have access to U.S. capital markets with IFRS-based financial statements.

- **April 2008:** The FASB and IASB agreed to accelerate the convergence process and focus on a subset of key convergence projects. Already-converged standards that you will encounter later in this textbook deal with such topics as earnings per share, share-based compensation, nonmonetary exchanges, inventory costs, and the calculation of fair value. **Where We're Headed** boxes throughout the text describe additional projects that are ongoing, and **Where We're Headed** supplements to chapters 5, 12, and 15 describe proposed converged standards relevant to revenue recognition, investments, and leases.

- **November 2008:** The SEC issues a *Roadmap* that listed necessary conditions (called "milestones") that must be achieved before the U.S. will shift to requiring use of IFRS by public companies. Milestones include completion of key convergence projects,

---

[19]See **www.iasplus.com/country/useias.htm**.

[20]For a comprehensive analysis of the pros and cons of U.S. adoption of IFRS, see L. Hail, C. Leuz and P. Wysocki, "Global Accounting Convergence and the Potential Adoption of IFRS in the US (Part 1): An Analysis of Economic and Policy Factors", *Accounting Horizons* 24 (No 3.), September 2010, pp. 355–394, and " . . . (Part 2): Political Factors and Future Scenarios for U.S. Accounting Standards", *Accounting Horizons* 24 (No. 4), December 2010, pp. 567–588

improving the structure and funding of the IASB, and updating the education and licensing of U.S. accountants.

- **May 2011:** The SEC issues a discussion paper describing a possible approach for incorporating IFRS into U.S. GAAP. That approach, since labled "condorsement", involves continuing the convergence process coupled with endorsement of additional International Financial Reporting Standards by the FASB for inclusion in U.S. GAAP if those standards are of sufficiently high quality. Under this approach, the SEC and FASB still have sovereignty over U.S. accounting standards, but those standards should largely converge to IFRS over time.

- **November 2011:** The SEC issued two studies comparing U.S. GAAP and IFRS and analyzing how IFRS are applied globally. In these studies, the SEC identifies key differences between U.S. GAAP and IFRS, and notes that U.S. GAAP provides significantly more guidance about particular transactions or industries. The SEC also notes some diversity in the application of IFRS that suggests the potential for non-comparability of financial statements across countries and industries.

- **December 2011:** The SEC postpones making a final determination concerning whether and how to incorporate IFRS into U.S. GAAP until sometime in 2012.

At the time this text is being written, it still is unclear whether or how IFRS will be incorporated into U.S. GAAP. The SEC might require (a) whole-scale adoption of IFRS by U.S. companies, (b) a standard-by-standard endorsement of IFRS standards in the U.S., or (c) a condorsement process like the SEC has suggested. Regardless, convergence already is gradually occurring through cooperation between the FASB and IASB.

SEC Chairman Schapiro has indicated that the first time U.S. companies could be required to report under IFRS would be no earlier than 2015. In the meantime, although U.S. companies continue to follow U.S. GAAP, you should be aware of important differences that exist between U.S. GAAP and IFRS. In fact, beginning in 2011, IFRS are tested on the CPA exam along with U.S. GAAP. Therefore, **International Financial Reporting Standards** boxes are included throughout the text to highlight circumstances in which IFRS differs from U.S. GAAP. Your instructor may assign end-of-chapter IFRS questions, exercises, problems, and cases that explore these differences. Throughout the remainder of the text, IFRS-related material is marked with the globe icon that you see to the left of this paragraph.

## The Establishment of Accounting Standards

**DUE PROCESS.**   When developing accounting standards, a standard setter must understand the nuances of the economic transactions the standards address and the views of key constituents concerning how accounting would best capture that economic reality. Therefore, the FASB undertakes a series of elaborate information-gathering steps before issuing an Accounting Standards Update. These steps include open hearings, deliberations, and requests for written comments from interested parties. Illustration 1–7 outlines the FASB's standard-setting process.

● LO1–4

**FINANCIAL Reporting Case**

Q2, p. 3

**Illustration 1–7**
The FASB's Standard-Setting Process

The FASB undertakes a series of information-gathering steps before issuing an Accounting Standards Update.

| Step | Explanation |
|---|---|
| 1. | The Board receives requests/recommendations for possible projects and reconsideration of existing standards from various sources. |
| 2. | The FASB Chairman decides whether to add a project to the technical agenda, subject to oversight by the Foundation's Board of Trustees and after appropriate consultation with FASB Members and others. |
| 3. | The Board deliberates at one or more public meetings the various issues identified and analyzed by the staff. |
| 4. | The Board issues an Exposure Draft. (In some projects, a Discussion Paper may be issued to obtain input at an early stage that is used to develop an Exposure Draft.) |
| 5. | The Board holds a public roundtable meeting on the Exposure Draft, if necessary. |
| 6. | The staff analyzes comment letters, public roundtable discussion, and any other information. The Board redeliberates the proposed provisions at public meetings. |
| 7. | The Board issues an Accounting Standards Update describing amendments to the Accounting Standards Codification. |

These steps are the FASB's attempt to acquire information to help determine the preferred method of accounting. However, as a practical matter this information gathering also exposes the FASB to much political pressure by various interest groups who want an accounting treatment that serves their economic best interest. As you will see later in this chapter, the FASB's concepts statements indicate that standards should present information in a neutral manner, rather than being designed to favor particular economic consequences, but sometimes politics intrudes on the standard-setting process.

**POLITICS IN STANDARD SETTING.**    A change in accounting standards can result in a substantial redistribution of wealth within our economy. Therefore, it is no surprise that the FASB has had to deal with intense political pressure over controversial accounting standards, and sometimes has changed standards in response to that pressure.

One example of the effect of politics on standard setting occurred in the mid-1990's with respect to accounting for employee stock options. The accounting standards in place at that time typically did not recognize compensation expense if a company paid their employees with stock options rather than cash. Yet, the company was sacrificing something of value to compensate its employees. Therefore, the FASB proposed that companies recognize compensation expense in an amount equal to the fair value of the options, with some of the expense recognized in each of the periods in which the employee earned the options. Numerous companies (particularly in California's Silicon Valley, where high-tech companies had been compensating employees with stock options to a great extent) applied intense political pressure against this proposal, and eventually the FASB backed down and required only disclosure of options-related compensation expense in the notes to the financial statements. Nearly a decade later, this contentious issue resurfaced in a more amenable political climate, and the FASB issued a standard requiring expense recognition as originally proposed. This issue is discussed at greater length in Chapter 19.

Another example of politics in standard setting relates to accounting for business combinations. GAAP used to allow two separate and distinct methods of accounting for business combinations: the pooling of interests method and the purchase method. A key issue involved goodwill, an intangible asset that arises only in business combinations accounted for using the purchase method. Under the then-existing standards, goodwill was amortized (expensed) over its estimated useful life. To avoid that amortization expense, many companies incurred costs to structure their business combinations as a pooling of interests. The FASB proposed eliminating the pooling method. As you can guess, that proposal met with strong opposition. Companies that were actively engaged in business acquisitions argued that they would not undertake business combinations important to economic growth if they were required to use the purchase method, due to the negative impact on earnings caused by goodwill amortization. Eventually the FASB compromised.[21] In the final standard issued in 2001, only the purchase method, now called the acquisition method, is acceptable, but to soften the impact, the resulting goodwill is *not* amortized.[22] We discuss goodwill and its measurement in Chapters 10 and 11.

A recent example of the political process at work in standard setting is the controversy surrounding the implementation of the fair value accounting standard issued in 2007. Many financial assets and liabilities are reported at fair value in the balance sheet, and many types of fair value changes are included in net income. Some have argued that fair values were estimated in a manner that exacerbated the financial crisis of 2008–2009 by forcing financial institutions to take larger than necessary write-downs of financial assets in the illiquid markets that existed at that time. As discussed further in Chapter 12, pressure from lobbyists and politicians influenced the FASB to revise its guidance on recognizing investment losses in these situations, and ongoing pressure remains to reduce the extent to which fair value changes are included in the determination of net income.

---

[21]Jonathan Weil, "FASB Backs Down on Goodwill-Accounting Rules," *The Wall Street Journal* (December 7, 2000).

[22]FASB ASC 805: Business Combinations (previously "Business Combinations," *Statement of Financial Accounting Standards No. 141 (revised)* (Norwalk, Conn.: FASB, 2007)), and FASB ASC 350: Intangibles—Goodwill and Other (previously "Goodwill and Other Intangible Assets," *Statement of Financial Accounting Standards No. 142* (Norwalk, Conn.: FASB, 2001)).

# International Financial Reporting Standards

**Politics in International Standard Setting.** Political pressures on the IASB's standard-setting process are severe. One source of pressure comes from the international business community. Unlike the FASB, which is funded through fees paid by companies listing securities on stock exchanges, the IASB receives much of its funding through voluntary donations by accounting firms and corporations, and there is concern that this financial support may compromise the IASB's independence. In fact, one of the milestones specified by the SEC for the eventual adoption of IFRS in the U.S. is that the IASB's independence be increased by creating a funding mechanism more like the FASB's.

Another source of political pressure arises from the fact that politicians from countries that use IFRS lobby for the standards they prefer. The European Union (EU) is a particularly important adopter of IFRS and utilizes a formal evaluation process for determining whether an IFRS standard will be endorsed for use in EU countries. Economic consequences for EU member nations are an important consideration in that process. For example, in 2003 and 2004 French banks lobbied against some aspects of accounting for financial instruments stridently enough that the EU eventually "carved out" two key provisions before endorsing the relevant accounting standard (IAS 39).[24] Similarly, in 2008 the EU successfully pressured the IASB to suspend its due process and immediately allow reclassification of investments so that EU banks could avoid recognizing huge losses during a financial crisis.[25] Highlighting the importance of politics in the IASB, as of July 1, 2011, the chairman of the IASB is Hans Hoogervorst, a Dutch securities regulator with much diplomatic experience but no formal accounting background. Although the IASB's vice-chairman, Ian Mackintosh, has a long career in accounting and standard setting, the appointment of a nonaccountant as IASB Chairman perhaps signals a priority on political considerations.

● LO1–11

> **Charlie McCreevy, European Commissioner for Internal Markets and Services**
> Accounting is now far too important to be left solely to . . . accountants![23]

# Encouraging High-Quality Financial Reporting

Numerous factors affect the quality of financial reporting. In this section, we discuss the role of the auditor, recent reforms in financial reporting, and the debate about whether accounting standards should emphasize rules or underlying principles.

● LO1–5

## The Role of the Auditor

It is the responsibility of management to apply GAAP appropriately. Another group, auditors, serves as an independent intermediary to help ensure that management has in fact appropriately applied GAAP in preparing the company's financial statements. Auditors examine (audit) financial statements to express a professional, independent opinion about whether the statements fairly present the company's financial position, its results of operations, and its cash flows in compliance with GAAP. Audits add credibility to the financial statements, increasing the confidence of those who rely on the information. Auditors, therefore, play an important role in the capital markets.

The report of the independent auditors of **Dell Inc.**'s financial statements is in the annual report information in Appendix B located at the back of the text. In that report, the accounting

**FINANCIAL Reporting Case**

Q3, p. 3

*Auditors* express an opinion on the compliance of financial statements with GAAP.

---

[23]Charlie McCreevy, Keynote Address, "Financial Reporting in a Changing World" Conference, Brussels, 5/7/2009.

[24]Stephen A. Zeff, "IFRS Developments in the USA and EU, and Some Implications for Australia," *Australian Accounting Review* 18 (2008), pp. 275–282.

[25]Sarah Deans and Dane Mott, "Lowering Standards," www.morganmarkets.com, 10/14/2008.

firm of **PricewaterhouseCoopers LLP** stated that "In our opinion, the consolidated financial statements listed in the accompanying index present fairly . . . , in conformity with accounting principles generally accepted in the United States of America." This is known as a clean opinion. Had there been any material departures from GAAP or other problems that caused the auditors to question the fairness of the statements, the report would have been modified to inform readers. Normally, companies correct any material misstatements that auditors identify in the course of an audit, so companies usually receive clean opinions. The audit report for public companies also provides the auditors' opinion on the effectiveness of the company's internal control over financial reporting. We discuss this second opinion in the next section.

In most states, only individuals licensed as **certified public accountants (CPAs)** can represent that the financial statements have been audited in accordance with generally accepted auditing standards. Requirements to be licensed as a CPA vary from state to state, but all states specify education, testing, and experience requirements. The testing requirement is to pass the Uniform CPA Examination.

## Financial Reporting Reform

The dramatic collapse of **Enron** in 2001 and the dismantling of the international public accounting firm of **Arthur Andersen** in 2002 severely shook U.S. capital markets. The credibility of the accounting profession itself as well as of corporate America was called into question. Public outrage over accounting scandals at high-profile companies like **WorldCom, Xerox, Merck, Adelphia Communications**, and others increased the pressure on lawmakers to pass measures that would restore credibility and investor confidence in the financial reporting process.

> **Paul Sarbanes—U.S. Senator**
> We confront an increasing crisis of confidence with the public's trust in our markets. If this continues, I think it poses a real threat to our economic health.[26]

Driven by these pressures, Congress acted swiftly and passed the *Public Company Accounting Reform and Investor Protection Act of 2002,* commonly referred to as the *Sarbanes-Oxley Act* or *SOX* for the two congressmen who sponsored the bill. SOX applies to public securities-issuing entities. It provides for the regulation of auditors and the types of services they furnish to clients, increases accountability of corporate executives, addresses conflicts of interest for securities analysts, and provides for stiff criminal penalties for violators. Illustration 1–8 outlines key provisions of the Act.

Section 404 is perhaps the most controversial provision of SOX. It requires that company management document internal controls and report on their adequacy. Auditors also must express an opinion on whether the company has maintained effective control over financial reporting.

No one argues the importance of adequate internal controls, but many argued that the benefits of Section 404 did not justify the costs of complying with it. Research provides evidence that 404 reports affect investors' risk assessments and companies' stock prices, indicating these reports are seen as useful by investors.[27] Unfortunately, it is not possible to quantify the more important benefit of potentially avoiding business failures like Enron by focusing attention on the implementation and maintenance of adequate internal controls.

The costs of 404 compliance initially were quite steep. For example, one survey of Fortune 1,000 companies estimated that large companies spent, on average, approximately $8.5 million and $4.8 million (including internal costs and auditor fees) during the first two years of the act to comply with 404 reporting requirements.[28] As expected, the costs dropped significantly in the second year, and likely continued to drop as the efficiency of internal control audits increased. Fortunately, many companies now perceive that the benefits of these internal control reports exceed their costs.[29]

We revisit Section 404 in Chapter 7 in the context of an introduction to internal controls.

*Auditors offer credibility to financial statements.*

*Certified public accountants (CPAs) are licensed by states to provide audit services.*

Sarbanes-Oxley

---

[26]James Kuhnhenn, "Bush Vows to Punish Corporate Lawbreakers," *San Jose Mercury News* (July 9, 2002), p. 8A.

[27]Hollis Ashbaugh Skaife, Daniel W. Collins, William R. Kinney, Jr., and Ryan LaFond. "The Effect of SOX Internal Control Deficiencies on Firm Risk and Cost of Equity," *Journal of Accounting Research* 47 (2009), pp. 1–43.

[28]"Sarbanes-Oxley 404 Costs and Implementation Issues: Spring 2006 Survey Update," CRA International (April 17, 2006).

[29]Protiviti, Inc., *2011 Sarbanes-Oxley Compliance Survey* (June, 2011).

**Key Provisions of the Sarbanes-Oxley Act:**

- **Oversight board.** The five-member (two accountants) Public Company Accounting Oversight Board has the authority to establish standards dealing with auditing, quality control, ethics, independence and other activities relating to the preparation of audit reports, or can choose to delegate these responsibilities to the AICPA. Prior to the act, the AICPA set auditing standards. The SEC has oversight and enforcement authority.

- **Corporate executive accountability.** Corporate executives must personally certify the financial statements and company disclosures with severe financial penalties and the possibility of imprisonment for fraudulent misstatement.

- **Nonaudit services.** The law makes it unlawful for the auditors of public companies to perform a variety of nonaudit services for audit clients. Prohibited services include bookkeeping, internal audit outsourcing, appraisal or valuation services, and various other consulting services. Other nonaudit services, including tax services, require pre-approval by the audit committee of the company being audited.

- **Retention of work papers.** Auditors of public companies must retain all audit or review work papers for seven years or face the threat of a prison term for willful violations.

- **Auditor rotation.** Lead audit partners are required to rotate every five years. Mandatory rotation of audit firms came under consideration.

- **Conflicts of interest.** Audit firms are not allowed to audit public companies whose chief executives worked for the audit firm and participated in that company's audit during the preceding year.

- **Hiring of auditor.** Audit firms are hired by the audit committee of the board of directors of the company, not by company management.

- **Internal control.** Section 404 of the act requires that company management document and assess the effectiveness of all internal control processes that could affect financial reporting. The PCAOB's *Auditing Standard No. 2* (since replaced by *Auditing Standard No. 5*) requires that the company auditors express an opinion on whether the company has maintained effective internal control over financial reporting.

**Illustration 1–8**

Public Company Accounting Reform and Investor Protection Act of 2002 (Sarbanes-Oxley)

# A Move Away from Rules-Based Standards?

The accounting scandals at Enron and other companies involved managers using elaborately structured transactions to try to circumvent specific rules in accounting standards. One consequence of those scandals was a rekindled debate over **principles-based**, or more recently termed **objectives-oriented**, versus **rules-based** accounting standards. In fact, a provision of the Sarbanes-Oxley Act required the SEC to study the issue and provide a report to Congress on its findings. That report, issued in July 2003, recommended that accounting standards be developed using an objectives-oriented approach.[30]

A principles-based, or objectives-oriented, approach to standard-setting stresses professional judgment, as opposed to following a list of rules.

An objectives-oriented approach to standard setting emphasizes using professional judgment, as opposed to following a list of rules, when choosing how to account for a transaction. Proponents of an objectives-oriented approach argue that a focus on professional judgment means that there are few rules to sidestep, and we are more likely to arrive at an appropriate accounting treatment. Detractors, on the other hand, argue that the absence of detailed rules opens the door to even more abuse, because management can use the latitude provided by objectives to justify their preferred accounting approach. Even in the absence of intentional misuse, reliance on professional judgment might result in different interpretations for similar transactions, raising concerns about comparability. Also, detailed rules help auditors withstand pressure from clients who want a more favorable accounting treatment, and help companies ensure that they are complying with GAAP and avoid litigation or SEC inquiry. For these reasons, it's challenging to avoid providing detailed rules in the U.S. reporting environment. Given ongoing efforts to converge FASB and IASB standards, it is likely that this debate will continue.

Regardless of whether accounting standards are based more on rules or on objectives, prior research highlights that there is some potential for abuse, either by structuring

---

[30]"Study Pursuant to Section 108 (d) of the Sarbanes-Oxley Act of 2002 on the Adoption by the United States Financial Reporting System of a Principles-Based Accounting System," Securities and Exchange Commission (July 2003).

transactions around precise rules or opportunistically interpreting underlying principles.[31] The key is whether management is dedicated to high-quality financial reporting. It appears that poor ethical values on the part of management are at the heart of accounting abuses and scandals like **Enron** and **WorldCom**, so we now turn to a discussion of ethics in the accounting profession.

## Ethics in Accounting

*Ethics* **deals with the ability to distinguish right from wrong.**

**Ethics** is a term that refers to a code or moral system that provides criteria for evaluating right and wrong. An ethical dilemma is a situation in which an individual or group is faced with a decision that tests this code. Many of these dilemmas are simple to recognize and resolve. For example, have you ever been tempted to call your professor and ask for an extension on the due date of an assignment by claiming a pretended illness? Temptation like this will test your personal ethics.

Accountants, like others in the business world, are faced with many ethical dilemmas, some of which are complex and difficult to resolve. For instance, the capital markets' focus on near-term profits may tempt a company's management to bend or even break accounting rules to inflate reported net income. In these situations, technical competence is not enough to resolve the dilemma.

**ETHICS AND PROFESSIONALISM.** One characteristic that distinguishes a profession from other occupations is the acceptance by its members of a responsibility for the interests of those it serves. Ethical behavior is expected of those engaged in a profession. That expectation often is articulated in a code of ethics. For example, law and medicine are professions that have their own codes of professional ethics. These codes provide guidance and rules to members in the performance of their professional responsibilities.

Public accounting has achieved widespread recognition as a profession. The AICPA, the national organization of certified public accountants, has its own Code of Professional Conduct that prescribes the ethical conduct members should strive to achieve. Similarly, the **Institute of Management Accountants (IMA)**—the primary national organization of accountants working in industry and government—has its own code of ethics, as does the **Institute of Internal Auditors**—the national organization of accountants providing internal auditing services for their own organizations.

**ANALYTICAL MODEL FOR ETHICAL DECISIONS.** Ethical codes are informative and helpful, but the motivation to behave ethically must come from within oneself and not just from the fear of penalties for violating professional codes. Presented below is a sequence of steps that provide a framework for analyzing ethical issues. These steps can help you apply your own sense of right and wrong to ethical dilemmas:[32]

**Step 1.** Determine the facts of the situation. This involves determining the who, what, where, when, and how.

**Step 2.** Identify the ethical issue and the stakeholders. Stakeholders may include shareholders, creditors, management, employees, and the community.

**Step 3.** Identify the values related to the situation. For example, in some situations confidentiality may be an important value that might conflict with the right to know.

**Step 4.** Specify the alternative courses of action.

**Step 5.** Evaluate the courses of action specified in step 4 in terms of their consistency with the values identified in step 3. This step may or may not lead to a suggested course of action.

---

[31]Mark W. Nelson, John A. Elliott, and Robin L. Tarpley, "Evidence From Auditors About Managers' and Auditors Earnings Management Decisions," *The Accounting Review* 77 (2002), pp. 175–202.

[32]Adapted from Harold Q. Langenderfer and Joanne W. Rockness, "Integrating Ethics into the Accounting Curriculum: Issues, Problems, and Solutions," *Issues in Accounting Education* (Spring 1989). These steps are consistent with those provided by the American Accounting Association's Advisory Committee on Professionalism and Ethics in their publication *Ethics in the Accounting Curriculum: Cases and Readings, 1990.*

**Step 6.**  Identify the consequences of each possible course of action. If step 5 does not provide a course of action, assess the consequences of each possible course of action for all of the stakeholders involved.

**Step 7.**  Make your decision and take any indicated action.

Ethical dilemmas are presented throughout the text. These dilemmas are designed to raise your awareness of accounting issues with ethical ramifications. The analytical steps outlined above provide a framework you can use to evaluate these situations. In addition, your instructor may assign end-of-chapter ethics cases for further discussion and application.

# Ethical Dilemma

You recently have been employed by a large retail chain that sells sporting goods. One of your tasks is to help prepare periodic financial statements for external distribution. The chain's largest creditor, National Savings & Loan, requires quarterly financial statements, and you are currently working on the statements for the three-month period ending June 30, 2013.

During the months of May and June, the company spent $1,200,000 on a hefty radio and TV advertising campaign. The $1,200,000 included the costs of producing the commercials as well as the radio and TV time purchased to air the commercials. All of the costs were charged to advertising expense. The company's chief financial officer (CFO) has asked you to prepare a June 30 adjusting entry to remove the costs from advertising expense and to set up an asset called *prepaid advertising* that will be expensed in July. The CFO explained that "This advertising campaign has led to significant sales in May and June and I think it will continue to bring in customers through the month of July. By recording the ad costs as an asset, we can match the cost of the advertising with the additional July sales. Besides, if we expense the advertising in May and June, we will show an operating loss on our income statement for the quarter. The bank requires that we continue to show quarterly profits in order to maintain our loan in good standing."

# THE CONCEPTUAL FRAMEWORK

**PART B**

● LO1–6

**FINANCIAL Reporting Case**

Q4, p. 3

The conceptual framework does not prescribe GAAP. It provides an underlying foundation for accounting standards.

Sturdy buildings are built on sound foundations. The U.S. Constitution is the foundation for the laws of our land. The **conceptual framework** has been described as an "Accounting Constitution" because it provides the underlying foundation for U.S. accounting standards. More formally, it is a coherent system of interrelated objectives and fundamentals that is intended to lead to consistent standards and that prescribes the nature, function, and limits of financial accounting and reporting. The fundamentals are the underlying concepts of accounting that guide the selection of events to be accounted for, the measurement of those events, and the means of summarizing and communicating them to interested parties.[33] The conceptual framework provides structure and direction to financial accounting and reporting but does not directly prescribe GAAP.

The FASB disseminates this framework through Statements of Financial Accounting Concepts *(SFACs). SFAC 1* and *SFAC 2* deal with the Objectives and Qualitative Characteristics of financial information, respectively. *SFAC 3,* describing the elements of financial statements, was superseded by *SFAC 6.* The objectives of financial reporting for nonprofit organizations are the subject of *SFAC 4* and are not covered in this text. Concept Statements 5 and 7 deal with recognition and measurement.

Earlier in the chapter we discussed the ongoing efforts of standard setters to converge U.S. GAAP and International Financial Reporting Standards. As part of that process, the FASB and the IASB are working together to develop a common and improved conceptual

---

[33]"Conceptual Framework for Financial Accounting and Reporting: Elements of Financial Statements and Their Measurement," *Discussion Memorandum* (Stamford, Conn.: FASB, 1976), p. 2.

framework that will provide the foundation for developing principles-based, common standards. Only the first phase of the project is complete. That phase contains two chapters which replace *SFAC 1* and *SFAC 2,* and was issued as *SFAC 8* in 2010.[34] As the project progresses, prior Concepts Statements will be replaced by new chapters in *SFAC 8.* It likely will take several years before the entire project is completed.

In the remainder of this section we discuss the components of the conceptual framework that influence financial statements as depicted in Illustration 1–9. The financial statements and their elements are most informative when they possess specific qualitative characteristics. Proper recognition and measurement of financial information rely on several assumptions and principles that underlie the financial reporting process.

## Illustration 1–9

The Conceptual Framework

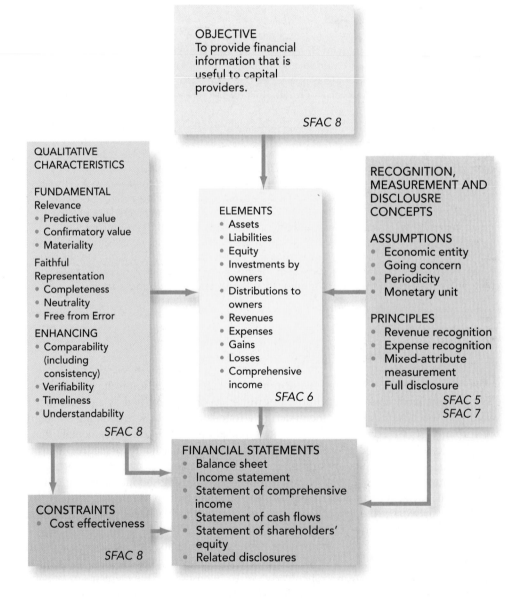

Our discussions of the objective and qualitative characteristics of financial reporting information are based on *SFAC 8,* while the remainder of our conceptual framework coverage relies on the relevant FASB Concept Statements still in effect. We discuss and illustrate the financial statements themselves in subsequent chapters.

---

[34]"Conceptual Framework for Financial Reporting: Chapter 1, The Objective of General Purpose Financial Reporting, and Chapter 3, Qualitative Characteristics of Useful Financial Information," *Statement of Financial Accounting Concepts No. 8* (Norwalk, Conn.: FASB, 2010).

# International Financial Reporting Standards

**Role of the conceptual framework.** The conceptual frameworks in U.S. GAAP and IFRS are very similar, and are converging even more with ongoing efforts by the FASB and IASB. However, in U.S. GAAP, the conceptual framework primarily provides guidance to standard setters to help them develop high-quality standards. In IFRS the conceptual framework guides standard setting, but in addition it is supposed to provide a basis for practitioners to make accounting judgments when another IFRS standard does not apply. Also, IFRS emphasizes the overarching concept of the financial statements providing a "true and fair representation" of the company. U.S. GAAP does not include a similar requirement, but U.S. auditing standards require this consideration.

● LO1–11

# Objective of Financial Reporting

The objective of general purpose financial reporting is to provide financial information about companies that is useful to capital providers in making decisions. For example, investors decide whether to buy, sell, or hold equity or debt securities, and creditors decide whether to provide or settle loans.[35] Information that is useful to capital providers may also be useful to other users of financial reporting information, such as regulators or taxing authorities.

● LO1–7

   Both investors and creditors are directly interested in the amount, timing, and uncertainty of a company's future cash flows. Information about a company's economic resources (assets) and claims against resources (liabilities) also is useful. Not only does this information about resources and claims provide insight into future cash flows, it also helps decision makers identify the company's financial strengths and weaknesses and assess liquidity and solvency.

# Qualitative Characteristics of Financial Reporting Information

What characteristics should information have to best meet the objective of financial reporting? Illustration 1–10 indicates the desirable qualitative characteristics of financial reporting information, presented in the form of a hierarchy of their perceived importance. Notice that these characteristics are intended to enhance the **decision usefulness** of information.

**Illustration 1–10**   Hierarchy of Qualitative Characteristics of Financial Information

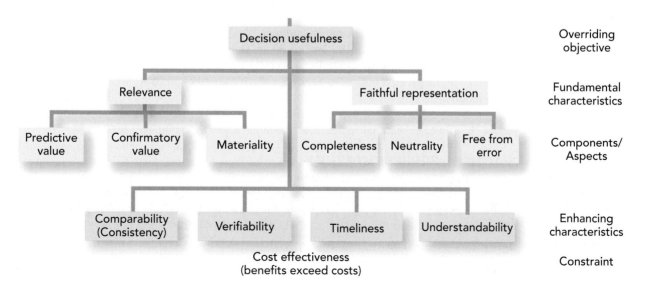

---

[35]Ibid., par. OB2.

# Fundamental Qualitative Characteristics

**To be useful for decision making, information should possess the qualities of *relevance* and *faithful representation*.**

For financial information to be useful, it should possess the fundamental decision-specific qualities of relevance and faithful representation. Both are critical. Information is of little value if it's not relevant. And even if information is relevant, it is not as useful if it doesn't faithfully represent the economic phenomenon it purports to represent. Let's look closer at each of these two qualitative characteristics, including the components that make those characteristics desirable. We also consider other characteristics that enhance usefulness.

**RELEVANCE.** Obviously, to make a difference in the decision process, information must be relevant to the decision. Relevance in the context of financial reporting means that the information must possess predictive value and/or confirmatory value, typically both. For example, current-period net income has predictive value if it helps users predict a company's future cash flows, and it has confirmatory value if it helps investors confirm or change their prior assessments regarding a company's cash-flow generating ability.

Predictive and confirmatory value are central to the concept of "earnings quality," the ability of reported earnings (income) to predict a company's future earnings. We revisit this concept frequently throughout this textbook in order to explore the impact on earnings quality of various topics under discussion. For instance, in Chapter 4 we discuss the contents of the income statement and certain classifications used in that statement to help analysts separate a company's transitory earnings from its permanent earnings. This separation is critical to a meaningful prediction of future earnings because it's permanent earnings that are likely to recur. In later chapters, we look at how various financial reporting decisions affect earnings quality.

**Information is *material* if it has an effect on decisions.**

Financial information is material if omitting it or misstating it could affect users' decisions. Materiality is an aspect of relevance that depends on a company's particular situation and is based on the nature or magnitude of the item that is being reported. If information is immaterial, it's not relevant.

One consequence of considering materiality is that GAAP need not be followed if an item is immaterial. For example, GAAP requires that receivables be measured at their "net realizable value." If bad debts are anticipated, they should be estimated and subtracted from the face amount of receivables for balance sheet measurement.[36] However, if the amount of anticipated bad debts is not considered to be large enough to affect decisions made by users, it's OK to wait and just record the effects of bad debts when the receivable has gone bad rather than having to estimate bad debts for existing receivables.[37]

The threshold for materiality often depends on the *relative* dollar amount of the transaction. For example, $10,000 in total anticipated bad debts for a multibillion dollar company like **Dell** would not be considered material. This same $10,000 amount, however, might easily be material for a neighborhood pizza parlor. Because of the context-specific nature of materiality, the FASB has been reluctant to establish any quantitative materiality guidelines. The threshold for materiality has been left to the subjective judgment of the company preparing the financial statements and its auditors.

**Professional judgment determines what amount is material in each situation.**

Materiality often relates to the nature of the item as well. It depends on qualitative as well as quantitative considerations. For example, an illegal payment of a $10,000 bribe to an official of a foreign government to secure a valuable contract probably would be considered material qualitatively even if the amount is small relative to the size of the company. Similarly, a small dollar amount that changes a net loss to a net income for the reporting period could be viewed as material to financial statement users for qualitative reasons.[38]

**Faithful representation means agreement between a measure and a real-world phenomenon that the measure is supposed to represent.**

**FAITHFUL REPRESENTATION.** Faithful representation exists when there is agreement between a measure or description and the phenomenon it purports to represent. For example, assume that the term *inventory* in the balance sheet of a retail company is understood by external users to represent items that are intended for sale in the ordinary course of business. If inventory includes, say, machines used to produce inventory, then it lacks faithful representation.

---

[36]This is called the *allowance method* of accounting for bad debts.
[37]This is called the *direct write-off method* of accounting for bad debts.
[38]Conceptual Framework for Financial Reporting: Chapter 1, The Objective of General Purpose Financial Reporting, and Chapter 3, Qualitative Characteristics of Useful Financial Information, Statement of Financial Accounting Concepts No. 8 (Norwalk, Conn.: FASB, 2010).

To break it down further, faithful representation requires that information be *complete, neutral,* and *free from error.* A depiction of an economic phenomenon is complete if it includes all the information necessary for faithful representation of the economic phenomena that it purports to represent.[39] Omitting a portion of that information can cause it to be false or misleading and thus not helpful.

A financial accounting standard, and the standard-setting process, is "neutral" if it is free from bias. You learned earlier that changes in accounting standards can lead to adverse economic consequences for certain companies and that political pressure is sometimes brought to bear on the standard-setting process in hopes of achieving particular outcomes. Accounting standards should be established with the goal of providing high-quality information, and should try not to achieve particular social outcomes or favor particular groups or companies. The FASB faces a difficult task in maintaining neutrality in the face of economic consequences and resulting political pressures.

Representational faithfulness also is enhanced if information is free from error, meaning that there are no errors or omissions in the description of the amount or the process used to report the amount. Uncertainty is a fact of life when we measure many items of financial information included in financial statements. Estimates are common, and some inaccuracy is likely. An estimate is represented faithfully if it is described clearly and accurately as being an estimate, and financial statement users are given enough information to understand the potential for inaccuracy that exists.

Many accountants have recommended that we deal with the potential for error by employing conservatism. Conservatism means that accountants require greater verification before recognizing good news than bad news. The result is that losses are reflected in net income more quickly than are gains, and net assets tend to be biased downwards.

*SFAC 8* explicitly rejects conservatism as a desirable characteristic of accounting information, stating that conservatism undermines representational faithfulness by being inconsistent with neutrality. Nevertheless, some accounting practices, such as the lower-of-cost-or-market method for measuring inventory (Chapter 9), appear to be generated by a desire to be conservative. One justification for these practices is that investors and creditors who lose money on their investments are less likely to sue the company if bad news has been exaggerated and good news underestimated. Another justification is that conservative accounting can trigger debt covenants that allow creditors to protect themselves from bad management. So, despite the lack of support for conservatism in the conceptual framework, it is likely to persist as an important consideration in accounting practice and in the application of some accounting standards.

## Enhancing Qualitative Characteristics

Illustration 1–10 identifies four *enhancing* qualitative characteristics, *comparability (including consistency), verifiability, timeliness,* and *understandability.*

Comparability helps users see similarities and differences between events and conditions. We already have discussed the importance of investors and creditors being able to compare information *among companies* to make their resource allocation decisions. Closely related to comparability is the notion that consistency of accounting practices over time permits valid comparisons *among different reporting periods.* The predictive and confirmatory value of information is enhanced if users can compare the performance of a company over time.[40] In the **Dell** financial statements and disclosure notes, notice that disclosure Note 1 includes a summary of significant accounting policies. If Dell were to change one of these policies, new numbers might not be comparable to numbers measured under a previous policy. To be sure readers are aware of the change, Dell would need to provide full disclosure in the notes to the financial statements.

Verifiability implies that different knowledgeable and independent measurers would reach consensus regarding whether information is a faithful representation of what it is intended to

*A depiction is complete if it includes all information necessary for faithful representation.*

*Neutrality implies freedom from bias.*

*Representational faithfulness is enhanced if information is free from error.*

*Conservatism is inconsistent with neutrality.*

*Accounting information should be comparable across different companies and over different time periods.*

*Accounting information is consistent if it is measured and reported the same way in each time period.*

*Information is verifiable if different measurers would reach consensus about whether it is representationally faithful.*

---

[39]Ibid., par. QC13.

[40]Companies occasionally do change their accounting practices, which makes it difficult for users to make comparisons among different reporting periods. Chapter 4 and Chapter 20 describe the disclosures that a company makes in this situation to restore consistency among periods.

depict. Direct verification involves observing the item being depicted. For example, the historical cost of a parcel of land to be reported in a company's balance sheet usually is highly verifiable. The cost can be traced to an exchange transaction, the purchase of the land. On the other hand, the fair value of that land is much more difficult to verify. Appraisers could differ in their assessment of fair value. Verification of their estimates would be indirect, involving examination of their valuation models and assessments of the reasonableness of model inputs. The term *objectivity* often is linked to verifiability. The historical cost of the land is objective and easy to verify, but the land's fair value is subjective, and may be influenced by the measurer's past experience and biases. A measurement that is subjective is more difficult to verify, which may make users doubt its representational faithfulness.

**Information is *timely* if it is available to users before a decision is made.**

**Timeliness** also is important for information to be useful. Information is timely when it's available to users early enough to allow them to use it in their decision process. The need for timely information requires that companies provide information on a periodic basis. To enhance timeliness, the SEC requires its registrants to submit financial statement information on a quarterly as well as on an annual basis for each fiscal year.

**Information is *understandable* if users can comprehend it.**

**Understandability** means that users must be able to comprehend the information within the context of the decision being made. This is a user-specific quality because users will differ in their ability to comprehend any set of information. The overriding objective of financial reporting is to provide comprehensible information to those who have a *reasonable understanding* of business and economic activities and are diligent in studying the information.

## Key Constraint: Cost Effectiveness

Most of us learn early in life that we can't get everything we want. The latest electronic gadget may have all the qualitative characteristics that current technology can provide, but limited resources may lead us to buy a model with fewer bells and whistles. **Cost effectiveness** constrains the accounting choices we make. The benefits of endowing financial information with all the qualitative characteristics we've discussed must exceed the costs of doing so.

**Information is *cost effective* only if the benefit of increased *decision usefulness* exceeds the costs of providing that information.**

The costs of providing financial information include those of gathering, processing, and disseminating information. There also are costs to users when interpreting information. In addition, costs include possible adverse economic consequences of implementing accounting standards. For example, consider the requirement that companies that have more than one operating segment must disclose certain disaggregated financial information.[41] In addition to the costs of information gathering, processing, and communicating that information, many companies feel that this reporting requirement imposes what could be called *competitive disadvantage costs*. These companies are concerned that their competitors will gain some advantage from having access to the disaggregated data.

**The costs of providing financial information include any possible adverse economic consequences of accounting standards.**

The perceived benefit from this or any accounting standard is increased *decision usefulness* of the information provided, which, ideally, improves the resource allocation process. It is inherently impossible to quantify this benefit. The elaborate information-gathering process undertaken by the FASB in setting accounting standards is an attempt to assess both costs and benefits of a proposed accounting standard, even if in a subjective, nonquantifiable manner.

## Elements of Financial Statements

**The 10 elements of financial statements defined in *SFAC 6* describe financial position and periodic performance.**

*SFAC 6* defines 10 elements of financial statements. These elements are "the building blocks with which financial statements are constructed—the classes of items that financial statements comprise."[42] They focus directly on items related to reporting financial position and measuring performance. The *accrual accounting* model actually is embodied in the element definitions. For now, we list and define the elements in Illustration 1–11. You will learn much more about these elements in subsequent chapters.

---

[41]FASB ASC 280: Segment Reporting (previously "Disclosures about Segments of an Enterprise and Related Information," *Statement of Financial Accounting Standards No. 131* (Norwalk, Conn.: FASB, 1997)).

[42]"Elements of Financial Statements," *Statement of Financial Accounting Concepts No. 6* (Stamford, Conn.: FASB, 1985), par. 5.

| Elements of Financial Statements | |
|---|---|
| **Assets** | Probable future economic benefits obtained or controlled by a particular entity as a result of past transactions or events. |
| **Liabilities** | Probable future sacrifices of economic benefits arising from present obligations of a particular entity to transfer assets or provide services to other entities in the future as a result of past transactions or events. |
| **Equity (or net assets)** | Called shareholders' equity or stockholders' equity for a corporation, it is the residual interest in the assets of an entity that remains after deducting its liabilities. |
| **Investments by owners** | Increases in equity of a particular business enterprise resulting from transfers to it from other entities of something of value to obtain or increase ownership interests in it. |
| **Distributions to owners** | Decreases in equity of a particular enterprise resulting from transfers to owners. |
| **Comprehensive income** | The change in equity of a business enterprise during a period from transactions and other events and circumstances from nonowner sources. It includes all changes in equity during a period except those resulting from investments by owners and distributions to owners. |
| **Revenues** | Inflows or other enhancements of assets of an entity or settlements of its liabilities during a period from delivering or producing goods, rendering services, or other activities that constitute the entity's ongoing major or central operations. |
| **Expenses** | Outflows or other using up of assets or incurrences of liabilities during a period from delivering or producing goods, rendering services, or other activities that constitute the entity's ongoing major or central operations. |
| **Gains** | Increases in equity from peripheral or incidental transactions of an entity. |
| **Losses** | Represent decreases in equity arising from peripheral or incidental transactions of an entity. |

**Illustration 1–11**

Elements of Financial Statements

# Underlying Assumptions

Though not emphasized in the FASB's concepts statements, four basic assumptions underlie GAAP: (1) the economic entity assumption, (2) the going concern assumption, (3) the periodicity assumption, and (4) the monetary unit assumption. These assumptions identify the entity that is being reported on, the assumption that the entity will continue to exist, and the frequency and denomination in which reports occur.

● LO1–8

## Economic Entity Assumption

An essential assumption is that all economic events can be identified with a particular **economic entity**. Investors desire information about an economic entity that corresponds to their ownership interest. For example, if you were considering buying some ownership stock in **Google**, you would want information on the various operating units that constitute Google. You would need information not only about its United States operations but also about its European and other international operations. The financial information for the various companies (subsidiaries) in which Google owns a controlling interest (greater than 50% ownership of voting stock) should be combined with that of Google (the parent) to provide a complete picture. The parent and its subsidiaries are separate *legal* entities but one *accounting* entity.

The *economic entity assumption* presumes that economic events can be identified specifically with an economic entity.

Another key aspect of this assumption is the distinction between the economic activities of owners and those of the company. For example, the economic activities of a sole proprietorship, Uncle Jim's Restaurant, should be separated from the activities of its owner, Uncle Jim. Uncle Jim's personal residence, for instance, is not an asset of the business.

## Going Concern Assumption

**Financial statements of a company presume the business is a *going concern*.**

Another necessary assumption is that, in the absence of information to the contrary, we anticipate that a business entity will continue to operate indefinitely. Accountants realize that the going concern assumption does not always hold since there certainly are many business failures. However, this assumption is critical to many broad and specific accounting principles. For example, the assumption provides justification for measuring many assets based on their historical costs. If it were known that an enterprise would cease operations in the near future, assets and liabilities would be measured at their current liquidation values. Similarly, when we depreciate a building over an estimated life of 40 years, we assume the business will operate that long.

## Periodicity Assumption

**The *periodicity assumption* allows the life of a company to be divided into artificial time periods to provide timely information.**

The periodicity assumption relates to the qualitative characteristic of *timeliness*. External users need *periodic* information to make decisions. This need for periodic information requires that the economic life of a company (presumed to be indefinite) be divided into artificial time periods for financial reporting. Corporations whose securities are publicly traded are required to provide financial information to the SEC on a quarterly and annual basis.[43] Financial statements often are prepared on a monthly basis for banks and others that might need more timely information.

For many companies, the annual time period (the fiscal year) is the calendar year. However, other companies have chosen a fiscal year that does not correspond to the calendar year. The accounting profession and the SEC advocate that companies adopt a fiscal year that corresponds to their natural business year. A natural business year is the 12-month period that ends when the business activities of a company reach their lowest point in the annual cycle. For example, many retailers, **Walmart** for example, have adopted a fiscal year ending on January 31. Business activity in January generally is quite slow following the very busy Christmas period. We can see from the Dell financial statements that the company's fiscal year ends at the end of January. The **Campbell Soup Company**'s fiscal year ends in July; **Clorox**'s in June; and **Monsanto**'s in August.

## Monetary Unit Assumption

**The *monetary unit assumption* states that financial statement elements should be measured in a particular monetary unit (in the United States, the U.S. dollar).**

The monetary unit or measurement scale used in financial statements is nominal units of money, without any adjustment for changes in purchasing power. In the United States, the U.S. dollar is the monetary unit used in financial statements. In the EU, the euro is the monetary unit. Other countries use other currencies as their monetary units.

One problem with use of a monetary unit like the dollar or the euro is that it is presumed to be stable over time. That is, the value of the dollar, in terms of its ability to purchase certain goods and services, is assumed to be constant over time. This assumption obviously does not strictly hold. The U.S. economy has experienced periods of rapidly changing prices. To the extent that prices are unstable, and machines, trucks, and buildings were purchased at different times, the monetary unit used to measure them is not the same. The effect of changing prices on financial information generally is discussed elsewhere in your accounting curriculum, often in an advanced accounting course.

Illustration 1–12 summaries the four assumptions underlying GAAP.

---

[43]The report that must be filed for the first three quarters of each fiscal year is Form 10-Q and the annual report is Form 10-K.

| Assumptions | Description |
|---|---|
| Economic entity | All economic events can be identified with a particular economic entity. |
| Going concern | In the absence of information to the contrary, it is anticipated that a business entity will continue to operate indefinitely. |
| Periodicity | The life of a company can be divided into artificial time periods to provide timely information to external users. |
| Monetary unit | In the United States, financial statement elements should be measured in terms of the U.S. dollar. |

**Illustration 1–12**

Summary of Assumptions Underlying GAAP

# Recognition, Measurement, and Disclosure Concepts

Now that we have identified the various elements and underlying assumptions of the financial statements, we discuss *when* the elements should be recognized (recorded) and how they should be *measured* and *disclosed*. For example, an asset was previously defined as a probable future economic benefit obtained or controlled by a company as a result of past transactions or events. But *when* should the asset be recorded, at *what* amount, and what other important information about the asset should be provided in the financial statements? *SFAC 5* addresses these issues. Recognition refers to the process of admitting information into the financial statements. Measurement is the process of associating numerical amounts with the elements. Disclosure refers to the process of including additional pertinent information in the financial statements and accompanying notes.

● LO1–9

## Recognition

**GENERAL RECOGNITION CRITERIA.**   According to *SFAC 5*, an item should be recognized in the basic financial statements when it meets the following four criteria, subject to a cost effectiveness constraint and materiality threshold:

1. *Definition.* The item meets the definition of an element of financial statements.
2. *Measurability.* The item has a relevant attribute measurable with sufficient reliability.
3. *Relevance.* The information about it is capable of making a difference in user decisions.
4. *Reliability.* The information is representationally faithful, verifiable, and neutral.[44]

Recognition criteria

These obviously are very general guidelines. *SFAC 5* provides further guidance with respect to revenue and expense recognition, and you will learn about more specific guidelines throughout this book.

**REVENUE RECOGNITION: REALIZATION.**   Revenues are inflows of assets resulting from providing a product or service to a customer. An income statement should report the results of these activities only for the time period specified in the financial statements. Therefore, the *timing* of revenue recognition is a key element of earnings measurement. Not adhering to revenue recognition criteria could result in overstating revenue and hence net income in one reporting period and, consequently, understating revenue and net income in another period.

According to the *realization principle*, revenue should be recognized when the earnings process is virtually complete and collection is reasonably assured.

   The realization principle requires that two criteria be satisfied before revenue can be recognized:

1. The earnings process is judged to be complete or virtually complete.
2. There is reasonable certainty as to the collectibility of the asset to be received (usually cash).

---

[44]"Recognition and Measurement in Financial Statements," *Statement of Financial Accounting Concepts No. 5* (Stamford, Conn.: FASB, 1984), par. 63. *SFAC 8* has replaced reliability with faithful representation as the second primary qualitative characteristic of financial information.

These criteria help ensure that a company doesn't record revenue until it has performed all or most of its earnings activities for a financially capable buyer. Notice that these criteria allow for the implementation of the accrual accounting model. Revenue should be recognized in the period it is earned, *not necessarily in the period in which cash is received.*

The timing of revenue recognition also affects the timing of asset recognition. When revenue is recognized by crediting a revenue account, the corresponding debit typically increases some asset, usually cash or an account receivable.

*Both revenue recognition criteria usually are met at the point-of-sale.*

The primary earnings activity that triggers the recognition of revenue is known as the *critical event.* The critical event for many businesses occurs at the **point-of-sale**. This usually occurs when the goods or services sold to the buyer are *delivered* (i.e., title is transferred). However, some revenue-producing activities require revenue recognition over time, rather than at one particular point in time. For example, banks earn interest revenue associated with loans outstanding with the passage of time. We discuss revenue recognition in considerable depth in Chapter 5, and discuss upcoming changes to revenue recognition requirements in the Addendum to Chapter 5.

**EXPENSE RECOGNITION: MATCHING.** Expenses were defined earlier in the chapter as "outflows or other using up of assets or incurrences of liabilities." When are expenses recognized? In practice, expense recognition often matches revenues and expenses that arise from the same transactions or other events. There is a cause-and-effect relationship between revenue and expense recognition implicit in this approach. In a given period, revenue is recognized according to the realization principle, and the **matching principle** then requires that all expenses incurred in generating that revenue also be recognized.[45] The net result is a measure—net income—that identifies the amount of profit or loss for the period provided by operations.

*According to the matching principle, expenses should be recognized in the period in which they produce revenues.*

Although these concepts are straightforward, their implementation can be difficult, because many expenses are not incurred *directly* to produce a particular amount of revenue. Instead, the association between revenue and many expenses is indirect. Therefore, expense recognition is implemented by one of four different approaches, depending on the nature of the specific expense:[46]

- **Based on an exact cause-and-effect relationship.** This approach is appropriate for *cost of goods sold,* as one example. There is a definite cause-and-effect relationship between **Dell Inc.**'s revenue from the sale of personal computers and the costs to produce those computers. Commissions paid to salespersons for obtaining revenues also is an example of an expense recognized based on this approach.

- **By associating an expense with the revenues recognized in a specific time period.** Many expenses can be related only to periods of time during which revenue is earned. For example, the monthly salary paid to an office worker is not directly related to any specific revenue event. Instead, the employee provides benefits to the company for that one month that *indirectly* relate to the revenue recognized in that same period.

- **By a systematic and rational allocation to specific time periods.** Some costs are incurred to acquire assets that provide benefits to the company for more than one reporting period, so we recognize expenses over those time periods. For example, straight-line depreciation is a "systematical and rational" way to allocate the cost of equipment to the periods in which that equipment is used to produce revenue.

---

[45]Although the term *matching principle* is used frequently to refer to this expense recognition practice, the conceptual framework does not include that term. Rather, *SFACs 5* and *6* discuss matching as a result of recognizing expenses and revenues that arise from the same underlying transactions or events. Standard setters are reluctant to apply matching more broadly, because they are concerned that doing so could result in inappropriately recognizing as assets some amounts that do not provide "probable future economic benefits," and therefore don't meet the definition of an asset. We discuss this topic more in the "Evolving GAAP" section at the end of this chapter.

[46]"Elements of Financial Statements—a replacement of FASB Concepts Statement No. 3 (incorporating an amendment of FASB Concepts Statement No. 2)" *Statement of Financial Accounting Concepts No. 6* (Norwalk, Conn.: FASB, 1985).

- **In the period incurred, without regard to related revenues.** Sometimes costs are incurred, but it is impossible to determine in which period or periods, if any, related revenues will occur. For example, let's say Google spends $1 million for a series of television commercials. It's difficult to determine when, how much, or even whether additional revenues occur as a result of that particular series of ads. As a result, we recognize advertising expenditures as expenses in the period incurred.

The timing of expense recognition also affects the timing of asset and liability recognition and de-recognition. When we debit an expense, the corresponding credit usually either decreases an asset (for example, decreasing cash because it was used to pay an employee's salary) or increases a liability (for example, increasing salaries payable to accrue wages that will be paid at a later date).

## Measurement

If an amount is to be recognized, it also must be measured. As indicated in *SFAC 5,* GAAP currently employs a "mixed attribute" measurement model. If you look at a balance sheet, for instance, you might see land measured at historical cost, accounts receivable at net realizable value, a liability at the present value of cash payments, and an investment at fair value. The attribute chosen to measure a particular item should be the one that maximizes the combination of relevance and representational faithfulness. *SFAC 5* lists five measurement attributes employed in GAAP:

1. Historical cost
2. Net realizable value
3. Current cost
4. Present (or discounted) value of future cash flows
5. Fair value

These different measurement attributes often indicate the same amount, particularly when the amount is initially recognized. However, sometimes they differ in important ways.

**HISTORICAL COST.**   We often measure assets and liabilities based on their *original transaction value,* that is, their *historical cost.* Some accountants refer to this practice as applying the *historical cost principle.* For an asset, historical cost equals the value of what is given in exchange (usually cash) for the asset at its initial acquisition. For liabilities, it is the current cash equivalent received in exchange for assuming the liability. Historical cost for long-lived, revenue-producing assets such as equipment typically is adjusted subsequent to its initial measurement by recognizing depreciation or amortization.

> *Historical cost* bases measurements on the amount given or received in the exchange transaction.

Why base measurement on historical costs? First, historical cost provides important cash flow information as it represents the cash or cash equivalent paid for an asset or received in exchange for the assumption of a liability. Second, because historical cost valuation is the result of an exchange transaction between two independent parties, the agreed-upon exchange value is objective and highly verifiable.

**NET REALIZABLE VALUE.**   Some assets are measured at their *net realizable value,* which is the amount of cash into which an asset is expected to be converted in the ordinary course of business. For example, if customers purchased goods or services on account for $10,000, and if $2,000 in bad debts were anticipated, net receivables should be valued at $8,000, the net realizable value. Departures from historical cost measurement such as this provide useful information to aid in the prediction of future cash flows.

> *Net realizable value* bases measurements on the amount of cash into which the asset or liability will be converted in the ordinary course of business.

**CURRENT COST**   Some inventories are reported at their current replacement cost, which is measured by the cost that would be incurred to purchase or reproduce the goods. This topic is discussed further in Chapter 9.

*Present value* bases measurement on future cash flows discounted for the time value of money.

**PRESENT VALUE.** Because of its importance to many accounting measurements, *present value* is the focus of an FASB concept statement, *SFAC 7,* which provides a framework for using future cash flows as the basis for accounting measurement and also asserts that the objective in valuing an asset or liability using present value is to approximate its fair value.[47] We explore the topic of present value in more depth in Chapter 6 and the application of present value in accounting measurement in subsequent chapters.

*Fair value* bases measurements on the price that would be received to sell assets or transfer liabilities in an orderly market transaction.

**FAIR VALUE.** We measure many financial assets and liabilities at *fair value* (called *current market value* originally in *SFAC 5*). Also, we use fair values when determining whether the value of nonfinancial assets like property, plant, equipment and intangible assets has been impaired. Given the complexity and growing importance of this measurement attribute, we discuss it in some detail.

Fair value is defined as:

---

The price that would be received to sell assets or paid to transfer a liability in an orderly transaction between market participants at the measurement date.

---

A key aspect of this definition is its focus on the perspective of *market participants.* For instance, if a company buys a competitor's patent, not intending to use it but merely to keep the competitor from using it, the company still will have to assign a value to the asset because a market participant would find value in using the patent.

Fair value can be measured using:
1. Market approaches.
2. Income approaches.
3. Cost approaches.

The FASB has provided a framework for measuring fair value whenever fair value is called for in applying generally accepted accounting principles.[48] The IASB recently converged to use the same framework.[49] In the framework, three types of valuation techniques can be used to measure fair value. *Market approaches* base valuation on market information. For example, the value of a share of a company's stock that's not traded actively could be estimated by multiplying the earnings of that company by the P/E (price of shares/earnings) multiples of similar companies. *Income approaches* estimate fair value by first estimating future amounts (for example, earnings or cash flows) and then mathematically converting those amounts to a single present value. You will see how to apply such techniques in Chapter 6 when we discuss time value of money concepts. *Cost approaches* determine value by estimating the amount that would be required to buy or construct an asset of similar quality and condition. A firm can use one or more of these valuation approaches, depending on availability of information, and should try to use them consistently unless changes in circumstances require a change in approach.

To increase consistency and comparability in applying this definition, the framework provides a "hierarchy" that prioritizes the inputs companies should use when determining fair value. The priority is based on three broad preference levels. The higher the level (Level 1 is the highest), the more preferable the input. The framework encourages companies to strive to obtain the highest level input available for each situation. Illustration 1–13 describes the type of inputs and provides an example for each level.

Companies also must provide detailed disclosures about their use of fair value measurements. The disclosures include a description of the inputs used to measure fair value. For recurring fair value measurements that rely on significant *unobservable* inputs (within Level 3 of the fair value hierarchy), companies should disclose the effect of the measurements on earnings (or changes in net assets) for the period.

You are not yet familiar with some of the examples mentioned in Illustration 1–13, but as you progress through the book, you will encounter many instances in which we use fair value for valuation purposes. Refer back to this discussion and speculate on the level of input that would be available to a company in these situations. When a company has the option to measure financial assets or liabilities at fair value (discussed next), we address the choices available to the company in those situations.

---

[47]"Using Cash Flow Information and Present Value in Accounting Measurements," *Statement of Financial Accounting Concepts No. 7* (Norwalk, Conn.: FASB, 2000).

[48]FASB ASC 820: Fair Value Measurements and Disclosures (previously "Fair Value Measurements," *Statement of Financial Accounting Standards No. 157* (Norwalk, Conn.: FASB, 2006)).

[49]"Fair Value Measurement," *International Financial Reporting Standard No. 13* (London, UK: IASCF, 2011).

## Illustration 1–13  Fair Value Hierarchy

| Fair Value Hierarchy | | |
| --- | --- | --- |
| Level | Inputs | Example |
| **1**<br>**Most Desirable** | Quoted market prices in active markets for identical assets or liabilities. | In Chapter 12 you will learn that certain investments in marketable securities are reported at their *fair values*. Fair value in this case would be measured using the quoted market price from the NYSE, NASDAQ, or other exchange on which the security is traded. |
| **2** | Inputs other than quoted prices that are *observable* for the asset or liability. These inputs include quoted prices for *similar* assets or liabilities in active or inactive markets and inputs that are derived principally from or corroborated by observable related market data. | In Chapter 10 we discuss how companies sometimes acquire assets with consideration other than cash. In any noncash transaction, each element of the transaction is recorded at its *fair value*. If one of the assets in the exchange is a building, for instance, then quoted market prices for similar buildings recently sold could be used to value the building or, if there were no similar buildings recently exchanged from which to obtain a comparable market price, valuation could be based on the price per square foot derived from observable market data. |
| **3**<br>**Least Desirable** | *Unobservable* inputs that reflect the entity's own assumptions about the assumptions market participants would use in pricing the asset or liability developed based on the best information available in the circumstances. | Asset retirement obligations (AROs), discussed in Chapter 10, are measured at *fair value*. Neither Level 1 nor Level 2 inputs would be possible in most ARO valuation situations. Fair value would be estimated using Level 3 inputs to include the present value of expected cash flows estimated using the entity's own data if there is no information that indicates that market participants would use different assumptions. |

The use of the fair value measurement attribute is increasing, both under U.S GAAP and IFRS. This trend, though, is controversial. Proponents of fair value cite its relevance and are convinced that historical cost information may not be useful for many types of decisions. Opponents of fair value counter that estimates of fair value may lack representational faithfulness, particularly when based on inputs from Level 3 in the fair value hierarchy, and that managers might be tempted to exploit the unverifiability of such inputs to manipulate earnings. They argue that accounting should emphasize verifiability by recognizing only those gains and other increases in fair value that actually have been realized in transactions or are virtually certain to exist.

**FAIR VALUE OPTION.**    Usually the measurement attribute we use for a particular financial statement item is not subject to choice. However, GAAP gives a company the option to report some or all of its *financial* assets and liabilities at fair value.[50] For example, in Chapter 14 you will learn that a company normally would report bonds payable at historical cost (adjusted for unamortized premium or discount), but the fair value option allows that company to choose instead to report the bonds payable at fair value. If a company chooses the fair value option, future changes in fair value are reported as gains and losses in the income statement.

*GAAP gives a company the option to value financial assets and liabilities at fair value.*

Why allow the fair value option for financial assets and liabilities, and not for, say, buildings or land? Financial assets and liabilities are cash and other assets and liabilities that convert directly into known amounts of cash. These include investments in stocks and bonds of other entities, notes receivable and payable, bonds payable, and derivative securities.[51] Some of these financial assets and liabilities currently are *required* under GAAP to be reported

---

[50]FASB ASC 825–10–25–1: Financial Instruments—Overall—Recognition—Fair Value Option (previously "The Fair Value Option for Financial Assets and Financial Liabilities," *Statement of Financial Accounting Standards No. 159* (Norwalk, Conn.: FASB, 2007)).

[51]The fair value option does not apply to certain specified financial instruments, including pension obligations and assets or liabilities arising from leases.

at fair value, and others are not, leading to some potential inconsistencies in how similar or related items are treated. The fair value option provides companies a way to reduce volatility in reported earnings without having to comply with complex hedge accounting standards. It also helps in the convergence with international accounting standards we discussed earlier in the chapter as the IASB also has adopted a fair value option for financial instruments.

It is not necessary that the company elect the fair value option to report all of its financial instruments at fair value or even all instruments of a particular type at fair value. Companies can "mix and match" on an instrument-by-instrument basis. However, a company is not allowed to switch methods once a method is chosen.

We will revisit the fair value option in subsequent chapters that address the key financial assets and liabilities that now can be measured at fair value. You'll find it easier to understand the concepts introduced in this chapter in the context of the financial assets and liabilities affected: investments (Chapter 12) and bonds payable (Chapter 14).[52]

## Disclosure

> The *full-disclosure principle* requires that any information useful to decision makers be provided in the financial statements, subject to the cost effectiveness constraint.

Remember, the purpose of accounting is to provide information that is useful to decision makers. So, naturally, if there is accounting information not included in the primary financial statements that would benefit users, that information should be provided too. The full-disclosure principle means that the financial reports should include any information that could affect the decisions made by external users. Of course, the benefits of that information, as noted earlier, should exceed the costs of providing the information. Such information is disclosed in a variety of ways, including:

1. **Parenthetical comments** or **modifying comments** placed on the face of the financial statements.
2. **Disclosure notes** conveying additional insights about company operations, accounting principles, contractual agreements, and pending litigation.
3. **Supplemental schedules and tables** that report more detailed information than is shown in the primary financial statements.

We find examples of these disclosures in the **Dell Inc.** financial statements in Appendix B located at the back of the text. A parenthetical or modifying comment is provided in the stockholders' equity section of the balance sheet with disclosure of the number of shares of stock authorized, issued, and outstanding, and the statements include several notes. We discuss and illustrate disclosure requirements as they relate to specific financial statement elements in later chapters as those elements are discussed.

Illustration 1–14 provides an overview of key recognition, measurement and disclosure concepts.

## Evolving GAAP

Earlier in this chapter you learned that the convergence of accounting standards with international standards is having a profound effect on financial reporting in the United States. More broadly, U.S. and international GAAP have been evolving over time from an emphasis on revenues and expenses to an emphasis on assets and liabilities. Of course, you know from introductory accounting that the balance sheet and income statement are intertwined and must reconcile with each other. For example, the revenues reported in the income statement depict inflows of assets whose balances at a particular point in time are reported in the balance sheet. But which comes first, identifying revenues and expenses, or identifying assets and liabilities? That emphasis can affect accounting standards in important ways. To help you understand the changes taking place, we start by discussing the revenue/expense approach and then discuss the asset/liability approach.

---

[52]As discussed in further detail in the Addendum to Chapter 12, the overhaul of accounting for financial instruments being completed by the FASB and IASB includes removal of the fair value option.

| Concept | Description |
|---|---|
| Recognition | General criteria:<br>1. Meets the definition of an element<br>2. Has a measurement attribute<br>3. Is relevant<br>4. Is reliable (representationally faithful)<br>Examples of recognition timing:<br>1. Revenue realization<br>2. Expense matching |
| Measurement | Mixed attribute model in which the attribute used to measure an item is chosen to maximize relevance and representational faithfulness. These attributes include:<br>1. Historical cost<br>2. Net realizable value<br>3. Current cost<br>4. Present (or discounted) value of future cash flows<br>5. Fair value |
| Disclosure | Financial reports should include all information that could affect the decisions made by external users.<br>Examples of disclosures:<br>1. Parenthetical amounts<br>2. Notes to the financial statements<br>3. Supplemental schedules and tables |

**Illustration 1—14**

Summary of Recognition, Measurement, and Disclosure Concepts

● **LO1–10**

With the *revenue/expense approach,* recognition and measurement of revenues and expenses are emphasized.

Under the **revenue/expense approach**, we emphasize principles for recognizing revenues and expenses, with some assets and liabilities recognized as necessary to make the balance sheet reconcile with the income statement. For example, when accounting for a sales transaction our focus would be on whether revenue has been earned, and if we determine that to be the case, we would record an asset (usually cash or accounts receivable) that is associated with the revenue.[53] We would identify the expenses necessary to earn that revenue, and then would adjust assets and liabilities accordingly. Much of our accounting for revenues and expenses follows this revenue/expense approach. Key to the revenue/expense approach are the realization principle and the matching principle discussed previously in this chapter.

With the *asset/liability approach,* recognition and measurement of assets and liabilities drives revenue and expense recognition.

Under the **asset/liability approach**, on the other hand, we first recognize and measure the assets and liabilities that exist at a balance sheet date and, secondly, recognize and measure the revenues, expenses, gains and losses needed to account for the changes in these assets and liabilities from the previous measurement date. Proponents of this approach point out that, since revenues and expenses are defined in terms of inflows and outflows of assets and liabilities, the fundamental concepts underlying accounting are assets and liabilities. Therefore, we should try to recognize and measure assets and liabilities appropriately, and as a result will also capture their inflows and outflows in a manner that provides relevant and representationally faithful information about revenues and expenses.

For example, when accounting for a sales transaction, our focus would be on whether a potential accounts receivable meets the definition of an asset (a probable future economic benefit). We would consider such factors as whether the receivable is supported by an enforceable contract and whether the seller has performed its obligations enough to be able to expect receipt of cash flows. The key would be determining if the seller has an asset, and then recognizing whatever amount of revenue is implied by the inflow of that asset. Also, we would not attempt to match expenses to revenues. Rather, we would determine those net assets that had decreased as part of operations during the period, and

---

[53]Some assets and liabilities aren't related to revenue or expense. For example, issuance of shares of stock increases cash as well as shareholders' equity. The treatment of these sorts of transactions is not affected by whether GAAP emphasizes revenues and expenses or assets and liabilities.

recognize those decreases as expenses. In subsequent chapters you will see that recent standards involving accounting for revenue, investments, and income taxes follow this asset/liability approach.

These changes are controversial. It may seem like it shouldn't matter whether standard setters use the revenue/expense or asset/liability approach, given that both approaches affect both the income statement and balance sheet, and it is true that these approaches often will result in the same accounting outcomes. For example, whether matching is a principle used to determine when expenses are recognized, or a result of recognizing that assets were consumed as part of the economic activity that occurred in a particular period in which revenue was also recognized, we typically still will see expenses recognized in the periods in which they are incurred to produce revenues. However, the particular approach used by a standard setter can affect recognition and measurement in important ways. In particular, the asset/liability approach encourages us to focus on accurately measuring assets and liabilities. It perhaps is not surprising, then, that a focus on assets and liabilities has led standard setters to lean more and more toward fair value measurement. The future changes to the conceptual framework discussed in the following Where We're Headed box are likely to continue this emphasis on the asset/liability approach.

## Where We're Headed

The FASB and IASB are working together to develop a common and improved conceptual framework. The project has eight phases, and the Boards currently are working on the first four. Phase A, "Objective and Qualitative Characteristics," has been completed and resulted in the issuance of *SFAC 8*. That material is incorporated in this and subsequent chapters where applicable. There is no timetable for the completion of the remaining phases. However, the Boards have reached some tentative conclusions highlighted below.

**Phase B: Elements and Recognition.** The Boards have tentatively adopted working definitions for assets and liabilities that differ from those contained in *SFAC 6*.

|  | SFAC 6 | Phase B |
|---|---|---|
| Assets | Probable future economic benefits obtained or controlled by a particular entity as a result of past transactions or events. | A present economic resource to which an entity has a right or other access that others do not have. |
| Liabilities | Probable future sacrifices of economic benefits arising from present obligations of a particular entity to transfer assets or provide services to other entities in the future as a result of past transactions or events. | A present economic obligation for which the entity is the obligor. |

*SFAC 6* identifies more elements than does the IASB's framework, and the two frameworks define common elements differently. The Boards are working toward a common set of elements and definitions.

**Phase C: Measurement.** The objective of Phase C is to provide guidance for selecting measurement bases that satisfy the objective and qualitative characteristics of financial reporting. No tentative conclusions have been reached on this issue.

**Phase D: Reporting Entity.** The objective of Phase D is to determine what constitutes a reporting entity for the purposes of financial reporting. The Board issued an exposure draft for this phase in March of 2010. The Board's preliminary view is that *control* is a key aspect in determining what constitutes a reporting entity. The Board defines "control" as the ability to direct the activities of the entity to generate benefits for (or limit losses to) itself.

# Financial Reporting Case Solution

1. **What should you tell your friend about the presence of accounting standards in the United States? Who has the authority for standard setting? Who has the responsibility?** *(p. 8)*   In the United States we have a set of standards known as generally accepted accounting principles (GAAP). GAAP is a dynamic set of both broad and specific guidelines that companies should follow when measuring and reporting the information in their financial statements and related notes. The Securities and Exchange Commission has the authority to set accounting standards for companies whose securities are publicly traded but always has delegated the primary responsibility to the accounting profession. At present, the Financial Accounting Standards Board is the private sector body responsible for standard setting.

2. **What is the economic and political environment in which standard setting occurs?** *(p. 13)*   The setting of accounting and reporting standards often has been characterized as a *political process.* Standards, particularly changes in standards, can have significant differential effects on companies, investors and creditors, and other interest groups. A change in an accounting standard or the introduction of a new standard can result in a substantial redistribution of wealth within our economy. The FASB's due process is designed to obtain information from all interested parties to help determine the appropriate accounting approach, but standards are supposed to be neutral with respect to the interests of various parties. Nonetheless, both the FASB and IASB sometimes come under political pressure that sways the results of the standard-setting process.

3. **What is the relationship among management, auditors, investors, and creditors that tends to preclude the "What would you like it to be?" attitude?** *(p. 15)*   It is the responsibility of management to apply accounting standards when communicating with investors and creditors through financial statements. Auditors serve as independent intermediaries to help ensure that the management-prepared statements are presented fairly in accordance with GAAP. In providing this assurance, the auditor precludes the "What would you like it to be?" attitude.

4. **In general, what is the conceptual framework that underlies accounting principles?** *(p. 19)*   The conceptual framework is a coherent system of interrelated objectives and fundamentals that can lead to consistent standards and that prescribe the nature, function, and limits of financial accounting and reporting. The fundamentals are the underlying concepts of accounting, concepts that guide the selection of events to be accounted for, the measurement of those events, and the means of summarizing and communicating them to interested parties. ●

# The Bottom Line

● **LO1–1**   Financial accounting is concerned with providing relevant financial information to various external users. However, the primary focus is on the financial information provided by profit-oriented companies to their present and potential investors and creditors. *(p. 4)*

● **LO1–2**   Cash basis accounting provides a measure of periodic performance called *net operating cash flow,* which is the difference between cash receipts and cash disbursements from transactions related to providing goods and services to customers. Accrual accounting provides a measure of performance called *net income,* which is the difference between revenues and expenses. Periodic net income is considered a better indicator of future operating cash flows than is current net operating cash flows. *(p. 6)*

● **LO1–3**   Generally accepted accounting principles (GAAP) comprise a dynamic set of both broad and specific guidelines that companies follow when measuring and reporting the information in their financial statements and related notes. The Securities and Exchange Commission (SEC) has the authority to set accounting standards in the United States. However, the SEC has always delegated the task to a private sector body, at this time the Financial Accounting Standards Board (FASB). The International Accounting

Standards Board (IASB) sets global accounting standards and works with national accounting standard setters to achieve convergence in accounting standards around the world. (*p. 8*)

● **LO1–4** Accounting standards can have significant differential effects on companies, investors, creditors, and other interest groups. Various interested parties sometimes lobby standard setters for their preferred outcomes. For this reason, the setting of accounting standards often has been characterized as a political process. (*p. 13*)

● **LO1–5** Factors encouraging high-quality financial reporting include conceptually based financial accounting standards, external auditors, financial reporting reforms (such as the Sarbanes-Oxley Act), ethical management, and professional accounting organizations that prescribe ethical conduct and license practitioners. (*p. 15*)

● **LO1–6** The FASB's conceptual framework is a set of cohesive objectives and fundamental concepts on which financial accounting and reporting standards can be based. (*p. 19*)

● **LO1–7** The objective of financial reporting is to provide useful financial information to capital providers. The primary decision-specific qualities that make financial information useful are relevance and faithful representation. To be relevant, information must possess predictive value and/or confirmatory value, and all material information should be included. Completeness, neutrality, and freedom from error enhance faithful representation. The 10 elements of financial statements are assets, liabilities, equity, investments by owners, distributions to owners, revenues, expenses, gains, losses, and comprehensive income. (*p. 21*)

● **LO1–8** The four basic assumptions underlying GAAP are (1) the economic entity assumption, (2) the going concern assumption, (3) the periodicity assumption, and (4) the monetary unit assumption. (*p. 25*)

● **LO1–9** Recognition determines whether an item is reflected in the financial statements, and measurement determines the amount of the item. Measurement involves choice of a monetary unit and choice of a measurement attribute. In the United States, the monetary unit is the dollar. Various measurement attributes are used in GAAP, including historical cost, net realizable value, present value, and fair value. (*p. 27*)

● **LO1–10** A revenue/expense approach to financial reporting emphasizes recognition and measurement of revenues (typically using the realization principle) and expenses (typically applying the matching principle), while an asset/liability approach emphasizes recognition and measurement of assets and liabilities. (*p. 33*)

● **LO1–11** IFRS and U.S. GAAP are similar in the organizations that support standard setting and in the presence of ongoing political pressures on the standard-setting process. U.S. GAAP and IFRS also have similar conceptual frameworks, although the role of the conceptual framework in IFRS is to provide guidance to preparers as well as to standard setters, while the role of the conceptual framework in U.S. GAAP is more to provide guidance to standard setters. (*pp. 15 and 21*) ●

# Questions For Review of Key Topics

**Q 1–1** What is the function and primary focus of financial accounting?

**Q 1–2** What is meant by the phrase *efficient allocation of resources?* What mechanism fosters the efficient allocation of resources in the United States?

**Q 1–3** Identify two important variables to be considered when making an investment decision.

**Q 1–4** What must a company do in the long run to be able to provide a return to investors and creditors?

**Q 1–5** What is the primary objective of financial accounting?

**Q 1–6** Define net operating cash flows. Briefly explain why periodic net operating cash flows may not be a good indicator of future operating cash flows.

**Q 1–7** What is meant by GAAP? Why should all companies follow GAAP in reporting to external users?

**Q 1–8** Explain the roles of the SEC and the FASB in the setting of accounting standards.

**Q 1–9** Explain the role of the auditor in the financial reporting process.

**Q 1–10** List three key provisions of the Sarbanes-Oxley Act of 2002. Order your list from most important to least important in terms of the likely long-term impact on the accounting profession and financial reporting.

**Q 1–11** Explain what is meant by *adverse economic consequences* of new or changed accounting standards.

**Q 1–12** Why does the FASB undertake a series of elaborate information-gathering steps before issuing a substantive accounting standard?

**Q 1–13** What is the purpose of the FASB's conceptual framework project?

**Q 1–14** Discuss the terms *relevance* and *faithful representation* as they relate to financial accounting information.

**Q 1–15** What are the components of relevant information? What are the components of faithful representation?

**Q 1–16** Explain what is meant by: The benefits of accounting information must exceed the costs.

**Q 1–17** What is meant by the term *materiality* in financial reporting?

Q 1–18   Briefly define the financial accounting elements: (1) assets, (2) liabilities, (3) equity, (4) investments by owners, (5) distributions to owners, (6) revenues, (7) expenses, (8) gains, (9) losses, and (10) comprehensive income.

Q 1–19   What are the four basic assumptions underlying GAAP?

Q 1–20   What is the going concern assumption?

Q 1–21   Explain the periodicity assumption.

Q 1–22   What are four key accounting practices that often are referred to as principles in current GAAP?

Q 1–23   What are two important reasons to base the valuation of assets and liabilities on their historical cost?

Q 1–24   Describe the two criteria that must be satisfied before revenue can be recognized.

Q 1–25   What are the four different approaches to implementing the matching principle? Give an example of an expense that is recognized under each approach.

Q 1–26   In addition to the financial statement elements arrayed in the basic financial statements, what are some other ways to disclose financial information to external users?

Q 1–27   Briefly describe the inputs that companies should use when determining fair value. Organize your answer according to preference levels, from highest to lowest priority.

Q 1–28   What measurement attributes are commonly used in financial reporting?

Q 1–29   Distinguish between the revenue/expense and the asset/liability approaches to setting financial reporting standards.

**IFRS**   Q 1–30   What are the functions of the conceptual framework under IFRS?

**IFRS**   Q 1–31   What is the standard-setting body responsible for determining IFRS? How does it obtain its funding?

**IFRS**   Q 1–32   In late 2011, what further information did the SEC provide about its plans with respect to future convergence between U.S. GAAP and IFRS?

## Brief Exercises

**BE 1–1**
Accrual
accounting
● LO1–2

Cash flows during the first year of operations for the Harman-Kardon Consulting Company were as follows: Cash collected from customers, $340,000; Cash paid for rent, $40,000; Cash paid to employees for services rendered during the year, $120,000; Cash paid for utilities, $50,000.

In addition, you determine that customers owed the company $60,000 at the end of the year and no bad debts were anticipated. Also, the company owed the gas and electric company $2,000 at year-end, and the rent payment was for a two-year period. Calculate accrual net income for the year.

**BE 1–2**
Financial statement
elements
● LO1–7

For each of the following items, identify the appropriate financial statement element or elements: (1) probable future sacrifices of economic benefits; (2) probable future economic benefits owned by the company; (3) inflows of assets from ongoing, major activities; (4) decrease in equity from peripheral or incidental transactions.

**BE 1–3**
Basic assumptions
and principles
● LO1–7 through
LO1–9

Listed below are several statements that relate to financial accounting and reporting. Identify the basic assumption, broad accounting principle, or pervasive constraint that applies to each statement.

1. **Sirius Satellite Radio Inc.** files its annual and quarterly financial statements with the SEC.
2. The president of **Applebee's International, Inc.**, travels on the corporate jet for business purposes only and does not use the jet for personal use.
3. Jackson Manufacturing does not recognize revenue for unshipped merchandise even though the merchandise has been manufactured according to customer specifications.
4. Lady Jane Cosmetics depreciates the cost of equipment over their useful lives.

**BE 1–4**
Basic assumptions
and principles
● LO1–7 through
LO1–9

Identify the basic assumption or broad accounting principle that was violated in each of the following situations.

1. Astro Turf Company recognizes an expense, cost of goods sold, in the period the product is manufactured.
2. McCloud Drug Company owns a patent that it purchased three years ago for $2 million. The controller recently revalued the patent to its approximate market value of $8 million.
3. Philips Company pays the monthly mortgage on the home of its president, Larry Crosswhite, and charges the expenditure to miscellaneous expense.

**BE 1–5**
Basic assumptions
and principles
● LO1–7 through
LO1–9

For each of the following situations, (1) indicate whether you agree or disagree with the financial reporting practice employed and (2) state the basic assumption, pervasive constraint, or accounting principle that is applied (if you agree), or violated (if you disagree).

1. Winderl Corporation did not disclose that it was the defendant in a material lawsuit because the trial was still in progress.
2. Alliant Semiconductor Corporation files quarterly and annual financial statements with the SEC.

3. Reliant Pharmaceutical paid rent on its office building for the next two years and charged the entire expenditure to rent expense.

4. Rockville Engineering records revenue only after products have been shipped, even though customers pay Rockville 50% of the sales price in advance.

**BE 1–6**
**IFRS**
● **LO1–11**

 **IFRS**

Indicate the organization related to IFRS that performs each of the following functions:

1. Obtains funding for the IFRS standard-setting process.
2. Determines IFRS.
3. Encourages cooperation among securities regulators to promote effective and efficient capital markets.
4. Provides input about the standard-setting agenda.
5. Provides implementation guidance about relatively narrow issues.

# Exercises

An alternate exercise and problem set is available on the text website: www.mhhe.com/spiceland7e

**E 1–1**
**Accrual accounting**
● **LO1–2**

Listed below are several transactions that took place during the first two years of operations for the law firm of Pete, Pete, and Roy.

|  | Year 1 | Year 2 |
|---|---|---|
| Amounts billed to customers for services rendered | $170,000 | $220,000 |
| Cash collected from customers | 160,000 | 190,000 |
| Cash disbursements: |  |  |
| Salaries paid to employees for services rendered during the year | 90,000 | 100,000 |
| Utilities | 30,000 | 40,000 |
| Purchase of insurance policy | 60,000 | –0– |

In addition, you learn that the company incurred utility costs of $35,000 in year 1, that there were no liabilities at the end of year 2, no anticipated bad debts on receivables, and that the insurance policy covers a three-year period.

**Required:**

1. Calculate the net operating cash flow for years 1 and 2.
2. Prepare an income statement for each year similar to Illustration 1–3 on page xxx according to the accrual accounting model.
3. Determine the amount of receivables from customers that the company would show in its year 1 and year 2 balance sheets prepared according to the accrual accounting model.

**E 1–2**
**Accrual accounting**
● **LO1–2**

Listed below are several transactions that took place during the second two years of operations for RPG Consulting.

|  | Year 2 | Year 3 |
|---|---|---|
| Amounts billed to customers for services rendered | $350,000 | $450,000 |
| Cash collected from credit customers | 260,000 | 400,000 |
| Cash disbursements: |  |  |
| Payment of rent | 80,000 | –0– |
| Salaries paid to employees for services rendered during the year | 140,000 | 160,000 |
| Travel and entertainment | 30,000 | 40,000 |
| Advertising | 15,000 | 35,000 |

In addition, you learn that the company incurred advertising costs of $25,000 in year 2, owed the advertising agency $5,000 at the end of year 1, and there were no liabilities at the end of year 3. Also, there were no anticipated bad debts on receivables, and the rent payment was for a two-year period, year 2 and year 3.

**Required:**

1. Calculate accrual net income for both years.
2. Determine the amount due the advertising agency that would be shown as a liability on the RPG's balance sheet at the end of year 2.

**E 1–3**
**FASB codification research**
● **LO1–3**

The *FASB Accounting Standards Codification* represents the single source of authoritative U.S. generally accepted accounting principles.

**Required:**

1. Obtain the relevant authoritative literature on fair value measurements using the FASB's Codification Research System at the FASB website (www.fasb.org). Identify the Codification topic number that provides guidance on fair value measurements.

2. What is the specific citation that lists the disclosures required in the notes to the financial statements for each major category of assets and liabilities measured at fair value?

3. List the disclosure requirements.

**E 1–4**
FASB codification research
● LO1–3

Access the FASB's Codification Research System at the FASB website (**www.fasb.org**). Determine the specific citation for each of the following items:

1. The topic number for business combinations.

2. The topic number for related party disclosures.

3. The topic, subtopic, and section number for the initial measurement of internal-use software.

4. The topic, subtopic, and section number for the subsequent measurement of asset retirement obligations.

5. The topic, subtopic, and section number for the recognition of stock compensation.

**E 1–5**
Participants in establishing GAAP
● LO1–3

Three groups that participate in the process of establishing GAAP are users, preparers, and auditors. These groups are represented by various organizations. For each organization listed below, indicate which of these groups it primarily represents.

1. Securities and Exchange Commission

2. Financial Executives International

3. American Institute of Certified Public Accountants

4. Institute of Management Accountants

5. Association of Investment Management and Research

**E 1–6**
Financial statement elements
● LO1–7

For each of the items listed below, identify the appropriate financial statement element or elements.

1. Obligation to transfer cash or other resources as a result of a past transaction.

2. Dividends paid by a corporation to its shareholders.

3. Inflow of an asset from providing a good or service.

4. The financial position of a company.

5. Increase in equity during a period from nonowner transactions.

6. Increase in equity from peripheral or incidental transaction.

7. Sale of an asset used in the operations of a business for less than the asset's book value.

8. The owners' residual interest in the assets of a company.

9. An item owned by the company representing probable future benefits.

10. Revenues plus gains less expenses and losses.

11. An owner's contribution of cash to a corporation in exchange for ownership shares of stock.

12. Outflow of an asset related to the production of revenue.

**E 1–7**
Concepts; terminology; conceptual framework
● LO1–7

Listed below are several terms and phrases associated with the FASB's conceptual framework. Pair each item from List A (by letter) with the item from List B that is most appropriately associated with it.

| List A | List B |
| --- | --- |
| _____ 1. Predictive value | a. Decreases in equity resulting from transfers to owners. |
| _____ 2. Relevance | b. Requires consideration of the costs and value of information. |
| _____ 3. Timeliness | c. Important for making interfirm comparisons. |
| _____ 4. Distribution to owners | d. Applying the same accounting practices over time. |
| _____ 5. Confirmatory value | e. Users understand the information in the context of the decision being made. |
| _____ 6. Understandability | f. Agreement between a measure and the phenomenon it purports to represent. |
| _____ 7. Gain | g. Information is available prior to the decision. |
| _____ 8. Faithful representation | h. Pertinent to the decision at hand. |
| _____ 9. Comprehensive income | i. Implies consensus among different measurers. |
| _____10. Materiality | j. Information confirms expectations. |
| _____11. Comparability | k. The change in equity from nonowner transactions. |
| _____12. Neutrality | l. The process of admitting information into financial statements. |
| _____13. Recognition | m. The absence of bias. |
| _____14. Consistency | n. Results if an asset is sold for more than its book value. |
| _____15. Cost effectiveness | o. Information is useful in predicting the future. |
| _____16. Verifiability | p. Concerns the relative size of an item and its effect on decisions. |

**E 1–8**
**Qualitative characteristics**
● **LO1–7**

Phase A of the joint FASB and IASB conceptual framework project stipulates the desired fundamental and enhancing qualitative characteristics of accounting information. Several constraints impede achieving these desired characteristics. Answer each of the following questions related to these characteristics and constraints.

1. Which component would allow a company to record the purchase of a $120 printer as an expense rather than capitalizing the printer as an asset?

2. Donald Kirk, former chairman of the FASB, once noted that " . . . there must be public confidence that the standard-setting system is credible, that selection of board members is based on merit and not the influence of special interests . . ." Which characteristic is implicit in Mr. Kirk's statement?

3. Allied Appliances, Inc., changed its revenue recognition policies. Which characteristic is jeopardized by this change?

4. National Bancorp, a publicly traded company, files quarterly and annual financial statements with the SEC. Which characteristic is relevant to the timing of these periodic filings?

5. In general, relevant information possesses which qualities?

6. When there is agreement between a measure or description and the phenomenon it purports to represent, information possesses which characteristic?

7. Jeff Brown is evaluating two companies for future investment potential. Jeff's task is made easier because both companies use the same accounting methods when preparing their financial statements. Which characteristic does the information Jeff will be using possess?

8. A company should disclose information only if the perceived benefits of the disclosure exceed the costs of providing the information. Which constraint does this statement describe?

**E 1–9**
**Basic assumptions, principles, and constraints**
● **LO1–7 through LO1–9**

Listed below are several terms and phrases associated with basic assumptions, broad accounting principles, and constraints. Pair each item from List A (by letter) with the item from List B that is most appropriately associated with it.

| List A | List B |
|---|---|
| _____ 1. Matching principle | a. The enterprise is separate from its owners and other entities. |
| _____ 2. Periodicity | b. A common denominator is the dollar. |
| _____ 3. Historical cost principle | c. The entity will continue indefinitely. |
| _____ 4. Materiality | d. Record expenses in the period the related revenue is recognized. |
| _____ 5. Realization principle | e. The original transaction value upon acquisition. |
| _____ 6. Going concern assumption | f. All information that could affect decisions should be reported. |
| _____ 7. Monetary unit assumption | g. The life of an enterprise can be divided into artificial time periods. |
| _____ 8. Economic entity assumption | h. Criteria usually satisfied at point of sale. |
| _____ 9. Full-disclosure principle | i. Concerns the relative size of an item and its effect on decisions. |

**E 1–10**
**Basic assumptions and principles**
● **LO1–7 through LO1–9**

Listed below are several statements that relate to financial accounting and reporting. Identify the basic assumption, broad accounting principle, or component that applies to each statement.

1. Jim Marley is the sole owner of Marley's Appliances. Jim borrowed $100,000 to buy a new home to be used as his personal residence. This liability was not recorded in the records of Marley's Appliances.

2. **Apple Inc.** distributes an annual report to its shareholders.

3. **Hewlett-Packard Corporation** depreciates machinery and equipment over their useful lives.

4. Crosby Company lists land on its balance sheet at $120,000, its original purchase price, even though the land has a current fair value of $200,000.

5. **Honeywell Corporation** records revenue when products are delivered to customers, even though the cash has not yet been received.

6. Liquidation values are not normally reported in financial statements even though many companies do go out of business.

7. **IBM Corporation**, a multibillion dollar company, purchased some small tools at a cost of $800. Even though the tools will be used for a number of years, the company recorded the purchase as an expense.

**E 1–11**
**Basic assumptions and principles**
● **LO1–8, LO1–9**

Identify the basic assumption or broad accounting principle that was violated in each of the following situations.

1. Pastel Paint Company purchased land two years ago at a price of $250,000. Because the value of the land has appreciated to $400,000, the company has valued the land at $400,000 in its most recent balance sheet.

2. Atwell Corporation has not prepared financial statements for external users for over three years.

3. The Klingon Company sells farm machinery. Revenue from a large order of machinery from a new buyer was recorded the day the order was received.

4. Don Smith is the sole owner of a company called Hardware City. The company recently paid a $150 utility bill for Smith's personal residence and recorded a $150 expense.

5. Golden Book Company purchased a large printing machine for $1,000,000 (a material amount) and recorded the purchase as an expense.

6. Ace Appliance Company is involved in a major lawsuit involving injuries sustained by some of its employees in the manufacturing plant. The company is being sued for $2,000,000, a material amount, and is not insured. The suit was not disclosed in the most recent financial statements because no settlement had been reached.

**E 1–12**
**Basic assumptions and principles**
● **LO1–7 through LO1–9**

For each of the following situations, indicate whether you agree or disagree with the financial reporting practice employed and state the basic assumption, component, or accounting principle that is applied (if you agree) or violated (if you disagree).

1. Wagner Corporation adjusted the valuation of all assets and liabilities to reflect changes in the purchasing power of the dollar.

2. Spooner Oil Company changed its method of accounting for oil and gas exploration costs from successful efforts to full cost. No mention of the change was included in the financial statements. The change had a material effect on Spooner's financial statements.

3. Cypress Manufacturing Company purchased machinery having a five-year life. The cost of the machinery is being expensed over the life of the machinery.

4. Rudeen Corporation purchased equipment for $180,000 at a liquidation sale of a competitor. Because the equipment was worth $230,000, Rudeen valued the equipment in its subsequent balance sheet at $230,000.

5. Davis Bicycle Company received a large order for the sale of 1,000 bicycles at $100 each. The customer paid Davis the entire amount of $100,000 on March 15. However, Davis did not record any revenue until April 17, the date the bicycles were delivered to the customer.

6. Gigantic Corporation purchased two small calculators at a cost of $32.00. The cost of the calculators was expensed even though they had a three-year estimated useful life.

7. Esquire Company provides financial statements to external users every three years.

**E 1–13**
**Basic assumptions and principles**
● **LO1–7 through LO1–9**

For each of the following situations, state whether you agree or disagree with the financial reporting practice employed, and briefly explain the reason for your answer.

1. The controller of the Dumars Corporation increased the carrying value of land from its original cost of $2 million to its recently appraised value of $3.5 million.

2. The president of Vosburgh Industries asked the company controller to charge miscellaneous expense for the purchase of an automobile to be used solely for personal use.

3. At the end of its 2013 fiscal year, Dower, Inc., received an order from a customer for $45,350. The merchandise will ship early in 2014. Because the sale was made to a long-time customer, the controller recorded the sale in 2013.

4. At the beginning of its 2013 fiscal year, Rossi Imports paid $48,000 for a two-year lease on warehouse space. Rossi recorded the expenditure as an asset to be expensed equally over the two-year period of the lease.

5. The Reliable Tire Company included a note in its financial statements that described a pending lawsuit against the company.

6. The Hughes Corporation, a company whose securities are publicly traded, prepares monthly, quarterly, and annual financial statements for internal use but disseminates to external users only the annual financial statements.

**E 1–14**
**Basic assumptions and principles**
● **LO1–7 through LO1–9**

Listed below are the basic assumptions, broad accounting principles, and constraints discussed in this chapter.

| | |
|---|---|
| a. Economic entity assumption | g. Matching principle |
| b. Going concern assumption | h. Full-disclosure principle |
| c. Periodicity assumption | i. Cost effectiveness |
| d. Monetary unit assumption | j. Materiality |
| e. Historical cost principle | k. Conservatism |
| f. Realization principle | |

Identify by letter the assumption, principle, or constraint that relates to each statement or phrase below.

_____ 1. Revenue is recognized only after certain criteria are satisfied.

_____ 2. Information that could affect decision making should be reported.

_____ 3. Cause-and-effect relationship between revenues and expenses.

_____ 4. The basis for measurement of many assets and liabilities.

_____ 5. Relates to the qualitative characteristic of timeliness.

_____ 6. All economic events can be identified with a particular entity.

_____ 7. The benefits of providing accounting information should exceed the cost of doing so.

_____ 8. A consequence is that GAAP need not be followed in all situations.

_____ 9. Not a qualitative characteristic, but a practical justification for some accounting choices.

_____10. Assumes the entity will continue indefinitely.

_____11. Inflation causes a violation of this assumption.

**E 1–15**
**Multiple choice; concept statements, basic assumptions, principles**
● **LO1–6 through LO1–9**

Determine the response that best completes the following statements or questions.

1. The primary objective of financial reporting is to provide information
   a. About a firm's management team.
   b. Useful to capital providers.
   c. Concerning the changes in financial position resulting from the income-producing efforts of the entity.
   d. About a firm's financing and investing activities.

2. *Statements of Financial Accounting Concepts* issued by the FASB
   a. Represent GAAP.
   b. Have been superseded by *SFASs*.
   c. Are subject to approval of the SEC.
   d. Identify the conceptual framework within which accounting standards are developed.

3. In general, revenue is recognized as earned when the earning process is virtually complete and
   a. The sales price has been collected.
   b. A purchase order has been received.
   c. There is reasonable certainty as to the collectibility of the asset to be received.
   d. A contract has been signed.

4. In depreciating the cost of an asset, accountants are most concerned with
   a. Conservatism.
   b. The realization principle.
   c. Full disclosure.
   d. The matching principle.

5. The primary objective of the matching principle is to
   a. Provide full disclosure.
   b. Record expenses in the period that related revenues are recognized.
   c. Provide timely information to decision makers.
   d. Promote comparability between financial statements of different periods.

6. The separate entity assumption states that, in the absence of contrary evidence, all entities will survive indefinitely.
   a. True
   b. False

# CPA and CMA Exam Questions

**CPA Exam Questions**

**KAPLAN**

The following questions are adapted from a variety of sources including questions developed by the AICPA Board of Examiners and those used in the Kaplan CPA Review Course to study the environment and theoretical structure of financial accounting while preparing for the CPA examination. Determine the response that best completes the statements or questions.

● **LO1–7**

1. Which of the following is *not* a qualitative characteristic of accounting information according to the FASB's conceptual framework?
   a. Auditor independence.
   b. Neutrality.
   c. Timeliness.
   d. Predictive value.

● **LO1–7**

2. According to the conceptual framework, neutrality is a characteristic of
   a. Understandability.
   b. Faithful representation.
   c. Relevance.
   d. Both relevance and faithful representation.

● **LO1–3**

3. The Financial Accounting Standards Board (FASB)
   a. Is a division of the Securities and Exchange Commission (SEC).
   b. Is a private body that helps set accounting standards in the United States.

c. Is responsible for setting auditing standards that all auditors must follow.

d. Consists entirely of members of the American Institute of Certified Public Accountants.

● LO1–7

4. Confirmatory value is an ingredient of the primary quality of

|  | Relevance | Faithful Representation |
|---|---|---|
| a. | Yes | No |
| b. | No | Yes |
| c. | Yes | Yes |
| d. | No | No |

● LO1–7

5. Predictive value is an ingredient of

|  | Faithful Representation | Relevance |
|---|---|---|
| a. | Yes | No |
| b. | No | No |
| c. | Yes | Yes |
| d. | No | Yes |

● LO1–7

6. Completeness is an ingredient of the primary quality of

a. Verifiability.

b. Faithful representation.

c. Relevance.

d. Understandability.

● LO1–1

7. The objective of financial reporting for business enterprises is based on

a. Generally accepted accounting principles.

b. The needs of the users of the information.

c. The need for conservatism.

d. None of above.

● LO1–7

8. According to the FASB's conceptual framework, comprehensive income includes which of the following?

|  | Operating Income | Investments by Owners |
|---|---|---|
| a. | No | Yes |
| b. | No | No |
| c. | Yes | Yes |
| d. | Yes | No |

Beginning in 2011, International Financial Reporting Standards are tested on the CPA exam along with U.S. GAAP. The following questions deal with the application of IFRS.

● LO1–11

● IFRS

9. The equivalent to the FASB's Financial Accounting Standards Advisory Council (FASAC) for the IASB is:

a. International Financial Reporting Interpretations Committee (IFRIC).

b. International Organization of Securities Commissions (IOSCO).

c. International Financial Accounting Advisory Council (IFAAC).

d. Standards Advisory Council (SAC).

● LO1–11

● IFRS

10. Which of the following is not a function of the IASB's conceptual framework?

a. The conceptual framework provides guidance to standard setters to help them develop high quality standards.

b. The conceptual framework provides guidance to practitioners when individual standards to not apply.

c. The conceptual framework includes specific implementation guidance to enable consistent application of particular complex standards.

d. The conceptual framework emphasizes a "true and fair representation" of the company.

● LO1–11

● IFRS

11. Late in 2011, the SEC indicated what future direction concerning convergence of U.S. GAAP and IFRS?

a. The U.S. will continue to work with the IASB on convergence efforts, and the SEC will reassess whether adoption of IFRS is appropriate after several more years.

b. The U.S. will follow a "condorsement approach", whereby the U.S. endorses IFRS standards as they are issued and works to converge existing standards prior to adopting IFRS.

c. The U.S. will continue working on convergence projects with a goal to eventually adopt IFRS, and in the meantime large U.S. companies will be allowed to report under IFRS if they so choose.

d. None of the above.

CMA Exam
Questions

The following questions dealing with the environment and theoretical structure of financial accounting are adapted from questions that previously appeared on Certified Management Accountant (CMA) examinations. The CMA designation sponsored by the Institute of Management Accountants (www.imanet.org) provides members with an objective measure of knowledge and competence in the field of management accounting. Determine the response that best completes the statements or questions.

● LO1–3

1. Accounting standard setting in the United States is
   a. Done primarily by the Securities and Exchange Commission.
   b. Done primarily by the private sector.
   c. The responsibility of the public sector.
   d. Done primarily by the International Accounting Standards Committee.

● LO1–7

2. Verifiability as used in accounting includes
   a. Determining the revenue first, then determining the costs incurred in earning that revenue.
   b. The entity's giving the same treatment to comparable transactions from period to period.
   c. Similar results being obtained by both the accountant and an independent party using the same measurement methods.
   d. The disclosure of all facts that may influence the judgment of an informed reader.

● LO1–7

3. Recognition is the process of formally recording and reporting an item in the financial statements. In order for a revenue item to be recognized, it must be all of the following except
   a. Measurable.
   b. Relevant.
   c. Material.
   d. Realized or realizable.

# Broaden Your Perspective

Apply your critical-thinking ability to the knowledge you've gained. These cases will provide you an opportunity to develop your research, analysis, judgment, and communication skills. You will also work with other students, integrate what you've learned, apply it in real world situations, and consider its global and ethical ramifications. This practice will broaden your knowledge and further develop your decision-making abilities.

**Judgment
Case 1–1**
The development of accounting standards
● LO1–3

In 1934, Congress created the Securities and Exchange Commission (SEC) and gave the commission both the power and responsibility for setting accounting and reporting standards in the United States.

**Required:**
1. Explain the relationship between the SEC and the various private sector standard-setting bodies that have, over time, been delegated the responsibility for setting accounting standards.
2. Can you think of any reasons why the SEC has delegated this responsibility rather than set standards directly?

**Research
Case 1–2**
Accessing SEC information through the Internet
● LO1–3

Internet access to the World Wide Web has provided a wealth of information accessible with our personal computers. Many chapters in this text contain Real World Cases that require you to access the web to research an accounting issue. The purpose of this case is to introduce you to the Internet home page of the Securities and Exchange Commission (SEC) and its EDGAR database.

**Required:**
1. Access the SEC home page on the Internet. The web address is www.sec.gov.
2. Choose the subaddress "About the SEC." What are the two basic objectives of the 1933 Securities Act?
3. Return to the SEC home page and access EDGAR. Describe the contents of the database.

**Research
Case 1–3**
Accessing FASB information through the Internet
● LO1–4

The purpose of this case is to introduce you to the information available on the website of the Financial Accounting Standards Board (FASB).

**Required:**
Access the FASB home page on the Internet. The web address is www.fasb.org. Answer the following questions.
1. Describe the mission of the FASB.
2. Who are the current Board members of the FASB? Briefly describe their backgrounds.
3. How are topics added to the FASB's technical agenda?

**Research Case 1–4**
Accessing IASB information through the Internet
● LO1–3

The purpose of this case is to introduce you to the information available on the website of the International Accounting Standards Board (IASB).

**Required:**
Access the IASB home page on the Internet. The web address is **www.iasb.org**. Answer the following questions.
1. Describe the mission of the IASB.
2. The IASB has how many board members?
3. Who is the current chairman of the IASB?
4. Where is the IASB located?

**Research Case 1–5**
Accounting standards in China
● LO1–3, LO1–4

Economic reforms in the People's Republic of China are moving that nation toward a market-driven economy. China's accounting practices must also change to accommodate the needs of potential investors. In an article entitled "Institutional Factors Influencing China's Accounting Reforms and Standards," Professor Bing Xiang analyzes the changes in the accounting environment of China during the recent economic reforms and their implications for the development of accounting reforms.

**Required:**
1. In your library or from some other source, locate the indicated article in *Accounting Horizons,* June 1998.
2. Briefly describe the economic reforms that led to the need for increased external financial reporting in China.
3. Conformity with International Accounting Standards was specified as an overriding objective in formulating China's accounting standards. What is the author's opinion of this objective?

**Communication Case 1–6**
Relevance and reliability
● LO1–7

Some theorists contend that companies that create pollution should report the social cost of that pollution in income statements. They argue that such companies are indirectly subsidized as the cost of pollution is borne by society while only production costs (and perhaps minimal pollution fines) are shown in the income statement. Thus, the product sells for less than would be necessary if all costs were included.

Assume that the FASB is considering a standard to include the social costs of pollution in the income statement. The process would require considering both relevance and faithful representation of the information produced by the new standard. Your instructor will divide the class into two to six groups depending on the size of the class. The mission of your group is to explain how the concepts of relevance and faithful representation relate to this issue.

**Required:**
Each group member should consider the question independently and draft a tentative answer prior to the class session for which the case is assigned.

In class, each group will meet for 10 to 15 minutes in different areas of the classroom. During that meeting, group members will take turns sharing their suggestions for the purpose of arriving at a single group treatment.

After the allotted time, a spokesperson for each group (selected during the group meetings) will share the group's solution with the class. The goal of the class is to incorporate the views of each group into a consensus answer to the question.

**Communication Case 1–7**
Accounting standard setting
● LO1–4

One of your friends is a financial analyst for a major stock brokerage firm. Recently she indicated to you that she had read an article in a weekly business magazine that alluded to the political process of establishing accounting standards. She had always assumed that accounting standards were established by determining the approach that conceptually best reflected the economics of a transaction.

**Required:**
Write a one to two-page article for a business journal explaining what is meant by the political process for establishing accounting standards. Be sure to include in your article a discussion of the need for the FASB to balance accounting considerations and economic consequences.

**Ethics Case 1–8**
The auditors' responsibility
● LO1–4

It is the responsibility of management to apply accounting standards when communicating with investors and creditors through financial statements. Another group, auditors, serves as an independent intermediary to help ensure that management has in fact appropriately applied GAAP in preparing the company's financial statements. Auditors examine (audit) financial statements to express a professional, independent opinion. The opinion reflects the auditors' assessment of the statements' fairness, which is determined by the extent to which they are prepared in compliance with GAAP.

Some feel that it is impossible for an auditor to give an independent opinion on a company's financial statements because the auditors' fees for performing the audit are paid by the company. In addition to the audit fee, quite often the auditor performs other services for the company such as preparing the company's income tax returns.

**Required:**
How might an auditor's ethics be challenged while performing an audit?

**Judgment Case 1–9**
Qualitative characteristics
● LO1–7

Generally accepted accounting principles do not require companies to disclose forecasts of any financial variables to external users. A friend, who is a finance major, is puzzled by this and asks you to explain why such relevant information is not provided to investors and creditors to help them predict future cash flows.

**Required:**
Explain to your friend why this information is not routinely provided to investors and creditors.

**Judgment Case 1–10**
GAAP, comparability, and the role of the auditor
● LO1–4, LO1–7

Mary McQuire is trying to decide how to invest her money. A friend recommended that she buy the stock of one of two corporations and suggested that she should compare the financial statements of the two companies before making a decision.

**Required:**
1. Do you agree that Mary will be able to compare the financial statements of the two companies?
2. What role does the auditor play in ensuring comparability of financial statements between companies?

**Judgment Case 1–11**
Cost effectiveness
● LO1–7

Phase A of the joint FASB and IASB conceptual framework project includes a discussion of the constraint cost effectiveness. Assume that the FASB is considering revising an important accounting standard.

**Required:**
1. What is the desired benefit from revising an accounting standard?
2. What are some of the possible costs that could result from a revision of an accounting standard?
3. What does the FASB do in order to assess possible benefits and costs of a proposed revision of an accounting standard?

**Judgment Case 1–12**
The realization principle
● LO1–9

A new client, the Wolf Company, asks your advice concerning the point in time that the company should recognize revenue from the rental of its office buildings. Renters usually pay rent on a quarterly basis at the beginning of the quarter. The owners contend that the critical event that motivates revenue recognition should be the date the cash is received from renters. After all, the money is in hand and is very seldom returned.

**Required:**
1. Describe the two criteria that must be satisfied before revenue can be recognized.
2. Do you agree or disagree with the position of the owners of Wolf Company? Support your answer.

**Analysis Case 1–13**
The matching principle
● LO1–9

Revenues measure the accomplishments of a company during the period. Expenses are then matched with revenues to produce a periodic measure of performance called *net income.*

**Required:**
1. Explain what is meant by the phrase *matched with revenues.*
2. Describe the four approaches used to implement the matching principle and label them 1 through 4.
3. For each of the following, identify which matching approach should be used to recognize the cost as expense.
   a. The cost of producing a product.
   b. The cost of advertising.
   c. The cost of monthly rent on the office building.
   d. The salary of an office employee.
   e. Depreciation on an office building.

**Judgment Case 1–14**
Capitalize or expense?
● LO1–9

When a company makes an expenditure that is neither a payment to a creditor nor a distribution to an owner, management must decide if the expenditure should be capitalized (recorded as an increase in an asset) or expensed (recorded as an expense thereby decreasing owners' equity).

**Required:**
1. Which factor or factors should the company consider when making this decision?
2. Which key accounting principle is involved?
3. Are there any constraints that could cause the company to alter its decision?

**Real World Case 1–15**
Elements; disclosures; The Gap Inc.
● LO1–7, LO1–9

Selected financial statements from a recent annual report of **The Gap Inc.** follow. Use these statements to answer the following questions.

**Required:**
1. What amounts did Gap report for the following items for the 2010 fiscal year ended January 29, 2011?
   a. Total net revenues
   b. Total operating expenses
   c. Net income (earnings)

d. Total assets

e. Total stockholders' equity

Real World Financials 2. How many shares of common stock did the company have issued on January 29, 2011?

3. Why do you think Gap reports more than one year of data in its financial statements?

### THE GAP INC.
### Consolidated Balance Sheets

| ($ and shares in millions except par value) | January 29, 2011 | January 30, 2010 |
|---|---|---|
| **Assets** | | |
| Current assets: | | |
| Cash and cash equivalents | $ 1,561 | $ 2,348 |
| Short-term investments | 100 | 225 |
| Merchandise inventory | 1,620 | 1,477 |
| Other current assets | 645 | 614 |
| Total current assets | 3,926 | 4,664 |
| Property and equipment, net | 2,563 | 2,628 |
| Other long-term assets | 576 | 693 |
| Total assets | $ 7,065 | $ 7,985 |
| **Liabilities and Stockholders' Equity** | | |
| Current liabilities: | | |
| Accounts payable | $ 1,049 | $ 1,027 |
| Accrued expenses and other current liabilities | 996 | 1,063 |
| Income taxes payable | 50 | 41 |
| Total current liabilities | 2,095 | 2,131 |
| Lease incentives and other long-term liabilities | 890 | 963 |
| Commitments and contingencies (see Notes 9 and 13) | | |
| Stockholders' equity: | | |
| Common stock $0.05 par value | | |
| Authorized 2,300 shares; Issued 1,106 for all periods presented; Outstanding 588 and 676 shares | 55 | 55 |
| Additional paid-in capital | 2,939 | 2,935 |
| Retained earnings | 11,767 | 10,815 |
| Accumulated other comprehensive earnings | 185 | 155 |
| Treasury stock, at cost (518 and 430 shares) | (10,866) | (9,069) |
| Total stockholders' equity | 4,080 | 4,891 |
| Total liabilities and stockholders' equity | $ 7,065 | $ 7,985 |

### THE GAP INC.
### Consolidated Statements of Income

| | Fiscal Year | | |
|---|---|---|---|
| ($ and shares in millions except per share amounts) | 2010 | 2009 | 2008 |
| Net sales | $14,664 | $14,197 | $14,526 |
| Cost of goods sold and occupancy expenses | 8,775 | 8,473 | 9,079 |
| Gross profit | 5,889 | 5,724 | 5,447 |
| Operating expenses | 3,921 | 3,909 | 3,899 |
| Operating income | 1,968 | 1,815 | 1,548 |
| Interest expense (reversal) | (8) | 6 | 1 |
| Interest income | (6) | (7) | (37) |
| Income before income taxes | 1,982 | 1,816 | 1,584 |
| Income taxes | 778 | 714 | 617 |
| Net income | $ 1,204 | $ 1,102 | $  967 |
| Weighted-average number of shares—basic | 636 | 694 | 716 |
| Weighted-average number of shares—diluted | 641 | 699 | 719 |
| Earnings per share—basic | $1.89 | $1.59 | $1.35 |
| Earnings per share—diluted | $1.88 | $1.58 | $1.34 |
| Cash dividends declared and paid per share | $0.40 | $0.34 | $0.34 |

**Judgment
Case 1–16**
Convergence
● LO1–11

IFRS

Consider the question of whether the United States should converge accounting standards with IFRS.

**Required:**

1. Make a list of arguments that favor convergence.

2. Make a list of arguments that favor nonconvergence.

3. Indicate your own conclusion regarding whether the United States should converge with IFRS, and indicate the primary considerations that determined your conclusion.

# Air France–KLM Case

**AIRFRANCE /**

Air France–KLM (AF), a French company, prepares its financial statements according to International Financial Reporting Standards. AF's annual report for the year ended March 31, 2011, which includes financial statements and disclosure notes, is provided with all new textbooks. This material also is included in AF's "Registration Document 2010–11," dated June 15, 2011 and is available at **www.airfranceklm.com**.

● LO1–11

IFRS

**Required:**

1. What amounts did AF report for the following items for the 2011 fiscal year ended March 31, 2011?

   a. Total revenues

   b. Income from current operations

   c. Net income (AF equity holders)

   d. Total assets

   e. Total equity

2. What was AF's basic earnings per share for the 2011 fiscal year?

3. Examine Note 3.1.1 of AF's annual report. What accounting principles were used to prepare AF's financial statements? Under those accounting principles, could AF's financial information differ from that of a company that exactly followed IFRS as published by the IASB? Explain.

# 2

# Review of the Accounting Process

**LEARNING OBJECTIVES**

**After studying this chapter, you should be able to:**

- **LO2–1** Analyze routine economic events—transactions—and record their effects on a company's financial position using the accounting equation format. (p. 52)
- **LO2–2** Record transactions using the general journal format. (p. 56)
- **LO2–3** Post the effects of journal entries to general ledger accounts and prepare an unadjusted trial balance. (p. 63)
- **LO2–4** Identify and describe the different types of adjusting journal entries. (p. 66)
- **LO2–5** Record adjusting journal entries in general journal format, post entries, and prepare an adjusted trial balance. (p. 67)
- **LO2–6** Describe the four basic financial statements. (p. 75)
- **LO2–7** Explain the closing process. (p. 79)
- **LO2–8** Convert from cash basis net income to accrual basis net income. (p. 83)

## FINANCIAL REPORTING CASE

### Engineering Profits

After graduating from college last year, two of your engineering-major friends started an Internet consulting practice. They began operations on July 1 and felt they did quite well during their first year. Now they would like to borrow $20,000 from a local bank to buy new computing equipment and office furniture. To support their loan application, the friends presented the bank with the following income statement for their first year of operations ending June 30:

| Consulting revenue | | $96,000 |
|---|---|---|
| Operating expenses: | | |
| Salaries | $32,000 | |
| Rent | 9,000 | |
| Supplies | 4,800 | |
| Utilities | 3,000 | |
| Advertising | 1,200 | (50,000) |
| Net income | | $46,000 |

The bank officer noticed that there was no depreciation expense in the income statement and has asked your friends to revise the statement after making year-end adjustments. After agreeing to help, you discover the following information:

a. The friends paid $80,000 for equipment when they began operations. They think the equipment will be useful for five years.

b. They pay $500 a month to rent office space. In January, they paid a full year's rent in advance. This is included in the $9,000 rent expense.

c. Included in consulting revenue is $13,000 they received from a customer in June as a deposit for work to be performed in August.

By the time you finish this chapter, you should be able to respond appropriately to the questions posed in this case. Compare your response to the solution provided at the end of the chapter.

**QUESTIONS**

**1.** What purpose do adjusting entries serve? (p. 67)

**2.** What year-end adjustments are needed to revise the income statement? Did your friends do as well their first year as they thought? (p. 67)

A solid foundation is vital to a sound understanding of intermediate accounting. So, we review the fundamental accounting process here to serve as a framework for the new concepts you will learn in this course.

Chapter 1 introduced the theoretical structure of financial accounting and the environment within which it operates. The primary function of financial accounting—to provide financial information to external users that possesses the fundamental decision-specific qualities of relevance and faithful representation—is accomplished by periodically disseminating financial statements and related notes. In this chapter we review the *process* used to identify, analyze, record, summarize, and then report the economic events affecting a company's financial position.

Keep in mind as you study this chapter that the accounting information systems businesses actually use are quite different from company to company. Larger companies generally use more complex systems than smaller companies use. The types of economic events affecting companies also cause differences in systems. We focus on the many features that tend to be common to all accounting systems.

**Computers are used to process accounting information. In this chapter we provide an overview of the basic model that underlies computer software programs.**

It is important to understand that this chapter and its appendixes are not intended to describe actual accounting systems. In most business enterprises, the sheer volume of data that must be processed precludes a manual accounting system. Fortunately, the computer provides a solution. *We describe and illustrate a manual accounting information system to provide an overview of the basic model that underlies the computer software programs actually used to process accounting information.*

Electronic data processing is fast, accurate, and affordable. Many large and medium-sized companies own or rent their own mainframe computers and company-specific data processing systems. Smaller companies can take advantage of technology with relatively inexpensive desktop and laptop computers and generalized data software packages such as QuickBooks and Peachtree Accounting Software. Enterprise Resource Planning (ERP) systems are now being installed in companies of all sizes. The objective of ERP is to create a customized software program that integrates all departments and functions across a company onto a single computer system that can serve the information needs of those different departments, including the accounting department.

# The Basic Model

The first objective of any accounting system is to identify the **economic events** that can be expressed in financial terms by the system.[1] An economic event for accounting purposes is any event that *directly* affects the financial position of the company. Recall from Chapter 1 that financial position comprises assets, liabilities, and owners' equity. Broad and specific accounting principles determine which events should be recorded, when the events should be recorded, and the dollar amount at which they should be measured.

**Economic events cause changes in the financial position of the company.**

Economic events can be classified as either external events or internal events. **External events** involve an exchange between the company and a separate economic entity. Examples are purchasing merchandise inventory for cash, borrowing cash from a bank, and paying salaries to employees. In each instance, the company receives something (merchandise, cash, and services) in exchange for something else (cash, assumption of a liability, and cash).

**External events involve an exchange between the company and another entity.**

On the other hand, **internal events** directly affect the financial position of the company but don't involve an exchange transaction with another entity. Examples are the depreciation of machinery and the use of supplies. As we will see later in the chapter, these events must be recorded to properly reflect a company's financial position and results of operations in accordance with the accrual accounting model.

**Internal events do not involve an exchange transaction but do affect the company's financial position.**

## The Accounting Equation

● LO2–1     The **accounting equation** underlies the process used to capture the effect of economic events.

$$\text{Assets} = \text{Liabilities} + \text{Owners' Equity}$$

---

[1]There are many economic events that affect a company *indirectly* and are not recorded. For example, when the Federal Reserve changes its discount rate, it is an important economic event that can affect the company in many ways, but it is not recorded by the company.

This general expression portrays the equality between the total economic resources of an entity (its assets)—shown on the left side of the equation—and the total claims against the entity (liabilities and equity)—shown on the right side. In other words, the resources of an enterprise are provided by creditors and owners.

The equation also implies that each economic event affecting this equation will have a dual effect because resources always must equal claims. For illustration, consider the events (we refer to these throughout the text as **transactions**) in Illustration 2–1.

> *Each event, or transaction, has a dual effect on the accounting equation.*

**Illustration 2–1**

Transaction Analysis

1. **An attorney invested $50,000 to open a law office.**
   An investment by the owner causes both assets and owners' equity to increase.

   | Assets | = | Liabilities | + | Owners' Equity |
   |---|---|---|---|---|
   | +$50,000 (cash) | | | | +$50,000 (investment by owner) |

2. **$40,000 was borrowed from a bank and a note payable was signed.**
   This transaction causes assets and liabilities to increase. A bank loan increases cash and creates an obligation to repay it.

   | Assets | = | Liabilities | + | Owners' Equity |
   |---|---|---|---|---|
   | +$40,000 (cash) | | +$40,000 (note payable) | | |

3. **Supplies costing $3,000 were purchased on account.**
   Buying supplies on credit also increases both assets and liabilities.

   | Assets | = | Liabilities | + | Owners' Equity |
   |---|---|---|---|---|
   | +$3,000 (supplies) | | +$3,000 (accounts payable) | | |

   Transactions 4, 5, and 6 are revenue and expense transactions. Revenues and expenses (and gains and losses) are events that cause owners' equity to change. Revenues and gains describe inflows of assets, causing owners' equity to increase. Expenses and losses describe outflows of assets (or increases in liabilities), causing owners' equity to decrease.

4. **Services were performed on account for $10,000.**

   | Assets | = | Liabilities | + | Owners' Equity |
   |---|---|---|---|---|
   | +$10,000 (receivables) | | | | +$10,000 (revenue) |

5. **Salaries of $5,000 were paid to employees.**

   | Assets | = | Liabilities | + | Owners' Equity |
   |---|---|---|---|---|
   | −$5,000 (cash) | | | | −$5,000 (expense) |

6. **$500 of supplies were used.**

   | Assets | = | Liabilities | + | Owners' Equity |
   |---|---|---|---|---|
   | −$500 (supplies) | | | | −$500 (expense) |

7. **$1,000 was paid on account to the supplies vendor.**
   This transaction causes assets and liabilities to decrease.

   | Assets | = | Liabilities | + | Owners' Equity |
   |---|---|---|---|---|
   | −$1,000 (cash) | | −$1,000 (accounts payable) | | |

Each transaction is analyzed to determine its effect on the equation and on the specific financial position elements.

The accounting equation can be expanded to include a column for each type of asset and liability and for each type of change in owners' equity.

> *Owners' equity for a corporation, called shareholders' equity, is classified by source as either paid-in capital or retained earnings.*

As discussed in Chapter 1, owners of a corporation are its shareholders, so owners' equity for a corporation is referred to as shareholders' equity. Shareholders' equity for a corporation arises primarily from two sources: (1) amounts *invested* by shareholders in the corporation and (2) amounts *earned* by the corporation (on behalf of its shareholders). These are reported as (1) **paid-in capital** and (2) **retained earnings**. Retained earnings equals net income less distributions to shareholders (primarily dividends) since the inception of the corporation. Illustration 2–2 shows the basic accounting equation for a corporation with shareholders' equity expanded to highlight its composition. We use the corporate format throughout the remainder of the chapter.

**Illustration 2–2**

Accounting Equation for a Corporation

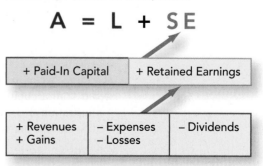

## Account Relationships

The *double-entry system* is used to process transactions.

All transactions could be recorded in columnar fashion as increases or decreases to elements of the accounting equation. However, even for a very small company with few transactions, this would become cumbersome. So, most companies use a process called the double-entry system. The term *double-entry* refers to the dual effect that each transaction has on the accounting equation.

A *general ledger* is a collection of storage areas, called *accounts,* used to keep track of increases and decreases in financial position elements.

Elements of the accounting equation are represented by accounts which are contained in a general ledger. Increases and decreases in each element of a company's financial position are recorded in these accounts. A separate account is maintained for individual assets and liabilities, retained earnings, and paid-in capital. Also, to accumulate information needed for the income statement, we use separate accounts to keep track of the changes in retained earnings caused by revenues, expenses, gains, and losses. The number of accounts depends on the complexity of the company's operations.

An account includes the account title, an account number to aid the processing task, and columns or fields for increases, decreases, the cumulative balance, and the date. For instructional purposes we use T-accounts instead of formal ledger accounts. A T-account has space at the top for the account title and two sides for recording increases and decreases.

In the double-entry system, *debit* means *left* side of an account and *credit* means *right* side of an account.

| Account Title |
|---|
| |

For centuries, accountants have effectively used a system of debits and credits to increase and decrease account balances in the ledger. Debits merely represent the *left* side of the account and credits the *right* side, as shown below.

Asset *increases* are entered on the *debit* side of accounts and *decreases* are entered on the *credit* side. Liability and equity account *increases* are *credits* and *decreases* are *debits.*

| Account Title | |
|---|---|
| debit side | credit side |

Whether a debit or a credit represents an increase or a decrease depends on the type of account. Accounts on the left side of the accounting equation (assets) are *increased* (+) by *debit* entries and *decreased* (−) by *credit* entries. Accounts on the right side of the accounting equation (liabilities and shareholders' equity) are *increased* (+) by *credit* entries and *decreased* (−) by *debit* entries. This arbitrary, but effective, procedure ensures that for each transaction the net impact on the left sides of accounts always equals the net impact on the right sides of accounts.

For example, consider the bank loan in our earlier illustration. An asset, cash, increased by $40,000. Increases in assets are *debits*. Liabilities also increased by $40,000. Increases in liabilities are *credits*.

| **Assets** | | = | **Liabilities** | | + | **Owners' Equity** |
|---|---|---|---|---|---|---|
| **Cash** | | | **Note Payable** | | | |
| debit | credit | | debit | credit | | |
| + 40,000 | | | | 40,000 + | | |

The debits equal the credits in every transaction (dual effect), so both before and after a transaction the accounting equation is in balance.

Prior exposure to the terms debit and credit probably comes from your experience with a bank account. For example, when a bank debits your checking account for service charges, it decreases your account balance. When you make a deposit, the bank credits your account, increasing your account balance. You must remember that from the bank's perspective, your bank account balance is a liability—it represents the amount that the bank owes you. Therefore, when the bank debits your account, it is decreasing its liability. When the bank credits your account, its liability increases.

Illustration 2–3 illustrates the relationship among the accounting equation, debits and credits, and the increases and decreases in financial position elements.

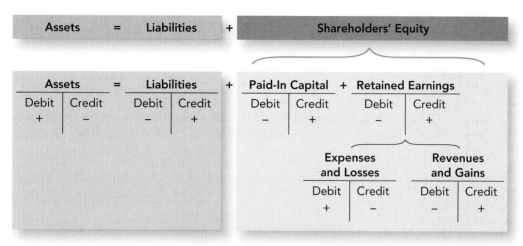

**Illustration 2–3**
Accounting Equation,
Debits and Credits,
Increases and Decreases

Notice that increases and decreases in retained earnings are recorded *indirectly*. For example, an expense represents a decrease in retained earnings, which requires a debit. That debit, however, is recorded in an appropriate expense account rather than in retained earnings itself. This allows the company to maintain a separate record of expenses incurred during an accounting period. The debit to retained earnings for the expense is recorded in a closing entry (reviewed later) at the end of the period, only after the expense total is reflected in the income statement. Similarly, an increase in retained earnings due to revenue is recorded indirectly with a credit to a revenue account, which is later reflected as a credit to retained earnings.

The general ledger accounts serve as control accounts. Subsidiary accounts associated with a particular general ledger control account are maintained in separate subsidiary ledgers. For example, a subsidiary ledger for accounts receivable contains individual account receivable accounts for each of the company's credit customers and the total of all subsidiary accounts would equal the amount in the control account. Subsidiary ledgers are discussed in more detail in Appendix 2C.

Each general ledger account can be classified as either *permanent* or *temporary*. **Permanent accounts** represent assets, liabilities, and shareholders' equity at a point in time. **Temporary accounts** represent changes in the retained earnings component of shareholders' equity for a corporation caused by revenue, expense, gain, and loss transactions. It would be cumbersome to record each revenue/expense, gain/loss transaction directly into the retained earnings account. The different types of events affecting retained earnings should be kept separate to facilitate the preparation of the financial statements. The balances in these temporary accounts are periodically, usually once a year, closed (zeroed out), and the net effect is recorded in the permanent retained earnings account. The temporary accounts need to be zeroed out to measure income on an annual basis. This closing process is discussed in a later section of this chapter.

*Permanent accounts represent the basic financial position elements of the accounting equation.*

*Temporary accounts keep track of the changes in the retained earnings component of shareholders' equity.*

# The Accounting Processing Cycle

Now that we've reviewed the basics of the double-entry system, let's look closer at the process used to identify, analyze, record, and summarize transactions and prepare financial statements. This section deals only with *external transactions,* those that involve an exchange transaction with another entity. Internal transactions are discussed in a later section.

The 10 steps in the accounting processing cycle are listed in Illustration 2–4. Steps 1–4 take place during the accounting period while steps 5–8 occur at the end of the accounting period. Steps 9 and 10 are required only at the end of the year.

We now discuss these steps in order.

The first step in the process is to *identify* external transactions affecting the accounting equation. An accountant usually does not directly witness business transactions. A mechanism is needed to relay the essential information about each transaction to the accountant. **Source documents** such as sales invoices, bills from suppliers, and cash register tapes serve this need.

**STEP 1**

Obtain information about transactions from *source documents.*

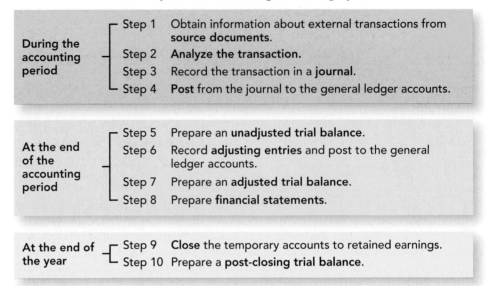

**Illustration 2–4**

The Accounting
Processing Cycle

**The Steps of the Accounting Processing Cycle**

| | | |
|---|---|---|
| **During the accounting period** | Step 1 | Obtain information about external transactions from source documents. |
| | Step 2 | **Analyze the transaction.** |
| | Step 3 | Record the transaction in a **journal**. |
| | Step 4 | **Post** from the journal to the general ledger accounts. |
| **At the end of the accounting period** | Step 5 | Prepare an **unadjusted trial balance**. |
| | Step 6 | Record **adjusting entries** and post to the general ledger accounts. |
| | Step 7 | Prepare an **adjusted trial balance**. |
| | Step 8 | Prepare **financial statements**. |
| **At the end of the year** | Step 9 | **Close** the temporary accounts to retained earnings. |
| | Step 10 | Prepare a **post-closing trial balance**. |

These source documents usually identify the date and nature of each transaction, the participating parties, and the monetary terms. For example, a sales invoice identifies the date of sale, the customer, the specific goods sold, the dollar amount of the sale, and the payment terms. With this information, the second step in the processing cycle, **transaction analysis**, can be accomplished. Transaction analysis is the process of reviewing the source documents to determine the dual effect on the accounting equation and the specific elements involved.

This process is summarized on the next page in Illustration 2–5 for the seven transactions described previously in Illustration 2–1. The item in each T-account is numbered to show the related transaction.

The third step in the process is to record the transaction in a **journal**. Journals provide a chronological record of all economic events affecting a firm. Each journal entry is expressed in terms of equal debits and credits to accounts affected by the transaction being recorded. Debits and credits represent increases or decreases to specific accounts, depending on the type of account, as explained earlier. For example, for credit sales, a debit to accounts receivable and a credit to sales revenue is recorded in a sales journal.

A sales journal is an example of a **special journal** used to record a repetitive type of transaction. Appendix 2C discusses the use of special journals in more depth. In this chapter and throughout the text, we use the **general journal** format to record all transactions.

● LO2–2     Any type of transaction can be recorded in a general journal. It has a place for the date of the transaction, a place for account titles, account numbers, and supporting explanations, as well as a place for debit entries, and a place for credit entries. A simplified journal entry is used throughout the text that lists the account titles to be debited and credited and the dollar amounts. A common convention is to list the debited accounts first, indent the credited accounts, and use the first of two columns for the debit amounts and the second column for the credit amounts. An explanation is entered for each journal entry (for ease in this example the explanation is located in the margin). For example, the **journal entry** for the bank loan in Illustration 2–1, which requires a debit to cash and a credit to note payable, is recorded as follows:

**STEP 2**

Analyze the transaction.

**STEP 3**

Record the transaction in a *journal*.

To record the borrowing of cash and the signing of a note payable.

| | | |
|---|---|---|
| Cash .......................................................................................... | 40,000 | |
|    Note payable .......................................................................... | | 40,000 |

**STEP 4**

*Post* from the journal to the general ledger accounts.

Step 4 is to periodically transfer or *post* the debit and credit information from the journal to individual ledger accounts. Recall that a ledger is simply a collection of all of the company's various accounts. Each account provides a summary of the effects of all events and transactions on that individual account. This process is called **posting**. Posting involves transferring debits and credits recorded in individual journal entries to the specific accounts

# Illustration 2–5 Transaction Analysis, the Accounting Equation, and Debits and Credits

| Transaction | Transaction Analysis | Accounting Equation | | | Account Entry |
|---|---|---|---|---|---|
| | | **Assets** = | **Liabilities** + | **Owners' Equity** | |
| 1. An attorney invested $50,000 to open a law office. | Assets (cash) and owners' equity each increased by $50,000. | +50,000 | | +50,000 | **Cash** / **Owners' Equity**<br>1. 50,000 \| 50,000  1. |
| | Cumulative balances | 50,000 = | | 50,000 | |
| 2. $40,000 was borrowed from a bank and a note payable was signed. | Assets (cash) and liabilities (note payable) each increased by $40,000. | +40,000 | +40,000 | | **Cash** / **Note Payable**<br>1. 50,000 \|  2. 40,000 \| 40,000  2. |
| | Cumulative balances | 90,000 = | 40,000 + | 50,000 | |
| 3. Supplies costing $3,000 were purchased on account. | Assets (supplies) and liabilities (accounts payable) each increased by $3,000. | +3,000 | +3,000 | | **Supplies** / **Accounts Payable**<br>3. 3,000 \|  \| 3,000  3. |
| | Cumulative balances | 93,000 = | 43,000 + | 50,000 | |
| 4. Services were performed on account for $10,000. | Assets (accounts receivable) and owners' equity (revenue) each increased by $10,000. | +10,000 | | +10,000 | **Accounts Receivable** / **Owners' Equity (Revenue)**<br>4. 10,000 \|  \| 10,000  4. |
| | Cumulative balances | 103,000 = | 43,000 + | 60,000 | |
| 5. Salaries of $5,000 were paid to employees. | Assets (cash) decreased and owners' equity decreased (salaries expense increased) by $5,000. | −5,000 | | −5,000 | **Cash** / **Owners' Equity (Salaries Expense)**<br>1. 50,000 \| 5,000  5.  2. 40,000 \|  5. 5,000 \| |
| | Cumulative balances | 98,000 = | 43,000 + | 55,000 | |
| 6. $500 of supplies were used. | Assets (supplies) decreased and owners' equity decreased (supplies expense increased) by $500. | −500 | | −500 | **Supplies** / **Owners' Equity (Supplies Expense)**<br>3. 3,000 \| 500  6.  6. 500 \| |
| | Cumulative balances | 97,500 = | 43,000 + | 54,500 | |
| 7. $1,000 was paid on account to the supplies vendor. | Assets (cash) and liabilities (accounts payable) each decreased by $1,000. | −1,000 | −1,000 | | **Cash** / **Accounts Payable**<br>1. 50,000 \| 5,000  5.  2. 40,000 \| 1,000  7.  7. 1,000 \| 3,000  3. |
| | Cumulative balances | 96,500 = | 42,000 + | 54,500 | |

affected. As discussed earlier in the chapter, most accounting systems today are computerized. For these systems, the journal input information creates a stored journal and simultaneously posts each entry to the ledger accounts.

These first four steps in the processing cycle are illustrated using the external transactions in Illustration 2–6 which occurred during the month of July 2013, the first month of operations for Dress Right Clothing Corporation. The company operates a retail store that sells men's and women's clothing. Dress Right is organized as a corporation so owners' equity is classified by source as either paid-in capital or retained earnings.

**Illustration 2–6**

External Transactions for July 2013

| July | 1 | Two individuals each invested $30,000 in the corporation. Each investor was issued 3,000 shares of common stock. |
|------|---|---|
| | 1 | Borrowed $40,000 from a local bank and signed two notes. The first note for $10,000 requires payment of principal and 10% interest in six months. The second note for $30,000 requires the payment of principal in two years. Interest at 10% is payable each year on July 1, 2014, and July 1, 2015. |
| | 1 | Paid $24,000 in advance for one year's rent on the store building. |
| | 1 | Purchased furniture and fixtures from Acme Furniture for $12,000 cash. |
| | 3 | Purchased $60,000 of clothing inventory on account from the Birdwell Wholesale Clothing Company. |
| | 6 | Purchased $2,000 of supplies for cash. |
| | 4–31 | During the month, sold merchandise costing $20,000 for $35,000 cash. |
| | 9 | Sold clothing on account to St. Jude's School for Girls for $3,500. The clothing cost $2,000. |
| | 16 | Subleased a portion of the building to a jewelry store. Received $1,000 in advance for the first two months' rent beginning on July 16. |
| | 20 | Paid Birdwell Wholesale Clothing $25,000 on account. |
| | 20 | Paid salaries to employees for the first half of the month, $5,000. |
| | 25 | Received $1,500 on account from St. Jude's. |
| | 30 | The corporation paid its shareholders a cash dividend of $1,000. |

The local bank requires that Dress Right furnish financial statements on a monthly basis. The transactions listed in the illustration are used to demonstrate the accounting processing cycle for the month of July 2013.

For each transaction, a source document provides the necessary information to complete steps two and three in the processing cycle, transaction analysis, and recording the appropriate journal entry. Each transaction listed in Illustration 2–6 is analyzed below, preceded by the necessary journal entry.

**To record the issuance of common stock.**

**July 1**
| Cash ................................................................................................ | 60,000 | |
| Common stock ............................................................................ | | 60,000 |

This first transaction is an investment by owners that increases an asset, cash, and also increases shareholders' equity. Increases in assets are recorded as debits and increases in shareholders' equity are recorded as credits. We use the paid-in capital account called common stock because stock was issued in exchange for cash paid in.[2]

**To record the borrowing of cash and the signing of notes payable.**

**July 1**
| Cash ................................................................................................ | 40,000 | |
| Notes payable ............................................................................ | | 40,000 |

This transaction causes increases in both cash and the liability, notes payable. Increases in assets are debits and increases in liabilities are credits. The notes require payment of $40,000 in

---

[2]The different types of stock are discussed in Chapter 18.

principal and $6,500 ([$10,000 $\times$ 10% $\times$ $\frac{6}{12}$ = $500] + [$30,000 $\times$ 10% $\times$ 2 years = $6,000])
in interest. However, at this point we are concerned only with the external transaction that
occurs when the cash is borrowed and the notes are signed. Later we discuss how the interest is recorded.

| July 1 | | |
|---|---|---|
| Prepaid rent ................................................................................. | 24,000 | |
|    Cash ................................................................................ | | 24,000 |

To record the payment of one year's rent in advance.

This transaction increased an asset called prepaid rent, which is debited, and decreased
the asset cash (a credit). Dress Right acquired the right to use the building for one full year.
This is an asset because it represents a future benefit to the company. As we will see later,
this asset expires over the one-year rental period.

| July 1 | | |
|---|---|---|
| Furniture and fixtures ................................................................. | 12,000 | |
|    Cash ................................................................................ | | 12,000 |

To record the purchase of furniture and fixtures.

This transaction increases one asset, furniture and fixtures, and decreases another, cash.

| July 3 | | |
|---|---|---|
| Inventory ..................................................................................... | 60,000 | |
|    Accounts payable ............................................................. | | 60,000 |

To record the purchase of merchandise inventory.

This purchase of merchandise on account is recorded by a debit to inventory, an asset,
and a credit to accounts payable, a liability. Increases in assets are debits, and increases in
liabilities are credits.

The Dress Right Clothing Company uses the *perpetual inventory system* to keep track
of its merchandise inventory. This system requires that the cost of merchandise purchased
be recorded in inventory, an asset account. When inventory is sold, the inventory account is
decreased by the cost of the item sold. The alternative method, the periodic system, is briefly
discussed on the next page, and Chapters 8 and 9 cover the topic of inventory in depth.

| July 6 | | |
|---|---|---|
| Supplies ....................................................................................... | 2,000 | |
|    Cash ................................................................................ | | 2,000 |

To record the purchase of supplies.

The acquisition of supplies is recorded as a debit to the asset account supplies (an increase)
and a credit to the asset cash (a decrease). Supplies are recorded as an asset because they
represent future benefits.

| July 4–31 | | |
|---|---|---|
| Cash ............................................................................................. | 35,000 | |
|    Sales revenue .................................................................... | | 35,000 |
| Cost of goods sold (expense) .................................................... | 20,000 | |
|    Inventory .......................................................................... | | 20,000 |

To record the month's cash sales and the cost of those sales.

During the month of July, cash sales to customers totaled $35,000. The company's
assets (cash) increase by this amount as does shareholders' equity. This increase in equity is
recorded by a credit to the temporary account sales revenue.

At the same time, an asset, inventory, decreases and retained earnings decreases. Recall
that expenses are outflows or using up of assets from providing goods and services. Dress
Right incurred an expense equal to the cost of the inventory sold. The temporary account
cost of goods sold increases. However, this increase in an expense represents a *decrease* in

shareholders' equity—retained earnings—and accordingly the account is debited. Both of these transactions are *summary* transactions. Normally each sale made during the month requires a separate and similar entry in a special journal which is discussed in Appendix 2C.

**To record a credit sale and the cost of that sale.**

**July 9**

| | | |
|---|---|---|
| Accounts receivable .................................................................................... | 3,500 | |
|    Sales revenue ......................................................................................... | | 3,500 |
| Cost of goods sold .................................................................................... | 2,000 | |
|    Inventory ................................................................................................ | | 2,000 |

This transaction is similar to the cash sale above. The only difference is that the asset acquired in exchange for merchandise is accounts receivable rather than cash.

# Additional Consideration

**Periodic Inventory System**

The principal alternative to the perpetual inventory system is the periodic system. This system requires that the cost of merchandise purchased be recorded in a temporary account called *purchases.* When inventory is sold, the inventory account is not decreased and cost of goods sold is not recorded. Cost of goods sold for a period is determined and the inventory account is adjusted only at the end of a reporting period.

For example, the purchase of $60,000 of merchandise on account by Dress Right Clothing is recorded as follows:

| | | |
|---|---|---|
| Purchases ..................................................................... | 60,000 | |
|    Accounts payable .................................................................. | | 60,000 |

No cost of goods sold entry is recorded when sales are made in the periodic system.

At the end of July, the amount of ending inventory is determined (either by means of a physical count of goods on hand or by estimation) to be $38,000 and cost of goods sold for the month is determined as follows:

| | |
|---|---|
| Beginning inventory | –0– |
| Plus: Purchases | 60,000 |
| Less: Ending inventory | (38,000) |
| Cost of goods sold | 22,000 |

The following journal entry records cost of goods sold for the period and adjusts the inventory account to the actual amount on hand (in this case from zero to $38,000):

| | | |
|---|---|---|
| Cost of goods sold.................................................................. | 22,000 | |
| Inventory ................................................................................ | 38,000 | |
|    Purchases.............................................................................. | | 60,000 |

Inventory is discussed in depth in Chapters 8 and 9.

**To record the receipt of rent in advance.**

**July 16**

| | | |
|---|---|---|
| Cash ................................................................................................................ | 1,000 | |
|    Unearned rent revenue (liability) ...................................................... | | 1,000 |

Cash increases by $1,000 so the cash account is debited. At this point, Dress Right does not recognize revenue even though cash has been received. Recall that the first criterion required for revenue recognition as stated in the realization principle is that the "earnings process is judged to be complete or virtually complete." Dress Right does not earn the revenue until it has provided the jewelry store with the use of facilities; that is, the revenue is earned as the rental period expires. On receipt of the cash, a liability called *unearned rent revenue* increases and is credited. This liability represents Dress Right's obligation to provide the use of facilities to the jewelry store.

| July 20 | | |
|---|---|---|
| Accounts payable | 25,000 | |
| Cash | | 25,000 |

*To record the payment of accounts payable.*

This transaction decreases both an asset (cash) and a liability (accounts payable). A debit decreases, the liability and a credit decreases the asset.

| July 20 | | |
|---|---|---|
| Salaries expense | 5,000 | |
| Cash | | 5,000 |

*To record the payment of salaries for the first half of the month.*

Employees were paid for services rendered during the first half of the month. The cash expenditure did not create an asset since no future benefits resulted. Cash decreases and is credited; shareholders' equity decreases and is debited. The debit is recorded in the temporary account salaries expense.

| July 25 | | |
|---|---|---|
| Cash | 1,500 | |
| Accounts receivable | | 1,500 |

*To record receipt of cash on account.*

This transaction is an exchange of one asset, accounts receivable, for another asset, cash.

| July 30 | | |
|---|---|---|
| Retained earnings | 1,000 | |
| Cash | | 1,000 |

*To record the payment of a cash dividend.*

The payment of a cash dividend is a distribution to owners that reduces both cash and retained earnings.

# Additional Consideration

An alternative method of recording a cash dividend is to debit a temporary account called dividends. In that case, the dividends account is later closed (transferred) to retained earnings along with the other temporary accounts at the end of the fiscal year. The journal entry to record the dividend using this approach is

| Dividends | 1,000 | |
|---|---|---|
| Cash | | 1,000 |

We discuss and illustrate the closing process later in the chapter.

Illustration 2–7 summarizes each of the transactions just discussed as they would appear in a general journal. In addition to the date, account titles, and debit and credit columns, the journal also has a column titled Post Ref. (Posting Reference). This usually is a number assigned to the general ledger account that is being debited or credited. For purposes of this illustration, all asset accounts have been assigned numbers in the 100s, all liabilities are 200s, permanent shareholders' equity accounts are 300s, revenues are 400s, and expenses are 500s.

**Illustration 2–7**
The General Journal

| General Journal | | | | Page 1 |
|---|---|---|---|---|
| **Date 2013** | **Account Title and Explanation** | **Post Ref.** | **Debit** | **Credit** |
| July  1 | Cash | 100 | 60,000 | |
| | Common stock | 300 | | 60,000 |
| | *To record the issuance of common stock.* | | | |
| 1 | Cash | 100 | 40,000 | |
| | Notes payable | 220 | | 40,000 |
| | *To record the borrowing of cash and the signing of notes payable.* | | | |
| 1 | Prepaid rent | 130 | 24,000 | |
| | Cash | 100 | | 24,000 |
| | *To record the payment of one year's rent in advance.* | | | |
| 1 | Furniture and fixtures | 150 | 12,000 | |
| | Cash | 100 | | 12,000 |
| | *To record the purchase of furniture and fixtures.* | | | |
| 3 | Inventory | 140 | 60,000 | |
| | Accounts payable | 210 | | 60,000 |
| | *To record the purchase of merchandise inventory.* | | | |
| 6 | Supplies | 125 | 2,000 | |
| | Cash | 100 | | 2,000 |
| | *To record the purchase of supplies.* | | | |
| 4–31 | Cash | 100 | 35,000 | |
| | Sales revenue | 400 | | 35,000 |
| | *To record cash sales for the month.* | | | |
| 4–31 | Cost of goods sold | 500 | 20,000 | |
| | Inventory | 140 | | 20,000 |
| | *To record the cost of cash sales.* | | | |
| 9 | Accounts receivable | 110 | 3,500 | |
| | Sales revenue | 400 | | 3,500 |
| | *To record credit sale.* | | | |
| 9 | Cost of goods sold | 500 | 2,000 | |
| | Inventory | 140 | | 2,000 |
| | *To record the cost of a credit sale.* | | | |
| 16 | Cash | 100 | 1,000 | |
| | Unearned rent revenue | 230 | | 1,000 |
| | *To record the receipt of rent in advance.* | | | |
| 20 | Accounts payable | 210 | 25,000 | |
| | Cash | 100 | | 25,000 |
| | *To record the payment of accounts payable.* | | | |
| 20 | Salaries expense | 510 | 5,000 | |
| | Cash | 100 | | 5,000 |
| | *To record the payment of salaries for the first half of the month.* | | | |
| 25 | Cash | 100 | 1,500 | |
| | Accounts receivable | 110 | | 1,500 |
| | *To record the receipt of cash on account.* | | | |
| 30 | Retained earnings | 310 | 1,000 | |
| | Cash | 100 | | 1,000 |
| | *To record the payment of a cash dividend.* | | | |

The ledger accounts also contain a posting reference, usually the page number of the journal in which the journal entry was recorded. This allows for easy cross-referencing between the journal and the ledger. Page 1 is used for Illustration 2–7.

Step 4 in the processing cycle is to transfer (post) the debit/credit information from the journal to the general ledger accounts. Illustration 2–8 contains the ledger accounts (in T-account form) for Dress Right *after* all the general journal transactions have been posted. The reference GJ1 next to each of the posted amounts indicates that the source of the entry is page 1 of the general journal. An alternative is to number each of the entries in chronological order and reference them by number.

● LO2–3

**Illustration 2–8**

General Ledger Accounts

### Balance Sheet Accounts

**Cash    100**

| | | | | |
|---|---|---|---|---|
| July 1 GJ1 | 60,000 | 24,000 | July 1 GJ1 | |
| 1 GJ1 | 40,000 | 12,000 | 1 GJ1 | |
| 4–31GJ1 | 35,000 | 2,000 | 6 GJ1 | |
| 16 GJ1 | 1,000 | 25,000 | 20 GJ1 | |
| 25 GJ1 | 1,500 | 5,000 | 20 GJ1 | |
| | | 1,000 | 30 GJ1 | |
| July 31 Bal. | 68,500 | | | |

**Prepaid Rent    130**

| | | | |
|---|---|---|---|
| July 1 GJ1 | 24,000 | | |
| July 31 Bal. | 24,000 | | |

**Accounts Receivable    110**

| | | | |
|---|---|---|---|
| July 9 GJ1 | 3,500 | 1,500    July 25 GJ1 | |
| July 31 Bal. | 2,000 | | |

**Inventory    140**

| | | | |
|---|---|---|---|
| July 3 GJ1 | 60,000 | 20,000 | July 4–31 |
| | | 2,000 | 9 GJ1 |
| July 31 Bal. | 38,000 | | |

**Supplies    125**

| | | |
|---|---|---|
| July 6 GJ1 | 2,000 | |
| July 31 Bal. | 2,000 | |

**Furniture and Fixtures    150**

| | | |
|---|---|---|
| July 1 GJ1 | 12,000 | |
| July 31 Bal. | 12,000 | |

**Accounts Payable    210**

| | | | |
|---|---|---|---|
| July 20 GJ1 | 25,000 | 60,000 | July 3 GJ1 |
| | | 35,000 | July 31 Bal. |

**Notes Payable    220**

| | | |
|---|---|---|
| | 40,000 | July 1 GJ1 |
| | 40,000 | July 31 Bal. |

**Unearned Rent Revenue    230**

| | | |
|---|---|---|
| | 1,000 | July 16 GJ1 |
| | 1,000 | July 31 Bal. |

**Common Stock    300**

| | | |
|---|---|---|
| | 60,000 | July 1 GJ1 |
| | 60,000 | July 31 Bal. |

**Retained Earnings    310**

| | | | |
|---|---|---|---|
| July 30 GJ1 | 1,000 | | |
| July 31 Bal. | 1,000 | | |

### Income Statement Accounts

**Sales Revenue    400**

| | | |
|---|---|---|
| | 35,000 | July 4–31 GJ1 |
| | 3,500 | 9 GJ1 |
| | 38,500 | July 31 Bal. |

**Cost of Goods Sold    500**

| | | | |
|---|---|---|---|
| July 4–31 GJ1 | 20,000 | | |
| 9 GJ1 | 2,000 | | |
| July 31 Bal. | 22,000 | | |

**Salaries Expense    510**

| | | |
|---|---|---|
| July 20 GJ1 | 5,000 | |
| July 31 Bal. | 5,000 | |

**STEP 5**

*Prepare an unadjusted trial balance.*

Before financial statements are prepared and before adjusting entries (internal transactions) are recorded at the end of an accounting period, an **unadjusted trial balance** usually is prepared—step 5. A trial balance is simply a list of the general ledger accounts, listed in the order that they appear in the ledger, along with their balances at a particular date. Its purpose is to allow us to check for completeness and to prove that the sum of the accounts with debit balances equals the sum of the accounts with credit balances, that is, the accounting equation is in balance. The fact that the debits and credits are equal, though, does not necessarily ensure that the equal balances are correct. The trial balance could contain offsetting errors. As we will see later in the chapter, this trial balance also facilitates the preparation of adjusting entries.

The unadjusted trial balance at July 31, 2013, for the Dress Right Clothing Corporation appears in Illustration 2–9. Notice that retained earnings has a debit balance of $1,000. This reflects the payment of the cash dividend to shareholders. The increases and decreases in retained earnings from revenue, expense, gain and loss transactions are recorded indirectly in temporary accounts. Before the start of the next year, these increases and decreases are transferred to the retained earnings account.

**Illustration 2–9**

Unadjusted Trial Balance

**At any time, the total of all debit balances should equal the total of all credit balances.**

| **DRESS RIGHT CLOTHING CORPORATION**<br>**Unadjusted Trial Balance**<br>**July 31, 2013** | | |
|---|---|---|
| **Account Title** | **Debits** | **Credits** |
| Cash | 68,500 | |
| Accounts receivable | 2,000 | |
| Supplies | 2,000 | |
| Prepaid rent | 24,000 | |
| Inventory | 38,000 | |
| Furniture and fixtures | 12,000 | |
| Accounts payable | | 35,000 |
| Notes payable | | 40,000 |
| Unearned rent revenue | | 1,000 |
| Common stock | | 60,000 |
| Retained earnings | 1,000 | |
| Sales revenue | | 38,500 |
| Cost of goods sold | 22,000 | |
| Salaries expense | 5,000 | |
| Totals | 174,500 | 174,500 |

## Concept Review Exercise

**JOURNAL ENTRIES FOR EXTERNAL TRANSACTIONS**

The Wyndham Wholesale Company began operations on August 1, 2013. The following transactions occur during the month of August.

a. Owners invest $50,000 cash in the corporation in exchange for 5,000 shares of common stock.

b. Equipment is purchased for $20,000 cash.

c. On the first day of August, $6,000 rent on a building is paid for the months of August and September.

d. Merchandise inventory costing $38,000 is purchased on account. The company uses the perpetual inventory system.

e. $30,000 is borrowed from a local bank, and a note payable is signed.

f. Credit sales for the month are $40,000. The cost of merchandise sold is $22,000.

g. $15,000 is collected on account from customers.

h. $20,000 is paid on account to suppliers of merchandise.

i. Salaries of $7,000 are paid to employees for August.

j. A bill for $2,000 is received from the local utility company for the month of August.

k. $20,000 cash is loaned to another company, evidenced by a note receivable.

l. The corporation pays its shareholders a cash dividend of $1,000.

**Required:**

1. Prepare a journal entry for each transaction.

2. Prepare an unadjusted trial balance as of August 31, 2013.

**Solution:**

1. Prepare a journal entry for each transaction.

  a. The issuance of common stock for cash increases both cash and shareholders' equity (common stock).

| | | |
|---|---|---|
| Cash ............................................................................................... | 50,000 | |
| Common stock ............................................................................. | | 50,000 |

  b. The purchase of equipment increases equipment and decreases cash.

| | | |
|---|---|---|
| Equipment ..................................................................................... | 20,000 | |
| Cash ............................................................................................ | | 20,000 |

  c. The payment of rent in advance increases prepaid rent and decreases cash.

| | | |
|---|---|---|
| Prepaid rent .................................................................................. | 6,000 | |
| Cash ............................................................................................ | | 6,000 |

  d. The purchase of merchandise on account increases both inventory and accounts payable.

| | | |
|---|---|---|
| Inventory ....................................................................................... | 38,000 | |
| Accounts payable ........................................................................ | | 38,000 |

  e. Borrowing cash and signing a note increases both cash and note payable.

| | | |
|---|---|---|
| Cash ............................................................................................... | 30,000 | |
| Note payable ............................................................................... | | 30,000 |

  f. The sale of merchandise on account increases both accounts receivable and sales revenue. Also, cost of goods sold increases and inventory decreases.

| | | |
|---|---|---|
| Accounts receivable ..................................................................... | 40,000 | |
| Sales revenue ............................................................................. | | 40,000 |
| Cost of goods sold ....................................................................... | 22,000 | |
| Inventory ..................................................................................... | | 22,000 |

  g. The collection of cash on account increases cash and decreases accounts receivable.

| | | |
|---|---|---|
| Cash ............................................................................................... | 15,000 | |
| Accounts receivable ................................................................... | | 15,000 |

  h. The payment of suppliers on account decreases both accounts payable and cash.

| | | |
|---|---|---|
| Accounts payable .......................................................................... | 20,000 | |
| Cash ............................................................................................ | | 20,000 |

i. The payment of salaries for the period increases salaries expense (decreases retained earnings) and decreases cash.

| | | |
|---|---|---|
| Salaries expense .............................................................................. | 7,000 | |
| Cash .......................................................................................... | | 7,000 |

j. The receipt of a bill for services rendered increases both an expense (utilities expense) and accounts payable. The expense decreases retained earnings.

| | | |
|---|---|---|
| Utilities expense .............................................................................. | 2,000 | |
| Accounts payable .......................................................................... | | 2,000 |

k. The lending of cash to another entity and the signing of a note increases note receivable and decreases cash.

| | | |
|---|---|---|
| Note receivable ............................................................................... | 20,000 | |
| Cash .......................................................................................... | | 20,000 |

l. Cash dividends paid to shareholders reduce both retained earnings and cash.

| | | |
|---|---|---|
| Retained earnings[3] ......................................................................... | 1,000 | |
| Cash .......................................................................................... | | 1,000 |

2. Prepare an unadjusted trial balance as of August 31, 2013.

| Account Title | Debits | Credits |
|---|---|---|
| Cash | 21,000 | |
| Accounts receivable | 25,000 | |
| Prepaid rent | 6,000 | |
| Inventory | 16,000 | |
| Note receivable | 20,000 | |
| Equipment | 20,000 | |
| Accounts payable | | 20,000 |
| Note payable | | 30,000 |
| Common stock | | 50,000 |
| Retained earnings | 1,000 | |
| Sales revenue | | 40,000 |
| Cost of goods sold | 22,000 | |
| Salaries expense | 7,000 | |
| Utilities expense | 2,000 | |
| Totals | 140,000 | 140,000 |

## Adjusting Entries

● LO2–4

**STEP 6**

Record *adjusting entries* and post to the ledger accounts.

Step 6 in the processing cycle is to record in the general journal and post to the ledger accounts the effect of *internal events* on the accounting equation. These transactions do not involve an exchange transaction with another entity and, therefore, are not initiated by a source document. They are recorded *at the end of any period when financial statements are prepared.* These transactions are commonly referred to as **adjusting entries**.

Even when all transactions and events are analyzed, corrected, journalized, and posted to appropriate ledger accounts, some account balances will require updating. Adjusting entries

---

[3]An alternative is to debit a temporary account—dividends—that is closed to retained earnings at the end of the fiscal year along with the other temporary accounts.

are required to implement the *accrual accounting model.* More specifically, these entries are required to satisfy the *realization principle* and the *matching principle.* Adjusting entries help ensure that all revenues earned in a period are recognized in that period, regardless of when the cash is received. Also, they enable a company to recognize all expenses incurred during a period, regardless of when cash payment is made. As a result, a period's income statement provides a more complete measure of a company's operating performance and a better measure for predicting future operating cash flows. The balance sheet also provides a more complete assessment of assets and liabilities as sources of future cash receipts and disbursements. You might think of adjusting entries as a method of bringing the company's financial information up to date before preparing the financial statements.

Adjusting entries are necessary for three situations:

1. Prepayments, sometimes referred to as *deferrals.*
2. Accruals.
3. Estimates.

## Prepayments

Prepayments occur when the cash flow *precedes* either expense or revenue recognition. For example, a company may buy supplies in one period but use them in a later period. The cash outflow creates an asset (supplies) which then must be expensed in a future period as the asset is used up. Similarly, a company may receive cash from a customer in one period but provide the customer with a good or service in a future period. For instance, magazine publishers usually receive cash in advance for magazine subscriptions. The cash inflow creates a liability (unearned revenue) that is recognized as revenue in a future period when it is earned.

**PREPAID EXPENSES.** Prepaid expenses are the costs of assets acquired in one period and expensed in a future period. Whenever cash is paid, and it is not to (1) satisfy a liability or (2) pay a dividend or return capital to owners, it must be determined whether or not the payment creates future benefits or whether the payment benefits only the current period. The purchase of machinery, equipment, or supplies or the payment of rent in advance are examples of payments that create future benefits and should be recorded as assets. The benefits provided by these assets expire in future periods and their cost is expensed in future periods as related revenues are recognized.

To illustrate this concept, assume that a company paid a radio station $2,000 in July for advertising. If that $2,000 were for advertising provided by the radio station during the month of July, the entire $2,000 would be expensed in the same period as the cash disbursement. If, however, the $2,000 was a payment for advertising to be provided in a future period, say the month of August, then the cash disbursement creates an asset called *prepaid advertising.* An adjusting entry is required at the end of August to increase advertising expense (decrease shareholders' equity) and to decrease the asset prepaid advertising by $2,000. Assuming that the cash disbursement records a debit to an asset, as in this example, the adjusting entry for a prepaid expense is, therefore, a *debit to an expense* and a *credit to an asset.*

The unadjusted trial balance can provide a starting point for determining which adjusting entries are required for a period, particularly for prepayments. Review the July 31, 2013, unadjusted trial balance for the Dress Right Clothing Corporation in Illustration 2–9 on page 64 and try to anticipate the required adjusting entries for prepaid expenses.

The first asset that requires adjustment is supplies, $2,000 of which were purchased during July. This transaction created an asset as the supplies will be used in future periods. The company could either track the supplies used or simply count the supplies at the end of the period and determine the dollar amount of supplies remaining. Assume that Dress Right determines that at the end of July, $1,200 of supplies remain. The following adjusting journal entry is required.

| July 31 | | |
|---|---|---|
| Supplies expense ............................................................ | 800 | |
|     Supplies ............................................................ | | 800 |

---

**Supplies**

| | | |
|---|---|---|
| Beg. bal. | 0 | |
| | 2,000 | 800 |
| End bal. | 1,200 | |

**Supplies Expense**

| | | |
|---|---|---|
| Beg. bal. | 0 | |
| | 800 | |
| End bal. | 800 | |

*To record the cost of expired rent for the month of July.*

**Prepaid Rent**

| | | |
|---|---|---|
| Beg. bal. | 0 | |
| | 24,000 | 2,000 |
| End bal. | 22,000 | |

**Rent Expense**

| | | |
|---|---|---|
| Beg. bal. | 0 | |
| | 2,000 | |
| End bal. | 2,000 | |

*To record depreciation of furniture and fixtures for the month of July.*

*Unearned revenues represent liabilities recorded when cash is received from customers in advance of providing a good or service.*

After this entry is recorded and posted to the ledger accounts, the supplies (asset) account is reduced to a $1,200 debit balance, and the supplies expense account will have an $800 debit balance.

The next prepaid expense requiring adjustment is rent. Recall that at the beginning of July, the company paid $24,000 to its landlord representing one year's rent in advance. As it is reasonable to assume that the rent services provided each period are equal, the monthly rent is $2,000. At the end of July 2013, one month's prepaid rent has expired and must be recognized as expense.

| July 31 | | |
|---|---|---|
| Rent expense ($24,000 ÷ 12) ........................................................ | 2,000 | |
| Prepaid rent ............................................................. | | 2,000 |

After this entry is recorded and posted to the ledger accounts, the prepaid rent account will have a debit balance of $22,000, representing 11 remaining months at $2,000 per month, and the rent expense account will have a $2,000 debit balance.

The final prepayment involves the asset represented by furniture and fixtures that was purchased for $12,000. This asset has a long life but nevertheless will expire over time. For the previous two adjusting entries, it was fairly straightforward to determine the amount of the asset that expired during the period.

However, it is difficult, if not impossible, to determine how much of the benefits from using the furniture and fixtures expired during any particular period. Recall from Chapter 1 that one approach to implementing the matching principle is to recognize an expense "by a systematic and rational allocation to specific time periods."

Assume that the furniture and fixtures have a useful life of five years (60 months) and will be worthless at the end of that period, and that we choose to allocate the cost equally over the period of use. The amount of monthly expense, called *depreciation expense,* is $200 ($12,000 ÷ 60 months = $200), and the following adjusting entry is recorded.

| July 31 | | |
|---|---|---|
| Depreciation expense ................................................ | 200 | |
| Accumulated depreciation—furniture and fixtures .................... | | 200 |

The entry reduces an asset, furniture and fixtures, by $200. However, the asset account is not reduced directly. Instead, the credit is to an account called *accumulated depreciation.* This is a contra account to furniture and fixtures. The normal balance in a contra asset account will be a credit, that is, "contra," or opposite, to the normal debit balance in an asset account. The purpose of the contra account is to keep the original cost of the asset intact while reducing it indirectly. In the balance sheet, furniture and fixtures is reported net of accumulated depreciation. This topic is covered in depth in Chapter 11.

After this entry is recorded and posted to the ledger accounts, the accumulated depreciation account will have a credit balance of $200 and the depreciation expense account will have a $200 debit balance. If a required adjusting entry for a prepaid expense is not recorded, net income, assets, and shareholders' equity (retained earnings) will be overstated.

**UNEARNED REVENUES.**     Unearned revenues are created when a company receives cash from a customer in one period for goods or services that are to be provided in a future period. The cash receipt, an external transaction, is recorded as a debit to cash and a credit to a liability. This liability reflects the company's obligation to provide goods or services in the future.

To illustrate an unearned revenue transaction, assume that during the month of June a magazine publisher received $24 in cash for a 24-month subscription to a monthly magazine. The subscription begins in July. On receipt of the cash, the publisher records a liability, unearned subscription revenue, of $24. Subsequently, revenue of $1 is earned as each monthly magazine is published and mailed to the customer. An adjusting entry is required each month to increase shareholders' equity (revenue) to recognize the $1 in revenue earned and to decrease the liability. Assuming that the cash receipt entry included a credit to a liability, the adjusting entry for unearned revenues, therefore, is a *debit to a liability,* in this case unearned subscription revenue, and a *credit to revenue.*

> The adjusting entry required when unearned revenues are earned is a *debit to a liability* and a *credit to revenue.*

Once again, the unadjusted trial balance provides information concerning unearned revenues. For Dress Right Clothing Corporation, the only unearned revenue in the trial balance is unearned rent revenue. Recall that the company subleased a portion of its building to a jewelry store for $500 per month. On July 16, the jewelry store paid Dress Right $1,000 in advance for the first two months' rent. The transaction was recorded as a debit to cash and a credit to unearned rent revenue.

At the end of July, how much of the $1,000 has been earned? Approximately one-half of one month's rent has been earned, or $250, requiring the following adjusting journal entry.

| July 31 | | |
|---|---|---|
| Unearned rent revenue ................................................................. | 250 | |
| Rent revenue .................................................................... | | 250 |

> To record previously unearned rent revenue earned during July.

After this entry is recorded and posted to the ledger accounts, the unearned rent revenue account is reduced to a credit balance of $750 for the remaining one and one-half months' rent, and the rent revenue account will have a $250 credit balance. If this entry is not recorded, net income and shareholders' equity (retained earnings) will be understated, and liabilities will be overstated.

**Unearned Rent Revenue**

| | 0 Beg. bal. |
|---|---|
| 250 | 1,000 |
| | 750 End bal. |

**Rent Revenue**

| | 0 Beg. bal. |
|---|---|
| | 250 |
| | 250 End bal. |

### ALTERNATIVE APPROACH TO RECORD PREPAYMENTS.
The same end result can be achieved for prepayments by recording the external transaction directly into an expense or revenue account. In fact, many companies prefer this approach. For simplicity, bookkeeping instructions may require all cash payments for expenses to be debited to the appropriate expense account and all cash receipts for revenues to be credited to the appropriate revenue account. The adjusting entry then records the *unexpired* prepaid expense (asset) or *unearned* revenue (liability) as of the end of the period.

For example, on July 1, 2013, Dress Right paid $24,000 in cash for one year's rent on its building. The entry included a debit to prepaid rent. The company could have debited rent expense instead.

**Rent Expense**

| Beg. bal. | 0 | |
|---|---|---|
| | 24,000 | 22,000 |
| End bal. | 2,000 | |

| **Alternative Approach** | | |
|---|---|---|
| **July 1** | | |
| Rent expense ............................................................... | 24,000 | |
| Cash ............................................................... | | 24,000 |

The adjusting entry then records the amount of prepaid rent as of the end of July, $22,000, and reduces rent expense to $2,000, the cost of rent for the month of July.

**Prepaid Rent**

| Beg. bal. | 0 | |
|---|---|---|
| | 22,000 | |
| End bal. | 22,000 | |

| **Alternative Approach** | | |
|---|---|---|
| **July 31** | | |
| Prepaid rent ............................................................... | 22,000 | |
| Rent expense ............................................................... | | 22,000 |

The net effect of handling the transactions in this manner is the same as the previous treatment. Either way, the prepaid rent account will have a debit balance at the end of July of $22,000, and the rent expense account will have a debit balance of $2,000. What's important is that an adjusting entry is recorded to ensure the appropriate amounts are reflected in both the expense and asset *before financial statements are prepared.*

Similarly, the July 16 cash receipt from the jewelry store representing an advance for two months' rent could have been recorded by Dress Right as a credit to rent revenue instead of unearned rent revenue (a liability).

**Rent Revenue**

| | | |
|---|---|---|
| | 0 | Beg. bal. |
| 750 | 1,000 | |
| | 250 | End bal. |

**Alternative Approach**

**July 16**

| | | |
|---|---|---|
| Cash ................................................................ | 1,000 | |
|    Rent revenue ................................................ | | 1,000 |

If Dress Right records the entire $1,000 as rent revenue in this way, it would then use the adjusting entry to record the amount of unearned revenue as of the end of July, $750, and reduce rent revenue to $250, the amount of revenue earned during the month of July.

**Unearned Rent Revenue**

| | | |
|---|---|---|
| | 0 | Beg. bal. |
| | 750 | |
| | 750 | End bal. |

**Alternative Approach**

**July 31**

| | | |
|---|---|---|
| Rent revenue ................................................... | 750 | |
|    Unearned rent revenue .................................. | | 750 |

## Accruals

*Accruals involve transactions where the cash outflow or inflow takes place in a period subsequent to expense or revenue recognition.*

**Accruals** occur when the cash flow comes *after* either expense or revenue recognition. For example, a company often uses the services of another entity in one period and pays for them in a subsequent period. An expense must be recognized in the period incurred and an accrued liability recorded. Also, goods and services often are provided to customers on credit. In such instances, a revenue is recognized in the period earned and an asset, a receivable, is recorded.

Many accruals involve external transactions that automatically are recorded from a source document. For example, a sales invoice for a credit sale provides all the information necessary to record the debit to accounts receivable and the credit to sales revenue. However, there are some accruals that involve internal transactions and thus require adjusting entries. Because accruals involve recognition of expense or revenue before cash flow, the unadjusted trial balance will not be as helpful in identifying required adjusting entries as with prepayments.

*Accrued liabilities represent liabilities recorded when an expense has been incurred prior to cash payment.*

**ACCRUED LIABILITIES.** For accrued liabilities, we are concerned with expenses incurred but not yet paid. Dress Right Clothing Corporation requires two adjusting entries for accrued liabilities at July 31, 2013.

The first entry is for employee salaries for the second half of July. Recall that on July 20 the company paid employees $5,000 for salaries for the first half of the month. Salaries for the second half of July will probably be paid in early August. Nevertheless, the company incurred an expense in July for services provided to it by its employees. Also, there exists an obligation at the end of July to pay the salaries earned by employees. An adjusting entry is required to increase salaries expense (decrease shareholders' equity) and to increase liabilities for the salaries payable. The adjusting entry for an accrued liability always includes a *debit to an expense,* and a *credit to a liability.* Assuming that salaries for the second half of July are $5,500, the following adjusting entry is recorded.

*The adjusting entry required to record an accrued liability is a debit to an expense and a credit to a liability.*

*To record accrued salaries at the end of July.*

**July 31**

| | | |
|---|---|---|
| Salaries expense........................................................... | 5,500 | |
|    Salaries payable........................................................ | | 5,500 |

**Salaries Payable**

| | | |
|---|---|---|
| | 0 | Beg. bal. |
| | 5,500 | |
| | 5,500 | End bal. |

After this entry is recorded and posted to the general ledger, the salaries expense account will have a debit balance of $10,500 ($5,000 + 5,500), and the salaries payable account will have a credit balance of $5,500.

The unadjusted trial balance does provide information about the second required accrued liability entry. In the trial balance we can see a balance in the notes payable account of $40,000. The company borrowed this amount on July 1, 2013, evidenced by two notes, each requiring the payment of 10% interest. Whenever the trial balance reveals interest-bearing debt, and interest is not paid on the last day of the period, an adjusting entry is required for the amount of interest that has built up (accrued) since the last payment date or the last date interest was accrued. In this case, we calculate interest as follows:

$$\text{Principal} \times \text{Interest rate} \times \text{Time} = \text{Interest}$$
$$\$40,000 \times \quad 10\% \quad \times \quad \frac{1}{12} = \$333 \text{ (rounded)}$$

*Interest rates always are stated as the annual rate.* Therefore, the above calculation uses this annual rate multiplied by the principal amount multiplied by the amount of time outstanding, in this case one month or one-twelfth of a year.

| Salaries Expense | | |
|---|---|---|
| Beg. bal. | 0 | |
| July 20 | 5,000 | |
| | | 5,500 |
| End bal. | 10,500 | |

| **July 31** | | |
|---|---|---|
| Interest expense ........................................................................ | 333 | |
|     Interest payable ............................................................ | | 333 |

*To accrue interest expense for July on notes payable.*

After this entry is recorded and posted to the ledger accounts, the interest expense account will have a debit balance of $333, and the interest payable account will have a credit balance of $333. Failure to record a required adjusting entry for an accrued liability will cause net income and shareholders' equity (retained earnings) to be overstated, and liabilities to be understated.[4]

**ACCRUED RECEIVABLES.** Accrued receivables involve the recognition of revenue earned *before* cash is received. An example of an internal accrued revenue event is the recognition of interest earned on a loan to another entity. For example, assume that Dress Right loaned another corporation $30,000 at the beginning of August, evidenced by a note receivable. Terms of the note call for the payment of principal, $30,000, and interest at 8% in three months. An external transaction records the cash disbursement—a debit to note receivable and a credit to cash of $30,000.

*Accrued receivables involve situations when the revenue is earned in a period prior to the cash receipt.*

What adjusting entry would be required at the end of August? Dress Right needs to record the interest revenue earned but not yet received along with the corresponding receivable. Interest receivable increases and interest revenue (shareholders' equity) also increases. The adjusting entry for accrued receivables always includes a *debit to an asset,* a receivable, and a *credit to revenue.* In this case, at the end of August Dress Right recognizes $200 in interest revenue ($30,000 \times 8\% \times \frac{1}{12}$) and makes the following adjusting entry. If this entry is not recorded, net income, assets, and shareholders' equity (retained earnings) will be understated.

*The adjusting entry required to record an accrued revenue is a debit to an asset, a receivable, and a credit to revenue.*

| **August 31** | | |
|---|---|---|
| Interest receivable ...................................................................... | 200 | |
|     Interest revenue .......................................................... | | 200 |

*To accrue interest revenue earned in August on note receivable.*

There are no accrued revenue adjusting entries required for Dress Right at the end of July.

The required adjusting entries for prepayments and accruals are recapped with the aid of T-accounts in Illustration 2–10. In each case an expense or revenue is recognized in a period that differs from the period in which cash was paid or received. These adjusting entries are necessary to properly measure operating performance and financial position on an accrual basis.

---

[4]Dress Right Clothing is a corporation. Corporations are income-tax-paying entities. Income taxes—federal, state, and local—are assessed on an annual basis and payments are made throughout the year. An additional adjusting entry would be required for Dress Right to accrue the amount of estimated income taxes payable that are applicable to the month of July. Accounting for income taxes is introduced in Chapter 4 and covered in depth in Chapter 16.

**Illustration 2–10**

Adjusting Entries

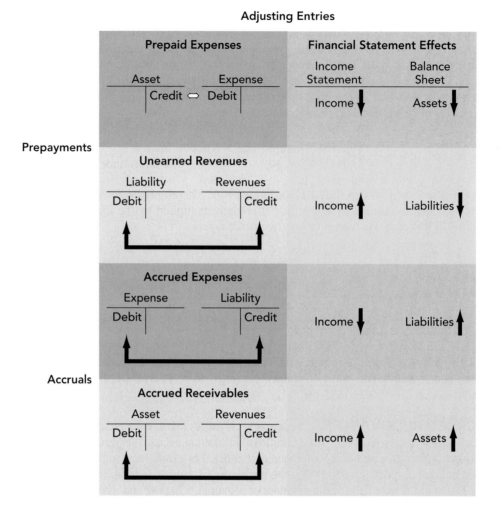

**Estimates**

Accountants often must make *estimates* in order to comply with the accrual accounting model.

A third classification of adjusting entries is estimates. Accountants often must make estimates of future events to comply with the accrual accounting model. For example, the calculation of depreciation expense requires an estimate of expected useful life of the asset being depreciated as well as its expected residual value. We discussed the adjusting entries for depreciation expense in the context of its being a prepayment, but it also could be thought of as an estimate.

One adjusting-entry situation involving an estimate that does not fit neatly into either the prepayment or accrual classification is bad debts. Accounting for bad debts requires a company to estimate the amount of accounts receivable that ultimately will prove to be uncollectible and to reduce accounts receivable by that estimated amount. This is neither a prepayment nor an accrual because it does not involve the payment of cash either before or after income is reduced. We explore accounts receivable and bad debts in depth in Chapter 7.

Illustration 2–11 recaps the July 31, 2013, adjusting entries for Dress Right Clothing Corporation as they would appear in a general journal. The journal entries are numbered (1) to (6) corresponding to the number used in the worksheet illustrated in Appendix 2A.

After the adjusting entries are posted to the general ledger accounts, the next step—step 7—in the processing cycle is to prepare an adjusted trial balance. The term adjusted refers to the fact that adjusting entries have now been posted to the accounts. Recall that the column titled Post Ref. (Posting Reference) is the number assigned to the general ledger account that is being debited or credited. Illustration 2–12 shows the July 31, 2013, adjusted trial balance for Dress Right Clothing Corporation.

**Illustration 2—11**
The General Journal—
Adjusting Entries

**DRESS RIGHT CLOTHING CORPORATION**

**General Journal**                                                                Page 2

| Date 2013 | | Account Title and Explanation | Post. Ref. | Debit | Credit |
|---|---|---|---|---|---|
| July | 31 | Supplies expense | 520 | 800 | |
| (1) | | Supplies | 125 | | 800 |
| | | *To record the cost of supplies used during the month of July.* | | | |
| (2) | 31 | Rent expense | 530 | 2,000 | |
| | | Prepaid rent | 130 | | 2,000 |
| | | *To record the cost of expired rent for the month of July.* | | | |
| (3) | 31 | Depreciation expense | 540 | 200 | |
| | | Accumulated depreciation—furniture and fixtures | 155 | | 200 |
| | | *To record depreciation of furniture and fixtures for the month of July.* | | | |
| (4) | 31 | Unearned rent revenue | 230 | 250 | |
| | | Rent revenue | 410 | | 250 |
| | | *To record previously unearned rent revenue earned during July.* | | | |
| (5) | 31 | Salaries expense | 510 | 5,500 | |
| | | Salaries payable | 230 | | 5,500 |
| | | *To record accrued salaries at the end of July.* | | | |
| (6) | 31 | Interest expense | 550 | 333 | |
| | | Interest payable | 240 | | 333 |
| | | *To accrue interest expense for July on notes payable.* | | | |

**Illustration 2—12**
Adjusted Trial Balance

**STEP 7**

Prepare an *adjusted trial balance.*

**DRESS RIGHT CLOTHING CORPORATION**
**Adjusted Trial Balance**
**July 31, 2013**

| Account Title | Debits | Credits |
|---|---|---|
| Cash | 68,500 | |
| Accounts receivable | 2,000 | |
| Supplies | 1,200 | |
| Prepaid rent | 22,000 | |
| Inventory | 38,000 | |
| Furniture and fixtures | 12,000 | |
| Accumulated depreciation—furniture and fixtures | | 200 |
| Accounts payable | | 35,000 |
| Notes payable | | 40,000 |
| Unearned rent revenue | | 750 |
| Salaries payable | | 5,500 |
| Interest payable | | 333 |
| Common stock | | 60,000 |
| Retained earnings | 1,000 | |
| Sales revenue | | 38,500 |
| Rent revenue | | 250 |
| Cost of goods sold | 22,000 | |
| Salaries expense | 10,500 | |
| Supplies expense | 800 | |
| Rent expense | 2,000 | |
| Depreciation expense | 200 | |
| Interest expense | 333 | |
| Totals | 180,533 | 180,533 |

# Concept Review Exercise

**ADJUSTING ENTRIES**

The Wyndham Wholesale Company needs to prepare financial statements at the end of August 2013 for presentation to its bank. An unadjusted trial balance as of August 31, 2013, was presented in a previous concept review exercise on page 66.

The following information also is available:

a. The note payable requires the entire $30,000 in principal plus interest at 10% to be paid on July 31, 2014. The date of the loan is August 1, 2013.

b. Depreciation on the equipment for the month of August is $500.

c. The note receivable is dated August 16, 2013. The note requires the entire $20,000 in principal plus interest at 12% to be repaid in four months (the loan was outstanding for one-half month during August).

d. The prepaid rent of $6,000 represents rent for the months of August and September.

**Required:**

1. Prepare any necessary adjusting entries at August 31, 2013.

2. Prepare an adjusted trial balance as of August 31, 2013.

3. What is the total net effect on income (overstated or understated) if the adjusting entries are not made?

**Solution:**

1. Prepare any necessary adjusting entries at August 31, 2013.

   a. An adjusting entry is required to accrue the interest expense on the note payable for the month of August. Accrued interest is calculated as follows:

$$\$30,000 \times 10\% \times \tfrac{1}{12} = \$250$$

| | | |
|---|---|---|
| Interest expense ............................................................................ | 250 | |
|     Interest payable .................................................................... | | 250 |

   b. Depreciation expense on the equipment must be recorded.

| | | |
|---|---|---|
| Depreciation expense ..................................................................... | 500 | |
|     Accumulated depreciation—equipment ..................................... | | 500 |

   c. An adjusting entry is required for the one-half month of accrued interest revenue earned on the note receivable. Accrued interest is calculated as follows:

$$\$20,000 \times 12\% \times \tfrac{1}{12} \times \tfrac{1}{2} = \$100$$

| | | |
|---|---|---|
| Interest receivable ......................................................................... | 100 | |
|     Interest revenue .................................................................... | | 100 |

   d. An adjusting entry is required to recognize the amount of prepaid rent that expired during August.

| | | |
|---|---|---|
| Rent expense ................................................................................. | 3,000 | |
|     Prepaid rent .......................................................................... | | 3,000 |

2. Prepare an adjusted trial balance as of August 31, 2013.

| Account Title | Debits | Credits |
|---|---|---|
| Cash | 21,000 | |
| Accounts receivable | 25,000 | |
| Prepaid rent | 3,000 | |
| Inventory | 16,000 | |
| Interest receivable | 100 | (continued) |

| (concluded) | **Account Title** | **Debits** | **Credits** |
|---|---|---|---|
| | Note receivable | 20,000 | |
| | Equipment | 20,000 | |
| | Accumulated depreciation—equipment | | 500 |
| | Accounts payable | | 20,000 |
| | Interest payable | | 250 |
| | Note payable | | 30,000 |
| | Common stock | | 50,000 |
| | Retained earnings | 1,000 | |
| | Sales revenue | | 40,000 |
| | Interest revenue | | 100 |
| | Cost of goods sold | 22,000 | |
| | Salaries expense | 7,000 | |
| | Utilities expense | 2,000 | |
| | Interest expense | 250 | |
| | Depreciation expense | 500 | |
| | Rent expense | 3,000 | |
| | Totals | 140,850 | 140,850 |

3. What is the effect on income (overstated or understated), if the adjusting entries are not made?

| **Adjusting Entry** | **Income overstated (understated)** |
|---|---|
| Interest expense | 250 |
| Depreciation expense | 500 |
| Interest revenue | (100) |
| Rent expense | 3,000 |
| Net effect, income overstated by | $3,650 |

We now turn our attention to the preparation of financial statements.

# Preparing the Financial Statements

The purpose of each of the steps in the processing cycle to this point is to provide information for step 8—preparation of the **financial statements**. The adjusted trial balance contains the necessary information. After all, the financial statements are the primary means of communicating financial information to external parties.

● LO2–6

**STEP 8**
Preparation of *financial statements.*

## The Income Statement

The purpose of the **income statement** is to summarize the profit-generating activities of a company that occurred during a particular period of time. It is a *change* statement in that it reports the changes in shareholders' equity (retained earnings) that occurred during the period as a result of revenues, expenses, gains, and losses. Illustration 2–13 shows the income statement for Dress Right Clothing Corporation for the month of July 2013.

The income statement indicates a profit for the month of July of $2,917. During the month, the company was able to increase its net assets (equity) from activities related to selling its product. Dress Right is a corporation and subject to the payment of income tax on its profits. We ignore this required accrual here and address income taxes in a later chapter.

The components of the income statement usually are classified, that is, grouped according to common characteristics. A common classification scheme is to separate operating items from nonoperating items, as we do in Dress Right's income statement. Operating items include revenues and expenses directly related to the principal revenue-generating activities of the company. For example, operating items for a manufacturing company include sales

The *income statement* is a *change* statement that summarizes the profit-generating transactions that caused shareholders' equity (retained earnings) to change during the period.

**Illustration 2–13**

Income Statement

**DRESS RIGHT CLOTHING CORPORATION**
**Income Statement**
**For the Month of July 2013**

| | | |
|---|---:|---:|
| Sales revenue | | $38,500 |
| Cost of goods sold | | 22,000 |
| Gross profit | | 16,500 |
| Operating expenses: | | |
| Salaries | $10,500 | |
| Supplies | 800 | |
| Rent | 2,000 | |
| Depreciation | 200 | |
| Total operating expenses | | 13,500 |
| Operating income | | 3,000 |
| Other income (expense): | | |
| Rent revenue | 250 | |
| Interest expense | (333) | (83) |
| Net income | | $ 2,917 |

revenues from the sale of products and all expenses related to this activity. Companies that sell products like Dress Right often report a subtotal within operating income, sales less cost of goods sold, called *gross profit*. Nonoperating items include certain gains and losses and revenues and expenses from peripheral activities. For Dress Right Clothing, rent revenue and interest expense are nonoperating items because they do not relate to the principal revenue-generating activity of the company, selling clothes. In Chapter 4 we discuss the format and content of the income statement in more depth.

## The Statement of Comprehensive Income

The purpose of the statement of comprehensive income is to report the changes in shareholders' equity during the period that were not a result of transactions with owners. A few types of gains and losses, called other comprehensive income (OCI) or loss items, are excluded from the determination of net income and the income statement, but are included in the broader concept of comprehensive income. Comprehensive income can be reported in one of two ways: (1) in a single, continuous statement of comprehensive income, or (2) in two separate, but consecutive statements.[5]

In the single statement approach, net income is a subtotal within the statement followed by these OCI items, culminating in a final total of comprehensive income. In the two statement approach, a company presents an income statement immediately followed by a statement of comprehensive income. The statement of comprehensive income begins with net income as the first component followed by OCI items to arrive at comprehensive income. Obviously, the approaches are quite similar; in the separate statement approach, we separate the continuous statement into two parts, but the content is the same.

Dress Right Clothing has no OCI items so the company presents only an income statement in Illustration 2–13. An entity that has no OCI items is not required to report OCI or comprehensive income. We discuss comprehensive income and the alternative approaches to its presentation in more depth in Chapter 4.

The *balance sheet* is a position statement that presents an organized list of assets, liabilities and equity at a particular point in time.

## The Balance Sheet

The purpose of the balance sheet is to present the financial position of the company on a particular date. Unlike the income statement, which is a change statement reporting events

[5]FASB ASC 220-10-45-1: Comprehensive Income—Overall—Other Presentation Matters [Accounting Standards Update No. 2011-05 (Norwalk, Conn.: FASB, June 2011)].

that occurred *during a period of time,* the balance sheet is a statement that presents an organized list of assets, liabilities, and shareholders' equity *at a point in time.* To provide a quick overview, Illustration 2–14 shows the balance sheet for Dress Right at July 31, 2013.

<table>
<tr><td colspan="3" align="center">**DRESS RIGHT CLOTHING CORPORATION**<br>**Balance Sheet**<br>**At July 31, 2013**<br>**Assets**</td></tr>
<tr><td>Current assets:</td><td></td><td></td></tr>
<tr><td>Cash</td><td></td><td>$ 68,500</td></tr>
<tr><td>Accounts receivable</td><td></td><td>2,000</td></tr>
<tr><td>Supplies</td><td></td><td>1,200</td></tr>
<tr><td>Inventory</td><td></td><td>38,000</td></tr>
<tr><td>Prepaid rent</td><td></td><td>22,000</td></tr>
<tr><td>Total current assets</td><td></td><td>131,700</td></tr>
<tr><td>Property and equipment:</td><td></td><td></td></tr>
<tr><td>Furniture and fixtures</td><td>$12,000</td><td></td></tr>
<tr><td>Less: Accumulated depreciation</td><td>200</td><td>11,800</td></tr>
<tr><td>Total assets</td><td></td><td>$143,500</td></tr>
<tr><td colspan="3" align="center">**Liabilities and Shareholders' Equity**</td></tr>
<tr><td>Current liabilities:</td><td></td><td></td></tr>
<tr><td>Accounts payable</td><td></td><td>$ 35,000</td></tr>
<tr><td>Salaries payable</td><td></td><td>5,500</td></tr>
<tr><td>Unearned rent revenue</td><td></td><td>750</td></tr>
<tr><td>Interest payable</td><td></td><td>333</td></tr>
<tr><td>Note payable</td><td></td><td>10,000</td></tr>
<tr><td>Total current liabilities</td><td></td><td>51,583</td></tr>
<tr><td>Long-term liabilities:</td><td></td><td></td></tr>
<tr><td>Note payable</td><td></td><td>30,000</td></tr>
<tr><td>Shareholders' equity:</td><td></td><td></td></tr>
<tr><td>Common stock, 6,000 shares issued and outstanding</td><td>$60,000</td><td></td></tr>
<tr><td>Retained earnings</td><td>1,917*</td><td></td></tr>
<tr><td>Total shareholders' equity</td><td></td><td>61,917</td></tr>
<tr><td>Total liabilities and shareholders' equity</td><td></td><td>$143,500</td></tr>
</table>

*Beginning retained earnings + Net income – Dividends
    0        +   $2,917  –  1,000  = $1,917

**Illustration 2–14**

Balance Sheet

As we do in the income statement, we group the balance sheet elements into meaningful categories. For example, most balance sheets include the classifications of **current assets** and **current liabilities**. Current assets are those assets that are cash, will be converted into cash, or will be used up within one year or the operating cycle, whichever is longer. Current liabilities are those liabilities that will be satisfied within one year or the operating cycle, whichever is longer. For a manufacturing company, the operating cycle refers to the period of time necessary to convert cash to raw materials, raw materials to a finished product, the finished product to receivables, and then finally receivables back to cash. For most companies, this period is less than a year.

Balance sheet items usually are classified (grouped) according to common characteristics.

Examples of assets not classified as current include property and equipment and long-term receivables and investments. The only noncurrent asset that Dress Right has at July 31, 2013, is furniture and fixtures, which is classified under the property and equipment category.

All liabilities not classified as current are listed as long term. Dress Right's liabilities at July 31, 2013, include the $30,000 note payable due to be paid in 23 months. This liability is classified as long term.

Shareholders' equity lists the *paid-in capital* portion of equity—common stock—and *retained earnings.* Notice that the income statement we looked at in Illustration 2–13 ties in to the balance sheet through retained earnings. Specifically, the revenue, expense, gain, and loss transactions that make up net income in the income statement ($2,917) become the major components of retained earnings. Later in the chapter we discuss the closing process we use to transfer, or close, these *temporary* income statement accounts to the *permanent* retained earnings account.

During the month, retained earnings, which increased by the amount of net income, also decreased by the amount of the cash dividend paid to shareholders, $1,000. The net effect of these two changes is an increase in retained earnings from zero at the beginning of the period to $1,917 ($2,917 − 1,000) at the end of the period and also is reported in the statement of shareholders' equity in Illustration 2–16 on page 79.

## The Statement of Cash Flows

The purpose of the *statement of cash flows* is to summarize the transactions that caused cash to change during the period.

Similar to the income statement, the statement of cash flows also is a change statement. The purpose of the statement is to report the events that caused cash to change during the period. The statement classifies all transactions affecting cash into one of three categories: (1) operating activities, (2) investing activities, and (3) financing activities. Operating activities are inflows and outflows of cash related to transactions entering into the determination of net income. Investing activities involve the acquisition and sale of (1) long-term assets used in the business and (2) nonoperating investment assets. Financing activities involve cash inflows and outflows from transactions with creditors and owners.

The statement of cash flows for Dress Right for the month of July 2013 is shown in Illustration 2–15. As this is the first period of operations for Dress Right, the cash balance at the beginning of the period is zero. The net increase in cash of $68,500, therefore, equals the ending balance of cash disclosed in the balance sheet.

**Illustration 2–15**

Statement of Cash Flows

**DRESS RIGHT CLOTHING CORPORATION**
**Statement of Cash Flows**
**For the Month of July 2013**

| | | |
|---|---:|---:|
| **Cash Flows from Operating Activities** | | |
| Cash inflows: | | |
| From customers | $36,500 | |
| From rent | 1,000 | |
| Cash outflows: | | |
| For rent | (24,000) | |
| For supplies | (2,000) | |
| To suppliers of merchandise | (25,000) | |
| To employees | (5,000) | |
| Net cash flows from operating activities | | $(18,500) |
| **Cash Flows from Investing Activities** | | |
| Purchase of furniture and fixtures | | (12,000) |
| **Cash Flows from Financing Activities** | | |
| Issue of common stock | $60,000 | |
| Increase in notes payable | 40,000 | |
| Payment of cash dividend | (1,000) | |
| Net cash flows from financing activities | | 99,000 |
| **Net increase in cash** | | $ 68,500 |

There are two generally accepted formats that can be used to report operating activities, the direct method and the indirect method. In Illustration 2–15 we use the direct method. These two methods are discussed and illustrated in subsequent chapters.

## The Statement of Shareholders' Equity

The final statement, the statement of shareholders' equity, also is a change statement. Its purpose is to disclose the sources of the changes in the various permanent shareholders' equity accounts that occurred during the period from investments by owners, distributions to owners, net income, and other comprehensive income. Illustration 2–16 shows the statement of shareholders' equity for Dress Right for the month of July 2013.[6]

*The statement of shareholders' equity discloses the sources of changes in the permanent shareholders' equity accounts.*

**Illustration 2–16**
Statement of Shareholders' Equity

**DRESS RIGHT CLOTHING CORPORATION**
**Statement of Shareholders' Equity**
**For the Month of July 2013**

| | Common Stock | Retained Earnings | Total Shareholders' Equity |
|---|---|---|---|
| Balance at July 1, 2013 | $   –0– | $  –0– | $    –0– |
| Issue of common stock | 60,000 | | 60,000 |
| Net income for July 2013 | | 2,917 | 2,917 |
| Less: Dividends | | (1,000) | (1,000) |
| Balance at July 31, 2013 | $60,000 | $1,917 | $61,917 |

The individual profit-generating transactions causing retained earnings to change are summarized in the income statement. Therefore, the statement of shareholders' equity only shows the net effect of these transactions on retained earnings, in this case an increase of $2,917. In addition, the company paid its shareholders a cash dividend that reduced retained earnings.

# The Closing Process

At the end of any interim reporting period, the accounting processing cycle is now complete. An interim reporting period is any period when financial statements are produced other than at the end of the fiscal year. However, at the end of the fiscal year, two final steps are necessary, closing the temporary accounts—step 9—and preparing a post-closing trial balance—step 10.

**STEP 9**
*Close* the temporary accounts to retained earnings (at year-end only).

● LO2–7

The closing process serves a *dual purpose:* (1) the temporary accounts (revenues, expenses, gains and losses) are reduced to *zero balances,* ready to measure activity in the upcoming accounting period, and (2) these temporary account balances are *closed (transferred) to retained earnings* to reflect the changes that have occurred in that account during the period. Often, an intermediate step is to close revenues and expenses to income summary, and then income summary is closed to retained earnings. The use of the income summary account is just a bookkeeping convenience that provides a check that all temporary accounts have been properly closed (that is, the balance equals net income or loss).

To illustrate the closing process, assume that the fiscal year-end for Dress Right Clothing Corporation is July 31. Using the adjusted trial balance in Illustration 2–12, we can prepare the following general journal entries.

*To close the revenue accounts to income summary.*

| July 31 | | |
|---|---|---|
| Sales revenue .................................................................. | 38,500 | |
| Rent revenue .................................................................. | 250 | |
|    Income summary ......................................................... | | 38,750 |

---

[6]Some companies choose to disclose the changes in the retained earnings component of shareholders' equity in a separate statement or in a combined statement of income and retained earnings.

The first closing entry transfers the revenue account balances to income summary. Because revenue accounts have credit balances, they are debited to bring them to zero. After this entry is posted to the accounts, both revenue accounts have a zero balance.

**To close the expense accounts to income summary.**

**July 31**

| | | |
|---|---|---|
| Income summary | 35,833 | |
| Cost of goods sold | | 22,000 |
| Salaries expense | | 10,500 |
| Supplies expense | | 800 |
| Rent expense | | 2,000 |
| Depreciation expense | | 200 |
| Interest expense | | 333 |

The second closing entry transfers the expense account balances to income summary. As expense accounts have debit balances, they are credited to bring them to zero. After this entry is posted to the accounts, the expense accounts have a zero balance and the income summary account has a credit balance equal to net income for the period, in this case $2,917.

**Income Summary**

| | | | |
|---|---|---|---|
| Expenses | 35,833 | 38,750 | Revenues |
| | | 2,917 | Net income |

**To close the income summary account to retained earnings.**

**July 31**

| | | |
|---|---|---|
| Income summary | 2,917 | |
| Retained earnings | | 2,917 |

After this entry is posted to the accounts, the temporary accounts have zero balances and retained earnings has increased by the amount of the net income. It is important to remember that the temporary accounts are closed only at year-end and not at the end of any interim period. Closing the temporary accounts during the year would make it difficult to prepare the annual income statement.

# Additional Consideration

A previous additional consideration indicated that an alternative method of recording a cash dividend is to debit a temporary account called dividends, rather than debiting retained earnings. If this approach is used, an additional closing entry is required to close the dividend account to retained earnings, as follows:

| | | |
|---|---|---|
| Retained earnings | 1,000 | |
| Dividends | | 1,000 |

As you can see, the net result of a cash dividend is the same—a reduction in retained earnings and a reduction in cash.

**STEP 10**

Prepare a *post-closing trial balance* (at year-end only).

After the closing entries are posted to the ledger accounts, a **post-closing trial balance** is prepared. The purpose of this trial balance is to verify that the closing entries were prepared and posted correctly and that the accounts are now ready for next year's transactions. Illustration 2–17 shows the post-closing trial balance for Dress Right at July 31, 2013, assuming a July 31 fiscal year-end.

Illustration 2–17

Post-Closing Trial Balance

### DRESS RIGHT CLOTHING CORPORATION
### Post-Closing Trial Balance
### July 31, 2013

| Account Title | Debits | Credits |
|---|---|---|
| Cash | 68,500 | |
| Accounts receivable | 2,000 | |
| Supplies | 1,200 | |
| Prepaid rent | 22,000 | |
| Inventory | 38,000 | |
| Furniture and fixtures | 12,000 | |
| Accumulated depreciation—furniture and fixtures | | 200 |
| Accounts payable | | 35,000 |
| Notes payable | | 40,000 |
| Unearned rent revenue | | 750 |
| Salaries payable | | 5,500 |
| Interest payable | | 333 |
| Common stock | | 60,000 |
| Retained earnings | | 1,917 |
| Totals | 143,700 | 143,700 |

## Concept Review Exercise

**FINANCIAL STATEMENT PREPARATION AND CLOSING**

Refer to the August 31, 2013, adjusted trial balance of the Wyndham Wholesale Company presented in a previous concept review exercise on pages 74 and 75.

**Required:**

1. Prepare an income statement and a statement of shareholders' equity for the month ended August 31, 2013, and a classified balance sheet as of August 31, 2013.

2. Assume that August 31 is the company's fiscal year-end. Prepare the necessary closing entries and a post-closing trial balance.

**Solution:**

1. Prepare an income statement and a statement of shareholders' equity for the month ended August 31, 2013, and a classified balance sheet as of August 31, 2013.

### WYNDHAM WHOLESALE COMPANY
### Income Statement
### For the Month of August 2013

| | | |
|---|---|---|
| Sales revenue | | $40,000 |
| Cost of goods sold | | 22,000 |
| Gross profit | | 18,000 |
| Operating expenses: | | |
|    Salaries | $7,000 | |
|    Utilities | 2,000 | |
|    Depreciation | 500 | |
|    Rent | 3,000 | |
|     Total operating expenses | | 12,500 |
| Operating income | | 5,500 |
| Other income (expense): | | |
|    Interest revenue | 100 | |
|    Interest expense | (250) | (150) |
| Net income | | $ 5,350 |

**WYNDHAM WHOLESALE COMPANY**
**Statement of Shareholders' Equity**
**For the Month of August 2013**

| | Common Stock | Retained Earnings | Total Shareholders' Equity |
|---|---|---|---|
| Balance at August 1, 2013 | $  –0– | $  –0– | $  –0– |
| Issue of common stock | 50,000 | | 50,000 |
| Net income for August 2013 | | 5,350 | 5,350 |
| Less: Dividends | | (1,000) | (1,000) |
| Balance at August 31, 2013 | $50,000 | $4,350 | $54,350 |

**WYNDHAM WHOLESALE COMPANY**
**Balance Sheet**
**At August 31, 2013**
**Assets**

| | | |
|---|---|---|
| Current assets: | | |
| Cash | | $ 21,000 |
| Accounts receivable | | 25,000 |
| Inventory | | 16,000 |
| Interest receivable | | 100 |
| Note receivable | | 20,000 |
| Prepaid rent | | 3,000 |
| Total current assets | | 85,100 |
| Property and equipment: | | |
| Equipment | $20,000 | |
| Less: Accumulated depreciation | 500 | 19,500 |
| Total assets | | $104,600 |

**Liabilities and Shareholders' Equity**

| | | |
|---|---|---|
| Current liabilities: | | |
| Accounts payable | | $ 20,000 |
| Interest payable | | 250 |
| Note payable | | 30,000 |
| Total current liabilities | | 50,250 |
| Shareholders' equity: | | |
| Common stock, 5,000 shares issued and outstanding | $50,000 | |
| Retained earnings | 4,350 | |
| Total shareholders' equity | | 54,350 |
| Total liabilities and shareholders' equity | | $104,600 |

2. Assume that August 31 is the company's fiscal year-end. Prepare the necessary closing entries and a post-closing trial balance.

| | | |
|---|---|---|
| To close the revenue accounts to income summary. | **August 31** | |
| | Sales revenue ................................................................ | 40,000 |
| | Interest revenue ............................................................ | 100 |
| | Income summary ......................................................... | 40,100 |
| To close the expense accounts to income summary. | **August 31** | |
| | Income summary ............................................................ | 34,750 |
| | Cost of goods sold .................................................... | 22,000 |
| | Salaries expense ......................................................... | 7,000 |
| | Utilities expense ........................................................ | 2,000 |
| | Depreciation expense ................................................ | 500 |
| | Rent expense .............................................................. | 3,000 |
| | Interest expense ......................................................... | 250 |
| | | (continued) |

(concluded)

**August 31**

| | Debit | Credit |
|---|---|---|
| Income summary ............................................................................... | 5,350 | |
|    Retained earnings ....................................................................... | | 5,350 |

To close the income summary account to retained earnings.

**Post-Closing Trial Balance**

| Account Title | Debits | Credits |
|---|---|---|
| Cash | 21,000 | |
| Accounts receivable | 25,000 | |
| Prepaid rent | 3,000 | |
| Inventory | 16,000 | |
| Interest receivable | 100 | |
| Note receivable | 20,000 | |
| Equipment | 20,000 | |
| Accumulated depreciation—equipment | | 500 |
| Accounts payable | | 20,000 |
| Interest payable | | 250 |
| Note payable | | 30,000 |
| Common stock | | 50,000 |
| Retained earnings | | 4,350 |
| Totals | 105,100 | 105,100 |

# Conversion from Cash Basis to Accrual Basis

● LO2–8

In Chapter 1, we discussed and illustrated the differences between cash and accrual accounting. Cash basis accounting produces a measure called *net operating cash flow*. This measure is the difference between cash receipts and cash disbursements during a reporting period from transactions related to providing goods and services to customers. On the other hand, the accrual accounting model measures an entity's accomplishments and resource sacrifices during the period, regardless of when cash is received or paid. At this point, you might wish to review the material in Chapter 1 on pages 6 through 8 to reinforce your understanding of the motivation for using the accrual accounting model.

Adjusting entries, for the most part, are conversions from cash basis to accrual basis. Prepayments and accruals occur when cash flow precedes or follows expense or revenue recognition.

Accountants sometimes are called upon to convert cash basis financial statements to accrual basis financial statements, particularly for small businesses. You now have all of the tools you need to make this conversion. For example, if a company paid $20,000 cash for insurance during the fiscal year and you determine that there was $5,000 in prepaid insurance at the beginning of the year and $3,000 at the end of the year, then you can determine (accrual basis) *insurance expense* for the year. Prepaid insurance decreased by $2,000 during the year, so insurance expense must be $22,000 ($20,000 in cash paid *plus* the decrease in prepaid insurance). You can visualize as follows:

| Prepaid Insurance | |
|---|---|
| Balance, beginning of year | $ 5,000 |
| Plus: Cash paid | 20,000 |
| Less: Insurance expense | ? |
| Balance, end of year | $ 3,000 |

Insurance expense of $22,000 completes the explanation of the change in the balance of prepaid insurance. Prepaid insurance of $3,000 is reported as an asset in an accrual basis balance sheet.

Suppose a company paid $150,000 for salaries to employees during the year and you determine that there were $12,000 and $18,000 in salaries payable at the beginning and end of the year, respectively. What was salaries expense for the year?

| Salaries Payable | |
|---|---:|
| Balance, beginning of year | $ 12,000 |
| Plus: Salaries expense | ? |
| Less: Cash paid | 150,000 |
| Balance, end of year | $ 18,000 |

Salaries payable increased by $6,000 during the year, so *salaries expense* must be $156,000 ($150,000 in cash paid *plus* the increase in salaries payable). Salaries payable of $18,000 is reported as a liability in an accrual basis balance sheet.

Using T-accounts is a convenient approach for converting from cash to accrual accounting.

| Salaries Payable | | Salaries Expense |
|---|---|---|
| | 12,000 Beg. balance | |
| Cash paid  150,000 | | ? |
| | ?  Salaries expense | |
| | 18,000 End balance | |

The debit to salaries expense and credit to salaries payable must have been $156,000 to balance the salaries payable account.

For another example using T-accounts, assume that the amount of cash collected from customers during the year was $220,000, and you know that accounts receivable at the beginning of the year was $45,000 and $33,000 at the end of the year. You can use T-accounts to determine that *sales revenue* for the year must have been $208,000, the necessary debit to accounts receivable and credit to sales revenue to balance the accounts receivable account.

| Accounts Receivable | | Sales Revenue |
|---|---|---|
| Beg. balance  45,000 | | |
| Credit sales  ? | | ?  Credit sales |
| | 220,000 Cash collections | |
| End balance  33,000 | | |

Now suppose that, on occasion, customers pay in advance of receiving a product or service. Recall from our previous discussion of adjusting entries that this event creates a liability called unearned revenue. Assume the same facts in the previous example except you also determine that unearned revenues were $10,000 and $7,000 at the beginning and end of the year, respectively. A $3,000 decrease in unearned revenues means that the company earned an additional $3,000 in sales revenue for which the cash had been collected in a previous year. So, *sales revenue* for the year must have been $211,000, the $208,000 determined in the previous example *plus* the $3,000 decrease in unearned revenue.

Illustration 2–18 provides another example of converting from cash basis net income to accrual basis net income.

Notice a pattern in the adjustments to cash net income. When converting from cash to accrual income, we add increases and deduct decreases in assets. For example, an increase in accounts receivable means that the company earned more revenue than cash collected, requiring the addition to cash basis income. Conversely, we add decreases and deduct increases in accrued liabilities. For example, a decrease in interest payable means that the company incurred less interest expense than the cash interest it paid, requiring the addition to cash basis income. These adjustments are summarized in Illustration 2–19.

Most companies keep their books on an accrual basis.[7] A more important conversion for these companies is from the accrual basis to the cash basis. This conversion,

**Most companies must convert from an accrual basis to a cash basis when preparing the statement of cash flows.**

---

[7]Generally accepted accounting principles require the use of the accrual basis. Some small, nonpublic companies might use the cash basis in preparing their financial statements as an other comprehensive basis of accounting.

**Illustration 2–18**

Cash to Accrual

The Krinard Cleaning Services Company maintains its records on the cash basis, with one exception. The company reports equipment as an asset and records depreciation expense on the equipment. During 2013, Krinard collected $165,000 from customers, paid $92,000 in operating expenses, and recorded $10,000 in depreciation expense, resulting in net income of $63,000. The owner has asked you to convert this $63,000 in net income to full accrual net income. You are able to determine the following information about accounts receivable, prepaid expenses, accrued liabilities, and unearned revenues:

|  | January 1, 2013 | December 31, 2013 |
|---|---|---|
| Accounts receivable | $16,000 | $25,000 |
| Prepaid expenses | 7,000 | 4,000 |
| Accrued liabilities | | |
| (for operating expenses) | 2,100 | 1,400 |
| Unearned revenues | 3,000 | 4,200 |

Accrual net income is $68,500, determined as follows:

| | | |
|---|---|---|
| Cash basis net income | | $63,000 |
| Add: | Increase in accounts receivable | 9,000 |
| Deduct: | Decrease in prepaid expenses | (3,000) |
| Add: | Decrease in accrued liabilities | 700 |
| Deduct: | Increase in unearned revenues | (1,200) |
| Accrual basis net income | | $68,500 |

**Illustration 2–19**

Converting Cash Basis to Accrual Basis Income

| Converting Cash Basis Income to Accrual Basis Income | | |
|---|---|---|
| | **Increases** | **Decreases** |
| **Assets** | Add | Deduct |
| **Liabilities** | Deduct | Add |

essential for the preparation of the statement of cash flows, is discussed and illustrated in Chapters 4 and 21. The lessons learned here, though, will help you with that conversion. For example, if sales revenue for the period is $120,000 and beginning and ending accounts receivable are $20,000 and $24,000, respectively, how much cash did the company collect from its customers during the period? The answer is $116,000. An increase in accounts receivable of $4,000 means that the company collected $4,000 less from customers than accrual sales revenue, and cash basis income is $4,000 less than accrual basis income.

# Financial Reporting Case Solution

1. **What purpose do adjusting entries serve?** *(p. 67)* Adjusting entries help ensure that only revenues actually earned in a period are recognized in that period, regardless of when cash is received. In this instance, for example, $13,000 cash has been received for services that haven't yet been performed. Also, adjusting entries enable a company to recognize all expenses incurred during a period, regardless of when cash is paid. Without depreciation, the friends' cost of using the equipment is not taken into account. Conversely, without adjustment, the cost of rent is overstated by $3,000 paid in advance for part of next year's rent.

   With adjustments, we get an accrual income statement that provides a more complete measure of a company's operating performance and a better measure for predicting future operating cash flows. Similarly, the balance sheet provides a more complete assessment of assets and liabilities as sources of future cash receipts and disbursements.

**2. What year-end adjustments are needed to revise the income statement? Did your friends do as well their first year as they thought?** *(p. 67)*   Three year-end adjusting entries are needed:

| | | |
|---|---:|---:|
| 1. Depreciation expense ($80,000 ÷ 5 years) ......................................... | 16,000 | |
|     Accumulated depreciation—equipment ...................................... | | 16,000 |
| 2. Prepaid rent ($500 × 6 months [July–Dec.]) ............................... | 3,000 | |
|     Rent expense ............................................................ | | 3,000 |
| 3. Consulting revenue ........................................................ | 13,000 | |
|     Unearned consulting revenue .................................................. | | 13,000 |

No, your friends did not fare as well as their cash based statement would have indicated. With appropriate adjustments, their net income is actually only $20,000:

| | | |
|---|---:|---:|
| Consulting revenue ($96,000 − 13,000) | | $83,000 |
| Operating expenses: | | |
| Salaries | $32,000 | |
| Rent ($9,000 − 3,000) | 6,000 | |
| Supplies | 4,800 | |
| Utilities | 3,000 | |
| Advertising | 1,200 | |
| Depreciation | 16,000 | 63,000 |
| Net income | | $20,000 |

## The Bottom Line

● **LO2–1**   The accounting equation underlies the process used to capture the effect of economic events. The equation (Assets = Liabilities + Owners' Equity) implies an equality between the total economic resources of an entity (its assets) and the total claims against the entity (liabilities and equity). It also implies that each economic event affecting this equation will have a dual effect because resources always must equal claims. (*p. 52*)

● **LO2–2**   After determining the dual effect of external events on the accounting equation, the transaction is recorded in a journal. A journal is a chronological list of transactions in debit/credit form. (*p. 56*)

● **LO2–3**   The next step in the processing cycle is to periodically transfer, or *post*, the debit and credit information from the journal to individual general ledger accounts. A general ledger is simply a collection of all of the company's various accounts. Each account provides a summary of the effects of all events and transactions on that individual account. The process of entering items from the journal to the general ledger is called *posting*. An unadjusted trial balance is then prepared. (*p. 63*)

● **LO2–4**   The next step in the processing cycle is to record the effect of *internal events* on the accounting equation. These transactions are commonly referred to as *adjusting entries*. Adjusting entries can be classified into three types: (1) prepayments, (2) accruals, and (3) estimates. Prepayments are transactions in which the cash flow *precedes* expense or revenue recognition. Accruals involve transactions where the cash outflow or inflow takes place in a period *subsequent* to expense or revenue recognition. Estimates for items such as future bad debts on receivables often are required to comply with the accrual accounting model. (*p. 66*)

● **LO2–5**   Adjusting entries are recorded in the general journal and posted to the ledger accounts at the end of any period when financial statements must be prepared for external use. After these entries are posted to the general ledger accounts, an adjusted trial balance is prepared. (*p. 67*)

● **LO2–6**   The adjusted trial balance is used to prepare the financial statements. The basic financial statements are: (1) the income statement, (2) the statement of comprehensive income, (3) the balance sheet, (4) the statement of cash flows, and (5) the statement of shareholders' equity. The purpose of the income statement is to summarize the profit-generating activities of the company that occurred during a particular period of time. A company also must report its other comprehensive income (OCI) or loss items either in a single, continuous statement or in a separate statement of comprehensive income. In the single statement approach, net income is a subtotal within the statement followed by these OCI items, culminating in a final total of comprehensive income. In the two statement approach, a company presents an income statement immediately followed by a statement of comprehensive income. The statement of comprehensive income begins with net income as the first component followed by OCI items to arrive at comprehensive income. The balance sheet presents the financial position of the company on a particular date. The statement of cash flows discloses the events that caused cash to change during the reporting period. The statement of shareholders' equity discloses the sources of the changes in the various permanent shareholders' equity accounts that occurred during the period. (*p. 75*)

● **LO2–7**    At the end of the fiscal year, a final step in the accounting processing cycle, closing, is required. The closing process serves a *dual purpose:* (1) the temporary accounts (revenues and expenses) are reduced to *zero balances,* ready to measure activity in the upcoming accounting period, and (2) these temporary account balances are *closed (transferred) to retained earnings* to reflect the changes that have occurred in that account during the period. Often, an intermediate step is to close revenues and expenses to *income summary;* then *income summary* is closed to *retained earnings.* (*p. 79*)

● **LO2–8**    Cash basis accounting produces a measure called *net operating cash flow.* This measure is the difference between cash receipts and cash disbursements during a reporting period from transactions related to providing goods and services to customers. On the other hand, the accrual accounting model measures an entity's accomplishments and resource sacrifices during the period, regardless of when cash is received or paid. Accountants sometimes are called upon to convert cash basis financial statements to accrual basis financial statements, particularly for small businesses. (*p. 83*) ●

## Use of a Worksheet

**APPENDIX 2A**

A **worksheet** often is used to organize the accounting information needed to prepare adjusting and closing entries and the financial statements. It is an informal tool only and is not part of the accounting system. There are many different ways to design and use worksheets. We will illustrate a representative method using the financial information for the Dress Right Clothing Corporation presented in the chapter. Computerized programs such as Lotus 1-2-3 and Excel facilitate the use of worksheets.

*A worksheet can be used as a tool to facilitate the preparation of adjusting and closing entries and the financial statements.*

Illustration 2A–1 presents the completed worksheet. The worksheet is utilized in conjunction with step 5 in the processing cycle, preparation of an unadjusted trial balance.

**Illustration 2A–1**    Worksheet, Dress Right Clothing Corporation, July 31, 2013

| Account Title | Unadjusted Trial Balance Dr. | Unadjusted Trial Balance Cr. | Adjusting Entries Dr. | | Adjusting Entries Cr. | | Adjusted Trial Balance Dr. | Adjusted Trial Balance Cr. | Income Statement Dr. | Income Statement Cr. | Balance Sheet Dr. | Balance Sheet Cr. |
|---|---|---|---|---|---|---|---|---|---|---|---|---|
| Cash | 68,500 | | | | | | 68,500 | | | | 68,500 | |
| Accounts receivable | 2,000 | | | | | | 2,000 | | | | 2,000 | |
| Supplies | 2,000 | | | | (1) | 800 | 1,200 | | | | 1,200 | |
| Prepaid rent | 24,000 | | | | (2) | 2,000 | 22,000 | | | | 22,000 | |
| Inventory | 38,000 | | | | | | 38,000 | | | | 38,000 | |
| Furniture & fixtures | 12,000 | | | | | | 12,000 | | | | 12,000 | |
| Accumulated depreciation – | | | | | | | | | | | | |
|     furniture & fixtures | | 0 | | | (3) | 200 | | 200 | | | | 200 |
| Accounts payable | | 35,000 | | | | | | 35,000 | | | | 35,000 |
| Note payable | | 40,000 | | | | | | 40,000 | | | | 40,000 |
| Unearned rent revenue | | 1,000 | (4) | 250 | | | | 750 | | | | 750 |
| Salaries payable | | 0 | | | (5) | 5,500 | | 5,500 | | | | 5,500 |
| Interest payable | | 0 | | | (6) | 333 | | 333 | | | | 333 |
| Common stock | | 60,000 | | | | | | 60,000 | | | | 60,000 |
| Retained earnings | | 1,000 | | | | | | 1,000 | | | | 1,000 |
| Sales revenue | | 38,500 | | | | | | 38,500 | | 38,500 | | |
| Rent revenue | | 0 | | | (4) | 250 | | 250 | | 250 | | |
| Cost of goods sold | 22,000 | | | | | | 22,000 | | 22,000 | | | |
| Salaries expense | 5,000 | | (5) | 5,500 | | | 10,500 | | 10,500 | | | |
| Supplies expense | 0 | | (1) | 800 | | | 800 | | 800 | | | |
| Rent expense | 0 | | (2) | 2,000 | | | 2,000 | | 2,000 | | | |
| Depreciation expense | 0 | | (3) | 200 | | | 200 | | 200 | | | |
| Interest expense | 0 | | (6) | 333 | | | 333 | | 333 | | | |
|     Totals | 174,500 | 174,500 | | 9,083 | | 9,083 | 180,533 | 180,533 | | | | |
| | | | | | | | | | | | | |
| Net Income | | | | | | | | | 2,917 | | 2,917 | |
|     Totals | | | | | | | | | 38,750 | 38,750 | 144,700 | 144,700 |

Sheet1    Sheet2    Sheet3

The first step is to enter account titles in column A and the unadjusted account balances in columns B and C.

**Step 1.** The account titles as they appear in the general ledger are entered in column A and the balances of these accounts are copied onto columns B and C, entitled Unadjusted Trial Balance. The accounts are copied in the same order as they appear in the general ledger, which usually is assets, liabilities, shareholders' equity permanent accounts, revenues, and expenses. The debit and credit columns are totaled to make sure that they balance. This procedure is repeated for each set of columns in the worksheet to check for accuracy.

The second step is to determine end-of-period adjusting entries and enter them in columns E and G.

**Step 2.** The end-of-period adjusting entries are determined and entered directly on the worksheet in columns E and G, entitled Adjusting Entries. The adjusting entries for Dress Right Clothing Corporation were discussed in detail in the chapter and exhibited in general journal form in Illustration 2–11 on page 73. You should refer back to this illustration and trace each of the entries to the worksheet. For worksheet purposes, the entries have been numbered from (1) to (6) for easy referencing.

For example, entry (1) records the cost of supplies used during the month of July with a debit to supplies expense and a credit to supplies for $800. A (1) is placed next to the $800 in the debit column in the supplies expense row as well as next to the $800 in the credit column in the supplies row. This allows us to more easily reconstruct the entry for general journal purposes and locate errors if the debit and credit columns do not balance.

The third step adds or deducts the effects of the adjusting entries on the account balances.

**Step 3.** The effects of the adjusting entries are added to or deducted from the account balances listed in the Unadjusted Trial Balance columns and copied across to columns H and I, entitled Adjusted Trial Balance. For example, supplies had an unadjusted balance of $2,000. Adjusting entry (1) credited this account by $800, reducing the balance to $1,200.

The fourth step is to transfer the temporary retained earnings account balances to columns J and K.

**Step 4.** The balances in the temporary retained earnings accounts, revenues and expenses, are transferred to columns J and K, entitled Income Statement. The difference between the total debits and credits in these columns is equal to net income or net loss. In this case, because credits (revenues) exceed debits (expenses), a net income of $2,917 results. To balance the debits and credits in this set of columns, a $2,917 debit entry is made in the line labeled Net income.

The fifth step is to transfer the balances in the permanent accounts to columns L and M.

**Step 5.** The balances in the permanent accounts are transferred to columns L and M, entitled Balance Sheet. To keep the debits and credits equal in the worksheet, a $2,917 credit must be recorded to offset the $2,917 debit recorded in step 4 and labeled as net income. This credit represents the fact that when the temporary accounts are closed out to retained earnings, a $2,917 credit to retained earnings will result. The credit in column M, therefore, represents an increase in retained earnings for the period, that is, net income.

After the worksheet is completed, the financial statements can be prepared directly from columns J–M. The financial statements for Dress Right Clothing Corporation are shown in Illustrations 2–13 through 2–16. The accountant must remember to then record the adjusting entries in the general journal and post them to the general ledger accounts. An adjusted trial balance should then be prepared, which should be identical to the one in the worksheet. At fiscal year-end, the income statement columns can then be used to prepare closing entries. ●

# APPENDIX 2B    Reversing Entries

Accountants sometimes use **reversing entries** at the beginning of a reporting period. These optional entries remove the effects of some of the adjusting entries made at the end of the previous reporting period for the sole purpose of simplifying journal entries made during the new period. If the accountant does use reversing entries, these entries are recorded in the general journal and posted to the general ledger accounts on the first day of the new period.

Reversing entries are used most often with accruals. For example, the following adjusting entry for accrued salaries was recorded at the end of July 2013 for the Dress Right Clothing Corporation in the chapter:

To record accrued salaries at the end of July.

| July 31 | | |
|---|---|---|
| Salaries expense ............................................................... | 5,500 | |
| Salaries payable ............................................................. | | 5,500 |

If reversing entries are not used, when the salaries actually are paid in August, the accountant needs to remember to debit salaries payable and not salaries expense.

The account balances before and after salary payment can be seen below with the use of T-accounts.

| Salaries Expense | | | | Salaries Payable | | |
|---|---|---|---|---|---|---|
| Bal. July 31 | 10,500 | | | | 5,500 | Bal. July 31 |
| | | | (Cash Payment) 5,500 | | | |
| | | | | | –0– | Balance |

*If the accountant for Dress Right employs reversing entries,* the following entry is made on August 1, 2013:

| August 1 | | | To reverse accrued salaries expense recorded at the end of July. |
|---|---|---|---|
| Salaries payable ................................................................. | 5,500 | | |
|     Salaries expense ........................................................... | | 5,500 | |

This entry reduces the salaries payable account to zero and reduces the salary expense account by $5,500. When salaries actually are paid in August, the debit is to salaries expense, thus increasing the account by $5,500.

| Salaries Expense | | | | Salaries Payable | | |
|---|---|---|---|---|---|---|
| Bal. July 31 | 10,500 | | | | 5,500 | Bal. July 31 |
| | | 5,500 | (Reversing entry) | 5,500 | | |
| (Cash payment) | 5,500 | | | | | |
| Balance | 10,500 | | | | –0– | Balance |

We can see that balances in the accounts after cash payment is made are identical. The use of reversing entries for accruals, which is optional, simply allows cash payments or cash receipts to be entered directly into the temporary expense or revenue accounts without regard to the accruals made at the end of the previous period.

Reversing entries also can be used with prepayments and unearned revenues. For example, earlier in the chapter Dress Right Clothing Corporation used the following entry to record the purchase of supplies on July 6:

| July 6 | | | To record the purchase of supplies. |
|---|---|---|---|
| Supplies ................................................................................. | 2,000 | | |
|     Cash .............................................................................. | | 2,000 | |

If reversing entries are not used, an adjusting entry is needed at the end of July to record the amount of supplies consumed during the period. In the illustration, Dress Right recorded this adjusting entry at the end of July:

| July 31 | | | To record the cost of supplies used during the month of July. |
|---|---|---|---|
| Supplies expense ................................................................. | 800 | | |
|     Supplies ......................................................................... | | 800 | |

T-accounts help us visualize the account balances before and after the adjusting entry.

| Supplies | | | | Supplies Expense | | |
|---|---|---|---|---|---|---|
| (Cash payment) 2,000 | | | | | | |
| | | 800 | (Adjusting entry) | 800 | | |
| Bal. July 31 | 1,200 | | | Bal. July 31 | 800 | |

*If the accountant for Dress Right employs reversing entries,* the purchase of supplies is recorded as follows:

**To record the purchase of supplies.**

| July 6 | | |
|---|---|---|
| Supplies expense ......................................................................... | 2,000 | |
| Cash ................................................................................. | | 2,000 |

The adjusting entry then is used to establish the balance in the supplies account at $1,200 (amount of supplies still on hand at the end of the month) and reduce the supplies expense account from the amount purchased to the amount used.

**To record the cost of supplies on hand at the end of July.**

| July 31 | | |
|---|---|---|
| Supplies (balance on hand) ................................................. | 1,200 | |
| Supplies expense ($2,000 − 800) ................................. | | 1,200 |

T-accounts make the process easier to see before and after the adjusting entry:

| Supplies | | Supplies Expense | |
|---|---|---|---|
| | 1,200 | (Cash payment) 2,000 | |
| | | (Adjusting entry) | 1,200 |
| Bal. July 31   1,200 | | Bal. July 31   1,200 | |

Notice that the ending balances in both accounts are the same as when reversing entries are not used. Up to this point, this approach is the alternate approach to recording prepayments discussed on page 69. The next step is an optional expediency.

On August 1, the following reversing entry can be recorded:

**To reverse the July adjusting entry for supplies on hand.**

| August 1 | | |
|---|---|---|
| Supplies expense ......................................................................... | 1,200 | |
| Supplies ................................................................................. | | 1,200 |

This entry reduces the supplies account to zero and increases the supplies expense account to $2,000. Subsequent purchases would then be entered into the supplies expense account and future adjusting entries would record the amount of supplies still on hand at the end of the period. At the end of the fiscal year, the supplies expense account, along with all other temporary accounts, is closed to retained earnings.

Using reversing entries for prepayments, which is optional, simply allows cash payments to be entered directly into the temporary expense accounts without regard to whether only the current, or both the current and future periods, are benefitted by the expenditure. Adjustments are then made at the end of the period to reflect the amount of the unexpired benefit (asset). ●

# APPENDIX 2C    Subsidiary Ledgers and Special Journals

## Subsidiary Ledgers

**Accounting systems employ a *subsidiary ledger* which contains a group of subsidiary accounts associated with particular general ledger control accounts.**

The general ledger contains what are referred to as *control accounts.* In addition to the general ledger, a subsidiary ledger contains a group of subsidiary accounts associated with a particular general ledger control account. For example, there will be a subsidiary ledger for accounts receivable that keeps track of the increases and decreases in the account receivable balance for each of the company's customers purchasing goods or services on credit. After all of the postings are made from the appropriate journals, the balance in the accounts receivable control account should equal the sum of the balances in the accounts receivable subsidiary ledger accounts. Subsidiary ledgers also are used for accounts payable, property and equipment, investments, and other accounts.

## Special Journals

An actual accounting system employs many different types of journals. The purpose of each journal is to record, in chronological order, the dual effect of a transaction in debit/credit form. The chapter used the general journal format to record each transaction. However, even for small companies with relatively few transactions, the general journal is used to record only a few types of transactions.[8]

The majority of transactions are recorded in special journals. These journals capture the dual effect of *repetitive* types of transactions. For example, cash receipts are recorded in a cash receipts journal, cash disbursements in a cash disbursements journal, credit sales in a sales journal, and the purchase of merchandise on account in a purchases journal.

Special journals simplify the recording process in the following ways:

1. Journalizing the effects of a particular transaction is made more efficient through the use of specifically designed formats.
2. Individual transactions are not posted to the general ledger accounts but are accumulated in the special journals and a summary posting is made on a periodic basis.
3. The responsibility for recording journal entries for the repetitive types of transactions is placed on individuals who have specialized training in handling them.

The concepts of subsidiary ledgers and special journals are illustrated using the *sales journal* and the *cash receipts journal.*

*For most external transactions, special journals are used to capture the dual effect of the transaction in debit/credit form.*

## Sales Journal

The purpose of the sales journal is to record all credit sales. Cash sales are recorded in the cash receipts journal. Every entry in the sales journal has exactly the same effect on the accounts; the sales revenue account is credited and the accounts receivable control account is debited. Therefore, there is only one column needed to record the debit/credit effect of these transactions. Other columns are needed to capture information for updating the accounts receivable subsidiary ledger. Illustration 2C–1 presents the sales journal for Dress Right Clothing Corporation for the month of August 2013.

*All credit sales are recorded in the sales journal.*

|  |  |  |  | Page 1 |
| --- | --- | --- | --- | --- |
| Date | Accounts Receivable Subsidiary Account No. | Customer Name | Sales Invoice No. | Cr. Sales Revenue (400) Dr. Accounts Receivable (110) |
| **2013** |  |  |  |  |
| Aug.  5 | 801 | Leland High School | 10-221 | 1,500 |
| 9 | 812 | Mr. John Smith | 10-222 | 200 |
| 18 | 813 | Greystone School | 10-223 | 825 |
| 22 | 803 | Ms. Barbara Jones | 10-224 | 120 |
| 29 | 805 | Hart Middle School | 10-225 | 650 |
|  |  |  |  | 3,295 |

## Illustration 2C–1

Sales Journal, Dress Right Clothing Corporation, August 2013

During the month of August, the company made five credit sales, totaling $3,295. This amount is posted as a debit to the accounts receivable control account, account number 110, and a credit to the sales revenue account, account number 400. The T-accounts for accounts receivable and sales revenue appear below. The reference SJ1 refers to page 1 of the sales journal.

### General Ledger

| Accounts Receivable      110 |  |  | Sales Revenue      400 |  |
| --- | --- | --- | --- | --- |
| July 31 Balance  2,000 |  |  |  |  |
| Aug. 31 SJ1    3,295 |  |  | 3,295 | Aug. 31 SJ1 |

---

[8]For example, end-of-period adjusting entries would be recorded in the general journal.

In a computerized accounting system, as each transaction is recorded in the sales journal, the subsidiary ledger accounts for the customer involved will automatically be updated. For example, the first credit sale of the month is to Leland High School for $1,500. The sales invoice number for this sale is 10-221 and the customer's subsidiary account number is 801. As this transaction is entered, the subsidiary account 801 for Leland High School is debited for $1,500.

**Accounts Receivable Subsidiary Ledger**

| Leland High School | | 801 |
|---|---|---|
| August 5 SJ1 | 1,500 | |

As cash is collected from this customer, the cash receipts journal records the transaction with a credit to the accounts receivable control account and a debit to cash. At the same time, the accounts receivable subsidiary ledger account number 801 also is credited. After the postings are made from the special journals, the balance in the accounts receivable control account should equal the sum of the balances in the accounts receivable subsidiary ledger accounts.

## Cash Receipts Journal

All cash receipts are recorded in the *cash receipts journal*.

The purpose of the **cash receipts journal** is to record all cash receipts, regardless of the source. Every transaction recorded in this journal produces a debit entry to the cash account with the credit to various other accounts. Illustration 2C–2 shows a cash receipts journal using transactions of the Dress Right Clothing Corporation for the month of August 2013.

**Illustration 2C–2**

Cash Receipts Journal, Dress Right Clothing Corporation, August 2013

| | | | | | | Page 1 |
|---|---|---|---|---|---|---|
| Date | Explanation or Account Name | Dr. Cash (100) | Cr. Accounts Receivable (110) | Cr. Sales Revenue (400) | Cr. Other | Other Accounts |
| **2013** | | | | | | |
| Aug. 7 | Cash sale | 500 | | 500 | | |
| 11 | Borrowed cash | 10,000 | | | 10,000 | Note payable (220) |
| 17 | Leland High School | 750 | 750 | | | |
| 20 | Cash sale | 300 | | 300 | | |
| 25 | Mr. John Smith | 200 | 200 | | | |
| | | 11,750 | 950 | 800 | 10,000 | |

Because every transaction results in a debit to the cash account, No. 100, a column is provided for that account. At the end of August, an $11,750 debit is posted to the general ledger cash account with the source labeled CR1, cash receipts journal, page 1.

Because cash and credit sales are common, separate columns are provided for these accounts. At the end of August, a $950 credit is posted to the accounts receivable general ledger account, No. 110, and an $800 credit is posted to the sales revenue account, No. 400. Two additional credit columns are provided for uncommon cash receipt transactions, one for the credit amount and one for the account being credited. We can see that in August, Dress Right borrowed $10,000 requiring a credit to the note payable account, No. 220.

In addition to the postings to the general ledger control accounts, each time an entry is recorded in the accounts receivable column, a credit is posted to the accounts receivable subsidiary ledger account for the customer making the payment. For example, on August 17, Leland High School paid $750 on account. The subsidiary ledger account for Leland High School is credited for $750.

**Accounts Receivable Subsidiary Ledger**

| Leland High School | | 801 | |
|---|---|---|---|
| August 5 SJ1 | 1,500 | | |
| | | 750 | August 17 CR1 |

# Questions For Review of Key Topics

Q 2–1    Explain the difference between external events and internal events. Give an example of each type of event.

Q 2–2    Each economic event or transaction will have a dual effect on financial position. Explain what is meant by this dual effect.

Q 2–3    What is the purpose of a journal? What is the purpose of a general ledger?

Q 2–4    Explain the difference between permanent accounts and temporary accounts. Why does an accounting system include both types of accounts?

Q 2–5    Describe how debits and credits affect assets, liabilities, and permanent owners' equity accounts.

Q 2–6    Describe how debits and credits affect temporary owners' equity accounts.

Q 2–7    What is the first step in the accounting processing cycle? What role do source documents fulfill in this step?

Q 2–8    Describe what is meant by transaction analysis.

Q 2–9    Describe what is meant by posting, the fourth step in the processing cycle.

Q 2–10    Describe the events that correspond to the following two journal entries:

| | | |
|---|---|---|
| 1. Inventory .................................................................. | 20,000 | |
|    Accounts payable ................................................ | | 20,000 |
| 2. Accounts receivable ................................................. | 30,000 | |
|    Sales revenue ..................................................... | | 30,000 |
|    Cost of goods sold ............................................. | 18,000 | |
|     Inventory ...................................................... | | 18,000 |

Q 2–11    What is an unadjusted trial balance? An adjusted trial balance?

Q 2–12    Define adjusting entries and discuss their purpose.

Q 2–13    Define closing entries and their purpose.

Q 2–14    Define prepaid expenses and provide at least two examples.

Q 2–15    Unearned revenues represent liabilities recorded when cash is received from customers in advance of providing a good or service. What adjusting journal entry is required at the end of a period to recognize the amount of unearned revenues that were earned during the period?

Q 2–16    Define accrued liabilities. What adjusting journal entry is required to record accrued liabilities?

Q 2–17    Describe the purpose of each of the five primary financial statements.

Q 2–18    [Based on Appendix A] What is the purpose of a worksheet? In a columnar worksheet similar to Illustration 2A–1, what would be the result of incorrectly transferring the balance in a liability account to column K, the credit column under income statement?

Q 2–19    [Based on Appendix B] Define reversing entries and discuss their purpose.

Q 2–20    [Based on Appendix C] What is the purpose of special journals? In what ways do they simplify the recording process?

Q 2–21    [Based on Appendix C] Explain the difference between the general ledger and a subsidiary ledger.

# Brief Exercises

**BE 2–1**
Transaction analysis
● LO2–1

The Marchetti Soup Company entered into the following transactions during the month of June: (1) purchased inventory on account for $165,000 (assume Marchetti uses a perpetual inventory system); (2) paid $40,000 in salaries to employees for work performed during the month; (3) sold merchandise that cost $120,000 to credit customers for $200,000; (4) collected $180,000 in cash from credit customers; and (5) paid suppliers of inventory $145,000. Analyze each transaction and show the effect of each on the accounting equation for a corporation.

**BE 2–2**
Journal entries
● LO2–2

Prepare journal entries for each of the transactions listed in BE 2–1.

**BE 2–3**
T-accounts
● LO2–3

Post the journal entries prepared in BE 2–2 to T-accounts. Assume that the opening balances in each of the accounts is zero except for cash, accounts receivable, and accounts payable that had opening balances of $65,000, $43,000, and $22,000, respectively.

**BE 2–4**
Journal entries
● LO2–2

Prepare journal entries for each of the following transactions for a company that has a fiscal year-end of December 31: (1) on October 1, $12,000 was paid for a one-year fire insurance policy; (2) on June 30 the company lent its chief financial officer $10,000; principal and interest at 6% are due in one year; and (3) equipment costing $60,000 was purchased at the beginning of the year for cash.

**BE 2–5**
Adjusting entries
● LO2–5

Prepare the necessary adjusting entries at December 31 for each of the items listed in BE 2–4. Depreciation on the equipment is $12,000 per year.

**BE 2–6**
Adjusting
entries; income
determination
● LO2–4, LO2–5

If the adjusting journal entries prepared in BE 2–5 were not made, would net income be higher or lower and by how much?

**BE 2–7**
Adjusting entries
● LO2–5

Prepare the necessary adjusting entries at its year-end of December 31, 2013, for the Jamesway Corporation for each of the following situations. No adjusting entries were made during the year.

1. On December 20, 2013, Jamesway received a $4,000 payment from a customer for services to be rendered early in 2014. Service revenue was credited.

2. On December 1, 2013, the company paid a local radio station $2,000 for 40 radio ads that were to be aired, 20 per month, throughout December and January. Prepaid advertising was debited.

3. Employee salaries for the month of December totaling $16,000 will be paid on January 7, 2014.

4. On August 31, 2013, Jamesway borrowed $60,000 from a local bank. A note was signed with principal and 8% interest to be paid on August 31, 2014.

**BE 2–8**
Income
determination
● LO2–4

If none of the adjusting journal entries prepared in BE 2–7 were made, would assets, liabilities, and shareholders' equity on the 12/31/13 balance sheet be higher or lower and by how much?

**BE 2–9**
Financial
statements
● LO2–6

The following account balances were taken from the 2013 adjusted trial balance of the Bowler Corporation: sales revenue, $325,000; cost of goods sold, $168,000; salaries expense; $45,000; rent expense, $20,000; depreciation expense, $30,000; and miscellaneous expense, $12,000. Prepare an income statement for 2013.

**BE 2–10**
Financial
statements
● LO2–6

The following account balances were taken from the 2013 post-closing trial balance of the Bowler Corporation: cash, $5,000; accounts receivable, $10,000; inventory, $16,000; machinery and equipment, $100,000; accumulated depreciation—machinery and equipment, $40,000; accounts payable, $20,000; salaries payable, $12,000; retained earnings, $9,000; and common stock, $50,000. Prepare a 12/31/13 balance sheet.

**BE 2–11**
Closing entries
● LO2–7

The year-end adjusted trial balance of the Timmons Tool and Die Corporation included the following account balances: retained earnings, $220,000; sales revenue, $850,000; cost of goods sold, $580,000; salaries expense, $180,000; rent expense, $40,000; and interest expense, $15,000. Prepare the necessary closing entries.

**BE 2–12**
Cash versus
accrual
accounting
● LO2–8

Newman Consulting Company maintains its records on a cash basis. During 2013 the following cash flows were recorded: cash received from customers, $420,000; and cash paid for salaries, utilities, and advertising, $240,000, $35,000, and $12,000, respectively. You also determine that customers owed the company $52,000 and $60,000 at the beginning and end of the year, respectively, and that the company owed the utility company $6,000 and $4,000 at the beginning and end of the year, respectively. Determine accrual net income for the year.

# Exercises

An alternate exercise and problem set is available on the text website: www.mhhe.com/spiceland7e

**E 2–1**
Transaction
analysis
● LO2–1

The following transactions occurred during March 2013 for the Wainwright Corporation. The company owns and operates a wholesale warehouse.

1. Issued 30,000 shares of common stock in exchange for $300,000 in cash.

2. Purchased equipment at a cost of $40,000. $10,000 cash was paid and a note payable was signed for the balance owed.

3. Purchased inventory on account at a cost of $90,000. The company uses the perpetual inventory system.

4. Credit sales for the month totaled $120,000. The cost of the goods sold was $70,000.

5. Paid $5,000 in rent on the warehouse building for the month of March.
6. Paid $6,000 to an insurance company for fire and liability insurance for a one-year period beginning April 1, 2013.
7. Paid $70,000 on account for the merchandise purchased in 3.
8. Collected $55,000 from customers on account.
9. Recorded depreciation expense of $1,000 for the month on the equipment.

**Required:**
Analyze each transaction and show the effect of each on the accounting equation for a corporation.
*Example:*

Assets    = Liabilities + Paid-In Capital + Retained Earnings
1.   +300,000 (cash)                    + 300,000 (common stock)

---

**E 2–2**
**Journal entries**
● **LO2–2**

Prepare journal entries to record each of the transactions listed in Exercise 2–1.

---

**E 2–3**
**T-accounts and trial balance**
● **LO2–3**

Post the journal entries prepared in Exercise 2–2 to T-accounts. Assume that the opening balances in each of the accounts is zero. Prepare a trial balance from the ending account balances.

---

**E 2–4**
**Journal entries**
● **LO2–2**

The following transactions occurred during the month of June 2013 for the Stridewell Corporation. The company owns and operates a retail shoe store.

1. Issued 100,000 shares of common stock in exchange for $500,000 cash.
2. Purchased furniture and fixtures at a cost of $100,000. $40,000 was paid in cash and a note payable was signed for the balance owed.
3. Purchased inventory on account at a cost of $200,000. The company uses the perpetual inventory system.
4. Credit sales for the month totaled $280,000. The cost of the goods sold was $140,000.
5. Paid $6,000 in rent on the store building for the month of June.
6. Paid $3,000 to an insurance company for fire and liability insurance for a one-year period beginning June 1, 2013.
7. Paid $120,000 on account for the merchandise purchased in 3.
8. Collected $55,000 from customers on account.
9. Paid shareholders a cash dividend of $5,000.
10. Recorded depreciation expense of $2,000 for the month on the furniture and fixtures.
11. Recorded the amount of prepaid insurance that expired for the month.

**Required:**
Prepare journal entries to record each of the transactions and events listed above.

---

**E 2–5**
**The accounting processing cycle**
● **LO2–2 through LO2–7**

Listed below are several terms and phrases associated with the accounting processing cycle. Pair each item from List A (by letter) with the item from List B that is most appropriately associated with it.

| List A | List B |
|---|---|
| _____ 1. Source documents | a. Record of the dual effect of a transaction in debit/credit form. |
| _____ 2. Transaction analysis | b. Internal events recorded at the end of a reporting period. |
| _____ 3. Journal | c. Primary means of disseminating information to external decision makers. |
| _____ 4. Posting | d. To zero out the owners' equity temporary accounts. |
| _____ 5. Unadjusted trial balance | e. Determine the dual effect on the accounting equation. |
| _____ 6. Adjusting entries | f. List of accounts and their balances before recording adjusting entries. |
| _____ 7. Adjusted trial balance | g. List of accounts and their balances after recording closing entries. |
| _____ 8. Financial statements | h. List of accounts and their balances after recording adjusting entries. |
| _____ 9. Closing entries | i. A means of organizing information: not part of the formal accounting system. |
| _____ 10. Post-closing trial balance | j. Transferring balances from the journal to the ledger. |
| _____ 11. Worksheet | k. Used to identify and process external transactions. |

**E 2–6**
**Debits and credits**
● **LO2–2**

Indicate whether a *debit* will increase (I) or decrease (D) each of the following accounts listed in items 1 through 16:

| Increase (I) or Decrease (D) | Account |
|---|---|
| 1. _____ | Inventory |
| 2. _____ | Depreciation expense |
| 3. _____ | Accounts payable |
| 4. _____ | Prepaid rent |
| 5. _____ | Sales revenue |
| 6. _____ | Common stock |
| 7. _____ | Wages payable |
| 8. _____ | Cost of goods sold |
| 9. _____ | Utility expense |
| 10. _____ | Equipment |
| 11. _____ | Accounts receivable |
| 12. _____ | Utilities payable |
| 13. _____ | Rent expense |
| 14. _____ | Interest expense |
| 15. _____ | Interest revenue |
| 16. _____ | Gain on sale of equipment |

**E 2–7**
**Transaction analysis; debits and credits**
● **LO2–2**

Some of the ledger accounts for the Sanderson Hardware Company are numbered and listed below. For each of the October 2013 transactions numbered 1 through 12 below, indicate by account number which accounts should be debited and which should be credited. The company uses the perpetual inventory system. Assume that appropriate adjusting entries were made at the end of September.

| | | |
|---|---|---|
| (1) Accounts payable | (2) Equipment | (3) Inventory |
| (4) Accounts receivable | (5) Cash | (6) Supplies |
| (7) Supplies expense | (8) Prepaid rent | (9) Sales revenue |
| (10) Retained earnings | (11) Note payable | (12) Common stock |
| (13) Unearned revenue | (14) Rent expense | (15) Wages payable |
| (16) Cost of goods sold | (17) Wage expense | (18) Interest expense |

| | Account(s) Debited | Account(s) Credited |
|---|---|---|
| *Example:* Purchased inventory for cash | 3 | 5 |

1. Paid a cash dividend.
2. Paid rent for the next three months.
3. Sold goods to customers on account.
4. Purchased inventory on account.
5. Purchased supplies for cash.
6. Paid employees wages for September.
7. Issued common stock in exchange for cash.
8. Collected cash from customers for goods sold in 3.
9. Borrowed cash from a bank and signed a note.
10. At the end of October, recorded the amount of supplies that had been used during the month.
11. Received cash for advance payment from customer.
12. Accrued employee wages for October.

**E 2–8**
**Adjusting entries**
● **LO2–5**

Prepare the necessary adjusting entries at December 31, 2013, for the Falwell Company for each of the following situations. Assume that no financial statements were prepared during the year and no adjusting entries were recorded.

1. A three-year fire insurance policy was purchased on July 1, 2013, for $12,000. The company debited insurance expense for the entire amount.
2. Depreciation on equipment totaled $15,000 for the year.
3. Employee salaries of $18,000 for the month of December will be paid in early January 2014.
4. On November 1, 2013, the company borrowed $200,000 from a bank. The note requires principal and interest at 12% to be paid on April 30, 2014.
5. On December 1, 2013, the company received $3,000 in cash from another company that is renting office space in Falwell's building. The payment, representing rent for December and January, was credited to unearned rent revenue.

**E 2–9**
Adjusting entries
● LO2–5

Prepare the necessary adjusting entries at December 31, 2013, for the Microchip Company for each of the following situations. Assume that no financial statements were prepared during the year and no adjusting entries were recorded.

1. On October 1, 2013, Microchip lent $90,000 to another company. A note was signed with principal and 8% interest to be paid on September 30, 2014.

2. On November 1, 2013, the company paid its landlord $6,000 representing rent for the months of November through January. Prepaid rent was debited.

3. On August 1, 2013, collected $12,000 in advance rent from another company that is renting a portion of Microchip's factory. The $12,000 represents one year's rent and the entire amount was credited to rent revenue.

4. Depreciation on machinery is $4,500 for the year.

5. Vacation pay for the year that had been earned by employees but not paid to them or recorded is $8,000.

6. Microchip began the year with $2,000 in its asset account, supplies. During the year, $6,500 in supplies were purchased and debited to supplies. At year-end, supplies costing $3,250 remain on hand.

**E 2–10**
Adjusting entries; solving for unknowns
● LO2–4, LO2–5

The Eldorado Corporation's controller prepares adjusting entries only at the end of the fiscal year. The following adjusting entries were prepared on December 31, 2013:

| | Debit | Credit |
|---|---|---|
| Interest expense | 7,200 | |
| Interest payable | | 7,200 |
| Rent expense | 35,000 | |
| Prepaid rent | | 35,000 |
| Interest receivable | 500 | |
| Interest revenue | | 500 |

Additional information:

1. The company borrowed $120,000 on March 31, 2013. Principal and interest are due on March 31, 2014. This note is the company's only interest-bearing debt.

2. Rent for the year on the company's office space is $60,000. The rent is paid in advance.

3. On October 31, 2013, Eldorado lent money to a customer. The customer signed a note with principal and interest at 6% due in one year.

**Required:**
Determine the following:

1. What is the interest rate on the company's note payable?

2. The 2013 rent payment was made at the beginning of which month?

3. How much did Eldorado lend its customer on October 31?

**E 2–11**
Financial statements and closing entries
● LO2–6, LO2–7

The December 31, 2013, adjusted trial balance for the Blueboy Cheese Corporation is presented below.

| Account Title | Debits | Credits |
|---|---|---|
| Cash | 21,000 | |
| Accounts receivable | 300,000 | |
| Prepaid rent | 10,000 | |
| Inventory | 50,000 | |
| Equipment | 600,000 | |
| Accumulated depreciation—equipment | | 250,000 |
| Accounts payable | | 60,000 |
| Note payable (due in six months) | | 60,000 |
| Salaries payable | | 8,000 |
| Interest payable | | 2,000 |
| Common stock | | 400,000 |
| Retained earnings | | 100,000 |
| Sales revenue | | 800,000 |
| Cost of goods sold | 480,000 | |
| Salaries expense | 120,000 | |
| Rent expense | 30,000 | |
| Depreciation expense | 60,000 | |
| Interest expense | 4,000 | |
| Advertising expense | 5,000 | |
| Totals | 1,680,000 | 1,680,000 |

**Required:**

1. Prepare an income statement for the year ended December 31, 2013, and a classified balance sheet as of December 31, 2013.

2. Prepare the necessary closing entries at December 31, 2013.

**E 2–12**
**Closing entries**
● **LO2–7**

American Chip Corporation's fiscal year-end is December 31. The following is a partial adjusted trial balance as of December 31, 2013.

| Account Title | Debits | Credits |
|---|---|---|
| Retained earnings | | 80,000 |
| Sales revenue | | 750,000 |
| Interest revenue | | 3,000 |
| Cost of goods sold | 420,000 | |
| Salaries expense | 100,000 | |
| Rent expense | 15,000 | |
| Depreciation expense | 30,000 | |
| Interest expense | 5,000 | |
| Insurance expense | 6,000 | |

**Required:**
Prepare the necessary closing entries at December 31, 2013.

**E 2–13**
**Closing entries**
● **LO2–7**

Presented below is income statement information of the Schefter Corporation for the year ended December 31, 2013.

| | | | |
|---|---|---|---|
| Sales revenue | $492,000 | Cost of goods sold | $284,000 |
| Salaries expense | 80,000 | Insurance expense | 12,000 |
| Interest revenue | 6,000 | Interest expense | 4,000 |
| Advertising expense | 10,000 | Income tax expense | 30,000 |
| Gain on sale of investments | 8,000 | Depreciation expense | 20,000 |

**Required:**
Prepare the necessary closing entries at December 31, 2013.

**E 2–14**
**Cash versus accrual accounting; adjusting entries**
● **LO2–4, LO2–5, LO2–8**

The Righter Shoe Store Company prepares monthly financial statements for its bank. The November 30 and December 31, 2013, trial balances contained the following account information:

| | Nov. 30 Dr. | Nov. 30 Cr. | Dec. 31 Dr. | Dec. 31 Cr. |
|---|---|---|---|---|
| Supplies | 1,500 | | 3,000 | |
| Prepaid insurance | 6,000 | | 4,500 | |
| Wages payable | | 10,000 | | 15,000 |
| Unearned rent revenue | | 2,000 | | 1,000 |

The following information also is known:
a.  The December income statement reported $2,000 in supplies expense.
b.  No insurance payments were made in December.
c.  $10,000 was paid to employees during December for wages.
d.  On November 1, 2013, a tenant paid Righter $3,000 in advance rent for the period November through January. Unearned rent revenue was credited.

**Required:**
1.  What was the cost of supplies purchased during December?
2.  What was the adjusting entry recorded at the end of December for prepaid insurance?
3.  What was the adjusting entry recorded at the end of December for accrued wages?
4.  What was the amount of rent revenue earned in December? What adjusting entry was recorded at the end of December for unearned rent?

**E 2–15**
**External transactions and adjusting entries**
● **LO2–2, LO2–5**

The following transactions occurred during 2013 for the Beehive Honey Corporation:

| | |
|---|---|
| Feb. 1 | Borrowed $12,000 from a bank and signed a note. Principal and interest at 10% will be paid on January 31, 2014. |
| Apr. 1 | Paid $3,600 to an insurance company for a two-year fire insurance policy. |
| July 17 | Purchased supplies costing $2,800 on account. The company records supplies purchased in an asset account. At the December 31, 2013, year-end, supplies costing $1,250 remained on hand. |
| Nov. 1 | A customer borrowed $6,000 and signed a note requiring the customer to pay principal and 8% interest on April 30, 2014. |

**Required:**
1.  Record each transaction in general journal form. Omit explanations.
2.  Prepare any necessary adjusting entries at the December 31, 2013, year-end. No adjusting entries were made during the year for any item.

**E 2–16**
**Accrual**
**accounting**
**income**
**determination**
● **LO2–4, LO2–8**

During the course of your examination of the financial statements of the Hales Corporation for the year ended December 31, 2013, you discover the following:

a.  An insurance policy covering three years was purchased on January 1, 2013, for $6,000. The entire amount was debited to insurance expense and no adjusting entry was made for this item.

b.  During 2013, the company received a $1,000 cash advance from a customer for merchandise to be manu-factured and shipped in 2014. The $1,000 was credited to sales revenue. No entry was made for the cost of merchandise.

c.  There were no supplies listed in the balance sheet under assets. However, you discover that supplies costing $750 were on hand at December 31.

d.  Hales borrowed $20,000 from a local bank on October 1, 2013. Principal and interest at 12% will be paid on September 30, 2014. No accrual was made for interest.

e.  Net income reported in the 2013 income statement is $30,000 before reflecting any of the above items.

**Required:**
Determine the proper amount of net income for 2013.

**E 2–17**
**Cash versus**
**accrual accounting**
● **LO2–8**

Stanley and Jones Lawn Service Company (S&J) maintains its books on a cash basis. However, the company recently borrowed $100,000 from a local bank and the bank requires S&J to provide annual financial statements prepared on an accrual basis. During 2013, the following cash flows were recorded:

| | | |
|---|---|---|
| Cash collected from customers | | $320,000 |
| Cash paid for: | | |
| Salaries | $180,000 | |
| Supplies | 25,000 | |
| Rent | 12,000 | |
| Insurance | 6,000 | |
| Miscellaneous | 20,000 | 243,000 |
| Net operating cash flow | | $ 77,000 |

You are able to determine the following information about accounts receivable, prepaid expenses, and accrued liabilities:

| | January 1, 2013 | December 31, 2013 |
|---|---|---|
| Accounts receivable | $32,000 | $27,000 |
| Prepaid insurance | –0– | 2,000 |
| Supplies | 1,000 | 1,500 |
| Accrued liabilities | | |
| (for miscellaneous expenses) | 2,400 | 3,400 |

In addition, you learn that the bank loan was dated September 30, 2013, with principal and interest at 6% due in one year. Depreciation on the company's equipment is $10,000 for the year.

**Required:**
Prepare an accrual basis income statement for 2013. (Ignore income taxes.)

**E 2–18**
**Cash versus**
**accrual**
**accounting**
● **LO2–8**

Haskins and Jones, Attorneys-at-Law, maintain its books on a cash basis. During 2013, the company collected $545,000 in fees from its clients and paid out $412,000 in expenses. You are able to determine the following information about accounts receivable, prepaid expenses, unearned fee revenue, and accrued liabilities:

| | January 1, 2013 | December 31, 2013 |
|---|---|---|
| Accounts receivable | $62,000 | $55,000 |
| Prepaid insurance | 4,500 | 6,000 |
| Prepaid rent | 9,200 | 8,200 |
| Unearned fee revenue | 9,200 | 11,000 |
| Accrued liabilities | | |
| (for various expenses) | 12,200 | 15,600 |

In addition, 2013 depreciation expense on furniture and fixtures is $22,000.

**Required:**
Determine accrual basis net income for 2013.

**E 2–19**
**Worksheet**
● **Appendix 2A**

The December 31, 2013, unadjusted trial balance for the Wolkstein Drug Company is presented below. December 31 is the company's fiscal year-end.

| Account Title | Debits | Credits |
|---|---|---|
| Cash | 20,000 | |
| Accounts receivable | 35,000 | |
| Prepaid rent | 5,000 | |
| Inventory | 50,000 | |
| Equipment | 100,000 | |
| Accumulated depreciation—equipment | | 30,000 |
| Accounts payable | | 25,000 |
| Wages payable | | –0– |
| Common stock | | 100,000 |
| Retained earnings | | 29,000 |
| Sales revenue | | 323,000 |
| Cost of goods sold | 180,000 | |
| Wage expense | 71,000 | |
| Rent expense | 30,000 | |
| Depreciation expense | –0– | |
| Utility expense | 12,000 | |
| Advertising expense | 4,000 | |
| Totals | 507,000 | 507,000 |

The following year-end adjusting entries are required:

a. Depreciation expense for the year on the equipment is $10,000.

b. Accrued wages payable at year-end should be $4,000.

**Required:**

1. Prepare and complete a worksheet similar to Illustration 2A–1.

2. Prepare an income statement for 2013 and a balance sheet as of December 31, 2013.

**E 2–20**
Reversing entries
● Appendix 2B

The employees of Xitrex, Inc., are paid each Friday. The company's fiscal year-end is June 30, which falls on a Wednesday for the current year. Wages are earned evenly throughout the five-day workweek, and $10,000 will be paid on Friday, July 2.

**Required:**

1. Prepare an adjusting entry to record the accrued wages as of June 30, a reversing entry on July 1, and an entry to record the payment of wages on July 2.

2. Prepare journal entries to record the accrued wages as of June 30 and the payment of wages on July 2 assuming a reversing entry is not made.

**E 2–21**
Reversing entries
● Appendix 2B

Refer to Exercise 2–9 and respond to the following requirements.

**Required:**

1. If Microchip's accountant employed reversing entries for accruals, which adjusting entries would she likely reverse at the beginning of the following year?

2. Prepare the adjusting entries at the end of 2013 for the adjustments you identified in requirement 1.

3. Prepare the appropriate reversing entries at the beginning of 2014.

**E 2–22**
Reversing entries
● Appendix 2B

Refer to Exercise 2–9 and respond to the following requirements.

**Required:**

1. If Microchip's accountant employed reversing entries for prepaid expenses, which transactions would be affected?

2. Prepare the original transactions creating the prepaid expenses and the adjusting entries at the end of 2013 for the transactions you identified in requirement 1.

3. Prepare the appropriate reversing entries at the beginning of 2014.

**E 2–23**
Special journals
● Appendix 2C

The White Company's accounting system consists of a general journal (GJ), a cash receipts journal (CR), a cash disbursements journal (CD), a sales journal (SJ), and a purchases journal (PJ). For each of the following, indicate which journal should be used to record the transaction.

| Transaction | Journal |
|---|---|
| 1. Purchased merchandise on account. | _____ |
| 2. Collected an account receivable. | _____ |
| 3. Borrowed $20,000 and signed a note. | _____ |
| 4. Recorded depreciation expense. | _____ |

(continued)

(concluded)

    5. Purchased equipment for cash.          _____

    6. Sold merchandise for cash (the sale only, not the cost of the merchandise).   _____

    7. Sold merchandise on credit (the sale only, not the cost of the merchandise).   _____

    8. Recorded accrued wages payable.   _____

    9. Paid employee wages.   _____

   10. Sold equipment for cash.   _____

   11. Sold equipment on credit.   _____

   12. Paid a cash dividend to shareholders.   _____

   13. Issued common stock in exchange for cash.   _____

   14. Paid accounts payable.   _____

**E 2–24**
**Special journals**
● **Appendix 2C**

The accounting system of K and M Manufacturing consists of a general journal (GJ), a cash receipts journal (CR), a cash disbursements journal (CD), a sales journal (SJ), and a purchases journal (PJ). For each of the following, indicate which journal should be used to record the transaction.

| Transaction | Journal |
|---|---|
| 1. Paid interest on a loan. | _____ |
| 2. Recorded depreciation expense. | _____ |
| 3. Purchased furniture for cash. | _____ |
| 4. Purchased merchandise on account. | _____ |
| 5. Sold merchandise on credit (the sale only, not the cost of the merchandise). | _____ |
| 6. Sold merchandise for cash (the sale only, not the cost of the merchandise). | _____ |
| 7. Paid rent. | _____ |
| 8. Recorded accrued interest payable. | _____ |
| 9. Paid advertising bill. | _____ |
| 10. Sold machinery on credit. | _____ |
| 11. Collected cash from customers on account. | _____ |
| 12. Paid employees wages. | _____ |
| 13. Collected interest on a note receivable. | _____ |

# CPA Review Questions

**CPA Exam Questions**

The following questions are adapted from a variety of sources including questions developed by the AICPA Board of Examiners and those used in the Kaplan CPA Review Course to study accounting changes and errors processing while preparing for the CPA examination. Determine the response that best completes the statements or questions.

● **LO2–1**

1. JME Corporation bills its customers when services are rendered and recognizes revenue at the same time. This event causes an
   a. Increase in assets.
   b. Increase in net income.
   c. Increase in retained earnings.
   d. All of the above.

● **LO2–5**

2. Fay Corp. pays its outside salespersons fixed monthly salaries as well as commissions on net sales. Sales commissions are paid in the month following the month of sale, while the fixed salaries are expensed but considered advances against commissions. However, if salespersons' fixed salaries exceed their sales commissions earned for a month, such excess is not returned to the company. Pertinent data for the month of March for the three salespersons are as follows:

| Salesperson | Fixed Salary | Net Sales | Commission Rate |
|---|---|---|---|
| A | $10,000 | $ 200,000 | 4% |
| B | 14,000 | 400,000 | 6% |
| C | 18,000 | 600,000 | 6% |
| Totals | $42,000 | $1,200,000 | |

What amount should Fay accrue as a debit to sales commissions expense and a credit to sales commissions payable at March 31?

a. $26,000
b. $28,000
c. $68,000
d. $70,000

● LO2–8    3. Compared to the accrual basis of accounting, the cash basis of accounting produces a lower amount of income by the net decrease during the accounting period of

|  | Accounts Receivable | Accrued Liabilities |
|---|---|---|
| a. | Yes | No |
| b. | No | Yes |
| c. | Yes | Yes |
| d. | No | No |

● LO2–8    4. On April 1 Ivy Corp. began operating a service company with an initial cash investment by shareholders of $1,000,000. The company provided $3,200,000 of services in April and received full payment in May. Ivy also incurred expenses of $1,500,000 in April that were paid in June. During May, Ivy paid its shareholders cash dividends of $500,000. What was the company's income before income taxes for the two months ended May 31 under the following methods of accounting?

|  | Cash Basis | Accrual Basis |
|---|---|---|
| a. | $3,200,000 | $1,700,000 |
| b. | $2,700,000 | $1,200,000 |
| c. | $1,700,000 | $1,700,000 |
| d. | $3,200,000 | $1,200,000 |

● LO2–8    5. Under East Co.'s accounting system, all insurance premiums paid are debited to prepaid insurance. During the year, East records monthly estimated charges to insurance expense with credits to prepaid insurance. Additional information for the year ended December 31 is as follows:

| Prepaid insurance at January 1 | $105,000 |
|---|---|
| Insurance expense recognized during the year | 437,500 |
| Prepaid insurance at December 31 | 122,500 |

What was the total amount of cash paid by East for insurance premiums during the year?

a. $332,500
b. $420,000
c. $437,500
d. $455,000

# Problems

 connect
|ACCOUNTING

**An alternate exercise and problem set is available on the text website:** www.mhhe.com/spiceland7e

P 2–1
Accounting
cycle through
unadjusted trial
balance
● LO2–2, LO2–3

Halogen Laminated Products Company began business on January 1, 2013. During January, the following transactions occurred:

Jan.  1    Issued common stock in exchange for $100,000 cash.
     2    Purchased inventory on account for $35,000 (the perpetual inventory system is used).
     4    Paid an insurance company $2,400 for a one-year insurance policy.
    10    Sold merchandise on account for $12,000. The cost of the merchandise was $7,000.
    15    Borrowed $30,000 from a local bank and signed a note. Principal and interest at 10% is to be repaid in six months.
    20    Paid employees $6,000 wages for the first half of the month.
    22    Sold merchandise for $10,000 cash. The cost of the merchandise was $6,000.
    24    Paid $15,000 to suppliers for the merchandise purchased on January 2.
    26    Collected $6,000 on account from customers.
    28    Paid $1,000 to the local utility company for January gas and electricity.
    30    Paid $4,000 rent for the building. $2,000 was for January rent, and $2,000 for February rent.

**Required:**

1. Prepare general journal entries to record each transaction. Omit explanations.
2. Post the entries to T-accounts.
3. Prepare an unadjusted trial balance as of January 30, 2013.

**P 2–2**
Accounting
cycle through
unadjusted trial
balance
● LO2–2, LO2–3

The following is the post-closing trial balance for the Whitlow Manufacturing Corporation as of December 31, 2012.

| Account Title | Debits | Credits |
|---|---|---|
| Cash | 5,000 | |
| Accounts receivable | 2,000 | |
| Inventory | 5,000 | |
| Equipment | 11,000 | |
| Accumulated depreciation—equipment | | 3,500 |
| Accounts payable | | 3,000 |
| Common stock | | 10,000 |
| Retained earnings | | 6,500 |
| Sales revenue | | –0– |
| Cost of goods sold | –0– | |
| Wage expense | –0– | |
| Rent expense | –0– | |
| Advertising expense | –0– | |
| Totals | 23,000 | 23,000 |

The following transactions occurred during January 2013:

Jan. 1   Sold merchandise for cash, $3,500. The cost of the merchandise was $2,000. The company uses the perpetual inventory system.

    2   Purchased equipment on account for $5,500 from the Strong Company.

    4   Received a $150 bill from the local newspaper for an advertisement that appeared in the paper on January 2.

    8   Sold merchandise on account for $5,000. The cost of the merchandise was $2,800.

  10   Purchased merchandise on account for $9,500.

  13   Purchased equipment for cash, $800.

  16   Paid the entire amount due to the Strong Company.

  18   Received $4,000 from customers on account.

  20   Paid $800 to the owner of the building for January's rent.

  30   Paid employees $3,000 for salaries for the month of January.

  31   Paid a cash dividend of $1,000 to shareholders.

**Required:**

1. Set up T-accounts and enter the beginning balances as of January 1, 2013.
2. Prepare general journal entries to record each transaction. Omit explanations.
3. Post the entries to T-accounts.
4. Prepare an unadjusted trial balance as of January 31, 2013.

**P 2–3**
Adjusting entries
● LO2–5

Pastina Company manufactures and sells various types of pasta to grocery chains as private label brands. The company's fiscal year-end is December 31. The unadjusted trial balance as of December 31, 2013, appears below.

| Account Title | Debits | Credits |
|---|---|---|
| Cash | 30,000 | |
| Accounts receivable | 40,000 | |
| Supplies | 1,500 | |
| Inventory | 60,000 | |
| Note receivable | 20,000 | |
| Interest receivable | –0– | |

(continued)

(concluded)

| Account Title | Debits | Credits |
|---|---|---|
| Prepaid rent | 2,000 | |
| Prepaid insurance | –0– | |
| Equipment | 80,000 | |
| Accumulated depreciation—equipment | | 30,000 |
| Accounts payable | | 31,000 |
| Wages payable | | –0– |
| Note payable | | 50,000 |
| Interest payable | | –0– |
| Unearned revenue | | –0– |
| Common stock | | 60,000 |
| Retained earnings | | 24,500 |
| Sales revenue | | 148,000 |
| Interest revenue | | –0– |
| Cost of goods sold | 70,000 | |
| Wage expense | 18,900 | |
| Rent expense | 11,000 | |
| Depreciation expense | –0– | |
| Interest expense | –0– | |
| Supplies expense | 1,100 | |
| Insurance expense | 6,000 | |
| Advertising expense | 3,000 | |
| Totals | 343,500 | 343,500 |

Information necessary to prepare the year-end adjusting entries appears below.

1. Depreciation on the equipment for the year is $10,000.
2. Employee wages are paid twice a month, on the 22nd for wages earned from the 1st through the 15th, and on the 7th of the following month for wages earned from the 16th through the end of the month. Wages earned from December 16 through December 31, 2013, were $1,500.
3. On October 1, 2013, Pastina borrowed $50,000 from a local bank and signed a note. The note requires interest to be paid annually on September 30 at 12%. The principal is due in 10 years.
4. On March 1, 2013, the company lent a supplier $20,000 and a note was signed requiring principal and interest at 8% to be paid on February 28, 2014.
5. On April 1, 2013, the company paid an insurance company $6,000 for a two-year fire insurance policy. The entire $6,000 was debited to insurance expense.
6. $800 of supplies remained on hand at December 31, 2013.
7. A customer paid Pastina $2,000 in December for 1,500 pounds of spaghetti to be manufactured and delivered in January 2014. Pastina credited sales revenue.
8. On December 1, 2013, $2,000 rent was paid to the owner of the building. The payment represented rent for December and January 2014, at $1,000 per month.

**Required:**
Prepare the necessary December 31, 2013, adjusting journal entries.

**P 2–4**
**Accounting cycle; adjusting entries through post-closing trial balance**
● **LO2–3, LO2–5 through LO2–7**

Refer to Problem 2–3 and complete the following steps:
1. Enter the unadjusted balances from the trial balance into T-accounts.
2. Post the adjusting entries prepared in Problem 2–3 to the accounts.
3. Prepare an adjusted trial balance.
4. Prepare an income statement and a statement of shareholders' equity for the year ended December 31, 2013, and a classified balance sheet as of December 31, 2013. Assume that no common stock was issued during the year and that $4,000 in cash dividends were paid to shareholders during the year.
5. Prepare closing entries and post to the accounts.
6. Prepare a post-closing trial balance.

P 2–5
Adjusting entries
● LO2–5

Howarth Company's fiscal year-end is December 31. Below are the unadjusted and adjusted trial balances for December 31, 2013.

| Account Title | Unadjusted | | Adjusted | |
|---|---|---|---|---|
| | Debits | Credits | Debits | Credits |
| Cash | 50,000 | | 50,000 | |
| Accounts receivable | 35,000 | | 35,000 | |
| Prepaid rent | 2,000 | | 1,200 | |
| Supplies | 1,500 | | 800 | |
| Inventory | 60,000 | | 60,000 | |
| Note receivable | 30,000 | | 30,000 | |
| Interest receivable | –0– | | 1,500 | |
| Equipment | 45,000 | | 45,000 | |
| Accumulated depreciation—equipment | | 15,000 | | 21,500 |
| Accounts payable | | 34,000 | | 34,000 |
| Wages payable | | –0– | | 6,200 |
| Note payable | | 50,000 | | 50,000 |
| Interest payable | | –0– | | 2,500 |
| Unearned rent revenue | | –0– | | 2,000 |
| Common stock | | 46,000 | | 46,000 |
| Retained earnings | | 20,000 | | 20,000 |
| Sales revenue | | 244,000 | | 244,000 |
| Rent revenue | | 6,000 | | 4,000 |
| Interest revenue | | –0– | | 1,500 |
| Cost of goods sold | 126,000 | | 126,000 | |
| Wage expense | 45,000 | | 51,200 | |
| Rent expense | 11,000 | | 11,800 | |
| Depreciation expense | –0– | | 6,500 | |
| Supplies expense | 1,100 | | 1,800 | |
| Interest expense | 5,400 | | 7,900 | |
| Advertising expense | 3,000 | | 3,000 | |
| Totals | 415,000 | 415,000 | 431,700 | 431,700 |

**Required:**
Prepare the adjusting journal entries that were made at December 31, 2013.

P 2–6
Accounting cycle
● LO2–2 through
LO2–7

The general ledger of the Karlin Company, a consulting company, at January 1, 2013, contained the following account balances:

| Account Title | Debits | Credits |
|---|---|---|
| Cash | 30,000 | |
| Accounts receivable | 15,000 | |
| Equipment | 20,000 | |
| Accumulated depreciation | | 6,000 |
| Salaries payable | | 9,000 |
| Common stock | | 40,500 |
| Retained earnings | | 9,500 |
| Total | 65,000 | 65,000 |

The following is a summary of the transactions for the year:
a. Sales of services, $100,000, of which $30,000 was on credit.
b. Collected on accounts receivable, $27,300.
c. Issued shares of common stock in exchange for $10,000 in cash.
d. Paid salaries, $50,000 (of which $9,000 was for salaries payable).
e. Paid miscellaneous expenses, $24,000.
f. Purchased equipment for $15,000 in cash.
g. Paid $2,500 in cash dividends to shareholders.

**Required:**

1. Set up the necessary T-accounts and enter the beginning balances from the trial balance.
2. Prepare a general journal entry for each of the summary transactions listed above.
3. Post the journal entries to the accounts.
4. Prepare an unadjusted trial balance.
5. Prepare and post adjusting journal entries. Accrued salaries at year-end amounted to $1,000. Depreciation for the year on the equipment is $2,000.
6. Prepare an adjusted trial balance.
7. Prepare an income statement for 2013 and a balance sheet as of December 31, 2013.
8. Prepare and post closing entries.
9. Prepare a post-closing trial balance.

**P 2–7**

**Adjusting entries and income effects**

● **LO2–4, LO2–5**

The information necessary for preparing the 2013 year-end adjusting entries for Vito's Pizza Parlor appears below. Vito's fiscal year-end is December 31.

a. On July 1, 2013, purchased $10,000 of **IBM Corporation** bonds at face value. The bonds pay interest twice a year on January 1 and July 1. The annual interest rate is 12%.

b. Vito's depreciable equipment has a cost of $30,000, a five-year life, and no salvage value. The equipment was purchased in 2011. The straight-line depreciation method is used.

c. On November 1, 2013, the bar area was leased to Jack Donaldson for one year. Vito's received $6,000 representing the first six months' rent and credited unearned rent revenue.

d. On April 1, 2013, the company paid $2,400 for a two-year fire and liability insurance policy and debited insurance expense.

e. On October 1, 2013, the company borrowed $20,000 from a local bank and signed a note. Principal and interest at 12% will be paid on September 30, 2014.

f. At year-end, there is a $1,800 debit balance in the supplies (asset) account. Only $700 of supplies remain on hand.

**Required:**

1. Prepare the necessary adjusting journal entries at December 31, 2013.
2. Determine the amount by which net income would be misstated if Vito's failed to make these adjusting entries. (Ignore income tax expense.)

**P 2–8**

**Adjusting entries**

● **LO2–5**

Excalibur Corporation manufactures and sells video games for personal computers. The unadjusted trial balance as of December 31, 2013, appears below. December 31 is the company's fiscal year-end. The company uses the perpetual inventory system.

| Account Title | Debits | Credits |
|---|---|---|
| Cash | 23,300 | |
| Accounts receivable | 32,500 | |
| Supplies | –0– | |
| Prepaid rent | –0– | |
| Inventory | 65,000 | |
| Equipment | 75,000 | |
| Accumulated depreciation—equipment | | 10,000 |
| Accounts payable | | 26,100 |
| Wages payable | | 3,000 |
| Note payable | | 30,000 |
| Common stock | | 80,000 |
| Retained earnings | | 16,050 |
| Sales revenue | | 180,000 |
| Cost of goods sold | 95,000 | |
| Interest expense | –0– | |
| Wage expense | 32,350 | |
| Rent expense | 14,000 | |
| Supplies expense | 2,000 | |
| Utility expense | 6,000 | |
| Totals | 345,150 | 345,150 |

Information necessary to prepare the year-end adjusting entries appears below.

1. The equipment was purchased in 2011 and is being depreciated using the straight-line method over an eight-year useful life with no salvage value.
2. Accrued wages at year-end should be $4,500.

3. The company borrowed $30,000 on September 1, 2013. The principal is due to be repaid in 10 years. Interest is payable twice a year on each August 31 and February 28 at an annual rate of 10%.

4. The company debits supplies expense when supplies are purchased. Supplies on hand at year-end cost $500.

5. Prepaid rent at year-end should be $1,000.

**Required:**
Prepare the necessary December 31, 2013, adjusting entries.

**P 2–9**
Accounting cycle; unadjusted trial balance through closing
● LO2–3, LO2–5, LO2–7

The unadjusted trial balance as of December 31, 2013, for the Bagley Consulting Company appears below. December 31 is the company's fiscal year-end.

| Account Title | Debits | Credits |
|---|---|---|
| Cash | 8,000 | |
| Accounts receivable | 9,000 | |
| Prepaid insurance | 3,000 | |
| Land | 200,000 | |
| Buildings | 50,000 | |
| Accumulated depreciation—buildings | | 20,000 |
| Equipment | 100,000 | |
| Accumulated depreciation—equipment | | 40,000 |
| Accounts payable | | 35,050 |
| Salaries payable | | –0– |
| Unearned rent revenue | | –0– |
| Common stock | | 200,000 |
| Retained earnings | | 56,450 |
| Sales revenue | | 90,000 |
| Interest revenue | | 3,000 |
| Rent revenue | | 7,500 |
| Salaries expense | 37,000 | |
| Depreciation expense | –0– | |
| Insurance expense | –0– | |
| Utility expense | 30,000 | |
| Maintenance expense | 15,000 | |
| Totals | 452,000 | 452,000 |

**Required:**
1. Enter the account balances in T-accounts.
2. From the trial balance and information given, prepare adjusting entries and post to the accounts.
   a. The buildings have an estimated useful life of 50 years with no salvage value. The company uses the straight-line depreciation method.
   b. The equipment is depreciated at 10 percent of original cost per year.
   c. Prepaid insurance expired during the year, $1,500.
   d. Accrued salaries at year-end, $1,500.
   e. Unearned rent revenue at year-end should be $1,200.
3. Prepare an adjusted trial balance.
4. Prepare closing entries.
5. Prepare a post-closing trial balance.

**P 2–10**
Accrual accounting; financial statements
● LO2–4, LO2–6, LO2–8

McGuire Corporation began operations in 2013. The company purchases computer equipment from manufacturers and then sells to retail stores. During 2013, the bookkeeper used a check register to record all cash receipts and cash disbursements. No other journals were used. The following is a recap of the cash receipts and disbursements made during the year.

| Cash receipts: | |
|---|---|
| Sale of common stock | $ 50,000 |
| Collections from customers | 320,000 |
| Borrowed from local bank on April 1, note signed requiring principal and interest at 12% to be paid on March 31, 2014 | 40,000 |
| Total cash receipts | $410,000 |

(continued)

(concluded)

| Cash disbursements: | |
|---|---|
| Purchase of merchandise | $220,000 |
| Payment of salaries | 80,000 |
| Purchase of equipment | 30,000 |
| Payment of rent on building | 14,000 |
| Miscellaneous expenses | 10,000 |
| Total cash disbursements | $354,000 |

You are called in to prepare financial statements at December 31, 2013. The following additional information was provided to you:

1. Customers owed the company $22,000 at year-end.
2. At year-end, $30,000 was still due to suppliers of merchandise purchased on credit.
3. At year-end, merchandise inventory costing $50,000 still remained on hand.
4. Salaries owed to employees at year-end amounted to $5,000.
5. On December 1, $3,000 in rent was paid to the owner of the building used by McGuire. This represented rent for the months of December through February.
6. The equipment, which has a 10-year life and no salvage value, was purchased on January 1, 2013. Straight-line depreciation is used.

**Required:**
Prepare an income statement for 2013 and a balance sheet as of December 31, 2013.

**P 2–11**
**Cash versus accrual accounting**
● LO2–8

Selected balance sheet information for the Wolf Company at November 30, and December 31, 2013, is presented below. The company uses the perpetual inventory system and all sales to customers are made on credit.

| | Nov. 30 | | Dec. 31 | |
|---|---|---|---|---|
| | **Dr.** | **Cr.** | **Dr.** | **Cr.** |
| Accounts receivable | 10,000 | | 3,000 | |
| Prepaid insurance | 5,000 | | 7,500 | |
| Inventory | 7,000 | | 6,000 | |
| Accounts payable | | 12,000 | | 15,000 |
| Wages payable | | 5,000 | | 3,000 |

The following cash flow information also is available:

a. Cash collected from credit customers, $80,000.
b. Cash paid for insurance, $5,000.
c. Cash paid to suppliers of inventory, $60,000 (the entire accounts payable amounts relate to inventory purchases).
d. Cash paid to employees for wages, $10,000.

**Required:**
1. Determine the following for the month of December:
   a. Sales revenue.
   b. Cost of goods sold.
   c. Insurance expense.
   d. Wage expense.
2. Prepare a summary journal entry to record the month's sales and cost of those sales.

**P 2–12**
**Cash versus accrual accounting**
● LO2–8

Zambrano Wholesale Corporation maintains its records on a cash basis. At the end of each year the company's accountant obtains the necessary information to prepare accrual basis financial statements. The following cash flows occurred during the year ended December 31, 2013:

| Cash receipts: | |
|---|---|
| From customers | $675,000 |
| Interest on note | 4,000 |
| Loan from a local bank | 100,000 |
| Total cash receipts | $779,000 |
| Cash disbursements: | |
| Purchase of merchandise | $390,000 |
| Annual insurance payment | 6,000 |
| Payment of salaries | 210,000 |
| Dividends paid to shareholders | 10,000 |
| Annual rent payment | 24,000 |
| Total cash disbursements | $640,000 |

Selected balance sheet information:

|  | 12/31/12 | 12/31/13 |
|---|---|---|
| Cash | $25,000 | $164,000 |
| Accounts receivable | 62,000 | 92,000 |
| Inventory | 80,000 | 62,000 |
| Prepaid insurance | 2,500 | ? |
| Prepaid rent | 11,000 | ? |
| Interest receivable | 3,000 | ? |
| Note receivable | 50,000 | 50,000 |
| Equipment | 100,000 | 100,000 |
| Accumulated depreciation—equipment | (40,000) | (50,000) |
| Accounts payable (for merchandise) | 110,000 | 122,000 |
| Salaries payable | 20,000 | 24,000 |
| Note payable | –0– | 100,000 |
| Interest payable | –0– | ? |

Additional information:

1. On March 31, 2012, Zambrano lent a customer $50,000. Interest at 8% is payable annually on each March 31. Principal is due in 2016.

2. The annual insurance payment is made in advance on April 30. The policy period begins on May 1.

3. On October 31, 2013, Zambrano borrowed $100,000 from a local bank. Principal and interest at 6% are due on October 31, 2014.

4. Annual rent on the company's facilities is paid in advance on June 30. The rental period begins on July 1.

**Required:**

1. Prepare an accrual basis income statement for 2013 (ignore income taxes).

2. Determine the following balance sheet amounts on December 31, 2013:

    a. Prepaid insurance.

    b. Prepaid rent.

    c. Interest receivable.

    d. Interest payable.

**P 2–13**
**Worksheet**
● **Appendix 2A**

Using the information from Problem 2–8, prepare and complete a worksheet similar to Illustration 2A–1. Use the information in the worksheet to prepare an income statement and a statement of shareholders' equity for 2013 and a balance sheet as of December 31, 2013. Cash dividends paid to shareholders during the year amounted to $6,000. Also prepare the necessary closing entries assuming that adjusting entries have been correctly posted to the accounts.

## Broaden Your Perspective

Apply your critical-thinking ability to the knowledge you've gained. These cases will provide you an opportunity to develop your research, analysis, judgment, and communication skills. You also will work with other students, integrate what you've learned, apply it in real world situations, and consider its global and ethical ramifications. This practice will broaden your knowledge and further develop your decision-making abilities.

**Judgment**
**Case 2–1**
Cash versus
accrual
accounting;
adjusting entries;
Chapters 1 and 2
● **LO2–4, LO2–8**

You have recently been hired by Davis & Company, a small public accounting firm. One of the firm's partners, Alice Davis, has asked you to deal with a disgruntled client, Mr. Sean Pitt, owner of the city's largest hardware store. Mr. Pitt is applying to a local bank for a substantial loan to remodel his store. The bank requires accrual based financial statements but Mr. Pitt has always kept the company's records on a cash basis. He does not see the purpose of accrual based statements. His most recent outburst went something like this: "After all, I collect cash from customers, pay my bills in cash, and I am going to pay the bank loan with cash. And, I already show my building and equipment as assets and depreciate them. I just don't understand the problem."

**Required:**

1. Explain the difference between a cash basis and an accrual basis measure of performance.

2. Why, in most cases, does accrual basis net income provide a better measure of performance than net operating cash flow?

3. Explain the purpose of adjusting entries as they relate to the difference between cash and accrual accounting.

**Judgment Case 2–2**

Cash versus accrual accounting

● LO2–8

Refer to Case 2–1 above. Mr. Pitt has relented and agrees to provide you with the information necessary to convert his cash basis financial statements to accrual basis statements. He provides you with the following transaction information for the fiscal year ending December 31, 2013:

1. A comprehensive insurance policy requires a payment every year for the upcoming year. The last payment of $12,000 was made on September 1, 2013.

2. Mr. Pitt allows customers to pay using a credit card. At the end of the current year, various credit card companies owed Mr. Pitt $6,500. At the end of last year, customer credit card charges outstanding were $5,000.

3. Employees are paid once a month, on the 10th of the month following the work period. Cash disbursements to employees were $8,200 and $7,200 for January 10, 2014, and January 10, 2013, respectively.

4. Utility bills outstanding totaled $1,200 at the end of 2013 and $900 at the end of 2012.

5. A physical count of inventory is always taken at the end of the fiscal year. The merchandise on hand at the end of 2013 cost $35,000. At the end of 2012, inventory on hand cost $32,000.

6. At the end of 2012, Mr. Pitt did not have any bills outstanding to suppliers of merchandise. However, at the end of 2013, he owed suppliers $4,000.

**Required:**

1. Mr. Pitt's 2013 cash basis net income (including depreciation expense) is $26,000. Determine net income applying the accrual accounting model.

2. Explain the effect on Mr. Pitt's balance sheet of converting from cash to accrual. That is, would assets, liabilities, and owner's equity be higher or lower and by what amounts?

**Communication Case 2–3**

Adjusting entries

● LO2–4

"I don't understand," complained Chris, who responded to your bulletin board posting in your responsibilities as a tutor. The complaint was in response to your statements that recording adjusting entries is a critical step in the accounting processing cycle, and the two major classifications of adjusting entries are prepayments and accruals.

**Required:**

Respond to Chris.

1. When do prepayments occur? Accruals?

2. Describe the appropriate adjusting entry for prepaid expenses and for unearned revenues. What is the effect on net income, assets, liabilities, and shareholders' equity of not recording a required adjusting entry for prepayments?

3. Describe the required adjusting entry for accrued liabilities and for accrued receivables. What is the effect on net income, assets, liabilities, and shareholders' equity of not recording a required adjusting entry for accruals?

# 3

# The Balance Sheet and Financial Disclosures

**OVERVIEW** — Chapter 1 stressed the importance of the financial statements in helping investors and creditors predict future cash flows. The balance sheet, along with accompanying disclosures, provides relevant information useful in helping investors and creditors not only to predict future cash flows, but also to make the related assessments of liquidity and long-term solvency.

The purpose of this chapter is to provide an overview of the balance sheet and financial disclosures and to explore how this information is used by decision makers.

**LEARNING OBJECTIVES** — **After studying this chapter, you should be able to:**

● **LO3–1** Describe the purpose of the balance sheet and understand its usefulness and limitations. (*p. 115*)

● **LO3–2** Identify and describe the various balance sheet asset classifications. (*p. 117*)

● **LO3–3** Identify and describe the two balance sheet liability classifications. (*p. 120*)

● **LO3–4** Explain the purpose of financial statement disclosures. (*p. 124*)

● **LO3–5** Explain the purpose of the management discussion and analysis disclosure. (*p. 128*)

● **LO3–6** Explain the purpose of an audit and describe the content of the audit report. (*p. 130*)

● **LO3–7** Describe the techniques used by financial analysts to transform financial information into forms more useful for analysis. (*p. 132*)

● **LO3–8** Identify and calculate the common liquidity and financing ratios used to assess risk. (*p. 134*)

● **LO3–9** Discuss the primary differences between U.S. GAAP and IFRS with respect to the balance sheet, financial disclosures, and segment reporting. (*pp. 122* and *141*)

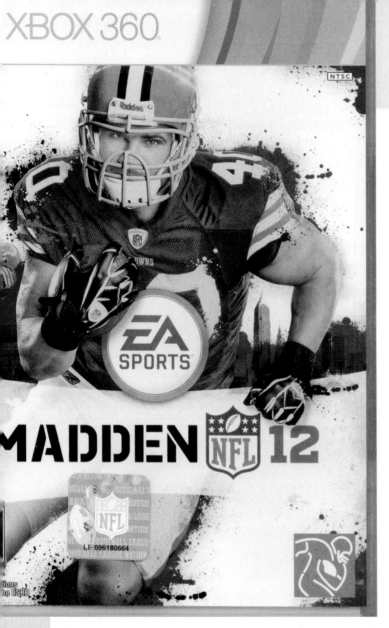

## FINANCIAL REPORTING CASE

### What's It Worth?

"I can't believe it. Why don't you accountants prepare financial statements that are relevant?" Your friend Jerry is a finance major and is constantly badgering you about what he perceives to be a lack of relevance of financial statements prepared according to generally accepted accounting principles. "For example, take a look at this balance sheet for **Electronic Arts** that I just downloaded off the Internet. Electronic Arts is the company in California that produces all those cool video games like Battlefield 2, NBA Live, and Madden NFL. Anyway, the shareholders' equity of the company according to the 2011 balance sheet is about $2.5 billion. But if you multiply the number of outstanding shares by the most recent stock price per share, the company's market value is three times that amount. I thought financial statements were supposed to help investors and creditors value a company." You decide to look at the company's balance sheet and try to set Jerry straight.

By the time you finish this chapter, you should be able to respond appropriately to the questions posed in this case. Compare your response to the solution provided at the end of the chapter.

QUESTIONS

1. Respond to Jerry's criticism that shareholders' equity does not represent the market value of the company. What information does the balance sheet provide? (p. 115)

2. The usefulness of the balance sheet is enhanced by classifying assets and liabilities according to common characteristics. What are the classifications used in Electronic Arts' balance sheets and what elements do those categories include? (p. 116)

**ELECTRONIC ARTS INC.
AND SUBSIDIARIES
Consolidated Balance Sheets**
(In millions, except par value data)

| Assets | March 31, 2011 | March 31, 2010 |
|---|---|---|
| Current assets: | | |
| Cash and cash equivalents | $1,579 | $1,273 |
| Short-term investments | 497 | 432 |
| Marketable equity securities | 161 | 291 |
| Receivables, net of allowances of $304 and $217, respectively | 335 | 206 |
| Inventories | 77 | 100 |
| Deferred income taxes, net | 56 | 44 |
| Other current assets | 327 | 239 |
| Total current assets | 3,032 | 2,585 |
| Property and equipment, net | 513 | 537 |
| Goodwill | 1,110 | 1,093 |
| Acquisition-related intangibles, net | 144 | 204 |
| Deferred income taxes, net | 49 | 52 |
| Other assets | 80 | 175 |
| Total Assets | $4,928 | $4,646 |
| **Liabilities and Stockholders' Equity** | | |
| Current liabilities: | | |
| Accounts payable | $ 228 | $ 91 |
| Accrued and other current liabilities | 768 | 717 |
| Deferred net revenue (packaged goods and digital content) | 1,005 | 766 |
| Total current liabilities | 2,001 | 1,574 |
| Income tax obligations | 192 | 242 |
| Deferred income taxes, net | 37 | 2 |
| Other liabilities | 134 | 99 |
| Total liabilities | 2,364 | 1,917 |
| Commitments and contingencies (See Note 10) | | |
| Stockholders' equity: | | |
| Preferred stock, $0.01 par value. 10 shares authorized | — | — |
| Common stock, $0.01 par value. 1,000 shares authorized; 333 and 330 shares issued and outstanding, respectively | 3 | 3 |
| Paid-in capital | 2,495 | 2,375 |
| Retained earnings (accumulated deficit) | (153) | 123 |
| Accumulated other comprehensive income | 219 | 228 |
| Total stockholders' equity | 2,564 | 2,729 |
| Total Liabilities and Stockholders' Equity | $4,928 | $4,646 |

The balance sheet, along with accompanying disclosures, provides a wealth of information to external decision makers. The information provided is useful not only in the prediction of future cash flows but also in the related assessments of liquidity and long-term solvency.

This chapter begins our discussion of the financial statements by providing an overview of the balance sheet and the financial disclosures that accompany the financial statements. The first part of the chapter describes the usefulness and limitations of the balance sheet and illustrates the content of the statement. The second part illustrates financial statement disclosures presented to external users in addition to the basic financial statements. In the third part we discuss how this information can be used by decision makers to assess business risk. That discussion introduces some common financial ratios used to assess liquidity and long-term solvency.

Chapter 4 continues this discussion of the financial statements with its coverage of the income statement, statement of comprehensive income, and the statement of cash flows.

# THE BALANCE SHEET

The purpose of the balance sheet, sometimes referred to as the statement of financial position, is to report a company's financial position on a particular date. Unlike the income statement, which is a change statement reporting events that occurred *during a period of time,* the balance sheet presents an organized array of assets, liabilities, and shareholders' equity *at a point in time.* It is a freeze frame or snapshot of financial position at the end of a particular day marking the end of an accounting period.

● LO3–1

## Usefulness and Limitations

An important limitation of the balance sheet is that *it does not portray the market value of the entity* as a going concern, nor its liquidation value. Many assets, like land and buildings for example, are measured at their historical costs rather than their fair values. Relatedly, many company resources including its trained employees, its experienced management team, and its reputation are not recorded as assets at all. Also, many items and amounts reported in the balance sheet are heavily reliant on estimates rather than determinable amounts. For example, companies estimate the amount of receivables they will be able to actually collect and the amount of warranty costs they will eventually incur for products already sold. For these and other reasons, a company's book value, its assets minus its liabilities as shown in the balance sheet, usually will not directly measure the company's market value (number of shares of common stock outstanding multiplied by the price per share).

**FINANCIAL Reporting Case**

Q1, p. 113

Assets minus liabilities, measured according to GAAP, is not likely to be representative of the market value of the entity.

Consider for example that early in 2011, the 30 companies constituting the Dow Jones Industrial Average had an average ratio of market value to book value of approximately 3.5. The ratio for IBM, one of the world's largest technology companies, was almost 9.0. Can you think of a reason why IBM's market value would be nine times higher than its book value? A significant reason is the way we account for research and development costs. IBM invests considerable amounts, over $6 billion in 2010 alone, on research and development of new products. Quite a few of these products that the company has developed over the years have been market successes, and yet the costs to discover and develop them are not represented in the balance sheet. We expense research and development costs in the period incurred rather than capitalize them as assets for the balance sheet.

During the financial crisis of 2008–2009 we saw stock prices plummet resulting in historic declines in the market to book ratio for most companies. For example, in 2007 the average ratio of market to book for the 30 Dow Jones Industrial Average companies was 4.46, almost twice the early 2009 average. Particularly hard hit were financial services companies. Early in 2009, both Bank of America and Citigroup had market to book ratios significantly less than 1.0. Later in 2009, Citigroup was replaced and is no longer one of the Dow Jones Industrial 30 companies.

Despite these limitations, the balance sheet does have significant value. An important feature of the statement is that it describes many of the resources a company has available for generating future cash flows. Another way the statement's content is informative is in combination with income statement items. For example, the relation between net income and assets provides a measure of return that is useful in predicting future profitability. In fact, many of the amounts reported in either of the two statements are more informative when viewed relative to an amount from the other statement.[1]

The balance sheet provides information useful for assessing future cash flows, liquidity, and long-term solvency.

The balance sheet does not simply list assets and liabilities. Instead, assets and liabilities are classified (grouped) according to common characteristics. These classifications, which we explore in the next section, along with related disclosure notes, help the balance sheet to provide additional important information about liquidity and long-term solvency. Liquidity refers to the period of time before an asset is converted to cash or until a liability is paid. This information is useful in assessing a company's ability to pay its *current* obligations.

---

[1]We explore some of these relationships in Chapter 5.

**Long-term solvency** refers to the riskiness of a company with regard to the amount of liabilities in its capital structure. Other things being equal, the risk to an investor or creditor increases as the percentage of liabilities, relative to equity, increases.

Solvency also provides information about *financial flexibility*—the ability of a company to alter cash flows in order to take advantage of unexpected investment opportunities and needs. For example, the higher the percentage of a company's liabilities to its equity, the more difficult it typically will be to borrow additional funds either to take advantage of a promising investment opportunity or to meet obligations. In general, the less financial flexibility, the more risk there is that an enterprise will fail. In a subsequent section of this chapter, we introduce some common ratios used to assess liquidity and long-term solvency.

In summary, even though the balance sheet does not *directly measure* the market value of the entity, it provides valuable information that can be used to help *judge* market value.

# Classifications

**FINANCIAL Reporting Case**

Q2, p. 113

The key classification of assets and liabilities in the balance sheet is the current versus noncurrent distinction.

**Illustration 3–1** Classification of Elements within a Balance Sheet

| Assets |
| --- |
| Current assets |
| Investments |
| Property, plant, and equipment |
| Intangible assets |
| Other assets |
| Liabilities |
| Current liabilities |
| Long-term liabilities |
| Shareholders' Equity |
| Paid-in capital |
| Retained earnings |

Current assets include cash and all other assets expected to become cash or be consumed within one year or the *operating cycle,* whichever is longer.

The usefulness of the balance sheet is enhanced when assets and liabilities are grouped according to common characteristics. *The broad distinction made in the balance sheet is the current versus noncurrent classification of both assets and liabilities.* The remainder of Part A provides an overview of the balance sheet. We discuss each of the three primary elements of the balance sheet (assets, liabilities, and shareholders' equity) in the order they are reported in the statement as well as the classifications typically made within the elements. The balance sheet elements were defined in Chapter 1 as follows:

**Assets** are probable future economic benefits obtained or controlled by a particular entity as a result of past transactions or events.

**Liabilities** are probable future sacrifices of economic benefits arising from present obligations of a particular entity to transfer assets or provide services to other entities in the future as a result of past transactions or events.

**Equity** (or net assets), called **shareholders' equity** or **stockholders' equity** for a corporation, is the residual interest in the assets of an entity that remains after deducting liabilities.

Illustration 3–1 lists the balance sheet elements along with their subclassifications.

We intentionally avoid detailed discussion of the question of valuation in order to focus on an overview of the balance sheet. In later chapters we look closer at the nature and valuation of the specific assets and liabilities.

## Assets

**CURRENT ASSETS.** Current assets include cash and other assets that are reasonably expected to be converted to cash or consumed within the coming year, or within the normal operating cycle of the business if that's longer than one year. The **operating cycle** for a typical manufacturing company refers to the period of time necessary to convert cash to raw materials, raw materials to a finished product, the finished product to receivables, and then finally receivables back to cash. This concept is illustrated in Illustration 3–2.

In some businesses, such as shipbuilding or distilleries, the operating cycle extends far beyond one year. For example, if it takes two years to build an oil-carrying supertanker, then the shipbuilder will classify as current those assets that will be converted to cash or consumed within two years. But for most businesses the operating cycle will be shorter than one year. In these situations the one-year convention is used to classify both assets and liabilities. Where a company has no clearly defined operating cycle, the one-year convention is used.

Illustration 3–3 presents the current asset sections of **Dell Inc.**'s 2011 and 2010 balance sheets (statements of financial position) that also can be located in the company's financial statements in Appendix B at the back of the text. In keeping with common practice, the individual current assets are listed in the order of their liquidity (nearness to cash).

**Cash and Cash Equivalents.** The most liquid asset, cash, is listed first. Cash includes cash on hand and in banks that is available for use in the operations of the business and such items as bank drafts, cashier's checks, and money orders. **Cash equivalents** frequently include certain negotiable items such as commercial paper, money market funds, and U.S. treasury bills. These are highly liquid investments that can be quickly converted into cash. Most companies draw a distinction between investments classified as cash equivalents and the next category of current assets, short-term investments, according to the scheduled maturity of the investment. It is common practice to classify investments that have a maturity date of three months or less from the date of purchase as cash equivalents. **Dell Inc.**'s policy follows this practice and is disclosed in the summary of significant accounting policies disclosure note. The portion of the note from the company's 2011 financial statements is shown in Illustration 3–4.

**Illustration 3–2** Operating Cycle of a Typical Manufacturing Company

1. Use cash to acquire raw materials
2. Convert raw materials to finished product
3. Deliver product to customer
4. Collect cash from customer

● LO3–2

**Illustration 3–3**

Current Assets—Dell Inc.

Real World Financials

| (In millions) | January 28, 2011 | January 29, 2010 |
|---|---|---|
| **Assets** | | |
| Current assets: | | |
| Cash and cash equivalents | $13,913 | $10,635 |
| Short-term investments | 452 | 373 |
| Accounts receivable, net | 6,493 | 5,837 |
| Financing receivables, net | 3,643 | 2,706 |
| Inventories, net | 1,301 | 1,051 |
| Other current assets | 3,219 | 3,643 |
| Total current assets | 29,021 | 24,245 |

**Illustration 3–4**

Disclosure of Cash Equivalents—Dell Inc.

Real World Financials

**Note 1—Description of Business and Summary of Significant Accounting Policies**
*Cash and Cash Equivalents*
All highly liquid investments, including credit card receivables, due from banks, with original maturities of three months or less at date of purchase are carried at cost and are considered to be cash equivalents. All other investments not considered to be cash equivalents are separately categorized as investments.

Cash that is restricted for a special purpose and not available for current operations should not be classified as a current asset. For example, if cash is being accumulated to repay a debt due in five years, the cash is classified as investments, a noncurrent asset.[2]

**Short-Term Investments.** Liquid investments not classified as cash equivalents are reported as either **short-term investments**, sometimes called *temporary investments* or *short-term marketable securities*. Investments in stock and debt securities of other corporations are included as short-term investments *if* the company has the ability and intent to sell those securities within the next 12 months or operating cycle, whichever is longer. If, for example, a company owns 1,000 shares of **IBM Corporation** stock and intends to hold those shares for several years, the stock is a long-term investment and should be classified as a noncurrent asset, investments.

*Investments* are classified as current if management has the ability and intent to liquidate the investment in the near term.

---

[2]If the debt is due in the next year and classified as a current liability, then the cash also would be classified as current.

For reporting purposes, investments in debt and equity securities are classified in one of three categories: (1) held to maturity, (2) trading securities, or (3) securities available for sale. We discuss these different categories and their accounting treatment in Chapter 12.

**Accounts Receivable.** Accounts receivable result from the sale of goods or services on credit. Notice in Illustration 3–3 that Dell's accounts receivable and financing receivables (discussed in Chapter 7) are valued net, that is, less an allowance for uncollectible accounts (the amount not expected to be collected). Accounts receivable often are referred to as *trade receivables* because they arise in the course of a company's normal trade. *Nontrade receivables* result from loans or advances by the company to individuals and other entities. When receivables are supported by a formal agreement or note that specifies payment terms they are called notes receivable.

Accounts receivable usually are due in 30 to 60 days, depending on the terms offered to customers and are, therefore, classified as current assets. Any receivable, regardless of the source, not expected to be collected within one year or the operating cycle, whichever is longer, is classified as a noncurrent asset, investments.

*Inventories* consist of assets that a retail or wholesale company acquires for resale or goods that manufacturers produce for sale.

**Inventories.** Inventories include goods awaiting sale (finished goods), goods in the course of production (work in process), and goods to be consumed directly or indirectly in production (raw materials). Inventory for a wholesale or retail company consists only of finished goods, but the inventory of a manufacturer will include all three types of goods. Occasionally, a manufacturing company will report all three types of inventory directly in the balance sheet. More often, only the total amount of inventories is shown in the balance sheet and the balances of each type are shown in a disclosure note. For example, the note shown in Illustration 3–5 lists the components of inventory in the 2011 financial statements of **Dell Inc.**

**Illustration 3–5**

Inventories Disclosure—
Dell Inc.

Real World Financials

**Note 12—Supplemental Consolidated Financial Information (in part)**

| | January 28, 2011 | January 29, 2010 |
|---|---|---|
| Inventories, net: | | |
| Production materials | $ 593 | $ 487 |
| Work-in-process | 232 | 168 |
| Finished goods | 476 | 396 |
| Total | $1,301 | $1,051 |

Inventories are reported as current assets because they normally are sold within the operating cycle.

**Prepaid Expenses.** Recall from Chapter 2 that a prepaid expense represents an asset recorded when an expense is paid in advance, creating benefits beyond the current period. Examples are prepaid rent and prepaid insurance. Even though these assets are not converted to cash, they would involve an outlay of cash if not prepaid.

Whether a prepaid expense is current or noncurrent depends on when its benefits will be realized. For example, if rent on an office building were prepaid for one year, then the entire prepayment is classified as a current asset. However, if rent were prepaid for a period extending beyond the coming year, a portion of the prepayment is classified as an other asset, a noncurrent asset.[3] **Dell Inc.** includes prepaid expenses in the other current assets category. Other current assets also include assets—such as nontrade receivables—that, because their amounts are not material, did not warrant separate disclosure.

When assets are expected to provide economic benefits beyond the next year, or operating cycle, they are reported as *noncurrent assets.* Typical classifications of noncurrent assets are (1) investments, (2) property, plant, and equipment, and (3) intangible assets.

---

[3]Companies often include prepayments for benefits extending beyond one year as current assets when the amounts are not material.

**INVESTMENTS.** Most companies occasionally acquire assets that are not used directly in the operations of the business. These assets include investments in equity and debt securities of other corporations, land held for speculation, noncurrent receivables, and cash set aside for special purposes (such as for future plant expansion). These assets are classified as noncurrent because management does not intend to convert the assets into cash in the next year (or the operating cycle if that's longer).

*Investments* are assets not used directly in operations.

**PROPERTY, PLANT, AND EQUIPMENT.** Virtually all companies own assets classified as property, plant, and equipment. The common characteristics these assets share are that they are *tangible, long-lived,* and *used in the operations of the business.* Property, plant, and equipment, along with intangible assets, often are the primary revenue-generating assets of the business.

Tangible, long-lived assets used in the operations of the business are classified as *property, plant, and equipment.*

Property, plant, and equipment includes land, buildings, equipment, machinery, and furniture, as well as natural resources, such as mineral mines, timber tracts, and oil wells. These various assets usually are reported as a single amount in the balance sheet, with details provided in a note. They are reported at original cost less accumulated depreciation (or depletion for natural resources) to date. Quite often, a company will present only the net amount of property, plant, and equipment in the balance sheet and provide details in a disclosure note. Land often is listed as a separate item in this classification because it has an unlimited useful life and thus is not depreciated.

**INTANGIBLE ASSETS.** Some assets used in the operations of a business have no physical substance. These are appropriately called intangible assets. Generally, these represent the ownership of an exclusive right to something such as a product, a process, or a name. This right can be a valuable resource in generating future revenues. Patents, copyrights, and franchises are examples. They are reported in the balance sheet net of accumulated amortization. Some companies include intangible assets as part of property, plant, and equipment, while others report them either in a separate intangible asset classification or as other noncurrent assets.

*Intangible assets* generally represent exclusive rights that a company can use to generate future revenues.

Quite often, much of the value of intangibles is not reported in the balance sheet. For example, it would not be unusual for the historical cost of a patent to be significantly lower than its market value. As we discuss in Chapter 10, for internally developed intangibles, the costs that are included as part of historical cost are limited. Specifically, none of the research and development costs incurred in developing the intangible asset are included in cost.

**OTHER ASSETS.** Balance sheets often include a catch-all classification of noncurrent assets called other assets. This classification includes long-term prepaid expenses, called *deferred charges,* and any noncurrent asset not falling in one of the other classifications. For instance, if a company's noncurrent investments are not material in amount, they might be reported in the other asset classification rather than in a separate investments category.

Illustration 3–6 reproduces the noncurrent asset section of **Dell Inc.**'s 2011 and 2010 balance sheets. For Dell, noncurrent assets include property, plant, and equipment, investments, long-term financing receivables, goodwill (an intangible asset), purchased intangible assets, and other noncurrent assets.

| | January 28, 2011 | January 29, 2010 |
|---|---|---|
| (In millions) | | |
| **Assets** | | |
| Property, plant, and equipment, net | 1,953 | 2,181 |
| Investments | 704 | 781 |
| Long-term financing receivables, net | 799 | 332 |
| Goodwill | 4,365 | 4,074 |
| Purchased intangible assets, net | 1,495 | 1,694 |
| Other noncurrent assets | 262 | 345 |

**Illustration 3–6**

Noncurrent Assets— Dell Inc.

Real World Financials

We've seen how assets are grouped into current and noncurrent categories and that noncurrent assets always are subclassified further. Let's now turn our attention to liabilities. These, too, are separated into current and noncurrent (long-term) categories.

## Liabilities

● LO3–3  Liabilities represent obligations to other entities. The information value of reporting these amounts is enhanced by classifying them as current liabilities and long-term liabilities. Illustration 3–7 shows the liability section of Dell Inc.'s 2011 and 2010 balance sheets.

**Illustration 3–7**

Liabilities—Dell Inc.

Real World Financials

| (In millions) | January 28, 2011 | January 29, 2010 |
|---|---|---|
| **Liabilities** | | |
| Current liabilities: | | |
| Short-term debt | $   851 | $   663 |
| Accounts payable | 11,293 | 11,373 |
| Accrued and other | 4,181 | 3,884 |
| Short-term deferred services revenue | 3,158 | 3,040 |
| Total current liabilities | 19,483 | 18,960 |
| Long-term debt | 5,146 | 3,417 |
| Long-term deferred service revenue | 3,518 | 3,029 |
| Other noncurrent liabilities | 2,686 | 2,605 |
| Total liabilities | 30,833 | 28,011 |

**Current liabilities are expected to be satisfied within one year or the operating cycle, whichever is longer.**

**CURRENT LIABILITIES.**  Current liabilities are those obligations that are expected to be satisfied through the use of current assets or the creation of other current liabilities. So, this classification includes all liabilities that are expected to be satisfied within one year or the operating cycle, whichever is longer. An exception is a liability that management intends to refinance on a long-term basis. For example, if management intends to refinance a six-month note payable by substituting a two-year note payable and has the ability to do so, then the liability would not be classified as current even though it's due within the coming year. This exception is discussed in more detail in Chapter 13.

**Current liabilities usually include *accounts* and *notes payable, unearned revenues, accrued liabilities,* and the *current maturities of long-term debt.***

The most common current liabilities are accounts payable, notes payable (short-term borrowings), unearned revenues, accrued liabilities, and the currently maturing portion of long-term debt. **Accounts payable** are obligations to suppliers of merchandise or of services purchased on open account, with payment usually due in 30 to 60 days. **Notes payable** are written promises to pay cash at some future date (I.O.U.s). Unlike accounts payable, notes usually require the payment of explicit interest in addition to the original obligation amount. Notes maturing in the next year or operating cycle, whichever is longer, will be classified as current liabilities. **Unearned revenues**, sometimes called deferred revenues as in Dell's balance sheet, represent cash received from a customer for goods or services to be provided in a future period.

**Accrued liabilities** represent obligations created when expenses have been incurred but will not be paid until a subsequent reporting period. Examples are accrued salaries payable, accrued interest payable, and accrued taxes payable. **Dell Inc.**'s accrued liabilities include accrued warranty liabilities, accrued income and other taxes, accrued compensation, and other.

Long-term notes, loans, mortgages, and bonds payable usually are reclassified and reported as current liabilities as they become payable within the next year (or operating cycle if that's longer).[4] Likewise, when long-term debt is payable in installments, the installment payable currently is reported as a current liability. For example, a $1,000,000 note payable requiring $100,000 in principal payments to be made in each of the next 10 years

---

[4]Payment can be with current assets or the creation of other current liabilities.

is classified as a $100,000 current liability—**current maturities of long-term debt**—and a $900,000 long-term liability.

Chapter 13 provides a more detailed analysis of current liabilities.

**LONG-TERM LIABILITIES.**     Long-term liabilities are obligations that will *not* be satisfied in the next year or operating cycle, whichever is longer. They do not require the use of current assets or the creation of current liabilities for payment. Examples are long-term notes, bonds, pension obligations, and lease obligations.

But simply classifying a liability as long-term doesn't provide complete information to external users. For instance, long-term could mean anything from 2 to 20, 30, or 40 years. Payment terms, interest rates, and other details needed to assess the impact of these obligations on future cash flows and long-term solvency are reported in a disclosure note.

**Dell Inc.** reports long-term debt, long-term deferred services revenue, and other noncurrent liabilities at the end of its 2011 fiscal year. A disclosure note indicates that other noncurrent liabilities include warranty liabilities, income and other taxes payable, and other. Long-term liabilities are discussed in subsequent chapters.

> *Current liabilities include the current maturities of long-term debt.*

> *Noncurrent, or long-term liabilities, usually are those payable beyond the current year.*

## Shareholders' Equity

Recall from our discussions in Chapters 1 and 2 that owners' equity is simply a residual amount derived by subtracting liabilities from assets. For that reason, it's sometimes referred to as net assets. Also recall that owners of a corporation are its shareholders, so owners' equity for a corporation is referred to as shareholders' equity or stockholders' equity. Shareholders' equity for a corporation arises primarily from two sources: (1) amounts *invested* by shareholders in the corporation, and (2) amounts *earned* by the corporation (on behalf of its shareholders). These are reported as (1) **paid-in capital** and (2) **retained earnings**. Retained earnings represents the accumulated net income earned since the inception of the corporation and not (yet) paid to shareholders as dividends.

Illustration 3–8 presents the shareholders' equity section of **Dell Inc.**'s 2011 and 2010 fiscal year-end balance sheets.

> *Shareholders' equity is composed of paid-in capital (invested capital) and retained earnings (earned capital).*

| (In millions) | January 28, 2011 | January 29, 2010 |
|---|---|---|
| **Stockholders' equity:** | | |
| Common stock and capital in excess of $.01 par value; shares authorized: 7,000; shares issued: 3,369 and 3,351, respectively; shares outstanding; 1,918 and 1,957, respectively | 11,797 | 11,472 |
| Treasury stock, at cost: 976 and 919 shares, respectively | (28,704) | (27,904) |
| Retained earnings | 24,744 | 22,110 |
| Accumulated other comprehensive loss | (71) | (37) |
| Total stockholders' equity | 7,766 | 5,641 |

**Illustration 3–8**

Shareholders' Equity— Dell Inc.

Real World Financials

From the inception of the corporation through January 28, 2011, Dell has accumulated net income, less dividends, of $24,744 million which is reported as *retained earnings.* The company's *paid-in capital* is represented by common stock and additional paid-in capital less treasury stock, which collectively represent cash invested by shareholders in exchange for ownership interests. Information about the number of shares the company has authorized and how many shares have been issued and are outstanding also must be disclosed.

In addition to paid-in capital and retained earnings, shareholders' equity may include a few other equity components. For example, Dell reports accumulated other comprehensive loss. Accumulated other comprehensive income (loss) is discussed in Chapters 4, 12, and 18. Other equity components are addressed in later chapters, Chapter 18 in particular. We also discuss the concept of par value in Chapter 18.

# International Financial Reporting Standards

● LO3–9

**Balance Sheet Presentation.** There are more similarities than differences in balance sheets prepared according to U.S. GAAP and those prepared applying IFRS. Some of the differences are:

- International standards specify a minimum list of items to be presented in the balance sheet. U.S. GAAP has no minimum requirements.
- *IAS No.1, revised,*[5] changed the title of the balance sheet to *statement of financial position*, although companies are not required to use that title. Some U.S. companies use the statement of financial position title as well.
- Under U.S. GAAP, we present current assets and liabilities before noncurrent assets and liabilities. *IAS No. 1* doesn't prescribe the format of the balance sheet, but balance sheets prepared using IFRS often report noncurrent items first. A recent survey of large companies that prepare their financial statements according to IFRS reports that in 2009, 73% of the surveyed companies list noncurrent items first.[6] For example, the balance sheet of Sanofi-Aventis, a French pharmaceutical company, included in a recent half-year report, presented assets, liabilities, and equity in the following order:

Real World Financials

**Sanofi-Aventis**
**Balance Sheet (condensed)**
**At June 30**

| (€ in millions) | 2011 |
| --- | --- |
| Noncurrent assets (including property, plant, and equipment) | €76,958 |
| Current assets | 22,592 |
| Assets held for sale or exchange | 44 |
| Total assets | €99,594 |
| | |
| Shareholders' equity | €52,599 |
| Noncurrent liabilities | 30,943 |
| Current liabilities | 16,038 |
| Liabilities related to assets held for sale or exchange | 14 |
| Total liabilities and equity | €99,594 |

# Where We're Headed

● LO3–9

**The FASB and IASB are working together on a standard that would have a dramatic impact on the format of financial statements.**

**Demonstrating the cohesiveness among the financial statements is a key objective of the Financial Statement Presentation project.**

The FASB and IASB are working together on a project, Financial Statement Presentation, to establish a common standard for presenting information in the financial statements, including classifying and displaying line items and aggregating line items into subtotals and totals. This standard would have a dramatic impact on the format of financial statements. An important part of the proposal involves the organization of elements of the balance sheet (statement of financial position), statement of comprehensive income (including the income statement), and statement of cash flows into a common set of classifications.

Each of the financial statements would include classifications by operating, investing, and financing activities, providing a "cohesive" financial picture that stresses the relationships among the financial statements. Recall from your previous accounting education and from our brief discussion in Chapter 2, that this is the way we currently classify activities in the statement of cash flows.

(continued)

---

[5]"Financial Statement Presentation," *International Accounting Standard No. 1* (IASCF), as amended effective January 1, 2011.
[6]*IFRS Accounting Trends and Techniques*—2010 (New York, AICPA, 2010), p.133.

(concluded)

For each statement, though, operating and investing activities would be included within a new category, "business" activities. Each statement also would include three additional groupings: discontinued operations, income taxes, and equity (if needed). The new look for the balance sheet (statement of financial position) would be:

**Statement of Financial Position**

**Business**
- Operating assets and liabilities
- Investing assets and liabilities

**Financing**
- Debt
- Equity

**Income Taxes**

**Discontinued Operations**

The project has multiple phases and it is uncertain when it will be completed.

# Concept Review Exercise

The following is a post-closing trial balance for the Sepia Paint Corporation at December 31, 2013, the end of the company's fiscal year:

**BALANCE SHEET CLASSIFICATION**

| Account Title | Debits | Credits |
| --- | --- | --- |
| Cash | 80,000 | |
| Accounts receivable | 200,000 | |
| Allowance for uncollectible accounts | | 20,000 |
| Inventories | 300,000 | |
| Prepaid expenses | 30,000 | |
| Note receivable (due in one month) | 60,000 | |
| Investments | 50,000 | |
| Land | 120,000 | |
| Buildings | 550,000 | |
| Machinery | 500,000 | |
| Accumulated depreciation—buildings and machinery | | 450,000 |
| Patent (net of amortization) | 50,000 | |
| Accounts payable | | 170,000 |
| Salaries payable | | 40,000 |
| Interest payable | | 10,000 |
| Note payable | | 100,000 |
| Bonds payable (due in 10 years) | | 500,000 |
| Common stock, no par | | 400,000 |
| Retained earnings | | 250,000 |
| Totals | 1,940,000 | 1,940,000 |

The $50,000 balance in the investment account consists of marketable equity securities of other corporations. The company's intention is to hold the securities for at least three years. The $100,000 note payable is an installment loan. $10,000 of the principal, plus interest, is due on each July 1 for the next 10 years. At the end of the year, 100,000 shares of common stock were issued and outstanding. The company has 500,000 shares of common stock authorized.

**Required:**

Prepare a classified balance sheet for the Sepia Paint Corporation at December 31, 2013.

Solution:

**SEPIA PAINT CORPORATION**
**Balance Sheet**
**At December 31, 2013**

### Assets

**Current assets:**

| | | |
|---|---|---|
| Cash | | $ 80,000 |
| Accounts receivable | $ 200,000 | |
| Less: Allowance for uncollectible amounts | (20,000) | 180,000 |
| Note receivable | | 60,000 |
| Inventories | | 300,000 |
| Prepaid expenses | | 30,000 |
| Total current assets | | 650,000 |
| Investments | | 50,000 |

**Property, plant, and equipment:**

| | | |
|---|---|---|
| Land | 120,000 | |
| Buildings | 550,000 | |
| Machinery | 500,000 | |
| | 1,170,000 | |
| Less: Accumulated depreciation | (450,000) | |
| Net property, plant, and equipment | | 720,000 |

**Intangible assets:**

| | | |
|---|---|---|
| Patent | | 50,000 |
| Total assets | | $1,470,000 |

### Liabilities and Shareholders' Equity

**Current liabilities:**

| | | |
|---|---|---|
| Accounts payable | | $ 170,000 |
| Salaries payable | | 40,000 |
| Interest payable | | 10,000 |
| Current maturities of long-term debt | | 10,000 |
| Total current liabilities | | 230,000 |

**Long-term liabilities:**

| | | |
|---|---|---|
| Note payable | $ 90,000 | |
| Bonds payable | 500,000 | |
| Total long-term liabilities | | 590,000 |

**Shareholders' equity:**

| | | |
|---|---|---|
| Common stock, no par, 500,000 shares authorized, 100,000 shares issued and outstanding | 400,000 | |
| Retained earnings | 250,000 | |
| Total shareholders' equity | | 650,000 |
| Total liabilities and shareholders' equity | | $1,470,000 |

The usefulness of the balance sheet, as well as the other financial statements, is significantly enhanced by financial statement disclosures. We now turn our attention to these disclosures.

## PART B    FINANCIAL DISCLOSURES

● LO3–4    Financial statements are included in the annual report a company mails to its shareholders. They are, though, only part of the information provided. Critical to understanding the financial statements and to evaluating a firm's performance and financial health are additional disclosures included as part of the financial statements.

Financial statement disclosures are provided (1) by including additional information, often parenthetically, on the face of the statement following a financial statement item and (2) in disclosure notes that often include supporting schedules. Common examples of disclosures included on the face of the balance sheet are the allowance for uncollectible accounts and information about common stock. Disclosure notes, discussed and illustrated in the next section, are the most common means of providing these additional disclosures. The specific format of disclosure is generally not important, only that the information is, in fact, disclosed.

**The full-disclosure principle requires that financial statements provide all material relevant information concerning the reporting entity.**

# Disclosure Notes

Disclosure notes typically span several pages and either explain or elaborate upon the data presented in the financial statements themselves, or provide information not directly related to any specific item in the statements. Throughout this text you will encounter examples of items that usually are disclosed this way. For instance, the fair values of financial instruments and "off-balance-sheet" risk associated with financial instruments are disclosed in notes. Information providing details of many financial statement items is provided using disclosure notes. Some examples include:

- Pension plans
- Leases
- Long-term debt
- Investments
- Income taxes
- Property, plant, and equipment
- Employee benefit plans

Disclosure notes must include certain specific notes such as a summary of significant accounting policies, descriptions of subsequent events, and related third-party transactions, but many notes are fashioned to suit the disclosure needs of the particular reporting enterprise. Actually, any explanation that contributes to investors' and creditors' understanding of the results of operations, financial position, and cash flows of the company should be included. Let's take a look at just a few disclosure notes.

## Summary of Significant Accounting Policies

There are many areas where management chooses from among equally acceptable alternative accounting methods. For example, management chooses whether to use accelerated or straight-line depreciation, whether to use FIFO, LIFO, or average cost to measure inventories, and whether the completed contract or percentage-of-completion method best reflects the performance of construction operations. The company also defines which securities it considers to be cash equivalents and its policies regarding the timing of recognizing revenues. Typically, the first disclosure note consists of a summary of significant accounting policies that discloses the choices the company makes.[7] Illustration 3–9 shows you a portion of a typical summary note from a recent annual report of the **Starbucks Corporation**.

The *summary of significant accounting policies* conveys valuable information about the company's choices from among various alternative accounting methods.

Studying this note is an essential step in analyzing financial statements. Obviously, knowing which methods were used to derive certain accounting numbers is critical to assessing the adequacy of those amounts.

## Subsequent Events

When an event that has a material effect on the company's financial position occurs after the fiscal year-end but before the financial statements are issued or "available to be issued," the

---

[7]FASB ASC 235–10–50: Notes to Financial Statements—Overall—Disclosure (previously "Disclosure of Accounting Policies," *Accounting Principles Board Opinion No. 22* (New York: AICPA, 1972)).

**Illustration 3–9** Summary of Significant Accounting Policies—Starbucks Corporation

### Note 1: Summary of Accounting Policies (in part)

#### Principles of Consolidation

The consolidated financial statements reflect the financial position and operating results of Starbucks, which includes wholly owned subsidiaries and investees controlled by the Company.

#### Cash Equivalents

The Company considers all highly liquid instruments with a maturity of three months or less at the time of purchase to be cash equivalents.

#### Inventories

Inventories are stated at the lower of cost (primarily moving average cost) or market. The Company records inventory reserves for obsolete and slow-moving items and for estimated shrinkage between physical inventory counts.

#### Property, Plant, and Equipment

Property, plant, and equipment are carried at cost less accumulated depreciation. Depreciation of property, plant, and equipment which includes assets under leases, is provided on the straight-line method over estimated useful lives, generally ranging from two to seven years for equipment and 30 to 40 years for buildings. Leasehold improvements are amortized over the shorter of their estimated useful lives or the related lease life, generally 10 years.

#### Revenue Recognition

Company-operated retail store revenues are recognized when payment is tendered at the point of sale. Revenues from the Company's store value cards, such as the Starbucks Card, and gift certificates are recognized when tendered for payment, or upon redemption. Outstanding customer balances are included in Deferred revenue on the consolidated balance sheets.

---

**Real World Financials**

A *subsequent event* is a significant development that occurs after a company's fiscal year-end but before the financial statements are issued or available to be issued.

event is described in a *subsequent event* disclosure note.[8] Examples include the issuance of debt or equity securities, a business combination or the sale of a business, the sale of assets, an event that sheds light on the outcome of a loss contingency, or any other event having a material effect on operations. Illustration 3–10 illustrates the required disclosure by showing a note that Wal-Mart Stores, Inc., included in its January 31, 2011, financial statements, announcing both an increase in the company's annual dividend and the uncertainty of the damages to the company's business in Japan following the March 2011 earthquake.

We cover subsequent events in more depth in Chapter 13.

**Illustration 3–10**

Subsequent Event— Wal-Mart Stores, Inc.

Real World Financials

### 14 Subsequent Events (in part)

#### Dividends Declared

On March 3, 2011, our Board of Directors approved an increase in the annual dividend for fiscal 2012 to $1.46 per share, an increase of approximately 21% over the dividends paid in fiscal 2011. Dividends per share were $1.21 and $1.09 in fiscal 2011 and 2010, respectively. For the fiscal year ending January 31, 2012, the annual dividend will be paid in four quarterly installments.

#### Earthquake in Japan

On March 11, 2011, an earthquake of 9.0 magnitude occurred near the Northeastern coast of Japan, creating extremely destructive tsunami waves. The earthquake and tsunami waves caused extensive damage in Northeastern Japan and also affected other regions in Japan through a lack of electricity, water and transportation. We are currently unable to estimate the value of damages and the corresponding insurance recovery regarding our business in Japan, although we do not believe that any damages would be material to our financial position.

### Noteworthy Events and Transactions

Some transactions and events occur only occasionally, but when they do occur are potentially important to evaluating a company's financial statements. In this category are related-party transactions, errors and irregularities, and illegal acts. The more frequent of these is related-party transactions.

---

[8]Financial statements are viewed as issued if they have been widely distributed to financial statement users in a format consistent with GAAP. Some entities (for example, private companies) don't widely distribute their financial statements to users. For those entities, the key date for subsequent events is not the date of issuance but rather the date upon which the financial statements are "available to be issued," which occurs when the financial statements are complete, in a format consistent with GAAP, and have obtained the necessary approvals for issuance. Companies must disclose the date through which subsequent events have been evaluated. (FASB ASC 855: Subsequent Events (previously "Subsequent Events," *Statement of Financial Accounting Standards No. 165* (Stamford, Conn.: FASB, 2009))).

Sometimes a company will engage in transactions with owners, management, families of owners or management, affiliated companies, and other parties that can significantly influence or be influenced by the company. The potential problem with **related-party transactions** is that their economic substance may differ from their legal form. For instance, borrowing or lending money at an interest rate that differs significantly from the market interest rate is an example of a transaction that could result from a related-party involvement. As a result of the potential for misrepresentation, financial statement users are particularly interested in more details about these transactions.

When related-party transactions occur, companies must disclose the nature of the relationship, provide a description of the transactions, and report the dollar amounts of transactions and any amounts due from or to related parties.[9] Illustration 3–11 shows a disclosure note from a recent annual report of **Guess, Inc.**, the contemporary apparel and accessories company. The note describes the charter of aircraft from a trust organized for the benefit of executives of the company.

> The economic substance of *related-party* transactions should be disclosed, including dollar amounts involved.

### 11. Related-Party Transactions (in part)

The Company and its subsidiaries periodically enter into transactions with other entities or individuals that are considered related parties, including certain transactions with entities affiliated with trusts for the respective benefit of Maurice and Paul Marciano, who are executives of the Company, Armand Marciano, their brother and former executive of the Company, and certain of their children (the "Marciano Trusts").

### Aircraft Arrangements

The Company periodically charters aircraft owned by MPM Financial, LLC ("MPM Financial"), an entity affiliated with the Marciano Trusts, through independent third party management companies contracted by MPM Financial to manage its aircraft. Under an informal arrangement with MPM Financial and the third party management companies, the Company has chartered and may from time to time continue to charter aircraft owned by MPM Financial at a discount from the third party management companies' preferred customer hourly charter rates. The total fees paid under these arrangements for fiscal 2011, fiscal 2010 and fiscal 2009 were approximately $1.1 million, $0.4 million and $0.9 million, respectively.

**Illustration 3–11**

Related-Party Transactions Disclosure—Guess, Inc.

**Real World Financials**

More infrequent are errors, irregularities, and illegal acts; however, when they do occur, their disclosure is important. The distinction between errors and **irregularities** is that errors are unintentional while irregularities are *intentional* distortions of financial statements.[10] Obviously, management fraud might cause a user to approach financial analysis from an entirely different and more cautious viewpoint.

Closely related to irregularities are **illegal acts** such as bribes, kickbacks, illegal contributions to political candidates, and other violations of the law. Accounting for illegal practices has been influenced by the Foreign Corrupt Practices Act passed by Congress in 1977. The Act is intended to discourage illegal business practices through tighter controls and also encourage better disclosure of those practices when encountered. The nature of such disclosures should be influenced by the materiality of the impact of illegal acts on amounts disclosed in the financial statements.[11] However, the SEC issued guidance expressing its view that exclusive reliance on quantitative benchmarks to assess materiality in preparing financial statements is inappropriate.[12] A number of other factors, including whether the item in question involves an unlawful transaction, should also be considered when determining materiality.

As you might expect, any disclosures of related-party transactions, irregularities, and illegal acts can be quite sensitive. Although auditors must be considerate of the privacy of the parties involved, that consideration cannot be subordinate to users' needs for full disclosure.

---

[9]FASB ASC 850–10–50: Related Party Disclosures—Overall—Disclosure (previously "Related Party Disclosures," *Statement of Financial Accounting Standards No. 57* (Stamford, Conn.: FASB, 1982)).

[10]"The Auditor's Responsibility to Detect and Report Errors and Irregularities," *Statement on Auditing Standards No. 53* (New York: AICPA, 1988).

[11]"Illegal Acts by Clients," *Statement on Auditing Standards No. 54* (New York: AICPA, 1988).

[12]FASB ASC 250–10–S99–1, SAB Topic 1.M: Assessing Materiality (originally "Materiality," *Staff Accounting Bulletin No. 99* (Washington, D.C.: SEC, August 1999)).

Disclosure notes for some financial statement elements are required. Others are provided when required by specific situations in the interest of full disclosure.

We've discussed only a few of the disclosure notes most frequently included in annual reports. Other common disclosures include details concerning earnings per share calculations, income taxes, property and equipment, contingencies, long-term debt, leases, pensions, stock options, changes in accounting methods, fair values of financial instruments, and exposure to market risk and credit risk. We discuss and illustrate these in later chapters in the context of related financial statement elements.

# Management Discussion and Analysis

● LO3–5

The management discussion and analysis provides a biased but informed perspective of a company's (a) operations, (b) liquidity, and (c) capital resources.

In addition to the financial statements and accompanying disclosure notes, each annual report of a public company requires a fairly lengthy discussion and analysis provided by the company's management. In this section, management provides its views on significant events, trends, and uncertainties pertaining to the company's (a) operations, (b) liquidity, and (c) capital resources. Although the management discussion and analysis (MD&A) section may embody management's biased perspective, it can offer an informed insight that might not be available elsewhere. Illustration 3–12 contains part of the liquidity and capital resources portion of **PetSmart, Inc.**'s MDA that followed a discussion of operations in its annual report for the fiscal year ended January 30, 2011.

**Illustration 3–12**

Management Discussion and Analysis—PetSmart, Inc.

Real World Financials

---

**Management Discussion and Analysis of Financial Condition and Results of Operations**
(In part: Liquidity and Capital Resources only)

*Cash Flow*

We believe that our operating cash flow and cash on hand will be adequate to meet our operating, investing and financing needs in the foreseeable future. In addition, we also have access to our $350.0 million revolving credit facility, although there can be no assurance of our ability to access these markets on commercially acceptable terms in the future. We expect to continuously assess the economic environment and market conditions to guide our decisions regarding our uses of cash, including capital expenditures, investments, dividends and the purchase of our common stock.

*Common Stock Purchase Program*

In June 2010, the Board of Directors replaced the $350.0 million program with a new share purchase program authorizing the purchase of up to $400.0 million of our common stock through January 29, 2012. During the thirteen weeks ended January 30, 2011, we purchased 2.6 million shares of common stock for $99.9 million. Since the inception of the $400.0 million authorization in June 2010, we have purchased 4.2 million shares of common stock for $156.2 million. As of January 30, 2011, $243.8 million remained available under the $400.0 million program.

*Common Stock Dividends*

We presently believe our ability to generate cash allows us to invest in the growth of the business and, at the same time, distribute a quarterly dividend. Our credit facility and letter of credit facility permit us to pay dividends, so long as we are not in default and the payment of dividends would not result in default. During 2010, 2009, and 2008, we paid aggregate dividends of $0.45 per share, $0.26 per share, and $0.12 per share, respectively.

*Operating Capital and Capital Expenditure Requirements*

Substantially all our stores are leased facilities. We opened 46 new stores and closed 8 stores in 2010. Generally, each new store requires capital expenditures of approximately $1.0 million for fixtures, equipment and leasehold improvements, approximately $0.3 million for inventory and approximately $0.1 million for preopening costs. We expect total capital spending to be approximately $130.0 to $140.0 million for 2011, based on our plan to open 45 to 50 net new stores and 8 to 10 new PetsHotels, continuing our investment in the development of our information systems, adding to our services capacity with the expansion of certain grooming salons, remodeling or replacing certain store assets and continuing our store refresh program.

# Management's Responsibilities

Management prepares and is responsible for the financial statements and other information in the annual report. To enhance the awareness of the users of financial statements concerning the relative roles of management and the auditor, annual reports of public companies include a management's responsibilities section that asserts the responsibility of management for the information contained in the annual report as well as an assessment of the company's internal control procedures.

Illustration 3–13 contains the statement of responsibility disclosure for **Home Depot, Inc.** included with the company's financial statements for the year ended January 30, 2011. Recall from our discussion of financial reporting reform in Chapter 1, that the *Sarbanes-Oxley Act of 2002* requires corporate executives to personally certify the financial statements. Submission of false statements carries a penalty of up to 20 years in jail. The illustration also contains Management's Report on Internal Control Over Financial Reporting. Francis S. Blake, Home Depot's chairman and chief executive officer, and Carol B. Tomé, the company's chief financial officer and executive vice president, signed the required certifications as well as these statements of responsibility.

### Illustration 3–13

Management's Responsibilities—Home Depot, Inc.

**Real World Financials**

The *management's responsibilities* section avows the responsibility of management for the company's *financial* statements and internal control system.

---

**Management's Responsibility for Financial Statements**

The financial statements presented in this Annual Report have been prepared with integrity and objectivity and are the responsibility of the management of The Home Depot, Inc. These financial statements have been prepared in conformity with U.S. generally accepted accounting principles and properly reflect certain estimates and judgments based upon the best available information.

The financial statements of the Company have been audited by KPMG LLP, an independent registered public accounting firm. Their accompanying report is based upon an audit conducted in accordance with the standards of the Public Company Accounting Oversight Board (United States).

The Audit Committee of the Board of Directors, consisting solely of outside directors, meets five times a year with the independent registered public accounting firm, the internal auditors and representatives of management to discuss auditing and financial reporting matters. In addition, a telephonic meeting is held prior to each quarterly earnings release. The Audit Committee retains the independent registered public accounting firm and regularly reviews the internal accounting controls, the activities of the independent registered public accounting firm and internal auditors and the financial condition of the Company. Both the Company's independent registered public accounting firm and the internal auditors have free access to the Audit Committee.

**Management's Report on Internal Control over Financial Reporting**

Our management is responsible for establishing and maintaining adequate internal control over financial reporting, as such term is defined in Rules 13a–15(f) promulgated under the Securities Exchange Act of 1934, as amended (the "Exchange Act"). Under the supervision and with the participation of our management, including our Chief Executive Officer and Chief Financial Officer, we conducted an evaluation of the effectiveness of our internal control over financial reporting as of January 30, 2011 based on the framework in *Internal Control—Integrated Framework* issued by the Committee of Sponsoring Organizations of the Treadway Commission (COSO). Based on our evaluation, our management concluded that our internal control over financial reporting was effective as of January 30, 2011, in providing reasonable assurance regarding the reliability of financial reporting and the preparation of financial statements for external purposes in accordance with generally accepted accounting principles. The effectiveness of our internal control over financial reporting as of January 30, 2011, has been audited by KPMG LLP, an independent registered public accounting firm, as stated in their report which is included on page 30 in this Form 10-K.

Francis S. Blake
Chairman & Chief Executive Officer

Carol B. Tomé
Chief Financial Officer & Executive Vice President

# Auditors' Report

● LO3–6

**The auditors' report provides the analyst with an independent and professional opinion about the fairness of the representations in the financial statements and about the effectiveness of internal controls.**

Auditors examine financial statements and the internal control procedures designed to support the content of those statements. Their role is to attest to the fairness of the financial statements based on that examination. The auditors' attest function results in an opinion stated in the auditors' report.

One step in financial analysis should be an examination of the auditors' report, which is issued by the CPAs who audit the financial statements and inform users of the audit findings. Every audit report of a public company looks similar to the one prepared by KPMG LLP for the financial statements of J. Crew Group, Inc., as shown in Illustration 3–14.

**Illustration 3–14**

Auditors' Report—
J. Crew Group, Inc.

Real World Financials

---

**Report of Independent Registered Public Accounting Firm**

**The Board of Directors and Stockholders**
**J.Crew Group, Inc.:**

We have audited the accompanying consolidated balance sheets of J.Crew Group, Inc. and subsidiaries ("Group") as of January 29, 2011 and January 30, 2010, and the related consolidated statements of operations, changes in stockholders' equity, and cash flows for each of the years in the three-year period ended January 29, 2011. In connection with our audits of the consolidated financial statements, we also have audited financial statement schedule II. These consolidated financial statements and the financial statement schedule are the responsibility of the Company's management. Our responsibility is to express an opinion on these consolidated financial statements and the financial statement schedule based on our audits.

We conducted our audits in accordance with the standards of the Public Company Accounting Oversight Board (United States). Those standards require that we plan and perform the audit to obtain reasonable assurance about whether the financial statements are free of material misstatement. An audit includes examining, on a test basis, evidence supporting the amounts and disclosures in the financial statements. An audit also includes assessing the accounting principles used and significant estimates made by management, as well as evaluating the overall financial statement presentation. We believe that our audits provide a reasonable basis for our opinion.

In our opinion, the consolidated financial statements referred to above present fairly, in all material respects, the financial position of Group as of January 29, 2011 and January 30, 2010 and the results of its operations and its cash flows for each of the years in the three-year period ended January 29, 2011, in conformity with U.S. generally accepted accounting principles. Also, in our opinion, the related financial statement schedule, when considered in relation to the consolidated financial statements taken as a whole, presents fairly, in all material respects, the information set forth therein.

We also have audited, in accordance with the standards of the Public Company Accounting Oversight Board (United States), Group's internal control over financial reporting as of January 29, 2011, based on the criteria established in Internal Control–Integrated Framework issued by the Committee of Sponsoring Organizations of the Treadway Commission (COSO), and our report dated March 21, 2011 expressed an unqualified opinion on the effectiveness of Group's internal control over financial reporting.

KPMG LLP
New York, New York
March 21, 2011

---

The reason for the similarities is that auditors' reports of public companies must be in compliance with the specifications of the PCAOB.[13] In most cases, including the report for J. Crew, the auditors will be satisfied that the financial statements "present fairly" the financial position, results of operations, and cash flows and are "in conformity with accounting principles generally accepted in the United States of America." These situations prompt an unqualified opinion. Notice that the last paragraph in J. Crew's report references the auditors' separate report on the effectiveness of the company's internal control over financial reporting.

---

[13]"An Audit of Internal Control over Financial Reporting That Is Integrated with An Audit of Financial Statements," *Auditing Standard No. 5* (Washington, D.C., PCAOB, 2007).

Sometimes circumstances cause the auditors' report to include an explanatory paragraph in addition to the standard wording, even though the report is unqualified. Most notably, these include:

- *Lack of consistency* due to a change in accounting principle such that comparability is affected even though the auditor concurs with the desirability of the change.
- *Uncertainty* as to the ultimate resolution of a contingency for which a loss is material in amount but not necessarily probable or probable but not estimable.
- *Emphasis* of a matter concerning the financial statements that does not affect the existence of an unqualified opinion but relates to a significant event such as a related-party transaction.

Some audits result in the need to issue other than an unqualified opinion due to exceptions such as (a) nonconformity with generally accepted accounting principles, (b) inadequate disclosures, and (c) a limitation or restriction of the scope of the examination. In these situations the auditor will issue a (an):

> The auditors' report calls attention to problems that might exist in the financial statements.

- *Qualified opinion* This contains an exception to the standard unqualified opinion but not of sufficient seriousness to invalidate the financial statements as a whole.
- *Adverse opinion* This is necessary when the exceptions (a) and (b) above are so serious that a qualified opinion is not justified. Adverse opinions are rare because auditors usually are able to persuade management to rectify problems to avoid this undesirable report.
- *Disclaimer* An auditor will disclaim an opinion for item (c) above such that insufficient information has been gathered to express an opinion.

During the course of each audit, the auditor is required to evaluate the company's ability to continue for a reasonable time as a going concern. If the auditor determines there is significant doubt, an explanation of the potential problem must be included in the auditors' report.[14]

> The auditor should assess the firm's ability to continue as a going concern.

Obviously, the auditors' report is most informative when any of these deviations from the standard unqualified opinion are present. These departures from the norm should raise a red flag to a financial analyst and prompt additional search for information.

As an example, a recent auditors' report of **Blockbuster Inc.** included a going concern paragraph shown in Illustration 3–15.

The accompanying consolidated financial statements have been prepared assuming that the Company will continue as a going concern. As discussed in Note 1 to the consolidated financial statements, the Company has incurred a net loss from operations for the year ended January 3, 2010 and has a stockholders' deficit as of January 3, 2010. In addition, the increasingly competitive industry conditions under which the Company operates have negatively impacted the Company's results of operations and cash flows and may continue to in the future. These factors raise substantial doubt about the Company's ability to continue as a going concern. Management's plans in regard to these matters are also described in Note 1. The financial statements do not include any adjustments that might result from the outcome of this uncertainty.

**Illustration 3–15**

Going Concern Paragraph—Blockbuster Inc.

Real World Financials

# Compensation of Directors and Top Executives

In the early 1990s, the compensation large U.S. corporations paid their top executives became an issue of considerable public debate and controversy. Shareholders, employees, politicians, and the public in general began to question the huge pay packages received by company officials at the same time that more and more rank-and-file employees were being laid off as a result of company cutbacks. Contributing to the debate was the realization that the compensation gap between executives and lower-level employees was much wider than

---

[14]"The Auditor's Consideration of an Entity's Ability to Continue as a Going Concern," *Statement on Auditing Standards No. 59* (New York: AICPA, 1988).

in Japan and most other industrial countries. During this time, it also became apparent that discovering exactly how much compensation corporations paid their top people was nearly impossible.

Part of the problem stemmed from the fact that disclosures of these amounts were meager; but a large part of the problem was that a substantial portion of executive pay often is in the form of stock options. Executive stock options give their holders the right to buy stock at a specified price, usually equal to the market price when the options are granted. When stock prices rise, executives can exercise their options and realize a profit. In some cases, options have made executive compensation seem extremely high. Stock options are discussed in depth in Chapter 19.

To help shareholders and others sort out the content of executive pay packages and better understand the commitments of the company in this regard, SEC requirements provide for more disclosures on compensation to directors and executives, and in particular, concerning stock options. The **proxy statement** that must be sent each year to all shareholders, usually in the same mailing with the annual report, invites shareholders to the meeting to elect board members and to vote on issues before the shareholders or to vote using an enclosed proxy card. The proxy statement also includes compensation and stock option information for directors and top executives. Illustration 3–16 shows a portion of **Best Buy Co. Inc.**'s 2011 summary compensation table included in a recent proxy statement.

> The *proxy statement* contains disclosures on compensation to directors and executives.

**Illustration 3–16** Summary Compensation Table—Best Buy Co. Inc.

**Summary Compensation Table (in part)**

| Name and Title | Fiscal Year | Salary and Bonus | Stock Awards | Option Awards | Non-Equity Incentive Plan Compensation | All Other Compensation | Total Compensation |
|---|---|---|---|---|---|---|---|
| Brian J. Dunn<br>Chief Executive Officer | 2011 | $1,061,540 | $ — | $3,206,125 | $746,667 | $15,168 | $5,029,500 |
| James L. Muehlbauer<br>Executive VP Chief Financial Officer | 2011 | 662,308 | — | 1,172,700 | 290,500 | 16,801 | 2,142,309 |
| Shari L. Ballard<br>Executive Vice President | 2011 | 680,770 | — | 864,835 | 298,958 | 14,928 | 1,859,491 |
| Michael A. Vitelli<br>Executive Vice President | 2011 | 661,540 | — | 864,835 | 291,667 | 18,110 | 1,836,152 |
| Carol A. Surace<br>Executive Vice President | 2011 | 1,057,308 | 1,196,000 | 789,393 | 166,833 | 65,172 | 3,274,706 |

Real World Financials

## PART C

# RISK ANALYSIS
## Using Financial Statement Information

The overriding objective of financial reporting is providing information that investors and creditors can use to make decisions. Nevertheless, it's sometimes easy to lose sight of that objective while dealing with the intricacies that specific concepts and procedures can involve. In this part of the chapter we provide an overview of financial statement analysis

● LO3–7

and then demonstrate the use of ratios, a popular financial statement analysis technique, to analyze risk.

Investors, creditors, and others use information that companies provide in corporate financial reports to make decisions. Although the financial reports focus primarily on the past performance and the present financial condition of the reporting company, information users are most interested in the outlook for the future. Trying to gain a glimpse of the future from past and present data entails using various tools and techniques to formulate predictions. This is the goal of financial statement analysis.

Financial statements are not presented in isolation. Every financial statement issued is accompanied by the corresponding financial statement of the preceding year, and often the previous two years. These are called comparative financial statements. They enable investors, creditors, and other users to compare year-to-year financial position, results of operations, and cash flows. These comparative data help an analyst detect and predict trends. Because operations often expand and contract in a cyclical fashion, analysis of any one year's data may not provide an accurate picture of a company.

*Comparative financial statements* allow financial statement users to compare year-to-year financial position, results of operations, and cash flows.

Some analysts enhance their comparison by expressing each item as a percentage of that same item in the financial statements of another year (base amount) in order to more easily see year-to-year changes. This is referred to as horizontal analysis. Similarly, vertical analysis involves expressing each item in the financial statements as a percentage of an appropriate corresponding total, or base amount, but within the same year. For example, cash, inventory, and other assets can be restated as a percentage of total assets; net income and each expense can be restated as a percentage of revenues.

Regardless of the specific technique used, the essential point is that accounting numbers are virtually meaningless in isolation. Their value derives from comparison with other numbers. The most common way of comparing accounting numbers to evaluate the performance and risk of a firm is ratio analysis.

No accounting numbers are meaningful in and of themselves.

We use ratios every day. Batting averages indicate how well our favorite baseball players are performing. We evaluate basketball players by field goal percentage and rebounds per game. Speedometers measure the speed of our cars in terms of miles per hour. We compare grocery costs on the basis of price per pound or ounce. In each of these cases, the ratio is more meaningful than a single number by itself. Do 45 hits indicate satisfactory performance? It depends on the number of at-bats. Is $2 a good price for cheese? It depends on how many ounces the $2 buys. Ratios make these measurements meaningful.

Likewise, we can use ratios to help evaluate a firm's performance and financial position. Is net income of $4 million a cause for shareholders to celebrate? Probably not if shareholders' equity is $10 billion. But if shareholders equity is $10 million, that's a 40% return on equity! Although ratios provide more meaningful information than absolute numbers alone, the ratios are most useful when analyzed relative to some standard of comparison. That standard of comparison may be previous performance of the same company, the performance of a competitor company, or an industry average for the particular ratio.

Evaluating information in ratio form allows analysts to control for size differences over time and among firms.

Accountants should be conversant with ratio analysis for at least three reasons. First, when preparing financial statements, accountants should be familiar with the ways users will use the information provided to make better decisions concerning what and how to report. Second, when accountants participate in company decisions concerning operating and financing alternatives, they may find ratio analysis helpful in evaluating available choices. Third, during the planning stages of an audit, independent auditors often use ratio analysis. This analysis assists in identifying potential audit problems and determining the specific audit procedures that should be performed.

We introduce ratios related to risk analysis in this chapter and ratios related to profitability analysis in Chapter 5. You will also employ ratios in Decision Makers' Perspective sections of many of the chapters in this text. Analysis cases that benefit from ratio analysis are included in many of these chapters as well.

Investors and creditors use financial information to assess the future risk and return of their investments in business enterprises. The balance sheet provides information useful to this assessment. A key element of risk analysis is investigating a company's ability to pay its obligations when they come due. This type of risk often is referred to as default risk. Another aspect of risk is operational risk, which relates more to how adept a company is at withstanding various events and circumstances that might impair its ability to earn profits. Obviously, these two types of risk are not completely independent of one another. Inability to earn profits certainly increases a company's chances of defaulting on its obligations. Conversely, regardless of a company's long-run prospects for generating profits, if it can't meet its obligations, the company's operations are at risk.

Assessing risk necessarily involves consideration of a variety of economywide risk factors such as inflation, interest rates, and the general business climate. Industrywide influences including competition, labor conditions, and technological forces also affect a company's risk profile. Still other risk factors are specific to the company itself. Financial ratios often are used in risk analysis to investigate a company's liquidity and long-term solvency. As we discuss some of the more common ratios in the following paragraphs, keep in mind the inherent relationship between risk and return and thus between our risk analysis in this chapter and our profitability analysis in Chapter 5.

## Liquidity Ratios

● LO3–8

Liquidity refers to the readiness of assets to be converted to cash. By comparing a company's liquid assets with its short-term obligations, we can obtain a general idea of the firm's ability to pay its short-term debts as they come due. Usually, current assets are thought of as the most liquid of a company's assets. Obviously, though, some are more liquid than others, so it's important also to evaluate the specific makeup of current assets. Two common measures of liquidity are (1) the current ratio and (2) the acid-test ratio (or quick ratio) calculated as follows:

$$\text{Current ratio} = \frac{\text{Current assets}}{\text{Current liabilities}}$$

$$\text{Acid-test ratio (or quick ratio)} = \frac{\text{Quick assets}}{\text{Current liabilities}}$$

*Working capital,* the difference between current assets and current liabilities, is a popular measure of a company's ability to satisfy its short-term obligations.

**CURRENT RATIO.** Implicit in the definition of a current liability is the relationship between current assets and current liabilities. The difference between current assets and current liabilities is called working capital. By comparing a company's obligations that will shortly become due with the company's cash and other assets that, by definition, are expected to shortly be converted to cash, the analysis offers some indication as to ability to pay those debts. Although used in a variety of decisions, it is particularly useful to those considering whether to extend short-term credit. The current ratio is computed by dividing current assets by current liabilities. A current ratio of 2 indicates that the company has twice as many current assets available as current liabilities.

Dell Inc.'s working capital (in millions) at the end of its January 28, 2011, fiscal year is $9,538, consisting of current assets of $29,021 (Illustration 3–3 on page 117) minus current liabilities of $19,483 (Illustration 3–7 on page 120). The current ratio can be computed as follows:

$$\text{Current ratio} = \frac{\$29,021}{\$19,483} = 1.49$$

**Working capital may not present an accurate or complete picture of a company's liquidity.**

Care should be taken, however, in assessing liquidity based solely on working capital. Liabilities usually are paid with cash, not other components of working capital. A company could have difficulty paying its liabilities even with a current ratio significantly greater than 1.0. For example, if a significant portion of current assets consisted of inventories, and inventories usually are not converted to cash for several months, there could be a problem in paying accounts payable due in 30 days. On the other hand, a current ratio of less than 1.0 doesn't necessarily mean the company will have difficulty meeting its current obligations. A line of credit, for instance, which the company can use to borrow funds, provides financial flexibility. That also must be considered in assessing liquidity.

# Ethical Dilemma

The Raintree Cosmetic Company has several loans outstanding with a local bank. The debt agreements all contain a covenant stipulating that Raintree must maintain a current ratio of at least .9. Jackson Phillips, company controller, estimates that the 2013 year-end current assets and current liabilities will be $2,100,000 and $2,400,000, respectively. These estimates provide a current ratio of only .875. Violation of the debt agreement will increase Raintree's borrowing costs as the loans are renegotiated at higher rates.

Jackson proposes to the company president that Raintree purchase inventory of $600,000 on credit before year-end. This will cause both current assets and current liabilities to increase by the same amount, but the current ratio will increase to .9. The extra $600,000 in inventory will be used over the later part of 2014. However, the purchase will cause warehousing costs and financing costs to increase.

Jackson is concerned about the ethics of his proposal. What do you think?

**ACID-TEST RATIO (OR QUICK RATIO).**   Some analysts like to modify the current ratio to consider only current assets that are readily available to pay current liabilities. One such variation in common use is the acid-test ratio. This ratio excludes inventories and prepaid items from current assets before dividing by current liabilities. The numerator, then, consists of cash, short-term investments, and accounts receivable, the "quick assets." By eliminating current assets less readily convertible into cash, the acid-test ratio provides a more rigorous indication of liquidity than does the current ratio.

Dell Inc.'s quick assets at the end of its January 28, 2011, fiscal year (in millions) total $24,501 ($13,913 + 452 + 6,493 + 3,643). The acid-test ratio can be computed as follows:

> The *acid-test ratio* provides a more stringent indication of a company's ability to pay its current obligations.

$$\text{Acid-test ratio} = \frac{\$24,501}{\$19,483} = 1.26$$

Are these liquidity ratios adequate? It's generally difficult to say without some point of comparison. As indicated previously, common standards for such comparisons are industry averages for similar ratios or ratios of the same company in prior years. Industry averages for the above two ratios are as follows:

**Industry Average**
Current ratio = 1.39
Acid-test ratio = 1.04

Dell's ratios are higher than the industry average. What if the ratios were lower? Would that indicate a liquidity problem? Not necessarily, but it would raise a red flag that calls for caution in analyzing other areas. Remember that each ratio is but one piece of the entire puzzle. For instance, profitability is perhaps the best indication of liquidity in the long run. We discuss ratios that measure profitability in Chapter 5.

Also, management may be very efficient in managing current assets so that, let's say, receivables are collected faster than normal or inventory is sold faster than normal, making those assets more liquid than they otherwise would be. Higher turnover ratios, relative to those of a competitor or the industry, generally indicate a more liquid position for a given level of the current ratio. We discuss these turnover ratios in Chapter 5.

> Liquidity ratios should be assessed in the context of both profitability and efficiency of managing assets.

## Financing Ratios

Investors and creditors, particularly long-term creditors, are vitally interested in a company's long-term solvency and stability. Financing ratios provide some indication of the riskiness of a company with regard to its ability to pay its long-term debts. Two common financing ratios are (1) the debt to equity ratio and (2) the times interest earned ratio. These ratios are calculated as follows:

$$\text{Debt to equity ratio} = \frac{\text{Total liabilities}}{\text{Shareholders' equity}}$$

$$\text{Times interest earned ratio} = \frac{\text{Net income} + \text{Interest expense} + \text{Income taxes}}{\text{Interest expense}}$$

The *debt to equity ratio* indicates the extent of reliance on creditors, rather than owners, in providing resources.

**DEBT TO EQUITY RATIO.** The debt to equity ratio compares resources provided by creditors with resources provided by owners. It is calculated by dividing total liabilities (current and noncurrent) by total shareholders' equity (including retained earnings).[15]

The ratio provides a measure of creditors' protection in the event of insolvency. Other things being equal, the higher the ratio, the higher the risk. The higher the ratio, the greater the creditor claims on assets, so the higher the likelihood an individual creditor would not be paid in full if the company is unable to meet its obligations. Relatedly, a high ratio indicates not only more fixed interest obligations, but probably a higher *rate* of interest as well because lenders tend to charge higher rates as the level of debt increases.

Dell Inc.'s liabilities at the end of its January 28, 2011, fiscal year (in millions) total $30,833 (Illustration 3–7 on page 120), and stockholders' equity totals $7,766 (Illustration 3–8 on page 121). The debt to equity ratio can be computed as follows:

$$\text{Debt to equity ratio} = \frac{\$30,833}{\$\ 7,766} = 3.97$$

As with all ratios, the debt to equity ratio is more meaningful if compared to some standard such as an industry average or a competitor. For example, the debt to equity ratio for **Hewlett-Packard (HP)**, a major competitor, is 2.1, significantly lower than Dell's ratio, indicating that Dell has more liabilities in its capital structure than does HP. Does this mean that Dell's default risk is more than that of HP? Other things equal—yes. Is that good? Not necessarily. As discussed in the next section, it may be that debt is being underutilized by Hewlett-Packard. More debt might increase the potential for return to shareholders, but the price would be higher risk. This is a fundamental trade-off faced by virtually all firms when trying to settle on the optimal capital structure.

The makeup of liabilities also is important. For example, Dell's liabilities include $6,676 million of unearned (deferred) services revenue, representing 22% of total liabilities. Recall that unearned revenues are liabilities recorded when cash is received from customers in advance of providing a good or service. Dell will satisfy these liabilities not by paying cash, but by providing a service to its customers.

**Relationship Between Risk and Profitability.** The proportion of debt in the capital structure also is of interest to shareholders. After all, shareholders receive no return on their investments until after all creditor claims are paid. Therefore, the higher the debt to equity ratio, the higher the risk to shareholders. On the other hand, by earning a return on borrowed funds that exceeds the cost of borrowing the funds, a company can provide its shareholders with a total return higher than it could achieve by employing equity funds alone. This is referred to as favorable financial leverage.

The debt to equity ratio indicates the extent of trading on the equity by using *financial leverage*.

For illustration, consider a newly formed corporation attempting to determine the appropriate mix of debt and equity. The initial capitalization goal is $50 million. The capitalization mix alternatives have been narrowed to two: (1) $10 million in debt and $40 million in equity and (2) $30 million in debt and $20 million in equity.

Also assume that regardless of the capitalization mix chosen, the corporation will be able to generate a 16% annual return, *before payment of interest and income taxes,* on the $50 million in assets acquired. In other words, income before interest and taxes will be $8 million (16% × $50 million). If the interest rate on debt is 8% and the income tax rate is 40%, comparative net income for the first year of operations for the two capitalization alternatives can be calculated as follows:

---

[15]A commonly used variation of the debt to equity ratio is found by dividing total liabilities by *total assets* (or total equities), rather than by shareholders' equity only. Of course, in this configuration the ratio measures precisely the same attribute of the firm's capital structure but can be interpreted as the percentage of a company's total assets provided by funds from creditors, rather than by owners.

| | Alternative 1 | Alternative 2 |
|---|---|---|
| Income before interest and income taxes | $8,000,000 | $8,000,000 |
| Less: Interest expense | (800,000)[a] | (2,400,000)[b] |
| Income before income taxes | $7,200,000 | $5,600,000 |
| Less: Income tax expense (40%) | (2,880,000) | (2,240,000) |
| Net income | $4,320,000 | $3,360,000 |

[a]8% × $10,000,000
[b]8% × $30,000,000

Choose Alternative 1? Probably not. Although alternative 1 provides a higher net income, the return on the shareholders' equity (net income divided by shareholders' equity) is higher for alternative 2. Here's why:

| | Alternative 1 | Alternative 2 |
|---|---|---|
| Return on shareholders' equity[16] = | $\dfrac{\$4,320,000}{\$40,000,000}$ | $\dfrac{\$3,360,000}{\$20,000,000}$ |
| = | 10.8% | 16.8% |

**Favorable financial leverage means earning a return on borrowed funds that exceeds the cost of borrowing the funds.**

Alternative 2 generated a higher return for each dollar invested by shareholders. This is because the company leveraged its $20 million equity investment with additional debt. Because the cost of the additional debt (8%) is less than the return on assets invested (16%), the return to shareholders is higher. This is the essence of favorable financial leverage.

Be aware, though, leverage is not always favorable; the cost of borrowing the funds might exceed the returns they provide. If the return on assets invested turned out to be less than expected, the additional debt could result in a lower return on equity for alternative 2. If, for example, the return on assets invested (before interest and income taxes) had been 6%, rather than 16%, alternative 1 would have provided the better return on equity:

| | Alternative 1 | Alternative 2 |
|---|---|---|
| Income before interest and income taxes | $3,000,000 | $3,000,000 |
| Less: Interest expense | (800,000)[a] | (2,400,000)[b] |
| Income before income taxes | $2,200,000 | $ 600,000 |
| Less: Income tax expense (40%) | (880,000) | (240,000) |
| Net income | $1,320,000 | $ 360,000 |

[a]8% × $10,000,000
[b]8% × $30,000,000

| | Alternative 1 | Alternative 2 |
|---|---|---|
| Return on shareholders' equity[17] = | $\dfrac{\$1,320,000}{\$40,000,000}$ | $\dfrac{\$360,000}{\$20,000,000}$ |
| = | 3.3% | 1.8% |

---

[16]If return is calculated on *average* shareholders' equity, we're technically assuming that all income is paid to shareholders in cash dividends, so that beginning, ending, and average shareholders' equity are the same. If we assume *no* dividends are paid, rates of return would be

| | Alternative 1 | Alternative 2 |
|---|---|---|
| Return on shareholders' equity = | $\dfrac{\$4,320,000}{(\$44,320,000 + 40,000,000)/2}$ | $\dfrac{\$3,360,000}{(\$20,000,000 + 23,360,000)/2}$ |
| = | 10.25% | 15.50% |

In any case our conclusions are the same.

[17]If we assume *no* dividends are paid, rates of return would be

| | Alternative 1 | Alternative 2 |
|---|---|---|
| Return on shareholders' equity = | $\dfrac{\$1,320,000}{(\$41,320,000 + 40,000,000)/2}$ | $\dfrac{\$360,000}{(\$20,000,000 + 20,360,000)/2}$ |
| = | 3.25% | 1.78% |

In any case our conclusions are the same.

So, shareholders typically are faced with a trade-off between the risk that high debt denotes and the potential for a higher return from having the higher debt. In any event, the debt to equity ratio offers a basis for making the choice.

The *times interest earned ratio* indicates the margin of safety provided to creditors.

**TIMES INTEREST EARNED RATIO.**  Another way to gauge the ability of a company to satisfy its fixed debt obligations is by comparing interest charges with the income available to pay those charges. The times interest earned ratio is designed to do this. It is calculated by dividing income before subtracting interest expense and income taxes by interest expense.

Bondholders, noteholders, and other creditors can measure the margin of safety they are accorded by a company's earnings. If income is many times greater than interest expense, creditors' interests are more protected than if income just barely covers this expense. For this purpose, income should be the amount available to pay interest, which is income before subtracting interest and income taxes, calculated by adding back to net income the interest and income taxes that were deducted.

As an example, Dell Inc.'s financial statements for the fiscal year ended January 28, 2011, report the following:

|  | ($ in millions) |
| --- | --- |
| Net income | $2,635 |
| Interest expense | 199 |
| Income taxes | 715 |
| Income before interest and taxes | $3,549 |

The times interest earned ratio can be computed as follows:

$$\text{Times interest earned ratio} = \frac{\$3,549}{\$199} = 18$$

The ratio of 18 times indicates a considerable margin of safety for creditors. Income could decrease many times and the company would still be able to meet its interest payment obligations.[18] Dell is a highly profitable company with little interest-bearing debt. In comparison, the average times interest earned ratio for the S&P 500 companies is approximately 17 times, similar to Dell's ratio.

Especially when viewed alongside the debt-equity ratio, the coverage ratio seems to indicate a comfortable safety cushion for creditors. It also indicates a degree of financial mobility if the company were to decide to raise new debt funds to "trade on the equity" and attempt to increase the return to shareholders through favorable financial leverage.

## Financial Reporting Case Solution

**1. Respond to Jerry's criticism that shareholders' equity does not represent the market value of the company. What information does the balance sheet provide?** *(p. 115)*  Jerry is correct. The financial statements are supposed to help investors and creditors value a company. However, the balance sheet is not intended to portray the market value of the entity. The assets of a company minus its liabilities as shown in the balance sheet (shareholders' equity) usually will not equal the company's market value for several reasons. For example, many assets are measured at their historical costs rather than their fair values. Also, many company resources, including its trained employees, its experienced management team, and its reputation are not recorded as assets at all. The balance sheet must be used in conjunction with other financial statements, disclosure notes, and other publicly available information.

The balance sheet does, however, provide valuable information that can be used by investors and creditors to help determine market value. After all, it is the balance sheet that describes many of the resources a company has available for generating future cash

---

[18]Of course, interest is paid with cash, not with "income." The times interest earned ratio often is calculated by using cash flow from operations before subtracting either interest payments or tax payments as the numerator and interest payments as the denominator.

flows. The balance sheet also provides important information about liquidity and long-term solvency.

2. **The usefulness of the balance sheet is enhanced by classifying assets and liabilities according to common characteristics. What are the classifications used in Electronic Arts' balance sheets and what elements do those categories include?** *(p. 116)*    Electronic Arts' balance sheets contain the following classifications:

Assets:

- *Current assets* include cash and several other assets that are reasonably expected to be converted to cash or consumed within the coming year, or within the normal operating cycle of the business if that's longer than one year.
- *Property and equipment* are the tangible long-lived assets used in the operations of the business. This category includes land, buildings, equipment, machinery, and furniture, as well as natural resources.
- *Goodwill* is a unique intangible asset in that its cost can't be directly associated with any specifically identifiable right and is not separable from the company as a whole. It represents the unique value of the company as a whole over and above all identifiable tangible and intangible assets.
- *Acquisition-related intangibles* are assets that represent exclusive rights to something such as a product, a process, or a name. Patents, copyrights, and franchises are examples. These intangible assets were acquired by purchasing other companies.
- *Deferred income taxes* result from temporary differences between taxable income and accounting income.
- *Other assets* is a "catch-all" classification of noncurrent assets and could include long-term prepaid expenses and any noncurrent asset not included in one of the other categories.

Liabilities:

- *Current liabilities* are those obligations that are expected to be satisfied through the use of current assets or the creation of other current liabilities. Usually, this means liabilities that are expected to be paid within one year, or the operating cycle if that's longer than one year.
- *Long-term liabilities* are payable further in the future and include bonds, deferred income taxes, and pension obligations. Electronic Arts lists *income tax obligations, deferred income taxes,* and *other liabilities* as its long-term liabilities.

Shareholders' equity:

- *Common stock* and *paid-in capital* collectively equal the amounts invested by shareholders in the corporation.
- *Retained earnings (accumulated deficit)* represents the accumulated net income earned or net loss incurred since inception of the corporation less dividends paid out to shareholders. If this amount is negative, as it is on March 31, 2011, it is called *accumulated deficit.*
- *Accumulated other comprehensive income* is the cumulative amount of other comprehensive income items. This topic is addressed in subsequent chapters. ●

## The Bottom Line

● **LO3–1**    The balance sheet is a position statement that presents an organized array of assets, liabilities, and shareholders' equity at a particular point in time. The statement does not portray the market value of the entity. However, the information in the statement can be useful in assessing market value, as well as in providing important information about liquidity and long-term solvency. *(p. 115)*

● **LO3–2**    Current assets include cash and other assets that are reasonably expected to be converted to cash or consumed during one year or within the normal operating cycle of the business if the operating cycle is longer than one year. All other assets are classified as various types of noncurrent assets. In addition to cash and cash equivalents, current assets include short-term investments, accounts receivable, inventories, and prepaid expenses. Other asset classifications include investments; property, plant, and equipment; intangible assets; and other assets. (*p. 117*)

● **LO3–3** Current liabilities are those obligations that are expected to be satisfied through the use of current assets or the creation of other current liabilities. All other liabilities are classified as long term. Current liabilities include notes and accounts payable, unearned revenues, accrued liabilities, and the current maturities of long-term debt. Long-term liabilities include long-term notes, loans, mortgages, bonds, pension and lease obligations, as well as deferred income taxes. (*p. 120*)

● **LO3–4** Financial statement disclosures are used to convey additional information about the account balances in the basic financial statements as well as to provide supplemental information. This information is disclosed, often parenthetically in the basic financial statements, or in disclosure notes that often include supporting schedules. (*p. 124*)

● **LO3–5** Annual reports of public companies will include management's discussion and analysis of key aspects of the company's business. The purpose of this disclosure is to provide external parties with management's insight into certain transactions, events, and circumstances that affect the enterprise, including their financial impact. (*p. 128*)

● **LO3–6** The purpose of an audit is to provide a professional, independent opinion as to whether or not the financial statements are prepared in conformity with generally accepted accounting principles. The standard audit report of a public company contains four paragraphs; the first two deal with the scope of the audit and the third paragraph states the auditors' opinion regarding the financial statements. The fourth paragraph provides the auditors' opinion on the effectiveness of the company's internal control. (*p. 130*)

● **LO3–7** Financial analysts use various techniques to transform financial information into forms more useful for analysis. Horizontal analysis and vertical analysis provide a useful way of analyzing year-to-year changes. Ratio analysis allows analysts to control for size differences over time and among firms while investigating important relationships among financial variables. (*p. 132*)

● **LO3–8** The balance sheet provides information that can be useful in assessing risk. A key element of risk analysis is investigating a company's ability to pay its obligations when they come due. Liquidity ratios and financing ratios provide information about a company's ability to pay its obligations. (*p. 134*)

● **LO3–9** There are more similarities than differences in balance sheets and financial disclosures prepared according to U.S. GAAP and those prepared applying IFRS. Balance sheet presentation is one important difference. Under U.S. GAAP, we present current assets and liabilities before noncurrent assets and liabilities. IFRS doesn't prescribe the format of the balance sheet, but balance sheets prepared using IFRS often report noncurrent items first. Reportable segment disclosures also are similar. However, IFRS requires an additional disclosure, the amount of segment liabilities (Appendix 3). (*pp. 122 and 141*) ●

# APPENDIX 3 | Reporting Segment Information

**Many companies operate in several business segments as a strategy to achieve growth and to reduce operating risk through diversification.**

Financial analysis of diversified companies is especially difficult. Consider, for example, a company that operates in several distinct business segments including computer peripherals, home health care systems, textiles, and consumer food products. The results of these distinctly different activities will be aggregated into a single set of financial statements, making difficult an informed projection of future performance. It may well be that the five-year outlook differs greatly among the areas of the economy represented by the different segments. To make matters worse for an analyst, the integrated financial statements do not reveal the relative investments in each of the business segments nor the success the company has had within each area. Given the fact that so many companies these days have chosen to balance their operating risks through diversification, aggregated financial statements pose a widespread problem for analysts, lending and credit officers, and other financial forecasters.

**Segment reporting facilitates the financial statement analysis of diversified companies.**

## Reporting by Operating Segment

To address the problem, the accounting profession requires companies engaged in more than one significant business to provide supplemental information concerning individual operating segments. The supplemental disaggregated data do not include complete financial statements for each reportable segment, only certain specified items.

### WHAT IS A REPORTABLE OPERATING SEGMENT?

According to U.S. GAAP guidelines, a *management approach* is used in determining which segments of a company are reportable. This approach is based on the way that management organizes the segments within the enterprise for making operating decisions and assessing performance. The segments are, therefore, evident from the structure of the enterprise's internal organization.

More formally, the following characteristics define an operating segment:[19]
An operating segment is a component of an enterprise:

- That engages in business activities from which it may earn revenues and incur expenses (including revenues and expenses relating to transactions with other components of the same enterprise).
- Whose operating results are regularly reviewed by the enterprise's chief operating decision maker to make decisions about resources to be allocated to the segment and assess its performance.
- For which discrete financial information is available.

The FASB hopes that this approach provides insights into the risk and opportunities management sees in the various areas of company operations. Also, reporting information based on the enterprise's internal organization should reduce the incremental cost to companies of providing the data. In addition, there are quantitative thresholds for the definition of an operating segment to limit the number of reportable segments. Only segments of certain size (10% or more of total company revenues, assets, or net income) must be disclosed. However, a company must account for at least 75% of consolidated revenue through segment disclosures.

### WHAT AMOUNTS ARE REPORTED BY AN OPERATING SEGMENT?

For areas determined to be reportable operating segments, the following disclosures are required:

   a. General information about the operating segment.
   b. Information about reported segment profit or loss, including certain revenues and expenses included in reported segment profit or loss, segment assets, and the basis of measurement.
   c. Reconciliations of the totals of segment revenues, reported profit or loss, assets, and other significant items to corresponding enterprise amounts.
   d. Interim period information.[20]

Illustration 3A–1 shows the business segment information reported by **3M Co.** in its 2010 annual report.

# International Financial Reporting Standards

**Segment Reporting.** U.S. GAAP requires companies to report information about reported segment profit or loss, including certain revenues and expenses included in reported segment profit or loss, segment assets, and the basis of measurement. The international standard on segment reporting, *IFRS No. 8*,[21] requires that companies also disclose total *liabilities* of its reportable segments.

● LO3–9

---

[19]FASB ASC 280–10–50–1: Segment Reporting—Overall—Disclosure (previously "Disclosures about Segments of an Enterprise and Related Information," *Statement of Financial Accounting Standards No. 131* (Norwalk, Conn.: FASB, 1997), par. 10).
[20]FASB ASC 280–10–50–20 through 26 and 280–10–50–32: Segment Reporting—Overall—Disclosure (previously "Disclosures about Segments of an Enterprise and Related Information," *Statement of Financial Accounting Standards No. 131* (Norwalk, Conn.: FASB, 1997), par. 25).
[21]"Operating Segments," *International Financial Reporting Standard No. 8* (IASCF), as amended effective January 1, 2011.

**Business Segment Information**
($ in millions)

| | | Net Sales | Operating Income | Assets | Depr. and Amort. | Capital Expendit. |
|---|---|---|---|---|---|---|
| Industrial and | 2010 | $ 8,581 | $ 1,799 | $ 6,813 | $ 331 | $ 343 |
| Transportation | 2009 | 7,232 | 1,259 | 6,441 | 333 | 235 |
| | 2008 | 8,294 | 1,568 | 6,373 | 288 | 355 |
| Health Care | 2010 | 4,521 | 1,364 | 4,190 | 131 | 78 |
| | 2009 | 4,294 | 1,350 | 3,218 | 143 | 125 |
| | 2008 | 4,303 | 1,175 | 3,096 | 146 | 169 |
| Display and Graphics | 2010 | 3,884 | 946 | 3,729 | 187 | 185 |
| | 2009 | 3,132 | 590 | 3,564 | 174 | 160 |
| | 2008 | 3,268 | 583 | 3,479 | 220 | 305 |
| Consumer and Office | 2010 | 3,853 | 840 | 2,149 | 100 | 69 |
| | 2009 | 3,471 | 748 | 1,819 | 88 | 43 |
| | 2008 | 3,578 | 683 | 1,815 | 79 | 87 |
| Safety, Security and | 2010 | 3,308 | 707 | 3,995 | 168 | 130 |
| Protection Services | 2009 | 3,064 | 724 | 3,206 | 169 | 93 |
| | 2008 | 3,330 | 689 | 3,127 | 147 | 107 |
| Electro and | 2010 | 2,922 | 631 | 2,135 | 96 | 98 |
| Communications | 2009 | 2,276 | 322 | 2,067 | 102 | 60 |
| | 2008 | 2,835 | 540 | 2,186 | 127 | 143 |
| Corporate and | 2010 | (407) | (369) | 7,145 | 107 | 188 |
| Unallocated/Elimina- | 2009 | (346) | (179) | 6,935 | 148 | 187 |
| tion of Dual Credit | 2008 | (339) | (20) | 5,717 | 146 | 305 |
| Total Company | 2010 | $26,662 | $ 5,918 | $30,156 | $1,120 | $1,091 |
| | 2009 | 23,123 | 4,814 | 27,250 | 1,157 | 903 |
| | 2008 | 25,269 | 5,218 | 25,793 | 1,153 | 1,471 |

## REPORTING BY GEOGRAPHIC AREA

In today's global economy it is sometimes difficult to distinguish domestic and foreign companies. Most large U.S. firms conduct significant operations in other countries in addition to having substantial export sales from this country. Differing political and economic environments from country to country means risks and associated rewards sometimes vary greatly among the various operations of a single company. For instance, manufacturing facilities in a South American country embroiled in political unrest pose different risks from having a plant in Vermont, or even Canada. Without disaggregated financial information, these differences cause problems for analysts.

U.S. GAAP requires an enterprise to report certain geographic information unless it is impracticable to do so. This information includes:

a. Revenues from external customers (1) attributed to the enterprise's country of domicile and (2) attributed to all foreign countries in total from which the enterprise derives revenues, and

b. Long-lived assets other than financial instruments, long-term customer relationships of a financial institution, mortgage and other servicing rights, deferred policy acquisition costs, and deferred tax assets (1) located in the enterprise's country of domicile and (2) located in all foreign countries in total in which the enterprise holds assets.[22]

---

[22]FASB ASC 280–10–50–41: Segment Reporting—Overall—Disclosure (previously "Disclosures about Segments of an Enterprise and Related Information," *Statement of Financial Accounting Standards No. 131* (Norwalk, Conn.: FASB, 1997), par. 38).

3M reported its geographic area information separately in a table reproduced in Illustration 3A–2. Notice that both the business segment (Illustration 3A–1) and geographic information disclosures include a reconciliation to company totals. For example, in both illustrations, year 2010 net sales of both the segments and the geographic areas are reconciled to the company's total net sales of $26,662 ($ in millions).

## Illustration 3A–2    Geographic Area Information Disclosure—3M Company

**Geographic Areas**
($ in millions)

| | | United States | Asia Pacific | Europe, Middle East, and Africa | Latin America and Canada | Other Unallocated | Total Company |
|---|---|---|---|---|---|---|---|
| Net sales | 2010 | $9,210 | $8,259 | $6,259 | $2,950 | $(16) | $26,662 |
| | 2009 | 8,509 | 6,120 | 5,972 | 2,516 | 6 | 23,123 |
| | 2008 | 9,179 | 6,423 | 6,941 | 2,723 | 3 | 25,269 |
| Operating income | 2010 | 1,636 | 2,400 | 1,112 | 797 | (27) | 5,918 |
| | 2009 | 1,640 | 1,528 | 1,003 | 631 | 12 | 4,814 |
| | 2008 | 1,578 | 1,662 | 1,294 | 693 | (9) | 5,218 |
| Property, plant, and equipment | 2010 | 3,888 | 1,605 | 1,239 | 547 | — | 7,279 |
| | 2009 | 3,809 | 1,366 | 1,318 | 507 | — | 7,000 |

Real World Financials

For another example of both business segment and geographic area disclosures, see the **Dell Inc.** segment information reported in the financial statements in Appendix B at the back of the text.

## INFORMATION ABOUT MAJOR CUSTOMERS

Some companies in the defense industry derive substantial portions of their revenues from contracts with the Defense Department. When cutbacks occur in national defense or in specific defense systems, the impact on a company's operations can be considerable. Obviously, financial analysts are extremely interested in information concerning the extent to which a company's prosperity depends on one or more major customers such as in the situation described here. For this reason, if 10% or more of the revenue of an enterprise is derived from transactions with a single customer, the enterprise must disclose that fact, the total amount of revenue from each such customer, and the identity of the operating segment or segments earning the revenue. The identity of the major customer or customers need not be disclosed, although companies routinely provide that information. In its 2010 annual report, 3M did not report any major customer information. As an example of this type of disclosure, **Procter & Gamble Company**'s business segment disclosure included information on its largest customer, **Walmart**, as shown in Illustration 3A–3 ●

> **Revenues from major customers must be disclosed.**

**Note 12. Segment Information (in part)**
Our largest customer, Wal-Mart Stores, Inc. and its affiliates, accounted for 15% of consolidated net sales in 2011 and 16% in 2010 and 2009.

## Illustration 3A–3
Major Customer Disclosure—Procter & Gamble Company

Real World Financials

# Questions For Review of Key Topics

Q 3–1    Describe the purpose of the balance sheet.

Q 3–2    Explain why the balance sheet does not portray the market value of the entity.

Q 3–3    Define current assets and list the typical asset categories included in this classification.

Q 3–4    Define current liabilities and list the typical liability categories included in this classification.

Q 3–5    Describe what is meant by an operating cycle for a typical manufacturing company.

Q 3–6    Explain the difference(s) between investments in equity securities classified as current assets versus those classified as noncurrent assets.

Q 3–7    Describe the common characteristics of assets classified as property, plant, and equipment and identify some assets included in this classification.

Q 3–8    Distinguish between property, plant, and equipment and intangible assets.

Q 3–9    Explain how each of the following liabilities would be classified in the balance sheet:
- A note payable of $100,000 due in five years.
- A note payable of $100,000 payable in annual installments of $20,000 each, with the first installment due next year.

Q 3–10    Define the terms *paid-in-capital* and *retained earnings.*

Q 3–11    Disclosure notes are an integral part of the information provided in financial statements. In what ways are the notes critical to understanding the financial statements and to evaluating the firm's performance and financial health?

Q 3–12    A summary of the company's significant accounting policies is a required disclosure. Why is this disclosure important to external financial statement users?

Q 3–13    Define a subsequent event.

Q 3–14    Every annual report of a public company includes an extensive discussion and analysis provided by the company's management. Specifically, which aspects of the company must this discussion address? Isn't management's perspective too biased to be of use to investors and creditors?

Q 3–15    The auditors' report provides the analyst with an independent and professional opinion about the fairness of the representations in the financial statements. What are the four main types of opinion an auditor might issue? Describe each.

Q 3–16    What is a proxy statement? What information does it provide?

Q 3–17    Define the terms *working capital, current ratio,* and *acid-test ratio* (or *quick ratio*).

Q 3–18    Show the calculation of the following financing ratios: (1) the debt to equity ratio, and (2) the times interest earned ratio.

**IFRS**    Q 3–19    Where can we find authoritative guidance for balance sheet presentation under IFRS?

**IFRS**    Q 3–20    Describe at least two differences between U.S. GAAP and IFRS in balance sheet presentation.

Q 3–21    (Based on Appendix 3) Segment reporting facilitates the financial statement analysis of diversified companies. What determines whether an operating segment is a reportable segment for this purpose?

Q 3–22    (Based on Appendix 3) For segment reporting purposes, what amounts are reported by each operating segment?

**IFRS**    Q 3–23    (Based on Appendix 3) Describe any differences in segment disclosure requirements between U.S. GAAP and IFRS.

# Brief Exercises

**BE 3–1**
Current versus noncurrent classification
● LO3–2, LO3–3

Indicate whether each of the following assets and liabilities should be classified as current or noncurrent: (a) accounts receivable; (b) prepaid rent for the next six months; (c) note receivable due in two years; (d) note payable due in 90 days; (e) note payable due in five years; and (f) patent.

**BE 3–2**
Balance sheet classification
● LO3–2, LO3–3

The trial balance for K and J Nursery, Inc., listed the following account balances at December 31, 2013, the end of its fiscal year: cash, $16,000; accounts receivable, $11,000; inventories, $25,000; equipment (net), $80,000; accounts payable, $14,000; wages payable, $9,000; interest payable, $1,000; note payable (due in 18 months), $30,000; common stock, $50,000. Calculate total current assets and total current liabilities that would appear in the company's year-end balance sheet.

**BE 3–3**
Balance sheet classification
● LO3–2, LO3–3

Refer to the situation described in BE 3–2. Determine the year-end balance in retained earnings for K and J Nursery, Inc.

**BE 3–4**
Balance sheet classification
● LO3–2, LO3–3

Refer to the situation described in BE 3–2. Prepare a classified balance sheet for K and J Nursery, Inc. The equipment originally cost $140,000.

**BE 3–5**
Balance sheet classification
● LO3–2, LO3–3

The following is a December 31, 2013, post-closing trial balance for Culver City Lighting, Inc. Prepare a classified balance sheet for the company.

| Account Title | Debits | Credits |
|---|---|---|
| Cash | 55,000 | |
| Accounts receivable | 39,000 | |
| Inventories | 45,000 | |
| Prepaid insurance | 15,000 | |
| Equipment | 100,000 | |
| Accumulated depreciation—equipment | | 34,000 |
| Patent, net | 40,000 | |
| Accounts payable | | 12,000 |
| Interest payable | | 2,000 |
| Note payable (due in 10, equal annual installments) | | 100,000 |
| Common stock | | 70,000 |
| Retained earnings | | 76,000 |
| Totals | 294,000 | 294,000 |

**BE 3–6**
Balance sheet classification
● LO3–2, LO3–3

You have been asked to review the December 31, 2013, balance sheet for Champion Cleaning. After completing your review, you list the following three items for discussion with your superior:

1. An investment of $30,000 is included in current assets. Management has indicated that it has no intention of liquidating the investment in 2014.

2. A $100,000 note payable is listed as a long-term liability, but you have determined that the note is due in 10, equal annual installments with the first installment due on March 31, 2014.

3. Unearned revenue of $60,000 is included as a current liability even though only two-thirds will be earned in 2014.

Determine the appropriate classification of each of these items.

**BE 3–7**
Balance sheet preparation; missing elements
● LO3–2, LO3–3

The following information is taken from the balance sheet of Raineer Plumbing: cash and cash equivalents, $40,000; accounts receivable, $120,000; inventories, ?; total current assets, $235,000; property, plant, and equipment (net), ?; total assets, $400,000; accounts payable, $32,000; note payable (due in two years), $50,000; common stock; $100,000; and retained earnings, ?. Determine the missing amounts.

**BE 3–8**
Financial statement disclosures
● LO3–4

For each of the following note disclosures, indicate whether the disclosure would likely appear in (A) the summary of significant accounts policies or (B) a separate note: (1) depreciation method; (2) contingency information; (3) significant issuance of common stock after the fiscal year-end; (4) cash equivalent designation; (5) long-term debt information; and (6) inventory costing method.

**BE 3–9**
Calculating ratios
● LO3–8

Refer to the trial balance information in BE 3–5. Calculate the (a) current ratio, (b) acid-test ratio, and (c) debt to equity ratio.

**BE 3–10**
Effect of decisions on ratios
● LO3–8

At the end of 2013, Barker Corporation's preliminary trial balance indicated a current ratio of 1.2. Management is contemplating paying some of its accounts payable balance before the end of the fiscal year. Explain the effect this transaction would have on the current ratio. Would your answer be the same if the preliminary trial balance indicated a current ratio of .8?

**BE 3–11**
Calculating ratios; solving for unknowns
● LO3–8

The current asset section of Stibbe Pharmaceutical Company's balance sheet included cash of $20,000 and accounts receivable of $40,000. The only other current asset is inventories. The company's current ratio is 2.0 and its acid-test ratio is 1.5. Determine the ending balance in inventories and total current liabilities.

# Exercises

An alternate exercise and problem set is available on the text website: www.mhhe.com/spiceland7e

**E 3–1**
Balance sheet; missing elements
● LO3–2, LO3–3, LO3–8

The following December 31, 2013, fiscal year-end account balance information is available for the Stonebridge Corporation:

| | |
|---|---|
| Cash and cash equivalents | $ 5,000 |
| Accounts receivable (net) | 20,000 |
| Inventories | 60,000 |
| Property, plant, and equipment (net) | 120,000 |
| Accounts payable | 44,000 |
| Wages payable | 15,000 |
| Paid-in-capital | 100,000 |

The only asset not listed is short-term investments. The only liabilities not listed are a $30,000 note payable due in two years and related accrued interest of $1,000 due in four months. The current ratio at year-end is 1.5:1.

**Required:**
Determine the following at December 31, 2013:
1. Total current assets
2. Short-term investments
3. Retained earnings

**E 3–2**
**Balance sheet classification**
● **LO3–2, LO3–3**

The following are the typical classifications used in a balance sheet:

| | |
|---|---|
| a. Current assets | f. Current liabilities |
| b. Investments and funds | g. Long-term liabilities |
| c. Property, plant, and equipment | h. Paid-in-capital |
| d. Intangible assets | i. Retained earnings |
| e. Other assets | |

**Required:**
For each of the following balance sheet items, use the letters above to indicate the appropriate classification category. If the item is a contra account, place a minus sign before the chosen letter.

1. _____ Equipment
2. _____ Accounts payable
3. _____ Allowance for uncollectible accounts
4. _____ Land, held for investment
5. _____ Note payable, due in 5 years
6. _____ Unearned rent revenue
7. _____ Note payable, due in 6 months
8. _____ Income less dividends, accumulated
9. _____ Investment in XYZ Corp., long-term
10. _____ Inventories
11. _____ Patent
12. _____ Land, in use
13. _____ Accrued liabilities
14. _____ Prepaid rent
15. _____ Common stock
16. _____ Building, in use
17. _____ Cash
18. _____ Taxes payable

**E 3–3**
**Balance sheet classification**
● **LO3–2, LO3–3**

The following are the typical classifications used in a balance sheet:

| | |
|---|---|
| a. Current assets | f. Current liabilities |
| b. Investments and funds | g. Long-term liabilities |
| c. Property, plant, and equipment | h. Paid-in-capital |
| d. Intangible assets | i. Retained earnings |
| e. Other assets | |

**Required:**
For each of the following 2013 balance sheet items, use the letters above to indicate the appropriate classification category. If the item is a contra account, place a minus sign before the chosen letter.

1. _____ Accrued interest payable
2. _____ Franchise
3. _____ Accumulated depreciation
4. _____ Prepaid insurance, for 2014
5. _____ Bonds payable, due in 10 years
6. _____ Current maturities of long-term debt
7. _____ Note payable, due in three months
8. _____ Long-term receivables
9. _____ Bond sinking fund, will be used to retire bonds in 10 years
10. _____ Supplies
11. _____ Machinery
12. _____ Land, in use
13. _____ Unearned revenue
14. _____ Copyrights
15. _____ Preferred stock
16. _____ Land, held for speculation
17. _____ Cash equivalents
18. _____ Wages payable

**E 3–4**
**Balance sheet preparation**
● **LO3–2, LO3–3**

The following is a December 31, 2013, post-closing trial balance for the Jackson Corporation.

| Account Title | Debits | Credits |
|---|---|---|
| Cash | 40,000 | |
| Accounts receivable | 34,000 | |
| Inventories | 75,000 | |
| Prepaid rent | 16,000 | |
| Marketable securities (short term) | 10,000 | |
| Machinery | 145,000 | |
| Accumulated depreciation—machinery | | 11,000 |
| Patent (net of amortization) | 83,000 | |
| Accounts payable | | 8,000 |
| Wages payable | | 4,000 |
| Taxes payable | | 32,000 |

(continued)

| | | |
|---|---|---|
| (concluded) | Bonds payable (due in 10 years) | 200,000 |
| | Common stock | 100,000 |
| | Retained earnings | 48,000 |
| | Totals | 403,000    403,000 |

**Required:**
Prepare a classified balance sheet for Jackson Corporation at December 31, 2013.

**E 3–5**
**Balance sheet**
**preparation**
● **LO3–2, LO3–3**

The following is a December 31, 2013, post-closing trial balance for the Valley Pump Corporation.

| Account Title | Debits | Credits |
|---|---|---|
| Cash | 25,000 | |
| Accounts receivable | 56,000 | |
| Inventories | 81,000 | |
| Interest payable | | 10,000 |
| Marketable securities | 44,000 | |
| Land | 120,000 | |
| Buildings | 300,000 | |
| Accumulated depreciation—buildings | | 100,000 |
| Equipment | 75,000 | |
| Accumulated depreciation—equipment | | 25,000 |
| Copyright (net of amortization) | 12,000 | |
| Prepaid expenses | 32,000 | |
| Accounts payable | | 65,000 |
| Unearned revenues | | 20,000 |
| Notes payable | | 250,000 |
| Allowance for uncollectible accounts | | 5,000 |
| Common stock | | 200,000 |
| Retained earnings | | 70,000 |
| Totals | 745,000 | 745,000 |

**Additional Information:**
1. The $120,000 balance in the land account consists of $100,000 for the cost of land where the plant and office buildings are located. The remaining $20,000 represents the cost of land being held for speculation.
2. The $44,000 in the marketable securities account represents an investment in the common stock of another corporation. Valley intends to sell one-half of the stock within the next year.
3. The notes payable account consists of a $100,000 note due in six months and a $150,000 note due in three annual installments of $50,000 each, with the first payment due in August of 2014.

**Required:**
Prepare a classified balance sheet for the Valley Pump Corporation at December 31, 2013.

**E 3–6**
**Balance sheet;**
**Current versus**
**noncurrent**
**classification**
● **LO3–2, LO3–3**

Presented below is a partial trial balance for the Kansas Instruments Corporation at December 31, 2013.

| Account Title | Debits | Credits |
|---|---|---|
| Cash | 20,000 | |
| Accounts receivable | 130,000 | |
| Raw materials | 24,000 | |
| Note receivable | 100,000 | |
| Interest receivable | 3,000 | |
| Interest payable | | 5,000 |
| Marketable securities | 32,000 | |
| Land | 50,000 | |
| Buildings | 1,300,000 | |
| Accumulated depreciation—buildings | | 620,000 |
| Work in process | 42,000 | |
| Finished goods | 89,000 | |
| Equipment | 300,000 | |
| Accumulated depreciation—equipment | | 130,000 |
| Patent (net of amortization) | 120,000 | |
| Prepaid rent (for the next two years) | 60,000 | |
| Unearned revenue | | 36,000 |
| Accounts payable | | 180,000 |
| Note payable | | 400,000 |
| Cash restricted for payment of note payable | 80,000 | |
| Allowance for uncollectible accounts | | 13,000 |
| Sales revenue | | 800,000 |
| Cost of goods sold | 450,000 | |
| Rent expense | 28,000 | |

**Additional Information:**

1. The note receivable, along with any accrued interest, is due on November 22, 2014.

2. The note payable is due in 2017. Interest is payable annually.

3. The marketable securities consist of treasury bills, all of which mature in the next year.

4. Unearned revenue will be earned equally over the next two years.

**Required:**

Determine the company's working capital (current assets minus current liabilities) at December 31, 2013.

**E 3–7**
**Balance sheet preparation; errors**
● **LO3–2, LO3–3**

The following balance sheet for the Los Gatos Corporation was prepared by a recently hired accountant. In reviewing the statement you notice several errors.

**LOS GATOS CORPORATION**
**Balance Sheet**
**At December 31, 2013**

**Assets**

| | |
|---|---:|
| Cash | $ 40,000 |
| Accounts receivable | 80,000 |
| Inventories | 55,000 |
| Machinery (net) | 120,000 |
| Franchise (net) | 30,000 |
| Total assets | $325,000 |

**Liabilities and Shareholders' Equity**

| | |
|---|---:|
| Accounts payable | $ 50,000 |
| Allowance for uncollectible accounts | 5,000 |
| Note payable | 55,000 |
| Bonds payable | 110,000 |
| Shareholders' equity | 105,000 |
| Total liabilities and shareholders' equity | $325,000 |

**Additional Information:**

1. Cash includes a $20,000 bond sinking fund to be used for repayment of the bonds payable in 2017.

2. The cost of the machinery is $190,000.

3. Accounts receivable includes a $20,000 note receivable from a customer due in 2016.

4. The note payable includes accrued interest of $5,000. Principal and interest are both due on February 1, 2014.

5. The company began operations in 2008. Income less dividends since inception of the company totals $35,000.

6. 50,000 shares of no par common stock were issued in 2008. 100,000 shares are authorized.

**Required:**

Prepare a corrected, classified balance sheet.

**E 3–8**
**Balance sheet; current versus noncurrent classification**
● **LO3–2, LO3–3**

Cone Corporation is in the process of preparing its December 31, 2013, balance sheet. There are some questions as to the proper classification of the following items:

a. $50,000 in cash set aside in a savings account to pay bonds payable. The bonds mature in 2017.

b. Prepaid rent of $24,000, covering the period January 1, 2014, through December 31, 2015.

c. Note payable of $200,000. The note is payable in annual installments of $20,000 each, with the first install-ment payable on March 1, 2014.

d. Accrued interest payable of $12,000 related to the note payable.

e. Investment in marketable securities of other corporations, $80,000. Cone intends to sell one-half of the secu-rities in 2014.

**Required:**

Prepare a partial classified balance sheet to show how each of the above items should be reported.

**E 3–9**
**Balance sheet preparation; cash versus accrual accounting; Chapters 2 and 3**
● **LO3–2, LO3–3**

The following is the balance sheet of Korver Supply Company at December 31, 2012.

**KORVER SUPPLY COMPANY**
**Balance Sheet**
**At December 31, 2012**

**Assets**

| | |
|---|---:|
| Cash | $120,000 |
| Accounts receivable | 300,000 |
| Inventories | 200,000 |
| Furniture and fixtures, net | 150,000 |
| Total assets | $770,000 |

(continued)

(concluded)

**Liabilities and Shareholders' Equity**

| | |
|---|---:|
| Accounts payable (for merchandise) | $190,000 |
| Note payable | 200,000 |
| Interest payable | 6,000 |
| Common stock | 100,000 |
| Retained earnings | 274,000 |
| Total liabilities and shareholders' equity | $770,000 |

Transactions during 2013 were as follows:

| | |
|---|---:|
| 1. Sales to customers on account | $800,000 |
| 2. Cash collected from customers | 780,000 |
| 3. Purchase of merchandise on account | 550,000 |
| 4. Cash payment to suppliers | 560,000 |
| 5. Cost of merchandise sold | 500,000 |
| 6. Cash paid for operating expenses | 160,000 |
| 7. Cash paid for interest on note | 12,000 |

The note payable is dated June 30, 2012 and is due on June 30, 2014. Interest at 6% is payable annually on June 30. Depreciation on the furniture and fixtures for the year is $20,000. The furniture and fixtures originally cost $300,000.

**Required:**
Prepare a classified balance sheet at December 21, 2013 (ignore income taxes).

**E 3–10**
**Financial statement disclosures**
● **LO3–4**

The following are typical disclosures that would appear in the notes accompanying financial statements. For each of the items listed, indicate where the disclosure would likely appear—either in (A) the significant accounting policies note or (B) a separate note.

| | |
|---|---|
| 1. Inventory costing method | A |
| 2. Information on related party transactions | —— |
| 3. Composition of property, plant, and equipment | —— |
| 4. Depreciation method | —— |
| 5. Subsequent event information | —— |
| 6. Basis of revenue recognition on long-term contracts | —— |
| 7. Important merger occurring after year-end | —— |
| 8. Composition of receivables | —— |

**E 3–11**
**Disclosure notes**
● **LO3–4**

Hallergan Company produces car and truck batteries that it sells primarily to auto manufacturers. Dorothy Hawkins, the company's controller, is preparing the financial statements for the year ended December 31, 2013. Hawkins asks for your advice concerning the following information that has not yet been included in the statements. The statements will be issued on February 28, 2014.

1. Hallergan leases its facilities from the brother of the chief executive officer.
2. On January 8, 2014, Hallergan entered into an agreement to sell a tract of land that it had been holding as an investment. The sale, which resulted in a material gain, was completed on February 2, 2014.
3. Hallergan uses the straight-line method to determine depreciation on all of the company's depreciable assets.
4. On February 8, 2014, Hallergan completed negotiations with its bank for a $10,000,000 line of credit.
5. Hallergan uses the first-in, first-out (FIFO) method to value inventory.

**Required:**
For each of the above items, discuss any additional disclosures that Hawkins should include in Hallergan's financial statements.

**E 3–12**
**Financial statement disclosures**
● **LO3–4**

Parkman Sporting Goods is preparing its annual report for its 2013 fiscal year. The company's controller has asked for your help in determining how best to disclose information about the following items:

1. A related-party transaction.
2. Depreciation method.
3. Allowance for uncollectible accounts.
4. Composition of investments.
5. Composition of long-term debt.
6. Inventory costing method.
7. Number of shares of common stock authorized, issued, and outstanding.
8. Employee benefit plans.

**Required:**
Indicate whether the above items should be disclosed (A) in the summary of significant accounting policies note, (B) in a separate disclosure note, or (C) on the face of the balance sheet.

**E 3–13**
FASB codification research
● LO3–4

The *FASB Accounting Standards Codification* represents the single source of authoritative U.S. generally accepted accounting principles.

**Required:**
1. Obtain the relevant authoritative literature on the disclosure of accounting policies using the FASB's Codification Research System at the FASB website (www.fasb.org). Identify the topic number that provides guidance on information contained in the notes to the financial statements.
2. What is the specific citation that requires a company to identify and describe in the notes to the financial statements the accounting principles and methods used to prepare the financial statements?
3. Describe the disclosure requirements.

**E 3–14**
FASB codification research
● LO3–2, LO3–4

Access the FASB's Codification Research System at the FASB website (www.fasb.org). Determine the specific citation for each of the following items:
1. What is the balance sheet classification for a note payable due in six months that was used to purchase a building?
2. Which assets may be excluded from current assets?
3. Should a note receivable from a related party be included in the balance sheet with notes receivable or accounts receivable from customers?
4. What items are nonrecognized subsequent events that require a disclosure in the notes to the financial statements?

**E 3–15**
Concepts; terminology
● LO3–2 through LO3–4, LO3–6

Listed below are several terms and phrases associated with the balance sheet and financial disclosures. Pair each item from List A (by letter) with the item from List B that is most appropriately associated with it.

| List A | List B |
|---|---|
| ___ 1. Balance sheet | a. Will be satisfied through the use of current assets. |
| ___ 2. Liquidity | b. Items expected to be converted to cash or consumed within one year or the operating cycle, whichever is longer. |
| ___ 3. Current assets | |
| ___ 4. Operating cycle | c. The statements are presented fairly in conformity with GAAP. |
| ___ 5. Current liabilities | d. An organized array of assets, liabilities, and equity. |
| ___ 6. Cash equivalent | e. Important to a user in comparing financial information across companies. |
| ___ 7. Intangible asset | |
| ___ 8. Working capital | f. Scope limitation or a departure from GAAP. |
| ___ 9. Accrued liabilities | g. Recorded when an expense is incurred but not yet paid. |
| ___ 10. Summary of significant accounting policies | h. Relates to the amount of time before an asset is converted to cash or a liability is paid. |
| ___ 11. Subsequent events | i. Occurs after the fiscal year-end but before the statements are issued. |
| ___ 12. Unqualified opinion | j. Cash to cash. |
| ___ 13. Qualified opinion | k. One-month U.S. Treasury bill. |
| | l. Current assets minus current liabilities. |
| | m. Lacks physical substance. |

**E 3–16**
Calculating ratios
● LO3–8

The 2013 balance sheet for Hallbrook Industries, Inc., is shown below.

**HALLBROOK INDUSTRIES, INC.**
**Balance Sheet**
**December 31, 2013**
($ in 000s)

**Assets**

| | |
|---|---:|
| Cash | $ 200 |
| Short-term investments | 150 |
| Accounts receivable | 200 |
| Inventories | 350 |
| Property, plant, and equipment (net) | 1,000 |
| Total assets | $1,900 |

**Liabilities and Shareholders' Equity**

| | |
|---|---:|
| Current liabilities | $ 400 |
| Long-term liabilities | 350 |
| Paid-in capital | 750 |
| Retained earnings | 400 |
| Total liabilities and shareholders' equity | $1,900 |

The company's 2013 income statement reported the following amounts ($ in 000s):

| | |
|---|---:|
| Net sales | $4,600 |
| Interest expense | 40 |
| Income tax expense | 100 |
| Net income | 160 |

**Required:**
Determine the following ratios for 2013:

1. Current ratio
2. Acid-test ratio
3. Debt to equity ratio
4. Times interest earned ratio

**E 3–17**
**Calculating ratios;**
**Best Buy**
● **LO3–8**

Real World Financials

**Best Buy Co, Inc.**, is a leading retailer specializing in consumer electronics. A condensed income statement and balance sheet for the fiscal year ended February 26, 2011, are shown below.

**Best Buy Co., Inc.**
**Balance Sheet**
**At February 26, 2011**
($ in millions)
**Assets**

| | |
|---|---:|
| Current assets: | |
| Cash and cash equivalents | $ 1,103 |
| Short-term investments | 22 |
| Accounts receivable, net | 2,348 |
| Merchandise inventories | 5,897 |
| Other current assets | 1,103 |
| Total current assets | 10,473 |
| Noncurrent assets | 7,376 |
| Total assets | $17,849 |

**Liabilities and Shareholders' Equity**

| | |
|---|---:|
| Current liabilities: | |
| Accounts payable | $ 4,894 |
| Other current liabilities | 3,769 |
| Total current liabilities | 8,663 |
| Long-term liabilities | 1,894 |
| Shareholders' equity | 7,292 |
| Total liabilities and shareholders' equity | $17,849 |

**Best Buy Co., Inc.**
**Income Statement**
**For the Year Ended February 26, 2011**
($ in millions)

| | |
|---|---:|
| Revenues | $50,272 |
| Costs and expenses | 48,158 |
| Operating income | 2,114 |
| Other income (expense)* | (34) |
| Income before income taxes | 2,080 |
| Income tax expense | 714 |
| Net income including noncontrolling interests | 1,366 |
| Net income attributable to noncontrolling interests | (89) |
| Net income | $ 1,277 |

*Includes $87 of interest expense.

Liquidity and financing ratios for the industry are as follows:

| | **Industry Average** |
|---|:---:|
| Current ratio | 1.25 |
| Acid-test ratio | .63 |
| Debt to equity | .63 |
| Times interest earned | .89 times |

**Required:**

1. Determine the following ratios for Best Buy for its fiscal year ended February, 26, 2011:
   a. Current ratio
   b. Acid-test ratio
   c. Debt to equity ratio
   d. Times interest earned ratio
2. Using the ratios from requirement 1, assess Best Buy's liquidity and solvency relative to its industry.

**E 3–18**
Calculating
ratios; solve for
unknowns
● LO3–8

The current asset section of the Excalibur Tire Company's balance sheet consists of cash, marketable securities, accounts receivable, and inventories. The December 31, 2013, balance sheet revealed the following:

| | |
|---|---|
| Inventories | $ 840,000 |
| Total assets | $2,800,000 |
| Current ratio | 2.25 |
| Acid-test ratio | 1.2 |
| Debt to equity ratio | 1.8 |

**Required:**

Determine the following 2013 balance sheet items:
1. Current assets
2. Shareholders' equity
3. Noncurrent assets
4. Long-term liabilities

**E 3–19**
Calculating
ratios; solve for
unknowns
● LO3–8

The current asset section of Guardian Consultant's balance sheet consists of cash, accounts receivable, and prepaid expenses. The 2013 balance sheet reported the following: cash, $1,300,000; prepaid expenses, $360,000; noncurrent assets, $2,400,000; and shareholders' equity, $2,500,000. The current ratio at the end of the year was 2.0 and the debt to equity ratio was 1.4.

**Required:**

Determine the following 2013 amounts and ratios:
1. Current liabilities.
2. Long-term liabilities.
3. Accounts receivable.
4. The acid-test ratio.

**E 3–20**
Effect of
management
decisions on
ratios
● LO3–8

Most decisions made by management impact the ratios analysts use to evaluate performance. Indicate (by letter) whether each of the actions listed below will immediately increase (I), decrease (D), or have no effect (N) on the ratios shown. Assume each ratio is less than 1.0 before the action is taken.

| Action | Current Ratio | Acid-Test Ratio | Debt to Equity Ratio |
|---|---|---|---|
| 1. Issuance of long-term bonds | ____ | ____ | ____ |
| 2. Issuance of short-term notes | ____ | ____ | ____ |
| 3. Payment of accounts payable | ____ | ____ | ____ |
| 4. Purchase of inventory on account | ____ | ____ | ____ |
| 5. Purchase of inventory for cash | ____ | ____ | ____ |
| 6. Purchase of equipment with a 4-year note | ____ | ____ | ____ |
| 7. Retirement of bonds | ____ | ____ | ____ |
| 8. Sale of common stock | ____ | ____ | ____ |
| 9. Write-off of obsolete inventory | ____ | ____ | ____ |
| 10. Purchase of short-term investment for cash | ____ | ____ | ____ |
| 11. Decision to refinance on a long-term basis some currently maturing debt | ____ | ____ | ____ |

**E 3–21**
Segment
reporting
● Appendix 3

The Canton Corporation operates in four distinct business segments. The segments, along with 2013 information on revenues, assets and net income, are listed below ($ in millions):

| Segment | Revenues | Assets | Net Income |
|---|---|---|---|
| Pharmaceuticals | $2,000 | $1,000 | $200 |
| Plastics | 3,000 | 1,500 | 270 |
| Farm equipment | 2,500 | 1,250 | 320 |
| Electronics | 500 | 250 | 40 |
| Total company | $8,000 | $4,000 | $830 |

**Required:**

1. For which segments must Canton report supplementary information according to U.S. GAAP?
2. What amounts must be reported for the segments you identified in requirement 1?

**E 3–22**
Segment reporting
● **Appendix 3**
LO3–9

 **IFRS**

Refer to Exercise 3–21.

**Required:**

How might your answers differ if Canton Corporation prepares its segment disclosure according to International Financial Reporting Standards?

# CPA and CMA Review Questions

**CPA Exam Questions**

The following questions are adapted from a variety of sources including questions developed by the AICPA Board of Examiners and those used in the Kaplan CPA Review Course to study balance sheet presentation, financial disclosures, and liquidity ratios while preparing for the CPA examination. Determine the response that best completes the statements or questions.

● LO3–2

1. In Merf's April 30, 2013, balance sheet, a note receivable was reported as a noncurrent asset and the related accrued interest for eight months was reported as a current asset. Which of the following descriptions would fit Merf's receivable classification?
   a. Both principal and interest amounts are due on August 31, 2013, and August 31, 2014.
   b. Principal is due August 31, 2014, and interest is due August 31, 2013, and August 31, 2014.
   c. Principal and interest are due December 31, 2013.
   d. Both principal and interest amounts are due on December 31, 2013, and December 31, 2014.

● LO3–3

2. Mill Co.'s trial balance included the following account balances at December 31, 2013:

| | |
|---|---|
| Accounts payable | $15,000 |
| Bond payable, due 2014 | 22,000 |
| Dividends payable 1/31/14 | 8,000 |
| Notes payable, due 2015 | 20,000 |

   What amount should be included in the current liability section of Mill's December 31, 2013, balance sheet?
   a. $45,000
   b. $51,000
   c. $65,000
   d. $78,000

● LO3–4

3. Which of the following would be disclosed in the summary of significant accounting policies disclosure note?

| | Composition of Plant Assets | Inventory Pricing |
|---|---|---|
| a. | No | Yes |
| b. | Yes | No |
| c. | Yes | Yes |
| d. | No | No |

● LO3–6

4. How are management's responsibility and the auditor's report represented in the standard auditor's report?

| | Management's Responsibility | Auditor's Responsibility |
|---|---|---|
| a. | Implicitly | Explicitly |
| b. | Implicitly | Implicitly |
| c. | Explicitly | Explicitly |
| d. | Explicitly | Implicitly |

● LO3–8

5. At December 30, Vida Co. had cash of $200,000, a current ratio of 1.5:1, and a quick ratio of .5:1. On December 31, all the cash was used to reduce accounts payable. How did this cash payment affect the ratios?

| | Current Ratio | Quick Ratio |
|---|---|---|
| a. | Increased | No effect |
| b. | Increased | Decreased |
| c. | Decreased | Increased |
| d. | Decreased | No effect |

● LO3–8

6. Zenk Co. wrote off obsolete inventory of $100,000 during 2013. What was the effect of this write-off on Zenk's ratio analysis?

    a. Decrease in the current ratio but not the quick ratio.
    b. Decrease in the quick ratio but not in the current ratio.
    c. Increase in the current ratio but not in the quick ratio.
    d. Increase in the quick ratio but not in the current ratio.

Beginning in 2011, International Financial Reporting Standards are tested on the CPA exam along with U.S. GAAP. The following questions deal with the application of IFRS.

● LO3–9

● IFRS

7. Noncurrent assets must be reported before current assets in a balance sheet reported by a company using:

    a. IFRS.
    b. U.S. GAAP.
    c. Both U.S. GAAP and IFRS.
    d. Neither U.S. GAAP nor IFRS.

● LO3–9
● Appendix 3

● IFRS

8. Total liabilities of a company's reportable segments must be reported when the company provides supplemental information on operating segments using:

    a. IFRS.
    b. U.S. GAAP.
    c. Both U.S. GAAP and IFRS.
    d. Neither U.S. GAAP nor IFRS.

**CMA Exam Questions**

The following questions dealing with balance sheet presentation, financial disclosures, and liquidity ratios are adapted from questions that previously appeared on Certified Management Accountant (CMA) examinations. The CMA designation sponsored by the Institute of Management Accountants (**www.imanet.org**) provides members with an objective measure of knowledge and competence in the field of management accounting. Determine the response that best completes the statements or questions.

● LO3–4

1. The Financial Accounting Standards Board has provided guidance on disclosures of transactions between related parties, for example, transactions between subsidiaries of a common parent. GAAP regarding related-party transactions requires all of the following disclosures except

    a. The nature of the relationship involved.
    b. A description of the transactions for each period an income statement is presented.
    c. The dollar amounts of transactions for each period an income statement is presented.
    d. The effect on the cash flow statement for each period a cash flow statement is presented.

● LO3–5

2. The Management's Discussion and Analysis (MD&A) section of an annual report

    a. Includes the company president's letter.
    b. Covers three financial aspects of a firm's business: liquidity, capital resources, and results of operations.
    c. Is a technical analysis of past results and a defense of those results by management.
    d. Covers marketing and product line issues.

● LO3–8

3. Windham Company has current assets of $400,000 and current liabilities of $500,000. Windham Company's current ratio would be increased by

    a. The purchase of $100,000 of inventory on account.
    b. The payment of $100,000 of accounts payable.
    c. The collection of $100,000 of accounts receivable.
    d. Refinancing a $100,000 long-term loan with short-term debt.

## Problems

An alternate exercise and problem set is available on the text website: www.mhhe.com/spiceland7e

P 3–1
Balance sheet preparation
● LO3–2, LO3–3

Presented below is a list of balance sheet accounts presented in alphabetical order.

| | |
|---|---|
| Accounts payable | Cash |
| Accounts receivable | Common stock |
| Accumulated depreciation—buildings | Copyright |
| Accumulated depreciation—equipment | Equipment |
| Allowance for uncollectible accounts | Interest receivable (due in three months) |
| Bond sinking fund | Inventories |
| Bonds payable (due in 10 years) | Land (in use) |
| Buildings | Long-term investments |

(continued)

(concluded)

| Notes payable (due in 6 months) | Rent payable (current) |
|---|---|
| Notes receivable (due in 2 years) | Retained earnings |
| Patent | Short-term investments |
| Preferred stock | Taxes payable |
| Prepaid expenses | Wages payable |

**Required:**
Prepare a classified balance sheet ignoring monetary amounts.

**P 3–2**
Balance sheet
preparation;
missing elements
● LO3–2, LO3–3

The data listed below are taken from a balance sheet of Trident Corporation. Some amounts, indicated by question marks, have been intentionally omitted.

|  | ($ in 000s) |
|---|---|
| Cash and cash equivalents | $  239,186 |
| Short-term investments | 353,700 |
| Accounts receivable (net of allowance) | 504,944 |
| Inventories | ? |
| Prepaid expenses (current) | 83,259 |
| Total current assets | 1,594,927 |
| Long-term receivables | 110,800 |
| Property and equipment (net) | ? |
| Total assets | ? |
| Notes payable and short-term debt | 31,116 |
| Accounts payable | ? |
| Accrued liabilities | 421,772 |
| Other current liabilities | 181,604 |
| Total current liabilities | 693,564 |
| Long-term debt and deferred taxes | ? |
| Total liabilities | 956,140 |
| Shareholders' equity | 1,370,627 |

**Required:**
1. Determine the missing amounts.
2. Prepare Trident's classified balance sheet.

**P 3–3**
Balance sheet
preparation
● LO3–2, LO3–3

The following is a December 31, 2013, post-closing trial balance for Almway Corporation.

| Account Title | Debits | Credits |
|---|---|---|
| Cash | 45,000 |  |
| Investments | 110,000 |  |
| Accounts receivable | 60,000 |  |
| Inventories | 200,000 |  |
| Prepaid insurance | 9,000 |  |
| Land | 90,000 |  |
| Buildings | 420,000 |  |
| Accumulated depreciation—buildings |  | 100,000 |
| Equipment | 110,000 |  |
| Accumulated depreciation—equipment |  | 60,000 |
| Patents (net of amortization) | 10,000 |  |
| Accounts payable |  | 75,000 |
| Notes payable |  | 130,000 |
| Interest payable |  | 20,000 |
| Bonds payable |  | 240,000 |
| Common stock |  | 300,000 |
| Retained earnings |  | 129,000 |
| Totals | 1,054,000 | 1,054,000 |

**Additional Information:**
1. The investment account includes an investment in common stock of another corporation of $30,000 which management intends to hold for at least three years. The balance of these investments is intended to be sold in the coming year.
2. The land account includes land which cost $25,000 that the company has not used and is currently listed for sale.
3. The cash account includes $15,000 set aside in a fund to pay bonds payable that mature in 2016 and $23,000 set aside in a three-month Treasury bill.

4. The notes payable account consists of the following:

   a. a $30,000 note due in six months.

   b. a $50,000 note due in six years.

   c. a $50,000 note due in five annual installments of $10,000 each, with the next installment due February 15, 2014.

5. The $60,000 balance in accounts receivable is net of an allowance for uncollectible accounts of $8,000.

6. The common stock account represents 100,000 shares of no par value common stock issued and outstanding. The corporation has 500,000 shares authorized.

**Required:**
Prepare a classified balance sheet for the Almway Corporation at December 31, 2013.

**P 3–4**
Balance sheet preparation
● LO3–2, LO3–3

The following is a December 31, 2013, post-closing trial balance for the Weismuller Publishing Company.

| Account Title | Debits | Credits |
| --- | --- | --- |
| Cash | 65,000 | |
| Accounts receivable | 160,000 | |
| Inventories | 285,000 | |
| Prepaid expenses | 148,000 | |
| Machinery and equipment | 320,000 | |
| Accumulated depreciation—equipment | | 110,000 |
| Investments | 140,000 | |
| Accounts payable | | 60,000 |
| Interest payable | | 20,000 |
| Unearned revenue | | 80,000 |
| Taxes payable | | 30,000 |
| Notes payable | | 200,000 |
| Allowance for uncollectible accounts | | 16,000 |
| Common stock | | 400,000 |
| Retained earnings | | 202,000 |
| Totals | 1,118,000 | 1,118,000 |

**Additional Information:**

1. Prepaid expenses include $120,000 paid on December 31, 2013, for a two-year lease on the building that houses both the administrative offices and the manufacturing facility.

2. Investments include $30,000 in Treasury bills purchased on November 30, 2013. The bills mature on January 30, 2014. The remaining $110,000 includes investments in marketable equity securities that the company intends to sell in the next year.

3. Unearned revenue represents customer prepayments for magazine subscriptions. Subscriptions are for periods of one year or less.

4. The notes payable account consists of the following:

   a. a $40,000 note due in six months.

   b. a $100,000 note due in six years.

   c. a $60,000 note due in three annual installments of $20,000 each, with the next installment due August 31, 2014.

5. The common stock account represents 400,000 shares of no par value common stock issued and outstanding. The corporation has 800,000 shares authorized.

**Required:**
Prepare a classified balanced sheet for the Weismuller Publishing Company at December 31, 2013.

**P 3–5**
Balance sheet preparation
● LO3–2, LO3–3

The following is a June 30, 2013, post-closing trial balance for Excell Company.

| Account Title | Debits | Credits |
| --- | --- | --- |
| Cash | 83,000 | |
| Short-term investments | 65,000 | |
| Accounts receivable | 280,000 | |
| Prepaid expenses | 32,000 | |
| Land | 75,000 | |
| Buildings | 320,000 | |
| Accumulated depreciation—buildings | | 160,000 |
| Equipment | 265,000 | |
| Accumulated depreciation—equipment | | 120,000 |
| Accounts payable | | 173,000 |

(continued)

(concluded)

| | | |
|---|---|---|
| Accrued expenses | | 45,000 |
| Notes payable | | 100,000 |
| Mortgage payable | | 250,000 |
| Common stock | | 100,000 |
| Retained earnings | | 172,000 |
| Totals | 1,120,000 | 1,120,000 |

**Additional Information:**

1. The short-term investments account includes $18,000 in U.S. treasury bills purchased in May. The bills mature in July.

2. The accounts receivable account consists of the following:

| | |
|---|---|
| a. Amounts owed by customers | $225,000 |
| b. Allowance for uncollectible accounts—trade customers | (15,000) |
| c. Nontrade note receivable (due in three years) | 65,000 |
| d. Interest receivable on note (due in four months) | 5,000 |
| Total | $280,000 |

3. The notes payable account consists of two notes of $50,000 each. One note is due on September 30, 2013, and the other is due on November 30, 2014.

4. The mortgage payable is payable in *semiannual* installments of $5,000 each plus interest. The next payment is due on October 31, 2013. Interest has been properly accrued and is included in accrued expenses.

5. Five hundred thousand shares of no par common stock are authorized, of which 200,000 shares have been issued and are outstanding.

6. The land account includes $50,000 representing the cost of the land on which the company's office building resides. The remaining $25,000 is the cost of land that the company is holding for investment purposes.

**Required:**
Prepare a classified balance sheet for the Excell Company at June 30, 2013.

**P 3–6**
Balance sheet
preparation;
disclosures
● **LO3–2 through LO3–4**

The following is a December 31, 2013, post-closing trial balance for the Vosburgh Electronics Corporation.

| Account Title | Debits | Credits |
|---|---|---|
| Cash | 67,000 | |
| Short-term investments | 182,000 | |
| Accounts receivable | 123,000 | |
| Long-term investments | 35,000 | |
| Inventories | 215,000 | |
| Loans to employees | 40,000 | |
| Prepaid expenses (for 2014) | 16,000 | |
| Land | 280,000 | |
| Building | 1,550,000 | |
| Machinery and equipment | 637,000 | |
| Patent | 152,000 | |
| Franchise | 40,000 | |
| Note receivable | 250,000 | |
| Interest receivable | 12,000 | |
| Accumulated depreciation—building | | 620,000 |
| Accumulated depreciation—equipment | | 210,000 |
| Accounts payable | | 189,000 |
| Dividends payable (payable on 1/16/14) | | 10,000 |
| Interest payable | | 16,000 |
| Taxes payable | | 40,000 |
| Unearned revenue | | 60,000 |
| Notes payable | | 300,000 |
| Allowance for uncollectible accounts | | 8,000 |
| Common stock | | 2,000,000 |
| Retained earnings | | 146,000 |
| Totals | 3,599,000 | 3,599,000 |

**Additional Information:**

1. The common stock represents 1 million shares of no par stock authorized, 500,000 shares issued and outstanding.

2. The loans to employees are due on June 30, 2014.

3. The note receivable is due in installments of $50,000, payable on each September 30. Interest is payable annually.

4. Short-term investments consist of marketable equity securities that the company plans to sell in 2014 and $50,000 in treasury bills purchased on December 15 of the current year that mature on February 15, 2014. Long-term investments consist of marketable equity securities that the company does not plan to sell in the next year.

5. Unearned revenue represents customer payments for extended service contracts. Eighty percent of these contracts expire in 2014, the remainder in 2015.

6. Notes payable consists of two notes, one for $100,000 due on January 15, 2015, and another for $200,000 due on June 30, 2016.

**Required:**

1. Prepare a classified balance sheet for Vosburgh at December 31, 2013.

2. Identify the items that would require additional disclosure, either on the face of the balance sheet or in a disclosure note.

**P 3–7**
Balance sheet
preparation;
errors
● LO3–2, LO3–3

The following balance sheet for the Hubbard Corporation was prepared by the company:

### HUBBARD CORPORATION
### Balance Sheet
### At December 31, 2013

#### Assets

| | |
|---|---:|
| Buildings | $ 750,000 |
| Land | 250,000 |
| Cash | 60,000 |
| Accounts receivable (net) | 120,000 |
| Inventories | 240,000 |
| Machinery | 280,000 |
| Patent (net) | 100,000 |
| Investment in marketable equity securities | 60,000 |
| Total assets | $1,860,000 |

#### Liabilities and Shareholders' Equity

| | |
|---|---:|
| Accounts payable | $ 215,000 |
| Accumulated depreciation | 255,000 |
| Notes payable | 500,000 |
| Appreciation of inventories | 80,000 |
| Common stock, authorized and issued 100,000 shares of no par stock | 430,000 |
| Retained earnings | 380,000 |
| Total liabilities and shareholders' equity | $1,860,000 |

**Additional Information:**

1. The buildings, land, and machinery are all stated at cost except for a parcel of land that the company is holding for future sale. The land originally cost $50,000 but, due to a significant increase in market value, is listed at $120,000. The increase in the land account was credited to retained earnings.

2. Marketable equity securities consist of stocks of other corporations and are recorded at cost, $20,000 of which will be sold in the coming year. The remainder will be held indefinitely.

3. Notes payable are all long-term. However, a $100,000 note requires an installment payment of $25,000 due in the coming year.

4. Inventories are recorded at current resale value. The original cost of the inventories is $160,000.

**Required:**

Prepare a corrected classified balance sheet for the Hubbard Corporation at December 31, 2013.

**P 3–8**
Balance sheet;
errors; missing
amounts
● LO3–2, LO3–3

The following incomplete balance sheet for the Sanderson Manufacturing Company was prepared by the company's controller. As accounting manager for Sanderson, you are attempting to reconstruct and revise the balance sheet.

**Sanderson Manufacturing Company**
**Balance Sheet**
**At December 31, 2013**
($ in 000s)

**Assets**

| | |
|---|---:|
| Current assets: | |
| Cash | $ 1,250 |
| Accounts receivable | 3,500 |
| Allowance for uncollectible accounts | (400) |
| Finished goods inventory | 6,000 |
| Prepaid expenses | 1,200 |
| Total current assets | 11,550 |
| Noncurrent assets: | |
| Investments | 3,000 |
| Raw materials and work in process inventory | 2,250 |
| Equipment | 15,000 |
| Accumulated depreciation—equipment | (4,200) |
| Patent | ? |
| Total assets | $    ? |

**Liabilities and Shareholders' Equity**

| | | |
|---|---:|---:|
| Current liabilities: | | |
| Accounts payable | | $ 5,200 |
| Note payable | | 4,000 |
| Interest payable—note | | 100 |
| Unearned revenue | | 3,000 |
| Total current liabilities | | 12,300 |
| Long-term liabilities: | | |
| Bonds payable | | 5,500 |
| Interest payable—bonds | | 200 |
| Shareholders' equity: | | |
| Common stock | $ ? | |
| Retained earnings | ? | ? |
| Total liabilities and shareholders' equity | | ? |

**Additional Information ($ in 000s):**

1. Certain records that included the account balances for the patent and shareholders' equity items were lost. However, the controller told you that a complete, preliminary balance sheet prepared before the records were lost showed a debt to equity ratio of 1.2. That is, total liabilities are 120% of total shareholders' equity. Retained earnings at the beginning of the year was $4,000. Net income for 2013 was $1,560 and $560 in cash dividends were declared and paid to shareholders.

2. Management intends to sell the investments in the next six months.

3. Interest on both the note and the bonds is payable annually.

4. The note payable is due in annual installments of $1,000 each.

5. Unearned revenue will be earned equally over the next two fiscal years.

6. The common stock represents 400,000 shares of no par stock authorized, 250,000 shares issued and outstanding.

**Required:**

Prepare a complete, corrected, classified balance sheet.

**P 3–9**
**Balance sheet preparation**
● **LO3–2, LO3–3**

Presented below is the balance sheet for HHD, Inc., at December 31, 2013.

| | | | |
|---|---:|---|---:|
| Current assets | $ 600,000 | Current liabilities | $ 400,000 |
| Investments | 500,000 | Long-term liabilities | 1,100,000 |
| Property, plant, and equipment | 2,000,000 | Shareholders' equity | 1,800,000 |
| Intangible assets | 200,000 | | |
| Total assets | $3,300,000 | Total liabilities and shareholders' equity | $3,300,000 |

The captions shown in the summarized statement above include the following:

a. Current assets: cash, $150,000; accounts receivable, $200,000; inventories, $225,000; and prepaid insurance, $25,000.

b. Investments: investments in common stock, short term, $90,000, and long term, $160,000; and bond sinking fund, $250,000.

c. Property, plant, and equipment: buildings, $1,500,000 less accumulated depreciation, $600,000; equipment, $500,000 less accumulated depreciation, $200,000; and land, $800,000.

d. Intangible assets: patent, $110,000; and copyright, $90,000.

e. Current liabilities: accounts payable, $100,000; notes payable, short term, $150,000, and long term, $90,000; and taxes payable, $60,000.

f. Long-term liabilities: bonds payable due 2018.

g. Shareholders' equity: common stock, $1,000,000; retained earnings, $800,000. Five hundred thousand shares of no par common stock are authorized, of which 200,000 shares were issued and are outstanding.

**Required:**
Prepare a corrected classified balance sheet for HHD, Inc., at December 31, 2013.

**P 3–10**
**Balance sheet preparation**
● **LO3–2, LO3–3**

Melody Lane Music Company was started by John Ross early in 2013. Initial capital was acquired by issuing shares of common stock to various investors and by obtaining a bank loan. The company operates a retail store that sells records, tapes, and compact discs. Business was so good during the first year of operations that John is considering opening a second store on the other side of town. The funds necessary for expansion will come from a new bank loan. In order to approve the loan, the bank requires financial statements.

John asks for your help in preparing the balance sheet and presents you with the following information for the year ending December 31, 2013:

a. Cash receipts consisted of the following:

| | |
|---|---|
| From customers | $360,000 |
| From issue of common stock | 100,000 |
| From bank loan | 100,000 |

b. Cash disbursements were as follows:

| | |
|---|---|
| Purchase of inventory | $300,000 |
| Rent | 15,000 |
| Salaries | 30,000 |
| Utilities | 5,000 |
| Insurance | 3,000 |
| Purchase of equipment and furniture | 40,000 |

c. The bank loan was made on March 31, 2013. A note was signed requiring payment of interest and principal on March 31, 2014. The interest rate is 12%.

d. The equipment and furniture were purchased on January 3, 2013, and have an estimated useful life of 10 years with no anticipated salvage value. Depreciation per year is $4,000.

e. Inventories on hand at the end of the year cost $100,000.

f. Amounts owed at December 31, 2013, were as follows:

| | |
|---|---|
| To suppliers of inventory | $20,000 |
| To the utility company | 1,000 |

g. Rent on the store building is $1,000 per month. On December 1, 2013, four months' rent was paid in advance.

h. Net income for the year was $76,000. Assume that the company is not subject to federal, state, or local income tax.

i. One hundred thousand shares of no par common stock are authorized, of which 20,000 shares were issued and are outstanding.

**Required:**
Prepare a balance sheet at December 31, 2013.

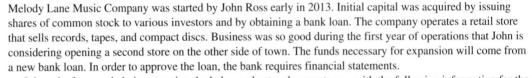

**Broaden Your Perspective**

Apply your critical-thinking ability to the knowledge you've gained. These cases will provide you an opportunity to develop your research, analysis, judgment, and communication skills. You also will work with other students, integrate what you've learned, apply it in real world situations, and consider its global and ethical ramifications. This practice will broaden your knowledge and further develop your decision-making abilities.

**Communication Case 3–1**
Current versus noncurrent classification
● LO3–2

A first-year accounting student is confused by a statement made in a recent class. Her instructor stated that the assets listed in the balance sheet of the **IBM Corporation** include computers that are classified as current assets as well as computers that are classified as noncurrent assets. In addition, the instructor stated that investments in marketable securities of other corporations could be classified in the balance sheet as either current or noncurrent assets.

**Required:**

Explain to the student the distinction between current and noncurrent assets pertaining to the IBM computers and the investments in marketable securities.

**Analysis Case 3–2**
Current versus noncurrent classification
● LO3–2, LO3–3

The usefulness of the balance sheet is enhanced when assets and liabilities are grouped according to common characteristics. The broad distinction made in the balance sheet is the current versus noncurrent classification of both assets and liabilities.

**Required:**

1. Discuss the factors that determine whether an asset or liability should be classified as current or noncurrent in a balance sheet.
2. Identify six items that under different circumstances could be classified as either current or noncurrent. Indicate the factors that would determine the correct classification.

**Communication Case 3–3**
FASB codification research; inventory or property, plant, and equipment
● LO3–2

The Red Hen Company produces, processes, and sells fresh eggs. The company is in the process of preparing financial statements at the end of its first year of operations and has asked for your help in determining the appropriate treatment of the cost of its egg-laying flock. The estimated life of a laying hen is approximately two years, after which they are sold to soup companies.

The controller considers the company's operating cycle to be two years and wants to present the cost of the egg-producing flock as inventory in the current asset section of the balance sheet. He feels that the hens are "goods awaiting sale." The chief financial officer does not agree with this treatment. He thinks that the cost of the flock should be classified as property, plant, and equipment because the hens are used in the production of product—the eggs.

The focus of this case is the balance sheet presentation of the cost of the egg-producing flock. Your instructor will divide the class into two to six groups depending on the size of the class. The mission of your group is to reach consensus on the appropriate presentation.

**Required:**

1. Each group member should deliberate the situation independently and draft a tentative argument prior to the class session for which the case is assigned.
2. In class, each group will meet for 10 to 15 minutes in different areas of the classroom. During that meeting, group members will take turns sharing their suggestions for the purpose of arriving at a single group treatment.
3. After the allotted time, a spokesperson for each group (selected during the group meetings) will share the group's solution with the class. The goal of the class is to incorporate the views of each group into a consensus approach to the situation.

**IFRS Case 3–4**
Balance sheet presentation; Vodafone Group, Plc.
● LO3–2, LO3–3, LO3–9

IFRS

Real World Financials

**Vodafone Group, Plc.**, a U.K. company, is the largest mobile telecommunications network company in the world. The company prepares its financial statements in accordance with International Financial Reporting Standards. Below are partial company balance sheets (statements of financial position) included in a recent annual report:

| Vodafone Group, Plc. Consolidated Statements of Financial Position At March 31 | | |
|---|---|---|
| | 2011 | 2010 |
| | £m | £m |
| **Noncurrent assets** | | |
| Goodwill | 45,236 | 51,838 |
| Other intangible assets | 23,322 | 22,420 |
| Property, plant, and equipment | 20,181 | 20,642 |
| Investments in associates | 38,105 | 36,377 |
| Other investments | 1,381 | 7,591 |
| Deferred tax assets | 2,018 | 1,033 |
| Post employment benefits | 97 | 34 |
| Trade and other receivables | 3,877 | 2,831 |
| | 134,217 | 142,766 |

(continued)

| (concluded) | 2011 | 2010 |
|---|---|---|
| | £m | £m |
| **Current assets** | | |
| Inventory | 537 | 433 |
| Taxation recoverable | 281 | 191 |
| Trade and other receivables | 9,259 | 8,784 |
| Other investments | 674 | 388 |
| Cash and cash equivalents | 6,252 | 4,423 |
| | 17,003 | 14,219 |
| **Total assets** | 151,220 | 156,985 |
| | | |
| Equity (details provided in complete statement) | 87,561 | 90,810 |
| **Noncurrent liabilities** | | |
| Long-term borrowings | 28,375 | 28,632 |
| Taxation liabilities | 350 | — |
| Deferred tax liabilities | 6,486 | 7,377 |
| Postemployment benefits | 87 | 237 |
| Provisions | 482 | 497 |
| Trade and other payables | 804 | 816 |
| | 36,584 | 37,559 |
| **Current liabilities** | | |
| Short-term borrowings | 9,906 | 11,163 |
| Taxation liabilities | 1,912 | 2,874 |
| Provisions | 559 | 497 |
| Trade and other payables | 14,698 | 14,082 |
| | 27,075 | 28,616 |
| **Total equity and liabilities** | 151,220 | 156,985 |

**Required:**

1. Describe the differences between Vodafone's balance sheets and a typical U.S. company balance sheet.

2. What type of liabilities do you think are included in the *provisions* category in Vodafone's balance sheets?

**Judgment Case 3–5**
Balance sheet; errors
● LO3–2 through LO3–4

You recently joined the internal auditing department of Marcus Clothing Corporation. As one of your first assignments, you are examining a balance sheet prepared by a staff accountant.

**MARCUS CLOTHING CORPORATION**
**Balance Sheet**
**At December 31, 2013**

**Assets**

| Current assets: | | |
|---|---|---|
| Cash | | $ 137,000 |
| Accounts receivable, net | | 80,000 |
| Note receivable | | 53,000 |
| Inventories | | 240,000 |
| Investments | | 66,000 |
| Total current assets | | 576,000 |
| Other assets: | | |
| Land | $200,000 | |
| Equipment, net | 320,000 | |
| Prepaid expenses | 27,000 | |
| Patent | 22,000 | |
| Total other assets | | 569,000 |
| Total assets | | $1,145,000 |

**Liabilities and Shareholders' Equity**

| Current liabilities: | | |
|---|---|---|
| Accounts payable | | $ 125,000 |
| Salaries payable | | 32,000 |
| Total current liabilities | | 157,000 |

(continued)

| (concluded) | Long-term liabilities: | | |
|---|---|---|---|
| | Note payable | $100,000 | |
| | Bonds payable | 300,000 | |
| | Interest payable | 20,000 | |
| | Total long-term liabilities | | 420,000 |
| | Shareholders' equity: | | |
| | Common stock | 500,000 | |
| | Retained earnings | 68,000 | |
| | Total shareholders' equity | | 568,000 |
| | Total liabilities and shareholders' equity | | $1,145,000 |

In the course of your examination you uncover the following information pertaining to the balance sheet:

1. The company rents its facilities. The land that appears in the statement is being held for future sale.
2. The note receivable is due in 2015. The balance of $53,000 includes $3,000 of accrued interest. The next interest payment is due in July 2014.
3. The note payable is due in installments of $20,000 per year. Interest on both the notes and bonds is payable annually.
4. The company's investments consist of marketable equity securities of other corporations. Management does not intend to liquidate any investments in the coming year.

**Required:**

Identify and explain the deficiencies in the statement prepared by the company's accountant. Include in your answer items that require additional disclosure, either on the face of the statement or in a note.

**Judgment Case 3–6**
Financial disclosures
● LO3–4

You recently joined the auditing staff of Best, Best, and Krug, CPAs. You have been assigned to the audit of Clearview, Inc., and have been asked by the audit senior to examine the balance sheet prepared by Clearview's accountant.

**CLEARVIEW, INC.**
**Balance Sheet**
**At December 31, 2013**
($ in millions)

**Assets**

| | | |
|---|---|---|
| Current assets: | | |
| Cash | | $ 10.5 |
| Accounts receivable | | 112.1 |
| Inventories | | 220.6 |
| Prepaid expenses | | 5.5 |
| Total current assets | | 348.7 |
| Investments | | 22.0 |
| Property, plant, and equipment, net | | 486.9 |
| Total assets | | $857.6 |

**Liabilities and Shareholders' Equity**

| | | |
|---|---|---|
| Current liabilities: | | |
| Accounts payable | | $ 83.5 |
| Accrued taxes and interest | | 25.5 |
| Current maturities of long-term debt | | 20.0 |
| Total current liabilities | | 129.0 |
| Long-term liabilities: | | 420.0 |
| Total liabilities | | 549.0 |
| Shareholders' equity: | | |
| Common stock | $100.0 | |
| Retained earnings | 208.6 | |
| Total shareholders' equity | | 308.6 |
| Total liabilities and shareholders' equity | | $857.6 |

**Required:**

Identify the items in the statement that most likely would require further disclosure either on the face of the statement or in a note. Further identify those items that would require disclosure in the significant accounting policies note.

**Real World Case 3–7**

Balance sheet and significant accounting policies disclosure; Walmart

● LO3–2 through LO3–4, LO3–8

Real World Financials

The balance sheet and disclosure of significant accounting policies taken from the 2011 annual report of **Wal-Mart Stores, Inc.**, appear below. Use this information to answer the following questions:

1. What are the asset classifications contained in Walmart's balance sheet?
2. What amounts did Walmart report for the following items for 2011:
   a. Total assets
   b. Current assets
   c. Current liabilities
   d. Total shareholders' equity
   e. Retained earnings
   f. Inventories
3. What is the par value of Walmart's common stock? How many shares of common stock are authorized, issued, and outstanding at the end of 2011?
4. Compute Walmart's current ratio for 2011.
5. Identify the following items:
   a. The company's inventory valuation method.
   b. The definition of cash equivalents.

### WAL-MART STORES, INC.
#### Consolidated Balance Sheets
(Amounts in millions except per share data)

| As of January 31, | 2011 | 2010 As Adjusted |
|---|---|---|
| **Assets** | | |
| Current assets: | | |
| Cash and cash equivalents | $ 7,395 | $ 7,907 |
| Receivables, net | 5,089 | 4,144 |
| Inventories | 36,318 | 32,713 |
| Prepaid expenses and other | 2,960 | 3,128 |
| Current assets of discontinued operations | 131 | 140 |
| Total current assets | 51,893 | 48,032 |
| Property and equipment: | | |
| Land | 24,386 | 22,591 |
| Buildings and improvements | 79,051 | 73,657 |
| Fixtures and equipment | 38,290 | 34,035 |
| Transportation equipment | 2,595 | 2,355 |
| Construction in process | 4,262 | 5,210 |
| Property and equipment | 148,584 | 137,848 |
| Less accumulated depreciation | (43,486) | (38,304) |
| Property and equipment, net | 105,098 | 99,544 |
| Property under leases: | | |
| Property under leases | 5,905 | 5,669 |
| Less accumulated amortization | (3,125) | (2,906) |
| Property under leases, net | 2,780 | 2,763 |
| Goodwill | 16,763 | 16,126 |
| Other assets and deferred charges | 4,129 | 3,942 |
| Total assets | $180,663 | $170,407 |
| **Liabilities and Shareholders' Equity** | | |
| Current liabilities: | | |
| Short-term borrowings | $ 1,031 | $ 523 |
| Accounts payable | 33,557 | 30,451 |
| Accrued liabilities | 18,701 | 18,734 |
| Accrued income taxes | 157 | 1,347 |

(continued)

(concluded)

| | | |
|---|---:|---:|
| Long-term debt due within one year | 4,655 | 4,050 |
| Obligations under capital due within one year | 336 | 346 |
| Current liabilities of discontinued operations | 47 | 92 |
| Total current liabilities | 58,484 | 55,543 |
| Long-term debt | 40,692 | 33,231 |
| Long-term obligations under leases | 3,150 | 3,170 |
| Deferred income taxes and other | 6,682 | 5,508 |
| Redeemable noncontrolling interest | 408 | 307 |
| Commitments and contingencies | | |
| Shareholders' equity: | | |
| Preferred stock ($0.10 par value; 100 shares authorized, none issued) | — | — |
| Common stock ($0.10 par value; 11,000 shares authorized, 3,516 and 3,786 issued and outstanding at January 31, 2011 and 2010, respectively) | 352 | 378 |
| Capital in excess of par value | 3,577 | 3,803 |
| Retained earnings | 63,967 | 66,357 |
| Accumulated other comprehensive income (loss) | 646 | (70) |
| Total Walmart shareholders' equity | 68,542 | 70,468 |
| Noncontrolling interest | 2,705 | 2,180 |
| Total equity | 71,247 | 72,648 |
| Total liabilities and shareholders' equity | $180,663 | $170,407 |

## NOTES TO CONSOLIDATED FINANCIAL STATEMENTS
## WAL-MART STORES, INC.

### 1 Summary of Significant Accounting Policies (in part)

*Cash and Cash Equivalents*
The Company considers investments with a maturity of three months or less when purchased to be cash equivalents.

*Inventories*
The Company values inventories at the lower of cost or market as determined primarily by the retail method of accounting, using the last-in, first-out ("LIFO") method for substantially all of the Walmart U.S. segment's merchandise inventories. Inventories for the Walmart International operations are primarily valued by the retail method of accounting, using the first-in, first-out ("FIFO") method. At January 31, 2011 and 2010, our inventories valued at LIFO approximate those inventories as if they were valued at FIFO.

*Revenue Recognition*
The Company recognizes sales revenue net of sales taxes and estimated sales returns at the time it sells merchandise to the customer. Customer purchases of shopping cards are not recognized as revenue until the card is redeemed and the customer purchases merchandise by using the shopping card. The Company also recognizes revenue from service transactions at the time the service is performed. Generally, revenue from services is classified as a component of net sales on our consolidated statements of income.

**Judgment Case 3–8**
Post fiscal year-end events
● LO3–4

The fiscal year-end for the Northwest Distribution Corporation is December 31. The company's 2013 financial statements were issued on March 15, 2014. The following events occurred between December 31, 2013, and March 15, 2014.

1. On January 22, 2014, the company negotiated a major merger with Blandon Industries. The merger will be completed by the middle of 2014.

2. On February 3, 2014, Northwest negotiated a $10 million long-term note with the Credit Bank of Ohio. The amount of the note is material.

3. On February 25, 2014, a flood destroyed one of the company's manufacturing plants causing $600,000 of uninsured damage.

**Required:**

Determine the appropriate treatment of each of these events in the 2013 financial statements of Northwest Distribution Corporation.

**Research Case 3–9**
FASB codification; locate and extract relevant information and cite authoritative support for a financial reporting issue; related-party disclosures; Enron Corporation

● LO3–4

Real World Financials

**Enron Corporation** was a darling in the energy-provider arena, and in January 2001 its stock price rose above $100 per share. A collapse of investor confidence in 2001 and revelations of accounting irregularities led to one of the largest bankruptcies in U.S. history. By the end of the year, Enron's stock price had plummeted to less than $1 per share. Investigations and lawsuits followed. One problem area concerned transactions with related parties that were not adequately disclosed in the company's financial statements. Critics stated that the lack of information about these transactions made it difficult for analysts following Enron to identify problems the company was experiencing.

**Required:**

1. Obtain the relevant authoritative literature on related-party transactions using the FASB's Codification Research System. You might gain access at the FASB website (**www.fasb.org**). What is the specific citation that outlines the required information on related-party disclosures that must be included in the notes to the financial statements?

2. Describe the disclosures required for related-party transactions.

3. Use EDGAR (**www.sec.gov**) or another method to locate the December 31, 2000, financial statements of Enron. Search for the related-party disclosure. Briefly describe the relationship central to the various transactions described.

4. Why is it important that companies disclose related-party transactions? Use the Enron disclosure of the sale of dark fiber inventory in your answer.

**Real World Case 3–10**
Disclosures; proxy statement; Nordstrom

● LO3–4, LO3–6

Real World Financials

EDGAR, the Electronic Data Gathering, Analysis, and Retrieval system, performs automated collection, validation, indexing, and forwarding of submissions by companies and others who are required by law to file forms with the SEC. All publicly traded domestic companies use EDGAR to make the majority of their filings. (Some foreign companies file voluntarily.) Form 10-K, which includes the annual report, is required to be filed on EDGAR. The SEC makes this information available on the Internet.

**Required:**

1. Access EDGAR on the Internet. The web address is **www.sec.gov**.

2. Search for **Nordstrom, Inc.**, a leading clothing department store chain. Access the 10-K for the fiscal year ended January 29, 2011. Search or scroll to find the disclosure notes and audit report.

3. Answer the following questions:

   a. Describe the subsequent events disclosed by the company.

   b. Which firm is the company's auditor? What type of audit opinion did the auditor render?

4. Access the proxy statement filed with the SEC on March 31, 2011 (the proxy statement designation is Def 14A), locate the executive officers summary compensation table and answer the following questions:

   a. What is the principal position of Michael G. Koppel?

   b. What was the salary paid to Mr. Koppel during the year ended January 29, 2011?

**Judgment Case 3–11**
Debt versus equity

● LO3–7

A common problem facing any business entity is the debt versus equity decision. When funds are required to obtain assets, should debt or equity financing be used? This decision also is faced when a company is initially formed. What will be the mix of debt versus equity in the initial capital structure? The characteristics of debt are very different from those of equity as are the financial implications of using one method of financing as opposed to the other.

Cherokee Plastics Corporation is formed by a group of investors to manufacture household plastic products. Their initial capitalization goal is $50,000,000. That is, the incorporators have decided to raise $50,000,000 to acquire the initial assets of the company. They have narrowed down the financing mix alternatives to two:

1. All equity financing.

2. $20,000,000 in debt financing and $30,000,000 in equity financing.

No matter which financing alternative is chosen, the corporation expects to be able to generate a 10% annual return, before payment of interest and income taxes, on the $50,000,000 in assets acquired. The interest rate on debt would be 8%. The effective income tax rate will be approximately 50%.

Alternative 2 will require specified interest and principal payments to be made to the creditors at specific dates. The interest portion of these payments (interest expense) will reduce the taxable income of the corporation and hence the amount of income tax the corporation will pay. The all-equity alternative requires no specified payments to be made to suppliers of capital. The corporation is not legally liable to make distributions to its owners. If the board of directors does decide to make a distribution, it is not an expense of the corporation and does not reduce taxable income and hence the taxes the corporation pays.

**Required:**

1. Prepare abbreviated income statements that compare first-year profitability for each of the two alternatives.

2. Which alternative would be expected to achieve the highest first-year profits? Why?

3. Which alternative would provide the highest rate of return on shareholders' equity? Why?

4. What other related implications of the decision should be considered?

**Analysis Case 3–12**
Obtain and critically evaluate an actual annual report

● LO3–4, LO3–6 through LO3–8

Real World Financials

Financial reports are the primary means by which corporations report their performance and financial condition. Financial statements are one component of the annual report mailed to their shareholders and to interested others.

**Required:**

Obtain an annual report from a corporation with which you are familiar. Using techniques you learned in this chapter and any analysis you consider useful, respond to the following questions:

1. Do the firm's auditors provide a clean opinion on the financial statements?

2. Has the company made changes in any accounting methods it uses?

3. Have there been any subsequent events, errors and irregularities, illegal acts, or related-party transactions that have a material effect on the company's financial position?

4. What are two trends in the company's operations or capital resources that management considers significant to the company's future?

5. Is the company engaged in more than one significant line of business? If so, compare the relative profitability of the different segments.

6. How stable are the company's operations?

7. Has the company's situation deteriorated or improved with respect to liquidity, solvency, asset management, and profitability?

**Note:** You can obtain a copy of an annual report from a local company, from a friend who is a shareholder, from the investor relations department of the corporation, from a friendly stockbroker, or from EDGAR (Electronic Data Gathering, Analysis, and Retrieval) on the Internet (www.sec.gov).

**Analysis Case 3–13**
Obtain and compare annual reports from companies in the same industry

● LO3–4, LO3–7, LO3–8

Real World Financials

Insight concerning the performance and financial condition of a company often comes from evaluating its financial data in comparison with other firms in the same industry.

**Required:**

Obtain annual reports from three corporations in the same primary industry. Using techniques you learned in this chapter and any analysis you consider useful, respond to the following questions:

1. Are there differences in accounting methods that should be taken into account when making comparisons?

2. How do earnings trends compare in terms of both the direction and stability of income?

3. Which of the three firms had the greatest earnings relative to resources available?

4. Which corporation has made most effective use of financial leverage?

5. Of the three firms, which seems riskiest in terms of its ability to pay short-term obligations? Long-term obligations?

**Note:** You can obtain copies of annual reports from friends who are shareholders, from the investor relations department of the corporations, from a friendly stockbroker, or from EDGAR (Electronic Data Gathering, Analysis, and Retrieval) on the Internet (www.sec.gov).

**Analysis Case 3–14**
Balance sheet information

● LO3–2 through LO3–4

Refer to the financial statements and related disclosure notes of **Dell Inc.** in Appendix B located at the back of the text.

**Required:**

1. What categories does the company use to classify its assets? Its liabilities?

2. Why are investments shown as a current asset?

3. Explain the current liability "deferred services revenue."

4. What purpose do the disclosure notes serve?

5. What method does the company use to depreciate its property and equipment?

6. Does the company report any subsequent events or related party transactions in its disclosure notes?

**Analysis Case 3–15**
Segment reporting concepts

● Appendix 3 LO3–9

IFRS

Levens Co. operates in several distinct business segments. The company does not have any reportable foreign operations or major customers.

**Required:**

1. What is the purpose of operating segment disclosures?

2. Define an operating segment.

3. List the amounts to be reported by operating segment.

4. How would your answer to requirement 3 differ if Levens Co. prepares its segment disclosure according to International Financial Reporting Standards?

**Ethics Case 3–16**
Segment
reporting
● Appendix 3

You are in your third year as an accountant with McCarver-Lynn Industries, a multidivisional company involved in the manufacturing, marketing, and sales of surgical prosthetic devices. After the fiscal year-end, you are working with the controller of the firm to prepare supplemental business segment disclosures. Yesterday you presented her with the following summary information:

| | | | | | | ($ in millions) |
|---|---|---|---|---|---|---|
| | **Domestic** | **Union of South Africa** | **Egypt** | **France** | **Denmark** | **Total** |
| Revenues | $ 845 | $222 | $265 | $343 | $311 | $1,986 |
| Capital expenditures | 145 | 76 | 88 | 21 | 42 | 372 |
| Assets | 1,005 | 301 | 290 | 38 | 285 | 1,919 |

Upon returning to your office after lunch, you find the following memo:

*Nice work. Let's combine the data this way:*

| | | | | ($ in millions) |
|---|---|---|---|---|
| | **Domestic** | **Africa** | **Europe** | **Total** |
| Revenues | $ 845 | $487 | $654 | $1,986 |
| Capital expenditures | 145 | 164 | 63 | 372 |
| Assets | 1,005 | 591 | 323 | 1,919 |

*Some of our shareholders might react unfavorably to our recent focus on South African operations.*

**Required:**

Do you perceive an ethical dilemma? What would be the likely impact of following the controller's suggestions? Who would benefit? Who would be injured?

# Air France–KLM Case

 AIRFRANCE ✈

● LO3–9

🌐 IFRS

Air France–KLM (AF), a French company, prepares its financial statements according to International Financial Reporting Standards. AF's annual report for the year ended March 31, 2011, which includes financial statements and disclosure notes, is provided with all new textbooks. This material also is included in AF's "Registration Document 2010–11," dated June 15, 2011 and is available at **www.airfranceklm.com.**

**Required:**

Describe the apparent differences in the order of presentation of the components of the balance sheet between IFRS as applied by Air France–KLM (AF) and a typical balance sheet prepared in accordance with U.S. GAAP.

# The Income Statement, Comprehensive Income, and the Statement of Cash Flows

The purpose of the income statement is to summarize the profit-generating activities that occurred during a particular reporting period. Comprehensive income includes net income as well as a few gains and losses that are not part of net income and are considered other comprehensive income items instead.

The purpose of the statement of cash flows is to provide information about the cash receipts and cash disbursements of an enterprise that occurred during the period.

This chapter has a twofold purpose: (1) to consider important issues dealing with the content, presentation, and disclosure of net income and other components of comprehensive income and (2) to provide an *overview* of the statement of cash flows, which is covered in depth in Chapter 21.

**After studying this chapter, you should be able to:**

- **LO4–1** Discuss the importance of income from continuing operations and describe its components. (*p. 172*)
- **LO4–2** Describe earnings quality and how it is impacted by management practices to manipulate earnings. (*p. 177*)
- **LO4–3** Discuss the components of operating and nonoperating income and their relationship to earnings quality. (*p. 178*)
- **LO4–4** Define what constitutes discontinued operations and describe the appropriate income statement presentation for these transactions. (*p. 184*)
- **LO4–5** Define extraordinary items and describe the appropriate income statement presentation for these transactions. (*p. 188*)
- **LO4–6** Define earnings per share (EPS) and explain required disclosures of EPS for certain income statement components. (*p. 192*)
- **LO4–7** Explain the difference between net income and comprehensive income and how we report components of the difference. (*p. 192*)
- **LO4–8** Describe the purpose of the statement of cash flows. (*p. 198*)
- **LO4–9** Identify and describe the various classifications of cash flows presented in a statement of cash flows. (*p. 198*)
- **LO4–10** Discuss the primary differences between U.S. GAAP and IFRS with respect to the income statement, statement of comprehensive income, and statement of cash flows. (*pp. 177, 184, 189, 194, 199, and 204*)

# FINANCIAL REPORTING CASE

## Alberto-Culver Company

Your friend, Becky Morgan, just received a generous gift from her grandfather. Accompanying a warm letter were 200 shares of stock of the **Alberto-Culver Company**, a global manufacturer of beauty and health care products, along with the most recent quarterly financial statements of the company. Becky knows that you are an accounting major and pleads with you to explain some items in the company's income statement. "I remember studying the income statement in my introductory accounting course," says Becky, "but I am still confused. What is this item *discontinued operations?* How about *restructuring costs?* These don't sound good. Are they something I should worry about? We studied earnings per share briefly, but what does *diluted earnings per share* mean?" You agree to try to help.

### ALBERTO-CULVER COMPANY & SUBSIDIARIES
### Income Statements
### Year Ended September 30
($ in thousands, except per share data)

|  | 2010 | 2009 |
|---|---|---|
| Sales | $1,597,233 | $1,433,980 |
| Cost of products sold | 762,557 | 698,778 |
| Gross profit | 834,676 | 735,202 |
| Marketing, selling and administrative expenses | 609,407 | 545,261 |
| Restructuring costs | 5,101 | 6,776 |
| Operating income | 220,168 | 183,165 |
| Interest expense (income) net | 2,324 | (2,673) |
| Income from continuing operations before income taxes | 217,844 | 185,838 |
| Provision for income taxes | 62,708 | 68,005 |
| Income from continuing operations | 155,136 | 117,833 |
| Income from discontinued operations, net of income taxes | 174 | 1,541 |
| Net income | $ 155,310 | $ 119,374 |
| Basic earnings per share: |  |  |
|    Continuing operations | $    1.58 | $    1.21 |
|    Discontinued operations | .01 | .01 |
|    Net income | $    1.59 | $    1.22 |
| Diluted earnings per share: |  |  |
|    Continuing operations | $    1.55 | $    1.19 |
|    Discontinued operations | .01 | .01 |
|    Net income | $    1.56 | $    1.20 |

**By the time you finish this chapter, you should be able to respond appropriately to the questions posed in this case. Compare your response to the solution provided at the end of the chapter.**

**QUESTIONS**

1. How would you explain restructuring costs to Becky? Are restructuring costs something Becky should worry about? (p. 179)

2. Explain to Becky what is meant by discontinued operations and describe to her how that item is reported in an income statement. (p. 184)

**3.** In addition to discontinued operations, what other events sometimes are reported separately in the income statement that you might tell Becky about? Why are these items reported separately? (*p. 188*)

**4.** Describe to Becky the difference between basic and diluted earnings per share. (*p. 192*)

In Chapter 1 we discussed the critical role of financial accounting information in allocating resources within our economy. Ideally, resources should be allocated to private enterprises that will (1) provide the goods and services our society desires and (2) at the same time provide a fair rate of return to those who supply the resources. A company will be able to achieve these goals only if it can use the resources society provides to generate revenues from selling products and services that exceed the expenses necessary to provide those products and services (that is, generate a profit).

> The income statement displays a company's operating performance, that is, its net profit or loss, during the reporting period.

The purpose of the **income statement**, sometimes called the **statement of operations** or **statement of earnings**, is to summarize the profit-generating activities that occurred during a particular reporting period. Many investors and creditors perceive it as the statement most useful for predicting future profitability (future cash-generating ability).

A few types of gains and losses are excluded from the determination of net income and the income statement but are included in the broader concept of **comprehensive income**. We refer to these as items of **other comprehensive income (OCI) or loss**. Comprehensive income can be reported in one of two ways: (1) in a single, continuous **statement of comprehensive income** or (2) in two separate but consecutive statements—an income statement and a statement of comprehensive income that begins with net income and then reports OCI items to combine for comprehensive income.

The purpose of the **statement of cash flows** is to provide information about the cash receipts and cash disbursements of an enterprise that occurred during a period. In describing cash flows, the statement provides valuable information about the operating, investing, and financing activities that occurred during the period.

> The *income statement* and *statement of cash flows* report changes that occurred during a particular reporting period.

Unlike the balance sheet, which is a position statement, the income statement and the statement of cash flows are *change* statements. The income statement reports the changes in shareholders' equity (retained earnings) that occurred during the reporting period as a result of revenues, expenses, gains, and losses. The statement of cash flows also is a change statement, disclosing the events that caused cash to change during the period.

This chapter is divided into two parts. The first part describes the content and presentation of the income statement and comprehensive income as well as related disclosure issues. The second part provides an overview of the statement of cash flows.

## PART A    THE INCOME STATEMENT AND COMPREHENSIVE INCOME

Before we discuss the specific components of an income statement in much depth, let's take a quick look at the general makeup of the statement. Illustration 4–1 offers a statement for a hypothetical manufacturing company that you can refer to as we proceed through the chapter. At this point, our objective is only to gain a general perspective on the items reported and classifications contained in corporate income statements.

Let's first look closer at the components of net income. At the end of this part, we'll see how net income fits within the concept of comprehensive income and how comprehensive income is reported.

● LO4–1

## Income from Continuing Operations

> Income from continuing operations includes the revenues, expenses, gains and losses that will probably continue in future periods.

The need to provide information to help analysts predict future cash flows emphasizes the importance of properly reporting the amount of income from the entity's continuing operations. Clearly, it is the operating transactions that probably will continue into the future that are the best predictors of future cash flows. The components of **income from continuing operations** are revenues, expenses (including income taxes), gains, and losses, excluding those related to discontinued operations and extraordinary items.[1]

---

[1]These two separately reported items are addressed in a subsequent section.

**Illustration 4–1**
Income Statement

**Income Statements**
(In millions, except earnings per share)

| | | Years Ended June 30 | |
|---|---|---|---|
| | | **2013** | **2012** |
| Income from Continuing Operations | Sales revenue | $1,450.6 | $1,380.0 |
| | Cost of goods sold | 832.6 | 800.4 |
| | Gross profit | 618.0 | 579.6 |
| | Operating expenses: | | |
| | Selling | 123.5 | 110.5 |
| | General and administrative | 147.8 | 139.1 |
| | Research and development | 55.0 | 65.0 |
| | Restructuring costs | 125.0 | — |
| | Total operating expenses | 451.3 | 314.6 |
| | Operating income | 166.7 | 265.0 |
| | Other income (expense): | | |
| | Interest income | 12.4 | 11.1 |
| | Interest expense | (25.9) | (24.8) |
| | Gain on sale of investments | 18.0 | 19.0 |
| | Income from continuing operations before income taxes and extraordinary item | 171.2 | 270.3 |
| | Income tax expense | 59.9 | 94.6 |
| | Income from continuing operations before extraordinary item | 111.3 | 175.7 |
| Separately Reported Items | Discontinued operations: | | |
| | Loss from operations of discontinued component (including gain on disposal in 2013 of $47) | (7.6) | (45.7) |
| | Income tax benefit | 2.0 | 13.0 |
| | Loss on discontinued operations | (5.6) | (32.7) |
| | Income before extraordinary item | 105.7 | 143.0 |
| | Extraordinary gain, net of $11 in income tax expense | — | 22.0 |
| | Net income | $ 105.7 | $ 165.0 |
| Earnings per Share | **Earnings per common share—basic:** | | |
| | Income from continuing operations before extraordinary item | $ 2.14 | $ 3.38 |
| | Discontinued operations | (.11) | (.62) |
| | Extraordinary gain | — | .42 |
| | Net income | $ 2.03 | $ 3.18 |
| | **Earnings per common share—diluted:** | | |
| | Income from continuing operations before extraordinary item | $ 2.06 | $ 3.25 |
| | Discontinued operations | (.11) | (.62) |
| | Extraordinary gain | — | .42 |
| | Net income | $ 1.95 | $ 3.05 |

## Revenues, Expenses, Gains, and Losses

Revenues are inflows of resources resulting from providing goods or services to customers. For merchandising companies like **Walmart**, the main source of revenue is sales revenue derived from selling merchandise. Service firms such as **FedEx** and **State Farm Insurance** generate revenue by providing services.

Expenses are outflows of resources incurred while generating revenue. They represent the costs of providing goods and services. The *matching principle* is a key player in the way we measure expenses. We attempt to establish a causal relationship between revenues and expenses. If causality can be determined, expenses are reported in the same period that the related revenue is recognized. If a causal relationship cannot be established, we relate the expense to a particular period, allocate it over several periods, or expense it as incurred.

Gains and losses are increases or decreases in equity from peripheral or incidental transactions of an entity. In general, these gains and losses result from changes in equity that do not result directly from operations but nonetheless are related to those activities. For example, gains and losses from the routine sale of equipment, buildings, or other operating assets and from the sale of investment assets normally would be included in income from continuing operations. Later in the chapter we discuss certain gains and losses that are excluded from continuing operations.

## Income Tax Expense

*Income tax expense* is shown as a separate expense in the income statement.

Income taxes represent a major expense to a corporation, and accordingly, income tax expense is given special treatment in the income statement. Income taxes are levied on taxpayers in proportion to the amount of taxable income that is reported to taxing authorities. Like individuals, corporations are income-tax-paying entities.[2] Because of the importance and size of income tax expense (sometimes called *provision for income taxes*), it always is reported as a separate expense in corporate income statements.

Federal, state, and sometimes local taxes are assessed annually and usually are determined by first applying a designated percentage (or percentages), the tax rate (or rates), to taxable income. Taxable income comprises revenues, expenses, gains, and losses as measured according to the regulations of the appropriate taxing authority.

While the actual measurement of income tax expense can be complex, at this point we can consider income tax expense to be a simple percentage of income before taxes.

Many of the components of taxable income and income reported in the income statement coincide. But sometimes tax rules and GAAP differ with respect to when and even whether a particular revenue or expense is included in income. When tax rules and GAAP differ regarding the timing of revenue or expense recognition, the actual payment of taxes may occur in a period different from when income tax expense is reported in the income statement. A common example is when a corporation takes advantage of tax laws by legally deducting more depreciation in the early years of an asset's life on its federal income tax return than it reports in its income statement. The amount of tax actually paid in the early years is less than the amount that is found by applying the tax rate to the reported GAAP income before taxes. We discuss this and other issues related to accounting for income taxes in Chapter 16. At this point, consider income tax expense to be simply a percentage of income before taxes.

## Operating versus Nonoperating Income

A distinction often is made between *operating* and *nonoperating* income.

Many corporate income statements distinguish between operating income and nonoperating income. Operating income includes revenues and expenses directly related to the primary revenue-generating activities of the company. For example, operating income for a manufacturing company includes sales revenues from selling the products it manufactures as well as all expenses related to this activity. Similarly, operating income might also include gains and losses from selling equipment and other assets used in the manufacturing process.[3]

Nonoperating income relates to peripheral or incidental activities of the company. For example, a manufacturer would include interest and dividend revenue, gains and losses from selling investments, and interest expense in nonoperating income. *Other income (expense)* often is the classification heading companies use in the income statement for nonoperating items. On the other hand, a financial institution like a bank would consider those items to be a part of operating income because they relate to the principal revenue-generating activities for that type of business.

---

[2] Partnerships are not tax-paying entities. Their taxable income or loss is included in the taxable income of the individual partners.
[3] FASB ASC 360–10–45–5: Property, plant, and equipment—Overall—Other Presentation Matters (previously "Accounting for the Impairment of Long-Lived Assets and for Long-Lived Assets to Be Disposed Of," *Statement of Financial Accounting Standards No. 144* (Norwalk, Conn.: FASB, 2001)).

Illustration 4–2 presents the 2011, 2010, and 2009 income statements for **Dell Inc.** Notice that Dell distinguishes between operating income and nonoperating income (labeled Interest and other, net). Nonoperating revenues, expenses, gains and losses, and income tax expense (called Income tax provision) are added to or subtracted from operating income to arrive at net income. As Dell has no separately reported items, *income from continuing operations equals net income.*[4]

**Consolidated Statements of Income**

(In millions, except per share amounts)

| | Fiscal Year Ended | | |
|---|---|---|---|
| | January 28, 2011 | January 29, 2010 | January 30, 2009 |
| Net revenue: | | | |
| Products | $50,002 | $43,697 | $52,337 |
| Services, including software related | 11,492 | 9,205 | 8,764 |
| Total net revenue | 61,494 | 52,902 | 61,101 |
| Cost of net revenue: | | | |
| Products | 42,068 | 37,534 | 44,670 |
| Services, including software related | 8,030 | 6,107 | 5,474 |
| Total cost of net revenue | 50,098 | 43,641 | 50,144 |
| Gross margin | 11,396 | 9,261 | 10,957 |
| Operating expenses: | | | |
| Selling, general, and administrative | 7,302 | 6,465 | 7,102 |
| Research, development, and engineering | 661 | 624 | 665 |
| Total operating expenses | 7,963 | 7,089 | 7,767 |
| Operating income | 3,433 | 2,172 | 3,190 |
| Interest and other, net | (83) | (148) | 134 |
| Income before income taxes | 3,350 | 2,024 | 3,324 |
| Income tax provision | 715 | 591 | 846 |
| Net income | $ 2,635 | $ 1,433 | $ 2,478 |
| Earnings per common share: | | | |
| Basic | $ 1.36 | $ .73 | $ 1.25 |
| Diluted | $ 1.35 | $ .73 | $ 1.25 |

**Illustration 4–2**

Income Statement— Dell Inc.

Real World Financials

Now let's consider the formats used to report the components of net income.

## Income Statement Formats

No specific standards dictate how income from continuing operations must be displayed, so companies have considerable latitude in how they present the components of income from continuing operations. This flexibility has resulted in a variety of income statement presentations. However, we can identify two general approaches, the single-step and the multiple-step formats, that might be considered the two extremes, with the income statements of most companies falling somewhere in between.

The single-step format first lists all the revenues and gains included in income from continuing operations. Then, expenses and losses are grouped, subtotaled, and subtracted—in a single step—from revenues and gains to derive income from continuing operations. In a departure from that, though, companies usually report income tax expense as a separate last item in the statement. Operating and nonoperating items are not separately classified. Illustration 4–3 shows an example of a single-step income statement for a hypothetical manufacturing company, Maxwell Gear Corporation.

A *single-step* income statement format groups all revenues and gains together and all expenses and losses together.

___
[4]In a later section we discuss items that are reported separately from continuing operations.

**Illustration 4–3**

Single-Step Income
Statement

**MAXWELL GEAR CORPORATION**
**Income Statement**
**For the Year Ended December 31, 2013**

| | | |
|---|---:|---:|
| Revenues and gains: | | |
| Sales | | $573,522 |
| Interest and dividends | | 26,400 |
| Gain on sale of investments | | 5,500 |
| Total revenues and gains | | 605,422 |
| Expenses and losses: | | |
| Cost of goods sold | $302,371 | |
| Selling | 47,341 | |
| General and administrative | 24,888 | |
| Research and development | 16,300 | |
| Interest | 14,522 | |
| Total expenses and losses | | 405,422 |
| Income before income taxes | | 200,000 |
| Income tax expense | | 80,000 |
| Net income | | $120,000 |

A *multiple-step* income statement format includes a number of intermediate subtotals before arriving at income from continuing operations.

The **multiple-step** format reports a series of intermediate subtotals such as gross profit, operating income, and income before taxes. The overview income statements presented in Illustration 4–1 and the **Dell Inc.** income statements in Illustration 4–2 are variations of the multiple-step format. Illustration 4–4 presents a multiple-step income statement for the Maxwell Gear Corporation.

**Illustration 4–4**

Multiple-Step Income
Statement

**MAXWELL GEAR CORPORATION**
**Income Statement**
**For the Year Ended December 31, 2013**

| | | |
|---|---:|---:|
| Sales revenue | | $573,522 |
| Cost of goods sold | | 302,371 |
| Gross profit | | 271,151 |
| Operating expenses: | | |
| Selling | $47,341 | |
| General and administrative | 24,888 | |
| Research and development | 16,300 | |
| Total operating expenses | | 88,529 |
| Operating income | | 182,622 |
| Other income (expense): | | |
| Interest and dividend revenue | 26,400 | |
| Gain on sale of investments | 5,500 | |
| Interest expense | (14,522) | |
| Total other income, net | | 17,378 |
| Income before income taxes | | 200,000 |
| Income tax expense | | 80,000 |
| Net income | | $120,000 |

An advantage of the single-step format is its simplicity. Revenues and expenses are not classified or prioritized. A primary advantage of the multiple-step format is that, by separately classifying operating and nonoperating items, it provides information that might be useful in analyzing trends. Similarly, the classification of expenses by function also provides useful information. For example, reporting gross profit for merchandising companies highlights the important relationship between sales revenue and cost of goods sold. It is important to note that this issue is one of presentation. The bottom line, net income, is the same regardless of the format used. A recent survey of income statements of 500 large public companies indicates that the multiple-step format is used more than five times as often as the single-step format[5] We use the multiple-step format for illustration purposes throughout the remainder of this chapter.

# International Financial Reporting Standards

● LO4–10

**Income Statement Presentation.** There are more similarities than differences between income statements prepared according to U.S. GAAP and those prepared applying international standards. Some of the differences are:

- International standards require certain minimum information to be reported on the face of the income statement. U.S. GAAP has no minimum requirements.

- International standards allow expenses to be classified either by function (e.g., cost of goods sold, general and administrative, etc.), or by natural description (e.g., salaries, rent, etc.). SEC regulations require that expenses be classified by function.

- In the United States, the "bottom line" of the income statement usually is called either *net income* or *net loss*. The descriptive term for the bottom line of the income statement prepared according to international standards is either *profit* or *loss*.

- As we discuss later in the chapter, we report "extraordinary items" separately in an income statement prepared according to U.S. GAAP. International standards prohibit reporting "extraordinary items."

Before we investigate separately reported items, let's take a closer look at the components of both operating and nonoperating income and their relationship to earnings quality.

# Earnings Quality

● LO4–2

Financial analysts are concerned with more than just the bottom line of the income statement—net income. The presentation of the components of net income and the related supplemental disclosures provide clues to the user of the statement in an assessment of *earnings quality*. Earnings quality is used as a framework for more in-depth discussions of operating and nonoperating income.

The term **earnings quality** refers to the ability of reported earnings (income) to predict a company's future earnings. After all, an income statement simply reports on events that already have occurred. The relevance of any historical-based financial statement hinges on its predictive value. To enhance predictive value, analysts try to separate a company's *transitory earnings* effects from its *permanent earnings*. Transitory earnings effects result from transactions or events that are not likely to occur again in the foreseeable future or that are likely to have a different impact on earnings in the future. Later in the chapter we address two items that, because of their transitory nature, are required to be reported separately at the bottom of the income statement. Analysts begin their assessment of permanent earnings with income before these two items, that is, income from continuing operations.

It would be a mistake, though, to assume income from continuing operations reflects permanent earnings entirely. In other words, there may be transitory earnings effects included in income from continuing operations. In a sense, the phrase *continuing* may be misleading.

> Earnings quality refers to the ability of reported earnings (income) to predict a company's future earnings.

## Manipulating Income and Income Smoothing

An often-debated contention is that, within GAAP, managers have the power, to a limited degree, to manipulate reported company income. And the manipulation is not always in the

[5]*Accounting Trends and Techniques—2011* (New York: AICPA, 2011), p. 305.

direction of higher income. One author states that "Most executives prefer to report earnings that follow a smooth, regular, upward path. They hate to report declines, but they also want to avoid increases that vary wildly from year to year; it's better to have two years of 15% earnings increases than a 30% gain one year and none the next. As a result, some companies 'bank' earnings by understating them in particularly good years and use the banked profits to polish results in bad years."[6]

Many believe that corporate earnings management practices reduce the quality of reported earnings.

**Arthur Levitt, Jr.**
While the problem of earnings management is not new, it has swelled in a market that is unforgiving of companies that miss their estimates. I recently read of one major U.S. company that failed to meet its so-called numbers by one penny and lost more than six percent of its stock value in one day.[7]

Many believe that manipulating income reduces earnings quality because it can mask permanent earnings. A 1998 *BusinessWeek* issue was devoted entirely to the topic of earnings management. The issue, entitled "Corporate Earnings: Who Can You Trust," contains articles that are highly critical of corporate America's earnings manipulation practices. Arthur Levitt, Jr., former Chairman of the Securities and Exchange Commission, has been outspoken in his criticism of corporate earnings management practices and their effect on earnings quality. In an article appearing in the *CPA Journal*, he states,

Increasingly, I have become concerned that the motivation to meet Wall Street earnings expectations may be overriding commonsense business practices. Too many corporate managers, auditors, and analysts are participants in a game of nods and winks. In the zeal to satisfy consensus earnings estimates and project a smooth earnings path, wishful thinking may be winning the day over faithful representation. As a result, I fear that we are witnessing an erosion in the *quality of earnings,* and therefore, the quality of financial reporting. Managing may be giving way to manipulation; integrity may be losing out to illusion. (emphasis added)[8]

How do managers manipulate income? Two major methods are (1) income shifting and (2) income statement classification. Income shifting is achieved by accelerating or delaying the recognition of revenues or expenses. For example, a practice called "channel stuffing" accelerates revenue recognition by persuading distributors to purchase more of your product than necessary near the end of a reporting period. The most common income statement classification manipulation involves the inclusion of recurring operating expenses in "special charge" categories such as restructuring costs (discussed below). This practice sometimes is referred to as "big bath" accounting, a reference to cleaning up company balance sheets. Asset reductions, or the incurrence of liabilities, for these restructuring costs result in large reductions in income that might otherwise appear as normal operating expenses either in the current or future years.

Mr. Levitt called for changes by standard setters to improve the transparency of financial statements. He did not want to eliminate necessary flexibility in financial reporting, but wanted to make it easier for financial statement users to "see through the numbers" to the future. A key to a meaningful assessment of a company's future profitability is to understand the events reported in the income statement and their relationship with future earnings. Let's now revisit the components of operating income.

## Operating Income and Earnings Quality

● LO4–3  Should all items of revenue and expense included in operating income be considered indicative of a company's permanent earnings? No, not necessarily. Sometimes, for example, operating expenses include some unusual items that may or may not continue in the future. Look closely at the 2010 and 2009 partial income statements of **JDS Uniphase Corporation**, a leading provider of optical products for telecommunications service providers, presented in Illustration 4–5. What items appear unusual? Certainly "Impairment of goodwill," "Impairment of long-lived assets" and "Restructuring costs" require further investigation. We discuss restructuring costs first.

---

[6]Ford S. Worthy, "Manipulating Profits: How It's Done," *Fortune,* June 25, 1984, p. 50.
[7]Arthur Levitt, Jr., "The Numbers Game," *The CPA Journal,* December 1998, p. 16.
[8]Ibid., p. 14.

**Income Statements (in part)**

($ in millions)

| | Years Ended | |
|---|---|---|
| | July 3, 2010 | June 27, 2009 |
| Net revenue | $1,363.9 | $1,283.3 |
| Cost of sales | 816.8 | 796.7 |
| Gross profit | 547.1 | 486.6 |
| Operating expenses: | | |
| Research and development | 174.9 | 167.1 |
| Selling, general and administrative | 380.9 | 399.0 |
| Amortization of intangibles | 27.8 | 27.0 |
| Impairment of goodwill | — | 741.7 |
| Impairment of long-lived assets | — | 13.2 |
| Restructuring costs | 17.7 | 38.5 |
| Total operating expenses | 601.3 | 1,386.5 |
| Operating loss | (54.2) | (899.9) |

**Illustration 4–5**

Partial Income Statement— JDS Uniphase Corporation

Real World Financials

**RESTRUCTURING COSTS.** It's not unusual for a company to reorganize its operations to attain greater efficiency. When this happens, the company often incurs significant associated restructuring costs. Facility closings and related employee layoffs translate into costs incurred for severance pay and relocation costs. Restructuring costs are incurred in connection with:

A program that is planned and controlled by management, and materially changes either the scope of a business undertaken by an entity, or the manner in which that business is conducted.[9]

Restructuring costs appear frequently in corporate income statements. In fact, a recent survey reports that in 2010, of the 500 companies surveyed, 41% included restructuring costs in their income statements.[10] For instance, consider again our JDS Uniphase Corporation example. A disclosure note accompanying the company's financial statements indicates workforce reductions as well as manufacturing transfer costs resulting from plant closures and consolidation of operations. Illustration 4–6 reports a portion of the disclosure note related to the restructuring costs.

**FINANCIAL Reporting Case**

Q1, p. 171

*Restructuring costs* include costs associated with shutdown or relocation of facilities or downsizing of operations.

**Restructuring Costs (in part)**
During fiscal 2010, the Company reported $17.7 million in restructuring related charges. The charges were primarily a result of (i) $7.1 million for severance and benefits primarily in the Communications Test and measurement segment . . .; (ii) $8.5 million for manufacturing transfer costs primarily in the Communications and Commercial Optical Products segments, which were the result of a production site closure in California, the consolidation of Lasers manufacturing operations at a contract manufacturer in Asia, the transfer of certain production processes into existing sites in California, and the reduction in force of the Company's manufacturing support organization across all sites.

**Illustration 4–6**

Disclosure of Restructuring Costs— JDS Uniphase Corporation

Real World Financials

Restructuring costs are recognized in the period the exit or disposal cost obligation actually is incurred. As an example, suppose terminated employees are to receive termination benefits, but only after they remain with the employer beyond a minimum retention

GAAP requires that restructuring costs be recognized only in the period incurred.

[9]FASB ASC 420–10–20: Exit or Disposal Cost Obligations—Overall—Glossary (previously "Accounting for Costs Associated with Exit or Disposal Activities," *Statement of Financial Accounting Standards No. 146* (Norwalk, Conn.: FASB, 2002)).
[10]*Accounting Trends and Techniques—2011* (New York: AICPA, 2011), p. 326.

period. In that case, a liability for termination benefits, and corresponding expense, should be accrued in the period(s) the employees render their service. On the other hand, if future service beyond a minimum retention period is not required, the liability and corresponding expense for benefits are recognized at the time the company communicates the arrangement to employees. In both cases, the liability and expense are recorded at the point they are deemed incurred. Similarly, costs associated with closing facilities and relocating employees are recognized when goods or services associated with those activities are received.

**Fair value is the objective for the initial measurement of a liability associated with restructuring costs.**

GAAP also establishes that fair value is the objective for initial measurement of the liability, and that a liability's fair value often will be measured by determining the present value of future estimated cash outflows. We discuss such present value calculations at length in later chapters, particularly in Chapters 6 and 14. Because some restructuring costs require estimation, actual costs could differ. Also, the costs might not occur until a subsequent reporting period. As we discuss later in this chapter and throughout the text, when an estimate is changed, the company should record the effect of the change in the period the estimate is changed rather than by restating prior years' financial statements to correct the estimate. On occasion, this process has resulted in a negative expense amount for restructuring costs due to the overestimation of costs in a prior reporting period.

**Should restructuring costs be considered part of a company's permanent earnings stream?**

Now that we understand the nature of restructuring costs, we can address the important question: Should investors attempting to forecast future earnings consider these costs to be part of a company's permanent earnings stream, or are they transitory in nature? There is no easy answer. For example, JDS Uniphase incurred restructuring costs in both 2010 and 2009. Will the company incur these costs again in the near future? Consider the following facts. During the 10-year period from 2001 through 2010, the Dow Jones Industrial 30 companies reported 114 restructuring charges in their collective income statements. That's an average of 3.8 per company. But the average is deceiving. Five of the 30 companies reported no restructuring charges during that period, while three of the 30 companies reported restructuring charges in each of the 10 years. The inference: an analyst must interpret restructuring charges in light of a company's past history. In general, the more frequently these sorts of unusual charges occur, the more appropriate it is that analysts include them in the company's permanent earnings stream. Information in disclosure notes describing the restructuring and management plans related to the business involved also can be helpful.

> **Arthur Levitt, Jr.**
> When a company decides to restructure, management and employees, investors and creditors, customers and suppliers all want to understand the expected effects. We need, of course, to ensure that financial reporting provides this information. But this should not lead to flushing all the associated costs—and maybe a little extra—through the financial statements.[11]

Two other expenses in JDS Uniphase's income statements that warrant additional scrutiny are *impairment of goodwill* and *impairment of long-lived assets*. These expenses involve what is referred to as asset impairment losses or charges. Any long-lived asset, whether tangible or intangible, should have its balance reduced if there has been a significant impairment of value. We explore property, plant, and equipment and intangible assets in Chapters 10 and 11. After discussing this topic in more depth in those chapters, we revisit the concept of earnings quality as it relates to asset impairment.

Is it possible that financial analysts might look favorably at a company in the year it incurs a substantial restructuring charge or other unusual expense such as an asset impairment loss? Perhaps so, if they view management as creating higher profits in future years through operating efficiencies. Would analysts then reward that company again in future years when those operating efficiencies materialize? Certainly this double halo effect might provide an attractive temptation to the management of some companies.

**Unusual or infrequent items included in operating income require investigation to determine their permanent or transitory nature.**

These aren't the only components of operating expenses that call into question this issue of earnings quality. For example, in Chapter 9 we discuss the write-down of inventory to comply with the lower-of-cost-or-market rule. Earnings quality also is influenced by the way a company records income from investments (Chapter 12) and accounts for its pension plans (Chapter 17).

---

[11] Arthur Levitt, Jr. "The Numbers Game," *The CPA Journal*, December 1998, p. 16.

Earnings quality is affected by revenue issues as well. As an example, suppose that toward the end of its fiscal year, a company loses a major customer that can't be replaced. That would mean the current year's revenue numbers include a transitory component equal to the revenue generated from sales to the lost customer. Of course, in addition to its effect on revenues, losing the customer would have implications for the transitory/permanent nature of expenses and net income.

Another revenue issue affecting earnings quality is the timing of revenue recognition. Companies face continual pressure to meet their earnings expectations. That pressure often has led to premature revenue recognition, reducing the quality of reported earnings.

Accelerating revenue recognition has caused problems for many companies. For example, in 2008, **International Rectifier Corporation**, a manufacturer of power management products, was named defendant in a federal class action suit related to numerous irregularities including premature revenue recognition. The company admitted shipping products and recording sales with no obligation by customers to receive and pay for the products.

*Real World Financials*

We explore these issues in Chapter 5, when we discuss revenue recognition in considerable depth, and in Chapter 13, when we discuss liabilities that companies must record when they receive payment prior to having actually earned the related revenue. Now, though, let's discuss earnings quality issues related to *nonoperating* items.

## Nonoperating Income and Earnings Quality

Most of the components of earnings in an income statement relate directly to the ordinary, continuing operations of the company. Some, though, such as interest and gains or losses are only tangentially related to normal operations. These we refer to as nonoperating items. Some nonoperating items have generated considerable discussion with respect to earnings quality, notably gains and losses generated from the sale of investments. For example, as the stock market boom reached its height late in the year 2000, many companies recorded large gains from sale of investments that had appreciated significantly in value. How should those gains be interpreted in terms of their relationship to future earnings? Are they transitory or permanent? Let's consider an example.

*Gains and losses from the sale of investments often can significantly inflate or deflate current earnings.*

**Intel Corporation** is the world's largest manufacturer of semiconductors. Illustration 4–7 shows the nonoperating section of Intel's income statements for the 2000 and 1999 fiscal years. In 2000, income before taxes increased by approximately 35% from the prior year. But notice that the *gains on investments, net* (net means net of losses) increased from $883 million to over $3.7 billion, accounting for a large portion of the increase in income. Some analysts questioned the quality of Intel's 2000 earnings because of these large gains.

| Income Statements (in part)<br>(in millions) | | |
|---|---|---|
| | **Years Ended December 30** | |
| | **2000** | **1999** |
| Operating income | 10,395 | 9,767 |
| Gains on investments, net | 3,759 | 883 |
| Interest and other, net | 987 | 578 |
| Income before taxes | 15,141 | 11,228 |

**Illustration 4–7**

Income Statements (in part)—Intel Corporation

*Real World Financials*

Consider **Hecla Mining**, a precious metals company. In one fiscal year, the company reported income before income taxes of $61.8 million. Included in this amount was a $36.4 million gain on the sale of investments, representing 59% of total before-tax income. Can Hecla sustain these gains? Should they be considered part of permanent earnings or are they transitory? There are no easy answers to these questions. It's interesting to note that in the prior two years Hecla reported no investment gains.

*Many companies voluntarily provide* pro forma earnings—*management's assessment of permanent earnings.*

Companies often voluntarily provide a **pro forma earnings** number when they announce annual or quarterly earnings. Supposedly, these pro forma earnings numbers are management's view of "permanent earnings," in the sense of being a better long-run performance measure. For example, in January 2011, **Google Inc.** announced that its income for the fourth quarter of 2010 was $2.54 billion or $7.95 per share. At the same time, the company announced that its *pro forma net income* (for which Google excluded stock-based compensation expense) for the quarter was $2.85 billion or $8.75 per share. These pro forma earnings numbers are controversial because determining which items to exclude is at the discretion of management. Therefore, management could mislead investors. Nevertheless, these disclosures do represent management's perception of what its permanent earnings are and provides additional information to the financial community.

The Sarbanes-Oxley Act addressed pro forma earnings in its Section 401. One of the act's important provisions requires that if pro forma earnings are included in any periodic or other report filed with the SEC or in any public disclosure or press release, the company also must provide a reconciliation with earnings determined according to generally accepted accounting principles.[12]

We now turn our attention to two income statement items—discontinued operations and extraordinary items—that, because of their nature, are more obviously not part of a company's permanent earnings and, appropriately, are excluded from continuing operations.

# Separately Reported Items

The information in the income statement is useful if it can help users predict the future. Toward this end, users should be made aware of events reported in the income statement that are not likely to occur again in the foreseeable future.

There are two types of events that, if they have a material effect[13] on the income statement, require separate reporting below income from continuing operations as well as separate disclosure: (1) discontinued operations, and (2) extraordinary items.[14] Although a company has considerable flexibility in reporting income from *continuing operations,* the presentation order of these items is mandated as follows:[15]

| | |
|---|---|
| Income from continuing operations before income taxes and extraordinary items | $xxx |
| Income tax expense | xx |
| Income from continuing operations before extraordinary items | xxx |
| Discontinued operations, net of $xx in tax | xx |
| Extraordinary items, net of $xx in tax[16] | xx |
| **Net income** | **$xxx** |

The objective is to separately report all of the income effects of these items. That's why we include the income tax effect of each item in this separate presentation rather than report them as part of income tax expense. The process of associating income tax effects with the income statement components that create them is referred to as *intraperiod tax allocation.* We address this process in the next section.

## Intraperiod Income Tax Allocation

**Intraperiod tax allocation** associates (allocates) income tax expense (or income tax benefit if there is a loss) with each major component of income that causes it.[17] More specifically,

---

[12]The Congress of the United States of America, *The Sarbanes-Oxley Act of 2002,* Section 401 (b) (2), Washington, D.C., 2004.

[13]We discussed the concept of materiality in Chapter 1. If the effect on the income statement is not material, these items are included in income from continuing operations.

[14]FASB ASC 225–20–45: Income Statement—Extraordinary Items—Other Presentation Matters, and FASB ASC 205–20–45: Presentation of Financial Statement—Discontinued Operations—Other Presentation Matters (previously "Reporting Results of Operations," *Accounting Principles Board Opinion No. 30* (New York: AICPA, 1973)).

[15]The presentation of these separately reported items is the same for single-step and multiple-step income statement formats. The single-step versus multiple-step distinction applies to items included in income from continuing operations.

[16]Companies that report discontinued operations and extraordinary items sometimes show a subtotal after discontinued operations. This is not required.

[17]*Intraperiod* tax allocation refers to the association of income tax with various components of net income within the income statement. *Interperiod* tax allocation, covered in Chapter 16, refers to allocating income taxes between two or more reporting periods by recognizing deferred tax assets and liabilities.

income tax is allocated to income from continuing operations and each of the two separately reported items. For example, assume a company experienced an extraordinary gain during the year.[18] The amount of income tax expense deducted to arrive at income from continuing operations is the amount of income tax expense that the company would have incurred *if there were no extraordinary gain*. The effect on income taxes caused by the extraordinary item is deducted directly from the extraordinary gain in the income statement. Illustration 4–8 demonstrates this concept.

---

The Maxwell Gear Corporation had income from continuing operations before income tax expense of $200,000 and an extraordinary gain of $60,000 in 2013. The income tax rate is 40% on all items of income or loss. Therefore, the company's total income tax expense is $104,000 (40% × $260,000).

**Illustration 4–8**

Intraperiod Tax Allocation

---

How should the company allocate the tax expense between income from continuing operations and the extraordinary gain? A partial income statement, beginning with income from continuing operations before income tax expense, *ignoring* intraperiod tax allocation, is shown in Illustration 4–8A.

---

**Incorrect Presentation**

| | |
|---|---:|
| Income before income taxes and extraordinary item | $200,000 |
| Income tax expense | (104,000) |
| Income before extraordinary item | 96,000 |
| Extraordinary gain (gross) | 60,000 |
| Net income | $156,000 |

**Illustration 4–8A**

Income Statement Presented *Incorrectly*— No Intraperiod Tax Allocation (extraordinary gain)

---

The deficiency of this presentation is that the apparent contribution to net income of (a) income before the extraordinary gain (that is, income from continuing operations) and (b) the extraordinary gain is misleading. If the extraordinary gain had not occurred, income tax expense would not have been $104,000 but rather $80,000 (40% × $200,000). Similarly, the net benefit of the extraordinary gain is not $60,000, but rather $36,000 ($60,000 minus 40% × $60,000). The total tax expense of $104,000 must be *allocated*, $80,000 to continuing operations and $24,000 (40% × $60,000) to the extraordinary gain. The appropriate income statement presentation appears in Illustration 4–8B.

---

**Correct Presentation**

| | |
|---|---:|
| Income before income taxes and extraordinary item | $200,000 |
| Income tax expense | (80,000) |
| Income before extraordinary item | 120,000 |
| Extraordinary gain, net of $24,000 tax expense | 36,000 |
| Net income | $156,000 |

**Illustration 4–8B**

Income Statement Presented *Correctly*— Intraperiod Tax Allocation (extraordinary gain)

---

Net income is $156,000 either way. Intraperiod tax allocation is not an issue of measurement but an issue of presentation. The $120,000 income before extraordinary gain properly reflects income from continuing operations *including* the appropriate tax effects. Also, notice that income tax expense represents taxes that relate to the total of all of the revenue, expense, gain, and loss items included in continuing operations. Each of the items following continuing operations (discontinued operations and extraordinary items) are presented *net of their tax effect*. No individual items included in the computation of income from continuing operations are reported net of tax.

**The two items reported separately below income from continuing operations are presented net of the related income tax effect.**

---

[18]The criteria for classifying gains and losses as extraordinary are discussed in a later section of this chapter.

In the illustration, the extraordinary gain caused additional income tax expense to be incurred. What if the company had experienced an extraordinary loss of $60,000 instead of an extraordinary gain? In that case, rather than creating additional tax, the loss actually decreases tax due to its reducing taxable income by $60,000. The company's total income tax expense would be $56,000 [40% × ($200,000 − 60,000)].

The extraordinary loss *decreased* the amount of tax the company otherwise would have had to pay by $24,000. This is commonly referred to as a *tax benefit.* A partial income statement, beginning with income from continuing operations before income tax expense, *ignoring* intraperiod tax allocation is shown in Illustration 4–8C.

**Illustration 4–8C**

Income Statement Presented *Incorrectly*— No Intraperiod Tax Allocation (extraordinary loss)

| **Incorrect Presentation** | |
| --- | --- |
| Income before income taxes and extraordinary item | $200,000 |
| Income tax expense | (56,000) |
| Income before extraordinary item | 144,000 |
| Extraordinary loss (gross) | (60,000) |
| Net income | $ 84,000 |

Once again, income before the extraordinary loss (that is, income from continuing operations) is misleading. If the extraordinary loss had not occurred, income tax expense would not have been $56,000 but rather $80,000 (40% × $200,000). The total tax expense of $56,000 must be *allocated,* $80,000 tax expense to continuing operations and $24,000 tax benefit to the extraordinary loss. The appropriate income statement presentation appears in Illustration 4–8D.

**Illustration 4–8D**

Income Statement Presented *Correctly*— Intraperiod Tax Allocation (extraordinary loss)

| **Correct Presentation** | |
| --- | --- |
| Income before income taxes and extraordinary item | $200,000 |
| Income tax expense | (80,000) |
| Income before extraordinary item | 120,000 |
| Extraordinary loss, net of $24,000 tax benefit | (36,000) |
| Net income | $ 84,000 |

Now that we have seen how to report items net of their related tax effects, let's look closer at the two items reported net of tax below income from continuing operations: discontinued operations and extraordinary items.

## Discontinued Operations

● LO4–4

**FINANCIAL Reporting Case**

Q2, p. 171

**Time Warner, Inc.,** is a leading media and entertainment company. Prior to 2009, the company operated the following business segments: AOL, cable, filmed entertainment, networks, and publishing. In 2009, the company sold its cable business. **The Procter & Gamble Company** is perhaps best known for providing a wide variety of consumer packaged goods to consumers. Prior to 2010, the company also operated a global pharmaceuticals business. But the company sold the pharmaceuticals business during its 2010 fiscal year. Time Warner's sale of its cable business and Proctor & Gamble's sale of its pharmaceutical business are examples of **discontinued operations.**

**WHAT CONSTITUTES AN OPERATION?**    For purposes of reporting discontinued operations, in 2001 the FASB issued a standard that defined an operation as a *component of an entity* whose operations and cash flows can be clearly distinguished, operationally and for financial reporting purposes, from the rest of the entity. International standards also defined a discontinued operation as a discontinued component of an entity. However, what constitutes a "component" of an entity differed significantly between U.S. GAAP and *IFRS No. 5.*[19]

As part of the continuing process to converge U.S. GAAP and international standards, the FASB and IASB have been working together to develop a common definition and a common set of disclosures for discontinued operations. At the time this text was published, a final Accounting Standards Update had not been issued, but the two Boards had expressed a new direction in an Exposure Draft of a new ASU.

The proposed ASU defines a discontinued operation as a "component" that either (a) has been disposed of or (b) is classified as held for sale, and represents one of the following:

1. a separate major line of business or major geographical area of operations,
2. part of a single coordinated plan to dispose of a separate major line of business or geographical area of operations, or
3. a business that meets the criteria to be classified as held for sale on acquisition.[20]

Many were critical of prior guidance, feeling its definition of a component of the entity was too broad. In addition to achieving convergence with international standards, the new guidance is expected to reduce the number of business segments that require separate income statement presentation as a discontinued operation.

**REPORTING DISCONTINUED OPERATIONS.**   By definition, the income or loss stream from a discontinued operation no longer will continue. An analyst concerned with Time Warner's and Procter & Gamble's future profitability is more interested in the results of their operations that will continue. It is informative, then, for companies to separate the effects of the discontinued operations from the results of operations that will continue. This information might have a significant impact on the analyst's assessment of future profitability.

For this reason, the revenues, expenses, gains, losses, and income tax related to a *discontinued* operation must be removed from *continuing* operations and reported separately for all years presented.[21] A key for assessing profitability is comparing the company's performance from *continuing* operations from year to year and from company to company.

Sometimes a discontinued component actually has been sold by the end of a reporting period. Often, though, the component is being held for sale, but the disposal transaction has not yet been completed as of the end of the reporting period. We consider these two possibilities next.

> The net-of-tax income effects of a discontinued operation are reported separately in the income statement, below income from continuing operations.

**When the component has been sold.**   When the discontinued component is sold before the end of the reporting period, the reported income effects of a discontinued operation will include two elements:

1. Income or loss from operations (revenues, expenses, gains, and losses) of the component from the beginning of the reporting period to the disposal date.
2. Gain or loss on disposal of the component's assets.

These two elements can be combined or reported separately, net of their tax effects. If combined, the gain or loss component must be indicated. In our illustrations to follow, we combine the income effects. Illustration 4–9 describes a situation in which the discontinued component is sold before the end of the reporting period.

Notice that a tax *benefit* occurs because a *loss* reduces taxable income, saving the company $880,000. On the other hand, had there been *income* from operations of $2,200,000, the $880,000 income tax effect would have represented additional income tax expense.

For comparison purposes, the net of tax income or loss from operations of the discontinued component for any prior years included in the comparative income statements also are separately reported as discontinued operations.

---

[19]"Non-current Assets Held for Sale and Discontinued Operations," *International Financial Reporting Standard No. 5* (IASCF), as amended effective January 1, 2011.

[20]"FAS 144—Reporting Discontinued Operations—Joint Project of the IASB and FASB," *Project Update* (Norwalk, Conn.: FASB, July 29, 2010).

[21]For example, even though Time Warner did not sell its cable business until 2009, it's important for comparative purposes to separate the effects for any prior years presented. This allows an apples-to-apples comparison of income from *continuing* operations. So, in its 2009 three-year comparative income statements, the 2008 and 2007 income statements were reclassified and the income from discontinued operations presented as a separately reported item. In addition, there was a disclosure note to inform readers that prior years were reclassified.

**Illustration 4–9**
Discontinued
Operations—
Gain on Disposal

The Duluth Holding Company has several operating divisions. In October 2013, management decided to sell one of its divisions that qualifies as a separate component according to generally accepted accounting principles. The division was sold on December 18, 2013, for a net selling price of $14,000,000. On that date, the assets of the division had a book value of $12,000,000. For the period January 1 through disposal, the division reported a pretax loss from operations of $4,200,000. The company's income tax rate is 40% on all items of income or loss. Duluth generated after-tax profits of $22,350,000 from its continuing operations.

Duluth's income statement for the year 2013, beginning with income from continuing operations, would be reported as follows:

| | | |
|---|---|---|
| Income from continuing operations | | $22,350,000 |
| Discontinued operations: | | |
|   Loss from operations of discontinued component | | |
|     (including gain on disposal of $2,000,000*) | $(2,200,000)† | |
|   Income tax benefit | 880,000‡ | |
| Loss on discontinued operations | | (1,320,000) |
| Net income | | $21,030,000 |

\* Net selling price of $14 million less book value of $12 million
† Loss from operations of $4.2 million less gain on disposal of $2 million
‡ $2,200,000 × 40%

If a component to be discontinued has not yet been sold, its income effects, including any impairment loss, usually still are reported separately as discontinued operations.

**When the component is considered held for sale.**   What if a company has decided to discontinue a component but, when the reporting period ends, the component has not yet been sold? If the situation indicates that the component is likely to be sold within a year, the component is considered "held for sale."[22] In that case, the income effects of the discontinued operation still are reported, but the two components of the reported amount are modified as follows:

1. Income or loss from operations (revenues, expenses, gains and losses) of the component from the beginning of the reporting period *to the end of the reporting period.*
2. An "impairment loss" if the carrying value (book value) of the assets of the component is more than fair value minus cost to sell.

The two income elements can be combined or reported separately, net of their tax effects. In addition, if the amounts are combined and there is an impairment loss, the loss must be disclosed, either parenthetically on the face of the statement or in a disclosure note. Consider the example in Illustration 4–10.

A disclosure note would provide additional details about the discontinued component, including the identity of the component, the major classes of assets and liabilities of the component, the reason for the discontinuance, and the expected manner of disposition. Also, the net-of-tax income or loss from operations of the component being discontinued is also reported separate from continuing operations for any prior year that is presented for comparison purposes along with the 2013 income statement.

In Illustration 4–10, if the fair value of the division's assets minus cost to sell exceeded the book value of $12,000,000, there is no impairment loss and the income effects of the discontinued operation would include only the loss from operations of $4,200,000, less the income tax benefit.[23]

The balance sheet is affected, too. The assets and liabilities of the component considered held for sale are reported at the lower of their carrying amount (book value) or fair value minus cost to sell. And, because it's not in use, an asset classified as held for sale is no longer reported as part of property, plant, and equipment or intangible assets and is not depreciated or amortized.

---

[22]Six criteria are used to determine whether the component is likely to be sold and therefore considered "held for sale." You can find these criteria in FASB ASC 360–10–45–9: Property, Plant, and Equipment—Overall—Other Presentation Matters—Long-Lived Assets Classified as Held for Sale (previously "Accounting for the Impairment or Disposal of Long-Lived Assets," *Statement of Financial Accounting Standards No. 144* (Norwalk, Conn.: FASB, 2001), par. 30).

[23]In the following year when the component is sold, the income effects also must be reported as a discontinued operation.

**Illustration 4–10**
Discontinued
Operations—
Impairment Loss

The Duluth Holding Company has several operating divisions. In October 2013, management decided to sell one of its divisions that qualifies as a separate component according to generally accepted accounting principles. On December 31, 2013, the end of the company's fiscal year, the division had not yet been sold. On that date, the assets of the division had a book value of $12,000,000 and a fair value, minus anticipated cost to sell, of $9,000,000. For the year, the division reported a pre-tax loss from operations of $4,200,000. The company's income tax rate is 40% on all items of income or loss. Duluth generated after-tax profits of $22,350,000 from its continuing operations.

Duluth's income statement for 2013, beginning with income from continuing operations, would be reported as follows:

| | | |
|---|---:|---:|
| Income from continuing operations | | $22,350,000 |
| Discontinued operations: | | |
| Loss from operations of discontinued component (including impairment loss of $3,000,000\*) | $(7,200,000)† | |
| Income tax benefit | 2,880,000‡ | |
| Loss on discontinued operations | | (4,320,000) |
| Net income | | $18,030,000 |

\*Book value of $12 million less fair value net of cost to sell of $9 million
†Loss from operations of $4.2 million plus impairment loss of $3 million
‡$7,200,000 × 40%

As an example, **Phoenix Footwear Group** specializes in quality comfort women's and men's footwear. Late in its fiscal year ended January 1, 2011, the company adopted a plan to cease operating PGX Canada, its Canadian distribution company, and at year-end this business was considered held for sale. This was one of three businesses considered held for sale at year-end. The current asset and current liability sections of the year-end balance sheet reported $404 thousand in "Current assets of discontinued operations," and $412 thousand in "Current liabilities of discontinued operations," respectively. Information about these assets was included in the disclosure note shown in Illustration 4–11.

**4. Discontinued Operations (in part)**
Assets and liabilities of Tommy Bahama, Chambers, and PXG Canada businesses included in the Consolidated Balance Sheet are summarized as follows:

| ($ in thousands) | January 1, 2011 |
|---|---:|
| Assets: | |
| Accounts receivable | $ 139 |
| Inventories, net | 213 |
| Other current assets | 52 |
| Total current assets | $ 404 |
| | |
| Liabilities: | |
| Accounts payable | $ 179 |
| Accrued liabilities | 233 |
| Total current liabilities | $ 412 |

Notice that the assets and liabilities held for sale are classified as *current* because the company expects to sell or liquidate the businesses within one year.

**Interim reporting.**   Remember that companies whose ownership shares are publicly traded in the United States must file quarterly reports with the Securities and Exchange Commission. If a component of an entity is considered held for sale at the end of a quarter, the income effects of the discontinued component must be separately reported in the quarterly income statement. These effects would include the income or loss from operations for the quarter as well as an impairment loss if the component's assets have a book value more than fair value minus cost to sell. If the assets are impaired and written down, any gain or loss on disposal in a subsequent quarter is determined relative to the new, written-down book value.

Let's now turn our attention to the second separately reported item, extraordinary gains and losses.

## Extraordinary Items

● LO4–5

*Extraordinary items* are material gains and losses that are both *unusual in nature* and *infrequent in occurrence.*

Occasionally, an unusual event may occur that materially affects the current year's income but is highly unlikely to occur again in the foreseeable future. If such an item is allowed to simply alter net income without pointing out its extraordinary nature, earnings quality is seriously compromised and investors and creditors may be misled into basing predictions of future income on current income that includes the nonrecurring event. For that reason, **extraordinary items** are "red flagged" in an income statement by being reported separately, net of tax, and appropriately labeled. Extraordinary items are material events and transactions that are both:

1. Unusual in nature
2. Infrequent in occurrence[24]

These criteria must be considered in light of the environment in which the entity operates. There obviously is a considerable degree of subjectivity involved in the determination. The concepts of unusual and infrequent require judgment. In making these judgments, an accountant should keep in mind the overall objective of the income statement. The key question is how the event relates to a firm's future profitability. If it is judged that the event, because of its unusual nature and infrequency of occurrence, *is not likely to occur again,* separate reporting is warranted.

Companies often experience *unexpected* events that are not considered extraordinary items. The loss of a major customer and the death of the company president are unexpected events that likely will affect a company's future but are both normal risks of operating a business that could recur in the future. Other gains and losses from unexpected events that are *not* considered extraordinary include the effects of a strike, including those against competitors and major suppliers, and the adjustment of accruals on long-term contracts.[25]

A key point in the definition of an extraordinary item is that determining whether an event satisfies *both* criteria depends on the environment in which the firm operates. The environment includes factors such as the type of products or services sold and the geographical location of the firm's operations. What is extraordinary for one firm may not be extraordinary for another firm. For example, a loss caused by a tornado in Missouri may not be judged to be extraordinary. However, tornado damage in another state may indeed be unusual and infrequent.

The determination of whether an item is unusual and infrequent should consider the environment in which the company operates.

Companies frequently sell subsidiary companies or their partial ownership interest in companies. Generally, the gain or loss is reported as a nonoperating item in the income statement or as a discontinued operation if the subsidiary is considered a component of the entity according to generally accepted accounting principles. In contrast, though, consider the disclosure note from a quarterly financial statement of **Verizon Communications, Inc.,** shown in Illustration 4–12.

Why was the loss on sale of the company's 28.5% interest in a Venezuelan company considered an extraordinary item? The unusual nature of the forced sale, the nationalization (expropriation) of CANTV by a foreign government, resulted in the conclusion by Verizon that such a loss was unlikely to occur again in the foreseeable future.

Logic and reasoning must be applied to the determination of whether or not an event is extraordinary. Keep in mind that the income statement should be a guide to predicting the

---

[24]FASB ASC 225–20–45–2: Income Statement—Extraordinary and Unusual Items—Other Presentation Matters (previously "Reporting Results of Operations," *Accounting Principles Board Opinion No. 30* (New York: AICPA, 1973), par. 20).

[25]FASB ASC 225–20–45–4: Income Statement—Extraordinary and Unusual Items—Other Presentation Matters (previously "Reporting Results of Operations," *Accounting Principles Board Opinion No. 30* (New York: AICPA, 1973), par. 23).

**Illustration 4–12**
Extraordinary Loss
Disclosure—Verizon
Communications, Inc.

**Real World Financials**

> **Extraordinary Item (in part)**
> In January of the current year, the Bolivarian Republic of Venezuela declared its intent
> to nationalize certain companies, including CANTV. In February, we entered into a
> Memorandum of Understanding (MOU) with the Republic. The MOU provides that the
> Republic will offer to purchase all of the equity securities of CANTV, including our 28.5%
> interest . . . at a price equivalent to $17.85 . . . Based upon the terms of the MOU and
> our current investment balance in CANTV, we recorded an extraordinary loss on our
> investment of $131 million, net of tax, or $.05 per diluted shares, in the first quarter.

future. If it is extremely unlikely that a material gain or loss will occur again in the future, the quality of earnings is improved and the usefulness of the income statement in predicting the future is enhanced if the income effects of that gain or loss are reported separately.

As shown previously on page 182, the net-of-tax effects of extraordinary gains and losses are presented in the income statement below discontinued operations. In addition, a disclosure note is necessary to describe the nature of the event and the tax effects, if they are not indicated on the face of the income statement.

> Extraordinary gains and losses are presented, net of tax, in the income statement below discontinued operations.

# International Financial Reporting Standards

> **Extraordinary Items.** U.S. GAAP provides for the separate reporting, as an extraordinary item, of a material gain or loss that is unusual in nature and infrequent in occurrence. In 2003, the IASB revised *IAS No. 1*.[26] The revision states that neither the income statement nor any notes may contain any items called "extraordinary."

● LO4–10

A recent survey of 500 large public companies reported that only 24 of the companies disclosed an extraordinary gain or loss in their 2010 income statements.[27] Losses from two 21st century "extraordinary" events, the September 11, 2001, terrorist attacks and Hurricane Katrina in 2005, were not reported as extraordinary items. The treatment of these two events, the scarcity of extraordinary gains and losses reported in corporate income statements, and the desire to converge U.S. and international accounting standards could guide the FASB to the elimination of the extraordinary item classification.[28]

> Very few extraordinary gains and losses are reported in corporate income statements.
>
> The extraordinary item classification could soon be eliminated.

## Unusual or Infrequent Items

If the income effect of an event is material and the event is either unusual or infrequent—but not both—the item should be *included in continuing operations* but reported as a separate income statement component. Recall the JDS Uniphase Corporation example in Illustration 4–5 on page 179. Restructuring costs and the impairment of goodwill and long-lived assets included in that company's continuing operations are examples of this type of event. The events may be unusual or infrequent, but, by their nature, they could occur again in the foreseeable future. However, rather than include these items with other gains and losses or with other expenses, they are reported as a separate line item in the income statement.[29] This method of reporting, including note disclosure, enhances earnings quality by providing information to the statement user to help assess the events' relationship with future profitability.

> The income effect of an event that is either unusual or infrequent should be reported as a separate component of continuing operations.

In the next section, we briefly discuss the way various types of accounting changes are reported.

---

[26]"Financial Statement Presentation," *International Accounting Standard No. 1* (IASCF), as amended effective January 1, 2011.
[27]*Accounting Trends and Techniques—2011* (New York: AICPA, 2011), p. 418.
[28]For a thorough discussion of this topic, see Massoud, Raiborn and Humphrey, "Extraordinary Items: Time to Eliminate the Classification," *The CPA Journal* (February 2007).
[29]These items are *not* reported net of tax. Only the two separately reported items—discontinued operations and extraordinary items—are reported net of tax.

# Accounting Changes

Accounting changes fall into one of three categories: (1) a change in an accounting principle, (2) a change in estimate, or (3) a change in reporting entity. The correction of an error is another adjustment that is accounted for in the same way as certain accounting changes. A brief overview of a change in accounting principle, a change in estimate, and correction of errors is provided here. We cover accounting changes in detail, including changes in reporting entities, in subsequent chapters, principally in Chapter 20.

## Change in Accounting Principle

A change in accounting principle refers to a change from one acceptable accounting method to another. There are many situations that allow alternative treatments for similar transactions. Common examples of these situations include the choice among FIFO, LIFO, and average cost for the measurement of inventory and among alternative revenue recognition methods. New accounting standard updates issued by the FASB also may require companies to change their accounting methods.

**VOLUNTARY CHANGES IN ACCOUNTING PRINCIPLES.** Occasionally, a company will change from one generally accepted treatment to another. When these changes in accounting principles occur, information lacks consistency, hampering the ability of external users to compare financial information among reporting periods. If, for example, inventory and cost of goods sold are measured in one reporting period using the LIFO method, but are measured using the FIFO method in a subsequent period, inventory, cost of goods sold, and hence net income for the two periods are not comparable. Difficulties created by inconsistency and lack of comparability are alleviated by the way we report voluntary accounting changes.

GAAP requires that voluntary accounting changes be accounted for retrospectively.[30] That is, we recast prior years' financial statements when we report those statements again (in comparative statements, for example) to appear as if the new accounting method had been used in those periods. For each year in the comparative statements reported, we revise the balance of each account affected to make those statements appear as if the newly adopted accounting method had been applied all along. Then, a journal entry is created to adjust all account balances affected to what those amounts would have been. An adjustment is made to the beginning balance of retained earnings for the earliest period reported in the comparative statements of shareholders' equity to account for the cumulative income effect of changing to the new principle in periods prior to those reported.[31]

We will see these aspects of accounting for the change in accounting principle demonstrated in Chapter 9 in the context of our discussion of inventory methods. We'll also discuss changes in accounting principles in depth in Chapter 20.

**MANDATED CHANGES IN ACCOUNTING PRINCIPLES.** When a new FASB accounting standard update mandates a change in accounting principle, the board often allows companies to choose among multiple ways of accounting for the changes. One approach generally allowed is to account for the change retrospectively, exactly as we account for voluntary changes in principles. The FASB may also allow companies to report the cumulative effect on the income of previous years from having used the old method rather than the new method in the income statement of the year of change as a separately reported item below extraordinary items. Other approaches might also be allowed. Therefore, when a mandated change in accounting principle occurs, it is important to check the accounting standards update to determine how companies might account for the change.

> **Voluntary changes in accounting principles are accounted for retrospectively by revising prior years' financial statements.**

---

[30]FASB ASC 250–10–45–5: Accounting Changes and Error Corrections—Overall—Other Presentation Matters (previously "Accounting Changes and Error Corrections—a replacement of APB Opinion No. 20 and FASB Statement No. 3," *Statement of Financial Accounting Standard No. 154* (Norwalk, Conn.: FASB, 2005)).

[31]Sometimes a lack of information makes it impracticable to report a change retrospectively so the new method is simply applied prospectively, that is, we simply use the new method from now on. Also, if a new standard specifically requires prospective accounting, that requirement is followed.

## Change in Depreciation, Amortization, or Depletion Method

A change in depreciation, amortization, or depletion method is considered to be a change in accounting estimate that is achieved by a change in accounting principle. We account for this change prospectively, almost exactly as we would any other change in estimate. One difference is that most changes in estimate don't require a company to justify the change. However, this change in estimate is a result of changing an accounting principle and therefore requires a clear justification as to why the new method is preferable. Chapter 11 provides an illustration of a change in depreciation method.

*Changes in depreciation, amortization, or depletion methods are accounted for the same way as a change in an accounting estimate.*

## Change in Accounting Estimate

Estimates are a necessary aspect of accounting. A few of the more common accounting estimates are the amount of future bad debts on existing accounts receivable, the useful life and residual value of a depreciable asset, and future warranty expenses.

*A change in accounting estimate is reflected in the financial statements of the current period and future periods.*

Because estimates require the prediction of future events, it's not unusual for them to turn out to be wrong. When an estimate is modified as new information comes to light, accounting for the change in estimate is quite straightforward. We do not revise prior years' financial statements to reflect the new estimate. Instead, we merely incorporate the new estimate in any related accounting determinations from that point on, that is, we account for a change in accounting estimate prospectively.[32] If the effect of the change is material, a disclosure note is needed to describe the change and its effect on both net income and earnings per share. Chapters 11 and 20 provide illustrations of changes in accounting estimates.

# Correction of Accounting Errors

Errors occur when transactions are either recorded incorrectly or not recorded at all. We briefly discuss the correction of errors here as an overview and in later chapters in the context of the effect of errors on specific chapter topics. In addition, Chapter 20 provides comprehensive coverage of the correction of errors.

Accountants employ various control mechanisms to ensure that transactions are accounted for correctly. In spite of this, errors occur. When errors do occur, they can affect any one or several of the financial statement elements on any of the financial statements a company prepares. In fact, many kinds of errors simultaneously affect more than one financial statement. When errors are discovered, they should be corrected.

Most errors are discovered in the same year that they are made. These errors are simple to correct. The original erroneous journal entry is reversed and the appropriate entry is recorded. If an error is discovered in a year subsequent to the year the error is made, the accounting treatment depends on whether or not the error is material with respect to its effect on the financial statements. In practice, the vast majority of errors are not material and are, therefore, simply corrected in the year discovered. However, material errors that are discovered in subsequent periods require a prior period adjustment.

## Prior Period Adjustments

Assume that after its financial statements are published and distributed to shareholders, Roush Distribution Company discovers a material error in the statements. What does it do? Roush must make a **prior period adjustment**.[33] Roush would record a journal entry that adjusts any balance sheet accounts to their appropriate levels and would account for the income effects of the error by increasing or decreasing the beginning retained earnings balance in a statement of shareholders' equity. Remember, net income in prior periods was closed to retained earnings so, by adjusting retained earnings, the prior period adjustment accounts for the error's effect on prior periods' net income.

---

[32]If the original estimate had been based on erroneous information or calculations or had not been made in good faith, the revision of that estimate would constitute the correction of an error.

[33]FASB ASC 250–10–45–23: Accounting Changes and Error Corrections—Overall—Other Presentation Matters (previously "Prior Period Adjustments," *Statement of Financial Accounting Standards No. 16* (Norwalk, Conn.: FASB, 1977)).

Simply reporting a corrected retained earnings amount might cause misunderstanding for someone familiar with the previously reported amount. Explicitly reporting a prior period adjustment in the statement of shareholders' equity (or statement of retained earnings if that's presented instead) highlights the adjustment and avoids this confusion.

In addition to reporting the prior period adjustment to retained earnings, previous years' financial statements that are incorrect as a result of the error are retrospectively restated to reflect the correction. Also, a disclosure note communicates the impact of the error on prior periods' net income.

# Earnings per Share Disclosures

● LO4–6

**FINANCIAL Reporting Case**

Q4, p. 172

All corporations whose common stock is publicly traded must disclose EPS.

As we discussed in Chapter 3, financial statement users often use summary indicators, called *ratios,* to more efficiently make comparisons among different companies and over time for the same company. Besides highlighting important relationships among financial statement variables, ratios also accommodate differences in company size.

One of the most widely used ratios is earnings per share (EPS), which shows the amount of income earned by a company expressed on a per share basis. Public companies report basic EPS and, if there are certain potentially dilutive securities, diluted EPS, on the face of the income statement. Basic EPS is computed by dividing income available to common shareholders (net income less any preferred stock dividends) by the weighted-average number of common shares outstanding (weighted by time outstanding) for the period. For example, suppose the Fetzer Corporation reported net income of $600,000 for its fiscal year ended December 31, 2013. Preferred stock dividends of $75,000 were declared during the year. Fetzer had one million shares of common stock outstanding at the beginning of the year and issued an additional one million shares on March 31, 2013. Basic EPS of $.30 per share for 2013 is computed as follows:

$$\frac{\$600,000 - 75,000}{\underset{\substack{\text{Shares} \\ \text{at Jan. 1}}}{1,000,000} + \underset{\text{New shares}}{1,000,000\ (^9/_{12})}} = \frac{\$525,000}{1,750,000} = \$0.30$$

DELL

Diluted EPS reflects the potential dilution that could occur for companies that have certain securities outstanding that are convertible into common shares or stock options that could create additional common shares if the options were exercised. These items could cause EPS to decrease (become diluted). Because of the complexity of the calculation and the importance of EPS to investors, we devote a substantial portion of Chapter 19 to this topic. At this point, we focus on the financial statement presentation of EPS. In Illustration 4–2 on page 175, Dell Inc. discloses both basic and diluted EPS in its income statements for all years presented.

Companies must disclose per share amounts for (1) income before any separately reported items, (2) each separately reported item, and (3) net income (loss).

When the income statement includes one or more of the separately reported items, we report per-share amounts for both income (loss) from continuing operations and net income (loss), as well as for each separately reported item. We see this demonstrated in income statements of Charming Shoppes, Inc., a specialty retailer of plus-size women's apparel that includes the Lane Bryant brand, partially reproduced in Illustration 4–13.

# Comprehensive Income

● LO4–7

Accounting professionals have engaged in an ongoing debate concerning which transactions should be included as components of periodic income. For instance, some argue that certain changes in shareholders' equity besides those attributable to traditional net income should be included in the determination of income. In what might be viewed as a compromise, the FASB decided to maintain the traditional view of net income, but to require companies also to report an expanded version of income called comprehensive income to include four types of gains and losses that traditionally hadn't been included in income statements. Let's consider what that means.

**Illustration 4–13**

EPS Disclosures—
Charming Shoppes, Inc

Real World Financials

**CHARMING SHOPPES, INC.**
**Consolidated Statements of Operations (in part)**

| ($ in thousands, except per share data) | Year Ended | | |
|---|---|---|---|
| | January 30, 2010 | January 31, 2009 | February 2, 2008 |
| Loss from continuing operations before extraordinary item | $(77,962) | $(180,351) | $ (4,163) |
| Loss from discontinued operations, net of tax | | (74,922) | (85,039) |
| Extraordinary item, net of tax | — | — | 912 |
| Net loss | $(77,962) | $(255,273) | $(88,290) |
| **Basic earnings (loss) per share:** | | | |
| Loss from continuing operations before extraordinary item | $ (.67) | $ (1.57) | $ (.03) |
| Loss from discontinued operations | — | (.65) | (.70) |
| Extraordinary item | — | — | .01 |
| Net loss | $ (.67) | $ (2.22) | $ (.72) |
| **Diluted earnings (loss) per share:** | | | |
| Loss from continuing operations before extraordinary item | $ (.67) | $ (1.57) | $ (.03) |
| Loss from discontinued operations | — | (.65) | (.70) |
| Extraordinary gain | — | — | .01 |
| Net loss | $ (.67) | $ (2.22) | $ (.72) |

## Other Comprehensive Income

The calculation of net income omits certain types of gains and losses that are included in comprehensive income. As one example, in Chapter 12 you will learn that certain investments are reported in the balance sheet at their fair values, but that the gains and losses resulting from adjusting those investments to fair value might not be included in net income. Instead, they are reported as a separate component of shareholders' equity, other comprehensive income (OCI) (loss).

*Comprehensive income is the total change in equity for a reporting period other than from transactions with owners.*

Companies must report both net income and comprehensive income and reconcile the difference between the two.[34] Be sure to remember that net income actually is a part of comprehensive income. The reconciliation simply extends net income to include other comprehensive income items, reported net of tax, as shown in Illustration 4–14.

The actual terminology used by companies for the four other comprehensive income items varies considerably. For instance, deferred gains (losses) from derivatives are sometimes called *derivative mark-to-market adjustments* or *changes in fair value of derivatives*, and gains (losses) from foreign currency translation are often identified as *foreign currency translation adjustments.*

## Flexibility in Reporting

The information in the income statement and other comprehensive income items shown in Illustration 4–14 can be presented either (1) in a single, continuous statement of comprehensive income or (2) in two separate, but consecutive statements, an income statement and a statement of comprehensive income. Each component of other comprehensive income can be displayed net of tax, as in Illustration 4–14, or alternatively, before tax with one amount shown for the aggregate income tax expense (or benefit).[35]

*Reporting comprehensive income can be accomplished with a single, continuous statement or in two separate, but consecutive statements.*

---

[34]FASB ASC 220-10-45-1A and 1B: Comprehensive Income–Overall–Other Presentation Matters (previously "Reporting Comprehensive Income," *Statement of Financial Accounting Standards No. 130* (Norwalk, Conn.: FASB, 1997)).
[35]GAAP does not require the reporting of comprehensive earnings per share.

## Illustration 4–14
Comprehensive Income

Comprehensive income includes net income as well as other gains and losses that change shareholders' equity but are not included in traditional net income.

| | ($ in millions) |
|---|---|
| Net income | $xxx |
| Other comprehensive income: | |
| Net unrealized holding gains (losses) on investments (net of tax)* | $x |
| Gains (losses) from and amendments to postretirement benefit plans (net of tax)† | (x) |
| Deferred gains (losses) from derivatives (net of tax)‡ | (x) |
| Gains (losses) from foreign currency translation (net of tax)§ | x    xx |
| Comprehensive income | $xxx |

*Changes in the market value of certain investments (described in Chapter 12).
†Gains and losses due to revising assumptions or market returns differing from expectations and prior service cost from amending the plan (described in Chapter 17).
‡When a derivative designated as a cash flow hedge is adjusted to fair value, the gain or loss is deferred as a component of comprehensive income and included in earnings later, at the same time as earnings are affected by the hedged transaction (described in the Derivatives Appendix to the text).
§Gains or losses from changes in foreign currency exchange rates. The amount could be an addition to or reduction in shareholders' equity. (This item is discussed elsewhere in your accounting curriculum.)

Companies such as **McAfee, Inc.**, and **The Standard Register Company**, choose to present comprehensive income in a single statement. On the other hand, in its 2011 financial statements, **Astro-Med Inc.**, a manufacturer of a broad range of specialty technology products, chose to use the separate statement approach, as shown in Illustration 4–15.

## Illustration 4–15
Comprehensive Income Presented as a Separate Statement—Astro-Med Inc.

**Real World Financials**

| **ASTRO-MED INC.** **Consolidated Statements of Comprehensive Income** **For the Year Ended January 31,** | | | |
|---|---|---|---|
| ($ in thousands) | **2011** | **2010** | **2009** |
| Net income | $2,062 | $2,766 | $2,964 |
| Other comprehensive income (loss): | | | |
| Foreign currency translation adjustments, net of tax | (66) | 328 | (627) |
| Unrealized gain (loss) on securities, net of tax | 15 | (12) | (21) |
| Other comprehensive income (loss) | (51) | 316 | (648) |
| Comprehensive income | $2,011 | $3,082 | $2,316 |

● LO4–10

# International Financial Reporting Standards

**Comprehensive Income. Both U.S. GAAP and IFRS allow companies to report comprehensive income in either a single statement of comprehensive income or in two separate statements.**

Other comprehensive income items are similar under the two sets of standards. However, an additional OCI item, *changes in revaluation surplus*, is possible under IFRS. In Chapter 10 you will learn that *IAS No. 16*[36] permits companies to value property, plant, and equipment at (1) cost less accumulated depreciation or (2) fair value (revaluation). *IAS No. 38*[37] provides a similar option for the valuation of intangible assets. U.S. GAAP prohibits revaluation.

If the revaluation option is chosen and fair value is higher than book value, the difference, changes in revaluation surplus, is reported as *other comprehensive income* and then accumulates in a revaluation surplus account in equity.

---

[36]"Property, Plant and Equipment," *International Accounting Standard No. 16* (IASCF), as amended effective January 1, 2011.
[37]"Intangible Assets," *International Accounting Standard No. 38* (IASCF), as amended effective January 1, 2011.

## Accumulated Other Comprehensive Income

In addition to reporting OCI that occurs in the current reporting period, we must also report these amounts on a cumulative basis in the balance sheet. This is consistent with the way we report net income that occurs in the current reporting period in the income statement and also report accumulated net income (that hasn't been distributed as dividends) in the balance sheet as retained earnings. Similarly, we report OCI as it occurs in the current reporting period and also report accumulated other comprehensive income (AOCI) in the balance sheet. This is demonstrated in Illustration 4–16 for Astro-Med Inc.

> The cumulative total of OCI (or comprehensive loss) is reported as accumulated other comprehensive income (AOCI), an additional component of shareholders' equity that is displayed separately.

**ASTRO-MED INC.**
**Consolidated Balance Sheets (in part)**
**Years Ended January 31**

| ($ in thousands) | 2011 | 2010 |
|---|---|---|
| Shareholders' equity: | | |
| Common stock | 433 | 416 |
| Additional paid-in capital | 36,586 | 34,713 |
| Retained earnings | 26,843 | 26,817 |
| Accumulated other comprehensive income | 266 | 317 |
| Treasury stock | (9,840) | (8,030) |
| Total shareholders' equity | $54,288 | $54,233 |

**Illustration 4–16**

Shareholders' Equity—Astro-Med Inc.

Real World Financials

Referring to the numbers reported in Illustration 4–15, we can reconcile the changes in both retained earnings and AOCI:

| ($ in thousands) | Retained Earnings | Accumulated Other Comprehensive Income |
|---|---|---|
| Balance, 1/31/10 | $26,817 | $317 |
| Add: Net income | 2,062 | |
| Deduct: Dividends | (2,036) | |
| Other comprehensive loss | | (51) |
| Balance, 1/31/11 | $26,843 | $266 |

> AOCI decreased by $51 thousand, from $317 thousand to $266 thousand.

To further understand the relationship between net income and other comprehensive income, consider another example. Suppose Philips Corporation began 2013 with retained earnings of $600 million and accumulated other comprehensive income of $34 million. Let's also assume that net income for 2013, before considering the gain discussed below, is $100 million, of which $40 million was distributed to shareholders as dividends. Now assume that Philips purchased shares of IBM stock for $90 million during the year and sold them at year-end for $100 million. In that case, Philips would include the realized gain of $10 million in determining net income. If the income tax rate is 40%, net income includes a $6 million net-of-tax gain from the sale. This means that shareholders' equity, specifically retained earnings, also will include the $6 million.

| ($ in millions) | Retained Earnings | Accumulated Other Comprehensive Income |
|---|---|---|
| Balance, 12/31/12 | $600 | $34 |
| Net income ($100 + 6) | 106 | |
| Dividends | (40) | |
| Other comprehensive income | | –0– |
| Balance, 12/31/13 | $666 | $34 |

On the other hand, what if the shares are not sold before the end of the fiscal year but the year-end fair value is $100 million and Philips accounts for the shares as an other comprehensive income item? In that case, the *unrealized* gain of $10 million is not included in net income. Instead, $6 million net-of-tax gain is considered a component of *other comprehensive income (loss)* for 2013 and results in an increase in *accumulated other comprehensive income (loss)*, rather than retained earnings, in the 2013 balance sheet. The total of retained earnings and accumulated other comprehensive income is $700 million either way, as demonstrated below.

If the shares are not sold, the *unrealized* gain is part of other comprehensive income.

| ($ in millions) | Retained Earnings | Accumulated Other Comprehensive Income |
|---|---|---|
| Balance, 12/31/12 | $600 | $34 |
| Net income | 100 | |
| Dividends | (40) | |
| Other comprehensive income | | 6 |
| Balance, 12/31/13 | $660 | $40 |

Net income and comprehensive income are identical for an enterprise that has no other comprehensive income items. When this occurs for all years presented, a statement of comprehensive income is not required. Components of other comprehensive income are described in subsequent chapters.

## Concept Review Exercise

**INCOME STATEMENT PRESENTATION; COMPREHENSIVE INCOME**

The Barrington Construction Company builds office buildings. It also owns and operates a chain of motels throughout the Northwest. On September 30, 2013, the company decided to sell the entire motel business for $40 million. The sale was completed on December 15, 2013. Income statement information for 2013 is provided below for the two components of the company.

|  | ($ in millions) | |
|---|---|---|
|  | **Construction Component** | **Motel Component** |
| Sales revenue | $450.0 | $200.0 |
| Operating expenses | 226.0 | 210.0 |
| Other income (loss)* | 16.0 | (30.0) |
| Income (loss) before income taxes | $240.0 | $ (40.0) |
| Income tax expense (benefit)† | 96.0 | (16.0) |
| Net income (loss) | $144.0 | $ (24.0) |

*For the motel component, the entire Other income (loss) amount represents the loss on sale of assets of the component for $40 million when their book value was $70 million.
†A 40% tax rate applies to all items of income or loss.

In addition to the revenues and expenses of the construction and motel components, Barrington experienced a before-tax loss of $20 million to its construction business from damage to buildings and equipment caused by volcanic activity at Mount St. Helens. The event was considered unusual and infrequent. Also, in 2013 the company had pretax net unrealized holding gains on investment securities of $3 million and a foreign currency translation adjustment gain of $1 million.

**Required:**
1. Prepare a single, continuous 2013 statement of comprehensive income for the Barrington Construction Company including EPS disclosures. There were 100 million shares of common stock outstanding throughout 2013. The company had no potential

common shares outstanding. Use the multiple-step approach for the income statement portion of the statement.

2. Prepare a separate 2013 statement of comprehensive income.

**Solution:**

1. Prepare a single, continuous 2013 statement of comprehensive income.

**BARRINGTON CONSTRUCTION COMPANY**
**Statement of Comprehensive Income**
**For the Year Ended December 31, 2013**
($ in millions, except per share amounts)

| | | |
|---|---|---|
| Sales revenue | | $450.0 |
| Operating expenses | | 226.0 |
| Operating income | | 224.0 |
| Other income | | 16.0 |
| Income from continuing operations before income taxes and extraordinary item | | 240.0 |
| Income tax expense | | 96.0 |
| Income from continuing operations before extraordinary item | | 144.0 |
| Discontinued operations: | | |
| Loss from operations of discontinued motel component (including loss on disposal of $30) | $(40) | |
| Income tax benefit | 16 | |
| Loss on discontinued operations | | (24.0) |
| Income before extraordinary item | | 120.0 |
| Extraordinary loss from volcano damage, net of $8.0 tax benefit | | (12.0) |
| Net income | | $108.0 |
| Other comprehensive income: | | |
| Unrealized gains on investment securities, net of tax | 1.8 | |
| Foreign currency translation gain, net of tax | .6 | |
| Total other comprehensive income | | 2.4 |
| Comprehensive income | | $110.4 |
| **Earnings per share:** | | |
| Income from continuing operations before extraordinary item | | $ 1.44 |
| Discontinued operations | | (.24) |
| Extraordinary loss | | (.12) |
| Net income | | $ 1.08 |

2. Prepare a separate 2013 statement of comprehensive income.

**BARRINGTON CONSTRUCTION COMPANY**
**Statement of Comprehensive Income**
**For the Year Ended December 31, 2013**
($ in millions)

| | | |
|---|---|---|
| Net income | | $108.0 |
| Other comprehensive income: | | |
| Unrealized gains on investment securities, net of tax | 1.8 | |
| Foreign currency translation gain, net of tax | .6 | |
| Total other comprehensive income | | 2.4 |
| Comprehensive income | | $110.4 |

Now that we have discussed the presentation and content of the income statement, we turn our attention to the statement of cash flows.

# THE STATEMENT OF CASH FLOWS

● LO4–8

*A statement of cash flows is presented for each period for which results of operations are provided.*

In addition to the income statement and the balance sheet, a statement of cash flows (SCF) is an essential component within the set of basic financial statements.[38] Specifically, when a balance sheet and an income statement are presented, a statement of cash flows is required for each income statement period. The purpose of the SCF is to provide information about the cash receipts and cash disbursements of an enterprise that occurred during a period. Similar to the income statement, it is a *change* statement, summarizing the transactions that caused cash to change during a reporting period. The term *cash* refers to *cash plus cash equivalents.* Cash equivalents, discussed in Chapter 3, include highly liquid (easily converted to cash) investments such as Treasury bills. Chapter 21 is devoted exclusively to the SCF. A brief overview is provided here.

## Usefulness of the Statement of Cash Flows

We discussed the difference between cash and accrual accounting in Chapter 1. It was pointed out and illustrated that over short periods of time, operating cash flows may not be indicative of the company's long-run cash-generating ability, and that accrual-based net income provides a more accurate prediction of future operating cash flows. Nevertheless, information about cash flows from operating activities, when combined with information about cash flows from other activities, can provide information helpful in assessing future profitability, liquidity, and long-term solvency. After all, a company must pay its debts with cash, not with income.

Of particular importance is the amount of cash generated from operating activities. In the long run, a company must be able to generate positive cash flow from activities related to selling its product or service. These activities must provide the necessary cash to pay debts, provide dividends to shareholders, and provide for future growth.

## Classifying Cash Flows

● LO4–9

A list of cash flows is more meaningful to investors and creditors if they can determine the type of transaction that gave rise to each cash flow. Toward this end, the statement of cash flows classifies all transactions affecting cash into one of three categories: (1) operating activities, (2) investing activities, and (3) financing activities.

### Operating Activities

*Operating activities are inflows and outflows of cash related to the transactions entering into the determination of net operating income.*

The inflows and outflows of cash that result from activities reported in the income statement are classified as cash flows from operating activities. In other words, this classification of cash flows includes the elements of net income reported on a cash basis rather than an accrual basis.[39]

Cash inflows include cash received from:

1. Customers from the sale of goods or services.
2. Interest and dividends from investments.

These amounts may differ from sales and investment income reported in the income statement. For example, sales revenue measured on the accrual basis reflects revenue earned during the period, not necessarily the cash actually collected. Revenue will not equal cash collected from customers if receivables from customers or unearned revenue changed during the period.

Cash outflows include cash paid for:

1. The purchase of inventory.
2. Salaries, wages, and other operating expenses.
3. Interest on debt.
4. Income taxes.

---

[38]FASB ASC 230–10–45: Statement of Cash Flows—Overall—Other Presentation Matters (previously "Statement of Cash Flows," *Statement of Financial Accounting Standards No. 95* (Norwalk, Conn.: FASB, 1987)).

[39]Cash flows related to gains and losses from the sale of assets shown in the income statement are reported as investing activities in the SCF.

Likewise, these amounts may differ from the corresponding accrual expenses reported in the income statement. Expenses are reported when incurred, not necessarily when cash is actually paid for those expenses. Also, some revenues and expenses, like depreciation expense, don't affect cash at all and aren't included as cash outflows from operating activities.

The difference between the inflows and outflows is called *net cash flows from operating activities*. This is equivalent to net income if the income statement had been prepared on a cash basis rather than an accrual basis.

# International Financial Reporting Standards

**Classification of Cash Flows.** Like U.S. GAAP, international standards also require a statement of cash flows. Consistent with U.S. GAAP, cash flows are classified as operating, investing, or financing. However, the U.S. standard designates cash outflows for interest payments and cash inflows from interest and dividends received as operating cash flows. Dividends paid to shareholders are classified as financing cash flows.

● LO4–10

*IAS No. 7,*[40] on the other hand, allows more flexibility. Companies can report interest and dividends paid as either operating or financing cash flows and interest and dividends received as either operating or investing cash flows. Interest and dividend payments usually are reported as financing activities. Interest and dividends received normally are classified as investing activities.

### Typical Classification of Cash Flows from Interest and Dividends

| U.S. GAAP | IFRS |
|---|---|
| *Operating Activities* | *Operating Activities* |
| Dividends received | |
| Interest received | |
| Interest paid | |
| *Investing Activities* | *Investing Activities* |
| | Dividends received |
| | Interest received |
| *Financing Activities* | *Financing Activities* |
| Dividends paid | Dividends paid |
| | Interest paid |

**Siemens AG**, a German company, prepares its financial statements according to IFRS. In the statement of cash flows for quarter ended March 31, 2011, the company reported interest and dividends received as operating cash flows, as would a U.S. company. However, Siemens classified interest paid as a financing cash flow.

Real World Financials

### SIEMENS AG
### Statement of Cash Flows (partial)
### For the Three Months Ended March 31, 2011

(€ in millions)

| | |
|---|---:|
| Cash flows from financing activities: | |
| Proceeds from re-issuance of treasury stock | 109 |
| Repayment of long-term debt | (13) |
| Change in short-term debt and other | 85 |
| Interest paid | (72) |
| Dividends paid | (2,356) |
| Dividends paid to minority shareholders | (81) |
| Financing discontinued operations | (401) |
| Net cash used in financing activities—continuing operations | (2,729) |

---

[40]"Statement of Cash Flows," *International Accounting Standard No. 7* (IASCF), as amended effective January 1, 2011.

By the *direct method*, the cash effect of each operating activity is reported directly in the SCF.

By the *indirect method*, cash flow from operating activities is derived indirectly by starting with reported net income and adding or subtracting items to convert that amount to a cash basis.

**DIRECT AND INDIRECT METHODS OF REPORTING.** Two generally accepted formats can be used to report operating activities, the direct method and the indirect method. Under the **direct method**, the cash effect of each operating activity is reported directly in the statement. For example, *cash received from customers* is reported as the cash effect of sales activities. Income statement transactions that have no cash flow effect, such as depreciation, are simply not reported.

By the **indirect method**, on the other hand, we arrive at net cash flow from operating activities indirectly by starting with reported net income and working backwards to convert that amount to a cash basis. Two types of adjustments to net income are needed. First, components of net income that do not affect cash are reversed. That means that noncash revenues and gains are subtracted, while noncash expenses and losses are added. For example, depreciation expense does not reduce cash, but it is subtracted in the income statement. To reverse this, then, we add back depreciation expense to net income to arrive at the amount that we would have had if depreciation had not been subtracted.

Second, we make adjustments for changes in operating assets and liabilities during the period that indicate that amounts included as components of net income are not the same as cash flows for those components. For instance, suppose accounts receivable increases during the period because cash collected from customers is less than sales revenue. This increase in accounts receivable would then be subtracted from net income to arrive at *cash flow from operating activities*. In the indirect method, positive adjustments to net income are made for decreases in related assets and increases in related liabilities, while negative adjustments are made for increases in those assets and decreases in those liabilities.

To contrast the direct and indirect methods further, consider the example in Illustration 4–17.

## Illustration 4–17

Contrasting the Direct and Indirect Methods of Presenting Cash Flows from Operating Activities

Net income is $35,000, but cash flow from these same activities is not necessarily the same amount.

Changes in assets and liabilities can indicate that cash inflows are different from revenues and cash outflows are different from expenses.

Arlington Lawn Care (ALC) began operations at the beginning of 2013. ALC's 2013 income statement and its year-end balance sheet are shown below ($ in thousands).

**ARLINGTON LAWN CARE**
**Income Statement**
**For the Year Ended December 31, 2013**

| | | |
|---|---:|---:|
| Service revenue | | $90 |
| Operating expenses: | | |
| General and administrative | $32* | |
| Depreciation | 8 | |
| Total operating expenses | | 40 |
| Income before income taxes | | 50 |
| Income tax expense | | 15 |
| Net income | | $35 |

*Includes $6 in insurance expense

**ARLINGTON LAWN CARE**
**Balance Sheet**
**At December 31, 2013**

| Assets | | Liabilities and Shareholders' Equity | |
|---|---:|---|---:|
| Current assets: | | Current liabilities: | |
| Cash | $ 54 | Accounts payable** | $ 7 |
| Accounts receivable | 12 | Income taxes payable | 15 |
| Prepaid insurance | 4 | Total current liabilities | 22 |
| Total current assets | 70 | Shareholders' equity: | |
| Equipment | 40 | Common stock | 50 |
| Less: Accumulated depreciation | (8) | Retained earnings | 30*** |
| Total assets | $102 | Total liabilities and shareholders' equity | $102 |

**For general and administrative expenses
***Net income of $35 less $5 in cash dividends paid

**DIRECT METHOD.**   Let's begin with the direct method of presentation. We illustrated this method previously in Chapter 2. In that chapter, specific cash transactions were provided and we simply included them in the appropriate cash flow category in the SCF. Here, we start with account balances, so the direct method requires a bit more reasoning.

From the income statement, we see that ALC's net income has four components. Three of those—service revenue, general and administrative expenses, and income tax expense—affect cash flows, but not by the accrual amounts reported in the income statement. One component—depreciation—reduces net income but not cash; it's simply an allocation over time of a prior year's expenditure for a depreciable asset. So, to report these operating activities on a cash basis, rather than an accrual basis, we take the three items that affect cash and adjust the amounts to reflect cash inflow rather than revenue earned and cash outflows rather than expenses incurred. Let's start with service revenue.

Service revenue is $90,000, but ALC did not collect that much cash from its customers. We know that because accounts receivable increased from $0 to $12,000, ALC must have collected to date only $78,000 of the amount earned.

| Accounts receivable | | | |
|---|---|---|---|
| Beg. bal. | 0 | | |
| Revenue | 90 | | |
| | | 78 | Cash |
| End bal. | 12 | | |

Similarly, general and administrative expenses of $32,000 were incurred, but $7,000 of that hasn't yet been paid. We know that because accounts payable increased by $7,000. Also, prepaid insurance increased by $4,000 so ALC must have paid $4,000 more cash for insurance coverage than the amount that expired and was reported as insurance expense. That means cash paid thus far for general and administrative expenses was only $29,000 ($32,000 less the $7,000 increase in accounts payable plus the $4,000 increase in prepaid insurance). The other expense, income tax, was $15,000, but that's the amount by which income taxes payable increased so no cash has yet been paid for income taxes.

We can report ALC's cash flows from operating activities using the direct method as shown in Illustration 4–17A.

---

**ARLINGTON LAWN CARE**
**Statement of Cash Flows**
**For the Year Ended December 31, 2013**

( $ in thousands)

| | |
|---|---|
| Cash Flows from Operating Activities | |
| Cash received from customers* | $78 |
| Cash paid for general and administrative expenses** | (29) |
| Net cash flows from operating activities | $49 |

*Service revenue of $90 thousand, less increase of $12 thousand in accounts receivable.

**General and administrative expenses of $32 thousand, less increase of $7 thousand in accounts payable, plus increase of $4 thousand in prepaid insurance.

**Illustration 4–17A**

Direct Method of Presenting Cash Flows from Operating Activities

By the direct method, we report the components of net income on a cash basis.

---

**INDIRECT METHOD.**   To report operating cash flows using the indirect method, we take a different approach. We start with ALC's net income but realize that the $35,000 includes both cash and noncash components. We need to adjust net income, then, to eliminate the noncash effects so that we're left with only the cash flows. We start by eliminating the only noncash component of net income in our illustration—depreciation expense. Depreciation of $8,000 was subtracted in the income statement, so we simply add it back in to eliminate it.

That leaves us with the three components that do affect cash but not by the amounts reported. For those, we need to make adjustments to net income to cause it to reflect cash flows rather than accrual amounts. For instance, we saw earlier that only $78,000 cash was received from customers even though $90,000 in revenue is reflected in net income. That means we need to include an adjustment to reduce net income by $12,000, the increase in accounts receivable. In a similar manner, we include adjustments for the changes in accounts payable, income taxes payable, and prepaid insurance to cause net income to reflect cash payments rather than expenses incurred. For accounts payable and taxes payable, because more was subtracted in the income statement than cash paid for the expenses related to these two liabilities, we need to add back the differences. Note that if these liabilities had

Depreciation expense does not reduce cash, but is subtracted in the income statement. So, we add back depreciation expense to net income to eliminate it.

We make adjustments for changes in assets and liabilities that indicate that components of net income are not the same as cash flows.

decreased, we would have subtracted, rather than added, the changes. For prepaid insurance, because less was subtracted in the income statement than cash paid, we need to subtract the difference—the increase in prepaid insurance. If this asset had decreased, we would have added, rather than subtracted, the change.

Cash flows from operating activities using the indirect method are shown in Illustration 4–17B.

## Illustration 4–17B

Indirect Method of Presenting Cash Flows from Operating Activities

By the indirect method, we start with net income and work backwards to convert that amount to a cash basis.

### ARLINGTON LAWN CARE
### Statement of Cash Flows
### For the Year Ended December 31, 2013

($ in thousands)

| Cash Flows from Operating Activities | | |
|---|---|---|
| Net income | | $35 |
| Adjustments for noncash effects: | | |
| Depreciation expense | $ 8 | |
| Changes in operating assets and liabilities: | | |
| Increase in prepaid insurance | (4) | |
| Increase in accounts receivable | (12) | |
| Increase in accounts payable | 7 | |
| Increase in income taxes payable | 15 | 14 |
| Net cash flows from operating activities | | $49 |

Both the direct and the indirect methods produce the same net cash flows from operating activities ($49 thousand in our illustration); they are merely alternative approaches to reporting the cash flows. The FASB, in promulgating GAAP for the statement of cash flows, stated its preference for the direct method. However, while both methods are used in practice, the direct method is infrequently used.

The choice of presentation method for cash flow from operating activities has no effect on how investing activities and financing activities are reported. We now look at how cash flows are classified into those two categories.

## Investing Activities

Investing activities involve the acquisition and sale of (1) long-term assets used in the business and (2) nonoperating investment assets.

Cash flows from investing activities include inflows and outflows of cash related to the acquisition and disposition of long-lived assets used in the operations of the business (such as property, plant, and equipment) and investment assets (except those classified as cash equivalents and trading securities). The purchase and sale of inventories are not considered investing activities. Inventories are purchased for the purpose of being sold as part of the company's operations, so their purchase and sale are included with operating activities rather than investing activities.

Cash outflows from investing activities include cash paid for:

1. The purchase of long-lived assets used in the business.
2. The purchase of investment securities like stocks and bonds of other entities (other than those classified as cash equivalents and trading securities).
3. Loans to other entities.

Later, when the assets are disposed of, cash inflow from the sale of the assets (or collection of loans and notes) also is reported as cash flows from investing activities. As a result, cash inflows from these transactions are considered investing activities:

1. The sale of long-lived assets used in the business.
2. The sale of investment securities (other than cash equivalents and trading securities).
3. The collection of a nontrade receivable (excluding the collection of interest, which is an operating activity).

*Net cash flows from investing activities* represents the difference between the inflows and outflows. The only investing activity indicated in Illustration 4–17 is ALC's investment of $40,000 cash for equipment.

## Financing Activities

Financing activities relate to the external financing of the company. Cash inflows occur when cash is borrowed from creditors or invested by owners. Cash outflows occur when cash is paid back to creditors or distributed to owners. The payment of interest to a creditor, however, is classified as an operating activity.

*Financing activities involve cash inflows and outflows from transactions with creditors (excluding trade creditors) and owners.*

Cash inflows include cash received from:

1. Owners when shares are sold to them.
2. Creditors when cash is borrowed through notes, loans, mortgages, and bonds.

Cash outflows include cash paid to:

1. Owners in the form of dividends or other distributions.
2. Owners for the reacquisition of shares previously sold.
3. Creditors as repayment of the principal amounts of debt (excluding trade payables that relate to operating activities).

*Net cash flows from financing activities* is the difference between the inflows and outflows. The only financing activities indicated in Illustration 4–17 are ALC's receipt of $50,000 cash from issuing common stock and the payment of $5,000 in cash dividends.

## Noncash Investing and Financing Activities

As we just discussed, the statement of cash flows provides useful information about the investing and financing activities in which a company is engaged. Even though these primarily result in cash inflows and cash outflows, there may be significant investing and financing activities occurring during the period that do not involve cash flows at all. In order to provide complete information about these activities, any significant *noncash* investing and financing activities (that is, noncash exchanges) are reported either on the face of the SCF or in a disclosure note. An example of a significant noncash investing and financing activity is the acquisition of equipment (an investing activity) by issuing either a long-term note payable or equity securities (a financing activity).

*Significant investing and financing transactions not involving cash also are reported.*

The 2013 statement of cash flows for ALC, beginning with net cash flows from operating activities, is shown in Illustration 4–18.

**Illustration 4–18**

Statement of Cash Flows (beginning with net cash flows from operating activities)

**ARLINGTON LAWN CARE**
**Statement of Cash Flows (in part)**
**For the Year Ended December 31, 2013**

|  |  | ($ in thousands) |
|---|---|---|
| Net cash flows from operating activities |  | $49 |
| **Cash flows from investing activities:** |  |  |
| Purchase of equipment |  | (40) |
| **Cash flows from financing activities:** |  |  |
| Sale of common stock | $50 |  |
| Payment of cash dividends | (5) |  |
| Net cash flows from financing activities |  | 45 |
| Net increase in cash |  | 54 |
| Cash balance, January 1 |  | 0 |
| Cash balance, December 31 |  | $54 |

We know $40 thousand was paid to buy equipment because that balance sheet account increased from no balance to $40 thousand. Likewise, because common stock increased from zero to $50 thousand, we include that amount as a cash inflow from financing activities. Finally, Illustration 4–17 told us that $5 thousand was paid as a cash dividend, also a financing activity.

## Where We're Headed

● LO4–10

The FASB and IASB are working together on a standard that would have a dramatic impact on the format of financial statements.

Demonstrating the cohesiveness among the financial statements is a key objective of the Financial Statement Presentation project.

The FASB and IASB are working together on a project, Financial Statement Presentation, to establish a common standard for presenting information in the financial statements, including classifying and displaying line items and aggregating line items into subtotals and totals. This standard would have a dramatic impact on the format of financial statements. An important part of the proposal involves the organization of elements of the balance sheet (statement of financial position), statement of comprehensive income (including the income statement), and statement of cash flows (SCF) into a common set of classifications.

The income statement (statement of comprehensive income) and the statement of cash flows are slated to change in several ways. First, though, we should note that the SCF would retain the three major classifications of cash flows. The income statement (and balance sheet as well) also would include classifications by operating, investing, and financing activities, providing a "cohesive" financial picture that stresses the relationships among the financial statements.

For each statement, though, operating and investing activities would be included within a new category, "business" activities. Each statement also would include three additional groupings: discontinued operations, income taxes, and equity (if needed). The new look for the statement of comprehensive income and the statement of cash flows would be:

| Statement of Comprehensive Income | Statement of Cash Flows |
|---|---|
| **Business** <br> • Operating income and expenses <br> • Investing income and expenses | **Business** <br> • Operating cash flows <br> • Investing cash flows |
| **Financing** <br> • Debt expense | **Financing** <br> • Debt cash flows <br> • Equity cash flows |
| **Multi-category transactions** <br> **Income Taxes** | **Multi-category transactions** <br> **Income Taxes** |
| **Discontinued Operations (net of tax)** | **Discontinued Operations** |
| **Other Comprehensive Income (net of tax)** | |

The proposed new standard would require the direct method.

One change planned for the statement of cash flows is to no longer permit a choice between the direct method and the indirect method, but to require the direct method, reasoning that it provides more useful information to investors. Another change is to eliminate the concept of cash equivalents in favor of cash only. Also, while we still will have operating, investing, and financing activities, some cash flows will switch categories. Under the new "management approach," cash flows will be classified based on how related assets and liabilities are used by management. For instance, expenditures for property, plant, and equipment likely would be classified as operating, because those assets are used in the "core" business. Investing activities would be limited primarily to investments in stock, bonds, and other securities. The multicategory sections primarily encompass the acquisition and sale of other companies since they include assets and liabilities in different categories.

## Concept Review Exercise

**STATEMENT OF CASH FLOWS**

Dublin Enterprises, Inc. (DEI), owns a chain of retail electronics stores located in shopping malls. The following are the company's 2013 income statement and comparative balance sheets ($ in millions):

**Income Statement**
**For the Year Ended December 31, 2013**

| | | |
|---|---:|---:|
| Revenue | | $2,100 |
| Cost of goods sold | | 1,400 |
| Gross profit | | 700 |
| Operating expenses: | | |
| Selling and administrative | $ 355 | |
| Depreciation | 85 | |
| Total operating expenses | | 440 |
| Income before income taxes | | 260 |
| Income tax expense | | 78 |
| Net income | | $ 182 |

| Comparative Balance Sheets | 12/31/13 | 12/31/12 |
|---|---:|---:|
| Assets: | | |
| Cash | $ 300 | $ 220 |
| Accounts receivable (net) | 227 | 240 |
| Inventory | 160 | 120 |
| Property, plant & equipment | 960 | 800 |
| Less: Accumulated depreciation | (405) | (320) |
| Total assets | $1,242 | $1,060 |
| | | |
| Liabilities and shareholders' equity: | | |
| Accounts payable | $ 145 | $ 130 |
| Payables for selling and admin. expenses | 147 | 170 |
| Income taxes payable | 95 | 50 |
| Long-term debt | –0– | 100 |
| Common stock | 463 | 400 |
| Retained earnings | 392 | 210 |
| Total liabilities and shareholders' equity | $1,242 | $1,060 |

**Required:**

1. Prepare DEI's 2013 statement of cash flows using the direct method.
2. Prepare the cash flows from operating activities section of DEI's 2013 statement of cash flows using the indirect method.

**Solution**

1. Prepare DEI's 2013 statement of cash flows using the direct method.

**DUBLIN ENTERPRISES, INC.**
**Statement of Cash Flows**
**For the Year Ended December 31, 2013**
($ in millions)

| | | |
|---|---:|---:|
| **Cash Flows from Operating Activities** | | |
| Collections from customers[1] | $2,113 | |
| Purchase of inventory[2] | (1,425) | |
| Payment of selling and administrative expenses[3] | (378) | |
| Payment of income taxes[4] | (33) | |
| Net cash flows from operating activities | | $277 |

[1]Sales revenue of $2,100 million, plus $13 million decrease in accounts receivable (net).
[2]Cost of goods sold of $1,400 million, plus $40 million increase in inventory, less $15 million increase in accounts payable.
[3]Selling and administrative expenses of $355 million, plus $23 million decrease in payables for selling and administrative expenses.
[4]Income tax expense of $78 million, less $45 million increase in income taxes payable.

(continued)

(concluded)

| Cash Flows from Investing Activities | | |
|---|---|---|
| Purchase of property, plant, and equipment | | (160) |
| **Cash Flows from Financing Activities** | | |
| Issuance of common stock | 63 | |
| Payment on long-term debt | (100) | |
| Net cash flows from financing activities | | (37) |
| Net increase in cash | | 80 |
| Cash, January 1 | | 220 |
| Cash, December 31 | | $300 |

2. Prepare the cash flows from operating activities section of DEI's 2013 statement of cash flows using the indirect method.

**DUBLIN ENTERPRISES, INC.**
**Statement of Cash Flows**
**For the Year Ended December 31, 2013**
($ in millions)

| Cash Flows from Operating Activities | | |
|---|---|---|
| Net Income | $182 | |
| *Adjustments for noncash effects:* | | |
| Depreciation expense | 85 | |
| *Changes in operating assets and liabilities:* | | |
| Decrease in accounts receivable (net) | 13 | |
| Increase in inventory | (40) | |
| Increase in accounts payable | 15 | |
| Increase in income taxes payable | 45 | |
| Decrease in payables for selling and administrative expenses | (23) | |
| Net cash flows from operating activities | | $277 |

# Financial Reporting Case Solution

1. **How would you explain restructuring costs to Becky? Are restructuring costs something Becky should worry about?** *(p. 179)*   Restructuring costs include employee severance and termination benefits plus other costs associated with the shutdown or relocation of facilities or downsizing of operations. Restructuring costs are not necessarily bad. In fact, the objective is to make operations more efficient. The costs are incurred now in hopes of better earnings later.

2. **Explain to Becky what is meant by discontinued operations and describe to her how that item is reported in an income statement.** *(p. 184)*   A discontinued operation occurs when a company decides to discontinue a separate component. The net-of-tax effect of discontinued operations is separately reported below income from continuing operations. If the component has been disposed of by the end of the reporting period, the income effects include: (1) income or loss from operations of the discontinued component from the beginning of the reporting period through the disposal date and (2) gain or loss on disposal of the component's assets. If the component has not been disposed of by the end of the reporting period, the income effects include: (1) income or loss from operations of the discontinued component from the beginning of the reporting period through the end of the reporting period, and (2) an impairment loss if the fair value minus cost to sell of the component's assets is less than their carrying amount (book value).

3. **In addition to discontinued operations, what other events sometimes are reported separately in the income statement that you might tell Becky about? Why are these items reported separately?** *(p. 188)*    In addition to discontinued operations, extraordinary items also are reported separately in the income statement when they are present. The predictive ability of an income statement is significantly enhanced if normal and recurrent transactions are separated from unusual and nonrecurrent items. The income statement is a historical report, summarizing the most recent profit-generating activities of a company. The information in the statement is useful if it can help users predict the future. Toward this end, users should be made aware of events reported in the income statement that are not likely to occur again in the foreseeable future.

4. **Describe to Becky the difference between basic and diluted earnings per share.** *(p. 192)*    Basic earnings per share is computed by dividing income available to common shareholders (net income less any preferred stock dividends) by the weighted-average number of common shares outstanding for the period. Diluted earnings per share reflects the potential dilution that could occur for companies that have certain securities outstanding that are convertible into common shares or stock options that could create additional common shares if the options were exercised. These items could cause earnings per share to decrease (become diluted). Because of the complexity of the calculation and the importance of earnings per share to investors, the text devotes a substantial portion of Chapter 19 to this topic. ●

# The Bottom Line

● **LO4–1**    The components of income from continuing operations are revenues, expenses (including income taxes), gains, and losses, excluding those related to discontinued operations and extraordinary items. Companies often distinguish between operating and nonoperating income within continuing operations. *(p. 172)*

● **LO4–2**    The term *earnings quality* refers to the ability of reported earnings (income) to predict a company's future earnings. The relevance of any historical-based financial statement hinges on its predictive value. To enhance predictive value, analysts try to separate a company's *transitory earnings* effects from its *permanent earnings.* Many believe that manipulating income reduces earnings quality because it can mask permanent earnings. Two major methods used by managers to manipulate earnings are (1) income shifting and (2) income statement classification. *(p. 177)*

● **LO4–3**    Analysts begin their assessment of permanent earnings with income from continuing operations. It would be a mistake to assume income from continuing operations reflects permanent earnings entirely. In other words, there may be transitory earnings effects included in both operating and nonoperating income. *(p. 178)*

● **LO4–4**    A discontinued operation refers to the disposal or planned disposal of a component of the entity. The net-of-tax effect of discontinued operations is separately reported below income from continuing operations. *(p. 184)*

● **LO4–5**    Extraordinary items are material gains and losses that are both unusual in nature and infrequent in occurrence. The net-of-tax effects of extraordinary items are presented in the income statement below discontinued operations, if any. *(p. 188)*

● **LO4–6**    Earnings per share (EPS) is the amount of income achieved during a period expressed per share of common stock outstanding. The EPS must be disclosed for income from continuing operations and for each item below continuing operations. *(p. 192)*

● **LO4–7**    The FASB's Concept Statement 6 defines the term *comprehensive income* as the change in equity from nonowner transactions. The calculation of net income, however, excludes certain transactions that are included in comprehensive income. To convey the relationship between the two measures, companies must report both net income and comprehensive income and reconcile the difference between the two. The presentation can be (1) in a single, continuous statement of comprehensive income, or (2) in two separate, but consecutive statements—an income statement and a statement of comprehensive income. *(p. 192)*

● **LO4–8** When a company provides a set of financial statements that reports both financial position and results of operations, a statement of cash flows is reported for each period for which results of operations are provided. The purpose of the statement is to provide information about the cash receipts and cash disbursements that occurred during the period. (*p. 198*)

● **LO4–9** To enhance the usefulness of the information, the statement of cash flows classifies all transactions affecting cash into one of three categories: (1) operating activities, (2) investing activities, or (3) financing activities. (*p. 198*)

● **LO4–10** There are more similarities than differences between income statements and statements of cash flows prepared according to U.S. GAAP and those prepared applying international standards. However, we report extraordinary items separately in an income statement prepared according to U.S. GAAP, but international standards prohibit reporting extraordinary items. In a statement of cash flows, some differences are possible in the classifications of interest and divided revenue, interest expense, and dividends paid. (*pp. 177, 184, 189, 194, 199, and 204*) ●

# Questions For Review of Key Topics

| | |
|---|---|
| Q 4–1 | The income statement is a change statement. Explain what is meant by this. |
| Q 4–2 | What transactions are included in income from continuing operations? Briefly explain why it is important to segregate income from continuing operations from other transactions affecting net income. |
| Q 4–3 | Distinguish between operating and nonoperating income in relation to the income statement. |
| Q 4–4 | Briefly explain the difference between the single-step and multiple-step income statement formats. |
| Q 4–5 | Explain what is meant by the term *earnings quality*. |
| Q 4–6 | What are restructuring costs and where are they reported in the income statement? |
| Q 4–7 | Define intraperiod tax allocation. Why is the process necessary? |
| Q 4–8 | How are discontinued operations reported in the income statement? |
| Q 4–9 | Define extraordinary items. |
| Q 4–10 | How should extraordinary gains and losses be reported in the income statement? |
| Q 4–11 | What is meant by a change in accounting principle? Describe the accounting treatment for a voluntary change in accounting principle. |
| Q 4–12 | Accountants very often are required to make estimates, and very often those estimates prove incorrect. In what period(s) is the effect of a change in an accounting estimate reported? |
| Q 4–13 | The correction of a material error discovered in a year subsequent to the year the error was made is considered a prior period adjustment. Briefly describe the accounting treatment for prior period adjustments. |
| Q 4–14 | Define earnings per share (EPS). For which income statement items must EPS be disclosed? |
| Q 4–15 | Define comprehensive income. What are the two ways companies can present comprehensive income? |
| Q 4–16 | Describe the purpose of the statement of cash flows. |
| Q 4–17 | Identify and briefly describe the three categories of cash flows reported in the statement of cash flows. |
| Q 4–18 | Explain what is meant by noncash investing and financing activities pertaining to the statement of cash flows. Give an example of one of these activities. |
| Q 4–19 | Distinguish between the direct method and the indirect method for reporting the results of operating activities in the statement of cash flows. |
| IFRS   Q 4–20 | Identify any differences between U.S. GAAP and International Financial Reporting Standards (IFRS) in the number of possible separately reported items that could appear in income statements. |
| IFRS   Q 4–21 | Describe the potential statement of cash flows classification differences between U.S. GAAP and IFRS. |

# Brief Exercises

| | |
|---|---|
| **BE 4–1**<br>Single-step<br>income<br>statement<br>● **LO4–1** | The adjusted trial balance of Pacific Scientific Corporation on December 31, 2013, the end of the company's fiscal year, contained the following income statement items ($ in millions): sales revenue, $2,106; cost of goods sold, $1,240; selling expenses, $126; general and administrative expenses, $105; interest expense, $35; and gain on sale of investments, $45. Income tax expense has not yet been accrued. The income tax rate is 40%. Prepare a single-step income statement for 2013. Ignore EPS disclosures. |

**BE 4–2**
Multiple-step income statement
● LO4–1, LO4–3

Refer to the situation described in BE 4–1. If the company's accountant prepared a multiple-step income statement, what amount would appear in that statement for (a) operating income and (b) nonoperating income?

**BE 4–3**
Multiple-step income statement
● LO4–1, LO4–3

Refer to the situation described in BE 4–1. Prepare a multiple-step income statement for 2013. Ignore EPS disclosures.

**BE 4–4**
Multiple-step income statement
● LO4–1, LO4–3

The following is a partial year-end adjusted trial balance.

| Account Title | Debits | Credits |
|---|---|---|
| Sales revenue | | 300,000 |
| Loss on sale of investments | 22,000 | |
| Interest revenue | | 4,000 |
| Loss from flood damage (unusual and infrequent) | 50,000 | |
| Cost of goods sold | 160,000 | |
| General and administrative expenses | 40,000 | |
| Restructuring costs | 50,000 | |
| Selling expenses | 25,000 | |
| Income tax expense | 0 | |

Income tax expense has not yet been accrued. The income tax rate is 40%. Determine the following:
(a) operating income (loss), (b) income (loss) before any separately reported items, and (c) net income (loss).

**BE 4–5**
Extraordinary item
● LO4–5

Memorax Company earned before-tax income of $790,000 for its 2013 fiscal year. During the year the company experienced a $520,000 loss from earthquake damage that it considered to be an extraordinary item. This loss is not included in the $790,000 before-tax income figure. The company's income tax rate is 40%. Prepare the lower portion of the 2013 income statement beginning with $790,000.

**BE 4–6**
Separately reported items
● LO4–3, LO4–5, LO4–6

The following are partial income statement account balances taken from the December 31, 2013, year-end trial balance of White and Sons, Inc.: restructuring costs, $300,000; interest revenue, $40,000; loss from earthquake (unusual and infrequent), $400,000; and loss on sale of investments, $50,000. Income tax expense has not yet been accrued. The income tax rate is 40%. Prepare the lower portion of the 2013 income statement beginning with $850,000 income before income taxes and extraordinary item. Include appropriate basic EPS disclosures. The company had 100,000 shares of common stock outstanding throughout the year.

**BE 4–7**
Discontinued operations
● LO4–4

On December 31, 2013, the end of the fiscal year, California Microtech Corporation completed the sale of its semiconductor business for $10 million. The business segment qualifies as a component of the entity according to GAAP. The book value of the assets of the segment was $8 million. The loss from operations of the segment during 2013 was $3.6 million. Pretax income from continuing operations for the year totaled $5.8 million. The income tax rate is 30%. Prepare the lower portion of the 2013 income statement beginning with pretax income from continuing operations. Ignore EPS disclosures.

**BE 4–8**
Discontinued operations
● LO4–4

Refer to the situation described in BE 4–7. Assume that the semiconductor segment was not sold during 2013 but was held for sale at year-end. The estimated fair value of the segment's assets, less costs to sell, on December 31 was $10 million. Prepare the lower portion of the 2013 income statement beginning with pretax income from continuing operations. Ignore EPS disclosures.

**BE 4–9**
Discontinued operations
● LO4–4

Refer to the situation described in BE 4–8. Assume instead that the estimated fair value of the segment's assets, less costs to sell, on December 31 was $7 million rather than $10 million. Prepare the lower portion of the 2013 income statement beginning with pretax income from continuing operations. Ignore EPS disclosures.

**BE 4–10**
Comprehensive income
● LO4–7

O'Reilly Beverage Company reported net income of $650,000 for 2013. In addition, the company deferred a $60,000 pretax loss on derivatives and had pretax net unrealized holding gains on investment securities of $40,000. Prepare a separate statement of comprehensive income for 2013. The company's income tax rate is 40%.

**BE 4–11**
Statement of
cash flows; direct
method
● LO4–9

The following are summary cash transactions that occurred during the year for Hilliard Healthcare Co. (HHC):

| Cash received from: | |
| --- | --- |
| Customers | $660,000 |
| Interest on note receivable | 12,000 |
| Collection of note receivable | 100,000 |
| Sale of land | 40,000 |
| Issuance of common stock | 200,000 |
| Cash paid for: | |
| Interest on note payable | 18,000 |
| Purchase of equipment | 120,000 |
| Operating expenses | 440,000 |
| Dividends to shareholders | 30,000 |

Prepare the cash flows from operating activities section of HHC's statement of cash flows using the direct method.

**BE 4–12**
Statement of cash
flows; investing
and financing
activities
● LO4–9

Refer to the situation described in BE 4–11. Prepare the cash flows from investing and financing activities sections of HHC's statement of cash flows.

**BE 4–13**
Statement of
cash flows;
indirect method
● LO4–9

Net income of Mansfield Company was $45,000. The accounting records reveal depreciation expense of $80,000 as well as increases in prepaid rent, salaries payable, and income taxes payable of $60,000, $15,000, and $12,000, respectively. Prepare the cash flows from operating activities section of Mansfield's statement of cash flows using the indirect method.

**BE 4–14**
IFRS; Statement
of cash flows
● LO4–9, LO4–10

 **IFRS**

Refer to the situation described in BE 4–11 and BE 4–12. How might your solution to those brief exercises differ if Hilliard Healthcare Co. prepares its statement of cash flows according to International Financial Reporting Standards?

---

## Exercises                                         |ACCOUNTING

An alternate exercise and problem set is available on the text website: www.mhhe.com/spiceland7e

**E 4–1**
Income
statement format;
single step and
multiple step
● LO4–1, LO4–6

The following is a partial trial balance for the Green Star Corporation as of December 31, 2013:

| Account Title | Debits | Credits |
| --- | --- | --- |
| Sales revenue | | 1,300,000 |
| Interest revenue | | 30,000 |
| Gain on sale of investments | | 50,000 |
| Cost of goods sold | 720,000 | |
| Selling expenses | 160,000 | |
| General and administrative expenses | 75,000 | |
| Interest expense | 40,000 | |
| Income tax expense | 130,000 | |

100,000 shares of common stock were outstanding throughout 2013.

**Required:**
1. Prepare a single-step income statement for 2013, including EPS disclosures.
2. Prepare a multiple-step income statement for 2013, including EPS disclosures.

**E 4–2**
Income
statement format;
single step and
multiple step
● LO4–1, LO4–3,
  LO4–5, LO4–6

The following is a partial trial balance for General Lighting Corporation as of December 31, 2013:

| Account Title | Debits | Credits |
|---|---|---|
| Sales revenue | | 2,350,000 |
| Rental revenue | | 80,000 |
| Loss on sale of investments | 22,500 | |
| Loss from flood damage (event is both unusual and infrequent) | 120,000 | |
| Cost of goods sold | 1,200,300 | |
| Loss from write-down of inventory due to obsolescence | 200,000 | |
| Selling expenses | 300,000 | |
| General and administrative expenses | 150,000 | |
| Interest expense | 90,000 | |

300,000 shares of common stock were outstanding throughout 2013. Income tax expense has not yet been accrued. The income tax rate is 40%.

**Required:**
1. Prepare a single-step income statement for 2013, including EPS disclosures.
2. Prepare a multiple-step income statement for 2013, including EPS disclosures.

**E 4–3**
Multiple-step
continuous
statement of
comprehensive
income
● LO4–1, LO4–5,
  LO4–6, LO4–7

The trial balance for Lindor Corporation, a manufacturing company, for the year ended December 31, 2013, included the following income accounts:

| Account Title | Debits | Credits |
|---|---|---|
| Sales revenue | | 2,300,000 |
| Gain on litigation settlement (unusual and infrequent) | | 400,000 |
| Cost of goods sold | 1,400,000 | |
| Selling and administrative expenses | 420,000 | |
| Interest expense | 40,000 | |
| Unrealized holding gains on investment securities | | 80,000 |

The trial balance does not include the accrual for income taxes. Lindor's income tax rate is 30%. One million shares of common stock were outstanding throughout 2013.

**Required:**
Prepare a single, continuous multiple-step statement of comprehensive income for 2013, including appropriate EPS disclosures.

**E 4–4**
Income
statement
presentation;
intraperiod tax
allocation
● LO4–1, LO4–5,
  LO4–6

The following *incorrect* income statement was prepared by the accountant of the Axel Corporation:

**AXEL CORPORATION**
**Income Statement**
**For the Year Ended December 31, 2013**

| | | |
|---|---:|---:|
| Revenues and gains: | | |
| Sales | | $592,000 |
| Interest and dividends | | 32,000 |
| Gain from litigation settlement | | 86,000 |
| Total revenues and gains | | 710,000 |
| Expenses and losses: | | |
| Cost of goods sold | $325,000 | |
| Selling expenses | 67,000 | |
| Administrative expenses | 87,000 | |
| Interest | 26,000 | |
| Restructuring costs | 55,000 | |
| Income taxes | 60,000 | |
| Total expenses and losses | | 620,000 |
| Net Income | | $ 90,000 |
| Earnings per share | | $ 0.90 |

**Required:**
Prepare a multiple-step income statement for 2013 applying generally accepted accounting principles. The income tax rate is 40%. The gain from litigation settlement is considered an unusual and infrequent event and the amount is material.

**E 4–5**
**Discontinued operations**
● **LO4–4, LO4–6**

Chance Company had two operating divisions, one manufacturing farm equipment and the other office supplies. Both divisions are considered separate components as defined by generally accepted accounting principles. The farm equipment component had been unprofitable, and on September 1, 2013, the company adopted a plan to sell the assets of the division. The actual sale was completed on December 15, 2013, at a price of $600,000. The book value of the division's assets was $1,000,000, resulting in a before-tax loss of $400,000 on the sale.

The division incurred a before-tax operating loss from operations of $130,000 from the beginning of the year through December 15. The income tax rate is 40%. Chance's after-tax income from its continuing operations is $350,000.

**Required:**
Prepare an income statement for 2013 beginning with income from continuing operations. Include appropriate EPS disclosures assuming that 100,000 shares of common stock were outstanding throughout the year.

**E 4–6**
**Income statement presentation; discontinued operations; restructuring charges**
● **LO4–1, LO4–3, LO4–4**

Esquire Comic Book Company had income before tax of $1,000,000 in 2013 *before* considering the following material items:
1. Esquire sold one of its operating divisions, which qualified as a separate component according to generally accepted accounting principles. The before-tax loss on disposal was $350,000. The division generated before-tax income from operations from the beginning of the year through disposal of $500,000. Neither the loss on disposal nor the operating income is included in the $1,000,000 before-tax income the company generated from its other divisions.
2. The company incurred restructuring costs of $80,000 during the year.

**Required:**
Prepare a 2013 income statement for Esquire beginning with income from continuing operations. Assume an income tax rate of 40%. Ignore EPS disclosures.

**E 4–7**
**Discontinued operations; disposal in subsequent year**
● **LO4–4**

Kandon Enterprises, Inc., has two operating divisions; one manufactures machinery and the other breeds and sells horses. Both divisions are considered separate components as defined by generally accepted accounting principles. The horse division has been unprofitable, and on November 15, 2013, Kandon adopted a formal plan to sell the division. The sale was completed on April 30, 2014. At December 31, 2013, the component was considered held for sale.

On December 31, 2013, the company's fiscal year-end, the book value of the assets of the horse division was $250,000. On that date, the fair value of the assets, less costs to sell, was $200,000. The before-tax loss from operations of the division for the year was $140,000. The company's effective tax rate is 40%. The after-tax income from continuing operations for 2013 was $400,000.

**Required:**
1. Prepare a partial income statement for 2013 beginning with income from continuing operations. Ignore EPS disclosures.
2. Repeat requirement 1 assuming that the estimated net fair value of the horse division's assets was $400,000, instead of $200,000.

**E 4–8**
**Discontinued operations; disposal in subsequent year; solving for unknown**
● **LO4–4**

On September 17, 2013, Ziltech, Inc. entered into an agreement to sell one of its divisions that qualifies as a component of the entity according to generally accepted accounting principles. By December 31, 2013, the company's fiscal year-end, the division had not yet been sold, but was considered held for sale. The net fair value (fair value minus costs to sell) of the division's assets at the end of the year was $11 million. The pretax income from operations of the division during 2013 was $4 million. Pretax income from continuing operations for the year totaled $14 million. The income tax rate is 40%. Ziltech reported net income for the year of $7.2 million.

**Required:**
Determine the book value of the division's assets on December 31, 2013.

**E 4–9**
**Earnings per share**
● **LO4–6**

The Esposito Import Company had 1 million shares of common stock outstanding during 2013. Its income statement reported the following items: income from continuing operations, $5 million; loss from discontinued operations, $1.6 million; extraordinary gain, $2.2 million. All of these amounts are net of tax.

**Required:**
Prepare the 2013 EPS presentation for the Esposito Import Company.

**E 4–10**
**Comprehensive income**
● **LO4–7**

The Massoud Consulting Group reported net income of $1,354,000 for its fiscal year ended December 31, 2013. In addition, during the year the company experienced a foreign currency translation adjustment gain of $240,000 and had unrealized losses on investment securities of $80,000. The company's effective tax rate on all items affecting comprehensive income is 30%. Each component of other comprehensive income is displayed net of tax.

**Required:**
Prepare a separate statement of comprehensive income for 2013.

**E 4–11**
**Statement of cash flows; classifications**
● **LO4–9**

The statement of cash flows classifies all cash inflows and outflows into one of the three categories shown below and lettered from a through c. In addition, certain transactions that do not involve cash are reported in the statement as noncash investing and financing activities, labeled d.

a.  Operating activities
b.  Investing activities
c.  Financing activities
d.  Noncash investing and financing activities

**Required:**
For each of the following transactions, use the letters above to indicate the appropriate classification category.

1.  ____Purchase of equipment for cash.
2.  ____Payment of employee salaries.
3.  ____Collection of cash from customers.
4.  ____Cash proceeds from a note payable.
5.  ____Purchase of common stock of another corporation for cash.
6.  ____Issuance of common stock for cash.
7.  ____Sale of machinery for cash.
8.  ____Payment of interest on note payable.
9.  ____Issuance of bonds payable in exchange for land and building.
10.  ____Payment of cash dividends to shareholders.
11.  ____Payment of principal on note payable.

**E 4–12**
**Statement of cash flows preparation**
● **LO4–9**

The following summary transactions occurred during 2013 for Bluebonnet Bakers:

| Cash Received from: | |
|---|---:|
| Customers | $380,000 |
| Interest on note receivable | 6,000 |
| Principal on note receivable | 50,000 |
| Sale of investments | 30,000 |
| Proceeds from note payable | 100,000 |
| **Cash Paid for:** | |
| Purchase of inventory | 160,000 |
| Interest on note payable | 5,000 |
| Purchase of equipment | 85,000 |
| Salaries to employees | 90,000 |
| Principal on note payable | 25,000 |
| Payment of dividends to shareholders | 20,000 |

The balance of cash and cash equivalents at the beginning of 2013 was $17,000.

**Required:**
Prepare a statement of cash flows for 2013 for Bluebonnet Bakers. Use the direct method for reporting operating activities.

**E 4–13**
**IFRS; statement of cash flows**
● **LO4–9, LO4–10**

 **IFRS**

Refer to the situation described in Exercise 4–12.

**Required:**
How might your solution differ if Bluebonnet Bakers prepares the statement of cash flows according to International Financial Reporting Standards?

**E 4–14**
**Indirect method; reconciliation of net income to net cash flows from operating activities**
● **LO4–9**

The accounting records of Hampton Company provided the data below ($ in 000s).

| | |
|---|---:|
| Net income | $17,300 |
| Depreciation expense | 7,800 |
| Increase in accounts receivable | 4,000 |
| Decrease in inventory | 5,500 |
| Decrease in prepaid insurance | 1,200 |
| Decrease in salaries payable | 2,700 |
| Increase in interest payable | 800 |

**Required:**
Prepare a reconciliation of net income to net cash flows from operating activities.

**E 4–15**
**Statement of cash flows; directly from transactions**
● LO4–9

The following transactions occurred during March 2013 for the Wainwright Corporation. The company owns and operates a wholesale warehouse. [These are the same transactions analyzed in Exercise 2–1, when we determined their effect on elements of the accounting equation.]

1. Issued 30,000 shares of capital stock in exchange for $300,000 in cash.
2. Purchased equipment at a cost of $40,000. $10,000 cash was paid and a note payable was signed for the balance owed.
3. Purchased inventory on account at a cost of $90,000. The company uses the perpetual inventory system.
4. Credit sales for the month totaled $120,000. The cost of the goods sold was $70,000.
5. Paid $5,000 in rent on the warehouse building for the month of March.
6. Paid $6,000 to an insurance company for fire and liability insurance for a one-year period beginning April 1, 2013.
7. Paid $70,000 on account for the merchandise purchased in 3.
8. Collected $55,000 from customers on account.
9. Recorded depreciation expense of $1,000 for the month on the equipment.

**Required:**
1. Analyze each transaction and classify each as a financing, investing, and/or operating activity (a transaction can represent more than one type of activity). In doing so, also indicate the cash effect of each, if any. If there is no cash effect, simply place a check mark (√) in the appropriate column(s).
   *Example:*

| Financing | Investing | Operating |
|---|---|---|
| 1. $300,000 | | |

2. Prepare a statement of cash flows, using the direct method to present cash flows from operating activities. Assume the cash balance at the beginning of the month was $40,000.

**E 4–16**
**Statement of cash flows; indirect method**
● LO4–9

Cemptex Corporation prepares its statement of cash flows using the indirect method to report operating activities. Net income for the 2013 fiscal year was $624,000. Depreciation and amortization expense of $87,000 was included with operating expenses in the income statement. The following information describes the changes in current assets and liabilities other than cash:

| | |
|---|---|
| Decrease in accounts receivable | $22,000 |
| Increase in inventories | 9,200 |
| Increase prepaid expenses | 8,500 |
| Increase in salaries payable | 10,000 |
| Decrease in income taxes payable | 14,000 |

**Required:**
Prepare the operating activities section of the 2013 statement of cash flows.

**E 4–17**
**IFRS; statement of cash flows**
● LO4–9, LO4–10

🌐 **IFRS**

The statement of cash flows for the year ended December 31, 2013, for Bronco Metals is presented below.

**BRONCO METALS**
**Statement of Cash Flows**
**For the Year Ended December 31, 2013**

| | | |
|---|---|---|
| Cash flows from operating activities: | | |
| Collections from customers | $ 353,000 | |
| Interest on note receivable | 4,000 | |
| Dividends received from investments | 2,400 | |
| Purchase of inventory | (186,000) | |
| Payment of operating expenses | (67,000) | |
| Payment of interest on note payable | (8,000) | |
| Net cash flows from operating activities | | $ 98,400 |
| Cash flows from investing activities: | | |
| Collection of note receivable | 100,000 | |
| Purchase of equipment | (154,000) | |
| Net cash flows from investing activities | | (54,000) |

(continued)

(concluded)

| Cash flows from financing activities: | | |
|---|---|---|
| Proceeds from issuance of common stock | 200,000 | |
| Dividends paid | (40,000) | |
| Net cash flows from financing activities | | 160,000 |
| Net increase in cash | | 204,400 |
| Cash and cash equivalents, January 1 | | 28,600 |
| Cash and cash equivalents, December 31 | | $233,000 |

**Required:**

Prepare the statement of cash flows assuming that Bronco prepares its financial statements according to International Financial Reporting Standards. Where IFRS allows flexibility, use the classification used most often in IFRS financial statements.

**E 4–18**
**Statement of cash flows; indirect method**
● **LO4–9**

Presented below is the 2013 income statement and comparative balance sheet information for Tiger Enterprises.

### TIGER ENTERPRISES
### Income Statement
### For the Year Ended December 31, 2013

| ($ in thousands) | | |
|---|---|---|
| Sales revenue | | $7,000 |
| Operating expenses: | | |
| Cost of goods sold | $3,360 | |
| Depreciation | 240 | |
| Insurance | 100 | |
| Administrative and other | 1,800 | |
| Total operating expenses | | 5,500 |
| Income before income taxes | | 1,500 |
| Income tax expense | | 600 |
| Net income | | $ 900 |

| Balance Sheet Information ($ in thousands) | Dec. 31, 2013 | Dec. 31, 2012 |
|---|---|---|
| **Assets:** | | |
| Cash | $ 300 | $ 200 |
| Accounts receivable | 750 | 830 |
| Inventory | 640 | 600 |
| Prepaid insurance | 50 | 20 |
| Plant and equipment | 2,100 | 1,800 |
| Less: Accumulated depreciation | (840) | (600) |
| Total assets | $3,000 | $2,850 |
| **Liabilities and Shareholders' Equity:** | | |
| Accounts payable | $ 300 | $ 360 |
| Payables for administrative and other expenses | 300 | 400 |
| Income taxes payable | 200 | 150 |
| Note payable (due 12/31/2014) | 800 | 600 |
| Common stock | 900 | 800 |
| Retained earnings | 500 | 540 |
| Total liabilities and shareholders' equity | $3,000 | $2,850 |

**Required:**

Prepare Tiger's statement of cash flows, using the indirect method to present cash flows from operating activities. (Hint: You will have to calculate dividend payments.)

**E 4–19**
**Statement of cash flows; direct method**
● **LO4–9**

Refer to the situation described in Exercise 4–18.

**Required:**

Prepare the cash flows from operating activities section of Tiger's 2013 statement of cash flows using the direct method. Assume that all purchases and sales of inventory are on account, and that there are no anticipated bad debts for accounts receivable. (Hint: Use T-accounts for the pertinent items to isolate the information needed for the statement.)

**E 4–20**
**FASB codification research**
● **LO4–6**

The *FASB Accounting Standards Codification* represents the single source of authoritative U.S. generally accepted accounting principles.

**Required:**

1. Obtain the relevant authoritative literature on earnings per share using the FASB's Codification Research System at the FASB website (www.fasb.org). Identify the Codification topic number that provides the accounting for earnings per share.

2. What is the specific citation that describes the additional information for earnings per share that must be included in the notes to the financial statements?

3. Describe the required disclosures.

**E 4–21**
**FASB codification research**
● LO4–5, LO4–6, LO4–7, LO4–9

Access the FASB's Codification Research System at the FASB website (www.fasb.org). Determine the specific citation for each of the following items:

1. The criteria for determining if a gain or loss should be reported as an extraordinary item.

2. The calculation of the weighted average number of shares for basic earnings per share purposes.

3. The alternative formats permissible for reporting comprehensive income.

4. The classifications of cash flows required in the statement of cash flows.

**E 4–22**
**Concepts; terminology**
● LO4–1 through LO4–9

Listed below are several terms and phrases associated with income statement presentation and the statement of cash flows. Pair each item from List A (by letter) with the item from List B that is most appropriately associated with it.

| List A | List B |
|---|---|
| _____ 1. Intraperiod tax allocation | a. Unusual, infrequent, and material gains and losses. |
| _____ 2. Comprehensive income | b. Starts with net income and works backwards to convert to cash. |
| _____ 3. Extraordinary items | c. Reports the cash effects of each operating activity directly on the statement. |
| _____ 4. Operating income | d. Correction of a material error of a prior period. |
| _____ 5. A discontinued operation | e. Related to the external financing of the company. |
| _____ 6. Earnings per share | f. Associates tax with income statement item. |
| _____ 7. Prior period adjustment | g. Total nonowner change in equity. |
| _____ 8. Financing activities | h. Related to the transactions entering into the determination of net income. |
| _____ 9. Operating activities (SCF) | i. Related to the acquisition and disposition of long-term assets. |
| _____ 10. Investing activities | j. Required disclosure for publicly traded corporation. |
| _____ 11. Direct method | k. A component of an entity. |
| _____ 12. Indirect method | l. Directly related to principal revenue-generating activities. |

# CPA and CMA Review Questions

**CPA Exam Questions**

● LO4–4

The following questions are adapted from a variety of sources including questions developed by the AICPA Board of Examiners and those used in the Kaplan CPA Review Course to study the income statement and statement of cash flows while preparing for the CPA examination. Determine the response that best completes the statements or questions.

1. Roco Company manufactures both industrial and consumer electronics. Due to a change in its strategic focus, the company decided to exit the consumer electronics business, and in 2013 sold the division to Sunny Corporation. The consumer electronics division qualifies as a component of the entity according to GAAP. How should Roco report the sale in its 2013 income statement?

   a. Include in income from continuing operations as a nonoperating gain or loss.
   b. As an extraordinary item.
   c. As a discontinued operation, reported below income from continuing operations.
   d. None of the above.

● LO4–3, LO4–4, LO4–5

2. Bridge Company's results for the year ended December 31, 2013, include the following material items:

| | |
|---|---|
| Sales revenue | $5,000,000 |
| Cost of goods sold | 3,000,000 |
| Administrative expenses | 1,000,000 |
| Gain on sale of equipment | 200,000 |
| Loss on discontinued operations | 400,000 |
| Loss from earthquake damage (unusual and infrequent event) | 500,000 |
| Understatement of depreciation expense in 2012 caused by mathematical error | 250,000 |

Bridge Company's income from continuing operations before income taxes for 2013 is:
a. $700,000
b. $950,000
c. $1,000,000
d. $1,200,000

● LO4–4, LO4–5

3. In Baer Food Co.'s 2013 single-step income statement, the section titled "Revenues" consisted of the following:

| | |
|---|---:|
| Net sales revenue | $187,000 |
| Income on discontinued operations including gain on disposal of $21,000 and net taxes of $6,000 | 12,000 |
| Interest revenue | 10,200 |
| Gain on sale of equipment | 4,700 |
| Extraordinary gain net of $750 tax effect | 1,500 |
| Total revenues | $215,400 |

In the revenues section of the 2013 income statement, Baer Food should have reported total revenues of
a. $201,900
b. $203,700
c. $215,400
d. $216,300

● LO4–4

4. On November 30, 2013, Pearman Company committed to a plan to sell a division that qualified as a component of the entity according to GAAP, and was properly classified as held for sale on December 31, 2013, the end of the company's fiscal year. The division was tested for impairment and a $400,000 loss was indicated. The division's loss from operations for 2013 was $1,000,000. The final sale was expected to occur on February 15, 2014. What before-tax amount(s) should Pearman report as loss on discontinued operations in its 2013 income statement?
a. $1,400,000 loss.
b. $400,000 loss.
c. None.
d. $400,000 impairment loss included in continuing operations and a $1,000,000 loss from discontinued operations.

● LO4–9

5. Which of the following items is *not* considered an operating cash flow in the statement of cash flows?
a. Dividends paid to stockholders.
b. Cash received from customers.
c. Interest paid to creditors.
d. Cash paid for salaries.

● LO4–9

6. Which of the following items is *not* considered an investing cash flow in the statement of cash flows?
a. Purchase of equipment.
b. Purchase of securities.
c. Issuing common stock for cash.
d. Sale of land.

Beginning in 2011, International Financial Reporting Standards are tested on the CPA exam along with U.S. GAAP. The following questions deal with the application of IFRS.

● LO4–10

● IFRS

7. Under *both* U.S. GAAP and IFRS, which one of the following items is reported separately in the income statement, net of tax?
a. Restructuring costs.
b. Discontinued operations.
c. Extraordinary gains and losses.
d. None of the above.

● LO4–10

● IFRS

8. In a statement of cash flows prepared under IFRS, interest paid
a. Must be classified as an operating cash flow.
b. Can be classified as either an operating cash flow or an investing cash flow.
c. Can be classified as either an operating cash flow or a financing cash flow.
d. Can be classified as either an investing cash flow or a financing cash flow.

**CMA Exam Questions**

The following questions dealing with the income statement are adapted from questions that previously appeared on Certified Management Accountant (CMA) examinations. The CMA designation sponsored by the Institute of Management Accountants (www.imanet.org) provides members with an objective measure of knowledge and competence in the field of management accounting. Determine the response that best completes the statements or questions.

● **LO4–1**

1. Which one of the following items is included in the determination of income from continuing operations?
   a. Discontinued operations.
   b. Extraordinary loss.
   c. Cumulative effect of a change in an accounting principle.
   d. Unusual loss from a write-down of inventory.

● **LO4–3**

2. In a multiple-step income statement for a retail company, all of the following are included in the operating section except
   a. Sales.
   b. Cost of goods sold.
   c. Dividend revenue.
   d. Administrative and selling expenses.

● **LO4–5**

3. When reporting extraordinary items,
   a. Each item (net of tax) is presented on the face of the income statement separately as a component of net income for the period.
   b. Each item is presented exclusive of any related income tax.
   c. Each item is presented as an unusual item within income from continuing operations.
   d. All extraordinary gains or losses that occur in a period are summarized as total gains and total losses and then offset to present the net extraordinary gain or loss.

# Problems

An alternate exercise and problem set is available on the text website: **www.mhhe.com/spiceland7e**

**P 4–1**
Comparative income statements; multiple-step format

● **LO4–1, LO4–3 through LO4–5, LO4–6**

Selected information about income statement accounts for the Reed Company is presented below (the company's fiscal year ends on December 31):

|  | 2013 | 2012 |
|---|---|---|
| Sales | $4,400,000 | $3,500,000 |
| Cost of goods sold | 2,860,000 | 2,000,000 |
| Administrative expenses | 800,000 | 675,000 |
| Selling expenses | 360,000 | 312,000 |
| Interest revenue | 150,000 | 140,000 |
| Interest expense | 200,000 | 200,000 |
| Loss on sale of assets of discontinued component | 50,000 | — |

On July 1, 2013, the company adopted a plan to discontinue a division that qualifies as a component of an entity as defined by GAAP. The assets of the component were sold on September 30, 2013, for $50,000 less than their book value. Results of operations for the component (*included* in the above account balances) were as follows:

|  | 1/1/13–9/30/13 | 2012 |
|---|---|---|
| Sales | $400,000 | $500,000 |
| Cost of goods sold | (290,000) | (320,000) |
| Administrative expenses | (50,000) | (40,000) |
| Selling expenses | (20,000) | (30,000) |
| Operating income before taxes | $ 40,000 | $110,000 |

In addition to the account balances above, several events occurred during 2013 that have *not* yet been reflected in the above accounts:

1. A fire caused $50,000 in uninsured damages to the main office building. The fire was considered to be an infrequent but not unusual event.

2. An earthquake caused $100,000 in property damage to one of Reed's factories. The amount of the loss is material and the event is considered unusual and infrequent.

3. Inventory that had cost $40,000 had become obsolete because a competitor introduced a better product. The inventory was sold as scrap for $5,000.

4. Income taxes have not yet been accrued.

**Required:**
Prepare a multiple-step income statement for the Reed Company for 2013, showing 2012 information in comparative format, including income taxes computed at 40% and EPS disclosures assuming 300,000 shares of common stock.

**P 4–2**
Discontinued
operations
● LO4–4

The following condensed income statements of the Jackson Holding Company are presented for the two years ended December 31, 2013 and 2012:

|  | 2013 | 2012 |
|---|---|---|
| Sales | $15,000,000 | $9,600,000 |
| Cost of goods sold | 9,200,000 | 6,000,000 |
| Gross profit | 5,800,000 | 3,600,000 |
| Operating expenses | 3,200,000 | 2,600,000 |
| Operating income | 2,600,000 | 1,000,000 |
| Gain on sale of division | 600,000 | — |
|  | 3,200,000 | 1,000,000 |
| Income tax expense | 1,280,000 | 400,000 |
| Net income | $ 1,920,000 | $ 600,000 |

On October 15, 2013, Jackson entered into a tentative agreement to sell the assets of one of its divisions. The division qualifies as a component of an entity as defined by GAAP. The division was sold on December 31, 2013, for $5,000,000. Book value of the division's assets was $4,400,000. The division's contribution to Jackson's operating income before-tax for each year was as follows:

| 2013 | $400,000 loss |
|---|---|
| 2012 | $300,000 loss |

Assume an income tax rate of 40%.

**Required:**
1. Prepare revised income statements according to generally accepted accounting principles, beginning with income from continuing operations before income taxes. Ignore EPS disclosures.
2. Assume that by December 31, 2013, the division had not yet been sold but was considered held for sale. The fair value of the division's assets on December 31 was $5,000,000. How would the presentation of discontinued operations be different from your answer to requirement 1?
3. Assume that by December 31, 2013, the division had not yet been sold but was considered held for sale. The fair value of the division's assets on December 31 was $3,900,000. How would the presentation of discontinued operations be different from your answer to requirement 1?

**P 4–3**
Income
statement
presentation
● LO4–4, LO4–5

For the year ending December 31, 2013, Micron Corporation had income from continuing operations before taxes of $1,200,000 before considering the following transactions and events. All of the items described below are before taxes and the amounts should be considered material.
1. During 2013, one of Micron's factories was damaged in an earthquake. As a result, the firm recognized a loss of $800,000. The event is considered unusual and infrequent.
2. In November 2013, Micron sold its Waffle House restaurant chain that qualified as a component of an entity. The company had adopted a plan to sell the chain in May 2013. The income from operations of the chain from January 1, 2013, through November was $160,000 and the loss on sale of the chain's assets was $300,000.
3. In 2013, Micron sold one of its six factories for $1,200,000. At the time of the sale, the factory had a carrying value of $1,100,000. The factory was not considered a component of the entity.
4. In 2011, Micron's accountant omitted the annual adjustment for patent amortization expense of $120,000. The error was not discovered until December 2013.

**Required:**
1. Prepare Micron's income statement, beginning with income from continuing operations before taxes, for the year ended December 31, 2013. Assume an income tax rate of 30%. Ignore EPS disclosures.
2. Briefly explain the motivation for segregating certain income statement events from income from continuing operations.

**P 4–4**
Income
statement
presentation;
unusual items
● LO4–3, LO4–5

The preliminary 2013 income statement of Alexian Systems, Inc., is presented below:

**ALEXIAN SYSTEMS, INC.**
**Income Statement**
**For the Year Ended December 31, 2013**
($ in millions, except earnings per share)

| Revenues and gains: | |
|---|---|
| Net sales | $ 425 |
| Interest | 3 |
| Other income | 126 |
| Total revenues and gains | 554 |

(continued)

(concluded)

| Expenses: | |
|---|---|
| Cost of goods sold | 270 |
| Selling and administrative | 154 |
| Income taxes | 52 |
| Total expenses | 476 |
| Net Income | $ 78 |
| Earnings per share | $3.90 |

**Additional Information:**

1.  Selling and administrative expenses include $26 million in restructuring costs.

2.  Included in other income is an extraordinary gain of $120 million. The remaining $6 million is from the gain on sale of investments.

3.  Cost of goods sold was increased by $5 million to correct an error in the calculation of 2012's ending inventory. The amount is material.

**Required:**

For each of the three additional facts listed above, discuss the appropriate presentation of the item described. Do not prepare a revised statement.

**P 4–5**
Income statement presentation; unusual items
● **LO4–1, LO4–3, LO4–5, LO4–6**

[This is a variation of the previous problem focusing on income statement presentation.]

**Required:**

Refer to the information presented in Problem 4–4. Prepare a revised income statement for 2013 reflecting the additional facts. Use a multiple-step format. Assume that an income tax rate of 40% applies to all income statement items, and that 20 million shares of common stock were outstanding throughout the year.

**P 4–6**
Income statement presentation
● **LO4–1, LO4–3 through LO4–5, LO4–6**

Rembrandt Paint Company had the following income statement items for the year ended December 31, 2013 ($ in 000s):

| | | | |
|---|---|---|---|
| Net sales | $18,000 | Cost of goods sold | $10,500 |
| Interest income | 200 | Selling and administrative expenses | 2,500 |
| Interest expense | 350 | Restructuring costs | 800 |
| Extraordinary gain | 3,000 | | |

In addition, during the year the company completed the disposal of its plastics business and incurred a loss from operations of $1.6 million and a gain on disposal of the component's assets of $2 million. 500,000 shares of common stock were outstanding throughout 2013. Income tax expense has not yet been accrued. The income tax rate is 30% on all items of income (loss).

**Required:**

Prepare a multiple-step income statement for 2013, including EPS disclosures.

**P 4–7**
Income statement presentation; statement of comprehensive income; unusual items
● **LO4–1, LO4–3, LO4–4, LO4–5, LO4–6, LO4–7**

The following income statement items appeared on the adjusted trial balance of Schembri Manufacturing Corporation for the year ended December 31, 2013 ($ in 000s): sales revenue, $15,300; cost of goods sold, $6,200; selling expenses, $1,300; general and administrative expenses, $800; interest revenue, $85; interest expense, $180. Income taxes have not yet been accrued. The company's income tax rate is 40% on all items of income or loss. These revenue and expense items appear in the company's income statement every year. The company's controller, however, has asked for your help in determining the appropriate treatment of the following nonrecurring transactions that also occurred during 2013 ($ in 000s). All transactions are material in amount.

1.  Investments were sold during the year at a loss of $220. Schembri also had unrealized gains of $320 for the year on investments.

2.  One of the company's factories was closed during the year. Restructuring costs incurred were $1,200.

3.  An earthquake destroyed a warehouse causing $2,000 in damages. The event is considered to be unusual and infrequent.

4.  During the year, Schembri completed the sale of one of its operating divisions that qualifies as a component of the entity according to GAAP. The division had incurred a loss from operations of $560 in 2013 prior to the sale, and its assets were sold at a gain of $1,400.

5.  In 2013, the company's accountant discovered that depreciation expense in 2012 for the office building was understated by $200.

6.  Foreign currency translation losses for the year totaled $240.

**Required:**
1. Prepare Schembri's single, continuous multiple-step statement of comprehensive income for 2013, including basic earnings per share disclosures. One million shares of common stock were outstanding at the beginning of the year and an additional 400,000 shares were issued on July 1, 2013.
2. Prepare a separate statement of comprehensive income for 2013.

**P 4–8**
Multiple-step statement of income and comprehensive income
● LO4–1, LO4–3, LO4–5, LO4–7

Duke Company's records show the following account balances at December 31, 2013:

| | |
|---|---|
| Sales | $15,000,000 |
| Cost of goods sold | 9,000,000 |
| General and administrative expenses | 1,000,000 |
| Selling expenses | 500,000 |
| Interest expense | 700,000 |

Income tax expense has not yet been determined. The following events also occurred during 2013. All transactions are material in amount.
1. $300,000 in restructuring costs were incurred in connection with plant closings.
2. The company operates a factory in South America. During the year, the foreign government took over (expropriated) the factory and paid Duke $1,000,000, which was one-fourth of the book value of the assets involved. The factory is not a component of the entity and the event is considered to be unusual and infrequent.
3. Inventory costing $400,000 was written off as obsolete. Material losses of this type are not considered to be unusual.
4. It was discovered that depreciation expense for 2012 was understated by $50,000 due to a mathematical error.
5. The company experienced a foreign currency translation adjustment loss of $200,000 and had unrealized gains on investments of $180,000.

**Required:**
Prepare a single, continuous multiple-step statement of comprehensive income for 2013. The company's effective tax rate on all items affecting comprehensive income is 40%. Each component of other comprehensive income should be displayed net of tax. Ignore EPS disclosures.

**P 4–9**
Statement of cash flows
● LO4–9

The Diversified Portfolio Corporation provides investment advice to customers. A condensed income statement for the year ended December 31, 2013, appears below:

| | |
|---|---|
| Service revenue | $900,000 |
| Operating expenses | 700,000 |
| Income before income taxes | 200,000 |
| Income tax expense | 80,000 |
| Net income | $120,000 |

The following balance sheet information also is available:

| | 12/31/13 | 12/31/12 |
|---|---|---|
| Cash | $275,000 | $ 70,000 |
| Accounts receivable | 120,000 | 100,000 |
| Accounts payable (operating expenses) | 70,000 | 60,000 |
| Income taxes payable | 10,000 | 15,000 |

In addition, the following transactions took place during the year:
1. Common stock was issued for $100,000 in cash.
2. Long-term investments were sold for $50,000 in cash. The original cost of the investments also was $50,000.
3. $80,000 in cash dividends was paid to shareholders.
4. The company has no outstanding debt, other than those payables listed above.
5. Operating expenses include $30,000 in depreciation expense.

**Required:**
1. Prepare a statement of cash flows for 2013 for the Diversified Portfolio Corporation. Use the direct method for reporting operating activities.
2. Prepare the cash flows from operating activities section of Diversified's 2013 statement of cash flows using the indirect method.

P 4–10
Integration
of financial
statements;
Chapters 3 and 4
● LO4–9

The chief accountant for Grandview Corporation provides you with the company's 2013 statement of cash flows and income statement. The accountant has asked for your help with some missing figures in the company's comparative balance sheets. These financial statements are shown next ($ in millions).

**GRANDVIEW CORPORATION**
**Statement of Cash Flows**
**For the Year Ended December 31, 2013**

| | | |
|---|---:|---:|
| **Cash Flows from Operating Activities:** | | |
| Collections from customers | $71 | |
| Payment to suppliers | (30) | |
| Payment of general & administrative expenses | (18) | |
| Payment of income taxes | (9) | |
| Net cash flows from operating activities | | $14 |
| **Cash Flows from Investing Activities:** | | |
| Sale of investments | | 65 |
| **Cash Flows from Financing Activities:** | | |
| Issuance of common stock | 10 | |
| Payment of dividends | (3) | |
| Net cash flows from financing activities | | 7 |
| Net increase in cash | | $86 |

**GRANDVIEW CORPORATION**
**Income Statement**
**For the Year Ended December 31, 2013**

| | | |
|---|---:|---:|
| Sales revenue | | $80 |
| Cost of goods sold | | 32 |
| Gross profit | | 48 |
| Operating expenses: | | |
| General and administrative | $18 | |
| Depreciation | 10 | |
| Total operating expenses | | 28 |
| Operating income | | 20 |
| Other income: | | |
| Gain on sale of investments | | 15 |
| Income before income taxes | | 35 |
| Income tax expense | | 7 |
| Net income | | $28 |

**GRANDVIEW CORPORATION**
**Balance Sheets**
**At December 31**

| | 2013 | 2012 |
|---|---:|---:|
| **Assets:** | | |
| Cash | $145 | $ ? |
| Accounts receivable | ? | 84 |
| Investments | — | 50 |
| Inventory | 60 | ? |
| Property, plant & equipment | 150 | 150 |
| Less: Accumulated depreciation | (65) | ? |
| Total assets | ? | ? |
| **Liabilities and Shareholders' Equity:** | | |
| Accounts payable to suppliers | $ 40 | $ 30 |
| Payables for selling & admin. expenses | 9 | 9 |
| Income taxes payable | 22 | ? |
| Common stock | 240 | 230 |
| Retained earnings | ? | 47 |
| Total liabilities and shareholders' equity | ? | ? |

**Required:**
1. Calculate the missing amounts.
2. Prepare the operating activities section of Grandview's 2013 statement of cash flows using the indirect method.

**P 4–11**
Statement of
cash flows;
indirect method
● LO4–9

Presented below are the 2013 income statement and comparative balance sheets for Santana Industries.

**SANTANA INDUSTRIES**
**Income Statement**
**For the Year Ended December 31, 2013**
($ in thousands)

| | | |
|---|---:|---:|
| Sales revenue | $14,250 | |
| Service revenue | 3,400 | |
| Total revenue | | $17,650 |
| Operating expenses: | | |
| Cost of goods sold | 7,200 | |
| Selling | 2,400 | |
| General and administrative | 1,500 | |
| Total operating expenses | | 11,100 |
| Operating income | | 6,550 |
| Interest expense | | 200 |
| Income before income taxes | | 6,350 |
| Income tax expense | | 2,500 |
| Net income | | $ 3,850 |

| Balance Sheet Information ($ in thousands) | Dec. 31, 2013 | Dec. 31, 2012 |
|---|---:|---:|
| **Assets:** | | |
| Cash | $ 7,350 | $ 2,200 |
| Accounts receivable | 2,500 | 2,200 |
| Inventory | 4,000 | 3,000 |
| Prepaid rent | 150 | 300 |
| Plant and equipment | 14,500 | 12,000 |
| Less: Accumulated depreciation | (5,100) | (4,500) |
| Total assets | $23,400 | $15,200 |
| **Liabilities and Shareholders' Equity:** | | |
| Accounts payable | $ 1,400 | $ 1,100 |
| Interest payable | 100 | 0 |
| Unearned service revenue | 800 | 600 |
| Income taxes payable | 550 | 800 |
| Loan payable (due 12/31/2012) | 5,000 | 0 |
| Common stock | 10,000 | 10,000 |
| Retained earnings | 5,550 | 2,700 |
| Total liabilities and shareholders' equity | $23,400 | $15,200 |

Additional information for the 2013 fiscal year ($ in thousands):
1. Cash dividends of $1,000 were declared and paid.
2. Equipment costing $4,000 was purchased with cash.
3. Equipment with a book value of $500 (cost of $1,500 less accumulated depreciation of $1,000) was sold for $500.
4. Depreciation of $1,600 is included in operating expenses.

**Required:**
Prepare Santana Industries' 2013 statement of cash flows, using the indirect method to present cash flows from operating activities.

# Broaden Your Perspective

Apply your critical-thinking ability to the knowledge you've gained. These cases will provide you an opportunity to develop your research, analysis, judgment, and communication skills. You also will work with other students, integrate what you've learned, apply it in real world situations, and consider its global and ethical ramifications. This practice will broaden your knowledge and further develop your decision-making abilities.

**Judgment Case 4–1**
Earnings quality
● LO4–2, LO4–3

The financial community in the United States has become increasingly concerned with the quality of reported company earnings.

**Required:**

1. Define the term *earnings quality*.
2. Explain the distinction between permanent and transitory earnings as it relates to the concept of earnings quality.
3. How do earnings management practices affect the quality of earnings?
4. Assume that a manufacturing company's annual income statement included a large gain from the sale of investment securities. What factors would you consider in determining whether or not this gain should be included in an assessment of the company's permanent earnings?

**Judgment Case 4–2**
Restructuring costs
● LO4–3

The appearance of restructuring costs in corporate income statements increased significantly in the 1980s and 1990s and continues to be relevant today.

**Required:**

1. What types of costs are included in restructuring costs?
2. When are restructuring costs recognized?
3. How would you classify restructuring costs in a multi-step income statement?
4. What factors would you consider in determining whether or not restructuring costs should be included in an assessment of a company's permanent earnings?

**Judgment Case 4–3**
Earnings management
● LO4–2, LO4–3

Companies often are under pressure to meet or beat Wall Street earnings projections in order to increase stock prices and also to increase the value of stock options. Some resort to earnings management practices to artificially create desired results.

**Required:**

Is *earnings management* always intended to produce higher income? Explain.

**Real World Case 4–4**
Earnings quality and pro forma earnings
● LO4–3

Companies often voluntarily provide a pro forma earnings number when they announce annual or quarterly earnings.

**Required:**

1. What is meant by the term *pro forma earnings* in this context?
2. How do pro forma earnings relate to the concept of earnings quality?

**Communication Case 4–5**
Income statement presentation of gain
● LO4–5

McMinville Corporation manufactures paper products. In 2009, the company purchased several large tracts of timber for $22 million with the intention of harvesting the timber rather than buying this critical raw material from outside suppliers. However, in 2013, McMinville abandoned the idea and all of the timber tracts were sold for $31 million. Net income for 2013, before considering this event, is $17.5 million and the company's effective tax rate is 30%.

The focus of this case is the income statement presentation of the gain on the sale of the timber tracts. Your instructor will divide the class into two to six groups depending on the size of the class. The mission of your group is to reach consensus on the appropriate income statement presentation of the gain.

**Required:**

Each group member should deliberate the situation independently and draft a tentative argument prior to the class session for which the case is assigned.

In class, each group will meet for 10 to 15 minutes in different areas of the classroom. During that meeting, group members will take turns sharing their suggestions for the purpose of arriving at a single group treatment.

After the allotted time, a spokesperson for each group (selected during the group meetings) will share the group's solution with the class. The goal of the class is to incorporate the views of each group into a consensus approach to the situation.

**Communication Case 4–6**
Income statement presentation
● LO4–5

Real World Financials

Carter Hawley Hale Stores (CHHS), Inc., was one of the largest department store retailers in the United States. At the end of fiscal 1989, the company operated 113 stores in the Sunbelt regions of the country. The company's divisions included The Broadway, with 43 stores in Southern California and 11 stores in the southwest, and Emporium, with 22 stores in the greater San Francisco Bay Area.

On October 17, 1989, a 7.1 Richter scale earthquake caused significant amounts of monetary damage to the San Francisco Bay Area. This was the largest earthquake to hit the Bay Area since the quake of 1906 destroyed much of San Francisco. California is lined with many active earthquake faults. Hundreds of small earthquakes occur each year throughout the state.

The Emporium division of CHHS suffered extensive damage as a result of the October 17 earthquake. Twelve of the twenty-two stores were closed for varying periods of time, with the Oakland store hardest hit. In total, uninsured damage was $27.5 million ($16.5 million after tax benefits).

For the fiscal year ending August 4, 1990, CHHS reported an after-tax loss of $9.47 million *before* considering the earthquake loss. Total revenues for the year were $2.857 billion.

**Required:**

Assume that you are the CHHS controller. The chief financial officer of CHHS has asked you to prepare a short report (1–2 pages) in memo form giving your recommendation as to the proper reporting of the earthquake damage costs in the income statement for the year ending August 4, 1990. Explain why your recommendation is appropriate. Be sure to include in your report any references to authoritative pronouncements that support your recommendation.

**Ethics Case 4–7**
Income statement presentation of unusual loss
● LO4–3, LO4–5

After a decade of consistent income growth, the Cranor Corporation sustained a before-tax loss of $8.4 million in 2013. The loss was primarily due to $10 million in expenses related to a product recall. Cranor manufactures medical equipment, including x-ray machines. The recall was attributable to a design flaw in the manufacture of the company's new line of machines.

The company controller, Jim Dietz, has suggested that the loss should be included in the 2013 income statement as an extraordinary item. "If we report it as an extraordinary item, our income from continuing operations will actually show an increase from the prior year. The stock market will appreciate the continued growth in ongoing profitability and will discount the one-time loss. And our bonuses are tied to income from continuing operations, not net income."

The chief executive officer asked Jim to justify this treatment. "I know we have had product recalls before and, of course, they do occur in our industry," Jim replied, "but we have never had a recall of this magnitude, and we fixed the design flaw and upgraded our quality control procedures."

**Required:**

Discuss the ethical dilemma faced by Jim Dietz and the company's chief executive officer.

**Research Case 4–8**
FASB codification; locate and extract relevant information and cite authoritative support for a financial reporting issue; restructuring costs; exit or disposal cost obligations
● LO4–2, LO4–3

The accrual of restructuring costs creates obligations (liabilities) referred to as *exit or disposal cost obligations.*

**Required:**

1. Obtain the relevant authoritative literature on exit or disposal cost obligations using the FASB's Codification Research System. You might gain access at the FASB website (www.fasb.org). What is the Codification topic number that addresses this issue?

2. What is the specific citation that addresses the initial measurement of these obligations?

3. How are these obligations and related costs to be measured?

4. What is the specific citation that describes the disclosure requirements in the notes to the financial statements for exit or disposal obligations?

5. List the required disclosures.

**Judgment Case 4–9**
Income statement presentation
● LO4–3 through LO4–5

Each of the following situations occurred during 2013 for one of your audit clients:

1. The write-off of inventory due to obsolescence.

2. Discovery that depreciation expenses were omitted by accident from 2012's income statement.

3. The useful lives of all machinery were changed from eight to five years.

4. The depreciation method used for all equipment was changed from the declining-balance to the straight-line method.

5. Ten million dollars face value of bonds payable were repurchased (paid off) prior to maturity resulting in a material loss of $500,000. The company considers the event unusual and infrequent.

6. Restructuring costs were incurred.

7. The Stridewell Company, a manufacturer of shoes, sold all of its retail outlets. It will continue to manufacture and sell its shoes to other retailers. A loss was incurred in the disposition of the retail stores. The retail stores are considered a component of the entity.

8. The inventory costing method was changed from FIFO to average cost.

**Required:**

1. For each situation, identify the appropriate reporting treatment from the list below (consider each event to be material):

   a. As an extraordinary item.

   b. As an unusual or infrequent gain or loss.

   c. As a prior period adjustment.

   d. As a change in accounting principle.

   e. As a discontinued operation.

   f. As a change in accounting estimate.

   g. As a change in accounting estimate achieved by a change in accounting principle.

2. Indicate whether each situation would be included in the income statement in continuing operations (CO) or below continuing operations (BC), or if it would appear as an adjustment to retained earnings (RE). Use the format shown below to answer requirements 1 and 2.

| Situation | Treatment (a–g) | Financial Statement Presentation (CO, BC, or RE) |
|---|---|---|
| 1. | | |
| 2. | | |
| 3. | | |
| 4. | | |
| 5. | | |
| 6. | | |
| 7. | | |
| 8. | | |

**Judgment Case 4–10**
Income statement presentation
● LO4–3 through LO4–5

The following events occurred during 2013 for various audit clients of your firm. Consider each event to be independent and the effect of each event to be material.

1. A manufacturing company recognized a loss on the sale of investments.

2. An automobile manufacturer sold all of the assets related to its financing component. The operations of the financing business is considered a component of the entity.

3. A company changed its depreciation method from the double-declining-balance method to the straight-line method.

4. Due to obsolescence, a company engaged in the manufacture of high-technology products incurred a loss on the write-down of inventory.

5. One of your clients discovered that 2012's depreciation expense was overstated. The error occurred because of a miscalculation of depreciation for the office building.

6. A cosmetics company decided to discontinue the manufacture of a line of women's lipstick. Other cosmetic lines will be continued. A loss was incurred on the sale of assets related to the lipstick product line. The operations of the discontinued line is not considered a component of the entity.

**Required:**

Discuss the 2013 financial statement presentation of each of the above events. Do not consider earnings per share disclosures.

**IFRS Case 4–11**
Statement of cash flows; GlaxoSmithKline Plc.
● LO4–9, LO4–10

🌐 IFRS

Real World Financials

GlaxoSmithKline Plc. (GSK) is a global pharmaceutical and consumer health-related products company located in the United Kingdom. The company prepares its financial statements in accordance with International Financial Reporting Standards. Below is a portion of the company's statements of cash flows included in recent financial statements:

| GLAXOSMITHKLINE PLC. Consolidated Statements of Cash Flows (in part) For the Years Ended December 31 | | | | |
|---|---|---|---|---|
| | Notes | 2010 £m | 2009 £m | 2008 £m |
| **Cash flow from investing activities** | | | | |
| Purchase of property, plant and equipment | | (1,014) | (1,418) | (1,437) |
| Proceeds from sale of property, plant and equipment | | 92 | 48 | 20 |
| Purchase of intangible assets | | (621) | (455) | (632) |
| Proceeds from sale of intangible assets | | 126 | 356 | 171 |

(continued)

(concluded)

| | | | | |
|---|---|---:|---:|---:|
| Purchase of equity investments | | (279) | (154) | (87) |
| Proceeds from sale of equity investments | | 27 | 59 | 42 |
| Share transactions with minority shareholders | | | | |
| Purchase of businesses, net of cash acquired | 38 | (354) | (2,792) | (454) |
| Disposal of businesses and interest in associates | | — | 178 | — |
| Investments in associates and joint ventures | 38 | (61) | (29) | (9) |
| Decrease/(increase) in liquid investments | | 91 | 87 | 905 |
| Interest received | | 107 | 90 | 320 |
| Dividends from associates and joint ventures | | 18 | 17 | 12 |
| Net cash outflow from investing activities | | (1,868) | (4,013) | (1,149) |
| **Cash flow from financing activities** | | | | |
| Proceeds from own shares for employee share options | | 17 | 13 | 9 |
| Shares acquired by ESOP Trusts | | (16) | (57) | (19) |
| Issue of share capital | 33 | 62 | 43 | 62 |
| Purchase of own shares for cancellation | | — | — | (3,706) |
| Purchase of Treasury shares | | | | |
| Increase in long-term loans | | — | 1,358 | 5,523 |
| Repayment of long-term loans | | | | |
| Net (repayment of)/increase in short-term loans | | | | |
| Net repayment of obligations under finance leases | | (45) | (48) | (48) |
| Interest paid | | (775) | (780) | (730) |
| Dividends paid to shareholders | | (3,205) | (3,003) | (2,929) |
| Dividends paid to minority interests | | | | |
| Other financing cash flows | | (201) | (109) | 68 |
| Net cash outflow from financing activities | | (5,571) | (2,774) | (4,908) |
| Increase/(decrease) in cash and bank overdrafts | 37 | (642) | 1,054 | 1,148 |

**Required:**

Identify the items in the above statements that would be reported differently if GlaxoSmithKline prepared its financial statements according to U.S. GAAP rather than IFRS.

**Judgment Case 4–12**
Income statement presentation; unusual items; comprehensive income
● LO4–3 through LO4–5, LO4–7

Norse Manufacturing Inc. prepares an annual single, continuous statement of income and comprehensive income. The following situations occurred during the company's 2013 fiscal year:

1. Restructuring costs were incurred due to the closing of a factory.
2. Investments were sold, and a loss was recognized.
3. Gains from foreign currency translation were recognized.
4. Interest expense was incurred.
5. A division was sold that qualifies as a separate component of the entity according to GAAP.
6. Obsolete inventory was written off.
7. The controller discovered an error in the calculation of 2012's patent amortization expense.
8. A volcano destroyed a storage facility on a South Sea island. The event is considered to be unusual and infrequent in occurrence.

**Required:**

1. For each situation, identify the appropriate reporting treatment from the list below (consider each event to be material).
   a. As a component of operating income.
   b. As a nonoperating income item (other income or expense).
   c. As a separately reported item.
   d. As an other comprehensive income item.
   e. As an adjustment to retained earnings.
2. Identify the situations that would be reported net-of-tax.

**Judgment Case 4–13**
Management incentives for change
● LO4–2

It has been suggested that not all accounting choices are made by management in the best interest of fair and consistent financial reporting.

**Required:**

What motivations can you think of for management's choice of accounting methods?

**Research Case 4–14**
Pro forma earnings
● LO4–3

Companies often voluntarily provide a pro forma earnings number when they announce annual or quarterly earnings. These pro forma earnings numbers are controversial as they represent management's view of permanent earnings. The Sarbanes-Oxley Act (SOX), issued in 2002, requires that if pro forma earnings are included in any periodic or other report filed with the SEC or in any public disclosure or press release, the company also must provide a reconciliation with earnings determined according to GAAP.

Professors Entwistle, Feltham, and Mbagwu, in "Financial Reporting Regulation and the Reporting of Pro Forma Earnings," examine whether firms changed their reporting practice in response to the pro forma regulations included in SOX.

**Required:**

1. In your library or from some other source, locate the indicated article in *Accounting Horizons,* March 2006.
2. What sample of firms did the authors use in their examination?
3. What percent of firms reported pro forma earnings in 2001? In 2003?
4. What percent of firms had pro forma earnings greater than GAAP earnings in 2001? In 2003?
5. What was the most frequently reported adjusting item in 2001? In 2003?
6. What are the authors' main conclusions of the impact of SOX on pro forma reporting?

**Integrating Case 4–15**
Balance sheet and income statement;
Chapters 3 and 4
● LO4–3, LO4–5

Rice Corporation is negotiating a loan for expansion purposes and the bank requires financial statements. Before closing the accounting records for the year ended December 31, 2013, Rice's controller prepared the following financial statements:

**RICE CORPORATION**
**Balance Sheet**
**At December 31, 2013**
($ in 000s)

| | |
|---|---:|
| **Assets** | |
| Cash | $ 275 |
| Marketable securities | 78 |
| Accounts receivable | 487 |
| Inventories | 425 |
| Allowance for uncollectible accounts | (50) |
| Property and equipment, net | 160 |
| Total assets | $1,375 |
| **Liabilities and Shareholders' Equity** | |
| Accounts payable and accrued liabilities | $ 420 |
| Notes payable | 200 |
| Common stock | 260 |
| Retained earnings | 495 |
| Total liabilities and shareholders' equity | $1,375 |

**RICE CORPORATION**
**Income Statement**
**For the Year Ended December 31, 2013**
($ in 000s)

| | | |
|---|---:|---:|
| Net sales | | $1,580 |
| Expenses: | | |
| Cost of goods sold | $755 | |
| Selling and administrative | 385 | |
| Miscellaneous | 129 | |
| Income taxes | 100 | |
| Total expenses | | 1,369 |
| Net income | | $ 211 |

**Additional Information:**

1. The company's common stock is traded on an organized stock exchange.
2. The investment portfolio consists of short-term investments valued at $57,000. The remaining investments will not be sold until the year 2015.
3. Miscellaneous expense represents the before-tax loss from damages caused by an earthquake. The event is considered to be both unusual and infrequent.
4. Notes payable consist of two notes:

   Note 1: $80,000 face value dated September 30, 2013. Principal and interest at 10% are due on September 30, 2014.

Note 2: $120,000 face value dated April 30, 2013. Principal is due in two equal installments of $60,000 plus interest on the unpaid balance. The two payments are scheduled for April 30, 2014, and April 30, 2015.

Interest on both loans has been correctly accrued and is included in accrued liabilities on the balance sheet and selling and administrative expenses on the income statement.

5. Selling and administrative expenses include a $90,000 charge incurred by the company in restructuring some of its operations. The amount of the charge is material.

**Required:**

Identify and explain the deficiencies in the presentation of the statements prepared by the company's controller. Do not prepare corrected statements. Include in your answer a list of items which require additional disclosure, either on the face of the statement or in a note.

**Analysis
Case 4–16**
Income statement information
● LO4–1

**DELL**

Refer to the income statements of Dell Inc. included in the company's financial statements in Appendix B at the back of the text.

**Required:**

1. What was the percentage increase or decrease in the company's net income from 2010 to 2011? From 2009 to 2010?

2. Using 2011 data, what is the company's approximate income tax rate?

3. Using 2011 data, what is the percentage of net income relative to revenue dollars?

**Real World
Case 4–17**
Income statement information
● LO4–1, LO4–3
  through LO4–5

Real World Financials

EDGAR, the Electronic Data Gathering, Analysis, and Retrieval system, performs automated collection, validation, indexing, and forwarding of submissions by companies and others who are required by law to file forms with the U.S. Securities and Exchange Commission (SEC). All publicly traded domestic companies use EDGAR to make the majority of their filings. (Some foreign companies file voluntarily.) Form 10-K, which includes the annual report, is required to be filed on EDGAR. The SEC makes this information available on the Internet.

**Required:**

1. Access EDGAR on the Internet. The web address is www.sec.gov.

2. Search for a public company with which you are familiar. Access the most recent 10-K filing. Search or scroll to find the financial statements and related notes.

3. Answer the following questions related to the company's income statement:
   a. Does the company use the single-step or multiple-step format, or a variation?
   b. Does the income statement contain any separately reported items in any year presented (discontinued operation or extraordinary item)? If it does, describe the event that caused the item. (Hint: there should be a related disclosure note.)
   c. Describe the trend in net income over the years presented.

4. Repeat requirements 2 and 3 for two additional companies.

# Air France–KLM Case

**AIRFRANCE /**

● LO4–10

Air France–KLM (AF), a French company, prepares its financial statements according to International Financial Reporting Standards. AF's annual report for the year ended March 31, 2011, which includes financial statements and disclosure notes, is provided with all new textbooks. This material also is included in AF's "Registration Document 2010–11," dated June 15, 2011 and is available at www.airfranceklm.com.

**Required:**

1. How does AF classify operating expenses in its income statement? How are these expenses typically classified in a U.S. company income statement?

2. How does AF classify interest paid, interest received, and dividends received in its statement of cash flows? What other alternatives, if any, does the company have for the classification of these items? How are these items classified under U.S. GAAP?

# CPA Simulation 4–1

**Bart Company**
Income statement presentation

**CPA Review**

Test your knowledge of the concepts discussed in this chapter, practice critical professional skills necessary for career success, and prepare for the computer-based CPA exam by accessing our CPA simulations at the text website: www.mhhe.com/spiceland7e.

The Bart Company simulation tests your knowledge of the contents and presentation of the income statement.

# 5

# Income Measurement and Profitability Analysis

The focus of this chapter is revenue recognition. We first discuss the general circumstance in which revenue is recognized when a good or service is delivered. Then we discuss circumstances in which revenue should be deferred until after delivery or should be recognized prior to delivery. The chapter also includes an Appendix describing requirements for interim financial reporting and a Where We're Headed Supplement explaining in detail a proposed Accounting Standards Update (hereafter, "the proposed ASU") that the FASB and IASB plan to issue in 2012 that substantially changes how we account for revenue recognition.

**After studying this chapter, you should be able to:**

- **LO5–1** Discuss the timing of revenue recognition, list the two general criteria that must be satisfied before revenue can be recognized, and explain why these criteria usually are satisfied when products or services are delivered. (p. 232)

- **LO5–2** Discuss the principal/agent distinction that determines the amount of revenue to record. (p. 237)

- **LO5–3** Describe the installment sales and cost recovery methods of recognizing revenue and explain the unusual conditions under which these methods might be used. (p. 239)

- **LO5–4** Discuss the implications for revenue recognition of allowing customers the right of return. (p. 243)

- **LO5–5** Identify situations requiring recognition of revenue over time and demonstrate the percentage-of-completion and completed contract methods of recognizing revenue for long-term contracts. (p. 244)

- **LO5–6** Discuss the revenue recognition issues involving multiple-deliverable contracts, software, and franchise sales. (pp. 258 and 260)

- **LO5–7** Identify and calculate the common ratios used to assess profitability. (p. 263)

- **LO5–8** Discuss the primary differences between U.S. GAAP and IFRS with respect to revenue recognition. (pp. 235, 255, 260, 262 and 272)

## FINANCIAL REPORTING CASE

### You Don't Have to Be a Rocket Scientist

"Good news! I got the job," she said, closing the door behind her.

Your sister, an aerospace engineer, goes on to explain that she accepted a position at Lockheed Martin Corporation, a world leader in the design, development, manufacture, and servicing of aircraft, spacecraft and launch vehicles, missiles, electronics, and informa-

tion and telecommunication systems. She will supervise a long-term government contract beginning Tuesday.

"I got the salary I was asking for too," she continued. "Mr. Watson, my supervisor, also said I'll be getting a bonus tied to the gross profit on the project. It didn't hit me until I left his office, though, that this project will take two and a half years to complete. I hope I don't have to wait that long to get my bonus." Pointing to a page where she's circled part of a disclosure note, your sister hands you Lockheed's annual report. "I can't believe they wait that long to record income on all these multiyear projects. You're the accountant in the family; is that what this note is telling us?"

*Sales and earnings (in part)*
We record net sales and estimated profits on a percentage-of-completion (POC) basis for cost reimbursable and fixed-price design, development, and production (DD&P) contracts. . . .

---

**By the time you finish this chapter, you should be able to respond appropriately to the questions posed in this case. Compare your response to the solution provided at the end of the chapter.**

**QUESTIONS**

1. Does your sister have to wait two and a half years to get her bonus? Explain. (*p. 238*)

2. How are gross profits recognized using the percentage-of-completion method? (*p. 245*)

3. Are there other situations in which revenue is recognized at times other than when a product is delivered? (*p. 248*)

# REVENUE RECOGNITION

In Chapter 4 we discussed the *nature of income* and its presentation in the income statement. In this chapter we turn our attention to the *measurement* of periodic accounting income. Of primary interest here is the timing of revenue recognition.

What is revenue? According to the FASB, "Revenues are inflows or other enhancements of assets of an entity or settlements of its liabilities (or a combination of both) from delivering or producing goods, rendering services, or other activities that constitute the entity's ongoing major or central operations."[1] In other words, revenue tracks the inflow of net assets that occurs when a business provides goods or services to its customers.

Why is the timing of revenue recognition so important? An income statement should report the results of operations only for the time period specified in the report. That is, a one-year income statement should report the company's accomplishments and sacrifices (revenues and expenses) only for that one-year period.[2] Revenue recognition criteria help ensure that a proper cutoff is made each period and that no more than one year's activity is reported in the annual income statement. Revenues reflect positive inflows from activities that eventually generate cash flows. By comparing these activity levels period to period, a user can better assess future activities and thus future cash flows.

> Revenue recognition criteria help ensure that an income statement reflects the actual accomplishments of a company for the period.

Our objective, then, is to recognize revenue in the period or periods that the revenue-generating activities of the company are performed. But we also must consider that recognizing revenue presumes that an asset (usually cash) has been received or will be received in exchange for the goods or services sold. Our judgment as to the collectibility of the cash from the sale of a product or service will, therefore, affect the timing of revenue recognition. These two concepts of performance and collectibility are captured by the general guidelines for revenue recognition in the realization principle.

● LO5–1

The **realization principle** requires that two criteria be satisfied before revenue can be recognized (recorded):[3]

1. The earnings process is judged to be complete or virtually complete (the earnings process refers to the activity or activities performed by the company to generate revenue).

2. There is reasonable certainty as to the collectibility of the asset to be received (usually cash).

Even with these guidelines, revenue recognition continues to be a controversial issue. Premature revenue recognition reduces the quality of reported earnings, particularly if those revenues never materialize. Many sad stories have surfaced involving companies forced to revise earnings numbers downward due to a restatement of revenues. The case of **Krispy Kreme Doughnuts** offers a prime example. In January 2005, the company announced that it would be restating its earnings for the last three quarters of fiscal 2004. Investors were already alarmed by the recent filing of a lawsuit that alleged the company routinely padded sales by doubling shipments to wholesale customers at the end of the quarter. In the two-day period following the announced restatement, the company's stock price dropped over 20% in value!

> **Arthur Levitt, Jr.**
> Lastly, companies try to boost earnings by manipulating the recognition of revenue. Think about a bottle of fine wine. You wouldn't pop the cork on that bottle before it was ready. But some companies are doing this with their revenue . . .[4]

---

[1]"Elements of Financial Statements," *Statement of Financial Concepts No. 6* (Stamford, Conn.: FASB, 1985, par. 78).

[2]In addition to reporting on an annual basis, companies often provide information quarterly and, on occasion, monthly. The SEC requires its registrants to provide information on a quarterly and annual basis. This information, referred to as *interim financial statements*, pertains to any financial report covering a period of less than one year. The key accounting issues related to the presentation of interim statements are discussed in Appendix 5.

[3]These criteria are addressed in SFAC 5, "Recognition and Measurement in Financial Statements," *Statement of Financial Accounting Concepts No. 5* (Stamford, Conn.: FASB, 1984).

[4]Arthur Levitt, Jr., "The Numbers Game," *The CPA Journal,* December 1998, p. 18.

As part of its crackdown on earnings management, the SEC issued additional guidance, summarized in *Staff Accounting Bulletin (SAB) No. 101* and later in *SAB No. 104,*[5] indicating the SEC's views on revenue. The *SABs* provide additional criteria for judging whether or not the realization principle is satisfied:

1. Persuasive evidence of an arrangement exists.
2. Delivery has occurred or services have been rendered.
3. The seller's price to the buyer is fixed or determinable.
4. Collectibility is reasonably assured.

In addition to these four criteria, the *SABs* also pose a number of revenue recognition questions relating to each of the criteria. The questions provide the facts of the scenario and then the SEC offers its interpretive response. These responses and supporting explanations provide guidance to companies with similar revenue recognition issues. For example, the following question relates to the delivery and performance criteria necessary to recognize revenue on a transaction commonly referred to as a "Bill and Hold" sale:

---

**Facts:** Company A receives purchase orders for products it manufactures. At the end of its fiscal quarters, customers may not yet be ready to take delivery of the products for various reasons. These reasons may include, but are not limited to, a lack of available space for inventory, having more than sufficient inventory in their distribution channel, or delays in customers' production schedules.

**Questions:** May Company A recognize revenue for the sale of its products once it has completed manufacturing if it segregates the inventory of the products in its own warehouse from its own products? May Company A recognize revenue for the sale if it ships the products to a third-party warehouse but (1) Company A retains title to the product and (2) payment by the customer is dependent upon ultimate delivery to a customer-specified site?

---

How would you answer these questions? The SEC's response is that, generally, revenue should not be recognized upon shipment to a third-party warehouse. Delivery generally is not considered to have occurred unless the end customer takes title and assumes the risk and rewards of ownership of the specific products in the customer's purchase order or sales agreement. Typically this occurs when a product is delivered to the customer's delivery site and accepted by the customer.[6]

Soon after *SAB No. 101* was issued, many companies changed their revenue recognition methods. In most cases, the changes resulted in a deferral of revenue recognition. As a case in point, consider the change made by **Brown & Sharpe Manufacturing Company**, a multinational manufacturer of metrology products, described in a disclosure note, displayed in Illustration 5–1.

**2. Accounting Change (in part)**
In 2000, the Company adopted *SEC Staff Accounting Bulletin No. 101 (SAB 101)*. As a result of adopting *SAB 101*, the Company changed the way it recognizes revenue for machines sold to customers. Prior to the adoption of *SAB 101*, the Company recognized revenue when the machines were shipped and title passed to the customer. Effective as of January 1, 2001, the Company recognizes revenue for machines sold to customers once the performance of machines is accepted by the customers.

**Illustration 5–1**

Disclosure of Change in Revenue Recognition Policy—Brown & Sharpe Manufacturing Company

Real World Financials

Although this example relates to product delivery, much of *SAB 101* and *104* are related to service revenue. We discuss some of these issues later in the chapter.

---

[5]FASB ASC 605–10–S99: Revenue Recognition–Overall–SEC Materials (originally "Revenue Recognition in Financial Statements," *Staff Accounting Bulletin No. 101* (Washington, D.C.: SEC, December 1999) and *Staff Accounting Bulletin No. 104* (Washington, D.C.: SEC, December 2003)).
[6]Ibid., p. 5.

# Ethical Dilemma

The Precision Parts Corporation manufactures automobile parts. The company has reported a profit every year since the company's inception in 1980. Management prides itself on this accomplishment and believes one important contributing factor is the company's incentive plan that rewards top management a bonus equal to a percentage of operating income *if the operating income goal for the year is achieved.* However, 2013 has been a tough year, and prospects for attaining the income goal for the year are bleak.

Tony Smith, the company's chief financial officer, has determined a way to increase December sales by an amount sufficient to boost operating income over the goal for the year and earn bonuses for all top management. A reputable customer ordered $120,000 of parts to be shipped on January 15, 2014. Tony told the rest of top management "I know we can get that order ready by December 31 even though it will require some production line overtime. We can then just leave the order on the loading dock until shipment. I see nothing wrong with recognizing the sale in 2013, since the parts will have been manufactured and we do have a firm order from a reputable customer." The company's normal procedure is to ship goods f.o.b. destination and to recognize sales revenue when the customer receives the parts.

Illustration 5–2 relates various revenue-recognition methods to critical steps in the earnings process, and Illustration 5–3 provides a more detailed overview of the methods used in current practice. As noted in the chapter supplement, some of these methods change with new FASB guidance, but adoption of the new revenue recognition standard is not likely to be required before 2015 at the earliest, so it is important to understand current practice.

Recall that the realization principle indicates that the central issues for recognizing revenue are (a) judging when the earnings process is substantially complete and (b) whether there is reasonable certainty as to the collectibility of the cash to be received. Often this decision is straightforward and tied to delivery of the product from the seller to the buyer. At delivery, the earnings process is virtually complete and the seller receives either cash or a receivable. At other times, though, recognizing revenue upon delivery may be inappropriate. It may be that revenue should be deferred to a point *after* delivery because the seller is unable to estimate whether the buyer will return the product or pay the receivable. Or, sometimes revenue should be recognized at a point *prior* to delivery because the earnings process occurs over multiple reporting periods and the company can better inform financial statement users by making reliable estimates of revenue and cost prior to delivery.

Now let's consider specific revenue recognition methods in more detail. We start with revenue recognition at delivery, then discuss circumstances where revenue recognition must be postponed until after delivery, and then discuss circumstances that allow revenue recognition prior to delivery.

**Illustration 5–2**

Relation between Earnings Process and Revenue Recognition Methods

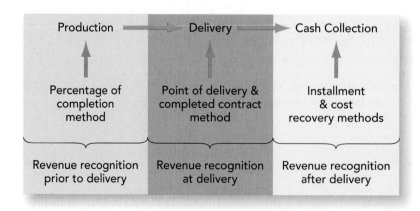

**Illustration 5–3**
Revenue Recognition Methods

| Nature of the Revenue | Usually Recognize Revenue for: | |
| --- | --- | --- |
| | Sale of a Product | Sale of a Service |
| **Revenue Recognition Prior to Delivery** | | |
| Dependable estimates of progress are available. | Each period during the earnings process (e.g., long-term construction contract) in proportion to its percentage of completion (percentage-of-completion method) | Not applicable |
| Dependable estimates of progress are not available. | At the completion of the project (completed contract method) | Not applicable |
| **Revenue Recognition at Delivery** | When product is delivered and title transfers | As the service is provided or the key activity is performed |
| **Revenue Recognition After Delivery, Because:** | | |
| • Payments are significantly uncertain | When cash is collected (installment sales or cost recovery method) | When cash is collected |
| • Reliable estimates of product returns are unavailable | When critical event occurs that reduces product return uncertainty | Not applicable |
| • The product sold is out on consignment | When the consignee sells the product to the ultimate consumer | Not applicable |

When revenue is being earned in a multi-period contract, sometimes it is more meaningful to recognize revenue over time in proportion to the percentage of work completed.

We usually recognize revenue at or near the completion of the earnings process.

If collectibility is an issue, we defer revenue recognition until we can reasonably estimate the amount to be received.

# International Financial Reporting Standards

**Revenue Recognition Concepts.** *IAS No. 18* governs most revenue recognition under IFRS. Similar to U.S. GAAP, it defines revenue as "the gross inflow of economic benefits during the period arising in the course of the ordinary activities of an entity when those inflows result in increases in equity, other than increases relating to contributions from equity participants."[7] IFRS allows revenue to be recognized when the following conditions have been satisfied:

● LO5–8

(a) The amount of revenue and costs associated with the transaction can be measured reliably,

(b) It is probable that the economic benefits associated with the transaction will flow to the seller,

(c) (for sales of goods) the seller has transferred to the buyer the risks and rewards of ownership, and doesn't effectively manage or control the goods,

(d) (for sales of services) the stage of completion can be measured reliably.

These general conditions typically will lead to revenue recognition at the same time and in the same amount as would occur under U.S. GAAP, but there are exceptions. For example, later in this chapter we discuss differences between IFRS and U.S. GAAP that may affect the timing of revenue recognition with respect to multiple-deliverable contracts. More generally, IFRS has much less industry-specific guidance than does U.S. GAAP, leading to fewer exceptions to applying these revenue recognition conditions.

---

[7]"Revenue," *International Accounting Standard No. 18* (IASCF), as amended effective January 1, 2011, par. 7.

# Revenue Recognition at Delivery

## Product Revenue

While revenue usually is earned during a period of time, it often is recognized at one specific point in time when both revenue recognition criteria are satisfied.

Consider the timing of revenue recognition for a typical manufacturing company that sells its products on credit. Illustration 5–2 shows three alternative points in time during the earnings process that could be considered the critical event for revenue recognition. It should be pointed out that revenue actually is earned *throughout* the earnings process. The critical event is the point in time when the realization principle is satisfied.[8]

Let's first consider the date production ends. At that point, it might be said that the earnings process is virtually complete. After all, the majority of the costs that must be expended to generate revenue have been incurred. The product has been produced and the remaining tasks are to sell the product and collect the asset to be exchanged for the product, which is usually cash.

Revenue from the sale of products usually is recognized at the point of product delivery.

However, at this point there usually exist significant uncertainties. We don't know if the product will be sold, the selling price, the buyer, or the collectibility of the asset to be received. Because of these uncertainties, revenue recognition usually is delayed until the point of sale, at product delivery. The product delivery date occurs when legal title to the goods passes from seller to buyer, which depends on the terms of the sales agreement. If the goods are shipped *f.o.b. (free on board) shipping point,* then legal title to the goods changes hands at the point of shipment, when the seller delivers the goods to the common carrier (for example, a trucking company), and the purchaser is responsible for shipping costs and transit insurance. On the other hand, if the goods are shipped *f.o.b. destination,* the seller is responsible for shipping, and legal title does not pass until the goods arrive at the customer's location.[9]

The point of delivery refers to the date legal title to the product passes from seller to buyer.

The basic journal entries to record revenue upon delivery should look familiar. As an example, assume that Taft Company sells a supercomputer for $5,000,000 that cost $4,100,000 to produce. The journal entries to record the sale, assuming that Taft uses the perpetual inventory method, would be

| | | |
|---|---|---|
| Accounts receivable ......................................................... | 5,000,000 | |
|     Revenue ....................................................................... | | 5,000,000 |
| Cost of goods sold ........................................................... | 4,100,000 | |
|     Inventory ..................................................................... | | 4,100,000 |

This sale yields gross profit of $900,000 ($5,000,000 − 4,100,000).

At the product delivery date we know the product has been sold, the price, and the buyer. However, usually the buyer is given a length of time, say 30 days, to pay for the goods after they have been delivered. Therefore, the only remaining uncertainty at the time of delivery involves the ultimate cash collection, which usually can be accounted for by estimating and recording allowances for possible return of the product and for uncollectibility of the cash, that is, bad debts. Both of these estimates are discussed in Chapter 7. As we discuss later in this chapter, significant uncertainty at point of product delivery related to either collectibility or product return causes a delay in revenue recognition.

## Service Revenue

Service revenue, too, often is recognized at a point in time if there is one final activity that is deemed critical to the earnings process. In this case, all revenue is deferred until this final activity has been performed. For example, a moving company will pack, load, transport, and deliver household goods for a fixed fee. Although packing, loading, and transporting all are important to the earning process, delivery is the culminating event of the earnings

---

[8]As you will learn later in this chapter when we discuss the percentage-of-completion method, revenue can be recognized during the earnings process rather than at one particular point in time as long as particular criteria have been met.
[9]We discuss this aspect of title transfer further in Chapter 7.

process. So, the entire service fee is recognized as revenue after the goods have been delivered. **FedEx** recognizes revenue in this manner. The Company's Summary of Significant Accounting Policies disclosure note indicates that "Revenue is recognized upon delivery of shipments." As with the sale of product, estimates of uncollectible amounts must be made for service revenue provided to customers on a credit basis.

However, in many instances, service revenue activities occur over extended periods, so recognizing revenue at any single date within one period would be inappropriate. Instead, it's more meaningful to recognize revenue over time as the service is performed.

As an example, consider the revenue a property owner earns when renting office space. If a landlord charges a tenant $12,000 in rent for the upcoming year, it would seem logical to recognize $1,000 of rent revenue each month over the one-year period (i.e., straight-line method) since similar services are performed throughout the period. The landlord recognizes rent revenue in proportion to the passage of time. Likewise, **Gold's Gym** will recognize revenue from a two-year membership ratably over the 24-month membership period. If the customer pays in advance in such cases, the seller debits cash and credits a liability (unearned revenue) because the seller is holding the customer's cash and has the obligation to provide the service. The seller only reduces that liability when the service has been provided and therefore revenue has been earned. We discuss unearned revenue liabilities and customer advances more in Chapter 13.

A similar situation occurs if you buy a season pass to Disney World. When would **Walt Disney Co.** recognize revenue for the cash it collects for the sale of a 365-day pass? Rationalizing that a pass can be used any number of times during the season, thus making it difficult to determine when service is provided, many companies once recognized all revenue from the sale of season passes on the date of sale. However, the SEC's *Staff Accounting Bulletins No. 101* and *104,* discussed earlier in the chapter, motivated most of these companies to change to recognizing revenue throughout the service period. For example, Illustration 5–4 provides a disclosure note **Walt Disney Co.** included in a recent annual report. Notice that the company recognizes revenue *over time,* based on the anticipated usage of the season pass over the operating season.

> Service revenue often is recognized over time, in proportion to the amount of service performed.

**Revenue Recognition (in part)**
Revenues from advance theme park ticket sales are recognized when the tickets are used. For non-expiring, multi-day tickets, revenues are recognized over a three-year time period based on estimated usage, which is derived from historical usage patterns.

**Illustration 5–4**

Disclosure of Revenue Recognition Policy—Walt Disney Co.

**Real World Financials**

## Is the Seller a Principal or an Agent?

Regardless of whether we are dealing with a product or a service, an important consideration is whether the seller is acting as a "principal" or as an "agent." Here's the difference. A principal has primary responsibility for delivering a product or service, and typically is vulnerable to risks associated with delivering the product or service and collecting payment from the customer. In contrast, an agent doesn't primarily deliver goods or services, but acts as a facilitator that earns a commission for helping sellers transact with buyers.

If the company is a principal, the company should recognize as revenue the gross (total) amount received from a customer. If instead the company is an agent, it recognizes as revenue only the *net* commission it receives for facilitating the sale.

There are many examples of agents in business. One you're familiar with is a real estate agent. Real estate agents don't own the houses they sell, but rather charge a commission to help home owners transact with home buyers. Similarly, online auction houses like **eBay**, travel facilitators like **Expedia, Inc.** and **priceline.com**, and broad web-based retailers like **Amazon.com** act as agents for a variety of sellers. Complicating matters, these same companies also act as *principals* on some other arrangements, selling their own products and services directly to customers. For example, eBay acts as an agent by linking sellers with buyers, but acts as a principal when selling its PayPal transaction-processing service.

● LO5–2

An *agent* doesn't control goods or services, but rather facilitates transfers between sellers and buyers.

Companies use a number of indicators to help determine if they are principals or agents with respect to a particular transaction. Indicators that the company is a principal include the following:

- The company is primarily responsible for providing the product or service to the customer.
- The company owns inventory prior to a customer ordering it and after a customer returns it.
- The company has discretion in setting prices and identifying suppliers.[10]

**An agent only records its commission as revenue.**

The reason the principal versus agent distinction is important is because, if the company is a principal, it records (a) the sales price to customers as revenue and (b) the cost of the item sold as cost of goods sold. On the other hand, if the company is an agent, it records as revenue only the commission it earns on the transaction. In Illustration 5–5 we see the difference in accounting by principals and agents.

**Illustration 5–5**

Comparison of Revenue Recognition by Principals and Agents

Ima Buyer purchases a television from an online retailer for $375. Let's consider accounting for that sale by two retailers: PrinCo and AgenCo:

- PrinCo obtains TVs directly from a supplier for $250, has the TVs shipped to its distribution center in Kansas, and then ships individual TVs to buyers when a sale is made. PrinCo offers occasional price discounts according to its marketing strategy. Because PrinCo is responsible for fulfilling the contract, bears the risk of holding inventory, and has latitude in setting sales prices, the evidence suggests that PrinCo is a principal in this transaction.

- AgenCo serves as a web portal by which multiple TV manufacturers can offer their products for sale. The manufacturers ship directly to buyers when a sale is made. AgenCo earns a flat 50% of the wholesale price set by the manufacturers as a commission. Given that AgenCo is not primarily responsible for fulfilling the contract, bears no inventory risk, has no latitude in setting sales prices, and is paid on commission, the evidence suggests AgenCo is an agent in this transaction.

The first part of the income statement for each retailer is shown below. Notice that the same amount of gross profit, $125, is recognized by the principal and the agent. What differs are the amounts of revenue and expense that are recognized and reported.

| A Principal Records Gross Revenue (PrinCo) | | An Agent Records Net Revenue (AgenCo) | |
|---|---|---|---|
| Revenue | $375 | | |
| Less: Cost of goods sold | 250 | | |
| Gross profit | $125 | Revenue | $125 |

We see from Illustration 5–5 that reporting revenue gross versus net can have a significant effect on a company's revenue. Particularly for start-up or growth-oriented companies that may be valued more on growth in revenue, rather than on growth in net income, determining whether a company should be considered a principal or an agent is critical.

# Revenue Recognition after Delivery

**FINANCIAL Reporting Case**

Q3, p. 231

Recognizing revenue when goods and services are delivered as described in the previous section assumes we are able to make reasonable estimates of amounts due from customers that potentially might be uncollectible. For product sales, this also includes amounts not collectible due to customers returning the products they purchased. Otherwise, we would violate one of the requirements of the revenue realization principle we discussed earlier— that there must be reasonable certainty as to the collectibility of cash from the customer. In this section we address a few situations in which uncertainties are so severe that they could cause a delay in recognizing revenue from a sale of a product or service. For each of these

---

[10]FASB ASC 605–45–45: Revenue Recognition–Principal Agent Considerations–Other Presentation Matters (originally *EITF 99-19: Reporting Revenue Gross as a Principal versus Net as an Agent* (Stamford, Conn.: FASB, 2000)).

situations, notice that the accounting is essentially the same—*deferring* recognition of the gross profit arising from a sale of a product or service until uncertainties have been resolved.

## Installment Sales

Customers sometimes are allowed to pay for purchases in installments over a long period of time. Many large retail stores, such as **Sears** and **J.C. Penney**, sell products on an installment plan. Increasing the length of time allowed for payment usually increases the uncertainty about whether the store actually will collect a receivable. Is the uncertainty sufficient in an installment sale to cause these companies to delay recognizing revenue and related expenses beyond the point of sale? Usually, it's not.

● LO5–3

In most situations, the increased uncertainty concerning the collection of cash from installment sales can be accommodated satisfactorily by estimating uncollectible amounts. If, however, the installment sale creates significant uncertainty concerning cash collection, making impossible a reasonable assessment of future bad debts, then revenue and expense recognition should be delayed. For example, real estate sales often are made on an installment basis with relatively small down payments and long payment periods, perhaps 25 years or more. These payment characteristics, combined with the general speculative nature of many of these transactions, may translate into extreme uncertainty concerning the collectibility of the installment receivable.[11] In fact, GAAP requires that the installment sales method (discussed below) be applied to a retail land sale that meets certain criteria.[12]

At times, revenue recognition is delayed due to a high degree of uncertainty related to ultimate cash collection.

When extreme uncertainty exists regarding the ultimate collectibility of cash, we delay recognizing revenue and related expenses using one of two accounting techniques, the **installment sales method** or the **cost recovery method**. *We emphasize that these methods should be used only in situations involving exceptional uncertainty.* As an example, consider **Nathan's Famous, Inc.**, which operates company-owned stores and franchise stores specializing in selling hot dogs. Illustration 5–6 shows part of the revenue recognition disclosure note included with Nathan's 2011 financial statements.

The *installment sales* and *cost recovery* methods are only used in unusual circumstances.

**Sales of Restaurants (in part)**
The Company recognizes profit on sales of restaurants or real estate under the full accrual method, the installment method and the deposit method (deferring revenue when a deposit is made until the earnings process is complete), depending on the specific terms of each sale. Profit recognition by the full accrual method is appropriate provided (a) the profit is determinable, that is, the collectibility of the sales price is reasonably assured or the amount that will not be collectible can be estimated, and (b) the earnings process is virtually complete, that is, the seller is not obliged to perform significant activities after the sale to earn the profit. Unless both conditions exist, recognition of all or part of the profit shall be postponed and other methods of profit recognition shall be followed.

**Illustration 5–6**

Disclosure of Revenue Recognition Policy— Nathan's Famous, Inc.

**Real World Financials**

**INSTALLMENT SALES METHOD.**   To deal with the uncertainty of collection, the installment sales method recognizes revenue and costs only when cash payments are received. Each payment is assumed to be composed of two components: (1) a partial recovery of the cost of the item sold and (2) a gross profit component. These components are determined by the gross profit percentage applicable to the sale. For example, if the gross profit percentage (gross profit ÷ sales price) is 40%, then 60% of each dollar collected represents cost recovery and the remaining 40% is gross profit. Consider the example in Illustration 5–7.

**Illustration 5–7**

Installment Sales Method

On November 1, 2013, the Belmont Corporation, a real estate developer, sold a tract of land for $800,000. The sales agreement requires the customer to make four equal annual payments of $200,000 plus interest on each November 1, beginning November 1, 2013. The land cost $560,000 to develop. The company's fiscal year ends on December 31.

---

[11]For income tax purposes, the installment sales method applies only to gains from the sale of certain types of properties. The tax law requires the use of the installment sales method for these transactions unless a taxpayer elects not to use the method.
[12]FASB ASC 360–20: Property, Plant, and Equipment—Real Estate Sales (previously "Accounting for Sales of Real Estate," *Statement of Financial Accounting Standards No. 66* (Stamford, Conn.: FASB, 1982)).

The gross profit of $240,000 ($800,000 − 560,000) represents 30% of the sales price ($240,000 ÷ $800,000). The collection of cash and the recognition of gross profit under the installment method are summarized below. In this example, we ignore the collection of interest charges and the recognition of interest revenue to concentrate on the collection of the $800,000 sales price and the recognition of gross profit on the sale.

| | | Amount Allocated to: | |
|---|---|---|---|
| **Date** | **Cash Collected** | **Cost (70%)** | **Gross Profit (30%)** |
| Nov. 1, 2013 | $200,000 | $140,000 | $ 60,000 |
| Nov. 1, 2014 | 200,000 | 140,000 | 60,000 |
| Nov. 1, 2015 | 200,000 | 140,000 | 60,000 |
| Nov. 1, 2016 | 200,000 | 140,000 | 60,000 |
| Totals | $800,000 | $560,000 | $240,000 |

The gross profit recognized in a period will be equal to the gross profit percentage multiplied by the period's cash collection. The following journal entries are recorded (interest charges ignored):

**Make Installment Sale:**
**November 1, 2013**

| | | |
|---|---|---|
| Installment receivables ............................................................. | 800,000 | |
|     Inventory ......................................................................... | | 560,000 |
|     Deferred gross profit ...................................................... | | 240,000 |
| *To record installment sale.* | | |

The first entry records the installment receivable and the reduction of inventory. The difference between the $800,000 selling price and the $560,000 cost of sales represents the gross profit on the sale of $240,000. As gross profit will be recognized in net income only as collections are received, it is recorded initially in an account called *deferred gross profit.* This is a contra account to the installment receivable. The deferred gross profit account will be reduced to zero as collections are received.[13]

**Collect Cash:**
**November 1, 2013**

| | | |
|---|---|---|
| Cash ........................................................................................ | 200,000 | |
|     Installment receivables .................................................... | | 200,000 |
| *To record cash collection from installment sale.* | | |
| Deferred gross profit ............................................................. | 60,000 | |
|     Realized gross profit ....................................................... | | 60,000 |
| *To recognize gross profit from installment sale.* | | |

The second set of entries records the collection of the first installment and recognizes the gross profit component of the payment, $60,000. Realized gross profit gets closed to income summary as part of the normal year-end closing process and is included in net income in the income statement. Journal entries to record the remaining three payments on November 1, 2014, 2015, and 2016, are identical.

---

[13]Accountants sometimes record installment sales in the following manner:

| | | |
|---|---|---|
| Installment receivables ............................................. | 800,000 | |
|     Installment sales ................................................. | | 800,000 |
| *To record installment sales.* | | |
| Cost of installment sales............................................ | 560,000 | |
|     Inventory............................................................ | | 560,000 |
| *To record the cost of installment sales.* | | |

Then at the end of the period, the following adjusting/closing entry is recorded:

| | | |
|---|---|---|
| Installment sales ....................................................... | 800,000 | |
|     Cost of installment sales...................................... | | 560,000 |
|     Deferred gross profit on installment sales.............. | | 240,000 |

The text entries concentrate on the effect of the transactions and avoid this unnecessary procedural complexity.

At the end of 2013, the balance sheet would report the following:

| | |
|---|---|
| Installment receivables ($800,000 − 200,000) | $600,000 |
| Less: Deferred gross profit ($240,000 − 60,000) | (180,000) |
| Installment receivables (net) | $420,000 |

The net amount of the receivable reflects the portion of the remaining payments to be received that represents cost recovery (70% × $600,000). The installment receivables are classified as current assets if they will be collected within one year (or within the company's operating cycle, if longer); otherwise, they are classified as noncurrent assets.

The income statement for 2013 would report gross profit from installment sales of $60,000. Sales and cost of goods sold associated with installment sales usually are not reported in the income statement under the installment method, just the resulting gross profit. However, if those amounts aren't included in the income statement in the period in which the installment sale is made, they need to be included in the notes to the financial statements, along with the amount of gross profit that has not yet been recognized.

# Additional Consideration

We discuss in significant depth in Chapter 7 the problem of accounting for bad debts. However, bad debts related to receivables on sales accounted for using the installment method create a unique problem. A company uses the installment method because it can't reliably estimate bad debts. Therefore, the company doesn't explicitly recognize bad debts or create an allowance for uncollectible accounts in the installment method. Rather, bad debts are dealt with implicitly by deferring gross profit until cash is collected. If the cash never is collected, the related deferred gross profit never gets included in net income. To illustrate, assume that in the example described in Illustration 5–7, the Belmont Corporation collected the first payment but the customer was unable to make the remaining payments. Typically, the seller would repossess the item sold and make the following journal entry:

| | | |
|---|---|---|
| Repossessed inventory.............................................. | 420,000 | |
| Deferred gross profit........................................... | 180,000 | |
|     Installment receivable.................................... | | 600,000 |

This entry removes the receivable and the remaining deferred gross profit and records the repossessed land in an inventory account. This example assumes that the repossessed land's current fair value is equal to the net receivable of $420,000. If the land's fair value at the date of repossession is less than $420,000, a loss on repossession is recorded (debited).

**COST RECOVERY METHOD.**   In situations where there is an extremely high degree of uncertainty regarding the ultimate cash collection on an installment sale, an even more conservative approach, the **cost recovery method**, can be used. This method defers all gross profit recognition until the cost of the item sold has been recovered. The gross profit recognition pattern applying the cost recovery method to the Belmont Corporation situation used in Illustration 5–7 is shown below.

> The *cost recovery method* defers all gross profit recognition until cash equal to the cost of the item sold has been received.

| Date | Cash Collected | Cost Recovery | Gross Profit Recognized |
|---|---|---|---|
| Nov. 1, 2013 | $200,000 | $200,000 | $ –0– |
| Nov. 1, 2014 | 200,000 | 200,000 | –0– |
| Nov. 1, 2015 | 200,000 | 160,000 | 40,000 |
| Nov. 1, 2016 | 200,000 | –0– | 200,000 |
| Totals | $800,000 | $560,000 | $240,000 |

The journal entries using this method are similar to those for the installment sales method except that $40,000 in gross profit is recognized in 2015 and $200,000 in 2016.

The cost recovery method's initial journal entry is identical to the installment sales method.

**Make Installment Sale:**

**November 1, 2013**

| | | |
|---|---|---|
| Installment receivables............................................................. | 800,000 | |
|   Inventory.......................................................................... | | 560,000 |
|   Deferred gross profit ..................................................... | | 240,000 |
| *To record installment sale.* | | |

**Collect Cash:**

**November 1, 2013, 2014, 2015, and 2016**

| | | |
|---|---|---|
| Cash....................................................................................... | 200,000 | |
|   Installment receivables................................................... | | 200,000 |
| *To record cash collection from installment sale.* | | |

**November 1, 2013 and 2014**

No entry for gross profit.

When payments are received, gross profit is recognized only after cost has been fully recovered.

**November 1, 2015**

| | | |
|---|---|---|
| Deferred gross profit ......................................................... | 40,000 | |
|   Realized gross profit ...................................................... | | 40,000 |
| *To recognize gross profit from installment sale.* | | |

**November 1, 2016**

| | | |
|---|---|---|
| Deferred gross profit ......................................................... | 200,000 | |
|   Realized gross profit ...................................................... | | 200,000 |
| *To recognize gross profit from installment sale.* | | |

Why not use the installment sales method or cost recovery method for all installment sales? Because doing so would violate the realization principle and be inconsistent with accrual accounting. If bad debts can be reasonably estimated, there is no reason to delay revenue recognition.

## Concept Review Exercise

**INSTALLMENT SALES**

Boatwright Implements, Inc., manufactures and sells farm machinery. For most of its sales, revenue and cost of sales are recognized at the delivery date. In 2013 Boatwright sold a cotton baler to a new customer for $100,000. The cost of the machinery was $60,000. Payment will be made in five annual installments of $20,000 each, with the first payment due in 2013. Boatwright usually does not allow its customers to pay in installments. Due to the unusual nature of the payment terms and the uncertainty of collection of the installment payments, Boatwright is considering alternative methods of recognizing profit on this sale.

**Required:**

Ignoring interest charges, prepare a table showing the gross profit to be recognized from 2013 through 2017 on the cotton-baler sale using the following three methods:

1. Point of delivery revenue recognition.
2. The installment sales method.
3. The cost recovery method.

**Solution:**

| | Point of Delivery | Installment Sales Method (40% × cash collection) | Cost Recovery Method |
|---|---|---|---|
| 2013 | $40,000 | $ 8,000 | $    –0– |
| 2014 | –0– | 8,000 | –0– |
| 2015 | –0– | 8,000 | –0– |
| 2016 | –0– | 8,000 | 20,000 |
| 2017 | –0– | 8,000 | 20,000 |
| Totals | $40,000 | $40,000 | $40,000 |

# Right of Return

Retailers usually give their customers the right to return merchandise if they are not satisfied. In most situations, even though the right to return merchandise exists, revenues and expenses can be appropriately recognized at point of delivery. Based on past experience, a company usually can estimate the returns that will result for a given volume of sales. These estimates are used to reduce both sales and cost of goods sold in anticipation of returns. The purpose of the estimates is to avoid overstating gross profit in the period of sale and understating gross profit in the period of return. The specific accounting treatment for sales returns is illustrated in Chapter 7 in conjunction with discussing the valuation of accounts receivable.

Because the return of merchandise can negate the benefits of having made a sale, the seller must meet specific criteria before revenue is recognized in situations when the right of return exists. The most critical of these criteria is that the seller must be able to make reliable estimates of future returns.[14] In some situations, these criteria are not satisfied at the point of delivery of the product. For example, manufacturers of semiconductors like **Intel Corporation** and **Motorola Corporation** usually sell their products through independent distributor companies. Economic factors, competition among manufacturers, and rapid obsolescence of the product motivate these manufacturers to grant the distributors the right of return if they are unable to sell the semiconductors. So, revenue recognition often is deferred beyond the delivery point to the date the products actually are sold by the distributor to an end user. The disclosure note shown in Illustration 5–8 appeared in a recent annual report of Intel Corporation.

● LO5–4

> **Revenue Recognition**
> We recognize net product revenue when the earnings process is complete, as evidenced by an agreement with the customer, transfer of title, and acceptance, if applicable, as well as fixed pricing and probable collectability. . . . Because of frequent sales price reductions and rapid technology obsolescence in the industry, we defer product revenue and related costs of sales from sales made to distributors under agreements allowing price protection or right of return until the distributors sell the merchandise.

**Illustration 5–8**

Disclosure of Revenue Recognition Policy—Intel Corporation

**Real World Financials**

For Intel, the event critical to revenue recognition is *not* the delivery of the product to a distributor but the ultimate sale of the product by the distributor to an end user.

Alternatively, the right of return could be specified contractually as expiring on some future date, and revenue recognition could be deferred to that date. Regardless, the accounting treatment in these situations would be similar to that used for the installment sales and cost recovery methods. The difference is that the journal entries we use to move deferred gross profit to realized gross profit would be recorded in whatever period that returns can be estimated reliably or the right of return no longer exists.

Similarly, sometimes, a sales agreement requires additional, important performance steps to be performed by the seller. In this case, the earnings process is not virtually complete until those steps are performed, but as in the case of significant uncertainty about cash collection, revenue recognition must be deferred. Illustration 5–1 on page 233 illustrates a situation where the seller, Brown & Sharpe, delays revenue recognition beyond delivery of machines until the performance of the machines has been accepted by the buyer. Customer acceptance is an important part of the agreement between buyer and seller.

Any time a company recognizes revenue at a point other than the point of delivery, the revenue recognition method used is disclosed in the summary of significant accounting policies. Intel's disclosure note is an example. As another example, Illustration 5–9 shows a disclosure note included with the 2011 first quarter financial statements of **Helicos Biosciences Corporation**, a producer of genetic analysis instrumentation for research, pharmaceutical, and medical applications.

---

[14]Other, less critical criteria are listed in FASB ASC 605–15–25: Revenue Recognition–Products–Recognition (previously "Revenue Recognition When Right of Return Exists," *Statement of Financial Accounting Standards No. 48* (Stamford, Conn.: FASB, 1981)).

**Illustration 5–9**

Disclosure of Revenue Recognition Policy— Helicos Biosciences Corporation

Real World Financials

> **2. Summary of Significant Accounting Policies: Revenue Recognition (in part)**
> The Company recognizes revenue in accordance with accounting guidance on revenue recognition in financial statements. . . . This guidance requires that persuasive evidence of a sales arrangement exists, delivery of goods occurs through transfer of title and risk and rewards of ownership, the selling price is fixed or determinable and collectability is reasonably assured. . . . In instances where the Company sells an instrument with specified acceptance criteria, the Company will defer revenue recognition until such acceptance has been obtained.

As the note indicates, some of Helicos's revenue is delayed beyond the point of product delivery. Until the product has been installed and meets customer acceptance criteria, there is a high degree of uncertainty concerning the possibility the product might be returned, so Helicos has not completed its obligation to its customer until acceptance has occurred.

# Consignment Sales

Consigned inventory stays in the balance sheet of the consignor until an arms-length transaction transfers title to a buyer.

Sometimes a company arranges for another company to sell its product under consignment. The "consignor" physically transfers the goods to the other company (the consignee), but the consignor retains legal title. If the consignee can't find a buyer within an agreed-upon time, the consignee returns the goods to the consignor. However, if a buyer is found, the consignee remits the selling price (less commission and approved expenses) to the consignor.

Because the consignor retains the risks and rewards of ownership of the product and title does not pass to the consignee, the consignor does not record a sale (revenue and related expenses) until the consignee sells the goods and title passes to the eventual customer. Of course, that means goods on consignment still are part of the consignor's inventory. As an example, **Boston Scientific Corporation** earns revenue from selling single-use medical devices. Some of the company's product is sold using consignment arrangements. Illustration 5–10 shows a portion of the revenue recognition disclosure note that Boston Scientific included in a recent annual report.

**Illustration 5–10**

Disclosure of Revenue Recognition Policy— Boston Scientific Corporation

Real World Financials

> **Note 1: Business and Summary of Significant Accounting Policies: *Revenue Recognition* (in part)**
> We consider revenue to be realized or realizable and earned when all of the following criteria are met: persuasive evidence of a sales arrangement exists; delivery has occurred or services have been rendered; the price is fixed or determinable; and collectibility is reasonably assured. We generally meet these criteria at the time of shipment, unless a consignment arrangement exists or we are required to provide additional services. We recognize revenue from consignment arrangements based on product usage, or implant, which indicates that the sale is complete.

Up until now, we've focused on revenue-generating activities in which some specific event (e.g., delivery, collection, product performance, and resale) indicates that the earnings process is substantially completed and significant uncertainties have been alleviated, prompting us to recognize revenue and related expenses. We now turn our attention to situations in which it's desirable to recognize revenue over more than one reporting period— before a specific event indicates the earnings process is substantially completed.

# Revenue Recognition Prior to Delivery

● **LO5–5**

The types of companies that make use of long-term contracts are many and varied. A recent survey of reporting practices of 500 large public companies indicates that approximately one in every six companies engages in long-term contracts.[15] And they are not just construction

---

[15]*Accounting Trends and Techniques—2011* (New York: AICPA, 2011), p. 410.

companies. In fact, even services such as research, installation, and consulting often are contracted for on a long-term basis. Illustration 5–11 lists just a sampling of companies that use long-term contracts, many of which you might recognize.

**Illustration 5–11**

Companies Engaged in Long-Term Contracts

| Company | Type of Industry or Product |
| --- | --- |
| Oracle Corp. | Computer software, license and consulting fees |
| Lockheed Martin Corporation | Aircraft, missiles, and spacecraft |
| Hewlett-Packard | Information technology |
| Northrop Grumman Newport News | Shipbuilding |
| Nortel Networks Corp. | Networking solutions and services to support the Internet |
| SBA Communications Corp. | Telecommunications |
| Layne Christensen Company | Water supply services and geotechnical construction |
| Kaufman & Broad Home Corp. | Commercial and residential construction |
| Raytheon Company | Defense electronics |
| Foster Wheeler Corp. | Construction, petroleum and chemical facilities |
| Halliburton | Construction, energy services |
| Allied Construction Products Corp. | Large metal stamping presses |

The general revenue recognition criteria described in the realization principle suggest that revenue should be recognized when a long-term project is finished (that is, when the earnings process is virtually complete). This is known as the **completed contract method** of revenue recognition. The problem with this method is that all revenues, expenses, and resulting income from the project are recognized in the period in which the project is completed; no revenues or expenses are reported in the income statements of earlier reporting periods in which much of the work may have been performed. Net income should provide a measure of periodic accomplishment to help predict future accomplishments. Clearly, income statements prepared using the completed contract method do not fairly report each period's accomplishments when a project spans more than one reporting period. Much of the earnings process is far removed from the point of delivery.

The **percentage-of-completion method** of revenue recognition for long-term construction and other projects is designed to help address this problem. By this approach, we recognize revenues (and expenses) over time by allocating a share of the project's expected revenues and expenses to each period in which the earnings process occurs, that is, the contract period. Although the contract usually specifies total revenues, the project's expenses are not known until completion. Consequently, it's necessary for a company to estimate the project's future costs at the end of each reporting period in order to estimate total gross profit to be earned on the project.

Because the percentage-of-completion method does a better job of recognizing revenue in the periods in which revenue is earned, U.S. and international GAAP require the use of that method unless it's not possible to make reliable estimates of revenues, expenses, and progress toward completion.[16] Companies prefer the percentage-of-completion method as well because it allows earlier revenue and profit recognition than does the completed contract method. For both reasons, the percentage-of-completion method is more prevalent in practice. However, much of the accounting is the same under either method, so we start by discussing the similarities between the two methods, and then the differences. You'll see that we recognize the same total amounts or revenue and profit over the life of the contract under either method. Only the timing of recognition differs.

The *completed contract method* recognizes revenue at a point in time when the earnings process is complete.

**FINANCIAL Reporting Case**

Q1, p. 231

The *percentage-of-completion method* allocates a share of a project's revenues and expenses to each reporting period as construction occurs.

---

[16]Specifically, U.S. GAAP requires that the percentage-of-completion method be used whenever (1) reasonable estimates can be made of revenues and costs; (2) the contract specifies the parties' rights, consideration to be paid, and payment terms; and (3) both the purchaser and seller have the ability and expectation to fulfill their obligations under the contract [FASB ASC 605–35–25: Revenue Recognition–Construction-Type and Production-Type Contracts–Recognition (previously "Accounting for Performance of Construction-Type and Certain Production-Type Contracts," *Statement of Position 81-1* (New York: AICPA, 1981))]. Similar criteria are included in IAS No. 11, "Construction Contracts" (IASCF, as amended, effective January 1, 2011, paragraph 23).

Illustration 5–12 provides information to compare accounting for long-term contracts using the completed contract and percentage-of-completion methods.

## Illustration 5–12
Completed Contract and Percentage-of-Completion Methods Compared

At the beginning of 2013, the Harding Construction Company received a contract to build an office building for $5 million. The project is estimated to take three years to complete. According to the contract, Harding will bill the buyer in installments over the construction period according to a prearranged schedule. Information related to the contract is as follows:

|  | 2013 | 2014 | 2015 |
|---|---|---|---|
| Construction costs incurred during the year | $1,500,000 | $1,000,000 | $1,600,000 |
| Construction costs incurred in prior years | –0– | 1,500,000 | 2,500,000 |
| Cumulative construction costs | 1,500,000 | 2,500,000 | 4,100,000 |
| Estimated costs to complete at end of year | 2,250,000 | 1,500,000 | –0– |
| Total estimated and actual construction costs | $3,750,000 | $4,000,000 | $4,100,000 |
| Billings made during the year | $1,200,000 | $2,000,000 | $1,800,000 |
| Cash collections during year | 1,000,000 | 1,400,000 | 2,600,000 |

Construction costs include the labor, materials, and overhead costs directly related to the construction of the building. Notice how the total of estimated and actual construction costs changes from period to period. Cost revisions are typical in long-term contracts in which costs are estimated over long periods of time.

**ACCOUNTING FOR THE COST OF CONSTRUCTION AND ACCOUNTS RECEIVABLE.** Summary journal entries for both the percentage-of-completion and completed contract methods are shown in Illustration 5–12A for construction costs, billings, and cash receipts.

## Illustration 5–12A    Journal Entries—Costs, Billings, and Cash Receipts

|  | 2013 | | 2014 | | 2015 | |
|---|---|---|---|---|---|---|
| Construction in progress ....................... | 1,500,000 | | 1,000,000 | | 1,600,000 | |
| Cash, materials, etc. ........................... | | 1,500,000 | | 1,000,000 | | 1,600,000 |
| *To record construction costs.* | | | | | | |
| Accounts receivable ............................. | 1,200,000 | | 2,000,000 | | 1,800,000 | |
| Billings on construction contract ........ | | 1,200,000 | | 2,000,000 | | 1,800,000 |
| *To record progress billings.* | | | | | | |
| Cash........................................................ | 1,000,000 | | 1,400,000 | | 2,600,000 | |
| Accounts receivable ........................... | | 1,000,000 | | 1,400,000 | | 2,600,000 |
| *To record cash collections.* | | | | | | |

**Accounting for costs, billings, and cash receipts are the same for both the percentage-of-completion and completed contract methods.**

With both the completed contract and percentage-of-completion methods, all costs incurred in the construction process are initially recorded in an asset account called **construction in progress**. This asset account is equivalent to work-in-process inventory in a manufacturing company. This is logical since the construction project is essentially an inventory item in process for the contractor.

Notice that periodic billings are credited to **billings on construction contract**. This account is a contra account to the construction in progress asset. At the end of each period, the balances in these two accounts are compared. If the net amount is a debit, it is reported in the balance sheet as an asset. Conversely, if the net amount is a credit, it is reported as a liability.[17]

---

[17]If the company is engaged in more than one long-term contract, all contracts for which construction in progress exceeds billings are grouped together and all contracts for which billings exceed construction in progress also are grouped together. This would result in the presentation of both an asset and a liability in the balance sheet.

To understand why we use the billings on construction contract account (or *billings* for short), consider a key difference between accounting for a long-term contract and accounting for a typical sale in which revenue is recognized upon delivery. Recall our earlier example in which Taft Company gives up its physical asset (inventory; in this instance a supercomputer) and recognizes cost of goods sold at the same time it gets a financial asset (an account receivable) and recognizes revenue. So, first a physical asset is in the balance sheet, and then a financial asset, but the two are not in the balance sheet at the same time.

*Construction in progress is the contractor's work-in-process inventory.*

Now consider our Harding Construction example. Harding is creating a physical asset (construction in progress) in the same periods it recognizes a financial asset (first recognizing accounts receivable when the customer is billed and then recognizing cash when the receivable is collected). Having both the physical asset and the financial asset in the balance sheet at the same time constitutes double counting the same arrangement. The billings account solves this problem. Whenever an account receivable is recognized, the other side of the journal entry increases the billings account, which is contra to (and thus reduces) construction in progress. As a result, the financial asset (accounts receivable) increases and the physical asset (the net amount of construction in progress and billings) decreases, and no double counting occurs.

*The billings on construction contract account prevents "double counting" assets by reducing construction in progress whenever an accounts receivable is recognized.*

**GROSS PROFIT RECOGNITION—GENERAL APPROACH.**    Now let's consider recognition of gross profit. The top portion of Illustration 5–12B shows the journal entry to recognize revenue, cost of construction (think of this as cost of goods sold), and gross profit under the completed contract method, while the bottom portion shows the journal entries that achieve this for the percentage-of-completion method. At this point focus on the structure of the journal entries (what is debited and credited). We'll discuss how to calculate the specific amounts later in the chapter.

## Illustration 5–12B   Journal Entries—Profit Recognition

|  | 2013 | 2014 | 2015 |
|---|---|---|---|
| **Completed Contract** |  |  |  |
| Construction in progress (gross profit) ............ |  |  | 900,000 |
| Cost of construction ........................................ |  |  | 4,100,000 |
|    Revenue from long-term contracts .............. |  |  | 5,000,000 |
| *To record gross profit.* |  |  |  |
|  |  |  |  |
| **Percentage-of-Completion** |  |  |  |
| Construction in progress (gross profit) ............ | 500,000 | 125,000 | 275,000 |
| Cost of construction ........................................ | 1,500,000 | 1,000,000 | 1,600,000 |
|    Revenue from long-term contracts .............. | 2,000,000 | 1,125,000 | 1,875,000 |
| *To record gross profit.* |  |  |  |

It's important to understand two key aspects of Illustration 5–12B. First, the same amounts of revenue, cost, and gross profit are recognized under both the completed contract and percentage-of-completion methods. The only difference is timing. To check this, sum all of the revenue recognized for both methods over the three years:

*The same total amount of revenue is recognized under both the completed contract and the percentage-of-completion methods, but the timing of recognition differs.*

|  | **Percentage-of-Completion** | **Completed Contract** |
|---|---|---|
| Revenue recognized: |  |  |
|    2013 | $2,000,000 | –0– |
|    2014 | 1,125,000 | –0– |
|    2015 | 1,875,000 | $5,000,000 |
| Total revenue | $5,000,000 | $5,000,000 |

Second, notice that in both methods we add gross profit (the difference between revenue and cost) to the construction in progress asset. That seems odd—why add *profit* to what is essentially an *inventory* account? The key here is that, when Harding recognizes gross profit, Harding is acting like it has sold some portion of the asset to the customer, but Harding keeps the asset in Harding's own balance sheet (in the construction in progress account)

Construction in progress includes profits and losses on the contract that have been recognized to date.

until delivery to the customer. Putting recognized gross profit into the construction in progress account just updates that account to reflect the total value (cost + gross profit = sales price) of the customer's asset. However, don't forget that the billings account is contra to the construction in progress account. Over the life of the construction project, Harding will bill the customer for the entire sales price of the asset. Therefore, at the end of the contract, the construction in progress account (containing total cost and gross profit) and the billings account (containing all amounts billed to the customer) will have equal balances that exactly offset to create a net value of zero.

The same journal entry is recorded to close out the billings and construction in progress accounts under the completed contract and percentage-of-completion methods.

The only task remaining is for Harding to officially transfer title to the finished asset to the customer. At that time, Harding will prepare a journal entry that removes the contract from its balance sheet by debiting billings and crediting construction in progress for the entire value of the contract. As shown in Illustration 5–12C, the same journal entry is recorded to close out the billings on construction contract and construction in progress accounts under the completed contract and percentage-of-completion methods.

**Illustration 5–12C**

Journal Entry to Close Billings and Construction in Progress Accounts

| | 2013 | 2014 | 2015 | |
| --- | --- | --- | --- | --- |
| Billings on construction contract ....... | | | 5,000,000 | |
|   Construction in progress .............. | | | | 5,000,000 |
| *To close accounts.* | | | | |

Now that we've seen how gross profit is recognized for long-term contracts, let's consider how the timing of that recognition differs between the completed contract and percentage-of-completion methods.

**FINANCIAL Reporting Case**

Q3, p. 231

Under the completed contract method, profit is not recognized until the project is completed.

### TIMING OF GROSS PROFIT RECOGNITION UNDER THE COMPLETED CONTRACT METHOD.

The timing of gross profit recognition under the completed contract method is simple. As the name implies, all revenues and expenses related to the project are recognized when the contract is completed. As shown in Illustration 5–12B and in the T-accounts below, completion occurs in 2015 for our Harding example. Prior to then, construction in progress includes only costs, showing a balance of $1,500,000 and $2,500,000 of cost at the end of 2013 and 2014, respectively, and including $4,100,000 of cost when the project is completed in 2015. Harding includes an additional $900,000 of gross profit in construction in progress when the project is completed in 2015 because the asset is viewed as "sold" on that date. The company records revenue of $5,000,000, cost of construction (similar to cost of goods sold) of $4,100,000, and the resulting $900,000 gross profit on that date.

Under the completed contract method, construction in progress is updated to include gross profit at the end of the life of the contract.

**Completed Contract**

| | Construction in Progress | | Billings on Construction Contract | |
| --- | --- | --- | --- | --- |
| 2013 construction costs | 1,500,000 | | 1,200,000 | 2013 billings |
| End balance, 2013 | 1,500,000 | | 2,000,000 | 2014 billings |
| 2014 construction costs | 1,000,000 | | 1,800,000 | 2015 billings |
| | | | 5,000,000 | Balance, before closing |
| End balance, 2014 | 2,500,000 | | | |
| 2015 construction costs | 1,600,000 | | | |
| 2015 gross profit | 900,000 | | | |
| Balance, before closing | 5,000,000 | | | |

Under the percentage-of-completion method, profit is recognized over the life of the project as the project is completed.

### TIMING OF GROSS PROFIT RECOGNITION UNDER THE PERCENTAGE-OF-COMPLETION METHOD.

Using the percentage-of-completion method we recognize a portion of the estimated gross profit each period based on progress to date. How should progress to date be estimated?

One approach is to use *output* measures like units of production. For example, with a multi-year contract to deliver airplanes we might recognize progress according to the number of planes delivered. Another example of an output measure is recognizing portions of revenue associated with achieving particular milestones specified in a sales contract. Accounting guidance[18] states a preference for output measures when they can be established, arguing that they are more directly and reliably related to assessing progress than are input measures.

Another approach is to use an *input* measure like the "**cost-to-cost ratio**," by which progress to date is estimated by calculating the percentage of estimated total cost that has been incurred to date. Similar input measures might be used instead, like the number of labor hours incurred to date compared to estimated total hours. One advantage of input measures is that they capture progress on long-term contracts that may not translate easily into simple output measures. For example, a natural output measure for highway construction might be finished miles of road, but that measure could be deceptive if not all miles of road require the same effort. A highway contract for the state of Arizona would likely pay the contractor more for miles of road blasted through the mountains than for miles paved across flat desert, and a cost-to-cost approach reflects that difference. Research suggests that the cost-to-cost input measure is most common in practice.[19]

> Progress to date can be estimated using input and output measures.

> A common input measure is a *cost-to-cost ratio*.

Regardless of the specific approach used to estimate progress to date, under the percentage-of-completion method we determine the amount of gross profit recognized in each period using the following logic:

$$\begin{pmatrix} \text{Gross profit} \\ \text{recognized this} \\ \text{period} \end{pmatrix} = \left( \begin{array}{c} \text{Total estimated} \\ \text{gross profit} \end{array} \times \begin{array}{c} \text{Percentage completed} \\ \text{to date} \end{array} \right) - \begin{pmatrix} \text{Gross profit} \\ \text{recognized in} \\ \text{prior periods} \end{pmatrix}$$

where total estimated gross profit = total estimated revenue − total estimated cost.

Illustration 5–12D shows the calculation of gross profit for each of the years for our Harding Construction Company example, with progress to date estimated using the cost-to-cost ratio. Refer to the bottom part of Illustration 5–12B to see the journal entries used to recognize gross profit in each period, and the T-accounts on the next page to see that the gross profit recognized in each period is added to the construction in progress account.

| | 2013 | 2014 | 2015 |
|---|---|---|---|
| **Contract price** (A) | $5,000,000 | $5,000,000 | $5,000,000 |
| **Construction costs:** | | | |
| Construction costs incurred during the year | $1,500,000 | $1,000,000 | $1,600,000 |
| Construction costs incurred in prior years | –0– | 1,500,000 | 2,500,000 |
| Actual costs to date | $1,500,000 | $2,500,000 | $4,100,000 |
| Estimated remaining costs to complete | 2,250,000 | 1,500,000 | –0– |
| Total cost (estimated + actual) (B) | $3,750,000 | $4,000,000 | $4,100,000 |
| **Total gross profit** (A − B) | $1,250,000 | $1,000,000 | $ 900,000 |
| *Multiplied by:* | × | × | × |
| **Percentage of completion:** | $\left(\dfrac{\$1,500,000}{\$3,750,000}\right)$ | $\left(\dfrac{\$2,500,000}{\$4,000,000}\right)$ | $\left(\dfrac{\$4,100,000}{\$4,100,000}\right)$ |
| $\dfrac{\text{Actual costs to date}}{\text{Total cost (est. + actual)}}$ | = 40% | = 62.5% | = 100% |
| *Equals:* | | | |
| **Gross profit earned to date** | $ 500,000 | $ 625,000 | $ 900,000 |
| *Less:* | | | |
| **Gross profit recognized in prior periods** | –0– | (500,000) | (625,000) |
| *Equals:* | | | |
| **Gross profit recognized currently** | $ 500,000 | $ 125,000 | $ 275,000 |

**Illustration 5–12D**

Percentage-of-Completion Method—Allocation of Gross Profit to Each Period

---

[18]FASB ASC 605–35–25–71: Revenue Recognition–Construction–Type and Production-Type Contracts–Recognition–Input and Output Measures (previously "Accounting for Performance of Construction-Type and Certain Production-Type Contracts," *Statement of Position No. 81-1* (New York: AICPA, 1981)).
[19]R. K. Larson and K. L. Brown, 2004, "Where Are We with Long-Term Contract Accounting?" *Accounting Horizons,* September, pp. 207–219.

**Percentage-of-Completion**

| | Construction in Progress | | | Billings on Construction Contract | |
|---|---|---|---|---|---|
| 2013 construction costs | 1,500,000 | | | 1,200,000 | 2013 billings |
| 2013 gross profit | 500,000 | | | 2,000,000 | 2014 billings |
| End balance, 2013 | 2,000,000 | | | 1,800,000 | 2015 billings |
| 2014 construction costs | 1,000,000 | | | 5,000,000 | Balance, before closing |
| 2014 gross profit | 125,000 | | | | |
| End balance, 2014 | 3,125,000 | | | | |
| 2015 construction costs | 1,600,000 | | | | |
| 2015 gross profit | 275,000 | | | | |
| Balance, before closing | 5,000,000 | | | | |

**Under the percentage-of-completion method, construction in progress is updated each period to include gross profit.**

Income statements are more informative if the sales revenue and cost components of gross profit are reported rather than the net figure alone. So, the income statement for each year will report the appropriate revenue and cost of construction amounts. For example, in 2013, the gross profit of $500,000 consists of revenue of $2,000,000 (40% of the $5,000,000 contract price) less the $1,500,000 cost of construction. In subsequent periods, we calculate revenue by multiplying the percentage of completion by the contract price and then subtracting revenue recognized in prior periods, similar to the way we calculate gross profit each period. The cost of construction, then, is the difference between revenue and gross profit. In most cases, cost of construction also equals the construction costs incurred during the period.[20] The table in Illustration 5–12E shows the revenue and cost of construction recognized in each of the three years of our example. Of course, as you can see in this illustration, we could have initially determined the gross profit by first calculating revenue and then subtracting cost of construction.[21]

**In the income statement, we separate the gross profit into its two components: revenue and cost of construction.**

**Illustration 5–12E**

Percentage-of-Completion Method— Allocation of Revenue and Cost of Construction to Each Period

| **2013** | | |
|---|---|---|
| Revenue recognized ($5,000,000 × 40%) | | $2,000,000 |
| Cost of construction | | (1,500,000) |
| Gross profit | | $ 500,000 |
| **2014** | | |
| Revenue recognized to date ($5,000,000 × 62.5%) | $3,125,000 | |
| Less: revenue recognized in 2013 | 2,000,000 | |
| Revenue recognized | | $1,125,000 |
| Cost of construction | | (1,000,000) |
| Gross profit | | $ 125,000 |
| **2015** | | |
| Revenue recognized to date ($5,000,000 × 100%) | $5,000,000 | |
| Less: revenue recognized in 2013 and 2014 | 3,125,000 | |
| Revenue recognized | | $1,875,000 |
| Cost of construction | | (1,600,000) |
| Gross profit | | $ 275,000 |

---

[20]Cost of construction does not equal the construction costs incurred during the year when a loss is projected on the entire project. This situation is illustrated later in the chapter.

[21]As a practical matter, if the percentage of completion figure is rounded we may calculate different amounts of revenue by (a) directly calculating revenue using the percentage of completion, and (b) indirectly calculating revenue by first calculating gross profit using the percentage of completion and then calculating revenue by adding gross profit to cost of construction. In that case, given that gross profit is defined as revenue minus cost, it is best to use approach (a) and first calculate revenue directly, solving for gross profit by subtracting cost of construction from revenue.

# A Comparison of the Completed Contract and Percentage-of-Completion Methods

**INCOME RECOGNITION.**   Illustration 5–12B shows journal entries that would determine the amount of revenue, cost, and therefore gross profit that would appear in the income statement under the percentage-of-completion and completed contract methods. Comparing the gross profit patterns produced by each method of revenue recognition demonstrates the essential difference between them:

The same total amount of profit or loss is recognized under both the completed contract and the percentage-of-completion methods, but the timing of recognition differs.

|  | Percentage-of-Completion | Completed Contract |
| --- | --- | --- |
| Gross profit recognized: |  |  |
| 2013 | $500,000 | –0– |
| 2014 | 125,000 | –0– |
| 2015 | 275,000 | $900,000 |
| Total gross profit | $900,000 | $900,000 |

Although both methods yield identical gross profit of $900,000 for the entire 3-year period, the timing differs. The completed contract method defers all gross profit to 2015, when the project is completed. Obviously, the percentage-of-completion method provides a better measure of the company's economic activity and progress over the three-year period. That's why the percentage-of-completion method is preferred, and, as mentioned previously, the completed contract method should be used only when the company is unable to make dependable estimates of future revenue and costs necessary to apply the percentage-of-completion method.[22]

**BALANCE SHEET RECOGNITION.**   The balance sheet presentation for the construction-related accounts by both methods is shown in Illustration 5–12F. The balance in the construction in progress account differs between methods because of the earlier gross profit recognition that occurs under the percentage-of-completion method.

**Illustration 5–12F**

Balance Sheet Presentation

| Balance Sheet (End of Year) | | |
| --- | --- | --- |
|  | **2013** | **2014** |
| **Percentage-of-Completion:** |  |  |
| *Current assets:* |  |  |
| Accounts receivable | $200,000 | $800,000 |
| Costs and profit ($2,000,000) in excess of billings ($1,200,000) | 800,000 |  |
| *Current liabilities:* |  |  |
| Billings ($3,200,000) in excess of costs and profit ($3,125,000) |  | $ 75,000 |
| **Completed Contract:** |  |  |
| *Current assets:* |  |  |
| Accounts receivable | $200,000 | $800,000 |
| Costs ($1,500,000) in excess of billings ($1,200,000) | 300,000 |  |
| *Current liabilities:* |  |  |
| Billings ($3,200,000) in excess of costs ($2,500,000) |  | $700,000 |

In the balance sheet, the construction in progress (CIP) account (containing costs and profit) is offset against the billings on construction contract account, with CIP > Billings shown as an asset and Billings > CIP shown as a liability. Because a company may have some contracts that have a net asset position and others that have a net liability position, we usually will see both net assets and net liabilities shown in a balance sheet at the same time.

*Construction in progress in excess of billings* essentially represents an unbilled receivable. Companies include it in their balance sheets as a component of accounts receivable, as part of

Billings on construction contracts are subtracted from construction in progress to determine balance sheet presentation.

---

[22]For income tax purposes, the completed contract method may be used for home construction contracts and certain other real estate construction contracts. All other contracts must use the percentage-of-completion method.

inventory, or on its own line. The construction company is incurring construction costs (and recognizing gross profit using the percentage-of-completion method) for which it will be paid by the buyer. If the construction company bills the buyer an amount exactly equal to these costs (and profits recognized) then the accounts receivable balance properly reflects the claims of the construction company. If, however, the amount billed is less than the costs incurred (plus profits recognized) the difference represents the remaining claim to cash—an asset.

On the other hand, *Billings in excess of construction in progress* essentially indicates that the overbilled accounts receivable overstates the amount of the claim to cash earned to that date and must be reported as a liability. This is similar to the unearned revenue liability that is recorded when a customer pays for a product or service in advance. The advance is properly shown as a liability representing the obligation to provide the good or service in the future.

### LONG-TERM CONTRACT LOSSES.

The Harding Construction Company example above involves a situation in which a profit was realized on the construction contract. Unfortunately, losses sometimes occur on long-term contracts.

**Periodic loss occurs for profitable project.** When using the percentage-of-completion method, a loss sometimes must be recognized in at least one period over the life of the project even though the project as a whole is expected to be profitable. We determine the loss in precisely the same way we determined the profit in profitable years. For example, assume the same $5 million contract for Harding Construction Company described in Illustration 5–12 but with the following cost information:

|  | 2013 | 2014 | 2015 |
|---|---|---|---|
| Construction costs incurred during the year | $1,500,000 | $1,260,000 | $1,840,000 |
| Construction costs incurred in prior years | –0– | 1,500,000 | 2,760,000 |
| Cumulative construction costs | 1,500,000 | 2,760,000 | 4,600,000 |
| Estimated costs to complete at end of year | 2,250,000 | 1,840,000 | –0– |
| Total estimated and actual construction costs | $3,750,000 | $4,600,000 | $4,600,000 |

At the end of 2013, gross profit of $500,000 (revenue of $2,000,000 less cost of construction of $1,500,000) is recognized as previously determined.

At the end of 2014, the company now forecasts a total profit of $400,000 ($5,000,000 − 4,600,000) on the project and, at that time, the project is estimated to be 60% complete ($2,760,000 ÷ 4,600,000). Applying this percentage to the anticipated gross profit of $400,000 results in a gross profit *to date* of $240,000. But remember, a gross profit of $500,000 was recognized in 2013.

This situation is treated as a *change in accounting estimate* because it resulted from a change in the estimation of costs to complete at the end of 2013. Actual total costs to complete—$4,600,000—were much higher than the 2013 year-end estimate of $3,750,000. Recall from our discussion of changes in accounting estimates in Chapter 4 that we don't go back and restate the prior year's gross profit. Instead, the 2014 income statement would report *a loss of $260,000* ($500,000 − 240,000) so that the cumulative amount recognized to date totals $240,000 of gross profit. The loss consists of 2014 revenue of $1,000,000 (computed as $5,000,000 × 60% = $3,000,000 revenue to be recognized by end of 2014 less 2013 revenue of $2,000,000) less cost of construction of $1,260,000 (cost incurred in 2014). The following journal entry records the loss in 2014:

| | | |
|---|---|---|
| Cost of construction ................................................................ | 1,260,000 | |
|     Revenue from long-term contracts (below) ........................... | | 1,000,000 |
|     Construction in progress (loss) ............................................. | | 260,000 |

The 2015 gross profit comprises $2,000,000 in revenue ($5,000,000 less revenue of $3,000,000 recognized in 2013 and 2014) and $1,840,000 in cost of construction (cost incurred in 2015). The 2015 income statement would report a gross profit of $160,000:

| | |
|---|---|
| Revenue | $2,000,000 |
| Less: Cost of construction | (1,840,000) |
| Gross profit | $ 160,000 |

Of course, when using the completed contract method, no profit or loss is recorded in 2013 or 2014. Instead, a $400,000 gross profit (revenue of $5,000,000 and cost of construction of $4,600,000) is recognized in 2015.

**Loss is projected on the entire project.**   If an overall loss is projected on the entire contract, the total loss must be recognized in the period in which that projection occurs, regardless of whether the percentage-of-completion or completed contract method is being used. Again consider the Harding Construction Company example but with the following cost information:

| | 2013 | 2014 | 2015 |
|---|---|---|---|
| Construction costs incurred during the year | $1,500,000 | $1,260,000 | $2,440,000 |
| Construction costs incurred in prior years | –0– | 1,500,000 | 2,760,000 |
| Cumulative construction costs | 1,500,000 | 2,760,000 | 5,200,000 |
| Estimated costs to complete at end of year | 2,250,000 | 2,340,000 | –0– |
| Total estimated and actual construction costs | $3,750,000 | $5,100,000 | $5,200,000 |

At the end of 2014, revised costs indicate a loss of $100,000 for the entire project ($5,000,000 − 5,100,000). In this situation, the *total* anticipated loss must be recognized in 2014 for both the percentage-of-completion method and the completed contract method. As a gross profit of $500,000 was recognized in 2013 using the percentage-of-completion method, *a $600,000 loss is recognized in 2014* so that the cumulative amount recognized to date totals a $100,000 loss. Once again, this situation is treated as a change in accounting estimate, with no restatement of 2013 income. If the completed contract method is used, because no gross profit is recognized in 2013, the $100,000 loss for the project is recognized in 2014 by debiting loss from long-term contracts and crediting construction in progress for $100,000.

> An estimated loss on a long-term contract is fully recognized in the first period the loss is anticipated, regardless of the revenue recognition method used.

Why recognize the estimated overall loss of $100,000 in 2014, rather than at the end of the contract? If the loss was not recognized in 2014, construction in progress would be valued at an amount greater than the company expects to realize from the contract. To avoid that problem, the construction in progress account is reduced to $2,660,000 ($2,760,000 in costs to date less $100,000 estimated total loss). This amount combined with the estimated costs to complete of $2,340,000 equals the realizable contract price of $5,000,000. Recognizing losses on long-term projects in the period the losses become known is equivalent to measuring inventory at the lower of cost or market.

The pattern of gross profit (loss) over the contract period for the two methods is summarized in the following table. Notice that an unanticipated increase in costs of $100,000 causes a further loss of $100,000 to be recognized in 2015.

| | Percentage-of-Completion | Completed Contract |
|---|---|---|
| Gross profit (loss) recognized: | | |
| 2013 | $ 500,000 | –0– |
| 2014 | (600,000) | $(100,000) |
| 2015 | (100,000) | (100,000) |
| Total project loss | $(200,000) | $(200,000) |

The table in Illustration 5–12G shows the revenue and cost of construction recognized in each of the three years using the percentage-of-completion method.

Revenue is recognized in the usual way by multiplying a percentage of completion by the total contract price. In situations where a loss is expected on the entire project, cost of construction for the period will no longer be equal to cost incurred during the period. The easiest way to compute cost of construction is to add the amount of the recognized loss to

**Illustration 5–12G**

Percentage-of-Completion Method: Allocation of Revenue and Cost of Construction to Each Period—Loss on Entire Project

| | | |
|---|---|---|
| **2013** | | |
| Revenue recognized ($5,000,000 × 40%) | | $2,000,000 |
| Costs of construction | | (1,500,000) |
| Gross profit | | $ 500,000 |
| **2014** | | |
| Revenue recognized to date ($5,000,000 × 54.12%)* | $2,706,000 | |
| Less: Revenue recognized in 2013 | (2,000,000) | |
| Revenue recognized | | $ 706,000 |
| Cost of construction† | | (1,306,000) |
| Loss | | $ (600,000) |
| **2015** | | |
| Revenue recognized to date ($5,000,000 × 100%) | $5,000,000 | |
| Less: Revenue recognized in 2013 and 2014 | (2,706,000) | |
| Revenue recognized | | $2,294,000 |
| Cost of construction† | | (2,394,000) |
| Loss | | $ (100,000) |

*$2,760,000 ÷ $5,100,000 = 54.12%
†The difference between revenue and loss

the amount of revenue recognized. For example, in 2014 revenue recognized of $706,000 is added to the loss of $600,000 to arrive at the cost of construction of $1,306,000.[23]

The journal entries to record the losses in 2014 and 2015 are as follows:

Recognized losses on long-term contracts reduce the construction in progress account.

| | | |
|---|---|---|
| **2014** | | |
| Cost of construction ................................................................ | 1,306,000 | |
| Revenue from long-term contracts ......................................... | | 706,000 |
| Construction in progress (loss) ............................................... | | 600,000 |
| **2015** | | |
| Cost of construction ................................................................ | 2,394,000 | |
| Revenue from long-term contracts ......................................... | | 2,294,000 |
| Construction in progress (loss) ............................................... | | 100,000 |

Using the completed contract method, no revenue or cost of construction is recognized until the contract is complete. In 2014, a loss on long-term contracts (an income statement account) of $100,000 is recognized. In 2015, the income statement will report revenue of $5,000,000 and cost of construction of $5,100,000, thus reporting the additional loss of $100,000. The journal entries to record the losses in 2014 and 2015 are as follows:

| | | |
|---|---|---|
| **2014** | | |
| Loss on long-term contracts ..................................................... | 100,000 | |
| Construction in progress (loss) ............................................... | | 100,000 |
| **2015** | | |
| Cost of construction ................................................................ | 5,100,000 | |
| Revenue from long-term contracts ......................................... | | 5,000,000 |
| Construction in progress (loss) ............................................... | | 100,000 |

---

[23]The cost of construction also can be determined as follows:

| | | |
|---|---|---|
| Loss to date (100% recognized) | | $ 100,000 |
| Add: | | |
| Remaining total project cost, not including the loss | | |
| ($5,100,000 − 100,000) | $5,000,000 | |
| Multiplied by the percentage of completion | × .5412* | 2,706,000 |
| Total | | 2,806,000 |
| Less: Cost of construction recognized in 2011 | | (1,500,000) |
| Cost of construction recognized in 2012 | | $1,306,000 |

*$2,760,000 ÷ 5,100,000

You can see from this example that use of the percentage-of-completion method in this case produces a large overstatement of income in 2013 and a large understatement in 2014 caused by a change in the estimation of future costs. These estimate revisions happen occasionally. However, recall that if management believes they are unable to make dependable forecasts of future costs, the completed contract method should be used.

# International Financial Reporting Standards

**Long-Term Construction Contracts.** *IAS No. 11* governs revenue recognition for long-term construction contracts.[24] Like U.S. GAAP, that standard requires the use of the percentage-of-completion method when reliable estimates can be made. However, unlike U.S. GAAP, *IAS No. 11* requires the use of the cost recovery method rather than the completed contract method when reliable estimates can't be made.[25] Under the cost recovery method, contract costs are expensed as incurred, and an offsetting amount of contract revenue is recognized to the extent that it is probable that costs will be recoverable from the customer. No gross profit is recognized until all costs have been recovered, which is why this method is also sometimes called the "zero-profit method." Note that under both the completed contract and cost recovery methods no gross profit is recognized until the contract is essentially completed, but revenue and construction costs will be recognized earlier under the cost recovery method than under the completed contract method. Also, under both methods an expected loss is recognized immediately.

● LO5–8

To see this difference between the completed contract and cost recovery methods, here is a version of Illustration 5–12B that compares revenue, cost, and gross profit recognition under the two methods:

**IFRS ILLUSTRATION**

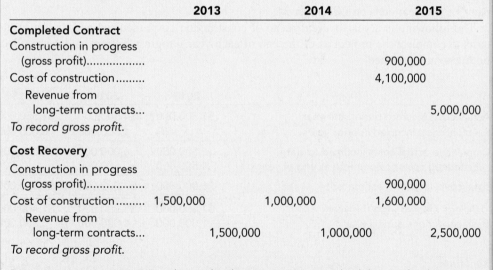

|  | 2013 | 2014 | 2015 |
|---|---|---|---|
| **Completed Contract** | | | |
| Construction in progress (gross profit)................. | | | 900,000 |
| Cost of construction......... | | | 4,100,000 |
| Revenue from long-term contracts... | | | 5,000,000 |
| *To record gross profit.* | | | |
| **Cost Recovery** | | | |
| Construction in progress (gross profit)................. | | | 900,000 |
| Cost of construction......... | 1,500,000 | 1,000,000 | 1,600,000 |
| Revenue from long-term contracts... | 1,500,000 | 1,000,000 | 2,500,000 |
| *To record gross profit.* | | | |

Revenue recognition occurs earlier under the cost recovery method than under the completed contract method, but gross profit recognition occurs at the end of the contract for both methods. As a result, gross profit as a percentage of revenue differs between the two methods at various points in the life of the contract.

---

[24]"Construction Contracts," *International Accounting Standard No. 11* (IASCF), as amended, effective January 1, 2011.

[25]Earlier in this chapter we referred to the "cost recovery method" in a different circumstance—when a company had already delivered a product to a customer but had to delay gross profit recognition until a point after delivery because of an inability to make reliable estimates of uncollectible accounts. In that case, gross profit only could be recognized after costs had been recovered (and cash collections exceeded cost of goods sold). IFRS' use of "cost recovery method" is similar, in that gross profit recognition is delayed until after cost has been recovered, but note that in this case the product is being constructed for the customer and therefore has not yet been delivered.

The first disclosure note to any set of financial statements usually is a summary of significant accounting policies. This note discloses the method the company uses to account for its long-term contracts. As an example of this, Illustration 5–13 shows the disclosure note that appeared in a recent annual report of **Fluor Corporation**.

## Illustration 5–13

Disclosure of Revenue Recognition Policy for Construction Contracts— Fluor Corporation

Real World Financials

> **Notes: Engineering and Construction Contracts (in part)**
>
> The company recognizes engineering and construction contract revenue using the percentage-of-completion method, based primarily on contract cost incurred to date compared to total estimated contract cost. . . . Contracts are generally segmented between types of services, such as engineering and construction, and accordingly, gross margin related to each activity is recognized as those separate services are rendered. Changes to total estimated contract cost or losses, if any, are recognized in the period in which they are determined. Pre-contract costs are expensed as incurred. Revenue recognized in excess of amounts billed is classified as a current asset under contract work in progress. Amounts billed to clients in excess of revenue recognized to date are classified as a current liability under advance billings on contracts.

# Concept Review Exercise

**LONG-TERM CONSTRUCTION CONTRACTS**

During 2013, the Samuelson Construction Company began construction on an office building for the City of Gernon. The contract price is $8,000,000 and the building will take approximately 18 months to complete. Completion is scheduled for early in 2015. The company's fiscal year ends on December 31.

The following is a year-by-year recap of construction costs incurred and the estimated costs to complete the project as of the end of each year. Progress billings and cash collections also are indicated.

|  | 2013 | 2014 | 2015 |
|---|---|---|---|
| Actual costs incurred during the year | $1,500,000 | $4,500,000 | $1,550,000 |
| Actual costs incurred in prior years | –0– | 1,500,000 | 6,000,000 |
| Cumulative actual costs incurred to date | 1,500,000 | 6,000,000 | 7,550,000 |
| Estimated costs to complete at end of year | 4,500,000 | 1,500,000 | –0– |
| Total costs (actual + estimated) | $6,000,000 | $7,500,000 | $7,550,000 |
| Billings made during the year | $1,400,000 | $5,200,000 | $1,400,000 |
| Cash collections during year | 1,000,000 | 4,000,000 | 3,000,000 |

**Required:**

1. Determine the amount of gross profit or loss to be recognized in each of the three years applying both the percentage-of-completion and completed contract methods.
2. Prepare the necessary summary journal entries for each of the three years to account for construction costs incurred, recognized revenue and cost of construction, contract billings, and cash collections and to close the construction accounts in 2015 using the percentage-of-completion method only.
3. Prepare a partial balance sheet for 2013 and 2014 to include all construction-related accounts using the percentage-of-completion method.

**Solution:**

1. Determine the amount of gross profit or loss to be recognized in each of the three years applying both the percentage-of-completion and completed contract methods.

## Percentage-of-Completion Method

| | 2013 | 2014 | 2015 |
|---|---|---|---|
| Contract price | $8,000,000 | $8,000,000 | $8,000,000 |
| Less: total cost* | 6,000,000 | $7,500,000 | 7,550,000 |
| Total estimated gross profit to date | 2,000,000 | 500,000 | 450,000 |
| Multiplied by % of completion** | 25% | 80% | 100% |
| Gross profit recognized to date | 500,000 | 400,000 | 450,000 |
| Less gross profit recognized in prior years | –0– | (500,000) | (400,000) |
| Gross profit (loss) recognized | $ 500,000 | $ (100,000) | $ 50,000 |

*Estimated in 2013 & 2014; Actual in 2015.
**Estimated percentage of completion:

| 2013 | 2014 | 2015 |
|---|---|---|
| $\frac{1,500,000}{6,000,000} = 25\%$ | $\frac{6,000,000}{7,500,000} = 80\%$ | Project complete |

## Completed Contract Method

| | 2013 | 2014 | 2015 |
|---|---|---|---|
| Gross profit recognized | –0– | –0– | $450,000 |

2. Prepare the necessary summary journal entries for each of the three years to account for construction costs incurred, recognized revenue and cost of construction, contract billings, and cash collections and to close the construction accounts in 2015 using the percentage-of-completion method only.

| | 2013 | | 2014 | | 2015 | |
|---|---|---|---|---|---|---|
| Construction in progress ..................... | 1,500,000 | | 4,500,000 | | 1,550,000 | |
| Cash, materials, etc. ....................... | | 1,500,000 | | 4,500,000 | | 1,550,000 |
| *To record construction costs.* | | | | | | |
| Construction in progress (gross profit) ... | 500,000 | | | | 50,000 | |
| Cost of construction ........................... | 1,500,000 | | | | 1,550,000 | |
| Revenue from long-term | | | | | | |
| contracts (below) .......................... | | 2,000,000 | | | | 1,600,000 |
| *To record gross profit.* | | | | | | |
| Cost of construction ......................... | | | 4,500,000 | | | |
| Revenue from long-term | | | | | | |
| contracts (below) .......................... | | | | 4,400,000 | | |
| Construction in progress (loss) .......... | | | | 100,000 | | |
| *To record loss.* | | | | | | |
| Accounts receivable ............................ | 1,400,000 | | 5,200,000 | | 1,400,000 | |
| Billings on construction contract ....... | | 1,400,000 | | 5,200,000 | | 1,400,000 |
| *To record progress billings.* | | | | | | |
| Cash ................................................ | 1,000,000 | | 4,000,000 | | 3,000,000 | |
| Accounts receivable ......................... | | 1,000,000 | | 4,000,000 | | 3,000,000 |
| *To record cash collections.* | | | | | | |
| Billings on construction contract .......... | | | | | 8,000,000 | |
| Construction in progress ................... | | | | | | 8,000,000 |
| *To close accounts.* | | | | | | |

| **Revenue recognized:** | | |
|---|---|---|
| **2013:** | $8,000,000 × 25% = | $2,000,000 |
| **2014:** | $8,000,000 × 80% = | $6,400,000 |
| | Less: Revenue recognized in 2013 | (2,000,000) |
| | Revenue recognized in 2014 | $4,400,000 |
| **2015:** | $8,000,000 × 100% = | $8,000,000 |
| | Less: Revenue recognized in 2013 and 2014 | (6,400,000) |
| | Revenue recognized in 2015 | $1,600,000 |

3. Prepare a partial balance sheet for 2013 and 2014 to include all construction-related accounts using the percentage-of-completion method.

**Balance Sheet**
**(End of Year)**

| | 2013 | 2014 |
|---|---|---|
| **Current assets:** | | |
| Accounts receivable | $400,000 | $1,600,000 |
| Costs and profit ($2,000,000) in excess of billings ($1,400,000) | 600,000 | |
| **Current liabilities:** | | |
| Billings ($6,600,000) in excess of costs and profit ($6,400,000) | | 200,000 |

# Industry-Specific Revenue Issues

● LO5–6

The previous sections addressed situations when revenue is recognized either at a point in time after the earnings process is virtually complete or over time during the earnings process. We now look at situations that require revenue recognition using a combination of the two approaches.

## Software and Other Multiple-Element Arrangements

The software industry is a key economic component of our economy. Microsoft alone reported revenues of almost $70 billion for its 2011 fiscal year. Yet, the recognition of software revenues has been a controversial accounting issue. The controversy stems from the way software vendors typically package their products. It is not unusual for these companies to sell multiple software element in a bundle for a lump-sum contract price. The bundle often includes product, upgrades, postcontract customer support, and other services. The critical accounting question concerns the timing of revenue recognition.

GAAP indicates that if a software arrangement includes multiple elements, the revenue from the arrangement should be allocated to the various elements based on "vendor-specific objective evidence" ("VSOE") of fair values of the individual elements. It doesn't matter what separate prices are indicated in the multiple-element contract. Rather, the VSOE of fair values are the sales prices of the elements when sold separately by that vendor. If VSOE doesn't exist, revenue recognition is deferred until VSOE is available or until all elements of the arrangement are delivered.[26]

Generally, a portion of the proceeds received from the sale of software is deferred and recognized as revenue in future periods.

For example, suppose that a vendor sold software to a customer for $90,000. As part of the contract, the vendor promises to provide "free" technical support over the next six months. However, the vendor sells the same software without technical support for $80,000, and the vendor sells a stand-alone six-month technical support contract for $20,000, so those products would sell for $100,000 if sold separately. Based on that VSOE, the software comprises 80% of the total fair values, and the technical support 20%. Prior to the AICPA guidance, some vendors were recognizing the entire $90,000 as revenue when the initial software was delivered. Now, the $90,000 contract price must be allocated based on VSOE. Therefore, the seller would recognize $72,000 ($90,000 × 80%) in revenue up front when the software is delivered, and defer the remaining $18,000 ($90,000 × 20%) and recognize it ratably over the next six

---

[26]FASB ASC 985–605–25: Software–Revenue Recognition–Recognition (previously "Software Revenue Recognition," *Statement of Position 97-2* (New York: AICPA, 1997), p. 14).

months as the technical support service is provided. If VSOE was not available, the vendor couldn't recognize any revenue initially, and instead would recognize the entire $90,000 ratably over the six-month period.

These revenue deferrals can be material. For example, in its 2011 balance sheet, Microsoft reported a liability for unearned (deferred) software revenue of over $17 billion.

In 2009, the FASB's Emerging Issues Task Force (EITF) issued guidance to broaden the application of this basic perspective to other arrangements that involve "multiple deliverables."[27] Examples of such arrangements are sales of appliances with maintenance contracts, cellular phone contracts that come with a "free phone," and even painting services that include sales of paint as well as labor. Other examples are products that contain both hardware and software essential to the functioning of the product, such as computers and smart phones that are always sold with an operating system. Now, as with software-only contracts, sellers allocate total revenue to the various parts of a multiple-deliverable arrangement on the basis of the relative stand-alone selling prices of the parts. Sellers must defer revenue recognition for parts that don't have stand-alone value, or whose value is contingent upon other undelivered parts. However, unlike software-only arrangements, sellers offering other multiple-deliverable contracts now are allowed to *estimate* selling prices when they lack VSOE from stand-alone sales prices. Using estimated selling prices allows earlier revenue recognition than would be allowed if sellers had to have VSOE in order to recognize revenue.

For some sellers this change had a huge effect. As an example, consider **Apple Inc.** and the highly successful iPhone. Prior to the change, Apple deferred revenue on iPhones and other products because it didn't have VSOE of the sales price of future software upgrades included with the phones. This practice resulted in over $12 billion of deferred (unearned) revenue as of the end of fiscal 2009. The excerpt from Apple's 2009 amended 10-K shown in Illustration 5–14 highlights that being able to use estimated selling prices to allocate revenue amongst multiple deliverables had a big effect on Apple's financial statements.

## Illustration 5–14

Disclosure of Revenue Recognition Policy for Multiple Deliverables— Apple, Inc.

**Real World Financials**

**Explanatory Note (in part)**
The new accounting principles generally require the Company to account for the sale of both iPhone and Apple TV as two deliverables. The first deliverable is the hardware and software delivered at the time of sale, and the second deliverable is the right included with the purchase of iPhone and Apple TV to receive on a when-and-if-available basis future unspecified software upgrades and features relating to the product's software. The new accounting principles result in the recognition of substantially all of the revenue and product costs from sales of iPhone and Apple TV at the time of sale. Additionally, the Company is required to estimate a standalone selling price for the unspecified software upgrade right included with the sale of iPhone and Apple TV and recognizes that amount ratably over the 24-month estimated life of the related hardware device. For all periods presented, the Company's estimated selling price for the software upgrade right included with each iPhone and Apple TV sold is $25 and $10, respectively. The adoption of the new accounting principles increased the Company's net sales by $6.4 billion, $5.0 billion and $572 million for 2009, 2008 and 2007, respectively. As of September 26, 2009, the revised total accumulated deferred revenue associated with iPhone and Apple TV sales to date was $483 million. . . .

After this accounting change, Apple recognizes almost all of the revenue associated with an iPhone at the time of sale. The only amount deferred is the small amount of revenue estimated for future software upgrade rights.

---

[27]FASB ASC 605–25–25: Revenue Recognition–Multiple-Element Arrangements–Recognition (originally *EITF 08-1: Revenue Arrangements with Multiple Deliverables* (Stamford, Conn.: FASB, 2009)), and *EITF 09-3: Applicability of AICPA Statement of Position 97-2 to Certain Arrangements That Include Software Elements* (Stamford, Conn.: FASB, 2009)).

# International Financial Reporting Standards

● LO5–8

> Multiple-Deliverable Arrangements. IFRS contains very little guidance about multiple-deliverable arrangements. *IAS No. 18* simply states that: ". . . in certain circumstances, it is necessary to apply the recognition criteria to the separately identifiable components of a single transaction in order to reflect the substance of the transaction" and gives a couple of examples.[28] Allocations of total revenue to individual components are based on fair value, with no requirements to focus on VSOE. Also, IFRS tends to encourage focus on the underlying economics of revenue transactions, so particular contractual characteristics like contingencies may matter less under IFRS than they do under U.S. GAAP.

## Franchise Sales

The use of franchise arrangements has become increasingly popular in the United States over the past 30 years. Many retail outlets for fast food, restaurants, motels, and auto rental agencies are operated as franchises. In the franchise arrangements, the **franchisor**, for example **McDonald's Corporation**, grants to the **franchisee**, quite often an individual, the right to sell the franchisor's products and use its name for a specified period of time. The restaurant where you ate your last Big Mac was probably owned and operated by an individual under a franchise agreement, not by McDonald's Corporation.

The fees to be paid by the franchisee to the franchisor usually comprise (1) the *initial franchise fee* and (2) *continuing franchise fees.* The services to be performed by the franchisor in exchange for the initial franchise fee, in addition to the right to use its name and sell its products, might include assistance in finding a location, constructing the facilities, and training employees. The initial franchise fee usually is a fixed amount, but it may be payable in installments.

> **FASB**
> Franchise fee revenue from an individual franchise sale ordinarily shall be recognized, with an appropriate provision for estimated uncollectible amounts, when all material services or conditions relating to the sale have been substantially performed or satisfied by the franchisor.[29]

The continuing franchise fees are paid to the franchisor for continuing rights as well as for advertising and promotion and other services provided over the life of the franchise agreement. These fees sometimes are a fixed annual or monthly amount, a percentage of the volume of business done by the franchise, or a combination of both.

The continuing franchise fees usually do not present any accounting difficulty and are recognized by the franchisor as revenue *over time* in the periods the services are performed by the franchisor, which generally corresponds to the periods they are received. The challenging revenue recognition issue pertains to the initial franchise fee. In the early 1960s and 1970s, many franchisors recognized the entire initial franchise fee as revenue in the period in which the contract was signed. In many cases, there were significant services to be performed and the fee was collectible in installments over an extended period of time creating uncertainty as to cash collection.

Specific guidelines for revenue recognition of the initial franchise fee are provided by GAAP. You should notice the similarity of these specific guidelines with those of the general revenue recognition guidelines we've discussed previously. A key to these conditions is the concept of *substantial performance.* It requires that substantially all of the initial services of the franchisor required by the franchise agreement be performed before the initial franchise fee can be recognized as revenue. The term *substantial* requires professional judgment on the part of the accountant. In situations when the initial franchise fee is collectible in installments, even after substantial performance has occurred, the installment sales or cost recovery methods should be used for profit recognition, if a reasonable estimate of uncollectibility cannot be made.

Consider the example in Illustration 5–15.

---

[28]"Revenue," *International Accounting Standard No. 18* (IASCF), as amended effective January 1, 2011, par. 13.
[29]FASB ASC 952–605–25: Franchisors–Revenue Recognition–Recognition (previously "Accounting for Franchise Fee Revenue," *Statement of Financial Accounting Standards No. 45* (Stamford, Conn.: FASB, 1981)).

On March 31, 2013, the Red Hot Chicken Wing Corporation entered into a franchise agreement with Thomas Keller. In exchange for an initial franchise fee of $50,000, Red Hot will provide initial services to include the selection of a location, construction of the building, training of employees, and consulting services over several years. $10,000 is payable on March 31, 2013, with the remaining $40,000 payable in annual installments which include interest at an appropriate rate. In addition, the franchisee will pay continuing franchise fees of $1,000 per month for advertising and promotion provided by Red Hot, beginning immediately after the franchise begins operations. Thomas Keller opened his Red Hot franchise for business on September 30, 2013.

**Illustration 5–15**

Franchise Sales

**INITIAL FRANCHISE FEE.** Assuming that the initial services to be performed by Red Hot subsequent to the contract signing are substantial but that collectibility of the installment receivable is reasonably certain, the following journal entry is recorded:

**March 31, 2013**

| | | |
|---|---|---|
| Cash ................................................................. | 10,000 | |
| Note receivable ................................................. | 40,000 | |
|     Unearned franchise fee revenue ............................. | | 50,000 |
| *To record franchise agreement and down payment.* | | |

Unearned franchise fee revenue is a liability. It would be reduced to zero and revenue would be recognized when the initial services have been performed. This could occur in increments or at one point in time, depending on the circumstances.[30] For example, in our illustration, if substantial performance was deemed to have occurred when the franchise began operations, the following entry would be recorded:

**Sept. 30, 2013**

| | | |
|---|---|---|
| Unearned franchise fee revenue ................................. | 50,000 | |
|     Franchise fee revenue ......................................... | | 50,000 |
| *To recognize franchise fee revenue.* | | |

If collectibility of the installment receivable is uncertain and there is no basis for estimating uncollectible amounts, the initial entry would record a credit to deferred franchise fee revenue, which is then recognized as being earned using either the installment sales or cost recovery methods.

**CONTINUING FRANCHISE FEES.** Continuing franchise fee revenue is recognized on a monthly basis as follows:

| | | |
|---|---|---|
| Cash (or accounts receivable) ....................................... | 1,000 | |
|     Service revenue ................................................. | | 1,000 |
| *To recognize continuing franchise fee revenue.* | | |

Expenses incurred by the franchisor in providing these continuing franchise services should be recognized in the same periods as the service revenue.

Other unique industry-specific revenue recognition situations exist besides those we have discussed. The FASB and AICPA have issued detailed revenue recognition guidance for such industries as insurance, record and music, cable television, and motion pictures.[31]

---

[30]Franchise agreements sometimes require that any payments made to the franchisor will be refunded if the franchise fails to open. If this condition is present, it would be an important factor in deciding whether to recognize revenue before the franchise opens.

[31]FASB ASC 944: Financial Services–Insurance (previously "Accounting and Reporting by Insurance Enterprises," *Statement of Financial Accounting Standards No. 60* (Stamford, Conn.: FASB, 1982)); FASB ASC 928—Entertainment–Music (previously "Financial Reporting in the Record and Music Industry," *Statement of Financial Accounting Standards No. 50* (Stamford, Conn.: FASB, 1981)); FASB ASC 922: Entertainment—Cable Television (previously "Financial Reporting by Cable Television Companies," *Statement of Financial Accounting Standards No. 51* (Stamford, Conn.: FASB, 1981)); FASB ASC 928: Entertainment–Films (previously "Accounting by Producers or Distributors of Films," *Statement of Position 00-2* (New York: AICPA, 2000)).

These industry standards are beyond the scope of this text. However, in each case, the objective is the same: to recognize revenue in the period or periods that the revenue-generating activities of the company are performed.

# Additional Consideration

In certain circumstances, revenue is recognized at the completion of the production process (before delivery). This approach generally is used by companies that deal in precious metals, and ". . . agricultural, mineral, and other products, units of which are interchangeable and have an immediate marketability at quoted prices. . . ."[32] This is called the *production basis* of recognizing revenue and is accomplished by writing inventory up from cost to market value.

Recall that in a typical manufacturing situation, revenue is not recognized at the completion of the production process due to significant uncertainty as to the collectibility of the asset to be received. We don't know if the product will be sold, nor the selling price, nor the buyer if eventually sold. These uncertainties are not significant when there is immediate marketability at quoted market prices for products like precious metals.

In cases when the production basis of recognizing revenue is used, full disclosure of the fact is required.

# Where We're Headed

**The FASB and IASB are working together on a comprehensive revenue-recognition standard.**

● LO5–8

The FASB and IASB are in the process of finalizing an Accounting Standards Update (ASU) that provides a new, comprehensive approach to revenue recognition. Why? Currently, the FASB has over 100 revenue-related standards that sometimes contradict each other and that treat similar economic events differently. The IASB has two primary standards (*IAS No. 11* and *IAS No. 18*) that also sometimes contradict each other and that don't offer guidance in some important areas (like multiple deliverables).[33] And, although both the FASB and IASB define revenue in terms of flows of assets and liabilities, the FASB guidance typically bases revenue recognition on the earnings process, while the IASB standards base it on the transfer of the risks and rewards of ownership, which can lead to different outcomes. So, the accounting guidance on revenue recognition could use some improvement.

The Boards' new approach is similar in many ways to the current U.S. guidance for recognizing revenue on multiple-deliverable contracts. The focus is on contracts between a seller and a buyer. A seller identifies all of its distinct performance obligations under a contract, determines the transaction price of the contract, and then allocates that price to the various performance obligations according to the estimated stand-alone selling prices of those obligations. The seller then recognizes revenue as each of those performance obligations is satisfied.

For many types of sales arrangements, adopting the proposed ASU will not change current practice. However, it will create consistency in revenue recognition across industries, and in some areas it will change practice considerably. For example, estimates of variable future payments will be included in revenue to a greater extent than exists currently, affecting revenue recognition on many contracts that peg future payments to future outcomes. Also, while companies still will estimate bad debts, an inability to estimate bad debts will not prevent revenue recognition, so the installment and cost-recovery methods will not exist.

The proposed ASU is being finalized at the time this text is being written. It is slated for issuance in late 2012, and adoption by companies will be required no sooner than 2015. We provide a detailed discussion of the proposed ASU in the chapter supplement.

---

[32]FASB ASC 330–10–35–16 : Inventory–Overall–Subsequent Measurement–Stating Inventories Above Cost (previously "Restatement and Revision of Accounting Research Bulletins," *Accounting Research Bulletin No. 43* (New York: AICPA, 1953), Chapter 4, par. 16).
[33]"Construction Contracts," *International Accounting Standard No. 11* (IASCF), as amended effective January 1, 2011, and "Revenue," *International Accounting Standard No. 18* (IASCF), as amended effective January 1, 2011.

# PROFITABILITY ANALYSIS

Chapter 3 provided an overview of financial statement analysis and introduced some of the common ratios used in risk analysis to investigate a company's liquidity and long-term solvency. We now introduce ratios related to profitability analysis.

● LO5–7

## Activity Ratios

One key to profitability is how well a company manages and utilizes its assets. Some ratios are designed to evaluate a company's effectiveness in managing assets. Of particular interest are the activity, or turnover ratios, of certain assets. The greater the number of times an asset turns over—the higher the ratio—the fewer assets are required to maintain a given level of activity (revenue). Given that a company incurs costs to finance its assets with debt (paying interest) or equity (paying dividends), high turnovers are usually attractive.

*Activity ratios* measure a company's efficiency in managing its assets.

Although, in concept, the activity or turnover can be measured for any asset, activity ratios are most frequently calculated for total assets, accounts receivable, and inventory. These ratios are calculated as follows:

$$\text{Asset turnover ratio} = \frac{\text{Net sales}}{\text{Average total assets}}$$

$$\text{Receivables turnover ratio} = \frac{\text{Net sales}}{\text{Average accounts receivable (net)}}$$

$$\text{Inventory turnover ratio} = \frac{\text{Cost of goods sold}}{\text{Average inventory}}$$

**ASSET TURNOVER.**   A broad measure of asset efficiency is the asset turnover ratio. The ratio is computed by dividing a company's net sales or revenues by the average total assets available for use during a period. The denominator, average assets, is determined by adding beginning and ending total assets and dividing by two. The asset turnover ratio provides an indication of how efficiently a company utilizes all of its assets to generate revenue.

The *asset turnover ratio* measures a company's efficiency in using assets to generate revenue.

**RECEIVABLES TURNOVER.**   The receivables turnover ratio is calculated by dividing a period's net credit sales by the average net accounts receivable. Because income statements seldom distinguish between cash sales and credit sales, this ratio usually is computed using total net sales as the numerator. The denominator, average accounts receivable, is determined by adding beginning and ending net accounts receivable (gross accounts receivable less allowance for uncollectible accounts) and dividing by two.[34]

The *receivables turnover ratio* offers an indication of how quickly a company is able to collect its accounts receivable.

The receivables turnover ratio provides an indication of a company's efficiency in collecting receivables. The ratio shows the number of times during a period that the average accounts receivable balance is collected. The higher the ratio, the shorter the average time between credit sales and cash collection.

A convenient extension is the average collection period. This measure is computed simply by dividing 365 days by the receivables turnover ratio. The result is an approximation of the number of days the average accounts receivable balance is outstanding.

$$\text{Average collection period} = \frac{365}{\text{Receivables turnover ratio}}$$

The *average collection period* indicates the average age of accounts receivable.

Monitoring the receivables turnover ratio (and average collection period) over time can provide useful information about a company's future prospects. For example, a decline in the receivables turnover ratio (an increase in the average collection period) could be an indication that sales are declining because of customer dissatisfaction with the company's products. Another possible explanation is that the company has changed its credit policy and is granting extended credit terms in order to maintain customers. Either explanation could

---

[34]Although *net* accounts receivable typically is used in practice for the denominator of receivables turnover, some prefer to use *gross* accounts receivable. Why? As the allowance for bad debts increases, net accounts receivable decreases, so if net accounts receivable is in the denominator, more bad debts have the effect of decreasing the denominator and therefore increasing receivables turnover. All else equal, an analyst would rather see receivables turnover improve because of more sales or less gross receivables, and not because of an increase in the allowance for bad debts.

signal a future increase in bad debts. Ratio analysis does not explain what is wrong. It does provide information that highlights areas for further investigation.

**INVENTORY TURNOVER.** An important activity measure for a merchandising company (a retail, wholesale, or manufacturing company) is the inventory turnover ratio. The ratio shows the number of times the average inventory balance is sold during a reporting period. It indicates how quickly inventory is sold. The more frequently a business is able to sell, or turn over, its inventory, the lower its investment in inventory must be for a given level of sales. The ratio is computed by dividing the period's cost of goods sold by the average inventory balance. The denominator, average inventory, is determined by adding beginning and ending inventory and dividing by two.[35]

A relatively high ratio, say compared to a competitor, usually is desirable. A high ratio indicates comparative strength, perhaps caused by a company's superior sales force or maybe a successful advertising campaign. However, it might also be caused by a relatively low inventory level, which could mean either very efficient inventory management or stockouts and lost sales in the future.

On the other hand, a relatively low ratio, or a decrease in the ratio over time, usually is perceived to be unfavorable. Too much capital may be tied up in inventory. A relatively low ratio may result from overstocking, the presence of obsolete items, or poor marketing and sales efforts.

Similar to the receivables turnover, we can divide the inventory turnover ratio into 365 days to compute the average days in inventory. This measure indicates the number of days it normally takes to sell inventory.

> The inventory turnover ratio measures a company's efficiency in managing its investment in inventory.

$$\text{Average days in inventory} = \frac{365}{\text{Inventory turnover ratio}}$$

## Profitability Ratios

A fundamental element of an analyst's task is to develop an understanding of a firm's profitability. Profitability ratios attempt to measure a company's ability to earn an adequate return relative to sales or resources devoted to operations. Resources devoted to operations can be defined as total assets or only those assets provided by owners, depending on the evaluation objective.

> Profitability ratios assist in evaluating various aspects of a company's profit-making activities.

Three common profitability measures are (1) the profit margin on sales, (2) the return on assets, and (3) the return on shareholders' equity. These ratios are calculated as follows:

$$\text{Profit margin on sales} = \frac{\text{Net income}}{\text{Net sales}}$$

$$\text{Return on assets} = \frac{\text{Net income}}{\text{Average total assets}}$$

$$\text{Return on shareholder's equity} = \frac{\text{Net income}}{\text{Average shareholders' equity}}$$

Notice that for all of the profitability ratios, our numerator is net income. Recall our discussion in Chapter 4 on earnings quality. The relevance of any historical-based financial statement hinges on its predictive value. To enhance predictive value, analysts often adjust net income in these ratios to separate a company's *transitory earnings* effects from its *permanent earnings*. Analysts begin their assessment of permanent earnings with income from continuing operations. Then, adjustments are made for any unusual, one-time gains or losses included in income from continuing operations. It is this adjusted number that they use as the numerator in these ratios.

> When calculating profitability ratios, analysts often adjust net income for any transitory income effects.

**PROFIT MARGIN ON SALES.** The profit margin on sales is simply net income divided by net sales. The ratio measures an important dimension of a company's profitability. It indicates the portion of each dollar of revenue that is available after all expenses have been covered. It offers a measure of the company's ability to withstand either higher expenses or lower revenues.

> The profit margin on sales measures the amount of net income achieved per sales dollar.

What is considered to be a desirable profit margin is highly sensitive to the nature of the business activity. For instance, you would expect a specialty shop to have a higher profit

---

[35]Notice the consistency in the measure used for the numerator and denominator of the two turnover ratios. For the receivables turnover ratio, both numerator and denominator are based on sales dollars, whereas they are both based on cost for the inventory turnover ratio.

margin than, say, Walmart. A low profit margin can be compensated for by a high asset turnover rate, and vice versa, which brings us to considering the trade-offs inherent in generating return on assets.

**RETURN ON ASSETS.**   The return on assets (ROA) ratio expresses income as a percentage of the average total assets available to generate that income. Because total assets are partially financed with debt and partially by equity funds, this is an inclusive way of measuring earning power that ignores specific sources of financing.

A company's return on assets is related to both profit margin and asset turnover. Specifically, profitability can be achieved by either a high profit margin, high turnover, or a combination of the two. In fact, the return on assets can be calculated by multiplying the profit margin and the asset turnover.

$$\textbf{Return on assets} \ = \textbf{Profit margin} \times \ \textbf{Asset turnover}$$

$$\frac{\text{Net income}}{\text{Average total assets}} = \frac{\text{Net income}}{\text{Net sales}} \times \frac{\text{Net sales}}{\text{Average total assets}}$$

> Profit margin and asset turnover combine to yield *return on assets,* which measures the return generated by a company's assets.

Industry standards are particularly important when evaluating asset turnover and profit margin. Some industries are characterized by low turnover but typically make up for it with higher profit margins. Others have low profit margins but compensate with high turnover. Grocery stores typically have relatively low profit margins but relatively high asset turnover. In comparison, a manufacturer of specialized equipment will have a higher profit margin but a lower asset turnover ratio.

**RETURN ON SHAREHOLDERS' EQUITY.**   Equity investors typically are concerned about the amount of profit that management can generate from the resources that owners provide. A closely watched measure that captures this concern is return on equity (ROE), calculated by dividing net income by average shareholders' equity.

> The *return on shareholders' equity* measures the return to suppliers of equity capital.

# Additional Consideration

The return on assets ratio often is computed as follows:

$$\text{Return on assets} = \frac{\text{Net income} + \text{Interest expense (1} - \text{Tax rate)}}{\text{Average total assets}}$$

The reason for adding back interest expense (net of tax) is that interest represents a return to suppliers of debt capital and should not be deducted in the computation of net income when computing the return on total assets. In other words, the numerator is the total amount of income available to both debt and equity capital.

In addition to monitoring return on equity, investors want to understand how that return can be improved. The DuPont framework provides a convenient basis for analysis that breaks return on equity into three key components:[36]

> The DuPont framework shows that return on equity depends on profitability, activity, and financial leverage.

- **Profitability,** measured by the profit margin (Net income ÷ Sales). As discussed already, a higher profit margin indicates that a company is generating more profit from each dollar of sales.

- **Activity,** measured by asset turnover (Sales ÷ Average total assets). As discussed already, higher asset turnover indicates that a company is using its assets efficiently to generate more sales from each dollar of assets.

- **Financial Leverage,** measured by the equity multiplier (Average total assets ÷ Average total equity). A high equity multiplier indicates that relatively more of the company's assets have been financed with debt. As indicated in Chapter 3, leverage can provide additional return to the company's equity holders.

---

[36]DuPont analysis is so named because the basic model was developed by F. Donaldson Brown, an electrical engineer who worked for DuPont in the early part of the 20th century.

In equation form, the DuPont framework looks like this:

**Return on equity = Profit margin × Asset turnover × Equity multiplier**

$$\frac{\text{Net income}}{\text{Avg. total equity}} = \frac{\text{Net income}}{\text{Total sales}} \times \frac{\text{Total sales}}{\text{Avg. total assets}} \times \frac{\text{Avg. total assets}}{\text{Avg. total equity}}$$

Notice that total sales and average total assets appear in the numerator of one ratio and the denominator of another, so they cancel to yield net income ÷ average total equity, or ROE.

We have already seen that ROA is determined by profit margin and asset turnover, so another way to compute ROE is by multiplying ROA by the equity multiplier:

**Return on equity = Return on assets × Equity multiplier**

$$\frac{\text{Net income}}{\text{Avg. total equity}} = \frac{\text{Net income}}{\text{Avg. total assets}} \times \frac{\text{Avg. total assets}}{\text{Avg. total equity}}$$

Because profit margin and asset turnover combine to create return on assets, the DuPont framework can also be viewed as indicating that return on equity depends on return on assets and financial leverage.

We can see from this equation that an equity multiplier of greater than 1 will produce a return on equity that is higher than the return on assets. However, as with all ratio analysis, there are trade-offs. If leverage is too high, creditors become concerned about the potential for default on the company's debt and require higher interest rates. Because interest is recognized as an expense, net income is reduced, so at some point the benefits of a higher equity multiplier are offset by a lower profit margin. Part of the challenge of managing a company is to identify the combination of profitability, activity, and leverage that produces the highest return for equity holders.

# Additional Consideration

Sometimes when return on equity is calculated, shareholders' equity is viewed more narrowly to include only common shareholders. In that case, preferred stock is excluded from the denominator, and preferred dividends are deducted from net income in the numerator. The resulting rate of return on common shareholders' equity focuses on profits generated on resources provided by common shareholders.

Illustration 5–16 provides a recap of the ratios we have discussed.

**Illustration 5–16**

Summary of Profitability Analysis Ratios

| **Activity ratios** | | |
|---|---|---|
| Asset turnover | = | $\dfrac{\text{Net sales}}{\text{Average total assets}}$ |
| Receivables turnover | = | $\dfrac{\text{Net sales}}{\text{Average accounts receivable (net)}}$ |
| Average collection period | = | $\dfrac{365}{\text{Receivables turnover ratio}}$ |
| Inventory turnover | = | $\dfrac{\text{Cost of goods sold}}{\text{Average inventory}}$ |
| Average days in inventory | = | $\dfrac{365}{\text{Inventory turnover ratio}}$ |
| **Profitability ratios** | | |
| Profit margin on sales | = | $\dfrac{\text{Net income}}{\text{Net sales}}$ |
| Return on assets | = | $\dfrac{\text{Net income}}{\text{Average total assets}}$ |
| Return on shareholders' equity | = | $\dfrac{\text{Net income}}{\text{Average shareholders' equity}}$ |
| **Leverage ratio** | | |
| Equity multiplier | = | $\dfrac{\text{Average total assets}}{\text{Average total equity}}$ |

# Profitability Analysis—An Illustration

To illustrate the application of the DuPont framework and the computation of the activity and profitability ratios, we analyze the 2011 financial statements of two well-known retailers, **Target Corporation** and **Wal-Mart Stores, Inc.**[37] The operations of these two companies are similar in terms of their focus on operating large general merchandising and food discount stores. Illustration 5–17A presents selected financial statement information for the two companies.

| | Target | | Walmart | |
|---|---|---|---|---|
| | **2011** | **2010** | **2011** | **2010** |
| Accounts receivable (net) | $ 6,153 | $ 6,966 | $ 5,089 | $ 4,144 |
| Inventories | $ 7,596 | $ 7,179 | $ 36,318 | $ 32,713 |
| Total assets | $43,705 | $44,533 | $180,663 | $170,407 |
| Total liabilities | $28,218 | $29,186 | $109,008 | $ 97,452 |
| Total shareholders' equity | $15,487 | $15,347 | $ 71,655 | $ 72,955 |
| Two-year averages: | | | | |
|   Accounts receivable (net) | | $ 6,560 | | $ 4,617 |
|   Inventories | | $ 7,388 | | $ 34,516 |
|   Total assets | | $44,119 | | $175,535 |
|   Total shareholders' equity | | $15,417 | | $ 72,305 |
| Income Statement—2011 | | | | |
|   Net sales | | $65,786 | | $421,849 |
|   Cost of goods sold | | $46,451 | | $315,287 |
|   Net Income (income from continuing operations for Walmart) | | $ 2,920 | | $ 16,389 |

**Illustration 5–17A**

Selected Financial Information for Target Corporation and Wal-Mart Stores, Inc.

**Real World Financials**

On the surface it appears that Walmart is far more profitable than Target. As shown in Illustration 5–17A, Walmart's 2011 net income was $16.389 billion, compared to Target's $2.920 billion. But that's not the whole story. Even though both are very large companies, Walmart is more than four times the size of Target in terms of total assets, so how can they be compared? Focusing on financial ratios helps adjust for size differences, and the DuPont framework helps identify the determinants of profitability from the perspective of shareholders.

Illustration 5–17B includes the DuPont analysis for Walmart and Target, as well as some additional activity ratios we've discussed. Walmart's return on assets (ROA) is higher than Target's (9.34% for Walmart compared to 6.62% for Target). Why? Remember that both profitability and activity combine to determine return on assets. Target's profit margin actually is a bit higher than Walmart's (4.44% compared to 3.89%), but Walmart's asset turnover is much higher than Target's (2.40 compared to 1.49). So, even though Target makes more profit on each sale, Walmart makes significantly more sales with its assets, and Walmart ends up coming out ahead on return on assets, both compared to Target and compared to the industry average.

The average days in inventory provides insight into Walmart's higher asset turnover. Inventory takes only 40 days on average before being sold by Walmart, compared with 47 for the industry average and 58 days for Target. Walmart also turns over its accounts receivable faster than Target does, but accounts receivable are small and don't matter much

---

[37]Walmart's financial statements are for the fiscal year ended January 31, 2011. Walmart refers to this as its 2011 fiscal year. Target's financial statements are for the fiscal year ended January 29, 2011. Target refers to this as its 2010 fiscal year, but for consistency with Walmart we refer to it as 2011.

**Illustration 5–17B**

DuPont Framework and Activity Ratios—Target Corporation and Wal-Mart Stores, Inc.

| | Target | | Walmart | | Industry Average* |
|---|---|---|---|---|---|
| **DuPont analysis:** | | | | | |
| Profit margin on sales | $\dfrac{\$2{,}920}{\$65{,}786}=$ | 4.44% | $\dfrac{\$16{,}389}{\$421{,}849}=$ | 3.89% | 3.43% |
| × | | × | | × | |
| Asset turnover | $\dfrac{\$65{,}786}{\$44{,}119}=$ | 1.49 | $\dfrac{\$421{,}849}{\$175{,}535}=$ | 2.40 | 2.19 |
| = | | = | | = | |
| Return on assets | $\dfrac{\$2{,}920}{\$44{,}119}=$ | 6.62% | $\dfrac{\$16{,}389}{\$175{,}535}=$ | 9.34% | 7.51% |
| × | | × | | × | |
| Equity Multiplier | $\dfrac{\$44{,}119}{\$15{,}417}=$ | 2.86 | $\dfrac{\$175{,}535}{\$72{,}305}=$ | 2.43 | 2.23 |
| = | | = | | = | |
| Return on shareholders' equity | $\dfrac{\$2{,}920}{\$15{,}417}=$ | 18.94% | $\dfrac{\$16{,}389}{\$72{,}305}=$ | 22.67% | 16.76% |
| **Other activity ratios:** | | | | | |
| Receivables turnover | $\dfrac{\$65{,}786}{\$6{,}560}=$ | 10.03 | $\dfrac{\$421{,}849}{\$4{,}617}=$ | 91.37 | 44.11 |
| Average collection period | $\dfrac{365}{10.03}=$ | 36.39 days | $\dfrac{365}{91.37}=$ | 3.99 days | 8.28 days |
| Inventory turnover | $\dfrac{\$46{,}451}{\$7{,}388}=$ | 6.29 | $\dfrac{\$315{,}287}{\$34{,}516}=$ | 9.13 | 7.73 |
| Average days in inventory | $\dfrac{365}{6.29}=$ | 58.03 days | $\dfrac{365}{9.13}=$ | 39.98 days | 47.24 days |

*Industry average based on sample of eleven discount retail companies.

for Walmart (Target offers a charge card and so maintains a higher receivable balance, on which it earns interest revenue).

What matters most to the shareholders of these companies is not return on assets, but the return on equity (ROE). Both beat the industry average, but Walmart also wins on this measure, with an ROE of 22.67% compared to Target's 18.94%. Target's equity multiplier is higher than Walmart's (2.86 for Target compared to 2.43 for Walmart), but that difference in leverage is not enough to make up for Walmart's much higher ROA.

A Target shareholder looking at these numbers might wonder how best to increase ROE. Should Target attempt to increase operational efficiency in hopes of approaching Walmart on the asset turnover dimension? Or, should Target attempt to increase profit margin? Given competitive pressures on retail pricing, can Target earn a much higher profit margin with its current product mix by including more upscale items in its inventory? Or, should Target attempt to increase leverage, such that debtholders are financing a greater percentage of assets?

The essential point of our discussion here, and in Part C of Chapter 3, is that raw accounting numbers alone mean little to decision makers. The numbers gain value when viewed in relation to other numbers. Similarly, the financial ratios formed by those relationships provide even greater perspective when compared with similar ratios of other companies, or relatedly, with averages for several companies in the same industry. Accounting information is useful in making decisions. Financial analysis that includes comparisons of financial ratios enhances the value of that information.

# Financial Reporting Case Solution

1. **Does your sister have to wait two and a half years to get her bonus? Explain.** *(p. 238)*   No. The *general* revenue recognition criteria would suggest that revenue and costs should be recognized when a project is finished. The difficulty this would create is that all revenues, expenses, and resulting profit from the project are recognized when the project is completed; no revenues or expenses would be reported in the income statements of earlier reporting periods in which much of the work may have been performed. The percentage-of-completion method of revenue recognition for long-term projects addresses this problem. A share of the project's profit is allocated to each period in which the earnings process occurs. This is two and a half years in this instance.

2. **How are gross profits recognized using the percentage-of-completion method?** *(p. 245)*   The percentage-of-completion method recognizes part of the estimated gross profit each period. The amount recognized is based on progress to date, which is estimated as the fraction of the project's cost incurred to date divided by total estimated costs. The estimated percentage of completion is multiplied by the revised project gross profit estimate. This yields the estimated gross profit earned from the beginning of the project. The gross profit recognized is calculated by subtracting from this amount the gross profit recognized in previous periods.

3. **Are there other situations in which revenue is recognized at times other than when a product is delivered?** *(p. 248)*   Yes, revenue recognition sometimes is delayed until after the product is delivered. These situations involve either the possibility of product returns or bad debts. In most cases, product returns and bad debt are estimated and revenues are recognized when a product is delivered. However, in situations involving an abnormal degree of uncertainty about cash collection caused by potential returns or bad debts, revenue recognition *after* delivery sometimes is appropriate. ●

# The Bottom Line

● **LO5–1**   The objective of revenue recognition is to recognize revenue in the period or periods that the revenue-generating activities of the company are performed. Also, judgment as to the collectibility of the cash from the sale of a product or service will impact the timing of revenue recognition. These two concepts of performance and collectibility are captured by the general guidelines for revenue recognition in the realization principle, which requires that revenue should be recognized only after (1) the earnings process is virtually complete and (2) there is reasonable certainty of collecting the asset to be received (usually cash) from the customer. For the sale of product, these criteria usually are satisfied at the point of product delivery. At that point, the majority of the productive activities have taken place and any remaining uncertainty concerning asset collection can be accounted for by estimating possible returns and bad debts. Also, service revenue often is recognized at a point in time if there is one final activity that is deemed critical to the earnings process. *(p. 232)*

● **LO5–2**   A *principal* has primary responsibility for delivering a product or service and recognizes as revenue the gross amount received from a customer. An *agent* doesn't primarily deliver goods or services, but acts as a facilitator that earns a commission for helping sellers transact with buyers and recognizes as revenue only the commission it receives for facilitating the sale. Various indicators can be used to determine which treatment is appropriate for a particular transaction. *(p. 237)*

● **LO5–3**   The installment sales method recognizes gross profit in collection periods by applying the gross profit percentage on the sale to the amount of cash actually received. The cost recovery method defers all gross profit recognition until cash has been received equal to the cost of the item sold. These methods of recognizing revenue should only be used in situations where there is an unusually high degree of uncertainty regarding the ultimate cash collection on an installment sale. *(p. 239)*

● **LO5–4**   In most situations, even though the right to return merchandise exists, revenues and expenses can be appropriately recognized at point of delivery. Based on past experience, a company usually can estimate the returns that will result for a given volume of sales. These estimates reduce both sales and cost of goods sold in anticipation of returns. Revenue cannot be recognized at the point of delivery unless the seller is able to make reliable estimates of future returns. Otherwise, revenue recognition is deferred beyond the delivery point. (*p. 243*)

● **LO5–5** Revenue recognition at a single point in time when the earnings process is virtually complete is inappropriate for certain types of service revenue activities and also, usually, for long-term contracts. The completed contract method recognizes revenues and expenses on long-term construction and other long-term contracts at a point in time when the project is complete. This method is only used in unusual situations. The preferable method for recognizing revenues and expenses for long-term contracts is the percentage-of-completion method, which recognizes revenues over time by assigning a share of the project's revenues and costs to each reporting period during the project. (*p. 244*)

● **LO5–6** Industry guidelines require that the lump-sum contract price for software be allocated to the various elements of the package based on the relative fair values of the individual elements. Generally, this results in a deferral of a portion of the proceeds that are then recognized as revenue in future periods. Other multiple-deliverable arrangements are accounted for in a similar manner. The use of franchise arrangements has become increasingly popular. The fees to be paid by the franchisee to the franchisor usually are composed of (1) the initial franchise fee and (2) continuing franchise fees. GAAP requires that the franchisor has substantially performed the services promised in the franchise agreement and that the collectibility of the initial franchise fee is reasonably assured before the initial fee can be recognized as revenue. The continuing franchise fees are recognized by the franchisor as revenue over time in the periods the services are performed by the franchisor. (*pp. 258 and 260*)

● **LO5–7** Activity and profitability ratios provide information about a company's profitability. Activity ratios include the receivables turnover ratio, the inventory turnover ratio, and the asset turnover ratio. Profitability ratios include the profit margin on sales, the return on assets, and the return on shareholders' equity. DuPont analysis explains return on stockholders' equity as determined by profit margin, asset turnover, and the extent to which assets are financed with equity versus debt. (*p. 263*)

● **LO5–8** For the most part, revenue recognition requirements are similar under U.S. GAAP and IFRS. U.S. GAAP is much more detailed, though, especially with respect to industry-specific guidance and multi-deliverable arrangements. In addition, when the percentage-of-completion method is not used to account for a long-term contract, U.S. GAAP requires the use of the completed contract method (in which revenue, cost, and gross profit are all typically recognized at the end of the contract), while IFRS requires the cost recovery method (in which revenue and cost are recognized over the life of the contract, but gross profit is recognized only after all costs have been recovered, which is typically at the end of the contract). As indicated in Appendix 5, IFRS views interim reports on a stand-alone basis rather than as an integral part of the annual report, as done in U.S. GAAP. As a result, interim period income under IFRS may be more volatile than under U.S. GAAP (*pp. 235, 255, 260, 262 and 272*) ●

# APPENDIX 5 | Interim Reporting

*Interim reports* **are issued for periods of less than a year, typically as quarterly financial statements.**

Financial statements covering periods of less than a year are called *interim reports.* Companies registered with the SEC, which includes most public companies, must submit quarterly reports, and you will see excerpts from these reports throughout this book.[38] Though there is no requirement to do so, most also send quarterly reports to their shareholders and typically include abbreviated, unaudited interim reports as supplemental information within their annual reports. For instance, Illustration 5A-1 shows the quarterly information disclosed in the 2011 annual report of **Dell Inc.**

For accounting information to be useful to decision makers, it must be available on a timely basis. One of the objectives of interim reporting is to enhance the timeliness of financial information. In addition, quarterly reports provide investors and creditors with additional insight on the seasonality of business operations that might otherwise get lost in annual reports.

**The fundamental debate regarding interim reporting centers on the choice between the** *discrete* **and** *integral part* **approaches.**

However, the downside to these benefits is the relative unreliability of interim reporting. With a shorter reporting period, questions associated with estimation and allocation are magnified. For example, certain expenses often benefit an entire year's operations and yet

---

[38]Quarterly reports are filed with the SEC on form 10-Q. Annual reports to the SEC are on form 10-K.

**Illustration 5A-1**  Interim Data in Annual Report—Dell Inc.

| | Fiscal Year 2011 | | | |
| --- | --- | --- | --- | --- |
| | First Quarter | Second Quarter | Third Quarter | Fourth Quarter |
| | (in millions, except per share data) | | | |
| Net revenue | $14,874 | $15,534 | $15,394 | $15,692 |
| Gross margin | 2,516 | 2,586 | 3,003 | 3,291 |
| Net income | 341 | 545 | 822 | 927 |
| Earnings per common share: | | | | |
| Basic | 0.17 | 0.28 | 0.42 | 0.48 |
| Diluted | 0.17 | 0.28 | 0.42 | 0.48 |
| Weighted-average shares outstanding: | | | | |
| Basic | 1,961 | 1,952 | 1,939 | 1,924 |
| Diluted | 1,973 | 1,960 | 1,949 | 1,938 |
| Stock sales price per share: | | | | |
| High | 17.52 | 16.46 | 14.89 | 14.70 |
| Low | 12.92 | 11.72 | 11.34 | 13.06 |

Real World Financials

are incurred primarily within a single interim period. Similarly, should smaller companies use lower tax rates in the earlier quarters and higher rates in later quarters as higher tax brackets are reached? Another result of shorter reporting periods is the intensified effect of major events such as discontinued operations or extraordinary items. A second quarter casualty loss, for instance, that would reduce annual profits by 10% might reduce second quarter profits by 40% or more. Is it more realistic to allocate such a loss over the entire year? These and similar questions tend to hinge on the way we view an interim period in relation to the fiscal year. More specifically, should each interim period be viewed as a *discrete* reporting period or as an *integral part* of the annual period?

## Reporting Revenues and Expenses

Existing practice and current reporting requirements for interim reporting generally follow the viewpoint that interim reports are an integral part of annual statements, although the discrete approach is applied to some items. Most revenues and expenses are recognized using the same accounting principles applicable to annual reporting. Some modifications are necessary to help cause interim statements to relate better to annual statements. This is most evident in the way costs and expenses are recognized. Most are recognized in interim periods as incurred. But when an expenditure clearly benefits more than just the period in which it is incurred, the expense should be allocated among the periods benefited on an allocation basis consistent with the company's annual allocation procedures. For example, annual repair expenses, property tax expense, and advertising expenses incurred in the first quarter that clearly benefit later quarters are assigned to each quarter through the use of accruals and deferrals. Costs and expenses subject to year-end adjustments, such as depreciation expense, are estimated and allocated to interim periods in a systematic way. Similarly, income tax expense at each interim date should be based on estimates of the effective tax rate for the whole year. This would mean, for example, that if the estimated effective rate has changed since the previous interim period(s), the tax expense period would be determined as the new rate times the cumulative pretax income to date, less the total tax expense reported in previous interim periods.

With only a few exceptions, the same accounting principles applicable to annual reporting are used for interim reporting.

## Reporting Unusual Items

On the other hand, major events such as discontinued operations or extraordinary items should be reported separately in the interim period in which they occur. That is, these amounts should not be allocated among individual quarters within the fiscal year. The same is true for items that are unusual or infrequent but not both. Treatment of these items is more consistent with the discrete view than the integral part view.

Discontinued operations, extraordinary items, and unusual items are reported entirely within the interim period in which they occur.

# International Financial Reporting Standards

● LO5–8

**Interim Reporting.** *IAS No. 34* requires that a company apply the same accounting policies in its interim financial statements as it applies in its annual financial statements. Therefore, IFRS takes much more of a discrete-period approach than does U.S. GAAP. For example, costs for repairs, property taxes, and advertising that do not meet the definition of an asset at the end of an interim period are expensed entirely in the period in which they occur under IFRS, but are accrued or deferred and then charged to each of the periods they benefit under U.S. GAAP. This difference would tend to make interim period income more volatile under IFRS than under U.S. GAAP. However, as in U.S. GAAP, income taxes are accounted for based on an estimate of the tax rate expected to apply for the entire year.[39]

## Earnings Per Share

**Quarterly EPS calculations follow the same procedures as annual calculations.**

A second item that is treated in a manner consistent with the discrete view is earnings per share. EPS calculations for interim reports follow the same procedures as annual calculations that you will study in Chapter 19. The calculations are based on conditions actually existing during the particular interim period rather than on conditions estimated to exist at the end of the fiscal year.

## Reporting Accounting Changes

**Accounting changes made in an interim period are reported by retrospectively applying the changes to prior financial statements.**

Recall from Chapter 4 that we account for a change in accounting principle retrospectively, meaning we recast prior years' financial statements when we report those statements again in comparative form. In other words, we make those statements appear as if the newly adopted accounting method had been used in those prior years. It's the same with interim reporting. We retrospectively report a change made during an interim period in similar fashion. Then in financial reports of subsequent interim periods of the same fiscal year, we disclose how that change affected (a) income from continuing operations, (b) net income, and (c) related per share amounts for the postchange interim period.

## Minimum Disclosures

Complete financial statements are not required for interim period reporting, but certain minimum disclosures are required as follows:[40]

- Sales, income taxes, extraordinary items, and net income.
- Earnings per share.
- Seasonal revenues, costs, and expenses.
- Significant changes in estimates for income taxes.
- Discontinued operations, extraordinary items, and unusual or infrequent items.
- Contingencies.
- Changes in accounting principles or estimates.
- Information about fair value of financial instruments and the methods and assumptions used to estimate fair values.
- Significant changes in financial position.

When fourth quarter results are not separately reported, material fourth quarter events, including year-end adjustments, should be reported in disclosure notes to annual statements. ●

---

[39]"Interim Financial Reporting," *International Accounting Standard No. 34* (IASCF), as amended effective January 1, 2011, par. 28–30.
[40]FASB ASC 270–10–50: Interim Reporting–Overall–Disclosure (previously "Interim Financial Reporting," *Accounting Principles Board Opinion No 28* (New York: AICPA, 1973)).

# Questions For Review of Key Topics

**Q 5–1**   What are the two general criteria that must be satisfied before a company can recognize revenue?

**Q 5–2**   Explain why, in most cases, a seller recognizes revenue when it delivers its product rather than when it produces the product.

**Q 5–3**   What is the difference between a principal and an agent for purposes of determining whether a company should report revenue on a gross or net basis?

**Q 5–4**   Revenue recognition for most installment sales occurs at the point of delivery of the product or service. Under what circumstances would a seller delay revenue recognition for installment sales beyond the delivery date?

**Q 5–5**   Distinguish between the installment sales method and the cost recovery method of accounting for installment sales.

**Q 5–6**   How does a company report deferred gross profit resulting from the use of the installment sales method in its balance sheet?

**Q 5–7**   Revenue recognition for most product sales that allow the right of return occurs at the point of product delivery. Under what circumstances would revenue recognition be delayed?

**Q 5–8**   Describe a consignment sale. When does a consignor recognize revenue for a consignment sale?

**Q 5–9**   Service revenue is recognized either at one point in time or over extended periods. Explain the rationale for recognizing revenue using these two approaches.

**Q 5–10**   Distinguish between the percentage-of-completion and completed contract methods of accounting for long-term contracts with respect to income recognition. Under what circumstances should a company use the completed contract method?

**IFRS**   **Q 5–11**   When percentage-of-completion accounting is not appropriate, U.S. GAAP requires the use of the completed contract method, while IFRS requires the use of the cost recovery method. Explain how the two methods affect recognition of revenue, cost of construction, and gross profit over the life of a profitable contract.

**Q 5–12**   Periodic billings to the customer for a long-term construction contract are recorded as billings on construction contract. How is this account reported in the balance sheet?

**Q 5–13**   When is an estimated loss on a long-term contract recognized using the percentage-of-completion method? The completed contract method?

**Q 5–14**   Briefly describe the guidelines for recognizing revenue from the sale of software and other multiple-deliverable arrangements.

**IFRS**   **Q 5–15**   Briefly describe how IFRS guidelines for recognizing revenue from multiple-deliverable arrangements differ from U.S. GAAP guidelines.

**Q 5–16**   Briefly describe the guidelines provided by GAAP for the recognition of revenue by a franchisor for an initial franchise fee.

**Q 5–17**   Show the calculation of the following activity ratios: (1) the receivables turnover ratio, (2) the inventory turnover ratio, and (3) the asset turnover ratio. What information about a company do these ratios offer?

**Q 5–18**   Show the calculation of the following profitability ratios: (1) the profit margin on sales, (2) the return on assets, and (3) the return on shareholders' equity. What information about a company do these ratios offer?

**Q 5–19**   Show the DuPont framework's calculation of the three components of return on shareholders' equity. What information about a company do these ratios offer?

**Q 5–20**   [Based on Appendix 5] Interim reports are issued for periods of less than a year, typically as quarterly financial statements. Should these interim periods be viewed as separate periods or integral parts of the annual period?

**IFRS**   **Q 5–21**   [Based on Appendix 5] What is the primary difference between interim reports under IFRS and U.S. GAAP?

# Brief Exercises

**BE 5–1**
Point of delivery
recognition
● LO5–1

On July 1, 2013, Apache Company sold a parcel of undeveloped land to a construction company for $3,000,000. The book value of the land on Apache's books was $1,200,000. Terms of the sale required a down payment of $150,000 and 19 annual payments of $150,000 plus interest at an appropriate interest rate due on each July 1 beginning in 2014. Apache has no significant obligations to perform services after the sale. How much gross profit will Apache recognize in both 2013 and 2014 assuming point of delivery profit recognition?

**BE 5–2**
Principal or agent
● LO5–2

Assume that **Amazon.com** sells the MacBook Pro, a computer brand produced by Apple. Amazon arranges its operations such that customers receive products from Apple Stores rather than Amazon. Customers purchase from Amazon using credit cards, and Amazon forwards cash to Apple less a fixed commission that Amazon keeps above the normal wholesale MacBook Pro price. In this arrangement, is Amazon a principal or an agent? Why? Given that answer, would Amazon recognize revenue for the entire sales price of the MacBook Pro or only the amount of the commission received in exchange for arranging sales for Apple Stores?

**BE 5–3**
Installment sales method
● LO5–3

Refer to the situation described in BE 5–1. How much gross profit will Apache recognize in both 2013 and 2014 applying the installment sales method?

**BE 5–4**
Cost recovery method
● LO5–3

Refer to the situation described in BE 5–1. How much gross profit will Apache recognize in both 2013 and 2014 applying the cost recovery method?

**BE 5–5**
Installment sales method
● LO5–3

Refer to the situation described in BE 5–1. What should be the balance in the deferred gross profit account at the end of 2014 applying the installment sales method?

**BE 5–6**
Right of return
● LO5–4

Meyer Furniture sells office furniture mainly to corporate clients. Customers who return merchandise within 90 days for any reason receive a full refund. Discuss the issues Meyer must consider in determining its revenue recognition policy.

**BE 5–7**
Percentage-of-completion method; profit recognition
● LO5–5

A construction company entered into a fixed-price contract to build an office building for $20 million. Construction costs incurred during the first year were $6 million and estimated costs to complete at the end of the year were $9 million. How much gross profit will the company recognize in the first year using the percentage-of-completion method? How much revenue will appear in the company's income statement?

**BE 5–8**
Percentage-of-completion method; balance sheet
● LO5–5

Refer to the situation described in BE 5–7. During the first year the company billed its customer $7 million, of which $5 million was collected before year-end. What would appear in the year-end balance sheet related to this contract?

**BE 5–9**
Completed contract method
● LO5–5

Refer to the situation described in BE 5–7. The building was completed during the second year. Construction costs incurred during the second year were $10 million. How much gross profit will the company recognize in the first year and in the second year applying the completed contract method?

**BE 5–10**
IFRS; cost recovery method
● LO5–5, LO5–8

IFRS

Refer to the situation described in BE 5–9. How much revenue, cost, and gross profit will the company recognize in the first and second year of the contract applying the cost recovery method that is required by IFRS?

**BE 5–11**
Percentage-of-completion and completed contract methods; loss on entire project
● LO5–5

Franklin Construction entered into a fixed-price contract to build a freeway-connecting ramp for $30 million. Construction costs incurred in the first year were $16 million and estimated remaining costs to complete at the end of the year were $17 million. How much gross profit or loss will Franklin recognize the first year applying the percentage-of-completion method? Applying the completed contract method?

**BE 5–12**
Revenue
recognition;
software contracts
● LO5–6

Orange, Inc., sells a LearnIt-Plus software package that consists of their normal LearnIt math tutorial program along with a one-year subscription to the online LearnIt Office Hours virtual classroom. LearnIt-Plus retails for $200. When sold separately, the LearnIt math tutorial sells for $150, and access to the LearnIt Office Hours sells for $100 per year. When should Orange recognize revenue for the parts of this arrangement? Would your answer change if Orange did not sell the LearnIt Office Hours separately, but believed it would price it at $100 per year if they ever decided to do so?

**BE 5–13**
Revenue
recognition;
software contracts
under IFRS
● LO5–6, LO5–8

 **IFRS**

Refer to the situation described in BE 5–12. How would your answer change if Orange reported under IFRS?

**BE 5–14**
Revenue
recognition;
franchise sales
● LO5–6

Collins, Inc., entered into a 10-year franchise agreement with an individual. For an initial franchise fee of $40,000, Collins agrees to assist in design and construction of the franchise location and in all other necessary start-up activities. Also, in exchange for advertising and promotional services, the franchisee agrees to pay continuing franchise fees equal to 5% of revenue generated by the franchise. When should Collins recognize revenue for the initial and continuing franchise fees?

**BE 5–15**
Receivables
and inventory
turnover ratios
● LO5–7

Universal Calendar Company began the year with accounts receivable and inventory balances of $100,000 and $80,000, respectively. Year-end balances for these accounts were $120,000 and $60,000, respectively. Sales for the year of $600,000 generated a gross profit of $200,000. Calculate the receivables and inventory turnover ratios for the year.

**BE 5–16**
Profitability ratios
● LO5–7

The 2013 income statement for Anderson TV and Appliance reported sales revenue of $420,000 and net income of $65,000. Average total assets for 2013 was $800,000. Shareholders' equity at the beginning of the year was $500,000 and $20,000 was paid to shareholders as dividends. There were no other shareholders' equity transactions that occurred during the year. Calculate the profit margin on sales, return on assets, and return on shareholders' equity for 2013.

**BE 5–17**
Profitability ratios
● LO5–7

Refer to the facts described in BE 5–16. Show the DuPont framework's calculation of the three components of the 2013 return on shareholders' equity for Anderson TV and Appliance.

**BE 5–18**
Inventory
turnover ratio
● LO5–7

During 2013, Rogue Corporation reported sales revenue of $600,000. Inventory at both the beginning and end of the year totaled $75,000. The inventory turnover ratio for the year was 6.0. What amount of gross profit did the company report in its income statement for 2013?

# Exercises

**An alternate exercise and problem set is available on the text website:** www.mhhe.com/spiceland7e

**E 5–1**
Service revenue
● LO5–1

Alpine West, Inc., operates a downhill ski area near Lake Tahoe, California. An all-day, adult ticket can be purchased for $55. Adult customers also can purchase a season pass that entitles the pass holder to ski any day during the season, which typically runs from December 1 through April 30. The season pass is nontransferable, and the $450 price is nonrefundable. Alpine expects its season pass holders to use their passes equally throughout the season. The company's fiscal year ends on December 31.

On November 6, 2013, Jake Lawson purchased a season ticket.

**Required:**
1. When should Alpine West recognize revenue from the sale of its season passes?
2. Prepare the appropriate journal entries that Alpine would record on November 6 and December 31.
3. What will be included in the 2013 income statement and 2013 balance sheet related to the sale of the season pass to Jake Lawson?

**E 5–2**
**Principal or agent**
● **LO5–2**

AuctionCo.com sells used products collected from different suppliers. Assume a customer ordered a used bicycle through AuctionCo.com for $30. The cost of this bicycle is $20 to AuctionCo.com. The bicycle will be shipped to the customer by the original bicycle owner.

**Required:**

1. Assume AuctionCo.com takes control of this used bicycle before sale. Under this assumption, how much revenue would the company recognize?
2. Assume AuctionCo.com never takes control of this used bicycle before sale. Under this assumption, how much revenue would the company recognize?
3. Which assumption do you think is more appropriate for the AuctionCo.com case? Explain.

**E 5–3**
**Installment sales method**
● **LO5–3**

Charter Corporation, which began business in 2013, appropriately uses the installment sales method of accounting for its installment sales. The following data were obtained for sales made during 2013 and 2014:

|  | 2013 | 2014 |
|---|---|---|
| Installment sales | $360,000 | $350,000 |
| Cost of installment sales | 234,000 | 245,000 |
| Cash collections on installment sales during: |  |  |
| 2013 | 150,000 | 100,000 |
| 2014 | — | 120,000 |

**Required:**

1. How much gross profit should Charter recognize in 2013 and 2014 from installment sales?
2. What should be the balance in the deferred gross profit account at the end of 2013 and 2014?

**E 5–4**
**Installment sales method; journal entries**
● **LO5–3**

[This is a variation of Exercise 5–3 focusing on journal entries.]

Charter Corporation, which began business in 2013, appropriately uses the installment sales method of accounting for its installment sales. The following data were obtained for sales during 2013 and 2014:

|  | 2013 | 2014 |
|---|---|---|
| Installment sales | $360,000 | $350,000 |
| Cost of installment sales | 234,000 | 245,000 |
| Cash collections on installment sales during: |  |  |
| 2013 | 150,000 | 100,000 |
| 2014 | — | 120,000 |

**Required:**

Prepare summary journal entries for 2013 and 2014 to account for the installment sales and cash collections. The company uses the perpetual inventory system.

**E 5–5**
**Installment sales; alternative recognition methods**
● **LO5–3**

On July 1, 2013, the Foster Company sold inventory to the Slate Corporation for $300,000. Terms of the sale called for a down payment of $75,000 and three annual installments of $75,000 due on each July 1, beginning July 1, 2014. Each installment also will include interest on the unpaid balance applying an appropriate interest rate. The inventory cost Foster $120,000. The company uses the perpetual inventory system.

**Required:**

1. Compute the amount of gross profit to be recognized from the installment sale in 2013, 2014, 2015, and 2016 using point of delivery revenue recognition. Ignore interest charges.
2. Repeat requirement 1 applying the installment sales method.
3. Repeat requirement 1 applying the cost recovery method.

**E 5–6**
**Journal entries; point of delivery, installment sales, and cost recovery methods**
● **LO5–1, LO5–3**

[This is a variation of Exercise 5–5 focusing on journal entries.]

On July 1, 2013, the Foster Company sold inventory to the Slate Corporation for $300,000. Terms of the sale called for a down payment of $75,000 and three annual installments of $75,000 due on each July 1, beginning July 1, 2014. Each installment also will include interest on the unpaid balance applying an appropriate interest rate. The inventory cost Foster $120,000. The company uses the perpetual inventory system.

**Required:**

1. Prepare the necessary journal entries for 2013 and 2014 using point of delivery revenue recognition. Ignore interest charges.
2. Repeat requirement 1 applying the installment sales method.
3. Repeat requirement 1 applying the cost recovery method.

**E 5–7**
Installment sales and cost recovery methods; solve for unknowns
● LO5–3

Wolf Computer Company began operations in 2013. The company allows customers to pay in installments for many of its products. Installment sales for 2013 were $1,000,000. If revenue is recognized at the point of delivery, $600,000 in gross profit would be recognized in 2013. If the company instead uses the cost recovery method, $100,000 in gross profit would be recognized in 2013.

**Required:**
1. What was the amount of cash collected on installment sales in 2013?
2. What amount of gross profit would be recognized if the company uses the installment sales method?

**E 5–8**
Installment sales; default and repossession
● LO5–3

Sanchez Development Company uses the installment sales method to account for some of its installment sales. On October 1, 2013, Sanchez sold a parcel of land to the Kreuze Corporation for $4 million. This amount was not considered significant relative to Sanchez's other sales during 2013. The land had cost Sanchez $1.8 million to acquire and develop. Terms of the sale required a down payment of $800,000 and four annual payments of $800,000 plus interest at an appropriate interest rate, with payments due on each October 1 beginning in 2014. Kreuze paid the down payment, but on October 1, 2014, defaulted on the remainder of the contract. Sanchez repossessed the land. On the date of repossession the land had a fair value of $1.3 million.

**Required:**
Prepare the necessary entries for Sanchez to record the sale, receipt of the down payment, and the default and repossession applying the installment sales method. Ignore interest charges.

**E 5–9**
Real estate sales; gain recognition
● LO5–1, LO5–3

On April 1, 2013, the Apex Corporation sold a parcel of underdeveloped land to the Applegate Construction Company for $2,400,000. The book value of the land on Apex's books was $480,000. Terms of the sale required a down payment of $120,000 and 19 annual payments of $120,000 plus interest at an appropriate interest rate due on each April 1 beginning in 2014. Apex has no significant obligations to perform services after the sale.

**Required:**
1. Prepare the necessary entries for Apex to record the sale, receipt of the down payment, and receipt of the first installment assuming that Apex is able to make a reliable estimate of possible uncollectible amounts (that is, point of delivery profit recognition is used). Ignore interest charges.
2. Repeat requirement 1 assuming that Apex cannot make a reliable estimate of possible uncollectible amounts and decides to use the installment sales method for profit recognition.

**E 5–10**
FASB codification research
● LO5–3, LO5–4, LO5–5

Access the *FASB's Codification Research System* at the FASB website (**www.fasb.org**).

**Required:**
Determine the specific citation for accounting for each of the following items:
1. When a provision for loss is recognized for a percentage-of-completion contract.
2. Circumstances indicating when the installment method or cost recovery method is appropriate for revenue recognition.
3. Criteria determining when a seller can recognize revenue at the time of sale from a sales transaction in which the buyer has the right to return the product.

**E 5–11**
Long-term contract; percentage-of-completion and completed contract methods
● LO5–5

Assume **Nortel Networks** contracted to provide a customer with Internet infrastructure for $2,000,000. The project began in 2013 and was completed in 2014. Data relating to the contract are summarized below:

|  | 2013 | 2014 |
|---|---|---|
| Costs incurred during the year | $ 300,000 | $1,575,000 |
| Estimated costs to complete as of 12/31 | 1,200,000 | –0– |
| Billings during the year | 380,000 | 1,620,000 |
| Cash collections during the year | 250,000 | 1,750,000 |

**Required:**
1. Compute the amount of gross profit or loss to be recognized in 2013 and 2014 using the percentage-of-completion method.
2. Compute the amount of gross profit or loss to be recognized in 2013 and 2014 using the completed contract method.
3. Prepare a partial balance sheet to show how the information related to this contract would be presented at the end of 2013 using the percentage-of-completion method.
4. Prepare a partial balance sheet to show how the information related to this contract would be presented at the end of 2013 using the completed contract method.

**E 5–12**
**Long-term contract; percentage of completion, completed contract and cost recovery methods**
● LO5–5, LO5–8

On June 15, 2013, Sanderson Construction entered into a long-term construction contract to build a baseball stadium in Washington D.C. for $220 million. The expected completion date is April 1 of 2015, just in time for the 2015 baseball season. Costs incurred and estimated costs to complete at year-end for the life of the contract are as follows ($ in millions):

|  | 2013 | 2014 | 2015 |
|---|---|---|---|
| Costs incurred during the year | $ 40 | $80 | $50 |
| Estimated costs to complete as of 12/31 | 120 | 60 | — |

**Required:**

1. Determine the amount of gross profit or loss to be recognized in each of the three years using the percentage-of-completion method.
2. How much revenue will Sanderson report in its 2013 and 2014 income statements related to this contract using the percentage-of-completion method?
3. Determine the amount of gross profit or loss to be recognized in each of the three years using the completed contract method.

● IFRS

4. Determine the amount of revenue, cost, and gross profit or loss to be recognized in each of the three years under IFRS, assuming that using the percentage-of-completion method is not appropriate.
5. Suppose the estimated costs to complete at the end of 2014 are $80 million instead of $60 million. Determine the amount of gross profit or loss to be recognized in 2014 using the percentage-of-completion method.

**E 5–13**
**Percentage-of-completion method; loss projected on entire project**
● LO5–5

On February 1, 2013, Arrow Construction Company entered into a three-year construction contract to build a bridge for a price of $8,000,000. During 2013, costs of $2,000,000 were incurred with estimated costs of $4,000,000 yet to be incurred. Billings of $2,500,000 were sent and cash collected was $2,250,000.

In 2014, costs incurred were $2,500,000 with remaining costs estimated to be $3,600,000. 2014 billings were $2,750,000 and $2,475,000 cash was collected. The project was completed in 2015 after additional costs of $3,800,000 were incurred. The company's fiscal year-end is December 31. Arrow uses the *percentage-of-completion* method.

**Required:**

1. Calculate the amount of gross profit or loss to be recognized in each of the three years.
2. Prepare journal entries for 2013 and 2014 to record the transactions described (credit various accounts for construction costs incurred).
3. Prepare a partial balance sheet to show the presentation of the project as of December 31, 2013 and 2014.

**E 5–14**
**Completed contract method; loss projected on entire project**
● LO5–5

[This is a variation of Exercise 5–13 focusing on the completed contract method.]

On February 1, 2013, Arrow Construction Company entered into a three-year construction contract to build a bridge for a price of $8,000,000. During 2013, costs of $2,000,000 were incurred with estimated costs of $4,000,000 yet to be incurred. Billings of $2,500,000 were sent and cash collected was $2,250,000.

In 2014, costs incurred were $2,500,000 with remaining costs estimated to be $3,600,000. 2014 billings were $2,750,000 and $2,475,000 cash was collected. The project was completed in 2015 after additional costs of $3,800,000 were incurred. The company's fiscal year-end is December 31. Arrow uses the *completed contract* method.

**Required:**

1. Calculate the amount of gross profit or loss to be recognized in each of the three years.
2. Prepare journal entries for 2013 and 2014 to record the transactions described (credit various accounts for construction costs incurred).
3. Prepare a partial balance sheet to show the presentation of the project as of December 31, 2013 and 2014.

**E 5–15**
**Income (loss) recognition; percentage-of-completion and completed contract methods compared**
● LO5–5

Brady Construction Company contracted to build an apartment complex for a price of $5,000,000. Construction began in 2013 and was completed in 2015. The following are a series of independent situations, numbered 1 through 6, involving differing costs for the project. All costs are stated in thousands of dollars.

| | Costs Incurred During Year | | | Estimated Costs to Complete (As of the End of the Year) | | |
|---|---|---|---|---|---|---|
| Situation | 2013 | 2014 | 2015 | 2013 | 2014 | 2015 |
| 1 | 1,500 | 2,100 | 900 | 3,000 | 900 | — |
| 2 | 1,500 | 900 | 2,400 | 3,000 | 2,400 | — |
| 3 | 1,500 | 2,100 | 1,600 | 3,000 | 1,500 | — |
| 4 | 500 | 3,000 | 1,000 | 3,500 | 875 | — |
| 5 | 500 | 3,000 | 1,300 | 3,500 | 1,500 | — |
| 6 | 500 | 3,000 | 1,800 | 4,600 | 1,700 | — |

**Required:**

Copy and complete the following table.

| | Gross Profit (Loss) Recognized | | | | | |
| | Percentage-of-Completion | | | Completed Contract | | |
| Situation | 2013 | 2014 | 2015 | 2013 | 2014 | 2015 |
|---|---|---|---|---|---|---|
| 1 | | | | | | |
| 2 | | | | | | |
| 3 | | | | | | |
| 4 | | | | | | |
| 5 | | | | | | |
| 6 | | | | | | |

**E 5–16**

**Percentage-of-completion method; solve for unknowns**

● **LO5–5**

In 2013, Long Construction Corporation began construction work under a three-year contract. The contract price is $1,600,000. Long uses the percentage-of-completion method for financial reporting purposes. The financial statement presentation relating to this contract at December 31, 2013, is as follows:

**Balance Sheet**

| | | |
|---|---|---|
| Accounts receivable (from construction progress billings) | | $30,000 |
| Construction in progress | $100,000 | |
| Less: Billings on construction contract | (94,000) | |
| Cost of uncompleted contracts in excess of billings | | 6,000 |

**Income Statement**

| | |
|---|---|
| Income (before tax) on the contract recognized in 2013 | $20,000 |

**Required:**

1. What was the cost of construction actually incurred in 2013?

2. How much cash was collected in 2013 on this contract?

3. What was the estimated cost to complete as of the end of 2013?

4. What was the estimated percentage of completion used to calculate income in 2013?

*(AICPA adapted)*

**E 5–17**

**FASB codification research**

● **LO5–5**

The *FASB Accounting Standards Codification* represents the single source of authoritative U.S. generally accepted accounting principles.

**Required:**

1. Obtain the relevant authoritative literature on the percentage-of-completion method using the FASB's Codification Research System at the FASB website (**www.fasb.org**). What is the specific citation that describes the circumstances and conditions under which it is preferable to use the percentage-of-completion method?

2. List the circumstances and conditions.

**E 5–18**

**Revenue recognition; software**

● **LO5–6**

Easywrite Software Company shipped software to a customer on July 1, 2013. The arrangement with the customer also requires the company to provide technical support over the next 12 months and to ship an expected software upgrade on January 1, 2014. The total contract price is $243,000, and Easywrite estimates that the individual fair values of the components of the arrangement if sold separately would be:

| | |
|---|---|
| Software | $210,000 |
| Technical support | 30,000 |
| Upgrade | 30,000 |

**Required:**

1. Determine the timing of revenue recognition for the $243,000.

2. Assume that the $243,000 contract price was paid on July 1, 2013. Prepare a journal entry to record the cash receipt. Do not worry about the cost of the items sold.

**E 5–19**

**Multiple-deliverable arrangements**

● **LO5–6**

Richardson Systems sells integrated bottling manufacturing systems that involve a conveyer, a labeler, a filler, and a capper. All of this equipment is sold separately by other vendors, and the fair values of the separate equipment are as follows:

| | |
|---|---|
| Conveyer | $20,000 |
| Labeler | 10,000 |
| Filler | 15,000 |
| Capper | 5,000 |
| Total | $50,000 |

Richardson sells the integrated system for $45,000. Each of the components is shipped separately to the customer for the customer to install.

**Required:**

1. Assume that each of the components can be used independently, even though Richardson sells them as an integrated system. How much revenue should be allocated to each component?

2. Now assume that the labeler, filler, and capper can't be used in production without the conveyer, and that the conveyer is the last component installed. How much revenue should be recognized at the time the conveyer is installed?

**E 5–20**
**Multiple-deliverable arrangements under IFRS**
● LO5–6, LO5–8

 **IFRS**

Assume the same facts as in E5–19, but that Richardson Systems reports under IFRS. How would your answers change? (Assume for requirement 2 that separate shipment is part of the normal course of Richardson's operations, and successful customer installation is highly probable.)

**E 5–21**
**Revenue recognition; franchise sales**
● LO5–6

On October 1, 2013, the Submarine Sandwich Company entered into a franchise agreement with an individual. In exchange for an initial franchise fee of $300,000, Submarine will provide initial services to the franchisee to include assistance in design and construction of the building, help in training employees, and help in obtaining financing. 10% of the initial franchise fee is payable on October 1, 2013, with the remaining $270,000 payable in nine equal annual installments beginning on October 1, 2014. These installments will include interest at an appropriate rate. The franchise opened for business on January 15, 2014.

**Required:**

Assume that the initial services to be performed by Submarine Sandwich subsequent to October 1, 2013, are substantial and that collectibility of the installment receivable is reasonably certain. Substantial performance of the initial services is deemed to have occurred when the franchise opened. Prepare the necessary journal entries for the following dates (ignoring interest charges):

1. October 1, 2013
2. January 15, 2014

**E 5–22**
**Concepts; terminology**
● LO5–3 through LO5–7

Listed below are several terms and phrases associated with revenue recognition and profitability analysis. Pair each item from List A (by letter) with the item from List B that is most appropriately associated with it.

| List A | List B |
|---|---|
| ___ 1. Inventory turnover | a. Net income divided by net sales. |
| ___ 2. Return on assets | b. Defers recognition until cash collected equals cost. |
| ___ 3. Return on shareholders' equity | c. Defers recognition until project is complete. |
| ___ 4. Profit margin on sales | d. Net income divided by assets. |
| ___ 5. Cost recovery method | e. Risks and rewards of ownership retained by seller. |
| ___ 6. Percentage-of-completion method | f. Contra account to construction in progress. |
| ___ 7. Completed contract method | g. Net income divided by shareholders' equity. |
| ___ 8. Asset turnover | h. Cost of goods sold divided by inventory. |
| ___ 9. Receivables turnover | i. Recognition is in proportion to work completed. |
| ___ 10. Right of return | j. Recognition is in proportion to cash received. |
| ___ 11. Billings on construction contract | k. Net sales divided by assets. |
| ___ 12. Installment sales method | l. Net sales divided by accounts receivable. |
| ___ 13. Consignment sales | m. Could cause the deferral of revenue recognition beyond delivery point. |

**E 5–23**
**Inventory turnover; calculation and evaluation**
● LO5–7

The following is a portion of the condensed income statement for Rowan, Inc., a manufacturer of plastic containers:

| | | |
|---|---|---|
| Net sales | | $2,460,000 |
| Less: Cost of goods sold: | | |
| Inventory, January 1 | $ 630,000 | |
| Net purchases | 1,900,000 | |
| Inventory, December 31 | (690,000) | 1,840,000 |
| Gross profit | | $ 620,000 |

**Required:**

1. Determine Rowan's inventory turnover.
2. What information does this ratio provide?

**E 5–24**
**Evaluating efficiency of asset management**
● LO5–7

The 2013 income statement of Anderson Medical Supply Company reported net sales of $8 million, cost of goods sold of $4.8 million, and net income of $800,000. The following table shows the company's comparative balance sheets for 2013 and 2012:

|  | ($ in 000s) | |
|---|---|---|
|  | **2013** | **2012** |
| **Assets** | | |
| Cash | $  300 | $  380 |
| Accounts receivable | 700 | 500 |
| Inventory | 900 | 700 |
| Property, plant, and equipment (net) | 2,400 | 2,120 |
| Total assets | $4,300 | $3,700 |
| **Liabilities and Shareholders' Equity** | | |
| Current liabilities | $  960 | $  830 |
| Bonds payable | 1,200 | 1,200 |
| Paid-in capital | 1,000 | 1,000 |
| Retained earnings | 1,140 | 670 |
| Total liabilities and shareholders' equity | $4,300 | $3,700 |

Some industry averages for Anderson's line of business are

| | |
|---|---|
| Inventory turnover | 5 times |
| Average collection period | 25 days |
| Asset turnover | 1.8 times |

**Required:**
Assess Anderson's asset management relative to its industry.

**E 5–25**
**Profitability ratios**
● LO5–7

The following condensed information was reported by Peabody Toys, Inc., for 2013 and 2012:

|  | ($ in 000s) | |
|---|---|---|
|  | **2013** | **2012** |
| **Income statement information** | | |
| Net sales | $5,200 | $4,200 |
| Net income | 180 | 124 |
| **Balance sheet information** | | |
| Current assets | $  800 | $  750 |
| Property, plant, and equipment (net) | 1,100 | 950 |
| Total assets | $1,900 | $1,700 |
| Current liabilities | $  600 | $  450 |
| Long-term liabilities | 750 | 750 |
| Paid-in capital | 400 | 400 |
| Retained earnings | 150 | 100 |
| Liabilities and shareholders' equity | $1,900 | $1,700 |

**Required:**
1. Determine the following ratios for 2013:
   a. Profit margin on sales.
   b. Return on assets.
   c. Return on shareholders' equity.
2. Determine the amount of dividends paid to shareholders during 2013.

**E 5–26**
**DuPont analysis**
● LO5–7

This exercise is based on the Peabody Toys, Inc., data from Exercise 5–25.

**Required:**
1. Determine the following components of the DuPont framework for 2013:
   a. Profit margin on sales.
   b. Asset turnover.
   c. Equity multiplier.
   d. Return on shareholders' equity.
2. Write an equation that relates these components in calculating ROE. Use the Peabody Toys data to show that the equation is correct.

**E 5–27**
Interim financial statements; income tax expense
● Appendix 5

Joplin Laminating Corporation reported income before income taxes during the first three quarters and management's estimates of the annual effective tax rate at the end of each quarter as shown below:

| | Quarter | | |
| --- | --- | --- | --- |
| | **First** | **Second** | **Third** |
| Income before income taxes | $50,000 | $40,000 | $100,000 |
| Estimated annual effective tax rate | 34% | 30% | 36% |

**Required:**
Determine the income tax expense to be reported in the income statement in each of the three quarterly reports.

**E 5–28**
Interim reporting; recognizing expenses
● Appendix 5

Security-Rand Corporation determines executive incentive compensation at the end of its fiscal year. At the end of the first quarter, management estimated that the amount will be $300 million. Depreciation expense for the year is expected to be $60 million. Also during the quarter, the company realized a gain of $23 million from selling two of its manufacturing plants.

**Required:**
What amounts for these items should be reported in the first quarter's income statement?

**E 5–29**
Interim financial statements; reporting expenses
● Appendix 5

Shields Company is preparing its interim report for the second quarter ending June 30. The following payments were made during the first two quarters:

**Required:**

| Expenditure | Date | Amount |
| --- | --- | --- |
| Annual advertising | January | $800,000 |
| Property tax for the fiscal year | February | 350,000 |
| Annual equipment repairs | March | 260,000 |
| Extraordinary casualty loss | April | 185,000 |
| One-time research and development fee to consultant | May | 96,000 |

For each expenditure indicate the amount that would be reported in the quarterly income statements for the periods ending March 31, June 30, September 30, and December 31.

**E 5–30**
Interim financial statements
● Appendix 5

IFRS

Assume the same facts as in E 5–29, but that Shields Company reports under IFRS. For each expenditure indicate the amount that would be reported in the quarterly income statements for the periods ending March 31, June 30, September 30, and December 31.

# CPA and CMA Review Questions

CPA Exam Questions

The following questions are adapted from a variety of sources including questions developed by the AICPA Board of Examiners and those used in the Kaplan CPA Review Course to study revenue recognition while preparing for the CPA examination. Determine the response that best completes the statements or questions.

● LO5–1

1. On October 1, 2013, Acme Fuel Co. sold 100,000 gallons of heating oil to Karn Co. at $3 per gallon. Fifty thousand gallons were delivered on December 15, 2013, and the remaining 50,000 gallons were delivered on January 15, 2014. Payment terms were 50% due on October 1, 2013, 25% due on first delivery, and the remaining 25% due on second delivery. What amount of revenue should Acme recognize from this sale during 2014?

   a. $ 75,000
   b. $150,000
   c. $225,000
   d. $300,000

● LO5–3

2. Since there is no reasonable basis for estimating the degree of collectibility, Astor Co. uses the installment sales method of revenue recognition for the following sales:

| | 2013 | 2014 |
|---|---|---|
| Sales | $600,000 | $900,000 |
| Collections from: | | |
| 2013 sales | 200,000 | 100,000 |
| 2014 sales | — | 300,000 |
| Accounts written off: | | |
| 2013 sales | 50,000 | 150,000 |
| 2014 sales | — | 50,000 |
| Gross profit percentage | 30% | 40% |

What amount should Astor report as deferred gross profit in its December 31, 2014, balance sheet for the 2013 and 2014 sales?

a. $225,000
b. $150,000
c. $160,000
d. $250,000

● LO5–3

3. Dolce Co., which began operations on January 1, 2013, appropriately uses the installment sales method of accounting to record revenues. The following information is available for the years ended December 31, 2013 and 2014:

| | 2013 | 2014 |
|---|---|---|
| Sales | $1,000,000 | $2,000,000 |
| Gross profit realized on sales made in: | | |
| 2013 | 150,000 | 90,000 |
| 2014 | — | 200,000 |
| Gross profit percentages | 30% | 40% |

What amount of installment accounts receivable should Dolce report in its December 31, 2014, balance sheet?

a. $1,700,000
b. $1,225,000
c. $1,300,000
d. $1,775,000

● LO5–5

4. Which of the following statements regarding the percentage-of-completion method of accounting is FALSE? The construction-in-progress account:

a. is shown net of advance billings as a liability if the amount is less than the amount of advance billings.
b. is an asset.
c. is shown net of advance billings on the balance sheet.
d. does not include the cumulative effect of gross profit recognition.

● LO5–5

5. The following data relates to a construction job started by Syl Co. during 2013:

| | |
|---|---|
| Total contract price | $100,000 |
| Actual costs during 2013 | 20,000 |
| Estimated remaining costs | 40,000 |
| Billed to customer during 2013 | 30,000 |
| Received from customer during 2013 | 10,000 |

Under the percentage-of-completion method, how much should Syl recognize as gross profit for 2013?

a. $26,667
b. $0
c. $13,333
d. $33,333

● LO5–5

6. Hansen Construction Inc. has consistently used the percentage-of-completion method of recognizing income. During 2013, Hansen started work on a $3,000,000 fixed-price construction contract. The accounting records disclosed the following data for the year ended December 31, 2013:

| | |
|---|---|
| Costs incurred | $ 930,000 |
| Estimated cost to complete | 2,170,000 |
| Progress billings | 1,100,000 |
| Collections | 700,000 |

How much loss should Hansen have recognized in 2013?

a. $180,000
b. $230,000
c. $30,000
d. $100,000

Beginning in 2011, International Financial Reporting Standards are tested on the CPA exam along with U.S. GAAP. The following questions deal with the application of IFRS.

● LO5–8

 **IFRS**

7. Which of the following is NOT a condition that must be satisfied under IFRS before revenue for a service can be recognized?

a. The stage of completion can be measured reliably.
b. It is probable that the economic benefits associated with the transaction will flow to the seller.
c. Cash collection is at least reasonably possible.
d. The amount of revenue and costs associated with the transaction can be measured reliably.

● LO5–8

 **IFRS**

8. O'Hara Company recognizes revenue on long-term construction contracts under IFRS. It cannot estimate progress toward completion accurately, and so uses the cost recovery method (also called the "zero profit method") to estimate revenue. O'Hara writes a contract to deliver an automated assembly line to Easley Motors. Easley will pay $2,000,000 to O'Hara, and O'Hara estimates the line will cost $1,500,000 to construct. The job is estimated to take three years to complete. In the first year of its contract with Easley Motors, O'Hara incurs $1,000,000 of cost, which O'Hara believes will eventually be recovered in the contract. How much revenue will O'Hara recognize in the first year of the contract?

a. $1,000,000
b. $0
c. $1,333,333
d. $666,667

● LO5–8

 **IFRS**

9. Which of the following is NOT true about revenue recognition for multiple deliverable contracts under IFRS?

a. *IAS No. 18* provides extensive guidance determining how contracts are to be separated into components for purposes of revenue recognition.
b. IFRS encourages focus on the economic substance of transactions, so some arrangements are likely to be accounted for differently than under U.S. GAAP.
c. Unlike U.S. GAAP, IFRS does not require VSOE for software contracts in order to separate contracts into multiple deliverables.
d. IFRS focuses on fair values to allocate total revenue to components.

● LO5–8
Appendix 5

 **IFRS**

10. Barrett Inc. paid $50,000 of property taxes in January that constitute the entire property tax bill for the year. Which of the following is true concerning how Barrett would account for those taxes in interim periods?

a. Under IFRS, Barrett would expense the entire $50,000 in the last quarter of the year.
b. Under U.S. GAAP, Barrett would expense the entire $50,000 of property taxes when the tax was paid in the first quarter of the year.
c. Under U.S. GAAP, Barrett would finish the first quarter of the year with a prepaid property taxes asset of $30,000.
d. Unlike IFRS, Barrett would start the third quarter of the year with a prepaid property tax asset of $0.

**CMA Exam Questions**

The following questions dealing with income measurement are adapted from questions that previously appeared on Certified Management Accountant (CMA) examinations. The CMA designation sponsored by the Institute of Management Accountants (www.imanet.org) provides members with an objective measure of knowledge and competence in the field of management accounting. Determine the response that best completes the statements or questions.

● LO5–1

1. On May 28, Markal Company purchased a tooling machine from Arens and Associates for $1,000,000 payable as follows: 50 percent at the transaction closing date and 50 percent due June 28. The cost of the machine to Arens is $800,000. Markal paid Arens $500,000 at the transaction closing date and took possession of the machine. On June 10, Arens determined that a change in the business environment has created a great deal of uncertainty regarding the collection of the balance due from Markal, and the amount is probably uncollectible. Arens and Markal have a fiscal year-end of May 31. The revenue recognized by Arens and Associates on May 28 is

a. $200,000
b. $800,000
c. $1,000,000
d. $0

● LO5–5

2. The percentage-of-completion method of accounting for long-term construction contracts is an exception to the
   a. Matching principle.
   b. Going-concern assumption.
   c. Economic-entity assumption.
   d. Point-of-sale recognition practice.

● LO5–5

3. Roebling Construction signed a $24 million contract on August 1, 2012, with the city of Candu to construct a bridge over the Vine River. Roebling's estimated cost of the bridge on that date was $18 million. The bridge was to be completed by April 2015. Roebling uses the percentage-of-completion method for income recognition. Roebling's fiscal year ends May 31. Data regarding the bridge contract are presented in the schedule below.

| | At May 31 ($000 omitted) | |
| --- | --- | --- |
| | **2013** | **2014** |
| Actual costs to date | $ 6,000 | $15,000 |
| Estimated costs to complete | 12,000 | 5,000 |
| Progress billings to date | 5,000 | 14,000 |
| Cash collected to date | 4,000 | 12,000 |

The gross profit or loss recognized in the fiscal year ended May 31, 2013, from this bridge contract is
   a. $6,000,000 gross profit.
   b. $2,000,000 gross profit.
   c. $3,000,000 gross profit.
   d. $1,000,000 gross profit.

# Problems

An alternate exercise and problem set is available on the text website: www.mhhe.com/spiceland7e

**P 5–1**
Income
statement
presentation;
installment
sales method
(Chapters 4 and 5)
● LO5–3

Reagan Corporation computed income from continuing operations before income taxes of $4,200,000 for 2013. The following material items have not yet been considered in the computation of income:

1. The company sold equipment and recognized a gain of $50,000. The equipment had been used in the manufacturing process and was replaced by new equipment.

2. In December, the company received a settlement of $1,000,000 for a lawsuit it had filed based on antitrust violations of a competitor. The settlement was considered to be an unusual and infrequent event.

3. Inventory costing $400,000 was written off as obsolete. Material losses of this type were incurred twice in the last eight years.

4. It was discovered that depreciation expense on the office building of $50,000 per year was not recorded in either 2012 or 2013.

In addition, you learn that *included* in revenues is $400,000 from installment sales made during the year. The cost of these sales is $240,000. At year-end, $100,000 in cash had been collected on the related installment receivables. Because of considerable uncertainty regarding the collectibility of receivables from these sales, the company's accountant should have used the installment sales method to recognize revenue and gross profit on these sales.

Also, the company's income tax rate is 40% and there were 1 million shares of common stock outstanding throughout the year.

**Required:**
Prepare an income statement for 2013 beginning with income from continuing operations before income taxes. Include appropriate EPS disclosures.

**P 5–2**
Installment sales
and cost recovery
methods
● LO5–3

Ajax Company appropriately accounts for certain sales using the installment sales method. The perpetual inventory system is used. Information related to installment sales for 2013 and 2014 is as follows:

| | 2013 | 2014 |
| --- | --- | --- |
| Sales | $300,000 | $400,000 |
| Cost of sales | 180,000 | 280,000 |
| Customer collections on: | | |
| 2013 sales | 120,000 | 100,000 |
| 2014 sales | — | 150,000 |

**Required:**

1. Calculate the amount of gross profit that would be recognized each year from installment sales.
2. Prepare all necessary journal entries for each year.
3. Repeat requirements 1 and 2 assuming that Ajax uses the cost recovery method to account for its installment sales.

**P 5–3**
Installment sales; alternative recognition methods
● LO5–3

**eXcel**

On August 31, 2013, the Silva Company sold merchandise to the Bendix Corporation for $500,000. Terms of the sale called for a down payment of $100,000 and four annual installments of $100,000 due on each August 31, beginning August 31, 2014. Each installment also will include interest on the unpaid balance applying an appropriate interest rate. The book value of the merchandise on Silva's books on the date of sale was $300,000. The perpetual inventory system is used. The company's fiscal year-end is December 31.

**Required:**

1. Prepare a table showing the amount of gross profit to be recognized in each of the five years of the installment sale applying each of the following methods:
   a. Point of delivery revenue recognition.
   b. Installment sales method.
   c. Cost recovery method.
2. Prepare journal entries for each of the five years applying the three revenue recognition methods listed in requirement 1. Ignore interest charges.
3. Prepare a partial balance sheet as of the end of 2013 and 2014 listing the items related to the installment sale applying each of the three methods listed in requirement 1.

**P 5–4**
Installment sales and cost recovery methods
● LO5–3

Mulcahey Builders (MB) remodels office buildings in low-income urban areas that are undergoing economic revitalization. MB typically accepts a 25% down payment when they complete a job and a note which requires that the remainder be paid in three equal installments over the next three years, plus interest. Because of the inherent uncertainty associated with receiving these payments, MB has historically used the cost recovery method to recognize revenue.

As of January 1, 2013, MB's outstanding gross installment accounts receivable (not net of deferred gross profit) consist of the following:

1. $400,000 due from the Bluebird Motel. MB completed the Bluebird job in 2011, and estimated gross profit on that job is 25%.
2. $150,000 due from the PitStop Gas and MiniMart. MB completed the PitStop job in 2010, and estimated gross profit on that job is 35%.

Dan Mulcahey has been considering switching from the cost recovery method to the installment sales method, because he wants to show the highest possible gross profit in 2013 and he understands that the installment sales method recognizes gross profit sooner than does the cost recovery method.

**Required:**

1. Calculate how much gross profit is expected to be earned on these jobs in 2013 under the cost recovery method, and how much would be earned if MB instead used the installment sales method. Ignore interest.
2. If Dan is primarily concerned about 2013, do you think he would be happy with a switch to the installment sales method? Explain.

**P 5–5**
Percentage-of-completion method
● LO5–5

**eXcel**

In 2013, the Westgate Construction Company entered into a contract to construct a road for Santa Clara County for $10,000,000. The road was completed in 2015. Information related to the contract is as follows:

|  | **2013** | **2014** | **2015** |
|---|---|---|---|
| Cost incurred during the year | $2,400,000 | $3,600,000 | $2,200,000 |
| Estimated costs to complete as of year-end | 5,600,000 | 2,000,000 | –0– |
| Billings during the year | 2,000,000 | 4,000,000 | 4,000,000 |
| Cash collections during the year | 1,800,000 | 3,600,000 | 4,600,000 |

Westgate uses the percentage-of-completion method of accounting for long-term construction contracts.

**Required:**

1. Calculate the amount of gross profit to be recognized in each of the three years.
2. Prepare all necessary journal entries for each of the years (credit *various accounts* for construction costs incurred).
3. Prepare a partial balance sheet for 2013 and 2014 showing any items related to the contract.
4. Calculate the amount of gross profit to be recognized in each of the three years assuming the following costs incurred and costs to complete information:

|  | **2013** | **2014** | **2015** |
|---|---|---|---|
| Costs incurred during the year | $2,400,000 | $3,800,000 | $3,200,000 |
| Estimated costs to complete as of year-end | 5,600,000 | 3,100,000 | –0– |

5. Calculate the amount of gross profit to be recognized in each of the three years assuming the following costs incurred and costs to complete information:

| | **2013** | **2014** | **2015** |
|---|---|---|---|
| Costs incurred during the year | $2,400,000 | $3,800,000 | $3,900,000 |
| Estimated costs to complete as of year-end | 5,600,000 | 4,100,000 | –0– |

**P 5–6**
Completed contract method
● **LO5–5**

[This is a variation of Problem 5–5 modified to focus on the completed contract method.]

**Required:**
Complete the requirements of Problem 5–5 assuming that Westgate Construction uses the completed contract method.

**P 5–7**
Construction accounting under IFRS
● **LO5–5, LO5–8**

🌐 **IFRS**

[This is a variation of the Problem 5–5 modified to focus on IFRS.]

**Required:**
Complete the requirements of Problem 5–5 assuming that Westgate Construction reports under IFRS and concludes that the percentage-of-completion method is not appropriate.

**P 5–8**
Construction accounting; loss projected on entire project
● **LO5–5**

Curtiss Construction Company, Inc., entered into a fixed-price contract with Axelrod Associates on July 1, 2013, to construct a four-story office building. At that time, Curtiss estimated that it would take between two and three years to complete the project. The total contract price for construction of the building is $4,000,000. Curtiss appropriately accounts for this contract under the completed contract method in its financial statements. The building was completed on December 31, 2015. Estimated percentage of completion, *accumulated* contract costs incurred, estimated costs to complete the contract, and *accumulated* billings to Axelrod under the contract were as follows:

| | **At 12-31-2013** | **At 12-31-2014** | **At 12-31-2015** |
|---|---|---|---|
| Percentage of completion | 10% | 60% | 100% |
| Costs incurred to date | $   350,000 | $2,500,000 | $4,250,000 |
| Estimated costs to complete | 3,150,000 | 1,700,000 | –0– |
| Billings to Axelrod, to date | 720,000 | 2,170,000 | 3,600,000 |

**Required:**
1. Prepare schedules to compute gross profit or loss to be recognized as a result of this contract for each of the three years.
2. Assuming Curtiss uses the percentage-of-completion method of accounting for long-term construction contracts, compute gross profit or loss to be recognized in each of the three years.
3. Assuming the percentage-of-completion method, compute the amount to be shown in the balance sheet at the end of 2013 and 2014 as either cost in excess of billings or billings in excess of costs.

*(AICPA adapted)*

**P 5–9**
Long-term contract; percentage-of-completion and completed contract methods
● **LO5–1, LO5–5**

☆

Citation Builders, Inc., builds office buildings and single-family homes. The office buildings are constructed under contract with reputable buyers. The homes are constructed in developments ranging from 10–20 homes and are typically sold during construction or soon after. To secure the home upon completion, buyers must pay a deposit of 10% of the price of the home with the remaining balance due upon completion of the house and transfer of title. Failure to pay the full amount results in forfeiture of the down payment. Occasionally, homes remain unsold for as long as three months after construction. In these situations, sales price reductions are used to promote the sale.

During 2013, Citation began construction of an office building for Altamont Corporation. The total contract price is $20 million. Costs incurred, estimated costs to complete at year-end, billings, and cash collections for the life of the contract are as follows:

| | **2013** | **2014** | **2015** |
|---|---|---|---|
| Costs incurred during the year | $ 4,000,000 | $ 9,500,000 | $4,500,000 |
| Estimated costs to complete as of year-end | 12,000,000 | 4,500,000 | — |
| Billings during the year | 2,000,000 | 10,000,000 | 8,000,000 |
| Cash collections during the year | 1,800,000 | 8,600,000 | 9,600,000 |

Also during 2013, Citation began a development consisting of 12 identical homes. Citation estimated that each home will sell for $600,000, but individual sales prices are negotiated with buyers. Deposits were received for eight of the homes, three of which were completed during 2013 and paid for in full for $600,000 each by the buyers. The completed homes cost $450,000 each to construct. The construction costs incurred during 2013 for the nine uncompleted homes totaled $2,700,000.

**Required:**

1. Briefly explain the difference between the percentage-of-completion and the completed contract methods of accounting for long-term construction contracts.

2. Answer the following questions assuming that Citation uses the completed contract method for its office building contracts:

   a. What is the amount of gross profit or loss to be recognized for the Altamont contract during 2013 and 2014?

   b. How much revenue related to this contract will Citation report in its 2013 and 2014 income statements?

   c. What will Citation report in its December 31, 2013, balance sheet related to this contract (ignore cash)?

3. Answer requirements 2a through 2c assuming that Citation uses the percentage-of-completion method for its office building contracts.

4. Assume that as of year-end 2014 the estimated cost to complete the office building is $9,000,000 and that Citation uses the percentage-of-completion method.

   a. What is the amount of gross profit or loss to be recognized for the Altamont contract during 2014?

   b. How much revenue related to this contract will Citation report in the 2014 income statement?

   c. What will Citation report in its 2014 balance sheet related to this contract (ignore cash)?

5. When should Citation recognize revenue for the sale of its single-family homes?

6. What will Citation report in its 2013 income statement and 2013 balance sheet related to the single-family home business (ignore cash in the balance sheet)?

**P 5–10**
Franchise sales;
installment sales
method
● LO5–3, LO5–6

Olive Branch Restaurant Corporation sells franchises throughout the western states. On January 30, 2013, the company entered into the following franchise agreement with Jim and Tammy Masters:

1. The initial franchise fee is $1.2 million. $200,000 is payable immediately and the remainder is due in 10, $100,000 installments plus 10% interest on the unpaid balance each January 30, beginning January 30, 2014. The 10% interest rate is an appropriate market rate.

2. In addition to allowing the franchisee to use the franchise name for the 10-year term of the agreement, in exchange for the initial fee Olive Branch agrees to assist the franchisee in selecting a location, obtaining financing, designing and constructing the restaurant building, and training employees.

3. All of the initial down payment of $200,000 is to be refunded by Olive Branch and the remaining obligation canceled if, for any reason, the franchisee fails to open the franchise.

4. In addition to the initial franchise fee, the franchisee is required to pay a monthly fee of 3% of franchise sales for advertising, promotion, menu planning, and other continuing services to be provided by Olive Branch over the life of the agreement. This fee is payable on the 10th of the following month.

Substantial performance of the initial services provided by Olive Branch, which are significant, is deemed to have occurred when the franchise opened on September 1, 2013. Franchise sales for the month of September 2013 were $40,000.

**Required:**

1. Assuming that collectibility of the installment receivable is reasonably certain, prepare the necessary journal entries for Olive Branch on the following dates (ignore interest charges on the installment receivable and the costs of providing franchise services):

   a. January 30, 2013
   b. September 1, 2013
   c. September 30, 2013
   d. January 30, 2014

2. Assume that significant uncertainty exists as to the collection of the installment receivable and that Olive Branch elects to recognize initial franchise fee revenue using the installment sales method. Prepare the necessary journal entries for the dates listed in requirement 1 (ignore interest charges on the installment receivable and the costs of providing franchise services).

3. Examine your answer to requirement 1a of this problem (the January 30, 2013, journal entry under the installment sales method). What is the effect of that journal entry on Olive Branch's balance sheet? (Ignore cash.) Briefly explain your answer.

**P 5–11**
Calculating
activity and
profitability ratios
● LO5–7

Financial statements for Askew Industries for 2013 are shown below:

### 2013 Income Statement

|  | ($ in 000s) |
|---|---|
| Sales | $ 9,000 |
| Cost of goods sold | (6,300) |
| Gross profit | 2,700 |
| Operating expenses | (2,000) |
| Interest expense | (200) |
| Tax expense | (200) |
| Net income | $   300 |

### Comparative Balance Sheets

|  | Dec. 31 | |
|---|---|---|
|  | **2013** | **2012** |
| **Assets** | | |
| Cash | $ 600 | $ 500 |
| Accounts receivable | 600 | 400 |
| Inventory | 800 | 600 |
| Property, plant, and equipment (net) | 2,000 | 2,100 |
|  | $4,000 | $3,600 |
| **Liabilities and Shareholders' Equity** | | |
| Current liabilities | $1,100 | $ 850 |
| Bonds payable | 1,400 | 1,400 |
| Paid-in capital | 600 | 600 |
| Retained earnings | 900 | 750 |
|  | $4,000 | $3,600 |

**Required:**
Calculate the following ratios for 2013.
1. Inventory turnover ratio
2. Average days in inventory
3. Receivables turnover ratio
4. Average collection period
5. Asset turnover ratio
6. Profit margin on sales
7. Return on assets
8. Return on shareholders' equity
9. Equity multiplier
10. Return on shareholders' equity (using the DuPont framework)

**P 5–12**
Use of ratios to
compare two
companies in the
same industry
● LO5–7

Presented below are condensed financial statements adapted from those of two actual companies competing in the pharmaceutical industry—**Johnson and Johnson (J&J)** and **Pfizer, Inc.** ($ in millions, except per share amounts).

**Required:**
Evaluate and compare the two companies by responding to the following questions.
   **Note:** Because two-year comparative statements are not provided, you should use year-end balances in place of average balances as appropriate.
1. Which of the two companies appears more efficient in collecting its accounts receivable and managing its inventory?
2. Which of the two firms had greater earnings relative to resources available?
3. Have the two companies achieved their respective rates of return on assets with similar combinations of profit margin and turnover?
4. From the perspective of a common shareholder, which of the two firms provided a greater rate of return?
5. From the perspective of a common shareholder, which of the two firms appears to be using leverage more effectively to provide a return to shareholders above the rate of return on assets?

## Balance Sheets

($ in millions, except per share data)

| | J&J | Pfizer |
|---|---|---|
| **Assets:** | | |
| Cash | $ 5,377 | $ 1,520 |
| Short-term investments | 4,146 | 10,432 |
| Accounts receivable (net) | 6,574 | 8,775 |
| Inventories | 3,588 | 5,837 |
| Other current assets | 3,310 | 3,177 |
| Current assets | 22,995 | 29,741 |
| Property, plant, and equipment (net) | 9,846 | 18,287 |
| Intangibles and other assets | 15,422 | 68,747 |
| Total assets | $48,263 | $116,775 |
| **Liabilities and Shareholders' Equity:** | | |
| Accounts payable | $ 4,966 | $ 2,601 |
| Short-term notes | 1,139 | 8,818 |
| Other current liabilities | 7,343 | 12,238 |
| Current liabilities | 13,448 | 23,657 |
| Long-term debt | 2,955 | 5,755 |
| Other long-term liabilities | 4,991 | 21,986 |
| Total liabilities | 21,394 | 51,398 |
| Capital stock (par and additional paid-in capital) | 3,120 | 67,050 |
| Retained earnings | 30,503 | 29,382 |
| Accumulated other comprehensive income (loss) | (590) | 195 |
| Less: treasury stock and other equity adjustments | (6,164) | (31,250) |
| Total shareholders' equity | 26,869 | 65,377 |
| Total liabilities and shareholders' equity | $48,263 | $116,775 |

## Income Statements

| | J&J | Pfizer |
|---|---|---|
| Net sales | $41,862 | $ 45,188 |
| Cost of goods sold | 12,176 | 9,832 |
| Gross profit | 29,686 | 35,356 |
| Operating expenses | 19,763 | 28,486 |
| Other (income) expense—net | (385) | 3,610 |
| Income before taxes | 10,308 | 3,260 |
| Tax expense | 3,111 | 1,621 |
| Net income | $ 7,197 | $ 1,639* |
| Basic net income per share | $ 2.42 | $ .22 |

* This is before income from discontinued operations.

**P 5–13**
**Creating a balance sheet from ratios;**
**Chapters 3 and 5**
● **LO5–7**

Cadux Candy Company's income statement for the year ended December 31, 2013, reported interest expense of $2 million and income tax expense of $12 million. Current assets listed in its balance sheet include cash, accounts receivable, and inventories. Property, plant, and equipment is the company's only noncurrent asset. Financial ratios for 2013 are listed below. Profitability and turnover ratios with balance sheet items in the denominator were calculated using year-end balances rather than averages.

| | |
|---|---|
| Debt to equity ratio | 1.0 |
| Current ratio | 2.0 |
| Acid-test ratio | 1.0 |
| Times interest earned ratio | 17 times |
| Return on assets | 10% |
| Return on shareholders' equity | 20% |
| Profit margin on sales | 5% |
| Gross profit margin | |
| (gross profit divided by net sales) | 40% |
| Inventory turnover | 8 times |
| Receivables turnover | 20 times |

**Required:**
Prepare a December 31, 2013, balance sheet for the Cadux Candy Company.

P 5–14
Compare two
companies in the
same industry;
Chapters 3 and 5
● LO5–7

Presented below are condensed financial statements adapted from those of two actual companies competing as
the primary players in a specialty area of the food manufacturing and distribution industry. ($ in millions, except
per share amounts.)

**Balance Sheets**

| Assets | Metropolitan | Republic |
|---|---|---|
| Cash | $  179.3 | $    37.1 |
| Accounts receivable (net) | 422.7 | 325.0 |
| Short-term investments | — | 4.7 |
| Inventories | 466.4 | 635.2 |
| Prepaid expenses and other current assets | 134.6 | 476.7 |
| Current assets | $1,203.0 | $1,478.7 |
| Property, plant, and equipment (net) | 2,608.2 | 2,064.6 |
| Intangibles and other assets | 210.3 | 464.7 |
| Total assets | $4,021.5 | $4,008.0 |
| **Liabilities and Shareholders' Equity** | | |
| Accounts payable | $  467.9 | $  691.2 |
| Short-term notes | 227.1 | 557.4 |
| Accruals and other current liabilities | 585.2 | 538.5 |
| Current liabilities | $1,280.2 | $1,787.1 |
| Long-term debt | 535.6 | 542.3 |
| Deferred tax liability | 384.6 | 610.7 |
| Other long-term liabilities | 104.0 | 95.1 |
| Total liabilities | $2,304.4 | $3,035.2 |
| Common stock (par and additional paid-in capital) | 144.9 | 335.0 |
| Retained earnings | 2,476.9 | 1,601.9 |
| Less: treasury stock | (904.7) | (964.1) |
| Total liabilities and shareholders' equity | $4,021.5 | $4,008.0 |

**Income Statements**

| | | |
|---|---|---|
| Net sales | $5,698.0 | $7,768.2 |
| Cost of goods sold | (2,909.0) | (4,481.7) |
| Gross profit | $2,789.0 | $3,286.5 |
| Operating expenses | (1,743.7) | (2,539.2) |
| Interest expense | (56.8) | (46.6) |
| Income before taxes | $  988.5 | $  700.7 |
| Tax expense | (394.7) | (276.1) |
| Net income | $  593.8 | $  424.6 |
| Net income per share | $    2.40 | $    6.50 |

**Required:**
Evaluate and compare the two companies by responding to the following questions.

   Note: Because comparative statements are not provided you should use year-end balances in place of average
balances as appropriate.

1. Which of the two firms had greater earnings relative to resources available?

2. Have the two companies achieved their respective rates of return on assets with similar combinations of profit
   margin and turnover?

3. From the perspective of a common shareholder, which of the two firms provided a greater rate of return?

4. Which company is most highly leveraged and which has made most effective use of financial leverage?

5. Of the two companies, which appears riskier in terms of its ability to pay short-term obligations?

6. How efficiently are current assets managed?

7. From the perspective of a creditor, which company offers the most comfortable margin of safety in terms of
   its ability to pay fixed interest charges?

**P 5–15**
Interim financial reporting

● Appendix 5

Branson Electronics Company is a small, publicly traded company preparing its first quarter interim report to be mailed to shareholders. The following information for the quarter has been compiled:

| | | |
|---|---:|---:|
| Revenues | | $180,000 |
| Cost of goods sold | | 35,000 |
| Operating expenses: | | |
| Fixed | $59,000 | |
| Variable | 48,000 | 107,000 |

Fixed operating expenses include payments of $50,000 to an advertising firm to promote the firm through various media throughout the year. The income tax rate for the firm's level of operations in the first quarter is 30%, but management estimates the effective rate for the entire year will be 36%.

**Required:**
Prepare the income statement to be included in Branson's first quarter interim report.

# Broaden Your Perspective

Apply your critical-thinking ability to the knowledge you've gained. These cases will provide you an opportunity to develop your research, analysis, judgment, and communication skills. You also will work with other students, integrate what you've learned, apply it in real world situations, and consider its global and ethical ramifications. This practice will broaden your knowledge and further develop your decision-making abilities.

**Real World Case 5–1**
Chainsaw Al; revenue recognition and earnings management

● LO5–1

In May 2001, the Securities and Exchange Commission sued the former top executives at Sunbeam, charging the group with financial reporting fraud that allegedly cost investors billions in losses. **Sunbeam Corporation** is a recognized designer, manufacturer, and marketer of household and leisure products, including Coleman, Eastpak, First Alert, Grillmaster, Mixmaster, Mr. Coffee, Oster, Powermate, and Campingaz. In the mid-1990s, Sunbeam needed help: its profits had declined by over 80% percent, and in 1996, its stock price was down over 50% from its high. To the rescue: Albert Dunlap, also known as "Chainsaw Al" based on his reputation as a ruthless executive known for his ability to restructure and turn around troubled companies, largely by eliminating jobs.

The strategy appeared to work. In 1997, Sunbeam's revenues had risen by 18 percent. However, in April 1998, the brokerage firm of **Paine Webber** downgraded Sunbeam's stock recommendation. Why the downgrade? Paine Webber had noticed unusually high accounts receivable, massive increases in sales of electric blankets in the third quarter 1997, which usually sell best in the fourth quarter, as well as unusually high sales of barbeque grills for the fourth quarter. Soon after, Sunbeam announced a first quarter loss of $44.6 million, and Sunbeam's stock price fell 25 percent.

It eventually came to light that Dunlap and Sunbeam had been using a "bill and hold" strategy with retail buyers. This involved selling products at large discounts to retailers before they normally would buy and then holding the products in third-party warehouses, with delivery at a later date.

Many felt Sunbeam had deceived shareholders by artificially inflating earnings and the company's stock price. A class-action lawsuit followed, alleging that Sunbeam and Dunlap violated federal securities laws, suggesting the motivation to inflate the earnings and stock price was to allow Sunbeam to complete hundreds of millions of dollars of debt financing in order to complete some ongoing mergers. Shareholders alleged damages when Sunbeam's subsequent earnings decline caused a huge drop in the stock price.

**Required:**
1. How might Sunbeam's 1997 "bill and hold" strategy have contributed to artificially high earnings in 1997?
2. How would the strategy have led to the unusually high accounts receivable Paine Webber noticed?
3. How might Sunbeam's 1997 "bill and hold" strategy have contributed to a 1998 earnings decline?
4. How does earnings management of this type affect earnings quality?

**Judgment Case 5–2**
Revenue recognition

● LO5–1

Revenue earned by a business enterprise is recognized for accounting purposes at different times, according to the circumstances. In some situations revenue is recognized approximately as it is earned in the economic sense. In other situations revenue is recognized at point of delivery.

**Required:**
1. Explain and justify why revenue often is recognized as earned at point of delivery.
2. Explain in what situations it would be useful to recognize revenue as the productive activity takes place.
3. At what times, other than those included in (1) and (2) above, may it be appropriate to recognize revenue?

**Judgment Case 5–3**
Service revenue

● LO5–1

Mega Fitness, Inc., operates fitness centers throughout the Western states. Members pay a nonrefundable, initial fee of $100, as well as a monthly fee of $40. As an option, a member could reduce the monthly fee to $30 by increasing the initial fee to $300. The monthly fee is billed to the member near the end of each month and is due by the 15th of the following month. The only cost incurred by Mega when a new member joins a center is the cost of issuing a laminated identification card with the member's picture. The card costs $3 to produce.

**Required:**

When should Mega Fitness recognize revenue for the initial fee and for the monthly fee?

**Judgment Case 5–4**
Revenue recognition; trade-ins
● LO5–1

Apex Computer Company manufactures and sells large mainframe computers. The computers range in price from $1 to $3 million and gross profit averages 40% of sales price. The company has a liberal trade-in policy. Customers are allowed to trade in their computers for a new generation machine anytime within three years of sale. The trade-in allowance granted will vary depending on the number of years between original sale and trade-in. However, in all cases, the allowance is expected to be approximately 25% higher than the prevailing market price of the computer.

As an example, in 2013 a customer who purchased a computer in 2011 for $2 million (the computer cost Apex $1,200,000 to manufacture) decided to trade it in for a new computer. The sales price of the new computer was $2.5 million and a trade-in allowance of $600,000 was granted on the old machine. As a result of the trade-in allowance, the customer had to pay only $1.9 million ($2.5 million less $600,000) for the new computer. The old computer taken back by Apex had a resale value of $480,000. The new computer cost $1.5 million to manufacture. The company accounted for the trade-in by recognizing revenue of $2,380,000 ($1.9 million received in cash + $480,000 value of old computer).

**Required:**

Does the company's revenue recognition policy for trade-ins seem appropriate? If not, describe the problem created by the liberal trade-in policy.

**Communication Case 5–5**
Revenue recognition
● LO5–1

Jerry's Ice Cream Parlor is considering a marketing plan to increase sales of ice cream cones. The plan will give customers a free ice cream cone if they buy 10 ice cream cones at regular prices. Customers will be issued a card that will be punched each time an ice cream cone is purchased. After 10 punches, the card can be turned in for a free cone.

Jerry Donovan, the company's owner, is not sure how the new plan will affect accounting procedures. He realizes that the company will be incurring costs each time a free ice cream cone is awarded, but there will be no corresponding revenue or cash inflow.

The focus of this case is the matching of revenues and expenses related to the free ice cream cones that will be awarded if the new plan is adopted. Your instructor will divide the class into two to six groups depending on the size of the class. The mission of your group is to reach consensus on the appropriate accounting treatment for the new plan.

**Required:**

1. Each group member should deliberate the situation independently and draft a tentative argument prior to the class session for which the case is assigned.

2. In class, each group will meet for 10–15 minutes in different areas of the classroom. During that meeting, group members will take turns sharing their suggestions for the purpose of arriving at a single group treatment.

3. After the allotted time, a spokesperson for each group (selected during the group meetings) will share the group's solution with the class. The goal of the class is to incorporate the views of each group into a consensus approach to the situation.

**Research Case 5–6**
Long-term contract accounting
● LO5–5

An article published in *Accounting Horizons* describes the current accounting practices and disclosures for long-term contracts for the Fortune 500 companies.

**Required:**

In your library or from some other source, locate the indicated article in *Accounting Horizons,* September 2004, and answer the following questions:

1. How many firms reported the use of one of the two long-term contract accounting methods?

2. Approximately half of the firms are in which industry?

3. How many firms reported the use of the percentage-of-completion method? The completed contract method?

4. What is the most frequently used approach to estimating a percentage-of-completion?

**Research Case 5–7**
Earnings management with respect to revenues
● LO5–1

An article published in *Accounting Horizons* describes various techniques that companies use to manage their earnings.

**Required:**

In your library or from some other source, locate the article "How Are Earnings Managed? Evidence from Auditors" in *Accounting Horizons,* 2003 (Supplement), and answer the following questions:

1. What are the four most common revenue-recognition abuses identified by auditors in that article? From the examples provided in the article, briefly explain each abuse.

2. What is the revenue-recognition abuse identified in the article related to the percentage-of-completion method?

3. Did revenue-recognition abuses tend to increase or decrease net income in the year they occurred?

4. Did auditors tend to require their clients to make adjustments that reduced the revenue-recognition abuses they detected?

**Ethics Case 5–8**
Revenue recognition
● LO5–1

Horizon Corporation manufactures personal computers. The company began operations in 2004 and reported profits for the years 2008 through 2011. Due primarily to increased competition and price slashing in the industry, 2012's income statement reported a loss of $20 million. Just before the end of the 2013 fiscal year, a memo from the company's chief financial officer to Jim Fielding, the company controller, included the following comments:

*If we don't do something about the large amount of unsold computers already manufactured, our auditors will require us to write them off. The resulting loss for 2013 will cause a violation of our debt covenants and force the company into bankruptcy. I suggest that you ship half of our inventory to J.B. Sales, Inc., in Oklahoma City. I know the company's president and he will accept the merchandise and acknowledge the shipment as a purchase. We can record the sale in 2013 which will boost profits to an acceptable level. Then J.B. Sales will simply return the merchandise in 2014 after the financial statements have been issued.*

**Required:**

Discuss the ethical dilemma faced by Jim Fielding.

**Judgment Case 5–9**
Revenue recognition; installment sale
● LO5–1, LO5–3

On October 1, 2013, the Marshall Company sold a large piece of machinery to the Hammond Construction Company for $80,000. The cost of the machine was $40,000. Hammond made a down payment of $10,000 and agreed to pay the remaining balance in seven equal monthly installments of $10,000, plus interest at 12% on the unpaid balance, beginning November 1.

**Required:**

1. Identify three alternative methods for recognizing revenue and costs for the situation described and compute the amount of gross profit that would be recognized in 2013 using each method.

2. Discuss the circumstances under which each of the three methods would be used.

**Judgment Case 5–10**
Revenue recognition; *SAB 101* questions; FASB codification
● LO5–1

As part of its crackdown on earnings management, the SEC issued *Staff Accounting Bulletins No.s 101 and 104* to provide additional guidance on when revenue should be recognized. Consider the following situations posed by the SEC and, for each, discuss whether or not you believe it is appropriate to recognize revenue. You might gain access to this literature through the FASB Codification Research System via the FASB website (www.fasb.org), the SEC (www.sec.gov), your school library, or some other source.

1. **Facts:** Company M is a discount retailer. It generates revenue from annual membership fees it charges customers to shop at its stores and from the sale of products at a discount price to those customers. The membership arrangements with retail customers require the customer to pay the entire membership fee (e.g., $35) at the outset of the arrangement. However, the customer has the unilateral right to cancel the arrangement at any time during its term and receive a full refund of the initial fee. Based on historical data collected over time for a large number of homogeneous transactions, Company M estimates that approximately 40% of the customers will request a refund before the end of the membership contract term. Company M's data for the past five years indicates that significant variations between actual and estimated cancellations have not occurred, and Company M does not expect significant variations to occur in the foreseeable future.

   **Question:** May Company M recognize revenue for the membership fees and accrue the costs to provide membership services at the outset of the arrangement?

2. **Facts:** Company Z enters into an arrangement with Customer A to deliver Company Z's products to Customer A on a consignment basis. Pursuant to the terms of the arrangement, Customer A is a consignee, and title to the products does not pass from Company Z to Customer A until Customer A consumes the products in its operations. Company Z delivers product to Customer A under the terms of their arrangement.

   **Question:** May Company Z recognize revenue upon delivery of its product to Customer A?

3. **Facts:** Company R is a retailer that offers "layaway" sales to its customers. Company R retains the merchandise, sets it aside in its inventory, and collects a cash deposit from the customer. Although Company R may set a time period within which the customer must finalize the purchase, Company R does not require the customer to enter into an installment note or other fixed payment commitment or agreement when the initial deposit is received. The merchandise generally is not released to the customer until the customer pays the full purchase price. In the event that the customer fails to pay the remaining purchase price, the customer forfeits its cash deposit. In the event the merchandise is lost, damaged, or destroyed, Company R either must refund the cash deposit to the customer or provide replacement merchandise.

   **Question:** When may Company R recognize revenue for merchandise sold under its layaway program?

**Research Case 5–11**
Locate and extract relevant information and authoritative support for a financial reporting issue; revenue recognition; right of return; FASB codification
● LO5–4

Many companies sell products allowing their customers the right to return merchandise if they are not satisfied. Because the return of merchandise can retroactively negate the benefits of having made a sale, the seller must meet certain criteria before revenue is recognized in situations when the right of return exists. Generally accepted accounting principles list the criteria, the most critical of which is that the seller must be able to make reliable estimates of future returns.

**Required:**

1. Obtain the relevant authoritative literature on accounting for the right to return merchandise using the FASB's Codification Research System. You might gain access at the FASB (**www.fasb.org**), from your school library, or some other source.
2. What factors do generally accepted accounting principles discuss that may impair the ability to make a reasonable estimate of returns? Cite the reference location regarding these factors.
3. List the criteria that must be met before revenue can be recognized when the right of return exists.
4. Using EDGAR (**www.sec.gov**) access the 10-K reports for the most recent fiscal year for **Hewlett-Packard Company** and for **Advanced Micro Devices, Inc**. Search for the revenue recognition policy to determine when these two companies recognize revenue for product sales allowing customers the right of return.
5. Using your answers to requirements 2 and 3, speculate as to why the two revenue recognition policies differ.

**Research Case 5–12**
FASB codification; locate and extract relevant information and authoritative support for a financial reporting issue; reporting revenue as a principal or as an agent
● LO5–1, LO5–2

The birth of the Internet in the 1990s led to the creation of a new industry of online retailers such as **Amazon**, **Overstock.com**, and **PC Mall, Inc**. Many of these companies often act as intermediaries between the manufacturer and the customer without ever taking possession of the merchandise sold. Revenue recognition for this type of transaction has been controversial.

Assume that **Overstock.com** sold you a product for $200 that cost $150. The company's profit on the transaction clearly is $50. Should Overstock recognize $200 in revenue and $150 in cost of goods sold (the gross method), or should it recognize only the $50 in gross profit (the net method) as commission revenue?

**Required:**

1. Obtain the relevant authoritative literature on reporting revenue at gross versus net using the FASB's Codification Research System. You might gain access at the FASB website (**www.fasb.org**), from your school library, or some other source. *Hint:* this guidance was originally issued in the Emerging Issues Task Force document EITF 99-19, and you can use the codification's "Cross Reference" function to identify where that EITF appears in the codification.
2. What factors does the authoritative literature discuss that will influence the choice of reporting method used by these companies? Cite the reference location and the specific titles pertaining to this reference location.
3. Using EDGAR (**www.sec.gov**), access **Google, Inc.**'s 2010 10-K. Locate the disclosure note that discusses the company's revenue recognition policy.
4. Does Google discuss determining whether they should report revenue on a gross versus net basis with respect to any of their products or services? What is the reason Google provides for its choices? Do you agree with Google's reasoning?

**Judgment Case 5–13**
Revenue recognition; service sales
● LO5–1, LO5–5

Each of the following situations concerns revenue recognition for services.

1. **Delta Airlines** books a reservation for a roundtrip flight to Orlando for Ming Tsai on April 12. Delta charges the $425 to Tsai's Visa card on April 13 and receives the cash from Visa on May 1. The roundtrip flight commences on May 15. The ticket is nonrefundable.
2. Highlife Ski Resort in Colorado sells a season pass to Larry Werner on October 15. Highlife usually opens its season just after Thanksgiving and stays open until approximately April 30.
3. Dixon Management requires tenants to sign a three-year lease and charges $5,000 per month for one floor in its midtown high-rise. In addition to the monthly fee, payable at the beginning of each month, tenants pay a nonrefundable fee of $12,000 to secure the lease.
4. Janora Hawkins, attorney, agrees to accept an accident victim's case. Hawkins will be paid on a contingency basis. That is, if she wins the case, she will receive 30% of the total settlement. The case commences on July 15 and is settled successfully on August 28. On September 15, Hawkins receives her contingency payment of $60,000.

**Required:**

For each of the above situations, determine the appropriate timing of revenue recognition.

**Judgment Case 5–14**
Revenue recognition; long-term construction contracts
● LO5–5

Two accounting students were discussing the alternative methods of accounting for long-term construction contracts. The discussion focused on which method was most like the typical revenue recognition method of recognizing revenue at point of product delivery. Bill argued that the completed contract method was preferable because it was analogous to recognizing revenue at the point of delivery. John disagreed and supported the percentage-of-completion method, stating that it was analogous to accruing revenue during the earnings process, that is, as the work was performed.

**Required:**

Discuss the arguments made by both students. Which argument do you support? Why?

**Communication Case 5–15**
Percentage-of-completion and completed contract methods
● LO5–5

Willingham Construction is in the business of building high-priced, custom, single-family homes. The company, headquartered in Anaheim, California, operates throughout the Southern California area. The construction period for the average home built by Willingham is six months, although some homes have taken as long as nine months.

You have just been hired by Willingham as the assistant controller and one of your first tasks is to evaluate the company's revenue recognition policy. The company presently uses the completed contract method for all of its projects and management is now considering a switch to the percentage-of-completion method.

**Required:**

Write a 1- to 2-page memo to Virginia Reynolds, company controller, describing the differences between the percentage-of-completion and completed contract methods. Be sure to include references to GAAP as they pertain to the choice of method. Do not address the differential effects on income taxes nor the effect on the financial statements of switching between methods.

**IFRS Case 5–16**
Comparison of revenue recognition in Sweden and the United States
● LO5–1, LO5–8

 **IFRS**

**Vodafone Group, Plc**, headquartered in the United Kingdom, is one of the world's largest telecommunications companies. Excerpts from the revenue recognition disclosure included in its 2011 annual report are reproduced below.

---

**Note 2: Significant accounting policies**

**Revenue**

Revenue is recognised to the extent the Group has delivered goods or rendered services under an agreement, the amount of revenue can be measured reliably and it is probable that the economic benefits associated with the transaction will flow to the Group. Revenue is measured at the fair value of the consideration received, exclusive of sales taxes and discounts.

The Group principally obtains revenue from providing the following telecommunication services: access charges, airtime usage, messaging, interconnect fees, data services and information provision, connection fees and equipment sales. Products and services may be sold separately or in bundled packages.

Revenue for access charges, airtime usage and messaging by contract customers is recognised as services are performed, with unbilled revenue resulting from services already provided accrued at the end of each period and unearned revenue from services to be provided in future periods deferred. Revenue from the sale of prepaid credit is deferred until such time as the customer uses the airtime, or the credit expires. Revenue from interconnect fees is recognised at the time the services are performed.

Revenue from data services and information provision is recognised when the Group has performed the related service and, depending on the nature of the service, is recognised either at the gross amount billed to the customer or the amount receivable by the Group as commission for facilitating the service. . .

Revenue for device sales is recognised when the device is delivered to the end customer and the sale is considered complete. For device sales made to intermediaries, revenue is recognised if the significant risks associated with the device are transferred to the intermediary and the intermediary has no general right of return. If the significant risks are not transferred, revenue recognition is deferred until sale of the device to an end customer by the intermediary or the expiry of the right of return.

---

**Required:**

On the basis of the information the disclosures provide, compare revenue recognition under IFRS (as applied by Vodafone) with that in the United States.

**IFRS Case 5–17**
Comparison of revenue recognition for construction contracts
● LO5–5, LO5–8

 **IFRS**

**ThyssenKrupp AG**, headquartered in Germany, is one of the world's largest technology companies, with 177,346 employees worldwide and primary segments in steel, technology, and capital goods and services.

**Required:**

1. Access ThyssenKrupp's most recent annual report using the Internet. Find the footnote describing significant accounting policies. Indicate the methods that ThyssenKrupp uses to account for long-term construction contracts when they can and cannot make an accurate estimate of the income on a construction contract.

2. If ThyssenKrupp was a U.S. company, how would you expect its accounting for these contracts to differ?

**Trueblood Accounting Case 5–18**
Revenue recognition for multiple-deliverable contracts involving software
● LO5–6

The following Trueblood case is recommended for use with this chapter. The case provides an excellent opportunity for class discussion, group projects, and writing assignments. The case, along with Professor's Discussion Material, can be obtained from the Deloitte Foundation at its website **www.deloitte.com/us/truebloodcases**.

### Case 10-11: *Eye Vision*

This case concerns the appropriate timing of revenue recognition for a bundled product and service.

**Trueblood Accounting Case 5–19**
Revenue recognition for multiple-deliverable contracts
● LO5–6

The following Trueblood case is recommended for use with this chapter. The case provides an excellent opportunity for class discussion, group projects, and writing assignments. The case, along with Professor's Discussion Material, can be obtained from the Deloitte Foundation at its website **www.deloitte.com/us/truebloodcases**.

### Case 07-3 Part 1: *Columbia On-Line Networks*

This case concerns recognizing revenue of arrangements that have multiple elements.

**Real World Case 5–20**
Revenue recognition; franchise sales
● LO5–6

EDGAR, the Electronic Data Gathering, Analysis, and Retrieval system, performs automated collection, validation, indexing, and forwarding of submissions by companies and others who are required by law to file forms with the U.S. Securities and Exchange Commission (SEC). All publicly traded domestic companies use EDGAR to make the majority of their filings. (Some foreign companies file voluntarily.) Form 10-K which includes the annual report, is required to be filed on EDGAR. The SEC makes this information available on the Internet.

**Required:**

1. Access EDGAR on the Internet. The web address is **www.sec.gov**.
2. Search for **Jack in the Box, Inc.** Access the most recent 10-K filing. Search or scroll to find the financial statements and related notes.
3. Answer the following questions related to the company's revenue recognition policies:
   a. When does the company recognize initial franchise license fee revenue?
   b. How are continuing fees determined?
4. Repeat requirements 2 and 3 for two additional companies that you suspect also earn revenues through the sale of franchise rights. Compare their revenue recognition policies with the policies of Jack in the Box.

**Real World Case 5–21**
Principal agent considerations
● LO5–2

EDGAR, the Electronic Data Gathering, Analysis, and Retrieval system, performs automated collection, validation, indexing, and forwarding of submissions by companies and others who are required by law to file forms with the U.S. Securities and Exchange Commission (SEC). All publicly traded domestic companies use EDGAR to make the majority of their filings. (Some foreign companies file voluntarily.) Form 10-K which includes the annual report, is required to be filed on EDGAR. The SEC makes this information available on the Internet.

**Required:**

1. Access EDGAR on the Internet. The web address is **www.sec.gov**.
2. Search for the most recent 10-K's of Orbitz and priceline.com. Search or scroll to find the revenue recognition note in the financial statements.
3. For each of the following types of revenue, indicate whether the amount shown on the income statement is "net" or "gross" as those terms have been used with respect to revenue recognition in our course, and briefly explain your answer.
   a. Orbitz's "merchant model" revenues.
   b. Orbitz's "retail model" revenues.
   c. priceline.com's "merchant revenues for 'Name Your Own Price'® services."
   d. priceline.com's "merchant revenues for 'Price-Disclosed Hotel' services."
   e. priceline.com's agency revenues.
4. Consider your responses to 3a through 3e. Does it look like there is the potential for noncomparability when readers consider Orbitz and priceline.com? Indicate "yes" or "no," and briefly explain your answer.

**Analysis
Case 5–22**

Evaluating profitability and asset management; obtain and compare annual reports from companies in the same industry

● LO5–7

Performance and profitability of a company often are evaluated using the financial information provided by a firm's annual report in comparison with other firms in the same industry. Ratios are useful in this assessment.

**Required:**

Obtain annual reports from two corporations in the same primary industry. Using techniques you learned in this chapter and any analysis you consider useful, respond to the following questions:

1. How do earnings trends compare in terms of both the direction and stability of income?
2. Which of the two firms had greater earnings relative to resources available?
3. How efficiently are current assets managed?
4. Has each of the companies achieved its respective rate of return on assets with similar combinations of profit margin and turnover?
5. Are there differences in accounting methods that should be taken into account when making comparisons?

   **Note:** You can obtain copies of annual reports from friends who are shareholders, the investor relations department of the corporations, from a friendly stockbroker, or from EDGAR (Electronic Data Gathering, Analysis, and Retrieval) on the Internet (www.sec.gov).

**Judgment
Case 5–23**

Relationships among ratios; Chapters 3 and 5

● LO5–7

You are a part-time financial advisor. A client is considering an investment in common stock of a waste recycling firm. One motivation is a rumor the client heard that the company made huge investments in a new fuel creation process. Unable to confirm the rumor, your client asks you to determine whether the firm's assets had recently increased significantly.

Because the firm is small, information is sparse. Last quarter's interim report showed total assets of $324 million, approximately the same as last year's annual report. The only information more current than that is a press release last week in which the company's management reported "record net income for the year of $21 million, representing a 14.0% return on shareholders' equity. Performance was enhanced by the Company's judicious use of financial leverage on a debt/equity ratio of 2 to 1."

**Required:**

Use the information available to provide your client with an opinion as to whether the waste recycling firm invested in the new fuel creation process during the last quarter of the year.

**Integrating
Case 5–24**

Using ratios to test reasonableness of data; Chapters 3 and 5

● LO5–7

You are a new staff accountant with a large regional CPA firm, participating in your first audit. You recall from your auditing class that CPAs often use ratios to test the reasonableness of accounting numbers provided by the client. Since ratios reflect the relationships among various account balances, if it is assumed that prior relationships still hold, prior years' ratios can be used to estimate what current balances should approximate. However, you never actually performed this kind of analysis until now. The CPA in charge of the audit of Covington Pike Corporation brings you the list of ratios shown below and tells you these reflect the relationships maintained by Covington Pike in recent years.

> Profit margin on sales = 5%
> Return on assets = 7.5%
> Gross profit margin = 40%
> Inventory turnover ratio = 6 times
> Receivables turnover ratio = 25 times
> Acid-test ratio = .9 to one
> Current ratio = 2 to 1
> Return on shareholders' equity = 10%
> Debt to equity ratio = $1/3$
> Times interest earned ratio = 12 times

Jotted in the margins are the following notes:

● Net income $15,000
● Only one short-term note ($5,000); all other current liabilities are trade accounts
● Property, plant, and equipment are the only noncurrent assets
● Bonds payable are the only noncurrent liabilities
● The effective interest rate on short-term notes and bonds is 8%
● No investment securities
● Cash balance totals $15,000

**Required:**

You are requested to approximate the current year's balances in the form of a balance sheet and income statement, to the extent the information allows. Accompany those financial statements with the calculations you use to estimate each amount reported.

# Air France—KLM Case

**AIRFRANCE** ⁄

● LO5–8

🌐 IFRS

Air France–KLM (AF), a French company, prepares its financial statements according to International Financial Reporting Standards. AF's annual report for the year ended March 31, 2011, which includes financial statements and disclosure notes, is provided with all new textbooks. This material also is included in AF's "Registration Document 2010–11," dated June 15, 2011 and is available at www.airfranceklm.com.

**Required:**

1. In note 3.6, AF indicates that "Upon issuance, both passenger and cargo tickets are recorded as "Deferred revenue on ticket sales" and that "Sales related to air transportation are recognized when the transportation service is provided."

   a. Examine AF's balance sheet. What is the total amount of deferred revenue on ticket sales as of March 31, 2011?

   b. When transportation services are provided with respect to the deferred revenue on ticket sales, what journal entry would AF make to reduce deferred revenue?

   c. Does AF's treatment of deferred revenue under IFRS appear consistent with how these transactions would be handled under U.S. GAAP? Explain.

2. AF has a frequent flyer program, "Flying Blue," which allows members to acquire "miles" as they fly on Air France or partner airlines that are redeemable for free flights or other benefits.

   a. How does AF account for these miles?

   b. Does AF report any liability associated with these miles as of March 31, 2011?

   c. Is AF's accounting approach under IFRS consistent with how U.S. GAAP accounts for multiple-deliverable contracts? Explain.

# REVENUE RECOGNITION
# Where We're Headed

**PREFACE** — The FASB and the IASB are collaborating on several major new standards designed in part to move U.S. GAAP and IFRS closer together (convergence). This reading is based on their joint Exposure Draft of a new revenue recognition Accounting Standards Update (ASU) and "tentative decisions" of the Boards after receiving feedback from the Exposure Draft as of the date this text went to press.[41]

Even after the proposed ASU is issued, previous GAAP will be relevant until the ASU becomes effective, and students taking the CPA or CMA exams will be responsible for the previous GAAP until six months after that effective date. Conversely, prior to the effective date of the proposed ASU it is useful for students to have an understanding of the new guidance on the horizon.

In June 2010 the FASB and IASB issued identical Exposure Drafts (ED) for a new ASU entitled "Revenue from Contracts with Customers," and followed up with another Exposure Draft in November of 2011.[42] The purpose of the proposed ASU is to improve revenue recognition guidance and in the process to eliminate current revenue recognition differences among industries and between U.S. GAAP and IFRS. It appears likely that the final ASU will become effective for fiscal years starting no sooner than 2015. This chapter supplement covers the main points of the proposed ASU. We focus in particular on important changes from current GAAP, identified with a *GAAP Change* note in the margin of the supplement.

The core revenue recognition principle and key application steps of the proposed ASU are shown in Illustration 5–18.

**Illustration 5–18**

Core Revenue Recognition Principle and Key Steps in Applying the Principle

*GAAP Change*

---

### Core Revenue Recognition Principle[43]

A company must recognize revenue when goods or services are transferred to customers in an amount that reflects the consideration the company expects to be entitled to receive in exchange for those goods or services.

### Key Steps in Applying The Principle

1. Identify a contract with a customer.
2. Identify the separate performance obligation(s) in the contract.
3. Determine the transaction price.
4. Allocate the transaction price to the separate performance obligations.
5. Recognize revenue when (or as) each performance obligation is satisfied.

---

[41]Because the proposed ASU had not been finalized as of the date this text went to press, it is possible that some aspects of the final ASU are different from what we show in this Supplement. Check the FASB Updates page (**http://lsb.scu.edu/jsepe/fasb-update-7e.htm**) to see if any changes have occurred.

[42]*Proposed Accounting Standards Update (Revised): Revenue Recognition (Topic 605)*, "Revenue from Contracts with Customers" (Norwalk, Conn: FASB, November 14, 2011).

[43]Ibid.

This approach may seem familiar—it is similar to what we use for "multiple-element contracts" in current U.S. GAAP. For many contracts, applying this approach is very straightforward and results in accounting that is very similar to what is required under current GAAP. As a simple example, assume Macy's sells a skirt to a woman named Susan for $75 that Macy's previously purchased from a wholesaler for $40. Given that the skirt is on sale, Macy's has a "no returns" policy. How would Macy's account for the sale?

1. **Identify the contract with a customer:** In this case, the contract is implicit but clear— Macy's delivers the skirt and Susan pays cash of $75.
2. **Identify the separate performance obligation(s) in the contract:** Macy's has only a single performance obligation—deliver the skirt.
3. **Determine the transaction price:** The price is $75.
4. **Allocate the transaction price to the separate performance obligations:** With only one performance obligation, no allocation is necessary.
5. **Recognize revenue when (or as) each performance obligation is satisfied:** Macy's satisfies its performance obligation when it delivers the skirt to Susan, and makes the following journal entries:

| | | |
|---|---:|---:|
| Cash ............................................................................................ | 75 | |
|     Revenue ................................................................................ | | 75 |
| Cost of goods sold ...................................................................... | 40 | |
|     Inventory ............................................................................... | | 40 |

Unfortunately, applying this revenue recognition approach in practice often is much more complicated, because different kinds of businesses use different arrangements to sell various combinations of goods and services. Let's walk through each of the five key steps in more detail.

## Step 1: Identify the Contract

Under the proposed ASU we recognize revenue associated with contracts that are legally enforceable. We normally think of a contract as being specified in a written document, but that doesn't have to be the case for revenue recognition to occur. Contracts can be oral rather than written. They can be explicit, but they also can be implicit based on the typical business practices that a company uses to sell products or services.

*Enforceable contracts can be explicit or implicit.*

When does an enforceable contract exist for purposes of revenue recognition?[44] As shown in Illustration 5–19, the contract must meet five criteria.

For purposes of applying revenue recognition criteria, a contract needs to have the following characteristics:

1. **Commercial substance.** The contract is expected to affect the seller's future cash flows.
2. **Approval.** Each party to the contract has approved the contract and is committed to satisfying their respective obligations.
3. **Rights.** Each party's rights are specified with regard to the goods or services to be transferred.
4. **Payment terms.** The terms and manner of payment are specified.
5. **Performance.** A contract does not exist if each party can terminate the contract without penalty before any obligations are performed.

**Illustration 5–19**

Criteria for Determining Whether a Contract Exists for Purposes of Revenue Recognition

*If an unperformed contract can be cancelled without penalty, a contract does not exist for purposes of revenue recognition.*

Illustration 5–20 shows these criteria applied to a TrueTech example that we will use throughout the remainder of this supplement.

---

[44]Our focus will be on accounting for a single contract. The proposed ASU requires sellers with multiple contracts to account for them as a single contract if (1) the contracts are negotiated as a package with a single commercial objective, (2) the transaction price of one contract depends on the price of the other contract, or (3) some or all of the goods or services promised in the contracts are a single performance obligation.

**Illustration 5–20**

Determining Whether a Contract Exists for Revenue Recognition Purposes

TrueTech Industries manufactures the Tri-Box System, a multiplayer gaming system allowing players to compete with each other over the Internet.

- The Tri-Box System has a wholesale price of $270 that includes the physical Tri-Box module as well as a one-year subscription to the Tri-Net of Internet-based games and other applications.
- TrueTech sells one-year subscriptions to the Tri-Net separately for $50 to owners of Tri-Box modules as well as owners of other gaming systems.
- TrueTech does not sell a Tri-Box module without the initial one-year Tri-Net subscription, but estimates that it would charge $250 per module if modules were sold alone.

CompStores orders 1,000 Tri-Box Systems at the normal wholesale price of $270.

- CompStores places its order on May 10, 2013, promising payment within 30 days after delivery. TrueTech or CompStores can cancel the order at any time prior to delivery without penalty.
- TrueTech delivers the Tri-Boxes to CompStores on May 20, 2013.

Is the TrueTech arrangement with CompStores a contract for purposes of revenue recognition? Yes, but only as of May 20, the date TrueTech delivers the systems to CompStores.

1. **Commercial substance.** The contract will affect TrueTech's cash flows.
2. **Approval.** TrueTech and CompStores both approved the contract.
3. **Rights.** Each party's rights are specified–TrueTech will deliver the Tri-Boxes and one-year subscriptions to Tri-Net; CompStores will pay $270 per unit.
4. **Payment terms.** The terms and manner of payment are specified—CompStores will pay the full balance within 30 days of delivery.
5. **Performance.** Prior to delivery, both parties can cancel the order without penalty, so the arrangement doesn't qualify as a contract for purposes of revenue recognition. Once TrueTech makes delivery, one party has performed a part of the contract, so the contract exists as of that date for purposes of revenue recognition.

Current GAAP requires persuasive evidence of an arrangement, which is similar to the idea of an enforceable contract in the proposed ASU, so for most arrangements this step will not change existing revenue recognition practice.

## Step 2: Identify the Performance Obligation(s)

Once a contract is identified, the next step is to determine what separate **performance obligation(s)** the seller must satisfy to fulfill the contract. A contract could obligate a seller to provide multiple goods and services. For example, when **Verizon** signs up a new cell phone customer, the sales contract could require delivery of a smart phone, delivery of the related software, and provision of a warranty on the phone, ongoing network access, and optional future upgrades.

*Performance obligations are promises to transfer goods and services to the buyer.*

Sellers account for performance obligations separately if the performance obligations are **distinct**. A performance obligation is distinct if either:

1. the seller regularly sells the good or service separately, or
2. a buyer could use the good or service on its own or in combination with goods or services the buyer could obtain elsewhere.

*Performance obligations are accounted for separately if they are distinct.*

In Illustration 5–21 we apply these criteria in determining the separate performance obligations for our TrueTech example.

If performance obligations are distinct, we account for them separately. The idea is to identify parts of contracts that can be viewed on a stand-alone basis, so that the financial statements can capture the transfer of separate goods and services and the profit margin that is attributable to each one.

Assume the same facts as in Illustration 5–20. What distinct performance obligations exist in the TrueTech contract with CompStores?

Although TrueTech does not sell the module separately, the module would have a function to the buyer in combination with games and subscription services the buyer could obtain elsewhere. The Tri-Net subscription is sold separately. Therefore, the module and subscription are distinct, and the contract has two separate performance obligations: (1) delivery of Tri-Box modules, and (2) fulfillment of Tri-Net subscriptions via access to the Tri-Net network over a one-year period.

**Illustration 5–21**
Determining If Performance Obligations Are Distinct

Sometimes, though, a *bundle* of goods and services is treated as a single performance obligation. That occurs if both of the following two criteria are met:

1. The goods or services in the bundle are highly interrelated and the seller provides a significant service of integrating the goods or services into the combined item(s) delivered to a customer.
2. The bundle of goods or services is significantly modified or customized to fulfill the contract.

> A bundle of goods and services is viewed as a single performance obligation if the seller provides a significant integration service and significantly modifies the bundle to fulfill the contract.

For example, when a construction company integrates many goods and services to provide a finished building, we view the construction company as providing an integration service that is a single performance obligation.

Also, if multiple distinct goods or services have the same pattern of transfer to the customer, the seller can treat them as a single performance obligation. The proposed ASU provides this alternative to sellers as a practical way to simplify accounting for these arrangements.

Several common aspects of contracts make it difficult to identify separate performance obligations: prepayments, right of return, warranties, and options. We discuss each in turn.

## PREPAYMENTS

Some contracts may require up front payments associated with particular initial activities (for example, registration fees to join health clubs and activation fees for cell phone service). Prepayments are *not* separate performance obligations because they aren't a promise to transfer a product or service to a customer. Instead, the upfront fee is an advance payment for future products or services and should be included in the transaction price, allocated to the various performance obligations in the contract and recognized as revenue when each performance obligation is satisfied.

> A *prepayment* is not a separate performance obligation.

## RIGHT OF RETURN

In some industries it's common for a seller to give customers the right to return merchandise. A right of return is not a separate performance obligation. Instead, it represents a failure to satisfy the performance obligation to deliver satisfactory goods. As a result, sellers need to estimate the amount of product that will be returned and account for those returns as a reduction in revenue and as a refund liability. We discuss accounting for returns further in Chapter 7.

> A *right of return* is not a separate performance obligation.

## WARRANTIES

Most products are sold with a quality assurance warranty that obligates the seller for some period of time after the sale to make repairs or replace products that are later demonstrated to be defective. Quality assurance warranties can be stated explicitly, or can be implicit because of normal business practice. Quality assurance warranties are not separate performance obligations. Rather, they are viewed as a cost of satisfying the performance obligation to deliver products of acceptable quality. Therefore, the seller recognizes in the period of sale an expense and related contingent liability for these warranties. For example, Dell reports a quality assurance warranty liability of $895 million as of the end of fiscal 2011. We discuss accounting for warranties further in Chapter 13.

> A *quality assurance warranty* is not a separate performance obligation.

An *extended warranty* is a separate performance obligation.

Other warranties are offered as an additional, extended service that covers new problems arising after the buyer takes control of the product. You probably have been offered extended warranties for an additional charge when you purchased electronics, appliances, automobiles, or other products. Unlike quality-assurance warranties, extended warranties *do* qualify as separate performance obligations because they represent additional services that could be (and often are) sold separately. Like other separate performance obligations, extended warranties are allocated a portion of the transaction price at the start of the contract, and then that portion of the transaction price is recognized as revenue over the extended warranty period. **Dell** reports a liability for deferred extended warranty revenue of $6,416 million as of the end of fiscal 2011.

It can be difficult to determine whether a warranty is only providing assurance that the product was delivered free from defects (and so is a quality assurance warranty and only accrued as a cost) or provides an additional service much like insurance (and so is an extended warranty that is treated as a separate performance obligation). The proposed ASU indicates that a warranty qualifies as a separate performance obligation if either (a) the buyer has the option to purchase the warranty separately from the seller or (b) the warranty provides a service to the customer beyond only assuring that the seller delivered a product or service that was free from defects.

## CUSTOMER OPTIONS FOR ADDITIONAL GOODS OR SERVICES

An *option* for additional goods and services is a separate performance obligation if it confers a material right to the buyer.

Some contracts involve the seller granting to the buyer an option to receive additional goods or services at no cost or at a discount. These options include software upgrades, customer loyalty programs (frequent flier miles, points), and contract renewal options. These sorts of options are separate performance obligations if they provide a material right to the buyer that the buyer would not receive otherwise.

*GAAP Change*

Depending on the industry, we treat customer options very differently under the proposed ASU than under current GAAP. For example, when you purchase a plane ticket, you might also have some number of miles added to a frequent flier plan that you have with the airline. Under current GAAP most airlines don't recognize frequent flier plans as creating separate performance obligations, and so don't allocate any revenue to them. Rather, airlines typically recognize all of the ticket revenue when customers take their flights, and only accrue an expense and liability for the estimated incremental cost of redeeming frequent flier miles. Under the proposed ASU, frequent flier miles create a separate performance obligation for the airline, because customers can redeem them for free airfare or discounts on other products or services that they could not obtain for the same price otherwise. Therefore, some of the price of the airline ticket is allocated to the miles and only recognized as revenue when the airline satisfies the performance obligation associated with the miles (for example, by the passenger redeeming the miles or the miles expiring).

On the other hand, as indicated earlier in Chapter 5, customer options for software upgrades are already treated as separate performance obligations by **Apple** and other smartphone venders, which is consistent with the proposed ASU. One goal of the ASU is to remove such between-industry differences in revenue recognition practice.

More generally, the proposed ASU may identify multiple performance obligations in arrangements that current GAAP treats as a single product or service. Complex contracts in telecommunications, pharmaceutical research, media distribution, and other industries will need to be reevaluated to determine which performance obligations are distinct under the ASU.

## Step 3: Determine the Transaction Price

The *transaction price* is the amount the seller expects to be entitled to receive from the buyer in exchange for providing goods and services.

Determining the transaction price is simple if the buyer pays a fixed amount immediately or in the near future (remember Macy's' sale of a skirt to Susan?). However, in some contracts this determination is more difficult. Specific complications we discuss are variable consideration, time value of money, and collectibility of the transaction price.

### VARIABLE CONSIDERATION

Sometimes a transaction price is uncertain because some of the price is to be paid to the seller depending on future events. Such variable consideration occurs in many industries, including construction (incentive payments), entertainment and media (royalties), health care (Medicare and Medicaid reimbursements), manufacturing (volume discounts), and telecommunications (rebates).

The seller should include variable consideration in the transaction price by estimating it as either the probability-weighted amount or the most likely amount, depending on which better predicts the amount that the seller will receive.[45] If there are many possible outcomes, a probability-weighted amount will be more appropriate. On the other hand, if there are only two outcomes, the most likely amount might be the best indication of the amount the seller will likely receive. Illustration 5–22 provides an example.

*Variable consideration is estimated as either the probability-weighted amount or the most likely amount.*

**Illustration 5–22**

Accounting for Variable Consideration

TrueTech enters into a contract with ProSport Gaming to add ProSport's online games to the Tri-Net network. ProSport will pay TrueTech an up front $300,000 fixed fee for six months of featured access, as well as a $200,000 bonus if Tri-Net users access ProSport products for at least 15,000 hours during the six-month period. TrueTech estimates a 75% chance that it will achieve the usage target and earn the $200,000 bonus.

TrueTech would make the following entry at contract inception to record receipt of the cash:

| | | |
|---|---|---|
| Cash ....................................... | 300,000 | |
| Unearned Revenue....... | | 300,000 |

**Probability-Weighted Amount**

A probability-weighted transaction price would be calculated as follows:

| Possible Amounts | Probabilities | | | Expected Amounts |
|---|---|---|---|---|
| $500,000 ($300,000 + 200,000) | × 75% | = | | $375,000 |
| $300,000 ($300,000 + 0) | × 25% | = | | 75,000 |
| Expected contract price at inception | | | | $450,000 |

**Most Likely Amount**

The most likely amount of bonus is $200,000, so a transaction price based on the most likely amount would be $300,000 + 200,000, or $500,000.

In this case, it is likely that TrueTech would use the estimate based on the most likely amount, $500,000, because only two outcomes are possible, and it is likely that the bonus will be received. In each successive month, TrueTech would recognize one month's revenue based on a total transaction price of $500,000, reducing unearned revenue and recognizing bonus receivable:

| | | |
|---|---|---|
| Unearned revenue ($300,000 ÷ 6 months)........ | 50,000 | |
| Bonus receivable (to balance) ............................ | 33,333 | |
| Revenue ($500,000 ÷ 6 months)[46].............. | | 83,333 |

After six months, TrueTech's Unearned revenue account would be reduced to a zero balance, and the Bonus receivable would have a balance of $200,000 ($33,333 × 6). At that point TrueTech would know if the usage of ProSport products had reached the bonus threshold and would make one of the following two journal entries:

| If TrueTech receives the bonus: | | If TrueTech does not receive bonus: | |
|---|---|---|---|
| Cash............................ 200,000 | | Revenue....................... 200,000 | |
| Bonus receivable..... | 200,000 | Bonus receivable...... | 200,000 |

This treatment of variable consideration is a significant departure from current GAAP, by which we typically only recognize revenue associated with variable consideration when the

*GAAP Change*

---

[45]Normally, sellers receive cash consideration, but sometimes sellers receive noncash consideration instead, like property or other assets. In those circumstances, the seller measures the noncash consideration at fair value.

[46]If TrueTech instead used the probability-weighted transaction price, the journal entries would be the same except that the amount of revenue recognized each month would be $75,000 ($450,000 ÷ 6 months) and the amount of bonus receivable accrued each month would be $25,000 (to balance).

uncertainty associated with the consideration has been resolved. Under the proposed ASU sellers might recognize revenue earlier and in different amounts than under current guidance.

## THE TIME VALUE OF MONEY

It's common for contracts to specify that payment occurs before or after delivery. A sale of a product on account, for instance, calls for the customer to pay for the product *after* it's been delivered. In that case, the seller can be viewed as loaning money to the buyer for the period in which the receivable is outstanding. On the other hand, when payment occurs significantly *before* delivery, the buyer can be viewed as loaning money to the seller in addition to buying goods or services from the seller.

If delivery and payment occur relatively near each other, the time value of money is not significant and it can be ignored. However, if the time value of money is significant, a sales transaction is viewed as including two parts: a delivery component (for goods or services) and a financing component (either interest paid to the buyer in the case of a prepayment or to the seller in the case of a receivable). Illustration 5–23 shows the accounting for the prepayment and receivable cases.

An obvious question is *when* a financing component is considered significant. Certainly, it's a matter of professional judgment, but there are indicators that might suggest

> The time value of money is not considered *significant* if delivery and payment occur within one year of each other.

## Illustration 5—23 Accounting for the Time Value of Money

On January 1, 2013, TrueTech enters into a contract with GameStop Stores to deliver four Tri-Box modules that have a fair value of $1,000.

- *Prepayment Case:* GameStop pays TrueTech $907 on January 1, 2013, and TrueTech agrees to deliver the modules on December 31, 2014. GameStop pays significantly in advance of delivery, such that TrueTech is viewed as borrowing money from GameStop and TrueTech incurs interest *expense*.
- *Receivable Case:* TrueTech delivers the modules on January 1, 2013, and GameStop agrees to pay TrueTech $1,000 on December 31, 2014. TrueTech delivers the modules significantly in advance of payment, such that TrueTech is viewed as loaning money to GameStop and TrueTech earns interest *revenue*.

The fiscal year-end for both companies is December 31. The time value of money in both cases is 5%. The following table compares TrueTech's accounting for the contract between the two cases (ignoring the entry for cost of goods sold):

| Prepayment (payment *before* delivery) | | | Receivable (payment *after* delivery) | | |
|---|---|---|---|---|---|
| **January 1, 2013** | | | **January 1, 2013** | | |
| *When prepayment occurs:* | | | *When delivery occurs:* | | |
| Cash............................................ | 907* | | Accounts receivable ................................ | 1,000 | |
|     Unearned revenue............................ | | 907 |     Revenue ........................................... | | 1,000 |
| **December 31, 2013** | | | **December 31, 2013** | | |
| *Accrual of year 1 interest expense:* | | | *Accrual of year 1 interest revenue:* | | |
| Interest expense ($907 × 5%)................. | 45 | | Accounts receivable ............................. | 50 | |
|     Unearned revenue............................ | | 45 |     Interest revenue ($1000 × 5%) ........ | | 50 |
| **December 31, 2014** | | | **December 31, 2014** | | |
| *When subsequent delivery occurs:* | | | *When subsequent payment occurs:* | | |
| Interest expense ($952 × 5%) ................ | 48 | | Cash....................................................... | 1,103** | |
| Unearned revenue................................. | 952 | |     Interest revenue ($1050 × 5%) ........ | | 53 |
|     Revenue ........................................... | | 1,000 |     Accounts receivable........................ | | 1,050 |

*$907 = $1000 × .90703 (present value of $1, n = 2, I = 5%; from Table 2)
**Note that in the prepayment case TrueTech receives less cash from GameStop than it receives in the receivables case. That is because TrueTech is paying interest to GameStop in the prepayment case, but is receiving interest from GameStop in the receivables case.

significance. If the customer would pay a substantially different amount if it paid cash at the time the good or service was delivered, the financing component is likely significant. Also, the financing component is more likely to be significant as the time between delivery and payment increases, or if the interest rate implicit in the contract is large. As a practical matter, sellers can assume the financing component is not significant if the period between delivery and payment is less than a year.

Current GAAP typically accounts for the time value of money for long-term receivables, but not for customer prepayments. For example, if the prepayment case in Illustration 5–23 were handled under current GAAP, the journal entry at delivery would not recognize any interest expense, and instead would simply debit unearned revenue and credit revenue for $907. Under the proposed ASU, the seller recognizes more revenue but also more interest expense than it does currently.

*GAAP Change*

We discuss the time value of money concept further in Chapter 6.

## COLLECTIBILITY OF THE TRANSACTION PRICE

Whenever sales are made on credit, there is some potential for bad debts. Under the proposed ASU, an estimate is made of the amount of bad debts, and that amount is treated as a contra-revenue, similar to how sales returns are treated in current GAAP. The estimated amount of bad debts is presented in the income statement as a separate line item immediately below gross revenue that reduces gross revenue to a net amount.

This treatment of collectibility of the transaction price differs from current GAAP in two important ways. First, under the proposed ASU, collectibility does not affect *whether* revenue is recognized. Current GAAP requires that there be reasonable certainty as to the collectibility of the asset to be received before revenue can be recognized. Otherwise, revenue is deferred and recognized under the installment method, cost recovery method, or when collectibility becomes reasonably assured. The ASU eliminates this criterion for revenue recognition, and as a consequence eliminates the installment and cost recovery methods.

*GAAP Change*

Second, under the proposed ASU, bad debts are shown as a contra-revenue, rather than as an expense. This change does not affect how bad debts are estimated, but does affect how they appear in the income statement. Under current GAAP bad debt expense is typically shown as part of selling, general, and administrative expenses ("SG&A"), below the gross profit line.[47] Under the proposed ASU, bad debts are deducted from gross revenue, similar to how sales returns are treated currently, before showing net revenue and before calculating gross profit.

We discuss accounting for bad debts further in Chapter 7.

## Step 4: Allocate the Transaction Price to the Performance Obligations

If an arrangement has more than one separate performance obligation, the seller allocates the transaction price to the separate performance obligations in proportion to the stand-alone selling price of the goods or services underlying those performance obligations.[48] If the seller can't observe actual stand-alone selling prices, the seller should estimate them. Illustration 5–24 provides an example.

The transaction price is allocated to separate performance obligations in proportion to their *relative stand-alone selling prices.*

Sometimes the stand-alone selling price of a good or service underlying a performance obligation is uncertain. In that case, a seller might estimate the stand-alone selling price of that performance obligation using the residual technique, by subtracting the stand-alone selling prices of the other performance obligations from the total contract price. Illustration 5–25 provides an example.

The *residual* technique is used to estimate a stand-alone selling price that is very uncertain.

---

[47]An exception is that recently GAAP changed to require some health care providers to display bad debts as a reduction of gross revenues, similar to how the proposed ASU would require bad debts to be displayed for all companies. This change is discussed more fully in "Presentation and Disclosure of Patient Service Revenue, Provision for Bad Debts, and the Allowance for Doubtful Accounts for Certain Health Care Entities" *Accounting Standards Update 2011-7* (Norwalk, Conn: FASB, 2011).

[48]A contractually stated "list price" doesn't necessarily represent a stand-alone selling price. The seller has to reference stand-alone selling prices, or estimate those prices.

**Illustration 5–24**

Allocating Transaction Price to Performance Obligations Based on Relative Selling Prices

Recall the initial data for the TrueTech example from Illustration 5–20:

- The Tri-Box System has a wholesale price of $270, which includes the physical Tri-Box console as well as a one-year subscription to the Tri-Net of Internet-based games and other applications.
- Owners of Tri-Box modules as well as other game consoles can purchase one-year subscriptions to the Tri-Net from TrueTech for $50.
- TrueTech does not sell a Tri-Box module without the initial one-year Tri-Net subscription, but estimates that it would charge $250 per unit if it chose to do so.

CompStores orders 1,000 Tri-Boxes at the normal wholesale price of $270. Because the standalone price of the Tri-Box module ($250) represents $5/6$ of the total fair values ($250 ÷ [$250 + 50]), and the Tri-Net subscription comprises $1/6$ of the total ($50 ÷ [$250 + 50]), we allocate $5/6$ of the transaction price to the Tri-Boxes and $1/6$ of the transaction price to the Tri-Net subscriptions. Accordingly, TrueTech would recognize the following journal entry (ignoring any entry to record the reduction in inventory and the corresponding cost of goods sold):

| | | |
|---|---|---|
| Accounts receivable ..................................................... | 270,000 | |
| Revenue ($270,000 × $5/6$) ......................................... | | 225,000 |
| Unearned revenue ($270,000 × $1/6$)....................... | | 45,000 |

TrueTech then converts the unearned revenue to revenue over the one-year term of the Tri-Net subscription as that revenue is earned.

**Illustration 5–25**

Allocating Transaction Price to Performance Obligations Using the Residual Technique

Assume the same facts as Illustration 5–24, except that there is no basis on which to estimate the value of the one-year Tri-Net subscription. In that case, the value of the subscription would be estimated as follows:

| | |
|---|---|
| Total price of Tri-Box with Tri-Net subscription | $270,000 |
| Estimated price of Tri-Box sold without subscription ($250 × 1,000) | 250,000 |
| Estimated price of Tri-Net subscription | $ 20,000 |

Based on these relative stand-alone selling prices, if CompStores orders 1,000 Tri-Boxes at the normal wholesale price of $270, TrueTech would recognize the following journal entry (ignoring any entry to record the reduction in inventory and corresponding cost of goods sold):

| | | |
|---|---|---|
| Accounts receivable ..................................................... | 270,000 | |
| Revenue ($270,000 × 250/270)............................. | | 250,000 |
| Unearned revenue ($270,000 × 20/250)............... | | 20,000 |

TrueTech would convert the unearned revenue to revenue over the one-year term of the Tri-Net subscription.

A contract might include a provision that specifies that the transaction price will change depending on some aspect of future performance. For example, the total price of a consulting service might depend on how successful that service is. Or, the contract price might be changed by mutual agreement. In general, the seller allocates resulting price changes to all the performance obligations in the contract in the same proportions that were used at the beginning of the contract. However, if the price change relates specifically to the seller's efforts to satisfy one particular performance obligation, the entire price change is allocated to that particular performance obligation only.[49]

Similarly, a contract might be modified by mutual agreement between the buyer and seller to add or change performance obligations. If goods and services yet to be transferred are distinct from previously satisfied performance obligations in the contract, the seller

---

[49]If an amount is allocated to a performance obligation that has already been completed, the amount is recognized by increasing or decreasing revenue.

allocates any remaining transaction price to the remaining performance obligations as if the prior contract was terminated and a new contract created. On the other hand, if remaining goods and services are not distinct, and instead are part of a single, partially satisfied performance obligation, the seller simply updates the transaction price and recognizes whatever amount of revenue is necessary to reflect the revised progress toward completion.

Overall, the allocation of transaction price to performance obligations required by the proposed ASU is very similar to what is used for multiple-element arrangements in current GAAP. However, important differences will occur in particular industries that currently have specialized revenue recognition approaches. For example, as discussed earlier in Chapter 5, current GAAP for software contracts requires vendor-specific objective evidence (VSOE) of stand-alone selling prices in order to allocate the transaction price to multiple deliverables. The proposed ASU would allow the use of estimated selling prices for these arrangements. Also, the proposed ASU would once again allow the residual technique for allocating revenue. GAAP disallowed that technique in 2009.[50]

*GAAP Change*

## Step 5: Recognize Revenue When (Or As) Each Performance Obligation Is Satisfied

In general, a seller recognizes revenue allocated to each performance obligation when it satisfies the performance obligation. We first discuss performance obligations that are satisfied over time, and then discuss performance obligations that are satisfied at a point in time. After that, we discuss an important limitation on the amount of revenue that can be recognized for goods and services during a long-term contract.

### PERFORMANCE OBLIGATIONS SATISFIED OVER TIME

Services such as lending money, performing audits, and providing consulting advice all are performed over a period of time. Also, many construction contracts are long-term in nature. So when can a seller recognize revenue over time, as such activities are performed, rather than waiting until performance has been completed?

**Performance obligations of services can be satisfied at one time or continuously.**

**Determining whether a performance obligation is satisfied over time.**   As shown in Illustration 5–26, the proposed ASU specifies criteria for determining whether a seller is satisfying a performance obligation over time.

---

**A performance obligation is satisfied *over time* if at least one of the following two criteria is met:**

1. **The seller is creating or enhancing an asset that the buyer controls as the service is performed.** This criterion captures many types of long-term construction arrangements in which the buyer owns the work-in-process as it is constructed by the seller.

OR

2. **The seller is not creating an asset that the buyer controls or that has alternative use to the seller, and *at least one* of the following conditions hold:**

   a. **The buyer simultaneously receives and consumes a benefit as the seller performs.** For example, this condition would be met by a technical support service that provides answers as questions are received.

   b. **Another seller would not need to reperform the tasks performed to date if that other seller were to fulfill the remaining obligation.** For example, a transportation company that ships goods across the country would qualify under this condition.

   c. **The seller has the right to payment for performance even if the buyer could cancel the contract, and it expects to fulfill the contract.** Many service contracts include this provision.

**Illustration 5–26**
Determining Whether a Performance Obligation Is Satisfied Over Time

When a performance obligation is satisfied over time, service revenue is recognized in proportion to the amount of service performed.

If a performance obligation meets at least one of the criteria listed in Illustration 5–26, we recognize revenue over time, in proportion to the amount of the performance obligation that

---

[50]The residual method is not currently permitted under GAAP as per *Accounting Standards Update 2009-13* codified in ASC 605-25-30-3

has been satisfied. For instance, if, say, one-third of a service has been performed, one-third of the performance obligation has been satisfied, so one-third of the revenue should be recognized. If none of the criteria in Illustration 5–26 is met, we recognize revenue at the point in time when the performance obligation has been completely satisfied.

The criteria in Illustration 5–26 seem broad enough to include many service contracts. So, what doesn't qualify? As an example, consider a market research firm that develops a market analysis for a consumer electronics company. The market research firm receives payment when the report is delivered to the customer, but other companies in the industry could purchase the market research. This case doesn't satisfy the first criterion in Illustration 5–26, because the buyer does not control the market research as it is being produced. It doesn't satisfy the second criterion in Illustration 5–26, because the seller has an alternate use for the report (the seller can sell it to other companies in the industry). Therefore, the performance obligation is not being satisfied over time, and the market research firm will wait until the report is delivered before recognizing revenue.

Long-term construction contracts typically are viewed as services that are provided continuously to the buyer.

Most long-term construction contracts qualify for revenue recognition over time under these criteria. Many contracts are structured such that the buyer owns the work-in-process (WIP) as it is constructed, which satisfies the first criterion. Also, even if the buyer doesn't own the WIP during construction, the second criterion is satisfied if the asset the seller is creating has no alternate use to the seller and another seller would not have to reperform the work done to date if that other seller were to finish the contract. If the construction contract qualifies for revenue recognition over time, the 'percentage-of-completion' method described in the chapter can be used to account simultaneously for the asset as it is being constructed and the accounts receivable due from the customer. If instead, revenue must be deferred until construction is completed, the completed contract method is used.

*GAAP Change*

The criteria for satisfying a performance obligation over time differ from current GAAP in important ways. For example, as discussed earlier in Chapter 5, under current GAAP a long-term construction contract is always accounted for under the percentage-of-completion method (which recognizes revenue over time) unless the seller can't make accurate estimates of revenues, costs, and progress toward completion. Under the proposed ASU, revenue recognition over time depends on various characteristics of the sales contract. So, the proposed ASU might allow revenue recognition over time when current GAAP would not. The reverse also could be true, with current GAAP allowing revenue recognition over time that the proposed ASU does not permit.

Also, the proposed ASU may encourage sellers to view as integration services some transactions that current GAAP typically views as product sales. For example, a manufacturing contract in which the manufacturer produces goods to a customer's specifications could be viewed as a manufacturing service. Depending on the specifics of the contract, the manufacturer could recognize revenue over time as the product is manufactured. Under current GAAP such manufacturers typically recognize revenue upon delivery.

**Determining progress toward completion.** The seller can recognize revenue over time only if it can reasonably measure progress toward completion. The seller needs to adopt a method for estimating how much transfer has occurred to determine how much revenue to recognize. As under current GAAP with respect to the percentage-of-completion method, sellers should choose a method that accurately depicts the transfer of goods or services while also being cost-effective to implement. As discussed in chapter 5, either output or input methods can be used for this purpose.

Input and output methods are used to estimate progress toward completion when performance obligations are satisfied over time.

Illustration 5–27 continues our TrueTech example from Illustration 5–24, showing how TrueTech recognizes revenue as its Tri-Net service obligation is satisfied over time.

Two other aspects of determining progress towards completion are emphasized in the proposed ASU. First, sometimes a contract involves a seller buying goods from another company and transferring them to a customer significantly prior to actually providing services to the customer. For example, a construction contractor might acquire materials and ship them to the job site well in advance of actually providing construction services. Second, sometimes a seller lacks the ability to make a reasonable estimate of its the progress towards completion, but expects to be able to at least recover its the costs on the contract. In each of those cases, the proposed ASU indicates that the seller should only recognize an amount of revenue equal to the cost of the goods. This approach is basically the "cost recovery" or "zero profit" method described in Chapter 5.

**Illustration 5–27**
Satisfying a Performance
Obligation Over Time

Recall that TrueTech recorded the following journal entry to recognize the sale of 1,000 Tri-Box systems:

| | | |
|---|---|---|
| Accounts receivable ($270 × 1,000)............................. | 270,000 | |
| Revenue ($270,000 × ⁵/₆)........................................ | | 225,000 |
| Unearned revenue ($270,000 × ¹/₆)........................ | | 45,000 |

TrueTech recognized $225,000 of revenue immediately because it had fulfilled the performance obligation to transfer 1,000 Tri-Box modules, but recognized an unearned revenue liability for $45,000 associated with the performance obligation to provide those customers access to the Tri-Net for a one-year period. The Tri-Net subscriptions qualify for revenue recognition over time under Illustration 5–26's criterion 2a ("The customer simultaneously receives and consumes a benefit as the seller performs"), because Tri-Net subscribers receive benefit each day by having access to the Tri-Net network. Therefore, in each of the 12 months following sale, TrueTech would make the following entry to recognize Tri-Net subscription revenue:

| | | |
|---|---|---|
| Unearned revenue ($45,000 × ¹/₁₂).............................. | 3,750 | |
| Revenue .................................................................. | | 3,750 |

After 12 months TrueTech will have recognized all of the Tri-Net subscription revenue associated with this contract and the unearned revenue liability would be reduced to zero.

## PERFORMANCE OBLIGATIONS SATISFIED AT A POINT IN TIME

If a performance obligation is not satisfied over time, it is satisfied at a single point in time, when the seller **transfers control** of goods to the buyer. Often transfer of control is obvious and coincides with delivery, as in our Macy's example when Susan leaves the store with her purchased skirt. In other circumstances, though, transfer of control is not as clear. Illustration 5–28 lists five key indicators that should be considered when judging whether control of a good has passed from the seller to the buyer, but sellers also should consider whether other indicators are appropriate.

*Performance obligations of goods are satisfied when the seller transfers control of goods to the buyer.*

**Illustration 5–28**
Key Indicators of
Transfer of Control

**Key indicators that control of a good has passed from the seller to the buyer:**

1. **Buyer has an unconditional obligation to pay.** An obligation to pay is unconditional if its only requirement is the passage of time.
2. **Buyer has legal title.** Legal title typically indicates which party has the ability to direct the use of, and receive the benefit from, a good.[51]
3. **Buyer has physical possession.** Buyers typically control the goods they possess.
4. **Buyer assumes risks and rewards of ownership.** Risks include suffering loss if the good is stolen or damaged; rewards include benefiting from increase in the value of the good.
5. **The buyer has accepted the asset.** Acceptance indicates the buyer has obtained the benefits of owning the asset.

Two common situations in which transfer of control is not the same as transfer of the physical goods are (1) bill-and-hold arrangements and (2) consignment sales. Bill-and-hold arrangements, in which a seller bills the buyer but does not ship the product until a later date, typically won't satisfy these indicators until shipment to the buyer actually occurs. Consignment sales, in which a seller ships inventory that it still owns to an intermediary for resale, typically won't satisfy these indicators until sale by the intermediary to a buyer occurs.

Some contractual arrangements involve one business paying a licensing fee for the right to use another business's intellectual property. These arrangements are common in the software, technology, media and entertainment (including motion pictures and music) industries. The performance obligation associated with a license or other rights of use is satisfied at the point in time that the buyer has the use of the rights. Therefore, the beginning of a license agreement is the point in time when revenue is recognized.

---

[51]In some circumstances sellers retain title in case the buyer does not follow through on some aspect of the contract. In those circumstances, retaining title is a "protective right" and doesn't necessarily indicate control.

## KEY LIMITATION ON CUMULATIVE AMOUNT OF REVENUE THAT CAN BE RECOGNIZED

When a contract includes uncertain consideration to be received from a customer, you learned earlier in this supplement that the transaction price is measured as either (a) the most likely amount or (b) a probability-weighted estimate of the amount that eventually should be received. Consequently, the transaction price includes uncertain amounts that are allocated to performance obligations and then recognized as revenue when the performance obligations are satisfied. However, the proposed ASU limits the cumulative amount of revenue that may be recognized under a contract to the amount to which the seller is reasonably assured to be entitled. Reasonable assurance exists only if the seller has experience or other evidence with similar types of performance obligations that can predict the amount of consideration to which the seller will be entitled when it satisfies the performance obligations. The word "entitled" is important, because it highlights that the uncertainty here is with the amounts the seller is owed, not uncertainty about whether the account will prove uncollectible. Circumstances in which a seller would *not* be reasonably assured to be entitled to an amount include:

- The customer could avoid paying an amount without breaching the contract (for example, not pay a sales-based royalty by not making sales).
- The seller lacks experience selling similar products and doesn't have evidence with which to estimate uncertain amounts.
- The uncertain amounts are very hard to estimate due to susceptibility to factors outside the seller's control, the uncertainty resolving only far in the future, or there being a high number of possible outcomes.

Illustration 5–29 demonstrates how this cumulative limitation would be applied.

**Illustration 5–29**

Applying the Cumulative Limitation on Revenue Recognition

> ChemCo sells Juniper Inc. a piece of specialized manufacturing equipment. The sales agreement specifies that Juniper will pay ChemCo a $50,000 fixed payment upon delivery of the equipment plus a 5% royalty on sales of products made using the equipment. ChemCo's probability-weighted estimate of royalties is $150,000, so the transaction price is estimated to be $200,000 ($50,000 + 150,000).
>
> Upon delivery of the equipment, ChemCo recognizes revenue of only $50,000, because it is not reasonably assured of receiving the other $150,000. ChemCo would recognize the remaining revenue as Juniper records sales and ChemCo becomes reasonably assured of being entitled to its 5% royalty on sold items.

This cumulative limitation actually reduces the difference between current GAAP and the proposed ASU. Current GAAP typically does not allow recognition of revenue associated with variable consideration until all relevant uncertainty has been resolved. The proposed ASU includes variable consideration in the transaction price and so includes it in revenue recognition. The cumulative limitation means that we would defer revenue recognition if an uncertain amount is very difficult to estimate or if the customer potentially could avoid owing it, similar to how we account for that circumstance under current GAAP.

## Additional Considerations

### CONTRACT ACQUISITION AND FULFILLMENT COSTS

For contracts lasting over one year, sellers are allowed to capitalize (record as an asset) incremental costs of obtaining a contract, such as sales commissions, that the company would not have incurred if it had not obtained the contract. Sellers also can capitalize other costs that relate directly to satisfying performance obligations under the contract in the future, so long as the seller expects those costs to be recovered. The resulting asset is amortized over the period the goods and services are transferred to the customer. Like other intangible assets, this one also is tested for impairment. We briefly discuss this intangible asset in Chapter 10 and its amortization and impairment testing in Chapter 11.

## ONEROUS PERFORMANCE OBLIGATIONS

Sometimes a seller anticipates losing money on a performance obligation. The proposed ASU may require the seller to recognize a liability and expense for such an *onerous* performance obligation under some circumstances. Specifically, if the onerous performance obligation is to be settled over a period of greater than one year, a liability and expense are recorded for an amount equal to the lowest cost of settling the performance obligation minus the amount of the transaction price that has been allocated to it. In subsequent periods the seller increases or decreases the liability (with an offsetting entry to expense) until the performance obligation eventually is satisfied. We also discuss accounting for onerous performance obligations in Chapter 13.

*Onerous* performance obligations satisfied over a period of time greater than one year produce a liability and expense.

## DISCLOSURE

The proposed ASU significantly expands the disclosure requirements associated with revenue recognition. For example, sellers must describe the significant judgments they use to (a) allocate transaction prices to performance obligations and (b) determine when performance obligations have been satisfied. Sellers also must disaggregate their revenue into categories, maybe product lines of goods or services, geographic regions, types of customers, or types of contracts. The choice of category should be the one that best indicates how the amount, timing, and uncertainty of the revenues and cash flows are affected by economic factors.

*GAAP Change*

A significant provision of the new guidance is the requirement for plentiful disclosures regarding a company's revenues.

Sellers should describe their outstanding performance obligations, discuss how performance obligations typically are satisfied, and describe important contractual terms like payment terms and policies for refunds, returns, and warranties. Sellers also must reconcile the beginning and ending balances of contract assets, contract liabilities, and liabilities for onerous performance obligations.

The objective of these disclosures is to help users of financial statements understand the amount, timing, and uncertainty of revenue and cash flows arising from contracts with customers. Of course, the downside of these disclosures is that sellers also are providing information to key competitors, suppliers, and customers.

## Concept Review Exercise

Four Flags Fitness sold 100 memberships with the following characteristics:

ACCOUNTING FOR REVENUE IN SINGLE-PERIOD CONTRACTS

- Members pay a $150 annual fee to cover the administrative costs of registering them in the Four Flags system.
- Members then pay an additional $400 in four equal quarterly installments of $100. The first installment is due at membership signing, and the other installments are due in 3, 6, and 9 months, paid by automatic withdrawal from bank accounts (so historically bad debts have been immaterial).
- Members have unlimited use of fitness equipment, spa and locker-rooms.
- Members also have access to Four Flags' health-oriented snack bar, but have the same access as and pay the same prices there that are paid by nonmembers.
- Each annual membership also includes a coupon for a complimentary session with a personal fitness trainer. Those sessions normally cost $50 per hour. On average 50 percent of members make use of a session.
- Each annual membership also includes access to the "Fit Buddies" website, featuring online content and social networking. Annual subscriptions to Fit Buddies cost $100 for nonmembers.
- Comparable gym memberships that lack complimentary fitness sessions or access to websites have an annual fee of $500.

**Required:**

1. Determine whether a gym membership constitutes a contract for purposes of applying revenue recognition criteria.

2. Identify the separate performance obligations in the contract.

3. Determine the transaction price.

4. Allocate the transaction price to the separate performance obligations, and prepare a journal entry to record the initial sale of 100 memberships.

5. Assume 14 members use their coupon for a complimentary session of fitness training. Prepare a journal entry to record the revenue earned at the end of one month.

**Solution:**

1. Determine whether each gym membership constitutes a contract for purposes of applying revenue recognition criteria.

   Applying the criteria in Illustration 2, each gym membership is a contract for purposes of applying revenue recognition criteria. Specifically:

   a. The contract will affect Four Flags' cash flows, so has commercial substance.

   b. Members and Four Flags both indicate contract approval.

   c. The contract clearly specifies contractual rights and obligations.

   d. The contract clearly specifies payment terms.

   e. Member prepayment constitutes performance by the member, so the contract is not wholly unperformed.

2. Identify the separate performance obligations in the contract.

   - Access to gym facilities, provision of a session of fitness training, and access to the Fit Buddies website all are separate performance obligations, as those services are sold separately.

   - Registering members in Four Flags' administrative system is not a performance obligation, as it does not transfer a service to a customer.

   - Access to the snack bar is not a performance obligation, as the access is not a material right beyond the rights of a nonmember.

3. Determine the transaction price.

   The transaction price is the probability-weighted expected consideration of $550 (the $150 up-front fee plus $400 to be paid in quarterly installments).

4. Allocate the transaction price to the separate performance obligations, and prepare a journal entry to record the initial sale of 100 memberships.

   The stand-alone selling price of access to gym facilities is $500. The probability-weighted stand-alone selling price of the training session is $25 ($50 × 50%). The stand-alone selling price of the website is $100. So, the total of the stand-alone selling prices is $625 ($500 + $25 + $100). Therefore, the total transaction price of $550 would be allocated as follows:

   Gym access: $550 × ($500 ÷ $625) = $440.
   Training coupon: $550 × ($25 ÷ $625) = $22.
   Fit Buddies access: $550 × ($100 ÷ $625) = $88.

| | | |
|---|---|---|
| Cash ([$150 initial fee + $100 Q1 fee] × 100) | 25,000 | |
| Accounts receivable ($100 × 3 payments × 100 members) | 30,000 | |
|     Unearned revenue, gym ($440 × 100 members) | | 44,000 |
|     Unearned revenue, Fit Buds ($88 × 100 members) | | 8,800 |
|     Unearned revenue, training ($22 × 100 members) | | 2,200 |

5. Assume 14 members use their coupon for a complimentary session of fitness training. Prepare a journal entry to record the revenue earned at the end of one month.

   The journal entry recognizes revenue for one month of gym access, one month of training access, and an appropriate proportion of training revenue (With 50% usage, we would anticipate 100 members × 50% = 50 coupons to be exercised, yielding proportion of 14 ÷ 50 = 28% of anticipated training coupons used to date).

| | |
|---|---:|
| Unearned revenue, gym ($44,000 ÷ 12) | 3,667 |
| Unearned revenue, Fit Buds ($8,800 ÷ 12) | 733 |
| Unearned revenue, training ($2,200 × 28%) | 616 |
| Revenue (to balance) | 5,016 |

Respond to the questions, brief exercises, exercises, and problems in this Supplement with the presumption that the guidance provided by the proposed Accounting Standards Update is being applied.

# Questions For Review of Key Topics

**Q 5–22** What are the five key steps to recognizing revenue?

**Q 5–23** What characteristics make a good or service a separate performance obligation?

**Q 5–24** When does an option granted with the sale of a good or service give rise to a separate performance obligation in the contract?

**Q 5–25** On what basis is the transaction price of a contract allocated to the contract's separate performance obligations?

**Q 5–26** What indicators suggest that a performance obligation has been satisfied with respect to a good (merchandise)?

**Q 5–27** What determines whether a company can recognize revenue over time when constructing an asset for a customer?

# Brief Exercises

**BE 5–19**
Definition of a contract

Richter Landscaping writes an agreement with a customer indicating that it will provide future landscaping services at a date and price to be determined. Does this agreement meet the definition of a contract? Briefly explain your answer.

**BE 5–20**
Separate performance obligation

A car dealer sells a particular brand of luxury sedan to individual affluent customers. Is each sedan a separate performance obligation? Briefly explain your answer.

**BE 5–21**
Separate performance obligation

McAfee sells a subscription to its anti-virus software along with a subscription renewal option that allows renewal at half the prevailing price for a new subscription. Are the software and subscription renewal option separate performance obligations? Briefly explain your answer.

**BE 5–22**
Variable consideration

Leo Consulting writes a contract with Highgate University to restructure Highgate's processes for purchasing goods and services from suppliers. The contract promises that Leo will earn a fixed fee of $25,000, and earn an additional $10,000 if Highgate achieves $100,000 of cost savings. Leo estimates that there is a 50% chance that Highgate will achieve $100,000 of cost savings. Assuming Leo determines transaction price as the probability-weighted amount of expected consideration, what transaction price would Leo estimate for this contract?

**BE 5–23**
Allocating transaction price

Sarjit Systems sold software to a customer for $90,000. As part of the contract, Sarjit promises to provide "free" technical support over the following six months. Sarjit sells the same software without technical support for $80,000 and a stand-alone six-month technical support contract for $20,000, so these products would sell for $100,000 if sold separately. Prepare Sarjit's journal entry to record the sale of the software (ignore any potential entry to revenue or cost of sales).

**BE 5–24**
Long-term contracts

Assume Estate Construction is constructing a building for CyberB, an online retailing company. Under the construction agreement, if for some reason Estate could not complete construction, CyberB would own the partially completed building and could retain another construction company to complete the job. When should Estate recognize revenue, as the building is constructed or after construction is completed? Explain your answer.

**BE 5–25**
Time value of money

Patterson, Inc. receives a $10,000 payment two years in advance of delivering a completed novel. A five percent interest rate applies. How much revenue would Patterson recognize associated with delivery of the novel, assuming delivery occurs on time?

## Exercises

**E 5–31**
**Options**

Clarks Inc., a shoe retailer, sells boots in different styles. In early November the company starts selling "SunBoots" to customers for $70 per pair. Clarks obtains the boots from wholesalers for $40 per pair. As part of the sales contract, Clarks gives customers who participate in an online survey a 30 percent discount voucher for any additional purchases in the next 30 days. Clarks anticipates that approximately 20 percent of customers will complete the survey and utilize the coupon, purchasing an average of $100 of goods. Clarks intends to offer a 10 percent discount on all sales during the next 30 days as part of a seasonal promotion during the Thanksgiving holidays.

**Required:**
1. Determine whether the discount voucher by Clarks is a separate performance obligation.
2. Prepare a journal entry to record the sale of 1,000 pairs of SunBoots.

**E 5–32**
**Separate performance obligation, option, upfront fee**

A New York City daily newspaper called "Manhattan Today" charges an annual subscription fee of $150. Customers prepay their subscriptions, and receive 260 issues for an annual subscription. To attract more subscribers, the company offered new subscribers a coupon to receive a 40 percent discount on a ride through Central Park on a horse-drawn carriage. The list price of a carriage ride is $130 per hour. The company estimates that approximately 30% of the vouchers will be redeemed.

**Required:**
1. Can Manhattan Today recognize any of the $150 subscription fee as revenue upon receipt? Explain.
2. When will Manhattan Today recognize revenue associated with the $150 subscription price?
3. What separate performance obligations exist in this contract?
4. Prepare the journal entry to recognize sale of one new subscription, clearly identifying the revenue or unearned revenue associated with each distinct performance obligation.

**E 5–33**
**Separate performance obligation, licensing**

**Pfizer**, a large research-based pharmaceutical company, enters into a contract with a start-up biotechnology company called HealthPro and promises:
1. To grant HealthPro the exclusive rights to use Pfizer's Technology A for the life of its patent. The license gives HealthPro the exclusive right to market, distribute, and manufacture Drug B as developed using Technology A.
2. To assign four full-time equivalent employees to perform research and development services for HealthPro in a specially designated Pfizer lab facility. The primary objective of these services is to receive regulatory approval to market and distribute Drug B using Technology A.

HealthPro is required to use Pfizer's lab to perform the research and development services necessary to develop Drug B using Technology A, because the know how and expertise related to Technology A are proprietary to Pfizer and not available elsewhere.

**Required:**
Determine which parts of this contract are separate performance obligations. Explain your reasoning for each obligation.

**E 5–34**
**Variable consideration**

Thomas Consultants provided Bran Construction with assistance with implementing various cost-savings initiatives. Thomas' contract specifies that it will receive a flat rate of $50,000 and an additional $20,000 if Bran reaches a prespecified target amount of cost savings. Thomas estimates that there is a 20% chance that Bran will achieve the cost-savings target.

**Required:**
1. Assuming Thomas uses a probability-weighted transaction price, calculate the amount of the transaction price.
2. Assuming Thomas uses the most likely value as the transaction price, calculate the amount of the transaction price.
3. Assuming Thomas is trying to apply the revenue recognition rules most appropriately, do you think the company is more likely to use the probability-weighted amount or the most likely value? Briefly explain your answer.
4. Assume that Thomas provides a plan for Bran, but Bran is responsible for implementing it. Also assume that Thomas delivers the plan in the first quarter of the year, but Bran will be implementing the plan and determining total cost savings over the entire year. Should Thomas recognize the entire transaction price when it delivers the plan? Briefly explain your reasoning.

**E 5–35**
**Variable consideration**

On January 1, Seneca Asset Management enters into a contract with a client to provide fund management services for one year. The client is required to pay a fixed amount of $100,000 at the end of each quarter, plus 10 percent of the increase in the fund's value relative to an observable index at the end of the year. Assume the fund increased by $800,000 over the course of the year.

**Required:**
1. Prepare the journal entry to record the first fixed payment.
2. Prepare the journal entry to record any additional revenue beyond the $100,000 fixed payment at the end of the fourth quarter

**E 5–36**
Satisfaction of performance obligation

McDonald's enters into a contract to sell Billy Bear dolls for Toys4U Stores. Based on the contract, McDonald's displays the dolls in selected stores. Toys4U is not paid until the dolls have been sold by McDonald's, and unsold dolls are returned to Toys4U.

**Required:**
Determine whether Toys4U has satisfied its performance obligation when it delivers the dolls to McDonald's. Explain your answer.

**E 5–37**
Satisfaction of performance obligation

Cutler Education Corporation developed a software product to help children under age 12 to learn mathematics. The software contains two separate parts: Basic Level (Level I) and Intermediate Level (Level II). The list price of the software contains the access code only for Level I. Parents are eligible to purchase the access code for a higher level only if their children pass an exam created by software. The accounting period ends December 31.

Kerry purchases the software at a price of $50 for his child, Tom, on December 1, 2012. Suppose Tom passed the Level I test on December 31, 2012, and Kerry immediately purchased the access code for Level II part for Tom for an additional $10. Cutler licensed Level II to Kerry on the same day, December 31, but provides him the access code to Level II on January 10, 2013.

**Required:**
When would Cutler recognize revenue for the sale of Level I and II software?

**E 5–38**
Time value of money

Stewart receives a $20,000 payment three years in advance of a scheduled appearance as a graduation speaker at a major state university. A four percent interest rate applies.

**Required:**
1. Prepare the journal entry to record Stewart's initial receipt of the $20,000 payment.
2. Prepare journal entries to record any interest revenue or expense recognized by Stewart for years one, two and three of the contract.
3. Prepare a journal entry to record revenue when Stewart delivers his graduation speech.

## Problems

**P 5–16**
Upfront fees, separate performance obligations

Fit & Slim is a health club that offers members various gym services. F&S accounts reports.

**Required:**
1. Assume F&S offers a deal whereby enrolling in a new membership also entitles the member to receive a voucher redeemable for 25 percent off a year's worth of premium yoga classes. A new membership costs $800, and a year's worth of premium yoga costs an additional $600. F&S estimates that approximately 40 percent of the vouchers will be redeemed. F&S offers a 10 percent discount on all courses as part of its seasonal promotion strategy.
   a. Identify the separate performance obligations in the new member deal.
   b. Allocate the contract price to the separate performance obligations.
   c. Prepare the journal entry to recognize revenue for the sale of a new membership. Clearly identify revenue or unearned revenue associated with each distinct performance obligation.
2. Assume F&S offers a "Fit 50" coupon book with 50 prepaid visits over the next year. F&S has learned that Fit 50 purchasers make an average of 40 visits before the coupon book expires. A customer purchases a Fit 50 book by paying $500 in advance, and for any additional visit over 50 during the year after the book is purchased, the customer can pay a $15 visitation fee. Depending on the season, F&S typically charges between $12 and $18 to nonmembers who wish to work out on a single day.
   a. Identify the separate performance obligations in the Fit 50 member deal.
   b. Allocate the contract price to the separate performance obligations.
   c. Prepare the journal entry to recognize revenue for the sale of a new Fit 50 book. When will F&S recognize revenue associated with people using its Fit 50 plans?

**P 5–17**
Satisfying performance obligations

Consider each of the following scenarios separately, assuming the company accounts for the arrangement:
   **Scenario 1:** Crown Construction Company enters into a contract with Star Hotel for building a highly sophisticated, customized conference room to be completed for a fixed price of $400,000. Nonrefundable progress payments are made on a monthly basis for work completed during the month. Legal title to the conference room

equipment is held by Crown until the end of the construction project, but if the contract is terminated before the conference room is finished, the Hotel retains the partially completed job and must pay for any work completed to date.

**Scenario 2:** Crown Company enters into a contract with Star Hotel for constructing and installing a standard designed gym for a fixed price of $400,000. Nonrefundable progress payments are made on a monthly basis for work completed during the month. Legal title to the gym passes to Star upon completion of the building process. If Star cancels the contract before the gym construction is completed, Crown removes all the installed equipment and Star must compensate Crown for any loss of profit on sale of the gym to another customer.

**Scenario 3:** On January 1, the CostDriver Company, a consulting firm, enters into a three-month contract with Coco Seafood Restaurant to analyze its cost structure in order to find a way to reduce operating costs and increase profits. CostDriver promises to share findings with the restaurant every two weeks and to provide the restaurant with a final analytical report at the end of the contract. This service is customized to Coco, and Cost-Driver would need to start from scratch if it provided a similar service to another client. Coco promises to pay $5,000 per month. If Coco chooses to terminate the contract, it is entitled to receive a summary report detailing analyses to that stage.

**Scenario 4:** Assume Trump International Tower (Phase II) is developing luxury residential real estate and begins to market individual apartments during their construction. The Tower enters into a contract with Edwards for the sale of a specific apartment. Edwards pays a deposit that is refundable only if the Tower fails to deliver the completed apartment in accordance with the contract. The remainder of the purchase price is paid on completion of the contract when Edwards obtains possession of the apartment.

**Required:**
For each of the scenarios, determine whether the seller should recognize revenue over time or when the product or service is completed. Explain your answer.

**P 5–18**
**Variable transaction price**

On January 1 Revis Consulting enters into a contract to complete a cost reduction program for Green Financial over a six-month period. Green will pay Revis $20,000 at the end of each month. If total cost savings reach a specific target, Green will pay an additional $10,000 to Revis at the end of the contract, but if total cost savings fall short, Revis will refund $10,000 to Green. Revis estimates an 80% chance that cost savings will reach the target and calculates the contract price based on the probability-weighted amounts of future payments to be received. Revis accounts for this arrangement.

**Required:**
Prepare the following journal entries for Revis:
1. The journal entry on January 31 to record the first month of revenue under the contract.
2. Assuming total cost savings exceed target, the journal entry on June 30 to record receipt of the bonus.
3. Assuming total cost savings fall short of target, the journal entry on June 30 to record payment of the penalty.

**P 5–19**
**Variable transaction price**

Velocity consulting firm enters into a contract to help Burger Boy, a fast-food restaurant, design a marketing strategy to compete with Burger King. The contract spans eight months. Burger Boy promises to pay $60,000 at the beginning of each month. At the end of the contract, Velocity either will give Burger Boy a refund of $20,000 or will be entitled to an additional $20,000 bonus, depending on whether sales at Burger Boy at the year-end has increased to a target level. At the inception of the contract, Velocity estimates an 80% chance that it will earn the $20,000 bonus. After four months, circumstances change and Velocity revises to 60% its estimate of the chance that it will earn the bonus. At the end of the contract, Velocity receives the additional consideration of $20,000. Velocity accounts for this arrangement.

**Required:**
1. Prepare a journal entry to record the revenue Velocity would recognize each month for the first four months.
2. Prepare a journal entry that the Velocity Company would make after four months to record the change in estimate associated with the likelihood that additional $20,000 would be received.
3. Prepare a journal entry to record the revenue that Velocity Company would recognize each month for the second four months.
4. Prepare a journal entry after eight months to record resolution of the uncertainty associated with receipt of the additional consideration of $20,000.

# 6

# Time Value of Money Concepts

**OVERVIEW** ——————— Time value of money concepts, specifically future value and present value, are essential in a variety of accounting situations. These concepts and the related computational procedures are the subjects of this chapter. Present values and future values of *single amounts* and present values and future values of *annuities* (series of equal periodic payments) are described separately but shown to be interrelated.

**LEARNING** ——————— **After studying this chapter, you should be able to:**

**OBJECTIVES**

- **LO6–1** Explain the difference between simple and compound interest. (*p. 322*)
- **LO6–2** Compute the future value of a single amount. (*p. 323*)
- **LO6–3** Compute the present value of a single amount. (*p. 324*)
- **LO6–4** Solve for either the interest rate or the number of compounding periods when present value and future value of a single amount are known. (*p. 326*)
- **LO6–5** Explain the difference between an ordinary annuity and an annuity due situation. (*p. 331*)
- **LO6–6** Compute the future value of both an ordinary annuity and an annuity due. (*p. 333*)
- **LO6–7** Compute the present value of an ordinary annuity, an annuity due, and a deferred annuity. (*p. 334*)
- **LO6–8** Solve for unknown values in annuity situations involving present value. (*p. 339*)
- **LO6–9** Briefly describe how the concept of the time value of money is incorporated into the valuation of bonds, long-term leases, and pension obligations. (*p. 342*)

## FINANCIAL REPORTING CASE

### The Winning Ticket

Al Castellano had been buying California State lottery tickets for 15 years at his neighborhood grocery store. On Sunday, June 24, 2001, his world changed. When he awoke, opened the local newspaper, and compared his lottery ticket numbers with Saturday night's winning numbers, he couldn't believe his eyes. All of the numbers on his ticket matched the winning numbers. He went outside for a walk, came back into the kitchen and checked the numbers again. He woke his wife Carmen, told her what had happened, and they danced through their apartment. Al, a 66-year-old retired supermarket clerk, and Carmen, a 62-year-old semiretired secretary, had won what at that time was the richest lottery in California's history, $141 million!

On Monday when Al and Carmen claimed their prize, their ecstasy waned slightly when they were informed that they would soon be receiving a check for approximately $43 million. When the Castellanos purchased the lottery ticket, they indicated that they would like to receive any lottery winnings in one lump payment rather than in 26 equal annual installments beginning now. They knew beforehand that the State of California is required to withhold 31% of lottery winnings for federal income tax purposes, but this reduction was way more than 31%.

Source: This case is adapted from an actual situation.

By the time you finish this chapter, you should be able to respond appropriately to the questions posed in this case. Compare your response to the solution provided at the end of the chapter.

QUESTIONS

1. Why were the Castellanos to receive $43 million rather than the $141 million lottery prize? (*p. 334*)

2. What interest rate did the State of California use to calculate the $43 million lump-sum payment? (*p. 340*)

3. What are some of the accounting applications that incorporate the time value of money into valuation? (*p. 342*)

# BASIC CONCEPTS
## Time Value of Money

> The *time value of money* means that money can be invested today to earn interest and grow to a larger dollar amount in the future.

The key to solving the problem described in the financial reporting case is an understanding of the concept commonly referred to as the **time value of money**. This concept means that money invested today will grow to a larger dollar amount in the future. For example, $100 invested in a savings account at your local bank yielding 6% annually will grow to $106 in one year. The difference between the $100 invested now—the present value of the investment—and its $106 future value represents the time value of money.

This concept has nothing to do with the worth or buying power of those dollars. Prices in our economy can change. If the inflation rate were higher than 6%, then the $106 you would have in the savings account actually would be worth less than the $100 you had a year earlier. The time value of money concept concerns only the growth in the dollar amounts of money.

> Time value of money concepts are useful in valuing several assets and liabilities.

The concepts you learn in this chapter are useful in solving business decisions such as the determination of the lottery award presented in the financial reporting case. More important, the concepts are necessary when valuing assets and liabilities for financial reporting purposes. Most accounting applications that incorporate the time value of money involve the concept of present value. The valuation of leases, bonds, pension obligations, and certain notes receivable and payable are a few prominent examples. It is important that you master the concepts and tools we review here as it is essential for the remainder of your accounting education.

### Simple versus Compound Interest

● **LO6–1**

> **Interest** is the amount of money paid or received in excess of the amount borrowed or lent.

**Interest** is the "rent" paid for the use of money for some period of time. In dollar terms, it is the amount of money paid or received in excess of the amount of money borrowed or lent. If you lent the bank $100 today and "received" $106 a year from now, your interest earned would be $6. Interest also can be expressed as a rate at which money will grow. In this case, that rate is 6%. It is this interest that gives money its time value.

**Simple interest** is computed by multiplying an initial investment times both the applicable interest rate and the period of time for which the money is used. For example, simple interest earned each year on a $1,000 investment paying 10% is $100 ($1,000 × 10%).

> **Compound interest** includes interest not only on the initial investment but also on the accumulated interest in previous periods.

**Compound interest** results in increasingly larger interest amounts for each period of the investment. The reason is that interest is now being earned not only on the initial investment amount but also on the accumulated interest earned in previous periods.

For example, Cindy Johnson invested $1,000 in a savings account paying 10% interest *compounded* annually. How much interest will she earn each year, and what will be her investment balance after three years?

| Date | **Interest**<br>**(Interest rate × Outstanding**<br>**balance = Interest)** | **Balance** |
| --- | --- | --- |
| Initial deposit | | $1,000 |
| End of year 1 | 10% × $1,000 = $100 | $1,100 |
| End of year 2 | 10% × $1,100 = $110 | $1,210 |
| End of year 3 | 10% × $1,210 = $121 | $1,331 |

With compound interest at 10% annually, the $1,000 investment would grow to $1,331 at the end of the three-year period. If Cindy withdrew the interest earned each year, she would earn only $100 in interest each year (the amount of simple interest). If the investment period had been 20 years, 20 calculations would be needed. However, calculators, computer programs, and compound interest tables make these calculations easier.

> Interest rates are typically stated as annual rates.

Most banks compound interest more frequently than once a year. Daily compounding is common for savings accounts. More rapid compounding has the effect of increasing the actual rate, which is called the **effective rate**, at which money grows per year. It is important to note that interest is typically stated as an annual rate regardless of the length of the compounding period involved. In situations when the compounding period is less than a year, the interest rate per compounding period is determined by dividing the annual rate by the number of periods. Assuming an annual rate of 12%:

| Compounded | Interest Rate Per Compounding Period |
|---|---|
| Semiannually | 12% ÷ 2 = 6% |
| Quarterly | 12% ÷ 4 = 3% |
| Monthly | 12% ÷ 12 = 1% |

As an example, now let's assume Cindy Johnson invested $1,000 in a savings account paying 10% interest *compounded* twice a year. There are two six-month periods paying interest at 5% (the annual rate divided by two periods). How much interest will she earn the first year, and what will be her investment balance at the end of the year?

| Date | Interest (Interest rate × Outstanding balance = Interest) | Balance |
|---|---|---|
| Initial deposit | | $1,000.00 |
| After six months | 5% × $1,000 = $50.00 | $1,050.00 |
| End of year 1 | 5% × $1,050 = $52.50 | $1,102.50 |

The $1,000 would grow by $102.50, the interest earned, to $1,102.50, $2.50 more than if interest were compounded only once a year. The effective annual interest rate, often referred to as the annual *yield,* is 10.25% ($102.50 ÷ $1,000).

> The *effective interest rate* is the rate at which money actually will grow during a full year.

# Valuing a Single Cash Flow Amount

## Future Value of a Single Amount

In the first Cindy example, in which $1,000 was invested for three years at 10% compounded annually, the $1,331 is referred to as the **future value (FV)**. A time diagram is a useful way to visualize this relationship, with 0 indicating the date of the initial investment.

● LO6–2

Future value of a single amount.

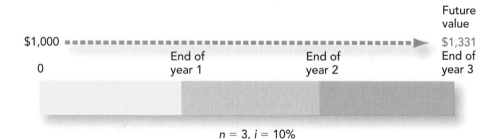

The future value after one year can be calculated as as $1,000 × 1.10 (1.00 + .10) = $1,100. After three years, the future value is $1,000 × 1.10 × 1.10 × 1.10 = $1,331. In fact, the future value of any invested amount can be determined as follows:

$$FV = I(1 + i)^n$$

where:    FV = Future value of the invested amount
          I = Amount invested at the beginning of the period
          $i$ = Interest rate
          $n$ = Number of compounding periods

> The *future value* of a single amount is the amount of money that a dollar will grow to at some point in the future.

The future value can be determined by using Table 1, Future Value of $1, located at the end of this textbook. The table contains the future value of $1 invested for various periods of time, *n,* and at various rates, *i.*

Use this table to determine the future value of any invested amount simply by multiplying it by the table value at the *intersection* of the column for the desired rate and the row for the number of compounding periods. Illustration 6–1 contains an excerpt from Table 1.

## Illustration 6–1

Future Value of $1 (excerpt from Table 1 located at the end of this textbook)

| | | Interest Rates (*i*) | | | | | |
|---|---|---|---|---|---|---|
| **Periods (*n*)** | **7%** | **8%** | **9%** | **10%** | **11%** | **12%** |
| 1 | 1.07000 | 1.08000 | 1.09000 | 1.10000 | 1.11000 | 1.12000 |
| 2 | 1.14490 | 1.16640 | 1.18810 | 1.21000 | 1.23210 | 1.25440 |
| 3 | 1.22504 | 1.25971 | 1.29503 | 1.33100 | 1.36763 | 1.40493 |
| 4 | 1.31080 | 1.36049 | 1.41158 | 1.46410 | 1.51807 | 1.57352 |
| 5 | 1.40255 | 1.46933 | 1.53862 | 1.61051 | 1.68506 | 1.76234 |

The table shows various values of $(1 + i)^n$ for different combinations of *i* and *n*. From the table you can find the future value factor for three periods at 10% to be 1.331. This means that $1 invested at 10% compounded annually will grow to approximately $1.33 in three years. So, the future value of $1,000 invested for three years at 10% is $1,331:

$$FV = I \times FV \text{ factor}$$
$$FV = \$1,000 \times 1.331^* = \$1,331$$
*Future value of $1; *n* = 3, *i* = 10%

The future value function in financial calculators or in computer spreadsheet programs calculates future values in the same way. Determining future values (and present values) electronically avoids the need for tables such as those in the chapter appendix. It's important to remember that the *n* in the future value formula refers to the number of compounding periods, not necessarily the number of years. For example, suppose you wanted to know the future value *two* years from today of $1,000 invested at 12% with *quarterly* compounding. The number of periods is therefore eight and the compounding rate is 3% (12% annual rate divided by four, the number of quarters in a year). The future value factor from Table 1 is 1.26677, so the future value is $1,266.77 ($1,000 × 1.26677).[1]

## Present Value of a Single Amount

● LO6–3

The present value of a single amount is today's equivalent to a particular amount in the future.

The example used to illustrate future value reveals that $1,000 invested today is equivalent to $1,100 received after one year, $1,210 after two years, or $1,331 after three years, assuming 10% interest compounded annually. Thus, the $1,000 investment (I) is the **present value (PV)** of the single sum of $1,331 to be received at the end of three years. It is also the present value of $1,210 to be received in two years and $1,100 in one year.

Remember that the future value of a present amount is the present amount *times* $(1 + i)^n$. Logically, then, that computation can be reversed to find the *present value* of a future amount to be the future amount *divided* by $(1 + i)^n$. We substitute PV for I (invested amount) in the future value formula above.

$$FV = PV (1 + i)^n$$

$$PV = \frac{FV}{(1 + i)^n}$$

In our example,

$$PV = \frac{\$1,331}{(1 + .10)^3} = \frac{\$1,331}{1.331} = \$1,000$$

---

[1]When interest is compounded more frequently than once a year, the effective annual interest rate, or yield, can be determined using the following equation:

$$\text{Yield} = (1 + \frac{i}{p})^p - 1$$

with *i* being the annual interest rate and *p* the number of compounding periods per year. In this example, the annual yield would be 12.55%, calculated as follows:

$$\text{Yield} = (1 + \frac{.12}{4})^4 - 1 = 1.1255 - 1 = .1255$$

Determining the yield is useful when comparing returns on investment instruments with different compounding period length.

Of course, dividing by $(1 + i)^n$ is the same as multiplying by its reciprocal, $1/(1 + i)^n$.

$$PV = \$1,331 \times \frac{1}{(1 + .10)^3} = \$1,331 \times .75131 = \$1,000$$

As with future value, these computations are simplified by using calculators, computer programs, or present value tables. Table 2, Present Value of $1, located at the end of this textbook provides the solutions of $1/(1 + i)^n$ for various interest rates ($i$) and compounding periods ($n$). These amounts represent the present value of $1 to be received at the *end* of the different periods. The table can be used to find the present value of any single amount to be received in the future by *multiplying* that amount by the value in the table that lies at the *intersection* of the column for the appropriate rate and the row for the number of compounding periods.[2] Illustration 6–2 contains an excerpt from Table 2.

| Periods (n) | Interest Rates (i) | | | | | |
|---|---|---|---|---|---|---|
|  | **7%** | **8%** | **9%** | **10%** | **11%** | **12%** |
| 1 | .93458 | .92593 | .91743 | .90909 | .90090 | .89286 |
| 2 | .87344 | .85734 | .84168 | .82645 | .81162 | .79719 |
| 3 | .81630 | .79383 | .77218 | .75131 | .73119 | .71178 |
| 4 | .76290 | .73503 | .70843 | .68301 | .65873 | .63552 |
| 5 | .71299 | .68058 | .64993 | .62092 | .59345 | .56743 |

**Illustration 6–2**

Present Value of $1 (excerpt from Table 2 located at the end of this textbook)

Notice that the farther into the future the $1 is to be received, the less valuable it is now. This is the essence of the concept of the time value of money. Given a choice between $1,000 now and $1,000 three years from now, you would choose to have the money now. If you have it now, you could put it to use. But the choice between, say, $740 now and $1,000 three years from now would depend on your time value of money. If your time value of money is 10%, you would choose the $1,000 in three years, because the $740 invested at 10% for three years would grow to only $984.94 [$740 × 1.331 (FV of $1, $i = 10\%$, $n = 3$)]. On the other hand, if your time value of money is 11% or higher, you would prefer the $740 now. Presumably, you would invest the $740 now and have it grow to $1,012.05 ($740 × 1.36763) in three years.

Using the present value table above, the present value of $1,000 to be received in three years assuming a time value of money of 10% is $751.31 [$1,000 × .75131 (PV of $1, $i = 10\%$ and $n = 3$)]. Because the present value of the future amount, $1,000, is higher than $740 we could have today, we again determine that with a time value of money of 10%, the $1,000 in three years is preferred to the $740 now.

In our earlier example, $1,000 now is equivalent to $1,331 in three years, assuming the time value of money is 10%. Graphically, the relation between the present value and the future value can be viewed this way:

| 0 | End of year 1 | End of year 2 | End of year 3 |
|---|---|---|---|
|  | $100 | $110 | $121 |

$1,000
PV ————————————————————————————————— $1,331
FV

While the calculation of future value of a single sum invested today requires the *inclusion* of compound interest, present value problems require the *removal* of compound interest. The process of computing present value *removes* the $331 of interest earned over the three-year period from the future value of $1,331, just as the process of computing

The calculation of future value requires the addition of interest, while the calculation of present value requires the removal of interest.

---

[2]The factors in Table 2 are the reciprocals of those in Table 1. For example, the future value factor for 10%, three periods is 1.331, while the present value factor is .75131. $1 ÷ 1.331 = $.75131, and $1 ÷ .75131 = $1.331.

future value *adds* $331 of interest to the present value of $1,000 to arrive at the future value of $1,331.

As we demonstrate later in this chapter and in subsequent chapters, present value calculations are incorporated into accounting valuation much more frequently than future value.

**Accountants use PV calculations much more frequently than FV.**

## Solving for Other Values When FV and PV are Known

● LO6–4   There are four variables in the process of adjusting single cash flow amounts for the time value of money: the present value (PV), the future value (FV), the number of compounding periods (*n*), and the interest rate (*i*). If you know any three of these, the fourth can be determined. Illustration 6–3 solves for an unknown interest rate and Illustration 6–4 determines an unknown number of periods.

### DETERMINING THE UNKNOWN INTEREST RATE

**Illustration 6–3**
Determining *i* When PV, FV, and *n* are Known

Suppose a friend asks to borrow $500 today and promises to repay you $605 two years from now. What is the annual interest rate you would be agreeing to?

The following time diagram illustrates the situation:

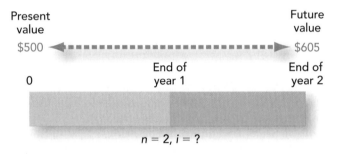

The interest rate is the discount rate that will provide a present value of $500 when discounting (determining present value) the $605 to be received in two years:

$$\$500 \text{ (present value)} = \$605 \text{ (future value)} \times ?*$$
*Present value of $1: n = 2, i = ?

**The unknown variable is the interest rate.**

Rearranging algebraically, we find that the present value table factor is .82645.

$$\$500 \text{ (present value)} \div \$605 \text{ (future value)} = .82645*$$
*Present value of $1: n = 2, i = ?

When you consult the present value table, Table 2, you search row two (*n* = 2) for this value and find it in the 10% column. So the effective interest rate is 10%. Notice that the computed factor value exactly equals the table factor value.[3]

### DETERMINING THE UNKNOWN NUMBER OF PERIODS

**Illustration 6–4**
Determining *n* When PV, FV, and *i* are Known

You want to invest $10,000 today to accumulate $16,000 for graduate school. If you can invest at an interest rate of 10% compounded annually, how many years will it take to accumulate the required amount?

---

[3]If the calculated factor lies between two table factors, interpolation is useful in finding the unknown value. For example, if the future value in our example is $600, instead of $605, the calculated PV factor is .83333 ($500 ÷ $600). This factor lies between the 9% factor of .84168 and the 10% factor of .82645. The total difference between these factors is .01523 (.84168 − .82645). The difference between the calculated factor of .83333 and the 10% factor of .82645 is .00688. This is 45% of the difference between the 9% and 10% factors:

$$\frac{.00688}{.01523} = .45$$

Therefore, the interpolated interest rate is 9.55% (10 − .45).

The following time diagram illustrates the situation:

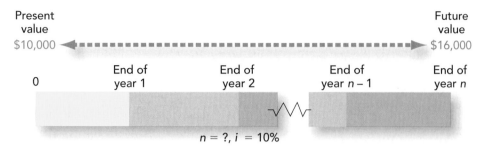

The number of years is the value of *n* that will provide a present value of $10,000 when discounting $16,000 at a rate of 10%:

$10,000 (present value) = $16,000 (future value) × ?*
*Present value of $1; *n* = ?, *i* = 10%

The unknown variable is the number of periods.

Rearranging algebraically, we find that the present value table factor is .625.

$10,000 (present value) ÷ $16,000 (future value) = .625*
*Present value of $1: *n* = ?, *i* = 10%

When you consult the present value table, Table 2, you search the 10% column (*i* = 10%) for this value and find .62092 in row five. So it would take approximately five years to accumulate $16,000 in the situation described.

# Additional Consideration

Solving for the unknown factor in either of these examples could just as easily be done using the future value tables. The number of years is the value of *n* that will provide a present value of $10,000 when discounting $16,000 at a discount rate of 10%.

$16,000 (future value) = $10,000 (present value) × ?*
*Future value of $1: *n* = ?, *i* = 10%

Rearranging algebraically, the future value table factor is 1.6.

$16,000 (future value) ÷ $10,000 (present value) = 1.6*
*Future value of $1: *n* = ?, *i* = 10%

When you consult the future value table, Table 1, you search the 10% column (*i* = 10%) for this value and find 1.61051 in row five. So it would take approximately five years to accumulate $16,000 in the situation described.

## Concept Review Exercise

Using the appropriate table, answer each of the following independent questions.

**VALUING A SINGLE CASH FLOW AMOUNT**

1. What is the future value of $5,000 at the end of six periods at 8% compound interest?

2. What is the present value of $8,000 to be received eight periods from today assuming a compound interest rate of 12%?

3. What is the present value of $10,000 to be received two *years* from today assuming an annual interest rate of 24% and *monthly* compounding?

4. If an investment of $2,000 grew to $2,520 in three periods, what is the interest rate at which the investment grew? Solve using both present and future value tables.

5. Approximately how many years would it take for an investment of $5,250 to accumulate to $15,000, assuming interest is compounded at 10% annually? Solve using both present and future value tables.

**Solution:**

1. FV = $5,000 × 1.58687* = $7,937
   *Future value of $1: $n = 6$, $i = 8\%$ (from Table 1)

2. PV = $8,000 × .40388* = $3,231
   *Present value of $1: $n = 8$, $i = 12\%$ (from Table 2)

3. PV = $10,000 × .62172* = $6,217
   *Present value of $1: $n = 24$, $i = 2\%$ (from Table 2)

4. Using present value table,

$$\frac{\$2,000}{\$2,520} = .7937*$$

   *Present value of $1: $n = 3$, $i = ?$ (from Table 2, i approximately **8%**)

   Using future value table,

$$\frac{\$2,520}{\$2,000} = 1.260*$$

   *Future value of $1: $n = 3$, $i = ?$ (from Table 1, i approximately **8%**)

5. Using present value table,

$$\frac{\$5,250}{\$15,000} = .35*$$

   *Present value of $1: $n = ?$, $i = 10\%$ (from Table 2, n approximately **11 years**)

   Using future value table,

$$\frac{\$15,000}{\$5,250} = 2.857*$$

   *Future value of $1: $n = ?$. $i = 10\%$ (from Table 1, n approximately **11 years**)

# Preview of Accounting Applications of Present Value Techniques—Single Cash Amount

Kile Petersen switched off his television set immediately after watching the Super Bowl game and swore to himself that this would be the last year he would watch the game on his 10-year-old 20-inch TV set. "Next year, a big screen TV," he promised himself. Soon after, he saw an advertisement in the local newspaper from Slim Jim's TV and Appliance offering a Philips 60-inch large screen television on sale for $1,800. And the best part of the deal was that Kile could take delivery immediately but would not have to pay the $1,800 for one whole year! "In a year, I can easily save the $1,800," he thought.

In the above scenario, the seller, Slim Jim's TV and Appliance, records a sale when the TV is delivered to Kile. How should the company value its receivable and corresponding sales revenue? We provide a solution to this question at the end of this section on page 330. The following discussion will help you to understand that solution.

*Most **monetary assets** and **monetary liabilities** are valued at the present value of future cash flows.*

Many assets and most liabilities are monetary in nature. Monetary assets include money and claims to receive money, the amount of which is fixed or determinable. Examples include cash and most receivables. Monetary liabilities are obligations to pay amounts of cash, the amount of which is fixed or determinable. Most liabilities are monetary. For example, if you borrow money from a bank and sign a note payable, the amount of cash to be repaid to the bank is fixed. Monetary receivables and payables are valued based on the fixed amount of cash to be received or paid in the future with proper reflection of the time value of money. In other words, we value most receivables and payables at the present value of future cash flows, reflecting an appropriate time value of money.[4]

The example in Illustration 6–5 demonstrates this concept.

---

[4]FASB ASC 835–30: Interest—Imputation of Interest (previously "Interest on Receivables and Payables," *Accounting Principles Board Opinion No. 21* (New York: AICPA, 1971)). As you will learn in Chapter 7, normal trade accounts receivable and accounts payable are valued at the amount expected to be received or paid, not the present value of those amounts. The difference between the amount expected to be received or paid and present values often is immaterial.

**Illustration 6–5**

Valuing a Note: One Payment, Explicit Interest

**Explicit Interest**
The Stridewell Wholesale Shoe Company manufactures athletic shoes for sale to retailers. The company recently sold a large order of shoes to Harmon Sporting Goods for $50,000. Stridewell agreed to accept a note in payment for the shoes requiring payment of $50,000 in one year plus interest at 10%.

How should Stridewell value the note receivable and corresponding sales revenue earned? How should Harmon value the note payable and corresponding inventory purchased? As long as the interest rate explicitly stated in the agreement properly reflects the time value of money, the answer is $50,000, the face value of the note. It's important to realize that this amount also equals the present value of future cash flows at 10%. Future cash flows equal $55,000, $50,000 in note principal plus $5,000 in interest ($50,000 × 10%). Using a time diagram:

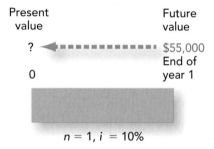

In equation form, we can solve for present value as follows:

$55,000 (future value) × .90909* = $50,000 (present value)
*Present value of $1: $n = 1, i = 10\%$

By calculating the present value of $55,000 to be received in one year, the interest of $5,000 is removed from the future value, resulting in a proper note receivable/sales revenue value of $50,000 for Stridewell and a $50,000 note payable/inventory value for Harmon.

While most notes, loans, and mortgages explicitly state an interest rate that will properly reflect the time value of money, there can be exceptions. Consider the example in Illustration 6–6.

**Illustration 6–6**

Valuing a Note: One Payment, No Explicit Interest

**No Explicit Interest**
The Stridewell Wholesale Shoe Company recently sold a large order of shoes to Harmon Sporting Goods. Terms of the sale require Harmon to sign a noninterest-bearing note of $60,500 with payment due in two years.

How should Stridewell and Harmon value the note receivable/payable and corresponding sales revenue/inventory? Even though the agreement states a noninterest-bearing note, the $60,500 does, in fact, include interest for the two-year period of the loan. We need to remove the interest portion of the $60,500 to determine the portion that represents the sales price of the shoes. We do this by computing the present value. The following time diagram illustrates the situation assuming that a rate of 10% reflects the appropriate interest rate for a loan of this type:

Present value
?

0

End of year 1

$60,500
Future value

End of year 2

$n = 2, i = 10\%$

Again, using the present value of $1 table,

$$\$60,500 \text{ (future value)} \times .82645^* = \$50,000 \text{ (present value)}$$
*Present value of $1: $n = 2$, $i = 10\%$

Both the note receivable for Stridewell and the note payable for Harmon initially will be valued at $50,000. The difference of $10,500 ($60,500 − 50,000) represents interest revenue/expense to be recognized over the life of the note. The appropriate journal entries are illustrated in later chapters.

Now can you answer the question posed in the scenario at the beginning of this section? Assuming that a rate of 10% reflects the appropriate interest rate in this situation, Slim Jim's TV and Appliance records a receivable and sales revenue of $1,636 which is the present value of the $1,800 to be received from Kile Petersen one year from the date of sale.

$$\$1,800 \text{ (future value)} \times .90909^* = \$1,636 \text{ (present value)}$$
*Present value of $1: $n = 1$, $i = 10\%$ (from Table 2)

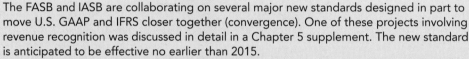

# Where We're Headed

The FASB and IASB are collaborating on several major new standards designed in part to move U.S. GAAP and IFRS closer together (convergence). One of these projects involving revenue recognition was discussed in detail in a Chapter 5 supplement. The new standard is anticipated to be effective no earlier than 2015.

In addition to requiring the time value of money to be appropriately accounted for with long-term receivables as in Illustration 6–6, the new standard also requires the time value of money to be accounted for with long-term (longer than one year) prepayments. For example, in Illustration 6–6, if Harmon Sporting Goods had prepaid Stridewell for delivery of the shoes in two years, Harmon is viewed as providing a two-year loan to Stridewell. Assuming that Harmon pays Stridewell $41,323, the present value of $50,000 for two-periods at 10%, Stridewell would record interest expense and Harmon interest revenue of $8,677 ($50,000 − 41,323) over the two-year period. When delivery occurs in two years, Stridewell records sales revenue of $50,000 and Harmon values the inventory acquired at $50,000.

See Illustration 5–23 in the supplement to Chapter 5 for a more detailed example.

# Expected Cash Flow Approach

*SFAC No. 7*

*SFAC No. 7* provides a framework for using future cash flows in accounting measurements.

Present value measurement has long been integrated with accounting valuation and is specifically addressed in several accounting standards. Because of its increased importance, the FASB issued *Statement of Financial Accounting Concepts No. 7*, "Using Cash Flow Information and Present Value in Accounting Measurements."[5] This statement provides a framework for using future cash flows as the basis for accounting measurement and asserts that the objective in valuing an asset or liability using present value is to approximate the fair value of that asset or liability. Key to that objective is determining the present value of future cash flows associated with the asset or liability, *taking into account any uncertainty concerning the amounts and timing of the cash flows.* Although future cash flows in many instances are contractual and certain, the amounts and timing of cash flows are less certain in other situations.

For example, lease payments are provided in the contract between lessor and lessee. On the other hand, the future cash flows to be paid to settle a pending lawsuit may be highly uncertain. Traditionally, the way uncertainty has been considered in present value calculations has been by discounting the "best estimate" of future cash flows applying a discount rate that has been adjusted to reflect the uncertainty or risk of those cash flows. With the approach

---

[5]"Using Cash Flow Information and Present Value in Accounting Measurements," *Statement of Financial Accounting Concepts No. 7* (Norwalk, Conn.: FASB, 2000). Recall that Concept Statements do not directly prescribe GAAP, but instead provide structure and direction to financial accounting.

described by *SFAC No. 7*, though, the adjustment for uncertainty or risk of cash flows is applied to the cash flows, not the discount rate. This new *expected cash flow approach* incorporates specific probabilities of cash flows into the analysis. Consider Illustration 6–7.

**Illustration 6–7**

Expected Cash Flow Approach

LDD Corporation faces the likelihood of having to pay an uncertain amount in five years in connection with an environmental cleanup. The future cash flow estimate is in the range of $100 million to $300 million with the following estimated probabilities:

| Loss Amount | Probability |
|---|---|
| $100 million | 10% |
| $200 million | 60% |
| $300 million | 30% |

The expected cash flow, then, is $220 million:

$$\$100 \times 10\% = \$\ 10 \text{ million}$$
$$200 \times 60\% = \ 120 \text{ million}$$
$$300 \times 30\% = \underline{\ \ 90 \text{ million}}$$
$$\$220 \text{ million}$$

If the company's credit-adjusted risk-free rate of interest is 5%, LDD will report a liability of $172,376,600, the present value of the expected cash outflow:

$$\$220,000,000$$
$$\underline{\times\ .78353^*}$$
$$\$172,376,600$$

*Present value of $1, n = 5, i = 5% (from Table 2)

Compare the approach described in Illustration 6–7 to the traditional approach that uses the present value of the most likely estimate of $200 million and ignores information about cash flow probabilities.

The discount rate used to determine present value when applying the expected cash flow approach should be the company's *credit-adjusted risk-free rate of interest*. Other elements of uncertainty are incorporated into the determination of the probability-weighted expected cash flows. In the traditional approach, elements of uncertainty are incorporated into a risk-adjusted discount rate.

The FASB expects that the traditional approach to calculating present value will continue to be used in many situations, particularly those where future cash flows are contractual. The board also believes that the expected cash flow approach is more appropriate in more complex situations. In fact, the board has incorporated the concepts developed in *SFAC No. 7* into standards on asset retirement obligations, impairment losses, and business combinations. In Chapter 10 we illustrate the use of the expected cash flow approach as it would be applied to the measurement of an asset retirement obligation. In Chapter 13, we use the approach to measure the liability associated with a loss contingency.

**SFAC No. 7**
"While many accountants do not routinely use the expected cash flow approach, expected cash flows are inherent in the techniques used in some accounting measurements, like pensions, other postretirement benefits, and some insurance obligations."[6]

The company's credit-adjusted risk-free rate of interest is used when applying the expected cash flow approach to the calculation of present value.

# BASIC ANNUITIES

**PART B**

The previous examples involved the receipt or payment of a single future amount. Financial instruments frequently involve multiple receipts or payments of cash. If the same amount is to be received or paid each period, the series of cash flows is referred to as an **annuity**. A common annuity encountered in practice is a loan on which periodic interest is paid in

● LO6–5

---

[6]Ibid., para. 48.

equal amounts. For example, bonds typically pay interest semiannually in an amount determined by multiplying a stated rate by a fixed principal amount. Some loans and most leases are paid in equal installments during a specified period of time.

An agreement that creates an annuity can produce either an **ordinary annuity** or an **annuity due** (sometimes referred to as an annuity in advance) situation. The first cash flow (receipt or payment) of an ordinary annuity is made one compounding period *after* the date on which the agreement begins. The final cash flow takes place on the *last* day covered by the agreement. For example, an installment note payable dated December 31, 2013, might require the debtor to make three equal annual payments, with the first payment due on December 31, 2014, and the last one on December 31, 2016. The following time diagram illustrates an ordinary annuity:

*In an ordinary annuity cash flows occur at the end of each period.*

*Ordinary annuity.*

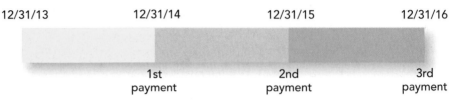

The first payment of an annuity due is made on the *first* day of the agreement, and the last payment is made one period *before* the end of the agreement. For example, a three-year lease of a building that begins on December 31, 2013, and ends on December 31, 2016, may require the first year's lease payment in advance on December 31, 2013. The third and last payment would take place on December 31, 2015, the beginning of the third year of the lease. The following time diagram illustrates this situation:

*In an annuity due cash flows occur at the beginning of each period.*

*Annuity due.*

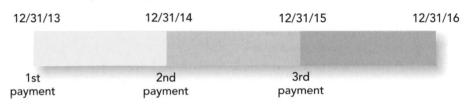

# Future Value of an Annuity

## Future Value of an Ordinary Annuity

Let's first consider the future value of an ordinary annuity in Illustration 6–8.

**Illustration 6–8**

Future Value of an Ordinary Annuity

> Sally Rogers wants to accumulate a sum of money to pay for graduate school. Rather than investing a single amount today that will grow to a future value, she decides to invest $10,000 a year over the next three years in a savings account paying 10% interest compounded annually. She decides to make the first payment to the bank one year from today.

The following time diagram illustrates this ordinary annuity situation. Time 0 is the start of the first period.

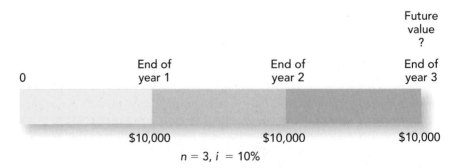

Using the FV of $1 factors from Table 1, we can calculate the future value of this annuity by calculating the future value of each of the individual payments as follows:

| | Payment | | FV of $1<br>i = 10% | | Future Value<br>(at the end of year 3) | n |
|---|---|---|---|---|---|---|
| First payment | $10,000 | × | 1.21 | = | $12,100 | 2 |
| Second payment | 10,000 | × | 1.10 | = | 11,000 | 1 |
| Third payment | 10,000 | × | 1.00 | = | 10,000 | 0 |
| Total | | | 3.31 | | $33,100 | |

From the time diagram, we can see that the first payment has two compounding periods to earn interest. The factor used, 1.21, is the FV of $1 invested for two periods at 10%. The second payment has one compounding period and the last payment does not earn any interest because it is invested on the last day of the three-year annuity period. Therefore, the factor used is 1.00.

In the future value of an ordinary annuity, the last cash payment will not earn any interest.

● LO6–6

This illustration shows that it's possible to calculate the future value of the annuity by separately calculating the FV of each payment and then adding these amounts together. Fortunately, that's not necessary. Table 3, Future Value of an Ordinary Annuity of $1, located at the end of this textbook, simplifies the computation by summing the individual FV of $1 factors for various factors of $n$ and $i$. Illustration 6–9 contains an excerpt from Table 3.

| | Interest Rates (i) | | | | | |
|---|---|---|---|---|---|---|
| Periods (n) | 7% | 8% | 9% | 10% | 11% | 12% |
| 1 | 1.0000 | 1.0000 | 1.0000 | 1.0000 | 1.0000 | 1.0000 |
| 2 | 2.0700 | 2.0800 | 2.0900 | 2.1000 | 2.1100 | 2.1200 |
| 3 | 3.2149 | 3.2464 | 3.2781 | 3.3100 | 3.3421 | 3.3744 |
| 4 | 4.4399 | 4.5061 | 4.5731 | 4.6410 | 4.7097 | 4.7793 |
| 5 | 5.7507 | 5.8666 | 5.9847 | 6.1051 | 6.2278 | 6.3528 |

**Illustration 6–9**

Future Value of an Ordinary Annuity of $1 (excerpt from Table 3 located at the end of this textbook)

The future value of $1 at the end of each of three periods invested at 10% is shown in Table 3 to be $3.31. We can simply multiply this factor by $10,000 to derive the FV of our ordinary annuity (FVA):

$$FVA = \$10,000 \text{ (annuity amount)} \times 3.31* = \$33,100$$
*Future value of an ordinary annuity of $1: n = 3, i = 10%

## Future Value of an Annuity Due

Let's modify the previous illustration to create an annuity due in Illustration 6–10.

Sally Rogers wants to accumulate a sum of money to pay for graduate school. Rather than investing a single amount today that will grow to a future value, she decides to invest $10,000 a year over the next three years in a savings account paying 10% interest compounded annually. She decides to make the first payment to the bank immediately. How much will Sally have available in her account at the end of three years?

**Illustration 6–10**

Future Value of an Annuity Due

The following time diagram depicts the situation. Again, note that 0 is the start of the first period.

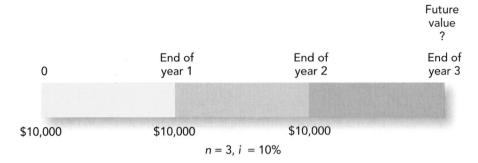

$$n = 3, i = 10\%$$

The future value can be found by separately calculating the FV of each of the three payments and then summing those individual future values:

In the future value of an annuity due, the last cash payment will earn interest.

|  | Payment | | FV of $1 i = 10% | | Future Value (at the end of year 3) | n |
|---|---|---|---|---|---|---|
| First payment | $10,000 | × | 1.331 | = | $13,310 | 3 |
| Second payment | 10,000 | × | 1.210 | = | 12,100 | 2 |
| Third payment | 10,000 | × | 1.100 | = | 11,000 | 1 |
| Total | | | 3.641 | | $36,410 | |

And, again, this same future value can be found by using the future value of an annuity due (FVAD) factor from Table 5, Future Value of an Annuity Due of $1, located at the end of this textbook, as follows:

$$\text{FVAD} = \$10,000 \text{ (annuity amount)} \times 3.641^* = \$36,410$$
*Future value of an annuity due of $1: n = 3, i = 10%

Of course, if *unequal* amounts are invested each year, we can't solve the problem by using the annuity tables. The future value of each payment would have to be calculated separately.

# Present Value of an Annuity

## Present Value of an Ordinary Annuity

● LO6–7    You will learn in later chapters that liabilities and receivables, with the exception of certain trade receivables and payables, are reported in financial statements at their present values. Most of these financial instruments specify equal periodic interest payments or installment payments. As a result, the most common accounting applications of the time value of money involve determining present value of annuities. As in the future value applications we discussed above, an annuity can be either an ordinary annuity or an annuity due. Let's look at an ordinary annuity first.

In Illustration 6–8 on page 332, we determined that Sally Rogers could accumulate $33,100 for graduate school by investing $10,000 at the end of each of three years at 10%. The $33,100 is the future value of the ordinary annuity described. Another alternative is to invest one single amount at the beginning of the three-year period. (See Illustration 6–11.) This single amount will equal the present value at the beginning of the three-year period of the $33,100 future value. It will also equal the present value of the $10,000 three-year annuity.

**FINANCIAL Reporting Case**

Q1, p. 321

**Illustration 6–11**

Present Value of an Ordinary Annuity

> Sally Rogers wants to accumulate a sum of money to pay for graduate school. She wants to invest a single amount today in a savings account earning 10% interest compounded annually that is equivalent to investing $10,000 at the end of each of the next three years.

The present value can be found by separately calculating the PV of each of the three payments and then summing those individual present values:

| | Payment | | PV of $1<br>i = 10% | | Present Value<br>(at the beginning of year 1) | n |
|---|---|---|---|---|---|---|
| First payment | $10,000 | × | .90909 | = | $ 9,091 | 1 |
| Second payment | 10,000 | × | .82645 | = | 8,264 | 2 |
| Third payment | 10,000 | × | .75131 | = | 7,513 | 3 |
| Total | | | 2.48685 | | $24,868 | |

A more efficient method of calculating present value is to use Table 4, Present Value of an Ordinary Annuity of $1, located at the end of this textbook. Illustration 6–12 contains an excerpt from Table 4.

| | Interest Rates (i) | | | | | |
|---|---|---|---|---|---|---|
| Periods (n) | 7% | 8% | 9% | 10% | 11% | 12% |
| 1 | 0.93458 | 0.92593 | 0.91743 | 0.90909 | 0.90090 | 0.89286 |
| 2 | 1.80802 | 1.78326 | 1.75911 | 1.73554 | 1.71252 | 1.69005 |
| 3 | 2.62432 | 2.57710 | 2.53129 | 2.48685 | 2.44371 | 2.40183 |
| 4 | 3.38721 | 3.31213 | 3.23972 | 3.16987 | 3.10245 | 3.03735 |
| 5 | 4.10020 | 3.99271 | 3.88965 | 3.79079 | 3.69590 | 3.60478 |

**Illustration 6–12**

Present Value of an Ordinary Annuity of $1 (excerpt from Table 4 located at the end of this textbook)

Using Table 4, we calculate the PV of the ordinary annuity (PVA) as follows:

PVA = $10,000 (annuity amount) × 2.48685* = $24,868
*Present value of an ordinary annuity of $1: n = 3, i = 10%

The relationship between the present value and the future value of the annuity can be depicted graphically as follows:

Present value $24,868

Future value $33,100

Relationship between present value and future value—ordinary annuity.

| 0 | End of<br>year 1 | End of<br>year 2 | End of<br>year 3 |
|---|---|---|---|

$10,000    $10,000    $10,000

n = 3, i = 10%

This can be interpreted in several ways:

1. $10,000 invested at 10% at the end of each of the next three years will accumulate to $33,100 at the end of the third year.
2. $24,868 invested at 10% now will grow to $33,100 after three years.
3. Someone whose time value of money is 10% would be willing to pay $24,868 now to receive $10,000 at the end of each of the next three years.
4. If your time value of money is 10%, you should be indifferent with respect to paying/receiving (a) $24,868 now, (b) $33,100 three years from now, or (c) $10,000 at the end of each of the next three years.

# Additional Consideration

We also can verify that these are the present value and future value of the same annuity by calculating the present value of a single cash amount of $33,100 three years hence:

PV = $33,100 (future value) × .75131* = $24,868
*Present value of $1: n = 3, i = 10%

## Present Value of an Annuity Due

**Illustration 6–13**

Present Value of an Annuity Due

In the previous illustration, suppose that the three equal payments of $10,000 are to be made at the *beginning* of each of the three years. Recall from Illustration 6–10 on page 333 that the future value of this annuity is $36,410. What is the present value?

The following time diagram depicts this situation:

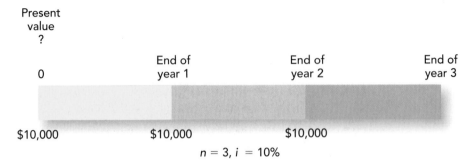

Present value of an annuity due.

Once again, using individual PV factors of $1 from Table 2, the PV of the annuity due can be calculated as follows:

| | Payment | | PV of $1 $i = 10\%$ | | Present Value (at the beginning of year 1) | $n$ |
|---|---|---|---|---|---|---|
| First payment | $10,000 | × | 1.00000 | = | $10,000 | 0 |
| Second payment | 10,000 | × | .90909 | = | 9,091 | 1 |
| Third payment | 10,000 | × | .82645 | = | 8,264 | 2 |
| Total | | | 2.73554 | | $27,355 | |

In the present value of an annuity due, no interest needs to be removed from the first cash payment.

The first payment does not contain any interest since it is made on the first day of the three-year annuity period. Therefore, the factor used is 1.00. The second payment has one compounding period and the factor used of .90909 is the PV factor of $1 for one period and 10%, and we need to remove two compounding periods of interest from the third payment. The factor used of .82645 is the PV factor of $1 for two periods and 10%.

The relationship between the present value and the future value of the annuity can be depicted graphically as follows:

Relationship between present value and future value—annuity due.

| Present value $27,355 | | | | Future value $36,410 |
|---|---|---|---|---|
| 0 | End of year 1 | End of year 2 | | End of year 3 |
| $10,000 | $10,000 | $10,000 | | |

$n = 3, i = 10\%$

Using Table 6, Present Value of an Annuity Due, located at the end of this book, we can more efficiently calculate the PV of the annuity due (PVAD):

$$\text{PVAD} = \$10,000 \text{ (annuity amount)} \times 2.73554^* = \$27,355$$

*Present value of an annuity due of $1: $n = 3, i = 10\%$

To better understand the relationship between Tables 4 and 6, notice that the PVAD factor for three periods, 10%, from Table 6 is 2.73554. This is simply the PVA factor for two periods, 10%, of 1.73554, plus 1.0. The addition of 1.0 reflects the fact that the first payment does not require the removal of any interest.

## Present Value of a Deferred Annuity

Accounting valuations often involve the present value of annuities in which the first cash flow is expected to occur more than one time period after the date of the agreement. As the inception of the annuity is deferred beyond a single period, this type of annuity is referred to as a **deferred annuity**.[7]

A *deferred annuity* exists when the first cash flow occurs more than one period after the date the agreement begins.

At January 1, 2013, you are considering acquiring an investment that will provide three equal payments of $10,000 each to be received at the end of three consecutive years. However, the first payment is not expected until *December 31, 2015*. The time value of money is 10%. How much would you be willing to pay for this investment?

**Illustration 6–14**

Deferred Annuity

The following time diagram depicts this situation:

Cash flows for a deferred annuity.

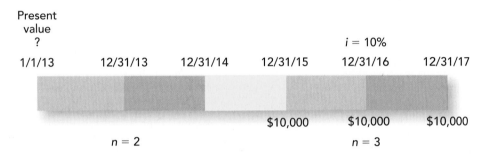

The present value of the deferred annuity can be calculated by summing the present values of the three individual cash flows, each discounted to today's PV:

|  | Payment |  | PV of $1 i = 10% |  | Present Value | n |
|---|---|---|---|---|---|---|
| First payment | $10,000 | × | .75131 | = | $ 7,513 | 3 |
| Second payment | 10,000 | × | .68301 | = | 6,830 | 4 |
| Third payment | 10,000 | × | .62092 | = | 6,209 | 5 |
|  |  |  |  |  | $20,552 |  |

A more efficient way of calculating the present value of a deferred annuity involves a two-step process:

1. Calculate the PV of the annuity as of the beginning of the annuity period.
2. Discount the single amount calculated in (1) to its present value *as of today.*

In this case, we compute the present value of the annuity as of December 31, 2014, by multiplying the annuity amount by the three-period ordinary annuity factor:

$$\text{PVA} = \$10,000 \text{ (annuity amount)} \times 2.48685^* = \$24,868$$
*Present value of an ordinary annuity of $1: n = 3, i = 10%

This is the present value as of December 31, 2014. This single amount is then reduced to present value as of January 1, 2013, by making the following calculation:

$$\text{PV} = \$24,868 \text{ (future amount)} \times .82645^* = \$20,552$$
*Present value of $1: n = 2, i = 10%

The following time diagram illustrates this two-step process:

---

[7]The future value of a deferred annuity is the same as the future amount of an annuity not deferred. That is because there are no interest compounding periods prior to the beginning of the annuity period.

**Present value of a deferred annuity—two-step process.**

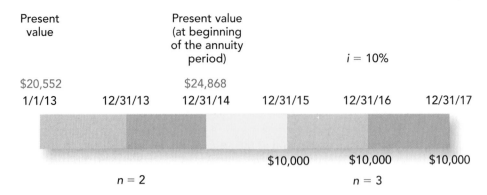

| Present value | | Present value (at beginning of the annuity period) | | i = 10% | |
|---|---|---|---|---|---|
| $20,552 | | $24,868 | | | |
| 1/1/13 | 12/31/13 | 12/31/14 | 12/31/15 | 12/31/16 | 12/31/17 |
| | | | $10,000 | $10,000 | $10,000 |
| | n = 2 | | | n = 3 | |

If you recall the concepts you learned in this chapter, you might think of other ways the present value of a deferred annuity can be determined. Among them:

1. Calculate the PV of an annuity due, rather than an ordinary annuity, and then discount that amount three periods rather than two:

$$PVAD = \$10,000 \text{ (annuity amount)} \times 2.73554^* = \$27,355$$
*Present value of an annuity due of $1: n = 3, i = 10%

This is the present value as of December 31, 2015. This single amount is then reduced to present value as of January 1, 2013 by making the following calculation:

$$PV = \$27,355 \times .75131^* = \$20,552$$
*Present value of $1: n = 3, i = 10%

2. From Table 4, subtract the two-period PVA factor (1.73554) from the five-period PVA factor (3.79079) and multiply the difference (2.05525) by $10,000 to get $20,552.

# Financial Calculators and Excel

As previously mentioned, financial calculators can be used to solve future and present value problems. For example, a Texas Instruments model BA-35 has the following pertinent keys:

| N | %I | PV | FV | PMT | CPT |

These keys are defined as follows:

N = number of periods
%I = interest rate
PV = present value
FV = future value
PMT = annuity payments
CPT = compute button

**Using a calculator:**
Enter: N 10 I 10
PMT 200
Output: PV 1,229

**Using Excel, enter:**
= PV(.10,10,200)
Output: 1,229

To illustrate its use, assume that you need to determine the present value of a 10-period ordinary annuity of $200 using a 10% interest rate. You would enter N 10, %I 10, PMT −200, then press CPT and PV to obtain the answer of $1,229.

Many professionals choose to use spreadsheet software, such as Excel, to solve time value of money problems. These spreadsheets can be used in a variety of ways. A template can be created using the formulas shown in Illustration 6–22 on page 345. An alternative is to use the software's built-in financial functions. For example, Excel has a function called PV that calculates the present value of an ordinary annuity. To use the function, you would select the pull-down menu for "Insert," click on "Function" and choose the category called "Financial." Scroll down to PV and double-click. You will then be asked to input the necessary variables—interest rate, the number of periods, and the payment amount.

In subsequent chapters we illustrate the use of both a calculator and Excel in addition to present value tables to solve present value calculations for selected examples and illustrations.

# Solving for Unknown Values in Present Value Situations

In present value problems involving annuities, there are four variables: (1) present value of an ordinary annuity (PVA) or present value of an annuity due (PVAD), (2) the amount of each annuity payment, (3) the number of periods, *n*, and (4) the interest rate, *i*. If you know any three of these, the fourth can be determined.

● **LO6–8**

> Assume that you borrow $700 from a friend and intend to repay the amount in four equal annual installments beginning one year from today. Your friend wishes to be reimbursed for the time value of money at an 8% annual rate. What is the required annual payment that must be made (the annuity amount), to repay the loan in four years?

**Illustration 6–15**

Determining the Annuity Amount When Other Variables Are Known

The following time diagram illustrates the situation:

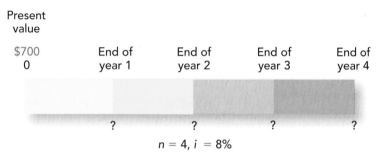

Determining the unknown annuity amount—ordinary annuity.

The required payment is the annuity amount that will provide a present value of $700 when discounting that amount at a discount rate of 8%:

$700 (present value) = 3.31213* × annuity amount

The unknown variable is the annuity amount.

Rearranging algebraically, we find that the annuity amount is $211.34.

$700 (present value) ÷ 3.31213* = $211.34 (annuity amount)
*Present value of an ordinary annuity of $1: *n* = 4, *i* = 8%

You would have to make four annual payments of $211.34 to repay the loan. Total payments of $845.36 (4 × $211.34) would include $145.36 in interest ($845.36 − 700.00).

> Assume that you borrow $700 from a friend and intend to repay the amount in equal installments of $100 per year over a period of years. The payments will be made at the end of each year beginning one year from now. Your friend wishes to be reimbursed for the time value of money at a 7% annual rate. How many years would it take before you repaid the loan?

**Illustration 6–16**

Determining n When Other Variables Are Known

Once again, this is an ordinary annuity situation because the first payment takes place one year from now. The following time diagram illustrates the situation:

Determining the unknown number of periods—ordinary annuity.

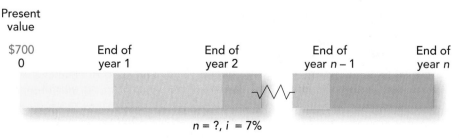

The number of years is the value of *n* that will provide a present value of $700 when discounting $100 at a discount rate of 7%:

| | |
|---|---|
| The unknown variable is the number of periods. | $700 (present value) = $100 (annuity amount) $\times$ ?*<br>*Present value of an ordinary annuity of $1: $n$ = ?, $i$ = 7% |

Rearranging algebraically, we find that the PVA table factor is 7.0.

$$\$700 \text{ (present value)} \div \$100 \text{ (annuity amount)} = 7.0*$$
*Present value of an ordinary annuity of $1: $n$ = ?, $i$ = 7%

When you consult the PVA table, Table 4, you search the 7% column ($i$ = 7%) for this value and find 7.02358 in row 10. So it would take approximately 10 years to repay the loan in the situation described.

**Illustration 6–17**

Determining *i* When Other Variables Are Known

Suppose that a friend asked to borrow $331 today (present value) and promised to repay you $100 (the annuity amount) at the end of each of the next four years. What is the annual interest rate implicit in this agreement?

**FINANCIAL Reporting Case**

Q2, p. 321

Determining the unknown interest rate— ordinary annuity.

First of all, we are dealing with an ordinary annuity situation as the payments are at the end of each period. The following time diagram illustrates the situation:

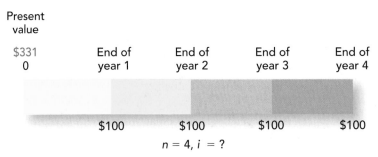

The interest rate is the discount rate that will provide a present value of $331 when discounting the $100 four-year ordinary annuity:

| | |
|---|---|
| The unknown variable is the interest rate. | $331 (present value) = $100 (annuity amount) $\times$ ?*<br>*Present value of an ordinary annuity of $1: $n$ = 4, $i$ = ? |

Rearranging algebraically, we find that the PVA table factor is 3.31.

$$\$331 \text{ (present value)} \div \$100 \text{ (annuity amount)} = 3.31*$$
*Present value of an ordinary annuity of $1: $n$ = 4, $i$ = ?

When you consult the PVA table, Table 4, you search row four ($n$ = 4) for this value and find it in the 8% column. So the effective interest rate is 8%.

**Illustration 6–18**

Determining *i* When Other Variables Are Known—Unequal Cash Flows

Suppose that you borrowed $400 from a friend and promised to repay the loan by making three annual payments of $100 at the end of each of the next three years plus a final payment of $200 at the end of year four. What is the interest rate implicit in this agreement?

Determining the unknown interest rate— unequal cash flow.

The following time diagram illustrates the situation:

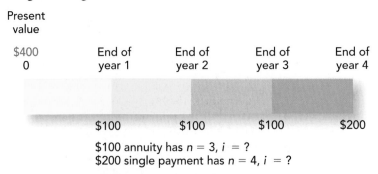

The interest rate is the discount rate that will provide a present value of $400 when discounting the $100 three-year ordinary annuity plus the $200 to be received in four years:

$400 (present value) = $100 (annuity amount) × ?* + $200 (single payment) × ?†

*Present value of an ordinary annuity of $1: $n = 3, i = ?$
†Present value of $1: $n = 4, i = ?$

The unknown variable is the interest rate.

This equation involves two unknowns and is not as easily solved as the two previous examples. One way to solve the problem is to trial-and-error the answer. For example, if we assumed $i$ to be 9%, the total PV of the payments would be calculated as follows:

$$PV = \$100 \, (2.53129^*) + \$200 \, (.70843^†) = \$395$$

*Present value of an ordinary annuity of $1: $n = 3, i = 9\%$
†Present value of $1: $n = 4, i = 9\%$

Because the present value computed is less than the $400 borrowed, using 9% removes too much interest. Recalculating PV with $i = 8\%$ results in a PV of $405. This indicates that the interest rate implicit in the agreement is between 8% and 9%.

## Concept Review Exercise

Using the appropriate table, answer each of the following independent questions.

**ANNUITIES**

1. What is the future value of an annuity of $2,000 invested at the *end* of each of the next six periods at 8% interest?
2. What is the future value of an annuity of $2,000 invested at the *beginning* of each of the next six periods at 8% interest?
3. What is the present value of an annuity of $6,000 to be received at the *end* of each of the next eight periods assuming an interest rate of 10%?
4. What is the present value of an annuity of $6,000 to be received at the *beginning* of each of the next eight periods assuming an interest rate of 10%?
5. Jane bought a $3,000 audio system and agreed to pay for the purchase in 10 equal annual installments of $408 beginning one year from today. What is the interest rate implicit in this agreement?
6. Jane bought a $3,000 audio system and agreed to pay for the purchase in 10 equal annual installments beginning one year from today. The interest rate is 12%. What is the amount of the annual installment?
7. Jane bought a $3,000 audio system and agreed to pay for the purchase by making nine equal annual installments beginning one year from today plus a lump-sum payment of $1,000 at the end of 10 periods. The interest rate is 10%. What is the required annual installment?
8. Jane bought an audio system and agreed to pay for the purchase by making four equal annual installments of $800 beginning one year from today plus a lump-sum payment of $1,000 at the end of five years. The interest rate is 12%. What was the cost of the audio system? (Hint: What is the present value of the cash payments?)
9. Jane bought an audio system and agreed to pay for the purchase by making five equal annual installments of $1,100 beginning four years from today. The interest rate is 12%. What was the cost of the audio system? (Hint: What is the present value of the cash payments?)

**Solution:**

1. FVA = $2,000 × 7.3359* = $14,672
   *Future value of an ordinary annuity of $1: $n = 6, i = 8\%$ (from Table 3)
2. FVAD = $2,000 × 7.9228* = $15,846
   *Future value of an annuity due of $1: $n = 6, i = 8\%$ (from Table 5)
3. PVA = $6,000 × 5.33493* = $32,010
   *Present value of ordinary annuity of $1: $n = 8, i = 10\%$ (from Table 4)

4. PVAD = $6,000 \times 5.86842^* = \$35,211$

   *Present value of an annuity due of $1: $n = 8$, $i = 10\%$ (from Table 6)

5. $\dfrac{\$3,000}{\$408} = 7.35^*$

   *Present value of an ordinary annuity of $1: $n = 10$, $i = ?$ (from Table 4, $i$ approximately 6%)

6. Each annuity payment $= \dfrac{\$3,000}{5.65022^*} = \$531$

   *Present value of an ordinary annuity of $1: $n = 10$, $i = 12\%$ (from Table 4)

7. Each annuity payment $= \dfrac{\$3,000 - [\text{PV of } \$1,000 \ (n = 10, i = 10\%)]}{5.75902^*}$

   Each annuity payment $= \dfrac{\$3,000 - (\$1,000 \times .38554^\dagger)}{5.75902^*}$

   Each annuity payment $= \dfrac{\$2,614}{5.75902^*} = \$454$

   *Present value of an ordinary annuity of $1: $n = 9$, $i = 10\%$ (from Table 4)
   †Present value of $1: $n = 10$, $i = 10\%$ (from Table 2)

8. PV $= \$800 \times 3.03735^* + \$1,000 \times .56743^\dagger = \$2,997$

   *Present value of an ordinary annuity of $1: $n = 4$, $i = 12\%$ (from Table 4)
   †Present value of $1: $n = 5$, $i = 12\%$ (from Table 2)

9. PVA $= \$1,100 \times 3.60478^* = \$3,965$

   *Present value of an ordinary annuity of $1: $n = 5$, $i = 12\%$ (from Table 4)

   This is the present value three years from today (the beginning of the five-year ordinary annuity). This single amount is then reduced to present value as of today by making the following calculation:

   PV $= \$3,965 \times .71178^\dagger = \$2,822$

   †Present value of $1: $n = 3$, $i = 12\%$, (from Table 2)

# Preview of Accounting Applications of Present Value Techniques—Annuities

The time value of money has many applications in accounting. Most of these applications involve the concept of present value. Because financial instruments typically specify equal periodic payments, these applications quite often involve annuity situations. For example, let's consider one accounting situation using both an ordinary annuity and the present value of a single amount (long-term bonds), one using an annuity due (long-term leases), and a third using a deferred annuity (pension obligations).

● LO6–9

## Valuation of Long-Term Bonds

**FINANCIAL Reporting Case**

Q3, p. 321

You will learn in Chapter 14 that a long-term bond usually requires the issuing (borrowing) company to repay a specified amount at maturity and make periodic stated interest payments over the life of the bond. The *stated* interest payments are equal to the contractual stated rate multiplied by the face value of the bonds. At the date the bonds are issued (sold), the marketplace will determine the price of the bonds based on the *market* rate of interest for investments with similar characteristics. The market rate at date of issuance may not equal the bonds' stated rate in which case the price of the bonds (the amount the issuing company actually is borrowing) will not equal the bonds' face value. Bonds issued at more than face value are said to be issued at a premium, while bonds issued at less than face value are said to be issued at a discount. Consider the example in Illustration 6–19.

On June 30, 2013, Fumatsu Electric issued 10% stated rate bonds with a face amount of $200 million. The bonds mature on June 30, 2033 (20 years). The market rate of interest for similar issues was 12%. Interest is paid semiannually (5%) on June 30 and December 31, beginning December 31, 2013. The interest payment is $10 million (5% × $200 million). What was the price of the bond issue? What amount of interest expense will Fumatsu record for the bonds in 2013?

**Illustration 6–19**
Valuing a Long-term
Bond Liability

To determine the price of the bonds, we calculate the present value of the 40-period annuity (40 semiannual interest payments of $10 million) and the lump-sum payment of $200 million paid at maturity using the semiannual market rate of interest of 6%. In equation form,

$$PVA = \$10 \text{ million (annuity amount)} \times 15.04630^* = \$150,463,000$$
$$PV = \$200 \text{ million (lump-sum)} \times .09722^\dagger = \underline{\phantom{000}19,444,000}$$
$$\text{Price of the bond issue} = \underline{\underline{\$169,907,000}}$$

*Present value of an ordinary annuity of $1: $n = 40$, $i = 6\%$
†Present value of $1: $n = 40$, $i = 6\%$

The bonds will sell for $169,907,000, which represents a discount of $30,093,000 ($200,000,000 − 169,907,000). The discount results from the difference between the semiannual stated rate of 5% and the market rate of 6%. Fumatsu records a $169,907,000 increase in cash and a corresponding liability for bonds payable.

Interest expense for the first six months is determined by multiplying the carrying value (book value) of the bonds ($169,907,000) by the semiannual effective rate (6%) as follows:

$$\$169,907,000 \times 6\% = \$10,194,420$$

The difference between interest expense ($10,194,420) and interest paid ($10,000,000) increases the carrying value of the bond liability. Interest for the second six months of the bond's life is determined by multiplying the new carrying value by the 6% semiannual effective rate.

We discuss the specific accounts used to record these transactions in Chapter 14.

## Valuation of Long-Term Leases

Companies frequently acquire the use of assets by leasing rather than purchasing them. Leases usually require the payment of fixed amounts at regular intervals over the life of the lease. You will learn in Chapter 15 that certain leases are treated in a manner similar to an installment purchase by the lessee. In other words, the lessee records an asset and corresponding lease liability at the present value of the lease payments. Consider the example in Illustration 6–20.

On January 1, 2013, the Stridewell Wholesale Shoe Company signed a 25-year lease agreement for an office building. Terms of the lease call for Stridewell to make annual lease payments of $10,000 at the beginning of each year, with the first payment due on January 1, 2013. Assuming an interest rate of 10% properly reflects the time value of money in this situation, how should Stridewell value the asset acquired and the corresponding lease liability?

**Illustration 6–20**
Valuing a Long-Term
Lease Liability

Once again, by computing the present value of the lease payments, we remove the portion of the payments that represents interest, leaving the portion that represents payment for the asset itself. Because the first payment is due immediately, as is common for leases, this is an annuity due situation. In equation form:

**Leases require the recording of an asset and corresponding liability at the present value of future lease payments.**

$$PVAD = \$10,000 \text{ (annuity amount)} \times 9.98474^* = \$99,847$$
*Present value of an annuity due of $1: $n = 25$, $i = 10\%$

Stridewell initially will value the leased asset and corresponding lease liability at $99,847.

**Journal entry at the inception of a lease.**

| Leased office building .................................................................... | 99,847 | |
| Lease payable .................................................................... | | 99,847 |

The difference between this amount and total future cash payments of $250,000 ($10,000 × 25) represents the interest that is implicit in this agreement. That difference is recorded as interest over the life of the lease.

## Valuation of Pension Obligations

Pension plans are important compensation vehicles used by many U.S. companies. These plans are essentially forms of deferred compensation as the pension benefits are paid to employees after they retire. You will learn in Chapter 17 that some pension plans create obligations during employees' service periods that must be paid during their retirement periods. These obligations are funded during the employment period. This means companies contribute cash to pension funds annually with the intention of accumulating sufficient funds to pay employees the retirement benefits they have earned. The amounts contributed are determined using estimates of retirement benefits. The actual amounts paid to employees during retirement depend on many factors including future compensation levels and length of life. Consider Illustration 6–21.

**Illustration 6–21**

Valuing a Pension Obligation

> On January 1, 2013, the Stridewell Wholesale Shoe Company hired Sammy Sossa. Sammy is expected to work for 25 years before retirement on December 31, 2037. Annual retirement payments will be paid at the end of each year during his retirement period, expected to be 20 years. The first payment will be on December 31, 2038. During 2013 Sammy earned an annual retirement benefit estimated to be $2,000 per year. The company plans to contribute cash to a pension fund that will accumulate to an amount sufficient to pay Sammy this benefit. Assuming that Stridewell anticipates earning 6% on all funds invested in the pension plan, how much would the company have to contribute at the end of 2013 to pay for pension benefits earned in 2013?

To determine the required contribution, we calculate the present value on December 31, 2013, of the deferred annuity of $2,000 that begins on December 31, 2038, and is expected to end on December 31, 2057.

The following time diagram depicts this situation:

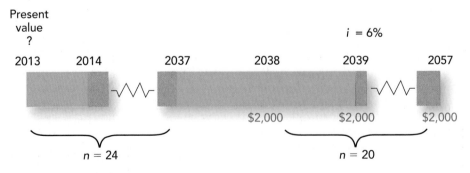

We can calculate the present value of the annuity using a two-step process. The first step computes the present value of the annuity as of December 31, 2037, by multiplying the annuity amount by the 20-period ordinary annuity factor:

$$PVA = \$2,000 \text{ (annuity amount)} \times 11.46992^* = \$22,940$$
*Present value of an ordinary annuity of $1: n = 20, i = 6%

This is the present value as of December 31, 2037. This single amount is then reduced to present value as of December 31, 2013, by a second calculation:

$$PV = \$22,940 \text{ (future amount)} \times .24698* = \$5,666$$
*Present value of $1: $n = 24$, $i = 6\%$

Stridewell would have to contribute $5,666 at the end of 2013 to fund the estimated pension benefits earned by its employee in 2013. Viewed in reverse, $5,666 invested now at 6% will accumulate a fund balance of $22,940 at December 31, 2037. If the fund balance remains invested at 6%, $2,000 can be withdrawn each year for 20 years before the fund is depleted.

Among the other situations you'll encounter using present value techniques are valuing notes (Chapters 10 and 14) and other postretirement benefits (Chapter 17).

# Summary of Time Value of Money Concepts

Illustration 6–22 summarizes the time value of money concepts discussed in this chapter.

| Concept | Summary | Formula | Table |
|---|---|---|---|
| Future value (FV) of $1 | The amount of money that a dollar will grow to at some point in the future. | $FV = \$1(1 + i)^n$ | 1 |
| Present value (PV) of $1 | The amount of money today that is equivalent to a given amount to be received or paid in the future. | $PV = \dfrac{\$1}{(1 + i)^n}$ | 2 |
| Future value of an ordinary annuity (FVA) of $1 | The future value of a series of equal-sized cash flows with the first payment taking place at the end of the first compounding period. | $FVA = \dfrac{(1 + i)^n - 1}{i}$ | 3 |
| Present value of an ordinary annuity (PVA) of $1 | The present value of a series of equal-sized cash flows with the first payment taking place at the end of the first compounding period. | $PVA = \dfrac{1 - \dfrac{1}{(1 + i)^n}}{i}$ | 4 |
| Future value of an annuity due (FVAD) of $1 | The future value of a series of equal-sized cash flows with the first payment taking place at the beginning of the annuity period. | $FVAD = \left[\dfrac{(1 + i)^n - 1}{i}\right] \times (1 + i)$ | 5 |
| Present value of an annuity due (PVAD) of $1 | The present value of a series of equal-sized cash flows with the first payment taking place at the beginning of the annuity period. | $PVAD = PVA = \left[\dfrac{1 - \dfrac{1}{(1 + i)^n}}{i}\right] \times (1 + i)$ | 6 |

**Illustration 6–22**

Summary of Time Value of Money Concepts

# Financial Reporting Case Solution

1. **Why were the Castellanos to receive $43 million rather than the $141 million lottery prize?** *(p. 334)*  The Castellanos chose to receive their lottery winnings in one lump payment immediately rather than in 26 equal annual installments beginning immediately. The state calculates the present value of the 26 equal payments, withholds the necessary federal income tax, and pays the Castellanos the remainder.

2. **What interest rate did the State of California use to calculate the $43 million lump-sum payment?** *(p. 340)*  The equal payment is determined by dividing $141 million by 26 periods:

| | |
|---|---:|
| $141 million ÷ 26 = | $5,423,077 |
| Less: 31% federal income tax | (1,681,154) |
| Net-of-tax payment | $3,741,923 |

Since the first payment is made immediately, this is an annuity due situation. We must find the interest rate that provides a present value of $43 million. There is no 26 period row in Table 6. We can subtract the first payment from the $43 million since it is paid immediately and solve using the 25-period ordinary annuity table (that is, the 25 remaining annual payments beginning in one year):

$$\text{PVA factor} = \frac{\$43,000,000 - 3,741,923}{\$3,741,923} = 10.4914*$$

*Present value of an ordinary annuity of $1: $n = 25$, $i = ?$ (from Table 4, $i$ = approximately 8%)

So, the interest rate used by the state was approximately 8%.

3. **What are some of the accounting applications that incorporate the time value of money into valuation?** *(p. 342)*  Accounting applications that incorporate the time value of money techniques into valuation include the valuation of long-term notes receivable and various long-term liabilities that include bonds, notes, leases, pension obligations, and postretirement benefits other than pensions. We study these in detail in later chapters. ●

# The Bottom Line

● **LO6–1**  A dollar today is worth more than a dollar to be received in the future. The difference between the present value of cash flows and their future value represents the time value of money. Interest is the rent paid for the use of money over time. *(p. 322)*

● **LO6–2**  The future value of a single amount is the amount of money that a dollar will grow to at some point in the future. It is computed by *multiplying* the single amount by $(1 + i)^n$, where $i$ is the interest rate and $n$ the number of compounding periods. The Future Value of $1 table allows for the calculation of future value for any single amount by providing the factors for various combinations of $i$ and $n$. *(p. 323)*

● **LO6–3**  The present value of a single amount is the amount of money today that is equivalent to a given amount to be received or paid in the future. It is computed by *dividing* the future amount by $(1 + i)^n$. The Present Value of $1 table simplifies the calculation of the present value of any future amount. *(p. 324)*

● **LO6–4**  There are four variables in the process of adjusting single cash flow amounts for the time value of money: present value (PV), future value (FV), $i$ and $n$. If you know any three of these, the fourth can be computed easily. *(p. 326)*

● **LO6–5**  An annuity is a series of equal-sized cash flows occurring over equal intervals of time. An ordinary annuity exists when the cash flows occur at the end of each period. An annuity due exists when the cash flows occur at the beginning of each period. *(p. 331)*

● **LO6–6**  The future value of an ordinary annuity (FVA) is the future value of a series of equalsized cash flows with the first payment taking place at the end of the first compounding period. The last payment will not earn any interest since it is made at the end of the annuity period. The future value of an annuity due (FVAD) is the future value of a series of equal-sized cash flows with the first payment taking place at the beginning of the annuity period (the beginning of the first compounding period). *(p. 333)*

● **LO6–7**  The present value of an ordinary annuity (PVA) is the present value of a series of equal-sized cash flows with the first payment taking place at the end of the first compounding period. The present value of an annuity due (PVAD) is the present value of a series of equal-sized cash flows with the first payment taking place at the beginning of the annuity period. The present value of a deferred annuity is the present value of a series of equal-sized cash flows with the first payment taking place more than one time period after the date of the agreement. *(p. 334)*

● **LO6–8**  In present value problems involving annuities, there are four variables: PVA or PVAD, the annuity amount, the number of compounding periods ($n$) and the interest rate ($i$). If you know any three of these, you can determine the fourth. *(p. 339)*

● **LO6–9**   Most accounting applications of the time value of money involve the present values of annuities. The initial valuation of long-term bonds is determined by calculating the present value of the periodic stated interest payments and the present value of the lump-sum payment made at maturity. Certain leases require the lessee to compute the present value of future lease payments to value the leased asset and corresponding lease obligation. Also, pension plans require the payment of deferred annuities to retirees. (*p. 342*) ●

## Questions For Review of Key Topics

Q 6–1    Define interest.

Q 6–2    Explain compound interest.

Q 6–3    What would cause the annual interest rate to be different from the annual effective rate or yield?

Q 6–4    Identify the three items of information necessary to calculate the future value of a single amount.

Q 6–5    Define the present value of a single amount.

Q 6–6    Explain the difference between monetary and nonmonetary assets and liabilities.

Q 6–7    What is an annuity?

Q 6–8    Explain the difference between an ordinary annuity and an annuity due.

Q 6–9    Explain the relationship between Table 2, Present Value of $1, and Table 4, Present Value of an Ordinary Annuity of $1.

Q 6–10    Prepare a time diagram for the present value of a four-year ordinary annuity of $200. Assume an interest rate of 10% per year.

Q 6–11    Prepare a time diagram for the present value of a four-year annuity due of $200. Assume an interest rate of 10% per year.

Q 6–12    What is a deferred annuity?

Q 6–13    Assume that you borrowed $500 from a friend and promised to repay the loan in five equal annual installments beginning one year from today. Your friend wants to be reimbursed for the time value of money at an 8% annual rate. Explain how you would compute the required annual payment.

Q 6–14    Compute the required annual payment in Question 6–13.

Q 6–15    Explain how the time value of money concept is incorporated into the valuation of certain leases.

## Brief Exercises

**BE 6–1**
Simple versus compound interest
● **LO6–1**

Fran Smith has two investment opportunities. The interest rate for both investments is 8%. Interest on the first investment will compound annually while interest on the second will compound quarterly. Which investment opportunity should Fran choose? Why?

**BE 6–2**
Future value; single amount
● **LO6–2**

Bill O'Brien would like to take his wife, Mary, on a trip three years from now to Europe to celebrate their 40th anniversary. He has just received a $20,000 inheritance from an uncle and intends to invest it for the trip. Bill estimates the trip will cost $23,500 and he believes he can earn 5% interest, compounded annually, on his investment. Will he be able to pay for the trip with the accumulated investment amount?

**BE 6–3**
Future value; solving for unknown; single amount
● **LO6–4**

Refer to the situation described in BE 6–2. Assume that the trip will cost $26,600. What interest rate, compounded annually, must Bill earn to accumulate enough to pay for the trip?

**BE 6–4**
Present value; single amount
● **LO6–3**

John has an investment opportunity that promises to pay him $16,000 in four years. He could earn a 6% annual return investing his money elsewhere. What is the maximum amount he would be willing to invest in this opportunity?

**BE 6–5**
Present value;
solving for
unknown; single
amount
● LO6–4

Refer to the situation described in BE 6–4. Suppose the opportunity requires John to invest $13,200 today. What is the interest rate John would earn on this investment?

**BE 6–6**
Future value;
ordinary annuity
● LO6–6

Leslie McCormack is in the spring quarter of her freshman year of college. She and her friends already are planning a trip to Europe after graduation in a little over three years. Leslie would like to contribute to a savings account over the next three years in order to accumulate enough money to take the trip. Assuming an interest rate of 4%, compounded quarterly, how much will she accumulate in three years by depositing $500 at the *end* of each of the next 12 quarters, beginning three months from now?

**BE 6–7**
Future value;
annuity due
● LO6–6

Refer to the situation described in BE 6–6. How much will Leslie accumulate in three years by depositing $500 at the *beginning* of each of the next 12 quarters?

**BE 6–8**
Present value;
ordinary annuity
● LO6–7

Canliss Mining Company borrowed money from a local bank. The note the company signed requires five annual installment payments of $10,000 beginning one year from today. The interest rate on the note is 7%. What amount did Canliss borrow?

**BE 6–9**
Present value;
annuity due
● LO6–7

Refer to the situation described in BE 6–8. What amount did Canliss borrow assuming that the first $10,000 payment was due immediately?

**BE 6–10**
Deferred annuity
● LO6–7

Refer to the situation described in BE 6–8. What amount did Canliss borrow assuming that the first of the five annual $10,000 payments was not due for three years?

**BE 6–11**
Solve for unknown;
annuity
● LO6–8

Kingsley Toyota borrowed $100,000 from a local bank. The loan requires Kingsley to pay 10 equal annual installments beginning one year from today. Assuming an interest rate of 8%, what is the amount of each annual installment payment?

**BE 6–12**
Price of a bond
● LO6–9

On December 31, 2013, Interlink Communications issued 6% stated rate bonds with a face amount of $100 million. The bonds mature on December 31, 2043. Interest is payable annually on each December 31, beginning in 2014. Determine the price of the bonds on December 31, 2013, assuming that the market rate of interest for similar bonds was 7%.

**BE 6–13**
Lease payment
● LO6–9

On September 30, 2013, Ferguson Imports leased a warehouse. Terms of the lease require Ferguson to make 10 annual lease payments of $55,000 with the first payment due immediately. Accounting standards require the company to record a lease liability when recording this type of lease. Assuming an 8% interest rate, at what amount should Ferguson record the lease liability on September 30, 2013, before the first payment is made?

# Exercises

**An alternate exercise and problem set is available on the text website: www.mhhe.com/spiceland7e**

**E 6–1**
Future value;
single amount
● LO6–2

Determine the future value of the following single amounts:

| | Invested Amount | Interest Rate | No. of Periods |
|---|---|---|---|
| 1. | $15,000 | 6% | 12 |
| 2. | 20,000 | 8 | 10 |
| 3. | 30,000 | 12 | 20 |
| 4. | 50,000 | 4 | 12 |

**E 6–2**
**Future value;**
**single amounts**
● **LO6–2**

Determine the future value of $10,000 under each of the following sets of assumptions:

| | Annual Rate | Period Invested | Interest Compounded |
|---|---|---|---|
| 1. | 10% | 10 years | Semiannually |
| 2. | 12 | 5 years | Quarterly |
| 3. | 24 | 30 months | Monthly |

**E 6–3**
**Present value;**
**single amounts**
● **LO6–3**

Determine the present value of the following single amounts:

| | Future Amount | Interest Rate | No. of Periods |
|---|---|---|---|
| 1. | $20,000 | 7% | 10 |
| 2. | 14,000 | 8 | 12 |
| 3. | 25,000 | 12 | 20 |
| 4. | 40,000 | 10 | 8 |

**E 6–4**
**Present value;**
**multiple, unequal**
**amounts**
● **LO6–3**

Determine the combined present value as of December 31, 2013, of the following four payments to be received at the end of each of the designated years, assuming an annual interest rate of 8%.

| Payment | Year Received |
|---|---|
| $5,000 | 2014 |
| 6,000 | 2015 |
| 8,000 | 2017 |
| 9,000 | 2019 |

**E 6–5**
**Noninterest-**
**bearing note;**
**single payment**
● **LO6–3**

The Field Detergent Company sold merchandise to the Abel Company on June 30, 2013. Payment was made in the form of a noninterest-bearing note requiring Abel to pay $85,000 on June 30, 2015. Assume that a 10% interest rate properly reflects the time value of money in this situation.

**Required:**
Calculate the amount at which Field should record the note receivable and corresponding sales revenue on June 30, 2013.

**E 6–6**
**Solving for**
**unknowns; single**
**amounts**
● **LO6–4**

For each of the following situations involving single amounts, solve for the unknown (?). Assume that interest is compounded annually. ($i$ = interest rate, and $n$ = number of years)

| | Present Value | Future Value | $i$ | $n$ |
|---|---|---|---|---|
| 1. | ? | $ 40,000 | 10% | 5 |
| 2. | $36,289 | 65,000 | ? | 10 |
| 3. | 15,884 | 40,000 | 8 | ? |
| 4. | 46,651 | 100,000 | ? | 8 |
| 5. | 15,376 | ? | 7 | 20 |

**E 6–7**
**Future value;**
**annuities**
● **LO6–6**

Wiseman Video plans to make four annual deposits of $2,000 each to a special building fund. The fund's assets will be invested in mortgage instruments expected to pay interest at 12% on the fund's balance. Using the appropriate annuity table, determine how much will be accumulated in the fund on December 31, 2016, under each of the following situations:

1. The first deposit is made on December 31, 2013, and interest is compounded annually.
2. The first deposit is made on December 31, 2012, and interest is compounded annually.
3. The first deposit is made on December 31, 2012, and interest is compounded quarterly.
4. The first deposit is made on December 31, 2012, interest is compounded annually, *and* interest earned is withdrawn at the end of each year.

**E 6–8**
**Present value;**
**annuities**
● **LO6–7**

Using the appropriate present value table and assuming a 12% annual interest rate, determine the present value on December 31, 2013, of a five-period annual annuity of $5,000 under each of the following situations:
1. The first payment is received on December 31, 2014, and interest is compounded annually.
2. The first payment is received on December 31, 2013, and interest is compounded annually.
3. The first payment is received on December 31, 2014, and interest is compounded quarterly.

**E 6–9**
**Solving for**
**unknowns;**
**annuities**
● **LO6–8**

For each of the following situations involving annuities, solve for the unknown (?). Assume that interest is compounded annually and that all annuity amounts are received at the *end* of each period. ($i$ = interest rate, and $n$ = number of years)

| | Present Value | Annuity Amount | i | n |
|---|---|---|---|---|
| 1. | ? | $ 3,000 | 8% | 5 |
| 2. | $242,980 | 75,000 | ? | 4 |
| 3. | 161,214 | 20,000 | 9 | ? |
| 4. | 500,000 | 80,518 | ? | 8 |
| 5. | 250,000 | ? | 10 | 4 |

**E 6–10**
Future value; solving for annuities and single amount
● LO6–4, LO6–8

John Rider wants to accumulate $100,000 to be used for his daughter's college education. He would like to have the amount available on December 31, 2018. Assume that the funds will accumulate in a certificate of deposit paying 8% interest compounded annually.

**Required:**
Answer each of the following independent questions.
1. If John were to deposit a single amount, how much would he have to invest on December 31, 2013?
2. If John were to make five equal deposits on each December 31, beginning on December 31, 2014, what is the required amount of each deposit?
3. If John were to make five equal deposits on each December 31, beginning on December 31, 2013, what is the required amount of each deposit?

**E 6–11**
Future and present value
● LO6–3, LO6–6, LO6–7

Answer each of the following independent questions.
1. Alex Meir recently won a lottery and has the option of receiving one of the following three prizes: (1) $64,000 cash immediately, (2) $20,000 cash immediately and a six-period annuity of $8,000 beginning one year from today, or (3) a six-period annuity of $13,000 beginning one year from today. Assuming an interest rate of 6%, which option should Alex choose?
2. The Weimer Corporation wants to accumulate a sum of money to repay certain debts due on December 31, 2022. Weimer will make annual deposits of $100,000 into a special bank account at the end of each of 10 years beginning December 31, 2013. Assuming that the bank account pays 7% interest compounded annually, what will be the fund balance after the last payment is made on December 31, 2022?

**E 6–12**
Deferred annuities
● LO6–7

Lincoln Company purchased merchandise from Grandville Corp. on September 30, 2013. Payment was made in the form of a noninterest-bearing note requiring Lincoln to make six annual payments of $5,000 on each September 30, beginning on September 30, 2016.

**Required:**
Calculate the amount at which Lincoln should record the note payable and corresponding purchases on September 30, 2013, assuming that an interest rate of 10% properly reflects the time value of money in this situation.

**E 6–13**
Solving for unknown annuity payment
● LO6–8

Don James purchased a new automobile for $20,000. Don made a cash down payment of $5,000 and agreed to pay the remaining balance in 30 monthly installments, beginning one month from the date of purchase. Financing is available at a 24% *annual* interest rate.

**Required:**
Calculate the amount of the required monthly payment.

**E 6–14**
Solving for unknown interest rate
● LO6–8

Lang Warehouses borrowed $100,000 from a bank and signed a note requiring 20 annual payments of $13,388 beginning one year from the date of the agreement.

**Required:**
Determine the interest rate implicit in this agreement.

**E 6–15**
Solving for unknown annuity amount
● LO6–8

Sandy Kupchack just graduated from State University with a bachelor's degree in history. During her four years at the university, Sandy accumulated $12,000 in student loans. She asks for your help in determining the amount of the *quarterly* loan payment. She tells you that the loan must be paid back in five years and that the annual interest rate is 8%. Payments begin in three months.

**Required:**
Determine Sandy's quarterly loan payment.

**E 6–16**
Deferred annuities; solving for annuity amount
● LO6–7, LO6–8

On April 1, 2013, John Vaughn purchased appliances from the Acme Appliance Company for $1,200. In order to increase sales, Acme allows customers to pay in installments and will defer any payments for six months. John will make 18 equal monthly payments, beginning October 1, 2013. The annual interest rate implicit in this agreement is 24%.

**Required:**
Calculate the monthly payment necessary for John to pay for his purchases.

**E 6–17**
Price of a bond
● LO6–9

On September 30, 2013, the San Fillipo Corporation issued 8% stated rate bonds with a face amount of $300 million. The bonds mature on September 30, 2033 (20 years). The market rate of interest for similar bonds was 10%. Interest is paid semiannually on March 31 and September 30.

**Required:**
Determine the price of the bonds on September 30, 2013.

**E 6–18**
Price of a bond;
interest expense
● LO6–9

On June 30, 2013, Singleton Computers issued 6% stated rate bonds with a face amount of $200 million. The bonds mature on June 30, 2028 (15 years). The market rate of interest for similar bond issues was 5% (2.5% semi-annual rate). Interest is paid semiannually (3%) on June 30 and December 31, beginning on December 31, 2013.

**Required:**
1. Determine the price of the bonds on June 30, 2013.
2. Calculate the interest expense Singleton reports in 2013 for these bonds.

**E 6–19**
Lease payments
● LO6–9

On June 30, 2013, Fly-By-Night Airlines leased a jumbo jet from Boeing Corporation. The terms of the lease require Fly-By-Night to make 20 annual payments of $400,000 on each June 30. Generally accepted accounting principles require this lease to be recorded as a liability for the present value of scheduled payments. Assume that a 7% interest rate properly reflects the time value of money in this situation.

**Required:**
1. At what amount should Fly-By-Night record the lease liability on June 30, 2013, assuming that the first payment will be made on June 30, 2014?
2. At what amount should Fly-By-Night record the lease liability on June 30, 2013, *before* any payments are made, assuming that the first payment will be made on June 30, 2013?

**E 6–20**
Lease payments;
solve for unknown
interest rate
● LO6–8, LO6–9

On March 31, 2013, Southwest Gas leased equipment from a supplier and agreed to pay $200,000 annually for 20 years beginning March 31, 2014. Generally accepted accounting principles require that a liability be recorded for this lease agreement for the present value of scheduled payments. Accordingly, at inception of the lease, Southwest recorded a $2,293,984 lease liability.

**Required:**
Determine the interest rate implicit in the lease agreement.

**E 6–21**
Concepts;
terminology
● LO6–1 through
LO6–3, LO6–5

Listed below are several terms and phrases associated with concepts discussed in the chapter. Pair each item from List A with the item from List B (by letter) that is most appropriately associated with it.

| List A | List B |
|---|---|
| ___ 1. Interest | a. First cash flow occurs one period after agreement begins. |
| ___ 2. Monetary asset | b. The rate at which money will actually grow during a year. |
| ___ 3. Compound interest | c. First cash flow occurs on the first day of the agreement. |
| ___ 4. Simple interest | d. The amount of money that a dollar will grow to. |
| ___ 5. Annuity | e. Amount of money paid/received in excess of amount |
| ___ 6. Present value of a single amount |    borrowed/lent. |
| ___ 7. Annuity due | f. Obligation to pay a sum of cash, the amount of which is fixed. |
| ___ 8. Future value of a single amount | g. Money can be invested today and grow to a larger amount. |
| ___ 9. Ordinary annuity | h. No fixed dollar amount attached. |
| ___10. Effective rate or yield | i. Computed by multiplying an invested amount by the interest rate. |
| ___11. Nonmonetary asset | j. Interest calculated on invested amount plus accumulated interest. |
| ___12. Time value of money | k. A series of equal-sized cash flows. |
| ___13. Monetary liability | l. Amount of money required today that is equivalent to a given |
| |    future amount. |
| | m. Claim to receive a fixed amount of money. |

# CPA and CMA Review Questions

**CPA Exam
Questions**

The following questions are used in the Kaplan CPA Review Course to study the time value of money while preparing for the CPA examination. Determine the response that best completes the statements or questions.

● LO6–3

1. An investment product promises to pay $25,458 at the end of nine years. If an investor feels this investment should produce a rate of return of 14 percent, compounded annually, what's the most the investor should be willing to pay for the investment?

| n | PV of $1 @ 14% |
|---|---|
| 8 | 0.3506 |
| 9 | 0.3075 |
| 10 | 0.2697 |

a. $6,866
b. $7,828
c. $8,926
d. $9,426

● LO6–7

2. On January 1, 2013, Ott Company sold goods to Fox Company. Fox signed a noninterest-bearing note requiring payment of $60,000 annually for seven years. The first payment was made on January 1, 2013. The prevailing rate of interest for this type of note at date of issuance was 10%. Information on present value factors is as follows:

| Periods | Present Value of 1 at 10% | Present Value of Ordinary Annuity of 1 at 10% |
|---|---|---|
| 6 | .56 | 4.36 |
| 7 | .51 | 4.87 |

Ott should record sales revenue in January 2013 of

a. $214,200
b. $261,600
c. $292,600
d. $321,600

● LO6–7

3. An annuity will pay eight annual payments of $100, with the first payment to be received one year from now. If the interest rate is 12 percent per year, what is the present value of this annuity? Use the appropriate table located at the end of the textbook to solve this problem.

a. $497
b. $556
c. $801
d. $897

● LO6–7

4. An annuity will pay four annual payments of $100, with the first payment to be received three years from now. If the interest rate is 12 percent per year, what is the present value of this annuity? Use the appropriate table located at the end of the textbook to solve this problem.

a. $181
b. $242
c. $304
d. $400

● LO6–7

5. Justin Banks just won the lottery and is trying to decide between the annual cash flow payment option of $100,000 per year for 15 years beginning today, and the lump-sum option. Justin can earn 8 percent investing his money. At what lump-sum payment amount would he be indifferent between the two alternatives? Use the appropriate table located at the end of the textbook to solve this problem.

a. $824,424
b. $855,948
c. $890,378
d. $924,424

● LO6–9

6. An investor purchases a 10-year, $1,000 par value bond that pays *annual* interest of $100. If the market rate of interest is 12 percent, what is the current market value of the bond?

a. $887
b. $950
c. $1,000
d. $1,100

● LO6–8

7. You borrow $15,000 to buy a car. The loan is to be paid off in monthly installments over five years at 12 percent interest annually. The first payment is due one month from today. If the present value of an ordinary annuity of $1 for 5 years @12% with monthly compounding is $44.955, what is the amount of each monthly payment?

a. $334
b. $456
c. $546
d. $680

**CMA Exam
Questions**

● LO6–2

The following questions dealing with the time value of money are adapted from questions that previously appeared on Certified Management Accountant (CMA) examinations. The CMA designation sponsored by the Institute of Management Accountants (www.imanet.org) provides members with an objective measure of knowledge and competence in the field of management accounting. Determine the response that best completes the statements or questions.

1. Janet Taylor Casual Wear has $75,000 in a bank account as of December 31, 2011. If the company plans on depositing $4,000 in the account at the end of each of the next 3 years (2012, 2013, and 2014) and all amounts in the account earn 8% per year, what will the account balance be at December 31, 2014? Ignore the effect of income taxes.

| | 8% Interest Rate Factors | |
| --- | --- | --- |
| Period | Future Value of an Amount of $1 | Future Value of an Ordinary Annuity of $1 |
| 1 | 1.08 | 1.00 |
| 2 | 1.17 | 2.08 |
| 3 | 1.26 | 3.25 |
| 4 | 1.36 | 4.51 |

   a. $ 87,000
   b. $ 88,000
   c. $ 96,070
   d. $107,500

● LO6–5, LO6–9

2. Essex Corporation is evaluating a lease that takes effect on March 1. The company must make eight equal payments, with the first payment due on March 1. The concept most relevant to the evaluation of the lease is

   a. The present value of an annuity due.
   b. The present value of an ordinary annuity.
   c. The future value of an annuity due.
   d. The future value of an ordinary annuity.

# Problems

**An alternate exercise and problem set is available on the text website: www.mhhe.com/spiceland7e**

**P 6–1
Analysis of
alternatives**
● LO6–3, LO6–7

Esquire Company needs to acquire a molding machine to be used in its manufacturing process. Two types of machines that would be appropriate are presently on the market. The company has determined the following:

Machine A could be purchased for $48,000. It will last 10 years with annual maintenance costs of $1,000 per year. After 10 years the machine can be sold for $5,000.

Machine B could be purchased for $40,000. It also will last 10 years and will require maintenance costs of $4,000 in year three, $5,000 in year six, and $6,000 in year eight. After 10 years, the machine will have no salvage value.

**Required:**
Determine which machine Esquire should purchase. Assume an interest rate of 8% properly reflects the time value of money in this situation and that maintenance costs are paid at the end of each year. Ignore income tax considerations.

**P 6–2
Present and
future value**
● LO6–6, LO6–7,
LO6–9

Johnstone Company is facing several decisions regarding investing and financing activities. Address each decision independently.

1. On June 30, 2013, the Johnstone Company purchased equipment from Genovese Corp. Johnstone agreed to pay Genovese $10,000 on the purchase date and the balance in five annual installments of $8,000 on each June 30 beginning June 30, 2014. Assuming that an interest rate of 10% properly reflects the time value of money in this situation, at what amount should Johnstone value the equipment?

2. Johnstone needs to accumulate sufficient funds to pay a $400,000 debt that comes due on December 31, 2018. The company will accumulate the funds by making five equal annual deposits to an account paying 6% interest compounded annually. Determine the required annual deposit if the first deposit is made on December 31, 2013.

3. On January 1, 2013, Johnstone leased an office building. Terms of the lease require Johnstone to make 20 annual lease payments of $120,000 beginning on January 1, 2013. A 10% interest rate is implicit in the lease agreement. At what amount should Johnstone record the lease liability on January 1, 2013, *before* any lease payments are made?

**P 6–3**
**Analysis of**
**alternatives**
● **LO6–3, LO6–7**

Harding Company is in the process of purchasing several large pieces of equipment from Danning Machine Corporation. Several financing alternatives have been offered by Danning:
1. Pay $1,000,000 in cash immediately.
2. Pay $420,000 immediately and the remainder in 10 annual installments of $80,000, with the first installment due in one year.
3. Make 10 annual installments of $135,000 with the first payment due immediately.
4. Make one lump-sum payment of $1,500,000 five years from date of purchase.

**Required:**
Determine the best alternative for Harding, assuming that Harding can borrow funds at an 8% interest rate.

**P 6–4**
**Investment**
**analysis**
● **LO6–3, LO6–7**

John Wiggins is contemplating the purchase of a small restaurant. The purchase price listed by the seller is $800,000. John has used past financial information to estimate that the net cash flows (cash inflows less cash outflows) generated by the restaurant would be as follows:

| Years | Amount |
|-------|--------|
| 1–6 | $80,000 |
| 7 | 70,000 |
| 8 | 60,000 |
| 9 | 50,000 |
| 10 | 40,000 |

If purchased, the restaurant would be held for 10 years and then sold for an estimated $700,000.

**Required:**
Assuming that John desires a 10% rate of return on this investment, should the restaurant be purchased? (Assume that all cash flows occur at the end of the year.)

**P 6–5**
**Investment**
**decision; varying**
**rates**
● **LO6–3, LO6–7**

John and Sally Claussen are contemplating the purchase of a hardware store from John Duggan. The Claussens anticipate that the store will generate cash flows of $70,000 per year for 20 years. At the end of 20 years, they intend to sell the store for an estimated $400,000. The Claussens will finance the investment with a variable rate mortgage. Interest rates will increase twice during the 20-year life of the mortgage. Accordingly, the Claussens' desired rate of return on this investment varies as follows:

| Years 1–5 | 8% |
|-----------|-----|
| Years 6–10 | 10% |
| Years 11–20 | 12% |

**Required:**
What is the maximum amount the Claussens should pay John Duggan for the hardware store? (Assume that all cash flows occur at the end of the year.)

**P 6–6**
**Solving for**
**unknowns**
● **LO6–3, LO6–8**

The following situations should be considered independently.
1. John Jamison wants to accumulate $60,000 for a down payment on a small business. He will invest $30,000 today in a bank account paying 8% interest compounded annually. Approximately how long will it take John to reach his goal?
2. The Jasmine Tea Company purchased merchandise from a supplier for $28,700. Payment was a noninterest-bearing note requiring Jasmine to make five annual payments of $7,000 beginning one year from the date of purchase. What is the interest rate implicit in this agreement?
3. Sam Robinson borrowed $10,000 from a friend and promised to pay the loan in 10 equal annual installments beginning one year from the date of the loan. Sam's friend would like to be reimbursed for the time value of money at a 9% annual rate. What is the annual payment Sam must make to pay back his friend?

**P 6–7**
**Solving for**
**unknowns**
● **LO6–8**

Lowlife Company defaulted on a $250,000 loan that was due on December 31, 2013. The bank has agreed to allow Lowlife to repay the $250,000 by making a series of equal annual payments beginning on December 31, 2014.

**Required:**
1. Calculate the required annual payment if the bank's interest rate is 10% and four payments are to be made.
2. Calculate the required annual payment if the bank's interest rate is 8% and five payments are to be made.
3. If the bank's interest rate is 10%, how many annual payments of $51,351 would be required to repay the debt?
4. If three payments of $104,087 are to be made, what interest rate is the bank charging Lowlife?

**P 6–8**
**Deferred annuities**
● **LO6–7**

On January 1, 2013, the Montgomery Company agreed to purchase a building by making six payments. The first three are to be $25,000 each, and will be paid on December 31, 2013, 2014, and 2015. The last three are to be $40,000 each and will be paid on December 31, 2016, 2017, and 2018. Montgomery borrowed other money at a 10% annual rate.

**Required:**
1. At what amount should Montgomery record the note payable and corresponding cost of the building on January 1, 2013?
2. How much interest expense on this note will Montgomery recognize in 2013?

**P 6–9**
**Deferred annuities**
● **LO6–7**

John Roberts is 55 years old and has been asked to accept early retirement from his company. The company has offered John three alternative compensation packages to induce John to retire:
1. $180,000 cash payment to be paid immediately.
2. A 20-year annuity of $16,000 beginning immediately.
3. A 10-year annuity of $50,000 beginning at age 65.

**Required:**
Which alternative should John choose assuming that he is able to invest funds at a 7% rate?

**P 6–10**
**Noninterest-bearing note; annuity and lump-sum payment**
● **LO6–3, LO6–7**

On January 1, 2013, The Barrett Company purchased merchandise from a supplier. Payment was a noninterest-bearing note requiring five annual payments of $20,000 on each December 31 beginning on December 31, 2013, and a lump-sum payment of $100,000 on December 31, 2017. A 10% interest rate properly reflects the time value of money in this situation.

**Required:**
Calculate the amount at which Barrett should record the note payable and corresponding merchandise purchased on January 1, 2013.

**P 6–11**
**Solving for unknown lease payment**
● **LO6–8, LO6–9**

Benning Manufacturing Company is negotiating with a customer for the lease of a large machine manufactured by Benning. The machine has a cash price of $800,000. Benning wants to be reimbursed for financing the machine at an 8% annual interest rate.

**Required:**
1. Determine the required lease payment if the lease agreement calls for 10 equal annual payments beginning immediately.
2. Determine the required lease payment if the first of 10 annual payments will be made one year from the date of the agreement.
3. Determine the required lease payment if the first of 10 annual payments will be made immediately and Benning will be able to sell the machine to another customer for $50,000 at the end of the 10-year lease.

**P 6–12**
**Solving for unknown lease payment; compounding periods of varying length**
● **LO6–8, LO6–9**

(This is a variation Problem 6–11 focusing on compounding periods of varying length.)
    Benning Manufacturing Company is negotiating with a customer for the lease of a large machine manufactured by Benning. The machine has a cash price of $800,000. Benning wants to be reimbursed for financing the machine at a 12% annual interest rate over the five-year lease term.

**Required:**
1. Determine the required lease payment if the lease agreement calls for 10 equal semiannual payments beginning six months from the date of the agreement.
2. Determine the required lease payment if the lease agreement calls for 20 equal quarterly payments beginning immediately.
3. Determine the required lease payment if the lease agreement calls for 60 equal monthly payments beginning one month from the date of the agreement. The present value of an ordinary annuity factor for $n = 60$ and $i = 1\%$ is 44.9550.

**P 6–13**
**Lease vs. buy alternatives**
● **LO6–3, LO6–7, LO6–9**

Kiddy Toy Corporation needs to acquire the use of a machine to be used in its manufacturing process. The machine needed is manufactured by Lollie Corp. The machine can be used for 10 years and then sold for $10,000 at the end of its useful life. Lollie has presented Kiddy with the following options:
1. *Buy machine.* The machine could be purchased for $160,000 in cash. All maintenance and insurance costs, which approximate $5,000 per year, would be paid by Kiddy.
2. *Lease machine.* The machine could be leased for a 10-year period for an annual lease payment of $25,000 with the first payment due immediately. All maintenance and insurance costs will be paid for by the Lollie Corp. and the machine will revert back to Lollie at the end of the 10-year period.

**Required:**

Assuming that a 12% interest rate properly reflects the time value of money in this situation and that all mainte-nance and insurance costs are paid at the end of each year, determine which option Kiddy should choose. Ignore income tax considerations.

**P 6–14**
Deferred
annuities;
pension
obligation
● LO6–7, LO6–9

Three employees of the Horizon Distributing Company will receive annual pension payments from the company when they retire. The employees will receive their annual payments for as long as they live. Life expectancy for each employee is 15 years beyond retirement. Their names, the amount of their annual pension payments, and the date they will receive their first payment are shown below:

| Employee | Annual Payment | Date of First Payment |
| --- | --- | --- |
| Tinkers | $20,000 | 12/31/16 |
| Evers | 25,000 | 12/31/17 |
| Chance | 30,000 | 12/31/18 |

**Required:**

1. Compute the present value of the pension obligation to these three employees as of December 31, 2013. Assume an 11% interest rate.

2. The company wants to have enough cash invested at December 31, 2016, to provide for all three employees. To accumulate enough cash, they will make three equal annual contributions to a fund that will earn 11% interest compounded annually. The first contribution will be made on December 31, 2013. Compute the amount of this required annual contribution.

**P 6–15**
Bonds and
leases; deferred
annuities
● LO6–3, LO6–7,
LO6–9

On the last day of its fiscal year ending December 31, 2013, the Sedgwick & Reams (S&R) Glass Company completed two financing arrangements. The funds provided by these initiatives will allow the company to expand its operations.

1. S&R issued 8% stated rate bonds with a face amount of $100 million. The bonds mature on December 31, 2033 (20 years). The market rate of interest for similar bond issues was 9% (4.5% semiannual rate). Interest is paid semiannually (4%) on June 30 and December 31, beginning on June 30, 2014.

2. The company leased two manufacturing facilities. Lease A requires 20 annual lease payments of $200,000 beginning on January 1, 2014. Lease B also is for 20 years, beginning January 1, 2014. Terms of the lease require 17 annual lease payments of $220,000 beginning on January 1, 2017. Generally accepted accounting principles require both leases to be recorded as liabilities for the present value of the scheduled payments. Assume that a 10% interest rate properly reflects the time value of money for the lease obligations.

**Required:**

What amounts will appear in S&R's December 31, 2013, balance sheet for the bonds and for the leases?

# Broaden Your Perspective

Apply your critical-thinking ability to the knowledge you've gained. These cases will provide you an opportunity to develop your research, analysis, judgment, and communication skills. You also will work with other students, inte-grate what you've learned, apply it in real world situations, and consider its global and ethical ramifications. This practice will broaden your knowledge and further develop your decision-making abilities.

**Ethics Case 6–1**
Rate of return
● LO6–1

The Damon Investment Company manages a mutual fund composed mostly of speculative stocks. You recently saw an ad claiming that investments in the funds have been earning a rate of return of 21%. This rate seemed quite high so you called a friend who works for one of Damon's competitors. The friend told you that the 21% return figure was determined by dividing the two-year appreciation on investments in the fund by the average invest-ment. In other words, $100 invested in the fund two years ago would have grown to $121 ($21 ÷ $100 = 21%).

**Required:**

Discuss the ethics of the 21% return claim made by the Damon Investment Company.

**Analysis
Case 6–2**
Bonus
alternatives;
present value
analysis
● LO6–3, LO6–7

Sally Hamilton has performed well as the chief financial officer of the Maxtech Computer Company and has earned a bonus. She has a choice among the following three bonus plans:

1. A $50,000 cash bonus paid now.

2. A $10,000 annual cash bonus to be paid each year over the next six years, with the first $10,000 paid now.

3. A three-year $22,000 annual cash bonus with the first payment due three years from now.

**Required:**

Evaluate the three alternative bonus plans. Sally can earn a 6% annual return on her investments.

**Communication Case 6–3**
Present value of annuities
● LO6–7

Harvey Alexander, an all-league professional football player, has just declared free agency. Two teams, the San Francisco 49ers and the Dallas Cowboys, have made Harvey the following offers to obtain his services:

> 49ers: $1 million signing bonus payable immediately and an annual salary of $1.5 million for the five-year term of the contract.
>
> Cowboys: $2.5 million signing bonus payable immediately and an annual salary of $1 million for the five-year term of the contract.

With both contracts, the annual salary will be paid in one lump sum at the end of the football season.

**Required:**

You have been hired as a consultant to Harvey's agent, Phil Marks, to evaluate the two contracts. Write a short letter to Phil with your recommendation including the method you used to reach your conclusion. Assume that Harvey has no preference between the two teams and that the decision will be based entirely on monetary considerations. Also assume that Harvey can invest his money and earn an 8% annual return.

**Analysis Case 6–4**
Present value of an annuity
● LO6–7

On a rainy afternoon two years ago, John Smiley left work early to attend a family birthday party. Eleven minutes later, a careening truck slammed into his SUV on the freeway causing John to spend two months in a coma. Now he can't hold a job or make everyday decisions and is in need of constant care. Last week, the 40-year-old Smiley won an out-of-court settlement from the truck driver's company. He was awarded payment for all medical costs and attorney fees, plus a lump-sum settlement of $2,330,716. At the time of the accident, John was president of his family's business and earned approximately $200,000 per year. He had anticipated working 25 more years before retirement.[8]

John's sister, an acquaintance of yours from college, has asked you to explain to her how the attorneys came up with the settlement amount. "They said it was based on his lost future income and a 7% rate of some kind," she explained. "But it was all 'legal-speak' to me."

**Required:**

How was the amount of the lump-sum settlement determined? Create a calculation that might help John's sister understand.

**Judgment Case 6–5**
Replacement decision
● LO6–3, LO6–7

Hughes Corporation is considering replacing a machine used in the manufacturing process with a new, more efficient model. The purchase price of the new machine is $150,000 and the old machine can be sold for $100,000. Output for the two machines is identical; they will both be used to produce the same amount of product for five years. However, the annual operating costs of the old machine are $18,000 compared to $10,000 for the new machine. Also, the new machine has a salvage value of $25,000, but the old machine will be worthless at the end of the five years.

**Required:**

Should the company sell the old machine and purchase the new model? Assume that an 8% rate properly reflects the time value of money in this situation and that all operating costs are paid at the end of the year. Ignore the effect of the decision on income taxes.

**Real World Case 6–6**
Zero-coupon bonds; Johnson & Johnson
● LO6–3, LO6–9

Real World Financials

**Johnson & Johnson** is one of the world's largest manufacturers of health care products. The company's 2010 financial statements included the following information in the long-term debt disclosure note:

|  | ($ in millions) **2010** |
| --- | --- |
| Zero-coupon convertible subordinated debentures, due 2020 | $194 |

The disclosure note stated that the debenture bonds were issued early in 2000 and have a maturity value of $272.5 million. The maturity value indicates the amount that Johnson & Johnson will pay bondholders in 2020. Each individual bond has a maturity value (face amount) of $1,000. Zero-coupon bonds pay no cash interest during the term to maturity. The company is "accreting" (gradually increasing) the issue price to maturity value using the bonds' effective interest rate computed on a semiannual basis.

**Required:**

1. Determine the effective interest rate on the bonds.
2. Determine the issue price in early 2000 of a single, $1,000 maturity-value bond.

**Real World Case 6–7**
Leases; Delta Airlines
● LO6–3, LO6–9

Real World Financials

**Delta Airlines** provides scheduled air transportation services in the United States. Like many airlines, Delta leases many of its planes from **Boeing Company**. In its long-term debt disclosure note included in the financial statements for the year ended December 31, 2010, the company listed $738 million in lease obligations. The existing leases had an approximate seven-year remaining life and future lease payments average approximately $153 million per year.

**Required:**

1. Determine the effective interest rate the company used to determine the lease liability assuming that lease payments are made at the end of each fiscal year.
2. Repeat requirement 1 assuming that lease payments are made at the beginning of each fiscal year.

---

[8]This case is based on actual events.

# 7

# Cash and Receivables

We begin our study of assets by looking at cash and receivables—the two assets typically listed first in a balance sheet. For cash, the key issues are internal control and classification in the balance sheet. For receivables, the key issues are valuation and the related income statement effects of transactions involving accounts receivable and notes receivable.

## LEARNING OBJECTIVES

After studying this chapter, you should be able to:

● **LO7–1** Define what is meant by internal control and describe some key elements of an internal control system for cash receipts and disbursements. (p. 360)

● **LO7–2** Explain the possible restrictions on cash and their implications for classification in the balance sheet. (p. 362)

● **LO7–3** Distinguish between the gross and net methods of accounting for cash discounts. (p. 365)

● **LO7–4** Describe the accounting treatment for merchandise returns. (p. 366)

● **LO7–5** Describe the accounting treatment of anticipated uncollectible accounts receivable. (p. 368)

● **LO7–6** Describe the two approaches to estimating bad debts. (p. 369)

● **LO7–7** Describe the accounting treatment of short-term notes receivable. (p. 374)

● **LO7–8** Differentiate between the use of receivables in financing arrangements accounted for as a secured borrowing and those accounted for as a sale. (p. 379)

● **LO7–9** Describe the variables that influence a company's investment in receivables and calculate the key ratios used by analysts to monitor that investment. (p. 388)

● **LO7–10** Discuss the primary differences between U.S. GAAP and IFRS with respect to cash and receivables. (pp. 363, 378, 397, and 398)

## FINANCIAL REPORTING CASE

### What Does It All Mean?

Your roommate, Todd Buckley, was surfing the net looking for information about his future employer, **Cisco Systems**. Todd, an engineering major, recently accepted a position with Cisco, the world's largest provider of hardware, software, and services that drive the Internet. He noticed an article on TheStreet.com entitled "Cisco Triples Bad-Account Provision." "This doesn't look good," Todd grumbled. "The article says that my new employer's deadbeat account column has more than tripled in the span of a year. I guess all those dot-com companies are not paying their bills. But this sentence is confusing. 'For the fiscal first quarter Cisco moved $275 million from operating cash to cover potential nonpayments from failed customers.' Did they actually move cash and if so, where did they move it and why?"

You studied accounting for bad debts in your intermediate accounting class and are confident you can help. After reading the article, you comfort Todd. "First of all, the term *provision* just means expense, and no, Cisco didn't move any cash. The company uses what is called the *allowance method* to account for its bad debts, and it looks like it simply recorded $275 million in expense for the quarter and increased the allowance for uncollectible accounts."

Todd was not happy with your answer. "Provisions! Allowance method! Uncollectible accounts! I want you to help me understand, not make things worse." "Okay," you offer, "let's start at the beginning."

**By the time you finish this chapter, you should be able to respond appropriately to the questions posed in this case. Compare your response to the solution provided at the end of the chapter.**

●————**QUESTIONS**

1. Explain the allowance method of accounting for bad debts. (*p. 368*)

2. What approaches might Cisco have used to arrive at the $275 million bad debt provision? (*p. 370*)

3. Are there any alternatives to the allowance method? (*p. 373*)

In the earlier chapters of this text, we studied the underlying measurement and reporting concepts for the basic financial statements presented to external decision makers. Now we turn our attention to the elements of those financial statements. Specifically, we further explore the elements of the balance sheet, and also consider the income statement effects of transactions involving these elements. We first address assets, then liabilities, and finally shareholders' equity. This chapter focuses on the current assets **cash and cash equivalents** and **receivables**.

# CASH AND CASH EQUIVALENTS

**Cash** includes currency and coins, balances in checking accounts, and items acceptable for deposit in these accounts, such as checks and money orders received from customers. These forms of cash represent amounts readily available to pay off debt or to use in operations, without any legal or contractual restriction.

Managers typically invest temporarily idle cash to earn interest on those funds rather than keep an unnecessarily large checking account. These amounts are essentially equivalent to cash because they can quickly become available for use as cash. So, short-term, highly liquid investments that can be readily converted to cash with little risk of loss are viewed as cash equivalents. For financial reporting we make no distinction between cash in the form of currency or bank account balances and amounts held in cash-equivalent investments.

A company's policy concerning which short-term, highly liquid investments it classifies as cash equivalents should be described in a disclosure note.

**Cash equivalents** include money market funds, treasury bills, and commercial paper. To be classified as cash equivalents, these investments must have a maturity date no longer than three months *from the date of purchase*. Companies are permitted flexibility in designating cash equivalents and must establish individual policies regarding which short-term, highly liquid investments are classified as cash equivalents. A company's policy should be consistent with the usual motivation for acquiring these investments. The policy should be disclosed in the notes to the financial statements. Illustration 7–1 shows a note from a 2011 quarterly report of **Mannatech Incorporated**, a manufacturer of dietary supplements and other wellness products, that provides a description of the company's cash equivalents.

**Illustration 7–1**

Disclosure of Cash Equivalents—Mannatech Incorporated

**Real World Financials**

**Note 1: Organization and Summary of Significant Accounting Policies (in part)** *Cash and Cash Equivalents*
The Company considers all highly liquid investments with original maturities of three months or less to be cash equivalents. The Company includes in its cash and cash equivalents credit card receivables due from its credit card processor, as the cash proceeds from credit card receivables are received within 24 to 72 hours.

Notice in the disclosure note that Mannatech includes credit card receivables as cash equivalents. These receivables typically are converted to cash within a few business days.

The measurement and reporting of cash and cash equivalents are largely straightforward because cash generally presents no measurement problems. It is the standard medium of exchange and the basis for measuring assets and liabilities. Cash and cash equivalents usually are combined and reported as a single amount in the balance sheet. However, cash that is not available for use in current operations because it is restricted for a special purpose usually is classified in one of the noncurrent asset categories. Restricted cash is discussed later in this chapter.

Credit and debit card receivables often are included in cash equivalents.

All assets must be safeguarded against possible misuse. However, cash is the most liquid asset and the asset most easily expropriated. As a result, a system of internal control of cash is a key accounting issue.

# Internal Control

The success of any business enterprise depends on an effective system of **internal control**. Internal control refers to a company's plan to (a) encourage adherence to company policies and procedures, (b) promote operational efficiency, (c) minimize errors and theft, and (d) enhance the reliability and accuracy of accounting data. From a financial accounting perspective, the focus is on controls intended to improve the accuracy and reliability of accounting information and to safeguard the company's assets.

● **LO7–1**

The Sarbanes-Oxley Act requires a company to document and assess its internal controls. Auditors express an opinion on management's assessment.

Recall from our discussion in Chapter 1 that Section 404 of the *Sarbanes-Oxley Act of 2002* requires that companies document their internal controls and assess their adequacy. The Public Company Accounting Oversight Board's *Auditing Standard No. 5* further requires the auditor to express its own opinion on whether the company has maintained effective internal control over financial reporting.

Many companies have incurred significant costs in an effort to comply with the requirements of Section 404.[1] A framework for designing an internal control system is provided

---

[1]In response to the high cost of 404 compliance, the PCAOB issued a second standard, *Auditing Standard No. 5,* to replace its Standard No. 2. The new standard emphasizes audit efficiency with a more focused, risk-based testing approach for material areas that is intended to reduce the total costs of 404 compliance.

by the **Committee of Sponsoring Organizations (COSO)** of the Treadway Commission.[2] Formed in 1985, the organization is dedicated to improving the quality of financial reporting through, among other things, effective internal controls.

COSO defines internal control as a process, undertaken by an entity's board of directors, management and other personnel, designed to provide reasonable assurance regarding the achievement of objectives in the following categories:

- Effectiveness and efficiency of operations.
- Reliability of financial reporting.
- Compliance with applicable laws and regulations.[3]

## Internal Control Procedures—Cash Receipts

As cash is the most liquid of all assets, a well-designed and functioning system of internal control must surround all cash transactions. **Separation of duties** is critical. Individuals that have physical responsibility for assets should not also have access to accounting records. So, employees who handle cash should not be involved in or have access to accounting records nor be involved in the reconciliation of cash book balances to bank balances.

Consider the cash receipt process. Most nonretail businesses receive payment for goods by checks received through the mail. An approach to internal control over cash receipts that utilizes separation of duties might include the following steps:

1. Employee A opens the mail each day and prepares a multicopy listing of all checks including the amount and payor's name.
2. Employee B takes the checks, along with one copy of the listing, to the person responsible for depositing the checks in the company's bank account.
3. A second copy of the check listing is sent to the accounting department where Employee C enters receipts into the accounting records.

Good internal control helps ensure accuracy as well as safeguard against theft. The bank-generated deposit slip can be compared with the check listing to verify that the amounts received were also deposited. And, because the person opening the mail is not the person who maintains the accounting records, it's impossible for one person to steal checks and alter accounting records to cover up their theft.

## Internal Control Procedures—Cash Disbursements

Proper controls for cash disbursements should be designed to prevent any unauthorized payments and ensure that disbursements are recorded in the proper accounts. Important elements of a cash disbursement control system include:

1. All disbursements, other than very small disbursements from petty cash, should be made by check. This provides a permanent record of all disbursements.
2. All expenditures should be *authorized* before a check is prepared. For example, a vendor invoice for the purchase of inventory should be compared with the purchase order and receiving report to ensure the accuracy of quantity, price, part numbers, and so on. This process should include verification of the proper ledger accounts to be debited.
3. Checks should be signed only by authorized individuals.

Once again, separation of duties is important. Responsibilities for check signing, check writing, check mailing, cash disbursement documentation, and recordkeeping should be separated whenever possible. That way, a single person can't write checks to himself and disguise that theft as a payment to an approved vendor.

> Employees involved in recordkeeping should not also have physical access to the assets.

[2]The sponsoring organizations include the AICPA, the Financial Executives International, the Institute of Internal Auditors, the American Accounting Association, and the Institute of Management Accountants.
[3]www.coso.org.

An important part of any system of internal control of cash is the periodic reconciliation of book balances and bank balances to the correct balance. In addition, a petty cash system is employed by many business enterprises. We cover these two topics in Appendix 7A.

# Restricted Cash and Compensating Balances

● LO7–2

We discussed the classification of assets and liabilities in Chapter 3. You should recall that only cash available for current operations or to satisfy current liabilities is classified as a current asset. Cash that is restricted in some way and not available for current use usually is reported as a noncurrent asset such as *investments and funds* or *other assets.*

Restrictions on cash can be informal, arising from management's intent to use a certain amount of cash for a specific purpose. For example, a company may set aside funds for future plant expansion. This cash, if material, should be classified as investments and funds or other assets. Sometimes restrictions are contractually imposed. Debt instruments, for instance, frequently require the borrower to set aside funds (often referred to as a sinking fund) for the future payment of a debt. In these instances, the restricted cash is classified as noncurrent investments and funds or other assets if the debt is classified as noncurrent. On the other hand, if the liability is current, the restricted cash also is classified as current. Disclosure notes should describe any material restrictions of cash.

Banks frequently require cash restrictions in connection with loans or loan commitments (lines of credit). Typically, the borrower is asked to maintain a specified balance in a low interest or noninterest-bearing account at the bank (creditor). The required balance usually is some percentage of the committed amount (say 2% to 5%). These are known as **compensating balances** because they compensate the bank for granting the loan or extending the line of credit.

The effect of a *compensating balance* is a higher effective interest rate on the debt.

A compensating balance results in the borrower's paying an effective interest rate higher than the stated rate on the debt. For example, suppose that a company borrows $10,000,000 from a bank at an interest rate of 12%. If the bank requires a compensating balance of $2,000,000 to be held in a noninterest-bearing checking account, the company really is borrowing only $8,000,000 (the loan less the compensating balance). This means an effective interest rate of 15% ($1,200,000 interest divided by $8,000,000 cash available for use).

A material compensating balance must be disclosed regardless of the classification of the cash.

The classification and disclosure of a compensating balance depends on the nature of the restriction and the classification of the related debt.[4] If the restriction is legally binding, the cash is classified as either current or noncurrent (investments and funds or other assets) depending on the classification of the related debt. In either case, note disclosure is appropriate.

If the compensating balance arrangement is informal with no contractual agreement that restricts the use of cash, the compensating balance can be reported as part of cash and cash equivalents, with note disclosure of the arrangement. Illustration 7–2 provides an example of a note disclosure of a compensating balance for **CNB Financial Services, Inc.,** a bank holding company incorporated in West Virginia.

**Illustration 7–2**

Disclosure of Compensating Balances—CNB Financial Services, Inc.

**Real World Financials**

> **Note 10—Lines of Credit (in part)**
> The Bank entered into an open-ended unsecured line of credit with Mercantile Safe Deposit and Trust Company for $3,000,000 for federal fund purchases. Funds issued under this agreement are at the Mercantile Safe Deposit and Trust Company federal funds rate effective at the time of borrowing. The line . . . has a compensating balance requirement of $250,000.

---

[4]FASB ASC 210–10–S99–2: SAB Topic 6.H–Balance Sheet—Overall—SEC Materials, *Accounting Series Release 148* (originally "Amendments to Regulations S-X and Related Interpretations and Guidelines Regarding the Disclosure of Compensating Balances and Short-Term Borrowing Arrangements," *Accounting Series Release No. 148,* Securities and Exchange Commission (November 13, 1973)).

# International Financial Reporting Standards

**Cash and Cash Equivalents.** In general, cash and cash equivalents are treated similarly under IFRS and U.S. GAAP. One difference relates to bank overdrafts, which occur when withdrawals from a bank account exceed the available balance. U.S. GAAP requires that overdrafts typically be treated as liabilities. In contrast, *IAS No. 7* allows bank overdrafts to be offset against other cash accounts when overdrafts are payable on demand and fluctuate between positive and negative amounts as part of the normal cash management program that a company uses to minimize its cash balance.[5] For example, LaDonia Company has two cash accounts with the following balances as of December 31, 2013:

- **LO7–10**

**IFRS ILLUSTRATION**

National Bank:   $300,000
Central Bank:     (15,000)

Under U.S. GAAP, LaDonia's 12/31/13 balance sheet would report a cash asset of $300,000 and an overdraft current liability of $15,000. Under IFRS, LaDonia would report a cash asset of $285,000.

## Decision Makers' Perspective

Cash often is referred to as a *nonearning* asset because it earns no interest. For this reason, managers invest idle cash in either cash equivalents or short-term investments, both of which provide a return. Management's goal is to hold the minimum amount of cash necessary to conduct normal business operations, meet its obligations, and take advantage of opportunities. Too much cash reduces profits through lost returns, while too little cash increases risk. This trade-off between risk and return is an ongoing choice made by management (internal decision makers). Whether the choice made is appropriate is an ongoing assessment made by investors and creditors (external decision makers).

A company must have cash available for the compensating balances we discussed in the previous section as well as for planned disbursements related to normal operating, investing, and financing cash flows. However, because cash inflows and outflows can vary from planned amounts, a company needs an additional cash cushion as a precaution against that contingency. The size of the cushion depends on the company's ability to convert cash equivalents and short-term investments into cash quickly, along with its short-term borrowing capacity.

**Companies hold cash to pay for planned and unplanned transactions and to satisfy compensating balance requirements.**

Liquidity is a measure of a company's cash position and overall ability to obtain cash in the normal course of business. A company is assumed to be liquid if it has sufficient cash or is capable of converting its other assets to cash in a relatively short period of time so that current needs can be met. Frequently, liquidity is measured with respect to the ability to pay currently maturing debt. The current ratio is one of the most common ways of measuring liquidity and is calculated by dividing current assets by current liabilities. By comparing liabilities that must be satisfied in the near term with assets that either are cash or will be converted to cash in the near term we have a base measure of a company's liquidity. We can refine the measure by adjusting for the implicit assumption of the current ratio that all current assets are equally liquid. In the acid-test or quick ratio, the numerator consists of "quick assets," which include only cash and cash equivalents, short-term investments, and accounts receivable. By eliminating inventories and prepaid expenses, the current assets that are less readily convertible into cash, we get a more precise indication of a company's short-term solvency than with the current ratio. We discussed and illustrated these liquidity ratios in Chapter 3.

We should evaluate the adequacy of any ratio in the context of the industry in which the company operates and other specific circumstances. Bear in mind, though, that industry averages are only one indication of acceptability and any ratio is but one indication of liquidity. Profitability, for instance, is perhaps the best long-run indication of liquidity. And

---

[5]"Statement of Cash Flows," *International Accounting Standard No. 7* (IASCF), as amended effective January 1, 2011, par. 8.

a company may be very efficient in managing its current assets so that, say, receivables are more liquid than they otherwise would be. The receivables turnover ratio we discuss in Part B of this chapter offers a measure of management's efficiency in this regard.

There are many techniques that a company can use to manage cash balances. A discussion of these techniques is beyond the scope of this text. However, it is sufficient here to understand that management must make important decisions related to cash that have a direct impact on a company's profitability and risk. Because the lack of prudent cash management can lead to the failure of an otherwise sound company, it is essential that managers as well as outside investors and creditors maintain close vigil over this facet of a company's health. ●

> A manager should actively monitor the company's cash position.

# PART B | CURRENT RECEIVABLES

**Receivables** represent a company's claims to the future collection of cash, other assets, or services. Receivables resulting from the sale of goods or services on account are called **accounts receivable** and often are referred to as *trade receivables. Nontrade receivables* are those other than trade receivables and include tax refund claims, interest receivable, and loans by the company to other entities including stockholders and employees. When a receivable, trade or nontrade, is accompanied by a formal promissory note, it is referred to as a note receivable. We consider notes receivable after first discussing accounts receivable.

As you study receivables, realize that one company's claim to the future collection of cash corresponds to another company's (or individual's) obligation to pay cash. One company's account receivable will be the mirror image of another company's account payable. Chapter 13 addresses accounts payable and other current liabilities.

> An account receivable and an account payable reflect opposite sides of the same transaction.

## Accounts Receivable

Most businesses provide credit to their customers, either because it's not practical to require immediate cash payment or to encourage customers to purchase the company's product or service. Accounts receivable are *informal* credit arrangements supported by an invoice and normally are due in 30 to 60 days after the sale. They almost always are classified as *current* assets because their normal collection period, even if longer than a year, is part of, and therefore less than, the operating cycle.

The point at which accounts receivable are recognized depends on the earnings process of the company. We discussed the realization principle in Chapter 5 and the criteria that must be met before revenue can be recognized. Recall that revenue can be recognized only after the earnings process is *virtually complete* and *collection* from the customer is *reasonably assured.* For the typical credit sale, these criteria are satisfied at the point of delivery of the product or service, so revenue and the related receivable are recognized at that time.

> Accounts receivable are current assets because, by definition, they will be converted to cash within the normal operating cycle.

> Typically, revenue and related accounts receivable are recognized at the point of delivery of the product or service.

### Initial Valuation of Accounts Receivable

We know from prior discussions that receivables should be recorded at the present value of future cash receipts using a realistic interest rate. So, a $10,000 sale on credit due in 30 days should result in a receivable valued at the present value of the $10,000. In other words, the interest portion of the $10,000 due in 30 days should be removed and recognized as interest revenue over the 30-day period, not as sales revenue at date of delivery of the product. If the monthly interest rate is 2%, the receivable would be valued at $9,804, calculated by multiplying the future cash payment of $10,000 by the present value of $1 factor for one period at 2% (.98039).

However, because the difference between the future and present values of accounts receivable often is immaterial, GAAP specifically excludes accounts receivable from the general rule that receivables be recorded at present value.[6] Therefore, accounts receivable initially are valued at the exchange price agreed on by the buyer and seller. In our example, both the account receivable and sales revenue would be recorded at $10,000. Let's discuss two aspects of accounts receivable related to their initial valuation—trade discounts and cash discounts.

> The typical account receivable is valued at the amount expected to be received, not the present value of that amount.

---

[6]FASB ASC 835–30–15–3: Interest—Imputation of Interest—Scope and Scope Exceptions (previously "Interest on Receivables and Payables," *Accounting Principles Board Opinion No. 21* (New York: AICPA, 1971)).

**TRADE DISCOUNTS.**   Companies frequently offer trade discounts to customers, usually a percentage reduction from the list price. Trade discounts can be a way to change prices
without publishing a new catalog or to disguise real prices from competitors. They also are
used to give quantity discounts to large customers. For example, a manufacturer might list
a machine part at $2,500 but sell it to a customer at a 10% discount. The trade discount of
$250 is not recognized directly when recording the transaction. The discount is recognized
indirectly by recording the sale at the net of discount price of $2,250, not at the list price.

**CASH DISCOUNTS.**   Be careful to distinguish a *trade* discount from a *cash* discount.
Cash discounts, often called *sales discounts,* represent reductions not in the selling price of
a good or service but in the amount to be paid by a credit customer if paid within a specified
period of time. It is a discount intended to provide incentive for quick payment.

*Cash discounts* reduce the amount to be paid if remittance is made within a specified short period of time.

● LO7–3

The *gross method* views cash discounts not taken as part of sales revenue.

   The amount of the discount and the time period within which it's available usually are
conveyed by terms like 2/10, n/30 (meaning a 2% discount if paid within 10 days, otherwise
full payment within 30 days). There are two ways to record cash discounts, the gross method
and the net method. Conceptually, the gross method views a discount not taken by the customer as part of sales revenue. On the other hand, the net method considers sales revenue
to be the net amount, after discount, and any discounts not taken by the customer as interest
revenue. The discounts are viewed as compensation to the seller for providing financing to
the customer. With both methods, sales revenue only ends up being reduced by sales discounts that are actually taken. Consider the example in Illustration 7–3.

**Illustration 7–3**
Cash Discounts

The Hawthorne Manufacturing Company offers credit customers a 2% cash discount if the
sales price is paid within 10 days. Any amounts not paid within 10 days are due in 30 days.
These repayment terms are stated as 2/10, n/30. On October 5, 2013, Hawthorne sold
merchandise at a price of $20,000. The customer paid $13,720 ($14,000 less the 2% cash
discount) on October 14 and the remaining balance of $6,000 on November 4.
   The appropriate journal entries to record the sale and cash collection, comparing the
gross and net methods are as follows:

| Gross Method | | | Net Method | | |
|---|---|---|---|---|---|
| **October 5, 2013** | | | **October 5, 2013** | | |
| Accounts receivable ........ | 20,000 | | Accounts receivable ....... | 19,600 | |
| Sales revenue .............. | | 20,000 | Sales revenue .............. | | 19,600 |
| **October 14, 2013** | | | **October 14, 2013** | | |
| Cash .............................. | 13,720 | | Cash .............................. | 13,720 | |
| Sales discounts ............... | 280 | | Accounts receivable .... | | 13,720 |
| Accounts receivable .... | | 14,000 | | | |
| **November 4, 2013** | | | **November 4, 2013** | | |
| Cash .............................. | 6,000 | | Cash .............................. | 6,000 | |
| Accounts receivable .... | | 6,000 | Accounts receivable .... | | 5,880 |
| | | | Interest revenue .......... | | 120 |

By either method, net sales is reduced by discounts *taken.*

Discounts *not* taken are included in sales revenue using the gross method and interest revenue using the net method.

   Notice that by using the gross method, we initially record the revenue and related receivable at the full $20,000 price. On remittance within the discount period, the $280 discount is
recorded as a debit to an account called *sales discounts.* This is a contra account to sales revenue and is deducted from sales revenue to derive the net sales reported in the income statement. For payments made after the discount period, cash is simply increased and accounts
receivable decreased by the gross amount originally recorded.

   Under the net method, we record revenue and the related accounts receivable at the
agreed-on price *less* the 2% discount applied to the entire price. Payments made within
the discount period are recorded as debits to cash and credits to accounts receivable for
the amount received. If a customer loses a discount by failing to pay within the discount
period, the discount not taken is recorded as interest revenue. In this case, $120 in cash
(2% × $6,000) is interest.

The *net method* considers cash discounts not taken as interest revenue.

Total revenue in the 2013 income statement would be the same by either method:

Revenue comparison of the gross method and the net method.

| | **Gross Method** | **Net Method** |
|---|---|---|
| Sales | $20,000 | $19,600 |
| Less: Sales discounts | (280) | –0– |
| Net sales revenue | 19,720 | 19,600 |
| Interest revenue | 0 | 120 |
| Total revenue | $19,720 | $19,720 |

Which is correct? Conceptually, the net method usually reflects the reality of the situation—the real price is $19,600 and $120 is an interest penalty for not paying promptly. The net price usually is the price expected by the seller because the discount usually reflects a hefty interest cost that prudent buyers are unwilling to bear. Consider Illustration 7–3. Although the discount rate is stated as 2%, the effective rate really is 37.23%. In order to save $2, the buyer must pay $98 twenty days earlier than otherwise due, effectively "investing" $98 to "earn" $2, a rate of return of 2.04% ($2/$98) for a 20-day period. To convert this 20-day rate to an annual rate, we multiply by 365/20:

$$2.04\% \times 365/20 = 37.23\% \text{ effective rate}$$

Understandably, most buyers try to take the discount if at all possible.

The difference between the two methods, in terms of the effect of the transactions on income, is in the timing of the recognition of any discounts not taken. The gross method recognizes discounts not taken as revenue when the sale is made. The net method recognizes them as revenue after the discount period has passed and the cash is collected. These two measurement dates could be in different reporting periods.

From a practical standpoint, the effect on the financial statements of the difference between the two methods usually is immaterial. As a result, most companies use the gross method because it's easier and doesn't require adjusting entries for discounts not taken.

## Subsequent Valuation of Accounts Receivable

Following the initial valuation of an account receivable, two situations possibly could cause the cash ultimately collected to be less than the initial valuation of the receivable: (1) the customer could return the product, or (2) the customer could default and not pay the agreed-upon sales price. When accounting for sales and accounts receivable, we anticipate these possibilities.

● LO7–4  **SALES RETURNS.** Customers frequently are given the right to return the merchandise they purchase if they are not satisfied. We discussed how this policy affects revenue recognition in Chapter 5. We now discuss it from the perspective of asset valuation.

Recognizing *sales returns* when they occur could result in an overstatement of income in the period of the related sale.

When merchandise is returned for a refund or for credit to be applied to other purchases, the situation is called a sales return. When practical, a dissatisfied customer might be given a special price reduction as an incentive to keep the merchandise purchased.[7] Returns are common and often substantial in some industries such as food products, publishing, and retailing. In these cases, recognizing returns and allowances only as they occur could cause profit to be overstated in the period of the sale and understated in the return period. For example, assume merchandise is sold to a customer for $10,000 in December 2013, the last month in the selling company's fiscal year, and that the merchandise cost $6,000. If all of the merchandise is returned in 2014 after financial statements for 2013 are issued, gross profit will be overstated in 2013 and understated in 2014 by $4,000. Assets at the end of 2013 also will be overstated by $4,000 because a $10,000 receivable would be recorded instead of $6,000 in inventory.

To avoid misstating the financial statements, sales revenue and accounts receivable should be reduced by the amount of returns in the period of sale if the amount of returns is

---

[7]Price reductions sometimes are referred to as *sales allowances* and are distinguished from situations when the products actually are returned for a refund or credit (sales returns).

anticipated to be material. We must account for all returns, including those that occur in the period of sale and those that are estimated to occur in future periods. The returns that occur in the period of sale are easy to account for, but the returns estimated for future periods are more difficult. We reduce sales revenue and accounts receivable for estimated returns by debiting a sales returns account (which is a contra account to sales revenue) and crediting an "allowance for sales returns" account (which is a contra account to accounts receivable). When returns actually occur in a following reporting period, the allowance for sales returns is debited and accounts receivable is credited. In this way, income is not reduced in the return period but in the period of the sales revenue.[8]

For an example, refer to Illustration 7–4. The perpetual inventory system records increases (debits) and decreases (credits) in the inventory account as they occur. The inventory of $78,000 in the first set of entries represents merchandise actually returned and on hand, while the inventory of $42,000 in the second set of entries represents an estimate of the cost of merchandise expected to be returned. This later amount is included in the period-end inventory in the company's balance sheet, even though the actual merchandise belongs to other entities, because ownership of the goods is expected to revert back to the company.

**Illustration 7–4**
Sales Returns

During 2013, its first year of operations, the Hawthorne Manufacturing Company sold merchandise on account for $2,000,000. This merchandise cost $1,200,000 (60% of the selling price). Industry experience indicates that 10% of all sales will be returned. Customers returned $130,000 in sales during 2013, prior to making payment.

The entries to record sales and merchandise returned during the year, *assuming that a perpetual inventory system is used,* are as follows:

**Sales**

| | | |
|---|---|---|
| Accounts receivable ................................................................. | 2,000,000 | |
|    Sales revenue ................................................................. | | 2,000,000 |
| Cost of goods sold (60% × $2,000,000) ........................................ | 1,200,000 | |
|    Inventory ..................................................................... | | 1,200,000 |

**Actual Returns**

| | | |
|---|---|---|
| Sales returns (actual returns) ..................................................... | 130,000 | |
|    Accounts receivable ......................................................... | | 130,000 |
| Inventory ......................................................................... | 78,000 | |
|    Cost of goods sold (60% × $130,000) ..................................... | | 78,000 |

At the end of 2013, the company would anticipate the remaining estimated returns using the following adjusting entries:

**Adjusting Entries**

| | | |
|---|---|---|
| Sales returns ([10% × $2,000,000] − $130,000) ............................... | 70,000 | |
|    Allowance for sales returns ................................................. | | 70,000 |
| Inventory—estimated returns ..................................................... | 42,000 | |
|    Cost of goods sold (60% × $70,000) ..................................... | | 42,000 |

If sales returns are material, they should be estimated and recorded in the same period as the related sales.

Assuming that the estimates of future returns are correct, the following (summary) journal entry would be recorded in 2014:

| | | |
|---|---|---|
| Allowance for sales returns ........................................................ | 70,000 | |
|    Accounts receivable ......................................................... | | 70,000 |

Sometimes a customer will return merchandise because it has been damaged during shipment or is defective. This possibility must be anticipated in a company's estimate of returns.

---

[8]Of course, if the allowance for sales returns is estimated incorrectly, income in both the period of the sale and the return will be misstated.

As you will study in Chapter 9, inventory is valued at the lower-of-cost-or-market. Therefore, damaged or defective merchandise returned from a customer must be written down to market value.[9]

What happens if the estimate of future returns turns out to be more or less than $70,000? Remember from previous discussions that when an estimate turns out to be wrong, we don't revise prior years' financial statements to reflect the new estimate. Instead, we merely incorporate the new estimate in any related accounting determinations from that point on. Suppose in our illustration that in 2014 actual returns from 2013 sales are $60,000, instead of $70,000. If that happens, the allowance account will have a $10,000 balance and the inventory account will have a $6,000 balance ($10,000 × 60%) representing inventory that was not returned as anticipated. These balances can be used to offset actual returns in 2014 from 2014 sales. As a result, the 2014 adjusting entry to record estimated returns would be $10,000 ($6,000 in cost of goods sold/inventory) less than if the 2013 estimate had been correct. Similarly, if actual returns are $80,000, the 2014 adjusting entry will be $10,000 ($6,000) higher than if the 2013 estimate had been correct.

How do companies estimate returns? Principally they rely on past history, taking into account any changes that might affect future experience. For example, changes in customer base, payment terms offered to customers, and overall economic conditions might suggest that future returns will differ from past returns. The task of estimating returns is made easier for many large retail companies whose fiscal year-end is the end of January. Since retail companies generate a large portion of their annual sales during the Christmas season, most returns from these sales would already have been accounted for by the end of January.

**AVX Corporation** is a leading manufacturer of electronic components. Illustration 7–5, drawn from AVX's 2011 annual report, describes the company's approach to estimating returns.

**Illustration 7–5**

Disclosure of Sales Returns Policy—AVX Corporation

Real World Financials

**Summary of Significant Accounting Policies (in part) Returns**
Sales revenue and cost of sales reported in the income statement are reduced to reflect estimated returns. We record an estimated sales allowance for returns at the time of sale based on using historical trends, current pricing and volume information, other market specific information and input from sales, marketing and other key management. The amount accrued reflects the return of value of the customer's inventory. These procedures require the exercise of significant judgments. We believe that these procedures enable us to make reliable estimates of future returns. Our actual results approximate our estimates. When the product is returned and verified, the customer is given credit against their accounts receivable.

In some industries, returns typically are small and infrequent. Companies in these industries usually simply record returns in the period they occur because the effect on income measurement and asset valuation is immaterial. In a few situations, significant uncertainty as to future collection is created by the right of return, because returns cannot be estimated reliably. In those cases, revenue recognition is deferred until the uncertainty is resolved. We discussed this possibility in Chapter 5.

● LO7–5 **UNCOLLECTIBLE ACCOUNTS RECEIVABLE.** Companies that extend credit to customers know that it's unlikely that all customers will fully pay their accounts. **Bad debt expense** is an inherent cost of granting credit. It's an operating expense incurred to make sales. As a result, even when specific customer accounts haven't been proven uncollectible by the end of the reporting period, the expense should be matched with sales revenue in the

[9]Another way to record these journal entries would be to set up an allowance for the entire amount of estimated returns when we record 2013 sales revenue, and then reduce the allowance when any actual returns occur in this or future periods. Under that approach, when we record sales revenue and cost of goods sold, we also debit sales returns and credit the allowance for sales returns for the entire amount of estimated returns (10% × $2,000,000 = $200,000), and debit inventory and credit cost of goods sold for 60% of that amount ($120,000). Then, when actual returns occurred, we would debit allowance for sales returns and credit accounts receivable, for a total of $130,000 in 2013 and $70,000 in 2014. Note that this approach takes us to the same outcomes in 2013 and 2014.

income statement for that period.[10] Likewise, as it's not expected that all accounts receivable will be collected, the balance sheet should report only the expected **net realizable value** of the asset, that is, the amount of cash the company expects to actually collect from customers.

Companies account for bad debts by recording an adjusting entry that debits bad debt expense and reduces accounts receivable indirectly by crediting a contra account (allowance for uncollectible accounts) to accounts receivable for an estimate of the amount that eventually will prove uncollectible. This approach to accounting for bad debts is known as the **allowance method**. Quite often, companies report the allowance for uncollectible accounts (often called the *allowance for doubtful accounts*) parenthetically or alongside the accounts receivable account title separated by a dash or a comma. Other times they will simply show the net balance in the balance sheet, and then describe the allowance in a footnote. For example, **Dell Inc.** reported the following under current assets in its comparative balance sheets for 2011 and 2010:

> Recognizing bad debt expense results in accounts receivable being reported at their *net realizable value*.

> The *allowance method* is an application of matching in accounting for bad debts.

|  | ($ in millions) | |
| --- | --- | --- |
|  | **January 28, 2011** | **January 29, 2010** |
| Accounts receivables, net | $6,493 | $5,837 |

Dell then included the note shown in Illustration 7–6 in its financial statements:

| **NOTE 17—SUPPLEMENTAL CONSOLIDATED FINANCIAL INFORMATION (partial)** | | |
| --- | --- | --- |
| **Supplemental Consolidated Statements of Financial Position Information:** | **January 28, 2011** | **January 29, 2010** |
|  | (in millions) | |
| *Accounts receivable, net* | | |
| Gross accounts receivable | $6,589 | $5,952 |
| Allowance for doubtful accounts | (96) | (115) |
| Total | $6,493 | $5,837 |

**Illustration 7–6**

Disclosure of Allowance for Doubtful Accounts— Dell, Inc.

Real World Financials

The $6,493 million figure at the end of 2011 is the company's estimate of the net realizable value of accounts receivable. Actual (gross) accounts receivable at the end of 2011 were $6,589 million ($6,493 + $96).

There are two ways commonly used to arrive at this estimate of future bad debts—the income statement approach and the balance sheet approach. Illustration 7–7 is used to demonstrate both approaches. As you proceed through the illustration, remember that the two approaches represent alternative ways to estimate the *amount* of future bad debts. Except for the amounts, the accounting entries are identical.

● **LO7–6**

| The Hawthorne Manufacturing Company sells its products offering 30 days' credit to its customers. During 2013, its first year of operations, the following events occurred: | |
| --- | --- |
| Sales on credit | $1,200,000 |
| Cash collections from credit customers | (895,000) |
| Accounts receivable, end of year | $  305,000 |
| There were no specific accounts determined to be uncollectible in 2013. The company anticipates that 2% of all credit sales will ultimately become uncollectible. | |

**Illustration 7–7**

Bad Debts

---

[10]Under the new revenue recognition standard currently being finalized by the FASB and IASB, bad debts are viewed as a contra-revenue (similar to sales returns) rather than as an expense, and are displayed in the statements of income and comprehensive income as a reduction of sales revenue to derive net revenue. Otherwise the approach for estimating and accounting for bad debts is unchanged. For more information about the proposed revenue recognition standard, see the addendum to Chapter 5 and *Proposed Accounting Standards Update (Revised): Revenue Recognition (Topic 605)*. "Revenue from Contracts with Customers." (Norwalk, Conn: FASB, November 14, 2011).

Using the *income statement approach,* the balance sheet amount is an incidental result of estimating bad debt expense as a percentage of net credit sales.

**FINANCIAL Reporting Case**

Q2, p. 359

### Income statement approach.

Using the income statement approach, we estimate bad debt expense as a percentage of each period's net credit sales. This percentage usually is determined by reviewing the company's recent history of the relationship between credit sales and actual bad debts. For a relatively new company, this percentage may be obtained by referring to other sources such as industry averages.

Under the income statement approach, the Hawthorne Manufacturing Company would make the following adjusting journal entry at the end of 2013:

| | | |
|---|---|---|
| Bad debt expense (2% × $1,200,000) ............................................... | 24,000 | |
| Allowance for uncollectible accounts ........................................... | | 24,000 |

In the current asset section of the 2013 balance sheet, accounts receivable would be reported *net* of the allowance, as follows:

| | |
|---|---|
| Accounts receivable | $305,000 |
| Less: Allowance for uncollectible accounts | (24,000) |
| Net accounts receivable | $281,000 |

It's important to notice that the income statement approach focuses on the current year's credit sales. The effect on the balance sheet—the allowance for uncollectible accounts and hence net accounts receivable—is an incidental result of estimating the expense. An alternative is to focus on the balance sheet amounts instead. We look at this approach next.

Using the *balance sheet approach,* bad debt expense is an incidental result of estimating the net realizable value of accounts receivable.

### Balance sheet approach.

Using the balance sheet approach to estimate future bad debts, we determine bad debt expense by estimating the net realizable value of accounts receivable to be reported in the balance sheet. Specifically, we determine what the ending balance of the allowance for uncollectible accounts should be, and then we record the amount of bad debt expense that's necessary to adjust the allowance to that desired balance.

For the Hawthorne Manufacturing Company example in Illustration 7–7, the company would estimate the amount of uncollectible accounts that will result from the $305,000 in accounts receivable outstanding at the end of 2013. This could be done by analyzing each customer account, by applying a percentage to the entire outstanding receivable balance, or by applying different percentages to accounts receivable balances depending on the length of time outstanding. This latter approach normally employs an accounts receivable aging schedule. For example, the aging schedule for Hawthorne's 2013 year-end accounts receivable is shown in Illustration 7–7A.

The schedule classifies the year-end receivable balances according to their length of time outstanding. Presumably, the longer an account has been outstanding the more likely it will prove uncollectible. Based on past experience or other sources of information, a percentage is applied to age group totals.

The 2013 entry to record bad debts adjusts the balance in the allowance for uncollectible accounts to this required amount of $25,500. Because it is the first year of operations for Hawthorne and the beginning balance in the allowance account is zero, the adjusting entry would *debit* bad debt expense and *credit* allowance for uncollectible accounts for $25,500.

To illustrate the concept further, let's suppose that this was not the first year of operations and the allowance account prior to the adjusting entry had a *credit* balance of $4,000. Then the amount of the entry would be $21,500—the amount necessary to adjust a credit balance of $4,000 to a credit balance of $25,500. Similarly, if the allowance account prior to the adjusting entry had a *debit* balance[11] of $4,000, then the amount of the entry would be $29,500.

| **Allowance** | |
|---|---|
| Beg. bal. | 4,000 |
| Adj. entry | 21,500 |
| Bal. | 25,500 |

---

[11]A debit balance could result if the amount of receivables actually written off (discussed below) during the period exceeds the beginning credit balance in the allowance account.

| Customer | Accounts Receivable 12/31/2013 | 0–60 Days | 61–90 Days | 91–120 Days | Over 120 Days |
|---|---|---|---|---|---|
| Axel Manufacturing Co. | $ 20,000 | $ 14,000 | $ 6,000 | | |
| Banner Corporation | 33,000 | | 20,000 | $10,000 | $ 3,000 |
| Dando Company | 60,000 | 50,000 | 10,000 | | |
| ˘˘˘˘ | ˘˘ | ˘˘ | ˘˘ | ˘˘ | ˘˘ |
| ˘˘˘˘ | ˘˘ | ˘˘ | ˘˘ | ˘˘ | ˘˘ |
| Xicon Company | 18,000 | 10,000 | 4,000 | 3,000 | 1,000 |
| Totals | $305,000 | $220,000 | $50,000 | $25,000 | $10,000 |

**Summary**

| Age Group | Amount | Estimated Percent Uncollectible | Estimated Allowance |
|---|---|---|---|
| 0–60 days | $220,000 | 5% | $11,000 |
| 61–90 days | 50,000 | 10% | 5,000 |
| 91–120 days | 25,000 | 20% | 5,000 |
| Over 120 days | 10,000 | 45% | 4,500 |
| Allowance for uncollectible accounts | | | $25,500 |

**Illustration 7–7A**

Accounts Receivable Aging Schedule

The schedule assumes older accounts are more likely to prove uncollectible.

Higher estimated default percentages are applied to groups of older receivables.

Some companies use a combination of approaches in estimating bad debts. For example, Hawthorne could decide to accrue bad debts on a monthly basis using the income statement approach and then employ the balance sheet approach at the end of the year based on an aging of receivables. Each month an adjusting entry would record a debit to bad debt expense and a credit to allowance for uncollectible accounts equal to 2% of credit sales. In our illustration, the monthly accruals for 2013 would result in the following account balances at the end of 2013:

| Accounts Receivable | |
|---|---|
| 305,000 | |

| Bad Debt Expense | |
|---|---|
| 24,000 | |

| Allowance for Uncollectible Accounts | |
|---|---|
| | 24,000 |

At the end of the year, if the aging revealed a required allowance of $25,500, the following adjusting entry would be recorded:

| | | |
|---|---|---|
| Bad debt expense ........................................................................ | 1,500 | |
|    Allowance for uncollectible accounts ......................................... | | 1,500 |

This entry adjusts the allowance account to the required amount.

In the 2013 balance sheet, accounts receivable would be reported net of the allowance, as follows:

| | |
|---|---|
| Accounts receivable | $305,000 |
| Less: Allowance for uncollectible accounts | (25,500) |
| Net accounts receivable | $279,500 |

**When accounts are deemed uncollectible.** The actual write-off of a receivable occurs when it is determined that all or a portion of the amount due will not be collected. Using the allowance method, the write-off is recorded as a debit to allowance for uncollectible accounts and a credit to accounts receivable. In our illustration, assume that actual bad debts in 2014 were $25,000. These write-offs would be recorded (in a summary journal entry) as follows:

| | | |
|---|---|---|
| Allowance for uncollectible accounts ............................................... | 25,000 | |
| Accounts receivable ................................................................. | | 25,000 |

*The write-off of an account receivable reduces both receivables and the allowance, thus having no effect on income or financial position.*

Net realizable value is not affected directly by the write-offs.

| | |
|---|---|
| Accounts receivable | $280,000 |
| Less: Allowance for uncollectible accounts | (500) |
| Net accounts receivable | $279,500 |

Of course, actual bad debts will tend to differ from estimates. However, the year in which the estimate is made, 2013 in this case, is unaffected by the incorrect estimate. If the prior year's estimate of bad debts is too low, then, using the balance sheet approach, bad debt expense in the subsequent year will be increased. If the estimate is too high, then bad debt expense in the subsequent year will be decreased. For example, in our illustration, the allowance at the end of 2013 is $25,500. Actual bad debts related to 2013 receivables are $25,000. 2013's financial information cannot be changed. Instead, the $500 credit balance in allowance for uncollectible accounts will cause 2014's bad debt expense to be less than if 2013's estimate of bad debts had been correct.

# Ethical Dilemma

The management of the Auto Parts Division of the Santana Corporation receives a bonus if the division's income achieves a specific target. For 2013 the target will be achieved by a wide margin. Mary Beth Williams, the controller of the division, has been asked by Philip Stanton, the head of the division's management team, to try to reduce this year's income and "bank" some of the profits for future years. Mary Beth suggests that the division's bad debt expense as a percentage of net credit sales for 2013 be increased from 3% to 5%. She believes that 3% is the more accurate estimate but knows that both the corporation's internal auditors as well as the external auditors allow some flexibility when estimates are involved. Does Mary Beth's proposal present an ethical dilemma?

*Recoveries of accounts receivable previously written off require the reinstatement of both the receivable and the allowance.*

**When previously written-off accounts are collected.** Occasionally, a receivable that has been written off will be collected in part or in full. When this happens, the receivable and the allowance should be reinstated. In other words, the entry to write off the account simply is reversed. The collection is then recorded the usual way as a debit to cash and a credit to accounts receivable. This process ensures that the company will have a complete record of the payment history of the customer. For example, assume that in our illustration, $1,200 that was previously written off is collected. The following journal entries record the event:

*To reinstate the receivable previously written off.*

| | | |
|---|---|---|
| Accounts receivable ........................................................................ | 1,200 | |
| Allowance for uncollectible accounts .......................................... | | 1,200 |
| *To reinstate the receivable previously written off.* | | |

*To record the cash collection.*

| | | |
|---|---|---|
| Cash ......................................................................................... | 1,200 | |
| Accounts receivable ................................................................. | | 1,200 |
| *To record the cash collection.* | | |

**Direct write-off of uncollectible accounts.** If uncollectible accounts are not anticipated or are immaterial, an allowance for uncollectible accounts is not appropriate. In these few cases, adjusting entries are not recorded and any bad debts that do arise simply are written off as bad debt expense. A $750 uncollectible account would be recorded as follows:

**FINANCIAL Reporting Case**

Q3, p. 359

| | | |
|---|---|---|
| Bad debt expense ........................................................................ | 750 | |
| Accounts receivable ................................................................ | | 750 |

This approach is known as the *direct write-off method*. Of course, if the sale that generated this receivable occurred in a previous reporting period, the matching principle is violated. Operating expenses would have been understated and assets overstated in that period. This is why the direct write-off method of accounting for uncollectible accounts is not permitted by GAAP except in limited circumstances. Specifically, the allowance method must be used if it is probable that a material amount of receivables will not be collected and the amount can be reasonably estimated.[12] For federal income tax purposes, however, the direct write-off method is the required method for most companies and the allowance method is not permitted.

Illustration 7–8 summarizes the key issues involving measuring and reporting accounts receivable.

The *direct write-off method* is used only rarely for financial reporting, but it is the required method for income tax purposes.

| | |
|---|---|
| **Recognition** | Depends on the earnings process; for most credit sales, revenue and the related receivables are recognized at the point of delivery. |
| **Initial valuation** | Initially recorded at the exchange price agreed upon by the buyer and seller. |
| **Subsequent valuation** | Initial valuation reduced to net realizable value by:<br>1. Allowance for sales returns<br>2. Allowance for uncollectible accounts:<br>   —The income statement approach<br>   —The balance sheet approach |
| **Classification** | Almost always classified as a current asset. |

**Illustration 7–8**

Measuring and Reporting Accounts Receivable

## Concept Review Exercise

The Hawthorne Manufacturing Company sells its products, offering 30 days' credit to its customers. Uncollectible amounts are estimated by accruing a monthly charge to bad debt expense equal to 2% of credit sales. At the end of the year, the allowance for uncollectible accounts is adjusted based on an aging of accounts receivable. The company began 2014 with the following balances in its accounts:

**UNCOLLECTIBLE ACCOUNTS RECEIVABLE**

| | |
|---|---|
| Accounts receivable | $305,000 |
| Allowance for uncollectible accounts | (25,500) |

During 2014, sales on credit were $1,300,000, cash collections from customers were $1,250,000, and actual write-offs of accounts were $25,000. An aging of accounts receivable at the end of 2014 indicates a required allowance of $30,000.

**Required:**

1. Determine the balances in accounts receivable and allowance for uncollectible accounts at the end of 2014.

2. Determine bad debt expense for 2014.

---

[12]FASB ASC 450–20–25–2: Contingencies—Loss Contingencies—Recognition (previously "Accounting for Contingencies," *Statement of Financial Accounting Standards No. 5* (Stamford, Conn.: FASB, 1975), par. 8).

3. Prepare journal entries for the accrual of bad debts (in summary form, with one entry covering all twelve months of the year), the write-off of receivables, and the year-end adjusting entry for bad debts.

**Solution:**

1. Determine the balances in accounts receivable and allowance for uncollectible accounts at the end of 2014.

Accounts receivable

| | |
|---|---:|
| Beginning balance | $ 305,000 |
| Add: Credit sales | 1,300,000 |
| Less: Cash collections | (1,250,000) |
| Write-offs | (25,000) |
| Ending balance | $ 330,000 |

Allowance for uncollectible accounts:

| | |
|---|---:|
| Beginning balance | $ 25,500 |
| Add: Bad debt expense recorded monthly (2% × $1,300,000) | 26,000 |
| Less: Write-offs | (25,000) |
| Balance before year-end adjustment | 26,500 |
| Year-end adjustment | 3,500* |
| Ending balance | $ 30,000 |

*Required allowance of $30,000 less $26,500 already in allowance account.

2. Determine bad debt expense for 2014.

Bad debt expense would be $29,500 (accrual of $26,000 plus year-end adjustment of an additional $3,500).

3. Prepare journal entries for the accrual of bad debts (in summary form), the write-off of receivables, and the year-end adjusting entry for bad debts.

| | | |
|---|---:|---:|
| Bad debt expense (2% × $1,300,000) ............................................... | 26,000 | |
| Allowance for uncollectible accounts ........................................ | | 26,000 |
| *Monthly accrual of 2% of credit sales—summary entry.* | | |
| | | |
| Allowance for uncollectible accounts ............................................. | 25,000 | |
| Accounts receivable ................................................................ | | 25,000 |
| *Write-off of accounts receivable as they are determined uncollectible.* | | |
| | | |
| Bad debt expense ........................................................................ | 3,500 | |
| Allowance for uncollectible accounts ........................................ | | 3,500 |
| *Year-end adjusting entry for bad debts.* | | |

# Notes Receivable

**Notes receivable** are formal credit arrangements between a creditor (lender) and a debtor (borrower). Notes arise from loans to other entities including affiliated companies and to stockholders and employees, from the extension of the credit period to trade customers, and occasionally from the sale of merchandise, other assets, or services. Notes receivable are classified as either current or noncurrent depending on the expected collection date(s).

● LO7–7

Our examples below illustrate short-term notes. When the term of a note is longer than a year, it is reported as a long-term note. Long-term notes receivable are discussed in conjunction with long-term notes payable in Chapter 14.

## Interest-Bearing Notes

The typical note receivable requires payment of a specified face amount, also called *principal*, at a specified maturity date or dates. In addition, interest is paid at a stated percentage of the face amount. Interest on notes is calculated as:

$$\text{Face amount} \times \text{Annual rate} \times \text{Fraction of the annual period}$$

For an example, consider Illustration 7–9.

**Illustration 7–9**

Note Receivable

The Stridewell Wholesale Shoe Company manufactures athletic shoes that it sells to retailers. On May 1, 2013, the company sold shoes to Harmon Sporting Goods. Stridewell agreed to accept a $700,000, 6-month, 12% note in payment for the shoes. Interest is payable at maturity.

Stridewell would account for the note as follows:*

**May 1, 2013**

| | | |
|---|---:|---:|
| Note receivable ............................................................................ | 700,000 | |
| Sales revenue ......................................................................... | | 700,000 |
| *To record the sale of goods in exchange for a note receivable.* | | |

**November 1, 2013**

| | | |
|---|---:|---:|
| Cash ($700,000 + $42,000) .......................................................... | 742,000 | |
| Interest revenue ($700,000 × 12% × $\frac{6}{12}$) ...................................... | | 42,000 |
| Note receivable ...................................................................... | | 700,000 |
| *To record the collection of the note at maturity.* | | |

*To focus on recording the note we intentionally omit the entry required for the cost of the goods sold if the perpetual inventory system is used.

If the sale in the illustration occurs on August 1, 2013, and the company's fiscal year-end is December 31, a year-end adjusting entry accrues interest earned.

**December 31, 2013**

| | | |
|---|---:|---:|
| Interest receivable ...................................................................... | 35,000 | |
| Interest revenue ($700,000 × 12% × $\frac{5}{12}$) ...................................... | | 35,000 |

The February 1 collection is then recorded as follows:

**February 1, 2014**

| | | |
|---|---:|---:|
| Cash ($700,000 + [$700,000 × 12% × $\frac{6}{12}$]) ...................................... | 742,000 | |
| Interest revenue ($700,000 × 12% × $\frac{1}{12}$) ...................................... | | 7,000 |
| Interest receivable (accrued at December 31) ............................ | | 35,000 |
| Note receivable ...................................................................... | | 700,000 |

## Noninterest-Bearing Notes

Sometimes a receivable assumes the form of a so-called **noninterest-bearing note**. The name is a misnomer, though. Noninterest-bearing notes actually do bear interest, but the interest is deducted (or discounted) from the face amount to determine the cash proceeds made available to the borrower at the outset. For example, the preceding note could be packaged as a $700,000 noninterest-bearing note, with a 12% discount rate. In that case, the $42,000 interest would be discounted at the outset rather than explicitly stated. As a result, the selling price of the shoes would have been only \$658,000. Assuming a May 1, 2013 sale, the transaction is recorded as follows:[13]

**The discount becomes interest revenue in a noninterest-bearing note.**

| **May 1, 2013** | | |
|---|---|---|
| Note receivable (face amount) .............................................................. | 700,000 | |
|     Discount on note receivable (\$700,000 × 12% × ⁶⁄₁₂) ........................ | | 42,000 |
|     Sales revenue (difference) ............................................................. | | 658,000 |
| **November 1, 2013** | | |
| Discount on note receivable ............................................................ | 42,000 | |
|     Interest revenue ......................................................................... | | 42,000 |
| Cash ......................................................................................... | 700,000 | |
|     Note receivable (face amount) ........................................................ | | 700,000 |

**When interest is discounted from the face amount of a note, the effective interest rate is higher than the stated discount rate.**

The discount on note receivable is a contra account to the note receivable account. That is, the note receivable would be reported in the balance sheet net (less) any remaining discount. The discount represents future interest revenue that will be recognized as it is earned over time. The sales revenue under this arrangement is only \$658,000, but the interest is calculated as the discount rate times the \$700,000 face amount. This causes the *effective* interest rate to be higher than the 12% stated rate.

| | |
|---|---|
| \$ 42,000 | Interest for 6 months |
| ÷ \$658,000 | Sales price |
| = 6.383% | Rate for 6 months |
| × 2* | To annualize the rate |
| = 12.766% | Effective interest rate |

*Two 6-month periods

**Using a calculator:**
Enter: N 1 I .06383
PMT − 700000
Output: PV 658,000

**Using Excel, enter:**
= PV(.06383,1,700000)
Output: 658,000

As we discussed earlier in the chapter, receivables, other than normal trade receivables, should be valued at the present value of future cash receipts. The present value of \$700,000 to be received in six months using an effective interest rate of 6.383% is \$658,000 (\$700,000 ÷ 1.06383 = \$658,000). The use of present value techniques for valuation purposes was introduced in Chapter 6, and we'll use these techniques extensively in subsequent chapters to value various long-term liabilities.

In the illustration, if the sale occurs on August 1, the December 31, 2013, the adjusting entry and the entry to record the cash collection on February 1, 2014, are recorded as follows:

| **December 31, 2013** | | |
|---|---|---|
| Discount on note receivable ............................................................... | 35,000 | |
|     Interest revenue (\$700,000 × 12% × ⁵⁄₁₂) ........................................... | | 35,000 |
| **February 1, 2014** | | |
| Discount on note receivable ............................................................... | 7,000 | |
|     Interest revenue (\$700,000 × 12% × ¹⁄₁₂) ........................................... | | 7,000 |
| Cash ......................................................................................... | 700,000 | |
|     Note receivable (face amount) ........................................................ | | 700,000 |

---

[13]The entries shown assume the note is recorded by the gross method. By the net method, the interest component is netted against the face amount of the note as follows:

| **May 1, 2013** | | |
|---|---|---|
| Note receivable ................................................................................. | 658,000 | |
|     Sales revenue .............................................................................. | | 658,000 |
| **November 1, 2013** | | |
| Cash ............................................................................................. | 700,000 | |
|     Note receivable ............................................................................ | | 658,000 |
|     Interest revenue (\$700,000 × 12% × ⁶⁄₁₂) ........................................... | | 42,000 |

In the December 31, 2013 balance sheet, the note receivable is shown at $693,000, face amount ($700,000) less remaining discount ($7,000).

Choice Hotels, Inc., accepts noninterest-bearing notes from franchisees that open new hotels. The 2011 disclosure note shown in Illustration 7–10 describes the company's accounting policy for these notes.

### Note 2: Notes Receivable (in part)

The Company has provided financing to franchisees in support of the development of properties in key markets. These notes include noninterest bearing receivables as well as notes bearing market interest and are due upon maturity. Noninterest bearing notes are recorded net of their unamortized discounts. At December 31, 2010 and 2009, all discounts were fully amortized. Interest income associated with these notes receivable is reflected in the accompanying consolidated statements of income under the caption interest and other investment (income) loss.

**Illustration 7–10**

Disclosure of Revenue Recognition for Franchise Agreements—Choice Hotels, Inc.

**Real World Financials**

**NOTES RECEIVED SOLELY FOR CASH.** If a note with an unrealistic interest rate—even a noninterest-bearing note—is received *solely* in exchange for cash, the cash paid to the issuer is considered to be its present value.[14] Even if this means recording interest at a ridiculously low or zero rate, the amount of cash exchanged is the basis for valuing the note. When a non-cash asset is exchanged for a note with a low stated rate, we can argue that its real value is less than it's purported to be, but we can't argue that the present value of a sum of cash currently exchanged is less than that sum. If the noninterest-bearing note in the previous example had been received solely in exchange for $700,000 cash, the transaction would be recorded as follows:

When a noninterest-bearing note is received solely in exchange for cash, the amount of cash exchanged is the basis for valuing the note.

| | | |
|---|---|---|
| Note receivable (face amount) ................................................. | 700,000 | |
| Cash (given) ........................................................................ | | 700,000 |

## Subsequent Valuation of Notes Receivable

Similar to accounts receivable, if a company anticipates bad debts on short-term notes receivable, it uses an allowance account to reduce the receivable to net realizable value. The process of recording bad debt expense is the same as with accounts receivable.

Long-term notes present a more significant measurement problem. The longer the duration of the note, the more likely are bad debts. One of the more difficult measurement problems facing banks and other lending institutions is the estimation of bad debts on their long-term notes (loans). As an example, Wells Fargo & Company, a large bank holding company, reported the following in the asset section of its March 31, 2011, quarter-end balance sheet:

| (in millions) | 3/31/2011 | 12/31/2010 |
|---|---|---|
| Loans | $751,155 | $757,267 |
| Allowance for loan losses | (21,983) | (23,022) |
| Net loans | $729,172 | $734,245 |

A disclosure note, reproduced in Illustration 7–11, describes Wells Fargo's loan loss policy.

---

[14]This assumes that no other present or future considerations are included in the agreement. For example, a noninterest-bearing note might be given to a vendor in exchange for cash *and* a promise to provide future inventories at prices lower than anticipated market prices. The issuer values the note at the present value of cash payments using a realistic interest rate, and the difference between present value and cash payments is recognized as interest revenue over the life of the note. This difference also increases future inventory purchases to realistic market prices.

**Illustration 7–11**

Disclosure of Allowance for Loan Losses—Wells Fargo & Company

Real World Financials

**Allowance for Credit Losses (ACL) (in part)**

The ACL is management's estimate of credit losses inherent in the loan portfolio, including unfunded credit commitments, at the balance sheet date. We have an established process to determine the adequacy of the allowance for credit losses that assesses the losses inherent in our portfolio and related unfunded credit commitments. While we attribute portions of the allowance to specific portfolio segments, the entire allowance is available to absorb credit losses inherent in the total loan portfolio and unfunded credit commitments.

GAAP requires that companies disclose the fair value of their notes receivable in the disclosure notes (they don't have to disclose the fair value of accounts receivable when the carrying value of the receivables approximates their fair value).[15] Also, GAAP recently changed to allow companies to choose to carry receivables at fair value in their balance sheets, with changes in fair value recognized as gains or losses in the income statements.[16] This "fair value option" is discussed in Chapter 12.

When it becomes probable that a creditor will be unable to collect all amounts due according to the contractual terms of a note, the receivable is considered **impaired**. When a creditor's investment in a note receivable becomes impaired for any reason, the receivable is remeasured as the discounted present value of currently expected cash flows at the loan's original effective rate. Impairments of receivables are discussed in Appendix 7B.

● LO7–10

# International Financial Reporting Standards

**Accounts Receivable.** Until recently, *IAS No. 39*[17] was the standard that specified appropriate accounting for accounts and notes receivables, under the category of Loans and Receivables. However, *IFRS No. 9*,[18] issued November 12, 2009, will be required after January 1, 2015, and earlier adoption is allowed. Therefore, until 2015 either standard could be in effect for a particular company that reports under IFRS (although countries in the European Union may not report under *IFRS No. 9*, as the European Commission has not yet ratified it). Still, both of the IFRS standards are very similar to U.S. GAAP with respect to accounting for accounts and notes receivable, with similar treatment of trade and cash discounts, sales returns, estimating bad debt expense, recognizing interest on notes receivable, and using an allowance for uncollectible accounts (which typically is called a "provision for bad debts" under IFRS).

A few key differences remain. IFRS and U.S. GAAP both allow a "fair value option" for accounting for receivables, but the IFRS standards restrict the circumstances in which that option is allowed (we discuss this more in Chapter 12). Also, *IAS No. 39* permits accounting for receivables as "available for sale" investments if that approach is elected upon initial recognition of the receivable. *IFRS No. 9* does not allow that option for receivables, and U.S. GAAP only allows "available for sale" accounting for investments in securities (we also discuss that approach further in Chapter 12). Finally, U.S. GAAP requires more disaggregation of accounts and notes receivable in the balance sheet or notes. For example, companies need to separately disclose accounts receivable from customers, from related parties, and from others. IFRS recommends but does not require separate disclosure.

---

[15]FASB ASC 825–10–50–10: Financial Instruments—Overall—Disclosure—Fair Value of Financial Instruments (previously "Disclosures about Fair Value of Financial Instruments" *Statement of Financial Accounting Standards No. 107* (Norwalk, Conn.: FASB, 1991)).

[16]FASB ASC 825–10–25: Financial Instruments—Overall—Recognition Fair Value Option (previously "The Fair Value Option for Financial Assets and Financial Liabilities" *Statement of Financial Accounting Standards No. 159* (Norwalk, Conn.: FASB, 2007)).

[17]"Financial Instruments: Recognition and Measurement," *International Accounting Standard No. 39* (IASCF), as amended effective January 1, 2011.

[18]"Financial Resources," *International Financial Reporting Standard No. 9* (IASCF), as amended effective January 1, 2011.

# Financing with Receivables

Financial institutions have developed a wide variety of ways for companies to use their receivables to obtain immediate cash. Companies can find this attractive because it shortens their operating cycles by providing cash immediately rather than having to wait until credit customers pay the amounts due. Also, many companies avoid the difficulties of servicing (billing and collecting) receivables by having financial institutions take on that role. Of course, financial institutions require compensation for providing these services, usually interest and/or a finance charge.

● **LO7–8**

The various approaches used to finance with receivables differ with respect to which rights and risks are retained by the *transferor* (the company who was the original holder of the receivables) and which are passed on to the *transferee* (the new holder, the financial institution). Despite this diversity, any of these approaches can be described as either:

1. *A secured borrowing.* Under this approach, the transferor (borrower) simply acts like it borrowed money from the transferee (lender), with the receivables remaining in the transferor's balance sheet and serving as collateral for the loan. On the other side of the transaction, the transferee recognizes a note receivable.
2. *A sale of receivables.* Under this approach, the transferor (seller) "derecognizes" (removes) the receivables from its balance sheet, acting like it sold them to the transferee (buyer). On the other side of the transaction, the transferee recognizes the receivables as assets in its balance sheet and measures them at their fair value.

Let's discuss each of these approaches in more detail as they apply to accounts receivable and notes receivable. Then we'll discuss the circumstances under which GAAP requires each approach.

## Secured Borrowing

Sometimes companies **pledge** accounts receivable as collateral for a loan. No particular receivables are associated with the loan. Rather, the entire receivables balance serves as collateral. The responsibility for collection of the receivables remains solely with the company. No special accounting treatment is needed for pledged receivables, but the arrangement should be described in a disclosure note. For example, Illustration 7–12 shows a portion of the long-term debt disclosure note included in the January 31, 2011 annual report of **Virco Mfg. Corporation**, a manufacturer of office furniture.

When companies *pledge* accounts receivable as collateral for debt, a disclosure note describes the arrangement.

**Note 5: Debt (in part)**

At January 31, 2011, the Company had outstanding borrowings pursuant to its revolving line of credit with Wells Fargo Bank. The revolving line typically provided for advances of up to 80% on eligible accounts receivable and 20%–60% on eligible inventory, subject to the specific terms of the facility.

**Illustration 7–12**

Disclosure of Receivables Used as Collateral—Virco Mfg. Corporation

**Real World Financials**

Alternatively, financing arrangements can require that companies **assign** particular receivables to serve as collateral for loans. You already may be familiar with the concept of assigning an asset as collateral if you or someone you know has a mortgage on a home. The bank or other financial institution holding the mortgage will require that, if the homeowner defaults on the mortgage payments, the home be sold and the proceeds used to pay off the mortgage debt. Similarly, in the case of an assignment of receivables, nonpayment of a debt will require the proceeds from collecting the assigned receivables to go directly toward repayment of the debt.

In these arrangements, the lender typically lends an amount of money that is less than the amount of receivables assigned by the borrower. The difference provides some protection for the lender to allow for possible uncollectible accounts. Also, the lender (sometimes called an *assignee*) usually charges the borrower (sometimes called an *assignor*) an up-front finance charge in addition to stated interest on the loan. The receivables might be collected either by the lender or the borrower, depending on the details of the arrangement. Illustration 7–13 provides an example.

## Illustration 7–13
Assignment of Accounts Receivable

On December 1, 2013, the Santa Teresa Glass Company borrowed $500,000 from Finance Bank and signed a promissory note. Interest at 12% is payable monthly. The company assigned $620,000 of its receivables as collateral for the loan. Finance Bank charges a finance fee equal to 1.5% of the accounts receivable assigned.

Santa Teresa Glass records the borrowing as follows:

| | | |
|---|---|---|
| Cash (difference) ............................................................. | 490,700 | |
| Finance charge expense* (1.5% × $620,000) ............................ | 9,300 | |
|     Liability—financing arrangement ......................................... | | 500,000 |

Santa Teresa will continue to collect the receivables, and will record any discounts, sales returns, and bad debt write-offs, but will remit the cash to Finance Bank, usually on a monthly basis. When $400,000 of the receivables assigned are collected in December, Santa Teresa Glass records the following entries:

| | | |
|---|---|---|
| Cash ............................................................................... | 400,000 | |
|     Accounts receivable ...................................................... | | 400,000 |
| | | |
| Interest expense ($500,000 × 12% × 1/12) .................................. | 5,000 | |
| Liability—financing arrangement ............................................. | 400,000 | |
|     Cash ........................................................................... | | 405,000 |

*In theory, this fee should be allocated over the entire period of the loan rather than recorded as an expense in the initial period. However, amounts usually are small and the loan period usually is short. For expediency, then, we expense the entire fee immediately.

**Accounts Receivable**

| | |
|---|---|
| 620,000 | |
| | 400,000 |
| 220,000 | |

**Note Payable**

| | |
|---|---|
| | 500,000 |
| 400,000 | |
| | 100,000 |

When companies *assign* particular accounts receivable as collateral for debt, the balances of the receivables and the debt are offset in the balance sheet.

In Santa Teresa's December 31, 2013, balance sheet, the company would report the receivables and note payable together as net accounts receivable:

| **Current assets:** | |
|---|---|
| Accounts receivable assigned | $220,000 |
| Less: Liability—financing arrangement | (100,000) |
| Equity in accounts receivable assigned | $120,000 |

Netting a liability against a related asset, also called offsetting, usually is not allowed by GAAP. However, in this case, we deduct the note payable from the accounts receivable assigned because, by contractual agreement, the note will be paid with cash collected from the receivables. In Santa Teresa's financial statements, the arrangement also is described in a disclosure note.

## Sale of Receivables

Accounts and notes receivable, like any other assets, can be sold at a gain or a loss. The basic accounting treatment for the sale of receivables is similar to accounting for the sale of other assets. The seller (transferor) (a) removes from the accounts the receivables (and any allowance for bad debts associated with them), (b) recognizes at fair value any assets acquired or liabilities assumed by the seller in the transaction, and (c) records the difference as a gain or loss.

The sale of accounts receivable is a popular method of financing. A technique once used by companies in a few industries or with poor credit ratings, the sale of receivables is now a common occurrence for many different types of companies. For example, **Toyota, Deere & Co.**, and **Raytheon** all sell receivables. The two most common types of selling arrangements are **factoring** and **securitization**. We'll now discuss each type.

Two popular arrangements used for the sale of receivables are *factoring* and *securitization*.

In a **factoring** arrangement, the company sells its accounts receivable to a financial institution. The financial institution typically buys receivables for cash, handles the billing and collection of the receivables, and charges a fee for this service. Actually, credit cards like **VISA** and **Mastercard** are forms of factoring arrangements. The seller relinquishes all rights to the future cash receipts in exchange for cash from the buyer (the *factor*).

As an example, Illustration 7–14 shows an excerpt from the website of **BusinessCash .Com**, a financial institution that offers factoring as one of its services.

**Accounts Receivable Factoring**

Accounts receivable factoring is the selling of your invoices (accounts receivable) for cash versus waiting 30–60 days to be paid by your customer. Factoring will get you the working capital you need now and improve your cash flow. We will advance 75%–90% against the invoice you generate and pay you the balance less our fee (typically 2%–4%) when the invoice is paid.

**Illustration 7–14**

Advertisement of Factoring Service— BusinessCash.Com

Real World Financials

Notice that the factor, BusinessCash.com, advances only between 75%–90% of the factored receivables. The remaining balance is retained as security until all of the receivables are collected and then remitted to the transferor, net of the factor's fee. The fee charged by this factor ranges from 2%–4%. The range depends on, among other things, the quality of the receivables and the length of time before payment is required.

Another popular arrangement used to sell receivables is **securitization**. In a typical accounts receivable securitization, the company creates a "special purpose entity" (SPE), usually a trust or a subsidiary. The SPE buys a pool of trade receivables, credit card receivables, or loans from the company, and then sells related securities, typically debt such as bonds or commercial paper, that are backed (collateralized) by the receivables. Securitizing receivables using an SPE can provide significant economic advantages, allowing companies to reach a large pool of investors and to obtain more favorable financing terms.[19]

As an example of a securitization, Illustration 7–15 shows a portion of the disclosure note included in a 2011 quarterly report of **Flextronics International Limited**, a worldwide leader in design, manufacturing and logistics services, describing the securitization of its trade accounts receivable.

**Note 6: TRADE RECEIVABLES SECURITIZATION (in part)**

The Company continuously sells a designated pool of trade receivables to an affiliated special purpose entity, which in turn sells an undivided ownership interest to an unaffiliated financial institution. The Company continues to service, administer and collect the receivables on behalf of the special purpose entity and receives a servicing fee of 1.00% of serviced receivables per annum.

**Illustration 7–15**

Description of Securitization Program— Flextronics International Limited

Real World Financials

The specifics of sale accounting vary depending on the particular arrangement between the seller and buyer (transferee).[20] One key feature is whether the receivables are transferred **without recourse** or **with recourse**.

**SALE WITHOUT RECOURSE.**    If a factoring arrangement is made **without recourse**, the buyer can't ask the seller for more money if the receivables prove to be uncollectible. Therefore, the buyer assumes the risk of bad debts. Illustration 7–16 on the next page provides an example of receivables factored without recourse.

Note that, in Illustration 7–16, the fair value ($50,000) of the last 10% of the receivables to be collected is less than 10% of the total book value of the receivables (10% × $600,000 = $60,000). That's typical, because the last receivables to be collected are likely to be reduced by sales returns and allowances, and therefore have a lower fair value.

*The buyer assumes the risk of uncollectibility when accounts receivable are sold* ***without recourse.***

[19]Because the SPE is a separate legal entity, it typically is viewed as "bankruptcy remote," meaning that the transferor's creditors can't access the receivables if the transferor goes bankrupt. This increases the safety of the SPE's assets and typically allows it to obtain more favorable financing terms than could the transferor.

[20]FASB ASC 860: Transfers and Servicing (previously "Accounting for Transfers of Financial Assets, an amendment of FASB Statement No. 140," *Statement of Financial Accounting Standards No. 166* (Norwalk, Conn.: FASB, 2009)).

**Illustration 7–16**

Accounts Receivable Factored without Recourse

In December 2013, the Santa Teresa Glass Company factored accounts receivable that had a book value of $600,000 to Factor Bank. The transfer was made without recourse. Under this arrangement, Santa Teresa transfers the $600,000 of receivables to Factor, and Factor immediately remits to Santa Teresa cash equal to 90% of the factored amount (90% × $600,000 = $540,000). Factor retains the remaining 10% to cover its factoring fee (equal to 4% of the total factored amount; 4% × $600,000 = $24,000) and to provide a cushion against potential sales returns and allowances. After Factor has collected cash equal to the amount advanced to Santa Teresa plus their factoring fee, Factor remits the excess to Santa Teresa. Therefore, under this arrangement Factor provides Santa Teresa with cash up-front and a "beneficial interest" in the transferred receivables equal to the fair value of the last 10% of the receivables to be collected (which management estimates to equal $50,000), less the 4% factoring fee.[21]

Santa Teresa Glass records the transfer as follows:

| | | |
|---|---|---|
| Cash (90% × $600,000) | 540,000 | |
| Loss on sale of receivables (to balance) | 34,000 | |
| Receivable from factor ($50,000 − 24,000 fee) | 26,000 | |
| Accounts receivable (book value sold) | | 600,000 |

**The seller retains the risk of uncollectibility when accounts receivable are sold *with recourse*.**

**SALE WITH RECOURSE.** When a company sells accounts receivable with recourse, the seller retains all of the risk of bad debts. In effect, the seller guarantees that the buyer will be paid even if some receivables prove to be uncollectible. In Illustration 7–16, even if the receivables were sold with recourse, Santa Teresa Glass still could account for the transfer as a sale so long as the conditions for sale treatment are met. The only difference is the additional requirement that Santa Teresa record the estimated fair value of its recourse obligation as a liability. The recourse obligation is the estimated amount that Santa Teresa will have to pay Factor Bank as a reimbursement for uncollectible receivables. Illustration 7–17 provides an example of receivables factored with recourse.

**Illustration 7–17**

Accounts Receivable Factored with Recourse

Assume the same facts as in Illustration 7–16, except that Santa Teresa sold the receivables to Factor *with recourse* and estimates the fair value of the recourse obligation to be $5,000. Santa Teresa records the transfer as follows:

| | | |
|---|---|---|
| Cash (90% × $600,000) | 540,000 | |
| Loss on sale of receivables (to balance) | 39,000 | |
| Receivable from factor ($50,000 − 24,000 fee) | 26,000 | |
| Recourse liability | | 5,000 |
| Accounts receivable (book value sold) | | 600,000 |

When comparing Illustrations 7–16 and 7–17, notice that the estimated recourse liability of $5,000 increases the loss on sale by $5,000. If the factor eventually collects all of the receivables, Santa Teresa eliminates the recourse liability and recognizes a gain.

## Transfers of Notes Receivable

We handle transfers of notes receivable in the same manner as transfers of accounts receivable. A note receivable can be used to obtain immediate cash from a financial institution either by pledging the note as collateral for a loan or by selling the note. Notes also can be securitized.

---

[21]Illustration 7–16 depicts an arrangement in which the factor's fee is paid out of the 10% of receivables retained by the factor. Alternatively, a factoring arrangement could be structured to have the factor's fee withheld from the cash advanced to the company at the start of the arrangement. In that case, in Illustration 7–16 the journal entry recorded by Santa Teresa would be:

| | | |
|---|---|---|
| Cash ([90% × $600,000] − $24,000 fee) | 516,000 | |
| Loss on sale of receivables (to balance) | 34,000 | |
| Receivable from factor | 50,000 | |
| Accounts receivable (book value sold) | | 600,000 |

The transfer of a note to a financial institution is referred to as **discounting**. The financial institution accepts the note and gives the seller cash equal to the maturity value of the note reduced by a discount. The discount is computed by applying a discount rate to the maturity value and represents the financing fee the financial institution charges for the transaction. Illustration 7–18 provides an example of the calculation of the proceeds received by the transferor.

The transfer of a note receivable to a financial institution is called *discounting*.

On December 31, 2013, the Stridewell Wholesale Shoe Company sold land in exchange for a nine-month, 10% note. The note requires the payment of $200,000 plus interest on September 30, 2014. The company's fiscal year-end is December 31. The 10% rate properly reflects the time value of money for this type of note. On March 31, 2014, Stridewell discounted the note at the Bank of the East. The bank's discount rate is 12%.

Because the note had been outstanding for three months before it's discounted at the bank, Stridewell first records the interest that has accrued prior to being discounted:

**March 31, 2014**

| | | |
|---|---|---|
| Interest receivable .......................................................... | 5,000 | |
| Interest revenue ($200,000 × 10% × $\frac{3}{12}$) ............................................. | | 5,000 |

Next, the value of the note if held to maturity is calculated. Then the discount for the time remaining to maturity is deducted to determine the cash proceeds from discounting the note:

| | |
|---|---|
| $200,000 | Face amount |
| 15,000 | Interest to maturity ($200,000 × 10% × $\frac{9}{12}$) |
| 215,000 | Maturity value |
| (12,900) | Discount ($215,000 × 12% × $\frac{6}{12}$) |
| $202,100 | Cash proceeds |

**Illustration 7–18**

Discounting a Note Receivable

STEP 1: Accrue interest earned on the note receivable prior to its being discounted.

STEP 2: Add interest to maturity to calculate maturity value.

STEP 3: Deduct discount to calculate cash proceeds.

Similar to accounts receivable, Stridewell potentially could account for the transfer as a sale or a secured borrowing. For example, Illustration 7–19 shows the appropriate journal entries to account for the transfer as a sale.

| | | |
|---|---|---|
| Cash (proceeds determined above) ............................................. | 202,100 | |
| Loss on sale of note receivable (difference) ............................................ | 2,900 | |
| Note receivable (face amount) ......................................................... | | 200,000 |
| Interest receivable (accrued interest determined above) ...................... | | 5,000 |

**Illustration 7–19**

Discounted Note Treated as a Sale

## Deciding Whether to Account for a Transfer as a Sale or a Secured Borrowing

Transferors usually prefer to use the sale approach rather than the secured borrowing approach to account for the transfer of a receivable, because the sale approach makes the transferor seem less leveraged, more liquid, and perhaps more profitable than does the secured borrowing approach. Illustration 7–20 explains why by describing particular effects on key accounting metrics.

So, when is a company allowed to account for the transfer of receivables as a sale? The most critical element is the extent to which the company (the transferor) *surrenders control over the assets transferred.* For some arrangements, surrender of control is clear (e.g., when a receivable is sold without recourse and without any other involvement by the transferor). However, for other arrangements this distinction is not obvious. Indeed, some companies appear to structure transactions in ways that qualify for sale treatment but retain enough involvement to have control. This led the FASB to provide guidelines designed to constrain inappropriate use of the sale approach. Specifically, the transferor (defined to include the company, its consolidated affiliates, and people acting on behalf of

**Illustration 7–20**

Why Do Transferors of Receivables Generally Want to Account for the Transfer as a Sale?

| Does the Accounting Approach: | Transfer of Receivables Accounted for as a: | | Why Sales Approach is Preferred by the Transferor: |
|---|---|---|---|
| | **Sale** | **Secured Borrowing** | |
| Derecognize A/R, reducing assets? | Yes | No | Sale approach produces lower total assets and higher return on assets (ROA) |
| Recognize liability for cash received? | No | Yes | Sale approach produces lower liabilities and less leverage (debt/equity) |
| Where is cash received shown in the statement of cash flows? | May be in operating or financing sections | Always in financing section | Sale approach can produce higher cash flow from operations at time of transfer |
| Recognize gain on transfer? | More likely | Less likely | Sale approach can produce higher income at time of transfer. |

the company) is determined to have surrendered control over the receivables if and only if all of the following conditions are met:[22]

If the transferor is deemed to have surrendered control over the transferred receivables, the arrangement is accounted for as a sale; otherwise as a secured borrowing.

a. The transferred assets have been isolated from the transferor—beyond the reach of the transferor and its creditors.
b. Each transferee has the right to pledge or exchange the assets it received.
c. The transferor does not maintain *effective control* over the transferred assets, for example, by structuring the transfer such that the assets are likely to end up returned to the transferor.

If all of these conditions are met, the transferor accounts for the transfer as a sale. If any of the conditions are *not* met, the transferor treats the transaction as a secured borrowing.

It is not surprising that some companies have aggressively tried to circumvent these conditions by creating elaborate transactions to qualify for sale treatment. The most famous recent case was Lehman Brothers' use of "Repo 105" transactions, discussed in Illustration 7–21.

**Illustration 7–21**

Repo 105 Transactions—Lehman Brothers

**Real World Financials**

Lehman Brothers' bankruptcy in 2008 was the largest ever to occur in the United States. One factor that likely contributed to investor losses was Lehman's use of "Repo 105" transactions that concealed how overburdened with liabilities the company had become. Here is how a Repo 105 transaction worked. Near the end of each quarter, Lehman would transfer financial assets like receivables to a bank or other financial institution in exchange for cash, and would account for that transfer as a sale of the financial assets. Lehman would use the cash obtained from the transfer to pay down liabilities, so the net effect of the transaction was to reduce assets, reduce liabilities, and therefore make Lehman appear less leveraged and less risky. However, Lehman also agreed to repurchase ("repo") the assets in the next quarter for an amount of cash that exceeded the amount it initially received. In substance, this transaction is a loan, since Lehman ended up retaining the financial assets and paying amounts equivalent to principal and interest. However, Lehman argued that the assets were beyond its *effective control*, because the cash it received for transferring the assets was insufficient to enable Lehman to repurchase those assets (the "105" in "Repo 105" refers to the assets being worth at least 105% of the cash Lehman was getting for them). Although Lehman's interpretation was supported by the GAAP in effect at the time, these transactions were very poorly disclosed, and when they eventually came to light, the financial markets and investing public reacted very negatively. In response to the Lehman debacle, the FASB has taken steps to close the loophole that allowed Repo 105 transactions to be accounted for as sales.[23]

---

[22]FASB ASC 860–10–40: Transfers and Servicing—Overall—Derecognition (previously "Accounting for Transfers and Servicing of Financial Assets and Extinguishments of Liabilities," *Statement of Financial Accounting Standards No. 140* (Norwalk, Conn.: FASB, 2000), as amended by *SFAS No. 166*).

[23]FASB ASC 860–10–55: Transfers and Servicing—Overall—Implementation Guidance and Illustrations (previously ASU 2011-03: Transfers and Servicing (Topic 860): *Reconsideration of Effective Control for Repurchase Agreements* (Norwalk, Conn.: FASB 2011)).

# Additional Consideration

**Participating Interests.** What if, rather than transferring all of a particular receivable, a company transfers only part of it? For example, what if a company transfers the right to receive future interest payments on a note, but retains the right to receive the loan principal? Recent changes in U.S. GAAP require that a partial transfer be treated as a secured borrowing unless the amount transferred qualifies as a "participating interest" as well as meeting the "surrender of control" requirements described above. Participating interests are defined as sharing proportionally in the cash flows of the receivable and having equal and substantial rights with respect to the receivable. Many common securitization arrangements do not qualify as participating interests, so this change in GAAP makes it harder for partial transfers to qualify for the sale approach.

Illustration 7–22 summarizes the decision process that is used to determine whether a transfer of a receivable is accounted for as a secured borrowing or a sale.

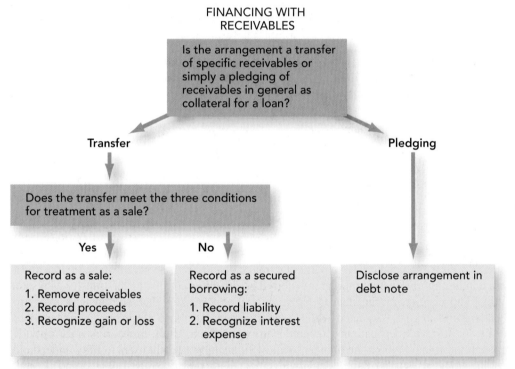

**Illustration 7–22**

Accounting for the Financing of Receivables

# Additional Consideration

**Dropping the Q.** Until recently, companies that securitized their receivables could avoid some consolidation rules by setting up a particular type of special purpose entity (SPE), called a "qualifying SPE" ("QSPE"), which operated solely to facilitate securitization transactions. The company would sell its receivables to its QSPE, often recognizing a gain on the sale, and the QSPE (not the company) would hold the receivables and related debt in the QSPE's balance sheet. Effective in 2010, the FASB eliminated the QSPE concept, leaving these SPEs vulnerable to consolidation requirements.[24] The FASB also tightened consolidation requirements with respect to these sorts of "variable interest entities."[25] Under these new standards, many companies had to consolidate their securitization

(continued)

---

[24]FASB ASC 860: Transfers and Servicing (previously "Accounting for Transfers of Financial Assets, an amendment of FASB Statement No. 140," *Statement of Financial Accounting Standards No. 166* (Norwalk, Conn.: FASB, 2009)).

[25]FASB ASC 810: Consolidation (previously "Amendments to FASB Interpretation No. 46R," *Statement of Financial Accounting Standards No. 167* (Norwalk, Conn.: FASB, 2009)).

(concluded)

SPE's, eliminating any transactions between the SPE and the company and treating their securitizations as secured borrowings.

How did companies respond to this change in accounting standards? Some companies modified their securitization arrangements to still achieve the off-balance-sheet accounting treatment they desired. The following excerpt from **Flextronics International Limited's** 2011 annual report provides an example:

### Note 8. Trade Receivables Securitization (in part)

Effective April 1, 2010, the Company adopted two new accounting standards, the first of which removed the concept of a qualifying special purpose entity and created more stringent conditions for reporting the transfer of a financial asset as a sale. The second standard amended the consolidation guidance for determining the primary beneficiary of a variable interest entity. . . .

Effective September 29, 2010, the securitization agreement was amended to provide for the sale by the special purpose entity of 100% of the eligible receivables to the unaffiliated financial institution. . . . Following the transfer of the receivables to the special purpose entity, the transferred receivables are isolated from the Company and its affiliates, and effective control of the transferred receivables is passed to the unaffiliated financial institution, which has the right to pledge or sell the receivables. As a result, although the Company still consolidates the special purpose entity, all of the receivables sold to the unaffiliated financial institution for cash are removed from the Condensed Consolidated Balance Sheet and the cash received is no longer accounted for as a secured borrowing.

On the other hand, other companies did not modify their securitization agreements, such that their asset securitizations started being treated as secured borrowings. As shown in Note 1 of its 2011 annual report (see top of p. 62 of the report), **Dell Inc.** is one such company.

## Disclosures

The amount of disclosures relevant to asset transfers increased dramatically in response to the 2008/2009 financial crisis. In particular, much disclosure is required when the transferor has continuing involvement in the transferred assets but accounts for the transfer as a sale. Why? Those are the circumstances under which it's most likely that the transferor may still bear significant risk associated with the arrangement, so those are the arrangements that analysts often view instead as a secured borrowing. As a result, transferors must provide enough information about the transfer to allow financial statement users to fully understand (a) the transfer, (b) any continuing involvement with the transferred assets, and (c) any ongoing risks to the transferor.

The company also has to provide information about the quality of the transferred assets. For example, for transferred receivables, the company needs to disclose the amount of receivables that are past due and any credit losses occurring during the period. Among the other information the company must disclose are:

- How fair values were estimated when recording the transaction.
- Any cash flows occurring between the transferor and the transferee.
- How any continuing involvement in the transferred assets will be accounted for on an ongoing basis.[26]

---

[26]FASB ASC 860–10–40: Transfers and Servicing—Overall—Derecognition (previously "Accounting for Transfers of Financial Assets, an amendment of FASB Statement No. 140," *Statement of Financial Accounting Standards No. 166* (Norwalk, Conn.: FASB, 2009), par. 17).

# International Financial Reporting Standards

**Transfers of Receivables.** *IAS No. 39*[27] and FASB ASC Topic 860[28] cover financing with receivables under IFRS and U.S. GAAP, respectively. The international and U.S. guidance often lead to similar accounting treatments. Both seek to determine whether an arrangement should be treated as a secured borrowing or a sale, and, having concluded which approach is appropriate, both account for the approaches in a similar fashion. Also, the recent change in U.S. GAAP that eliminated the concept of QSPEs is a big step toward convergence with IFRS, and is likely to reduce the proportion of U.S. securitizations that qualify for sale accounting.

● LO7–10

Where IFRS and U.S. GAAP most differ is in the conceptual basis for their choice of accounting approaches and in the decision process they require to determine which approach to use. As you have seen in this chapter, U.S. GAAP focuses on whether control of assets has shifted from the transferor to the transferee. In contrast, IFRS requires a more complex decision process. The company has to have transferred the rights to receive the cash flows from the receivable, and then considers whether the company has transferred "substantially all of the risks and rewards of ownership," as well as whether the company has transferred control. Under IFRS:

1. If the company *transfers* substantially all of the risks and rewards of ownership, the transfer is treated as a sale.

2. If the company *retains* substantially all of the risks and rewards of ownership, the transfer is treated as a secured borrowing.

3. If neither conditions 1 or 2 hold, the company accounts for the transaction as a sale if it has transferred control, and as a secured borrowing if it has retained control.

Whether risks and rewards have been transferred is evaluated by comparing how variability in the amounts and timing of the cash flows of the transferred asset affect the company before and after the transfer.

This is a broad overview of the IFRS guidance. Application of the detailed rules is complex, and depending on the specifics of an arrangement, a company could have different accounting under IFRS and U.S. GAAP.

# Where We're Headed

As indicated previously in this chapter, the FASB recently modified accounting for transfers of receivables. The board also indicated that those changes were a short-term solution and that it intended to work with the IASB to produce a standard that comprehensively addressed derecognition of assets and liabilities (which would include determining when transfers of receivables can be accounted for as sales). However, in 2010 the boards decided to focus on other convergence projects and so have not made recent progress on this one. Many differences between current IFRS and U.S. GAAP remain to be resolved before full convergence is achieved in this area.

The FASB and IASB both have projects under way relevant to transfers of receivables.

● LO7–10

## Concept Review Exercise

The Hollywood Lumber Company obtains financing from the Midwest Finance Company by factoring (or discounting) its receivables. During June 2013, the company factored $1,000,000 of accounts receivable to Midwest. The transfer was made *without* recourse. The factor, Midwest Finance, remits 80% of the factored receivables and retains 20%. When the

**FINANCING WITH RECEIVABLES**

[27]"Financial Instruments: Recognition and Measurement," *International Accounting Standard No. 39* (IASCF), as amended effective January 1, 2011.
[28]FASB ASC 860: Transfers and Servicing (previously "Accounting for Transfers of Financial Assets, an amendment of FASB Statement No. 140," *Statement of Financial Accounting Standards No. 166* (Norwalk, Conn.: FASB, 2009)).

receivables are collected by Midwest, the retained amount, less a 3% fee (3% of the total factored amount), will be remitted to Hollywood Lumber. Hollywood estimates that the fair value of the amount retained by Midwest is $180,000.

In addition, on June 30, 2013, Hollywood discounted a note receivable without recourse. The note, which originated on March 31, 2013, requires the payment of $150,000 *plus* interest at 8% on March 31, 2014. Midwest's discount rate is 10%. The company's fiscal year-end is December 31.

**Required:**

Prepare journal entries for Hollywood Lumber for the factoring of accounts receivable and the note receivable discounted on June 30. Assume that the required criteria are met and the transfers are accounted for as sales.

**Solution:**

| **The Factoring of Receivables** | | |
|---|---:|---:|
| Cash (80% × $1,000,000) | 800,000 | |
| Loss on sale of receivables (to balance) | 50,000 | |
| Receivable from factor ($180,000 – 30,000 fee) | 150,000 | |
| Accounts receivable (balance sold) | | 1,000,000 |

| **The Note Receivable Discounted** | | |
|---|---:|---:|
| Interest receivable | 3,000 | |
| Interest revenue ($150,000 × 8% × 3/12) | | 3,000 |
| Cash (proceeds determined below) | 149,850 | |
| Loss on sale of note receivable (difference) | 3,150 | |
| Note receivable (face amount) | | 150,000 |
| Interest receivable (accrued interest determined above) | | 3,000 |

**Add interest to maturity to calculate maturity value.**

**Deduct discount to calculate cash proceeds.**

| | |
|---:|---|
| $150,000 | Face amount |
| 12,000 | Interest to maturity ($150,000 × 8%) |
| 162,000 | Maturity value |
| (12,150) | Discount ($162,000 × 10% × 9/12) |
| $149,850 | Cash proceeds |

# Decision Makers' Perspective

● LO7–9

**Management must evaluate the costs and benefits of any change in credit and collection policies.**

**RECEIVABLES MANAGEMENT.**   A company's investment in receivables is influenced by several variables, including the level of sales, the nature of the product or service sold, and credit and collection policies. These variables are, of course, related. For example, a change in credit policies could affect sales. In fact, more liberal credit policies—allowing customers a longer time to pay or offering cash discounts for early payment—often are initiated with the specific objective of increasing sales volume.

Management's choice of credit and collection policies often involves trade-offs. For example, offering cash discounts may increase sales volume, accelerate customer payment, and reduce bad debts. These benefits are not without cost. The cash discounts reduce the amount of cash collected from customers who take advantage of the discounts. Extending payment terms also may increase sales volume. However, this creates an increase in the required investment in receivables and may increase bad debts.

The ability to use receivables as a method of financing also offers management alternatives. Assigning, factoring, and discounting receivables are alternative methods of financing operations that must be evaluated relative to other financing methods such as lines of credit or other types of short-term borrowing.

Investors, creditors, and financial analysts can gain important insights by monitoring a company's investment in receivables. Chapter 5 introduced the receivables turnover ratio and the related average collection period, ratios designed to monitor receivables. Recall that these ratios are calculated as follows:

$$\text{Receivables turnover ratio} = \frac{\text{Net sales}}{\text{Average accounts receivable (net)}}$$

$$\text{Average collection period} = \frac{365 \text{ days}}{\text{Receivables turnover ratio}}$$

The turnover ratio shows the number of times during a period that the average accounts receivable balance is collected, and the average collection period is an approximation of the number of days the average accounts receivable balance is outstanding.

As a company's sales grow, receivables also will increase. If the percentage increase in receivables is greater than the percentage increase in sales, the receivables turnover ratio will decline (the average collection period will increase). This could indicate customer dissatisfaction with the product or that the company has extended too generous payment terms in order to attract new customers, which, in turn, could increase sales returns and bad debts.

These ratios also can be used to compare the relative effectiveness of companies in managing the investment in receivables. Of course, it would be meaningless to compare the receivables turnover ratio of a computer products company such as **IBM** with that of, say, a food products company like **Hershey**. A company selling high-priced, low-volume products like mainframe computers generally will grant customers longer payment terms than a company selling lower priced, higher volume food products. Illustration 7–23 lists the 2011 receivables turnover ratio for some well-known companies. The differences are as expected, given the nature of the companies' products and operations. In particular, companies designing expensive products for medical and business applications turn over their receivables less frequently than do consumer-goods manufacturers and wholesalers.

| Company | 2011 Receivables Turnover Ratio |
|---|---|
| Medtronic (medical technology) | 4.45 |
| Autodesk (design software) | 6.55 |
| General Mills (wholesale consumer foods) | 13.50 |

**Illustration 7–23**
Receivables Turnover Ratios

To illustrate receivables analysis in more detail, let's compute the 2011 receivables turnover ratio and the average collection period for two companies in the software industry, **Symantec Corp.** and **CA, Inc.** (formerly Computer Associates, Inc.).

|  | ($ in millions) | | | |
|---|---|---|---|---|
|  | **Symantec Corp.** | | **CA, Inc.** | |
|  | **2011** | **2010** | **2011** | **2010** |
| Accounts receivable (net) | $1013 | $856 | $849 | $931 |
| Two-year averages |  | $934.5 |  | $ 890 |
| Net sales—2011 |  | $6,190 |  | $4,429 |

Balance sheet and income statement information—Symantec Corp. and CA, Inc.

| | **Symantec Corp.** | **CA, Inc.** | **Industry Average** |
|---|---|---|---|
| Receivables Turnover | $\dfrac{\$6,190}{\$934.5} = 6.62$ times | $\dfrac{\$4,429}{\$890} = 4.98$ times | 5.96 times |
| Average Collection Period | $= \dfrac{365}{6.62} = 55.14$ days | $\dfrac{365}{4.98} = 73.29$ days | 61.3 days |

Receivables turnover and average collection period—Symantec Corp. and CA, Inc.

On average, Symantec collects its receivables 18 days sooner than does CA, and six days faster than the industry average. A major portion of Symantec's sales of products like Norton antivirus software are made directly to consumers online who pay immediately with credit cards, significantly accelerating payment. CA, on the other hand, sells primarily to businesses, who take longer to pay.

> Bad debt expense is one of a variety of discretionary accruals that provide management with the opportunity to manipulate income.

**EARNINGS QUALITY.** Recall our discussion in Chapter 4 concerning earnings quality. We learned that managers have the ability, to a limited degree, to manipulate reported income and that many observers believe this practice diminishes earnings quality because it can mask "permanent" earnings. Former SEC Chairman Arthur Levitt listed discretionary accruals, which he called "Miscellaneous Cookie Jar Reserves," as one of the most popular methods companies use to manipulate income.

> **Arthur Levitt, Jr.**
> A third illusion played by some companies is using unrealistic assumptions to estimate . . . such items as sales returns, loan losses or warranty costs. In doing so, they stash accruals in cookie jars during good times and reach into them when needed in the bad times.[29]

**Dell Inc.** provides an example of a company that engaged in this sort of behavior. Dell had to restate four years of financial statements (from 2003 to 2007) after it discovered that executives had been using a variety of accounting techniques to achieve quarterly earnings targets. For example, revenue associated with software licenses and product warranties was being recognized too quickly, and extra warranty reserves were maintained that could be adjusted to compensate for earnings shortfalls.

Sometimes financial statement users can examine accounts receivable, the allowance for bad debts, and other accounts to detect low earnings quality. For example, in April 1998, **PaineWebber Inc.** downgraded its stock recommendation for **Sunbeam, Inc.**, after noticing unusually high accounts receivable and unexpected increases in sales of certain products. Also, Sunbeam's allowance for uncollectible accounts had shown large increases in prior periods. It eventually came to light that Sunbeam had been manipulating its income by using a "bill and hold" strategy with retail buyers. This involved selling products at large discounts to retailers before they normally would buy and then holding the products in third-party warehouses, with delivery at a later date.

Often times, though, financial statement users must rely on the company's internal control system to prevent fraud and preserve earnings quality, because the effects of poor accounting quality can be difficult for outsiders to detect. Dell's accounting problems were identified by an internal investigation that followed an SEC inquiry on another matter. Dell acknowledged that poor internal controls contributed to its problems. Dell's income manipulation was never extreme enough to be detected by outsiders, but strong internal controls could have prevented it from occurring at all.

Another area for accounting-quality concern is the sale method used to account for transfers of receivables. Recent research suggests that some companies manage earnings by distorting the fair value estimates that are made as part of recording securitizations.[30] Also, some firms classify cash flows associated with selling their accounts receivable in the operating section of the statement of cash flows, such that changes in the extent to which accounts receivable are sold can be used to manipulate cash flow from operations. In fact, evidence suggests that sophisticated investors and bond-rating agencies undo sales accounting to treat transfers of receivables as secured borrowings before assessing the riskiness of a company's debt.[31] As noted earlier in this chapter, recent changes in GAAP have made it more difficult for transfers to qualify for sales accounting, but Wall Street is very good at identifying clever ways to structure transactions around accounting standards, so it is important to be vigilant regarding the accounting for these transactions. ●

---

[29]Arthur Levitt, Jr., "The Numbers Game," *The CPA Journal,* December 1998, p. 16.

[30]P. M. Dechow, L. A. Myers, and C. Shakespeare, "Fair Value Accounting and Gains from Asset Securitizations: A Convenient Earnings Management Tool with Compensation Side-Benefits," *Journal of Accounting and Economics* 49, No. 2 (2010): 2–25.

[31]Other recent research provides evidence that investors treat securitizations as loans rather than asset sales, suggesting that they are unconvinced that a sale has truly taken place. For example, see W. R. Landsman, K. Peasnell, and C. Shakespeare, "Are Asset Securitizations Sales or Loans?" *The Accounting Review* 83, No. 5 (2008), pp. 1251–72.

# Financial Reporting Case Solution

1. **Explain the allowance method of accounting for bad debts.** *(p. 368)*   The allowance method estimates future bad debts in order to (1) match bad debt expense with related revenues and (2) report accounts receivable in the balance sheet at net realizable value. In an adjusting entry, we record bad debt expense and reduce accounts receivable indirectly by crediting a contra account to accounts receivable for an estimate of the amount that eventually will prove uncollectible.

2. **What approaches might Cisco have used to arrive at the $275 million bad debt provision?** *(p. 370)*   There are two ways commonly used to arrive at an estimate of future bad debts: the income statement approach and the balance sheet approach. Using the income statement approach, we estimate bad debt expense as a percentage of each period's net credit sales. The balance sheet approach determines bad debt expense by estimating the net realizable value of accounts receivable. In other words, the allowance for uncollectible accounts is determined and bad debt expense is an indirect outcome of adjusting the allowance account to the desired balance.

3. **Are there any alternatives to the allowance method?** *(p. 373)*   An alternative to the allowance method is the direct write-off method. Using this method, adjusting entries are not recorded and any bad debt that does arise simply is written off as bad debt expense. Of course, if the sale that generated this receivable occurred in a previous reporting period, this violates the matching principle. Operating expenses would have been understated and assets overstated that period. This is why the direct write-off method is not permitted by GAAP except in limited circumstances. ●

# The Bottom Line

● **LO7–1**    Internal control refers to the plan designed to encourage adherence to company policies and procedures; promote operational efficiency; minimize irregularities, errors, thefts or fraud; and maximize the reliability and accuracy of accounting data. Key elements of an internal control system for cash receipts and disbursements include separation of record keeping from control of cash duties and the periodic preparation of a bank reconciliation. *(p. 360)*

● **LO7–2**    Cash can be informally restricted by management for a particular purpose. Restrictions also can be contractually imposed. If restricted cash is available for current operations or to pay current liabilities, it's classified as a current asset; otherwise, it's classified as investments and funds or other assets. *(p. 362)*

● **LO7–3**    The gross method of accounting for cash discounts considers a discount not taken as part of sales revenue. The net method considers a discount not taken as interest revenue. *(p. 365)*

● **LO7–4**    When merchandise returns are anticipated, an allowance for sales returns should be recorded as a contra account to accounts receivable and sales revenue also should be reduced by the anticipated sales returns. *(p. 366)*

● **LO7–5**    Uncollectible accounts receivable should be anticipated in order to match bad debt expense with revenues generated. Likewise, accounts receivable should be reduced by an allowance for uncollectible accounts to report accounts receivable at net realizable value. *(p. 368)*

● **LO7–6**    There are two approaches to estimating future bad debts. The income statement approach estimates bad debt expense based on the notion that a certain percentage of each period's credit sales will prove to be uncollectible. The balance sheet approach to estimating future bad debts indirectly determines bad debt expense by directly estimating the net realizable value of accounts receivable at the end of the period. *(p. 369)*

● **LO7–7**    Notes receivable are formal credit arrangements between a creditor (lender) and a debtor (borrower). The typical note receivable requires the payment of a specified face amount, also called principal, at a specified maturity date or dates. In addition, interest is paid at a stated percentage of the face amount. Interest on notes is calculated by multiplying the face amount by the annual rate by the fraction of the annual period. *(p. 374)*

● **LO7–8**    A wide variety of methods exists for companies to use their receivables to obtain immediate cash. These methods can be described as either a secured borrowing or a sale of receivables. If three conditions indicating surrender of control are met, the transferor accounts for the transfer of receivables as a sale; otherwise as a secured borrowing. (*p. 379*)

● **LO7–9**    A company's investment in receivables is influenced by several related variables, to include the level of sales, the nature of the product or service, and credit and collection policies. Investors, creditors, and financial analysts can gain important insights by monitoring a company's investment in receivables. The receivables turnover and average collection period ratios are designed to monitor receivables. (*p. 388*)

● **LO7–10**    Accounting for cash and accounts receivable are similar under U.S. GAAP and IFRS. Other than some differences in terminology and balance sheet classifications, the most important differences involve accounting for transfers of receivables. Both IFRS and U.S. GAAP seek to distinguish between determining whether a sales treatment or secured borrowing treatment is appropriate, but they use different conceptual frameworks to guide that choice. U.S. GAAP focuses on whether control of the receivables is transferred, while IFRS use a more complex decision process that also considers whether substantially all of the risks and rewards of ownership have been transferred. Convergence efforts in this area are proceeding slowly. (*pp. 363, 378, 387, 397, and 398*) ●

# APPENDIX 7A  | Cash Controls

## Bank Reconciliation

One of the most important tools used in the control of cash is the **bank reconciliation**. Since all cash receipts are deposited into the bank account and cash disbursements are made by check, the bank account provides a separate record of cash. It's desirable to periodically compare the bank balance with the balance in the company's own records and reconcile any differences.

From your own personal experience, you know that the ending balance in your checking account reported on the monthly bank statement you receive rarely equals the balance you have recorded in your checkbook. Differences arise from two types of items: timing differences and errors.

*Timing differences* occur when the company and the bank record transactions at different times. At any point in time the company may have adjusted the cash balance for items of which the bank is not yet aware. Likewise, the bank may have adjusted its record of that balance by items of which the company is not yet aware. For example, checks written and cash deposits are not all processed by the bank in the same month that they are recorded by the company. Also, the bank may adjust the company's account for items such as service charges that the company is not aware of until the bank statement is received.

*Errors* can be made either by the company or the bank. For example, a check might be written for $210 but recorded on the company's books as a $120 disbursement; a deposit of $500 might be processed incorrectly by the bank as a $50 deposit. In addition to serving as a safeguard of cash, the bank reconciliation also uncovers errors such as these and helps ensure that the proper cash balance is reported in the balance sheet.

Bank reconciliations include adjustments to the balance per bank for timing differences involving transactions already reflected in the company's accounting records that have not yet been processed by the bank. These adjustments usually include *checks outstanding* and *deposits outstanding* (also called *deposits in transit*). In addition, the balance per bank would be adjusted for any bank errors discovered. These adjustments produce an adjusted bank balance that represents the corrected cash balance.

The balance per books is similarly adjusted for timing differences involving transactions already reflected by the bank of which the company is unaware until the bank statement is received. These would include service charges, charges for NSF (nonsufficient funds) checks, and collections made by the bank on the company's behalf. In addition, the balance per books is adjusted for any company errors discovered, resulting in an adjusted book balance that will also represent the corrected cash balance. *Each of these adjustments requires a journal entry to correct the book balance.* Only adjustments to the book balance require journal entries. Illustration 7A–1 recaps these reconciling items.

*Differences between the cash book and bank balance occur due to differences in the timing of recognition of certain transactions and errors.*

*STEP 1: Adjust the bank balance to the corrected cash balance.*

*STEP 2: Adjust the book balance to the corrected cash balance.*

**Step 1: Adjustments to Bank Balance:**

1. *Add deposits outstanding.* These represent cash amounts received by the company and debited to cash that have not been deposited in the bank by the bank statement cutoff date and cash receipts deposited in the bank near the end of the period that are not recorded by the bank until after the cutoff date.
2. *Deduct checks outstanding.* These represent checks written and recorded by the company as credits to cash that have not yet been processed by the bank before the cutoff date.
3. *Bank errors.* These will either be increases or decreases depending on the nature of the error.

**Step 2: Adjustments to Book Balance:**

1. *Add collections made by the bank* on the company's behalf and other increases in cash that the company is unaware of until the bank statement is received.
2. *Deduct service and other charges* made by the bank that the company is unaware of until the bank statement is received.
3. *Deduct NSF (nonsufficient funds) checks.* These are checks previously deposited for which the payors do not have sufficient funds in their accounts to cover the amount of the checks. The checks are returned to the company whose responsibility it is to seek payment from payors.
4. *Company errors.* These will either be increases or decreases depending on the nature of the error.

### Illustration 7A–1
Bank Reconciliation— Reconciling Items

**Bank balance**
+ Deposits outstanding
− Checks outstanding
± Errors
─────────
Corrected balance

**Book balance**
+ Collections by bank
− Service charges
− NSF checks
± Errors
─────────
Corrected balance

The two corrected balances must equal.

To demonstrate the bank reconciliation process, consider Illustration 7A–2.

### Illustration 7A–2
Bank Reconciliation

The Hawthorne Manufacturing Company maintains a general checking account at the First Pacific Bank. First Pacific provides a bank statement and canceled checks once a month. The cutoff date is the last day of the month. The bank statement for the month of May is summarized as follows:

| | |
|---|---|
| Balance, May 1, 2013 | $32,120 |
| Deposits | 82,140 |
| Checks processed | (78,433) |
| Service charges | (80) |
| NSF checks | (2,187) |
| Note payment collected by bank (includes $120 interest) | 1,120 |
| Balance, May 31, 2013 | $34,680 |

The company's general ledger cash account has a balance of $35,276 at the end of May. A review of the company records and the bank statement reveals the following:

1. Cash receipts not yet deposited totaled $2,965.
2. A deposit of $1,020 was made on May 31 that was not credited to the company's account until June.
3. All checks written in April have been processed by the bank. Checks written in May that had not been processed by the bank total $5,536.
4. A check written for $1,790 was incorrectly recorded by the company as a $790 disbursement. The check was for payment to a supplier of raw materials.

The bank reconciliation prepared by the company appears as follows:

| **Step 1: Bank Balance to Corrected Balance** | |
|---|---|
| Balance per bank statement | $34,680 |
| Add: Deposits outstanding | 3,985* |
| Deduct: Checks outstanding | (5,536) |
| Corrected cash balance | $33,129 |

(continued)

**Illustration 7A–2**
(concluded)

| Step 2: Book Balance to Corrected Balance | |
|---|---:|
| Balance per books | $35,276 |
| Add: Note collected by bank | 1,120 |
| Deduct: | |
| Service charges | (80) |
| NSF checks | (2,187) |
| Error—understatement of check | (1,000) |
| Corrected cash balance | $33,129 |

*$2,965 + 1,020 = $3,985

The next step is to prepare adjusting journal entries to reflect each of the adjustments to the balance per books. These represent amounts the company was not previously aware of until receipt of the bank statement. No adjusting entries are needed for the adjustments to the balance per bank because the company has already recorded these items. However, the bank needs to be notified of any errors discovered.

**To record the receipt of principal and interest on note collected directly by the bank.**

| | | |
|---|---:|---:|
| Cash .............................................................................................. | 1,120 | |
| Notes receivable ................................................................... | | 1,000 |
| Interest revenue ................................................................... | | 120 |

**To record credits to cash revealed by the bank reconciliation.**

| | | |
|---|---:|---:|
| Miscellaneous expense (bank service charges) ............................................. | 80 | |
| Accounts receivable (NSF checks) ............................................................. | 2,187 | |
| Accounts payable (error in check to supplier) ............................................. | 1,000 | |
| Cash ....................................................................................... | | 3,267 |

After these entries are posted, the general ledger cash account will equal the corrected balance of $33,129.

## Petty Cash

Most companies keep a small amount of cash on hand to pay for low-cost items such as postage, office supplies, delivery charges, and entertainment expenses. It would be inconvenient, time consuming, and costly to process a check each time these small payments are made. A petty cash fund provides a more efficient way to handle these payments.

A petty cash fund is established by transferring a specified amount of cash from the company's general checking account to an employee designated as the petty cash custodian. The amount of the fund should approximate the expenditures made from the fund during a relatively short period of time (say a week or a month). The custodian disburses cash from the fund when the appropriate documentation is presented, such as a receipt for the purchase of office supplies. At any point in time, the custodian should be in possession of cash and appropriate receipts that sum to the amount of the fund. The receipts serve as the basis for recording appropriate expenses each time the fund is replenished. Consider the example in Illustration 7A–3.

**The petty cash fund always should have cash and receipts that together equal the amount of the fund.**

**Illustration 7A–3**
Petty Cash Fund

On May 1, 2013, the Hawthorne Manufacturing Company established a $200 petty cash fund. John Ringo is designated as the petty cash custodian. The fund will be replenished at the end of each month. On May 1, 2013, a check is written for $200 made out to John Ringo, petty cash custodian. During the month of May, John paid bills totaling $160 summarized as follows:

| | |
|---|---:|
| Postage | $ 40 |
| Office supplies | 35 |
| Delivery charges | 55 |
| Entertainment | 30 |
| Total | $160 |

In journal entry form, the transaction to establish the fund would be recorded as follows:

| May 1, 2013 | | |
|---|---|---|
| Petty Cash ................................................................................................. | 200 | |
|     Cash (checking account) ...................................................................... | | 200 |

*A petty cash fund is established by writing a check to the custodian.*

No entries are recorded at the time the actual expenditures are made from the fund. The expenditures are recorded when reimbursement is requested at the end of the month. At that time, a check is written to John Ringo, petty cash custodian, for the total of the fund receipts, $160 in this case. John cashes the check and replenishes the fund to $200. In journal entry form, replenishing the fund would be recorded as follows:

| May 31, 2013 | | |
|---|---|---|
| Postage expense ...................................................................................... | 40 | |
| Office supplies expense .......................................................................... | 35 | |
| Delivery expense ..................................................................................... | 55 | |
| Entertainment expense .......................................................................... | 30 | |
|     Cash (checking account) ...................................................................... | | 160 |

*The appropriate expense accounts are debited when the petty cash fund is reimbursed.*

The petty cash account is not debited when replenishing the fund. If, however, the size of the fund is increased at time of replenishment, the account is debited for the increase. Similarly, petty cash would be credited if the size of the fund is decreased.

To maintain the control objective of separation of duties, the petty cash custodian should not be involved in the process of writing or approving checks, nor in recordkeeping. In addition, management should arrange for surprise counts of the fund. ●

## Accounting For Impairment of a Receivable and a Troubled Debt Restructuring[32]

# APPENDIX 7B

## Impairment of a Receivable

Earlier in this chapter you learned about the allowance method of accounting for bad debts. Because it is difficult to determine which individual receivables will ultimately prove uncollectible, the allowance method recognizes bad debt expense for a large group of receivables and reduces the book value of that group of receivables by establishing an allowance for uncollectible accounts. Later, when an individual receivable proves uncollectible, the receivable and the allowance are both reduced. The allowance method is used for many types of receivables, including normal trade receivables, notes receivable, and loans receivable.

However, for some receivables of a long-term nature, like notes receivable and loans receivable, it may become apparent over time to a creditor that an individual receivable has become impaired. For example, a bank may learn that one of its borrowers is having financial difficulties, or a bank may realize that borrowers in particular industries or countries are facing economic instability. In that case, a more precise estimate of an impairment loss for that receivable can be made.

An impairment loss on a receivable is recognized if the creditor (lender) believes it is probable that it will not receive all of the cash flows (principal and any interest payments) that have been promised by the debtor (borrower). In that case, the creditor remeasures the receivable based on the present value of currently expected cash flows, discounted at the loan's original effective interest rate.[33] The adjustment necessary to record the impaired receivable should seem familiar—a loss is included in current income by debiting bad debt expense (or a separate impairment loss account) and crediting the allowance for uncollectible accounts. Illustration 7B–1 provides an example.

---

[32]This appendix discusses accounting for the impairment of individual accounts and notes receivable, as specified in ASC 310–10–35: Receivables—Overall—Subsequent Measurement (previously "Accounting by Creditors for Impairment of a Loan–An amendment of FASB Statements No. 5 and 15," *Statement of Financial Accounting Standards No. 114* (Norwalk, Conn.: FASB, 1993)). When a receivable has been securitized, or when a company has elected to account for a receivable under the fair value option, the receivable is viewed as an investment and different GAAP applies, as described in Appendix 12B.

[33]Rather than calculating the present value of the loan, as a practical expediency the creditor can base the new value of the loan on the loan's market price or the fair value of collateral that supports the loan.

## Illustration 7B–1
### Receivable Impairment

Brillard Properties owes First Prudent Bank $30 million under a 10% note with two years remaining to maturity. Due to Brillard's financial difficulties, the previous year's interest ($3 million) was not paid. First Prudential estimates that it will not receive the $3 million of accrued interest, that it will receive only $2 million of interest in each of the next two years, and that it will receive only $25 million of principal at the end of two years.

### Analysis

**The discounted present value of the cash flows prior to the impairment is the same as the receivable's book value.**

| Previous Value | | | |
|---|---|---|---|
| Accrued interest | (10% × $30,000,000) | $ 3,000,000 | |
| Principal | | 30,000,000 | |
|   Book value of the receivable | | | $ 33,000,000 |

**The discounted present value of the cash flows after the impairment is less than book value.**

| New Value (based on estimated cash flows to be received) | | | |
|---|---|---|---|
| Present value of accrued interest to be received | = $ | 0 | |
| Present value of future interest | $ 2 million × 1.73554* = | $ 3,471,080 | |
| Present value of estimated principal | $25 million × 0.82645† = | 20,661,250 | |
|   Present value of the receivable | | | (24,132,330) |

**The difference is a loss, debited to bad debt expense.**

| Loss | | | $ 8,867,670 |
|---|---|---|---|

*Present value of an ordinary annuity of $1: $n = 2$, $i = 10\%$
†Present value of $1: $n = 2$, $i = 10\%$

### Journal Entry

| | | |
|---|---|---|
| Bad debt expense (to balance) ................................................. | 8,867,670 | |
|   Accrued interest receivable ................................................. | | 3,000,000 |
|   Allowance for uncollectible accounts | | |
|     ($30,000,000 − 24,132,330) ............................................. | | 5,867,670 |

In the future, if additional information indicates that conditions have changed, bad debt expense and the allowance for uncollectible accounts are increased or decreased as necessary to reflect the change.

You may be wondering whether recognizing an impairment loss leads to a double counting of bad debt expense. After all, the receivable first was included in a group of receivables for which bad debt expense was estimated, and then was singled out for recognition of an impairment loss. Creditors have to be careful to avoid this problem by excluding an impaired receivable from the rest of the receivables and estimating bad debt expense as appropriate for the rest of the receivables. That way, bad debt expense for the impaired receivable and the rest of the receivables is calculated separately, and there is no double counting.

## Troubled Debt Restructurings

**A *troubled debt restructuring* occurs when the creditor makes concessions to the debtor in response to the debtor's financial difficulties.**

Sometimes a creditor changes the original terms of a debt agreement in response to the debtor's financial difficulties. The creditor makes concessions to the debtor that make it easier for the debtor to pay, with the goal of maximizing the amount of cash that the creditor can collect. In that case, the new arrangement is referred to as a **troubled debt restructuring**. Because identifying an arrangement as a troubled debt restructuring requires recognizing any impairment loss associated with the arrangement, creditors might be reluctant to conclude that a troubled debt restructuring has occurred. The FASB recently provided clarification to help ensure that all troubled debt restructurings are properly identified.[34]

[34]A troubled debt restructuring occurs when a creditor makes concessions in response to a debtor's financial difficulties. These terms have been clarified recently (ASC 310–40–15: Receivables—Troubled Debt Restructurings by Creditors,—Scope and Scope Exceptions; previously "A Creditor's Determination of Whether a Restructuring is a Troubled Debt Restructuring," *Accounting Standards Update No. 2011–02* (Norwalk, Conn.: FASB, 2011)). A debtor is viewed as experiencing *financial difficulties* if it is probable that the debtor will default on any of its liabilities unless the creditor restructures the debt. A *concession* has occurred if, as a result of the restructuring, the creditor does not expect to collect all amounts due, including accrued interest. A concession also can occur if the creditor restructures the terms of the debt in a way that provides the debtor with funds at a better rate of interest than the debtor could receive if the debtor tried to obtain new debt with similar terms (for example, a similar payment schedule, collateral, and guarantees) as the restructured debt. But, not all changes are concessions. For example, a restructuring that results in an insignificant delay of payment is not a concession.

## WHEN THE RECEIVABLE IS CONTINUED, BUT WITH MODIFIED TERMS.

In a troubled debt restructuring, it's likely that the bank allows the receivable to continue but with the terms of the debt agreement modified to make it easier for the debtor to comply. The lender might agree to reduce or delay the scheduled interest payments. Or, it may agree to reduce or delay the maturity amount. Often a troubled debt restructuring will call for some combination of these concessions.

Consider again Illustration 7B–1. What if First Prudent Bank and Brillard Properties actually *renegotiated* Brillard's debt to (1) forgive the interest accrued from last year, (2) reduce the two remaining interest payments from $3 million each to $2 million each, and (3) reduce the face amount from $30 million to $25 million? In that case, First Prudent would account for its impairment loss in exactly the same way as shown in Illustration 7B–1. The only difference would be that, whereas we originally based calculations on First Prudent's estimates of future cash flows, we now base calculations on the cash flows that were specified in the restructured debt agreement.

## WHEN THE RECEIVABLE IS SETTLED OUTRIGHT.

Sometimes a receivable in a troubled debt restructuring is actually settled at the time of the restructuring by the debtor making a payment of cash, some other noncash assets, or even shares of the debtor's stock. In that case, the creditor simply records a loss for the difference between the carrying amount of the receivable and the fair value of the asset(s) or equity securities received. Illustration 7B–2 provides an example.

---

First Prudent Bank is owed $30 million by Brillard Properties under a 10% note with two years remaining to maturity. Due to Brillard's financial difficulties, the previous year's interest ($3 million) was not received. The bank agrees to settle the receivable (and accrued interest receivable) in exchange for property having a fair value of $20 million.

|  | ($ in millions) | |
|---|---|---|
| Land (fair value) | 20 | |
| Bad debt expense (to balance)* | 13 | |
|    Accrued interest receivable (10% × $30 million) | | 3 |
|    Note receivable (account balance) | | 30 |

*Rather than debiting bad debt expense, First Prudent might debit Loss on troubled debt restructuring.

**Illustration 7B–2**
Debt Settled at the Time of a Restructuring

# International Financial Reporting Standards

**● LO7–10**

**Impairments.** IFRS (IAS 39)[35] and U.S. GAAP (ASC 310)[36] generally provide similar treatments of impairments of receivables, but the specific impairment evaluation process and criteria are somewhat different regarding:

- Level of analysis:
  - Under U.S. GAAP we examine impairment of individual receivables. If impairment isn't indicated, we group the receivables with other receivables of similar risk characteristics when estimating bad debts for the group.
  - Under IFRS we first consider whether individually significant receivables are impaired. If impairment isn't indicated, the individually significant receivables are grouped with other receivables of similar risk characteristics to test impairment.

- Impairment indicators:
  - U.S. GAAP provides an illustrative list of information we might consider when evaluating receivables for impairment, and requires measurement of potential impairment if impairment (a) is viewed as probable and (b) can be estimated reliably.

(continued)

---

[35]"Financial Instruments: Recognition and Measurement," *International Accounting Standard No. 39* (IASCF), as amended effective January 1, 2011.
[36]FASB ASC 310–10–35: Receivables—Overall—Subsequent Measurement.

(concluded)

- º IFRS provides an illustrative list of "loss events" and requires measurement of an impairment if there is objective evidence that a loss event has occurred that has an impact on the future cash flows to be collected and that can be estimated reliably. Requiring the occurrence of a loss event may result in recognizing a loss later under IFRS than U.S. GAAP.

- Reversal of impairments: Under both U.S. GAAP and IFRS, if an impaired receivable's estimated future cash flows improve, the creditor recalculates the impairment and adjusts the valuation allowance up or down as appropriate. The net book value of the receivable can't exceed the original amount of the receivable (as adjusted for any normal amortization of any discount or premium). Reversals increase income (for example, by crediting bad debt expense in the period of reversal).

# Where We're Headed

**The FASB and IASB are working together on a new impairment model**

● LO7–10

The FASB and IASB are working jointly on a new model for recognizing impairments of receivables. The goal of the project is to base the accrual of impairment loss more on expected losses rather than only on probable losses, thereby providing more timely recognition of impairment losses and enhanced notification of financial statement users about credit-quality problems like those that occurred during the financial crisis of 2008/2009. The boards anticipate issuing an ASU sometime in 2012.

In this appendix we have focused on creditors' accounting for impairments and troubled debt restructurings. We discuss those topics from the standpoint of the debtor in Chapter 14, Appendix B. ●

# Questions For Review of Key Topics

Q 7–1    Define cash equivalents.

Q 7–2    Explain the primary functions of internal controls procedures in the accounting area. What is meant by separation of duties?

Q 7–3    What are the responsibilities of management described in Section 404 of the Sarbanes-Oxley Act? What are the responsibilities of the company's auditor?

Q 7–4    Define a compensating balance. How are compensating balances reported in financial statements?

**IFRS**    Q 7–5    Do U.S. GAAP and IFRS differ in how bank overdrafts are treated? Explain.

Q 7–6    Explain the difference between a trade discount and a cash discount.

Q 7–7    Distinguish between the gross and net methods of accounting for cash discounts.

Q 7–8    Briefly explain the accounting treatment for sales returns.

Q 7–9    Explain the typical way companies account for uncollectible accounts receivable (bad debts). When is it permissible to record bad debt expense only at the time when receivables actually prove uncollectible?

Q 7–10    Briefly explain the difference between the income statement approach and the balance sheet approach to estimating bad debts.

**IFRS**    Q 7–11    If a company has accounts receivable from ordinary customers and from related parties, can they combine those receivables in their financial statements under U.S. GAAP? Under IFRS?

Q 7–12    Is any special accounting treatment required for the assigning of accounts receivable in general as collateral for debt?

Q 7–13    Explain any possible differences between accounting for an account receivable factored with recourse compared with one factored without recourse.

IFRS    Q 7–14    Do U.S. GAAP and IFRS differ in the criteria they use to determine whether a transfer of receivables is treated as a sale? Explain.

Q 7–15    What is meant by the discounting of a note receivable? Describe the four-step process used to account for discounted notes.

Q 7–16    What are the key variables that influence a company's investment in receivables? Describe the two ratios used by financial analysts to monitor a company's investment in receivables.

Q 7–17    (Based on Appendix 7A) In a two-step bank reconciliation, identify the items that might be necessary to adjust the bank balance to the corrected cash balance. Identify the items that might be necessary to adjust the book balance to the corrected cash balance.

Q 7–18    (Based on Appendix 7A) How is a petty cash fund established? How is the fund replenished?

Q 7–19    (Based on Appendix 7B) Marshall Companies, Inc., holds a note receivable from a former subsidiary. Due to financial difficulties, the former subsidiary has been unable to pay the previous year's interest on the note. Marshall agreed to restructure the debt by both delaying and reducing remaining cash payments. The concessions impair the creditor's investment in the receivable. How is this impairment recorded?

IFRS    Q 7–20    (Based on Appendix 7B) Do U.S. GAAP and IFRS differ in the ability of a company to recognize in net income the recovery of impairment losses of accounts and notes receivable?

# Brief Exercises

**BE 7–1**
Internal control
● LO7–1

Janice Dodds opens the mail for the Ajax Plumbing Company. She lists all customer checks on a spreadsheet that includes the name of the customer and the check amount. The checks, along with the spreadsheet, are then sent to Jim Seymour in the accounting department who records the checks and deposits them daily in the company's checking account. How could the company improve its internal control procedure for the handling of its cash receipts?

**BE 7–2**
Bank overdrafts
● LO7–2, LO7–10

IFRS

Cutler Company has a cash account with a balance of $250,000 with Wright Bank and a cash account with an overdraft of $5,000 at Lowe Bank. What would the current assets section of Cutler's balance sheet include for "cash" under IFRS? Under U.S. GAAP?

**BE 7–3**
Cash and cash equivalents
● LO7–2

The following items appeared on the year-end trial balance of Consolidated Freight Corporation: cash in a checking account, U.S. Treasury bills that mature in six months, undeposited customer checks, cash in a savings account, and currency and coins. Which of these items would be included in the company's balance sheet as cash and cash equivalents?

**BE 7–4**
Cash discounts; gross method
● LO7–3

On December 28, 2013, Tristar Communications sold 10 units of its new satellite uplink system to various customers for $25,000 each. The terms of each sale were 1/10, n/30. Tristar uses the gross method to account for sales discounts. In what year will income before tax be affected by discounts, assuming that all customers paid the net-of-discount amount on January 6, 2014? By how much?

**BE 7–5**
Cash discounts; net method
● LO7–3

Refer to the situation described in BE 7–4. Answer the questions assuming that Tristar uses the net method to account for sales discounts.

**BE 7–6**
Sales returns
● LO7–4

During 2013, its first year of operations, Hollis Industries recorded sales of $10,600,000 and experienced returns of $720,000. Cost of goods sold totaled $6,360,000 (60% of sales). The company estimates that 8% of all sales will be returned. Prepare the year-end adjusting journal entries to account for anticipated sales returns.

**BE 7–7**
Accounts receivable classification
● LO7–5, LO7–10

IFRS

Singletary Associates has accounts receivable due from normal credit customers, and also has an account receivable due from a director of the company. Singletary would like to combine both of those receivables on one line in the current assets section of their balance sheet and in the footnotes. Is that permissible under U.S. GAAP? Under IFRS? Explain.

**BE 7–8**
Uncollectible accounts; income statement approach
● LO7–5, LO7–6

The following information relates to a company's accounts receivable: accounts receivable balance at the beginning of the year, $300,000; allowance for uncollectible accounts at the beginning of the year, $25,000 (credit balance); credit sales during the year, $1,500,000; accounts receivable written off during the year, $16,000; cash collections from customers, $1,450,000. Assuming the company estimates bad debts at an amount equal to 2% of credit sales, calculate (1) bad debt expense for the year and (2) the year-end balance in the allowance for uncollectible accounts.

**BE 7–9**
Uncollectible accounts; balance sheet approach
● LO7–5, LO7–6

Refer to the situation described in BE 7–8. Answer the two questions assuming the company estimates that future bad debts will equal 10% of the year-end balance in accounts receivable.

**BE 7–10**
Uncollectible accounts; solving for unknown
● LO7–5, LO7–6

A company's year-end balance in accounts receivable is $2,000,000. The allowance for uncollectible accounts had a beginning-of-year credit balance of $30,000. An aging of accounts receivable at the end of the year indicates a required allowance of $38,000. If bad debt expense for the year was $40,000, what was the amount of bad debts written off during the year?

**BE 7–11**
Uncollectible accounts; solving for unknown
● LO7–5, LO7–6

Refer to the situation described in BE 7–10. If credit sales for the year were $8,200,000 and $7,950,000 was collected from credit customers, what was the beginning-of-year balance in accounts receivable?

**BE 7–12**
Note receivable
● LO7–7

On December 1, 2013, Davenport Company sold merchandise to a customer for $20,000. In payment for the merchandise, the customer signed a 6% note requiring the payment of interest and principal on March 1, 2014. How much interest revenue will the company recognize during 2013? In 2014?

**BE 7–13**
Factoring of accounts receivable
● LO7–8

Logitech Corporation transferred $100,000 of accounts receivable to a local bank. The transfer was made without recourse. The local bank remits 85% of the factored amount to Logitech and retains the remaining 15%. When the bank collects the receivables, it will remit to Logitech the retained amount less a fee equal to 3% of the total amount factored. Logitech estimates a fair value of its 15% interest in the receivables of $11,000 (not including the 3% fee). What is the effect of this transaction on the company's assets, liabilities, and income before income taxes?

**BE 7–14**
Factoring of accounts receivable
● LO7–8

Refer to the situation described in BE 7–13. Assuming that the sale criteria are not met, describe how Logitech would account for the transfer.

**BE 7–15**
Transfers of accounts receivable
● LO7–8, LO7–10

IFRS

Huling Associates plans to transfer $300,000 of accounts receivable to Mitchell Inc. in exchange for cash. Huling has structured the arrangement so that it retains substantially all the risks and rewards of ownership but shifts control over the receivables to Mitchell. Assuming all other criteria are met for recognizing the transfer as a sale, how would Huling account for this transaction under IFRS? Under U.S. GAAP?

**BE 7–16**
Discounting a note
● LO7–8

On March 31, Dower Publishing discounted a $30,000 note at a local bank. The note was dated February 28 and required the payment of the principal amount and interest at 6% on May 31. The bank's discount rate is 8%. How much cash will Dower receive from the bank on March 31?

**BE 7–17**
Receivables turnover
● LO7–8

Camden Hardware's credit sales for the year were $320,000. Accounts receivable at the beginning and end of the year were $50,000 and $70,000, respectively. Calculate the accounts receivable turnover ratio and the average collection period for the year.

# Exercises

An alternate exercise and problem set is available on the text website: www.mhhe.com/spiceland7e

**E 7–1**
Cash and cash equivalents; restricted cash
● LO7–2

The controller of the Red Wing Corporation is in the process of preparing the company's 2013 financial statements. She is trying to determine the correct balance of cash and cash equivalents to be reported as a current asset in the balance sheet. The following items are being considered:

a.  Balances in the company's accounts at the First National Bank; checking $13,500, savings $22,100.

b.  Undeposited customer checks of $5,200.

c.  Currency and coins on hand of $580.

d.  Savings account at the East Bay Bank with a balance of $400,000. This account is being used to accumulate cash for future plant expansion (in 2015).

e.  $20,000 in a checking account at the East Bay Bank. The balance in the account represents a 20% compensating balance for a $100,000 loan with the bank. Red Wing may not withdraw the funds until the loan is due in 2016.

f.  U.S. Treasury bills; 2-month maturity bills totaling $15,000, and 7-month bills totaling $20,000.

**Required:**

1.  Determine the correct balance of cash and cash equivalents to be reported in the current asset section of the 2013 balance sheet.

2.  For each of the items not included in your answer to requirement 1, explain the correct classification of the item.

**E 7–2**
Cash and cash equivalents
● LO7–2

Delta Automotive Corporation has the following assets listed in its 12/31/2013 trial balance:

| | |
|---|---|
| Cash in bank—checking account | $22,500 |
| U.S. Treasury bills (mature in 60 days)* | 5,000 |
| Cash on hand (currency and coins) | 1,350 |
| U.S. Treasury bills (mature in six months)* | 10,000 |
| Undeposited customer checks | 1,840 |

*Purchased on 11/30/2013

**Required:**

1.  Determine the correct balance of cash and cash equivalents to be reported in the current asset section of the 2013 balance sheet.

2.  For each of the items not included in your answer to requirement 1, explain the correct classification of the item.

**E 7–3**
FASB codification research
● LO7–2, LO7–6, LO7–7

Access the *FASB's Codification Research System* at the FASB website (www.fasb.org).

**Required:**
Determine the specific citation for accounting for each of the following items:

1.  Accounts receivables from related parties should be shown separately from trade receivables.

2.  The definition of cash equivalents.

3.  The requirement to value notes exchanged for cash at the cash proceeds.

4.  The two conditions that must be met to accrue a loss on an accounts receivable.

**E 7–4**
Bank overdrafts
● LO7–2, LO7–10

● IFRS

Parker Inc. has the following cash balances:

| | |
|---|---|
| First Bank: | $150,000 |
| Second Bank: | (10,000) |
| Third Bank: | 25,000 |
| Fourth Bank: | (5,000) |

**Required:**

1.  Prepare the current assets and current liabilities section of Parker's 2013 balance sheet, assuming Parker reports under U.S. GAAP.

2.  Prepare the current assets and current liabilities section of Parker's 2013 balance sheet, assuming Parker reports under IFRS.

**E 7–5**
**Trade and cash discounts; the gross method and the net method compared**
● LO7–3

Tracy Company, a manufacturer of air conditioners, sold 100 units to Thomas Company on November 17, 2013. The units have a list price of $600 each, but Thomas was given a 30% trade discount. The terms of the sale were 2/10, n/30.

**Required:**

1. Prepare the journal entries to record the sale on November 17 (ignore cost of goods) and collection on November 26, 2013, assuming that the gross method of accounting for cash discounts is used.

2. Prepare the journal entries to record the sale on November 17 (ignore cost of goods) and collection on December 15, 2013, assuming that the gross method of accounting for cash discounts is used.

3. Repeat requirements 1 and 2 assuming that the net method of accounting for cash discounts is used.

**E 7–6**
**Cash discounts; the gross method**
● LO7–3

Harwell Company manufactures automobile tires. On July 15, 2013, the company sold 1,000 tires to the Nixon Car Company for $50 each. The terms of the sale were 2/10, n/30. Harwell uses the gross method of accounting for cash discounts.

**Required:**

1. Prepare the journal entries to record the sale on July 15 (ignore cost of goods) and collection on July 23, 2013.

2. Prepare the journal entries to record the sale on July 15 (ignore cost of goods) and collection on August 15, 2013.

**E 7–7**
**Cash discounts; the net method**
● LO7–3

[This is a variation of Exercise 7–6 modified to focus on the net method of accounting for cash discounts.] Harwell Company manufactures automobile tires. On July 15, 2013, the company sold 1,000 tires to the Nixon Car Company for $50 each. The terms of the sale were 2/10, n/30. Harwell uses the net method of accounting for cash discounts.

**Required:**

1. Prepare the journal entries to record the sale on July 15 (ignore cost of goods) and payment on July 23, 2013.

2. Prepare the journal entries to record the sale on July 15 (ignore cost of goods) and payment on August 15, 2013.

**E 7–8**
**Sales returns**
● LO7–4

Halifax Manufacturing allows its customers to return merchandise for any reason up to 90 days after delivery and receive a credit to their accounts. The company began 2013 with an allowance for sales returns of $300,000. During 2013, Halifax sold merchandise on account for $11,500,000. This merchandise cost Halifax $7,475,000 (65% of selling prices). Also during the year, customers returned $450,000 in sales for credit. Sales returns, estimated to be 4% of sales, are recorded as an adjusting entry at the end of the year.

**Required:**

1. Prepare the entry to record the merchandise returns and the year-end adjusting entry for estimated returns.

2. What is the amount of the year-end allowance for sales returns after the adjusting entry is recorded?

**E 7–9**
**FASB codification research**
● LO7–5

The *FASB Accounting Standards Codification* represents the single source of authoritative U.S. generally accepted accounting principles.

**Required:**

1. Obtain the relevant authoritative literature on accounting for accounts receivable using the FASB's Codification Research System at the FASB website (www.fasb.org). What is the specific citation that describes disclosure of accounting policies for credit losses and doubtful accounts?

2. List the disclosure requirements.

**E 7–10**
**Uncollectible accounts; allowance method vs. direct write-off method**
● LO7–5, LO7–6

Johnson Company uses the allowance method to account for uncollectible accounts receivable. Bad debt expense is established as a percentage of credit sales. For 2013, net credit sales totaled $4,500,000, and the estimated bad debt percentage is 1.5%. The allowance for uncollectible accounts had a credit balance of $42,000 at the beginning of 2013 and $40,000, after adjusting entries, at the end of 2013.

**Required:**

1. What is bad debt expense for 2013?

2. Determine the amount of accounts receivable written off during 2013.

3. If the company uses the direct write-off method, what would bad debt expense be for 2013?

**E 7–11**
**Uncollectible accounts; allowance method; balance sheet approach**
● LO7–5, LO7–6

Colorado Rocky Cookie Company offers credit terms to its customers. At the end of 2013, accounts receivable totaled $625,000. The allowance method is used to account for uncollectible accounts. The allowance for uncollectible accounts had a credit balance of $32,000 at the beginning of 2013 and $21,000 in receivables were written off during the year as uncollectible. Also, $1,200 in cash was received in December from a customer whose account previously had been written off. The company estimates bad debts by applying a percentage of 10% to accounts receivable at the end of the year.

**Required:**

1. Prepare journal entries to record the write-off of receivables, the collection of $1,200 for previously written off receivables, and the year-end adjusting entry for bad debt expense.

2. How would accounts receivable be shown in the 2013 year-end balance sheet?

**E 7–12**
Uncollectible accounts; allowance method and direct write-off method compared; solving for unknown
● LO7–6

Castle Company provides estimates for its uncollectible accounts. The allowance for uncollectible accounts had a credit balance of $17,280 at the beginning of 2013 and a $22,410 credit balance at the end of 2013 (after adjusting entries). If the direct write-off method had been used to account for uncollectible accounts (bad debt expense equals actual write-offs), the income statement for 2013 would have included bad debt expense of $17,100 and revenue of $2,200 from the collection of previously written off bad debts.

**Required:**
Determine bad debt expense for 2013 according to the allowance method.

**E 7–13**
Uncollectible accounts; allowance method; solving for unknowns; General Mills
● LO7–5, LO7–6

Real World Financials

General Mills reported the following information in its 2011 financial statements ($ in millions):

|  | **2011** | **2010** |
| --- | --- | --- |
| Balance Sheet: | | |
| Accounts receivable, net | $ 1,162.3 | $1,041.6 |
| 2011 Income statement: | | |
| Sales revenue | $14,880.2 | |

A note disclosed that the allowance for uncollectible accounts had a balance of $16.3 million and $15.8 million at the end of 2011 and 2010, respectively. Bad debt expense for 2011 was $12.7 million.

**Required:**
Determine the amount of cash collected from customers during 2011.

**E 7–14**
Note receivable
● LO7–7

On June 30, 2013, the Esquire Company sold some merchandise to a customer for $30,000. In payment, Esquire agreed to accept a 6% note requiring the payment of interest and principal on March 31, 2014. The 6% rate is appropriate in this situation.

**Required:**

1. Prepare journal entries to record the sale of merchandise (omit any entry that might be required for the cost of the goods sold), the December 31, 2013 interest accrual, and the March 31, 2014 collection.

2. If the December 31 adjusting entry for the interest accrual is not prepared, by how much will income before income taxes be over- or understated in 2013 and 2014?

**E 7–15**
Noninterest-bearing note receivable
● LO7–7

[This is a variation of Exercise 7–14 modified to focus on a noninterest-bearing note.]

On June 30, 2013, the Esquire Company sold some merchandise to a customer for $30,000 and agreed to accept as payment a noninterest-bearing note with an 8% discount rate requiring the payment of $30,000 on March 31, 2014. The 8% rate is appropriate in this situation.

**Required:**

1. Prepare journal entries to record the sale of merchandise (omit any entry that might be required for the cost of the goods sold), the December 31, 2013 interest accrual, and the March 31, 2014 collection.

2. What is the *effective* interest rate on the note?

**E 7–16**
Interest-bearing note receivable; solving for unknown rate
● LO7–7

On January 1, 2013, the Apex Company exchanged some shares of common stock it had been holding as an investment for a note receivable. The note principal plus interest is due on January 1, 2014. The 2013 income statement reported $2,200 in interest revenue from this note and a $6,000 gain on sale of investment in stock. The stock's book value was $16,000. The company's fiscal year ends on December 31.

**Required:**

1. What is the note's effective interest rate?

2. Reconstruct the journal entries to record the sale of the stock on January 1, 2013, and the adjusting entry to record interest revenue at the end of 2013. The company records adjusting entries only at year-end.

**E 7–17**
Assigning of specific accounts receivable
● LO7–8

On June 30, 2013, the High Five Surfboard Company had outstanding accounts receivable of $600,000. On July 1, 2013, the company borrowed $450,000 from the Equitable Finance Corporation and signed a promissory note. Interest at 10% is payable monthly. The company assigned specific receivables totaling $600,000 as collateral for the loan. Equitable Finance charges a finance fee equal to 1.8% of the accounts receivable assigned.

**Required:**
Prepare the journal entry to record the borrowing on the books of High Five Surfboard.

**E 7–18**
**Factoring of accounts receivable without recourse**
● **LO7–8**

Mountain High Ice Cream Company transferred $60,000 of accounts receivable to the Prudential Bank. The transfer was made *without recourse*. Prudential remits 90% of the factored amount to Mountain High and retains 10%. When the bank collects the receivables, it will remit to Mountain High the retained amount (which Mountain estimates has a fair value of $5,000) less a 2% fee (2% of the total factored amount).

**Required:**
Prepare the journal entry to record the transfer on the books of Mountain High assuming that the sale criteria are met.

**E 7–19**
**Factoring of accounts receivable with recourse**
● **LO7–8**

[This is a variation of Exercise 7–18 modified to focus on factoring with recourse.]
Mountain High Ice Cream Company transferred $60,000 of accounts receivable to the Prudential Bank. The transfer was made *with recourse*. Prudential remits 90% of the factored amount to Mountain High and retains 10% to cover sales returns and allowances. When the bank collects the receivables, it will remit to Mountain High the retained amount (which Mountain estimates has a fair value of $5,000). Mountain High anticipates a $3,000 recourse obligation. The bank charges a 2% fee (2% of $60,000), and requires that amount to be paid at the start of the factoring arrangement.

**Required:**
Prepare the journal entry to record the transfer on the books of Mountain High assuming that the sale criteria are met.

**E 7–20**
**Factoring of accounts receivable with recourse under IFRS**
● **LO7–8, LO7–10**
🌐 **IFRS**

[This is a variation of Exercise 7–19 modified to focus on factoring with recourse under IFRS.]
Mountain High Ice Cream Company reports under IFRS. Mountain High transferred $60,000 of accounts receivable to the Prudential Bank. The transfer was made *with recourse*. Prudential remits 90% of the factored amount to Mountain High and retains 10% to cover sales returns and allowances. When the bank collects the receivables, it will remit to Mountain High the retained amount (which Mountain estimates has a fair value of $5,000). Mountain High anticipates a $3,000 recourse obligation. The bank charges a 2% fee (2% of $60,000), and requires that amount to be paid at the start of the factoring arrangement. Mountain High has transferred control over the receivables, but determines that it still retains substantially all risks and rewards associated with them.

**Required:**
Prepare the journal entry to record the transfer on the books of Mountain High, considering whether the sale criteria under IFRS have been met.

**E 7–21**
**Discounting a note receivable**
● **LO7–8**

Selkirk Company obtained a $15,000 note receivable from a customer on January 1, 2013. The note, along with interest at 10%, is due on July 1, 2013. On February 28, 2013, Selkirk discounted the note at Unionville Bank. The bank's discount rate is 12%.

**Required:**
Prepare the journal entries required on February 28, 2013, to accrue interest and to record the discounting (round all calculations to the nearest dollar) for Selkirk. Assume that the discounting is accounted for as a sale.

**E 7–22**
**Concepts; terminology**
● **LO7–1 through LO7–8**

Listed below are several terms and phrases associated with cash and receivables. Pair each item from List A (by letter) with the item from List B that is most appropriately associated with it.

| List A | List B |
|--------|--------|
| _____ 1. Internal control | a. Restriction on cash. |
| _____ 2. Trade discount | b. Cash discount not taken is sales revenue. |
| _____ 3. Cash equivalents | c. Includes separation of duties. |
| _____ 4. Allowance for uncollectibles | d. Bad debt expense a % of credit sales. |
| _____ 5. Cash discount | e. Recognizes bad debts as they occur. |
| _____ 6. Balance sheet approach | f. Sale of receivables to a financial institution. |
| _____ 7. Income statement approach | g. Include highly liquid investments. |
| _____ 8. Net method | h. Estimate of bad debts. |
| _____ 9. Compensating balance | i. Reduction in amount paid by credit customer. |
| _____ 10. Discounting | j. Reduction below list price. |
| _____ 11. Gross method | k. Cash discount not taken is interest revenue. |
| _____ 12. Direct write-off method | l. Bad debt expense determined by estimating realizable value. |
| _____ 13. Factoring | m. Sale of note receivable to a financial institution. |

**E 7–23**
Receivables;
transaction
analysis
● LO7–3, LO7–5
  through LO7–8

Weldon Corporation's fiscal year ends December 31. The following is a list of transactions involving receivables that occurred during 2013:

| | | |
|---|---|---|
| Mar. 17 | Accounts receivable of $1,700 were written off as uncollectible. The company uses the allowance method. | |
| 30 | Loaned an officer of the company $20,000 and received a note requiring principal and interest at 7% to be paid on March 30, 2014. | |
| May 30 | Discounted the $20,000 note at a local bank. The bank's discount rate is 8%. The note was discounted without recourse and the sale criteria are met. | |
| June 30 | Sold merchandise to the Blankenship Company for $12,000. Terms of the sale are 2/10, n/30. Weldon uses the gross method to account for cash discounts. | |
| July 8 | The Blankenship Company paid its account in full. | |
| Aug. 31 | Sold stock in a nonpublic company with a book value of $5,000 and accepted a $6,000 non-interest-bearing note with a discount rate of 8%. The $6,000 payment is due on February 28, 2014. The stock has no ready market value. | |
| Dec. 31 | Bad debt expense is estimated to be 2% of credit sales for the year. Credit sales for 2013 were $700,000. | |

**Required:**
1. Prepare journal entries for each of the above transactions (round all calculations to the nearest dollar).
2. Prepare any additional year-end adjusting entries indicated.

**E 7–24**
Ratio analysis;
Microsoft
● LO7–9

Real World Financials

**Microsoft Corporation** reported the following information in its financial statements for three successive quarters during the 2011 fiscal year ($ in millions):

| | Three Months Ended | | |
|---|---|---|---|
| | 3/31/2011 (Q3) | 12/31/2010 (Q2) | 9/30/2010 (Q1) |
| Balance sheets: | | | |
| Accounts receivable, net | $10,033 | $12,874 | $ 9,646 |
| Income statements: | | | |
| Sales revenue | $16,428 | $19,953 | $16,195 |

**Required:**
Compute the receivables turnover ratio and the average collection period for the second and third quarters. Assume that each quarter consists of 91 days.

**E 7–25**
Ratio analysis;
solve for unknown
● LO7–9

The current asset section of the Moorcroft Outboard Motor Company's balance sheet reported the following amounts:

| | 12/31/2013 | 12/31/2012 |
|---|---|---|
| Accounts receivable, net | $400,000 | $300,000 |

The average collection period for 2013 is 50 days.

**Required:**
Determine net sales for 2013.

**E 7–26**
Petty cash
● Appendix 7A

Loucks Company established a $200 petty cash fund on October 2, 2013. The fund is replenished at the end of each month. At the end of October 2013, the fund contained $37 in cash and the following receipts:

| | |
|---|---|
| Office supplies | $76 |
| Lunch with client | 48 |
| Postage | 20 |
| Miscellaneous | 19 |

**Required:**
Prepare the necessary general journal entries to establish the petty cash fund on October 2 and to replenish the fund on October 31.

**E 7–27**
Petty cash
● Appendix 7A

The petty cash fund of Ricco's Automotive contained the following items at the end of September 2013:

| | | |
|---|---|---|
| Currency and coins | | $ 58 |
| Receipts for the following expenditures: | | |
| Delivery charges | $16 | |
| Printer paper | 11 | |
| Paper clips and rubber bands | 8 | 35 |
| An I.O.U. from an employee | | 25 |
| Postage | | 32 |
| Total | | $150 |

The petty cash fund was established at the beginning of September with a transfer of $150 from cash to the petty cash account.

**Required:**
Prepare the journal entry to replenish the fund at the end of September.

**E 7–28**
**Bank**
**reconciliation**
● **Appendix 7A**

Jansen Company's general ledger showed a checking account balance of $23,820 at the end of May 2013. The May 31 cash receipts of $2,340, included in the general ledger balance, were placed in the night depository at the bank on May 31 and were processed by the bank on June 1. The bank statement dated May 31, 2013, showed bank service charges of $38. All checks written by the company had been processed by the bank by May 31 and were listed on the bank statement except for checks totaling $1,890.

**Required:**
Prepare a bank reconciliation as of May 31, 2013. [*Hint:* You will need to compute the balance that would appear on the bank statement.]

**E 7–29**
**Bank**
**reconciliation and**
**adjusting entries**
● **Appendix 7A**

Harrison Company maintains a checking account at the First National City Bank. The bank provides a bank statement along with canceled checks on the last day of each month. The July 2013 bank statement included the following information:

| | |
|---|---:|
| Balance, July 1, 2013 | $ 55,678 |
| Deposits | 179,500 |
| Checks processed | (192,610) |
| Service charges | (30) |
| NSF checks | (1,200) |
| Monthly loan payment deducted directly by bank from account (includes $320 in interest) | (3,320) |
| Balance, July 31, 2013 | $ 38,018 |

The company's general ledger account had a balance of $38,918 at the end of July. Deposits outstanding totaled $6,300 and all checks written by the company were processed by the bank except for those totaling $8,420. In addition, a $2,000 July deposit from a credit customer was recorded as a $200 debit to cash and credit to accounts receivable, and a check correctly recorded by the company as a $30 disbursement was incorrectly processed by the bank as a $300 disbursement.

**Required:**
1. Prepare a bank reconciliation for the month of July.
2. Prepare the necessary journal entries at the end of July to adjust the general ledger cash account.

**E 7–30**
**Impairment**
**of securities**
**available-for-sale;**
**troubled debt**
**restructuring**
● **Appendix 7B**

At January 1, 2013, Clayton Hoists Inc. owed Third BancCorp $12 million, under a 10% note due December 31, 2014. Interest was paid last on December 31, 2011. Clayton was experiencing severe financial difficulties and asked Third BancCorp to modify the terms of the debt agreement. After negotiation Third BancCorp agreed to:

• Forgive the interest accrued for the year just ended.
• Reduce the remaining two years' interest payments to $1 million each.
• Reduce the principal amount to $11 million.

**Required:**
Prepare the journal entries by Third BancCorp necessitated by the restructuring of the debt at
1. January 1, 2013.
2. December 31, 2013.
3. December 31, 2014.

**E 7–31**
**Impairment**
**of securities**
**available-for-sale;**
**troubled debt**
**restructuring**
● **Appendix 7B**

At January 1, 2013, NCI Industries, Inc. was indebted to First Federal Bank under a $240,000, 10% unsecured note. The note was signed January 1, 2011, and was due December 31, 2014. Annual interest was last paid on December 31, 2011. NCI was experiencing severe financial difficulties and negotiated a restructuring of the terms of the debt agreement. First Federal agreed to reduce last year's interest and the remaining two years' interest payments to $11,555 each and delay all payments until December 31, 2014, the maturity date.

**Required:**
Prepare the journal entries by First Federal Bank necessitated by the restructuring of the debt at
1. January 1, 2013.
2. December 31, 2013.
3. December 31, 2014.

# CPA and CMA Review Questions

CPA Exam Questions

The following questions are adapted from a variety of sources including questions developed by the AICPA Board of Examiners and those used in the Kaplan CPA Review Course to study receivables while preparing for the CPA examination. Determine the response that best completes the statements or questions.

● LO7–5

1. At January 1, 2013, Simpson Co. had a credit balance of $260,000 in its allowance for uncollectible accounts. Based on past experience, 2 percent of Simpson's credit sales have been uncollectible. During 2013, Simpson wrote off $325,000 of accounts receivable. Credit sales for 2013 were $9,000,000. In its December 31, 2013, balance sheet, what amount should Simpson report as allowance for uncollectible accounts?
   a. $115,000
   b. $180,000
   c. $245,000
   d. $440,000

● LO7–5, LO7–6

2. The balance in accounts receivable at the beginning of 2013 was $600. During 2013, $3,200 of credit sales were recorded. If the ending balance in accounts receivable was $500 and $200 in accounts receivable were written off during the year, the amount of cash collected from customers was
   a. $3,100
   b. $3,200
   c. $3,300
   d. $3,800

● LO7–5

3. A company uses the allowance method to account for bad debts. What is the effect on each of the following accounts of the collection of an account previously written off?

| | Allowance for Uncollectible Accounts | Bad Debt Expense |
|---|---|---|
| a. | Increase | Decrease |
| b. | No effect | Decrease |
| c. | Increase | No effect |
| d. | No effect | No effect |

● LO7–4, LO7–5

4. The following information relates to Jay Co.'s accounts receivable for 2013:

| | |
|---|---|
| Accounts receivable balance, 1/1/2013 | $650,000 |
| Credit sales for 2013 | 2,700,000 |
| Sales returns during 2013 | 75,000 |
| Accounts receivable written off during 2013 | 40,000 |
| Collections from customers during 2013 | 2,150,000 |
| Allowance for uncollectible accounts balance, 12/31/2013 | 110,000 |

   What amount should Jay report for accounts receivable, before allowances, at December 31, 2013?
   a. $  925,000
   b. $1,085,000
   c. $1,125,000
   d. $1,200,000

● LO7–8

5. Gar Co. factored its receivables without recourse with Ross Bank. Gar received cash as a result of this transaction, which is best described as a
   a. Loan from Ross collateralized by Gar's accounts receivable.
   b. Loan from Ross to be repaid by the proceeds from Gar's accounts receivables.
   c. Sale of Gar's accounts receivable to Ross, with the risk of uncollectible accounts transferred to Ross.
   d. Sale of Gar's accounts receivable to Ross, with the risk of uncollectible accounts retained by Gar.

● LO7–5, LO7–6

6. The following information pertains to Tara Co.'s accounts receivable at December 31, 2013:

| Days Outstanding | Amount | Estimated % Uncollectible |
|---|---|---|
| 0–60 | $120,000 | 1% |
| 61–120 | 90,000 | 2% |
| Over 120 | 100,000 | 6% |
| | $310,000 | |

During 2013, Tara wrote off $7,000 in receivables and recovered $4,000 that had been written off in prior years. Tara's December 31, 2012, allowance for uncollectible accounts was $22,000. Under the aging method, what amount of allowance for uncollectible accounts should Tara report at December 31, 2013?

a. $ 9,000
b. $10,000
c. $13,000
d. $19,000

**● LO7–5, LO7–6**

7. West Company had the following account balances at December 31, 2013, before recording bad debt expense for the year:

| | |
|---|---:|
| Accounts receivable | $ 900,000 |
| Allowance for uncollectible accounts (credit balance) | 16,000 |
| Credit sales for 2013 | 1,750,000 |

West is considering the following methods of estimating bad debts for 2013:
- Based on 2% of credit sales
- Based on 5% of year-end accounts receivable

What amount should West charge to bad debt expense at the end of 2013 under each method?

| | Percentage of Credit Sales | Percentage of Accounts Receivable |
|---|---|---|
| a. | $35,000 | $29,000 |
| b. | $35,000 | $45,000 |
| c. | $51,000 | $29,000 |
| d. | $51,000 | $45,000 |

Beginning in 2011, International Financial Reporting Standards are tested on the CPA exam along with U.S. GAAP. The following questions deal with the application of IFRS to accounting for cash and receivables.

**● LO7–10**

**IFRS**

8. Shaefer Company prepares its financial statements according to International Financial Reporting Standards (IFRS). Shaefer sometimes has bank overdrafts that are payable on demand and that fluctuate as part of its cash management program. At the most recent financial reporting date, Shaefer had a €500,000 overdraft in one cash account and a positive balance of €3,000,000 in another cash account. Shaefer should report its cash balances as:

a. A cash asset of €3,000,000 and an overdraft liability of €500,000.
b. A cash asset of €2,500,000.
c. An overdraft liability of (€2,500,000).
d. None of the above.

**● LO7–10**

**IFRS**

9. Under IFRS, accounts receivable can be accounted for as "available for sale" investments if that approach is elected upon initial recognition of the receivable under:

a. *IASB No. 1.*
b. *IFRS No. 9.*
c. *IAS No. 39.*
d. None of the above.

**● LO7–10**

**IFRS**

10. Under IFRS, measurement of an impairment of a receivable is required if:

a. Cash payments have not been received for more than twelve months.
b. It is at least more likely than not that a future loss will occur, and the amount of discounted loss is measurable.
c. It is reasonably possible that prior events will give rise to a future loss that can be estimated with moderate reliability.
d. There is objective evidence that a loss event has occurred that has an impact on the future cash flows to be collected and that can be estimated reliably.

**CMA Exam Questions**

The following questions dealing with receivables are adapted from questions that previously appeared on Certified Management Accountant (CMA) examinations. The CMA designation sponsored by the Institute of Management Accountants (www.imanet.org) provides members with an objective measure of knowledge and competence in the field of management accounting. Determine the response that best completes the statements or questions.

**● LO7–5, LO7–6**

1. Bad debt expense must be estimated in order to satisfy the matching principle when expenses are recorded in the same periods as the related revenues. In estimating bad debt expense for a period, companies generally accrue

a. Either an amount based on a percentage of total sales or an amount based on a percentage of accounts receivable after adjusting for any balance in the allowance for doubtful accounts.
b. A percentage of total sales.
c. Either an amount based on a percentage of credit sales or an amount based on a percentage of accounts receivable after adjusting for any balance in the allowance for doubtful accounts.
d. An amount equal to last year's bad debt expense.

Questions 2 and 3 are based on the following information:

Madison Corporation uses the allowance method to value its accounts receivable and is making the annual adjustments at fiscal year-end, November 30. The proportion of uncollectible accounts is estimated based on past experience, which indicates 1.5% of net credit sales will be uncollectible. Total sales for the year were $2,000,000, of which $200,000 were cash transactions. Madison has determined that the Norris Corporation accounts receivable balance of $10,000 is uncollectible and will write off this account before year-end adjustments are made. Listed below are Madison's account balances at November 30 prior to any adjustments and the $10,000 write-off.

| | |
|---|---:|
| Sales | $2,000,000 |
| Accounts receivable | 750,000 |
| Sales discounts | 125,000 |
| Allowance for doubtful accounts | 16,500 |
| Sales returns and allowances | 175,000 |
| Bad debt expense | 0 |

● LO7–5    2. The entry to write off Norris Corporation's accounts receivable balance of $10,000 will

a. Increase total assets and decrease net income.
b. Decrease total assets and net income.
c. Have no effect on total assets and decrease net income.
d. Have no effect on total assets and net income.

● LO7–5    3. As a result of the November 30 adjusting entry to provide for bad debts, the allowance for doubtful accounts will

a. Increase by $30,000.
b. Increase by $25,500.
c. Increase by $22,500.
d. Decrease by $22,500.

# Problems

An alternate exercise and problem set is available on the text website: www.mhhe.com/spiceland7e

**P 7–1**
Uncollectible accounts; allowance method; income statement and balance sheet approach
● LO7–5, LO7–6

Swathmore Clothing Corporation grants its customers 30 days' credit. The company uses the allowance method for its uncollectible accounts receivable. During the year, a monthly bad debt accrual is made by multiplying 3% times the amount of credit sales for the month. At the fiscal year-end of December 31, an aging of accounts receivable schedule is prepared and the allowance for uncollectible accounts is adjusted accordingly.

At the end of 2012, accounts receivable were $574,000 and the allowance account had a credit balance of $54,000. Accounts receivable activity for 2013 was as follows:

| | |
|---|---:|
| Beginning balance | $ 574,000 |
| Credit sales | 2,620,000 |
| Collections | (2,483,000) |
| Write-offs | (68,000) |
| Ending balance | $ 643,000 |

The company's controller prepared the following aging summary of year-end accounts receivable:

| | Summary | |
|---|---|---|
| Age Group | Amount | Percent Uncollectible |
| 0–60 days | $430,000 | 4% |
| 61–90 days | 98,000 | 15 |
| 91–120 days | 60,000 | 25 |
| Over 120 days | 55,000 | 40 |
| Total | $643,000 | |

**Required:**

1. Prepare a summary journal entry to record the monthly bad debt accrual and the write-offs during the year.
2. Prepare the necessary year-end adjusting entry for bad debt expense.
3. What is total bad debt expense for 2013? How would accounts receivable appear in the 2013 balance sheet?

**P 7–2**
Uncollectible accounts; Amdahl
● LO7–5

Real World Financials

**Amdahl Corporation** manufactures large-scale, high performance computer systems. In a recent annual report, the balance sheet included the following information (dollars in thousands):

| | Current Year | Previous Year |
|---|---|---|
| Current assets: | | |
| Receivables, net of allowances of $5,042 and $6,590 in the previous year | $504,944 | $580,640 |

In addition, the income statement reported sales revenue of $2,158,755 ($ in thousands) for the current year. All sales are made on a credit basis. The statement of cash flows indicates that cash collected from customers during the current year was $2,230,065 ($ in thousands). There were no recoveries of accounts receivable previously written off.

**Required:**

1. Compute the following (dollar amounts in thousands):
   a. The amount of uncollectibles written off by Amdahl during the current year.
   b. The amount of bad debt expense that Amdahl would include in its income statement for the current year.
   c. The approximate percentage that Amdahl used to estimate uncollectibles for the current year, assuming that it uses the income statement approach.
2. Suppose that Amdahl had used the direct write-off method to account for uncollectibles. Compute the following (dollars in thousands):
   a. The accounts receivable information that would be included in the year-end balance sheet.
   b. The amount of bad debt expense that Amdahl would include in its income statement for the current year.

**P 7–3**
Bad debts;
Cirrus Logic
● LO7–5

Real World Financials

**Cirrus Logic, Inc.**, is a leading designer and manufacturer of advanced integrated circuits that integrate algorithms and mixed-signal processing for mass storage, communications, consumer electronics, and industrial markets. The company's 2011 financial statements contained the following information:

| | ($ in thousands) | |
|---|---|---|
| **Balance sheets** | **2011** | **2010** |
| Current assets: | | |
| Accounts receivable, net | $ 39,098 | $ 23,963 |
| **Income statements** | **2011** | **2010** |
| Net sales | $369,571 | $220,989 |

In addition, the statement of cash flows disclosed that accounts receivable increased during 2011 by $15,135 (in thousands). This indicates that cash received from customers was $15,135 (in thousands) less than accrual sales revenue. Also, a disclosure note reported that the allowance for uncollectible accounts (in thousands) was $421 and $488 at the end of 2011 and 2010, respectively

**Required:**

1. What is the amount of accounts receivable due from customers at the end of 2011 and 2010?
2. Assuming that all sales are made on a credit basis, determine the amount of bad debt expense for 2011 and the amount of actual bad debt write-offs made in 2011.

**P 7–4**
Uncollectible accounts
● LO7–5, LO7–6

Raintree Cosmetic Company sells its products to customers on a credit basis. An adjusting entry for bad debt expense is recorded only at December 31, the company's fiscal year-end. The 2012 balance sheet disclosed the following:

| Current assets: | |
|---|---|
| Receivables, net of allowance for uncollectible accounts of $30,000 | $432,000 |

During 2013, credit sales were $1,750,000, cash collections from customers $1,830,000, and $35,000 in accounts receivable were written off. In addition, $3,000 was collected from a customer whose account was written off in 2012. An aging of accounts receivable at December 31, 2013, reveals the following:

| Age Group | Percentage of Year-End Receivables in Group | Percent Uncollectible |
|---|---|---|
| 0–60 days | 65% | 4% |
| 61–90 days | 20 | 15 |
| 91–120 days | 10 | 25 |
| Over 120 days | 5 | 40 |

**Required:**

1. Prepare summary journal entries to account for the 2013 write-offs and the collection of the receivable previously written off.

2. Prepare the year-end adjusting entry for bad debts according to each of the following situations:

   a. Bad debt expense is estimated to be 3% of credit sales for the year.

   b. Bad debt expense is estimated by computing net realizable value of the receivables. The allowance for uncollectible accounts is estimated to be 10% of the year-end balance in accounts receivable.

   c. Bad debt expense is estimated by computing net realizable value of the receivables. The allowance for uncollectible accounts is determined by an aging of accounts receivable.

3. For situations (a)–(c) in requirement 2 above, what would be the net amount of accounts receivable reported in the 2013 balance sheet?

**P 7–5**
**Receivables;**
**bad debts**
**and returns;**
**Symantec**
● **LO7–4, LO7–5**

Real World Financials

**Symantec Corp.,** located in Cupertino, California, is one of the world's largest producers of security and systems management software. The company's consolidated balance sheets for the 2009 and 2008 fiscal years included the following ($ in thousands):

|  | 2009 | 2008 |
|---|---|---|
| **Current assets:** | | |
| Receivables, less allowances of $20,991 in 2009 and $23,314 in 2008 | $837,010 | $758,200 |

A disclosure note accompanying the financial statements reported the following ($ in thousands):

|  | Year Ended | |
|---|---|---|
|  | 2009 | 2008 |
|  | (In thousands) | |
| *Trade accounts receivable, net:* | | |
| Receivables | $858,001 | $781,514 |
| Less: allowance for doubtful accounts | (8,863) | (8,915) |
| Less: reserve for product returns | (12,128) | (14,399) |
| Trade accounts receivable, net: | $837,010 | $758,200 |

Assume that the company reported bad debt expense in 2009 of $1,500 and had products returned for credit totaling $3,155 (sales price). Net sales for 2009 were $6,149,800 (all numbers in thousands).

**Required:**

1. What is the amount of accounts receivable due from customers at the end of 2009 and 2008?
2. What amount of accounts receivable did Symantec write off during 2009?
3. What is the amount of Symantec's gross sales for the 2009 fiscal year?
4. Assuming that all sales are made on a credit basis, what is the amount of cash Symantec collected from customers during the 2009 fiscal year?

**P 7–6**
**Notes receivable;**
**solving for**
**unknowns**
● **LO7–7**

Cypress Oil Company's December 31, 2013, balance sheet listed $645,000 of notes receivable and $16,000 of interest receivable included in current assets. The following notes make up the notes receivable balance:

| Note 1 | Dated 8/31/2013, principal of $300,000 and interest at 10% due on 2/28/2014. |
|---|---|
| Note 2 | Dated 6/30/2013, principal of $150,000 and interest due 3/31/2014. |
| Note 3 | $200,000 face value noninterest-bearing note dated 9/30/2013, due 3/31/2014. Note was issued in exchange for merchandise. |

The company records adjusting entries only at year-end. There were no other notes receivable outstanding during 2013.

**Required:**

1. Determine the rate used to discount the noninterest-bearing note.
2. Determine the explicit interest rate on Note 2.
3. What is the amount of interest revenue that appears in the company's 2013 income statement related to these notes?

**P 7–7**
Factoring
versus assigning
of accounts
receivable
● LO7–8

Lonergan Company occasionally uses its accounts receivable to obtain immediate cash. At the end of June 2013, the company had accounts receivable of $780,000. Lonergan needs approximately $500,000 to capitalize on a unique investment opportunity. On July 1, 2013, a local bank offers Lonergan the following two alternatives:

a. Borrow $500,000, sign a note payable, and assign the entire receivable balance as collateral. At the end of each month, a remittance will be made to the bank that equals the amount of receivables collected plus 12% interest on the unpaid balance of the note at the beginning of the period.

b. Transfer $550,000 of specific receivables to the bank without recourse. The bank will charge a 2% finance charge on the amount of receivables transferred. The bank will collect the receivables directly from customers. The sale criteria are met.

**Required:**

1. Prepare the journal entries that would be recorded on July 1 for each of the alternatives.
2. Assuming that 80% of all June 30 receivables are collected during July, prepare the necessary journal entries to record the collection and the remittance to the bank.
3. For each alternative, explain any required note disclosures that would be included in the July 31, 2013, financial statements.

**P 7–8**
Factoring
of accounts
receivable;
without recourse
● LO7–8

Samson Wholesale Beverage Company regularly factors its accounts receivable with the Milpitas Finance Company. On April 30, 2013, the company transferred $800,000 of accounts receivable to Milpitas. The transfer was made without recourse. Milpitas remits 90% of the factored amount and retains 10%. When Milpitas collects the receivables, it remits to Samson the retained amount less a 4% fee (4% of the total factored amount). Samson estimates the fair value of the last 10% of its receivables to be $60,000.

**Required:**
Prepare journal entries for Samson Wholesale Beverage for the transfer of accounts receivable on April 30 assuming the sale criteria are met.

**P 7–9**
Cash and accounts
receivable under
IFRS
● LO7–2, LO7–5,
LO7–8, LO7–10

🌐 IFRS

The following facts apply to Walken Company during December 2013:

a. Walken began December with an accounts receivable balance (net of bad debts) of €25,000.
b. Walken had credit sales of €85,000.
c. Walken had cash collections of €30,000.
d. Walken factored €20,000 of net accounts receivable with Reliable Factor Company, transferring all risks and rewards associated with the receivable, and otherwise meeting all criteria necessary to qualify for treating the transfer of receivables as a sale.
e. Walken factored €15,000 of net accounts receivable with Dependable Factor Company, retaining all risks and rewards associated with the receivable, and otherwise meeting all criteria necessary to qualify for treating the transfer of receivables as a sale.
f. Walken did not recognize any additional bad debts expense, and had no write-offs of bad debts during the month.
g. At December 31, 2013, Walken had a balance of €40,000 of cash at M&V Bank and an overdraft of (€5000) at First National Bank. (That cash balance includes any effects on cash of the other transactions described in this problem.)

**Required:**
Prepare the cash and accounts receivable lines of the current assets section of Walken's balance sheet, as of December 31, 2013.

**P 7–10**
Miscellaneous
receivable
transactions
● LO7–3, LO7–4,
LO7–7, LO7–8

Evergreen Company sells lawn and garden products to wholesalers. The company's fiscal year-end is December 31. During 2013, the following transactions related to receivables occurred:

Feb. 28   Sold merchandise to Lennox, Inc. for $10,000 and accepted a 10%, 7-month note. 10% is an appropriate rate for this type of note.

Mar. 31   Sold merchandise to Maddox Co. and accepted a noninterest-bearing note with a discount rate of 10%. The $8,000 payment is due on March 31, 2014.

Apr. 3   Sold merchandise to Carr Co. for $7,000 with terms 2/10, n/30. Evergreen uses the gross method to account for cash discounts.

11   Collected the entire amount due from Carr Co.

17   A customer returned merchandise costing $3,200. Evergreen reduced the customer's receivable balance by $5,000, the sales price of the merchandise. Sales returns are recorded by the company as they occur.

30   Transferred receivables of $50,000 to a factor without recourse. The factor charged Evergreen a 1% finance charge on the receivables transferred. The sale criteria are met.

June 30   Discounted the Lennox, Inc., note at the bank. The bank's discount rate is 12%. The note was discounted without recourse.

Sep. 30   Lennox, Inc., paid the note amount plus interest to the bank.

**Required:**

1. Prepare the necessary journal entries for Evergreen for each of the above dates. For transactions involving the sale of merchandise, ignore the entry for the cost of goods sold (round all calculations to the nearest dollar).

2. Prepare any necessary adjusting entries at December 31, 2013. Adjusting entries are only recorded at year-end (round all calculations to the nearest dollar).

3. Prepare a schedule showing the effect of the journal entries in requirements 1 and 2 on 2013 income before taxes.

**P 7–11**
**Discounting a note receivable**
● LO7–7

Descriptors are provided below for six situations involving notes receivable being discounted at a bank. In each case, the maturity date of the note is December 31, 2013, and the principal and interest are due at maturity. For each, determine the proceeds received from the bank on discounting the note.

| Note | Note Face Value | Date of Note | Interest Rate | Date Discounted | Discount Rate |
|------|-----------------|--------------|---------------|-----------------|---------------|
| 1 | $50,000 | 3/31/2013 | 8% | 6/30/2013 | 10% |
| 2 | 50,000 | 3/31/2013 | 8 | 9/30/2013 | 10 |
| 3 | 50,000 | 3/31/2013 | 8 | 9/30/2013 | 12 |
| 4 | 80,000 | 6/30/2013 | 6 | 10/31/2013 | 10 |
| 5 | 80,000 | 6/30/2013 | 6 | 10/31/2013 | 12 |
| 6 | 80,000 | 6/30/2013 | 6 | 11/30/2013 | 10 |

**P 7–12**
**Accounts and notes receivable; discounting a note receivable; receivables turnover ratio**
● LO7–5, LO7–6, LO7–7, LO7–8, LO7–9

Chamberlain Enterprises Inc. reported the following receivables in its December 31, 2013, year-end balance sheet:

Current assets:
Accounts receivable, net of $24,000 in allowance for
uncollectible accounts ........................ $218,000
Interest receivable ............................... 6,800
Notes receivable ................................. 260,000

**Additional Information:**

1. The notes receivable account consists of two notes, a $60,000 note and a $200,000 note. The $60,000 note is dated October 31, 2013, with principal and interest payable on October 31, 2014. The $200,000 note is dated June 30, 2013, with principal and 6% interest payable on June 30, 2014.

2. During 2014, sales revenue totaled $1,340,000, $1,280,000 cash was collected from customers, and $22,000 in accounts receivable were written off. All sales are made on a credit basis. Bad debt expense is recorded at year-end by adjusting the allowance account to an amount equal to 10% of year-end accounts receivable.

3. On March 31, 2014, the $200,000 note receivable was discounted at the Bank of Commerce. The bank's discount rate is 8%. Chamberlain accounts for the discounting as a sale.

**Required:**

1. In addition to sales revenue, what revenue and expense amounts related to receivables will appear in Chamberlain's 2014 income statement?

2. What amounts will appear in the 2014 year-end balance sheet for accounts receivable?

3. Calculate the receivables turnover ratio for 2014.

**P 7–13**

Bank reconciliation and adjusting entries; cash and cash equivalents

● Appendix 7A

The bank statement for the checking account of Management Systems Inc. (MSI) showed a December 31, 2013, balance of $14,632.12. Information that might be useful in preparing a bank reconciliation is as follows:

a. Outstanding checks were $1,320.25.

b. The December 31, 2013, cash receipts of $575 were not deposited in the bank until January 2, 2014.

c. One check written in payment of rent for $246 was correctly recorded by the bank but was recorded by MSI as a $264 disbursement.

d. In accordance with prior authorization, the bank withdrew $450 directly from the checking account as payment on a mortgage note payable. The interest portion of that payment was $350. MSI has made no entry to record the automatic payment.

e. Bank service charges of $14 were listed on the bank statement.

f. A deposit of $875 was recorded by the bank on December 13, but it did not belong to MSI. The deposit should have been made to the checking account of MIS, Inc.

g. The bank statement included a charge of $85 for an NSF check. The check was returned with the bank statement and the company will seek payment from the customer.

h. MSI maintains a $200 petty cash fund that was appropriately reimbursed at the end of December.

i. According to instructions from MSI on December 30, the bank withdrew $10,000 from the account and purchased U.S. Treasury bills for MSI. MSI recorded the transaction in its books on December 31 when it received notice from the bank. Half of the Treasury bills mature in two months and the other half in six months.

**Required:**

1. Prepare a bank reconciliation for the MSI checking account at December 31, 2013. You will have to compute the balance per books.

2. Prepare any necessary adjusting journal entries indicated.

3. What amount would MSI report as cash and cash equivalents in the current asset section of the December 31, 2013, balance sheet?

**P 7–14**

Bank reconciliation and adjusting entries

● Appendix 7A

El Gato Painting Company maintains a checking account at American Bank. Bank statements are prepared at the end of each month. The November 30, 2013, reconciliation of the bank balance is as follows:

| | | |
|---|---:|---:|
| Balance per bank, November 30 | | $3,231 |
| Add: Deposits outstanding | | 1,200 |
| Less: Checks outstanding | | |
| #363 | $123 | |
| #365 | 201 | |
| #380 | 56 | |
| #381 | 86 | |
| #382 | 340 | (806) |
| Adjusted balance per bank, November 30 | | $3,625 |

The company's general ledger checking account showed the following for December:

| | |
|---|---:|
| Balance, December 1 | $ 3,625 |
| Receipts | 42,650 |
| Disbursements | (41,853) |
| Balance, December 31 | $ 4,422 |

The December bank statement contained the following information:

| | |
|---|---:|
| Balance, December 1 | $ 3,231 |
| Deposits | 43,000 |
| Checks processed | (41,918) |
| Service charges | (22) |
| NSF checks | (440) |
| Balance, December 31 | $ 3,851 |

The checks that were processed by the bank in December include all of the outstanding checks at the end of November except for check #365. In addition, there are some December checks that had not been processed by the bank by the end of the month. Also, you discover that check #411 for $320 was correctly recorded by the bank but was incorrectly recorded on the books as a $230 disbursement for advertising expense. Included in the bank's deposits is a $1,300 deposit incorrectly credited to the company's account. The deposit should have been posted to the credit of the Los Gatos Company. The NSF checks have not been redeposited and the company will seek payment from the customers involved.

**Required:**

1. Prepare a bank reconciliation for the El Gato checking account at December 31, 2013.
2. Prepare any necessary adjusting journal entries indicated.

**P 7–15**
Impairment
of securities
available-for-sale;
troubled debt
restructuring
● Appendix 7B

Rothschild Chair Company, Inc., was indebted to First Lincoln Bank under a $20 million, 10% unsecured note. The note was signed January 1, 2005, and was due December 31, 2016. Annual interest was last paid on December 31, 2011. At January 1, 2013, Rothschild Chair Company was experiencing severe financial difficulties and negotiated a restructuring of the terms of the debt agreement.

**Required:**

Prepare all journal entries by First Lincoln Bank to record the restructuring and any remaining transactions, for current and future years, relating to the debt under each of the independent circumstances below:

1. First Lincoln Bank agreed to settle the debt in exchange for land having a fair value of $16 million but carried on Rothschild Chair Company's books at $13 million.
2. First Lincoln Bank agreed to (a) forgive the interest accrued from last year, (b) reduce the remaining four interest payments to $1 million each, and (c) reduce the principal to $15 million.
3. First Lincoln Bank agreed to defer all payments (including accrued interest) until the maturity date and accept $27,775,000 at that time in settlement of the debt.

## Broaden Your Perspective

Apply your critical-thinking ability to the knowledge you've gained. These cases will provide you an opportunity to develop your research, analysis, judgment, and communication skills. You also will work with other students, integrate what you've learned, apply it in real world situations, and consider its global and ethical ramifications. This practice will broaden your knowledge and further develop your decision-making abilities.

**Judgment
Case 7–1**
Accounts and
notes receivable
● LO7–5, LO7–6,
LO7–8

Magrath Company has an operating cycle of less than one year and provides credit terms for all of its customers. On April 1, 2013, the company factored, without recourse, some of its accounts receivable. Magrath transferred the receivables to a financial institution, and will have no further association with the receivables.

Magrath uses the allowance method to account for uncollectible accounts. During 2013, some accounts were written off as uncollectible and other accounts previously written off as uncollectible were collected.

**Required:**

1. How should Magrath account for and report the accounts receivable factored on April 1, 2013? Why is this accounting treatment appropriate?
2. How should Magrath account for the collection of the accounts previously written off as uncollectible?
3. What are the two basic approaches to estimating uncollectible accounts under the allowance method? What is the rationale for each approach?

*(AICPA adapted)*

**Communication
Case 7–2**
Uncollectible
accounts
● LO7–5

You have been hired as a consultant by a parts manufacturing firm to provide advice as to the proper accounting methods the company should use in some key areas. In the area of receivables, the company president does not understand your recommendation to use the allowance method for uncollectible accounts. She stated, "Financial statements should be based on objective data rather than the guesswork required for the allowance method. Besides, since my uncollectibles are fairly constant from period to period, with significant variations occurring infrequently, the direct write-off method is just as good as the allowance method."

**Required:**

Draft a one-page response in the form of a memo to the president in support of your recommendation for the company to use the allowance method.

**Judgment
Case 7–3**
Accounts
receivable
● LO7–3, LO7–7,
LO7–8

Hogan Company uses the net method of accounting for sales discounts. Hogan offers trade discounts to various groups of buyers.

On August 1, 2013, Hogan factored some accounts receivable on a without recourse basis. Hogan incurred a finance charge.

Hogan also has some notes receivable bearing an appropriate rate of interest. The principal and total interest are due at maturity. The notes were received on October 1, 2013, and mature on September 30, 2014. Hogan's operating cycle is less than one year.

**Required:**

1. a. Using the net method, how should Hogan account for the sales discounts at the date of sale? What is the rationale for the amount recorded as sales under the net method?

   b. Using the net method, what is the effect on Hogan's sales revenues and net income when customers do not take the sales discounts?

2. What is the effect of trade discounts on sales revenues and accounts receivable? Why?

3. How should Hogan account for the accounts receivable factored on August 1, 2013? Why?

4. How should Hogan report the effects of the interest-bearing notes receivable in its December 31, 2013, balance sheet and its income statement for the year ended December 31, 2013? Why?

*(AICPA adapted)*

**Real World Case 7–4**
Sales returns;
Green Mountain Coffee Roasters
● LO7–4

Real World Financials

The following is an excerpt from Antar, Sam, "Is Green Mountain Coffee Roasters Shuffling the Beans to Beat Earnings Expectations*?" Phil's Stock World delivered by Newstex,* May 9, 2011.

On May 3, 2011, Green Mountain Coffee Roasters (NASDAQ: GMCR) beat analysts' earnings estimates by $0.10 per share for the thirteen-week period ended March 26, 2011. The next day, the stock price had risen to $11.91 per share to close at $75.98 per share, a staggering 18.5% increase over the previous day's closing stock price. CNBC Senior Stocks Commentator Herb Greenberg raised questions about the quality of Green Mountain Coffees earnings because its provision for sales returns dropped $22 million in the thirteen-week period. He wanted to know if there was a certain adjustment to reserves ("a reversal") that helped Green Mountain Coffee beat analysts' earnings estimates. . . .

During the thirteen-week period ended March 26, 2011, it was calculated that Green Mountain Coffee had a negative $22.259 million provision for sales returns. In its latest 10-Q report, Green Mountain Coffee disclosed that its provision for sales returns was $5.262 million for the twenty-six week period ending March 26, 2011, but the company did not disclose amounts for the thirteen-week period ended March 26, 2011. In its previous 10-Q report for the thirteen-week period ended December 25, 2010, Green Mountain Coffee disclosed that its provision for sales returns was $27.521 million. Therefore, the provision for sales returns for the thirteen-week period ended March 26, 2011 was a negative $22.259 million ($5.262 million minus $27.521 million).

**Required:**

1. Access EDGAR on the Internet. The web address is **www.sec.gov**.

2. Search for **Green Mountain Coffee Roasters, Inc.**'s 10-K for the fiscal year ended September 25, 2010 (filed December 9, 2010)**.** Answer the following questions related to the company's 2010 accounting for sales returns:

   a. What type of an account (for example, asset, contra-liability) is Sales Returns Reserve? Explain.

   b. Prepare a T-account for fiscal 2010's sales returns reserve. Include entries for the beginning and ending balance, acquisitions, amounts charged to cost and expense, and deductions.

   c. Prepare journal entries for amounts charged to cost and expense and for deductions. Provide a brief explanation of what each of those journal entries represents.

   d. For any of the amounts included in your journal entries that appear in Green Mountain's statement of cash flows on page F-8, explain why the amount appears as an increase or decrease to cash flows.

3. Now consider the information provided by Antar in the excerpt at the beginning of this case.

   a. Prepare a T-account for the first quarter of fiscal 2011's sales returns reserve. Assume amounts associated with acquisitions and deductions are zero, such that the only entry affecting the account during the first quarter of fiscal 2011 is to record amounts charged or recovered from cost and expense. Compute the ending balance of the account.

   b. Prepare a T-account for the second quarter of fiscal 2011's sales returns reserve. Assume amounts associated with acquisitions and deductions are zero, such that the only entry affecting the account during the first quarter of fiscal 2011 is to record amounts charged or recovered from cost and expense. Compute the ending balance of the account.

   c. Assume that actual returns were zero during the second quarter of fiscal 2011. Prepare a journal entry to record amounts charged or recovered from cost and expense during the second quarter of fiscal 2011. How would that journal entry affect 2011 net income?

   d. Speculate as to what might have caused the activity in Green Mountain's sales returns account during the second quarter of fiscal 2011. Consider how this result could occur unintentionally, or why it might occur intentionally as a way to manage earnings.

**Ethics Case 7–5**
Uncollectible
accounts
● LO7–5

You have recently been hired as the assistant controller for Stanton Industries, a large, publicly held manufacturing company. Your immediate superior is the controller who, in turn, is responsible to the vice president of finance.

The controller has assigned you the task of preparing the year-end adjusting entries. In the receivables area, you have prepared an aging of accounts receivable and have applied historical percentages to the balances of each of the age categories. The analysis indicates that an appropriate balance for the allowance for uncollectible accounts is $180,000. The existing balance in the allowance account prior to any adjusting entry is a $20,000 credit balance.

After showing your analysis to the controller, he tells you to change the aging category of a large account from over 120 days to current status and to prepare a new invoice to the customer with a revised date that agrees with the new aging category. This will change the required allowance for uncollectible accounts from $180,000 to $135,000. Tactfully, you ask the controller for an explanation for the change and he tells you "We need the extra income, the bottom line is too low."

**Required:**

1. What is the effect on income before taxes of the change requested by the controller?

2. Discuss the ethical dilemma you face. Consider your options and responsibilities along with the possible consequences of any action you might take.

**Judgment Case 7–6**
Internal control
● LO7–1

For each of the following independent situations, indicate the apparent internal control weaknesses and suggest alternative procedures to eliminate the weaknesses.

1. John Smith is the petty cash custodian. John approves all requests for payment out of the $200 fund, which is replenished at the end of each month. At the end of each month, John submits a list of all accounts and amounts to be charged and a check is written to him for the total amount. John is the only person ever to tally the fund.

2. All of the company's cash disbursements are made by check. Each check must be supported by an approved voucher, which is in turn supported by the appropriate invoice and, for purchases, a receiving document. The vouchers are approved by Dean Leiser, the chief accountant, after reviewing the supporting documentation. Betty Hanson prepares the checks for Leiser's signature. Leiser also maintains the company's check register (the cash disbursements journal) and reconciles the bank account at the end of each month.

3. Fran Jones opens the company's mail and makes a listing of all checks and cash received from customers. A copy of the list is sent to Jerry McDonald who maintains the general ledger accounts. Fran prepares and makes the daily deposit at the bank. Fran also maintains the subsidiary ledger for accounts receivable, which is used to generate monthly statements to customers.

**Real World Case 7–7**
Receivables; bad debts; Avon Products
● LO7–5

Real World Financials

EDGAR, the Electronic Data Gathering, Analysis, and Retrieval system, performs automated collection, validation, indexing, and forwarding of submissions by companies and others who are required by law to file forms with the U.S. Securities and Exchange Commission (SEC). All publicly traded domestic companies use EDGAR to make the majority of their filings. (Some foreign companies file voluntarily.) Form 10-K or 10-KSB, which include the annual report, is required to be filed on EDGAR. The SEC makes this information available on the Internet.

**Required:**

1. Access EDGAR on the Internet. The web address is **www.sec.gov**.

2. Search for **Avon Products, Inc.** Access the 10-K filing for the most recent fiscal year. Search or scroll to find the financial statements.

3. Answer the following questions related to the company's accounts receivable and bad debts:

   a. What is the amount of gross trade accounts receivable at the end of the year?

   b. What is the amount of bad debt expense for the year? (*Hint:* check the statement of cash flows.)

   c. Determine the amount of actual bad debt write-offs made during the year. Assume that all bad debts relate only to trade accounts receivable.

   d. Using only information from the balance sheets, income statements, and your answer to requirement 3(c), determine the amount of cash collected from customers during the year. Assume that all sales are made on a credit basis, that the company provides no allowances for sales returns, that no previously written-off receivables were collected, and that all sales relate to trade accounts receivable.

**Integrating Case 7–8**
Change in estimate of bad debts
● LO7–5

McLaughlin Corporation uses the allowance method to account for bad debts. At the end of the company's fiscal year, accounts receivable are analyzed and the allowance for uncollectible accounts is adjusted. At the end of 2013, the company reported the following amounts:

| | |
|---|---:|
| Accounts receivable | $10,850,000 |
| Less: Allowance for uncollectible accounts | (450,000) |
| Accounts receivable, net | $10,400,000 |

In 2014, it was determined that $1,825,000 of year-end 2013 receivables had to be written off as uncollectible. This was due in part to the fact that Hughes Corporation, a long-standing customer that had always paid its bills, unexpectedly declared bankruptcy in 2014. Hughes owed McLaughlin $1,400,000. At the end of 2013, none of the Hughes receivable was considered uncollectible.

**Required:**

Describe the appropriate accounting treatment and required disclosures for McLaughlin's underestimation of bad debts at the end of 2013.

**Analysis Case 7–9**
Financing with receivables
● LO7–8

Financial institutions have developed a wide variety of methods for companies to use their receivables to obtain immediate cash. The methods differ with respect to which rights and risks are retained by the transferor (the original holder of the receivable) and those passed on to the transferee (the new holder, usually a financial institution).

**Required:**

1. Describe the alternative methods available for companies to use their receivables to obtain immediate cash.
2. Discuss the alternative accounting treatments for these methods.

**Real World Case 7–10**
Financing with receivables; Sanofi-Aventis
● LO7–5, LO7–8, LO7–10

 IFRS

Search on the Internet for the 2010 annual report for **Sanofi-Aventis**. Find the accounts receivable disclosure note.

**Required:**

1. Sanofi-Aventis subtracts "impairment" from the gross value of accounts receivable to obtain the net value. Interpret the impairment of (€126) in 2010 in terms of how that amount would typically be described in U.S. GAAP.
2. To what extent does Sanofi-Aventis factor or securitize accounts receivable? How do you know?
3. Assume that Sanofi-Aventis decided to increase the extent to which it securitizes its accounts receivable, changing to a policy of securitizing accounts receivable immediately upon making a sale and treating the securitization as a sale of accounts receivable. Indicate the likely effect of that change in policy on:
   a. Accounts receivable in the period of the change.
   b. Cash flow from operations in the period of the change.
   c. Accounts receivable in subsequent periods.
   d. Cash flow from operations in subsequent periods.
4. Given your answers to requirement 3, could a company change the extent to which it factors or securitizes receivables to create one-time changes in its cash flow? Explain.

**Research Case 7–11**
Locate and extract relevant information and authoritative support for a financial reporting issue; financing with receivables
● LO7–8

You are spending the summer working for a local wholesale furniture company, Samson Furniture, Inc. The company is considering a proposal from a local financial institution, Old Reliant Financial, to factor Samson's receivables. The company controller is unfamiliar with the prevailing GAAP that deals with accounting for the transfer of financial assets and has asked you to do some research. The controller wants to make sure the arrangement with the financial institution is structured in such a way as to allow the factoring to be accounted for as a sale.

Old Reliant has offered to factor all of the company's receivables on a "without recourse" basis. Old Reliant will remit to Samson 90% of the factored amount, collect the receivables from Samson's customers, and retain the remaining 10% until all of the receivables have been collected. When Old Reliant collects all of the receivables, it will remit to Samson the retained amount, less a 4% fee (4% of the total factored amount).

**Required:**

1. Explain the meaning of the term *without recourse*.
2. Access the relevant authoritative literature on accounting for the transfer of financial assets using the FASB's Codification Research System. You might gain access at the FASB website (**www.fasb.org**), from your school library, or some other source. What conditions must be met for a transfer of receivables to be accounted for as a sale (or in accounting terms, "derecognized")? What is the specific citation that Samson would rely on in applying that accounting treatment?
3. Assuming that the conditions for treatment as a sale are met, prepare Samson's journal entry to record the factoring of $400,000 of receivables. Assume that the fair value of the last 10% of Samson's receivables is equal to $25,000.
4. An agreement that both entitles and obligates the transferor, Samson, to repurchase or redeem transferred assets from the transferee, Old Reliant, maintains the transferor's effective control over those assets and the transfer is accounted for as a secured borrowing, not a sale, if and only if what conditions are met?

**Analysis Case 7–12**
Compare receivables management using ratios; Del Monte Foods and Smithfield Foods
● LO7–9

The table below contains selected financial information included in the 2011 financial statements of **Del Monte Foods Co.** and **Smithfield Foods Inc.**

Real World Financials

| | ($ in millions) | | | |
| --- | --- | --- | --- | --- |
| | Del Monte | | Smithfield | |
| | **2011** | **2010** | **2011** | **2010** |
| **Balance sheet:** | | | | |
| Accounts receivable, net | $ 224.6 | $ 187.3 | $ 709.6 | $ 621.5 |
| **Income statement:** | | | | |
| Net sales | 3,627.0 | 3,739.8 | 12,202.7 | 11,202.6 |

**Required:**

1. Calculate the 2011 receivables turnover ratio and average collection period for both companies. Evaluate the management of each company's investment in receivables.

2. Obtain annual reports from three corporations in the same primary industry and compare the management of each company's investment in receivables.

   **Note:** You can obtain copies of annual reports from your library, from friends who are shareholders, from the investor relations department of the corporations, from a friendly stockbroker, or from EDGAR (Electronic Data Gathering, Analysis, and Retrieval) on the Internet (www.sec.gov).

**Analysis
Case 7–13**
Reporting cash
and receivables
● LO7–2, LO7–5

Refer to the financial statements and related disclosure notes of Dell Inc. included with all new copies of the text.

**Required:**

1. What is Dell's policy for designating investments as cash equivalents?

2. At the end of the 2011 fiscal year, how much cash was included in cash and cash equivalents?

3. Determine the gross amount of accounts receivable outstanding at January 30, 2011, and February 1, 2010.

# Air France–KLM Case

**AIRFRANCE /**

● LO7–8

🌐 IFRS

Air France–KLM (AF), a French company, prepares its financial statements according to International Financial Reporting Standards. AF's annual report for the year ended March 31, 2011, which includes financial statements and disclosure notes, is provided with all new textbooks. This material also is included in AF's "Registration Document 2010–11," dated June 15, 2011 and is available at www.airfranceklm.com.

**Required:**

1. In note 3.10.1, AF describes how it values trade receivables. How does the approach used by AF compare to U.S. GAAP?

2. In note 24, AF reconciles the beginning and ending balances of its valuation allowance for trade accounts receivable. Prepare a T-account for the valuation allowance and include entries for the beginning and ending balances and any reconciling items that affected the account during 2011.

3. Examine note 26. Does AF have any bank overdrafts? If so, are the overdrafts shown in the balance sheet the same way they would be shown under U.S. GAAP?

# 8

# Inventories: Measurement

**OVERVIEW** — The next two chapters continue our study of assets by investigating the measurement and reporting issues involving inventories and the related expense—cost of goods sold. Inventory refers to the assets a company (1) intends to sell in the normal course of business, (2) has in production for future sale, or (3) uses currently in the production of goods to be sold.

**LEARNING OBJECTIVES**

**After studying this chapter, you should be able to:**

- **LO8–1** Explain the difference between a perpetual inventory system and a periodic inventory system. (p. 424)

- **LO8–2** Explain which physical quantities of goods should be included in inventory. (p. 426)

- **LO8–3** Determine the expenditures that should be included in the cost of inventory. (p. 427)

- **LO8–4** Differentiate between the specific identification, FIFO, LIFO, and average cost methods used to determine the cost of ending inventory and cost of goods sold. (p. 430)

- **LO8–5** Discuss the factors affecting a company's choice of inventory method. (p. 437)

- **LO8–6** Understand supplemental LIFO disclosures and the effect of LIFO liquidations on net income. (p. 438)

- **LO8–7** Calculate the key ratios used by analysts to monitor a company's investment in inventories. (p. 444)

- **LO8–8** Determine ending inventory using the dollar-value LIFO inventory method. (p. 447)

- **LO8–9** Discuss the primary difference between U.S. GAAP and IFRS with respect to determining the cost of inventory. (p. 437)

# FINANCIAL REPORTING CASE

## Inventory Measurement at ConocoPhillips

A recent article in the financial section of your newspaper reported record profits generated by U.S. oil companies. When you showed the article to a friend, he laughed, "I'll bet U.S. oil companies use LIFO to value their inventories. That way they can report lower profits than they would if using another inventory method. If the profits are too high it could cause the government to jump in and impose an excess profits tax as it did in the 1980s." Curiosity aroused, you downloaded from the Internet a recent quarterly report of ConocoPhillips, one of the large U.S. oil companies. The report included the following disclosure:

**Note 3—Inventories**
Inventories consisted of the following ($ in millions):

|  | March 31 2011 | December 31 2010 |
| --- | --- | --- |
| Crude oil and petroleum products | $6,973 | $4,254 |
| Materials, supplies, and other | 971 | 943 |
| Total inventories | $7,944 | $5,197 |

Inventories valued on the last-in, first-out (LIFO) basis totaled $6,713 million and $4,051 million at March 31, 2011, and December 31, 2010, respectively. The excess of current replacement cost over LIFO cost of inventories amounted to $9,812 million and $6,794 million at March 31, 2011, and December 31, 2010, respectively.

In the company's annual financial statements, the summary of significant accounting policies reports that the LIFO method is used to value crude oil and petroleum products and the remaining inventories are valued under various methods, including FIFO and weighted average.

**By the time you finish this chapter, you should be able to respond appropriately to the questions posed in this case. Compare your response to the solution provided at the end of the chapter.**

QUESTIONS

**1.** What inventory methods does ConocoPhillips use to value its inventories? Is this permissible according to GAAP? (*p. 436*)

**2.** What is the purpose of disclosing the difference between the reported LIFO inventory amounts and replacement cost, assuming that replacement cost is equivalent to a FIFO basis? (*p. 438*)

**3.** Is your friend correct in his assertion that, by using LIFO, ConocoPhillips was able to report lower profits for the first quarter of 2011? (*p. 444*)

# RECORDING AND MEASURING INVENTORY

Inventory refers to the assets a company (1) intends to sell in the normal course of business, (2) has in production for future sale (work in process), or (3) uses currently in the production of goods to be sold (raw materials). The computers produced by **Apple Inc.** that are intended for sale to customers are inventory, as are partially completed components in the assembly lines of Apple's Cupertino facility, and the computer chips and memory modules that will go into computers produced later. The computers *used* by Apple to maintain its accounting system, however, are classified and accounted for as plant and equipment. Similarly, the stocks and bonds a securities dealer holds for sale are inventory, whereas Apple would classify the securities it holds as investments.

> **Inventories consist of assets that a retail or wholesale company acquires for resale or goods that manufacturers produce for sale.**

Proper accounting for inventories is essential for manufacturing, wholesale, and retail companies (enterprises that earn revenue by selling goods). Inventory usually is one of the most valuable assets listed in the balance sheet for these firms. Cost of goods sold—the expense recorded when inventory is sold—typically is the largest expense in the income statement. For example, a recent balance sheet for **Sara Lee Corporation** reported inventories of $976 million, which represented 21% of current assets. The company's income statement reported cost of goods sold of $5,868 million representing 73% of operating expenses.

> **An important objective in inventory accounting is to match the appropriate cost of goods sold with sales revenue.**

In this and the following chapter we discuss the measurement and reporting issues involving **inventory**, an asset, and the related expense, **cost of goods sold**. Inventory represents *quantities* of goods acquired, manufactured, or in the process of being manufactured. The inventory amount in the balance sheet at the end of an accounting period represents the cost of the inventory still on hand, and cost of goods sold in the income statement represents the cost of the inventory sold during the period. The historical cost principle and matching principle offer guidance for measuring inventory and cost of goods sold, but as we will see in this and the next chapter, it's usually difficult to measure inventory (cost of goods sold) at the exact cost of the actual physical quantities on hand (sold). Fortunately, accountants can use one of several techniques to approximate the desired result and satisfy our measurement objectives.

## Types of Inventory

### Merchandising Inventory

Wholesale and retail companies purchase goods that are primarily in finished form. These companies are intermediaries in the process of moving goods from the manufacturer to the end-user. They often are referred to as merchandising companies and their inventory as merchandise inventory. *The cost of merchandise inventory includes the purchase price plus any other costs necessary to get the goods in condition and location for sale.* We discuss the concept of condition and location and the types of costs that typically constitute inventory later in this chapter.

### Manufacturing Inventories

> **Inventory for a manufacturing company consists of *raw materials,* work in process, and finished goods.**

> **The cost of *work in process* and *finished goods* includes the cost of raw materials, direct labor, and an allocated portion of manufacturing overhead.**

Unlike merchandising companies, manufacturing companies actually produce the goods they sell to wholesalers, retailers, or other manufacturers. Inventory for a manufacturer consists of (1) raw materials, (2) work in process, and (3) finished goods. **Raw materials** represent the cost of components purchased from other manufacturers that will become part of the finished product. For example, Apple's raw materials inventory includes semiconductors, circuit boards, plastic, and glass that go into the production of personal computers.

**Work-in-process** inventory refers to the products that are not yet complete. The cost of work in process includes the cost of raw materials used in production, the cost of labor that can be directly traced to the goods in process, and an allocated portion of other manufacturing costs, called *manufacturing overhead.* Overhead costs include electricity and other utility costs to operate the manufacturing facility, depreciation of manufacturing equipment, and many other manufacturing costs that cannot be directly linked to the production of specific goods. Once the manufacturing process is completed, these costs that have accumulated in work in process are transferred to finished goods.

Manufacturing companies generally disclose, either in a note or directly in the balance sheet, the dollar amount of each inventory category. For example, Dell Inc.'s note disclosure of inventory categories was shown on page 118. Sara Lee Corporation reports inventory categories directly in the balance sheet, as shown in Illustration 8–1.

**Illustration 8–1**

Inventories Disclosure—Sara Lee Corporation

Real World Financials

| **Balance Sheet** | | |
| --- | --- | --- |
| | ($ in millions) | |
| | **2011** | **2010** |
| Current assets: | | |
| Inventories | | |
| Finished goods | $485 | $386 |
| Work in process | 36 | 31 |
| Materials and supplies | 455 | 278 |
| Total | $976 | $695 |

The inventory accounts and the cost flows for a typical manufacturing company are shown using T-accounts in Illustration 8–2. The costs of raw materials used, direct labor applied, and manufacturing overhead applied flow into work in process and then to finished goods. When the goods are sold, the cost of those goods flows to cost of goods sold.

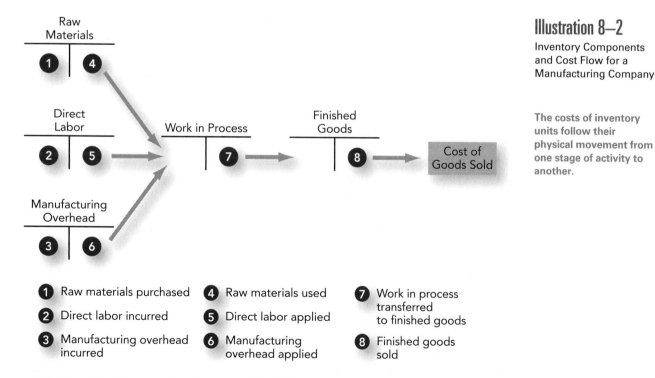

**Illustration 8–2**

Inventory Components and Cost Flow for a Manufacturing Company

The costs of inventory units follow their physical movement from one stage of activity to another.

1 Raw materials purchased
2 Direct labor incurred
3 Manufacturing overhead incurred
4 Raw materials used
5 Direct labor applied
6 Manufacturing overhead applied
7 Work in process transferred to finished goods
8 Finished goods sold

We focus in this text primarily on merchandising companies (wholesalers and retailers). Still, most of the accounting principles and procedures discussed here also apply to manufacturing companies. The unique problems involved with accumulating the direct costs of raw materials and labor and with allocating manufacturing overhead are addressed in managerial and cost accounting textbooks.

# Types of Inventory Systems

## Perpetual Inventory System

● **LO8–1**

*A perpetual inventory system* continuously records both changes in inventory quantity and inventory cost.

Two accounting systems are used to record transactions involving inventory: the **perpetual inventory system** and the **periodic inventory system**. The perpetual system was introduced in Chapter 2. The system is aptly termed perpetual because the account *inventory* is continually adjusted for each change in inventory, whether it's caused by a purchase, a sale, or a return of merchandise by the company to its supplier (a *purchase return* for the buyer, a *sales return* for the seller).[1] The cost of goods sold account, along with the inventory account, is adjusted each time goods are sold or are returned by a customer. This concept is applied to the Lothridge Wholesale Beverage Company for which inventory information is provided in Illustration 8–3. This hypothetical company also will be used in the next several illustrations.

**Illustration 8–3**

Perpetual Inventory System

The Lothridge Wholesale Beverage Company purchases soft drinks from producers and then sells them to retailers. The company begins 2013 with merchandise inventory of $120,000 on hand. During 2013 additional merchandise is purchased on account at a cost of $600,000. Sales for the year, all on account, totaled $820,000. The cost of the soft drinks sold is $540,000. Lothridge uses the perpetual inventory system to keep track of both inventory quantities and inventory costs. The system indicates that the cost of inventory on hand at the end of the year is $180,000.

The following summary journal entries record the inventory transactions for the Lothridge Company:

**2013**

| | | |
|---|---|---|
| Inventory | 600,000 | |
|    Accounts payable | | 600,000 |
| *To record the purchase of merchandise inventory.* | | |

**2013**

| | | |
|---|---|---|
| Accounts receivable | 820,000 | |
|    Sales revenue | | 820,000 |
| *To record sales on account.* | | |
| Cost of goods sold | 540,000 | |
|    Inventory | | 540,000 |
| *To record the cost of sales.* | | |

An important feature of a perpetual system is that it is designed to track inventory quantities from their acquisition to their sale. If the system is accurate, it allows management to determine how many goods are on hand on any date without having to take a physical count. However, physical counts of inventory usually are made anyway, either at the end of the fiscal year or on a sample basis throughout the year, to verify that the perpetual system is correctly tracking quantities. Differences between the quantity of inventory determined by the physical count and the quantity of inventory according to the perpetual system could be caused by system errors, theft, breakage, or spoilage. In addition to keeping up with inventory, a perpetual system also directly determines how many items are sold during a period.

*A perpetual inventory system tracks both inventory quantities and inventory costs.*

You are probably familiar with the scanning mechanisms used at grocery store checkout counters. The scanners not only record the sale on the cash register but also can be used to track the sale of merchandise for inventory management purposes. For a company to use the perpetual inventory system to record inventory and cost of goods sold transactions, merchandise cost data also must be included on the system. That is, when merchandise is purchased/sold, the system must be able to record not only the addition/reduction in inventory quantity but also the addition/reduction in the *cost* of inventory.

---

[1]We discussed accounting for sales returns in Chapter 7.

# Periodic Inventory System

A **periodic inventory system** is not designed to track either the quantity or cost of merchandise. The merchandise inventory account balance is not adjusted as purchases and sales are made but only periodically at the end of a reporting period. A physical count of the period's ending inventory is made and costs are assigned to the quantities determined. Merchandise purchases, purchase returns, purchase discounts, and freight-in (purchases plus freight-in less returns and discounts equals net purchases) are recorded in temporary accounts and the period's cost of goods sold is determined at the end of the period by combining the temporary accounts with the inventory account:

> A *periodic inventory system* adjusts inventory and records cost of goods sold only at the end of each reporting period.

Beginning inventory + Net purchases − Ending inventory = Cost of goods sold

> Cost of goods sold equation

The cost of goods sold equation assumes that all inventory quantities not on hand at the end of the period were sold. This may not be the case if inventory items were either damaged or stolen. If damaged and stolen inventory are identified, they must be removed from beginning inventory or purchases before calculating cost of goods sold and then classified as a separate expense item.

Illustration 8–4 looks at the periodic system using the Lothridge Wholesale Beverage Company example.

> **Illustration 8–4**
>
> Periodic Inventory System

The Lothridge Wholesale Beverage Company purchases soft drinks from producers and then sells them to retailers. The company begins 2013 with merchandise inventory of $120,000 on hand. During 2013, additional merchandise was purchased on account at a cost of $600,000. Sales for the year, all on account, totaled $820,000. Lothridge uses a periodic inventory system. A physical count determined the cost of inventory at the end of the year to be $180,000.

The following summary journal entries record the inventory transactions for 2013. Of course, each individual transaction would actually be recorded as incurred:

| 2013 | | |
|---|---|---|
| Purchases ................................................................. | 600,000 | |
|    Accounts payable ................................................. | | 600,000 |
| *To record the purchase of merchandise inventory.* | | |

| 2013 | | |
|---|---|---|
| Accounts receivable ................................................... | 820,000 | |
|    Sales revenue ...................................................... | | 820,000 |
| *To record sales on account.* | | |
| **No entry is recorded for the cost of inventory sold.** | | |

Because cost of goods sold isn't determined automatically and continually by the periodic system, it must be determined indirectly after a physical inventory count. Cost of goods sold for 2013 is determined as follows:

| | |
|---|---|
| Beginning inventory | $120,000 |
| Plus: Purchases | 600,000 |
| Cost of goods available for sale | 720,000 |
| Less: Ending inventory (per physical count) | (180,000) |
| Cost of goods sold | $540,000 |

The following journal entry combines the components of cost of goods sold into a single expense account and updates the balance in the inventory account:

| December 31, 2013 | | |
|---|---|---|
| Cost of goods sold ...................................................... | 540,000 | |
| Inventory (ending)....................................................... | 180,000 | |
|    Inventory (beginning) ............................................ | | 120,000 |
|    Purchases............................................................. | | 600,000 |
| *To adjust inventory, close the purchases account, and record cost of goods sold.* | | |

This entry adjusts the inventory account to the correct period-end amount, closes the temporary purchases account, and records the residual as cost of goods sold. Now let's compare the two inventory accounting systems.

## A Comparison of the Perpetual and Periodic Inventory Systems

Beginning inventory plus net purchases during the period is the *cost of goods available for sale*. The main difference between a perpetual and a periodic system is that the periodic system allocates cost of goods available for sale between ending inventory and cost of goods sold (periodically) *at the end of the period*. In contrast, the perpetual system performs this allocation by decreasing inventory and increasing cost of goods sold (perpetually) *each time goods are sold.*

The impact on the financial statements of choosing one system over the other generally is not significant. The choice between the two approaches usually is motivated by management control considerations as well as the comparative costs of implementation. Perpetual systems can provide more information about the dollar amounts of inventory levels on a continuous basis. They also facilitate the preparation of interim financial statements by providing fairly accurate information without the necessity of a physical count of inventory.

On the other hand, a perpetual system may be more expensive to implement than a periodic system. This is particularly true for inventories consisting of large numbers of low-cost items. Perpetual systems are more workable with inventories of high-cost items such as construction equipment or automobiles. However, with the help of computers and electronic sales devices such as cash register scanners, the perpetual inventory system is now available to many small businesses that previously could not afford them and is economically feasible for a broader range of inventory items than before.

The periodic system is less costly to implement during the period but requires a physical count before ending inventory and cost of goods sold can be determined. This makes the preparation of interim financial statements more costly unless an inventory estimation technique is used.[2] And, perhaps most importantly, the inventory monitoring features provided by a perpetual system are not available. However, it is important to remember that a perpetual system involves the tracking of both inventory quantities *and* costs. Many companies that determine costs only periodically employ systems to constantly monitor inventory quantities.

> A perpetual system provides more timely information but generally is more costly.

# What is Included in Inventory?

## Physical Quantities Included in Inventory

● LO8–2

Regardless of the system used, the measurement of inventory and cost of goods sold starts with determining the physical quantities of goods. Typically, determining the physical quantity that should be included in inventory is a simple matter because it consists of items in the possession of the company. However, in some situations the identification of items that should be included in inventory is more difficult. Consider, for example, goods in transit, goods on consignment, and sales returns.

**GOODS IN TRANSIT.** At the end of a reporting period, it's important to ensure a proper inventory cutoff. This means determining the ownership of goods that are in transit between the company and its customers as well as between the company and its suppliers. For example, in December 2013, the Lothridge Wholesale Beverage Company sold goods to the Jabbar Company. The goods were shipped on December 29, 2013, and arrived at Jabbar's warehouse on January 3, 2014. The fiscal year-end for both companies is December 31.

Should the merchandise shipped to Jabbar be recorded as a sale by Lothridge and a purchase by Jabbar in 2013 and thus included in Jabbar's 2013 ending inventory? Should recording the sale/purchase be delayed until 2014 and the merchandise be included in Lothridge's 2013 ending inventory? The answer depends on who owns the goods at December 31. Ownership depends on the terms of the agreement between the two companies. If the goods are shipped **f.o.b. (free on board) shipping point**, then legal title to the goods changes hands at the

> Inventory shipped *f.o.b. shipping point* is included in the purchaser's inventory as soon as the merchandise is shipped.

[2]In Chapter 9 we discuss inventory estimation techniques that avoid the necessity of a physical count to determine ending inventory and cost of goods sold.

point of shipment when the seller delivers the goods to the common carrier (for example, a trucking company), and the purchaser is responsible for shipping costs and transit insurance. In that case, Lothridge records the sale and inventory reduction in 2013 and Jabbar records a 2013 purchase and includes the goods in 2013 ending inventory even though the company is not in physical possession of the goods on the last day of the fiscal year.

On the other hand, if the goods are shipped **f.o.b. destination**, the seller is responsible for shipping and legal title does not pass until the goods arrive at their destination (the customer's location). In our example, if the goods are shipped f.o.b. destination, Lothridge includes the merchandise in its 2013 ending inventory and the sale is recorded in 2014. Jabbar records the purchase in 2014.

> Inventory shipped *f.o.b. destination* is included in the purchaser's inventory only after it reaches the purchaser's destination.

**GOODS ON CONSIGNMENT.**   Sometimes a company arranges for another company to sell its product under **consignment**. The goods are physically transferred to the other company (the consignee), but the transferor (consignor) retains legal title. If the consignee can't find a buyer, the goods are returned to the consignor. If a buyer is found, the consignee remits the selling price (less commission and approved expenses) to the consignor.

> Goods held on *consignment* are included in the inventory of the consignor until sold by the consignee.

As we discussed in Chapter 5, because risk is retained by the consignor, the sale is not complete (revenue is not recognized) until an eventual sale to a third party occurs. As a result, goods held on consignment generally are not included in the consignee's inventory. While in stock, they belong to the consignor and should be included in inventory of the consignor even though not in the company's physical possession. A sale is recorded by the consignor only when the goods are sold by the consignee and title passes to the customer.

**SALES RETURNS.**   Recall from our discussions in Chapters 5 and 7 that when the right of return exists, a seller must be able to estimate those returns before revenue can be recognized. The adjusting entry for estimated sales returns reduces sales revenue and accounts receivable. At the same time, cost of goods sold is reduced and inventory is increased (see Illustration 7–4 on page 367). As a result, a company includes in inventory the cost of merchandise it anticipates will be returned.

Now that we've considered which goods are part of inventory, let's examine the types of costs that should be associated with those inventory quantities.

## Expenditures Included in Inventory

As mentioned earlier, the cost of inventory includes all necessary expenditures to acquire the inventory and bring it to its desired *condition* and *location* for sale or for use in the manufacturing process. Obviously, the cost includes the purchase price of the goods. But usually the cost of acquiring inventory also includes freight charges on incoming goods borne by the buyer; insurance costs incurred by the buyer while the goods are in transit (if shipped f.o.b. shipping point); and the costs of unloading, unpacking, and preparing merchandise inventory for sale or raw materials inventory for use.[3] The costs included in inventory are called **product costs**. They are associated with products and *expensed as cost of goods sold only when the related products are sold.*[4]

> ● LO8–3
>
> Expenditures necessary to bring inventory to its *condition* and *location* for sale or use are included in its cost.

**FREIGHT-IN ON PURCHASES.**   Freight-in on purchases is commonly included in the cost of inventory. These costs clearly are necessary to get the inventory in location for sale or use and can generally be associated with particular goods. Freight costs are added to the inventory account in a perpetual system. In a periodic system, freight costs generally are added to a temporary account called **freight-in** or **transportation-in**, which is added to purchases in determining net purchases. The account is closed to cost of goods sold along with purchases and other components of cost of goods sold at the end of the reporting period. (See Illustration 8–6 on page 429.) From an accounting system perspective, freight-in also could be added to the purchases account. From a control perspective, by recording freight-in

> The cost of *freight-in* paid by the purchaser generally is part of the cost of inventory.

[3]Generally accepted accounting principles require that abnormal amounts of certain costs be recognized as current period expenses rather than being included in the cost of inventory, specifically idle facility costs, freight, handling costs, and waste materials (spoilage). FASB ASC 330–10–30: Inventory–Overall–Initial Measurement (previously "Inventory Costs—An Amendment of *ARB No. 43, Chapter 4," Statement of Financial Accounting Standards No. 151* (Norwalk, Conn.: FASB, 2004)).

[4]For practical reasons, though, some of these expenditures often are not included in inventory cost and are treated as **period costs.** They often are immaterial or it is impractical to associate the expenditures with particular units of inventory (for example, unloading and unpacking costs). Period costs are not associated with products and are expensed in the *period* incurred.

as a separate item, management can more easily track its freight costs. The same perspectives pertain to purchases returns and purchase discounts, which are discussed next.

Shipping charges on outgoing goods (freight-out) are not included in the cost of inventory. They are reported in the income statement either as part of cost of goods sold or as an operating expense, usually among selling expenses. If a company adopts a policy of not including shipping charges in cost of goods sold, both the amounts incurred during the period as well as the income statement classification of the expense must be disclosed.[5]

> **Shipping charges on outgoing goods are reported either as part of cost of goods sold or as an operating expense, usually among selling expenses.**

**PURCHASE RETURNS.** In Chapter 7 we discussed merchandise returns from the perspective of the selling company. We now address returns from the buyer's point of view. You may recall that the seller views a return as a reduction of net sales. Likewise, a buyer views a return as a reduction of net purchases. When the buyer returns goods to the seller, a **purchase return** is recorded. In a perpetual inventory system, this means a reduction in both inventory and accounts payable (if the account has not yet been paid) at the time of the return. In a periodic system an account called *purchase returns* temporarily accumulates these amounts. Purchase returns are subtracted from purchases when determining net purchases. The account is closed to cost of goods sold at the end of the reporting period.

> **A *purchase return* represents a reduction of net purchases.**

**PURCHASE DISCOUNTS.** Cash discounts also were discussed from the seller's perspective in Chapter 7. These discounts really are quick-payment discounts because they represent reductions in the amount to be paid by the buyer in the event payment is made within a specified period of time. The amount of the discount and the time period within which it's available are conveyed by terms like 2/10, n/30 (meaning a 2% discount if paid within 10 days, otherwise full payment within 30 days). As with the seller, the purchaser can record these **purchase discounts** using either the **gross method** or the **net method**. Consider Illustration 8–5, which is similar to the cash discount illustration in Chapter 7.

> **Purchase discounts represent reductions in the amount to be paid if remittance is made within a designated period of time.**

## Illustration 8–5
Purchase Discounts

On October 5, 2013, the Lothridge Wholesale Beverage Company purchased merchandise at a price of $20,000. The repayment terms are stated as 2/10, n/30. Lothridge paid $13,720 ($14,000 less the 2% cash discount) on October 14 and the remaining balance of $6,000 on November 4. Lothridge employs a periodic inventory system.

The gross and net methods of recording the purchase and cash payment are compared as follows:

| Gross Method | | | Net Method | | |
|---|---|---|---|---|---|
| **October 5, 2013** | | | **October 5, 2013** | | |
| Purchases*...................... | 20,000 | | Purchases*................... | 19,600 | |
| Accounts payable ...... | | 20,000 | Accounts payable..... | | 19,600 |
| **October 14, 2013** | | | **October 14, 2013** | | |
| Accounts payable .......... | 14,000 | | Accounts payable......... | 13,720 | |
| Purchase discounts*... | | 280 | Cash......................... | | 13,720 |
| Cash .......................... | | 13,720 | | | |
| **November 4, 2013** | | | **November 4, 2013** | | |
| Accounts payable .......... | 6,000 | | Accounts payable......... | 5,880 | |
| Cash .......................... | | 6,000 | Interest expense........... | 120 | |
| | | | Cash ......................... | | 6,000 |

*The inventory account is used in a perpetual system.

> **By either method, net purchases are reduced by discounts taken.**

> **Discounts not taken are included as purchases using the gross method and as interest expense using the net method.**

> **The *gross method* views discounts not taken as part of inventory cost.**

Conceptually, the gross method views a discount not taken as part of the cost of inventory. The net method considers the cost of inventory to include the net, after-discount amount, and any discounts not taken are reported as *interest expense.*[6] The discount is viewed as compensation to the seller for providing financing to the buyer.

---

[5]FASB ASC 605–45–50–2: Revenue Recognition–Principal Agent Considerations–Disclosure–Shipping and Handling Fees and Costs (previously "Accounting for Shipping and Handling Fees and Costs," *EITF Issue No. 00–10* (Norwalk, Conn.: FASB, 2000), par. 6).
[6]An alternative treatment is to debit an expense account called *purchase discounts lost* rather than interest expense. This enables a company to more easily identify the forgone discounts.

Purchase discounts recorded under the gross method are subtracted from purchases when determining net purchases. The account is a temporary account that is closed to cost of goods sold at the end of the reporting period. Under the perpetual inventory system, purchase discounts are treated as a reduction in the inventory account.

The effect on the financial statements of the difference between the two methods usually is immaterial. Net income over time will be the same using either method. There will, however, be a difference in gross profit between the two methods equal to the amount of discounts not taken. In the preceding illustration, $120 in discounts not taken is included as interest expense using the net method and cost of goods sold using the gross method.

Illustration 8–6 compares the perpetual and periodic inventory systems, using the net method.

The *net method* considers discounts not taken as interest expense.

**Illustration 8–6**

Inventory Transactions—Perpetual and Periodic Systems

The Lothridge Wholesale Beverage Company purchases soft drinks from producers and then sells them to retailers. The company began 2013 with merchandise inventory of $120,000 on hand. During 2013, additional merchandise is purchased on account at a cost of $600,000. Lothridge's suppliers offer credit terms of 2/10, n/30. All discounts were taken. Lothridge uses the net method to record purchase discounts. All purchases are made f.o.b. shipping point. Freight charges paid by Lothridge totaled $16,000. Merchandise with a net of discount cost of $20,000 was returned to suppliers for credit. Sales for the year, all on account, totaled $830,000. The cost of the soft drinks sold is $550,000. $154,000 of inventory remained on hand at the end of 2013.

The above transactions are recorded in summary form according to both the perpetual and periodic inventory systems as follows:

($ in 000s)

| Perpetual System | | | Periodic System | | |
|---|---|---|---|---|---|
| **Purchases** | | | | | |
| Inventory ($600 × 98%) ... | 588 | | Purchases ($600 × 98%) ......... | 588 | |
| Accounts payable ........ | | 588 | Accounts payable .............. | | 588 |
| **Freight** | | | | | |
| Inventory ......................... | 16 | | Freight-in ............................... | 16 | |
| Cash ............................. | | 16 | Cash .................................... | | 16 |
| **Returns** | | | | | |
| Accounts payable ............ | 20 | | Accounts payable ................... | 20 | |
| Inventory ..................... | | 20 | Purchase returns ................ | | 20 |
| **Sales** | | | | | |
| Accounts receivable ........ | 830 | | Accounts receivable .............. | 830 | |
| Sales revenue .............. | | 830 | Sales revenue ..................... | | 830 |
| Cost of goods sold .......... | 550 | | No entry | | |
| Inventory ..................... | | 550 | | | |
| **End of period** | | | | | |
| No entry | | | Cost of goods sold (below) .... | 550 ← | |
| | | | Inventory (ending) ................. | 154 | |
| | | | Purchase returns .................... | 20 | |
| | | | Inventory (beginning) .......... | | 120 |
| | | | Purchases ........................... | | 588 |
| | | | Freight-in ........................... | | 16 |

**Supporting Schedule:**

| | | |
|---|---|---|
| Cost of goods sold: | | |
| Beginning inventory .............. | | $120 |
| Purchases ............................. | $588 | |
| Less: Returns ...................... | (20) | |
| Plus: Freight-in ................... | 16 | |
| Net purchases ........................ | | 584 |
| Cost of goods available ........ | | 704 |
| Less: Ending inventory ........ | | (154) |
| Cost of goods sold ................ | | $550 ← |

# Inventory Cost Flow Assumptions

● LO8–4

Regardless of whether the perpetual or periodic system is used, it's necessary to assign dollar amounts to the physical quantities of goods sold and goods remaining in ending inventory. Unless each item of inventory is specifically identified and traced through the system, assigning dollars is accomplished by making an assumption regarding how units of goods (and their associated costs) flow through the system. We examine the common cost flow assumptions next. In previous illustrations, dollar amounts of the cost of goods sold and the cost of ending inventory were assumed known. However, if various portions of inventory are acquired at different costs, we need a way to decide which units were sold and which remain in inventory. Illustration 8–7 will help explain.

**Illustration 8–7**

Cost Flow

Goods available for sale include beginning inventory plus purchases.

The Browning Company began 2013 with $22,000 of inventory. The cost of beginning inventory is composed of 4,000 units purchased for $5.50 each. Merchandise transactions during 2013 were as follows:

**Purchases**

| Date of Purchase | Units | Unit Cost* | Total Cost |
|---|---|---|---|
| Jan. 17 | 1,000 | $6.00 | $ 6,000 |
| Mar. 22 | 3,000 | 7.00 | 21,000 |
| Oct. 15 | 3,000 | 7.50 | 22,500 |
| Totals | 7,000 | | $49,500 |

**Sales**

| Date of Sale | Units |
|---|---|
| Jan. 10 | 2,000 |
| Apr. 15 | 1,500 |
| Nov. 20 | 3,000 |
| Total | 6,500 |

*Includes purchase price and cost of freight.

As the data show, 7,000 units were purchased during 2013 at various prices and 6,500 units were sold. What is the cost of the 6,500 units sold? If all units, including beginning inventory, were purchased at the same price, then the answer would be simple. However, that rarely is the case.

The year started with 4,000 units, 7,000 units were purchased, and 6,500 units were sold. This means 4,500 units remain in ending inventory. This allocation of units available for sale is depicted in Illustration 8–7A.

**Illustration 8–7A**

Allocation of Units Available

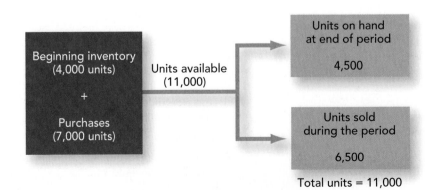

If a periodic system is used, what is the cost of the 4,500 units in ending inventory? In other words, which of the 11,000 (4,000 + 7,000) units available for sale were sold? Are they the more expensive ones bought toward the end of the year, or the less costly ones acquired before prices increased? Using the numbers given, let's consider the question as follows:

| | |
|---|---|
| Beginning inventory (4,000 units @ $5.50) | $22,000 |
| Plus: Purchases (7,000 units @ various prices) | 49,500 |
| Cost of goods available for sale (11,000 units) | $71,500 |
| Less: Ending inventory (4,500 units @ ?) | ? |
| Cost of goods sold (6,500 units @ ?) | ? |

The $71,500 in cost of goods available for sale must be allocated to ending inventory and cost of goods sold. The allocation decision is depicted in Illustration 8–7B.

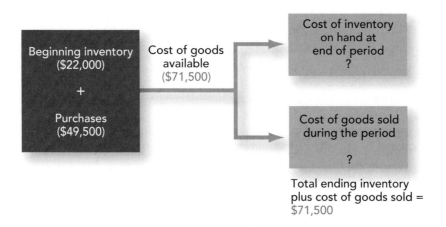

**Illustration 8–7B**
Allocation of Cost of Goods Available

Let's turn our attention now to the various inventory methods that can be used to achieve this allocation.

## Specific Identification

It's sometimes possible for each unit sold during the period or each unit on hand at the end of the period to be matched with its actual cost. Actual costs can be determined by reference to the invoice representing the purchase of the item. This method is used frequently by companies selling unique, expensive products with low sales volume which makes it relatively easy and economically feasible to associate each item with its actual cost. For example, automobiles have unique serial numbers that can be used to match a specific auto with the invoice identifying the actual purchase price.

The specific identification method, however, is not feasible for many types of products either because items are not uniquely identifiable or because it is too costly to match a specific purchase price with each item sold or each item remaining in ending inventory. Most companies use cost flow methods to determine cost of goods sold and ending inventory. Cost flow methods are based on assumptions about how inventory might flow in and out of a company. However, it's important to note that the actual flow of a company's inventory does not have to correspond to the cost flow assumed. The various motivating factors that influence management's choice among alternative methods are discussed later in this chapter. We now explore the three most common cost flow methods: average cost, first-in, first-out (FIFO) and last-in, first-out (LIFO).

## Average Cost

The average cost method assumes that cost of goods sold and ending inventory consist of a mixture of all the goods available for sale. The average unit cost applied to goods sold or to ending inventory is not simply an average of the various unit costs of purchases during the period but an average unit cost *weighted* by the number of units acquired at the various unit costs.

The *average cost method* assumes that items sold and items in ending inventory come from a mixture of all the goods available for sale.

In a periodic inventory system, the average cost is computed only at the end of the period.

**PERIODIC AVERAGE COST.**   In a periodic inventory system, this weighted average is calculated only at the end of the period as follows:

$$\text{Weighted-average unit cost} = \frac{\text{Cost of goods available for sale}}{\text{Quantity available for sale}}$$

The calculation of average cost is demonstrated in Illustration 8–7C using data from Illustration 8–7.

## Illustration 8–7C
Average Cost—Periodic Inventory System

| | |
|---|---:|
| Beginning inventory (4,000 units @ $5.50) | $22,000 |
| Plus: Purchases (7,000 units @ various prices) | 49,500 |
| Cost of goods available for sale (11,000 units) | 71,500 |
| Less: Ending inventory (determined below) | (29,250) |
| Cost of goods sold (6,500 units) | $42,250 |

**Cost of Ending Inventory:**

$$\text{Weighted-average unit cost} = \frac{\$71,500}{11,000 \text{ units}} = \$6.50$$

$$4,500 \text{ units} \times \$6.50 = \$29,250$$

Cost of goods sold also could be determined directly by multiplying the weighted-average unit cost of $6.50 by the number of units sold ($6.50 × 6,500 = $42,250).

In a perpetual inventory system, the average cost method is applied by computing a moving-average unit cost each time additional inventory is purchased.

**PERPETUAL AVERAGE COST.**   The weighted-average unit cost in a perpetual inventory system becomes a moving-average unit cost. A new weighted-average unit cost is calculated each time additional units are *purchased*. The new average is determined after each purchase by (1) summing the cost of the previous inventory balance and the cost of the new purchase, and (2) dividing this new total cost (cost of goods available for sale) by the number of units on hand (the inventory units that are available for sale). This average is then used to cost any units sold before the next purchase is made. The moving-average concept is applied in Illustration 8–7D.

## Illustration 8–7D    Average Cost—Perpetual Inventory System

| | Date | Purchased | Sold | Balance |
|---|---|---|---|---|
| | Beginning inventory | 4,000 @ $5.50 = $22,000 | | 4,000 @ $5.50 = $22,000 |
| | Jan. 10 | | 2,000 @ $5.50 = $11,000 | 2,000 @ $5.50 = $11,000 |
| | Jan. 17 | 1,000 @ $6.00 = $6,000 | | $11,000 + $6,000 = $17,000 |
| | | | | 2,000 + 1,000 = 3,000 units |
| Average cost per unit | → | $\left[\dfrac{\$17,000}{3,000 \text{ units}}\right] = \$5.667/\text{unit}$ | | |
| | Mar. 22 | 3,000 @ $7.00 = $21,000 | | $17,000 + $21,000 = $38,000 |
| Average cost per unit | → | $\left[\dfrac{\$38,000}{6,000 \text{ units}}\right] = \$6.333/\text{unit}$ | | 3,000 + 3,000 = 6,000 units |
| | Apr. 15 | | 1,500 @ $6.333 = $ 9,500 | 4,500 @ $6.333 = $28,500 |
| | Oct. 15 | 3,000 @ $7.50 = $22,500 | | $28,500 + $22,500 = $51,000 |
| Average cost per unit | → | $\left[\dfrac{\$51,000}{7,500 \text{ units}}\right] = \$6.80/\text{unit}$ | | 4,500 + 3,000 = 7,500 units |
| | Nov. 20 | | 3,000 @ $6.80 = $ 20,400 | 4,500 @ $6.80 = **$30,600** |
| | | Total cost of goods sold | = **$40,900** | |

On January 17 the new average of $5.667 (rounded) is calculated by dividing the $17,000 cost of goods available ($11,000 from beginning inventory + $6,000 purchased on January 17) by the 3,000 units available (2,000 units from beginning inventory + 1,000 units acquired on January 17). The average is updated to $6.333 (rounded) with the March 22 purchase. The 1,500 units sold on April 15 are then costed at the average cost of $6.333.

Periodic average cost and perpetual average cost generally produce different allocations to cost of goods sold and ending inventory.

## First-In, First-Out (FIFO)

The **first-in, first-out (FIFO) method** assumes that units sold are the first units acquired. Beginning inventory is sold first, followed by purchases during the period in the chronological order of their acquisition. In our illustration, 6,500 units were sold during 2013. Applying FIFO, these would be the 4,000 units in beginning inventory, the 1,000 units purchased on January 17, and 1,500 of the 3,000 units from the March 22 purchase. By default, ending inventory consists of the most recently acquired units. In this case, the 4,500 units in ending inventory consist of the 3,000 units purchased on October 15, and 1,500 of the 3,000 units purchased on March 22. Graphically, the flow is as follows:

The *first-in, first-out (FIFO) method* assumes that items sold are those that were acquired first.

Ending inventory applying FIFO consists of the most recently acquired items.

FIFO flow

**Units Available**

| | | |
|---|---|---|
| Beg. inv. | 4,000 | ⎫ |
| Jan. 17 | 1,000 | ⎬ 6,500 units sold |
| Mar. 22 | 1,500 | ⎭ |
| | | |
| Mar. 22 | 1,500 | ⎫ 4,500 units in ending inventory |
| Oct. 15 | 3,000 | ⎭ |
| Total | 11,000 | |

**PERIODIC FIFO.**   Recall that we determine physical quantities on hand in a periodic inventory system by taking a physical count. Costing the 4,500 units in ending inventory this way automatically gives us the cost of goods sold as well. Using the numbers from our illustration, we determine cost of goods sold to be $38,500 by subtracting the $33,000 ending inventory from $71,500 cost of goods available for sale as shown in Illustration 8–7E.

**Illustration 8–7E**

FIFO—Periodic Inventory System

| | | |
|---|---|---:|
| Beginning inventory (4,000 units @ $5.50) | | $22,000 |
| Plus: Purchases (7,000 units @ various prices) | | 49,500 |
| Cost of goods available for sale (11,000 units) | | 71,500 |
| Less: Ending inventory (determined below) | | (33,000) |
| Cost of goods sold (6,500 units) | | $38,500 |

**Cost of Ending Inventory:**

| Date of Purchase | Units | Unit Cost | Total Cost |
|---|---|---|---|
| Mar. 22 | 1,500 | $7.00 | $10,500 |
| Oct. 15 | 3,000 | 7.50 | 22,500 |
| Total | 4,500 | | $33,000 |

Of course, the 6,500 units sold could be costed directly as follows:

| Date of Purchase | Units | Unit Cost | Total Cost |
|---|---|---|---|
| Beg. inv. | 4,000 | $5.50 | $22,000 |
| Jan. 17 | 1,000 | 6.00 | 6,000 |
| Mar. 22 | 1,500 | 7.00 | 10,500 |
| Total | 6,500 | | $38,500 |

**PERPETUAL FIFO.**   The same ending inventory and cost of goods sold amounts are always produced in a perpetual inventory system as in a periodic inventory system when FIFO is used. This is because the same units and costs are first in and first out whether cost of goods sold is determined as each sale is made or at the end of the period as a residual amount. The application of FIFO in a perpetual system is shown in Illustration 8–7F.

**Illustration 8–7F**

FIFO—Perpetual Inventory System

| Date | Purchased | Sold | Balance |
|---|---|---|---|
| Beginning inventory | 4,000 @ $5.50 = $22,000 | | 4,000 @ $5.50 = $22,000 |
| Jan. 10 | | 2,000 @ $5.50 = $ 11,000 | 2,000 @ $5.50 = $11,000 |
| Jan. 17 | 1,000 @ $6.00 = $  6,000 | | 2,000 @ $5.50<br>1,000 @ $6.00 } $17,000 |
| Mar. 22 | 3,000 @ $7.00 = $21,000 | | 2,000 @ $5.50<br>1,000 @ $6.00<br>3,000 @ $7.00 } $38,000 |
| Apr. 15 | | 1,500 @ $5.50 = $  8,250 | 500 @ $5.50<br>1,000 @ $6.00<br>3,000 @ $7.00 } $29,750 |
| Oct. 15 | 3,000 @ $7.50 = $22,500 | | 500 @ $5.50<br>1,000 @ $6.00<br>3,000 @ $7.00<br>3,000 @ $7.50 } $52,250 |
| Nov. 20 | | 500 @ $5.50 +<br>1,000 @ $6.00 +<br>1,500 @ $7.00 = $ 19,250 | 1,500 @ $7.00<br>3,000 @ $7.50 } **$33,000** |
| | Total cost of goods sold | = **$38,500** | |

## Last-In, First-Out (LIFO)

*The last-in, first-out (LIFO) method assumes that items sold are those that were most recently acquired.*

The **last-in, first-out (LIFO) method** assumes that the units sold are the most recent units purchased. In our illustration, the 6,500 units assumed sold would be the 6,500 units acquired most recently: the 3,000 units acquired on October 15, the 3,000 units acquired on March 22, and 500 of the 1,000 units purchased on January 17. Ending inventory, then, consists of the units acquired first; in this case, the 4,000 units from beginning inventory and 500 of the 1,000 units purchased on January 17. Graphically, the flow is as follows:

*Ending inventory applying LIFO consists of the items acquired first.*

*LIFO flow*

| | **Units Available** | |
|---|---|---|
| Beg. inv. | 4,000 | } 4,500 units in ending inventory |
| Jan. 17 | 500 | |
| Jan. 17 | 500 | } 6,500 units sold |
| Mar. 22 | 3,000 | |
| Oct. 15 | 3,000 | |
| Total | 11,000 | |

**PERIODIC LIFO.**   The cost of ending inventory determined to be $25,000 (calculated below) by the LIFO assumption and using a periodic system is subtracted from cost of goods available for sale to arrive at the cost of goods sold of $46,500 as shown in Illustration 8–7G.

**Illustration 8–7G**

LIFO—Periodic Inventory System

| | | | |
|---|---|---|---|
| Beginning inventory (4,000 units @ $5.50) | | | $22,000 |
| Plus: Purchases (7,000 units @ various prices) | | | 49,500 |
| Cost of goods available for sale (11,000 units) | | | 71,500 |
| Less: Ending inventory (determined below) | | | (25,000) |
| Cost of goods sold (6,500 units) | | | $46,500 |

**Cost of Ending Inventory:**

| Date of Purchase | Units | Unit Cost | Total Cost |
|---|---|---|---|
| Beginning inventory | 4,000 | $5.50 | $22,000 |
| Jan. 17 | 500 | 6.00 | 3,000 |
| Total | 4,500 | | $25,000 |

The 6,500 sold could be costed directly as follows:

| Date of Purchase | Units | Unit Cost | Total Cost |
|---|---|---|---|
| Jan. 17 | 500 | $6.00 | $ 3,000 |
| Mar. 22 | 3,000 | 7.00 | 21,000 |
| Oct. 15 | 3,000 | 7.50 | 22,500 |
| Total | 6,500 | | $46,500 |

**PERPETUAL LIFO.** The application of LIFO in a perpetual system is shown in Illustration 8–7H. Each time inventory is purchased or sold, the LIFO layers are adjusted. For example, after the March 22 purchase, we have three layers of inventory at different unit costs listed in the chronological order of their purchase. When 1,500 units are sold on April 15, we assume they come from the most recent layer of 3,000 units purchased at $7.00.

**Illustration 8–7H**

LIFO—Perpetual Inventory System

| Date | Purchased | Sold | Balance |
|---|---|---|---|
| Beginning inventory | 4,000 @ $5.50 = $22,000 | | 4,000 @ $5.50 = $22,000 |
| Jan. 10 | | 2,000 @ $5.50 = $11,000 | 2,000 @ $5.50 = $11,000 |
| Jan. 17 | 1,000 @ $6.00 = $6,000 | | 2,000 @ $5.50<br>1,000 @ $6.00 } $17,000 |
| Mar. 22 | 3,000 @ $7.00 = $21,000 | | 2,000 @ $5.50<br>1,000 @ $6.00 } $38,000<br>3,000 @ $7.00 |
| Apr. 15 | | 1,500 @ $7.00 = $10,500 | 2,000 @ $5.50<br>1,000 @ $6.00 } $27,500<br>1,500 @ $7.00 |
| Oct. 15 | 3,000 @ $7.50 = $22,500 | | 2,000 @ $5.50<br>1,000 @ $6.00 } $50,000<br>1,500 @ $7.00<br>3,000 @ $7.50 |
| Nov. 20 | | 3,000 @ $7.50 = $22,500 | 2,000 @ $5.50<br>1,000 @ $6.00 } $27,500<br>1,500 @ $7.00 |
| | Total cost of goods sold | = $44,000 | |

Notice that the total cost of goods available for sale is allocated $44,000 to cost of goods sold by perpetual LIFO and $27,500 to ending inventory (the balance after the last transaction), which is different from the periodic LIFO result of $46,500 and $25,000.

Perpetual LIFO generally
results in cost of goods
sold and inventory
amounts that are
different from those
obtained by applying
periodic LIFO.

Unlike FIFO, applying LIFO in a perpetual inventory system will generally result in an ending inventory and cost of goods sold different from the allocation arrived at when applying LIFO in a periodic system. Periodic LIFO applies the last-in, first-out concept to total sales and total purchases only at the conclusion of the reporting period. Perpetual LIFO applies the same concept, but several times during the period—every time a sale is made.

For example, when 2,000 units are sold on January 10, perpetual LIFO costs those units at $5.50, the beginning inventory unit cost, because those were the last units acquired before the sale. Periodic LIFO, by contrast, would be applied at year-end. By the end of the year, enough purchases have been made that the beginning inventory would be assumed to remain intact, and the January 10 units sold would be costed at a price from the most recent acquisition before the end of the year.

## Comparison of Cost Flow Methods

Comparison of cost flow methods

The three cost flow methods are compared below assuming a periodic inventory system.

|  | Average | FIFO | LIFO |
|---|---|---|---|
| Cost of goods sold | $42,250 | $38,500 | $46,500 |
| Ending inventory | 29,250 | 33,000 | 25,000 |
| Total | $71,500 | $71,500 | $71,500 |

Notice that the average cost method in this example produces amounts that fall in between the FIFO and LIFO amounts for both cost of goods sold and ending inventory. This will usually be the case. Whether it will be FIFO or LIFO that produces the highest or lowest value of cost of goods sold and ending inventory depends on the pattern of the actual unit cost changes during the period.

During periods of generally rising costs, as in our example, FIFO results in a lower cost of goods sold than LIFO because the lower costs of the earliest purchases are assumed sold. LIFO cost of goods sold will include the more recent higher cost purchases. On the other hand, FIFO ending inventory includes the most recent higher cost purchases which results in a higher ending inventory than LIFO. LIFO ending inventory includes the lower costs of the earliest purchases. Conversely, if costs are declining, then FIFO will result in a higher cost of goods sold and lower ending inventory than LIFO.[7]

If unit costs are
increasing, LIFO will
result in a higher cost
of goods sold and lower
ending inventory than
FIFO.

Each of the three methods is permissible according to generally accepted accounting principles and frequently is used. Also, a company need not use the same method for its entire inventory. For example, **International Paper Company** uses LIFO for its raw materials and finished pulp and paper products, and both the FIFO and average cost methods for other inventories. Because of the importance of inventories and the possible differential effects of different methods on the financial statements, a company must identify in a disclosure note the method(s) it uses. The chapter's opening case included an example of this disclosure for **ConocoPhillips**, and you will encounter additional examples later in the chapter.

**FINANCIAL
Reporting Case**

Q1, p. 421

A company must disclose
the inventory method(s)
it uses.

Illustration 8–8 shows the results of a survey of inventory methods used by 500 large public companies in 2010.[8] FIFO is the most popular method, but both LIFO and average

**Illustration 8–8**

Inventory Cost Flow
Methods Used in Practice

| | 2010 | |
|---|---|---|
| | **# of Companies** | **% of Companies** |
| FIFO | 316 | 41% |
| LIFO | 166 | 22 |
| Average | 113 | 15 |
| Other* and not disclosed | 165 | 22 |
| Total | 760 | 100% |

*"Other" includes the specific identification method and miscellaneous less popular methods.

---

[7]The differences between the various methods also hold when a perpetual inventory system is used.
[8]*Accounting Trends and Techniques—2011* (New York, New York: AICPA, 2011), p. 174.

cost are used by many companies. Notice that the column total for the number of companies is greater than 500, indicating that many companies included in this sample do use multiple methods.

# International Financial Reporting Standards

**Inventory Cost Flow Assumptions.**    *IAS No. 2*[9] does not permit the use of LIFO. Because of this restriction, many U.S. multinational companies use LIFO only for their domestic inventories and FIFO or average cost for their foreign subsidiaries. A disclosure note included in a recent annual report of **General Mills** provides an example:

● LO8–9

Real World Financials

### Inventories (in part)

All inventories in the United States other than grain are valued at the lower of cost, using the last-in, first-out (LIFO) method, or market. . . . Inventories outside of the United States are valued at the lower of cost, using the first-in, first-out (FIFO) method, or market.

This difference could prove to be a significant impediment to U.S. convergence to international standards. Unless the U.S. Congress repeals the LIFO conformity rule (see page 438), convergence would cause many corporations to lose a valuable tax shelter, the use of LIFO for tax purposes. If these companies were immediately taxed on the difference between LIFO inventories and inventories valued using another method, it would cost companies billions of dollars. Some industries would be particularly hard hit. Most oil companies and auto manufacturers, for instance, use LIFO. The government estimates that the repeal of the LIFO method would increase federal tax revenues by $59 billion over a ten-year period.[10] The companies affected most certainly will lobby heavily to retain the use of LIFO for tax purposes.

## Decision Makers' Perspective—Factors Influencing Method Choice

What factors motivate companies to choose one method over another? What factors have caused the increased popularity of LIFO? Choosing among alternative accounting methods is a complex issue. Often such choices are not made in isolation but in such a way that the combination of inventory cost flow assumptions, depreciation methods, pension assumptions, and other choices meet a particular objective. Also, many believe managers sometimes make these choices to maximize their own personal benefits rather than those of the company or its external constituents. But regardless of the motive, the impact on reported numbers is an important consideration in each choice of method. The inventory choice determines (a) how closely reported costs reflect the actual physical flow of inventory, (b) the timing of reported income and income tax expense, and (c) how well costs are matched with associated revenues.

● LO8–5

**PHYSICAL FLOW.**    If a company wanted to choose a method that most closely approximates specific identification, then the actual physical flow of inventory in and out of the company would motivate the choice of method.

For example, companies often attempt to sell the oldest goods in inventory first for some of their products. This certainly is the case with perishable goods such as many grocery items. The FIFO method best mirrors the physical flow in these situations. The average cost method might be used for liquids such as chemicals where items sold are taken from a mixture of inventory acquired at different times and different prices. There are very few inventories that actually flow in a LIFO manner. It is important for you to understand that there is no requirement that companies choose an inventory method that approximates actual

*A company is not required to choose an inventory method that approximates actual physical flow.*

---

[9]"Inventories," *International Accounting Standard No. 2* (IASCF), as amended effective January 1, 2011.
[10]Marie Leone, "Sucking the LIFO Out of Inventory," *CFO Magazine*, July 15, 2010.

physical flow and few companies make the choice on this basis. In fact, as we discuss next, the effect of inventory method on income and income taxes is the primary motivation that influences method choice.

### INCOME TAXES AND NET INCOME.
If the unit cost of inventory changes during a period, the inventory method chosen can have a significant effect on the amount of income reported by the company to external parties and also on the amount of income taxes paid to the Internal Revenue Service (IRS) and state and local taxing authorities. Over the entire life of a company, cost of goods sold for all years will equal actual costs of items sold regardless of the inventory method used. However, as we have discussed, different inventory methods can produce significantly different results in each particular year.

When prices rise and inventory quantities are not decreasing, LIFO produces a higher cost of goods sold and therefore lower net income than the other methods. The company's income tax returns will report a lower taxable income using LIFO and lower taxes will be paid currently. Taxes are not reduced permanently, only deferred. The reduced amount will be paid to the taxing authorities when either the unit cost of inventory or the quantity of inventory subsequently declines. However, we know from our discussion of the time value of money that it is advantageous to save a dollar today even if it must be paid back in the future. In the past, high inflation (increasing prices) periods motivated many companies to switch to LIFO in order to gain this tax benefit.

A corporation's taxable income comprises revenues, expenses (including cost of goods sold), gains, and losses measured according to the regulations of the appropriate taxing authority. Income before tax as reported in the income statement does not always equal taxable income. In some cases, differences are caused by the use of different measurement methods.[11] However, IRS regulations, which determine federal taxable income, require that if a company uses LIFO to measure taxable income, the company also must use LIFO for external financial reporting. This is known as the **LIFO conformity rule** with respect to inventory methods.

Because of the LIFO conformity rule, to obtain the tax advantages of using LIFO in periods of rising prices, lower net income is reported to shareholders, creditors, and other external parties. The income tax motivation for using LIFO may be offset by a desire to report higher net income. Reported net income could have an effect on a corporation's share price,[12] on bonuses paid to management, or on debt agreements with lenders. For example, research has indicated that the managers of companies with bonus plans tied to income measures are more likely to choose accounting methods that maximize their bonuses (often those that increase net income).[13]

The LIFO conformity rule permits LIFO users to report non-LIFO inventory valuations in a supplemental disclosure note, but not on the face of the income statement. For example, Illustration 8–9 shows the note provided in a recent annual report of **Rite Aid Corporation**, a large drugstore chain, disclosing its use of LIFO to value its inventories.

● LO8–6   ### LIFO RESERVES.
Many companies use LIFO for external reporting and income tax purposes but maintain their internal records using FIFO or average cost. There is a variety of reasons, including: (1) the high recordkeeping costs for LIFO, (2) contractual agreements such as bonus or profit sharing plans that calculate net income with a method other than LIFO, and (3) using FIFO or average cost information for pricing decisions.

---

[11]For example, a corporation can take advantage of incentives offered by Congress by deducting more depreciation in the early years of an asset's life in its federal income tax return than it reports in its income statement.

[12]The concept of capital market efficiency has been debated for many years. In an efficient capital market, the market is not fooled by differences in accounting method choice that do not translate into real cash flow differences. The only apparent cash flow difference caused by different inventory methods is the amount of income taxes paid currently. In an efficient market, we would expect the share price of a company that switched its method to LIFO and saved tax dollars to increase even though it reported lower net income than if LIFO had not been adopted. Research on this issue is mixed. For example, see William E. Ricks, "Market's Response to the 1974 LIFO Adoptions," *Journal of Accounting Research* Autumn 1982; and Robert Moren Brown, "Short-Range Market Reaction to Changes to LIFO Using Preliminary Earnings Announcement Dates," *Journal of Accounting Research* Spring 1980.

[13]For example, see P. M. Healy, "The Effect of Bonus Schemes on Accounting Decisions," *Journal of Accounting and Economics* April 1985; and D. Dhaliwal, G. Salamon, and E. Smith, "The Effect of Owner Versus Management Control on the Choice of Accounting Methods," *Journal of Accounting and Economics* July 1982.

---

*Sidebar notes:*

Many companies choose LIFO in order to reduce income taxes in periods when prices are rising.

If a company uses LIFO to measure its taxable income, IRS regulations require that LIFO also be used to measure income reported to investors and creditors (the *LIFO conformity rule*).

**FINANCIAL Reporting Case**

Q2, p. 421

**Illustration 8–9**

Inventories Disclosure—
Rite Aid Corporation

Real World Financials

**Summary of Significant Accounting Policies (in part)**
**Inventories**
Inventories are stated at the lower of cost or market. The Company uses the Last-in, first-out (LIFO) method of accounting for substantially all of its inventories. At February 26, 2011 and February 27, 2010, inventories were $875 million and $831 million, respectively, lower than the amounts that would have been reported using the first-in, first-out (FIFO) method.

Generally, the conversion to LIFO from the internal records occurs at the end of the reporting period without actually entering the adjustment into the company's records. Some companies, though, enter the conversion adjustment—the difference between the internal method and LIFO—directly into the records as a "contra account" to inventory. This contra account is called either the LIFO reserve or the LIFO allowance.

For illustration, let's say that the Doubletree Corporation began 2013 with a balance of $475,000 in its LIFO reserve account, the difference between inventory valued internally using FIFO and inventory valued using LIFO. At the end of 2013, assume this difference increased to $535,000. The entry to record the increase in the reserve is:

| | | |
|---|---|---|
| Cost of goods sold ($535,000 – 475,000) ........................................... | 60,000 | |
| LIFO reserve ................................................................. | | 60,000 |

If the difference between inventory valued internally using FIFO and inventory valued using LIFO had decreased, this entry would be made in reverse. Companies such as Doubletree often use a disclosure note to show the difference between ending inventory valued using the internal method and the LIFO inventory amount reported in the balance sheet. As an example, **Casey's General Stores, Inc.**, operates convenience stores in 11 Midwest states. Illustration 8–10 shows the disclosure note from a recent annual report that indicated the composition of the company's inventories.

**Illustration 8–10**

Inventories Disclosure—
Casey's General
Stores, Inc.

Real World Financials

**Note 5: Inventories (in part)**
Inventories, which consist of merchandise and gasoline, are stated at the lower of cost or market. Cost is determined using the first-in, first-out (FIFO) method for gasoline and the last-in, first-out (LIFO) method for merchandise. Below is a summary of the inventory values at April 30, 2011, and 2010:

| ($ in thousands) | 2011 | 2010 |
|---|---|---|
| Gasoline | $ 81,964 | $ 54,439 |
| Merchandise | 113,934 | 102,344 |
| Merchandise LIFO reserve | (36,698) | (31,832) |
| Total inventory | $159,200 | $124,951 |

**LIFO LIQUIDATIONS.**    Earlier in the text, we demonstrated the importance of matching revenues and expenses in creating an income statement that is useful in predicting future cash flows. If prices change during a period, then LIFO generally will provide a better match of revenues and expenses. Sales reflect the most recent selling prices, and cost of goods sold includes the costs of the most recent purchases.

For the same reason, though, inventory costs in the balance sheet with LIFO generally are out of date because they reflect old purchase transactions. It is not uncommon for a company's LIFO inventory balance to be based on unit costs actually incurred several years earlier.

Proponents of LIFO argue that it results in a better match of revenues and expenses.

This distortion sometimes carries over to the income statement as well. When inventory quantities decline during a period, then these out-of-date inventory layers are liquidated and cost of goods sold will partially match noncurrent costs with current selling prices. If costs have been increasing (decreasing), LIFO liquidations produce higher (lower) net income than would have resulted if the liquidated inventory were included in cost of goods sold at current costs. The paper profits (losses) caused by including out of date, low (high) costs in cost of goods sold is referred to as the effect on income of liquidations of LIFO inventory.

To illustrate this problem, consider the example in Illustration 8–11.

**Illustration 8–11**
LIFO Liquidation

National Distributors, Inc. uses the LIFO inventory method. The company began 2013 with inventory of 10,000 units that cost $20 per unit. During 2013, 30,000 units were purchased for $25 each and 35,000 units were sold.

National's LIFO cost of goods sold for 2013 consists of:

| | |
|---|---|
| 30,000 units @ $25 per unit = | $750,000 |
| 5,000 units @ $20 per unit = | $100,000 |
| 35,000 | $850,000 |

Included in cost of goods sold are 5,000 units from beginning inventory that have now been liquidated. If the company had purchased at least 35,000 units, no liquidation would have occurred. Then cost of goods sold would have been $875,000 (35,000 units × $25 per unit) instead of $850,000. The difference between these two cost of goods sold figures is $25,000 ($875,000 – 850,000). This is the before tax income effect of the LIFO liquidation. Assuming a 40% income tax rate, the net effect of the liquidation is to increase net income by $15,000 [$25,000 × (1 – .40)]. The lower the costs of the units liquidated, the more severe the effect on income.

A company must disclose in a note any material effect of LIFO liquidation on net income. For example, Illustration 8–12 shows the disclosure note included with recent financial statements of SuperValue Inc., one of the largest grocery chains in the United States.

**Illustration 8–12**
LIFO Liquidation Disclosure—SuperValue Inc.

Real World Financials

**Summary of Significant Accounting Policies (in part)**
**Inventories**
During fiscal 2011, 2010, and 2009, inventory quantities in certain LIFO layers were reduced. These reductions resulted in a liquidation of LIFO inventory quantities carried at lower costs prevailing in prior years as compared with the cost of fiscal 2011, 2010, and 2009 purchases. As a result, cost of sales decreased by $11, $22, and $10 million in fiscal 2011, 2010, and 2009, respectively.

In our illustration, National Distributors, Inc. would disclose that LIFO liquidations increased income by $15,000 in 2013, assuming that this effect on income is considered material.

We've discussed several factors that influence companies in their choice of inventory method. A company could be influenced by the actual physical flow of its inventory, by the effect of inventory method on reported net income and the amount of income taxes payable currently, or by a desire to provide a better match of expenses with revenues. You've seen that the direction of the change in unit costs determines the effect of using different methods on net income and income taxes. While the United States has experienced persistent inflation for many years (increases in the general price-level), the prices of many goods and services have experienced periods of declining prices (for example, personal computers). ●

# Concept Review Exercise

**INVENTORY COST FLOW METHODS**

The Rogers Company began 2013 with an inventory of 10 million units of its principal product. These units cost $5 each. The following inventory transactions occurred during the first six months of 2013.

| Date | Transaction |
|------|-------------|
| Feb. 15 | Purchased, on account, 5 million units at a cost of $6.50 each. |
| Mar. 20 | Sold, on account, 8 million units at a selling price of $12 each. |
| Apr. 30 | Purchased, on account, 5 million units at a cost of $7 each. |

On June 30, 2013, 12 million units were on hand.

**Required:**

1. Prepare journal entries to record the above transactions. The company uses a periodic inventory system.
2. Prepare the required adjusting entry on June 30, 2013, applying each of the following inventory methods:
   a. Average
   b. FIFO
   c. LIFO
3. Repeat requirement 1 assuming that the company uses a perpetual inventory system.

**Solution:**

1. Prepare journal entries to record the above transactions. The company uses a periodic inventory system.

| **February 15** | ($ in millions) | |
|-----------------|-----------------|---|
| Purchases (5 million × $6.50) | 32.5 | |
|    Accounts payable | | 32.5 |
| *To record the purchase of inventory.* | | |
| **March 20** | | |
| Accounts receivable (8 million × $12) | 96 | |
|    Sales revenue | | 96 |
| *To record sales on account.* | | |
| **No entry is recorded for the cost of inventory sold.** | | |
| **April 30** | | |
| Purchases (5 million × $7) | 35 | |
|    Accounts payable | | 35 |
| *To record the purchase of inventory.* | | |

2. Prepare the required adjusting entry on June 30, 2013, applying each method.

| | | ($ in millions) | | | | |
|------|---------------|---------|---|------|---|------|
| **Date** | **Journal entry** | **Average** | | **FIFO** | | **LIFO** |
| June 30 | Cost of goods sold (determined below) | 47.0 | | 40.0 | | 54.5 |
| | Inventory (ending—determined below) | 70.5 | | 77.5 | | 63.0 |
| |    Inventory (beginning—[10 million @ $5]) | | 50.0 | | 50.0 | 50.0 |
| |    Purchases ($32.5 million + 35 million) | | 67.5 | | 67.5 | 67.5 |

Calculation of ending inventory and cost of goods sold:

a. Average:

| | ($ in millions) |
|------|------|
| Beginning inventory (10 million units @ $5.00) | $ 50.0 |
| Plus: Purchases (10 million units @ various prices) | 67.5 |
| Cost of goods available for sale (20 million units) | 117.5 |
| Less: Ending inventory (determined below) | (70.5) |
| Cost of goods sold | $ 47.0 |

Cost of ending inventory:

$$\text{Weighted-average unit cost} = \frac{\$117.5}{20 \text{ million units}} = \$5.875$$

$$12 \text{ million units} \times \$5.875 = \$70.5 \text{ million}$$

b. FIFO:

| | |
|---|---:|
| Cost of goods available for sale (20 million units) | $117.5 |
| Less: Ending inventory (determined below) | (77.5) |
| Cost of goods sold | $ 40.0 |

Cost of ending inventory:

| Date of Purchase | Units | Unit Cost | Total Cost |
|---|---|---|---|
| Beg. inv. | 2 million | $5.00 | 10.0 |
| Feb. 15 | 5 million | 6.50 | 32.5 |
| April 30 | 5 million | 7.00 | 35.0 |
| Total | 12 million | | $77.5 |

c. LIFO:

| | |
|---|---:|
| Cost of goods available for sale (20 million units) | $117.5 |
| Less: Ending inventory (determined below) | (63.0) |
| Cost of goods sold | $ 54.5 |

Cost of ending inventory:

| Date of Purchase | Units | Unit Cost | Total Cost |
|---|---|---|---|
| Beg. inv. | 10 million | $5.00 | $50.0 |
| Feb. 15 | 2 million | 6.50 | 13.0 |
| Total | 12 million | | $63.0 |

3. Repeat requirement 1 assuming that the company uses a perpetual inventory system.

| **February 15** | ($ in millions) | |
|---|---|---|
| Inventory (5 million × $6.50) ........................................................... | 32.5 | |
| Accounts payable ........................................................................... | | 32.5 |
| *To record the purchase of inventory.* | | |
| **April 30** | | |
| Inventory (5 million × $7.00) ........................................................... | 35.0 | |
| Accounts payable ........................................................................... | | 35.0 |
| *To record the purchase of inventory.* | | |

| Journal Entries—March 20 | ($ in millions) | | | | | |
|---|---|---|---|---|---|---|
| | **Average** | | **FIFO** | | **LIFO** | |
| Accounts receivable (8 million × $12) | 96.0 | | 96.0 | | 96.0 | |
| Sales revenue | | 96.0 | | 96.0 | | 96.0 |
| *To record sales on account.* | | | | | | |
| Cost of goods sold (determined below) | 44.0 | | 40.0 | | 47.5 | |
| Inventory | | 44.0 | | 40.0 | | 47.5 |
| *To record cost of goods sold.* | | | | | | |

Calculation of cost of goods sold:

a. Average:

Cost of goods sold:

($, except unit costs, in millions)

| Date | Purchased | Sold | Balance |
|---|---|---|---|
| Beg. inv. | 10 million @ $5.00 = $50.0 | | 10 million @ $5.00 = $50.0 |
| Feb. 15 | 5 million @ $6.50 = $32.5 | | $50 + $32.5 = $82.5 |
| | $\dfrac{\$82.5}{15 \text{ million units}} = \$5.50/\text{unit}$ | | |
| Mar. 20 | | 8 million @ $5.50 = $44.0 | |

b. FIFO:

Cost of goods sold:

| Units Sold | Cost of Units Sold | Total Cost |
|---|---|---|
| 8 million (from Beg. inv.) | $5.00 | $40.0 |

c. LIFO:

Cost of goods sold:

| Units Sold | Cost of Units Sold | Total Cost |
|---|---|---|
| 5 million (from Feb. 15 purchase) | $6.50 | $32.5 |
| 3 million (from Beg. inv.) | 5.00 | 15.0 |
| 8 million | | $47.5 |

# Decision Makers' Perspective

**INVENTORY MANAGEMENT.**   Managers closely monitor inventory levels to (1) ensure that the inventories needed to sustain operations are available, and (2) hold the cost of ordering and carrying inventories to the lowest possible level.[14] Unfortunately, these objectives often conflict with one another. Companies must maintain sufficient quantities of inventory to meet customer demand. However, maintaining inventory is costly. Fortunately, a variety of tools are available, including computerized inventory control systems and the outsourcing of inventory component production, to help balance these conflicting objectives.[15]

A **just-in-time (JIT) system** is another valuable technique that many companies have adopted to assist them with inventory management. JIT is a system used by a manufacturer to coordinate production with suppliers so that raw materials or components arrive just as they are needed in the production process. Have you ever ordered a personal computer from **Dell Inc.**? If so, the PC you received was not manufactured until you placed your order, and many of the components used in the production of your PC were not even acquired by Dell until then as well. This system enables Dell to maintain relatively low inventory balances. At the same time, the company's efficient production techniques, along with its excellent relationships with suppliers ensuring prompt delivery of components, enables Dell to quickly meet customer demand. In its January 28, 2011, fiscal year-end financial statements, Dell reported an inventory balance of $1.3 billion. With this relatively low investment in inventory, Dell was able to generate $50 billion in revenue from the sale of products.

A company should maintain sufficient inventory quantities to meet customer demand while at the same time minimizing inventory ordering and carrying costs.

---

[14]The cost of carrying inventory includes the possible loss from the write-down of obsolete inventory. We discuss inventory write-downs in Chapter 9. There are analytical models available to determine the appropriate amount of inventory a company should maintain. A discussion of these models is beyond the scope of this text.

[15]Eugene Brigham and Joel Houston, *Fundamentals of Financial Management,* 12th ed. (Florence, Kentucky: South-Western, 2010).

To appreciate the advantage this provides, compare these numbers with **Hewlett Packard (HP)**, a company that includes PCs among its wide variety of technology products. For its fiscal year ended October 31, 2010, HP reported product revenue of $85 billion. However, to achieve this level of sales, HP's investment in inventory was over $6 billion.

It is important for a financial analyst to evaluate a company's effectiveness in managing its inventory. As we discussed in Chapter 5, one key to profitability is how well a company utilizes its assets. This evaluation is influenced by the company's inventory method choice. The choice of inventory method is an important and complex management decision. The many factors affecting this decision were discussed in a previous section. The inventory method also affects the analysis of a company's liquidity and profitability by investors, creditors, and financial analysts. Analysts must make adjustments when evaluating companies that use different inventory methods. During periods of rising prices, we would expect a company using FIFO to report higher income than a LIFO or average cost company. If one of the companies being analyzed uses LIFO, precise adjustments can often be made using the supplemental disclosures provided by many LIFO companies. Recall that the LIFO conformity rule was liberalized to permit LIFO users to report in a note the effect of using a method other than LIFO for inventory valuation.

For example, the disclosure note shown in Illustration 8–9 on page 439 reveals that the **Rite Aid Corporation** uses the LIFO method. Additional information from the company's recent financial statements is provided below.

**FINANCIAL Reporting Case**

Q3, p. 421

| ($ in millions) | For the Year Ended | |
|---|---|---|
| | **February 26, 2011** | **February 27, 2010** |
| **Balance sheets:** | | |
| Inventories | $ 3,158 | $ 3,239 |
| **Income statements:** | | |
| Net sales | 25,215 | 25,669 |
| Cost of goods sold | 18,522 | 18,845 |

Supplemental LIFO disclosures can be used to convert LIFO inventories and cost of goods sold amounts.

Suppose an analyst wanted to compare Rite Aid with a competitor that used all FIFO, or that used both LIFO and FIFO. To compare apples with apples, we can convert Rite Aid's inventories and cost of goods sold (and the competitor's if necessary) to a 100% FIFO basis before comparing the two companies by using the information provided in Illustration 8–9. Inventories recorded at LIFO were lower by $875 million at February 26, 2011, and $831 million at February 27, 2010, than if they had been valued at FIFO:

| | **2011** | **2010** |
|---|---|---|
| Inventories (as reported) | $3,158 | $3,239 |
| Add: conversion to FIFO | 875 | 831 |
| Inventories (100% FIFO) | $4,033 | $4,070 |

If Rite Aid had used FIFO instead of LIFO, beginning inventory would have been $831 million higher, and ending inventory would have been higher by $875 million. As a result, cost of goods sold for the 2011 fiscal year would have been $44 million lower. This is because an increase in beginning inventory causes an *increase* in cost of goods sold, but an increase in ending inventory causes a *decrease* in cost of goods sold. Purchases for 2011 are the same regardless of the inventory valuation method used. Cost of goods sold, then, would have been $18,478 million ($18,522 – 44) if FIFO had been used for all inventories.

We can now use the 100% FIFO amounts to compare the two companies. Since cost of goods sold is lower by $44 million, income taxes and net income require similar adjustments before calculating a profitability ratio. Also, the converted inventory amounts can be used to compute liquidity ratios.

● LO8–7　One useful profitability indicator that involves cost of goods sold is **gross profit** or **gross margin**, which highlights the important relationship between net sales revenue and cost of goods sold. The **gross profit ratio** is computed as follows:

$$\text{Gross profit ratio} = \frac{\text{Gross profit}}{\text{Net sales}}$$

The higher the ratio, the higher is the markup a company is able to achieve on its products. For example, a product that costs $100 and sells for $150 provides a gross profit of $50 ($150 – 100) and the gross profit ratio is 33% ($50 ÷ $150). If that same product can be sold for $200, the gross profit increases to $100 and the gross profit ratio increases to 50% ($100 ÷ $200), so more dollars are available to cover expenses other than cost of goods sold.

The 2011 gross profit ($ in millions), for Rite Aid, using the 100% FIFO amounts, is $6,737 ($25,215 – 18,478), and the gross profit ratio is 26.7% ($6,737 ÷ $25,215). The same ratio for the drugstore industry is 17%, indicating that Rite Aid is able to sell its products at significantly higher markups than the average for its competitors. Rite Aid's percentage of each sales dollar available to cover remaining expenses and to provide a profit is over 50% higher than the industry average.

Monitoring this ratio over time can provide valuable insights. For example, a declining ratio might indicate that the company is unable to offset rising costs with corresponding increases in selling price, or perhaps that sales prices are declining without a commensurate reduction in costs. In either case, the decline in the ratio has important implications for future profitability.

In Chapter 5 we were introduced to an important ratio, the **inventory turnover ratio**, which is designed to evaluate a company's effectiveness in managing its investment in inventory. The ratio shows the number of times the average inventory balance is sold during a reporting period. The more frequently a business is able to sell or turn over its inventory, the lower its investment in inventory must be for a given level of sales. Usually, the higher the ratio the more profitable a company will be. Monitoring the inventory turnover ratio over time can highlight potential problems. A declining ratio generally is unfavorable and could be caused by the presence of obsolete or slow-moving products, or poor marketing and sales efforts.

Recall that the ratio is computed as follows:

$$\text{Inventory turnover ratio} = \frac{\text{Cost of goods sold}}{\text{Average inventory}}$$

If the analysis is prepared for the fiscal year reporting period, we can divide the inventory turnover ratio into 365 days to calculate the **average days in inventory**, which indicates the average number of days it normally takes the company to sell its inventory.

For Rite Aid, the inventory turnover ratio for the 2011 fiscal year, using the 100% FIFO amounts, is 4.56 ($18,478 ÷ [($4,033 + 4,070) ÷ 2]) and the average days in inventory is 80 days (365 ÷ 4.56). This compares to an industry average of 97 days. Rite Aid's products command a higher markup (higher gross profit ratio) and also turn over faster (lower average days in inventory) than the industry average.

Inventory increases that outrun increases in cost of goods sold might indicate difficulties in generating sales. These inventory buildups may also indicate that a company has obsolete or slow-moving inventory. This proposition was tested in an important academic research study. Professors Lev and Thiagarajan empirically demonstrated the importance of a set of 12 fundamental variables in valuing companies' common stock. The set of variables included inventory (change in inventory minus change in sales). The inventory variable was found to be a significant indicator of returns on investments in common stock, particularly during high and medium inflation years.[16]

**EARNINGS QUALITY.**    Changes in the ratios we discussed above often provide information about the quality of a company's current period earnings. For example, a slowing turnover ratio combined with higher than normal inventory levels may indicate the potential for decreased production, obsolete inventory, or a need to decrease prices to sell inventory (which will then decrease gross profit ratios and net income).

The *gross profit ratio* indicates the percentage of each sales dollar available to cover expenses other than cost of goods sold and to provide a profit.

---

[16]B. Lev and S. R. Thiagarajan, "Fundamental Information Analysis," *Journal of Accounting Research* (Autumn 1993). The main conclusion of the study was that fundamental variables, not just earnings, are useful in firm valuation, particularly when examined in the context of macroeconomic conditions such as inflation.

The choice of which inventory method to use also affects earnings quality, particularly in times of rapidly changing prices. Earlier in this chapter we discussed the effect of a LIFO liquidation on company profits. A LIFO liquidation profit (or loss) reduces the quality of current period earnings. Fortunately for analysts, companies must disclose these profits or losses, if material. In addition, LIFO cost of goods sold determined using a periodic inventory system is more susceptible to manipulation than is FIFO. Year-end purchases can have a dramatic effect on LIFO cost of goods sold in rapid cost-change environments. Recall again our discussion in Chapter 4 concerning earnings quality. Many believe that manipulating income reduces earnings quality because it can mask permanent earnings. Inventory write-downs and changes in inventory method are two additional inventory-related techniques a company could use to manipulate earnings. We discuss these issues in the next chapter. ●

## PART B

**METHODS OF SIMPLIFYING LIFO**

The LIFO method described and illustrated to this point is called *unit LIFO*[17] because the last-in, first-out concept is applied to individual units of inventory. One problem with unit LIFO is that it can be very costly to implement. It requires records of each unit of inventory. The costs of maintaining these records can be significant, particularly when a company has numerous individual units of inventory and when unit costs change often during a period.

> The recordkeeping costs of unit LIFO can be significant.

In the previous section, a second disadvantage of unit LIFO was identified—the possibility that LIFO layers will be liquidated if the quantity of a particular inventory unit declines below its beginning balance. Even if a company's total inventory quantity is stable or increasing, if the quantity of any particular inventory unit declines, unit LIFO will liquidate all or a portion of a LIFO layer of inventory. When inventory quantity declines in a period of rising costs, noncurrent lower costs will be included in cost of goods sold and matched with current selling prices, resulting in LIFO liquidation profit.

> Another disadvantage of unit LIFO is the possibility of LIFO liquidation.

This part of the chapter discusses techniques that can be used to significantly reduce the recordkeeping costs of LIFO and to minimize the probability of LIFO inventory layers being liquidated. Specifically, we discuss the use of inventory pools and the dollar-value LIFO method.

## LIFO Inventory Pools

The objectives of using **LIFO inventory pools** are to simplify recordkeeping by grouping inventory units into pools based on physical similarities of the individual units and to reduce the risk of LIFO layer liquidation. For example, a glass company might group its various grades of window glass into a single window pool. Other pools might be auto glass and sliding door glass. A lumber company might pool its inventory into hardwood, framing lumber, paneling, and so on.

> A pool consists of inventory units grouped according to natural physical similarities.

This allows a company to account for a few inventory pools rather than every specific type of inventory separately. Within pools, all purchases during a period are considered to have been made at the same time and at the same cost. Individual unit costs are converted to an average cost for the pool. If the quantity of ending inventory for the pool increases, then ending inventory will consist of the beginning inventory plus a single layer added during the period at the average acquisition cost for that pool.

> The average cost for all of the pool purchases during the period is applied to the current year's LIFO layer.

Here's an example. Let's say Diamond Lumber Company has a rough-cut lumber inventory pool that includes three types: oak, pine, and maple. The beginning inventory consisted of the following:

---

[17]Unit LIFO sometimes is called *specific goods LIFO*.

|  | Quantity (Board Feet) | Cost (Per Foot) | Total Cost |
|---|---|---|---|
| Oak | 16,000 | $2.20 | $35,200 |
| Pine | 10,000 | 3.00 | 30,000 |
| Maple | 14,000 | 2.40 | 33,600 |
|  | 40,000 |  | $98,800 |

The average cost for this pool is $2.47 per board foot ($98,800 ÷ 40,000 board feet). Now assume that during the next reporting period Diamond purchased 50,000 board feet of lumber as follows:

|  | Quantity (Board Feet) | Cost (Per Foot) | Total Cost |
|---|---|---|---|
| Oak | 20,000 | $2.25 | $ 45,000 |
| Pine | 14,000 | 3.00 | 42,000 |
| Maple | 16,000 | 2.50 | 40,000 |
|  | 50,000 |  | $127,000 |

The average cost for this pool is $2.54 per board foot ($127,000 ÷ 50,000 board feet). Assuming that Diamond sold 46,000 board feet during this period, the quantity of inventory for the pool increased by 4,000 board feet (50,000 purchased less 46,000 sold). The ending inventory will include the beginning inventory and a LIFO layer consisting of the 4,000 board feet increase. We would add this LIFO layer at the average cost of purchases made during the period, $2.54. The ending inventory of $108,960 now consists of two layers:

|  | Quantity (Board Feet) | Cost (Per Foot) | Total Cost |
|---|---|---|---|
| Beginning inventory | 40,000 | $2.47 | $ 98,800 |
| LIFO layer added | 4,000 | 2.54 | 10,160 |
| Ending inventory | 44,000 |  | $108,960 |

Despite the advantages of LIFO inventory pools, it's easy to imagine situations in which its benefits are not achieved. Suppose, for instance, that a company discontinues a certain product included in one of its pools. The old costs that existed in prior layers of inventory would be recognized as cost of goods sold and produce LIFO liquidation profit. Even if the product is replaced with another product, the replacement may not be similar enough to be included in the same inventory pool. In fact, the process itself of having to periodically redefine pools as changes in product mix occur can be expensive and time consuming. Next we discuss the dollar-value LIFO approach which helps overcome these problems.

# Dollar-Value LIFO

Dollar-value LIFO (DVL) gained such widespread popularity during the 1960s and 1970s that many LIFO applications are now based on this approach. DVL extends the concept of inventory pools by allowing a company to combine a large variety of goods into one pool. Physical units are not used in calculating ending inventory. Instead, the inventory is viewed as a quantity of value instead of a physical quantity of goods. Instead of layers of units from different purchases, the DVL inventory pool is viewed as comprising layers of dollar value from different years.

● LO8–8

Because the physical characteristics of inventory items are not relevant to DVL, an inventory pool is identified in terms of economic similarity rather than physical similarity. Specifically, a pool should consist of those goods that are likely to be subject to the same cost change pressures.

A DVL pool is made up of items that are likely to face the same cost change pressures.

## Advantages of DVL

The DVL method has important advantages. First, it simplifies the recordkeeping procedures compared to unit LIFO because no information is needed about unit flows. Second, it minimizes the probability of the liquidation of LIFO inventory layers, even more so than the use of pools alone, through the aggregation of many types of inventory into larger pools. In addition, the method can be used by firms that do not replace units sold with new units of the same kind. For firms whose products are subject to annual model changes, for example, the items in one year's inventory are not the same as those of the prior year. Under pooled LIFO, however, the new replacement items must be substantially identical to previous models to be included in the same pool. Under DVL, no distinction is drawn between the old and new merchandise on the basis of their physical characteristics, so a much broader range of goods can be included in the pool. That is, the acquisition of the new items is viewed as replacement of the dollar value of the old items. Because the old layers are maintained, this approach retains the benefits of LIFO by matching the most recent acquisition cost of goods with sales measured at current selling prices.

## Cost Indexes

In either the unit LIFO approach or the pooled LIFO approach, we determine whether a new LIFO layer was added by comparing the ending quantity with the beginning quantity. The focus is on *units* of inventory. Under DVL, we determine whether a new LIFO layer was added by comparing the ending dollar amount with the beginning dollar amount. The focus is on inventory *value,* not units. However, if the price level has changed, we need a way to determine whether an observed increase is a real increase (an increase in the quantity of inventory) or one caused by an increase in prices. So before we compare the beginning and ending inventory amounts, we need to deflate inventory amounts by any increase in prices so that both the beginning and ending amounts are measured in terms of the same price level. We accomplish this by using cost indexes. A cost index for a particular layer year is determined as follows:

$$\text{Cost index in layer year} = \frac{\text{Cost in layer year}}{\text{Cost in base year}}$$

The margin note beside this paragraph reads:

The cost index for the base year (the year DVL is initially adopted) is set at 1.00.

The base year is the year in which the DVL method is adopted and the layer year is any subsequent year in which an inventory layer is created. The cost index for the base year is set at 1.00. Subsequent years' indexes reflect cost changes relative to the base year. For example, if a "basket" of inventory items cost $120 at the end of the current year, and $100 at the end of the base year, the cost index for the current year would be: $120 ÷ $100 = 120%, or 1.20. This index simply tells us that costs in the layer year are 120% of what they were in the base year (i.e., costs increased by 20%).

There are several techniques that can be used to determine an index for a DVL pool. An external index like the Consumer Price Index or the Producer Price Index can be used. However, in most cases these indexes would not properly reflect cost changes for any individual DVL pool. Instead, most companies use an internally generated index. These indexes can be calculated using one of several techniques such as the *double-extension method* or the *link-chain method.* A discussion of these methods is beyond the scope of this text. In our examples and illustrations, we assume cost indexes are given.

## The DVL Inventory Estimation Technique

The margin note beside this paragraph reads:

The starting point in DVL is determining the current year's ending inventory valued at year-end costs.

DVL estimation begins with the determination of the current year's ending inventory valued in terms of year-end costs. It's not necessary for a company using DVL to track the item-by-item cost of purchases during the year. All that's needed is to take the physical quantities of goods on hand at the end of the year and apply year-end costs. Let's say the Hanes Company adopted the dollar-value LIFO method on January 1, 2013, when the inventory value was $400,000. The 2013 ending inventory valued at year-end costs is $441,000, and the cost index for the year is 1.05 (105%).

What is the 2013 ending inventory valued at DVL cost? The first step is to convert the ending inventory from year-end costs to base year costs so we can see if there was a real increase in inventory rather than an illusory one caused by price increases. We divide the ending inventory by the year's cost index to get an amount that can be compared directly with beginning inventory.

$$\text{Ending inventory at } base\ year \text{ cost} = \frac{\$441,000}{1.05} = \$420,000$$

STEP 1: Convert ending inventory valued at year-end cost to base year cost.

The $420,000 reflects the 2013 ending inventory deflated to base year cost.

Next we compare the $420,000 ending inventory at base year cost to the beginning inventory, also at base year cost, of $400,000. The $20,000 increase in base-year dollars signifies a real increase in inventory quantity during the year. Applying the LIFO concept, ending inventory at base year cost consists of the beginning inventory layer of $400,000 plus a $20,000 2013 layer. These are the hypothetical costs of the layers as if each was acquired at base year prices.

STEP 2: Identify the layers of ending inventory and the years they were created.

Once the layers are identified, each is restated to prices existing when the layers were acquired. Each layer is multiplied by the cost index for the year it was acquired. The costs are totaled to obtain ending inventory at DVL cost.[18]

| Date | Ending Inventory at Base Year Cost | × | Cost Index | = | Ending Inventory at DVL Cost |
|---|---|---|---|---|---|
| 1/1/13 | $400,000 | | 1.00 | | $400,000 |
| 2013 layer | 20,000 | | 1.05 | | 21,000 |
| Totals | $420,000 | | | | $421,000 |

STEP 3: Convert each layer's base year cost to layer year cost using the cost index for the year it was acquired.

If we determined that inventory quantity had decreased during the year, then there would have been no 2013 layer added. The most recently added layer, in this case the beginning inventory layer, would be decreased to the inventory valuation determined in step 1. Once a layer of inventory or a portion of a layer is used (that is, sold) it cannot be replaced. In our example, if the base year layer is reduced to $380,000, it will never be increased. Future increases in inventory quantity will result in new layers being added. This situation is illustrated in the concept review exercise that follows.

## Concept Review Exercise

On January 1, 2013, the Johnson Company adopted the dollar-value LIFO method. The inventory value on this date was $500,000. Inventory data for 2013 through 2016 are as follows:

**DOLLAR-VALUE LIFO**

| Date | Ending Inventory at Year-End Costs | Cost Index |
|---|---|---|
| 12/31/13 | $556,500 | 1.05 |
| 12/31/14 | 596,200 | 1.10 |
| 12/31/15 | 615,250 | 1.15 |
| 12/31/16 | 720,000 | 1.25 |

**Required:**
Calculate Johnson's ending inventory for the years 2013 through 2016.

---

[18]It is important to note that the costs of the year's layer are only an approximation of actual acquisition cost. DVL assumes that all inventory quantities added during a particular year were acquired at a single cost.

Solution:

### JOHNSON COMPANY

| Date | Ending Inventory at Year-End Cost | Step 1 Ending Inventory at Base Year Cost | Step 2 Inventory Layers at Base Year Cost | Step 3 Inventory Layers Converted to Acquisition Year Cost | Ending Inventory at DVL Cost |
|---|---|---|---|---|---|
| 1/1/13 | $500,000 (base year) | $\frac{\$500,000}{1.00} = \$500,000$ | $500,000 (base) | $500,000 \times 1.00 = \$500,000$ | **$500,000** |
| 12/31/13 | 556,500 | $\frac{\$556,500}{1.05} = \$530,000$ | $500,000 (base)<br>30,000 (2013) | $500,000 \times 1.00 = \$500,000$<br>$30,000 \times 1.05 = \quad 31,500$ | **531,500** |
| 12/31/14 | 596,200 | $\frac{\$596,200}{1.10} = \$542,000$ | $500,000 (base)<br>30,000 (2013)<br>12,000 (2014) | $500,000 \times 1.00 = \$500,000$<br>$30,000 \times 1.05 = \quad 31,500$<br>$12,000 \times 1.10 = \quad 13,200$ | **544,700** |
| 12/31/15 | 615,250 | $\frac{\$615,250}{1.15} = \$535,000^*$ | $500,000 (base)<br>30,000 (2013)<br>5,000 (2014) | $500,000 \times 1.00 = \$500,000$<br>$30,000 \times 1.05 = \quad 31,500$<br>$5,000 \times 1.10 = \quad 5,500$ | **537,000** |
| 12/31/16 | 720,000 | $\frac{\$720,000}{1.25} = \$576,000$ | $500,000 (base)<br>30,000 (2013)<br>5,000 (2014)<br>41,000 (2016) | $500,000 \times 1.00 = \$500,000$<br>$30,000 \times 1.05 = \quad 31,500$<br>$5,000 \times 1.10 = \quad 5,500$<br>$41,000 \times 1.25 = \quad 51,250$ | **588,250** |

*Since inventory declined during 2015 (from $542,000 to $535,000 at base year costs), no new layer is added. Instead the most recently acquired layer, 2014, is reduced to arrive at the $535,000 ending inventory at base year cost.

## Financial Reporting Case Solution

1. **What inventory methods does ConocoPhillips use to value its inventories? Is this permissible according to GAAP?** *(p. 436)* ConocoPhillips uses the LIFO inventory method to value the majority of its inventories. The cost of the remaining inventories is determined using various other methods, including FIFO and weighted average. Yes, each of these methods is permissible according to generally accepted accounting principles. A company need not use the same method for all of its inventories.

2. **What is the purpose of disclosing the difference between the reported LIFO inventory amounts and replacement cost, assuming that replacement cost is equivalent to a FIFO basis?** *(p. 438)* The LIFO conformity rule requires that if a company uses LIFO to measure taxable income, it also must use LIFO for external financial reporting. ConocoPhillips does this. However, the LIFO conformity rule allows LIFO users to report non-LIFO inventory valuations in a supplemental disclosure note, but not on the face of the income statement. The company's disclosure note offers this additional information.

3. **Is your friend correct in his assertion that, by using LIFO, Conoco-Phillips was able to report lower profits for the first quarter of 2011?** *(p. 444)* Yes. If ConocoPhillips had used FIFO instead of LIFO for its LIFO inventories, income before taxes for all prior years, including the first quarter of 2011, would have been higher by $9,812 million (the increase in March 31, 2011, ending inventory). For the first quarter of 2011 alone, income before taxes would have been higher by $3,018 million. Here's why. The increase in ending inventory of $9,812 million *decreases* cost of goods sold, but the increase in beginning inventory of $6,794 million *increases* cost of goods sold, resulting in a net decrease in cost of goods sold of $3,018 million. FIFO provides a lower cost of goods sold when costs are rising. During the first quarter of 2011, the price of crude oil rose from approximately $91 to $106 per barrel. ●

# The Bottom Line

● **LO8–1**  In a perpetual inventory system, inventory is continually adjusted for each change in inventory. Cost of goods sold is adjusted each time goods are sold or returned by a customer. A periodic inventory system adjusts inventory and records cost of goods sold only at the end of a reporting period. (*p. 424*)

● **LO8–2**  Generally, determining the physical quantity that should be included in inventory is a simple matter, because it consists of items in the possession of the company. However, at the end of a reporting period it's important to determine the ownership of goods that are in transit between the company and its customers as well as between the company and its suppliers. Also, goods on consignment should be included in inventory of the consignor even though the company doesn't have physical possession of the goods. In addition, a company anticipating sales returns includes in inventory the cost of merchandise it estimates will be returned. (*p. 426*)

● **LO8–3**  The cost of inventory includes all expenditures necessary to acquire the inventory and bring it to its desired condition and location for sale or use. Generally, these expenditures include the purchase price of the goods reduced by any returns and purchase discounts, plus freight-in charges. (*p. 427*)

● **LO8–4**  Once costs are determined, the cost of goods available for sale must be allocated between cost of goods sold and ending inventory. Unless each item is specifically identified and traced through the system, the allocation requires an assumption regarding the flow of costs. First-in, first-out (FIFO) assumes that units sold are the first units acquired. Last-in, first-out (LIFO) assumes that the units sold are the most recent units purchased. The average cost method assumes that cost of goods sold and ending inventory consist of a mixture of all the goods available for sale. (*p. 430*)

● **LO8–5**  A company's choice of inventory method will be influenced by (a) how closely cost flow reflects the actual physical flow of its inventory, (b) the timing of income tax expenses, and (c) how costs are matched with revenues. (*p. 437*)

● **LO8–6**  The LIFO conformity rule requires that if a company uses LIFO to measure taxable income, it also must use LIFO for external financial reporting. LIFO users often provide supplemental disclosures describing the effect on inventories of using another method on inventory valuation rather than LIFO. If a company uses LIFO and inventory quantities decline during a period, then out of date inventory layers are liquidated and the cost of goods sold will partially match noncurrent costs with current selling prices. If costs have been increasing (decreasing), LIFO liquidations produce higher (lower) net income than would have resulted if the liquidated inventory were included in cost of goods sold at current costs. The paper profits (losses) caused by including out of date, low (high) costs in cost of goods sold is referred to as the effect on income of liquidations of LIFO inventory. (*p. 438*)

● **LO8–7**  Investors, creditors, and financial analysts can gain important insights by monitoring a company's investment in inventories. The gross profit ratio, inventory turnover ratio, and average days in inventory are designed to monitor inventories. (*p. 444*)

● **LO8–8**  The dollar-value LIFO method converts ending inventory at year-end cost to base year cost using a cost index. After identifying the layers in ending inventory with the years they were created, each year's base year cost measurement is converted to layer year cost measurement using the layer year's cost index. The layers are then summed to obtain total ending inventory at cost. (*p. 447*)

● **LO8–9**  The primary difference between U.S. GAAP and IFRS with respect to determining the cost of inventory is that IFRS does not allow the use of the LIFO method to value inventory. (*p. 437*) ●

# Questions For Review of Key Topics

Q 8–1    Describe the three types of inventory of a manufacturing company.

Q 8–2    What is the main difference between a perpetual inventory system and a periodic inventory system?

Q 8–3    The Cloud Company employs a perpetual inventory system and the McKenzie Corporation uses a periodic system. Describe the differences between the two systems in accounting for the following events: (1) purchase of merchandise, (2) sale of merchandise, (3) return of merchandise to supplier, and (4) payment of freight charge on merchandise purchased. Indicate which accounts would be debited and credited for each event.

Q 8–4    The Bockner Company shipped merchandise to Laetner Corporation on December 28, 2013. Laetner received the shipment on January 3, 2014. December 31 is the fiscal year-end for both companies. The merchandise was shipped f.o.b. shipping point. Explain the difference in the accounting treatment of the merchandise if the shipment had instead been designated f.o.b. destination.

Q 8–5 What is a consignment arrangement? Explain the accounting treatment of goods held on consignment.

Q 8–6 Distinguish between the gross and net methods of accounting for purchase discounts.

Q 8–7 The Esquire Company employs a periodic inventory system. Indicate the effect (increase or decrease) of the following items on cost of goods sold:

1. Beginning inventory
2. Purchases
3. Ending inventory
4. Purchase returns
5. Freight-in

Q 8–8 Identify four methods of assigning cost to ending inventory and cost of goods sold and briefly explain the difference in the methods.

Q 8–9 It's common in the electronics industry for unit costs of raw materials inventories to decline over time. In this environment, explain the difference between LIFO and FIFO, in terms of the effect on income and financial position. Assume that inventory quantities remain the same for the period.

Q 8–10 Explain why proponents of LIFO argue that it provides a better match of revenue and expenses. In what situation would it not provide a better match?

Q 8–11 Explain what is meant by the Internal Revenue Service conformity rule with respect to the inventory method choice.

Q 8–12 Describe the ratios used by financial analysts to monitor a company's investment in inventories.

Q 8–13 What is a LIFO inventory pool? How is the cost of ending inventory determined when pools are used?

Q 8–14 Identify two advantages of dollar-value LIFO compared with unit LIFO.

Q 8–15 The Austin Company uses the dollar-value LIFO inventory method with internally developed price indexes. Assume that ending inventory at year-end cost has been determined. Outline the remaining steps used in the dollar-value LIFO computations.

IFRS Q 8–16 Identify any differences between U.S. GAAP and International Financial Reporting Standards in the methods allowed to value inventory.

## Brief Exercises

**BE 8–1**
Determining ending inventory; periodic system
● LO8–1

A company began its fiscal year with inventory of $186,000. Purchases and cost of goods sold for the year were $945,000 and $982,000, respectively. What was the amount of ending inventory?

**BE 8–2**
Perpetual system; journal entries
● LO8–1

Litton Industries uses a perpetual inventory system. The company began its fiscal year with inventory of $267,000. Purchases of merchandise on account during the year totaled $845,000. Merchandise costing $902,000 was sold on account for $1,420,000. Prepare the journal entries to record these transactions.

**BE 8–3**
Goods in transit
● LO8–2

Kelly Corporation shipped goods to a customer f.o.b. destination on December 29, 2013. The goods arrived at the customer's location in January. In addition, one of Kelly's major suppliers shipped goods to Kelly f.o.b. shipping point on December 30. The merchandise arrived at Kelly's location in January. Which shipments should be included in Kelly's December 31 inventory?

**BE 8–4**
Purchase discounts; gross method
● LO8–3

On December 28, 2013, Videotech Corporation (VTC) purchased 10 units of a new satellite uplink system from Tristar Communications for $25,000 each. The terms of each sale were 1/10, n/30. VTC uses the gross method to account for purchase discounts and a perpetual inventory system. VTC paid the net-of-discount amount on January 6, 2014. Prepare the journal entries on December 28 and January 6 to record the purchase and payment.

**BE 8–5**
Purchase discounts; net method
● LO8–3

Refer to the situation described in BE 8–4. Prepare the necessary journal entries assuming that VTC uses the net method to account for purchase discounts.

**BE 8–6**
Inventory cost
flow methods;
periodic system
● LO8–4

Samuelson and Messenger (S&M) began 2013 with 200 units of its one product. These units were purchased near the end of 2012 for $25 each. During the month of January, 100 units were purchased on January 8 for $28 each and another 200 units were purchased on January 19 for $30 each. Sales of 125 units and 100 units were made on January 10 and January 25, respectively. There were 275 units on hand at the end of the month. S&M uses a *periodic* inventory system. Calculate ending inventory and cost of goods sold for January using (1) FIFO, and (2) average cost.

**BE 8–7**
Inventory cost
flow methods;
perpetual system
● LO8–4

Refer to the situation described in BE 8–6. S&M uses a *perpetual* inventory system. Calculate ending inventory and cost of goods sold for January using (1) FIFO, and (2) average cost.

**BE 8–8**
LIFO method
● LO8–4

Esquire Inc. uses the LIFO method to value its inventory. Inventory at January 1, 2013, was $500,000 (20,000 units at $25 each). During 2013, 80,000 units were purchased, all at the same price of $30 per unit. 85,000 units were sold during 2013. Esquire uses a periodic inventory system. Calculate the December 31, 2013, ending inventory and cost of goods sold for 2013.

**BE 8–9**
LIFO method
● LO8–4

AAA Hardware uses the LIFO method to value its inventory. Inventory at the beginning of the year consisted of 10,000 units of the company's one product. These units cost $15 each. During the year, 60,000 units were purchased at a cost of $18 each and 64,000 units were sold. Near the end of the fiscal year, management is considering the purchase of an additional 5,000 units at $18. What would be the effect of this purchase on income before income taxes? Would your answer be the same if the company used FIFO instead of LIFO?

**BE 8–10**
LIFO liquidation
● LO8–6

Refer to the situation described in BE 8–8. Assuming an income tax rate of 40%, what is LIFO liquidation profit or loss that the company would report in a disclosure note accompanying its financial statements?

**BE 8–11**
Supplemental
LIFO disclosures;
SuperValue
● LO8–6

Real World Financials

SuperValue Inc., one of the largest grocery chains in the United States, reported inventories of $2,270 million and $2,342 million in its February 26, 2011, and February 27, 2010, balance sheets, respectively. Cost of goods sold for the fiscal year ended February 26, 2011, was $29,124 million. The company uses primarily the LIFO inventory method. A disclosure note reported that if FIFO had been used instead of LIFO, inventory would have been higher by $282 million and $264 million at the end of the February 26, 2011, and February 27, 2010, fiscal years, respectively. Calculate cost of goods sold for the February 26, 2011, fiscal year assuming SuperValue used FIFO instead of LIFO.

**BE 8–12**
Ratio analysis
● LO8–7

Selected financial statement data for Schmitzer Inc. is shown below:

|  | 2013 | 2012 |
| --- | --- | --- |
| Balance sheet: |  |  |
| Inventories | 60,000 | 48,000 |
| Ratios: |  |  |
| Gross profit ratio for 2013 | 40% |  |
| Inventory turnover ratio for 2013 | 5 |  |

What was the amount of net sales for 2013?

**BE 8–13**
Dollar-value LIFO
● LO8–8

At the beginning of 2013, a company adopts the dollar-value LIFO inventory method for its one inventory pool. The pool's value on that date was $1,400,000. The 2013 ending inventory valued at year-end costs was $1,664,000 and the year-end cost index was 1.04. Calculate the inventory value at the end of 2013 using the dollar-value LIFO method.

# Exercises

**An alternate exercise and problem set is available on the text website: www.mhhe.com/spiceland7e**

**E 8–1**
Perpetual
inventory system;
journal entries
● LO8–1

John's Specialty Store uses a perpetual inventory system. The following are some inventory transactions for the month of May 2013:

1. John's purchased merchandise on account for $5,000. Freight charges of $300 were paid in cash.
2. John's returned some of the merchandise purchased in (1). The cost of the merchandise was $600 and John's account was credited by the supplier.
3. Merchandise costing $2,800 was sold for $5,200 in cash.

**Required:**
Prepare the necessary journal entries to record these transactions.

**E 8–2**
Periodic
inventory system;
journal entries
● LO8–1

[This is a variation of Exercise 8-1 modified to focus on the periodic inventory system.]
John's Specialty Store uses a periodic inventory system. The following are some inventory transactions for the month of May 2013:

1. John's purchased merchandise on account for $5,000. Freight charges of $300 were paid in cash.
2. John's returned some of the merchandise purchased in (1). The cost of the merchandise was $600 and John's account was credited by the supplier.
3. Merchandise costing $2,800 was sold for $5,200 in cash.

**Required:**
Prepare the necessary journal entries to record these transactions.

**E 8–3**
Determining
cost of goods
sold; periodic
inventory system
● LO8–1

Askew Company uses a periodic inventory system. The June 30, 2013, year-end trial balance for the company contained the following information:

| Account | Debit | Credit |
|---|---|---|
| Merchandise inventory, 7/1/12 | 32,000 | |
| Sales | | 380,000 |
| Sales returns | 12,000 | |
| Purchases | 240,000 | |
| Purchase discounts | | 6,000 |
| Purchase returns | | 10,000 |
| Freight-in | 17,000 | |

In addition, you determine that the June 30, 2013, inventory balance is $40,000.

**Required:**
1. Calculate the cost of goods sold for the Askew Company for the year ending June 30, 2013.
2. Prepare the year-end adjusting entry to record cost of goods sold.

**E 8–4**
Perpetual
and periodic
inventory systems
compared
● LO8–1

The following information is available for the Johnson Corporation for 2013:

| | |
|---|---|
| Beginning inventory | $ 25,000 |
| Merchandise purchases (on account) | 155,000 |
| Freight charges on purchases (paid in cash) | 10,000 |
| Merchandise returned to supplier (for credit) | 12,000 |
| Ending inventory | 30,000 |
| Sales (on account) | 250,000 |
| Cost of merchandise sold | 148,000 |

**Required:**
Applying both a perpetual and a periodic inventory system, prepare the journal entries that summarize the transactions that created these balances. Include all end-of-period adjusting entries indicated.

**E 8–5**
Periodic
inventory system;
missing data
● LO8–1

The Playa Company uses a periodic inventory system. The following information is taken from Playa's records. Certain data have been intentionally omitted. ($ in thousands)

| | 2013 | 2014 | 2015 |
|---|---|---|---|
| Beginning inventory | ? | ? | 225 |
| Cost of goods sold | 627 | 621 | ? |
| Ending inventory | ? | 225 | 216 |
| Cost of goods available for sale | 876 | ? | 800 |
| Purchases (gross) | 630 | ? | 585 |
| Purchase discounts | 18 | 15 | ? |
| Purchase returns | 24 | 30 | 14 |
| Freight-in | 13 | 32 | 16 |

**Required:**
Determine the missing numbers. Show computations where appropriate.

**E 8–6**
**Goods in transit**
● **LO8–2**

The Kwok Company's inventory balance on December 31, 2013, was $165,000 (based on a 12/31/13 physical count) *before* considering the following transactions:

1. Goods shipped to Kwok f.o.b. destination on December 20, 2013, were received on January 4, 2014. The invoice cost was $30,000.
2. Goods shipped to Kwok f.o.b. shipping point on December 28, 2013, were received on January 5, 2014. The invoice cost was $17,000.
3. Goods shipped from Kwok to a customer f.o.b. destination on December 27, 2013, were received by the customer on January 3, 2014. The sales price was $40,000 and the merchandise cost $22,000.
4. Goods shipped from Kwok to a customer f.o.b. destination on December 26, 2013, were received by the customer on December 30, 2013. The sales price was $20,000 and the merchandise cost $13,000.
5. Goods shipped from Kwok to a customer f.o.b. shipping point on December 28, 2013, were received by the customer on January 4, 2014. The sales price was $25,000 and the merchandise cost $12,000.

**Required:**
Determine the correct inventory amount to be reported in Kwok's 2013 balance sheet.

**E 8–7**
**Goods in transit; consignment**
● **LO8–2**

The December 31, 2013, year-end inventory balance of the Raymond Corporation is $210,000. You have been asked to review the following transactions to determine if they have been correctly recorded.

1. Goods shipped to Raymond f.o.b. destination on December 26, 2013, were received on January 2, 2014. The invoice cost of $30,000 *is* included in the preliminary inventory balance.
2. At year-end, Raymond held $14,000 of merchandise on consignment from the Harrison Company. This merchandise *is* included in the preliminary inventory balance.
3. On December 29, merchandise costing $6,000 was shipped to a customer f.o.b. shipping point and arrived at the customer's location on January 3, 2014. The merchandise is *not* included in the preliminary inventory balance.
4. At year-end, Raymond had merchandise costing $15,000 on consignment with the Joclyn Corporation. The merchandise is *not* included in the preliminary inventory balance.

**Required:**
Determine the correct inventory amount to be reported in Raymond's 2013 balance sheet.

**E 8–8**
**Physical quantities and costs included in inventory**
● **LO8–2**

The Phoenix Corporation's fiscal year ends on December 31. Phoenix determines inventory quantity by a physical count of inventory on hand at the close of business on December 31. The company's controller has asked for your help in deciding if the following items should be included in the year-end inventory count.

1. Merchandise held on consignment for Trout Creek Clothing.
2. Goods shipped f.o.b. destination on December 28 that arrived at the customer's location on January 4.
3. Goods purchased from a vendor shipped f.o.b. shipping point on December 26 that arrived on January 3.
4. Goods shipped f.o.b. shipping point on December 28 that arrived at the customer's location on January 5.
5. Phoenix had merchandise on consignment at Lisa's Markets, Inc.
6. Goods purchased from a vendor shipped f.o.b. destination on December 27 that arrived on January 3.
7. Freight charges on goods purchased in 3.

**Required:**
Determine if each of the items above should be included or excluded from the company's year-end inventory.

**E 8–9**
**Purchase discounts; the gross method**
● **LO8–3**

On July 15, 2013, the Nixon Car Company purchased 1,000 tires from the Harwell Company for $50 each. The terms of the sale were 2/10, n/30. Nixon uses a periodic inventory system and the *gross* method of accounting for purchase discounts.

**Required:**
1. Prepare the journal entries to record the purchase on July 15 and payment on July 23, 2013.
2. Prepare the journal entry to record the payment on August 15, 2013.
3. If Nixon instead uses a perpetual inventory system, explain any changes to the journal entries created in requirements 1 and 2.

**E 8–10**
**Purchase discounts; the net method**
● **LO8–3**

[This is a variation of Exercise 8–9 modified to focus on the net method of accounting for purchase discounts.]
On July 15, 2013, the Nixon Car Company purchased 1,000 tires from the Harwell Company for $50 each. The terms of the sale were 2/10, n/30. Nixon uses a periodic inventory system and the *net* method of accounting for purchase discounts.

**Required:**

1. Prepare the journal entries to record the purchase on July 15 and payment on July 23, 2013.

2. Prepare the journal entry to record the payment on August 15, 2013.

3. If Nixon instead uses a perpetual inventory system, explain any changes to the journal entries created in requirements 1 and 2.

---

**E 8–11**
Trade and purchase discounts; the gross method and the net method compared
● LO8–3

Tracy Company, a manufacturer of air conditioners, sold 100 units to Thomas Company on November 17, 2013. The units have a list price of $500 each, but Thomas was given a 30% trade discount. The terms of the sale were 2/10, n/30. Thomas uses a periodic inventory system.

**Required:**

1. Prepare the journal entries to record the purchase by Thomas on November 17 and payment on November 26, 2013, using the gross method of accounting for purchase discounts.

2. Prepare the journal entry to record the payment on December 15, 2013, using the gross method of accounting for purchase discounts.

3. Repeat requirements 1 and 2 using the net method of accounting for purchase discounts.

---

**E 8–12**
FASB codification research
● LO8–2, LO8–3

Access the FASB's Codification Research System at the FASB website (www.fasb.org). Determine the specific citation for each of the following items:

1. Define the meaning of cost as it applies to the initial measurement of inventory.

2. Indicate the circumstances when it is appropriate to initially measure agricultural inventory at fair value.

3. What is a major objective of accounting for inventory?

4. Are abnormal freight charges included in the cost of inventory?

---

**E 8–13**
Inventory cost flow methods; periodic system
● LO8–1, LO8–4

Altira Corporation uses a periodic inventory system. The following information related to its merchandise inventory during the month of August 2013 is available:

| Aug. 1 | Inventory on hand—2,000 units; cost $6.10 each. |
| 8 | Purchased 10,000 units for $5.50 each. |
| 14 | Sold 8,000 units for $12.00 each. |
| 18 | Purchased 6,000 units for $5.00 each. |
| 25 | Sold 7,000 units for $11.00 each. |
| 31 | Inventory on hand—3,000 units. |

**Required:**
Determine the inventory balance Altira would report in its August 31, 2013, balance sheet and the cost of goods sold it would report in its August 2013 income statement using each of the following cost flow methods:

1. First-in, first-out (FIFO)

2. Last-in, first-out (LIFO)

3. Average cost

---

**E 8–14**
Inventory cost flow methods; perpetual system
● LO8–1, LO8–4

[This is a variation of Exercise 8–13 modified to focus on the perpetual inventory system and alternative cost flow methods.]
Altira Corporation uses a perpetual inventory system. The following transactions affected its merchandise inventory during the month of August 2013:

| Aug. 1 | Inventory on hand—2,000 units; cost $6.10 each. |
| 8 | Purchased 10,000 units for $5.50 each. |
| 14 | Sold 8,000 units for $12.00 each. |
| 18 | Purchased 6,000 units for $5.00 each. |
| 25 | Sold 7,000 units for $11.00 each. |
| 31 | Inventory on hand—3,000 units. |

**Required:**
Determine the inventory balance Altira would report in its August 31, 2013, balance sheet and the cost of goods sold it would report in its August 2013 income statement using each of the following cost flow methods:

1. First-in, first-out (FIFO)

2. Last-in, first-out (LIFO)

3. Average cost

**E 8–15**
Comparison of
FIFO and LIFO;
periodic system
● LO8–1, LO8–4

Alta Ski Company's inventory records contained the following information regarding its latest ski model. The company uses a periodic inventory system.

| | |
|---|---|
| Beginning inventory, January 1, 2013 | 600 units @ $80 each |
| Purchases: | |
|     January 15 | 1,000 units @ $95 each |
|     January 21 | 800 units @ $100 each |
| Sales: | |
|     January 5 | 400 units @ $120 each |
|     January 22 | 800 units @ $130 each |
|     January 29 | 400 units @ $135 each |
| Ending inventory, January 31, 2013 | 800 units |

**Required:**
1. Which method, FIFO or LIFO, will result in the highest cost of goods sold figure for January 2013? Why? Which method will result in the highest ending inventory balance? Why?
2. Compute cost of goods sold for January and the ending inventory using both the FIFO and LIFO methods.

**E 8–16**
Average cost
method; periodic
and perpetual
systems
● LO8–1, LO8–4

The following information is taken from the inventory records of the CNB Company:

| | |
|---|---|
| Beginning inventory, 9/1/13 | 5,000 units @ $10.00 |
| Purchases: | |
|     9/7 | 3,000 units @ $10.40 |
|     9/25 | 8,000 units @ $10.75 |
| Sales: | |
|     9/10 | 4,000 units |
|     9/29 | 5,000 units |
| 7,000 units were on hand at the end of September. | |

**Required:**
1. Assuming that CNB uses a periodic inventory system and employs the average cost method, determine cost of goods sold for September and September's ending inventory.
2. Repeat requirement 1 assuming that the company uses a perpetual inventory system.

**E 8–17**
FIFO, LIFO, and
average cost
methods
● LO8–1, LO8–4

Causwell Company began 2013 with 10,000 units of inventory on hand. The cost of each unit was $5.00. During 2013 an additional 30,000 units were purchased at a single unit cost, and 20,000 units remained on hand at the end of 2013 (20,000 units therefore were sold during 2013). Causwell uses a periodic inventory system. Cost of goods sold for 2013, applying the average cost method, is $115,000. The company is interested in determining what cost of goods sold would have been if the FIFO or LIFO methods were used.

**Required:**
1. Determine the cost of goods sold for 2013 using the FIFO method. [*Hint:* Determine the cost per unit of 2013 purchases.]
2. Determine the cost of goods sold for 2013 using the LIFO method.

**E 8–18**
Supplemental
LIFO disclosures;
LIFO reserve;
Steelcase
● LO8–6

Real World Financials

**Steelcase Inc.** is the global leader in providing furniture for office environments. The company uses the LIFO inventory method for external reporting and for income tax purposes but maintains its internal records using FIFO. The following disclosure note was included in a recent annual report:

**7. Inventories ($ in millions):**

| | February 25, 2011 | February 26, 2010 |
|---|---|---|
| Raw materials | $ 55.0 | $ 45.8 |
| Work-in-process | 13.9 | 11.9 |
| Finished goods | 79.1 | 62.0 |
| | 148.0 | 119.7 |
| LIFO reserve | (20.9) | (21.3) |
| | $127.1 | $ 98.4 |

The company's income statement reported cost of goods sold of $1,693.8 million for the fiscal year ended February 25, 2011.

**Required:**

1. Steelcase adjusts the LIFO reserve at the end of its fiscal year. Prepare the February 25, 2011, adjusting entry to make the cost of goods sold adjustment.

2. If Steelcase had used FIFO to value its inventories, what would cost of goods sold have been for the 2011 fiscal year?

3. Since its inception, what is the amount of income tax the company has saved by using LIFO instead of FIFO for tax purposes? Assume an effective income tax rate of 35%.

**E 8–19**
**LIFO liquidation**
● **LO8–1, LO8–4,**
**LO8–6**

The Reuschel Company began 2013 with inventory of 10,000 units at a cost of $7 per unit. During 2013, 50,000 units were purchased for $8.50 each. Sales for the year totaled 54,000 units leaving 6,000 units on hand at the end of 2013. Reuschel uses a periodic inventory system and the LIFO inventory cost method.

**Required:**

1. Calculate cost of goods sold for 2013.

2. From a financial reporting perspective, what problem is created by the use of LIFO in this situation? Describe the disclosure required to report the effects of this problem.

**E 8–20**
**FASB codification research**
● **LO8–6**

The *FASB Accounting Standards Codification* represents the single source of authoritative U.S. generally accepted accounting principles.

**Required:**

1. Obtain the relevant authoritative literature on the disclosure of accounting policies using the FASB's Codification Research System at the FASB website (**www.fasb.org**).

2. What is the specific citation that describes the disclosure requirements that must be made by publicly traded companies for a LIFO liquidation?

3. Describe the disclosure requirements.

**E 8–21**
**Ratio analysis; Home Depot and Lowe's**
● **LO8–7**

Real World Financials

The table below contains selected information from recent financial statements of **The Home Depot, Inc.**, and **Lowe's Companies, Inc.**, two companies in the home improvement retail industry ($ in millions):

| | Home Depot | | Lowe's | |
|---|---|---|---|---|
| | **1/30/11** | **1/31/10** | **1/28/11** | **1/29/10** |
| Net sales | $67,997 | $66,176 | $48,815 | $47,220 |
| Cost of goods sold | 44,693 | 43,764 | 31,663 | 30,757 |
| Year-end inventory | 10,625 | 10,188 | 8,321 | 8,249 |
| Industry averages: | | | | |
| Gross profit ratio | | 27% | | |
| Inventory turnover ratio | | 2.03 times | | |
| Average days in inventory | | 180 days | | |

**Required:**
Calculate the gross profit ratio, the inventory turnover ratio, and the average days in inventory for the two companies using the most recent fiscal year data. Compare your calculations for the two companies, taking into account the industry averages.

**E 8–22**
**Dollar-value LIFO**
● **LO8–8**

On January 1, 2013, the Haskins Company adopted the dollar-value LIFO method for its one inventory pool. The pool's value on this date was $660,000. The 2013 and 2014 ending inventory valued at year-end costs were $690,000 and $760,000, respectively. The appropriate cost indexes are 1.04 for 2013 and 1.08 for 2014.

**Required:**
Calculate the inventory value at the end of 2013 and 2014 using the dollar-value LIFO method.

**E 8–23**
**Dollar-value LIFO**
● **LO8–8**

Mercury Company has only one inventory pool. On December 31, 2013, Mercury adopted the dollar-value LIFO inventory method. The inventory on that date using the dollar-value LIFO method was $200,000. Inventory data are as follows:

| Year | Ending Inventory at Year-End Costs | Ending Inventory at Base Year Costs |
|---|---|---|
| 2014 | $231,000 | $220,000 |
| 2015 | 299,000 | 260,000 |
| 2016 | 300,000 | 250,000 |

**Required:**
Compute the inventory at December 31, 2014, 2015, and 2016, using the dollar-value LIFO method.

*(AICPA adapted)*

**E 8–24**
Concepts;
terminology

● LO8–1 through
  LO8–5

Listed below are several terms and phrases associated with inventory measurement. Pair each item from List A with the item from List B (by letter) that is most appropriately associated with it.

| List A | List B |
|---|---|
| _____ 1. Perpetual inventory system | a. Legal title passes when goods are delivered to common carrier. |
| _____ 2. Periodic inventory system | b. Goods are transferred to another company but title remains with transferor. |
| _____ 3. F.o.b. shipping point | c. Purchase discounts not taken are included in inventory cost. |
| _____ 4. Gross method | d. If LIFO is used for taxes, it must be used for financial reporting. |
| _____ 5. Net method | e. Assumes items sold are those acquired first. |
| _____ 6. Cost index | f. Assumes items sold are those acquired last. |
| _____ 7. F.o.b. destination | g. Purchase discounts not taken are considered interest expense. |
| _____ 8. FIFO | h. Used to convert ending inventory at year-end cost to base year cost. |
| _____ 9. LIFO | i. Continuously records changes in inventory. |
| _____ 10. Consignment | j. Assumes items sold come from a mixture of goods acquired during the period. |
| _____ 11. Average cost | k. Legal title passes when goods arrive at location. |
| _____ 12. IRS conformity rule | l. Adjusts inventory at the end of the period. |

# CPA and CMA Review Questions

**CPA Exam
Questions**

The following questions are adapted from a variety of sources including questions developed by the AICPA Board of Examiners and those used in the Kaplan CPA Review Course to study inventory while preparing for the CPA examination. Determine the response that best completes the statements or questions.

● LO8–2

1. Herc Co.'s inventory at December 31, 2013, was $1,500,000 based on a physical count priced at cost, and before any necessary adjustment for the following:

   • Merchandise costing $90,000, shipped f.o.b shipping point from a vendor on December 30, 2013, was received and recorded on January 5, 2014.
   • Goods in the shipping area were excluded from inventory although shipment was not made until January 4, 2014. The goods, billed to the customer f.o.b. shipping point on December 30, 2013, had a cost of $120,000.

   What amount should Herc report as inventory in its December 31, 2013, balance sheet?
   a. $1,500,000
   b. $1,590,000
   c. $1,700,000
   d. $1,710,000

● LO8–3

2. Dixon Menswear Shop regularly buys shirts from Colt Company. Dixon purchased shirts from Colt on May 27, and received an invoice with a list price amount of $3,600 and payment terms of 2/10, n/30. Dixon uses the net method to record purchases. Dixon should record the purchase at
   a. $3,430
   b. $3,500
   c. $3,528
   d. $3,600

● LO8–4

Questions 3 through 5 are based on the following information. Esquire Corp. uses the periodic inventory system. During its first year of operations, Esquire made the following purchases (list in chronological order of acquisition):
   • 20 units at $50
   • 35 units at $40
   • 85 units at $30

Sales for the year totaled 135 units, leaving 5 units on hand at the end of the year.

3. Ending inventory using the average cost method is

   a. $ 150

   b. $ 177

   c. $ 250

   d. $1,540

4. Ending inventory using the FIFO method is

   a. $ 150

   b. $ 177

   c. $ 250

   d. $1,540

5. Ending inventory using the LIFO method is

   a. $ 150

   b. $ 177

   c. $ 250

   d. $1,540

● LO8–4, LO8–5   6. Jamison Corporation's inventory cost in its balance sheet is lower using the first-in, first-out method than it would have been had it used the last-in, first-out method. Assuming no beginning inventory, what direction did the cost of purchases move during the period?

   a. Up.

   b. Down.

   c. Unchanged.

   d. Can't be determined.

● LO8–8   7. Dalton Company adopted the dollar-value LIFO inventory method on January 1, 2013. In applying the LIFO method, Dalton uses internal price indexes and the multiple-pools approach. The following data were available for Inventory Pool No. 1 for the two years following the adoption of LIFO:

|  | **Ending Inventory** | | |
| --- | --- | --- | --- |
|  | **At Current Year Cost** | **At Base Year Cost** | **Cost Index** |
| 1/1/13 | $100,000 | $100,000 | 1.00 |
| 12/31/13 | 126,000 | 120,000 | 1.05 |
| 12/31/14 | 140,800 | 128,000 | 1.10 |

Under the dollar-value LIFO method the inventory at December 31, 2014, should be

   a. $128,000

   b. $129,800

   c. $130,800

   d. $140,800

Beginning in 2011, International Financial Reporting Standards are tested on the CPA exam along with U.S. GAAP. The following question deals with the application of IFRS.

● LO8–9   8. Under IFRS, which of the following methods is not acceptable for the valuation of inventory?

● IFRS

   a. LIFO.

   b. FIFO.

   c. Average cost.

   d. Specific identification.

**CMA Exam Questions**

The following questions dealing with inventory are adapted from questions that previously appeared on Certified Management Accountant (CMA) examinations. The CMA designation sponsored by the Institute of Management Accountants (www.imanet.org) provides members with an objective measure of knowledge and competence in the field of management accounting. Determine the response that best completes the statements or questions.

● LO8–1, LO8–4   Questions 1 through 3 are based on the following information. Thomas Engine Company is a wholesaler of marine engine parts. The activity of carburetor 2642J during the month of March is presented below.

| Date | Balance or Transaction | Units | Unit Cost | Unit Sales Price |
|---|---|---|---|---|
| Mar 1 | Inventory | 3,200 | $64.30 | $86.50 |
| 4 | Purchase | 3,400 | 64.75 | 87.00 |
| 14 | Sales | 3,600 | | 87.25 |
| 25 | Purchase | 3,500 | 66.00 | 87.25 |
| 28 | Sales | 3,450 | | 88.00 |

1. If Thomas uses a first-in, first-out perpetual inventory system, the total cost of the inventory for carburetor 2642J at March 31 is
   a. $196,115
   b. $197,488
   c. $201,300
   d. $263,825

2. If Thomas uses a last-in, first-out periodic inventory system, the total cost of the inventory for carburetor 2642J at March 31 is
   a. $196,115
   b. $197,488
   c. $201,300
   d. $268,400

3. If Thomas uses a last-in, first-out perpetual inventory system, the total cost of the inventory for carburetor 2642J at March 31 is
   a. $196,200
   b. $197,488
   c. $263,863
   d. $268,400

# Problems

An alternate exercise and problem set is available on the text website: www.mhhe.com/spiceland7e

**P 8–1**
Various inventory transactions; journal entries
● **LO8–1 through LO8–3**

James Company began the month of October with inventory of $15,000. The following inventory transactions occurred during the month:
a. The company purchased merchandise on account for $22,000 on October 12, 2013. Terms of the purchase were 2/10, n/30. James uses the net method to record purchases. The merchandise was shipped f.o.b. shipping point and freight charges of $500 were paid in cash.
b. On October 18 the company returned merchandise costing $3,000. The return reduced the amount owed to the supplier. The merchandise returned came from beginning inventory, not from the October 12 purchase.
c. On October 31, James paid for the merchandise purchased on October 12.
d. During October merchandise costing $18,000 was sold on account for $28,000.
e. It was determined that inventory on hand at the end of October cost $16,060.

**Required:**
1. Assuming that the James Company uses a periodic inventory system, prepare journal entries for the above transactions including the adjusting entry at the end of October to record cost of goods sold.
2. Assuming that the James Company uses a perpetual inventory system, prepare journal entries for the above transactions.

**P 8–2**
Items to be included in inventory
● **LO8–2**

The following inventory transactions took place near December 31, 2013, the end of the Rasul Company's fiscal year-end:
1. On December 27, 2013, merchandise costing $2,000 was shipped to the Myers Company on consignment. The shipment arrived at Myers's location on December 29, but none of the merchandise was sold by the end of the year. The merchandise was *not* included in the 2013 ending inventory.

2. On January 5, 2014, merchandise costing $8,000 was received from a supplier and recorded as a purchase on that date and *not* included in the 2013 ending inventory. The invoice revealed that the shipment was made f.o.b. shipping point on December 28, 2013.

3. On December 29, 2013, the company shipped merchandise costing $12,000 to a customer f.o.b. destination. The goods, which arrived at the customer's location on January 4, 2014, were *not* included in Rasul's 2013 ending inventory. The sale was recorded in 2013.

4. Merchandise costing $4,000 was received on December 28, 2013, on consignment from the Aborn Company. A purchase was *not* recorded and the merchandise was *not* included in 2013 ending inventory.

5. Merchandise costing $6,000 was received and recorded as a purchase on January 8, 2014. The invoice revealed that the merchandise was shipped from the supplier on December 28, 2013, f.o.b. destination. The merchandise was *not* included in 2013 ending inventory.

**Required:**
State whether Rasul correctly accounted for each of the above transactions. Give the reason for your answer.

**P 8–3**
**Costs included in inventory**
● **LO8–2, LO8–3**

Reagan Corporation is a wholesale distributor of truck replacement parts. Initial amounts taken from Reagan's records are as follows:

| | |
|---|---|
| Inventory at December 31 (based on a physical count of goods in Reagan's warehouse on December 31) | $1,250,000 |
| Accounts payable at December 31: | |

| Vendor | Terms | Amount |
|---|---|---|
| Baker Company | 2%, 10 days, net 30 | $ 265,000 |
| Charlie Company | Net 30 | 210,000 |
| Dolly Company | Net 30 | 300,000 |
| Eagler Company | Net 30 | 225,000 |
| Full Company | Net 30 | — |
| Greg Company | Net 30 | — |
| Accounts payable, December 31 | | $1,000,000 |
| Sales for the year | | $9,000,000 |

**Additional Information:**

1. Parts held by Reagan on consignment from Charlie, amounting to $155,000, were included in the physical count of goods in Reagan's warehouse and in accounts payable at December 31.

2. Parts totaling $22,000, which were purchased from Full and paid for in December, were sold in the last week of the year and *appropriately* recorded as sales of $28,000. The parts were included in the physical count of goods in Reagan's warehouse on December 31 because the parts were on the loading dock waiting to be picked up by customers.

3. Parts in transit on December 31 to customers, shipped f.o.b. shipping point on December 28, amounted to $34,000. The customers received the parts on January 6 of the following year. Sales of $40,000 to the customers for the parts were recorded by Reagan on January 2.

4. Retailers were holding goods on consignment from Reagan, which had a cost of $210,000 and a retail value of $250,000.

5. Goods were in transit from Greg to Reagan on December 31. The cost of the goods was $25,000, and they were shipped f.o.b. shipping point on December 29.

6. A freight bill in the amount of $2,000 specifically relating to merchandise purchased in December, all of which was still in the inventory at December 31, was received on January 3. The freight bill was not included in either the inventory or in accounts payable at December 31.

7. All the purchases from Baker occurred during the last seven days of the year. These items have been recorded in accounts payable and accounted for in the physical inventory at cost before discount. Reagan's policy is to pay invoices in time to take advantage of all discounts, adjust inventory accordingly, and record accounts payable net of discounts.

**Required:**
Prepare a schedule of adjustments to the initial amounts using the format shown below. Show the effect, if any, of each of the transactions separately and if the transactions would have no effect on the amount shown, state *none*.

| | Inventory | Accounts Payable | Sales |
|---|---|---|---|
| Initial amounts | $1,250,000 | $1,000,000 | $ 9,000,000 |
| Adjustments—increase (decrease): | | | |
| 1. | | | |
| 2. | | | |
| 3. | | | |
| 4. | | | |
| 5. | | | |
| 6. | | | |
| 7. | | | |
| Total adjustments | | | |
| Adjusted amounts | $ | $ | $ |

*(AICPA adapted)*

**P 8–4**
**Various inventory transactions; determining inventory and cost of goods**
● **LO8–1 through LO8–4**

Johnson Corporation began 2013 with inventory of 10,000 units of its only product. The units cost $8 each. The company uses a periodic inventory system and the LIFO cost method. The following transactions occurred during 2013:

a. Purchased 50,000 additional units at a cost of $10 per unit. Terms of the purchases were 2/10, n/30, and 100% of the purchases were paid for within the 10-day discount period. The company uses the gross method to record purchase discounts. The merchandise was purchased f.o.b. shipping point and freight charges of $.50 per unit were paid by Johnson.

b. 1,000 units purchased during the year were returned to suppliers for credit. Johnson was also given credit for the freight charges of $.50 per unit it had paid on the original purchase. The units were defective and were returned two days after they were received.

c. Sales for the year totaled 45,000 units at $18 per unit.

d. On December 28, 2013, Johnson purchased 5,000 additional units at $10 each. The goods were shipped f.o.b. destination and arrived at Johnson's warehouse on January 4, 2014.

e. 14,000 units were on hand at the end of 2013.

**Required:**
1. Determine ending inventory and cost of goods sold for 2013.
2. Assuming that operating expenses other than those indicated in the above transactions amounted to $150,000, determine income before income taxes for 2013.

**P 8–5**
**Various inventory costing methods**
● **LO8–1, LO8–4**

Ferris Company began 2013 with 6,000 units of its principal product. The cost of each unit is $8. Merchandise transactions for the month of January 2013 are as follows:

| | **Purchases** | | |
|---|---|---|---|
| Date of Purchase | Units | Unit Cost* | Total Cost |
| Jan. 10 | 5,000 | $ 9 | $ 45,000 |
| Jan. 18 | 6,000 | 10 | 60,000 |
| Totals | 11,000 | | $105,000 |

*Includes purchase price and cost of freight.

| **Sales** | |
|---|---|
| Date of Sale | Units |
| Jan. 5 | 3,000 |
| Jan. 12 | 2,000 |
| Jan. 20 | 4,000 |
| Total | 9,000 |

8,000 units were on hand at the end of the month.

**Required:**
Calculate January's ending inventory and cost of goods sold for the month using each of the following alternatives:
1. FIFO, periodic system
2. LIFO, periodic system

3. LIFO, perpetual system

4. Average cost, periodic system

5. Average cost, perpetual system

**P 8–6**
Various inventory costing methods; gross profit ratio
● LO8–1, LO8–4, LO8–7

Topanga Group began operations early in 2013. Inventory purchase information for the quarter ended March 31, 2013, for Topanga's only product is provided below. The unit costs include the cost of freight. The company uses a periodic inventory system.

| Date of Purchase | Units | Unit Cost | Total Cost |
|---|---|---|---|
| Jan. 7 | 5,000 | $4.00 | $ 20,000 |
| Feb. 16 | 12,000 | 4.50 | 54,000 |
| March 22 | 17,000 | 5.00 | 85,000 |
| Totals | 34,000 | | $159,000 |

Sales for the quarter, all at $7.00 per unit, totaled 20,000 units leaving 14,000 units on hand at the end of the quarter.

**Required:**
1. Calculate the Topanga's gross profit ratio for the first quarter using:
   a. FIFO
   b. LIFO
   c. Average cost
2. Comment on the relative effect of each of the three inventory methods on the gross profit ratio.

**P 8–7**
Various inventory costing methods
● LO8–1, LO8–4

Carlson Auto Dealers Inc. sells a handmade automobile as its only product. Each automobile is identical; however, they can be distinguished by their unique ID number. At the beginning of 2013, Carlson had three cars in inventory, as follows:

| Car ID | Cost |
|---|---|
| 203 | $60,000 |
| 207 | 60,000 |
| 210 | 63,000 |

During 2013, each of the three autos sold for $90,000. Additional purchases (listed in chronological order) and sales for the year were as follows:

| Car ID | Cost | Selling Price |
|---|---|---|
| 211 | $63,000 | $ 90,000 |
| 212 | 63,000 | 93,000 |
| 213 | 64,500 | not sold |
| 214 | 66,000 | 96,000 |
| 215 | 69,000 | 100,500 |
| 216 | 70,500 | not sold |
| 217 | 72,000 | 105,000 |
| 218 | 72,300 | 106,500 |
| 219 | 75,000 | not sold |

**Required:**
1. Calculate 2013 ending inventory and cost of goods sold assuming the company uses the specific identification inventory method.
2. Calculate ending inventory and cost of goods sold assuming FIFO and a periodic inventory system.
3. Calculate ending inventory and cost of goods sold assuming LIFO and a periodic inventory system.
4. Calculate ending inventory and cost of goods sold assuming the average cost method and a periodic inventory system.

**P 8–8**
Supplemental LIFO disclosures; Caterpillar
● LO8–4, LO8–6

Caterpillar, Inc., is one of the world's largest manufacturers of construction, mining, and forestry machinery. The following disclosure note is included in the company's 2010 financial statements:

> **D. Inventories** ($ in millions)
>
> Inventories are stated at the lower of cost or market. Cost is principally determined using the last-in, first-out, (LIFO) method. The value of inventories on the LIFO basis represented about 70% of total inventories at December 31, 2010, 2009, and 2008.
>
> If the FIFO (first-in, first-out) method had been in use, inventories would have been $2,575 million, $3,022 million, and $3,216 million higher than reported at December 31, 2010, 2009, and 2008, respectively.

Real World Financials

If inventories valued at LIFO cost had been valued at FIFO cost, net income would have been $331 million lower in 2010 and $144 million lower in 2009.

**Required:**

1. Approximate the company's effective income tax rate for the year ended December 31, 2010.

2. Why might the information contained in the disclosure note be useful to a financial analyst?

3. Using the income tax rate calculated in 1, how much higher (lower) would retained earnings have been at the end of 2010 if Caterpillar had used the FIFO inventory method for all of its inventory?

**P 8–9**
**LIFO liquidation**
● **LO8–4, LO8–6**

Taylor Corporation has used a periodic inventory system and the LIFO cost method since its inception in 2006. The company began 2013 with the following inventory layers (listed in chronological order of acquisition):

| | |
|---|---:|
| 10,000 units @ $15 | $150,000 |
| 15,000 units @ $20 | 300,000 |
| Beginning inventory | $450,000 |

During 2013, 30,000 units were purchased for $25 per unit. Due to unexpected demand for the company's product, 2013 sales totaled 40,000 units at various prices, leaving 15,000 units in ending inventory.

**Required:**

1. Calculate cost of goods sold for 2013.

2. Determine the amount of LIFO liquidation profit that the company must report in a disclosure note to its 2013 financial statements. Assume an income tax rate of 40%.

3. If the company decided to purchase an additional 10,000 units at $25 per unit at the end of the year, how much income tax currently payable would be saved?

**P 8–10**
**LIFO liquidation**
● **LO8–4, LO8–6**

Cansela Corporation uses a periodic inventory system and the LIFO method to value its inventory. The company began 2013 with inventory of 4,500 units of its only product. The beginning inventory balance of $64,000 consisted of the following layers:

| | | |
|---|---|---:|
| 2,000 units at $12 per unit | = | $24,000 |
| 2,500 units at $16 per unit | = | 40,000 |
| | | $64,000 |

During the three years 2013–2015 the cost of inventory remained constant at $18 per unit. Unit purchases and sales during these years were as follows:

| | Purchases | Sales |
|---|---|---|
| 2013 | 10,000 | 11,000 |
| 2014 | 13,000 | 14,500 |
| 2015 | 12,000 | 13,000 |

**Required:**

1. Calculate cost of goods sold for 2013, 2014, and 2015.

2. Disregarding income tax, determine the LIFO liquidation profit or loss, if any, for each of the three years.

3. Prepare the company's LIFO liquidation disclosure note that would be included in the 2015 financial statements to report the effects of any liquidation on cost of goods sold and net income. Assume any liquidation effects are material and that Cansela's effective income tax rate is 40%. Cansela's 2015 financial statements include income statements for two prior years for comparative purposes.

**P 8–11**
Inventory cost flow methods: LIFO liquidation; ratios
● LO8–4, LO8–6, LO8–7

Cast Iron Grills, Inc., manufactures premium gas barbecue grills. The company uses a periodic inventory system and the LIFO cost method for its grill inventory. Cast Iron's December 31, 2013, fiscal year-end inventory consisted of the following (listed in chronological order of acquisition):

| Units | Unit Cost |
|---|---|
| 5,000 | $700 |
| 4,000 | 800 |
| 6,000 | 900 |

The replacement cost of the grills throughout 2014 was $1,000. Cast Iron sold 27,000 grills during 2014. The company's selling price is set at 200% of the current replacement cost.

**Required:**
1. Compute the gross profit (sales minus cost of goods sold) and the gross profit ratio for 2014 assuming that Cast Iron purchased 28,000 units during the year.
2. Repeat requirement 1 assuming that Cast Iron purchased only 15,000 units.
3. Why does the number of units purchased affect your answers to the above requirements?
4. Repeat requirements 1 and 2 assuming that Cast Iron uses the FIFO inventory cost method rather than the LIFO method.
5. Why does the number of units purchased have no effect on your answers to requirements 1 and 2 when the FIFO method is used?

**P 8–12**
Integrating problem; inventories and accounts receivable; Chapters 7 and 8
● LO8–4, LO8–6, LO8–7

Inverness Steel Corporation is a producer of flat-rolled carbon, stainless and electrical steels, and tubular products. The company's income statement for the 2013 fiscal year reported the following information ($ in millions):

| | |
|---|---|
| Sales | $6,255 |
| Cost of goods sold | 5,190 |

The company's balance sheets for 2013 and 2012 included the following information ($ in millions):

| | 2013 | 2012 |
|---|---|---|
| Current assets: | | |
| Accounts receivable, net | $703 | $583 |
| Inventories | 880 | 808 |

The statement of cash flows reported bad debt expense for 2013 of $8 million. The summary of significant accounting policies included the following notes ($ in millions):

**Accounts Receivable (in part)**
The allowance for uncollectible accounts was $10 and $7 at December 31, 2013 and 2012, respectively. All sales are on credit.

**Inventories**
Inventories are valued at the lower of cost or market. The cost of the majority of inventories is measured using the last in, first out (LIFO) method. Other inventories are measured principally at average cost and consist mostly of foreign inventories and certain raw materials. If the entire inventory had been valued on an average cost basis, inventory would have been higher by $480 and $350 at the end of 2013 and 2012, respectively.
   During 2013, 2012, and 2011, liquidation of LIFO layers generated income of $6, $7, and $25, respectively.

**Required:**
Using the information provided:
1. Determine the amount of accounts receivable Inverness wrote off during 2013.
2. Calculate the amount of cash collected from customers during 2013.
3. Calculate what cost of goods sold would have been for 2013 if the company had used average cost to value its entire inventory.

4. Calculate the following ratios for 2013:
   a. Receivables turnover ratio
   b. Inventory turnover ratio
   c. Gross profit ratio

5. Explain briefly what caused the income generated by the liquidation of LIFO layers. Assuming an income tax rate of 35%, what was the effect of the liquidation of LIFO layers on cost of goods sold in 2013?

---

**P 8–13**
Dollar-value LIFO
● LO8–8

On January 1, 2013, the Taylor Company adopted the dollar-value LIFO method. The inventory value for its one inventory pool on this date was $400,000. Inventory data for 2013 through 2015 are as follows:

| Date | Ending Inventory at Year-End Costs | Cost Index |
|---|---|---|
| 12/31/13 | $441,000 | 1.05 |
| 12/31/14 | 487,200 | 1.12 |
| 12/31/15 | 510,000 | 1.20 |

**Required:**
Calculate Taylor's ending inventory for 2013, 2014, and 2015.

---

**P 8–14**
Dollar-value LIFO
● LO8–8

Kingston Company uses the dollar-value LIFO method of computing inventory. An external price index is used to convert ending inventory to base year. The company began operations on January 1, 2013, with an inventory of $150,000. Year-end inventories at year-end costs and cost indexes for its one inventory pool were as follows:

| Year Ended December 31 | Ending Inventory at Year-End Costs | Cost Index (Relative to Base Year) |
|---|---|---|
| 2013 | $200,000 | 1.08 |
| 2014 | 245,700 | 1.17 |
| 2015 | 235,980 | 1.14 |
| 2016 | 228,800 | 1.10 |

**Required:**
Calculate inventory amounts at the end of each year.

---

**P 8–15**
Dollar-value LIFO
● LO8–8

On January 1, 2013, Avondale Lumber adopted the dollar-value LIFO inventory method. The inventory value for its one inventory pool on this date was $260,000. An internally generated cost index is used to convert ending inventory to base year. Year-end inventories at year-end costs and cost indexes for its one inventory pool were as follows:

| Year Ended December 31 | Inventory Year-End Costs | Cost Index (Relative to Base Year) |
|---|---|---|
| 2013 | $340,000 | 1.02 |
| 2014 | 350,000 | 1.06 |
| 2015 | 400,000 | 1.07 |
| 2016 | 430,000 | 1.10 |

**Required:**
Calculate inventory amounts at the end of each year.

---

**P 8–16**
Dollar-value
LIFO; solving for
unknowns
● LO8–8

At the beginning of 2013, Quentin and Kopps (Q&K) adopted the dollar-value LIFO (DVL) inventory method. On that date the value of its one inventory pool was $84,000. The company uses an internally generated cost index to convert ending inventory to base year. Inventory data for 2013 through 2016 are as follows:

| Year Ended December 31 | Ending Inventory at Year-End Costs | Ending Inventory at Base-Year Costs | Cost Index | Ending Inventory at DVL cost |
|---|---|---|---|---|
| 2013 | $100,800 | $ 96,000 | 1.05 | ? |
| 2014 | 136,800 | ? | 1.14 | ? |
| 2015 | 150,000 | 125,000 | ? | ? |
| 2016 | ? | ? | 1.25 | $133,710 |

**Required:**
Determine the missing amounts.

# Broaden Your Perspective

Apply your critical-thinking ability to the knowledge you've gained. These cases will provide you an opportunity to develop your research, analysis, judgment, and communication skills. You also will work with other students, integrate what you've learned, apply it in real world situations, and consider its global and ethical ramifications. This practice will broaden your knowledge and further develop your decision-making abilities.

**Judgment
Case 8–1**
Riding the
Merry-Go-Round
● LO8–7

Real World Financials

Merry-Go-Round Enterprises, the clothing retailer for dedicated followers of young men's and women's fashion, was looking natty as a company. It was March 1993, and the Joppa, Maryland-based outfit had just announced the acquisition of Chess King, a rival clothing chain, a move that would give it the biggest share of the young men's clothing market. Merry-Go-Round told brokerage firm analysts that the purchase would add $13 million, or 15 cents a share, to profits for the year. So some Wall Street analysts raised their earnings estimates for Merry-Go-Round. The company's stock rose $2.25, or 15 percent, to $17 on the day of the Chess King news. Merry-Go-Round was hot—$100 of its stock in January 1988 was worth $804 five years later. In 1993 the chain owned 1,460 stores in 44 states, mostly under the Cignal, Chess King, and Merry-Go-Round names.

Merry-Go-Round's annual report for the fiscal year ended January 30, 1993, reported a 15% sales growth, to $877.5 million from $761.2 million. A portion of the company's balance sheet is reproduced below:

| | Jan. 30, 1993 | Feb. 1, 1992 |
|---|---|---|
| **Assets** | | |
| Cash and cash equivalents | $40,115,000 | $29,781,000 |
| Marketable securities | — | 9,703 |
| Receivables | 6,466,000 | 6,195 |
| Merchandise inventories | 82,197,000 | 59,971,000 |

But Merry-Go-Round spun out. The company lost $544,000 in the first six months of 1993, compared with earnings of $13.5 million in the first half of 1992. In the fall of 1992, Leonard "Boogie" Weinglass, Merry-Go-Round's flamboyant founder and chairman who had started the company in 1968, boarded up his Merry-Go-Ranch in Aspen, Colorado, and returned to management after a 12-year hiatus. But the pony-tailed, shirtsleeved entrepreneur—the inspiration for the character Boogie in the movie *Diner*—couldn't save his company from bankruptcy. In January 1994, the company filed for Chapter 11 protection in Baltimore. Shares crumbled below $3.

**Required:**

In retrospect, can you identify any advance warning at the date of the financial statements of the company's impending bankruptcy?
[Adapted from Jonathan Burton, "Due Diligence," *Worth*, June 1994, pp. 89–96.]

**Real World
Case 8–2**
Physical
quantities and
costs included in
inventory; Sport
Chalet
● LO8–2

Real World Financials

Determining the physical quantity that should be included in inventory normally is a simple matter because that amount consists of items in the possession of the company. The cost of inventory includes all necessary expenditures to acquire the inventory and bring it to its desired *condition* and *location* for sale or for use in the manufacturing process.

**Required:**

1. Identify and describe the situations in which physical quantity included in inventory is more difficult than simply determining items in the possession of the company.

2. In addition to the direct acquisition costs such as the price paid and transportation costs to obtain inventory, what other expenditures might be necessary to bring the inventory to its desired condition and location?

3. Access EDGAR on the Internet. The web address is www.sec.gov. Search for **Sport Chalet Inc.**, a leading operator of full-service, specialty sporting goods stores in California and Nevada. Access the 10-K filing for the most recent fiscal year. Search or scroll to find the disclosure notes (footnotes). What costs does Sport Chalet include in its inventory?

**Judgment
Case 8–3**
The specific
identification
inventory
method;
inventoriable
costs
● LO8–3, LO8–4

Happlia Co. imports household appliances. Each model has many variations and each unit has an identification number. Happlia pays all costs for getting the goods from the port to its central warehouse in Des Moines. After repackaging, the goods are consigned to retailers. A retailer makes a sale, simultaneously buys the appliance from Happlia, and pays the balance due within one week.

To alleviate the overstocking of refrigerators at a Minneapolis retailer, some were reshipped to a Kansas City retailer where they were still held in inventory at December 31, 2013. Happlia paid the costs of this reshipment. Happlia uses the specific identification inventory costing method.

**Required:**

1. In regard to the specific identification inventory costing method:
   a. Describe its key elements.
   b. Discuss why it is appropriate for Happlia to use this method.
2. a. What general criteria should Happlia use to determine inventory carrying amounts at December 31, 2013?
   b. Give four examples of costs included in these inventory carrying amounts.
3. What costs should be reported in Happlia's 2013 income statement? Ignore lower of cost or market considerations.

*(AICPA adapted)*

**Communication Case 8–4**
LIFO versus FIFO
● LO8–4, LO8–5

You have just been hired as a consultant to Tangier Industries, a newly formed company. The company president, John Meeks, is seeking your advice as to the appropriate inventory method Tangier should use to value its inventory and cost of goods sold. Mr. Meeks has narrowed the choice to LIFO and FIFO. He has heard that LIFO might be better for tax purposes, but FIFO has certain advantages for financial reporting to investors and creditors. You have been told that the company will be profitable in its first year and for the foreseeable future.

**Required:**

Prepare a report for the president describing the factors that should be considered by Tangier in choosing between LIFO and FIFO.

**Communication Case 8–5**
LIFO versus FIFO
● LO8–4, LO8–5

An accounting intern for a local CPA firm was reviewing the financial statements of a client in the electronics industry. The intern noticed that the client used the FIFO method of determining ending inventory and cost of goods sold. When she asked a colleague why the firm used FIFO instead of LIFO, she was told that the client used FIFO to minimize its income tax liability. This response puzzled the intern because she thought that LIFO would minimize income tax liability.

**Required:**

What would you tell the intern to resolve the confusion?

**Judgment Case 8–6**
Goods in transit
● LO8–2

At the end of 2013, the Biggie Company performed its annual physical inventory count. John Lawrence, the manager in charge of the physical count, was told that an additional $22,000 in inventory that had been sold and was in transit to the customer should be included in the ending inventory balance. John was of the opinion that the merchandise shipped should be excluded from the ending inventory since Biggie was not in physical possession of the merchandise.

**Required:**

Discuss the situation and indicate why John's opinion might be incorrect.

**Ethics Case 8–7**
Profit manipulation
● LO8–4

In 2012 the Moncrief Company purchased from Jim Lester the right to be the sole distributor in the western states of a product called Zelenex. In payment, Moncrief agreed to pay Lester 20% of the gross profit recognized from the sale of Zelenex in 2013.

Moncrief uses a periodic inventory system and the LIFO inventory method. Late in 2013, the following information is available concerning the inventory of Zelenex:

| | |
|---|---|
| Beginning inventory, 1/1/13 (10,000 units @ $30) | $ 300,000 |
| Purchases (40,000 units @ $30) | 1,200,000 |
| Sales (35,000 units @ $60) | $2,100,000 |

By the end of the year, the purchase price of Zelenex had risen to $40 per unit. On December 28, 2013, three days before year-end, Moncrief is in a position to purchase 20,000 additional units of Zelenex at the $40 per unit price. Due to the increase in purchase price, Moncrief will increase the selling price in 2014 to $80 per unit. Inventory on hand before the purchase, 15,000 units, is sufficient to meet the next six months' sales and the company does not anticipate any significant changes in purchase price during 2014.

**Required:**

1. Determine the effect of the purchase of the additional 20,000 units on the 2013 gross profit from the sale of Zelenex and the payment due to Jim Lester.
2. Discuss the ethical dilemma Moncrief faces in determining whether or not the additional units should be purchased.

**Real World Case 8–8**
Effects of inventory valuation methods; supplemental LIFO disclosures; The Kroger Company
● LO8–4, LO8–6

Real World Financials

Income statement and balance sheet information abstracted from a recent annual report of The Kroger Company, one of the world's largest retailers, appears below:

**Balance Sheets**
($ in millions)

|  | January 29, 2011 | January 30, 2010 |
|---|---|---|
| Current assets: | | |
| Inventories | $4,966 | $4,935 |

**Income Statements**
($ in millions)

| | For the Year Ended | |
|---|---|---|
|  | January 29, 2011 | January 30, 2010 |
| Net sales | $82,189 | $76,733 |
| Cost of goods sold | 63,927 | 58,958 |
| Gross profit | $18,262 | $17,777 |

The significant accounting policies note disclosure contained the following:

**Inventories (in part)**

Inventories are stated at the lower of cost (principally on a LIFO basis) or market. In total, approximately 97% of inventories were valued using the LIFO method. Cost for the balance of the inventories, including substantially all fuel inventories, was determined using the first-in, first-out ("FIFO") method. Replacement cost was higher than the carrying amount by $827 million at January 29, 2011 and $770 million at January 30, 2010.

**Required:**

1. Why is Kroger disclosing the replacement cost of its LIFO inventory?
2. Assuming that year-end replacement cost figures approximate FIFO inventory values, estimate what the beginning and ending inventory balances for the fiscal year ended 1/29/11 would have been if Kroger had used FIFO for all of its inventories.
3. Estimate the effect on cost of goods sold (that is, would it have been greater or less and by how much?) for the fiscal year ended 1/29/11 if Kroger had used FIFO for all of its inventories.

**Real World Case 8–9**
Effects of inventory valuation methods; Whole Foods Market
● LO8–4, LO8–5, LO8–7

Real World Financials

EDGAR, the Electronic Data Gathering, Analysis, and Retrieval system, performs automated collection, validation, indexing, and forwarding of submission by companies and others who are required by law to file forms with the U.S. Securities and Exchange Commission (SEC). All publicly traded domestic companies use EDGAR to make the majority of their filings. (Some foreign companies file voluntarily.) Form 10-K, which includes the annual report, is required to be filed on EDGAR. The SEC makes this information available on the Internet.

**Required:**

1. Access EDGAR on the Internet. The web address is www.sec.gov.
2. Search for Whole Foods Market, Inc. Access the 10-K filing for the most recent fiscal year. Search or scroll to find the financial statements and related notes.
3. Answer the following questions related to the company's inventories:
   a. What method(s) does the company use to value its inventories?
   b. Calculate what cost of sales would have been for the year if the company had used FIFO to value its inventories.
   c. Calculate inventory turnover for the year using the reported numbers.

**Communication Case 8–10**
Dollar-value LIFO method
● LO8–8

Maxi Corporation uses the unit LIFO inventory method. The costs of the company's products have been steadily rising since the company began operations in 2003 and cost increases are expected to continue. The chief financial officer of the company would like to continue using LIFO because of its tax advantages. However, the controller, Sally Hamel, would like to reduce the recordkeeping costs of LIFO that have steadily increased over the years as new products have been added to the company's product line. Sally suggested the use of the dollar-value LIFO method. The chief financial officer has asked Sally to describe the dollar-value LIFO procedure.

**Required:**
Describe the dollar-value LIFO procedure.

**Research Case 8–11**
FASB codification; locate and extract relevant information and authoritative support for a financial reporting issue; product financing arrangement
● LO8–2, LO8–3

You were recently hired to work in the controller's office of the Balboa Lumber Company. Your boss, Alfred Eagleton, took you to lunch during your first week and asked a favor. "Things have been a little slow lately, and we need to borrow a little cash to tide us over. Our inventory has been building up and the CFO wants to pledge the inventory as collateral for a short-term loan. But I have a better idea." Mr. Eagleton went on to describe his plan. "On July 1, 2013, the first day of the company's third quarter, we will sell $100,000 of inventory to the Harbaugh Corporation for $160,000. Harbaugh will pay us immediately and then we will agree to repurchase the merchandise in two months for $164,000. The $4,000 is Harbaugh's fee for holding the inventory and for providing financing. I already checked with Harbaugh's controller and he has agreed to the arrangement. Not only will we obtain the financing we need, but the third quarter's before-tax profits will be increased by $56,000, the gross profit on the sale less the $4,000 fee. Go research the issue and make sure we would not be violating any specific accounting standards related to product financing arrangements."

**Required:**

1. Obtain the relevant authoritative literature on product financing arrangements using the FASB's Codification Research System. You might gain access at the FASB website (www.fasb.org). What is the specific citation that provides guidance for determining whether an arrangement involving the sale of inventory is "in substance" a financing arrangement?
2. What is the specific citation that addresses the recognition of a product financing arrangement?
3. Determine the appropriate treatment of product financing arrangements like the one proposed by Mr. Eagleton.
4. Prepare the journal entry for Balboa Lumber to record the "sale" of the inventory and subsequent repurchase.

**Analysis Case 8–12**
Compare inventory management using ratios; Saks and Dillards
● LO8–7

Real World Financials

The table below contains selected financial information included in the 2011 financial statements of Saks, Inc., and Dillards, Inc., two companies in the department store industry.

|  | ($ in millions) | | | |
|  | Saks, Inc. | | Dillards, Inc. | |
|  | 2011 | 2010 | 2011 | 2010 |
|---|---|---|---|---|
| **Balance sheet:** |  |  |  |  |
| Inventories | $  671 | $649 | $1,290 | $1,301 |
| **Income statement:** |  |  |  |  |
| Net sales | $2,786 |  | $6,121 |  |
| Cost of goods sold | 1,688 |  | 3,976 |  |

**Required:**

1. Calculate the 2011 gross profit ratio, inventory turnover ratio, and average days in inventory for both companies. Evaluate the management of each company's investment in inventory. Industry averages for these ratios are as follows:

| Gross profit | 24% |
|---|---|
| Inventory turnover | 2.84 times |
| Average days in inventory | 129 days |

2. Obtain annual reports from three corporations in an industry other than autos and compare the management of each company's investment in inventory.

**Note:** You can obtain copies of annual reports from your library, from friends who are shareholders, from the investor relations department of the corporations, from a friendly stockbroker, or from EDGAR (Electronic Data Gathering, Analysis, and Retrieval) on the Internet (www.sec.gov).

## Air France—Klm Case

 **AIRFRANCE**

● LO8–9

IFRS

Air France–KLM (AF), a French company, prepares its financial statements according to International Financial Reporting Standards. AF's annual report for the year ended March 31, 2011, which includes financial statements and disclosure notes, is provided with all new textbooks. This material also is included in AF's "Registration Document 2010–11," dated June 15, 2011 and is available at **www.airfranceklm.com**.

**Required:**

What method does the company use to value its inventory? What other alternatives are available under IFRS? Under U.S. GAAP?

## CPA Simulation 8–1

**Johnson Company**

Physical quantities and costs included in inventory.

**KAPLAN**

**CPA Review**

Test your knowledge of the concepts discussed in this chapter, practice critical professional skills necessary for career success, and prepare for the computer-based CPA exam by accessing our CPA simulations at the text website: **www.mhhe.com/spiceland7e**.

The Johnson Company simulation tests your knowledge of the physical quantities and costs that should be included in inventory.

# 9

# Inventories: Additional Issues

**OVERVIEW** ⎯⎯⎯⎯ We covered most of the principal measurement and reporting issues involving the asset inventory and the corresponding expense cost of goods sold in the previous chapter. In this chapter we complete our discussion of inventory measurement by explaining the lower-of-cost-or-market rule used to value inventories. In addition, we investigate inventory estimation techniques, methods of simplifying LIFO, changes in inventory method, and inventory errors.

**LEARNING** ⎯⎯⎯⎯ **After studying this chapter, you should be able to:**
**OBJECTIVES**

- **LO9–1** Understand and apply the lower-of-cost-or-market rule used to value inventories. (p. 476)

- **LO9–2** Estimate ending inventory and cost of goods sold using the gross profit method. (p. 484)

- **LO9–3** Estimate ending inventory and cost of goods sold using the retail inventory method, applying the various cost flow methods. (p. 486)

- **LO9–4** Explain how the retail inventory method can be made to approximate the lower-of-cost-or-market rule. (p. 489)

- **LO9–5** Determine ending inventory using the dollar-value LIFO retail inventory method. (p. 494)

- **LO9–6** Explain the appropriate accounting treatment required when a change in inventory method is made. (p. 497)

- **LO9–7** Explain the appropriate accounting treatment required when an inventory error is discovered. (p. 500)

- **LO9–8** Discuss the primary differences between U.S. GAAP and IFRS with respect to the lower-of-cost-or-market rule for valuing inventory. (p. 481)

## FINANCIAL REPORTING CASE

### Does It Count?

Today you drove over to **Sears** to pick up a few items. Yesterday, your accounting professor had discussed inventory measurement issues and the different methods (FIFO, LIFO, and average) used by companies to determine ending inventory and cost of goods sold. You can't imagine actually counting the inventory in all of the Sears stores around the country. "There must be some way Sears can avoid counting all of that inventory every time they want to produce financial statements," you tell your dog when you get home. "I think I'll go check their financial statements on the Internet to see what kind of inventory method they use." You find the following in the summary of significant accounting policies included in Sears's most recent financial statements:

#### Merchandise Inventories (in part):

Merchandise inventories are valued at the lower of cost or market. For Kmart and Sears Domestic, cost is primarily determined using the retail inventory method. Approximately 50% of consolidated merchandise inventories are valued using LIFO. To estimate the effects of inflation on inventories, we utilize external price indices determined by an outside source, the Bureau of Labor Statistics.

By the time you finish this chapter, you should be able to respond appropriately to the questions posed in this case. Compare your response to the solution provided at the end of the chapter.

**QUESTIONS**

1. Sears values its inventory at the lower of cost or market. What does that mean? Under what circumstances might Sears be justified in reporting its inventory at less than cost? (*p. 475*)

2. How does Sears avoid counting all its inventory every time it produces financial statements? What are external price indices used for? (*p. 494*)

# PART A

## REPORTING—LOWER OF COST OR MARKET

● LO9–1

In the previous chapter you learned that there are several methods a company could use to determine the cost of inventory at the end of a period and the corresponding cost of goods sold for the period. You also learned that it is important for a company to disclose the inventory method that it uses. Otherwise, investors and creditors would be unable to meaningfully compare accounting information from company to company. This disclosure typically is made in the summary of significant accounting policies accompanying the financial statements. **Coca-Cola Company**'s inventory method disclosure is shown in Illustration 9–1.

**Illustration 9–1**

Disclosure of Inventory Method—Coca-Cola Company

**Real World Financials**

**Inventories (in part)**

Inventories consists primarily of raw materials and packaging (which includes ingredients and supplies) and finished goods (which includes concentrates and syrups in our concentrate and foodservice operations, and finished beverages in our bottling and canning operations). Inventories are valued at the lower of cost or market. We determine cost on the basis of the average cost or first-in, first-out methods.

**FINANCIAL Reporting Case**

Q1, p. 475

The LCM approach to valuing inventory is required by GAAP.

**Real World Financials**

The disclosure indicates that Coca-Cola uses both the average cost and FIFO methods to determine the cost of its inventories. Notice that inventories actually are valued at the *lower of cost or market.* Assets are initially valued at their historical costs, but a departure from cost is warranted when the utility of an asset (its probable future economic benefits) is no longer as great as its cost. Accounts receivable, for example, are valued at net realizable value by reducing initial valuation with an allowance for uncollectible accounts.

The utility, or benefits, a company receives from inventory result from the ultimate sale of the goods. So deterioration, obsolescence, changes in price levels, or any situation that might compromise the inventory's salability impairs that utility. The **lower-of-cost-or-market (LCM)** approach to valuing inventory was developed to avoid reporting inventory at an amount greater than the benefits it can provide. Reporting inventories at LCM causes losses to be recognized in the period the value of inventory declines below its cost rather than in the period in which the goods ultimately are sold. LCM is not an optional approach to valuing inventory; it is required by GAAP.

The tremendous growth of the Internet that took place during the decade of the 90s allowed companies that produced products that support the Internet to become extremely profitable. **Cisco Systems, Inc.**, the world's largest networking products company, is one of those companies. In 1993, Cisco reported $649 million in sales revenue. By 2000, sales had reached nearly $19 billion! Growth rates of 50% year-to-year were commonplace. The company's market capitalization (price per share of common stock multiplied by the number of common shares outstanding) soared to over $500 billion. To keep pace with this growth in sales, inventories swelled from $71 million in 1993 to over $2.5 billion in 2000.

At the end of 2000, corporate spending on Internet infrastructure took a drastic downturn. Many dot-com companies went bankrupt, and companies like Cisco saw their fantastic growth rates nosedive. Early in 2001, the company reported its first-ever quarterly loss and, due to declining demand for its products, recorded an inventory write-down in excess of $2 billion. The company's once lofty market capitalization dropped to just over $100 billion.

**CISCO Posts $5BN Loss On Huge Write-Downs**
Technology giant Cisco Systems posted on Tuesday a third-quarter net loss of $2.69 billion, its first ever, following a write-down of inventory, restructuring costs and a sharp drop-off in corporate spending.

. . . and a write-down of over $2 billion for excess inventory.

Cisco said 80 percent of the inventory charge relates to raw materials, such as semiconductor memories, optical components, . . .

"Most of the excess inventory cannot be sold as it is custom built for Cisco," chief financial officer Mr. Larry Carter said in a conference call.[1]

---

[1]Fiona Buffini, "Cisco Posts $5bn Loss on Huge Writedowns," *Financial Review,* May 9, 2001.

# Determining Market Value

From the preceding discussion, you might interpret the term *market* to mean the amount that could be realized if the inventory were sold. However, generally accepted accounting principles define market for LCM purposes as the inventory's current replacement cost (by purchase or reproduction) except that market should not:

*Replacement cost (RC) generally means the cost to replace the item by purchase or manufacture.*

a. Exceed the net realizable value (that is, estimated selling price in the ordinary course of business less reasonably predictable costs of completion and disposal).

b. Be less than net realizable value reduced by an allowance for an approximately normal profit margin.

In effect, we have a ceiling and a floor between which market (that is, replacement cost) must fall. **Net realizable value (NRV)** represents the upper limit and **net realizable value less a normal profit margin (NRV − NP)** provides the lower limit. If **replacement cost (RC)** is within the range, it represents market; if it is above the ceiling or below the floor, the ceiling or the floor becomes market. As a result, the designated market value is the number that falls in the middle of the three possibilities: replacement cost, net realizable value, and net realizable value less a normal profit margin. The designated market value is compared with cost, and the lower of the two is used to value inventory.

*The ceiling of net realizable value (NRV) and the floor of net realizable value less a normal profit margin (NRV − NP) establish a range within which the market must fall.*

Illustration 9–2 portrays the lower-of-cost-or-market approach to inventory valuation.

## Lower-of-cost-or-market Approach to Valuing Inventory

**Illustration 9–2**

Lower-of-Cost-or-Market Approach to Valuing Inventory

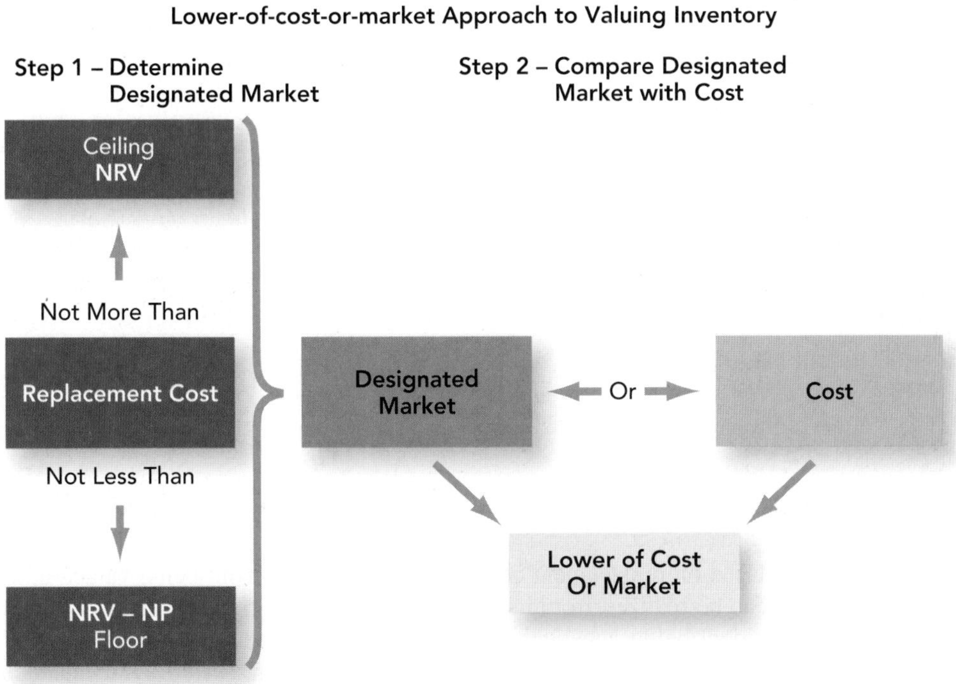

Let's see how the LCM rule is applied in Illustration 9–3 on the next page and then we will discuss its theoretical merit.

Notice that the designated market value is the middle amount of the three market possibilities. This number is then compared to cost and the lower of the two is the final inventory value. For item A, cost is lower than market. For each of the other items, the designated market is lower than cost, requiring an adjustment to the carrying value of inventory. We discuss the adjustment procedure later in the chapter. First though, let's consider the conceptual justification of the LCM rule.

**THEORETICAL MERITS.**   What is the logic for designating replacement cost as the principal meaning of market value in the LCM rule? First, a change in replacement cost usually is a good indicator of the direction of change in selling price. If replacement cost declines, selling price usually will decline, or already has declined. Another reason is that if previously acquired inventory is revalued at its replacement cost, then the profit margin realized on its sale will likely approximate the profit margin realizable on the sale of newly acquired items.

## Illustration 9–3
Lower of Cost or Market

The Collins Company has five inventory items on hand at the end of 2013. The year-end unit costs (determined by applying the average cost method), current unit selling prices, and estimated disposal (selling) costs for each of the items are presented below. The gross profit ratio for each of the products is 20% of selling price.

| Item | Cost | Replacement Cost | Selling Price | Estimated Disposal Costs |
|------|------|------------------|---------------|--------------------------|
| A | $ 50 | $55 | $100 | $15 |
| B | 100 | 90 | 120 | 20 |
| C | 80 | 70 | 85 | 20 |
| D | 90 | 37 | 100 | 24 |
| E | 95 | 92 | 110 | 24 |

The determination of inventory value is a two-step process: first, determine the designated market value and second, compare the designated market value to cost. The lower of the two is the LCM inventory value.

*Inventory is valued at the lower of cost or the designated market value.*

| Item | (1) RC | (2) NRV (The Ceiling) | (3) NRV − NP (The Floor) | (4) Designated Market Value [Middle Value of (1), (2) and (3)] | (5) Cost | Inventory Value [Lower of (4) and (5)] |
|------|--------|-----------------------|--------------------------|---------------------------------------------------------------|----------|-----------------------------------------|
| A | $55 | $ 85 | $65 | $65 | $ 50 | $50 |
| B | 90 | 100 | 76 | 90 | 100 | 90 |
| C | 70 | 65 | 48 | 65 | 80 | 65 |
| D | 37 | 76 | 56 | 56 | 90 | 56 |
| E | 92 | 86 | 64 | 86 | 95 | 86 |

RC = Current replacement cost.
NRV = Estimated selling price less estimated disposal costs.
NRV − NP = NRV less a normal profit margin.

Example for item B:

| | |
|---|---|
| Selling price | $120 |
| Less: Disposal costs | (20) |
| NRV | 100 |
| Less: Normal profit | (24) ($120 selling price × 20%) |
| NRV − NP | $ 76 |

The upper limit placed on replacement cost prevents inventory from being valued at an amount above what can be realized from its sale. The lower limit prevents inventory from being valued at an amount below what can be realized from its sale after considering normal profit margin. For example, consider item D in our illustration. If item D is valued at its replacement cost of $37 without considering the ceiling or floor, a loss of $53 ($90 cost less $37) would be recognized. If the item is subsequently sold at its current selling price less usual disposal costs (NRV = $76), then a gross profit of $39 ($76 less $37) would be recognized. This is much higher than its normal profit of $20 (20% × $100) and causes a shifting of income from the period the inventory loss is recognized to the period the item is sold. The ceiling and floor prohibit this kind of profit distortion.

*Some accountants complain that LCM promotes conservatism at the expense of consistency.*

On the other hand, critics of LCM contend that the method causes losses to be recognized that haven't actually occurred. Others maintain that it introduces needless inconsistency in order to be conservative. Inconsistency is created because LCM recognizes decreases in market value as they occur, but not increases.

The practice of recognizing decreases but not increases is not simply an application motivated by conservatism. Recall our discussions in previous chapters on revenue recognition and the realization principle. Recognizing increases in the value of inventory prior to sale would, in most cases, violate the realization principle. Assume that merchandise costing $100 has a net realizable value of $150. Recognizing the increase in value would increase pretax income by $50. This is equivalent to recognizing revenue of $150, cost of goods sold of $100, and gross profit of $50. Either way, pretax income is increased in a period prior to sale of the product. Prior to sale, there usually exists significant uncertainty as to the collectibility of the asset to be received. We don't know if the product will be sold, nor the selling price, or the buyer if eventually sold.

The LCM rules are intended as a guide rather than a literal rule. In practice, companies frequently define market as net realizable value. This is a number that often is easier to estimate than replacement cost. Also, assuming the NRV does not change, when the item is sold, there will be neither gross profit nor additional loss. The entire effect on income is recognized in the period the realizable value drops below cost.

# Ethical Dilemma

The Hartley Paper Company, owned and operated by Bill Hartley, manufactures and sells different types of computer paper. The company has reported profits in the majority of years since the company's inception in 1969 and is projecting a profit in 2013 of $65,000, down from $96,000 in 2012.

Near the end of 2013, the company is in the process of applying for a bank loan. The loan proceeds will be used to replace manufacturing equipment necessary to modernize the manufacturing operation. In preparing the financial statements for the year, the chief accountant, Don Davis, mentioned to Bill Hartley that approximately $40,000 of paper inventory has become obsolete and should be written off as a loss in 2013. Bill is worried that the write-down would lower 2013 income to a level that might cause the bank to refuse the loan. Without the loan, it would be difficult for the company to compete. This could cause decreased future business and employees might have to be laid off. Bill is considering waiting until 2014 to write down the inventory. Don Davis is contemplating his responsibilities in this situation.

## Applying Lower of Cost or Market

Lower of cost or market can be applied to individual inventory items, to logical categories of inventory, or to the entire inventory. A major product line can be considered a logical category of inventory. For income tax purposes, the lower-of-cost-or-market rule must be applied on an individual item basis.

Let's return to our illustration and assume the unit amounts pertain to 1,000 units of each inventory item. Also, let's say items A–B and items C–E are two collections of similar items that can be considered logical categories of inventory. Illustration 9–3A, on the next page, compares the LCM valuation accounting to each of three possible applications.

The final LCM inventory value is different for each of the three applications. The inventory value is $347,000 if LCM is applied to each item, $357,000 if it is applied to product line categories, and $362,000 if applied to the entire inventory. Applying LCM to groups of inventory items will usually cause a higher inventory valuation

> **LCM Application**
> The most common practice is to apply the *lower of cost or market rule* separately to each item of the inventory. However, if there is only one end-product category the cost utility of the total stock—the inventory in its entirety—may have the greatest significance for accounting purposes.
>
> Similarly, where more than one major product or operational category exists, the application of the *lower of cost or market, whichever is lower* rule to the total of items included in such major categories may result in the most useful determination of income.[2]

> **The LCM rule can be applied to individual inventory items, logical inventory categories, or the entire inventory.**

than if applied on an item-by-item basis because group application permits decreases in the market value of some items to be offset by increases in others. Each approach is acceptable but should be applied consistently from one period to another.

[2]FASB ASC 330–10–35–9 and 10: Inventory—Overall—Subsequent Measurement (previously "Restatement and Revision of Accounting Research Bulletins," *Accounting Research Bulletin* No. 43 (New York: AICPA, 1953), Ch. 4, par. 11).

**Illustration 9–3A**

LCM Determination—Application at Different Levels of Aggregation

| Item | Cost | Designated Market Value | Lower-of-Cost-or-Market By Individual Items | By Product Line | By Total Inventory |
|---|---|---|---|---|---|
| A | $ 50,000 | $ 65,000 | $ 50,000 | | |
| B | 100,000 | 90,000 | 90,000 | | |
| Total A + B | $150,000 | $155,000 | | $150,000 | |
| C | $ 80,000 | $ 65,000 | 65,000 | | |
| D | 90,000 | 56,000 | 56,000 | | |
| E | 95,000 | 86,000 | 86,000 | | |
| Total C, D, & E | $265,000 | $207,000 | | 207,000 | |
| Total | $415,000 | $362,000 | $347,000 | $357,000 | $362,000 |

## Adjusting Cost to Market

When a company applies the LCM rule and a material write-down of inventory is required, the company has two choices of how to report the reduction. One way found in practice is to report the loss as a separate item in the income statement. An alternative is to include the loss as part of the cost of goods sold.

| Loss on write-down of inventory ... xx | | Cost of goods sold .............. xx |
|---|---|---|
| Inventory* ............................. xx | or | Inventory* ...................... xx |

*Or, inventory can be reduced indirectly with a credit to an allowance account.

If inventory write-downs are commonplace for a company, it usually will include the losses as part of cost of goods sold. However, a write-down loss that is substantial and unusual should be reported as a separate item among operating expenses. Including these losses in cost of goods sold would distort the relationship between sales and cost of goods sold. Conceptually, cost of goods sold should include only the cost of goods actually sold during the period.

Recall from our introductory discussion to this chapter that **Cisco Systems, Inc.,** recorded an inventory write-down in excess of $2 billion. To understand how the relationship between sales and cost of goods sold can be distorted, let's consider the top part of the company's income statements for the first quarter of 2001 and 2000 shown in Illustration 9–4.

Using the information in the statements, the gross profit ratio dropped from 64% ($3,172 ÷ $4,933) in 2000 to 7% ($328 ÷ $4,728) in 2001. An analyst might conclude that

> **Recording Inventory Write-Downs**
> When substantial and unusual losses result from the application of cost or market, it will frequently be desirable to disclose the amount of the loss in the income statement as a separate charge separately identified from the consumed inventory costs described as cost of goods sold.[3]

**Illustration 9–4**

Partial Income Statements—Cisco Systems, Inc.

Real World Financials

| INCOME STATEMENTS (IN PART) For the Three Months Ended, ($ in millions) | | |
|---|---|---|
| | April 28, 2001 | April 29, 2000 |
| Net sales | $4,728 | $4,933 |
| Cost of sales | 4,400 | 1,761 |
| Gross profit | 328 | 3,172 |

[3]FASB ASC 330–10–50–2: Inventory—Overall—Disclosure—Losses from Application of Lower of Cost or Market (previously "Restatement and Revision of Accounting Research Bulletins," *Accounting Research Bulletin* No. 43 (New York: AICPA, 1953), Ch. 4, par. 14).

there was a significant deterioration in the markup the company was able to achieve on its products. However, this assessment is premature. A disclosure note included in the financial statements for the first quarter of 2001 reported that during the quarter Cisco recorded "an excess inventory charge of $2.25 billion classified as cost of sales." We get a more accurate portrayal of the company's gross profit ratio if we reduce the cost of goods sold by the inventory charge (write-down):

| | |
|---|---|
| Sales | $4,728 |
| Adjusted cost of sales ($4,400 − 2,250) | 2,150 |
| Adjusted gross profit | 2,578 |
| Adjusted gross profit ratio | 55% |

*Reporting a substantial and unusual loss from an inventory write-down as part of cost of goods sold distorts the relationship between sales and cost of goods sold.*

Cisco's gross profit ratio did decline from the prior year, but not nearly as drastically as the reported financial statement information would lead us to believe.

Regardless of which approach we use to report the write-down, the reduced inventory value becomes the new cost basis for subsequent reporting, and if the inventory value later recovers prior to its sale, we do not write it back up.[4]

# International Financial Reporting Standards

**Lower of cost or market.** You just learned that in the United States inventory is valued at the lower of cost or market, with market defined as replacement cost with a ceiling of net realizable value (NRV) and a floor of NRV less a normal profit margin. However, according to *IAS No. 2*,[5] inventory is valued at the lower of cost and net realizable value. In other words, "market" is always net realizable value under IFRS.

*IAS No. 2* also specifies that if circumstances indicate that an inventory write-down is no longer appropriate, it must be reversed. Reversals are not permitted under U.S. GAAP.

Under U.S. GAAP, the LCM rule can be applied to individual items, logical inventory categories, or the entire inventory. Using the international standard, the LCM assessment usually is applied to individual items, although using logical inventory categories is allowed under certain circumstances.

Consider the following illustration:

Biddle and White, LTD, prepares its financial statements according to IFRS. Using the data in Illustrations 9–3 and 9–3A, the company would determine the inventory carrying value at year-end, assuming the LCM rule is applied to individual items, as $377,000.

● LO9–8

**IFRS ILLUSTRATION**

| Item | Cost | NRV | LCM |
|---|---|---|---|
| A | $ 50,000 | $ 85,000 | $ 50,000 |
| B | 100,000 | 100,000 | 100,000 |
| C | 80,000 | 65,000 | 65,000 |
| D | 90,000 | 76,000 | 76,000 |
| E | 95,000 | 86,000 | 86,000 |
| Totals | $415,000 | | $377,000 |

Notice that the carrying value of $377,000 is larger than the $347,000 determined using U.S. GAAP. This normally will be the case because replacement cost usually is less than NRV. The entry to record the write-down is as follows:

| | | |
|---|---|---|
| Inventory write-down expense ($415,000 − 377,000) ........ | 38,000 | |
| Inventory valuation allowance ......................................... | | 38,000 |

*To record the write-down of inventory to market value.*

(continued)

[4]The SEC, in *Staff Accounting Bulletin* No. 100, "Restructuring and Impairment Charges" (Washington, D.C.: SEC, November, 1999), paragraph B.B., [FASB ASC 330–10–S35–1: SAB Topic 5.BB], reaffirmed the provisions of GAAP literature on this issue. For interim reporting purposes, however, recoveries of losses on the same inventory in subsequent interim periods of the same fiscal year through market price recoveries should be recognized as gains in the later interim period, not to exceed the previously recognized losses.
[5]"Inventories," *International Accounting Standard* No. 2 (IASCF), as amended effective January 1, 2011.

(concluded)

Because IFRS allows companies to reverse write-downs later if NRV increases, it's convenient to use an inventory valuation account in the above entry rather than reducing inventory directly. Reversals, then, are recorded by debiting the allowance account. IFRS does not require the write-down to be recorded in any specific income statement account.

**Siemens AG**, a German electronics and electrical engineering company, prepares its financial statements according to IFRS. The following disclosure note illustrates the valuation of inventory at the lower of cost and net realizable value.

**Inventories (in part)**
Inventory is valued at the lower of acquisition or production cost and net realizable value, cost being generally determined on the basis of an average or first-in, first-out method.

Real World Financials

# Additional Consideration

In very limited circumstances, businesses are allowed under GAAP to carry inventory at a market value above cost. This approach is restricted generally to companies that deal in precious metals, and ". . . agricultural, mineral, and other products, units of which are interchangeable and have an immediate marketability at quoted prices . . ."[6] Writing inventory up to market value means recognizing revenue for the increase. This is called the *production basis* of recognizing revenue. In rare cases when the method is appropriate, full disclosure of the fact that inventory is valued at market is required.

## Concept Review Exercise

**LOWER OF COST OR MARKET**

The Strand Company sells four products that can be grouped into two major categories. Information necessary to apply the LCM rule at the end of 2013 for each of the four products is presented below. The normal profit margin for each of the products is 25% of selling price. The company records any losses from adjusting cost to market as separate income statement items and reduces inventory directly.

| Product | Cost | Replacement Cost | Selling Price | Disposal Costs |
|---------|------|------------------|---------------|----------------|
| 101 | $ 80,000 | $ 85,000 | $160,000 | $30,000 |
| 102 | 175,000 | 160,000 | 200,000 | 25,000 |
| 201 | 160,000 | 140,000 | 180,000 | 50,000 |
| 202 | 45,000 | 20,000 | 60,000 | 22,000 |

Products 101 and 102 are in category A and products 201 and 202 are in category B.

**Required:**

1. Determine the designated market value for each of the four products according to the LCM rule.

2. Determine the amount of the loss from write-down of inventory that would be required, applying the LCM rule to:
   a. Individual items.
   b. Major categories.
   c. The entire inventory.

---

[6]FASB ASC 330–10–35–16: Inventory—Overall—Subsequent Measurement (previously "Restatement and Revision of Accounting Research Bulletins," *Accounting Research Bulletin* No. 43 (New York: AICPA, 1953), Ch. 4, par. 16).

**Solution:**

1. Determine the designated market value for each of the four products according to the LCM rule.

| Product | (1) RC | (2) NRV (Selling Price Less Disposal Costs) | (3) NRV − Normal profit (NP) | (4) Designated Market Value [Middle Value of (1), (2) & (3)] |
|---|---|---|---|---|
| 101 | $ 85,000 | $130,000 | $ 90,000 | $ 90,000 |
| 102 | 160,000 | 175,000 | 125,000 | 160,000 |
| 201 | 140,000 | 130,000 | 85,000 | 130,000 |
| 202 | 20,000 | 38,000 | 23,000 | 23,000 |

Calculation of NRV − NP:

| Product | NRV | NP | NRV − NP |
|---|---|---|---|
| 101 | $ 130,000 | $40,000 (25% × $160,000) | $ 90,000 |
| 102 | 175,000 | 50,000 (25% × $200,000) | 125,000 |
| 201 | 130,000 | 45,000 (25% × $180,000) | 85,000 |
| 202 | 38,000 | 15,000 (25% × $60,000) | 23,000 |

2. Determine the amount of the loss from write-down of inventory that would be required.

| Product | Cost | Designated Market Value | Lower-of-Cost-or-Market By Individual Products | By Category | By Total Inventory |
|---|---|---|---|---|---|
| 101 | $ 80,000 | $ 90,000 | $ 80,000 | | |
| 102 | 175,000 | 160,000 | 160,000 | | |
| Total 101 + 102 | $255,000 | $250,000 | | $250,000 | |
| 201 | $160,000 | $130,000 | 130,000 | | |
| 202 | 45,000 | 23,000 | 23,000 | | |
| Total 201 + 202 | $205,000 | $153,000 | | 153,000 | |
| Total | $460,000 | $403,000 | $393,000 | $403,000 | $403,000 |

The LCM value for both the category application and the entire inventory application are identical because, in this particular case, market is below cost for both of the categories.

Amount of loss from write-down using individual items:

$$\$460,000 - 393,000 = \mathbf{\$67,000}$$

Amount of loss from write-down using categories or the entire inventory:

$$\$460,000 - 403,000 = \mathbf{\$57,000}$$

# INVENTORY ESTIMATION TECHNIQUES

**PART B**

The Southern Wholesale Company distributes approximately 100 products throughout the state of Mississippi. Southern uses a periodic inventory system and takes a physical count of inventory once a year at the end of the year. A recent fire destroyed the entire inventory in one of Southern's warehouses. How can the company determine the dollar amount of inventory destroyed when submitting an insurance claim to obtain reimbursement for the loss?

Home Improvement Stores, Inc., sells over 1,000 different products to customers in each of its 17 retail stores. The company uses a periodic inventory system and takes a physical count of inventory once a year at its fiscal year-end. Home Improvement's bank has asked for monthly financial statements as a condition attached to a recent loan. Can the company avoid the costly procedure of counting inventory at the end of each month to determine ending inventory and cost of goods sold?

These are just two examples of situations when it is either impossible or infeasible to determine the dollar amount of ending inventory by taking a count of the physical quantity of inventory on hand at the end of a period. Fortunately, companies can estimate inventory in these situations by either the gross profit method or the retail inventory method.

# The Gross Profit Method

The **gross profit method**, also known as the **gross margin method**, is useful in situations where estimates of inventory are desirable. The technique is valuable in a variety of situations:

● LO9–2

1. In determining the cost of inventory that has been lost, destroyed, or stolen.
2. In estimating inventory and cost of goods sold for interim reports, avoiding the expense of a physical inventory count.
3. In auditors' testing of the overall reasonableness of inventory amounts reported by clients.
4. In budgeting and forecasting.

The *gross profit method* is not acceptable for the preparation of annual financial statements.

However, the gross profit method provides only an approximation of inventory and is not acceptable according to generally accepted accounting principles for annual financial statements.

The technique relies on a relationship you learned in the previous chapter—ending inventory and cost of goods sold always equal the cost of goods available for sale. Even when inventory is unknown, we can estimate it because accounting records usually indicate the cost of goods available for sale (beginning inventory plus net purchases), and the cost of goods sold can be estimated from available information. So by subtracting the cost of goods sold estimate from the cost of goods available for sale, we obtain an estimate of ending inventory. Let's compare that with the way inventory and cost of goods sold normally are determined.

Usually, in a periodic inventory system, ending inventory is known from a physical count and cost of goods sold is *derived* as follows:

| | |
|---|---|
| Beginning inventory | (from the accounting records) |
| Plus: Net purchases | (from the accounting records) |
| Goods available for sale | |
| Less: Ending inventory | (from a physical count) |
| Cost of goods sold | |

However, when using the gross profit method, the ending inventory is *not* known. Instead, the amount of sales is known—from which we can estimate the cost of goods sold—and ending inventory is the amount calculated.

| | |
|---|---|
| Beginning inventory | (from the accounting records) |
| Plus: Net purchases | (from the accounting records) |
| Goods available for sale | |
| Less: Cost of goods sold | (estimated) |
| Ending inventory | (estimated) |

So, a first step in estimating inventory is to estimate cost of goods sold. This estimate relies on the historical relationship among (a) net sales, (b) cost of goods sold, and (c) gross profit. Gross profit, you will recall, is simply net sales minus cost of goods sold. So, if we know what net sales are, and if we know what percentage of net sales the gross profit is, we can fairly accurately estimate cost of goods sold. Companies often sell products that have similar gross profit ratios. As a result, accounting records usually provide the information necessary to estimate the cost of ending inventory, even when a physical count is impractical. Let's use the gross profit method to solve the problem of Southern Wholesale Company introduced earlier in the chapter. Suppose the company began 2013 with inventory of $600,000, and on March 17 a warehouse fire destroyed the entire inventory. Company records indicate net purchases of $1,500,000 and net sales of $2,000,000 prior to the fire. The gross profit ratio in each of the previous three years has been very close to 40%. Illustration 9–5 shows how Southern can estimate the cost of the inventory destroyed for its insurance claim.

| | | |
|---|---:|---:|
| Beginning inventory (from records) | | $ 600,000 |
| Plus: Net purchases (from records) | | 1,500,000 |
| Goods available for sale | | 2,100,000 |
| Less: Cost of goods sold: | | |
| Net sales | $2,000,000 | |
| Less: Estimated gross profit of 40% | (800,000) | |
| Estimated cost of goods sold* | | (1,200,000) |
| Estimated ending inventory | | $ 900,000 |

*Alternatively, cost of goods sold can be calculated as $2,000,000 × (1 − .40) = $1,200,000.

**Illustration 9–5**

Gross Profit Method

## A Word of Caution

The gross profit method provides only an estimate. The key to obtaining good estimates is the reliability of the gross profit ratio. The ratio usually is estimated from relationships between sales and cost of goods sold. However, the current relationship may differ from the past. In that case, all available information should be used to make necessary adjustments. For example, the company may have made changes in the markup percentage of some of its products. Very often different products have different markups. In these situations, a blanket ratio should not be applied across the board. The accuracy of the estimate can be improved by grouping inventory into pools of products that have similar gross profit relationships rather than using one gross profit ratio for the entire inventory.

> The key to obtaining good estimates is the reliability of the gross profit ratio.

The company's cost flow assumption should be implicitly considered when estimating the gross profit ratio. For example, if LIFO is used and the relationship between cost and selling price has changed for recent acquisitions, this would suggest a ratio different from one where the average cost method was used. Another difficulty with the gross profit method is that it does not explicitly consider possible theft or spoilage of inventory. The method assumes that if the inventory was not sold, then it must be on hand at the end of the period. Suspected theft or spoilage would require an adjustment to estimates obtained using the gross profit method.

# Additional Consideration

The gross profit ratio is, by definition, a percentage of sales. Sometimes, though, the gross profit is stated as a percentage of cost instead. In that case, it is referred to as the markup on cost. For instance, a 66% markup on cost is equivalent to a gross profit ratio of 40%. Here's why:

A gross profit ratio of 40% can be formulated as:

$$\text{Sales} = \text{Cost} + \text{Gross profit}$$
$$100\% = 60\% + 40\%$$

Now, expressing gross profit as a percentage of cost we get:

$$\text{Gross profit \%} \div \text{Cost \%} = \text{Gross profit as a \% of cost}$$
$$40\% \div 60\% = 66\tfrac{2}{3}\%$$

(continued)

(concluded)

Conversely, gross profit as a percentage of cost can be converted to gross profit as a percentage of sales (the gross profit ratio) as follows:

$$\text{Gross profit as a \% of sales} = \frac{\text{Gross profit as a \% of cost}}{1 + \text{Gross profit as a \% of cost}}$$

$$\frac{66\tfrac{2}{3}\%}{1 + 66\tfrac{2}{3}\%} = 40\%$$

Be careful to note which way the percentage is being stated. If stated as a markup on cost, it can be converted to the gross profit ratio, and the gross profit method can be applied the usual way.

# The Retail Inventory Method

The retail inventory method is similar to the gross profit method in that it relies on the relationship between cost and selling price to estimate ending inventory and cost of goods sold.

● LO9–3

As the name implies, the method is used by many retail companies such as **Target**, **Walmart**, **Sears Holding Corporation**, **Saks**, and **Macy's**. Certain retailers like auto dealers and jewelry stores, whose inventory consists of few, high-priced items, can economically use the specific identification inventory method. However, high-volume retailers selling many different items at low unit prices find the retail inventory method ideal, although with the advent of bar coding on more and more retail merchandise, use of the method is declining. Similar to the gross profit method, its principal benefit is that a physical count of inventory is not required to estimate ending inventory and cost of goods sold.

The *retail inventory method* uses the *cost-to-retail percentage* based on a current relationship between cost and selling price.

The retail method tends to provide a more accurate estimate than the gross profit method because it's based on the current cost-to-retail percentage rather than on a historical gross profit ratio.

The increased reliability in the estimate of the cost percentage is achieved by comparing cost of goods available for sale with goods available for sale *at current selling prices*. So, to use the technique, a company must maintain records of inventory and purchases not only at cost, but also at current selling price. We refer to this as *retail information*. In its simplest form, the retail inventory method estimates the amount of ending inventory (at retail) by subtracting sales (at retail) from goods available for sale (at retail). This estimated ending inventory at retail is then converted to cost by multiplying it by the cost-to-retail percentage. This ratio is found by dividing goods available for sale at *cost* by goods available for sale at *retail*.

Let's use the retail inventory method to solve the problem of the Home Improvement Store introduced earlier in the chapter. Suppose the company's bank has asked for monthly financial statements as a condition attached to a loan dated May 31, 2013. To avoid a physical count of inventory, the company intends to use the retail inventory method to estimate ending inventory and cost of goods sold for the month of June. Using data available in its accounting records, Illustration 9–6 shows how Home Improvement can estimate ending inventory and cost of goods sold for June.

The retail inventory method can be used for financial reporting and income tax purposes.

Unlike the gross profit method, the retail inventory method is acceptable for external financial reporting if the results of applying the method are sufficiently close to what would have been achieved using a more rigorous determination of the cost of ending inventory. Also, it's allowed by the Internal Revenue Service as a method that can be used to determine cost of goods sold for income tax purposes.[7] Another advantage of the method is that different cost flow methods can be explicitly incorporated into the estimation technique. In other words, we can modify the application of the method to estimate ending inventory and cost

---

[7]The retail method is acceptable for external reporting and for tax purposes because it tends to provide a better estimate than the gross profit method. The retail method uses a current cost-to-retail percentage rather than a historical gross profit ratio.

|  | Cost | Retail |
|---|---|---|
| Beginning inventory | $ 60,000 | $100,000 |
| Plus: Net purchases | 287,200 | 460,000 |
| Goods available for sale | $347,200 | $560,000 |
| Cost-to-retail percentage: $\dfrac{\$347,200}{\$560,000} = 62\%$ |  |  |
| Less: Net sales |  | (400,000) |
| Estimated ending inventory at retail |  | $160,000 |
| Estimated ending inventory at cost (62% × $160,000) | (99,200) |  |
| Estimated cost of goods sold—goods available for sale (at cost) minus ending inventory (at cost) equals cost of goods sold | $248,000 |  |

**Illustration 9–6**
Retail Method

Goods available for sale (at retail) minus net sales equals estimated ending inventory (at retail).

of goods sold to approximate average cost, lower-of-average-cost-or-market (conventional method) and LIFO. (The FIFO retail method is possible but used less frequently in practice.) We illustrate these variations later in the chapter.

Like the gross profit method, the retail inventory method also can be used to estimate the cost of inventory lost, stolen, or destroyed; for testing the overall reasonableness of physical counts; in budgeting and forecasting as well as in generating information for interim financial statements. Even though the retail method provides fairly accurate estimates, a physical count of inventory usually is performed at least once a year to verify accuracy and detect spoilage, theft, and other irregularities.[8]

## Retail Terminology

Our example above is simplified in that we implicitly assumed that the selling prices of beginning inventory and of merchandise purchased did not change from date of acquisition to the end of the period. This frequently is an unrealistic assumption. The terms in Illustration 9–7 are associated with changing retail prices of merchandise inventory.

Changes in the selling prices must be included in the determination of ending inventory at retail.

| | |
|---|---|
| **Initial markup** | Original amount of markup from cost to selling price. |
| **Additional markup** | Increase in selling price subsequent to initial markup. |
| **Markup cancellation** | Elimination of an additional markup. |
| **Markdown** | Reduction in selling price below the original selling price. |
| **Markdown cancellation** | Elimination of a markdown. |

**Illustration 9–7**
Terminology Used in Applying the Retail Method

To illustrate, assume that a product purchased for $6 is initially marked up $4, from $6 to $10, the original selling price. If the selling price is subsequently increased to $12, the additional markup is $2. If the selling price is then subsequently decreased to $10.50, the markup cancellation is $1.50. We refer to the net effect of the additional changes ($2.00 − 1.50 = $.50) as the **net markup**. Illustration 9–8A depicts these events.

Now let's say the selling price of the product purchased for $6 and initially marked up to $10, is reduced to $7. The markdown is $3. If the selling price is later increased to $8, the markdown cancellation is $1. The net effect of the change ($3 − 1 = $2) is the **net markdown**. Illustration 9–8B depicts this possibility.

When applying the retail inventory method, *net markups and net markdowns must be included in the determination of ending inventory at retail*. We now continue our illustration of the retail inventory method, but expand it to incorporate markups and markdowns as well as to approximate cost by each of the alternative inventory cost flow methods.

*Net markups* and *net markdowns* are included in the retail column to determine ending inventory at retail.

---

[8]The retail inventory method also is allowable under IFRS. "Inventories," International Accounting Standard No. 2 (IASCF), as amended effective January 1, 2011, par. 22.

## Illustration 9–8A

Retail Inventory Method
Terminology

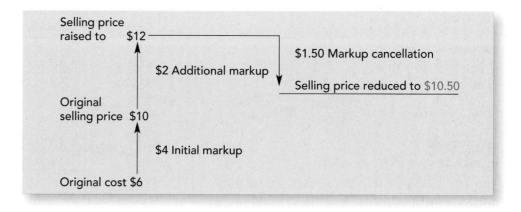

## Illustration 9–8B

Retail Inventory Method
Terminology

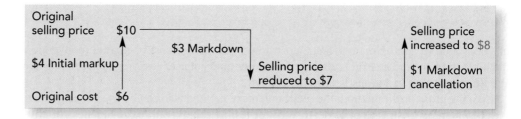

## Cost Flow Methods

Let's continue the Home Improvement Stores example into July with Illustration 9–9 and see how the retail inventory method can be used to approximate different cost flow assumptions. We'll also use the same illustration to see how the retail method can be modified to approximate lower of cost or market.

## Illustration 9–9

The Retail Inventory
Method—Various Cost
Flow Methods

Home Improvement Stores, Inc., uses a periodic inventory system and the retail inventory method to estimate ending inventory and cost of goods sold. The following data are available from the company's records for the month of July 2013:

| | Cost | Retail |
|---|---|---|
| Beginning inventory | $ 99,200 | $160,000 |
| Net purchases | 305,280[1] | 470,000[2] |
| Net markups | | 10,000 |
| Net markdowns | | 8,000 |
| Net sales | | 434,000[3] |

[1]Purchases at cost less returns, plus freight-in.
[2]Original selling price of purchased goods less returns at retail.
[3]Gross sales less returns.

**APPROXIMATING AVERAGE COST.** Recall that the average cost method assumes that cost of goods sold and ending inventory each consist of a *mixture* of all the goods available for sale. So when we use the retail method to approximate average cost, the cost-to-retail percentage should be based on the weighted averages of the costs and retail amounts for *all* goods available for sale. This is achieved by calculating the cost-to-retail percentage by dividing the total cost of goods available for sale by total goods available for sale at retail. When this average percentage is applied to ending inventory at retail, we get an estimate of ending inventory at average cost. If you look back to our simplified example for the month of June, you'll notice that we used this approach there. So, our ending inventory and cost of goods sold estimates for June were estimates of average cost.[9]

> To approximate average cost, the cost-to-retail percentage is determined for *all* goods available for sale.

---

[9]We also implicitly assumed no net markups or markdowns.

Now, we use the retail inventory method to approximate average costs for July. Notice in Illustration 9–10 that both markups and markdowns are included in the determination of goods available for sale at retail.

**Illustration 9–10**

Retail Method—
Average Cost

| | Cost | Retail |
|---|---|---|
| Beginning inventory | $ 99,200 | $160,000 |
| Plus: Net purchases | 305,280 | 470,000 |
| Net markups | | 10,000 |
| Less: Net markdowns | | (8,000) |
| Goods available for sale | 404,480 | 632,000 |

Cost-to-retail percentage: $\frac{\$404,480}{\$632,000} = 64\%$

| | | |
|---|---|---|
| Less: Net sales | | (434,000) |
| Estimated ending inventory at retail | | $198,000 |
| Estimated ending inventory at cost (64% × $198,000) | (126,720) | |
| Estimated cost of goods sold | $277,760 | |

**APPROXIMATING AVERAGE LCM—THE CONVENTIONAL RETAIL METHOD.** Recall from our discussion earlier in the chapter that, however costs are determined, inventory should be reported in the balance sheet at LCM. Fortunately, we can apply the retail inventory method in such a way that LCM is approximated. This method often is referred to as the **conventional retail method**. We apply the method by *excluding markdowns from the calculation of the cost-to-retail percentage*. Markdowns still are subtracted in the retail column but only after the percentage is calculated. To approximate lower of average cost or market, the retail method is modified as shown in Illustration 9–11.

● LO9–4

To approximate LCM, markdowns are not included in the calculation of the cost-to-retail percentage.

**Illustration 9–11**

Retail Method—
Average Cost, LCM

| | Cost | Retail |
|---|---|---|
| Beginning inventory | $ 99,200 | $160,000 |
| Plus: Net purchases | 305,280 | 470,000 |
| Net markups | | 10,000 |
| | | 640,000 |

Cost-to-retail percentage: $\frac{\$404,480}{\$640,000} = 63.2\%$

| | | |
|---|---|---|
| Less: Net markdowns | | (8,000) |
| Goods available for sale | 404,480 | 632,000 |
| Less: Net sales | | (434,000) |
| Estimated ending inventory at retail | | $198,000 |
| Estimated ending inventory at cost (63.2% × $198,000) | (125,136) | |
| Estimated cost of goods sold | $279,344 | |

Notice that by not subtracting net markdowns from the denominator, the cost-to-retail percentage is lower than it was previously (63.2% versus 64%). This always will be the case when markdowns exist. As a result, the cost approximation of ending inventory always will be less when markdowns exist. To understand why this lower amount approximates LCM, we need to realize that markdowns usually occur when obsolescence, spoilage, overstocking, price declines, or competition has lessened the utility of the merchandise. To recognize this decline in utility in the period it occurs, as LCM does, we exclude net markdowns from the calculation of the cost-to-retail (market) percentage. It should be emphasized that this approach provides only an *approximation* of what ending inventory might be as opposed to applying the LCM rule in the more exact way described earlier in the chapter.

Also notice that the ending inventory at retail is the same using both approaches ($198,000). This will be the case regardless of the cost flow method used because in all approaches this amount reflects the ending inventory at current retail prices.

The logic for using this approximation is that a markdown is evidence of a reduction in the utility of inventory.

The LCM variation is not generally used in combination with LIFO. This does not mean that a company using LIFO ignores the LCM rule. Any obsolete or slow-moving inventory that has not been marked down by year-end can be written down to market after the estimation of inventory using the retail method. This is usually not a significant problem. If prices are rising, LIFO ending inventory includes old lower priced items whose costs are likely to be lower than current market. The LCM variation could be applied to the FIFO method.

**THE LIFO RETAIL METHOD.**   The last-in, first-out (LIFO) method assumes that units sold are those most recently acquired. When there's a net increase in inventory quantity during a period, the use of LIFO results in ending inventory that includes the beginning inventory as well as one or more additional layers added during the period. When there's a net decrease in inventory quantity, LIFO layer(s) are liquidated. In applying LIFO to the retail method in the simplest way, we assume that the retail prices of goods remained stable during the period. This assumption, which is relaxed later in the chapter, allows us to look at the beginning and ending inventory in dollars to determine if inventory quantity has increased or decreased.

> **If inventory at retail increases during the year, a new layer is added.**

We'll use the numbers from our previous example to illustrate using the retail method to approximate LIFO so we can compare the results with those of the conventional retail method. Recall that beginning inventory at retail is $160,000 and ending inventory at retail is $198,000. If we assume stable retail prices, inventory quantity must have increased during the year. This means ending inventory includes the beginning inventory layer of $160,000 ($99,200 at cost) as well as some additional merchandise purchased during the period. To estimate total ending inventory at LIFO cost, we also need to determine the inventory layer added during the period. When using the LIFO retail method, we assume no more than one inventory layer is added per year if inventory increases.[10] Each layer will carry its own cost-to-retail percentage.

Illustration 9–12 shows how Home Improvement Stores would estimate total ending inventory and cost of goods sold for the period using the LIFO retail method. The beginning inventory layer carries a cost-to-retail percentage of 62% ($99,200 ÷ $160,000). The layer of inventory added during the period is $38,000 at retail, which is determined by subtracting beginning inventory at retail from ending inventory at retail ($198,000 − 160,000). This

**Illustration 9–12**
LIFO Retail Method

> **Beginning inventory is excluded from the calculation of the cost-to-retail percentage.**

| | Cost | Retail |
|---|---|---|
| Beginning inventory | $ 99,200 | $160,000 |
| Plus: Net purchases | 305,280 | 470,000 |
| Net markups | | 10,000 |
| Less: Net markdowns | | (8,000) |
| Goods available for sale (excluding beginning inventory) | 305,280 | 472,000 |
| Goods available for sale (including beginning inventory) | 404,480 | 632,000 |

Beginning inventory cost-to-retail percentage: $\dfrac{\$99,200}{\$160,000} = 62\%$

July cost-to-retail percentage: $\dfrac{\$305,280}{\$472,000} = 64.68\%$

| | | Retail |
|---|---|---|
| Less: Net sales | | (434,000) |
| Estimated ending inventory at retail | | $198,000 |

Estimated ending inventory at cost:

> **Each layer has its own cost-to-retail percentage.**

| | Retail | | Cost | |
|---|---|---|---|---|
| Beginning inventory | $160,000 | × 62.00% = | $ 99,200 | |
| Current period's layer | 38,000 | × 64.68% = | 24,578 | |
| Total | $198,000 | | $123,778 | (123,778) |
| Estimated cost of goods sold | | | | $280,702 |

---

[10]Of course, any number of layers at different costs can actually be added through the years. When using the regular LIFO method, rather than LIFO retail, we would keep track of each of those layers.

layer will be converted to cost by multiplying it by its own cost-to-retail percentage reflecting the *current* period's ratio of cost to retail amounts, in this case 64.68%.

The next period's (August's) beginning inventory will include the two distinct layers (June and July), each of which carries its own unique cost-to-retail percentage. Notice in the illustration that both net markups and net markdowns are included in the calculation of the current period's cost-to-retail percentage.

## Other Issues Pertaining to the Retail Method

To focus on the key elements of the retail method, we've so far ignored some of the details of the retail process. Fundamental elements such as returns and allowances, discounts, freight, spoilage, and shortages can complicate the retail method.

Recall that net purchases is found by adding freight-in to purchases and subtracting both purchase returns and purchase discounts. When these components are considered separately in the retail method, purchase returns are deducted from purchases on both the cost and retail side (at different amounts) and freight-in is added only to the cost side in determining net purchases. If the gross method is used to record purchases, purchase discounts taken also are deducted in determining the cost of net purchases.

Likewise, net sales is determined by subtracting sales returns from sales. However, sales discounts are *not* subtracted because to do so would cause the inventory to be overstated. Sales discounts do not represent an adjustment in selling price but a financial incentive for customers to pay early. On the other hand, when sales are recorded net of employee discounts, the discounts are *added* to net sales before sales are deducted in the retail column.

> If sales are recorded net of employee discounts, the discounts are added to sales.

For example, suppose an item of merchandise purchased for $6 is initially marked up to $10. Original selling price is therefore $10. When the item is sold, we deduct sales of $10 from the retail column. But if the item is sold to an employee for $7 (a $3 employee discount) and recorded as a $7 sale, the $3 employee discount must be added back to sales so the full $10 is deducted from goods available at retail to arrive at ending inventory at retail.

We also need to consider spoilage, breakage, and theft. So far we've assumed that by subtracting goods sold from goods available for sale, we find ending inventory. It's possible, though, that some of the goods available for sale were lost to such shortages and therefore do not remain in ending inventory.

To take these shortages into account when using the retail method, we deduct the retail value of inventory lost due to spoilage, breakage, or theft in the retail column. These losses are expected for most retail ventures so they are referred to as *normal shortages* (spoilage, breakage, etc.), and are deducted in the retail column *after* the calculation of the cost-to-retail percentage. Because these losses are anticipated, they are included implicitly in the determination of selling prices. Including normal spoilage in the calculation of the percentage would distort the normal relationship between cost and retail. *Abnormal shortages* should be deducted in both the cost and retail columns *before* the calculation of the cost-to-retail percentage. These losses are not anticipated and are not included in the determination of selling prices.

> Normal shortages are deducted in the retail column *after* the calculation of the cost-to-retail percentage.
>
> Abnormal shortages are deducted in both the cost and retail columns *before* the calculation of the cost-to-retail percentage.

We recap the treatment of special elements in the application of the retail method in Illustration 9–13 and illustrate the use of some of them in the concept review exercise that follows.

**Illustration 9–13**

Recap of Other Retail Method Elements

| Element | Treatment |
|---|---|
| **Before calculating the cost-to-retail percentage:** | |
| Freight-in | *Added* in the cost column. |
| Purchase returns | *Deducted* in both the cost and retail columns. |
| Purchase discounts taken (if gross method used to record purchases) | *Deducted* in the cost column. |
| Abnormal shortages (spoilage, breakage, theft) | *Deducted* in both the cost and retail columns. |
| **After calculating the cost-to-retail percentage:** | |
| Normal shortages (spoilage, breakage, theft) | *Deducted* in the retail column. |
| Employee discounts (if sales recorded net of discounts) | *Added* to net sales. |

## Concept Review Exercise

**RETAIL INVENTORY METHOD**

The Henderson Company uses the retail inventory method to estimate ending inventory and cost of goods sold. The following data for 2013 are available in Henderson's accounting records:

|  | Cost | Retail |
|---|---|---|
| Beginning inventory | $ 8,000 | $12,000 |
| Purchases | 68,000 | 98,000 |
| Freight-in | 3,200 | |
| Purchase returns | 3,000 | 4,200 |
| Net markups | | 6,000 |
| Net markdowns | | 2,400 |
| Normal spoilage | | 1,800 |
| Net sales | | 92,000 |

The company records sales net of employee discounts. These discounts for 2013 totaled $2,300.

**Required:**

1. Estimate Henderson's ending inventory and cost of goods sold for the year using the average cost method.
2. Estimate Henderson's ending inventory and cost of goods sold for the year using the conventional retail method (LCM, average cost).
3. Estimate Henderson's ending inventory and cost of goods sold for the year using the LIFO retail method.

**Solution:**

1. Estimate Henderson's ending inventory and cost of goods sold for the year using the average cost method.

|  |  | Cost | Retail |
|---|---|---|---|
| Beginning inventory | | $ 8,000 | $ 12,000 |
| Plus: Purchases | | 68,000 | 98,000 |
| Freight-in | | 3,200 | |
| Less: Purchase returns | | (3,000) | (4,200) |
| Plus: Net markups | | | 6,000 |
| Less: Net markdowns | | | (2,400) |
| Goods available for sale | | $76,200 | $109,400 |

Cost-to-retail percentage: $\dfrac{\$76,200}{\$109,400} = 69.65\%$

|  |  | | Retail |
|---|---|---|---|
| Less: Normal spoilage | | | (1,800) |
| Sales: | | | |
| Net sales | $92,000 | | |
| Add back employee discounts | 2,300 | | (94,300) |
| Estimated ending inventory at retail | | | $ 13,300 |

|  | Cost |
|---|---|
| Estimated ending inventory at cost (69.65% × $13,300) | (9,263) |
| Estimated cost of goods sold | $66,937 |

2. Estimate Henderson's ending inventory and cost of goods sold for the year using the conventional retail method (LCM, average cost).

|  | Cost | Retail |
|---|---|---|
| Beginning inventory | $ 8,000 | $ 12,000 |
| Plus:  Purchases | 68,000 | 98,000 |
| Freight-in | 3,200 | |
| Less:  Purchase returns | (3,000) | (4,200) |
| Plus:  Net markups | | 6,000 |
| | | 111,800 |

Cost-to-retail percentage: $\dfrac{\$76,200}{\$111,800} = 68.16\%$

|  | Cost | Retail |
|---|---|---|
| Less:  Net markdowns | | (2,400) |
| Goods available for sale | 76,200 | 109,400 |
| Less:  Normal spoilage | | (1,800) |
| Sales: | | |
| Net sales | $92,000 | |
| Add back employee discounts | 2,300 | (94,300) |
| Estimated ending inventory at retail | | $ 13,300 |
| Estimated ending inventory at cost (68.16% × $13,300) | (9,065) | |
| Estimated cost of goods sold | $67,135 | |

3. Estimate Henderson's ending inventory and cost of goods sold for the year using the LIFO retail method.

|  | Cost | Retail |
|---|---|---|
| Beginning inventory | $ 8,000 | $ 12,000 |
| Plus:  Purchases | 68,000 | 98,000 |
| Freight-in | 3,200 | |
| Less:  Purchase returns | (3,000) | (4,200) |
| Plus:  Net markups | | 6,000 |
| Less:  Net markdowns | | (2,400) |
| Goods available for sale (excluding beginning inventory) | 68,200 | 97,400 |
| Goods available for sale (including beginning inventory) | 76,200 | 109,400 |

Cost-to-retail percentage: $\dfrac{\$68,200}{\$97,400} = 70.02\%$

|  | Cost | Retail |
|---|---|---|
| Less:  Normal spoilage | | (1,800) |
| Sales: | | |
| Net sales | $92,000 | |
| Add back employee discounts | 2,300 | (94,300) |
| Estimated ending inventory at retail | | $ 13,300 |
| Estimated ending inventory at cost: | | |

|  | Retail | | Cost |
|---|---|---|---|
| Beginning inventory | $12,000 × 66.67%* | = | $8,000 |
| Current period's layer | 1,300 × 70.02% | = | 910 |
| Total | $13,300 | | $8,910 |

|  | | |
|---|---|---|
| Total | | (8,910) |
| Estimated cost of goods sold | | $67,290 |

*$8,000 ÷ $12,000 = 66.67%

## PART C

### DOLLAR-VALUE LIFO RETAIL

● LO9–5

In our earlier illustration of the LIFO retail method, we assumed that the retail prices of the inventory remained stable during the period. If you recall, we compared the ending inventory (at retail) with the beginning inventory (at retail) to see if inventory had increased. If the dollar amount of ending inventory exceeded the beginning amount, we assumed a new LIFO layer had been added. But this isn't necessarily true. It may be that the dollar amount of ending inventory exceeded the beginning amount simply because prices increased, without an actual change in the quantity of goods. So, to see if there's been a "real" increase in quantity, we need a way to eliminate the effect of any price changes before we compare the ending inventory with the beginning inventory. Fortunately, we can accomplish this by combining two methods we've already discussed—the LIFO retail method (Part B of this chapter) and dollar-value LIFO (previous chapter). The combination is called the **dollar-value LIFO retail method**.

To illustrate, we return to the Home Improvement Stores situation (Illustration 9–12) in which we applied LIFO retail. We keep the same inventory data, but change the illustration from the month of July to the fiscal year 2013. This allows us to build into Illustration 9–12A a significant change in retail prices over the year of 10% (an increase in the retail price index from 1 to 1.10). We follow the LIFO retail procedure up to the point of comparing the ending inventory with the beginning inventory. However, because prices have risen, the apparent increase in inventory is only partly due to an additional layer of inventory and partly due to the increase in retail prices. The real increase is found by deflating the ending inventory amount to beginning of the year prices before comparing beginning and

**FINANCIAL Reporting Case**

Q2, p. 475

Using the retail method to approximate LIFO is referred to as the *dollar-value LIFO retail method*.

### Illustration 9–12A

The Dollar-Value LIFO Retail Method

| | Cost | Retail |
|---|---|---|
| Beginning inventory | $ 99,200 | $160,000 |
| Plus:    Net purchases | 305,280 | 470,000 |
|             Net markups | | 10,000 |
| Less:   Net markdowns | | (8,000) |
| Goods available for sale (excluding beginning inventory) | 305,280 | 472,000 |
| Goods available for sale (including beginning inventory) | 404,480 | 632,000 |
| Base layer cost-to-retail percentage: $\frac{\$99,200}{\$160,000} = \underline{62\%}$ | | |
| 2013 layer cost-to-retail percentage: $\frac{\$305,280}{\$472,000} = \underline{64.68\%}$ | | |
| Less: Net sales | | (434,000) |
| Ending inventory at current year retail prices | | $198,000 |
| Estimated ending inventory at cost (calculated below) | (113,430) | |
| Estimated cost of goods sold | $291,050 | |

| Ending Inventory at Year-End Retail Prices | Step 1 Ending Inventory at Base Year Retail Prices | Step 2 Inventory Layers at Base Year Retail Prices | Step 3 Inventory Layers Converted to Cost |
|---|---|---|---|
| $198,000 ⟶ (determined above) | $\frac{\$198,000}{1.10} = \$180,000 \rightarrow$ | $180,000 | |
| | | 160,000 (base) × 1.00 × .62 | = $ 99,200 |
| | | $ 20,000 (2013) × 1.10 × .6468 = | 14,230 |
| Total ending inventory at dollar-value LIFO retail cost | | | $113,430 |

Base year retail amounts are converted to layer year retail and then to cost.

ending amounts. We did this with the dollar-value LIFO technique discussed in the previous chapter.[11]

In this illustration, a $20,000 year 2013 layer is added to the base layer. Two adjustments are needed to convert this amount to LIFO cost. Multiplying by the 2013 price index (1.10) converts it from its base year retail to 2013 retail. Multiplying by the 2013 cost-to-retail percentage (.6468) converts it from its 2013 retail to 2013 cost. The two steps are combined in our illustration. The base year inventory also is converted to cost. The two layers are added to derive ending inventory at dollar-value LIFO retail cost.

Each layer year carries its unique retail price index and its unique cost-to-retail percentage.

When additional layers are added in subsequent years, their LIFO amounts are determined the same way. For illustration, let's assume ending inventory in 2014 is $226,200 at current retail prices and the price level has risen to 1.16. Also assume that the cost-to-retail percentage for 2014 net purchases is 63%. In Illustration 9–12B, the ending inventory is converted to base year retail (step 1). This amount is apportioned into layers, each at base year retail (step 2). Layers then are converted to layer year costs (step 3).

**Illustration 9–12B**
The Dollar-Value LIFO Retail Inventory Method

| Ending Inventory at Year-End Retail Prices | Step 1 Ending Inventory at Base Year Retail Prices | Step 2 Inventory Layers at Base Year Retail Prices | Step 3 Inventory Layers Converted to LIFO Cost |
|---|---|---|---|
| $226,200 (assumed) | $\dfrac{\$226,200}{1.16}$ = $195,000 | → $195,000 | |
| | | 160,000 (base) × 1.00 × .62 | = $ 99,200 |
| | | 20,000 (2013) × 1.10 × .6468 | = 14,230 |
| | | $ 15,000 (2014) × 1.16 × .63 | = 10,962 |
| Total ending inventory at dollar-value LIFO retail cost | | | $124,392 |

Now, let's assume that ending inventory in 2014 is $204,160 at current retail prices (instead of $226,200) and the price level has risen to 1.16. Also assume that the cost-to-retail percentage for 2014 net purchases is 63%. Step 1 converts the ending inventory to a base year price of $176,000 ($204,160 ÷ 1.16). A comparison to the beginning inventory at base year prices of $180,000 ($160,000 base year layer + $20,000 2013 layer) indicates that inventory *decreased* during 2014. In this case, no 2014 layer is added and 2014 ending inventory at dollar-value LIFO retail of $110,584 is determined in Illustration 9–12C.

Base year retail amounts are converted to layer year retail and then to cost.

**Illustration 9–12C**
The Dollar-Value LIFO Retail Inventory Method

| Ending Inventory at Year-End Retail Prices | Step 1 Ending Inventory at Base Year Retail Prices | Step 2 Inventory Layers at Base Year Retail Prices | Step 3 Inventory Layers Converted to LIFO Cost |
|---|---|---|---|
| $204,160 (assumed) | $\dfrac{\$204,160}{1.16}$ = $176,000 | → $176,000 | |
| | | 160,000 (base) × 1.00 × .62 | = $ 99,200 |
| | | 16,000 (2013) × 1.10 × .6468 | = 11,384 |
| Total ending inventory at dollar-value LIFO retail cost | | | $110,584 |

A portion of the 2013 inventory layer has been liquidated—reduced from $20,000 to $16,000 at base year prices—to reduce total inventory at base year prices to $176,000.

---

[11]The index used here is analogous to the cost index used in regular DVL except that it reflects the change in retail prices rather than in acquisition costs.

As we mentioned earlier in this section, many high-volume retailers selling many different items use the retail method. **Target Corporation**, for example, uses the dollar-value LIFO variation of the retail method. Illustration 9–14 shows the inventory disclosure note included in the company's recent financial statements.

## Illustration 9–14

Disclosure of Inventory Method—Target Corporation

Real World Financials

> **Summary of Significant Accounting Policies Merchandise Inventories (in part)**
>
> Substantially all of our inventory and the related cost of sales are accounted for under the retail inventory accounting method (RIM) using the last-in, first-out (LIFO) method. Inventory is stated at the lower of LIFO cost or market. The LIFO provision is calculated based on inventory levels, markup rates and internally measured retail price indices.

Notice that Target uses internal indices to adjust for changing prices.

# Concept Review Exercise

**DOLLAR-VALUE LIFO RETAIL METHOD**

On January 1, 2013, the Nicholson Department Store adopted the dollar-value LIFO retail inventory method. Inventory transactions at both cost and retail and cost indexes for 2013 and 2014 are as follows:

|  | 2013 | | 2014 | |
|---|---|---|---|---|
|  | **Cost** | **Retail** | **Cost** | **Retail** |
| Beginning inventory | $16,000 | $24,000 | | |
| Net purchases | 42,000 | 58,500 | 45,000 | 58,700 |
| Net markups | | 3,000 | | 2,400 |
| Net markdowns | | 1,500 | | 1,100 |
| Net sales | | 56,000 | | 57,000 |
| Price index: | | | | |
| January 1, 2013 | 1.00 | | | |
| December 31, 2013 | 1.08 | | | |
| December 31, 2014 | 1.15 | | | |

**Required:**

Estimate the 2013 and 2014 ending inventory and cost of goods sold using the dollar-value LIFO retail inventory method.

**Solution:**

|  | 2013 | | 2014 | |
|---|---|---|---|---|
|  | **Cost** | **Retail** | **Cost** | **Retail** |
| Beginning inventory | $16,000 | $24,000 | $17,456 | $28,000 |
| Plus: Net purchases | 42,000 | 58,500 | 45,000 | 58,700 |
| Net markups | | 3,000 | | 2,400 |
| Less: Net markdowns | | (1,500) | | (1,100) |
| Goods available for sale (excluding beg. inv.) | 42,000 | 60,000 | 45,000 | 60,000 |
| Goods available for sale (including beg. inv.) | 58,000 | 84,000 | 62,456 | 88,000 |

Base layer

Cost-to-retail percentage: $\dfrac{\$16,000}{\$24,000} = 66.67\%$

2013

Cost-to-retail percentage: $\dfrac{\$42,000}{\$60,000} = 70\%$

(continued)

(concluded)

2014

Cost-to-retail percentage: $\dfrac{\$45,000}{\$60,000} = \underline{\underline{75\%}}$

| | | |
|---|---|---|
| Less: Net sales | (56,000) | (57,000) |
| Estimated ending inv. at current year retail prices | $28,000 | $31,000 |
| Less: Estimated ending inventory at cost (below) | (17,456) | (18,345) |
| Estimated cost of goods sold | $40,544 | $44,111 |

**2013**

| Ending Inventory at Year-End Retail Prices | Step 1 Ending Inventory at Base Year Retail Prices | Step 2 Inventory Layers at Base Year Retail Prices | Step 3 Inventory Layers Converted to Cost |
|---|---|---|---|
| $28,000 (above) | $\dfrac{\$28,000}{1.08} = 25,926$ | $24,000 (base) × 1.00 × 66.67% = | $16,000 |
| | | 1,926 (2013) × 1.08 × 70.00% = | 1,456 |
| Total ending inventory at dollar-value LIFO retail cost | | | $17,456 |

**2014**

| Ending Inventory at Year-End Retail Prices | Step 1 Ending Inventory at Base Year Retail Prices | Step 2 Inventory Layers at Base Year Retail Prices | Step 3 Inventory Layers Converted to Cost |
|---|---|---|---|
| $31,000 (above) | $\dfrac{\$31,000}{1.15} = \$26,957$ | $24,000 (base) × 1.00 × 66.67% = | $16,000 |
| | | 1,926 (2013) × 1.08 × 70.00% = | 1,456 |
| | | 1,031 (2014) × 1.15 × 75.00% = | 889 |
| Total ending inventory at dollar-value LIFO retail cost | | | $18,345 |

# CHANGE IN INVENTORY METHOD AND INVENTORY ERRORS
## Change in Inventory Method

Accounting principles should be applied consistently from period to period to allow for comparability of operating results. However, changes within a company as well as changes in the external economic environment may require a company to change an accounting method. As we mentioned in Chapter 8, high inflation in the 1970s motivated many companies to switch to the LIFO inventory method.

● LO9–6

Specific accounting treatment and disclosures are prescribed for companies that change accounting principles. Chapter 4 introduced the subject of accounting changes and Chapter 20 provides in-depth coverage of the topic. Here we provide an overview of how changes in inventory methods are reported.

### Most Inventory Changes

Recall from our brief discussion in Chapter 4 that most voluntary changes in accounting principles are reported retrospectively. This means reporting all previous periods' financial statements as if the new method had been used in all prior periods. Changes in inventory methods, other than a change to LIFO, are treated this way. We discuss the *to LIFO*

Changes in inventory methods, other than a change to LIFO, are accounted for retrospectively.

exception in the next section. In Chapter 4 we briefly discussed the steps a company undertakes to account for a change in accounting principle. We demonstrate those steps using a real world example in Illustrations 9–15 and 9–15A.

**Illustration 9–15**

Change in Inventory Method—McKesson Corporation

**Real World Financials**

**McKesson Corporation** is a Fortune 100 company producing products and services in the healthcare industry. In a note accompanying its 2011 financial statements, the company disclosed that it uses the LIFO inventory method for 87% of its inventories and FIFO for the remainder. The company's balance sheets reported inventories of $9,225 million and $9,441 million at the end of 2011 and 2010, respectively. The inventory disclosure note reports that if the FIFO method had been used to value the entire inventory, instead of just 13% of it, inventories would have been $9,321 million and $9,534 million at the end of 2011 and 2010, respectively. Partial income statements for 2011 and 2010 are as follows:

**McKESSON CORPORATION**
**Partial Income Statements**
**For the Years Ended March 31,**

|  | ($ in millions) | |
| --- | --- | --- |
|  | **2011** | **2010** |
| Sales revenue | $112,084 | $108,702 |
| Cost of goods sold | 106,114 | 103,026 |
| Gross profit | 5,970 | 5,676 |
| Operating expenses | 4,149 | 3,668 |
| Operating income | $  1,821 | $  2,008 |

Let's suppose that in 2011 McKesson decided to value all of its inventories using the FIFO method.

**Illustration 9–15A**

Income statements—100% FIFO

**McKESSON CORPORATION**
**Partial Income Statements**
**For the Years Ended March 31,**

|  | ($ in millions) | |
| --- | --- | --- |
|  | **2011** | **2010** |
| Sales revenue | $112,084 | $108,702 |
| Cost of goods sold | 106,111 | 103,018 |
| Gross profit | 5,973 | 5,684 |
| Operating expenses | 4,149 | 3,668 |
| Operating income | 1,824 | 2,016 |

McKesson would report 2011 cost of goods sold by its newly adopted method, 100% FIFO.

McKesson would increase the amount it reported last year for its cost of goods sold as if 100% FIFO had been used.

    The cost of goods sold of $106,111 million in 2011 is $3 million lower on a 100% FIFO basis. Here's why. McKesson's note reported that beginning inventory is $93 million higher ($9,534 − 9,441), and ending inventory also is higher by $96 million ($9,321 − 9,225). An increase in beginning inventory causes an *increase* in cost of goods sold, but an increase in ending inventory causes a *decrease* in cost of goods sold. The net effect of the two adjustments ($96 − 93) is the $3 million decrease in cost of goods sold.
    In a similar manner, the 2010 cost of goods sold would be adjusted to $103,018 million. A note included in McKesson's 2010 financial statements reports that 2009 ending inventory of $8,527 million would have been $8,612 million on an all FIFO basis. 2010's beginning inventory would have been $85 higher ($8,612 − 8,527) and ending inventory for 2010 would be $93 million higher ($9,534 − 9,441). The net effect of the two adjustments ($93 − 85) is that cost of goods sold would be $8 million lower.

**Step 1: Revise Comparative Financial Statements**

    The first step is to revise prior years' financial statements. That is, for each year reported in the comparative statements, McKesson makes those statements appear as if the newly adopted accounting method (100% FIFO) had been applied all along. In its balance sheets, McKesson would report 2011 inventory by its newly adopted method, 100% FIFO, and also would revise the amounts it reported last year for its 2010 inventory. In its income statements, cost of goods sold also would reflect the new method in both 2011 and 2010 as shown in Illustration 9–15A.

In its statements of shareholders' equity, McKesson would report retained earnings each year as if it had used FIFO all along, and for the earliest year reported, it would revise beginning retained earnings that year to reflect the cumulative income effect of the difference in inventory methods for all prior years. We see this step illustrated in Chapter 20 after you have studied the statement of shareholders' equity in more depth.

McKesson also would create a journal entry to adjust the book balances from their current amounts to what those balances would have been using 100% FIFO. Since differences in cost of goods sold and income are reflected in retained earnings, as are the income tax effects, the journal entry updates inventory, retained earnings, and the appropriate income tax account. We ignore the income tax effects here and include those effects in an illustration in Chapter 20. The journal entry below, *ignoring income taxes,* adjusts the 2011 beginning inventory to the 100% FIFO basis amount of $9,321 million.

> **Step 2: The appropriate accounts are adjusted.**

|  | ($ in millions) |  |
|---|---|---|
| Inventory ($9,321 − 9,225) ............................................................. | 96 |  |
| Retained earnings ................................................................. |  | 96 |

> **Inventory at the beginning of 2011 would be $96 million higher if FIFO is used to value the entire inventory.**

McKesson must provide in a disclosure note clear justification that the change to 100% FIFO is appropriate. The note also would indicate the effects of the change on (a) items not reported on the face of the primary statements, (b) any per share amounts affected for the current period and all prior periods, and (c) the cumulative effect of the change on retained earnings or other components of equity as of the beginning of the earliest period presented.

> **Step 3: A disclosure note provides additional information.**

We see an example of such a note in a recent annual report of **Charles & Colvard, Ltd.,** a jewelry manufacturer, when it changed its inventory method from FIFO to the average cost method. Illustration 9–16 shows the disclosure note that described the change.

**Inventories (in part)**

In April 2010, the Company changed its method of accounting for inventories from the first-in, first-out ("FIFO") method to the average cost method. The Company believes that the average cost method is preferable on the basis that it conforms to the manner in which the Company operationally manages its inventories and evaluates wholesale and retail pricing. In addition, the Company has expanded the focus of its business to include jewelry manufacturing in addition to loose-jewel manufacturing, and it now considers its peers to be jewelry manufacturers and retailers. Many of these peers utilize the average cost method for valuing their inventories, and this change makes the Company's inventory reporting more consistent to improve comparability among the peer companies. The change was effective January 1, 2010, and prior periods have been retrospectively adjusted for comparative purposes.

**Illustration 9–16**

Disclosure of Change in Inventory Method— Charles & Colvard, Ltd.

**Real World Financials**

Charles and Colvard's financial statements also included a note that disclosed the effect of the change on various financial statement items, including net income and earnings per share.

## Change to the LIFO Method

When a company changes *to the LIFO inventory method* from any other method, it usually is impossible to calculate the income effect on prior years. To do so would require assumptions as to when specific LIFO inventory layers were created in years prior to the change. As a result, a company changing to LIFO usually does not report the change retrospectively. Instead, the LIFO method simply is used from that point on. The base year inventory for all future LIFO determinations is the beginning inventory in the year the LIFO method is adopted.[12]

> **Accounting records usually are inadequate for a company changing to *LIFO* to report the change retrospectively.**

---

[12]A change to LIFO is handled the same way for income tax purposes.

A disclosure note is needed to explain (a) the nature of and justification for the change, (b) the effect of the change on current year's income and earnings per share, and (c) why retrospective application was impracticable. When **Seneca Foods Corporation** adopted the LIFO inventory method, it reported the change in the note shown in Illustration 9–17.

**Illustration 9–17**

Change in Inventory Method Disclosure—Seneca Foods Corporation

Real World Financials

### 10. Inventories (in part)

The Company decided to change its inventory valuation method from the lower of cost; determined under the FIFO method; or market, to the lower of cost; determined under the LIFO method or market. In the high inflation environment that the Company is experiencing, the Company believes that the LIFO inventory method is preferable over the FIFO method because it better compares the cost of current production to current revenue. Selling prices are established to reflect current market activity, which recognizes the increasing costs. Under FIFO, revenue and costs are not aligned. Under LIFO, the current cost of sales is matched to the current revenue.

The Company determined that retrospective application of LIFO for periods prior to the current fiscal year was impracticable because the period-specific information necessary to analyze inventories, including inventories acquired as part of the prior fiscal year's Signature acquisition, were not readily available and could not be precisely determined at the appropriate level of detail, including the commodity, size and item code information necessary to perform the detailed calculations required to retrospectively compute the internal LIFO indices applicable to prior fiscal years. The effect of this change was to reduce net earnings by $37,917,000 and $18,307,000 in the current and prior fiscal year, respectively, below that which would have been reported using the Company's previous inventory method. The reduction in earnings per share was $3.12 ($3.09 diluted) and $1.50 per share ($1.49 diluted) in the current and prior fiscal year, respectively.

As we discussed in Chapter 8, an important motivation for using LIFO in periods of rising costs is that it produces higher cost of goods sold and lowers income and income taxes. Notice in the Seneca Foods disclosure note that the switch to LIFO did cause a decrease in income and therefore income taxes in the year of the switch indicating an environment of increasing costs.

# Additional Consideration

When changing from one generally accepted accounting principle to another, a company must justify that the change results in financial information that more properly portrays operating results and financial position. For income tax purposes, a company generally must obtain consent from the Internal Revenue Service before changing an accounting method. A special form also must be filed with the IRS when a company intends to adopt the LIFO inventory method. When a company changes from LIFO for tax purposes, it can't change back to LIFO until five tax returns have been filed using the non-LIFO method.

## Inventory Errors

● LO9–7

Accounting errors must be corrected when they are discovered. In Chapter 4 we briefly discussed the correction of accounting errors and Chapter 20 provides in-depth coverage. Here we provide an overview of the accounting treatment and disclosures in the context of inventory errors. Inventory errors include the over- or understatement of ending inventory due to a mistake in physical count or a mistake in pricing inventory quantities. Also, errors include the over- or understatement of purchases which could be caused by the cutoff errors described in Chapter 8.

If an inventory error is discovered in the same accounting period it occurred, the original erroneous entry should simply be reversed and the appropriate entry recorded. This situation presents no particular reporting problem.

**For material errors, previous years' financial statements are retrospectively restated.**

If a *material* inventory error is discovered in an accounting period subsequent to the period in which the error was made, any previous years' financial statements that were incorrect as a result of the error are retrospectively restated to reflect the correction.[13] And, of course, any account balances that are incorrect as a result of the error are corrected by journal entry. If, due to an error affecting net income, retained earnings is one of the incorrect accounts, the correction is reported as a prior period adjustment to the beginning balance on the statement of shareholders' equity.[14] In addition, a disclosure note is needed to describe the nature of the error and the impact of its correction on net income, income before extraordinary items, and earnings per share.

When analyzing inventory errors, it's helpful to visualize the way cost of goods sold, net income, and retained earnings are determined (see Illustration 9–18). Beginning inventory and net purchases are *added* in the calculation of cost of goods sold. If either of these is overstated (understated) then cost of goods sold would be overstated (understated). On the other hand, ending inventory is *deducted* in the calculation of cost of goods sold, so if ending inventory is overstated (understated) then cost of goods sold is understated (overstated). Of course, errors that affect income also will affect income taxes. In the illustration that follows, we ignore the tax effects of the errors and focus on the errors themselves rather than their tax aspects.

*Incorrect balances are corrected.*

*A correction of retained earnings is reported as a prior period adjustment.*

*A disclosure note describes the nature and the impact of the error.*

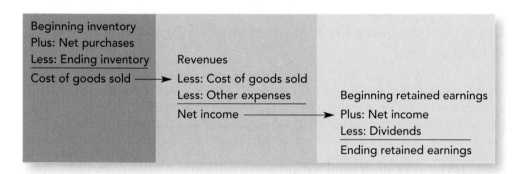

**Illustration 9–18**

Visualizing the Effect of Inventory Errors

Let's look at an example in Illustration 9–19.

**Illustration 9–19**

Inventory Error Correction

The Barton Company uses a periodic inventory system. At the end of 2012, a mathematical error caused an $800,000 overstatement of ending inventory. Ending inventories for 2013 and 2014 are correctly determined.

The way we correct this error depends on when the error is discovered. Assuming that the error is not discovered until after 2013, the 2012 and 2013 effects of the error, ignoring income tax effects, are shown below. The overstated and understated amounts are $800,000 in each instance.

**Analysis: U = Understated   O = Overstated**

| 2012 | | 2013 | |
|---|---|---|---|
| Beginning inventory | | Beginning inventory | O – 800,000 |
| Plus: Net purchases | | Plus: Net purchases | |
| Less: Ending inventory | O – 800,000 | Less: Ending inventory | |
| Cost of goods sold | U – 800,000 | Cost of goods sold | O – 800,000 |
| Revenues | | Revenues | |
| Less: Cost of goods sold | U – 800,000 | Less: Cost of goods sold | O – 800,000 |
| Less: Other expenses | | Less: Other expenses | |
| Net income | O – 800,000 | Net income | U – 800,000 |
| Retained earnings | O – 800,000 | Retained earnings | *corrected* |

---

[13]If the effect of the error is not material, it is simply corrected in the year of discovery.

[14]The prior period adjustment is applied to beginning retained earnings for the year following the error, or for the earliest year being reported in the comparative financial statements when the error occurs prior to the earliest year presented. The retained earnings balances in years after the first year also are adjusted to what those balances would be if the error had not occurred, but a company may choose not to explicitly report those adjustments as separate line items.

## When the Inventory Error Is Discovered the Following Year

*Previous years' financial statements are retrospectively restated.*

First, let's assume the error is discovered in 2013. The 2012 financial statements that were incorrect as a result of the error are retrospectively restated to reflect the correct inventory amount, cost of goods sold, net income, and retained earnings when those statements are reported again for comparative purposes in the 2013 annual report. The following journal entry, ignoring income taxes, corrects the error.

*A journal entry corrects any incorrect account balance.*

| | | |
|---|---|---|
| Retained earnings ............................................................ | 800,000 | |
| Inventory .................................................................... | | 800,000 |

*When retained earnings requires correction, a prior period adjustment is made on the statement of shareholders' equity.*

Because retained earnings is one of the accounts that is incorrect, when the error is discovered in 2013, the correction to that account is reported as a *prior period adjustment* to the 2013 beginning retained earnings balance in Barton's statement of shareholders' equity (or statement of retained earnings). Prior period adjustments do not flow through the income statement but directly adjust retained earnings. This adjustment is illustrated in Chapter 20.

## When the Inventory Error Is Discovered Subsequent to the Following Year

If the error isn't discovered until 2014, the 2013 financial statements also are retrospectively restated to reflect the correct cost of goods sold and net income even though no correcting entry would be needed at that point. Inventory and retained earnings would not require adjustment. The error has self-corrected and no prior period adjustment is needed.

*A disclosure note describes the nature of the error and the impact of the correction on income.*

Also, a disclosure note in Barton's annual report should describe the nature of the error and the impact of its correction on each year's net income (overstated by $800,000 in 2012; understated by $800,000 in 2013), income before extraordinary items (same as net income in this case), and earnings per share.

## Concept Review Exercise

**INVENTORY ERRORS**

In 2013, the controller of the Fleischman Wholesale Beverage Company discovered the following material errors related to the 2011 and 2012 financial statements:

a. Inventory at the end of 2011 was understated by $50,000.

b. Late in 2012, a $3,000 purchase was incorrectly recorded as a $33,000 purchase. The invoice has not yet been paid.

c. Inventory at the end of 2012 was overstated by $20,000.

The company uses a periodic inventory system.

**Required:**

1. Assuming that the errors were discovered after the 2012 financial statements were issued, analyze the effect of the errors on 2011 and 2012 cost of goods sold, net income, and retained earnings. Ignore income taxes.

2. Prepare a journal entry to correct the errors.

**Solution:**

1. **Analysis: U = Understated   O = Overstated**

| 2011 | | 2012 | |
|---|---|---|---|
| Beginning inventory | | Beginning inventory | U – 50,000 |
| Plus: Net purchases | | Plus: Net purchases | O – 30,000 |
| Less: Ending inventory | U – 50,000 | Less: Ending inventory | O – 20,000 |
| Cost of goods sold | O – 50,000 | Cost of goods sold | U – 40,000 |
| Revenues | | Revenues | |
| Less: Cost of goods sold | O – 50,000 | Less: Cost of goods sold | U – 40,000 |
| Less: Other expenses | | Less: Other expenses | |
| Net income | U – 50,000 | Net income | O – 40,000 |
| ↓ | | ↓ | |
| Retained earnings | U – 50,000 | Retained earnings | U – 10,000 |

2. Prepare a journal entry to correct the errors.

| | | |
|---|---|---|
| Accounts payable ........................................................................ | 30,000 | |
| Inventory ............................................................................. | | 20,000 |
| Retained earnings ................................................................ | | 10,000 |

# Earnings Quality

A change in the accounting method a company uses to value inventory is one way managers can artificially manipulate income. However, this method of income manipulation is transparent. As we learned in a previous section, the effect on income of switching from one inventory method to another must be disclosed. That disclosure restores comparability between periods and enhances earnings quality.

On the other hand, inventory write-downs are included in the broader category of "big bath" accounting techniques some companies use to manipulate earnings. By overstating the write-down, profits are increased in future periods as the inventory is used or sold. When the demand for many high technology products decreased significantly in late 2000 and early 2001, several companies, including **Sycamore Networks**, **Lucent Technologies**, and **JDS Uniphase**, recorded large inventory write-offs, some in the billions of dollars. In the introduction to this chapter, we discussed the over $2 billion inventory write-off recorded by **Cisco Systems**. Certainly, these write-offs reflected the existing economic environment. However, some analysts questioned the size of some of the write-offs. For example, William Schaff, an investment officer at Bay Isle Financial noted that Cisco's write-off was approximately equal to the balance of inventory on hand at the end of the previous quarter and about equal to the cost of goods actually sold during the quarter.

A financial analyst must carefully consider the effect of any significant asset write-down on the assessment of a company's permanent earnings.

> **William Schaff—Bay Isle Financial**
> I have nothing on which to base these theories other than the fact that writing off a whole quarter's inventory seems a bit much to just shrug off. It's very disturbing.[15]

Inventory write-downs often are cited as a method used to shift income between periods.

[15]William Schaff, "What Is the Definition of an Earnings Bath," *Information Week Online*, April 24, 2001.

# Financial Reporting Case Solution

1. **Sears values its inventory at the lower of cost or market. What does that mean? Under what circumstances might Sears be justified in reporting its inventory at less than cost?** *(p. 476)*   A departure from historical cost is warranted when the probable benefits to be received from any asset drop below the asset's cost. The benefits from inventory result from the ultimate sale of the goods. Deterioration, obsolescence, and

changes in price levels are situations that might cause the benefits to be received from sale to drop below cost. The lower-of-cost-or-market approach recognizes losses in the period when the value of the inventory declines below its cost rather than in the period in which the goods ultimately are sold.

2. **How does Sears avoid counting all its inventory every time it produces financial statements? What are external price indices used for?** *(p. 494)*    Sears uses the dollar-value LIFO retail inventory method. The retail inventory estimation technique avoids the counting of ending inventory by keeping track of goods available for sale not only at cost but also at retail prices. Each period's sales, at sales prices, are deducted from the retail amount of goods available for sale to arrive at ending inventory at retail. This amount is then converted to cost using a cost-to-retail percentage.

The dollar-value LIFO retail method uses a price index to first convert ending inventory at retail to base year prices. Yearly LIFO layers are then determined and each layer is converted to that year's current year retail prices using the year's price index and then to cost using the layer's cost-to-retail percentage. For the price index, Sears uses external indices rather than internally generated price indices. ●

## The Bottom Line

● **LO9–1**    Inventory is valued at the lower of cost or market (LCM). The designated market value in the LCM rule is the middle number of replacement cost (RC), net realizable value (NRV), and net realizable value less a normal profit margin (NRV − NP). *(p. 475)*

● **LO9–2**    The gross profit method estimates cost of goods sold which is then subtracted from cost of goods available for sale to estimate ending inventory. The estimate of cost of goods sold is determined by subtracting an estimate of gross profit from net sales. The estimate of gross profit is determined by multiplying the historical gross profit ratio times net sales. *(p. 484)*

● **LO9–3**    The retail inventory method determines the amount of ending inventory at retail by subtracting sales for the period from goods available for sale at retail. Ending inventory at retail is then converted to *cost* by multiplying it by the cost-to-retail percentage, which is based on a current relationship between cost and selling price. *(p. 486)*

● **LO9–4**    By the conventional retail method, we estimate average cost at lower of cost or market. Average cost is estimated by including beginning inventory in the calculation of the cost-to-retail percentage. LCM is estimated by excluding markdowns from the calculation. Markdowns are subtracted in the retail column after the percentage is calculated. *(p. 489)*

● **LO9–5**    By the LIFO retail method, ending inventory includes the beginning inventory plus the current year's layer. To determine layers, we compare ending inventory at retail to beginning inventory at retail and assume that no more than one inventory layer is added if inventory increases. Each layer carries its own cost-to-retail percentage which is used to convert each layer from retail to cost. The dollar-value LIFO retail inventory method combines the LIFO retail method and the dollar-value LIFO method (Chapter 8) to estimate LIFO from retail prices when the price level has changed. *(p. 494)*

● **LO9–6**    Most changes in inventory methods are reported retrospectively. This means revising all previous periods' financial statements to appear as if the newly adopted inventory method had been applied all along. An exception is a change to the LIFO method. In this case, it usually is impossible to calculate the income effect on prior years. To do so would require assumptions as to when specific LIFO inventory layers were created in years prior to the change. As a result, a company changing to LIFO usually does not report the change retrospectively. Instead, the LIFO method simply is used from that point on. *(p. 497)*

● **LO9–7**    If a material inventory error is discovered in an accounting period subsequent to the period in which the error is made, previous years' financial statements that were incorrect as a result of the error are retrospectively restated to reflect the correction. Account balances are corrected by journal entry. A correction of retained earnings is reported as a prior period adjustment to the beginning balance in the statement of shareholders' equity. In addition, a disclosure note is needed to describe the nature of the error and the impact of its correction on income. *(p. 500)*

● **LO9–8**    When applying the lower-of-cost-or-market rule for valuing inventory according to U.S. GAAP, market is defined as replacement cost with a ceiling of net realizable value (NRV) and a floor of NRV less a normal profit margin. However, according to *IAS No. 2,* inventory is valued at the lower of cost and net realizable value. *IAS No. 2* also specifies that if circumstances reveal that an inventory write-down is no longer appropriate, it must be reversed. Reversals are not permitted under U.S. GAAP. Under U.S. GAAP, the LCM rule can be applied to individual items, logical inventory categories, or the entire inventory. Using the international standard, the LCM assessment usually is applied to individual items, although using logical inventory categories is allowed under certain circumstances. (*p. 481*) ●

# Purchase Commitments

# APPENDIX 9

**Purchase commitments** are contracts that obligate a company to purchase a specified amount of merchandise or raw materials at specified prices on or before specified dates. Companies enter into these agreements to make sure they will be able to obtain important inventory as well as to protect against increases in purchase price. However, if the purchase price decreases before the agreement is exercised, the commitment has the disadvantage of requiring the company to purchase inventory at a higher than market price. If this happens, a loss on the purchase commitment is recorded.

> **Purchase commitments protect the buyer against price increases and provide a supply of product.**

Because purchase commitments create the possibility of this kind of loss, the loss occurs when the market price falls below the commitment price rather than when the inventory eventually is sold. This means recording the loss when the product is purchased or, if the commitment is still outstanding, at the end of the reporting period. In other words, purchases are recorded at market price when that price is lower than the contract price, and a loss is recognized for the difference. Also, losses are recognized for any purchase commitments outstanding at the end of a reporting period when market price is less than contract price. In effect, the LCM rule is applied to purchase commitments. This is best understood by the example in Illustration 9A–1.

> **Purchases made pursuant to a purchase commitment are recorded at the lower of contract price or market price on the date the contract is executed.**

> In July 2013, the Lassiter Company signed two purchase commitments. The first requires Lassiter to purchase inventory for $500,000 by November 15, 2013. The second requires the company to purchase inventory for $600,000 by February 15, 2014. Lassiter's fiscal year-end is December 31. The company uses a perpetual inventory system.

**Illustration 9A–1**
Purchase Commitments

## Contract Period within Fiscal Year

The contract period for the first commitment is contained within a single fiscal year. Lassiter would record the purchase at the contract price if the market price at date of acquisition is at least *equal to* the contract price of $500,000.[16]

| | | |
|---|---|---|
| Inventory (contract price) ................................................................. | 500,000 | |
| Cash (or accounts payable) ........................................................ | | 500,000 |

If the market price at acquisition is *less* than the contract price, inventory is recorded at the market price and a loss is recognized.[17] For example, if the market price is $425,000, the following entry records the purchase:

> **If market price on purchase date declines from year-end price, the purchase is recorded at the market price.**

| | | |
|---|---|---|
| Inventory (market price) ................................................................. | 425,000 | |
| Loss on purchase commitment ....................................................... | 75,000 | |
| Cash (or accounts payable) ........................................................ | | 500,000 |

> **If market price is less than the contract price, the purchase is recorded at the market price.**

The objective of this treatment is to associate the loss with the period in which the price declines rather than with the period in which the company eventually sells the inventory. This is the same objective as the LCM rule you studied in the chapter.

---

[16]In each of the following situations, if a periodic inventory system is used purchases is debited instead of inventory.
[17]Recall from the LCM discussion in the chapter that the preferred method of recording losses from inventory write-downs is to recognize the loss as a separate item in the income statement, rather than as an increase in cost of goods sold.

## Contract Period Extends beyond Fiscal Year

Now let's consider Lassiter's second purchase commitment that is outstanding at the end of the fiscal year 2013 (that is, the purchases have not yet been made). If the market price at the end of the year is at least *equal* to the contract price of $600,000, no entry is recorded. However, if the market price at year-end is *less* than the contract price, a loss must be recognized to satisfy the LCM objective of associating the loss with the period in which the price declines rather than with the period in which the company eventually sells the inventory. Let's say the year-end market price of the inventory for Lassiter's second purchase commitment is $540,000. The following adjusting entry is recorded:

**If the market price at year-end is less than the contract price a loss is recorded for the difference.**

| December 31, 2013 | | |
|---|---|---|
| Estimated loss on purchase commitment ($600,000 − 540,000) ........ | 60,000 | |
|    Estimated liability on purchase commitment ............................... | | 60,000 |

At this point, the loss is an *estimated* loss. The actual loss, if any, will not be known until the inventory actually is purchased. The best estimate of the market price on date of purchase is the current market price, in this case $540,000. Because no inventory has been acquired, we can't credit inventory for the LCM loss. Instead, a liability is credited because, in a sense, the loss represents an obligation to the seller of the inventory to purchase inventory above market price.

**A liability is credited for estimated losses on purchase commitments.**

The entry to record the actual purchase on or before February 15, 2014, will vary depending on the market price of the inventory at date of purchase. If the market price is unchanged or has increased from the year-end price, the following entry is made:

**If market price on purchase date has not declined from year-end price, the purchase is recorded at the year-end market price.**

| | | |
|---|---|---|
| Inventory (accounting cost) ................................................................. | 540,000 | |
| Estimated liability on purchase commitment .................................... | 60,000 | |
|    Cash (or accounts payable) ........................................................... | | 600,000 |

Even if the market price of the inventory increases, there is no recovery of the $60,000 loss recognized in 2013. Remember that when the LCM rule is applied, the reduced inventory value, in this case the reduced value of purchases, is considered to be the new cost and any recovery of value is ignored.

**If market price on purchase date has not declined from year-end price, the purchase is recorded at the year-end market price.**

If the market price declines even further from year-end levels, an additional loss is recognized. For example, if the market price of the inventory covered by the commitment declines to $510,000, the following entry is recorded:

| | | |
|---|---|---|
| Inventory (market price) ...................................................................... | 510,000 | |
| Loss on purchase commitment ($540,000 − 510,000) ...................... | 30,000 | |
| Estimated liability on purchase commitment .................................... | 60,000 | |
|    Cash (or accounts payable) ........................................................... | | 600,000 |

The total loss on this purchase commitment of $90,000 is thus allocated between 2013 and 2014 according to when the decline in value of the inventory covered by the commitment occurred.

If there are material amounts of purchase commitments outstanding at the end of a reporting period, the contract details are disclosed in a note. This disclosure is required even if no loss estimate has been recorded. ●

# Questions For Review of Key Topics

Q 9–1    Explain the lower-of-cost-or-market approach to valuing inventory.

Q 9–2    What is the meaning of market in the lower-of-cost-or-market rule?

Q 9–3    What are the various ways the LCM determination can be made?

Q 9–4    Describe the preferred method of adjusting from cost to market for material inventory write-downs.

Q 9–5    Explain the gross profit method of estimating ending inventory.

Q 9–6    The Rider Company uses the gross profit method to estimate ending inventory and cost of goods sold. The cost percentage is determined based on historical data. What factors could cause the estimate of ending inventory to be overstated?

Q 9–7    Explain the retail inventory method of estimating ending inventory.

Q 9–8    Both the gross profit method and the retail inventory method provide a way to estimate ending inventory. What is the main difference between the two estimation techniques?

Q 9–9    Define each of the following retail terms: initial markup, additional markup, markup cancellation, markdown, markdown cancellation.

Q 9–10    Explain how to estimate the average cost of inventory when using the retail inventory method.

Q 9–11    What is the conventional retail method?

Q 9–12    Explain the LIFO retail inventory method.

Q 9–13    Discuss the treatment of freight-in, net markups, normal spoilage, and employee discounts in the application of the retail inventory method.

Q 9–14    Explain the difference between the retail inventory method using LIFO and the dollar-value LIFO retail method.

Q 9–15    Describe the accounting treatment for a change in inventory method other than to LIFO.

Q 9–16    When a company changes its inventory method to LIFO, an exception is made for the way accounting changes usually are reported. Explain the difference in the accounting treatment of a change *to* the LIFO inventory method from other inventory method changes.

Q 9–17    Explain the accounting treatment of material inventory errors discovered in an accounting period subsequent to the period in which the error is made.

Q 9–18    It is discovered in 2013 that ending inventory in 2011 was understated. What is the effect of the understatement on the following:

| | |
|---|---|
| 2011: | Cost of goods sold |
| | Net income |
| | Ending retained earnings |
| 2012: | Net purchases |
| | Cost of goods sold |
| | Net income |
| | Ending retained earnings |

 **IFRS**    Q 9–19    Identify any differences between U.S. GAAP and IFRS when applying the lower-of-cost-or-market rule to inventory valuation.

Q 9–20    (Based on Appendix 9) Define purchase commitments. What is the advantage(s) of these agreements to buyers?

Q 9–21    (Based on Appendix 9) Explain how the lower-of-cost-or-market rule is applied to purchase commitments.

## Brief Exercises

**BE 9–1**
Lower of cost or market
● LO9–1

Ross Electronics has one product in its ending inventory. Per unit data consist of the following: cost, $20; replacement cost, $18; selling price, $30; disposal costs, $4. The normal profit margin is 30% of selling price. What unit value should Ross use when applying the LCM rule to ending inventory?

**BE 9–2**
Lower of cost or market
● LO9–1

SLR Corporation has 1,000 units of each of its two products in its year-end inventory. Per unit data for each of the products are as follows:

| | Product 1 | Product 2 |
|---|---|---|
| Cost | $50 | $30 |
| Replacement cost | 48 | 26 |
| Selling price | 70 | 36 |
| Disposal costs | 6 | 4 |
| Normal profit margin | 10 | 8 |

Determine the balance sheet carrying value of SLR's inventory assuming that the LCM rule is applied to individual products. What is the before-tax income effect of the LCM adjustment?

**BE 9–3**
IFRS; lower of
cost or market
● LO9–1, LO9–8

 **IFRS**

Refer to the situation described in BE 9–2. Determine the balance sheet carrying value of SLR's inventory assuming that the LCM rule is applied to individual products and that SLR prepares its financial statements according to IFRS. What is the before-tax income effect of the LCM adjustment?

**BE 9–4**
Gross profit
method
● LO9–2

On February 26 a hurricane destroyed the entire inventory stored in a warehouse owned by the Rockford Corporation. The following information is available from the records of the company's periodic inventory system: beginning inventory, $220,000; purchases and net sales from the beginning of the year through February 26, $400,000 and $600,000, respectively; gross profit ratio, 30%. Estimate the cost of the inventory destroyed by the hurricane using the gross profit method.

**BE 9–5**
Gross profit
method; solving
for unknown
● LO9–2

Adams Corporation estimates that it lost $75,000 in inventory from a recent flood. The following information is available from the records of the company's periodic inventory system: beginning inventory, $150,000; purchases and net sales from the beginning of the year through the date of the flood, $450,000 and $700,000, respectively. What is the company's gross profit ratio?

**BE 9–6**
Retail inventory
method; average
cost
● LO9–3

Kiddie World uses a periodic inventory system and the retail inventory method to estimate ending inventory and cost of goods sold. The following data are available for the quarter ending September 30, 2013:

|  | Cost | Retail |
|---|---|---|
| Beginning inventory | $300,000 | $ 450,000 |
| Net purchases | 861,000 | 1,210,000 |
| Freight-in | 22,000 |  |
| Net markups |  | 48,000 |
| Net markdowns |  | 18,000 |
| Net sales |  | 1,200,000 |

Estimate ending inventory and cost of goods sold (average cost).

**BE 9–7**
Retail inventory
method; LIFO
● LO9–3

Refer to the situation described in BE 9–6. Estimate ending inventory and cost of goods sold (LIFO).

**BE 9–8**
Conventional
retail method
● LO9–4

Refer to the situation described in BE 9–6. Estimate ending inventory and cost of goods sold using the conventional method (average cost and the LCM approximation).

**BE 9–9**
Conventional
retail method
● LO9–4

Roberson Corporation uses a periodic inventory system and the retail inventory method. Accounting records provided the following information for the 2013 fiscal year:

|  | Cost | Retail |
|---|---|---|
| Beginning inventory | $220,000 | $ 400,000 |
| Net purchases | 640,000 | 1,180,000 |
| Freight-in | 17,800 |  |
| Net markups |  | 16,000 |
| Net markdowns |  | 6,000 |
| Normal spoilage |  | 3,000 |
| Net sales |  | 1,300,000 |

The company records sales to employees net of discounts. These discounts totaled $15,000 for the year. Estimate ending inventory and cost of goods sold using the conventional method (average cost and the LCM approximation).

**BE 9–10**
Dollar-value
LIFO retail
● LO9–5

On January 1, 2013, Sanderson Variety Store adopted the dollar-value LIFO retail inventory method. Accounting records provided the following information:

|                              | Cost      | Retail    |
|------------------------------|-----------|-----------|
| Beginning inventory          | $ 40,800  | $ 68,000  |
| Net purchases                | 155,440   | 270,000   |
| Net markups                  |           | 6,000     |
| Net markdowns                |           | 8,000     |
| Net sales                    |           | 250,000   |
| Retail price index, end of year |        | 1.02      |

Calculate the inventory value at the end of the year using the dollar-value LIFO retail method.

**BE 9–11**
Dollar-value
LIFO retail
● LO9–5

This exercise is a continuation of BE 9–10. During 2014, purchases at cost and retail were $168,000 and $301,000, respectively. Net markups, net markdowns, and net sales for the year were $3,000, $4,000, and $280,000, respectively. The retail price index at the end of 2014 was 1.06. Calculate the inventory value at the end of 2014 using the dollar-value LIFO retail method.

**BE 9–12**
Change in inventory
costing methods
● LO9–6

In 2013, Hopyard Lumber changed its inventory method from LIFO to FIFO. Inventory at the end of 2012 of $127,000 would have been $145,000 if FIFO had been used. Inventory at the end of 2013 is $162,000 using the new FIFO method but would have been $151,000 if the company had continued to use LIFO. Describe the steps Hopyard should take to report this change. What is the effect of the change on 2013 cost of goods sold?

**BE 9–13**
Change in inventory
costing methods
● LO9–6

In 2013, Wade Window and Glass changed its inventory method from FIFO to LIFO. Inventory at the end of 2012 is $150,000. Describe the steps Wade Window and Glass should take to report this change.

**BE 9–14**
Inventory error
● LO9–7

In 2013, Winslow International, Inc.'s controller discovered that ending inventories for 2011 and 2012 were overstated by $200,000 and $500,000, respectively. Determine the effect of the errors on retained earnings at January 1, 2013. (Ignore income taxes.)

**BE 9–15**
Inventory error
● LO9–7

Refer to the situation described in BE 9–14. What steps would be taken to report the error in the 2013 financial statements?

## Exercises

An alternate exercise and problem set is available on the text website: www.mhhe.com/spiceland7e

**E 9–1**
Lower of cost
or market
● LO9–1

Herman Company has three products in its ending inventory. Specific per unit data for each of the products are as follows:

|                     | Product 1 | Product 2 | Product 3 |
|---------------------|-----------|-----------|-----------|
| Cost                | $20       | $ 90      | $50       |
| Replacement cost    | 18        | 85        | 40        |
| Selling price       | 40        | 120       | 70        |
| Disposal costs      | 6         | 40        | 10        |
| Normal profit margin| 5         | 30        | 12        |

**Required:**
What unit values should Herman use for each of its products when applying the LCM rule to ending inventory?

**E 9–2**
IFRS; Lower of
cost or market
● LO9–1, LO9–8

**IFRS**

Refer to the situation described in Exercise 9–1.

**Required:**
How might your solution differ if Herman Company prepares its financial statements according to International Financial Reporting Standards?

**E 9–3**
Lower of cost
or market
● LO9–1

Tatum Company has four products in its inventory. Information about the December 31, 2013, inventory is as follows:

| Product | Total Cost | Total Replacement Cost | Total Net Realizable Value |
|---------|-----------|------------------------|----------------------------|
| 101 | $120,000 | $110,000 | $100,000 |
| 102 | 90,000 | 85,000 | 110,000 |
| 103 | 60,000 | 40,000 | 50,000 |
| 104 | 30,000 | 28,000 | 50,000 |

The normal gross profit percentage is 25% of *cost*.

**Required:**
1. Determine the balance sheet inventory carrying value at December 31, 2013, assuming the LCM rule is applied to individual products.
2. Assuming that Tatum recognizes an inventory write-down as a separate income statement item, determine the amount of the loss.

**E 9–4**
**IFRS; lower of cost or market**
● **LO9–1, LO9–8**

 **IFRS**

Refer to the situation described in Exercise 9–3. Assume that Tatum Company prepares its financial statements according to IFRS.

**Required:**
1. Determine the balance sheet inventory carrying value at December 31, 2013, assuming Tatum applies the LCM rule to individual products.
2. Prepare a journal entry to record the inventory write-down, if necessary.

**E 9–5**
**Lower of cost or market**
● **LO9–1**

The inventory of Royal Decking consisted of five products. Information about the December 31, 2013, inventory is as follows:

| Product | Per Unit Cost | Replacement Cost | Selling Price |
|---------|------|------------------|---------------|
| A | $ 40 | $35 | $ 60 |
| B | 80 | 70 | 100 |
| C | 40 | 55 | 80 |
| D | 100 | 70 | 130 |
| E | 20 | 28 | 30 |

Disposal costs consist only of a sales commission equal to 10% of selling price and shipping costs equal to 5% of cost. The normal gross profit percentage is 30% of selling price.

**Required:**
What unit value should Royal Decking use for each of its products when applying the LCM rule to units of inventory?

**E 9–6**
**FASB codification research**
● **LO9–1**

The *FASB Accounting Standards Codification* represents the single source of authoritative U.S. generally accepted accounting principles.

**Required:**
1. Obtain the relevant authoritative literature on the lower-of-cost-or-market rule for valuing inventory using the FASB's Codification Research System at the FASB website (www.fasb.org). Identify the circumstances in which inventory is stated at the lower of cost or market.
2. What are the specific citations that discuss the level of aggregation that should be used in applying the LCM rule?
3. Summarize the discussion.

**E 9–7**
**FASB codification research**
● **LO9–1, LO9–3, LO9–6, LO9–7**

Access the FASB's Codification Research System at the FASB website (www.fasb.org). Determine the specific citation for each of the following items:
1. The income statement presentation of losses from the write-down of inventory.
2. The determination of market value for applying LCM to inventory.
3. The accounting treatment required for a correction of an inventory error in previously issued financial statements.
4. The use of the retail method to value inventory.

**E 9–8**
**Gross profit method**
● **LO9–2**

On September 22, 2013, a flood destroyed the entire merchandise inventory on hand in a warehouse owned by the Rocklin Sporting Goods Company. The following information is available from the records of the company's periodic inventory system:

| | |
|---|---|
| Inventory, January 1, 2013 | $140,000 |
| Net purchases, January 1 through September 22 | 370,000 |
| Net sales, January 1 through September 22 | 550,000 |
| Gross profit ratio | 25% |

**Required:**
Estimate the cost of inventory destroyed in the flood using the gross profit method.

**E 9–9**
**Gross profit method**
● **LO9–2**

On November 21, 2013, a fire at Hodge Company's warehouse caused severe damage to its entire inventory of Product Tex. Hodge estimates that all usable damaged goods can be sold for $12,000. The following information was available from the records of Hodge's periodic inventory system:

| | |
|---|---|
| Inventory, November 1 | $100,000 |
| Net purchases from November 1, to the date of the fire | 140,000 |
| Net sales from November 1, to the date of the fire | 220,000 |

Based on recent history, Hodge's gross profit ratio on Product Tex is 35% of net sales.

**Required:**
Calculate the estimated loss on the inventory from the fire, using the gross profit method.

*(AICPA adapted)*

**E 9–10**
**Gross profit method**
● **LO9–2**

A fire destroyed a warehouse of the Goren Group, Inc., on May 4, 2013. Accounting records on that date indicated the following:

| | |
|---|---|
| Merchandise inventory, January 1, 2013 | $1,900,000 |
| Purchases to date | 5,800,000 |
| Freight-in | 400,000 |
| Sales to date | 8,200,000 |

The gross profit ratio has averaged 20% of sales for the past four years.

**Required:**
Use the gross profit method to estimate the cost of the inventory destroyed in the fire.

**E 9–11**
**Gross profit method**
● **LO9–2**

Royal Gorge Company uses the gross profit method to estimate ending inventory and cost of goods sold when preparing monthly financial statements required by its bank. Inventory on hand at the end of October was $58,500. The following information for the month of November was available from company records:

| | |
|---|---|
| Purchases | $110,000 |
| Freight-in | 3,000 |
| Sales | 180,000 |
| Sales returns | 5,000 |
| Purchases returns | 4,000 |

In addition, the controller is aware of $8,000 of inventory that was stolen during November from one of the company's warehouses.

**Required:**
1. Calculate the estimated inventory at the end of November, assuming a gross profit ratio of 40%.
2. Calculate the estimated inventory at the end of November, assuming a markup on cost of 100%.

**E 9–12**
**Gross profit method; solving for unknown cost percentage**
● **LO9–2**

National Distributing Company uses a periodic inventory system to track its merchandise inventory and the gross profit method to estimate ending inventory and cost of goods sold for interim periods. Net purchases for the month of August were $31,000. The July 31 and August 31, 2013, financial statements contained the following information:

**Income Statements**
**For the Months Ending**

| | August 31, 2013 | July 31, 2013 |
|---|---|---|
| Net sales | $50,000 | $40,000 |

*(continued)*

(concluded)

**Balance Sheets**
**At**

|  | August 31, 2013 | July 31, 2013 |
|---|---|---|
| Assets: | | |
| Merchandise inventory | $28,000 | $27,000 |

**Required:**
Determine the company's cost percentage.

**E 9–13**
Retail inventory method; average cost
● LO9–3

San Lorenzo General Store uses a periodic inventory system and the retail inventory method to estimate ending inventory and cost of goods sold. The following data are available for the month of October 2013:

|  | Cost | Retail |
|---|---|---|
| Beginning inventory | $35,000 | $50,000 |
| Net purchases | 19,120 | 31,600 |
| Net markups | | 1,200 |
| Net markdowns | | 800 |
| Net sales | | 32,000 |

**Required:**
Estimate the average cost of ending inventory and cost of goods sold for October. Do not approximate LCM.

**E 9–14**
Conventional retail method
● LO9–4

Campbell Corporation uses the retail method to value its inventory. The following information is available for the year 2013:

|  | Cost | Retail |
|---|---|---|
| Merchandise inventory, January 1, 2013 | $190,000 | $280,000 |
| Purchases | 600,000 | 840,000 |
| Freight-in | 8,000 | |
| Net markups | | 20,000 |
| Net markdowns | | 4,000 |
| Net sales | | 800,000 |

**Required:**
Determine the December 31, 2013, inventory that approximates average cost, lower of cost or market.

**E 9–15**
Retail inventory method; LIFO
● LO9–3

Crosby Company owns a chain of hardware stores throughout the state. The company uses a periodic inventory system and the retail inventory method to estimate ending inventory and cost of goods sold. The following data are available for the three months ending March 31, 2013:

|  | Cost | Retail |
|---|---|---|
| Beginning inventory | $160,000 | $280,000 |
| Net purchases | 607,760 | 840,000 |
| Net markups | | 20,000 |
| Net markdowns | | 4,000 |
| Net sales | | 800,000 |

**Required:**
Estimate the LIFO cost of ending inventory and cost of goods sold for the three months ending March 31, 2013. Assume stable retail prices during the period.

**E 9–16**
Conventional retail method; normal spoilage
● LO9–4

Almaden Valley Variety Store uses the retail inventory method to estimate ending inventory and cost of goods sold. Data for 2013 are as follows:

|  | Cost | Retail |
|---|---|---|
| Beginning inventory | $ 12,000 | $ 20,000 |
| Purchases | 102,600 | 165,000 |
| Freight-in | 3,480 | |
| Purchase returns | 4,000 | 7,000 |
| Net markups | | 6,000 |
| Net markdowns | | 3,000 |
| Normal spoilage | | 4,200 |
| Net sales | | 152,000 |

**Required:**
Estimate the ending inventory and cost of goods sold for 2013, applying the conventional retail method (average, LCM).

**E 9–17**
**Conventional retail method; employee discounts**
● **LO9–3, LO9–4**

LeMay Department Store uses the retail inventory method to estimate ending inventory for its monthly financial statements. The following data pertain to one of its largest departments for the month of March 2013:

|  | Cost | Retail |
|---|---|---|
| Beginning inventory | $ 40,000 | $ 60,000 |
| Purchases | 207,000 | 400,000 |
| Freight-in | 14,488 |  |
| Purchase returns | 4,000 | 6,000 |
| Net markups |  | 5,800 |
| Net markdowns |  | 3,500 |
| Normal breakage |  | 6,000 |
| Net sales |  | 280,000 |
| Employee discounts |  | 1,800 |

Sales are recorded net of employee discounts.

**Required:**
1. Compute estimated ending inventory and cost of goods sold for March applying the conventional retail method (average, LCM).
2. Recompute the cost-to-retail percentage using the average cost method and ignoring LCM considerations.

**E 9–18**
**Retail inventory method; solving for unknowns**
● **LO9–3**

Adams Corporation uses a periodic inventory system and the retail inventory method to estimate ending inventory and cost of goods sold. The following data are available for the month of September 2013:

|  | Cost | Retail |
|---|---|---|
| Beginning inventory | $21,000 | $35,000 |
| Net purchases | 10,500 | ? |
| Net markups |  | 4,000 |
| Net markdowns |  | 1,000 |
| Net sales |  | ? |

The company used the average cost flow method and estimated inventory at the end of September to be $17,437.50. If the company had used the LIFO cost flow method, the cost-to-retail percentage would have been 50%.

**Required:**
Compute net purchases at retail and net sales for the month of September.

**E 9–19**
**Dollar-value LIFO retail**
● **LO9–5**

On January 1, 2013, the Brunswick Hat Company adopted the dollar-value LIFO retail method. The following data are available for 2013:

|  | Cost | Retail |
|---|---|---|
| Beginning inventory | $ 71,280 | $132,000 |
| Net purchases | 112,500 | 255,000 |
| Net markups |  | 6,000 |
| Net markdowns |  | 11,000 |
| Net sales |  | 232,000 |
| Retail price index, 12/31/13 |  | 1.04 |

**Required:**
Calculate the estimated ending inventory and cost of goods sold for 2013.

**E 9–20**
**Dollar-value LIFO retail**
● **LO9–5**

Canova Corporation adopted the dollar-value LIFO retail method on January 1, 2013. On that date, the cost of the inventory on hand was $15,000 and its retail value was $18,750. Information for 2013 and 2014 is as follows:

| Date | Ending Inventory at Retail | Retail Price Index | Cost-to-Retail Percentage |
|---|---|---|---|
| 12/31/13 | $25,000 | 1.25 | 82% |
| 12/31/14 | 28,600 | 1.30 | 85 |

**Required:**
1.  What is the cost-to-retail percentage for the inventory on hand at 1/1/13?
2.  Calculate the inventory value at the end of 2013 and 2014 using the dollar-value LIFO retail method.

**E 9–21**
**Dollar-value**
**LIFO retail**
● **LO9–5**

Lance-Hefner Specialty Shoppes decided to use the dollar-value LIFO retail method to value its inventory. Accounting records provide the following information:

|  | Cost | Retail |
| --- | --- | --- |
| Merchandise inventory, January 1, 2013 | $160,000 | $250,000 |
| Net purchases | 350,200 | 510,000 |
| Net markups |  | 7,000 |
| Net markdowns |  | 2,000 |
| Net sales |  | 380,000 |

Pertinent retail price indexes are as follows:

| January 1, 2013 | 1.00 |
| --- | --- |
| December 31, 2013 | 1.10 |

**Required:**
Determine ending inventory and cost of goods sold.

**E 9–22**
**Dollar-value LIFO**
**retail; solving for**
**unknowns**
● **LO9–5**

Bosco Company adopted the dollar-value LIFO retail method at the beginning of 2013. Information for 2013 and 2014 is as follows, with certain data intentionally omitted:

| Date | Inventory | | Retail Price Index | Cost-to-Retail Percentage |
| --- | --- | --- | --- | --- |
|  | Cost | Retail |  |  |
| Inventory, 1/1/13 | $21,000 | $28,000 | 1.00 | ? |
| Inventory, 12/31/13 | 22,792 | 33,600 | 1.12 | ? |
| 2014 net purchases | 60,000 | 88,400 |  |  |
| 2014 net sales |  | 80,000 |  |  |
| Inventory, 12/31/14 | ? | ? | 1.20 |  |

**Required:**
Determine the missing data.

**E 9–23**
**Change in**
**inventory costing**
**methods**
● **LO9–6**

In 2013, CPS Company changed its method of valuing inventory from the FIFO method to the average cost method. At December 31, 2012, CPS's inventories were $32 million (FIFO). CPS's records indicated that the inventories would have totaled $23.8 million at December 31, 2012, if determined on an average cost basis.

**Required:**
1.  Prepare the journal entry to record the adjustment. (Ignore income taxes.)
2.  Briefly describe other steps CPS should take to report the change.

**E 9–24**
**Change in**
**inventory costing**
**methods**
● **LO9–6**

Goddard Company has used the FIFO method of inventory valuation since it began operations in 2010. Goddard decided to change to the average cost method for determining inventory costs at the beginning of 2013. The following schedule shows year-end inventory balances under the FIFO and average cost methods:

| Year | FIFO | Average Cost |
| --- | --- | --- |
| 2010 | $45,000 | $54,000 |
| 2011 | 78,000 | 71,000 |
| 2012 | 83,000 | 78,000 |

**Required:**
1.  Ignoring income taxes, prepare the 2013 journal entry to adjust the accounts to reflect the average cost method.
2.  How much higher or lower would cost of goods sold be in the 2012 revised income statement?

**E 9–25**
**Error correction;**
**inventory error**
● **LO9–7**

During 2013, WMC Corporation discovered that its ending inventories reported in its financial statements were misstated by the following material amounts:

| 2011 | understated by | $120,000 |
| --- | --- | --- |
| 2012 | overstated by | 150,000 |

WMC uses a periodic inventory system and the FIFO cost method.

1. Determine the effect of these errors on retained earnings at January 1, 2013, before any adjustments. Explain your answer. (Ignore income taxes.)
2. Prepare a journal entry to correct the errors.
3. What other step(s) would be taken in connection with the correction of the errors?

**E 9–26**
Inventory errors
● LO9–7

For each of the following inventory errors occurring in 2013, determine the effect of the error on 2013's cost of goods sold, net income, and retained earnings. Assume that the error is not discovered until 2014 and that a periodic inventory system is used. Ignore income taxes.

U = understated    O = overstated    NE = no effect

| | Cost of Goods Sold | Net Income | Retained Earnings |
|---|:---:|:---:|:---:|
| 1. Overstatement of ending inventory | U | O | O |
| 2. Overstatement of purchases | | | |
| 3. Understatement of beginning inventory | | | |
| 4. Freight-in charges are understated | | | |
| 5. Understatement of ending inventory | | | |
| 6. Understatement of purchases | | | |
| 7. Overstatement of beginning inventory | | | |
| 8. Understatement of purchases plus understatement of ending inventory by the same amount | | | |

**E 9–27**
Inventory error
● LO9–7

In 2013, the internal auditors of Development Technologies, Inc. discovered that a $4 million purchase of merchandise in 2013 was recorded in 2012 instead. The physical inventory count at the end of 2012 was correct.

**Required:**
Prepare the journal entry needed in 2013 to correct the error. Also, briefly describe any other measures Development Technologies would take in connection with correcting the error. (Ignore income taxes.)

**E 9–28**
Inventory errors
● LO9–7

In 2013, the controller of Sytec Corporation discovered that $42,000 of inventory purchases were incorrectly charged to advertising expense in 2012. In addition, the 2012 year-end inventory count failed to include $30,000 of company merchandise held on consignment by Erin Brothers. Sytec uses a periodic inventory system. Other than the omission of the merchandise on consignment, the year-end inventory count was correct. The amounts of the errors are deemed to be material.

**Required:**
1. Determine the effect of the errors on retained earnings at January 1, 2013. Explain your answer. (Ignore income taxes.)
2. Prepare a journal entry to correct the errors.
3. What other step(s) would be taken in connection with the correction of the errors?

**E 9–29**
Concepts; terminology
● LO9–1 through LO9–7

Listed below are several terms and phrases associated with inventory measurement. Pair each item from List A with the item from List B (by letter) that is most appropriately associated with it.

| List A | List B |
|---|---|
| _____ 1. Gross profit ratio | a. Reduction in selling price below the original selling price. |
| _____ 2. Cost-to-retail percentage | b. Beginning inventory is not included in the calculation of the cost-to-retail percentage. |
| _____ 3. Additional markup | c. Deducted in the retail column after the calculation of the cost-to-retail percentage. |
| _____ 4. Markdown | d. Requires base year retail to be converted to layer year retail and then to cost. |
| _____ 5. Net markup | e. Gross profit divided by net sales. |
| _____ 6. Retail method, FIFO and LIFO | f. Material inventory error discovered in a subsequent year. |
| _____ 7. Conventional retail method | g. Must be added to sales if sales are recorded net of discounts. |
| _____ 8. Change from LIFO | h. Deducted in the retail column to arrive at goods available for sale at retail. |
| _____ 9. Dollar-value LIFO retail | i. Divide cost of goods available for sale by goods available at retail. |
| _____ 10. Normal spoilage | j. Average cost, LCM. |
| _____ 11. Requires retrospective restatement | k. Added to the retail column to arrive at goods available for sale. |
| _____ 12. Employee discounts | l. Increase in selling price subsequent to initial markup. |
| _____ 13. Net markdowns | m. Ceiling in the determination of market. |
| _____ 14. Net realizable value | n. Accounting change requiring retrospective treatment. |

**E 9–30**
**Purchase**
**commitments**
● **Appendix**

On October 6, 2013, the Elgin Corporation signed a purchase commitment to purchase inventory for $60,000 on or before March 31, 2014. The company's fiscal year-end is December 31. The contract was exercised on March 21, 2014, and the inventory was purchased for cash at the contract price. On the purchase date of March 21, the market price of the inventory was $54,000. The market price of the inventory on December 31, 2013, was $56,000. The company uses a perpetual inventory system.

**Required:**
1. Prepare the necessary adjusting journal entry (if any is required) on December 31, 2013.
2. Prepare the journal entry to record the purchase on March 21, 2014.

**E 9–31**
**Purchase**
**commitments**
● **Appendix**

In March 2013, the Phillips Tool Company signed two purchase commitments. The first commitment requires Phillips to purchase inventory for $100,000 by June 15, 2013. The second commitment requires the company to purchase inventory for $150,000 by August 20, 2013. The company's fiscal year-end is June 30. Phillips uses a periodic inventory system.

The first commitment is exercised on June 15, 2013, when the market price of the inventory purchased was $85,000. The second commitment was exercised on August 20, 2013, when the market price of the inventory purchased was $120,000.

**Required:**
Prepare the journal entries required on June 15, June 30, and August 20, 2013, to account for the two purchase commitments. Assume that the market price of the inventory related to the outstanding purchase commitment was $140,000 at June 30.

# CPA and CMA Review Questions

**CPA Exam**
**Questions**

The following questions are adapted from a variety of sources including questions developed by the AICPA Board of Examiners and those used in the Kaplan CPA Review Course to study inventory while preparing for the CPA examination. Determine the response that best completes the statements or questions.

● **LO9–1**

1. Kahn Co., in applying the lower of cost or market method, reports its inventory at replacement cost. Which of the following is correct?

|     | Cost is greater than replacement cost | NRV, less a normal profit margin, is greater than replacement cost |
| --- | --- | --- |
| a.  | Yes | Yes |
| b.  | No  | No  |
| c.  | Yes | No  |
| d.  | No  | Yes |

● **LO9–1**

2. Moss Co. has determined its year-end inventory on a FIFO basis to be $400,000. Information pertaining to that inventory is as follows:

| | |
| --- | --- |
| Estimated selling price | $408,000 |
| Estimated cost of disposal | 20,000 |
| Normal profit margin | 60,000 |
| Current replacement cost | 360,000 |

What should be the carrying value of Moss's inventory?
a. $328,000
b. $360,000
c. $388,000
d. $400,000

● **LO9–2**

3. On May 2, a fire destroyed the entire merchandise inventory on hand of Sanchez Wholesale Corporation. The following information is available:

| | |
| --- | --- |
| Sales, January 1 through May 2 | $360,000 |
| Inventory, January 1 | 80,000 |
| Merchandise purchases, January 1 through May 2 (including $40,000 of goods in transit on May 2, shipped f.o.b. shipping point) | 330,000 |
| Markup percentage on cost | 20% |

What is the estimated inventory on May 2 immediately prior to the fire?

a. $ 70,000
b. $ 82,000
c. $110,000
d. $122,000

● LO9–4

4. Hutch, Inc., uses the conventional retail inventory method to account for inventory. The following information relates to current year's operations:

| | Average | |
| --- | --- | --- |
| | Cost | Retail |
| Beginning inventory and purchases | $600,000 | $920,000 |
| Net markups | | 40,000 |
| Net markdowns | | 60,000 |
| Sales | | 780,000 |

What amount should be reported as cost of sales for the year?

a. $480,000
b. $487,500
c. $500,000
d. $525,000

● LO9–7

5. Bren Co.'s beginning inventory on January 1 was understated by $26,000, and its ending inventory on December 31 was overstated by $52,000. As a result, Bren's cost of goods sold for the year was

a. Understated by $26,000.
b. Overstated by $78,000.
c. Understated by $78,000.
d. Overstated by $26,000.

Beginning in 2011, International Financial Reporting Standards are tested on the CPA exam along with U.S. GAAP. The following questions deal with the application of IFRS.

● LO9–8

🌐 IFRS

6. A company determined the following values for its inventory at the end of its fiscal year:

| | |
| --- | --- |
| Historical cost | $100,000 |
| Replacement cost | 70,000 |
| Net realizable value | 90,000 |
| Net realizable value less a normal profit margin | 85,000 |
| Fair value | 95,000 |

Under IFRS, what amount should the company report as inventory in its balance sheet?

a. $70,000
b. $85,000
c. $90,000
d. $95,000

● LO9–8

🌐 IFRS

7. If circumstances indicate that an inventory write-down is no longer appropriate:

a. The write-down can be reversed under U.S. GAAP.
b. The write-down can be reversed under IFRS.
c. The write-down can be reversed under both U.S. GAAP and IFRS.
d. The write-down can't be reversed under either U.S. GAAP or IFRS.

**CMA Exam Questions**

The following questions dealing with inventory are adapted from questions that previously appeared on Certified Management Accountant (CMA) examinations. The CMA designation sponsored by the Institute of Management Accountants (www.imanet.org) provides members with an objective measure of knowledge and competence in the field of management accounting. Determine the response that best completes the statements or questions.

● LO9–4

1. The following FCL Corporation inventory information is available for the year ended December 31:

| | Cost | Retail |
| --- | --- | --- |
| Beginning inventory at 1/1 | $35,000 | $100,000 |
| Net purchases | 55,000 | 110,000 |
| Net markups | | 15,000 |
| Net markdowns | | 25,000 |
| Net sales | | 150,000 |

The December 31 ending inventory at cost using the conventional (lower of average cost or market) retail inventory method equals

a. $17,500
b. $20,000
c. $27,500
d. $50,000

● LO9–7

2. All sales and purchases for the year at Ross Corporation are credit transactions. Ross uses a perpetual inventory system. During the year, it shipped certain goods that were correctly excluded from ending inventory although the sale was not recorded. Which one of the following statements is correct?

a. Accounts receivable was not affected, inventory was not affected, sales were understated, and cost of goods sold was understated.
b. Accounts receivable was understated, inventory was not affected, sales were understated, and cost of goods sold was understated.
c. Accounts receivable was understated, inventory was overstated, sales were understated, and cost of goods sold was overstated.
d. Accounts receivable was understated, inventory was not affected, sales were understated, and cost of goods sold was not affected.

● LO9–7

3. During the year 1 year-end physical inventory count at Tequesta Corporation, $40,000 worth of inventory was counted twice. Assuming that the year 2 year-end inventory was correct, the result of the year 1 error was that

a. Year 1 retained earnings was understated, and year 2 ending inventory was correct.
b. Year 1 cost of goods sold was overstated, and year 2 income was understated.
c. Year 1 income was overstated, and year 2 ending inventory was overstated.
d. Year 1 cost of goods sold was understated, and year 2 retained earnings was correct.

# Problems

An alternate exercise and problem set is available on the text website: www.mhhe.com/spiceland7e

**P 9–1**
Lower of cost
or market
● LO9–1, LO9–8

IFRS

Decker Company has five products in its inventory. Information about the December 31, 2013, inventory follows.

| Product | Quantity | Unit Cost | Unit Replacement Cost | Unit Selling Price |
|---|---|---|---|---|
| A | 1,000 | $10 | $12 | $16 |
| B | 800 | 15 | 11 | 18 |
| C | 600 | 3 | 2 | 8 |
| D | 200 | 7 | 4 | 6 |
| E | 600 | 14 | 12 | 13 |

The selling cost for each product consists of a 15 percent sales commission. The normal profit percentage for each product is 40 percent of the selling price.

**Required:**

1. Determine the balance sheet inventory carrying value at December 31, 2013, assuming the LCM rule is applied to individual products.
2. Determine the balance sheet inventory carrying value at December 31, 2013, assuming the LCM rule is applied to the entire inventory. Also, assuming that Decker recognizes an inventory write-down as a separate income statement item, determine the amount of the loss.
3. Repeat requirement 1 assuming that Decker prepares its financial statements according to International Financial Reporting Standards.

**P 9–2**
Lower of cost
or market
● LO9–1

Almaden Hardware Store sells two distinct types of products, tools and paint products. Information pertaining to its 2013 year-end inventory is as follows:

| Inventory, by Product Type | Quantity | Per Unit Cost | Designated Market |
|---|---|---|---|
| Tools: | | | |
| Hammers | 100 | $ 5.00 | $5.50 |
| Saws | 200 | 10.00 | 9.00 |
| Screwdrivers | 300 | 2.00 | 2.60 |

(continued)

(concluded)

| Paint products: | | | |
|---|---|---|---|
| 1-gallon cans | 500 | 6.00 | 5.00 |
| Paint brushes | 100 | 4.00 | 4.50 |

**Required:**

1. Determine the balance sheet inventory carrying value at year-end, assuming the LCM rule is applied to (a) individual products, (b) product type, and (c) total inventory.

2. Assuming that the company recognizes an inventory write-down as a separate income statement item, for each of the LCM applications determine the amount of the loss.

**P 9–3**
**Gross profit method**
● **LO9–2**

Smith Distributors, Inc., supplies ice cream shops with various toppings for making sundaes. On November 17, 2013, a fire resulted in the loss of all of the toppings stored in one section of the warehouse. The company must provide its insurance company with an estimate of the amount of inventory lost. The following information is available from the company's accounting records:

| | Fruit Toppings | Marshmallow Toppings | Chocolate Toppings |
|---|---|---|---|
| Inventory, January 1, 2013 | $ 20,000 | $ 7,000 | $ 3,000 |
| Net purchases through Nov. 17 | 150,000 | 36,000 | 12,000 |
| Net sales through Nov. 17 | 200,000 | 55,000 | 20,000 |
| Historical gross profit ratio | 20% | 30% | 35% |

**Required:**

1. Calculate the estimated cost of each of the toppings lost in the fire.

2. What factors could cause the estimates to be over-or understated?

**P 9–4**
**Retail inventory method; various cost methods**
● **LO9–3, LO9–4**

Sparrow Company uses the retail inventory method to estimate ending inventory and cost of goods sold. Data for 2013 are as follows:

| | Cost | Retail |
|---|---|---|
| Beginning inventory | $ 90,000 | $180,000 |
| Purchases | 355,000 | 580,000 |
| Freight-in | 9,000 | |
| Purchase returns | 7,000 | 11,000 |
| Net markups | | 16,000 |
| Net markdowns | | 12,000 |
| Normal spoilage | | 3,000 |
| Abnormal spoilage | 4,800 | 8,000 |
| Sales | | 540,000 |
| Sales returns | | 10,000 |

The company records sales net of employee discounts. Discounts for 2013 totaled $4,000.

**Required:**

Estimate Sparrow's ending inventory and cost of goods sold for the year using the retail inventory method and the following applications:

1. Average cost

2. Conventional (average, LCM)

**P 9–5**
**Retail inventory method; conventional and LIFO**
● **LO9–3, LO9–4**

Alquist Company uses the retail method to estimate its ending inventory. Selected information about its year 2013 operations is as follows:

a. January 1, 2013, beginning inventory had a cost of $100,000 and a retail value of $150,000.

b. Purchases during 2013 cost $1,387,500 with an original retail value of $2,000,000.

c. Freight costs were $10,000 for incoming merchandise.

d. Net additional markups were $300,000 and net markdowns were $150,000.

e. Based on prior experience, shrinkage due to shoplifting was estimated to be $15,000 of retail value.

f. Merchandise is sold to employees at a 20% of selling price discount. Employee sales are recorded in a separate account at the net selling price. The balance in this account at the end of 2013 is $250,000.

g. Sales to customers totaled $1,750,000 for the year.

**Required:**

1. Estimate ending inventory and cost of goods sold using the conventional retail method (average, LCM).

2. Estimate ending inventory and cost of goods sold using the LIFO retail method. (Assume stable prices.)

**P 9–6**
**Retail inventory method; conventional**
● **LO9–4**

e**X**cel

Grand Department Store, Inc., uses the retail inventory method to estimate ending inventory for its monthly financial statements. The following data pertain to a single department for the month of October 2013:

**Inventory, October 1, 2013:**

| | |
|---|---:|
| At cost | $ 20,000 |
| At retail | 30,000 |
| Purchases (exclusive of freight and returns): | |
| At cost | 100,151 |
| At retail | 146,495 |
| Freight-in | 5,100 |
| Purchase returns: | |
| At cost | 2,100 |
| At retail | 2,800 |
| Additional markups | 2,500 |
| Markup cancellations | 265 |
| Markdowns (net) | 800 |
| Normal spoilage and breakage | 4,500 |
| Sales | 135,730 |

**Required:**

1. Using the conventional retail method, prepare a schedule computing estimated lower-of-cost-or-market inventory for October 31, 2013.

2. A department store using the conventional retail inventory method estimates the cost of its ending inventory as $29,000. An accurate physical count reveals only $22,000 of inventory at lower of cost or market. List the factors that may have caused the difference between computed inventory and the physical count.

*(AICPA adapted)*

**P 9–7**
**Retail method— average cost and LCM**
● **LO9–3, LO9–4**

Smith-Kline Company maintains inventory records at selling prices as well as at cost. For 2013, the records indicate the following data:

| | ($ in 000s) | |
|---|---:|---:|
| | **Cost** | **Retail** |
| Beginning inventory | $ 80 | $ 125 |
| Purchases | 671 | 1,006 |
| Freight-in on purchases | 30 | |
| Purchase returns | 1 | 2 |
| Net markups | | 4 |
| Net markdowns | | 8 |
| Net sales | | 916 |

**Required:**
Use the retail method to approximate cost of ending inventory in each of the following ways:
1. Average cost
2. Average (LCM) cost

**P 9–8**
**Dollar-value LIFO retail method**
● **LO9–5**

[This is a variation of the previous problem, modified to focus on the dollar-value LIFO retail method.] Smith-Kline Company maintains inventory records at selling prices as well as at cost. For 2013, the records indicate the following data:

| | ($ in 000s) | |
|---|---:|---:|
| | **Cost** | **Retail** |
| Beginning inventory | $ 80 | $ 125 |
| Purchases | 671 | 1,006 |
| Freight-in on purchases | 30 | |
| Purchase returns | 1 | 2 |
| Net markups | | 4 |
| Net markdowns | | 8 |
| Net sales | | 916 |

**Required:**
Assuming the price level increased from 1.00 at January 1 to 1.10 at December 31, 2013, use the dollar-value LIFO retail method to approximate cost of ending inventory and cost of goods sold.

**P 9–9**
Dollar-value
LIFO retail

● LO9–5

On January 1, 2013, HGC Camera Store adopted the dollar-value LIFO retail inventory method. Inventory transactions at both cost and retail, and cost indexes for 2013 and 2014 are as follows:

|  | 2013 | | 2014 | |
|---|---|---|---|---|
|  | **Cost** | **Retail** | **Cost** | **Retail** |
| Beginning inventory | $28,000 | $ 40,000 | | |
| Net purchases | 85,000 | 108,000 | 90,000 | 114,000 |
| Freight-in | 2,000 | | 2,500 | |
| Net markups | | 10,000 | | 8,000 |
| Net markdowns | | 2,000 | | 2,200 |
| Net sales to customers | | 100,000 | | 104,000 |
| Sales to employees (net of 20% discount) | | 2,400 | | 4,000 |
| Price Index: | | | | |
| January 1, 2013 | | | | 1.00 |
| December 31, 2013 | | | | 1.06 |
| December 31, 2014 | | | | 1.10 |

**Required:**
Estimate the 2013 and 2014 ending inventory and cost of goods sold using the dollar-value LIFO retail inventory method.

**P 9–10**
Retail inventory
method; various
applications

● LO9–3 through
LO9–5

Raleigh Department Store converted from the conventional retail method to the LIFO retail method on January 1, 2011, and is now considering converting to the dollar-value LIFO retail inventory method. Management requested, during your examination of the financial statements for the year ended December 31, 2013, that you furnish a summary showing certain computations of inventory costs for the past three years. Available information follows:

a.  The inventory at January 1, 2011, had a retail value of $45,000 and a cost of $27,500 based on the conventional retail method.

b.  Transactions during 2011 were as follows:

|  | Cost | Retail |
|---|---|---|
| Gross purchases | $282,000 | $490,000 |
| Purchase returns | 6,500 | 10,000 |
| Purchase discounts | 5,000 | |
| Gross sales | | 492,000 |
| Sales returns | | 5,000 |
| Employee discounts | | 3,000 |
| Freight-in | 26,500 | |
| Net markups | | 25,000 |
| Net markdowns | | 10,000 |

Sales to employees are recorded net of discounts.

c.  The retail value of the December 31, 2012, inventory was $56,100, the cost-to-retail percentage for 2012 under the LIFO retail method was 62%, and the appropriate price index was 102% of the January 1, 2012, price level.

d.  The retail value of the December 31, 2013, inventory was $48,300, the cost-to-retail percentage for 2013 under the LIFO retail method was 61%, and the appropriate price index was 105% of the January 1, 2012, price level.

**Required:**
1.  Prepare a schedule showing the computation of the cost of inventory at December 31, 2011, based on the conventional retail method.
2.  Prepare a similar schedule as in requirement 1 based on the LIFO retail method.
3.  Same requirement as (1) for December 31, 2012 and 2013, based on the dollar-value LIFO retail method.

*(AICPA adapted)*

**P 9–11**
Retail inventory
method; various
applications

● LO9–3 through
LO9–5

On January 1, 2013, Pet Friendly Stores adopted the retail inventory method. Inventory transactions at both cost and retail, and cost indexes for 2013 and 2014 are as follows:

| | 2013 | | 2014 | |
|---|---|---|---|---|
| | Cost | Retail | Cost | Retail |
| Beginning inventory | $ 90,000 | $150,000 | | |
| Purchases | 478,000 | 730,000 | 511,000 | 760,000 |
| Purchase returns | 2,500 | 3,500 | 2,200 | 4,000 |
| Freight-in | 6,960 | | 8,000 | |
| Net markups | | 8,500 | | 10,000 |
| Net markdowns | | 4,000 | | 6,000 |
| Net sales to customers | | 650,000 | | 680,000 |
| Sales to employees (net of 30% discount) | | 14,000 | | 17,500 |
| Normal spoilage | | 5,000 | | 6,600 |
| Price Index: | | | | |
| January 1, 2013 | 1.00 | | | |
| December 31, 2013 | 1.03 | | | |
| December 31, 2014 | 1.06 | | | |

**Required:**

1. Estimate the 2013 and 2014 ending inventory and cost of goods sold using the dollar-value LIFO retail method.

2. Estimate the 2013 ending inventory and cost of goods sold using the average cost method.

3. Estimate the 2013 ending inventory and cost of goods sold using the conventional retail method (average, LCM).

**P 9–12**
**Change in methods**
● **LO9–6**

Rockwell Corporation uses a periodic inventory system and has used the FIFO cost method since inception of the company in 1976. In 2013, the company decided to switch to the average cost method. Data for 2013 are as follows:

| | | |
|---|---|---|
| Beginning inventory, FIFO (5,000 units @ $30) | | $150,000 |
| Purchases: | | |
| 5,000 units @ $36 | $180,000 | |
| 5,000 units @ $40 | 200,000 | 380,000 |
| Cost of goods available for sale | | $530,000 |
| Sales for 2013 (8,000 units @ $70) | | $560,000 |

**Additional Information:**

a. The company's effective income tax rate is 40% for all years.

b. If the company had used the average cost method prior to 2013, ending inventory for 2012 would have been $130,000.

c. 7,000 units remained in inventory at the end of 2013.

**Required:**

1. Ignoring income taxes, prepare the 2013 journal entry to adjust the accounts to reflect the average cost method.

2. What is the effect of the change in methods on 2013 net income?

**P 9–13**
**Inventory errors**
● **LO9–7**

You have been hired as the new controller for the Ralston Company. Shortly after joining the company in 2013, you discover the following errors related to the 2011 and 2012 financial statements:

a. Inventory at 12/31/11 was understated by $6,000.

b. Inventory at 12/31/12 was overstated by $9,000.

c. On 12/31/12, inventory was purchased for $3,000. The company did not record the purchase until the inventory was paid for early in 2013. At that time, the purchase was recorded by a debit to purchases and a credit to cash.

The company uses a periodic inventory system.

**Required:**

1. Assuming that the errors were discovered after the 2012 financial statements were issued, analyze the effect of the errors on 2012 and 2011 cost of goods sold, net income, and retained earnings. (Ignore income taxes.)

2. Prepare a journal entry to correct the errors.

3. What other step(s) would be taken in connection with the errors?

**P 9–14**
**Inventory errors**
● **LO9–7**

The December 31, 2013, inventory of Tog Company, based on a physical count, was determined to be $450,000. Included in that count was a shipment of goods that cost $50,000 received from a supplier at the end of the month. The purchase was recorded and paid for in 2014. Another supplier shipment costing $20,000 was correctly recorded as a purchase in 2013. However, the merchandise, shipped FOB shipping point, was not received until 2014 and was incorrectly omitted from the physical count. A third purchase, shipped from a supplier FOB shipping point on December 28, 2013, did not arrive until January 3, 2014. The merchandise, which cost $80,000, was not included in the physical count and the purchase has not yet been recorded.

The company uses a periodic inventory system.

**Required:**

1. Determine the correct December 31, 2013, inventory balance and, assuming that the errors were discovered after the 2013 financial statements were issued, analyze the effect of the errors on 2013 cost of goods sold, net income, and retained earnings. (Ignore income taxes.)
2. Prepare a journal entry to correct the errors.

**P 9–15**
**Integrating problem; Chapters 8 and 9; inventory errors**
● **LO9–7**

Capwell Corporation uses a periodic inventory system. The company's ending inventory on December 31, 2013, its fiscal-year end, based on a physical count, was determined to be $326,000. Capwell's unadjusted trial balance also showed the following account balances: Purchases, $620,000; Accounts payable; $210,000; Accounts receivable, $225,000; Sales revenue, $840,000.

The internal audit department discovered the following items:

1. Goods valued at $32,000 held on consignment from Dix Company were included in the physical count but not recorded as a purchase.
2. Purchases from Xavier Corporation were incorrectly recorded at $41,000 instead of the correct amount of $14,000. The correct amount was included in the ending inventory.
3. Goods that cost $25,000 were shipped from a vendor on December 28, 2013, terms f.o.b. destination. The merchandise arrived on January 3, 2014. The purchase and related accounts payable were recorded in 2013.
4. One inventory item was incorrectly included in ending inventory as 100 units, instead of the correct amount of 1,000 units. This item cost $40 per unit.
5. The 2012 balance sheet reported inventory of $352,000. The internal auditors discovered that a mathematical error caused this inventory to be understated by $62,000. This amount is considered to be material.
6. Goods shipped to a customer f.o.b. destination on December 25, 2013, were received by the customer on January 4, 2014. The sales price was $40,000 and the merchandise cost $22,000. The sale and corresponding accounts receivable were recorded in 2013.
7. Goods shipped from a vendor f.o.b. shipping point on December 27, 2013, were received on January 3, 2014. The merchandise cost $18,000. The purchase was not recorded until 2014.

**Required:**

1. Determine the correct amounts for 2013 ending inventory, purchases, accounts payable, sales revenue, and accounts receivable.
2. Calculate cost of goods sold for 2013.
3. Describe the steps Capwell would undertake to correct the error in the 2012 ending inventory. What was the effect of the error on 2012 before-tax income?

**P 9–16**
**Purchase commitments**
● **Appendix**

In November 2013, the Brunswick Company signed two purchase commitments. The first commitment requires Brunswick to purchase 10,000 units of inventory at $10 per unit by December 15, 2013. The second commitment requires the company to purchase 20,000 units of inventory at $11 per unit by March 15, 2014. Brunswick's fiscal year-end is December 31. The company uses a periodic inventory system. Both contracts were exercised on their expiration date.

**Required:**

1. Prepare the journal entry to record the December 15 purchase for cash assuming the following alternative unit market prices on that date:
   a. $10.50
   b. $ 9.50
2. Prepare any necessary adjusting entry at December 31, 2013, for the second purchase commitment assuming the following alternative unit market prices on that date:
   a. $12.50
   b. $10.30
3. Assuming that the unit market price on December 31 was $10.30, prepare the journal entry to record the purchase on March 15, 2014, assuming the following alternative unit market prices on that date:
   a. $11.50
   b. $10.00

# Broaden Your Perspective

Apply your critical-thinking ability to the knowledge you've gained. These cases will provide you an opportunity to develop your research, analysis, judgment, and communication skills. You also will work with other students, integrate what you've learned, apply it in real world situations, and consider its global and ethical ramifications. This practice will broaden your knowledge and further develop your decision-making abilities.

**Judgment Case 9–1**
Inventoriable costs; lower of cost or market; retail inventory method
● LO9–1, LO9–3, LO9–4

Hudson Company, which is both a wholesaler and a retailer, purchases its inventories from various suppliers. Additional facts for Hudson's wholesale operations are as follows:

a. Hudson incurs substantial warehousing costs.

b. Hudson uses the lower-of-cost-or-market method. The replacement cost of the inventories is below the net realizable value and above the net realizable value less the normal profit margin. The original cost of the inventories is above replacement cost and below the net realizable value.

Additional facts for Hudson's retail operations are as follows:

a. Hudson determines the estimated cost of its ending inventories held for sale at retail using the conventional retail inventory method, which approximates lower of average cost or market.

b. Hudson incurs substantial freight-in costs.

c. Hudson has net markups and net markdowns.

**Required:**

1. Theoretically, how should Hudson account for the warehousing costs related to its wholesale inventories? Why?

2. a. In general, why is the lower-of-cost-or-market method used to value inventory?
   b. At which amount should Hudson's wholesale inventories be reported in the balance sheet?
   Explain the application of the lower-of-cost-or-market method in this situation.

3. In the calculation of the cost-to-retail percentage used to determine the estimated cost of its ending retail inventories, how should Hudson treat
   a. Freight-in costs?
   b. Net markups?
   c. Net markdowns?

4. Why does Hudson's retail inventory method approximate lower of average cost or market?

*(AICPA adapted)*

**Communication Case 9–2**
Lower of cost or market
● LO9–1

The lower-of-cost-or-market approach to valuing inventory is a departure from the accounting principle of reporting assets at their historical costs. There are those who believe that inventory, as well as other assets, should be valued at market, regardless of whether market is above or below cost.

The focus of this case is the justification for the lower-of-cost-or-market rule for valuing inventories. Your instructor will divide the class into two to six groups depending on the size of the class. The mission of your group is to defend the lower-of-cost-or-market approach against the alternatives of valuing inventory at either historical cost or market value.

**Required:**

1. Each group member should consider the situation independently and draft a tentative argument prior to the class session for which the case is assigned.

2. In class, each group will meet for 10 to 15 minutes in different areas of the classroom. During that meeting, group members will take turns sharing their suggestions for the purpose of arriving at a single group argument.

3. After the allotted time, a spokesperson for each group (selected during the group meetings) will share the group's solution with the class. The goal of the class is to incorporate the views of each group into a consensus approach to the situation.

**Integrating Case 9–3**
Unit LIFO and LCM
● LO9–1

York Co. sells one product, which it purchases from various suppliers. York's trial balance at December 31, 2013, included the following accounts:

| | |
|---|---|
| Sales (33,000 units @ $16) | $528,000 |
| Sales discounts | 7,500 |
| Purchases | 368,900 |
| Purchase discounts | 18,000 |
| Freight-in | 5,000 |
| Freight-out | 11,000 |

York Co.'s inventory purchases during 2013 were as follows:

|  | Units | Cost per Unit | Total Cost |
|---|---|---|---|
| Beginning inventory | 8,000 | $8.20 | $ 65,600 |
| Purchases, quarter ended March 31 | 12,000 | 8.25 | 99,000 |
| Purchases, quarter ended June 30 | 15,000 | 7.90 | 118,500 |
| Purchases, quarter ended September 30 | 13,000 | 7.50 | 97,500 |
| Purchases, quarter ended December 31 | 7,000 | 7.70 | 53,900 |
|  | 55,000 |  | $434,500 |

**Additional Information:**

a. York's accounting policy is to report inventory in its financial statements at the lower of cost or market, applied to total inventory. Cost is determined under the last-in, first-out (LIFO) method.

b. York has determined that, at December 31, 2013, the replacement cost of its inventory was $8 per unit and the net realizable value was $8.80 per unit. York's normal profit margin is $1.05 per unit.

**Required:**

1. Prepare York's schedule of cost of goods sold, with a supporting schedule of ending inventory. York uses the direct method of reporting losses from market decline of inventory.

2. Explain the rule of lower of cost or market and its application in this situation.

*(AICPA adapted)*

**Judgment Case 9–4**
The dollar-value LIFO method; the retail inventory method
● **LO9–3, LO9–4**

Huddell Company, which is both a wholesaler and retailer, purchases merchandise from various suppliers. The dollar-value LIFO method is used for the wholesale inventories.

Huddell determines the estimated cost of its retail ending inventories using the conventional retail inventory method, which approximates lower of average cost or market.

**Required:**

1. a. What are the advantages of using the dollar-value LIFO method as opposed to the traditional LIFO method

   b. How does the application of the dollar-value LIFO method differ from the application of the traditional LIFO method?

2. a. In the calculation of the cost-to-retail percentage used to determine the estimated cost of its ending inventories, how should Huddell use

   • Net markups?
   • Net markdowns?

   b. Why does Huddell's retail inventory method approximate lower of average cost or market?

*(AICPA adapted)*

**Communication Case 9–5**
Retail inventory method
● **LO9–3, LO9–4**

The Brenly Paint Company, your client, manufactures paint. The company's president, Mr. Brenly, decided to open a retail store to sell paint as well as wallpaper and other items that would be purchased from other suppliers. He has asked you for information about the retail method of estimating inventories at the retail store.

**Required:**

Prepare a report to the president explaining the retail method of estimating inventories.

**Analysis Case 9–6**
Change in inventory method
● **LO9–6**

Generally accepted accounting principles should be applied consistently from period to period. However, changes within a company, as well as changes in the external economic environment, may force a company to change an accounting method. The specific reporting requirements when a company changes from one generally accepted inventory method to another depend on the methods involved.

**Required:**

Explain the accounting treatment for a change in inventory method (a) not involving LIFO, (b) from the LIFO method, and (c) to the LIFO method. Explain the logic underlying those treatments. Also, describe how disclosure requirements are designed to address the departure from consistency and comparability of changes in accounting principle.

**Real World Case 9–7**
Change in inventory method; Duckwall-ALCO Stores, Inc.

● LO9–6

Real World Financials

**Duckwall-ALCO Stores, Inc.** operates general merchandise retail stores throughout the central portion of the U.S. The following disclosure notes were included in recent financial statements:

> ### Note 1. (c) Inventories (in part)
> In the fourth quarter of fiscal year 2011, the Company elected to change its method of accounting for inventory to the first-in, first-out (FIFO) method from the last-in, first-out (LIFO) method. The Company believes the FIFO method is preferable to the LIFO method as it better matches the current value of inventory in the company's balance sheet and provides a better matching of revenues and expenses.
>
> ### Note 2. Inventories (in part)
> In the fourth quarter of fiscal 2011, the Company elected to change its method of accounting for inventory from LIFO to FIFO. The Company applied this change in method of inventory by retrospectively adjusting the prior years' financial statements.

**Required:**
Why does GAAP require Duckwall-ALCO to retrospectively adjust prior periods' financial statements for this type of accounting change?

**Real World Case 9–8**
Various inventory issues; Chapters 8 and 9; Tops Holding Corporation

● LO9–1, LO9–5, LO9–6

Real World Financials

**Tops Holding Corporation**, the parent of Tops Markets, is a leading supermarket retailer in New York and Pennsylvania. Access the company's 10-K for the fiscal year ended January 1, 2011. You can find the 10-K by using EDGAR at www.sec.gov. Answer the following questions.

**Required:**
1. What inventory methods does Tops use to value its inventory?
2. When does the company take physical counts of its inventory?
3. A company that uses LIFO is allowed to provide supplemental disclosures reporting the effect of using another inventory method rather than LIFO. Using the supplemental LIFO disclosures provided by Tops, determine the income effect of using LIFO versus another method for the current fiscal year.
4. Calculate the company's inventory turnover ratio for the fiscal year ended January 1, 2011.
5. Assume that in the next fiscal year the company decides to switch to the average cost method. Describe the accounting treatment required for the switch.

**Communication Case 9–9**
Change in inventory method; disclosure note

● LO9–6

Mayfair Department Stores, Inc., operates over 30 retail stores in the Pacific Northwest. Prior to 2013, the company used the FIFO method to value its inventory. In 2013, Mayfair decided to switch to the dollar value LIFO retail inventory method. One of your responsibilities as assistant controller is to prepare the disclosure note describing the change in method that will be included in the company's 2013 financial statements. Kenneth Meier, the controller, provided the following information:
a. Internally developed retail price indexes are used to adjust for the effects of changing prices.
b. If the change had not been made, cost of goods sold for the year would have been $22 million lower. The company's income tax rate is 40% and there were 100 million shares of common stock outstanding during 2013.
c. The cumulative effect of the change on prior years' income is not determinable.
d. The reasons for the change were (a) to provide a more consistent matching of merchandise costs with sales revenue, and (b) the new method provides a more comparable basis of accounting with competitors that also use the LIFO method.

**Required:**
1. Prepare for Kenneth Meier the disclosure note that will be included in the 2013 financial statements.
2. Explain why the "cumulative effect of the change on prior years' income is not determinable."

**Judgment Case 9–10**
Inventory errors

● LO9–7

Some inventory errors are said to be self-correcting in that the error has the opposite financial statement effect in the period following the error, thereby correcting the original account balance errors.

**Required:**
Despite this self-correcting feature, discuss why these errors should not be ignored and describe the steps required to account for the error correction.

**Ethics Case 9–11**
Overstatement of ending inventory

● LO9–7

Danville Bottlers is a wholesale beverage company. Danville uses the FIFO inventory method to determine the cost of its ending inventory. Ending inventory quantities are determined by a physical count. For the fiscal year-end June 30, 2013, ending inventory was originally determined to be $3,265,000. However, on July 17, 2013,

John Howard, the company's controller, discovered an error in the ending inventory count. He determined that the correct ending inventory amount should be $2,600,000.

Danville is a privately owned corporation with significant financing provided by a local bank. The bank requires annual audited financial statements as a condition of the loan. By July 17, the auditors had completed their review of the financial statements which are scheduled to be issued on July 25. They did not discover the inventory error.

John's first reaction was to communicate his finding to the auditors and to revise the financial statements before they are issued. However, he knows that his and his fellow workers' profit-sharing plans are based on annual pretax earnings and that if he revises the statements, everyone's profit-sharing bonus will be significantly reduced.

**Required:**

1. Why will bonuses be negatively affected? What is the effect on pretax earnings?

2. If the error is not corrected in the current year and is discovered by the auditors during the following year's audit, how will it be reported in the company's financial statements?

3. Discuss the ethical dilemma John Howard faces.

**Analysis
Case 9–12**
Purchase
commitments
● **Appendix**

The management of the Esquire Oil Company believes that the wholesale price of heating oil that they sell to homeowners will increase again as the result of increased political problems in the Middle East. The company is currently paying $.80 a gallon. If they are willing to enter an agreement in November 2013 to purchase a million gallons of heating oil during the winter of 2014, their supplier will guarantee the price at $.80 per gallon. However, if the winter is a mild one, Esquire would not be able to sell a million gallons unless they reduced their retail price and thereby increase the risk of a loss for the year. On the other hand, if the wholesale price did increase substantially, they would be in a favorable position with respect to their competitors. The company's fiscal year-end is December 31.

**Required:**

Discuss the accounting issues related to the purchase commitment that Esquire is considering.

# Air France–KLM Case

**AIRFRANCE /**

● **LO9–8**

🌐 **IFRS**

**Air France–KLM (AF)**, a French company, prepares its financial statements according to International Financial Reporting Standards. AF's annual report for the year ended March 31, 2011, which includes financial statements and disclosure notes, is provided with all new textbooks. This material also is included in AF's "Registration Document 2010–11," dated June 15, 2011 and is available at **www.airfranceklm.com**.

**Required:**

AF's inventories are valued at the lower of cost and net realizable value. How does this approach differ from U.S. GAAP?

# CPA Simulation 9–1

**Jackson
Company**
Lower of cost
or market

**CPA Review**

Test your knowledge of the concepts discussed in this chapter, practice critical professional skills necessary for career success, and prepare for the computer-based CPA exam by accessing our CPA simulations at the text website: **www.mhhe.com/spiceland7e**.

The Jackson Company simulation tests your knowledge of the lower-of-cost-or-market rule for valuing inventory.

# Property, Plant, and Equipment and Intangible Assets: Acquisition and Disposition

**OVERVIEW** — This chapter and the one that follows address the measurement and reporting issues involving property, plant, and equipment and intangible assets, the tangible and intangible long-lived assets that are used in the production of goods and services. This chapter covers the valuation at date of acquisition and the disposition of these assets. In Chapter 11 we discuss the allocation of the cost of property, plant, and equipment and intangible assets to the periods benefited by their use, the treatment of expenditures made over the life of these assets to maintain and improve them, and impairment.

**LEARNING OBJECTIVES** — **After studying this chapter, you should be able to:**

- **LO10–1** Identify the various costs included in the initial cost of property, plant, and equipment, natural resources, and intangible assets. (*p. 532*)

- **LO10–2** Determine the initial cost of individual property, plant, and equipment and intangible assets acquired as a group for a lump-sum purchase price. (*p. 540*)

- **LO10–3** Determine the initial cost of property, plant, and equipment and intangible assets acquired in exchange for a deferred payment contract. (*p. 542*)

- **LO10–4** Determine the initial cost of property, plant, and equipment and intangible assets acquired in exchange for equity securities or through donation. (*p. 543*)

- **LO10–5** Calculate the fixed-asset turnover ratio used by analysts to measure how effectively managers use property, plant, and equipment. (*p. 545*)

- **LO10–6** Explain how to account for dispositions and exchanges for other nonmonetary assets. (*p. 546*)

- **LO10–7** Identify the items included in the cost of a self-constructed asset and determine the amount of capitalized interest. (*p. 551*)

- **LO10–8** Explain the difference in the accounting treatment of costs incurred to purchase intangible assets versus the costs incurred to internally develop intangible assets. (*p. 556*)

- **LO10–9** Discuss the primary differences between U.S. GAAP and IFRS with respect to the acquisition and disposition of property, plant, and equipment and intangible assets. (*pp. 540, 545, 561 and 562*)

# FINANCIAL REPORTING CASE

## A Disney Adventure

"Now I'm really confused," confessed Stan, your study partner, staring blankly at the Walt Disney Company balance sheet that your professor handed out last week. "I thought that interest is always expensed in the income statement. Now I see that Disney is capitalizing interest. I'm not even sure what *capitalize* means! And what about this other account called *goodwill?* What's that all about?" "If you hadn't missed class today, we wouldn't be having this conversation. Let's take a look at the Disney financial statements and the disclosure note on capitalized interest and I'll try to explain it all to you."

**Borrowings (in part):**
The Company capitalizes interest on assets constructed for its theme parks, resort and other property, and on theatrical and television productions in process. In 2011, 2010, and 2009, total interest capitalized was $91 million, $82 million, and $57 million, respectively.

---

By the time you finish this chapter, you should be able to respond appropriately to the questions posed in this case. Compare your response to the solution provided at the end of the chapter.

QUESTIONS

1. Describe to Stan what it means to capitalize an expenditure. What is the general rule for determining which costs are capitalized when property, plant, and equipment or an intangible asset is acquired? (*p. 532*)

2. Which costs might be included in the initial cost of equipment? (*p. 532*)

3. In what situations is interest capitalized rather than expensed? (*p. 551*)

4. What is the three-step process used to determine the amount of interest capitalized? (*p. 552*)

5. What is goodwill and how is it measured? (*p. 539*)

---

**General Motors Corporation** has significant investments in the production facilities it uses to manufacture the automobiles it sells. On the other hand, the principal revenue-producing assets of **Microsoft Corporation** are the copyrights on its computer software that permit it the exclusive rights to earn profits from those products. Timber reserves provide major revenues to **International Paper**. From a reporting perspective, we classify GM's production facilities as property, plant, and equipment;[1] Microsoft's copyrights as intangible assets; and International Paper's timber reserves as natural resources. Together, these three noncurrent assets constitute the *long-lived, revenue-producing assets* of a company. Unlike manufacturers, many service firms and merchandising companies rely primarily on people or investments in inventories rather than on property, plant, and equipment and intangible assets to generate revenues. Even nonmanufacturing firms, though, typically have at least modest investments in buildings and equipment.

---

[1] These are sometimes called *plant assets* or *fixed assets.*

The measurement and reporting issues pertaining to this group of assets include valuation at date of acquisition, disposition, the treatment of expenditures made over the life of these assets to maintain and improve them, the allocation of cost to reporting periods that benefit from their use, and impairment. The allocation of asset cost over time is called *depreciation* for plant and equipment, *amortization* for intangible assets, and *depletion* for natural resources. We focus on initial valuation and disposition in this chapter, and subsequent expenditures, cost allocation, and impairment in the next chapter.

# PART A

# VALUATION AT ACQUISITION

## Types of Assets

For financial reporting purposes, long-lived, revenue-producing assets typically are classified in two categories:

1. **Property, plant, and equipment.** Assets in this category include land, buildings, equipment, machinery, autos, and trucks. **Natural resources** such as oil and gas deposits, timber tracts, and mineral deposits also are included.
2. **Intangible assets.** Unlike property, plant, and equipment and natural resources, these lack physical substance and the extent and timing of their future benefits typically are highly uncertain. They include patents, copyrights, trademarks, franchises, and goodwill.

Of course, every company maintains its own unique mix of these assets. The way these assets are classified and combined for reporting purposes also varies from company to company. As an example, a recent balance sheet of **Semtech Corporation**, a leading supplier of analog and mixed-signal semiconductor products, reported net property, plant, and equipment of $56,778 thousand and $38,063 thousand at the end of fiscal 2011 and 2010, respectively. A disclosure note, shown in Illustration 10–1, provided the details.

**Illustration 10–1**

Property, Plant, and Equipment—Semtech Corporation

Real World Financials

| **Note 6. Property, Plant, and Equipment (in part):** | | |
|---|---|---|
| The following is a summary of property and equipment, at cost less accumulated depreciation: | | |
| | **January 30, 2011** | **January 31, 2010** |
| (In thousands) | | |
| Property | $ 5,991 | $ 5,991 |
| Buildings | 18,485 | 18,022 |
| Leasehold improvements | 2,718 | 1,701 |
| Machinery and equipment | 82,152 | 63,701 |
| Furniture and office equipment | 20,081 | 17,489 |
| Construction in progress | 4,594 | 1,964 |
| Property, plant, and equipment, gross | 134,021 | 108,868 |
| Less: accumulated depreciation | (77,243) | (70,805) |
| Property, plant, and equipment, net | $ 56,778 | $ 38,063 |

In practice, some companies report intangibles as part of property, plant, and equipment. Some include intangible assets in the other asset category in the balance sheet, and others show intangibles as a separate balance sheet category.

For example, **Layne Christensen Company**, a leading construction and exploration company, reported goodwill of $102,428 thousand and other intangible assets of $34,412 thousand in a recent balance sheet. A disclosure note, shown in Illustration 10–2, provided the details of the other intangible assets. We discuss goodwill, tradenames, patents, and other traditional intangible assets later in this part of the chapter. Technology and capitalized software are addressed in Part C of the chapter.

Before we examine in detail specific assets, you should find it helpful to study the overview provided by Illustration 10–3 on page 531.

**(5) Goodwill and Other Intangible Assets (in part)**
Goodwill and other intangible assets consisted of the following as of January 31:

| (in thousands) | 2011 | | 2010 | |
| --- | --- | --- | --- | --- |
| | **Gross Carrying Amount** | **Accumulated Amortization** | **Gross Carrying Amount** | **Accumulated Amortization** |
| Goodwill | $102,428 | $ — | $92,532 | $ — |
| Amortizable intangible assets: | | | | |
| Tradenames | $ 20,302 | $(3,896) | $18,962 | $(3,086) |
| Customer/contract-related | 3,220 | (488) | 332 | (332) |
| Patents | 6,992 | (1,155) | 3,152 | (755) |
| Non-competition agreements | 1,144 | (454) | 464 | (423) |
| Other | 2,754 | (1,966) | 2,754 | (1,419) |
| Total amortizable intangible assets | $ 34,412 | $(7,959) | $25,664 | $(6,015) |

**Illustration 10–2**

Intangible Assets—Layne Christensen Company

Real World Financials

**Illustration 10–3**    Property, Plant, and Equipment and Intangible Assets and Their Acquisition Costs

| Asset | Description | Typical Acquisition Costs |
| --- | --- | --- |
| **Property, plant, and equipment** | Productive assets that derive their value from long-term use in operations rather than from resale. | All expenditures necessary to get the asset in condition and location for its intended use. |
| Equipment | Broad term that includes machinery, computers and other office equipment, vehicles, furniture, and fixtures. | Purchase price (less discounts), taxes, transportation, installation, testing, trial runs, and reconditioning. |
| Land | Real property used in operations (land held for speculative investment or future use is reported as investments or other assets). | Purchase price, attorney's fees, title, recording fees, commissions, back taxes, mortgages, liens, clearing, filling, draining, and removing old buildings. |
| Land improvements | Enhancements to property such as parking lots, driveways, private roads, fences, landscaping, and sprinkler systems. | Separately identifiable costs. |
| Buildings | Structures that include warehouses, plant facilities, and office buildings. | Purchase price, attorney's fees, commissions, and reconditioning. |
| Natural resources | Productive assets that are physically consumed in operations such as timber, mineral deposits, and oil and gas reserves. | Acquisition, exploration, development, and restoration costs. |
| **Intangible Assets** | Productive assets that lack physical substance and have long-term but typically uncertain benefits. | All expenditures necessary to get the asset in condition and location for its intended use. |
| Patents | Exclusive 20-year right to manufacture a product or use a process. | Purchase price, legal fees, filing fees, not including internal R&D. |
| Copyrights | Exclusive right to benefit from a creative work such as a song, film, painting, photograph, or book. | Purchase price, legal fees, filing fees, not including internal R&D. |
| Trademarks (tradenames) | Exclusive right to display a word, a slogan, a symbol, or an emblem that distinctively identifies a company, product, or a service. | Purchase price, legal fees, filing fees, not including internal R&D. |
| Franchises | A contractual arrangement under which a franchisor grants the franchisee the exclusive right to use the franchisor's trademark or tradename and certain product rights. | Franchise fee plus any legal fees. |
| Goodwill | The unique value of the company as a whole over and above all identifiable assets. | Excess of the fair value of the consideration exchanged for the company over the fair value of the net assets acquired. |

# Costs to Be Capitalized

Property, plant, and equipment and intangible assets can be acquired through purchase, exchange, lease, donation, self-construction, or a business combination. We address acquisitions through leasing in Chapter 15 and acquisitions through business combinations later in this chapter and in Chapter 12.

The initial valuation of property, plant, and equipment and intangible assets usually is quite simple. We know from prior study that assets are valued on the basis of their original costs. In Chapter 8 we introduced the concept of condition and location in determining the cost of inventory. For example, if Thompson Company purchased inventory for $42,000 and incurred $1,000 in freight costs to have the inventory shipped to its location, the initial cost of the inventory is $43,000. This concept applies to the valuation of property, plant, and equipment and intangible assets as well. The initial cost of these assets includes the purchase price and all expenditures necessary to bring the asset to its desired condition and location for use. We discuss these additional expenditures in the next section.

Our objective in identifying the costs of an asset is to distinguish the expenditures that produce future benefits from those that produce benefits only in the current period. The costs in the second group are recorded as expenses, but those in the first group are *capitalized;* that is, they are recorded as an asset and expensed in future periods.[2] For example, the cost of a major improvement to a delivery truck that extends its useful life generally would be capitalized. On the other hand, the cost of an engine tune-up for the delivery truck simply allows the truck to continue its productive activity but does not increase future benefits. These maintenance costs would be expensed. Subsequent expenditures for these assets are discussed in Chapter 11.

The distinction is not trivial. This point was unmistakably emphasized in the summer of 2002 when **WorldCom, Inc.** disclosed that it had improperly capitalized nearly $4 billion in expenditures related to the company's telecom network. This massive fraud resulted in one of the largest financial statement restatements in history and triggered the collapse of the once powerful corporation. Capitalizing rather than expensing these expenditures caused a substantial overstatement of reported income for 2001 and the first quarter of 2002, in fact, producing impressive profits where losses should have been reported. If the deception had not been discovered, not only would income for 2001 and 2002 have been overstated, but income for many years into the future would have been understated as the fraudulent capitalized assets were depreciated. Of course, the balance sheet also would have overstated the assets and equity of the company.

## Property, Plant, and Equipment

**COST OF EQUIPMENT.** Equipment is a broad term that encompasses machinery used in manufacturing, computers and other office equipment, vehicles, furniture, and fixtures. The cost of equipment includes the purchase price plus any sales tax (less any discounts received from the seller), transportation costs paid by the buyer to transport the asset to the location in which it will be used, expenditures for installation, testing, legal fees to establish title, and any other costs of bringing the asset to its condition and location for use. To the extent that these costs can be identified and measured, they should be included in the asset's initial valuation rather than expensed currently.

Although most costs can be identified easily, others are more difficult. For example, the costs of training personnel to operate machinery could be considered a cost necessary to make the asset ready for use. However, because it is difficult to measure the amount of training costs associated with specific assets, these costs usually are expensed. Consider Illustration 10–4.

---

[2]Exceptions are land and certain intangible assets that have indefinite useful lives. Costs to acquire these assets also produce future benefits and therefore are capitalized, but unlike other property, plant, and equipment and intangible assets, their costs are not systematically expensed in future periods as depreciation or amortization.

**Illustration 10–4**

Initial Cost of Equipment

Central Machine Tools purchased an industrial lathe to be used in its manufacturing process. The purchase price was $62,000. Central paid a freight company $1,000 to transport the machine to its plant location plus $300 shipping insurance. In addition, the machine had to be installed and mounted on a special platform built specifically for the machine at a cost of $1,200. After installation, several trial runs were made to ensure proper operation. The cost of these trials including wasted materials was $600. At what amount should Central capitalize the lathe?

| | |
|---|---:|
| Purchase price | $62,000 |
| Freight and handling | 1,000 |
| Insurance during shipping | 300 |
| Special foundation | 1,200 |
| Trial runs | 600 |
| | $65,100 |

Each of the expenditures described was necessary to bring the machine to its condition and location for use and should be capitalized and then expensed in the future periods in which the asset is used.

**COST OF LAND.**   The cost of land also should include expenditures needed to get the land ready for its intended use. These include the purchase price plus closing costs such as fees for the attorney, real estate agent commissions, title and title search, and recording. If the property is subject to back taxes, liens, mortgages, or other obligations, these amounts are included also. In addition, any expenditures such as clearing, filling, draining, and even removing (razing) old buildings that are needed to prepare the land for its intended use are part of the land's cost. Proceeds from the sale of salvaged materials from old buildings torn down after purchase reduce the cost of land. Illustration 10–5 provides an example.

**Illustration 10–5**

Initial Cost of Land

The Byers Structural Metal Company purchased a six-acre tract of land and an existing building for $500,000. The company plans to raze the old building and construct a new office building on the site. In addition to the purchase price, the company made the following expenditures at closing of the purchase:

| | |
|---|---:|
| Title insurance | $ 3,000 |
| Commissions | 16,000 |
| Property taxes | 6,000 |

Shortly after closing, the company paid a contractor $10,000 to tear down the old building and remove it from the site. An additional $5,000 was paid to grade the land. The $6,000 in property taxes included $4,000 of delinquent taxes paid by Byers on behalf of the seller and $2,000 attributable to the portion of the current fiscal year after the purchase date. What should be the capitalized cost of the land?

| Capitalized cost of land: | |
|---|---:|
| Purchase price of land (and building to be razed) | $500,000 |
| Title insurance | 3,000 |
| Commissions | 16,000 |
| Delinquent property taxes | 4,000 |
| Cost of removing old building | 10,000 |
| Cost of grading | 5,000 |
| Total cost of land | $538,000 |

Two thousand dollars of the property taxes relate only to the current period and should be expensed. Other costs were necessary to acquire the land and are capitalized.

The costs of *land improvements* are capitalized and depreciated.

### LAND IMPROVEMENTS.
It's important to distinguish between the cost of land and the cost of land improvements because land has an indefinite life and land improvements usually have useful lives that are estimable. Examples of land improvements include the cost of parking lots, driveways, and private roads and the costs of fences and lawn and garden sprinkler systems. Costs of these assets are separately identified and capitalized. We depreciate their cost over periods benefited by their use.

### COST OF BUILDINGS.
The cost of acquiring a building usually includes realtor commissions and legal fees in addition to the purchase price. Quite often a building must be refurbished, remodeled, or otherwise modified to suit the needs of the new owner. These reconditioning costs are part of the building's acquisition cost. When a building is constructed rather than purchased, unique accounting issues are raised. We discuss these in the "Self-Constructed Assets" section of this chapter.

### COST OF NATURAL RESOURCES.
Natural resources that provide long-term benefits are reported as property, plant, and equipment. These include timber tracts, mineral deposits, and oil and gas deposits. They can be distinguished from other assets by the fact that their benefits are derived from their physical consumption. For example, mineral deposits are physically diminishing as the minerals are extracted from the ground and either sold or used in the production process.[3] On the contrary, equipment, land, and buildings produce benefits for a company through their *use* in the production of goods and services. Unlike those of natural resources, their physical characteristics usually remain unchanged during their useful lives.

The cost of a natural resource includes the *acquisition costs* for the use of land, the *exploration* and *development costs* incurred before production begins, and *restoration costs* incurred during or at the end of extraction.

Sometimes a company buys natural resources from another company. In that case, initial valuation is simply the purchase price plus any other costs necessary to bring the asset to condition and location for use. More frequently, though, the company will develop these assets. In this situation, the initial valuation can include (a) acquisition costs, (b) exploration costs, (c) development costs, and (d) restoration costs. Acquisition costs are the amounts paid to acquire the rights to explore for undiscovered natural resources or to extract proven natural resources. Exploration costs are expenditures such as drilling a well, or excavating a mine, or any other costs of searching for natural resources. Development costs are incurred after the resource has been discovered but before production begins. They include a variety of costs such as expenditures for tunnels, wells, and shafts. It is not unusual for the cost of a natural resource, either purchased or developed, also to include estimated restoration costs. These are costs to restore land or other property to its original condition after extraction of the natural resource ends. Because restoration expenditures occur later— after production begins—they initially represent an obligation incurred in conjunction with an asset retirement. Restoration costs are one example of *asset retirement obligations,* the topic of the next subsection.

On the other hand, the costs of heavy equipment and other assets a company uses during drilling or excavation usually are not considered part of the cost of the natural resource itself. Instead, they are considered depreciable plant and equipment. However, if an asset used in the development of a natural resource cannot be moved and has no alternative use, its depreciable life is limited by the useful life of the natural resource.

An asset retirement obligation (ARO) is measured at fair value and is recognized as a liability and corresponding increase in asset valuation.

### ASSET RETIREMENT OBLIGATIONS.
Sometimes a company incurs obligations associated with the disposition of property, plant, and equipment and natural resources, often as a result of acquiring those assets. For example, an oil and gas exploration company might be required to restore land to its original condition after extraction is completed. Before 2001, there was considerable diversity in the ways companies accounted for these obligations. Some companies recognized these asset retirement obligations (AROs) gradually over the life of the asset while others did not recognize the obligations until the asset was retired or sold.

Generally accepted accounting principles now require that an existing legal obligation associated with the retirement of a tangible, long-lived asset be recognized as a liability and

---

[3]Because of this characteristic, natural resources sometimes are called *wasting assets.*

measured at fair value, if value can be reasonably estimated. When the liability is credited, the offsetting debit is to the related asset.[4] These retirement obligations could arise in connection with several types of assets. We introduce the topic here because it often arises with natural resources. Let's consider some of the provisions of the standard that addresses these obligations.

**Scope.**   AROs arise only from *legal* obligations associated with the retirement of a tangible long-lived asset that result from the acquisition, construction, or development and (or) normal operation of a long-lived asset.

**Recognition.**   A retirement obligation might arise at the inception of an asset's life or during its operating life. For instance, an offshore oil-and-gas production facility typically incurs its removal obligation when it begins operating. On the other hand, a landfill or a mining operation might incur a reclamation obligation gradually over the life of the asset as space is consumed with waste or as the mine is excavated.

**Measurement.**   A company recognizes the fair value of an ARO in the period it's incurred. The liability increases the valuation of the related asset. Usually, the fair value is estimated by calculating the present value of estimated future cash outflows.

**Present value calculations.**   Traditionally, the way uncertainty has been considered in present value calculations has been by discounting the "best estimate" of future cash flows applying a discount rate that has been adjusted to reflect the uncertainty or risk of those cash flows. That's not the approach we take here. Instead, we follow the approach described in the FASB's *Concept Statement No. 7*[5] which is to adjust the cash flows, not the discount rate, for the uncertainty or risk of those cash flows. This expected cash flow approach incorporates specific probabilities of cash flows into the analysis. We use a discount rate equal to the *credit-adjusted risk free rate*. The higher a company's credit risk, the higher will be the discount rate. All other uncertainties or risks are incorporated into the cash flow probabilities. We first considered an illustration of this approach in Chapter 6. Illustration 10–6 demonstrates the approach in connection with the acquisition of a natural resource.

As we discuss in Chapter 11, the cost of the coal mine is allocated to future periods as *depletion* using a depletion rate based on the estimated amount of coal discovered. The $600,000 cost of the excavation equipment, less any anticipated residual value, is allocated to future periods as *depreciation.*

The difference between the asset retirement liability of $468,360 and the probability weighted expected cash outflow of $590,000 is recognized as accretion expense, an additional expense that accrues as an operating expense, over the three-year excavation period. This process increases the liability to $590,000 by the end of the excavation period.

*Accretion expense recognizes the addition to the asset retirement obligation.*

| Year | Accretion Expense | Increase in Balance | Asset Retirement Obligation |
|------|-------------------|---------------------|------------------------------|
|      |                   |                     | 468,360 |
| 1 | 8% (468,360) = 37,469 | 37,469 | 505,829 |
| 2 | 8% (505,829) = 40,466 | 40,466 | 546,295 |
| 3 | 8% (546,295) = 43,705* | 43,705 | 590,000 |

*rounded

If the actual restoration costs are more (less) than the $590,000, a loss (gain) on retirement of the obligation is recognized for the difference.

**SM Energy Company** is engaged in the exploration, development, acquisition, and production of natural gas and crude oil. For the three months ended March 31, 2011, SM reported $71 million in asset retirement obligations in its balance sheet. A disclosure note

*Real World Financials*

---

[4]FASB ASC 410–20–25: Asset Retirement and Environmental Obligations–Asset Retirement Obligations–Recognition (previously "Accounting for Asset Retirement Obligations," *Statement of Financial Accounting Standards No. 143* (Norwalk, Conn.: FASB, 2001)).
[5]"Using Cash Flow Information and Present Value in Accounting Measurements," *Statement of Financial Accounting Concepts No. 7* (Norwalk, Conn.: FASB, 2000).

**Illustration 10–6**

Cost of Natural
Resources

The Jackson Mining Company paid $1,000,000 for the right to explore for a coal deposit on 500 acres of land in Pennsylvania. Costs of exploring for the coal deposit totaled $800,000 and intangible development costs incurred in digging and erecting the mine shaft were $500,000. In addition, Jackson purchased new excavation equipment for the project at a cost of $600,000. After the coal is removed from the site, the equipment will be sold.

Jackson is required by its contract to restore the land to a condition suitable for recreational use after it extracts the coal. The company has provided the following three cash flow possibilities (A, B, and C) for the restoration costs to be paid in three years, after extraction is completed:

|   | Cash Outflow | Probability |
|---|---|---|
| A | $500,000 | 30% |
| B | 600,000 | 50% |
| C | 700,000 | 20% |

The company's credit-adjusted risk free interest rate is 8%.
Total capitalized cost for the coal deposit is:

| | |
|---|---|
| Purchase of rights to explore | $1,000,000 |
| Exploration costs | 800,000 |
| Development costs | 500,000 |
| Restoration costs | 468,360* |
| Total cost of coal deposit | $2,768,360 |

*Present value of expected cash outflow for restoration costs (asset retirement obligation):
$500,000 × 30% = $150,000
  600,000 × 50% =  300,000
  700,000 × 20% =  140,000
$590,000 × .79383 = $468,360
(.79383 is the present value of $1, $n = 3$, $i = 8\%$)

**Journal Entries:**

| | | |
|---|---|---|
| Coal mine (determined above) | 2,768,360 | |
|   Cash ($1,000,000 + 800,000 + 500,000) | | 2,300,000 |
|   Asset retirement liability (determined above) | | 468,360 |
| Excavation equipment | 600,000 | |
|   Cash (cost) | | 600,000 |

included in a recent annual report shown in Illustration 10–7 describes the company's policy and provides a summary of disclosure requirements.

**Illustration 10–7**

Disclosure of Asset
Retirement Obligations—
SM Energy Company

**Real World Financials**

**Note 9—Asset Retirement Obligations (in part)**
The Company recognizes an estimated liability for future costs associated with the abandonment of its oil and gas properties. A liability for the fair value of an asset retirement obligation and a corresponding increase to the carrying value of the related long-lived asset are recorded at the time a well is completed or acquired. The increase in carrying value is included in proved oil and gas properties in the consolidated balance sheets. The Company depletes the amount added to proved oil and gas property costs and recognizes accretion expense in connection with the discounted liability over the remaining estimated economic lives of the respective oil and gas properties. Cash paid to settle asset retirement obligations is included in the operating section of the Company's consolidated statement of cash flows.

The Company's estimated asset retirement obligation liability is based on historical experience in abandoning wells, estimated economic lives, estimates as to the cost to abandon the wells in the future and federal, and state regulatory requirements. The liability is discounted using a credit-adjusted risk-free rate estimated at the time the liability is incurred or revised. The credit-adjusted risk-free rates used to discount the Company's abandonment liabilities range from 6.5 percent to 12.0 percent. Revisions to the liability could occur due to changes in estimated abandonment costs or well economic lives, or if federal or state regulators enact new requirements regarding the abandonment of wells.

It is important to understand that asset retirement obligations could result from the acquisition of many different types of tangible assets, not just natural resources. For example, **Dow Chemical Company** reported a $99 million asset retirement liability in its 2010 balance sheet related to anticipated demolition and remediation activities at its manufacturing sites in the United States, Canada, Europe, Italy, and Brazil.

Sometimes, after exploration or development, it becomes apparent that continuing the project is economically infeasible. If that happens, any costs incurred are expensed rather than capitalized. An exception is in the oil and gas industry, where we have two generally accepted accounting alternatives for accounting for projects that prove unsuccessful. We discuss these alternatives in Appendix 10.

*Asset retirement obligations could result from the acquisition of many different types of tangible assets, not just natural resources.*

## Intangible Assets

Intangible assets are assets, other than financial assets, that lack physical substance. They include such items as patents, copyrights, trademarks, franchises, and goodwill. Despite their lack of physical substance, these assets can be extremely valuable resources for a company. For example, **Interbrand Sampson**, the world's leading branding consulting company, recently estimated the value of the **Coca-Cola** trademark to be $70 billion.[6] In general, intangible assets refer to the ownership of exclusive rights that provide benefits to the owner in the production of goods and services.

*Intangible assets generally represent exclusive rights that provide benefits to the owner.*

The issues involved in accounting for intangible assets are similar to those of property, plant, and equipment. One key difference, though, is that the future benefits that we attribute to intangible assets usually are much less certain than those attributed to tangible assets. For example, will the new toy for which a company acquires a patent be accepted by the market? If so, will it be a blockbuster like Silly Bandz or Rubik's Cube, or will it be only a moderate success? Will it have lasting appeal like Barbie dolls, or will it be a short-term fad? In short, it's often very difficult to anticipate the timing, and even the existence, of future benefits attributable to many intangible assets. In fact, this uncertainty is a discriminating characteristic of intangible assets that perhaps better distinguishes them from tangible assets than their lack of physical substance. After all, other assets, too, do not exist physically but are not considered intangible assets. Accounts receivable and prepaid expenses, for example, have no physical substance and yet are reported among tangible assets.

Companies can either (1) *purchase* intangible assets from other entities (existing patent, copyright, trademark, or franchise rights) or (2) *develop* intangible assets internally (say, develop a new product or process that is then patented). In either case, we amortize its cost, unless it has an indefinite useful life.[7] Also, just like property, plant, and equipment, intangibles are subject to asset impairment rules. We discuss amortization and impairment in Chapter 11. In this chapter, we consider the acquisition cost of intangible assets.

*Intangible assets with finite useful lives are amortized; intangible assets with indefinite useful lives are not amortized.*

The initial valuation of purchased intangible assets usually is quite simple. We value a purchased intangible at its original cost, which includes its purchase price and all other costs necessary to bring it to condition and location for intended use. For example, if a company purchases a patent from another entity, it might pay legal fees and filing fees in addition to the purchase price. We value intangible assets acquired in exchange for stock, or for other nonmonetary assets, or with deferred payment contracts exactly as we do property, plant, and equipment. Let's look briefly at the costs of purchasing some of the more common intangible assets.

*Purchased intangible assets are valued at their original cost.*

**PATENTS.**    A patent is an exclusive right to manufacture a product or to use a process. This right is granted by the U.S. Patent Office for a period of 20 years. In essence, the holder of a patent has a monopoly on the use, manufacture, or sale of the product or process. If a patent is purchased from an inventor or another individual or company, the amount paid is its initial valuation. The cost might also include such other costs as legal and filing fees to

---

[6]This $70 billion represents an estimate of the fair value to the company at the time the estimate was made, not the historical cost valuation that appears in the balance sheet of Coca-Cola.

[7]FASB ASC 350–30–35–1: Intangibles–Goodwill and Other–General Intangibles Other Than Goodwill–Subsequent Measurement, and FASB ASC 350–20–35–1: Intangibles–Goodwill and Other–Goodwill–Subsequent Measurement (previously "Goodwill and Other Intangible Assets," *Statement of Financial Accounting Standards No. 142* (Norwalk, Conn.: FASB, 2001)).

secure the patent. Holders of patents often need to defend a patent in court against infringement. Any attorney fees and other costs of successfully defending a patent are added to the patent account.

When a patent is *developed internally,* the research and development costs of doing so are expensed as incurred. We discuss research and development in more detail in a later section. We capitalize legal and filing fees to secure the patent, even if internally developed.

**COPYRIGHTS.**   A copyright is an exclusive right of protection given to a creator of a published work, such as a song, film, painting, photograph, or book. Copyrights are protected by law and give the creator the exclusive right to reproduce and sell the artistic or published work for the life of the creator plus 70 years. Accounting for the costs of copyrights is virtually identical to that of patents.

Trademarks or tradenames often are considered to have indefinite useful lives.

**TRADEMARKS.**   A trademark, also called tradename, is an exclusive right to display a word, a slogan, a symbol, or an emblem that distinctively identifies a company, a product, or a service. The trademark can be registered with the U.S. Patent Office which protects the trademark from use by others for a period of 10 years. The registration can be renewed for an indefinite number of 10-year periods, so a trademark is an example of an intangible asset whose useful life could be indefinite.

Real World Financials

Trademarks or tradenames often are acquired through a business combination. As an example, in 2002, **Hewlett-Packard Company (HP)** acquired all of the outstanding stock of **Compaq Computer Corporation** for $24 billion. Of that amount, $1.4 billion was assigned to the Compaq tradename. HP stated in a disclosure note that this ". . . intangible asset will not be amortized because it has an indefinite remaining useful life based on many factors and considerations, including the length of time that the Compaq name has been in use, the Compaq brand awareness and market position and the plans for continued use of the Compaq brand within a portion of HP's overall product portfolio."

Trademarks can be very valuable. The estimated value of $70 billion for the Coca-Cola trademark mentioned previously is a good example. Note that the cost of the trademark reported in the balance sheet is far less than the estimate of its worth to the company. The Coca-Cola Company's 2010 balance sheet disclosed all trademarks at a cost of only $6 billion.

*Franchise* operations are among the most common ways of doing business.

**FRANCHISES.**   A franchise is a contractual arrangement under which the franchisor grants the franchisee the exclusive right to use the franchisor's trademark or tradename and may include product and formula rights, within a geographical area, usually for a specified period of time. Many popular retail businesses such as fast food outlets, automobile dealerships, and motels are franchises. For example, the last time you ordered a hamburger at McDonald's, you were probably dealing with a franchise.

The owner of that McDonald's outlet paid **McDonald's Corporation** a fee in exchange for the exclusive right to use the McDonald's name and to sell its products within a specified geographical area. In addition, many franchisors provide other benefits to the franchisee, such as participating in the construction of the retail outlet, training of employees, and national advertising.

Payments to the franchisor usually include an initial payment plus periodic payments over the life of the franchise agreement. The franchisee capitalizes as an intangible asset the initial franchise fee plus any legal costs associated with the contract agreement. The franchise asset is then amortized over the life of the franchise agreement. The periodic payments usually relate to services provided by the franchisor on a continuing basis and are expensed as incurred.

Most purchased intangibles are *specifically identifiable.* That is, cost can be directly associated with a specific intangible right. An exception is goodwill, which we discuss next.

*Goodwill* can only be purchased through the acquisition of another company.

**GOODWILL.**   Goodwill is a unique intangible asset in that its cost can't be directly associated with any specifically identifiable right and it is not separable from the company itself. It represents the unique value of a company as a whole over and above its identifiable tangible and intangible assets. Goodwill can emerge from a company's clientele and reputation, its trained employees and management team, its favorable business location, and any other unique features of the company that can't be associated with a specific asset.

Because goodwill can't be separated from a company, it's not possible for a buyer to acquire it without also acquiring the whole company or a portion of it. Goodwill will appear as an asset in a balance sheet only when it was purchased in connection with the acquisition of control over another company. In that case, the capitalized cost of goodwill equals the fair value of the consideration exchanged (acquisition price) for the company less the fair value of the net assets acquired. The fair value of the net assets equals the fair value of all identifiable tangible and intangible assets less the fair value of any liabilities of the selling company assumed by the buyer. Goodwill is a residual asset; it's the amount left after other assets are identified and valued. Consider Illustration 10–8.

**FINANCIAL Reporting Case**

Q5, p. 529

*Goodwill* is the excess of the fair value of the consideration exchanged over the fair value of the net assets acquired.

## Illustration 10–8
Goodwill

The Smithson Corporation acquired all of the outstanding common stock of the Rider Corporation in exchange for $18 million cash.* Smithson assumed all of Rider's long-term debts which have a fair value of $12 million at the date of acquisition. The fair values of all identifiable assets of Rider are as follows ($ in millions):

| | |
|---|---|
| Receivables | $ 5 |
| Inventory | 7 |
| Property, plant, and equipment | 9 |
| Patent | 4 |
| Total | $25 |

The cost of the goodwill resulting from the acquisition is $5 million:

| | | |
|---|---|---|
| Fair value of consideration exchanged | | $18 |
| Less: Fair value of net assets acquired | | |
| Assets | $25 | |
| Less: Fair value of liabilities assumed | (12) | (13) |
| Goodwill | | $ 5 |

The Smithson Corporation records the acquisition as follows:

| | | |
|---|---|---|
| Receivables (fair value).................................................... | 5 | |
| Inventory (fair value)....................................................... | 7 | |
| Property, plant, and equipment (fair value) ..................... | 9 | |
| Patent (fair value) .......................................................... | 4 | |
| Goodwill (difference)....................................................... | 5 | |
| Liabilities (fair value) ................................................... | | 12 |
| Cash (acquisition price) ................................................ | | 18 |

*Determining the amount an acquirer is willing to pay for a company in excess of the identifiable net assets is a question of determining the value of a company as a whole. This question is addressed in most introductory and advanced finance textbooks.

Of course, a company can develop its own goodwill through advertising, training, and other efforts. In fact, most do. However, a company must expense all such costs incurred in the internal generation of goodwill. By not capitalizing these items, accountants realize that the matching principle is violated because many of these expenditures do result in significant future benefits. Also, it's difficult to compare two companies when one has acquired goodwill and the other has not. But imagine how difficult it would be to associate these expenditures with any objective measure of goodwill. In essence, we have a situation where the characteristic of faithful representation overshadows relevance.

Just like for other intangible assets that have indefinite useful lives, *we do not amortize goodwill.* This makes it imperative that companies make every effort to identify specific intangibles other than goodwill that they acquire in a business combination since goodwill is the amount left after other assets are identified.

Goodwill, along with other intangible assets with indefinite useful lives, is not amortized.

# Additional Consideration

It's possible for the fair value of net assets to exceed the fair value of the consideration exchanged for those net assets. A "bargain purchase" situation could result from an acquisition involving a "forced sale" in which the seller is acting under duress. The FASB previously required this excess, deemed *negative goodwill*, to be allocated as a pro rata reduction of the amounts that otherwise would have been assigned to particular assets acquired. This resulted in assets acquired being recorded at amounts less than their fair values. However, current GAAP makes it mandatory that assets and liabilities acquired in a business combination be valued at their fair values.[8] Any negative goodwill is reported as a gain in the year of the combination.

**In a business combination, an intangible asset must be recognized as an asset apart from goodwill if it arises from contractual or other legal rights or is separable.**

In keeping with that goal, GAAP provides guidelines for determining which intangibles should be separately recognized and valued. Specifically, an intangible should be recognized as an asset apart from goodwill if it arises from contractual or other legal rights or is capable of being separated from the acquired entity. Possibilities are patents, trademarks, copyrights, and franchise agreements, and such items as customer lists, license agreements, order backlogs, employment contracts, and noncompetition agreements.[9] In past years, some of these intangibles, if present in a business combination, often were included in the cost of goodwill.[10]

# Where We're Headed

● LO10–9

The FASB and IASB are collaborating on several major new standards designed in part to move U.S. GAAP and IFRS closer together (convergence). We discussed one of these projects—revenue recognition—in detail in a Chapter 5 supplement. Under the new standard update, which is anticipated to be effective no earlier than 2015, sellers are allowed to capitalize, as an intangible asset, the incremental costs of obtaining and fulfilling a long-term (longer than one year) contract. A sales commission is an example of a contract acquisition cost that could be capitalized, rather than expensed, under this new guidance. In a Where We're Headed box in Chapter 11 we discuss the amortization and impairment of these intangible assets.

# Lump-Sum Purchases

● LO10–2

It's not unusual for a group of assets to be acquired for a single sum. If these assets are indistinguishable, for example 10 identical delivery trucks purchased for a lump-sum price of $150,000, valuation is obvious. Each of the trucks would be valued at $15,000 ($150,000 ÷ 10). However, if the lump-sum purchase involves different assets, it's necessary to allocate the lump-sum acquisition price among the separate items. The assets acquired may have different characteristics and different useful lives. For example, the acquisition of a factory may include assets that are significantly different such as land, building, and equipment.

The allocation is made in proportion to the individual assets' relative fair values. This process is best explained by an example in Illustration 10–9.

---

[8]FASB ASC 805: Business Combinations (previously "Business Combinations," *Statement of Financial Accounting Standards No. 141 (revised)* (Norwalk, Conn.: FASB, 2007)).

[9]Ibid.

[10]An assembled workforce is an example of an intangible asset that is not recognized as a separate asset. A workforce does not represent a contractual or legal right, nor is it separable from the company as a whole.

The Smyrna Hand & Edge Tools Company purchased an existing factory for a single sum of $2,000,000. The price included title to the land, the factory building, and the manufacturing equipment in the building, a patent on a process the equipment uses, and inventories of raw materials. An independent appraisal estimated the fair values of the assets (if purchased separately) at $330,000 for the land, $550,000 for the building, $660,000 for the equipment, $440,000 for the patent and $220,000 for the inventories. The lump-sum purchase price of $2,000,000 is allocated to the separate assets as follows:

|  | **Fair Values** | |
|---|---|---|
| Land | $  330,000 | 15% |
| Building | 550,000 | 25 |
| Equipment | 660,000 | 30 |
| Patent | 440,000 | 20 |
| Inventories | 220,000 | 10 |
| Total | $2,200,000 | 100% |

| Land | (15% × $2,000,000) | 300,000 | |
|---|---|---|---|
| Building | (25% × $2,000,000) | 500,000 | |
| Equipment | (30% × $2,000,000) | 600,000 | |
| Patent | (20% × $2,000,000) | 400,000 | |
| Inventories | (10% × $2,000,000) | 200,000 | |
| Cash | | | 2,000,000 |

**Illustration 10–9**

Lump-Sum Purchase

The total purchase price is allocated in proportion to the relative fair values of the assets acquired.

The relative fair value percentages are multiplied by the lump-sum purchase price to determine the initial valuation of each of the separate assets. Notice that the lump-sum purchase includes inventories. The procedure used here to allocate the purchase price in a lump-sum acquisition pertains to any type of asset mix, not just to property, plant, and equipment and intangible assets.

# Ethical Dilemma

Grandma's Cookie Company purchased a factory building. The company controller, Don Nelson, is in the process of allocating the lump-sum purchase price between land and building. Don suggests to the company's chief financial officer, Judith Prince, that they fudge a little by allocating a disproportionately higher share of the price to land. Don reasons that this will reduce depreciation expense, boost income, increase their profit-sharing bonus, and hopefully, increase the price of the company's stock. Judith has some reservations about this because the higher reported income will also cause income taxes to be higher than they would be if a correct allocation of the purchase price is made.

What are the ethical issues? What stakeholders' interests are in conflict?

# Noncash Acquisitions

Companies sometimes acquire assets without paying cash but instead by issuing debt or equity securities, receiving donated assets, or exchanging other assets. *The controlling principle in each of these situations is that in any noncash transaction (not just those dealing with property, plant, and equipment and intangible assets), the components of the transaction are recorded at their fair values.* The first indicator of fair value is the fair value of the assets, debt, or equity securities given. Sometimes the fair value of the assets received is used when their fair value is more clearly evident than the fair value of the assets given.

Assets acquired in noncash transactions are valued at the fair value of the assets given or the fair value of the assets received, whichever is more clearly evident.

## Deferred Payments

● LO10–3    A company can acquire an asset by giving the seller a promise to pay cash in the future and thus creating a liability, usually a note payable. The initial valuation of the asset is, again, quite simple as long as the note payable explicitly requires the payment of interest at a realistic interest rate. For example, suppose a machine is acquired for $15,000 and the buyer signs a note requiring the payment of $15,000 sometime in the future *plus* interest in the meantime at a realistic interest rate. The machine would be valued at $15,000 and the transaction recorded as follows:

| | | |
|---|---|---|
| Machine................................................................................. | 15,000 | |
| Note payable ..................................................................... | | 15,000 |

We know from our discussion of the time value of money in Chapter 6 that most liabilities are valued at the present value of future cash payments, reflecting an appropriate time value of money. As long as the note payable explicitly contains a realistic interest rate, the present value will equal the face value of the note, $15,000 in our previous example. This also should be equal to the fair value of the machine purchased. On the other hand, when an interest rate is not specified or is unrealistic, determining the cost of the asset is less straightforward. In that case, the accountant should look beyond the form of the transaction and record its substance. Consider Illustration 10–10.

### Illustration 10–10
Asset Acquired with Debt—Present Value of Note Indicative of Fair Value

> On January 2, 2013, the Midwestern Steam Gas Corporation purchased an industrial furnace. In payment, Midwestern signed a noninterest-bearing note requiring $50,000 to be paid on December 31, 2014. If Midwestern had borrowed cash to buy the furnace, the bank would have required an interest rate of 10%.

**Some portion of the payment(s) required by a noninterest-bearing note in reality is interest.**

On the surface, it might appear that Midwestern is paying $50,000 for the furnace, the eventual cash payment. However, when you recognize that the agreement specifies no interest even though the payment won't be made for two years, it becomes obvious that a portion of the $50,000 payment is not actually payment for the furnace, but instead is interest on the note. At what amount should Midwestern value the furnace and the related note payable?

**Noncash transactions are recorded at the fair value of the items exchanged.**

The answer is fair value, as it is for any noncash transaction. This might be the fair value of the furnace or the fair value of the note. Let's say, in this situation, that the furnace is custom-built, so its cash price is unavailable. But Midwestern can determine the fair value of the note payable by computing the present value of the cash payments at the appropriate interest rate of 10%. The amount actually paid for the machine, then, is the present value of the cash flows called for by the loan agreement, discounted at the market rate—10% in this case.

$$PV = \$50,000 \, (.82645^*) = \$41,323$$
*Present value of $1: n = 2, i = 10% (from Table 2)

So the furnace should be recorded at its *real* cost, $41,323, as follows:[11]

**The economic essence of a transaction should prevail over its outward appearance.**

| | | |
|---|---|---|
| Furnance (determined above)................................................ | 41,323 | |
| Discount on note payable (difference).................................. | 8,677 | |
| Note payable (face amount) ............................................... | | 50,000 |

Notice that the note also is recorded at $41,323, its present value, but this is accomplished by using a contra account, called *discount on note payable,* for the difference between the face amount of the note ($50,000) and its present value ($41,323). The difference of $8,677

---

[11]The entry shown assumes the note is recorded using the gross method. By the net method, a discount account is not used and the note is simply recorded at present value.

| | | |
|---|---|---|
| Machine ........................................... | 41,323 | |
| Note payable .................................. | | 41,323 |

is the portion of the eventual $50,000 payment that represents interest and is recognized as interest expense over the life of the note.

Assuming that Midwestern's fiscal year-end is December 31 and that adjusting entries are recorded only at the end of each year, the company would record the following entries at the end of 2013 and 2014 to accrue interest and the payment of the note:

| | Note payable | |
|---|---|---|
| Jan. 1, 2013 | 50,000 | |
| | 50,000 | Dec. 31, 2014 |
| Bal. 12/31/14 | 0 | |

**December 31, 2013**

| | | |
|---|---|---|
| Interest expense ($41,323 × 10%) ................................................... | 4,132 | |
| Discount on note payable .......................................................... | | 4,132 |

| Discount on note payable | | |
|---|---|---|
| 8,677 | Jan. 1, 2013 | |
| Dec. 31, 2013 | 4,132 | |
| Dec. 31, 2014 | 4,545 | |
| 0 | Bal. 12/31/14 | |

**December 31, 2014**

| | | |
|---|---|---|
| Interest expense ([$41,323 + 4,132]* × 10%) .................................... | 4,545 | |
| Discount on note payable .......................................................... | | 4,545 |
| Note payable (face amount) ........................................................ | 50,000 | |
| Cash ................................................................................... | | 50,000 |

*The 2013 unpaid interest increases the amount owed by $4,132.

Sometimes, the fair value of an asset acquired in a noncash transaction is readily available from price lists, previous purchases, or otherwise. In that case, this fair value may be more clearly evident than the fair value of the note and it would serve as the best evidence of the exchange value of the transaction. As an example, let's consider Illustration 10–11.

**Illustration 10–11**
Noninterest-Bearing Note—Fair Value of Asset Is Known

On January 2, 2013, Dennison, Inc., purchased a machine and signed a noninterest-bearing note in payment. The note requires the company to pay $100,000 on December 31, 2015. Dennison is not sure what interest rate appropriately reflects the time value of money. However, price lists indicate the machine could have been purchased for cash at a price of $79,383.

Dennison records both the asset and liability at $79,383 on January 2:

| | | |
|---|---|---|
| Machine (cash price) ................................................. | 79,383 | |
| Discount on note payable (difference) ........................... | 20,617 | |
| Note payable (face amount) ..................................... | | 100,000 |

In this situation, we infer the present value of the note from the fair value of the asset. Again, the difference between the note's $79,383 present value and the cash payment of $100,000 represents interest. We can determine the interest rate that is implicit in the agreement as follows:

$$\$79,383 \text{ (present value)} = \$100,000 \text{ (face amount)} \times \text{PV factor}$$
$$\$79,383 \div \$100,000 = .79383^*$$

*Present value of $1: $n = 3$, $i = ?$ (from Table 2, $i = 8\%$)

We refer to the 8% rate as the *implicit rate of interest*. Dennison records interest each year at 8% in the same manner as demonstrated in Illustration 10–10 and discussed in greater depth in Chapter 14.

We now turn our attention to the acquisition of assets acquired in exchange for equity securities and through donation.

## Issuance of Equity Securities

The most common situation in which equity securities are issued for property, plant, and equipment and intangible assets occurs when small companies incorporate and the owner or owners contribute assets to the new corporation in exchange for ownership securities, usually common stock. Because the common shares are not publicly traded, it's difficult to determine their fair value. In that case, the fair value of the assets received by the corporation is probably the better indicator of the transaction's exchange value. In other situations, particularly those involving corporations whose stock is actively traded, the market value of the shares is the best indication of fair value. Consider Illustration 10–12.

● LO10–4

**Illustration 10–12**
Asset Acquired by
Issuing Equity Securities

> On March 31, 2013, the Elcorn Company issued 10,000 shares of its nopar common stock in exchange for land. On the date of the transaction, the fair value of the common stock, evidenced by its market price, was $20 per share. The journal entry to record this transaction is:
>
> | | | |
> |---|---:|---:|
> | Land ..................................................................................... | 200,000 | |
> |     Common stock (10,000 shares × $20) ................................... | | 200,000 |

*Assets acquired by issuing common stock are valued at the fair value of the securities or the fair value of the assets, whichever is more clearly evident.*

*Donated assets* are recorded at their fair values.

If the fair value of the common stock had not been reliably determinable, the value of the land as determined through an independent appraisal would be used as the cost of the land and the value of the common stock.

## Donated Assets

On occasion, companies acquire assets through donation. The donation usually is an enticement to do something that benefits the donor. For example, the developer of an industrial park might pay some of the costs of building a manufacturing facility to entice a company to locate in its park. Companies record assets donated by unrelated parties at their fair values based on either an available market price or an appraisal value. This should not be considered a departure from historical cost valuation. Instead, it is equivalent to the donor contributing cash to the company and the company using the cash to acquire the asset.

*Revenue is credited for the amount paid by an unrelated party.*

As the recipient records the asset at its fair value, what account receives the offsetting credit? Over the years, there has been disagreement over this question. Should the recipient increase its paid-in capital—the part of shareholders' equity representing investments in the firm? Or, should the donated asset be considered revenue? GAAP requires that donated assets be recorded as *revenue*.[12] Recall that revenues generally are inflows of assets from delivering or producing goods, rendering services, or from other activities that constitute the entity's ongoing major or central operations. The rationale is that the company receiving the donation is performing a service for the donor in exchange for the asset donated.

Corporations occasionally receive donations from governmental units. A local governmental unit might provide land or pay all or some of the cost of a new office building or manufacturing plant to entice a company to locate within its geographical boundaries. For example, the city of San Jose, California, paid a significant portion of the cost of a new office building for **IBM Corporation**. The new office building, located in downtown San Jose, brought jobs to a revitalized downtown area and increased revenues to the city. The City of San Jose did not receive an equity interest in IBM through its donation, but significantly benefited nevertheless.

Illustration 10–13 provides an example.

**Illustration 10–13**
Asset Donation

> Elcorn Enterprises decided to relocate its office headquarters to the city of Westmont. The city agreed to pay 20% of the $20 million cost of building the headquarters in order to entice Elcorn to relocate. The building was completed on May 3, 2013. Elcorn paid its portion of the cost of the building in cash. Elcorn records the transaction as follows:
>
> | | | |
> |---|---:|---:|
> | Building ............................................................................ | 20,000,000 | |
> |     Cash .............................................................................. | | 16,000,000 |
> |     Revenue—donation of asset (20% × $20 million) ........... | | 4,000,000 |

---

[12]FASB ASC 958–605–15–2 and FASB ASC 958–605–15–4: Not-for-Profit Entities–Revenue Recognition–Scope and Scope Exceptions–Contributions Received (previously "Accounting for Contributions Received and Contributions Made," *Statement of Financial Accounting Standards No. 116* (Norwalk, Conn.: FASB, 1993)).

# International Financial Reporting Standards

**Government Grants.** Both U.S. GAAP and IFRS require that companies value donated assets at their fair values. For government grants, though, the way that value is recorded is different under the two sets of standards. Unlike U.S. GAAP, donated assets are not recorded as revenue under IFRS. *IAS No. 20*[13] requires that government grants be recognized in income over the periods necessary to match them on a systematic basis with the related costs that they are intended to compensate. So, for example, *IAS No. 20* allows two alternatives for grants related to assets:

1. Deduct the amount of the grant in determining the initial cost of the asset.
2. Record the grant as a liability, deferred income, in the balance sheet and recognize it in the income statement systematically over the asset's useful life.

In Illustration 10–13, if a company chose the first option, the building would be recorded at $16 million. If instead the company chose the second option, the building would be recorded at $20 million, but rather than recognizing $4 million in revenue as with U.S. GAAP, a $4 million credit to deferred income would be recorded and recognized as income over the life of the building.

Siemens, a global electronics and electrical engineering company based in Germany, prepares its financial statements according to IFRS, and sometimes receives government grants for the purchase or production of fixed assets. The following disclosure note included with recent financial statements indicates that Siemens uses the first option, deducting the amount of the grant from the initial cost of the asset.

**Government Grants (in part)**
Grants awarded for the purchase or the production of fixed assets (grants related to assets) are generally offset against the acquisition or production costs of the respective assets and reduce future depreciations accordingly.

● **LO10–9**

**IFRS requires government grants to be recognized in income over the periods necessary to match them on a systematic basis with the related costs that they are intended to compensate.**

**IFRS ILLUSTRATION**

Real World Financials

Property, plant, and equipment and intangible assets also can be acquired in an exchange. Because an exchange transaction inherently involves a disposition of one asset as it is given up in exchange for another, we cover these transactions in Part B, Dispositions and Exchanges.

## Decision Makers' Perspective

The property, plant, and equipment and intangible asset acquisition decision is among the most significant decisions that management must make. A decision to acquire a new fleet of airplanes or to build or purchase a new office building or manufacturing plant could influence a company's performance for many years.

These decisions, often referred to as **capital budgeting** decisions, require management to forecast all future net cash flows (cash inflows minus cash outflows) generated by the asset(s). These cash flows are then used in a model to determine if the future cash flows are sufficient to warrant the capital expenditure. One such model, the net present value model, compares the present value of future net cash flows with the required initial acquisition cost of the asset(s). If the present value is higher than the acquisition cost, the asset is acquired. You have studied or will study capital budgeting in considerable depth in a financial management course. The introduction to the time value of money concept in Chapter 6 provided you with important tools necessary to evaluate capital budgeting decisions.

A key to profitability is how well a company manages and utilizes its assets. Financial analysts often use activity, or turnover, ratios to evaluate a company's effectiveness in managing assets. This concept was illustrated with receivables and inventory in previous chapters. Property, plant, and equipment (PP&E) usually are a company's primary revenue-generating assets. Their efficient use is critical to generating a satisfactory return to owners.

● **LO10–5**

---

[13]"Government Grants," *International Accounting Standard No. 20* (IASCF), as amended effective January 1, 2011.

The *fixed-asset turnover ratio* measures a company's effectiveness in managing property, plant, and equipment.

One ratio analysts often use to measure how effectively managers use PP&E is the fixed-asset turnover ratio. This ratio is calculated as follows:

$$\text{Fixed-asset turnover ratio} = \frac{\text{Net sales}}{\text{Average fixed assets}}$$

The ratio indicates the level of sales generated by the company's investment in fixed assets. The denominator usually is the book value (cost less accumulated depreciation and depletion) of property, plant, and equipment.[14]

As with other turnover ratios, we can compare a company's fixed-asset turnover with that of its competitors, with an industry average, or with the same company's ratio over time. Let's compare the fixed-asset turnover ratios for **The Gap, Inc.**, and **Ross Stores, Inc.**, two companies in the retail apparel industry.

**Real World Financials**

| | ($ in millions) | | | |
| --- | --- | --- | --- | --- |
| | **Gap** | | **Ross Stores** | |
| | **2011** | **2010** | **2011** | **2010** |
| Property, plant, and equipment (net) | $2,563 | $2,628 | $984 | $943 |
| Net sales—2011 | $14,664 | | $7,866 | |

The 2011 fixed-asset turnover for Gap is 5.65 ($14,664 ÷ [($2,563 + 2,628) ÷ 2]) compared to Ross Store's turnover of 8.16 ($7,866 ÷ [($984 ÷ 943) ÷ 2]). Ross Stores is able to generate $2.51 more in sales dollars than Gap for each dollar invested in fixed assets. ●

## PART B

● LO10–6

# DISPOSITIONS AND EXCHANGES

After using property, plant, and equipment and intangible assets, companies will sell, retire, or exchange those assets. Accounting for exchanges differs somewhat from accounting for sales and retirements because they involve both an acquisition and a disposition. So let's look first at sales and retirements and then we'll address accounting for exchanges. Be sure to note that in each case, the companies should record depreciation, depletion, or amortization up to the date of disposition or exchange.

### Dispositions

When selling property, plant, and equipment and intangible assets for monetary consideration (cash or a receivable), the seller recognizes a gain or loss for the difference between the consideration received and the book value of the asset sold. Let's look at Illustration 10–14.

**Illustration 10–14**

Sale of Property, Plant, and Equipment

A gain or loss is recognized for the difference between the consideration received and the asset's book value.

The Robosport Company sold for $6,000 machinery that originally cost $20,000. Depreciation of $12,000 had been recorded up to the date of sale. Since the $8,000 book value of the asset ($20,000 − 12,000) exceeds the $6,000 consideration Robosport received, the company recognizes a $2,000 loss. The sale is recorded as follows:

| | | |
| --- | --- | --- |
| Cash (selling price) | 6,000 | |
| Accumulated depreciation (account balance) | 12,000 | |
| Loss on disposal of machinery (difference) | 2,000 | |
| Machinery (account balance) | | 20,000 |

Retirements (or abandonments) are treated similarly. The only difference is that there will be no monetary consideration received. A loss is recorded for the remaining book value of the asset.

When property, plant, and equipment or an intangible asset is to be disposed of by sale in the near future, we classify it as "held for sale" and report it at the lower of its book value or

---

[14]If intangible assets are significant, their book value could be added to the denominator to produce a turnover that reflects all long-lived, revenue-producing assets. The use of book value provides an approximation of the company's current investment in these assets.

fair value less any cost to sell.[15] If the fair value less cost to sell is below book value, we recognize an impairment loss. Assets classified as held for sale are not depreciated or amortized. Recall from your study of discontinued operations in Chapter 4 that this treatment is the same one we employed in accounting for a component of an entity that is held for sale. We cover this topic in more depth in the impairment section of Chapter 11.

Property, plant, and equipment and intangible assets to be disposed of by sale are classified as held for sale and measured at the lower of book value or fair value less cost to sell.

# Additional Consideration

### Involuntary Conversions

Occasionally companies dispose of property, plant, and equipment and intangible assets unintentionally. These so-called involuntary conversions include destruction by fire, earthquake, flood, or other catastrophe and expropriation by a governmental body.

Usually, the company receives a cash settlement from an insurance company for destroyed assets or from the governmental body for expropriated assets. The company often immediately reinvests this cash in similar assets. Nevertheless, involuntary conversions are treated precisely the same as voluntary conversions. That is, the proceeds are recorded, the book value of the lost assets is removed, and a gain or loss is recognized for the difference.

# Exchanges

Sometimes a company will acquire an asset in exchange for an asset other than cash. This frequently involves a trade-in by which a new asset is acquired in exchange for an old asset, and cash is given to equalize the fair values of the assets exchanged. The basic principle followed in these nonmonetary asset[16] exchanges is to value the asset received at fair value. This can be the fair value of the asset(s) given up or the fair value of the asset(s) received plus (or minus) any cash exchanged. We first look to the fair value of the asset given up. However, in a trade-in, quite often the fair value of the new asset is more clearly evident than the second-hand value of the asset traded in. We recognize a gain or loss for the difference between the fair value of the asset given up and its book value. See the example in Illustration 10–15A.

The Elcorn Company traded its laser equipment for the newer air-cooled ion lasers manufactured by American Laser Corporation. The old equipment had a book value of $100,000 (cost of $500,000 less accumulated depreciation of $400,000) and a fair value of $150,000. To equalize the fair values of the assets exchanged, in addition to the old machinery, Elcorn paid American Laser $430,000 in cash. This means that the fair value of the new laser equipment is $580,000. We know this because American Laser was willing to trade the new lasers in exchange for old lasers worth $150,000 plus $430,000 cash. The following journal entry records the transaction:

**Illustration 10–15A**

Nonmonetary Asset Exchange

An asset received in an exchange of nonmonetary assets generally is valued at fair value.

| | | |
|---|---|---|
| Laser equipment—new (fair value: $150,000 + 430,000) ... | 580,000 | |
| Accumulated depreciation (account balance) ................... | 400,000 | |
|     Laser equipment—old (account balance) ...................... | | 500,000 |
|     Cash (amount paid) ....................................................... | | 430,000 |
|     Gain (to balance; also: $150,000 – 100,000) ................... | | 50,000 |

A gain is recognized when the fair value of an asset given is more than its book value.

The new laser equipment is recorded at $580,000, the fair value of the old equipment, $150,000, plus the cash given of $430,000. This also equals the fair value of the new lasers. Elcorn recognizes a gain of $50,000, which is simply the difference between the old equipment's fair value of $150,000 and its $100,000 book value as well as the amount needed to allow the debits to equal credits in the journal entry.

---

[15]FASB ASC 360–10–35–15: Property, Plant, and Equipment–Overall–Subsequent Measurement–Impairment or Disposal of Long-Lived Assets (previously "Accounting for the Impairment or Disposal of Long-lived Assets," *Statement of Financial Accounting Standards No. 144* (Norwalk, Conn.: FASB, 2001)).

[16]Monetary items are assets and liabilities whose *amounts are fixed*, by contract or otherwise, in terms of a specific number of dollars. Others are considered nonmonetary.

Let's modify the illustration slightly by assuming that the fair value of the old equipment is $75,000 instead of $150,000. Illustration 10–15B shows the journal entry to record the transaction.

**Illustration 10–15B**

Nonmonetary Asset Exchange

A loss is recognized when the fair value of an asset given is less than its book value.

The Elcorn Company traded its laser equipment for the newer air-cooled ion lasers manufactured by American Laser Corporation. The old equipment had a book value of $100,000 (cost of $500,000 less accumulated depreciation of $400,000) and a fair value of $75,000. To equalize the fair values of the assets exchanged, in addition to the old machinery, Elcorn paid American Laser $430,000 in cash. This means that the fair value of the new laser equipment is $505,000. We know this because American Laser was willing to trade the new lasers in exchange for old lasers worth $75,000 plus $430,000 in cash. The following journal entry records the transaction:

| | | |
|---|---:|---:|
| Laser equipment—new (fair value: $75,000 + 430,000) ......... | 505,000 | |
| Accumulated depreciation (account balance) ...................... | 400,000 | |
| Loss (to balance; also: $100,000 − 75,000) .......................... | 25,000 | |
|    Laser equipment—old (account balance) ........................... | | 500,000 |
|    Cash (amount paid) ............................................................. | | 430,000 |

The $25,000 difference between the equipment's fair value of $75,000 and its book value of $100,000 is recognized as a loss. The new equipment is valued at $505,000, the fair value of the old equipment of $75,000 plus the $430,000 cash given.

Gain or loss is the difference between fair value and book value of the asset given.

It's important to understand that the gain or loss recognized in these transactions is the difference between the fair value and book value of the asset given. *The amount of cash given or received has no effect on the amount of gain or loss recognized.* The cash given or received simply serves to equalize the fair value of the assets exchanged.

Until 2005, the accounting treatment of nonmonetary asset exchanges depended on a number of factors including (1) whether the assets exchanged were similar or dissimilar, (2) whether a gain or loss was indicated in the exchange, and (3) whether cash was given or received. A new accounting standard[17] simplified accounting for exchanges by requiring the use of fair value except in rare situations in which the fair value can't be determined or the exchange lacks commercial substance.[18]

Let's discuss these two rare situations.

## Fair Value Not Determinable

It would be unusual for a company to be unable to reasonably determine fair value of either asset in an exchange. Nevertheless, if the situation does occur, the company would simply use the book value of the asset given up, plus (minus) any cash given (received) to value the asset acquired. For example, if fair value had not been determinable in Illustration 10–15A, Elcorn would have recorded the exchange as follows:

If we can't determine the fair value of either asset in the exchange, the asset received is valued at the book value of the asset given.

| | | |
|---|---:|---:|
| Equipment—new (book value + cash: $100,000 + 430,000) ........ | 530,000 | |
| Accumulated depreciation (account balance) ............................ | 400,000 | |
|    Equipment—old (account balance) .......................................... | | 500,000 |
|    Cash (amount paid) ................................................................. | | 430,000 |

---

[17]FASB ASC 845: Nonmonetary Transactions (previously "Exchanges of Nonmonetary Assets an amendment of APB Opinion No. 29," *Statement of Financial Accounting Standards No. 153* (Norwalk, Conn.: FASB, 2004)).

[18]There is a third situation which precludes the use of fair value in a nonmonetary exchange. The transaction is an exchange of inventories to facilitate sales to customers other than the parties to the exchange.

The new equipment is valued at the book value of the old equipment ($100,000) plus the cash given ($430,000). No gain or loss is recognized.

## Exchange Lacks Commercial Substance

If we record an exchange at fair value, we recognize a gain or loss for the difference between the fair value and book value of the asset(s) given up. To preclude the possibility of a company exchanging appreciated assets solely to recognize a gain, fair value can be used only in gain situations that have "commercial substance."

A nonmonetary exchange is considered to have commercial substance if future cash flows will change as a result of the exchange. Most exchanges are for genuine business reasons and would not be transacted if there were no anticipated change in future cash flows. The exchange of old laser equipment for the *newer* model in Illustration 10–15A is an example of an exchange transacted for genuine business reasons.

> Commercial substance is present when future cash flows change as a result of the exchange.

**GAIN SITUATION.**    Suppose a company owned a tract of land that had a book value of $1 million and a fair value of $5 million. The only ways to recognize the $4 million appreciation are to either sell the land or to exchange the land for another nonmonetary asset for a genuine business purpose. For example, if the land were exchanged for a different type of asset, say a building, then future cash flows most likely will change, the exchange has commercial substance, fair value is used and the $4 million gain can be recognized. On the other hand, if the land were exchanged for a tract of land that has the identical characteristics as the land given, then it is unlikely that future cash flows would change. In this case, the exchange lacks commercial substance and the new land is valued at the book value of the old land. Illustration 10–16 provides an example.

The Elcorn Company traded a tract of land to Sanchez Development for a similar tract of land. The old land had a book value of $2,500,000 and a fair value of $4,500,000. To equalize the fair values of the assets exchanged, in addition to the land, Elcorn paid Sanchez $500,000 in cash. This means that the fair value of the land acquired is $5,000,000. The following journal entry records the transaction, *assuming that the exchange lacks commercial substance:*

| | | |
|---|---|---|
| Land—new (book value + cash: $2,500,000 + 500,000) .......... | 3,000,000 | |
| Land—old (account balance) ............................................. | | 2,500,000 |
| Cash (amount paid) ......................................................... | | 500,000 |

The new land is recorded at $3,000,000, the book value of the old land, $2,500,000, plus the cash given of $500,000. No gain is recognized.

**Illustration 10–16**

Nonmonetary Asset Exchange—Exchange Lacks Commercial Substance

**LOSS SITUATION.**    In Illustration 10–16, what if the fair value of the land given was less than its book value? It's unlikely that a company would enter into this type of transaction unless there was a good reason. The FASB's intent in including the commercial substance requirement for the use of fair value was to avoid companies' trading *appreciated* property for no genuine business reason other than to recognize the gain. This means that when a loss is indicated in a nonmonetary exchange, it's okay to record the loss and we use fair value to value the asset acquired.

> When the fair value of the asset given is less than its book value, we always use fair value to record the exchange.

# Additional Consideration

In Illustration 10–16, cash was given to equalize the fair values of the assets exchanged. What if cash was received? Suppose that $500,000 cash was *received* instead of given and that the fair value of the old land was $5,000,000. This means that the fair value of the land received is $4,500,000. In that case, part of the transaction is considered monetary and we would recognize a portion of the $2,500,000 gain ($5,000,000 − 2,500,000). The amount of gain recognized is equal to the proportion of cash received relative to total received:[19]

$$\frac{\$500,000}{\$500,000 + 4,500,000} = 10\%$$

Elcorn would recognize a $250,000 gain (10% × $2,500,000) and would value the land received at $2,250,000, the book value of the land given ($2,500,000), plus the gain recognized ($250,000), less the cash received ($500,000). The following journal entry records the transaction:

| | | |
|---|---|---|
| Land—new ($2,500,000 + 250,000 − 500,000) | 2,250,000 | |
| Cash | 500,000 | |
| Land—old | | 2,500,000 |
| Gain | | 250,000 |

# Concept Review Exercise

**EXCHANGES**

The MD Corporation recently acquired new equipment to be used in its production process. In exchange, the company traded in an existing asset that had an original cost of $60,000 and accumulated depreciation on the date of the exchange of $45,000. In addition, MD paid $40,000 cash to the equipment manufacturer. The fair value of the old equipment is $17,000.

**Required:**

1. Prepare the journal entry MD would use to record the exchange transaction assuming that the transaction has commercial substance.
2. Prepare the journal entry MD would use to record the exchange transaction assuming that the transaction does *not* have commercial substance.

**Solution:**

1. Prepare the journal entry MD would use to record the exchange transaction assuming that the transaction has commercial substance.

| | | |
|---|---|---|
| Equipment—new ($17,000 + 40,000) | 57,000 | |
| Accumulated depreciation (account balance) | 45,000 | |
| Cash (amount paid) | | 40,000 |
| Equipment—old (account balance) | | 60,000 |
| Gain ($17,000 fair value − $15,000 book value) | | 2,000 |

2. Prepare the journal entry MD would use to record the exchange transaction assuming that the transaction does *not* have commercial substance.

| | | |
|---|---|---|
| Equipment—new ($15,000 + 40,000) | 55,000 | |
| Accumulated depreciation (account balance) | 45,000 | |
| Cash (amount paid) | | 40,000 |
| Equipment—old (account balance) | | 60,000 |

---

[19]If the amount of monetary consideration received is deemed significant, the transaction is considered to be monetary and the entire gain is recognized. In other words, the transaction is accounted for as if it had commercial substance. GAAP defines "significance" in this situation as 25% or more of the fair value of the exchange. FASB ASC 845–10–25–6: Nonmonetary transactions–Overall–Recognition (previously "Interpretations of *APB Opinion No. 29*," *EITF Abstracts No. 01–02* (Norwalk, Conn.: FASB, 2002)).

# SELF-CONSTRUCTED ASSETS AND RESEARCH AND DEVELOPMENT

Two types of expenditures relating to property, plant, and equipment and intangible assets whose accounting treatment has generated considerable controversy are interest costs pertaining to self-constructed assets and amounts spent for research and development. We now consider those expenditures and why those controversies have developed.

# Self-Constructed Assets

A company might decide to construct an asset for its own use rather than buy an existing one. For example, a retailer like **Nordstrom** might decide to build its own store rather than purchase an existing building. A manufacturing company like **Intel** could construct its own manufacturing facility. In fact, Nordstrom and Intel are just two of the many companies that self-construct assets. Other recognizable examples include **Walt Disney**, **Sears**, and **Caterpillar**. Quite often these companies act as the main contractor and then subcontract most of the actual construction work.

● LO10–7

The critical accounting issue in these instances is identifying the cost of the self-constructed asset. The task is more difficult than for purchased assets because there is no external transaction to establish an exchange price. Actually, two difficulties arise in connection with assigning costs to self-constructed assets: (1) determining the amount of the company's indirect manufacturing costs (overhead) to be allocated to the construction and (2) deciding on the proper treatment of interest (actual or implicit) incurred during construction.

## Overhead Allocation

One difficulty of associating costs with self-constructed assets is the same difficulty encountered when determining cost of goods manufactured for sale. The costs of material and direct labor usually are easily identified with a particular construction project and are included in cost. However, the treatment of manufacturing overhead cost and its allocation between construction projects and normal production is a controversial issue.

The cost of a self-constructed asset includes identifiable materials and labor and a portion of the company's manufacturing overhead costs.

Some accountants advocate the inclusion of only the *incremental* overhead costs in the total cost of construction. That is, the asset's cost would include only those additional costs that are incurred because of the decision to construct the asset. This would exclude such indirect costs as depreciation and the salaries of supervisors that would be incurred whether or not the construction project is undertaken. If, however, a new construction supervisor was hired specifically to work on the project, then that salary would be included in asset cost.

Others advocate assigning overhead on the same basis that is used for a regular manufacturing process. That is, all overhead costs are allocated both to production and to self-constructed assets based on the relative amount of a chosen cost driver (for example, labor hours) incurred. This is known as the *full-cost approach* and is the generally accepted method used to determine the cost of a self-constructed asset.

## Interest Capitalization

To reiterate, the cost of an asset includes all costs necessary to get the asset ready for its intended use. Unlike one purchased from another company, a self-constructed asset requires time to create it. During this construction period, the project must be financed in some way. This suggests the question as to whether interest costs during the construction period are one of the costs of acquiring the asset itself or simply costs of financing the asset. On the one hand, we might point to interest charges to finance inventories during their period of manufacture or to finance the purchase of plant assets from others and argue that construction period interest charges are merely costs of financing the asset that should be expensed as incurred like all other interest costs. On the other hand, we might argue that self-constructed assets are different in that during the construction period, they are not yet ready for their intended use for producing revenues. And, so, in keeping with both the historical cost principle and the matching concept, all costs during this period, including interest, should be capitalized and then allocated as depreciation during later periods when the assets are providing benefits.

**FINANCIAL Reporting Case**

Q3, p. 529

Only assets that are constructed as discrete projects qualify for interest capitalization.

Only interest incurred during the construction period is eligible for capitalization.

The interest capitalization period begins when construction begins and the first expenditure is made as long as interest costs are actually being incurred.

*Average accumulated expenditures* approximates the average debt necessary for construction.

**QUALIFYING ASSETS.**   Generally accepted accounting principles are consistent with the second argument. Specifically, interest is capitalized during the construction period for (a) assets built for a company's own use as well as for (b) assets constructed *as discrete projects* for sale or lease (a ship or a real estate development, for example). This excludes from interest capitalization consideration inventories that are routinely manufactured in large quantities on a repetitive basis and assets that already are in use or are ready for their intended use.[20] Interest costs incurred during the productive life of the asset are expensed as incurred.

**PERIOD OF CAPITALIZATION.**   The capitalization period for a self-constructed asset starts with the first expenditure (materials, labor, or overhead) and ends either when the asset is substantially complete and ready for use or when interest costs no longer are being incurred. Interest costs incurred can pertain to borrowings other than those obtained specifically for the construction project. However, interest costs can't be imputed; actual interest costs must be incurred.

**AVERAGE ACCUMULATED EXPENDITURES.**   Because we consider interest to be a necessary cost of getting a self-constructed asset ready for use, the amount capitalized is only that portion of interest cost incurred during the construction period that *could have been avoided* if expenditures for the asset had not been made. In other words, if construction had not been undertaken, debt incurred for the project would not have been necessary and/or other interest-bearing debt could have been liquidated or employed elsewhere.

As a result, interest should be determined for only the construction expenditures *actually incurred* during the capitalization period. And unless all expenditures are made at the outset of the period, it's necessary to determine the *average* amount outstanding during the period. This is the amount of debt that would be required to finance the expenditures and thus the amount on which interest would accrue. For instance, if a company accumulated $1,500,000 of construction expenditures fairly evenly throughout the construction period, the average expenditures would be:

| | |
|---|---:|
| Total accumulated expenditures incurred evenly throughout the period | $1,500,000 |
| | ÷2 |
| Average accumulated expenditures | $  750,000 |

Average accumulated expenditures is determined by time-weighting individual expenditures made during the construction period.

At the beginning of the period, no expenditures have accumulated, so no interest has accrued (on the equivalent amount of debt). But, by the end of the period interest is accruing on the total amount, $1,500,000. On average, then, interest accrues on half the total or $750,000.

If expenditures are not incurred evenly throughout the period, a simple average is insufficient. In that case, a weighted average is determined by time-weighting individual expenditures or groups of expenditures by the number of months from their incurrence to the end of the construction period. This is demonstrated in Illustration 10–17.

**FINANCIAL Reporting Case**

Q4, p. 529

The weighted-average accumulated expenditures by the end of 2013 are:

| | | |
|---|---|---:|
| January 3, 2013 | $500,000 × $^{12}/_{12}$ = | $500,000 |
| March 31, 2013 | 400,000 × $^{9}/_{12}$ = | 300,000 |
| September 30, 2013 | 600,000 × $^{3}/_{12}$ = | 150,000 |
| Average accumulated expenditures for 2013 | = | $950,000 |

STEP 1: Determine the average accumulated expenditures.

Again notice that the average accumulated expenditures are less than the total accumulated expenditures of $1,500,000. If Mills had borrowed exactly the amount necessary to finance the project, it would not have incurred interest on a loan of $1,500,000 for the whole year but only on an average loan of $950,000. The next step is to determine the interest to be capitalized for the average accumulated expenditures.

[20]FASB ASC 835–20–25: Interest–Capitalization of Interest–Recognition (previously "Capitalization of Interest Costs," *Statement of Financial Accounting Standards No. 34* (Stamford, Conn.: FASB, 1979)).

**Illustration 10–17**

Interest Capitalization

On January 1, 2013, the Mills Conveying Equipment Company began construction of a building to be used as its office headquarters. The building was completed on June 30, 2014. Expenditures on the project, mainly payments to subcontractors, were as follows:

| | |
|---|---|
| January 3, 2013 | $   500,000 |
| March 31, 2013 | 400,000 |
| September 30, 2013 | 600,000 |
| Accumulated expenditures at December 31, 2013 (before interest capitalization) | $1,500,000 |
| January 31, 2014 | 600,000 |
| April 30, 2014 | 300,000 |

On January 2, 2013, the company obtained a $1 million construction loan with an 8% interest rate. The loan was outstanding during the entire construction period. The company's other interest-bearing debt included two long-term notes of $2,000,000 and $4,000,000 with interest rates of 6% and 12%, respectively. Both notes were outstanding during the entire construction period.

**INTEREST RATES.**  In this situation, debt financing was obtained specifically for the construction project, and the amount borrowed is sufficient to cover the average accumulated expenditures. To determine the interest capitalized, then, we simply multiply the construction loan rate of 8% by the average accumulated expenditures.

STEP 2: Calculate the amount of interest to be capitalized.

The amount of interest capitalized is determined by multiplying an interest rate by the average accumulated expenditures.

$$\text{Interest capitalized for 2013} = \$950,000 \times 8\% = \$76,000$$

Notice that this is the same answer we would get by assuming separate 8% construction loans were made for each expenditure at the time each expenditure was made:

| Loans | | Annual Rate | | Portion of Year Outstanding | | Interest |
|---|---|---|---|---|---|---|
| $500,000 | $\times$ | 8% | $\times$ | $^{12}\!/_{12}$ | = | $40,000 |
| 400,000 | $\times$ | 8% | $\times$ | $^{9}\!/_{12}$ | = | 24,000 |
| 600,000 | $\times$ | 8% | $\times$ | $^{3}\!/_{12}$ | = | 12,000 |
| Interest capitalized for 2013 | | | | | | $76,000 |

The interest of $76,000 is added to the cost of the building, bringing accumulated expenditures at December 31, 2013, to $1,576,000 ($1,500,000 + 76,000). The remaining interest cost incurred but not capitalized is expensed.

It should be emphasized that interest capitalization does not require that funds actually be borrowed for this specific purpose, only that the company does have outstanding debt. The presumption is that even if the company doesn't borrow specifically for the project, funds from other borrowings must be diverted to finance the construction. Either way—directly or indirectly—interest costs are incurred. In our illustration, for instance, even without the construction loan, interest would be capitalized because other debt was outstanding. The capitalized interest would be the average accumulated expenditures multiplied by the weighted-average rate on these other loans. The weighted-average interest rate on all debt other than the construction loan would be 10%, calculated as follows:[21]

| Loans | | Rate | | Interest |
|---|---|---|---|---|
| $2,000,000 | $\times$ | 6% | = | $120,000 |
| 4,000,000 | $\times$ | 12% | = | 480,000 |
| $6,000,000 | | | | $600,000 |

---

[21]The same result can be obtained simply by multiplying the individual debt interest rates by the relative amount of debt at each rate. In this case, one-third of total debt is at 6% and two-thirds of the total debt is at 12% [(1/3 × 6%) + (2/3 × 12%)].

$$\text{Weighted-average rate: } \frac{\$600,000}{\$6,000,000} = 10\%$$

This is a weighted average because total interest is $600,000 on total debt of $6,000,000.

# Additional Consideration

The weighted-average rate isn't used for 2013 in our illustration because the specific construction loan is sufficient to cover the average accumulated expenditures. If the specific construction loan had been insufficient to cover the average accumulated expenditures, its 8% interest rate would be applied to the average accumulated expenditures up to the amount of the specific borrowing, and any remaining average accumulated expenditures in excess of specific borrowings would be multiplied by the weighted-average rate on all other outstanding interest-bearing debt. Suppose, for illustration, that the 8% construction loan had been only $500,000 rather than $1,000,000. We would calculate capitalized interest using both the specific rate and the weighted-average rate:

|  | Average Accumulated Expenditures |  | Rate |  | Interest |
| --- | --- | --- | --- | --- | --- |
| Total | $950,000 |  |  |  |  |
| Specific borrowing | 500,000 | × | 8% | = | $40,000 |
| Excess | $450,000 | × | 10% | = | 45,000 |
| Capitalized interest |  |  |  |  | $85,000 |

In our illustration, it's necessary to use this approach in 2014.

**Interest capitalized is limited to interest incurred.**

It's possible that the amount of interest calculated to be capitalized exceeds the amount of interest actually incurred. If that's the case, we limit the interest capitalized to the actual interest incurred. In our illustration, total interest cost incurred during 2013 far exceeds the $76,000 of capitalized interest calculated, so it's not necessary to limit the capitalized amount.

**STEP 3: Compare calculated interest with actual interest incurred.**

| Loans |  | Annual Rate |  | Actual Interest |  | Calculated Interest |
| --- | --- | --- | --- | --- | --- | --- |
| $1,000,000 | × | 8% | = | $ 80,000 |  |  |
| 2,000,000 | × | 6% | = | 120,000 |  |  |
| 4,000,000 | × | 12% | = | 480,000 |  |  |
|  |  |  |  | $680,000 |  | $76,000 |

↑
Use lower amount

Continuing the example based on the information in Illustration 10–17, let's determine the amount of interest capitalized during 2014 for the building. The total accumulated expenditures by the end of the project are:

| Accumulated expenditures at the beginning of 2014 (including interest capitalization) | $1,576,000 |
| --- | --- |
| January 31, 2014 | 600,000 |
| April 30, 2014 | 300,000 |
| Accumulated expenditures at June 30, 2014 (before 2014 interest capitalization) | $2,476,000 |

The weighted-average accumulated expenditures by the end of the project are:

| | | | |
|---|---|---|---|
| January 1, 2014 | $1,576,000 × % = | $1,576,000 | STEP 1: Determine the average accumulated expenditures. |
| January 31, 2014 | 600,000 × % = | 500,000 | |
| April 30, 2014 | 300,000 × % = | 100,000 | |
| Average accumulated expenditures for 2014 | | $2,176,000 | |

Notice that the 2014 expenditures are weighted relative to the construction period of six months because the project was finished on June 30, 2014. Interest capitalized for 2014 would be $98,800, calculated as follows:

| | Average Accumulated Expenditures | | Annual Rate | | Fraction of Year | | | |
|---|---|---|---|---|---|---|---|---|
| | $2,176,000 | | | | | | | STEP 2: Calculate the amount of interest to be capitalized. |
| Specific borrowing | 1,000,000 | × | 8% | × | 6/12 | = | $40,000 | |
| Excess | $1,176,000 | × | 10% | × | 6/12 | = | 58,800 | |
| Capitalized interest | | | | | | | $98,800 | |

Multiplying by six-twelfths reflects the fact that the interest rates are annual rates (12-month rates) and the construction period is only 6 months.

| Loans | | Annual Rate | Actual Interest | Calculated Interest | |
|---|---|---|---|---|---|
| $1,000,000 | × | 8% × 6/12 = | $ 40,000 | | STEP 3: Compare calculated interest with actual interest incurred. |
| 2,000,000 | × | 6% × 6/12 = | 60,000 | | |
| 4,000,000 | × | 12% × 6/12 = | 240,000 | | |
| | | | $340,000 | $98,800 | |

Use lower amount

# Additional Consideration

To illustrate how the actual interest limitation might come into play, let's assume the nonspecific borrowings in our illustration were $200,000 and $400,000 (instead of $2,000,000 and $4,000,000). Our comparison would change as follows:

| Loans | | Annual Rate | Actual Interest | Calculated Interest |
|---|---|---|---|---|
| $1,000,000 | × | 8% × 6/12 = | $40,000 | |
| 2,000,000 | × | 6% × 6/12 = | 6,000 | |
| 4,000,000 | × | 12% × 6/12 = | 24,000 | |
| | | | $70,000 | $98,800 |

Use lower amount

For the first six months of 2014, $98,800 of interest would be capitalized, bringing the total capitalized cost of the building to $2,574,800 ($2,476,000 + 98,800), and $241,200 in interest would be expensed ($340,000 − 98,800).

The method of determining interest to capitalize that we've discussed is called the specific interest method because we use rates from specific construction loans to the extent of specific borrowings before using the average rate of other debt. Sometimes, though, it's difficult to associate specific borrowings with projects. In these situations, it's acceptable to just use the weighted-average rate on all interest-bearing debt, including all construction loans. This is known as the **weighted-average method**. In our illustration, for example, if the $1,000,000, 8% loan had not been specifically related to construction, we would calculate a single weighted-average rate as shown below.

**Weighted-average method**

| Loans | | Rate | | Interest |
|---|---|---|---|---|
| $1,000,000 | × | 8% | = | $ 80,000 |
| 2,000,000 | × | 6% | = | 120,000 |
| 4,000,000 | × | 12% | = | 480,000 |
| $7,000,000 | | | | $680,000 |

$$\text{Weighted-average rate: } \frac{\$680,000}{\$7,000,000} = 9.7\%$$

If we were using the weighted-average method rather than the specific interest method, we would simply multiply this single rate times the average accumulated expenditures to determine capitalizable interest.

**If material, the amount of interest capitalized during the period must be disclosed.**

**DISCLOSURE.** For an accounting period in which interest costs are capitalized, both the total amount of interest costs incurred and the amount that has been capitalized should be disclosed. Illustration 10–18 shows an interest capitalization disclosure note that was included in a recent annual report of **Wal-Mart Stores, Inc.**, the world's largest retailer.

**Illustration 10–18**

Capitalized Interest Disclosure—Wal-Mart Stores, Inc.

**Real World Financials**

**Capitalized Interest**

The interest costs associated with construction projects are capitalized and included as part of the cost of the project. When no debt is incurred specifically for a project, interest is capitalized on amounts expended on the project using our weighted-average cost of borrowing. Capitalization of interest ceases when the project is substantially complete. Interest costs capitalized on construction projects were $63 million, $85 million, and $88 million in fiscal 2011, 2010, and 2009, respectively.

## Research and Development (R&D)

● **LO10–8**

Prior to 1974, the practice was to allow companies to either expense or capitalize R&D costs, but GAAP now requires all research and development costs to be charged to expense when incurred.[22] This was a controversial change opposed by many companies that preferred delaying the recognition of these expenses until later years when presumably the expenditures bear fruit.

**Most R&D costs are expensed in the periods incurred.**

A company undertakes an R&D project because it believes the project will eventually provide benefits that exceed the current expenditures. Unfortunately, though, it's difficult to predict which individual research and development projects will ultimately provide benefits. In fact, only 1 in 10 actually reaches commercial production. Moreover, even for those projects that pan out, a direct relationship between research and development costs and specific future revenue is difficult to establish. In other words, even if R&D costs do lead to future benefits, it's difficult to objectively determine the size of the benefits and in which periods the costs should be expensed if they are capitalized. These are the issues that prompted the FASB to require immediate expensing.

**R&D costs entail a high degree of uncertainty of future benefits and are difficult to match with future revenues.**

The FASB's approach is certain in most cases to understate assets and overstate current expense because at least some of the R&D expenditures will likely produce future benefits.

---

[22]FASB ASC 730–10–25–1: Research and Development–Overall–Recognition (previously "Accounting for Research and Development Costs," *Statement of Financial Accounting Standards No. 2* (Stamford, Conn.: FASB, 1974), par. 12).

**DETERMINING R&D COSTS.**    GAAP distinguishes research and development as follows:

---

**Research** is planned search or critical investigation aimed at discovery of new knowledge with the hope that such knowledge will be useful in developing a new product or service or a new process or technique or in bringing about a significant improvement to an existing product or process.

**Development** is the translation of research findings or other knowledge into a plan or design for a new product or process or for a significant improvement to an existing product or process whether intended for sale or use.[23]

---

R&D costs include salaries, wages, and other labor costs of personnel engaged in R&D activities, the costs of materials consumed, equipment, facilities, and intangibles used in R&D projects, the costs of services performed by others in connection with R&D activities, and a reasonable allocation of indirect costs related to those activities. General and administrative costs should not be included unless they are clearly related to the R&D activity.

If an asset is purchased specifically for a single R&D project, its cost is considered R&D and expensed immediately even though the asset's useful life extends beyond the current year. However, the cost of an asset that has an alternative future use beyond the current R&D project is *not* a current R&D expense. Instead, the depreciation or amortization of these alternative-use assets is included as R&D expenses in the current and future periods the assets are used for R&D activities.

> R&D expense includes the depreciation and amortization of assets used in R&D activities.

In general, R&D costs pertain to activities that occur prior to the start of commercial production, and costs of starting commercial production and beyond are not R&D costs. Illustration 10–19 captures this concept with a time line beginning with the start of an R&D project and ending with the ultimate sale of a developed product or the use of a developed process. The illustration also provides examples of activities typically included as R&D and examples of activities typically excluded from R&D.[24]

| Start of R&D Activity | Start of Commercial Production | Sale of Product or Process |
|---|---|---|

**Illustration 10–19**
Research and Development Expenditures

| Examples of R&D Costs: | Examples of Non-R&D Costs: |
|---|---|
| • Laboratory research aimed at discovery of new knowledge | • Engineering follow-through in an early phase of commercial production |
| • Searching for applications of new research findings or other knowledge | • Quality control during commercial production including routine testing of products |
| • Design, construction, and testing of preproduction prototypes and models | • Routine ongoing efforts to refine, enrich, or otherwise improve on the qualities of an existing product |
| • Modification of the formulation or design of a product or process | • Adaptation of an existing capability to a particular requirement or customer's need as a part of a continuing commercial activity |

> Costs incurred *before* the start of commercial production are all expensed as R&D.

> Costs incurred *after* commercial production begins would be either expensed or included in the cost of inventory.

---

[23]Ibid., section 730–10–20 (previously par. 8 of *SFAS No. 2*).
[24]Ibid., section 730–10–55 (previously par. 9 of *SFAS No. 2*).

Costs incurred before the start of commercial production are all expensed as R&D. The costs incurred after commercial production begins would be either expensed or treated as manufacturing overhead and included in the cost of inventory. Let's look at an example in Illustration 10–20.

## Illustration 10–20
Research and Development Costs

The Askew Company made the following cash expenditures during 2013 related to the development of a new industrial plastic:

| | |
|---|---|
| R&D salaries and wages | $10,000,000 |
| R&D supplies consumed during 2013 | 3,000,000 |
| Purchase of R&D equipment | 5,000,000 |
| Patent filing and legal costs | 100,000 |
| Payments to others for services performed in connection with R&D activities | 1,200,000 |
| Total | $19,300,000 |

The project resulted in a new product to be manufactured in 2014. A patent was filed with the U.S. Patent Office. The equipment purchased will be employed in other projects. Depreciation on the equipment for 2013 was $500,000.

**Filing and legal costs for patents, copyrights, and other developed intangibles are capitalized and amortized in future periods.**

The salaries and wages, supplies consumed, and payments to others for R&D services are expensed in 2013 as R&D. The equipment is capitalized and the 2013 depreciation is expensed as R&D. Even though the costs to develop the patented product are expensed, the filing and legal costs for the patent are capitalized and amortized in future periods just as similar costs are capitalized for purchased intangibles. Amortization of the patent is discussed in Chapter 11.

The various expenditures would be recorded as follows:

| | | |
|---|---|---|
| R&D expense ($10,000,000 + 3,000,000 + 1,200,000) .................. | 14,200,000 | |
| Cash ......................................................................................... | | 14,200,000 |
| *To record R&D expenses.* | | |
| Equipment .................................................................................. | 5,000,000 | |
| Cash ......................................................................................... | | 5,000,000 |
| *To record the purchase of equipment.* | | |
| R&D expense ............................................................................. | 500,000 | |
| Accumulated depreciation—equipment ................................. | | 500,000 |
| *To record R&D depreciation.* | | |
| Patent ........................................................................................ | 100,000 | |
| Cash ......................................................................................... | | 100,000 |
| *To capitalize the patent filing and legal costs.* | | |

Expenditures reconciliation:

| | |
|---|---|
| Recorded as R&D | $14,200,000 |
| Capitalized as equipment | 5,000,000 |
| Capitalized as patent | 100,000 |
| Total expenditures | $19,300,000 |

**GAAP requires disclosure of total R&D expense incurred during the period.**

GAAP requires that total R&D expense incurred must be disclosed either as a line item in the income statement or in a disclosure note. For example, Microsoft reported over $9 billion of R&D expense on the face of its 2011 income statement. In our illustration, total R&D expense disclosed in 2013 would be $14,700,000 ($14,200,000 in expenditures and $500,000 in depreciation). Note that if Askew later sells this patent to another company for, say, $15 million, the buyer would capitalize the entire purchase price rather than only the filing and legal costs. Once again, the reason for the apparent inconsistency in accounting treatment of internally generated intangibles and externally purchased intangibles is the difficulty of associating costs and benefits.

**R&D PERFORMED FOR OTHERS.**    The principle requiring the immediate expensing of R&D does not apply to companies that perform R&D for other companies under contract. In these situations, the R&D costs are capitalized as inventory and carried forward into future years until the project is completed. Of course, justification is that the benefits of these expenditures are the contract fees that are determinable and are earned over the term of the project. Income from these contracts can be recognized using either the percentage-of-completion or completed contract method. We discussed these alternatives in Chapter 5.

Another exception pertains to a company that develops computer software. Expenditures made after the software is determined to be technologically feasible but before it is ready for commercial production are capitalized. Costs incurred before technological feasibility is established are expensed as incurred. We discuss software development costs below.

**START-UP COSTS.**    For the fiscal year ended December 31, 2010, **Chipotle Mexican Grill, Inc.**, opened 129 new restaurants. The company incurred a variety of one-time pre-opening costs for wages, benefits and travel for the training and opening teams, food and other restaurant operating costs totaling $7.8 million. In fact, whenever a company introduces a new product or service, or commences business in a new territory or with a new customer, it incurs similar start-up costs. As with R&D expenditures, a company must expense all the costs related to a company's start-up activities in the period incurred, rather than capitalize those costs as an asset. Start-up costs also include organization costs related to organizing a new entity, such as legal fees and state filing fees to incorporate.[25]

> Start-up costs are expensed in the period incurred.

# Additional Consideration

## Development Stage Enterprises

A development stage enterprise is a new business that has either not commenced its principal operations or has begun its principal operations but has not generated significant revenues. Years ago, many of these companies recorded an asset for the normal operating costs incurred during the development stage. This asset was then expensed over a period of time beginning with the commencement of operations.

GAAP requires that these enterprises comply with the same generally accepted accounting principles that apply to established operating companies in determining whether a cost is to be charged to expense when incurred or capitalized and expensed in future periods.[26] Therefore, normal operating costs incurred during the development stage are expensed, not capitalized. Development stage enterprises are allowed to provide items of supplemental information to help financial statement readers more readily assess their future cash flows.

**SOFTWARE DEVELOPMENT COSTS.**    The computer software industry has become a large and important U.S. business over the last two decades. Relative newcomers such as **Microsoft** and **Adobe Systems**, as well as traditional hardware companies like **IBM**, are leaders in this multibillion dollar industry. A significant expenditure for these companies is the cost of developing software. In the early years of the software industry, some software companies were capitalizing software development costs and expensing them in future periods and others were expensing these costs in the period incurred.

Now GAAP requires that companies record R&D as an expense, until **technological feasibility** of the software has been established, for costs they incur to develop or purchase computer

> GAAP requires the capitalization of software development costs incurred after technological feasibility is established.

---

[25]FASB ASC 720–15–25–1: Other Expenses–Start-Up Costs–Recognition (previously "Reporting on the Costs of Start-Up Activities," *Statement of Position 98-5* (New York: AICPA, 1998)).

[26]FASB ASC 915: Development Stage Entities (previously "Accounting and Reporting by Development Stage Enterprises," *Statement of Financial Accounting Standards No. 7* (Stamford, Conn.: FASB, 1975)).

software to be sold, leased, or otherwise marketed.[27] We account for the costs incurred to develop computer software *to be used internally* in a similar manner. Costs incurred during the preliminary project stage are expensed as R&D. After the application development stage is reached (for example, at the coding stage or installation stage), we capitalize any further costs.[28] We generally capitalize the costs of computer software *purchased* for internal use.

Technological feasibility is established "when the enterprise has completed all planning, designing, coding, and testing activities that are necessary to establish that the product can be produced to meet its design specifications including functions, features, and technical performance requirements."[29] Costs incurred after technological feasibility but before the software is available for general release to customers are capitalized as an intangible asset. These costs include coding and testing costs and the production of product masters. Costs incurred after the software release date usually are not R&D expenditures. Illustration 10–21 shows the R&D time line introduced earlier in the chapter modified to include the point at which technological feasibility is established. Only the costs incurred between technological feasibility and the software release date are capitalized.

**Illustration 10–21**

Research and Development Expenditures—Computer Software

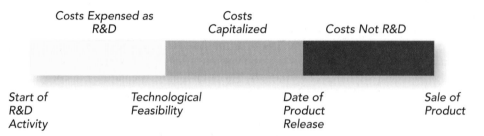

The amortization of capitalized computer software development costs begins when the product is available for general release to customers. The periodic amortization percentage is the greater of (1) the ratio of current revenues to current and anticipated revenues (percentage-of-revenue method) or (2) the straight-line percentage over the useful life of the asset, as shown in Illustration 10–22.

**Illustration 10–22**

Software Development Costs

The Astro Corporation develops computer software graphics programs for sale. A new development project begun in 2012 reached technological feasibility at the end of June 2013, and the product was available for release to customers early in 2014. Development costs incurred in 2013 prior to June 30 were $1,200,000 and costs incurred from June 30 to the product availability date were $800,000. 2014 revenues from the sale of the new product were $3,000,000 and the company anticipates an additional $7,000,000 in revenues. The economic life of the software is estimated at four years.

Astro Corporation would expense the $1,200,000 in costs incurred prior to the establishment of technological feasibility and capitalize the $800,000 in costs incurred between technological feasibility and the product availability date. 2014 amortization of the intangible asset, software development costs, is calculated as follows:

1. Percentage-of-revenue method:

$$\frac{\$3,000,000}{\$3,000,000 + 7,000,000} = 30\% \times \$800,000 = \$240,000$$

2. Straight-line method:

$$\tfrac{1}{4} \text{ or } 25\% \times \$800,000 = \$200,000.$$

The percentage-of-revenue method is used because it produces the greater amortization, $240,000.

---

[27]FASB ASC 985–20–25–1: Software–Costs of Software to be Sold, Leased, or Marketed–Recognition (previously "Accounting for the Costs of Computer Software to be Sold, Leased, or Otherwise Marketed," *Statement of Financial Accounting Standards No. 86* (Stamford, Conn.: FASB, 1985)).

[28]FASB ASC 350–40–25: Intangibles–Goodwill and Other–Internal-Use Software–Recognition (previously "Accounting for the Costs of Computer Software Developed or Obtained for Internal Use," *Statement of Position 98-1* (New York: AICPA, 1998)).

[29]FASB ASC 985–20–25–2: Software–Costs of Software to be Sold, Leased, or Marketed–Recognition (previously "Accounting for the Costs of Computer Software to be Sold, Leased, or Otherwise Marketed," *Statement of Financial Accounting Standards No. 86* (Stamford, Conn.: FASB, 1985), par. 4).

Illustration 10–23 shows the software disclosure included in a recent annual report of **CA, Inc.** The note provides a good summary of the accounting treatment of software development costs.

---

**Capitalized Development Costs (in part)**

Capitalized development costs in the accompanying Consolidated Balance Sheets include costs associated with the development of computer software to be sold, leased or otherwise marketed. Software development costs associated with new products and significant enhancements to existing software products are expensed as incurred until technological feasibility has been established. Annual amortization of capitalized software costs is the greater of the amount computed using the ratio that current gross revenues for a product bear to the total of current and anticipated future gross revenues for that product or the straight-line method over the remaining estimated economic life of the software product, generally estimated to be five years from the date the product became available for general release to customers.

**Illustration 10–23**

Software Disclosure— CA, Inc.

Real World Financials

---

Why do generally accepted accounting principles allow this exception to the general rule of expensing all R&D? We could attribute it to the political process. Software is a very important industry to our economy and perhaps its lobbying efforts resulted in the standard allowing software companies to capitalize certain R&D costs.

We could also attribute the exception to the nature of the software business. Recall that R&D costs in general are expensed in the period incurred for two reasons: (1) they entail a high degree of uncertainty of future benefits, and (2) they are difficult to match with future benefits. With software, there is an important identifiable engineering milestone, technological feasibility. When this milestone is attained, the probability of the software product's success increases significantly. And because the useful life of software is fairly short (one to four years in most cases), it is much easier to determine the periods of increased revenues than for R&D projects in other industries. Compare this situation with, say, the development of a new drug. Even after the drug has been developed, it must go through extensive testing to meet FDA (Food and Drug Administration) approval, which may never be attained. If attained, the useful life of the drug could be anywhere from a few months to many years.

# International Financial Reporting Standards

**Research and Development Expenditures.** Except for software development costs incurred after technological feasibility has been established, U.S. GAAP requires all research and development expenditures to be expensed in the period incurred. *IAS No. 38*[30] draws a distinction between research activities and development activities. Research expenditures are expensed in the period incurred. However, development expenditures that meet specified criteria are capitalized as an intangible asset. Under both U.S. GAAP and IFRS, any direct costs to secure a patent, such as legal and filing fees, are capitalized.

**Heineken,** a company based in Amsterdam, prepares its financial statements according to IFRS. The following disclosure note describes the company's adherence to *IAS No. 38*. The note also describes the criteria for capitalizing development expenditures as well as the types of expenditures capitalized.

**Software, Research and Development and Other Intangible Assets (in part)**
Expenditures on research activities, undertaken with the prospect of gaining new technical knowledge and understanding, are recognized in the income statement when incurred. Development activities involve a plan or design for the production of new or substantially improved products and processes. Development expenditures are capitalized only if development costs can be measured reliably, the product or process is technically and

● LO10–9

IFRS requires companies to capitalize development expenditures that meet specified criteria.

Real World Financials

(continued)

---

[30]"Intangible Assets," *International Accounting Standard No. 38* (IASCF), as amended effective January 1, 2011.

(concluded)

commercially feasible, future economic benefits are probable, and Heineken intends to and has sufficient resources to complete development and to use or sell the asset. The expenditures capitalized include the cost of materials, direct labor and overhead costs that are directly attributable to preparing the asset for its intended use, and capitalized borrowing costs.

Amortization of capitalized development costs begins when development is complete and the asset is available for use. Heineken disclosed that it amortizes its capitalized development costs using the straight-line method over an estimated 3-year useful life.

**PURCHASED RESEARCH AND DEVELOPMENT.** It's not unusual for one company to buy another company in order to obtain technology that the acquired company has developed or is in the process of developing. Any time a company buys another, it values the tangible and intangible assets acquired at fair value. When technology is involved, we distinguish between *developed technology* and *in-process research and development.* To do that, we borrow a criterion used in accounting for software development costs, and determine whether *technological feasibility* has been achieved. If so, the value of that technology is considered "developed," and we capitalize its fair value (record it as an asset) and amortize that amount over its useful life just like any other finite-life intangible asset.

> In business acquisitions, the fair value of in-process research and development is capitalized as an indefinite-life intangible asset.

We treat in-process R&D differently. GAAP requires the capitalization of the fair value of in-process R&D. But, unlike developed technology, we view it as an *indefinite-life* intangible asset.[31] As you will learn in Chapter 11, we don't amortize indefinite-life intangibles. Instead, we test them for impairment at least annually. If the R&D project is completed successfully, we switch to the way we account for developed technology and amortize the capitalized amount over the estimated period the product or process developed will provide benefits. If the project instead is abandoned, we expense the entire balance immediately. Research and development costs incurred after the acquisition to complete the project are expensed as incurred, consistent with the treatment of any other R&D expenditure not acquired in an acquisition.

> Real World Financials

As an example, during its fiscal year ended April 1, 2011, **Symantec Corporation**, a global provider of data security and storage systems, acquired the identity and authentication business of **VeriSign, Inc.**, for $1.29 billion. The fair values assigned included $354 million for finite-life life intangible assets (including $123 million in developed technology), $602 million for goodwill, and $274 million for indefinite-life intangibles (tradenames and trademarks). No in-process R&D was recorded.

# International Financial Reporting Standards

● LO10–9

**Software Development Costs.** The percentage we use to amortize computer software development costs under U.S. GAAP is the greater of (1) the ratio of current revenues to current and anticipated revenues or (2) the straight-line percentage over the useful life of the software. This approach is allowed under IFRS, but not required.

---

[31]FASB ASC 805: Business Combinations (previously "Business Combinations," *Statement of Financial Accounting Standards No. 141 (revised)* (Norwalk, Conn.: FASB, 2007)).

# Financial Reporting Case Solution

1. **Describe to Stan what it means to capitalize an expenditure. What is the general rule for determining which costs are capitalized when property, plant, and equipment or an intangible asset is acquired?** *(p. 532)*   To capitalize an expenditure simply means to record it as an asset. All expenditures other than payments to shareholders and debt repayments are either expensed as incurred or capitalized. In general, the choice is determined by whether the expenditure benefits more than just the current period. Exceptions to this general principle are discussed in the chapter. The initial cost of an asset includes all expenditures necessary to bring the asset to its desired condition and location for use.

2. **Which costs might be included in the initial cost of equipment?** *(p. 532)*   In addition to the purchase price, the cost of equipment might include the cost of transportation, installation, testing, and legal fees to establish title.

3. **In what situations is interest capitalized rather than expensed?** *(p. 551)*   Interest is capitalized only for assets constructed for a company's own use or for assets constructed as discrete products for sale or lease. For example, **Walt Disney** capitalizes interest on assets constructed for its theme parks, resorts and other property, and on theatrical and television productions in process. During the construction period, interest is considered a cost necessary to get the asset ready for its intended use.

4. **What is the three-step process used to determine the amount of interest capitalized?** *(p. 552)*   The first step is to determine the average accumulated expenditures for the period. The second step is to multiply the average accumulated expenditures by an appropriate interest rate or rates to determine the amount of interest capitalized. A final step compares the interest determined in step two with actual interest incurred. Interest capitalized is limited to the amount of interest incurred.

5. **What is goodwill and how is it measured?** *(p. 539)*   Goodwill represents the unique value of a company as a whole over and above its identifiable tangible and intangible assets. Because goodwill can't be separated from a company, it's not possible for a buyer to acquire it without also acquiring the whole company or a controlling portion of it. Goodwill will appear as an asset in a balance sheet only when it was purchased in connection with the acquisition of another company. In that case, the capitalized cost of goodwill equals the fair value of the consideration exchanged for the company less the fair value of the net assets acquired. Goodwill is a residual asset; it's the amount left after other assets are identified and valued. Just like for other intangible assets that have indefinite useful lives, we do not amortize goodwill. ●

# The Bottom Line

● **LO10–1**   The initial cost of property, plant, and equipment and intangible assets acquired in an exchange transaction includes the purchase price and all expenditures necessary to bring the asset to its desired condition and location for use. The cost of a natural resource includes the acquisition costs for the use of land, the exploration and development costs incurred before production begins, and restoration costs incurred during or at the end of extraction. Purchased intangible assets are valued at their original cost to include the purchase price and legal and filing fees. (*p. 532*)

● **LO10–2**   If a lump-sum purchase involves different assets, it is necessary to allocate the lump-sum acquisition price among the separate items according to some logical allocation method. A widely used allocation method is to divide the lump-sum purchase price according to the individual assets' relative fair values. (*p. 540*)

● **LO10–3**   Assets acquired in exchange for deferred payment contracts are valued at their fair value or the present value of payments using a realistic interest rate. (*p. 542*)

● **LO10–4** Assets acquired through the issuance of equity securities are valued at the fair value of the securities if known; if not known, the fair value of the assets received is used. Donated assets are valued at their fair value. (*p. 543*)

● **LO10–5** A key to profitability is how well a company manages and utilizes its assets. Financial analysts often use activity, or turnover, ratios to evaluate a company's effectiveness in managing its assets. Property, plant, and equipment (PP&E) usually are a company's primary revenue-generating assets. Their efficient use is critical to generating a satisfactory return to owners. One ratio that analysts often use to measure how effectively managers use PP&E is the fixed-asset turnover ratio. This ratio is calculated by dividing net sales by average fixed assets. (*p. 545*)

● **LO10–6** When an item of property, plant, and equipment or an intangible asset is sold, a gain or loss is recognized for the difference between the consideration received and the asset's book value. The basic principle used for nonmonetary exchanges is to value the asset(s) received based on the fair value of the asset(s) given up. In certain situations, the valuation of the asset(s) received is based on the book value of the asset(s) given up. (*p. 546*)

● **LO10–7** The cost of a self-constructed asset includes identifiable materials and labor and a portion of the company's manufacturing overhead costs. In addition, GAAP provides for the capitalization of interest incurred during construction. The amount of interest capitalized is equal to the average accumulated expenditures for the period multiplied by the appropriate interest rates, not to exceed actual interest incurred. (*p. 551*)

● **LO10–8** Research and development costs incurred to internally develop an intangible asset are expensed in the period incurred. Filing and legal costs for developed intangibles are capitalized. (*p. 556*)

● **LO10–9** Other than software development costs incurred after technological feasibility has been established, U.S. GAAP requires all research and development expenditures to be expensed in the period incurred. *IAS No. 38* draws a distinction between research activities and development activities. Research expenditures are expensed in the period incurred. However, development expenditures that meet specified criteria are capitalized as an intangible asset. *IAS No. 20* requires that government grants be recognized in income over the periods necessary to match them on a systematic basis with the related costs that they are intended to compensate. (*pp. 540, 545, 561,* and *562*) ●

# APPENDIX 10    Oil And Gas Accounting

Chapter 1 characterized the establishment of accounting and reporting standards as a political process. Standards, particularly changes in standards, can have significant differential effects on companies, investors and creditors, and other interest groups. The FASB must consider potential economic consequences of a change in an accounting standard or the introduction of a new standard. The history of oil and gas accounting provides a good example of this political process and the effect of possible adverse economic consequences on the standard-setting process.

There are two generally accepted methods that companies can use to account for oil and gas exploration costs. The **successful efforts method** requires that exploration costs that are known *not* to have resulted in the discovery of oil or gas (sometimes referred to as *dry holes*) be included as expenses in the period the expenditures are made. The alternative, the **full-cost method**, allows costs incurred in searching for oil and gas within a large geographical area to be capitalized as assets and expensed in the future as oil and gas from the successful wells are removed from that area. Both of these methods are widely used. Illustration 10A–1 compares the two alternatives.

Using the full-cost method, Shannon would capitalize the entire $20 million which is expensed as oil from the two successful wells is depleted. On the other hand, using the successful efforts method, the cost of the unsuccessful wells is expensed in 2013, and only the $4 million cost related to the successful wells is capitalized and expensed in future periods as the oil is depleted.

**Illustration 10A–1**
Oil and Gas Accounting

The Shannon Oil Company incurred $2,000,000 in exploration costs for each of 10 oil wells drilled in 2013 in west Texas. Eight of the 10 wells were dry holes.

The accounting treatment of the $20 million in total exploration costs will vary significantly depending on the accounting method used. The summary journal entries using each of the alternative methods are as follows:

| Successful Efforts | | Full Cost | |
|---|---|---|---|
| Oil deposit .................. | 4,000,000 | Oil deposit...... | 20,000,000 |
| Exploration expense .... | 16,000,000 | Cash ........... | 20,000,000 |
| Cash......................... | 20,000,000 | | |

In 1977 the FASB attempted to establish uniformity in the accounting treatment of oil and gas exploration costs. A standard was issued requiring all companies to use the successful efforts method.[32]

This Standard met with criticism from the oil and gas companies that were required to switch from full cost to successful efforts accounting. These companies felt that the switch would seriously depress their reported income over time. As a result, they argued, their ability to raise capital in the securities markets would be inhibited, which would result in a cutback of new exploration. The fear that the standard would cause domestic companies to significantly reduce oil and gas exploration and thus increase our dependence on foreign oil was compelling to the U.S. Congress, the SEC, and the Department of Energy.

Extensive pressure from Congress, the SEC, and affected companies forced the FASB to rescind the Standard. Presently, oil and gas companies can use either the successful efforts or full-cost method to account for oil and gas exploration costs. Of course, the method used must be disclosed. For example, Illustration 10A–2 shows how **Chevron Corp.** disclosed its use of the successful efforts method in a note to recent financial statements. ●

Many feared that the requirement to switch to successful efforts accounting would cause a significant cutback in the exploration for new oil and gas in the United States.

**Properties, Plant and Equipment**
The successful efforts method is used for crude oil and gas exploration and production activities.

**Illustration 10A–2**
Oil and Gas Accounting Disclosure—Chevron Corp.

Real World Financials

[32]The rescinded standard was "Financial Accounting and Reporting by Oil and Gas Producing Companies," *Statement of Financial Accounting Standards No. 19* (Stamford, Conn.: FASB, 1977). Authoritative guidance on this topic can now be found at FASB ASC 932: Extractive Activities–Oil and Gas.

# Questions For Review of Key Topics

**Q 10–1** Explain the difference between tangible and intangible long-lived, revenue-producing assets.

**Q 10–2** What is included in the original cost of property, plant, and equipment and intangible assets acquired in an exchange transaction?

**Q 10–3** Identify the costs associated with the initial valuation of a developed natural resource.

**Q 10–4** Briefly summarize the accounting treatment for intangible assets, explaining the difference between purchased and internally developed intangible assets.

**Q 10–5** What is goodwill and how is it measured?

**Q 10–6** Explain the method generally used to allocate the cost of a lump-sum purchase to the individual assets acquired.

**Q 10–7** When an asset is acquired and a note payable is assumed, explain how acquisition cost of the asset is determined when the interest rate for the note is less than the current market rate for similar notes.

**Q 10–8** Explain how assets acquired in exchange for equity securities are valued.

**Q 10–9** Explain how property, plant, and equipment and intangible assets acquired through donation are valued.

Q 10–10 When an item of property, plant, and equipment is disposed of, how is gain or loss on disposal computed?

Q 10–11 What is the basic principle for valuing property, plant, and equipment and intangible assets acquired in exchange for other nonmonetary assets?

Q 10–12 Identify the two exceptions to valuing property, plant, and equipment and intangible assets acquired in nonmonetary exchanges at the fair value of the asset(s) given up.

Q 10–13 In what situations is interest capitalized?

Q 10–14 Define average accumulated expenditures and explain how it is computed.

Q 10–15 Explain the difference between the specific interest method and the weighted-average method in determining the amount of interest to be capitalized.

Q 10–16 Define R&D according to U.S. GAAP.

Q 10–17 Explain the accounting treatment of equipment acquired for use in R&D projects.

Q 10–18 Explain the accounting treatment of costs incurred to develop computer software.

Q 10–19 Explain the difference in the accounting treatment of the cost of developed technology and the cost of in-process R&D in an acquisition.

**IFRS** Q 10–20 Identify any differences between U.S. GAAP and International Financial Reporting Standards in the treatment of research and development expenditures.

**IFRS** Q 10–21 Identify any differences between U.S. GAAP and International Financial Reporting Standards in the treatment of software development costs.

**IFRS** Q 10–22 Identify any differences between U.S. GAAP and International Financial Reporting Standards in accounting for government grants received.

Q 10–23 (Based on Appendix 10) Explain the difference between the successful efforts and the full-cost methods of accounting for oil and gas exploration costs.

## Brief Exercises

**BE 10–1**
Acquisition cost; machine
● LO10–1

Beaverton Lumber purchased a milling machine for $35,000. In addition to the purchase price, Beaverton made the following expenditures: freight, $1,500; installation, $3,000; testing, $2,000; personal property tax on the machine for the first year, $500. What is the initial cost of the machine?

**BE 10–2**
Acquisition cost; land and building
● LO10–1

Fullerton Waste Management purchased land and a warehouse for $600,000. In addition to the purchase price, Fullerton made the following expenditures related to the acquisition: broker's commission, $30,000; title insurance, $3,000; miscellaneous closing costs, $6,000. The warehouse was immediately demolished at a cost of $18,000 in anticipation of the building of a new warehouse. Determine the amounts Fullerton should capitalize as the cost of the land and the building.

**BE 10–3**
Lump-sum acquisition
● LO10–2

Refer to the situation described in BE 10–2. Assume that Fullerton decides to use the warehouse rather than demolish it. An independent appraisal estimates the fair values of the land and warehouse at $420,000 and $280,000, respectively. Determine the amounts Fullerton should capitalize as the cost of the land and the building.

**BE 10–4**
Cost of a natural resource
● LO10–1

Smithson Mining operates a silver mine in Nevada. Acquisition, exploration, and development costs totaled $5.6 million. After the silver is extracted in approximately five years, Smithson is obligated to restore the land to its original condition, including constructing a wildlife preserve. The company's controller has provided the following three cash flow possibilities for the restoration costs: (1) $500,000, 20% probability; (2) $550,000, 45% probability; and (3) $650,000, 35% probability. The company's credit-adjusted, risk-free rate of interest is 6%. What is the initial cost of the silver mine?

**BE 10–5**
Cost of a natural resource
● LO10–1

Refer to the situation described in BE 10–4. What is the carrying value of the asset retirement liability at the end of one year? Assuming that the actual restoration costs incurred after extraction is completed are $596,000, what amount of gain or loss will Smithson recognize on retirement of the liability?

**BE 10–6**
Goodwill
● LO10–1

Pro-tech Software acquired all of the outstanding stock of Reliable Software for $14 million. The book value of Reliable's net assets (assets minus liabilities) was $8.3 million. The fair values of Reliable's assets and liabilities equaled their book values with the exception of certain intangible assets whose fair values exceeded book values by $2.5 million. Calculate the amount paid for goodwill.

**BE 10–7**
Acquisition cost; noninterest-bearing note
● LO10–3

On June 30, 2013, Kimberly Farms purchased custom-made harvesting machinery from a local producer. In payment, Kimberly signed a noninterest-bearing note requiring the payment of $60,000 in two years. The fair value of the machinery is not known, but an 8% interest rate properly reflects the time value of money for this type of loan agreement. At what amount will Kimberly initially value the machinery? How much interest expense will Kimberly recognize in its income statement for this note for the year ended December 31, 2013?

**BE 10–8**
Acquisition cost; issuance of equity securities
● LO10–4

Shackelford Corporation acquired a patent from its founder, Jim Shackelford, in exchange for 50,000 shares of the company's nopar common stock. On the date of the exchange, the common stock had a fair value of $22 per share. Determine the cost of the patent.

**BE 10–9**
Fixed-asset turnover ratio; solve for unknown
● LO10–5

The balance sheets of Pinewood Resorts reported net fixed assets of $740,000 and $940,000 at the end of 2012 and 2013, respectively. The fixed-asset turnover ratio for 2013 was 3.25. Calculate Pinewood's net sales for 2013.

**BE 10–10**
Disposal of property, plant, and equipment
● LO10–6

Lawler Clothing sold manufacturing equipment for $16,000. Lawler originally purchased the equipment for $80,000, and depreciation through the date of sale totaled $71,000. What was the gain or loss on the sale of the equipment?

**BE 10–11**
Nonmonetary exchange
● LO10–6

Calaveras Tire exchanged machinery for two pickup trucks. The book value and fair value of the machinery were $20,000 (original cost of $65,000 less accumulated depreciation of $45,000) and $17,000, respectively. To equalize fair values, Calaveras paid $8,000 in cash. At what amount will Calaveras value the pickup trucks? How much gain or loss will the company recognize on the exchange? Assume the exchange has commercial substance.

**BE 10–12**
Nonmonetary exchange
● LO10–6

Refer to the situation described in BE 10–11. Answer the questions assuming that the fair value of the machinery was $24,000, instead of $17,000.

**BE 10–13**
Nonmonetary exchange
● LO10–6

Refer to the situation described in BE 10–12. Answer the questions assuming that the exchange lacks commercial substance.

**BE 10–14**
Interest capitalization
● LO10–7

A company constructs a building for its own use. Construction began on January 1 and ended on December 30. The expenditures for construction were as follows: January 1, $500,000; March 31, $600,000; June 30, $400,000; October 30, $600,000. To help finance construction, the company arranged a 7% construction loan on January 1 for $700,000. The company's other borrowings, outstanding for the whole year, consisted of a $3 million loan and a $5 million note with interest rates of 8% and 6%, respectively. Assuming the company uses the *specific interest method*, calculate the amount of interest capitalized for the year.

**BE 10–15**
Interest capitalization
● LO10–7

Refer to the situation described in BE 10–14. Assuming the company uses the *weighted-average method*, calculate the amount of interest capitalized for the year.

**BE 10–16**
Research and development
● LO10–8

Maxtor Technology incurred the following costs during the year related to the creation of a new type of personal computer monitor:

| | |
|---|---:|
| Salaries | $220,000 |
| Depreciation on R&D facilities and equipment | 125,000 |
| Utilities and other direct costs incurred for the R&D facilities | 66,000 |
| Patent filing and related legal costs | 22,000 |
| Payment to another company for performing a portion of the development work | 120,000 |
| Costs of adapting the new monitor for the specific needs of a customer | 80,000 |

What amount should Maxtor report as research and development expense in its income statement?

## Exercises

An alternate exercise and problem set is available on the text website: www.mhhe.com/spiceland7e

**E 10–1**
Acquisition costs;
land and building
● LO10–1

On March 1, 2013, Beldon Corporation purchased land as a factory site for $60,000. An old building on the property was demolished, and construction began on a new building that was completed on December 15, 2013. Costs incurred during this period are listed below:

| | |
|---|---:|
| Demolition of old building | $ 4,000 |
| Architect's fees (for new building) | 12,000 |
| Legal fees for title investigation of land | 2,000 |
| Property taxes on land (for period beginning March 1, 2013) | 3,000 |
| Construction costs | 500,000 |
| Interest on construction loan | 5,000 |

Salvaged materials resulting from the demolition of the old building were sold for $2,000.

**Required:**
Determine the amounts that Beldon should capitalize as the cost of the land and the new building.

**E 10–2**
Acquisition cost;
machinery
● LO10–1

Oaktree Company purchased a new machine and made the following expenditures:

| | |
|---|---:|
| Purchase price | $45,000 |
| Sales tax | 2,200 |
| Freight charges for shipment of machine | 700 |
| Insurance on the machine for the first year | 900 |
| Installation of machine | 1,000 |

The machine, including sales tax, was purchased on open account, with payment due in 30 days. The other expenditures listed above were paid in cash.

**Required:**
Prepare the necessary journal entries to record the above expenditures.

**E 10–3**
Acquisition
costs; lump-sum
acquisition
● LO10–1,
   LO10–2

Semtech Manufacturing purchased land and building for $4 million. In addition to the purchase price, Semtech made the following expenditures in connection with the purchase of the land and building:

| | |
|---|---:|
| Title insurance | $16,000 |
| Legal fees for drawing the contract | 5,000 |
| Pro-rated property taxes for the period | |
|    after acquisition | 36,000 |
| State transfer fees | 4,000 |

An independent appraisal estimated the fair values of the land and building, if purchased separately, at $3.3 and $1.1 million, respectively. Shortly after acquisition, Semtech spent $82,000 to construct a parking lot and $40,000 for landscaping.

**Required:**
1. Determine the initial valuation of each asset Semtech acquired in these transactions.
2. Repeat requirement 1, assuming that immediately after acquisition, Semtech demolished the building. Demolition costs were $250,000 and the salvaged materials were sold for $6,000. In addition, Semtech spent $86,000 clearing and grading the land in preparation for the construction of a new building.

**E 10–4**
Cost of a natural
resource
● LO10–1

Jackpot Mining Company operates a copper mine in central Montana. The company paid $1,000,000 in 2013 for the mining site and spent an additional $600,000 to prepare the mine for extraction of the copper. After the copper is extracted in approximately four years, the company is required to restore the land to its original condition, including repaving of roads and replacing a greenbelt. The company has provided the following three cash flow possibilities for the restoration costs:

| | Cash Outflow | Probability |
|---|---|---|
| 1 | $300,000 | 25% |
| 2 | 400,000 | 40% |
| 3 | 600,000 | 35% |

To aid extraction, Jackpot purchased some new equipment on July 1, 2013, for $120,000. After the copper is removed from this mine, the equipment will be sold. The credit-adjusted, risk-free rate of interest is 10%.

**Required:**
1. Determine the cost of the copper mine.
2. Prepare the journal entries to record the acquisition costs of the mine and the purchase of equipment.

**E 10–5**
**Intangibles**
● **LO10–1**

Freitas Corporation was organized early in 2013. The following expenditures were made during the first few months of the year:

| | |
|---|---|
| Attorneys' fees in connection with the organization of the corporation | $ 12,000 |
| State filing fees and other incorporation costs | 3,000 |
| Purchase of a patent | 20,000 |
| Legal and other fees for transfer of the patent | 2,000 |
| Purchase of furniture | 30,000 |
| Pre-opening salaries | 40,000 |
| Total | $107,000 |

**Required:**
Prepare a summary journal entry to record the $107,000 in cash expenditures.

**E 10–6**
**Goodwill**
● **LO10–1**

On March 31, 2013, Wolfson Corporation acquired all of the outstanding common stock of Barney Corporation for $17,000,000 in cash. The book values and fair values of Barney's assets and liabilities were as follows:

| | Book Value | Fair Value |
|---|---|---|
| Current assets | $ 6,000,000 | $ 7,500,000 |
| Property, plant, and equipment | 11,000,000 | 14,000,000 |
| Other assets | 1,000,000 | 1,500,000 |
| Current liabilities | 4,000,000 | 4,000,000 |
| Long-term liabilities | 6,000,000 | 5,500,000 |

**Required:**
Calculate the amount paid for goodwill.

**E 10–7**
**Goodwill**
● **LO10–1**

Johnson Corporation acquired all of the outstanding common stock of Smith Corporation for $11,000,000 in cash. The book value of Smith's net assets (assets minus liabilities) was $7,800,000. The fair values of all of Smith's assets and liabilities were equal to their book values with the following exceptions:

| | Book Value | Fair Value |
|---|---|---|
| Receivables | $1,300,000 | $1,100,000 |
| Property, plant, and equipment | 8,000,000 | 9,400,000 |
| Intangible assets | 200,000 | 1,200,000 |

**Required:**
Calculate the amount paid for goodwill.

**E 10–8**
**Lump-sum acquisition**
● **LO10–2**

Pinewood Company purchased two buildings on four acres of land. The lump-sum purchase price was $900,000. According to independent appraisals, the fair values were $450,000 (building A) and $250,000 (building B) for the buildings and $300,000 for the land.

**Required:**
Determine the initial valuation of the buildings and the land.

**E 10–9**
**Acquisition cost; noninterest-bearing note**
● **LO10–3**

On January 1, 2013, Byner Company purchased a used tractor. Byner paid $5,000 down and signed a noninterest-bearing note requiring $25,000 to be paid on December 31, 2015. The fair value of the tractor is not determinable. An interest rate of 10% properly reflects the time value of money for this type of loan agreement. The company's fiscal year-end is December 31.

**Required:**
1. Prepare the journal entry to record the acquisition of the tractor. Round computations to the nearest dollar.
2. How much interest expense will the company include in its 2013 and 2014 income statements for this note?
3. What is the amount of the liability the company will report in its 2013 and 2014 balance sheets for this note?

**E 10–10**
Acquisition costs; noninterest-bearing note
● LO10–1, LO10–3

Teradene Corporation purchased land as a factory site and contracted with Maxtor Construction to construct a factory. Teradene made the following expenditures related to the acquisition of the land, building, and machinery to equip the factory:

| | |
|---|---:|
| Purchase price of the land | $1,200,000 |
| Demolition and removal of old building | 80,000 |
| Clearing and grading the land before construction | 150,000 |
| Various closing costs in connection with acquiring the land | 42,000 |
| Architect's fee for the plans for the new building | 50,000 |
| Payments to Maxtor for building construction | 3,250,000 |
| Machinery purchased | 860,000 |
| Freight charges on machinery | 32,000 |
| Trees, plants, and other landscaping | 45,000 |
| Installation of a sprinkler system for the landscaping | 5,000 |
| Cost to build special platforms and install wiring for the machinery | 12,000 |
| Cost of trial runs to ensure proper installation of the machinery | 7,000 |
| Fire and theft insurance on the factory for the first year of use | 24,000 |

In addition to the above expenditures, Teradene purchased four forklifts from **Caterpillar**. In payment, Teradene paid $16,000 cash and signed a noninterest-bearing note requiring the payment of $70,000 in one year. An interest rate of 7% properly reflects the time value of money for this type of loan.

**Required:**
Determine the initial valuation of each of the assets Teradene acquired in the above transactions.

**E 10–11**
Acquisition cost; issuance of equity securities and donation
● LO10–4, LO10–9

 IFRS

On February 1, 2013, the Xilon Corporation issued 50,000 shares of its nopar common stock in exchange for five acres of land located in the city of Monrovia. On the date of the acquisition, Xilon's common stock had a fair value of $18 per share. An office building was constructed on the site by an independent contractor. The building was completed on November 2, 2013, at a cost of $6,000,000. Xilon paid $4,000,000 in cash and the remainder was paid by the city of Monrovia.

**Required:**
1. Prepare the journal entries to record the acquisition of the land and the building.
2. Assuming that Xilon prepares its financial statements according to International Financial Reporting Standards, explain the alternatives the company has for recording the acquisition of the office building.

**E 10–12**
Acquisition cost; acquisition by donation; government grant
● LO10–9

 IFRS

Cranston LTD. prepares its financial statements according to International Financial Reporting Standards. In October 2013, the company received a $2 million government grant. The grant represents 20% of the total cost of equipment that will be used to improve the roads in the local area. Cranston recorded the grant and the purchase of the equipment as follows:

| | | |
|---|---:|---:|
| Cash.................................. | 2,000,000 | |
| Revenue......................... | | 2,000,000 |
| Equipment........................ | 10,000,000 | |
| Cash............................. | | 10,000,000 |

**Required:**
1. Explain the alternative accounting treatments available to Cranston for accounting for this government grant.
2. Prepare any necessary correcting entries under each of the alternatives described in requirement 1.

**E 10–13**
Fixed-asset turnover ratio; Plantronics
● LO10–5

Real World Financials

**Plantronics, Inc.**, a leading worldwide manufacturer of communication and telephone headset systems, reported the following information in its 2011 financial statements ($ in thousands):

| | 2011 | 2010 |
|---|---:|---:|
| **Balance sheets** | | |
| Property, plant, and equipment (net) | $ 70,622 | $65,700 |
| **Income statement** | | |
| Net sales for 2011 | $683,602 | |

**Required:**
1. Calculate the company's 2011 fixed-asset turnover ratio.
2. How would you interpret this ratio?

**E 10–14**
Disposal of property, plant, and equipment
● LO10–6

Funseth Farms Inc. purchased a tractor in 2010 at a cost of $30,000. The tractor was sold for $3,000 in 2013. Depreciation recorded through the disposal date totaled $26,000.

**Required:**
1. Prepare the journal entry to record the sale.
2. Assuming that the tractor was sold for $10,000, prepare the journal entry to record the sale.

**E 10–15**
Nonmonetary exchange
● LO10–6

Cedric Company recently traded in an older model computer for a new model. The old model's book value was $180,000 (original cost of $400,000 less $220,000 in accumulated depreciation) and its fair value was $200,000. Cedric paid $60,000 to complete the exchange which has commercial substance.

**Required:**
Prepare the journal entry to record the exchange.

**E 10–16**
Nonmonetary exchange
● LO10–6

[This is a variation of the previous exercise.]

**Required:**
Assume the same facts as in Exercise 10–15, except that the fair value of the old equipment is $170,000. Prepare the journal entry to record the exchange.

**E 10–17**
Nonmonetary exchange
● LO10–6

The Bronco Corporation exchanged land for equipment. The land had a book value of $120,000 and a fair value of $150,000. Bronco paid the owner of the equipment $10,000 to complete the exchange which has commercial substance.

**Required:**
1. What is the fair value of the equipment?
2. Prepare the journal entry to record the exchange.

**E 10–18**
Nonmonetary exchange
● LO10–6

[This is a variation of the previous exercise.]

**Required:**
Assume the same facts as in Exercise 10–17 except that Bronco *received* $10,000 from the owner of the equipment to complete the exchange.
1. What is the fair value of the equipment?
2. Prepare the journal entry to record the exchange.

**E 10–19**
Nonmonetary exchange
● LO10–6

The Tinsley Company exchanged land that it had been holding for future plant expansion for a more suitable parcel located farther from residential areas. Tinsley carried the land at its original cost of $30,000. According to an independent appraisal, the land currently is worth $72,000. Tinsley gave $14,000 in cash to complete the transaction.

**Required:**
1. What is the fair value of the new parcel of land received by Tinsley?
2. Prepare the journal entry to record the exchange assuming the exchange has commercial substance.
3. Prepare the journal entry to record the exchange assuming the exchange lacks commercial substance.

**E 10–20**
Acquisition cost; multiple methods
● LO10–1, LO10–3, LO10–4, LO10–6

Connors Corporation acquired manufacturing equipment for use in its assembly line. Below are four *independent* situations relating to the acquisition of the equipment.
1. The equipment was purchased on account for $25,000. Credit terms were 2/10, n/30. Payment was made within the discount period and the company records the purchases of equipment net of discounts.
2. Connors gave the seller a noninterest-bearing note. The note required payment of $27,000 one year from date of purchase. The fair value of the equipment is not determinable. An interest rate of 10% properly reflects the time value of money in this situation.
3. Connors traded in old equipment that had a book value of $6,000 (original cost of $14,000 and accumulated depreciation of $8,000) and paid cash of $22,000. The old equipment had a fair value of $2,500 on the date of the exchange. The exchange has commercial substance.
4. Connors issued 1,000 shares of its nopar common stock in exchange for the equipment. The market value of the common stock was not determinable. The equipment could have been purchased for $24,000 in cash.

**Required:**
For each of the above situations, prepare the journal entry required to record the acquisition of the equipment. Round computations to the nearest dollar.

**E 10–21**
FASB codification research
● LO10–6

The *FASB Accounting Standards Codification* represents the single source of authoritative U.S. generally accepted accounting principles.

**Required:**
1. Obtain the relevant authoritative literature on nonmonetary exchanges using the FASB's Codification Research System at the FASB website (**www.fasb.org**). Identify the Codification topic number for nonmonetary transactions.
2. What are the specific citations that list the disclosure requirements for nonmonetary transactions?
3. Describe the disclosure requirements.

**E 10–22**
FASB codification research
● LO10–1,
  LO10–6,
  LO10–7,
  LO10–8

Access the FASB's Codification Research System at the FASB website (**www.fasb.org**). Determine the specific citation for each of the following items:
1. The disclosure requirements in the notes to the financial statements for depreciation on property, plant, and equipment.
2. The criteria for determining commercial substance in a nonmonetary exchange.
3. The disclosure requirements for interest capitalization.
4. The elements of costs to be included as R&D activities.

**E 10–23**
Interest capitalization
● LO10–7

On January 1, 2013, the Marjlee Company began construction of an office building to be used as its corporate headquarters. The building was completed early in 2014. Construction expenditures for 2013, which were incurred evenly throughout the year, totaled $6,000,000. Marjlee had the following debt obligations which were outstanding during all of 2013:

| | |
|---|---|
| Construction loan, 10% | $1,500,000 |
| Long-term note, 9% | 2,000,000 |
| Long-term note, 6% | 4,000,000 |

**Required:**
Calculate the amount of interest capitalized in 2013 for the building using the specific interest method.

**E 10–24**
Interest capitalization
● LO10–7

On January 1, 2013, the Shagri Company began construction on a new manufacturing facility for its own use. The building was completed in 2014. The only interest-bearing debt the company had outstanding during 2013 was long-term bonds with a book value of $10,000,000 and an effective interest rate of 8%. Construction expenditures incurred during 2013 were as follows:

| | |
|---|---|
| January 1 | $500,000 |
| March 1 | 600,000 |
| July 31 | 480,000 |
| September 30 | 600,000 |
| December 31 | 300,000 |

**Required:**
Calculate the amount of interest capitalized for 2013.

**E 10–25**
Interest capitalization
● LO10–7

On January 1, 2013, the Highlands Company began construction on a new manufacturing facility for its own use. The building was completed in 2014. The company borrowed $1,500,000 at 8% on January 1 to help finance the construction. In addition to the construction loan, Highlands had the following debt outstanding throughout 2013:

$5,000,000, 12% bonds
$3,000,000, 8% long-term note

Construction expenditures incurred during 2013 were as follows:

| | |
|---|---|
| January 1 | $ 600,000 |
| March 31 | 1,200,000 |
| June 30 | 800,000 |
| September 30 | 600,000 |
| December 31 | 400,000 |

**Required:**
Calculate the amount of interest capitalized for 2013 using the specific interest method.

**E 10–26**
Research and development
● LO10–8

In 2013, Space Technology Company modified its model Z2 satellite to incorporate a new communication device. The company made the following expenditures:

| | |
|---|---|
| Basic research to develop the technology | $2,000,000 |
| Engineering design work | 680,000 |
| Development of a prototype device | 300,000 |
| Acquisition of equipment | 60,000 |
| Testing and modification of the prototype | 200,000 |
| Legal and other fees for patent application on the new communication system | 40,000 |
| Legal fees for successful defense of the new patent | 20,000 |
| Total | $3,300,000 |

The equipment will be used on this and other research projects. Depreciation on the equipment for 2013 is $10,000.

During your year-end review of the accounts related to intangibles, you discover that the company has capitalized all of the above as costs of the patent. Management contends that the device simply represents an improvement of the existing communication system of the satellite and, therefore, should be capitalized.

**Required:**
Prepare correcting entries that reflect the appropriate treatment of the expenditures.

**E 10–27**
Research and development
● LO10–8

Delaware Company incurred the following research and development costs during 2013:

| | |
|---|---|
| Salaries and wages for lab research | $  400,000 |
| Materials used in R&D projects | 200,000 |
| Purchase of equipment | 900,000 |
| Fees paid to outsiders for R&D projects | 320,000 |
| Patent filing and legal costs for a developed product | 65,000 |
| Salaries, wages, and supplies for R&D work performed for another company under a contract | 350,000 |
| Total | $2,235,000 |

The equipment has a seven-year life and will be used for a number of research projects. Depreciation for 2013 is $120,000.

**Required:**
Calculate the amount of research and development expense that Delaware should report in its 2013 income statement.

**E 10–28**
IFRS; research and development
● LO10–8,
  LO10–9

🌐 **IFRS**

Janson Pharmaceuticals incurred the following costs in 2013 related to a new cancer drug:

| | |
|---|---|
| Research for new formulas | $2,425,000 |
| Development of a new formula | 1,600,000 |
| Legal and filing fees for a patent for the new formula | 60,000 |
| Total | $4,085,000 |

The development costs were incurred after technological and commercial feasibility was established and after the future economic benefits were deemed probable. The project was successfully completed and the new drug was patented before the end of the 2013 fiscal year.

**Required:**
1. Calculate the amount of research and development expense Janson should report in its 2013 income statement related to this project.
2. Repeat requirement 1 assuming that Janson prepares its financial statements according to International Financial Reporting Standards.

**E 10–29**
Concepts;
terminology
● LO10–1,
  LO10–4,
  LO10–6,
  LO10–7

Listed below are several terms and phrases associated with property, plant, and equipment and intangible assets. Pair each item from List A with the item from List B (by letter) that is most appropriately associated with it.

| List A | List B |
|---|---|
| _____ 1. Depreciation | a. Exclusive right to display a word, a symbol, or an emblem. |
| _____ 2. Depletion | b. Exclusive right to benefit from a creative work. |
| _____ 3. Amortization | c. Operational assets that represent rights. |
| _____ 4. Average accumulated expenditures | d. The allocation of cost for natural resources. |
| | e. Purchase price less fair value of net identifiable assets. |

(continued)

(concluded)

| | |
|---|---|
| _____ 5. Revenue—donation of asset | f. The allocation of cost for plant and equipment. |
| _____ 6. Nonmonetary exchange | g. Approximation of average amount of debt if all construction |
| _____ 7. Natural resources |     funds were borrowed. |
| _____ 8. Intangible assets | h. Account credited when assets are donated to a corporation. |
| _____ 9. Copyright | i. The allocation of cost for intangible assets. |
| _____10. Trademark | j. Basic principle is to value assets acquired using fair value of |
| _____11. Goodwill |     assets given. |
| | k. Wasting assets. |

**E 10–30**
**Software development costs**
● **LO10–8**

Early in 2013, the Excalibur Company began developing a new software package to be marketed. The project was completed in December 2013 at a cost of $6 million. Of this amount, $4 million was spent before technological feasibility was established. Excalibur expects a useful life of five years for the new product with total revenues of $10 million. During 2014, revenue of $3 million was recognized.

**Required:**
1. Prepare a journal entry to record the 2013 development costs.
2. Calculate the required amortization for 2014.
3. At what amount should the computer software costs be reported in the December 31, 2014, balance sheet?

**E 10–31**
**Full-cost and successful efforts methods compared**
● **Appendix**

The Manguino Oil Company incurred exploration costs in 2013 searching and drilling for oil as follows:

| | |
|---|---:|
| Well 101 | $ 50,000 |
| Well 102 | 60,000 |
| Well 103 | 80,000 |
| Wells 104–108 | 260,000 |
| Total | $450,000 |

It was determined that Wells 104–108 were dry holes and were abandoned. Wells 101, 102, and 103 were determined to have sufficient oil reserves to be commercially successful.

**Required:**
1. Prepare a summary journal entry to record the indicated costs assuming that the company uses the full-cost method of accounting for exploration costs. All of the exploration costs were paid in cash.
2. Prepare a summary journal entry to record the indicated costs assuming that the company uses the successful efforts method of accounting for exploration costs. All of the exploration costs were paid in cash.

# CPA and CMA Review Questions

**CPA Exam Questions**

The following questions are adapted from a variety of sources including questions developed by the AICPA Board of Examiners and those used in the Kaplan CPA Review Course to study property, plant, and equipment and intangible assets while preparing for the CPA examination. Determine the response that best completes the statements or questions.

● **LO10–1**

1. Simons Company purchased land to build a new factory. The following expenditures were made in conjunction with the land purchase:

   • Purchase price of the land, $150,000
   • Real estate commissions of 7% of the purchase price
   • Land survey, $5,000
   • Back taxes, $5,000

   What is the initial value of the land?
   a. $160,000
   b. $160,500
   c. $165,500
   d. $170,500

● **LO10–2**

2. During 2013, Burr Co. made the following expenditures related to the acquisition of land and the construction of a building:

| | |
|---|---:|
| Purchase price of land | $ 60,000 |
| Legal fees for contracts to purchase land | 2,000 |
| Architects' fees | 8,000 |
| Demolition of old building on site | 5,000 |
| Sale of scrap from old building | 3,000 |
| Construction cost of new building (fully completed) | 350,000 |

What amounts should be recorded as the initial values of the land and the building?

| | Land | Building |
|---|---|---|
| a. | $60,000 | $360,000 |
| b. | $62,000 | $360,000 |
| c. | $64,000 | $358,000 |
| d. | $65,000 | $362,000 |

● LO10–3

3. On December 31, 2013, Bart Inc. purchased a machine from Fell Corp. in exchange for a noninterest-bearing note requiring eight payments of $20,000. The first payment was made on December 31, 2013, and the remaining seven payments are due annually on each December 31, beginning in 2014. At the date of the transaction, the prevailing rate of interest for this type of note was 11%. Present value factors are as follows:

| Period | Present value of ordinary annuity of 1 at 11% | Present value of an annuity due of 1 at 11% |
|---|---|---|
| 7 | 4.712 | 5.231 |
| 8 | 5.146 | 5.712 |

The initial value of the machine is
a. $ 94,240
b. $102,920
c. $104,620
d. $114,240

● LO10–6

4. Amble Inc. exchanged a truck with a book value of $12,000 and a fair value of $20,000 for a truck and $5,000 cash. The exchange has commercial substance. At what amount should Amble record the truck received?
a. $12,000
b. $15,000
c. $20,000
d. $25,000

● LO10–7

5. Dahl Corporation has just built a machine to produce car doors. Dahl had to build this machine because it couldn't purchase one that met its specifications. The following are the costs related to the machine's construction and the first month of operations:

- Construction materials, $20,000
- Labor, $9,000 (construction, $3,000; testing, $1,000; operations, $5,000)
- Engineering fees, $5,000
- Utilities, $4,000 (construction, $1,000; testing, $1,000; operations, $2,000)

What is the initial value of the machine?
a. $28,000
b. $29,000
c. $31,000
d. $38,000

● LO10–7

6. Cole Co. began constructing a building for its own use in January 2013. During 2013, Cole incurred interest of $50,000 on specific construction debt, and $20,000 on other borrowings. Interest computed on the weighted-average amount of accumulated expenditures for the building during 2013 was $40,000. What amount of interest should Cole capitalize?
a. $20,000
b. $40,000
c. $50,000
d. $70,000

● LO10–8

7. On December 31, 2012, Bit Co. had capitalized costs for a new computer software product with an economic life of five years. Sales for 2013 were 30 percent of expected total sales of the software. At December 31, 2013,

the software had a fair value equal to 90 percent of the capitalized cost. What percentage of the original capitalized cost should be reported as the net amount in Bit's December 31, 2013, balance sheet?

a. 70%
b. 72%
c. 80%
d. 90%

● LO10–8

8. During the current year, Orr Company incurred the following costs:

| | |
|---|---|
| Research and development services performed by Key Corp. for Orr | $150,000 |
| Design, construction, and testing of preproduction prototypes and models | 200,000 |
| Testing in search for new products or process alternatives | 175,000 |

In its income statement for the current year, what amount should Orr report as research and development expense?

a. $150,000
b. $200,000
c. $350,000
d. $525,000

Beginning in 2011, International Financial Reporting Standards are tested on the CPA exam along with U.S. GAAP. The following questions deal with the application of IFRS to accounting for property, plant, and equipment.

● LO10–9

 IFRS

9. Under IFRS

a. research and development expenditures are expensed in the period incurred.
b. research and development expenditures are capitalized and amortized.
c. development expenditures that meet certain criteria are capitalized and amortized; research expenditures are expensed in the period incurred.
d. research expenditures that meet certain criteria are capitalized and amortized; development expenditures are expensed in the period incurred.

● LO10–9

 IFRS

10. In 2013 Sanford LTD. received a government grant of $100,000 to be used for the purchase of a machine. Sanford prepares its financial statements using IFRS. The grant must be recognized

a. as revenue in 2013.
b. as a reduction in the cost of the machine.
c. as deferred income in the balance sheet and then recognized in the income statement systematically over the asset's useful life.
d. either b or c.

**CMA Exam Questions**

The following questions dealing with property, plant, and equipment and intangible assets are adapted from questions that previously appeared on Certified Management Accountant (CMA) examinations. The CMA designation sponsored by the Institute of Management Accountants (www.imanet.org) provides members with an objective measure of knowledge and competence in the field of management accounting. Determine the response that best completes the statements or questions.

● LO10–1

1. Pearl Corporation acquired manufacturing machinery on January 1 for $9,000. During the year, the machine produced 1,000 units, of which 600 were sold. There was no work-in-process inventory at the beginning or at the end of the year. Installation charges of $300 and delivery charges of $200 were also incurred. The machine is expected to have a useful life of five years with an estimated salvage value of $1,500. Pearl uses the straight-line depreciation method. The original cost of the machinery to be recorded in Pearl's books is

a. $9,500
b. $9,300
c. $9,200
d. $9,000

● LO10–6

Questions 2 and 3 are based on the following information. Harper is contemplating exchanging a machine used in its operations for a similar machine on May 31. Harper will exchange machines with either Austin Corporation or Lubin Company. The data relating to the machines are presented below. Assume that the exchanges would have commercial substance.

| | Harper | Austin | Lubin |
|---|---|---|---|
| Original cost of the machine | $162,500 | $180,000 | $150,000 |
| Accumulated depreciation thru May 31 | 98,500 | 70,000 | 65,000 |
| Fair value at May 31 | 80,000 | 95,000 | 60,000 |

2. If Harper exchanges its used machine and $15,000 cash for Austin's used machine, the gain that Harper should recognize from this transaction for financial reporting purposes would be

    a. $0

    b. $2,526

    c. $15,000

    d. $16,000

3. If Harper exchanges its used machine for Lubin's used machine and also receives $20,000 cash, the gain that Harper should recognize from this transaction for financial reporting purposes would be

    a. $0

    b. $4,000

    c. $16,000

    d. $25,000

# Problems

An alternate exercise and problem set is available on the text website: www.mhhe.com/spiceland7e

**P 10–1**
Acquisition costs
● **LO10–1 through LO10–4**

Tristar Production Company began operations on September 1, 2013. Listed below are a number of transactions that occurred during its first four months of operations.

1. On September 1, the company acquired five acres of land with a building that will be used as a warehouse. Tristar paid $100,000 in cash for the property. According to appraisals, the land had a fair value of $75,000 and the building had a fair value of $45,000.

2. On September 1, Tristar signed a $40,000 noninterest-bearing note to purchase equipment. The $40,000 payment is due on September 1, 2014. Assume that 8% is a reasonable interest rate.

3. On September 15, a truck was donated to the corporation. Similar trucks were selling for $2,500.

4. On September 18, the company paid its lawyer $3,000 for organizing the corporation.

5. On October 10, Tristar purchased machinery for cash. The purchase price was $15,000 and $500 in freight charges also were paid.

6. On December 2, Tristar acquired various items of office equipment. The company was short of cash and could not pay the $5,500 normal cash price. The supplier agreed to accept 200 shares of the company's nopar common stock in exchange for the equipment. The fair value of the stock is not readily determinable.

7. On December 10, the company acquired a tract of land at a cost of $20,000. It paid $2,000 down and signed a 10% note with both principal and interest due in one year. Ten percent is an appropriate rate of interest for this note.

**Required:**
Prepare journal entries to record each of the above transactions.

**P 10–2**
Acquisition costs; land and building
● **LO10–1, LO10–2, LO10–7**

On January 1, 2013, the Blackstone Corporation purchased a tract of land (site number 11) with a building for $600,000. Additionally, Blackstone paid a real estate broker's commission of $36,000, legal fees of $6,000, and title insurance of $18,000. The closing statement indicated that the land value was $500,000 and the building value was $100,000. Shortly after acquisition, the building was razed at a cost of $75,000.

Blackstone entered into a $3,000,000 fixed-price contract with Barnett Builders, Inc., on March 1, 2013, for the construction of an office building on land site 11. The building was completed and occupied on September 30, 2014. Additional construction costs were incurred as follows:

| | |
|---|---|
| Plans, specifications, and blueprints | $12,000 |
| Architects' fees for design and supervision | 95,000 |

To finance the construction cost, Blackstone borrowed $3,000,000 on March 1, 2013. The loan is payable in 10 annual installments of $300,000 plus interest at the rate of 14%. Blackstone's average amounts of accumulated building construction expenditures were as follows:

| | |
|---|---|
| For the period March 1 to December 31, 2013 | $ 900,000 |
| For the period January 1 to September 30, 2014 | 2,300,000 |

**Required:**
1. Prepare a schedule that discloses the individual costs making up the balance in the land account in respect of land site 11 as of September 30, 2014.

2. Prepare a schedule that discloses the individual costs that should be capitalized in the office building account as of September 30, 2014.

*(AICPA adapted)*

**P 10–3**
Acquisition costs
● LO10–1,
LO10–4,
LO10–6

The plant asset and accumulated depreciation accounts of Pell Corporation had the following balances at December 31, 2012:

| | Plant Asset | Accumulated Depreciation |
|---|---|---|
| Land | $ 350,000 | $ — |
| Land improvements | 180,000 | 45,000 |
| Building | 1,500,000 | 350,000 |
| Machinery and equipment | 1,158,000 | 405,000 |
| Automobiles | 150,000 | 112,000 |

Transactions during 2013 were as follows:

a. On January 2, 2013, machinery and equipment were purchased at a total invoice cost of $260,000, which included a $5,500 charge for freight. Installation costs of $27,000 were incurred.

b. On March 31, 2013, a machine purchased for $58,000 in 2009 was sold for $36,500. Depreciation recorded through the date of sale totaled $24,650.

c. On May 1, 2013, expenditures of $50,000 were made to repave parking lots at Pell's plant location. The work was necessitated by damage caused by severe winter weather.

d. On November 1, 2013, Pell acquired a tract of land with an existing building in exchange for 10,000 shares of Pell's common stock that had a market price of $38 per share. Pell paid legal fees and title insurance totaling $23,000. Shortly after acquisition, the building was razed at a cost of $35,000 in anticipation of new building construction in 2014.

e. On December 31, 2013, Pell purchased a new automobile for $15,250 cash and trade-in of an old automobile purchased for $18,000 in 2009. Depreciation on the old automobile recorded through December 31, 2013, totaled $13,500. The fair value of the old automobile was $3,750.

**Required:**
1. Prepare a schedule analyzing the changes in each of the plant assets during 2013, with detailed supporting computations.
2. Prepare a schedule showing the gain or loss from each asset disposal that would be recognized in Pell's income statement for the year ended December 31, 2013.

*(AICPA adapted)*

**P 10–4**
Intangibles
● LO10–1,
LO10–8

The Horstmeyer Corporation commenced operations early in 2013. A number of expenditures were made during 2013 that were debited to one account called *intangible asset*. A recap of the $644,000 balance in this account at the end of 2013 is as follows:

| Date | Transaction | Amount |
|---|---|---|
| 2/3/13 | State incorporation fees and legal costs related to organizing the corporation | $ 7,000 |
| 3/1/13 | Fire insurance premium for three-year period | 6,000 |
| 3/15/13 | Purchased a copyright | 20,000 |
| 4/30/13 | Research and development costs | 40,000 |
| 6/15/13 | Legal fees for filing a patent on a new product resulting from an R&D project | 3,000 |
| 9/30/13 | Legal fee for successful defense of patent developed above | 12,000 |
| 10/13/13 | Entered into a 10-year franchise agreement with franchisor | 40,000 |
| Various | Advertising costs | 16,000 |
| 11/30/13 | Acquired all of the outstanding common stock of Stiltz Corp. | 500,000 |
| | Total | $644,000 |

The total amount paid for the Stiltz Corp. stock was debited to this account. The fair values of Stiltz Corp.'s assets and liabilities on the date of the acquisition were as follows:

| | |
|---|---|
| Receivables | $ 100,000 |
| Equipment | 350,000 |
| Patent | 150,000 |
| Total assets | 600,000 |
| Note payable assumed | (220,000) |
| Fair value of net assets | $ 380,000 |

**Required:**
Prepare the necessary journal entries to clear the intangible asset account and to set up accounts for separate intangible assets, other types of assets, and expenses indicated by the transactions.

**P 10–5**
Acquisition costs;
journal entries
● LO10–1,
   LO10–3,
   LO10–6,
   LO10–8

Consider each of the transactions below. All of the expenditures were made in cash.

1. The Edison Company spent $12,000 during the year for experimental purposes in connection with the development of a new product.

2. In April, the Marshall Company lost a patent infringement suit and paid the plaintiff $7,500.

3. In March, the Cleanway Laundromat bought equipment. Cleanway paid $6,000 down and signed a noninterest-bearing note requiring the payment of $18,000 in nine months. The cash price for this equipment was $23,000.

4. On June 1, the Jamsen Corporation installed a sprinkler system throughout the building at a cost of $28,000.

5. The Mayer Company, plaintiff, paid $12,000 in legal fees in November, in connection with a successful infringement suit on its patent.

6. The Johnson Company traded its old machine with an original cost of $7,400 and a book value of $3,000 plus cash of $8,000 for a new one that had a fair value of $10,000. The exchange has commercial substance.

**Required:**
Prepare journal entries to record each of the above transactions.

**P 10–6**
Nonmonetary
exchange
● LO10–6

Southern Company owns a building that it leases to others. The building's fair value is $1,400,000 and its book value is $800,000 (original cost of $2,000,000 less accumulated depreciation of $1,200,000). Southern exchanges this for a building owned by the Eastern Company. The building's book value on Eastern's books is $950,000 (original cost of $1,600,000 less accumulated depreciation of $650,000). Eastern also gives Southern $140,000 to complete the exchange. The exchange has commercial substance for both companies.

**Required:**
Prepare the journal entries to record the exchange on the books of both Southern and Eastern.

**P 10–7**
Nonmonetary
exchange
● LO10–6

On September 3, 2013, the Robers Company exchanged equipment with Phifer Corporation. The facts of the exchange are as follows:

|  | Robers' Asset | Phifer's Asset |
|---|---|---|
| Original cost | $120,000 | $140,000 |
| Accumulated depreciation | 55,000 | 63,000 |
| Fair value | 75,000 | 70,000 |

**Required:**
Record the exchange for both Robers and Phifer. The exchange has commercial substance for both companies.

**P 10–8**
Nonmonetary
exchange
● LO10–6

**Case A.** Kapono Farms exchanged an old tractor for a newer model. The old tractor had a book value of $12,000 (original cost of $28,000 less accumulated depreciation of $16,000) and a fair value of $9,000. Kapono paid $20,000 cash to complete the exchange. The exchange has commercial substance.

**Required:**
1. What is the amount of gain or loss that Kapono would recognize on the exchange? What is the initial value of the new tractor?

2. Repeat requirement 1 assuming that the fair value of the old tractor is $14,000 instead of $9,000.

**Case B.** Kapono Farms exchanged 100 acres of farmland for similar land. The farmland given had a book value of $500,000 and a fair value of $700,000. Kapono paid $50,000 cash to complete the exchange. The exchange has commercial substance.

**Required:**
1. What is the amount of gain or loss that Kapono would recognize on the exchange? What is the initial value of the new land?

2. Repeat requirement 1 assuming that the fair value of the farmland given is $400,000 instead of $700,000.

3. Repeat requirement 1 assuming that the exchange lacked commercial substance.

**P 10–9**
Interest
capitalization;
specific interest
method
● LO10–7

On January 1, 2013, the Mason Manufacturing Company began construction of a building to be used as its office headquarters. The building was completed on September 30, 2014.
   Expenditures on the project were as follows:

| | |
|---|---|
| January 1, 2013 | $1,000,000 |
| March 1, 2013 | 600,000 |
| June 30, 2013 | 800,000 |
| October 1, 2013 | 600,000 |
| January 31, 2014 | 270,000 |
| April 30, 2014 | 585,000 |
| August 31, 2014 | 900,000 |

On January 1, 2013, the company obtained a $3 million construction loan with a 10% interest rate. The loan was outstanding all of 2013 and 2014. The company's other interest-bearing debt included two long-term notes of $4,000,000 and $6,000,000 with interest rates of 6% and 8%, respectively. Both notes were outstanding during all of 2013 and 2014. Interest is paid annually on all debt. The company's fiscal year-end is December 31.

**Required:**
1. Calculate the amount of interest that Mason should capitalize in 2013 and 2014 using the specific interest method.
2. What is the total cost of the building?
3. Calculate the amount of interest expense that will appear in the 2013 and 2014 income statements.

**P 10–10**
Interest capitalization; weighted-average method
● LO10–7

[This is a variation of the previous problem, modified to focus on the weighted-average interest method.]

**Required:**
Refer to the facts in Problem 10–9 and answer the following questions:
1. Calculate the amount of interest that Mason should capitalize in 2013 and 2014 using the weighted-average method.
2. What is the total cost of the building?
3. Calculate the amount of interest expense that will appear in the 2013 and 2014 income statements.

**P 10–11**
Research and development
● LO10–8

In 2013, Starsearch Corporation began work on three research and development projects. One of the projects was completed and commercial production of the developed product began in December. The company's fiscal year-end is December 31. All of the following 2013 expenditures were included in the R&D expense account:

| | |
|---|---:|
| Salaries and wages for: | |
| Lab research | $  300,000 |
| Design and construction of preproduction prototype | 160,000 |
| Quality control during commercial production | 20,000 |
| Materials and supplies consumed for: | |
| Lab research | 60,000 |
| Construction of preproduction prototype | 30,000 |
| Purchase of equipment | 600,000 |
| Patent filing and legal fees for completed project | 40,000 |
| Payments to others for research | 120,000 |
| Total | $1,330,000 |

$200,000 of equipment was purchased solely for use in one of the projects. After the project is completed, the equipment will be abandoned. The remaining $400,000 in equipment will be used on future R&D projects. The useful life of equipment is five years. Assume that all of the equipment was acquired at the beginning of the year.

**Required:**
Prepare journal entries, reclassifying amounts in R&D expense, to reflect the appropriate treatment of the expenditures.

**P 10–12**
Acquisition costs; lump-sum acquisition; noninterest-bearing note; interest capitalization
● LO10–1, LO10–2, LO10–3, LO10–7

Early in its fiscal year ending December 31, 2013, San Antonio Outfitters finalized plans to expand operations. The first stage was completed on March 28 with the purchase of a tract of land on the outskirts of the city. The land and existing building were purchased for $800,000. San Antonio paid $200,000 and signed a noninterest-bearing note requiring the company to pay the remaining $600,000 on March 28, 2015. An interest rate of 8% properly reflects the time value of money for this type of loan agreement. Title search, insurance, and other closing costs totaling $20,000 were paid at closing.

During April, the old building was demolished at a cost of $70,000, and an additional $50,000 was paid to clear and grade the land. Construction of a new building began on May 1 and was completed on October 29. Construction expenditures were as follows:

| | |
|---|---:|
| May 30 | $1,200,000 |
| July 30 | 1,500,000 |
| September 1 | 900,000 |
| October 1 | 1,800,000 |

San Antonio borrowed $3,000,000 at 8% on May 1 to help finance construction. This loan, plus interest, will be paid in 2014. The company also had the following debt outstanding throughout 2013:

$2,000,000, 9% long-term note payable
$4,000,000, 6% long-term bonds payable

In November, the company purchased 10 identical pieces of equipment and office furniture and fixtures for a lump-sum price of $600,000. The fair values of the equipment and the furniture and fixtures were $455,000 and $245,000, respectively. In December, San Antonio paid a contractor $285,000 for the construction of parking lots and for landscaping.

**Required:**

1. Determine the initial values of the various assets that San Antonio acquired or constructed during 2013. The company uses the specific interest method to determine the amount of interest capitalized on the building construction.

2. How much interest expense will San Antonio report in its 2013 income statement?

# Broaden Your Perspective

**Apply your critical-thinking ability to the knowledge you've gained. These cases will provide you an opportunity to develop your research, analysis, judgment, and communication skills. You also will work with other students, integrate what you've learned, apply it in real world situations, and consider its global and ethical ramifications. This practice will broaden your knowledge and further develop your decision-making abilities.**

**Judgment
Case 10–1**
Acquisition costs
● LO10–1,
  LO10–3,
  LO10–6

A company may acquire property, plant, and equipment and intangible assets for cash, in exchange for a deferred payment contract, by exchanging other assets, or by a combination of these methods.

**Required:**

1. Identify six types of costs that should be capitalized as the cost of a parcel of land. For your answer, assume that the land has an existing building that is to be removed in the immediate future in order that a new building can be constructed on the site.

2. At what amount should a company record an asset acquired in exchange for a deferred payment contract?

3. In general, at what amount should assets received in exchange for other nonmonetary assets be valued? Specifically, at what amount should a company value a new machine acquired by exchanging an older, similar machine and paying cash?

*(AICPA adapted)*

**Research
Case 10–2**
FASB
codification;
locate and
extract relevant
information and
cite authoritative
support for
a financial
reporting issue;
restoration costs;
asset retirement
obligation
● LO10–1

Your client, Hazelton Mining, recently entered into an agreement to obtain the rights to operate a coal mine in West Virginia for $15 million. Hazelton incurred development costs of $6 million in preparing the mine for extraction, which began on July 1, 2013. The contract requires Hazelton to restore the land and surrounding area to its original condition after extraction is complete in three years.

The company controller, Alice Cushing, is not sure how to account for the restoration costs and has asked your advice. Alice is aware of an accounting standard addressing this issue, but is not sure of its provisions. She has narrowed down the possible cash outflows for the restoration costs to four possibilities:

| Cash Outflow | Probability |
|---|---|
| $3 million | 20% |
| 4 million | 30% |
| 5 million | 25% |
| 6 million | 25% |

Alice also informs you that the company's credit-adjusted risk-free interest rate is 9%. Before responding to Alice, you need to research the issue.

**Required:**

1. Obtain the relevant authoritative literature on accounting for asset retirement obligations using the FASB's Codification Research System. You might gain access at the FASB website (www.fasb.org). Explain the basic treatment of asset retirement obligations. What are the specific citations that you would rely on to determine (a) the accounting treatment for an asset retirement obligation and (b) how to measure the obligation?

2. Determine the capitalized cost of the coal mine.

3. Prepare a summary journal entry to record the acquisition costs of the mine.

4. How much accretion expense will the company record in its income statement for the 2013 fiscal year, related to this transaction? What are the specific citations from the FASB's Codification Research System that address (a) the calculation of accretion expense and (b) the classification of accretion expense in the income statement?

5. Explain to Alice how Hazelton would account for the restoration if the restoration costs differed from the recorded liability in three years. By way of explanation, prepare the journal entry to record the payment of the retirement obligation in three years assuming that the actual restoration costs were $4.7 million.

6. Describe to Alice the necessary disclosure requirements for the obligation. What is the specific citation from the FASB's Codification Research System that contains these disclosure requirements?

**Judgment Case 10–3**
Self-constructed assets
● LO10–7

Chilton Peripherals manufactures printers, scanners, and other computer peripheral equipment. In the past, the company purchased equipment used in manufacturing from an outside vendor. In March 2013, Chilton decided to design and build equipment to replace some obsolete equipment. A section of the manufacturing plant was set aside to develop and produce the equipment. Additional personnel were hired for the project. The equipment was completed and ready for use in September.

**Required:**

1. In general, what costs should be capitalized for a self-constructed asset?

2. Discuss two alternatives for the inclusion of overhead costs in the cost of the equipment constructed by Chilton. Which alternative is generally accepted for financial reporting purposes?

3. Under what circumstance(s) would interest be included in the cost of the equipment?

**Judgment Case 10–4**
Interest capitalization
● LO10–7

GAAP provides guidelines for the inclusion of interest in the initial cost of a self-constructed asset.

**Required:**

1. What assets qualify for interest capitalization? What assets do not qualify for interest capitalization?

2. Over what period should interest be capitalized?

3. Explain average accumulated expenditures.

4. Explain the two methods that could be used to determine the appropriate interest rate(s) to be used in capitalizing interest.

5. Describe the three steps used to determine the amount of interest capitalized during a reporting period.

**Research Case 10–5**
Goodwill
● LO10–1

Accounting for acquired goodwill has been a controversial issue for many years. In the United States, the amount of acquired goodwill is capitalized and not amortized. Globally, the treatment of goodwill varies significantly, with some countries not recognizing goodwill as an asset. Professors Johnson and Petrone, in "Is Goodwill an Asset?" discuss this issue.

**Required:**

1. In your library or from some other source, locate the indicated article in *Accounting Horizons,* September 1998.

2. Does goodwill meet the FASB's definition of an asset?

3. What are the key concerns of those that believe goodwill is not an asset?

**Real World Case 10–6**
Property, plant, and equipment; intangibles; Saks
● LO10–1

*Real World Financials*

Saks Incorporated, a major U.S. retailer, reported the following amounts in the asset section of its balance sheets for the years ended January 29, 2011, and January 30, 2010:

|  | ($ in thousands) | |
| --- | --- | --- |
|  | **January 29, 2011** | **January 30, 2010** |
| Property and equipment, net | $890,364 | $956,082 |

In addition, the 2011 statement of cash flows reported the following items ($ in thousands):

| | |
| --- | --- |
| Depreciation | $118,696 |
| Additions to property and equipment | 55,721 |
| Proceeds from the sale of property and equipment | 548 |

Also, the company wrote off $1,940 ($ in thousands) in property and equipment during 2011

**Required:**

What was the gain or loss Saks recognized in the year ended January 29, 2011, from the sale of property and equipment?

**Judgment Case 10–7**
Goodwill
● LO10–1

Athena Paper Corporation acquired for cash 100% of the outstanding common stock of Georgia, Inc., a supplier of wood pulp. The $4,500,000 amount paid was significantly higher than the book value of Georgia's net assets (assets less liabilities) of $2,800,000. The Athena controller recorded the difference of $1,700,000 as an asset, goodwill.

**Required:**

1. Discuss the meaning of the term *goodwill.*
2. In what situation would the Athena controller be correct in her valuation of goodwill?

**Judgment Case 10–8**
Research and development
● LO10–8

Prior to 1974, accepted practice was for companies to either expense or capitalize R&D costs. In 1974, the FASB issued a Standard that requires all research and development costs to be charged to expense when incurred. This was a controversial standard, opposed by many companies who preferred delaying the recognition of these expenses until later years when presumably the expenditures bear fruit.

Several research studies have been conducted to determine if the standard had any impact on the behavior of companies. One interesting finding was that, prior to 1974, companies that expensed R&D costs were significantly larger than those companies that capitalized R&D costs.

**Required:**

1. Explain the FASB's logic in deciding to require all companies to expense R&D costs in the period incurred.
2. Identify possible reasons to explain why, prior to 1974, companies that expensed R&D costs were significantly larger than those companies that capitalized R&D costs.

**Judgment Case 10–9**
Research and development
● LO10–8

Clonal, Inc., a biotechnology company, developed and patented a diagnostic product called Trouver. Clonal purchased some research equipment to be used exclusively for Trouver and subsequent research projects. Clonal defeated a legal challenge to its Trouver patent, and began production and marketing operations for the project.

Corporate headquarters' costs were allocated to Clonal's research division as a percentage of the division's salaries.

**Required:**

1. How should the equipment purchased for Trouver be reported in Clonal's income statements and statements of financial position?
2. a. Describe the matching principle.
   b. Describe the accounting treatment of research and development costs and consider whether this is consistent with the matching principle. What is the justification for the accounting treatment of research and development costs?
3. How should corporate headquarters' costs allocated to the research division be classified in Clonal's income statements? Why?
4. How should the legal expenses incurred in defending Trouver's patent be reported in Clonal's financial statements?

*(AICPA adapted)*

**Communication Case 10–10**
Research and development
● LO10–8

The focus of this case is the situation described in Case 10–9. What is the appropriate accounting for R&D costs? Do you believe that (1) capitalization is the correct treatment of R&D costs, (2) expensing is the correct treatment of R&D costs, or (3) that companies should be allowed to choose between expensing and capitalizing R&D costs?

**Required:**

1. Develop a list of arguments in support of your view prior to the class session for which the case is assigned. Do not be influenced by the method required by the FASB. Base your opinion on the conceptual merit of the options.
2. In class, your instructor will pair you (and everyone else) with a classmate who also has independently developed a position.
   a. You will be given three minutes to argue your view to your partner. Your partner likewise will be given three minutes to argue his or her view to you. During these three-minute presentations, the listening partner is not permitted to speak.
   b. Then after each person has had a turn attempting to convince his or her partner, the two partners will have a three-minute discussion in which they will decide which alternative is more convincing and arguments will be merged into a single view for each pair.
3. After the allotted time, a spokesperson for each of the three alternatives will be selected by the instructor. Each spokesperson will field arguments from the class as to the appropriate alternative. The class will then discuss the merits of the alternatives and attempt to reach a consensus view, though a consensus is not necessary.

**Communication
Case 10–11**
Research and
development
● LO10–8

Thomas Plastics is in the process of developing a revolutionary new plastic valve. A new division of the company was formed to develop, manufacture, and market this new product. As of year-end (December 31, 2013), the new product has not been manufactured for sale; however, prototype units were built and are in operation.

Throughout 2013, the new division incurred a variety of costs. These costs included expenses (including salaries of administrative personnel) and market research costs. In addition, approximately $500,000 in equipment (estimated useful life of 10 years) was purchased for use in developing and manufacturing the new valve. Approximately $200,000 of this equipment was built specifically for developing the design of the new product; the remaining $300,000 of the equipment was used to manufacture the preproduction prototypes and will be used to manufacture the new product once it is in commercial production.

The president of the company, Sally Rogers, has been told that research and development costs must be expensed as incurred, but she does not understand this treatment. She believes the research will lead to a profitable product and to increased future revenues. Also, she wonders how to account for the $500,000 of equipment purchased by the new division. "I thought I understood accounting," she growled. "Explain to me why expenditures that benefit our future revenues are expensed rather than capitalized!"

**Required:**

Write a one-to two-page report to Sally Rogers explaining the generally accepted accounting principles relevant to this issue. The report should also address the treatment of the equipment purchases.

*(AICPA adapted)*

**Ethics
Case 10–12**
Research and
development
● LO10–8

Mayer Biotechnical, Inc., develops, manufactures, and sells pharmaceuticals. Significant research and development (R&D) expenditures are made for the development of new drugs and the improvement of existing drugs. During 2013, $220 million was spent on R&D. Of this amount, $30 million was spent on the purchase of equipment to be used in a research project involving the development of a new antibiotic.

The controller, Alice Cooper, is considering capitalizing the equipment and depreciating it over the five-year useful life of the equipment at $6 million per year, even though the equipment likely will be used on only one project. The company president has asked Alice to make every effort to increase 2013 earnings because in 2014 the company will be seeking significant new financing from both debt and equity sources. "I guess we might use the equipment in other projects later," Alice wondered to herself.

**Required:**

1. Assuming that the equipment was purchased at the beginning of 2013, by how much would Alice's treatment of the equipment increase before tax earnings as opposed to expensing the equipment cost?

2. Discuss the ethical dilemma Alice faces in determining the treatment of the $30 million equipment purchase.

**IFRS Case 10–13**
Research and
development;
comparison of
U.S. GAAP and
IFRS; Roche
Group
● LO10–8,
  LO10–9

● IFRS

Roche Group, a Swiss company, is one of the largest pharmaceutical companies in the world. The company prepares its financial statements according to IFRS.

**Required:**

1. Use the Internet to locate Roche's most recent annual report. The address is **www.roche.com**. Locate the significant accounting policies disclosure note.

2. How does the company account for research and development expenditures? Does this policy differ from U.S. GAAP?

**Analysis
Case 10–14**
Fixed-asset
turnover ratio;
Bed Bath &
Beyond, Inc.
● LO10–5

Real World Financials

Bed Bath & Beyond Inc. is a leading retailer of domestic merchandise and home furnishings. The company's 2011 fixed-asset turnover ratio, using the average book value of property, plant, and equipment (PP&E) as the denominator, was approximately 7.8355. Additional information taken from the company's 2011 annual report is as follows:

| | ($ in thousands) |
|---|---|
| Book value of PP&E—beginning of 2011 | $1,119,292 |
| Purchases of PP&E during 2011 | 183,474 |
| Depreciation of PP&E for 2011 | 183,820 |

Equipment having a book value of $2,649 thousand was sold during 2011.

**Required:**

1. How is the fixed-asset turnover ratio computed? How would you interpret Bed Bath & Beyond's ratio of 7.8355?

2. Use the data to determine Bed Bath & Beyond's net sales for 2011.

3. Obtain annual reports from three corporations in the same primary industry as Bed Bath & Beyond (Cost Plus and Pier 1 Imports are two well-known companies in the same industry) and compare the management of each company's investment in property, plant, and equipment.

**Note:** You can obtain copies of annual reports from your library, from friends who are shareholders, from the investor relations department of the corporations, from a friendly stockbroker, or from EDGAR (Electronic Data Gathering, Analysis, and Retrieval) on the Internet (www.sec.gov).

**Judgment Case 10–15**
Computer software costs
● LO10–8

The Elegant Software Company recently completed the development and testing of a new software program that provides the ability to transfer data from among a variety of operating systems. The company believes this product will be quite successful and capitalized all of the costs of designing, developing, coding, and testing the software. These costs will be amortized over the expected useful life of the software on a straight-line basis.

**Required:**

1. Was Elegant correct in its treatment of the software development costs? Why?

2. Explain the appropriate method for determining the amount of periodic amortization for any capitalized software development costs.

**Real World Case 10–16**
Property, plant, and equipment; Home Depot
● LO10–1, LO10–7

Real World Financials

EDGAR, the Electronic Data Gathering, Analysis, and Retrieval system, performs automated collection, validation, indexing, and forwarding of submissions by companies and others who are required by law to file forms with the U.S. Securities and Exchange Commission (SEC). All publicly traded domestic companies use EDGAR to make the majority of their filings. (Some foreign companies file voluntarily.) Form 10-K, which includes the annual report, is required to be filed on EDGAR. The SEC makes this information available on the Internet.

**Required:**

1. Access EDGAR on the Internet. The web address is www.sec.gov.

2. Search for **Home Depot, Inc.** Access the 10-K filing for the most recent fiscal year. Search or scroll to find the financial statements and related notes.

3. Answer the following questions related to the company's property, plant, and equipment:

   a. Name the different types of assets the company lists in its balance sheet under property, plant, and equipment.

   b. How much cash was used for the acquisition of property, plant, and equipment during the year?

   c. What was the amount of interest capitalized during the year?

   d. Compute the fixed-asset turnover ratio for the fiscal year.

**Analysis Case 10–17**
Reporting property, plant, and equipment and intangible assets
● LO10–1, LO10–5

Refer to the financial statements and related disclosure notes of **Dell Inc.** in Appendix B located at the back of the text.

**Required:**

1. What categories of property, plant, and equipment and intangible assets does Dell report in its 2011 balance sheet?

2. How much cash was used in 2011 to purchase property and equipment? How does this compare with purchases in previous years?

3. The fixed-asset turnover ratio for **Hewlett-Packard Company**, a Dell competitor, is 10.91. How does this compare with Dell's ratio? What is the ratio intended to measure?

# Air France–KLM Case

**AIRFRANCE /**
● LO10–9
🌐 IFRS

**Air France–KLM (AF)**, a French company, prepares its financial statements according to International Financial Reporting Standards. AF's annual report for the year ended March 31, 2011, which includes financial statements and disclosure notes, is provided with all new textbooks. This material also is included in AF's "Registration Document 2010–11," dated June 15, 2011 and is available at www.airfranceklm.com.

**Required:**

1. What method does Air France-KLM use to amortize the cost of computer software development costs? How does this approach differ from U.S. GAAP?

2. AF does not report any research and development expenditures. If it did, its approach to accounting for research and development would be significantly different from U.S. GAAP. Describe the differences between IFRS and U.S. GAAP in accounting for research and development expenditures.

3. AF does not report the receipt of any governments grants. If it did, its approach to accounting for government grants would be significantly different from U.S. GAAP. Describe the differences between IFRS and U.S. GAAP in accounting for government grants. If AF received a grant for the purchase of assets, what alternative accounting treatments are available under IFRS?

## CPA Simulation 10–1

**Yamashita Corporation**

Interest capitalization

**CPA Review**

Test your knowledge of the concepts discussed in this chapter, practice critical professional skills necessary for career success, and prepare for the computer-based CPA exam by accessing our CPA simulations at the text website: **www.mhhe.com/spiceland7e**.

The Yamashita Company simulation tests your knowledge of accounting for interest capitalization.

# 11

# Property, Plant, and Equipment and Intangible Assets: Utilization and Impairment

## FINANCIAL REPORTING CASE

### What's in a Name?

"I don't understand this at all," your friend Penny Lane moaned. "Depreciation, depletion, amortization; what's the difference? Aren't they all the same thing?" Penny and you are part of a class team working on a case involving **Weyerhaeuser Company**, a large forest products company. Part of the project involves comparing reporting methods over a three-year period. "Look at these disclosure notes from last year's annual report. Besides mentioning those three terms, they also talk about asset impairment. How is that different?" Penny showed you the disclosure notes.

#### Property and Equipment and Timber and Timberlands (in part)

Depreciation is calculated using a straight-line method at rates based on estimated service lives. Logging railroads and truck roads are generally amortized—as timber is harvested—at rates based on the volume of timber estimated to be removed. We carry timber and timberlands at cost less depletion. To determine depletion rates, we divide the net carrying value by the related volume of timber estimated to be available over the growth cycle.

#### Impairment of Long-lived Assets (in part)

We review long-lived assets—including certain identifiable intangibles—for impairment whenever events or changes in circumstances indicate that the carrying amount of the assets may not be recoverable.

---

**By the time you finish this chapter, you should be able to respond appropriately to the questions posed in this case. Compare your response to the solution provided at the end of the chapter.**

● ─── QUESTIONS

1. Is Penny correct? Do the terms *depreciation, depletion,* and *amortization* all mean the same thing? (*p. 590*)

2. Weyerhaeuser determines depletion based on the "volume of timber estimated to be available." Explain this approach. (*p. 594*)

3. Explain how asset impairment differs from depreciation, depletion, and amortization. How do companies measure impairment losses for property, plant, and equipment and intangible assets with finite useful lives? (*p. 613*)

# PART A   DEPRECIATION, DEPLETION, AND AMORTIZATION

## Cost Allocation—an Overview

● LO11–1

Property, plant, and equipment and intangible assets are purchased with the expectation that they will provide future benefits, usually for several years. Specifically, they are acquired to be used as part of the revenue-generating operations. Logically, then, the costs of acquiring the assets should be allocated to expense during the reporting periods benefited by their use. That is, their costs are matched with the revenues they help generate.

Let's suppose that a company purchases a used delivery truck for $8,200 to be used to deliver product to customers. The company estimates that five years from the acquisition date the truck will be sold for $2,200. It is estimated, then, that $6,000 ($8,200 − 2,200) of the truck's purchase price will be used up (consumed) during a five-year useful life. The situation is portrayed in Illustration 11–1.

**Illustration 11–1**
Cost Allocation

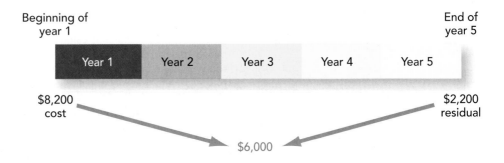

Theoretically, the matching principle requires that the $6,000 be allocated to the five individual years of asset use in direct proportion to the role the asset played in revenue production. However, very seldom is there a clear-cut relationship between the use of the asset and revenue production. In other words, we can't tell precisely the portion of the total benefits of the asset that was consumed in any particular period. As a consequence, we must resort to arbitrary allocation methods to approximate a matching of expense with revenue. Contrast this situation with the $24,000 prepayment of one year's rent on an office building at $2,000 per month. In that case, we know precisely that the benefits of the asset, prepaid rent, are consumed at a rate of $2,000 per month.

Cost allocation is known as **depreciation** for plant and equipment, **depletion** for natural resources, and **amortization** for intangibles. The process often is confused with measuring a decline in fair value of an asset. For example, let's say our delivery truck purchased for $8,200 can be sold for $5,000 at the end of one year but we intend to keep it for the full five-year estimated life. It has experienced a decline in value of $3,200 ($8,200 − 5,000). However, *depreciation is a process of cost allocation, not valuation.* We would not record depreciation expense of $3,200 for year one of the truck's life. Instead, we would distribute the cost of the asset, less any anticipated residual value, over the estimated useful life in a systematic and rational manner that attempts to match revenues with the *use* of the asset, not the decline in its value. After all, the truck is purchased to be used in operations, not to be sold.

The specific accounting treatment depends on the intended use of the asset. For assets used in the manufacture of a product, for example, depreciation, depletion, or amortization is considered a product cost to be included as part of the cost of inventory. Eventually, when the product is sold, it becomes part of the cost of goods sold. For assets *not* used in production, primarily plant and equipment and certain intangibles used in the selling and administrative functions of the company, periodic depreciation or amortization is reported as expense in the income statement. You might recognize this distinction as the difference between a product cost and a period cost. When a product cost is reported as an expense (cost of goods sold) depends on when the product is sold; when a period cost is reported as an expense depends on the reporting period in which it is incurred.

**FINANCIAL Reporting Case**

Q1, p. 589

Depreciation, depletion, and amortization are processes that attempt to satisfy the matching principle.

Depreciation, depletion, and amortization for an asset used to manufacture a product are included in the cost of inventory.

# Measuring Cost Allocation

The process of cost allocation requires that three factors be established at the time the asset is put into use. These factors are:

1. **Service life**—the estimated use that the company expects to receive from the asset.
2. **Allocation base**—the value of the usefulness that is expected to be consumed.
3. **Allocation method**—the pattern in which the usefulness is expected to be consumed.

Let's consider these one at a time.

## Service Life

The **service life**, or **useful life**, is the amount of use that the company expects to obtain from the asset before disposing of it. This use can be expressed in units of time, or in units of activity. For example, the estimated service life of a delivery truck could be expressed in terms of years or in terms of the number of miles that the company expects the truck to be driven before disposition. We use the terms service life and useful life interchangeably throughout the chapter.

Physical life provides the upper bound for service life of tangible, long-lived assets. Physical life will vary according to the purpose for which the asset is acquired and the environment in which it is operated. For example, a diesel powered electric generator may last for many years if it is used only as an emergency backup or for only a few years if it is used regularly.

The service life of a tangible asset may be less than physical life for a variety of reasons. For example, the expected rate of technological change may shorten service life. If suppliers are expected to develop new technologies that are more efficient, the company may keep an asset for a period of time much shorter than physical life. Likewise, if the company sells its product in a market that frequently demands new products, the machinery and equipment used to produce products may be useful only for as long as its output can be sold. Similarly, a mineral deposit might be projected to contain 4 million tons of a mineral, but it may be economically feasible with existing extraction methods to mine only 2 million tons. For intangible assets, legal or contractual life often is a limiting factor. For instance, a patent might be capable of providing enhanced profitability for 50 years, but the legal life of a patent is only 20 years.

Management intent also may shorten the period of an asset's usefulness below its physical, legal, or contractual life. For example, a company may have a policy of using its delivery trucks for a three-year period and then trading the trucks for new models.

Companies quite often disclose the range of service lives for different categories of assets. For example, Illustration 11–2 shows how **IBM Corporation** disclosed its service lives in a note accompanying recent financial statements.

> **Summary of Significant Accounting Policies (in part)**
> **Depreciation and Amortization**
> The estimated useful lives of certain depreciable assets are as follows: buildings, 30 to 50 years; building equipment, 10 to 20 years; land improvements, 20 years; plant, laboratory and office equipment, 2 to 20 years; and computer equipment, 1.5 to 5 years.

## Allocation Base

The total amount of cost to be allocated over an asset's service life is called its **allocation base**. The amount is the difference between the initial value of the asset at its acquisition (its cost) and its **residual value**. Residual or **salvage value** is the amount the company expects to receive for the asset at the end of its service life less any anticipated disposal costs. In our delivery truck example above, the allocation base is $6,000 ($8,200 cost less $2,200 anticipated residual value).

In certain situations, residual value can be estimated by referring to a company's prior experience or to publicly available information concerning resale values of various types of assets. For example, if a company intends to trade its delivery trucks in three years for

**The _service life,_ or _useful life,_ can be expressed in units of time or in units of activity.**

**Expected obsolescence can shorten service life below physical life.**

**Illustration 11–2**

Service Life Disclosure—
International Business
Machines Corporation

Real World Financials

**_Allocation base_ is the difference between the cost of the asset and its anticipated _residual value._**

the new model, approximations of the three-year residual value for that type of truck can be obtained from used truck values.

However, estimating residual value for many assets can be very difficult due to the uncertainty about the future. For this reason, along with the fact that residual values often are immaterial, many companies simply assume a residual value of zero. Companies usually do not disclose estimated residual values.

## Allocation Method

> The *allocation method* used should be systematic and rational and correspond to the pattern of asset use.

In determining how much cost to allocate to periods of an asset's use, a method should be selected that corresponds to the pattern of the loss of the asset's usefulness. Generally accepted accounting principles state that the chosen method should allocate the asset's cost "as equitably as possible to the periods during which services are obtained from [its] use." GAAP further specifies that the method should produce a cost allocation in a "systematic and rational manner."[1] The objective is to try to allocate cost to the period in an amount that is proportional to the amount of benefits generated by the asset during the period relative to the total benefits provided by the asset during its life.

In practice, there are two general approaches that attempt to obtain this systematic and rational allocation. The first approach allocates the cost base according to the *passage of time*. Methods following this approach are referred to as time-based methods. The second approach allocates an asset's cost base using a measure of the asset's *input* or *output*. This is an activity-based method. We compare these approaches first in the context of depreciation. Later we see that depletion of natural resources typically follows an activity-based approach and the amortization of intangibles typically follows a time-based approach.

# Depreciation

● LO11–2

To demonstrate and compare the most common depreciation methods, we refer to the situation described in Illustration 11–3.

**Illustration 11–3**

Depreciation Methods

The Hogan Manufacturing Company purchased a machine for $250,000. The company expects the service life of the machine to be five years. During that time, it is expected that the machine will produce 140,000 units. The anticipated residual value is $40,000. The machine was disposed of after five years of use. Actual production during the five years of the asset's life was:

| Year | Units Produced |
|------|----------------|
| 1 | 24,000 |
| 2 | 36,000 |
| 3 | 46,000 |
| 4 | 8,000 |
| 5 | 16,000 |
| Total | 130,000 |

## Time-Based Depreciation Methods

> The *straight-line depreciation method* allocates an equal amount of depreciable base to each year of the asset's service life.

**STRAIGHT-LINE METHOD.** By far the most easily understood and widely used depreciation method is straight line. By this approach, an equal amount of depreciable base is allocated to each year of the asset's service life. The depreciable base is simply divided by the number of years in the asset's life to determine annual depreciation. In our illustration, the straight-line annual depreciation is $42,000, calculated as follows:

$$\frac{\$250,000 - 40,000}{5 \text{ years}} = \$42,000 \text{ per year}$$

---

[1]FASB ASC 360–10–35–4: Property, Plant, and Equipment—Overall—Subsequent Measurement (previously "Restatement and Revision of Accounting Research Bulletins," *Accounting Research Bulletin No. 43* (New York: AICPA, 1953), Ch. 9).

**ACCELERATED METHODS.**    Using the straight-line method implicitly assumes that the benefits derived from the use of the asset are the same each year. In some situations it might be more appropriate to assume that the asset will provide greater benefits in the early years of its life than in the later years. In these cases, a more appropriate matching of depreciation with revenues is achieved with a declining pattern of depreciation, with higher depreciation in the early years of the asset's life and lower depreciation in later years. An accelerated depreciation method also would be appropriate when benefits derived from the asset are approximately equal over the asset's life, but repair and maintenance costs increase significantly in later years. The early years incur higher depreciation and lower repairs and maintenance expense, while the later years have lower depreciation and higher repairs and maintenance. Two commonly used ways to achieve such a declining pattern are the sum-of-the-years'-digits method and declining balance methods.

*Accelerated depreciation methods are appropriate when the asset is more useful in its earlier years.*

**Sum-of-the-years'-digits method.**    The sum-of-the-years'-digits (SYD) method has no logical foundation other than the fact that it accomplishes the objective of accelerating depreciation in a systematic manner. This is achieved by multiplying the depreciable base by a fraction that declines each year and results in depreciation that decreases by the same amount each year. The denominator of the fraction remains constant and is the sum of the digits from one to $n$, where $n$ is the number of years in the asset's service life. For example, if there are five years in the service life, the denominator is the sum of 1, 2, 3, 4, and 5, which equals 15.[2] The numerator decreases each year; it begins with the value of $n$ in the first year and decreases by one each year until it equals one in the final year of the asset's estimated service life. The annual fractions for an asset with a five-year life are: $\frac{5}{15}$, $\frac{4}{15}$, $\frac{3}{15}$, $\frac{2}{15}$, and $\frac{1}{15}$. We calculate depreciation for the five years of the machine's life using the sum-of-the-years'-digits method in Illustration 11–3A.

*The SYD method multiplies depreciable base by a declining fraction.*

## Illustration 11–3A    Sum-of-the-Years'-Digits Depreciation

| Year | Depreciable Base ($250,000 – 40,000) | × | Depreciation Rate per Year | = | Depreciation | Accumulated Depreciation | Book Value End of Year ($250,000 less Accum. Depreciation) |
|------|------|---|------|---|------|------|------|
| 1 | $210,000 | | $\frac{5}{15}$* | | $ 70,000 | $ 70,000 | $180,000 |
| 2 | 210,000 | | $\frac{4}{15}$ | | 56,000 | 126,000 | 124,000 |
| 3 | 210,000 | | $\frac{3}{15}$ | | 42,000 | 168,000 | 82,000 |
| 4 | 210,000 | | $\frac{2}{15}$ | | 28,000 | 196,000 | 54,000 |
| 5 | 210,000 | | $\frac{1}{15}$ | | 14,000 | 210,000 | 40,000 |
| Totals | | | $\frac{15}{15}$ | | $210,000 | | |

$$* \frac{n(n+1)}{2} = \frac{5(5+1)}{2} = 15$$

**Declining balance methods.**    As an alternative, an accelerated depreciation pattern can be achieved by various declining balance methods. Rather than multiplying a constant balance by a declining fraction as we do in SYD depreciation, we multiply a constant fraction by a declining balance each year. Specifically, we multiply a constant percentage rate times the decreasing book value (cost less accumulated depreciation), also referred to as carrying value, of the asset (not depreciable base) at the beginning of the year. Because the rate remains constant while the book value declines, annual depreciation is less each year.

The rates used are multiples of the straight-line rate. The straight-line rate is simply one, divided by the number of years in the asset's service life. For example, the straight-line rate for an asset with a five-year life is one-fifth, or 20%. Various multiples used in practice are

*Declining balance depreciation methods multiply beginning-of-year book value, not depreciable base, by an annual rate that is a multiple of the straight-line rate.*

[2]A formula useful when calculating the denominator is $n(n + 1)/2$.

125%, 150%, or 200% of the straight-line rate. When 200% is used as the multiplier, the method is known as the **double-declining-balance (DDB) method** because the rate used is twice the straight-line rate.

In our illustration, the double-declining-balance rate would be 40% (two times the straight-line rate of 20%). Depreciation is calculated in Illustration 11–3B for the five years of the machine's life using the double-declining-balance method.

### Illustration 11–3B

Double-Declining-Balance Depreciation

| Year | Book Value Beginning of Year | × | Depreciation Rate per Year | = | Depreciation | Accumulated Depreciation | Book Value End of Year ($250,000 less Accum. Depreciation) |
|---|---|---|---|---|---|---|---|
| 1 | $250,000 | | 40% | | $100,000 | $100,000 | $150,000 |
| 2 | 150,000 | | 40% | | 60,000 | 160,000 | 90,000 |
| 3 | 90,000 | | 40% | | 36,000 | 196,000 | 54,000 |
| 4 | 54,000 | | | | 14,000* | 210,000 | 40,000 |
| 5 | 40,000 | | | | — | | 40,000 |
| Total | | | | | $210,000 | | |

*Amount necessary to reduce book value to residual value.

Notice that in the fourth year depreciation expense is a plug amount that reduces book value to the expected residual value (book value beginning of year, $54,000, minus expected residual value, $40,000 = $14,000). There is no depreciation expense in year 5 since book value has already been reduced to the expected residual value. Declining balance methods often allocate the asset's depreciable base over fewer years than the expected service life.

**SWITCH FROM ACCELERATED TO STRAIGHT LINE.** The result of applying the double-declining-balance method in our illustration produces an awkward result in the later years of the asset's life. By using the double-declining-balance method in our illustration, no depreciation expense is recorded in year 5 even though the asset is still producing benefits. In practice, many companies switch to the straight-line method approximately halfway through an asset's useful life.

> It is not uncommon for a company to switch from accelerated to straight line approximately halfway through an asset's useful life as part of the company's planned depreciation approach.

In our illustration, the company would switch to straight line in either year 3 or year 4. Assuming the switch is made at the beginning of year 4, and the book value at the beginning of that year is $54,000, an additional $14,000 ($54,000 − 40,000 in residual value) of depreciation must be recorded. Applying the straight-line concept, $7,000 ($14,000 divided by two remaining years) in depreciation is recorded in both year 4 and year 5.

It should be noted that this switch to straight line is not a change in depreciation method. The switch is part of the company's planned depreciation approach. However, as you will learn later in the chapter, the accounting treatment is the same as a change in depreciation method.

## Activity-Based Depreciation Methods

> *Activity-based depreciation methods* estimate service life in terms of some measure of productivity.

The most logical way to allocate an asset's cost to periods of an asset's use is to measure the usefulness of the asset in terms of its productivity. For example, we could measure the service life of a machine in terms of its *output* (for example, the estimated number of units it will produce) or in terms of its *input* (for example, the number of hours it will operate). We have already mentioned that one way to measure the service life of a vehicle is to estimate the number of miles it will operate. The most common activity-based method is called the **units-of-production method**.

The measure of output used is the estimated number of units (pounds, items, barrels, etc.) to be produced by the machine. We could also use a measure of input such as the number of hours the machine is expected to operate. By the units-of-production method, we first compute the average depreciation rate per unit by dividing the depreciable base by the number

> **FINANCIAL Reporting Case**
>
> Q2, p. 589

of units expected to be produced. This per unit rate is then multiplied by the number of units produced each period. In our illustration, the depreciation rate per unit is $1.50, computed as follows:

$$\frac{\$250,000 - 40,000}{140,000 \text{ units}} = \$1.50 \text{ per unit}$$

> The *units-of-production method* computes a depreciation rate per measure of activity and then multiplies this rate by actual activity to determine periodic depreciation.

Each unit produced will require $1.50 of depreciation to be recorded. As we are estimating service life based on units produced rather than in years, depreciation is not constrained by time. However, total depreciation is constrained by the asset's cost and the anticipated residual value. In our illustration, suppose the company intended to dispose of the asset at the end of five years. Depreciation for year five must be modified. Depreciation expense would be an amount necessary to bring the book value of the asset down to residual value. Depreciation for the five years is determined in Illustration 11–3C using the units-of-production method. Notice that the last year's depreciation expense is a plug amount that reduces book value to the expected residual value.

**Illustration 11–3C**

Units-of-Production Depreciation

| Year | Units Produced | × Depreciation Rate per Unit = | Depreciation | Accumulated Depreciation | Book Value End of Year ($250,000 less Accum. Depreciation) |
|------|------|------|------|------|------|
| 1 | 24,000 | $1.50 | $ 36,000 | $ 36,000 | $214,000 |
| 2 | 36,000 | 1.50 | 54,000 | 90,000 | 160,000 |
| 3 | 46,000 | 1.50 | 69,000 | 159,000 | 91,000 |
| 4 | 8,000 | 1.50 | 12,000 | 171,000 | 79,000 |
| 5 | 16,000 | | 39,000* | 210,000 | 40,000 |
| Totals | 130,000 | | $210,000 | | |

*Amount necessary to reduce book value to residual value.

## Decision Makers' Perspective—Selecting A Depreciation Method

Illustration 11–3D compares periodic depreciation calculated using each of the alternatives we discussed and illustrated.

**Illustration 11–3D**  Comparison of Various Depreciation Methods

| Year | Straight Line | Sum-of-the-Years' Digits | Double-Declining Balance | Units of Production |
|------|------|------|------|------|
| 1 | $ 42,000 | $ 70,000 | $100,000 | $ 36,000 |
| 2 | 42,000 | 56,000 | 60,000 | 54,000 |
| 3 | 42,000 | 42,000 | 36,000 | 69,000 |
| 4 | 42,000 | 28,000 | 14,000 | 12,000 |
| 5 | 42,000 | 14,000 | 0 | 39,000 |
| Total | $210,000 | $210,000 | $210,000 | $210,000 |

> All methods provide the same total depreciation over an asset's life.

Theoretically, using an activity-based depreciation method provides a better matching of revenues and expenses. Clearly, the productivity of a plant asset is more closely associated with the benefits provided by that asset than the mere passage of time. Also, these methods allow for random patterns of depreciation to correspond with the random patterns of asset use.

However, activity-based methods quite often are either infeasible or too costly to use. For example, buildings don't have an identifiable measure of productivity. Even for machinery, there may be an identifiable measure of productivity such as machine hours or units produced, but it frequently is more costly to determine each period than it is to simply measure the passage of time. For these reasons, most companies use time-based depreciation methods.

Illustration 11–4 shows the results of a recent survey of depreciation methods used by large public companies.[3]

**Illustration 11–4**

Use of Various Depreciation Methods

| Depreciation Method | Number of Companies |
| --- | --- |
| Straight line | 492 |
| Declining balance | 10 |
| Sum-of-the-years'-digits | 2 |
| Accelerated method—not specified | 13 |
| Units of production | 15 |
| Group/composite | 4 |

Why do so many companies use the straight-line method as opposed to other time-based methods? Many companies perhaps consider the benefits derived from the majority of plant assets to be realized approximately evenly over these assets' useful lives. Certainly a contributing factor is that straight-line is the easiest method to understand and apply.

Another motivation is the positive effect on reported income. Straight-line depreciation produces a higher net income than accelerated methods in the early years of an asset's life. In Chapter 8 we pointed out that reported net income can affect bonuses paid to management or debt agreements with lenders.

Conflicting with the desire to report higher profits is the desire to reduce taxes by reducing taxable income. An accelerated method serves this objective by reducing taxable income more in the early years of an asset's life than straight line. You probably recall a similar discussion from Chapter 8 in which the benefits were described of using the LIFO inventory method during periods of increasing costs. However, remember that the LIFO conformity rule requires companies using LIFO for income tax reporting to also use LIFO for financial reporting. *No such conformity rule exists for depreciation methods.* Income tax regulations allow firms to use different approaches to computing depreciation in their tax returns and in their financial statements. The method used for tax purposes is therefore not a constraint in the choice of depreciation methods for financial reporting. As a result, most companies use the straight-line method for financial reporting and the Internal Revenue Service's prescribed accelerated method (discussed in Appendix 11A) for income tax purposes. For example, Illustration 11–5 shows **Merck & Co.**'s depreciation policy as reported in a disclosure note accompanying recent financial statements.

**Illustration 11–5**

Depreciation Method Disclosure—Merck & Co.

Real World Financials

**Summary of Accounting Policies (in part): Depreciation**

Depreciation is provided over the estimated useful lives of the assets, principally using the straight-line method. For tax purposes, accelerated methods are used.

It is not unusual for a company to use different depreciation methods for different classes of assets. For example, Illustration 11–6 illustrates the **International Paper Company** depreciation policy disclosure contained in a note accompanying recent financial statements.

---

[3]*Accounting Trends and Techniques—2011* (New York: AICPA, 2011), p. 394.

**Summary of Accounting Policies (in part):**
**Plants, Properties, and Equipment**

Plants, properties, and equipment are stated at cost, less accumulated depreciation. The units-of-production method of depreciation is used for major pulp and paper mills and the straight-line method is used for other plants and equipment. ●

**Illustration 11–6**

Depreciation Method Disclosure— International Paper Company

**Real World Financials**

# International Financial Reporting Standards

● LO11–10

**Depreciation.** *IAS No. 16* requires that each component of an item of property, plant, and equipment must be depreciated separately if its cost is significant in relation to the total cost of the item.[4] In the United States, component depreciation is allowed but is not often used in practice.

Consider the following illustration:

Cavandish LTD. purchased a delivery truck for $62,000. The truck is expected to have a service life of six years and a residual value of $12,000. At the end of three years, the oversized tires, which have a cost of $6,000 (included in the $62,000 purchase price), will be replaced.

Under U.S. GAAP, the typical accounting treatment is to depreciate the $50,000 ($62,000 − 12,000) depreciable base of the truck over its six-year useful life. Using IFRS, the depreciable base of the truck is $44,000 ($62,000 − 12,000 − 6,000) and is depreciated over the truck's six-year useful life, and the $6,000 cost of the tires is depreciated separately over a three-year useful life.

U.S. GAAP and IFRS determine depreciable base in the same way, by subtracting estimated residual value from cost. However, IFRS requires a review of residual values at least annually.

**Sanofi-Aventis**, a French pharmaceutical company, prepares its financial statements using IFRS. In its property, plant, and equipment note, the company discloses its use of the component-based approach to accounting for depreciation.

**IFRS ILLUSTRATION**

**Real World Financials**

**Property, plant, and equipment (in part)**

The component-based approach to accounting for property, plant, and equipment is applied. Under this approach, each component of an item of property, plant, and equipment with a cost which is significant in relation to the total cost of the item and which has a different useful life from the other components must be depreciated separately.

**Depreciation Methods.** *IAS No. 16* specifically mentions three depreciation methods: straight-line, units-of-production, and the diminishing balance method. The diminishing balance method is similar to the declining balance method sometimes used by U.S. companies. As in the U.S., the straight-line method is used by most companies. A recent survey of large companies that prepare their financial statement according to IFRS reports that in 2009, 93% of the surveyed companies used the straight-line method.[5]

## Concept Review Exercise

The Sprague Company purchased a fabricating machine on January 1, 2013, at a net cost of $130,000. At the end of its four-year useful life, the company estimates that the machine will be worth $30,000. Sprague also estimates that the machine will run for 25,000 hours during its four-year life. The company's fiscal year ends on December 31.

**DEPRECIATION METHODS**

**Required:**
Compute depreciation for 2013 through 2016 using each of the following methods:

1. Straight line.
2. Sum-of-the-years'-digits.

---

[4]"Property, Plant and Equipment," *International Accounting Standard No. 16* (IASCF), par. 42, as amended effective January 1, 2011.
[5]"*IFRS Accounting Trends and Techniques*" (New York, AICPA, 2010), p. 328.

3. Double-declining balance.

4. Units of production (using machine hours). Actual production was as follows:

| Year | Machine Hours |
|------|---------------|
| 2013 | 6,000 |
| 2014 | 8,000 |
| 2015 | 5,000 |
| 2016 | 7,000 |

**Solution:**

1. Straight line.

$$\frac{\$130,000 - 30,000}{4 \text{ years}} = \$25,000 \text{ per year}$$

2. Sum-of-the-years'-digits.

| Year | Depreciable Base | × | Depreciation Rate per Year | = | Depreciation |
|------|------------------|---|----------------------------|---|--------------|
| 2013 | $100,000 | | 4/10 | | $ 40,000 |
| 2014 | 100,000 | | 3/10 | | 30,000 |
| 2015 | 100,000 | | 2/10 | | 20,000 |
| 2016 | 100,000 | | 1/10 | | 10,000 |
| Total | | | | | $100,000 |

3. Double-declining balance.

| Year | Book Value Beginning of Year | × | Depreciation Rate per Year | = | Depreciation | Book Value End of Year |
|------|------------------------------|---|----------------------------|---|--------------|------------------------|
| 2013 | $130,000 | | 50% | | $ 65,000 | $65,000 |
| 2014 | 65,000 | | 50 | | 32,500 | 32,500 |
| 2015 | 32,500 | | | | 2,500* | 30,000 |
| 2016 | 30,000 | | | | — | 30,000 |
| Total | | | | | $100,000 | |

*Amount necessary to reduce book value to residual value.

4. Units of production (using machine hours).

| Year | Machine Hours | × | Depreciation Rate per Hour | = | Depreciation | Book Value End of Year |
|------|---------------|---|----------------------------|---|--------------|------------------------|
| 2013 | 6,000 | | $4* | | $ 24,000 | $106,000 |
| 2014 | 8,000 | | 4 | | 32,000 | 74,000 |
| 2015 | 5,000 | | 4 | | 20,000 | 54,000 |
| 2016 | 7,000 | | | | 24,000† | 30,000 |
| Total | | | | | $100,000 | |

*($130,000 − 30,000)/25,000 hours = $4 per hour.
†Amount necessary to reduce book value to residual value.

# Group and Composite Depreciation Methods

*Group and composite depreciation methods aggregate assets to reduce the recordkeeping costs of determining periodic depreciation.*

As you might imagine, depreciation records could become quite cumbersome and costly if a company has hundreds, or maybe thousands, of depreciable assets. However, the burden can be lessened if the company uses the group or composite method to depreciate assets collectively rather than individually. The two methods are the same except for the way the collection of assets is aggregated for depreciation. The **group depreciation method** defines the collection as depreciable assets that share similar service lives and other attributes. For example, group depreciation could be used for fleets of vehicles or collections of machinery. The

**composite depreciation method** is used when assets are physically dissimilar but are aggregated anyway to gain the convenience of a collective depreciation calculation. For instance, composite depreciation can be used for all of the depreciable assets in one manufacturing plant, even though individual assets in the composite may have widely diverse service lives.

Both approaches are similar in that they involve applying a single straight-line rate based on the average service lives of the assets in the group or composite.[6] The process is demonstrated using Illustration 11–7.

---

**Illustration 11–7**
Group Depreciation

The Express Delivery Company began operations in 2013. It will depreciate its fleet of delivery vehicles using the group method. The cost of vehicles purchased early in 2013, along with residual values, estimated lives, and straight-line depreciation per year by type of vehicle, are as follows:

| Asset | Cost | Residual Value | Depreciable Base | Estimated Life (yrs.) | Depreciation per Year (straight line) |
|-------|------|----------------|------------------|-----------------------|---------------------------------------|
| Vans | $150,000 | $30,000 | $120,000 | 6 | $20,000 |
| Trucks | 120,000 | 16,000 | 104,000 | 5 | 20,800 |
| Wagons | 60,000 | 12,000 | 48,000 | 4 | 12,000 |
| Totals | $330,000 | $58,000 | $272,000 | | $52,800 |

The *group depreciation* rate is determined by dividing the depreciation per year by the total cost. The group's *average service* life is calculated by dividing the depreciable base by the depreciation per year:

$$\text{Group depreciation rate} = \frac{\$52,800}{\$330,000} = 16\%$$

$$\text{Average service life} = \frac{\$272,000}{\$52,800} = 5.15 \text{ years (rounded)}$$

---

If there are no changes in the assets contained in the group, depreciation of $52,800 per year (16% × $330,000) will be recorded for 5.15 years. This means the depreciation in the sixth year will be $7,920 (.15 of a full year's depreciation = 15% × $52,800), which depreciates the cost of the group down to its estimated residual value. In other words, the group will be depreciated over the average service life of the assets in the group.

In practice, there very likely will be changes in the assets constituting the group as new assets are added and others are retired or sold. Additions are recorded by increasing the group asset account for the cost of the addition. Depreciation is determined by multiplying the group rate by the total cost of assets in the group for that period. Once the group or composite rate and the average service life are determined, they normally are continued despite the addition and disposition of individual assets. This implicitly assumes that the service lives of new assets approximate those of individual assets they replace.

Because depreciation records are not kept on an individual asset basis, dispositions are recorded under the assumption that the book value of the disposed item exactly equals any proceeds received and no gain or loss is recorded. For example, if a delivery truck in the above illustration that cost $15,000 is sold for $3,000 in the year 2016, the following journal entry is recorded:

**The depreciation rate is applied to the total cost of the group or composite for the period.**

**No gain or loss is recorded when a group or composite asset is retired or sold.**

| | | |
|---|---|---|
| Cash ................................................................................. | 3,000 | |
| Accumulated depreciation (difference) ........................................... | 12,000 | |
|    Vehicles ................................................................... | | 15,000 |

---

[6]A declining balance method could also be used with either the group or composite method by applying a multiple (e.g., 200%) to the straight-line group or composite rate.

Any actual gain or loss is included in the accumulated depreciation account. This practice generally will not distort income as the unrecorded gains tend to offset unrecorded losses.

The group and composite methods simplify the recordkeeping of depreciable assets. This simplification justifies any immaterial errors in income determination. Illustration 11–8 shows a disclosure note accompanying recent financial statements of the **El Paso Natural Gas Company (EPNG)** describing the use of the group depreciation method for its regulated property.

**Illustration 11–8**
Disclosure of
Depreciation Method—
El Paso Natural Gas
Company

Real World Financials

---

**Summary of Significant Accounting Policies (in part)**
**Property, Plant, and Equipment (in part)**

We use the group method to depreciate property, plant, and equipment. Under this method, assets with similar lives and characteristics are grouped and depreciated as one asset. We apply the FERC-accepted depreciation rate to the total cost of the group until its net book value equals its salvage value. For certain general plant and rights-of-way, we depreciate the asset to zero. The majority of our property, plant, and equipment are on our EPNG system which has depreciation rates ranging from one to 20 percent and the depreciable lives ranging from five to 92 years consistent with our rate settlements with the FERC.

When we retire property, plant, and equipment, we charge accumulated depreciation and amortization for the original cost of the assets in addition to the cost to remove, sell, or dispose of the assets, less their salvage value. We do not recognize a gain or loss unless we sell an entire operating unit, as defined by FERC.

---

Additional group-based depreciation methods, the retirement and replacement methods, are discussed in Appendix 11B.

# International Financial Reporting Standards

● LO11–10

**Valuation of Property, Plant, and Equipment.** As we've discussed, under U.S. GAAP a company reports property, plant, and equipment (PP&E) in the balance sheet at cost less accumulated depreciation (book value). *IAS No. 16*[7] allows a company to report property, plant, and equipment at that amount or, alternatively, at its fair value (revaluation). If a company chooses revaluation, all assets within a class of PP&E must be revalued on a regular basis. U.S. GAAP prohibits revaluation.

If the revaluation option is chosen, the way the company reports the difference between fair value and book value depends on which amount is higher:

- If fair value is higher than book value, the difference is reported as *other comprehensive income (OCI)* which then accumulates in a "revaluation surplus" (sometimes called revaluation reserve) account in equity.

- If book value is higher than fair value, the difference is reported as an *expense in the income statement*. An exception is when a revaluation surplus account relating to the same asset has a balance from a previous *increase* in fair value, that balance is eliminated before debiting revaluation expense.

Consider the following illustration:

**IFRS ILLUSTRATION**

Candless Corporation prepares its financial statements according to IFRS. At the beginning of its 2013 fiscal year, the company purchased equipment for $100,000. The equipment is expected to have a five-year useful life with no residual value, so depreciation for 2013 is $20,000. At the end of the year, Candless chooses to revalue the equipment as permitted by *IAS No. 16.* Assuming that the fair value of the equipment at year-end is $84,000, Candless records depreciation and the revaluation using the following journal entries:

(continued)

---

[7]"Property, Plant and Equipment," *International Accounting Standard No. 16* (IASCF), as amended effective January 1, 2011.

(continued)

| (a) Depreciation expense ($100,000 ÷ 5 years) | 20,000 | |
| Accumulated depreciation | | 20,000 |

After this entry, the book value of the equipment is $80,000; the fair value is $84,000. We use the ratio of the two amounts to adjust both the equipment and the accumulated depreciation accounts (and thus the book value) to fair value ($ in thousands):

| December 31, 2013 | Before Revaluation | | | | After Revaluation |
|---|---|---|---|---|---|
| Equipment | $100 | × | 84/80 | = | $105 |
| Accumulated depreciation | 20 | × | 84/80 | = | 21 |
| Book value | $ 80 | × | 84/80 | = | $ 84 |

The entries to revalue the equipment and the accumulated depreciation accounts (and thus the book value) are:

| (b) Equipment ($105,000 − 100,000) | 5,000 | |
| Accumulated depreciation ($21,000 − 20,000) | | 1,000 |
| Revaluation surplus—OCI ($84,000 − 80,000) | | 4,000 |

To record the revaluation of equipment to its fair value.

The new basis for the equipment is its fair value of $84,000 ($105,000 − 21,000), and the following years' depreciation is based on that amount. Thus, 2014 depreciation would be $84,000 divided by the four remaining years, or $21,000:[8]

| (a) Depreciation expense ($84,000 ÷ 4 years) | 21,000 | |
| Accumulated depreciation | | 21,000 |

After this entry, the book value of the equipment is $63,000. Let's say the fair value now is $57,000. We use the ratio of the two amounts (fair value of $57,000 divided by book value of $63,000) to adjust both the equipment and the accumulated depreciation accounts (and thus the book value) to fair value ($ in thousands):

| December 31, 2014 | Before Revaluation | | | | After Revaluation |
|---|---|---|---|---|---|
| Equipment | $105 | × | 57/63 | = | $95 |
| Accumulated depreciation ($21 + 21) | 42 | × | 57/63 | = | 38 |
| Book value | $ 63 | × | 57/63 | = | $57 |

The entries to revalue the equipment and the accumulated depreciation accounts (and thus the book value) are:

| (b) Revaluation surplus—OCI ($57,000 − 63,000 = $6,000; limit: $4,000 balance) | 4,000 | |
| Revaluation expense (to balance) | 2,000 | |
| Accumulated depreciation ($38,000 − 42,000) | 4,000 | |
| Equipment ($95,000 − 105,000) | | 10,000 |

A decrease in fair value, as occurred in 2014, is expensed unless it reverses a revaluation surplus account relating to the same asset, as in this illustration. So, of the $6,000 decrease in value ($63,000 book value less $57,000 fair value), $4,000 is debited to the previously created revaluation surplus and the remaining $2,000 is recorded as revaluation expense in the income statement.

**Investcorp**, a provider and manager of alternative investment products headquartered in London, prepares its financial statements according to IFRS. The following disclosure

Real World Financials

(continued)

---

[8]*IAS No. 16* allows companies to choose between the method illustrated here and an alternative. The second method eliminates the entire accumulated depreciation account and adjusts the asset account (equipment in this illustration) to fair value. Using either method the revaluation surplus (or expense) would be the same.

(concluded)

note included in a recent annual report discusses the company's decision to change its method of valuing its premises and equipment.

**Change in Accounting Policy**

During the current period, the Group changed its policy with respect of carrying value of premises and equipment. These assets have been revalued to their fair value in the current period and shall be carried at their revalued amount less any accumulated depreciation and cumulative impairment losses. The revaluation surplus has been recognized in other comprehensive income and included as separate component of equity as revaluation surplus.

The revaluation alternative is used infrequently. A recent survey of large companies that prepare their financial statements according to IFRS reports that in 2009, only 10 of the 160 surveyed companies used the revaluation alternative for at least one asset class.[9]

# Depletion of Natural Resources

● LO11–3

Allocation of the cost of natural resources is called **depletion**. Because the usefulness of natural resources generally is directly related to the amount of the resources extracted, the activity-based units-of-production method is widely used to calculate periodic depletion. Service life is therefore the estimated amount of natural resource to be extracted (for example, tons of mineral or barrels of oil).

Depletion base is cost less any anticipated residual value. Residual value could be significant if cost includes land that has a value after the natural resource has been extracted.

The example in Illustration 11–9 was first introduced in Chapter 10.

**Illustration 11–9**

Depletion of Natural Resources

The Jackson Mining Company paid $1,000,000 for the right to explore for a coal deposit on 500 acres of land in Pennsylvania. Costs of exploring for the coal deposit totaled $800,000 and intangible development costs incurred in digging and erecting the mine shaft were $500,000. In addition, Jackson purchased new excavation equipment for the project at a cost of $600,000. After the coal is removed from the site, the equipment will be sold for an anticipated residual value of $60,000.

The company geologist estimates that 1 million tons of coal will be extracted over the three-year period. During 2013, 300,000 tons were extracted. Jackson is required by its contract to restore the land to a condition suitable for recreational use after it extracts the coal.

In Chapter 10 on page 536 we determined that the capitalized cost of the natural resource, coal mine, including the restoration costs, is $2,768,360. Since there is no residual value to the land, the depletion base equals cost and the depletion rate per ton is calculated as follows:

Depletion of the cost of natural resources usually is determined using the units-of-production method.

$$\text{Depletion per ton} = \frac{\text{Depletion base}}{\text{Estimated extractable tons}}$$

$$\text{Depletion per ton} = \frac{\$2,768,360}{1,000,000 \text{ tons}} = \$2.76836 \text{ per ton}$$

For each ton of coal extracted, $2.768360 in depletion is recorded. In 2013, the following journal entry records depletion.

| | | |
|---|---|---|
| Depletion ($2.76836 × 300,000 tons) | 830,508 | |
| Coal mine | | 830,508 |

---

[9]*"IFRS Accounting Trends and Techniques"* (New York, AICPA, 2010), p. 171.

Notice that the credit is to the asset, coal mine, rather than to a contra account, accumulated depletion. Although this approach is traditional, the use of a contra account is acceptable.

Depletion is a product cost and is included in the cost of the inventory of coal, just as the depreciation on manufacturing equipment is included in inventory cost. The depletion is then included in cost of goods sold in the income statement when the coal is sold.

What about depreciation on the $600,000 cost of excavation equipment? If the equipment can be moved from the site and used on future projects, the equipment's depreciable base should be allocated over its useful life. If the asset is not movable, as in our illustration, then it should be depreciated over its useful life or the life of the natural resource, whichever is shorter.

Quite often, companies use the units-of-production method to calculate depreciation and amortization on assets used in the extraction of natural resources. The activity base used is the same as that used to calculate depletion, the estimated recoverable natural resource. In our illustration, the depreciation rate would be $.54 per ton, calculated as follows.

> The units-of-production method often is used to determine depreciation and amortization on assets used in the extraction of natural resources.

$$\text{Depreciation per ton} = \frac{\$600,000 - 60,000}{1,000,000 \text{ tons}} = \$.54 \text{ per ton}$$

In 2013, $162,000 in depreciation ($.54 × 300,000 tons) is recorded and also included as part of the cost of the coal inventory.

The summary of significant accounting policies disclosure accompanying recent financial statements of **ConocoPhilips** shown in Illustration 11–10 provides a good summary of depletion, amortization, and depreciation for natural resource properties.

---

**Summary of Significant Accounting Policies (in part)**

**Depletion and Amortization**—Leasehold costs of producing properties are depleted using the units-of-production method based on estimated proved oil and gas reserves. Amortization of intangible development costs is based on the units-of-production method using estimated proved developed oil and gas reserves.

**Depreciation and Amortization**—Depreciation and amortization of properties, plants and equipment on producing hydrocaron properties and certain pipeline assets, are determined by the units-of-production method.

**Illustration 11–10**

Depletion Method Disclosure—ConocoPhilips

Real World Financials

# Additional Consideration

**Percentage Depletion**

Depletion of cost less residual value required by GAAP should not be confused with percentage depletion (also called *statutory depletion*) allowable for income tax purposes for oil, gas, and most mineral natural resources. Under these tax provisions, a producer is allowed to deduct the greater of cost-based depletion or a fixed percentage of gross income as depletion expense. Over the life of the asset, depletion could exceed the asset's cost. The percentage allowed for percentage-based depletion varies according to the type of natural resource.

Because percentage depletion usually differs from cost depletion, a difference between taxable income and financial reporting income before tax results. These differences are discussed in Chapter 16.

# Amortization of Intangible Assets

Let's turn now to a third type of long-lived asset—intangible assets. As with other assets we have discussed, we allocate the cost of an intangible asset over its service or useful life. However, for the few intangible assets with indefinite useful lives, amortization is inappropriate.

● LO11–4

# International Financial Reporting Standards

● LO11–10

Real World Financials

**Biological Assets.** Living animals and plants, including the trees in a timber tract or in a fruit orchard, are referred to as *biological assets*. Under U.S. GAAP, a timber tract is valued at cost less accumulated depletion and a fruit orchard at cost less accumulated depreciation. Under IFRS, biological assets are valued at their fair value less estimated costs to sell, with changes in fair value included in the calculation of net income.[10]

**Mondi Limited,** an international paper and packing group headquartered in Johannesburg, South Africa, prepares its financial statements according to IFRS. The following disclosure note included in a recent annual report discusses the company's policy for valuing its forestry assets.

**Owned Forestry Assets (in part)**
Owned forestry assets are measured at fair value. The fair value is calculated by applying the expected selling price, less cost to harvest and deliver, to the estimated volume of timber on hand at each reporting date.
Changes in fair value are recognized in the consolidated income statement.

## Intangible Assets Subject to Amortization

The cost of an intangible asset with a *finite* useful life is *amortized*.

Allocating the cost of intangible assets is called amortization. For an intangible asset with a finite useful life, we allocate its capitalized cost less any estimated residual value to periods in which the asset is expected to contribute to the company's revenue-generating activities. This requires that we determine the asset's useful life, its amortization base (cost less estimated residual value), and the appropriate allocation method, similar to our depreciating tangible assets.

**USEFUL LIFE.** Legal, regulatory, or contractual provisions often limit the useful life of an intangible asset. On the other hand, useful life might sometimes be less than the asset's legal or contractual life. For example, the useful life of a patent would be considerably less than its legal life of 20 years if obsolescence were expected to limit the longevity of a protected product.

**RESIDUAL VALUE.** We discussed the cost of intangible assets in Chapter 10. The expected residual value of an intangible asset usually is zero. This might not be the case, though, if at the end of its useful life to the reporting entity the asset will benefit another entity. For example, if Quadra Corp. has a commitment from another company to purchase one of Quadra's patents at the end of its useful life at a determinable price, we use that price as the patent's residual value.

**ALLOCATION METHOD.** The method of amortization should reflect the pattern of use of the asset in generating benefits. Most companies use the straight-line method. We discussed and illustrated a unique approach to determining the periodic amortization of software development costs in Chapter 10. Recall that the periodic amortization percentage for software development costs is the *greater* of (1) the ratio of current revenues to current and anticipated revenues (percentage of revenue method), or (2) the straight-line percentage over the useful life of the asset.

**Intel Corporation** reported several intangible assets in a recent balance sheet. A note, shown in Illustration 11–11, disclosed the range of estimated useful lives and the use of the straight-line method of amortization.

---

[10]"Agriculture," *International Accounting Standard No. 41* (IASCF), as amended effective January 1, 2011.

**Summary of Significant Accounting Policies (in part)**
**Identified Intangible Assets**

Intellectual property assets primarily represent rights acquired under technology licenses and are generally amortized on a straight-line basis over periods of benefit, ranging from 3 to 17 years. We amortize acquisition-related developed technology based on economic benefit over the estimated useful life, ranging from 4 to 7 years. We amortize other intangible assets over periods ranging from 4 to 7 years.

**Illustration 11–11**

Intangible Asset Useful Life Disclosure—Intel Corporation

Real World Financials

Like depletion, amortization expense traditionally is credited to the asset account itself rather than to accumulated amortization. However, the use of a contra account is acceptable. Let's look at an example in Illustration 11–12.

**Illustration 11–12**

Amortization of Intangibles

Hollins Corporation began operations in 2013. Early in January, the company purchased a franchise from Ajax Industries for $200,000. The franchise agreement is for a period of 10 years. In addition, Hollins purchased a patent for $50,000. The remaining legal life of the patent is 13 years. However, due to expected technological obsolescence, the company estimates that the useful life of the patent is only 8 years. Hollins uses the straight-line amortization method for all intangible assets. The company's fiscal year-end is December 31.

The journal entries to record a full year of amortization for these intangibles are as follows:

| | | |
|---|---|---|
| Amortization expense ($200,000 ÷ 10 years) ................................... | 20,000 | |
| Franchise ......................................................................... | | 20,000 |
| *To record amortization of franchise.* | | |
| Amortization expense ($50,000 ÷ 8 years) ....................................... | 6,250 | |
| Patent ............................................................................ | | 6,250 |
| *To record amortization of patent.* | | |

Similar to depreciation, amortization is either a product cost or a period cost depending on the use of the asset. For intangibles used in the manufacture of a product, amortization is a product cost and is included in the cost of inventory (and doesn't become an expense until the inventory is sold). For intangible assets not used in production, such as the franchise cost in our illustration, periodic amortization is expensed in the period incurred.

## Intangible Assets Not Subject to Amortization

An intangible asset that is determined to have an indefinite useful life is not subject to periodic amortization. Useful life is considered indefinite if there is no foreseeable limit on the period of time over which the asset is expected to contribute to the cash flows of the entity.[11]

Indefinite does not necessarily mean permanent. For example, suppose Collins Corporation acquired a trademark in conjunction with the acquisition of a tire company. Collins plans to continue to produce the line of tires marketed under the acquired company's trademark. Recall from our discussion in Chapter 10 that trademarks have a legal life of 10 years, but the registration can be renewed for an indefinite number of 10-year periods. The life of the purchased trademark is initially considered to be indefinite and the cost of the trademark is not amortized. However, if after several years management decides to phase out production of the tire line over the next three years, Collins would amortize the remaining book value over a three-year period.

Recall the **Hewlett-Packard Company (HP)** acquisition of **Compaq Computer Corporation** discussed in Chapter 10. HP allocated $1.4 billion of the purchase price to Compaq's tradename, which is not being amortized. Illustration 11–13 provides another example in a disclosure made by **The Estee Lauder Companies Inc.**, in a recent annual report.

The cost of an intangible asset with an *indefinite* useful life is *not* amortized

Trademarks or tradenames often are considered to have indefinite useful lives.

---

[11]FASB ASC 350–30–35–4: Intangibles–Goodwill and Other—General Intangibles Other than Goodwill—Subsequent Measurement (previously "Goodwill and Other Intangible Assets," *Statement of Financial Accounting Standards No. 142* (Norwalk, Conn.: FASB, 2001), par. B45).

**Illustration 11–13**

Indefinite-Life Intangibles Disclosure—The Estee Lauder Companies Inc.

**Real World Financials**

> **Other Intangible Assets**
> Indefinite-lived intangible assets (e.g. trademarks) are not subject to amortization and are assessed at least annually for impairment during the fiscal fourth quarter, or more frequently if certain events or circumstances warrant.

Goodwill is an intangible asset whose cost is *not* expensed through periodic amortization.

Goodwill is the most common intangible asset with an indefinite useful life. Recall that goodwill is measured as the difference between the purchase price of a company and the fair value of all of the identifiable net assets (tangible and intangible assets minus the fair value of liabilities assumed). Does this mean that goodwill and other intangible assets with indefinite useful lives will remain in a company's balance sheet at their original capitalized values indefinitely? Not necessarily. Like other assets, intangibles are subject to the impairment of value rules we discuss in a subsequent section of this chapter. In fact, indefinite-life intangible assets must be tested for impairment annually, or more frequently if events or circumstances indicate that the asset might be impaired.

# International Financial Reporting Standards

● LO11–10

> **Valuation of Intangible Assets.** *IAS No. 38*[12] allows a company to value an intangible asset subsequent to initial valuation at (1) cost less accumulated amortization or (2) fair value, if fair value can be determined by reference to an active market. If revaluation is chosen, all assets within that class of intangibles must be revalued on a regular basis. Goodwill, however, cannot be revalued. U.S. GAAP prohibits revaluation of any intangible asset.
>
> Notice that the revaluation option is possible only if fair value can be determined by reference to an active market, making the option relatively uncommon. However, the option possibly could be used for intangibles such as franchises and certain license agreements.
>
> If the revaluation option is chosen, the accounting treatment is similar to the way we applied the revaluation option for property, plant, and equipment earlier in this chapter. Recall that the way the company reports the difference between fair value and book value depends on which amount is higher. If fair value is higher than book value, the difference is reported as other comprehensive income (OCI) and then accumulates in a revaluation surplus account in equity. On the other hand, if book value is higher than fair value, the difference is expensed.
>
> Consider the following illustration:

**IFRS ILLUSTRATION**

> Amershan LTD. prepares its financial statements according to IFRS. At the beginning of its 2013 fiscal year, the company purchased a franchise for $500,000. The franchise has a 10-year contractual life and no residual value, so amortization in 2013 is $50,000. The company does not use an accumulated amortization account and credits the franchise account directly when amortization is recorded. At the end of the year, Amershan chooses to revalue the franchise as permitted by *IAS No. 38*. Assuming that the fair value of the franchise, determined by reference to an active market, at year-end is $600,000, Amershan records amortization and the revaluation using the following journal entries:

To record the revaluation of franchise to its fair value.

| | | |
|---|---|---|
| Amortization expense ($500,000 ÷ 10 years) ................................... | 50,000 | |
|     Franchise .............................................................. | | 50,000 |
| Franchise ($600,000 − 450,000) ......................................... | 150,000 | |
|     Revaluation surplus—OCI ............................................ | | 150,000 |

> With the second entry Amershan increases the book value of the franchise from $450,000 ($500,000 − 50,000) to its fair value of $600,000 and records a revaluation surplus for the difference. The new basis for the franchise is its fair value of $600,000, and the following years' amortization is based on that amount. Thus, 2014 amortization would be $600,000 divided by the nine remaining years, or $66,667.

---

[12]"Intangible Assets," *International Accounting Standard No. 38* (IASCF), as amended effective January 1, 2011.

# Concept Review Exercise

**Part A:**

On March 29, 2013, the Horizon Energy Corporation purchased the mineral rights to a coal deposit in New Mexico for $2 million. Development costs and the present value of estimated land restoration costs totaled an additional $3.4 million. The company removed 200,000 tons of coal during 2013 and estimated that an additional 1,600,000 tons would be removed over the next 15 months.

**Required:**
Compute depletion on the mine for 2013.

**Solution:**

| Cost of Coal Mine: | ($ in millions) |
|---|---|
| Purchase price of mineral rights | $2.0 |
| Development and restoration costs | 3.4 |
| | $5.4 |

**Depletion:**

$$\text{Depletion per ton} = \frac{\$5.4 \text{ million}}{1.8 \text{ million tons*}} = \$3 \text{ per ton}$$

*200,000 + 1,600,000

$$2013 \text{ depletion} = \$3 \times 200,000 \text{ tons} = \$600,000$$

**Part B:**

On October 1, 2013, Advanced Micro Circuits, Inc., completed the purchase of Zotec Corporation for $200 million. Included in the allocation of the purchase price were the following identifiable intangible assets ($ in millions), along with the fair values and estimated useful lives:

| Intangible Asset | Fair value | Useful Life (in years) |
|---|---|---|
| Patent | $10 | 5 |
| Developed technology | 50 | 4 |
| Customer list | 10 | 2 |

In addition, the fair value of acquired tangible assets was $100 million. Goodwill was valued at $30 million. Straight-line amortization is used for all purchased intangibles.

During 2013, Advanced finished work on a software development project. Development costs incurred after technological feasibility was achieved and before the product release date totaled $2 million. The software was available for release to the general public on September 29, 2013. During the last three months of the year, revenue from the sale of the software was $4 million. The company estimates that the software will generate an additional $36 million in revenue over the next 45 months.

**Required:**
Compute amortization for purchased intangibles and software development costs for 2013.

**Solution:**

**Amortization of Purchased Intangibles:**

| Patent | $10 million / 5 = $2 million × 3/12 year = $.5 million |
|---|---|
| Developed technology | $50 million / 4 = $12.5 million × 3/12 year = $3.125 million |
| Customer list | $10 million / 2 = $5 million × 3/12 year = $1.25 million |
| Goodwill | The cost of goodwill is not amortized. |

**Amortization of Software Development Costs:**

(1) Percentage-of-revenue method:

$$\frac{\$4 \text{ million}}{(\$4 \text{ million} + 36 \text{ million})} = 10\% \times \$2 \text{ million} = \$200,000$$

(2) Straight-line:

$$\frac{3 \text{ months}}{48 \text{ months}} \text{ or } 6.25\% \times \$2 \text{ million} = \$125,000$$

Advanced will use the percentage-of-revenue method since it produces the greater amortization, $200,000.

## PART B

# ADDITIONAL ISSUES

In this part of the chapter, we discuss the following issues related to cost allocation:

1. Partial periods.
2. Changes in estimates.
3. Change in depreciation method.
4. Error correction.
5. Impairment of value.

# Partial Periods

Only in textbooks are property, plant, and equipment and intangible assets purchased and disposed of at the very beginning or very end of a company's fiscal year. When acquisition and disposal occur at other times, a company theoretically must determine how much depreciation, depletion, and amortization to record for the part of the year that each asset actually is used.

Let's repeat the Hogan Manufacturing Company illustration used earlier in the chapter but modify it in Illustration 11–14 to assume that the asset was acquired *during* the company's fiscal year.

**Illustration 11–14**

Depreciation Methods—
Partial Year

On April 1, 2013, the Hogan Manufacturing Company purchased a machine for $250,000. The company expects the service life of the machine to be five years and the anticipated residual value is $40,000. The machine was disposed of after five years of use. The company's fiscal year-end is December 31. Partial-year depreciation is recorded based on the number of months the asset is in service.

Notice that no information is provided on the estimated output of the machine. Partial-year depreciation presents a problem only when time-based depreciation methods are used. In an activity-based method, the rate per unit of output simply is multiplied by the actual output for the period, regardless of the length of that period.

Depreciation per year of the asset's life calculated earlier in the chapter for the various time-based depreciation methods is shown in Illustration 11–14A.

**Illustration 11–14A**

Yearly Depreciation

| Year | Straight Line | Sum-of-the-Years'-Digits | Double-Declining Balance |
|------|---------------|--------------------------|--------------------------|
| 1 | $ 42,000 | $ 70,000 | $100,000 |
| 2 | 42,000 | 56,000 | 60,000 |
| 3 | 42,000 | 42,000 | 36,000 |
| 4 | 42,000 | 28,000 | 14,000 |
| 5 | 42,000 | 14,000 | 0 |
| Total | $210,000 | $210,000 | $210,000 |

Illustration 11-14B shows how Hogan would depreciate the machinery by these three methods assuming an April 1 acquisition date.

## Illustration 11—14B    Partial-Year Depreciation

| Year | Straight Line | Sum-of-the-Years'-Digits | Double-Declining Balance |
|---|---|---|---|
| 2013 | $42,000 × ¾ = $ **31,500** | $70,000 × ¾ = $ **52,500** | $100,000 × ¾ = $ **75,000** |
| 2014 | $ **42,000** | $70,000 × ¼ = $ 17,500 | $100,000 × ¼ = $ 25,000 |
|  |  | +56,000 × ¾ =     42,000 | +60,000 × ¾ =     45,000 |
|  |  | $ **59,500** | $ **70,000*** |
| 2015 | $ **42,000** | $56,000 × ¼ = $ 14,000 | $60,000 × ¼ = $ 15,000 |
|  |  | +42,000 × ¾ =     31,500 | +36,000 × ¾ =     27,000 |
|  |  | $ **45,500** | $ **42,000** |
| 2016 | $ **42,000** | $42,000 × ¼ = $ 10,500 | $36,000 × ¼ = $ 9,000 |
|  |  | +28,000 × ¾ =     21,000 | +14,000 × ¾ =     10,500 |
|  |  | $ **31,500** | $ **19,500** |
| 2017 | $ **42,000** | $28,000 × ¼ = $ 7,000 | $14,000 × ¼ = $ **3,500** |
|  |  | +14,000 × ¾ =     10,500 |  |
|  |  | $ **17,500** |  |
| 2018 | $42,000 × ¼ = $ **10,500** | $14,000 × ¼ = $ **3,500** |  |
|  | Totals    **$210,000** | **$210,000** | **$210,000** |

*Could also be determined by multiplying the book value at the beginning of the year by twice the straight-line rate: ($250,000 − 75,000) × 40% = $70,000.

Notice that 2013 depreciation is three-quarters of the full year's depreciation for the first year of the asset's life, because the asset was used nine months, or ¾ of the year. The remaining one-quarter of the first year's depreciation is included in 2014's depreciation along with ¾ of the depreciation for the second year of the asset's life. This calculation is not necessary for the straight-line method because a full year's depreciation is the same for each year of the asset's life.

Usually, the above procedure is impractical or at least cumbersome. As a result, most companies adopt a simplifying assumption, or convention, for computing partial year's depreciation and use it consistently. A common convention is to record one-half of a full year's depreciation in the year of acquisition and another half year in the year of disposal. This is known as the **half-year convention**.[13]

# Changes in Estimates

The calculation of depreciation, depletion, or amortization requires estimates of both service life and residual value. It's inevitable that at least some estimates will prove incorrect. Chapter 4 briefly introduced the topic of changes in estimates along with coverage of changes in accounting principles and the correction of errors. Here and in subsequent sections of this chapter, we provide overviews of the accounting treatment and disclosures required for these changes and errors when they involve property, plant, and equipment and intangible assets.

● LO11–5

Changes in estimates are accounted for prospectively. When a company revises a previous estimate based on new information, prior financial statements are not restated. Instead, the company merely incorporates the new estimate in any related accounting determinations from then on. So, it usually will affect some aspects of both the balance sheet and the income statement in the current and future periods. A disclosure note should describe the effect of a change in estimate on income before extraordinary items, net income, and related pershare amounts for the current period.

A change in estimate should be reflected in the financial statements of the current period and future periods.

[13]Another common method is the modified half-year convention. This method records a full year's depreciation when the asset is acquired in the first half of the year or sold in the second half. No depreciation is recorded if the asset is acquired in the second half of the year or sold in the first half. These half-year conventions are simple and, in most cases, will not result in material differences from a more precise calculation.

Consider the example in Illustration 11–15.

**Illustration 11–15**

Change in Accounting Estimate

On January 1, 2011, the Hogan Manufacturing Company purchased a machine for $250,000. The company expects the service life of the machine to be five years and its anticipated residual value to be $40,000. The company's fiscal year-end is December 31 and the straight-line depreciation method is used for all depreciable assets. During 2013, the company revised its estimate of service life from five to eight years and also revised estimated residual value to $22,000.

For 2011 and 2012, depreciation is $42,000 per year [($250,000 − 40,000) ÷ 5 years] or $84,000 for the two years. However, with the revised estimate, depreciation for 2013 and subsequent years is determined by allocating the book value remaining at the beginning of 2013 less the revised residual value equally over the remaining service life of six years (8 − 2). The remaining book value at the beginning of 2013 is $166,000 ($250,000 − 84,000) and depreciation for 2013 and subsequent years is recorded as follows:

| | | |
|---|---|---|
| Depreciation expense (below) ........................................................ | 24,000 | |
|     Accumulated depreciation ...................................................... | | 24,000 |

| | | |
|---:|---:|---|
| | $250,000 | Cost |
| $42,000 | | Previous annual depreciation ($210,000 ÷ 5 years) |
| × 2 years | 84,000 | Depreciation to date (2011–2012) |
| | 166,000 | Book value as of 1/1/13 |
| | 22,000 | Less revised residual value |
| | 144,000 | Revised depreciable base |
| | ÷ 6 | Estimated remaining life (8 years − 2 years) |
| | $ 24,000 | New annual depreciation |

The asset's book value is depreciated down to the anticipated residual value of $22,000 at the end of the revised eight-year service life. In addition, a note discloses the effect of the change in estimate on income, if material. The before-tax effect is an increase in income of $18,000 (depreciation of $42,000 if the change had not been made, less $24,000 depreciation after the change).

**Zumiez Inc.** is a leading specialty retailer of action sports related apparel. The company recently revised its estimates of the service lives of its leasehold improvements. Illustration 11–16 shows the note that disclosed the change.

**Illustration 11–16**

Change in Estimate Disclosure—Zumiez Inc.

Real World Financials

**Fixed Assets (in part)**

In accordance with our fixed asset policy, we review the estimated useful lives of our fixed assets on an ongoing basis. This review indicated that the actual lives of leasehold improvements were longer than the estimated useful lives used for depreciation purposes in our consolidated financial statements. As a result, effective January 31, 2010, we changed our estimate of the useful lives of our leasehold improvements to the lesser of 10 years or the term of the lease to better reflect the estimated periods during which these assets will remain in service. The useful lives of leasehold improvements were previously estimated to be the lesser of 7 years or the term of the lease. For the fiscal year ended January 29, 2011, the effect of this change in estimate was to reduce depreciation expense by $4.2 million, increase net income by $2.7 million and increase basic and diluted earnings per share by $0.09.

# Change in Depreciation, Amortization, or Depletion Method

● LO11–6

Changes in depreciation, amortization, or depletion methods are accounted for the same way as a change in accounting estimate.

Generally accepted accounting principles require that a change in depreciation, amortization, or depletion method be considered a change in accounting estimate that is achieved by a change in accounting principle. We account for these changes prospectively, exactly as we would any other change in estimate. One difference is that most changes in estimate do not require a company to justify the change. However, this change in estimate is a result of changing an accounting principle and therefore requires a clear justification as to why the new method is preferable. Consider the example in Illustration 11–17.

On January 1, 2011, the Hogan Manufacturing Company purchased a machine for $250,000. The company expects the service life of the machine to be five years and its anticipated residual value to be $30,000. The company's fiscal year-end is December 31 and the double-declining-balance (DDB) depreciation method is used. During 2013, the company switched from the DDB to the straight-line method. In 2013, the adjusting entry is:

| | | |
|---|---|---|
| Depreciation expense (below) ................................................................ | 20,000 | |
|    Accumulated depreciation ..................................................................... | | 20,000 |

DDB depreciation:

| | | |
|---|---|---|
| 2011 | $100,000 | ($250,000 × 40%*) |
| 2012 | 60,000 | ([$250,000 − 100,000] × 40%*) |
| Total | $160,000 | |

*Double the straight-line rate for 5 years ([⅕ = 20%] × 2 = 40%)

| | |
|---|---|
| $250,000 | Cost |
| 160,000 | Depreciation to date, DDB (2011–2012) |
| 90,000 | Undepreciated cost as of 1/1/13 |
| 30,000 | Less residual value |
| 60,000 | Depreciable base |
| ÷ 3 yrs. | Remaining life (5 years − 2 years) |
| $ 20,000 | New annual depreciation |

A disclosure note reports the effect of the change on net income and earnings per share along with clear justification for changing depreciation methods.

**Illustration 11–17**

Change in Depreciation Method

Illustration 11–18 provides an example of a disclosure describing a recent change in depreciation method by **Composite Technology Corporation**, a producer of renewable energy products for the electrical utility industry.

**Change in Accounting Estimate (in part)**

Effective on October 1, 2009, the Company changed its method of depreciation for production machinery and equipment from the straight-line method to the units-of-production method. This change in depreciation method resulted from the use of new internally developed cost-effective machines that provided improved production rates, provided longer service lives and substantially increased production capacity. The new production machines actual pattern of consumption of the expected benefits is significantly less than straight-lining over time, therefore the units-of-production method was preferable and appropriate. In accordance with U.S. GAAP, the Company accounted for this change in accounting estimate prospectively beginning October 1, 2009. For the year ended September 30, 2010, the change in our method of depreciating production machinery and equipment resulted in lowering depreciation expense (included in Cost of Revenue), Net Loss from Continuing Operations and Net Loss by $184,000. For the year ended September 30, 2010, basic and diluted earnings per share from continuing operations and net loss were not affected.

**Illustration 11–18**

Change in Depreciation Method—Composite Technology Corporation

**Real World Financials**

Frequently, when a company changes depreciation method, the change will be effective only for assets placed in service after that date. Of course, that means depreciation schedules do not require revision because the change does not affect assets depreciated in prior periods. A disclosure note still is required to provide justification for the change and to report the effect of the change on the current year's income.

# Error Correction

Errors involving property, plant, and equipment and intangible assets include computational errors in the calculation of depreciation, depletion, or amortization and mistakes made in determining whether expenditures should be capitalized or expensed. These errors can affect many years. For example, let's say a major addition to equipment should be capitalized but

● LO11–7

incorrectly is expensed. Not only is income in the year of the error understated, but subsequent years' income is overstated because depreciation is omitted.

Recall from our discussion of inventory errors in Chapter 9 that if a material error is discovered in an accounting period subsequent to the period in which the error is made, any previous years' financial statements that were incorrect as a result of the error are retrospectively restated to reflect the correction. Any account balances that are incorrect as a result of the error are corrected by journal entry. If retained earnings is one of the incorrect accounts, the correction is reported as a *prior period adjustment* to the beginning balance in the statement of shareholders' equity.[14] In addition, a disclosure note is needed to describe the nature of the error and the impact of its correction on net income, income before extraordinary items, and earnings per share.

Here is a summary of the treatment of material errors occurring in a previous year:

- Previous years' financial statements are retrospectively restated.
- Account balances are corrected.
- If retained earnings requires correction, the correction is reported as a prior period adjustment.
- A note describes the nature of the error and the impact of the correction on income.

Consider Illustration 11–19. The 2011 and 2012 financial statements that were incorrect as a result of the error are *retrospectively restated* to report the addition to the patent and to reflect the correct amount of amortization expense, assuming both statements are reported again for comparative purposes in the 2013 annual report.

**Illustration 11–19**

Error Correction

Sometimes, the analysis is easier if you re-create the entries actually recorded incorrectly and those that would have been recorded if the error hadn't occurred, and then compare them.

In 2013, the controller of the Hathaway Corporation discovered an error in recording $300,000 in legal fees to successfully defend a patent infringement suit in 2011. The $300,000 was charged to legal fee expense but should have been capitalized and amortized over the five-year remaining life of the patent. Straight-line amortization is used by Hathaway for all intangibles.

**Analysis**

($ in thousands)

| | Correct (Should Have Been Recorded) | | | Incorrect (As Recorded) | | |
|---|---|---|---|---|---|---|
| 2011 | Patent .............. | 300 | | Expense ........................... | 300 | |
| | Cash ............. | | 300 | Cash .............................. | | 300 |
| 2011 | Expense ........... | 60 | | Amortization entry omitted | | |
| | Patent .......... | | 60 | | | |
| 2012 | Expense ........... | 60 | | Amortization entry omitted | | |
| | Patent .......... | | 60 | | | |

During the two-year period, amortization expense was *understated* by $120 thousand, but other expenses were *overstated* by $300 thousand, so net income during the period was *understated* by $180 thousand (ignoring income taxes). This means retained earnings is currently *understated* by that amount.

Patent is understated by $180 thousand.

| | ($ in thousands) | |
|---|---|---|
| Patent ........................................................................................... | 180 | |
|    Retained earnings ....................................................................... | | 180 |

*To correct incorrect accounts.*

Because retained earnings is one of the accounts incorrect as a result of the error, a correction to that account of $180,000 is reported as a prior period adjustment to the 2013

---

[14]The prior period adjustment is applied to beginning retained earnings for the year following the error, or for the earliest year being reported in the comparative financial statements when the error occurs prior to the earliest year presented. The retained earnings balances in years after the first year also are adjusted to what those balances would be if the error had not occurred, but a company may choose not to explicitly report those adjustments as separate line items.

beginning retained earnings balance in Hathaway's comparative statements of shareholders' equity. Assuming that 2012 is included with 2013 in the comparative statements, a correction would be made to the 2012 beginning retained earnings balance as well. That prior period adjustment, though, would be for the pre-2012 difference: $300,000 − 60,000 = $240,000.

Also, a disclosure note accompanying Hathaway's 2013 financial statements should describe the nature of the error and the impact of its correction on each year's net income (understated by $240,000 in 2011 and overstated by $60,000 in 2012), income before extraordinary items (same as net income), and earnings per share.

Chapter 20 provides in-depth coverage of changes in estimates and methods, and of accounting errors. We cover the tax effect of these changes and errors in that chapter.

# Impairment of Value

Depreciation, depletion, and amortization reflect a gradual consumption of the benefits inherent in property, plant, and equipment and intangible assets. An implicit assumption in allocating the cost of an asset over its useful life is that there has been no significant reduction in the anticipated total benefits or service potential of the asset. Situations can arise, however, that cause a significant decline or impairment of those benefits or service potentials. An extreme case would be the destruction of a plant asset—say a building destroyed by fire—before the asset is fully depreciated. The remaining carrying value of the asset in that case should be written off as a loss. Sometimes, though, the impairment of future value is more subtle.

● LO11–8

**FINANCIAL Reporting Case**

Q3, p. 589

The way we recognize and measure an impairment loss differs depending on whether the assets are to be held and used or are being held to be sold. Accounting is different, too, for assets with finite lives and those with indefinite lives. We consider those differences now.

## Assets to Be Held and Used

An increasingly common occurrence in practice is the partial write-down of property, plant, and equipment and intangible assets that remain in use. For example, in the second quarter of 2001, **American Airlines** reduced the carrying value (book value) of certain aircraft by $685 million. The write-down reflected the significant reduction in demand for air travel that occurred even before the September 11, 2001, terrorist attacks on the World Trade Center and the Pentagon.

Conceptually, there is considerable merit for a policy requiring the write-down of an asset when there has been a significant decline in value. A write-down can provide important information about the future cash flows that a company can generate from using the asset. However, in practice, this process is very subjective. Even if it appears certain that significant impairment of value has occurred, it often is difficult to measure the amount of the required write-down.

An asset held for use should be written down if there has been a significant impairment of value.

For example, let's say a company purchased $2,000,000 of equipment to be used in the production of a new type of laser printer. Depreciation is determined using the straight-line method over a useful life of six years and the residual value is estimated at $200,000. At the beginning of year 3, the machine's book value has been reduced by accumulated depreciation to $1,400,000 [$2,000,000 − ($300,000 × 2)]. At that time, new technology is developed causing a significant reduction in the selling price of the new laser printer as well as a reduction in anticipated demand for the product. Management estimates that the equipment will be useful for only two more years and will have no significant residual value.

This situation is not simply a matter of a change in the estimates of useful life and residual value. Management must decide if the events occurring in year 3 warrant a write-down of the asset below $1,400,000. A write-down would be appropriate if the company decided that it would be unable to fully recover this amount through future use.

For assets to be held and used, different guidelines apply to (1) property, plant, and equipment and intangible assets with finite useful lives (subject to depreciation, depletion, or amortization) and (2) intangible assets with indefinite useful lives (not subject to amortization).

**PROPERTY, PLANT, AND EQUIPMENT AND FINITE-LIFE INTANGIBLE ASSETS.** Generally accepted accounting principles provide guidelines for when to recognize and how to measure impairment losses of long-lived tangible assets and intangible assets with finite useful lives.[15] For purposes of this recognition and measurement, assets are grouped at the lowest level for which identifiable cash flows are largely independent of the cash flows of other assets.

**When to Test for Impairment.**    It would be impractical to test all assets or asset groups for impairment at the end of every reporting period. GAAP requires investigation of possible impairment only if events or changes in circumstances indicate that the book value of the asset or asset group may not be recoverable. This might happen from:

> Property, plant, and equipment and finite-life intangible assets are tested for impairment only when events or changes in circumstances indicate book value may not be recoverable.

a.  A significant decrease in market price.

b.  A significant adverse change in how the asset is being used or in its physical condition.

c.  A significant adverse change in legal factors or in the business climate.

d.  An accumulation of costs significantly higher than the amount originally expected for the acquisition or construction of an asset.

e.  A current-period loss combined with a history of losses or a projection of continuing losses associated with the asset.

f.  A realization that the asset will be disposed of significantly before the end of its estimated useful life.[16]

**Measurement.**    Determining whether to record an impairment loss and actually recording the loss is a two-step process. The first step is a *recoverability* test—an impairment loss is required only when the undiscounted sum of estimated future cash flows from an asset is less than the asset's book value. The *measurement* of impairment loss—step 2—is the difference between the asset's book value and its fair value. If an impairment loss is recognized, the written-down book value becomes the new cost base for future cost allocation. Later recovery of an impairment loss is prohibited.

> STEP 1—An impairment loss is required only when the undiscounted sum of future cash flows is less than book value.

Let's look closer at the measurement process (step two). Fair value is the amount at which the asset could be bought or sold in a current transaction between willing parties. Quoted market prices could be used if they're available. If fair value is not determinable, it must be estimated.

> STEP 2—The impairment loss is the excess of book value over fair value.

The process is best described by an example. Consider Illustration 11–20.

In the entry in Illustration 11–20, we reduce accumulated depreciation to zero and decrease the cost of the assets to their fair value of \$135 million (\$300 − 165). This adjusted amount serves as the revised basis for subsequent depreciation over the remaining useful life of the assets, just as if the assets had been acquired on the impairment date for their fair values.

> The present value of future cash flows often is used as a measure of fair value.

Because the fair value of the factory assets was not readily available to Dakota in Illustration 11–20, the \$135 million had to be estimated. One method that can be used to estimate fair value is to compute the discounted present value of future cash flows expected from the asset. Keep in mind that we use *undiscounted* estimates of cash flows in step one to determine whether an impairment loss is indicated, but *discounted* estimates of cash flows to determine the amount of the loss. In calculating present value, either a traditional approach or an expected cash flow approach can be used. The traditional approach is to incorporate risk and uncertainty into the discount rate. Recall from discussions in previous chapters that the expected cash flow approach incorporates risk and uncertainty instead into a determination of a probability-weighted cash flow expectation, and then discounts this expected cash flow using a risk-free interest rate. We discussed and illustrated the expected cash flow approach in previous chapters.

A disclosure note is needed to describe the impairment loss. The note should include a description of the impaired asset or asset group, the facts and circumstances leading to the impairment, the amount of the loss if not separately disclosed on the face of the income statement, and the method used to determine fair value.

**The Great Atlantic and Pacific Tea Company, Inc.**, is a large supermarket chain. Illustration 11–21 shows the company's disclosure note describing recent impairment losses. The note provides a summary of the process used to identify and measure impairment losses for property, plant, and equipment and finite-life intangible assets.

---

[15]FASB ASC 360–10–35–15 through 20: Property, Plant, and Equipment—Overall—Subsequent Measurement—Impairment or Disposal of Long-Lived Assets (previously "Accounting for the Impairment of Long-Lived Assets and for Long-Lived Assets to Be Disposed Of," *Statement of Financial Accounting Standards No. 144* (Norwalk, Conn.: FASB, 2001)).

[16]FASB ASC 360–10–35–21: Property, Plant, and Equipment—Overall—Subsequent Measurement—Impairment or Disposal of Long-Lived Assets (previously "Accounting for the Impairment of Long-Lived Assets and for Long-Lived Assets to Be Disposed Of," *Statement of Financial Accounting Standards No. 144* (Norwalk, Conn.: FASB, 2001), par.8).

The Dakota Corporation operates several factories that manufacture medical equipment. Near the end of the company's 2013 fiscal year, a change in business climate related to a competitor's innovative products indicated to management that the $170 million book value (original cost of $300 million less accumulated depreciation of $130 million) of the assets of one of Dakota's factories may not be recoverable.

Management is able to identify cash flows from this factory and estimates that future cash flows over the remaining useful life of the factory will be $150 million. The fair value of the factory's assets is not readily available but is estimated to be $135 million.

**Change in circumstances.** A change in the business climate related to a competitor's innovative products requires Dakota to investigate for possible impairment.

**Step 1. Recoverability.** Because the book value of $170 million exceeds the $150 million undiscounted future cash flows, an impairment loss is indicated.

**Step 2. Measurement of impairment loss.** The impairment loss is $35 million, determined as follows:

| | |
|---|---|
| Book value | $170 million |
| Fair value | 135 million |
| Impairment loss | $ 35 million |

The entry to record the loss is ($ in millions):

| | | |
|---|---|---|
| Loss on impairment ................... | 35 | |
| Accumulated depreciation .......... | 130 | |
| Factory assets ......................... | | 165 |

The loss normally is reported in the income statement as a separate component of operating expenses.

**Illustration 11–20**

Impairment Loss— Property, Plant, and Equipment

---

**Note 4 – Valuation of Long-Lived Assets (in part)**

We review the carrying values of our long-lived assets for possible impairment whenever events or changes in circumstances indicate that the carrying amount of assets may not be recoverable. Such review is primarily based upon groups of assets and the undiscounted estimated future cash flows from such assets to determine if the carrying value of such assets is recoverable from their respective cash flows. If such review indicates impairment exists, we measure such impairment as the difference between the fair value and carrying value of the assets.

**Impairments due to unrecoverable assets (in part)**

As a result of experiencing cash flow losses at certain stores, we determined that triggering events had occurred that required us to test the related long-lived assets for potential impairment. We recorded an impairment charge of $45.3 million during the fiscal year ended February 26, 2011 to partially write down these stores' long-lived assets.

**Illustration 11–21**

Asset Impairment Disclosure—The Great Atlantic and Pacific Tea Company Inc.

Real World Financials

# International Financial Reporting Standards

**Impairment of Value: Property, Plant, and Equipment and Finite-Life Intangible Assets.** Highlighted below are some important differences in accounting for impairment of value for property, plant, and equipment and finite-life intangible assets between U.S. GAAP and *IAS No. 36.*[17]

● LO11–10

| | U.S. GAAP | IFRS |
|---|---|---|
| **When to Test** | When events or changes in circumstances indicate that book value may not be recoverable. | Assets must be assessed for indicators of impairment at the end of each reporting period. Indicators of impairment are similar to U.S. GAAP. |

(continued)

---

[17]"Impairment of Assets," *International Accounting Standard No. 36* (IASCF), as amended effective January 1, 2011.

(concluded)

| | | |
|---|---|---|
| **Recoverability** | An impairment loss is required when an asset's book value exceeds the undiscounted sum of the asset's estimated future cash flows. | There is no equivalent recoverability test. An impairment loss is required when an asset's book value exceeds the higher of the asset's value-in-use (present value of estimated future cash flows) and fair value less costs to sell. |
| **Measurement** | The impairment loss is the difference between book value and fair value. | The impairment loss is the difference between book value and the "recoverable amount" (the higher of the asset's value-in-use and fair value less costs to sell). |
| **Subsequent Reversal of Loss** | Prohibited. | Required if the circumstances that caused the impairment are resolved. |

**IFRS ILLUSTRATION**

Let's look at an illustration highlighting the important differences described above. The Jasmine Tea Company has a factory that has significantly decreased in value due to technological innovations in the industry. Below are data related to the factory's assets:

| | ($ in millions) |
|---|---|
| Book value | $18.5 |
| Undiscounted sum of estimated future cash flows | 19.0 |
| Present value of future cash flows | 16.0 |
| Fair value less cost to sell (determined by appraisal) | 15.5 |

What amount of impairment loss should Jasmine Tea recognize, if any, under U.S. GAAP? Under IFRS?

**U.S. GAAP**    There is no impairment loss. The sum of undiscounted estimated future cash flows exceeds the book value.

**IFRS**    Jasmine should recognize an impairment loss of $2.5 million. Indicators of impairment are present and book value exceeds both value-in-use (present value of cash flows) and fair value less costs to sell. The recoverable amount is $16 million, the higher of value-in-use ($16 million) and fair value less costs to sell ($15.5 million). The impairment loss is the difference between book value of $18.5 million and the $16 million recoverable amount.

Real World Financials

Nokia, a Finnish company, prepares its financial statements according to IFRS. The following disclosure note describes the company's impairment policy:

**Impairment Review (in part)**

The Group assesses the carrying amount of identifiable intangible assets and long-lived assets if events or changes in circumstances indicate that such carrying amount may not be recoverable. Factors that trigger an impairment review include underperformance relative to historical or projected future results, significant changes in the manner of the use of the acquired assets or the strategy for the overall business and significant negative industry or economic trends.

The Group conducts its impairment testing by determining the recoverable amount for the asset. The recoverable amount of an asset is the higher of its fair value less costs to sell and its value in use. The recoverable amount is then compared to its carrying amount and an impairment loss is recognized if the recoverable amount is less than the carrying amount.

**INDEFINITE-LIFE INTANGIBLE ASSETS OTHER THAN GOODWILL.**    Intangible assets with indefinite useful lives should be tested for impairment annually, or more frequently if events or changes in circumstances indicate that the asset may be impaired. The measurement of an impairment loss for indefinite-life intangible assets other than goodwill is a one-step process. We compare the fair value of the asset with its book value. If book value exceeds fair value, an impairment loss is recognized for the difference. Notice that we omit the recoverability test with these assets. Because we anticipate cash flows to continue indefinitely, recoverability is not a good indicator of impairment.

*Intangible assets with indefinite useful lives should be tested for impairment at least annually.*

Similar to property, plant, and equipment and finite-life intangible assets, if an impairment loss is recognized, the written-down book value becomes the new cost base for future cost allocation. Recovery of the impairment loss is prohibited. Disclosure requirements also are similar.

If book value exceeds fair value, an impairment loss is recognized for the difference.

# International Financial Reporting Standards

**Impairment of Value: Indefinite-Life Intangible Assets Other than Goodwill.** Similar to U.S. GAAP, IFRS requires indefinite-life intangible assets other than goodwill to be tested for impairment at least annually. However, under U.S. GAAP, the impairment loss is measured as the difference between book value and fair value, while under IFRS the impairment loss is the difference between book value and the recoverable amount. The recoverable amount is the higher of the asset's value-in-use (present value of estimated future cash flows) and fair value less costs to sell.

● LO11–10

IFRS requires the reversal of an impairment loss if the circumstances that caused the impairment are resolved. Reversals are prohibited under U.S. GAAP.

Also, indefinite-life intangible assets may not be combined with other indefinite-life intangible assets for the required annual impairment test. Under U.S. GAAP, though, if certain criteria are met, indefinite-life intangible assets should be combined for the required annual impairment test.

**GOODWILL.**    Recall that goodwill is a unique intangible asset. Unlike other assets, its cost (a) can't be directly associated with any specific identifiable right and (b) is not separable from the company as a whole. Because of these unique characteristics, we can't measure the impairment of goodwill the same way as we do other assets. GAAP provides guidelines for impairment, which while similar to general impairment guidelines, are specific to goodwill.[18] Let's compare the two-step process for measuring goodwill impairment with the two-step process for measuring impairment for property, plant, and equipment and finite-life intangible assets.

In Step 1, for all classifications of assets, we decide whether a write-down due to impairment is required by determining whether the value of an asset has fallen below its book value. However, in this comparison, the value of assets for property, plant, and equipment and finite-life intangible assets is considered to be value-in-use as measured by the sum of undiscounted cash flows expected from the asset. But due to its unique characteristics, the value of goodwill is not associated with any specific cash flows and must be measured in a unique way. By its very nature, goodwill is inseparable from a particular *reporting unit*. So, for this step, we compare the value of the reporting unit itself with its book value. If the fair value of the reporting unit is less than its book value, an impairment loss is indicated. A reporting unit is an operating segment of a company or a component of an operating segment for which discrete financial information is available and segment management regularly reviews the operating results of that component.

STEP 1—A goodwill impairment loss is indicated when the fair value of the reporting unit is less than its book value.

If goodwill is tested for impairment at the same time as other assets of the reporting unit, the other assets must be tested first and any impairment loss and asset write-down recorded prior to testing goodwill.

In Step 2, for all classifications of property, plant, and equipment and intangible assets, if impairment is indicated from step 1, we measure the amount of impairment as the excess of the book value of the asset over its fair value. However, unlike for most other assets, the fair value of goodwill cannot be measured directly (market value, present value of associated cash flows, etc.) and so must be "implied" from the fair value of the reporting unit that acquired the goodwill.

STEP 2—A goodwill impairment loss is measured as the excess of the book value of the goodwill over its "implied" fair value.

The implied fair value of goodwill is calculated in the same way that goodwill is determined in a business combination. That is, it's a residual amount measured by subtracting the fair value of all identifiable net assets from the purchase price using the unit's previously determined fair value as the purchase price.[19]

---

[18]FASB ASC 350–20–35: Intangibles—Goodwill and Other—Goodwill—Subsequent Measurement (previously "Goodwill and Other Intangible Assets," *Statement of Financial Accounting Standards No. 142* (Norwalk, Conn.: FASB, 2001)).

[19]The impairment loss recognized cannot exceed the book value of goodwill.

**When to test for impairment.** Prior to 2012, companies were required to perform *step one* of the two-step test for goodwill impairment at least once a year, as well as in between annual test dates if something occurred that would indicate that the fair value of the reporting unit was below its book value. Then, if the first step indicated that the fair value of the reporting unit was indeed below book value, the company would perform *step two* to measure the amount of goodwill impairment.

In response to concerns about the cost and complexity of performing step one every year, the FASB issued an Accounting Standards Update (ASU) in 2011 that allows companies the option to decide whether step one is necessary.[20] Companies selecting this option will evaluate relevant events and circumstances to determine whether it is "more likely than not" (a likelihood of more than 50 percent) that the fair value of a reporting unit is now less than its book value. Only if that's determined to be the case will the company perform the first step of the two-step goodwill impairment test. A list of possible events and circumstances that a company should consider in this qualitative assessment is provided in the ASU.

A goodwill impairment example is provided in Illustration 11–22.

**Illustration 11–22**

Impairment Loss— Goodwill

In 2012, the Upjane Corporation acquired Pharmacopia Corporation for $500 million. Upjane recorded $100 million in goodwill related to this acquisition because the fair value of the net assets of Pharmacopia was $400 million. After the acquisition, Pharmacopia continues to operate as a separate company and is considered a reporting unit.

At the end of 2013, events and circumstances indicated that it is more likely than not that the fair value of Pharmacopia is less than its book value requiring Upjane to perform step one of the goodwill impairment test. The book value of Pharmacopia's net assets at the end of 2013 is $440 million, including the $100 million in goodwill. On that date, the fair value of Pharmacopia is estimated to be $360 million and the fair value of all of its identifiable tangible and intangible assets, excluding goodwill, is estimated to be $335 million.

**Step 1. Recoverability.** Because the book value of the net assets of $440 million exceeds the $360 million fair value of the reporting unit, an impairment loss is indicated.

**Step 2. Measurement of impairment loss.** The impairment loss is $75 million, determined as follows:

**Determination of implied goodwill:**

| | |
|---|---|
| Fair value of Pharmacopia | $360 million |
| Fair value of Pharmacopia's net assets (excluding goodwill) | 335 million |
| Implied value of goodwill | $ 25 million |

**Measurement of impairment loss:**

| | |
|---|---|
| Book value of goodwill | $100 million |
| Implied value of goodwill | 25 million |
| Impairment loss | $ 75 million |

The entry to record the loss is ($ in millions):

| | | |
|---|---|---|
| Loss on impairment of goodwill ................................................ | 75 | |
| Goodwill .................................................................... | | 75 |

The loss normally is reported in the income statement as a separate component of operating expenses.

The "implied" fair value of goodwill is a residual amount measured by subtracting the fair value of all identifiable net assets from the unit's fair value.

The acquiring company in a business combination often pays for the acquisition using its own stock. In the late 1990s, the stock prices of many companies were unusually high. These often-inflated stock prices meant high purchase prices for many acquisitions and, in many cases, incredibly high values allocated to goodwill. When stock prices retreated in 2000 and 2001, it became obvious that the book value of goodwill for many companies would never be recovered. Some examples of multibillion dollar goodwill impairment losses are shown in Illustration 11–23.

---

[20]FASB ASC 350–20–35–3: Intangibles—Goodwill and Other—Goodwill—Subsequent Measurement (previously "Goodwill and Other Intangible Assets," *Statement of Financial Accounting Standards No. 142* (Norwalk, Conn.: FASB, 2001)).

| Company | Goodwill Impairment Loss |
|---------|--------------------------|
| AOL Time Warner | $99 billion |
| JDS Uniphase | 50 billion |
| Nortel Networks | 12 billion |
| Lucent Technologies | 4 billion |
| Vivendi Universal SA | 15 billion (Euros) |

**Illustration 11–23**
Goodwill Impairment Losses

**The Clorox Company** provides a more recent example. In Illustration 11–24 we see the disclosure note that describes a $258 million impairment charge.

---

**Note 5. Goodwill, Trademarks, and Other Intangible Assets (in part)**

During the fiscal 2011 second quarter, the Company identified challenges in increasing sales for the Burt's Bees business in new international markets in accordance with projections, particularly in the European Union and Asia. Additionally, during the fiscal 2011 second quarter, the Company initiated its process for updating the three-year long-range financial and operating plan for the Burt's Bees business. In addition to slower than projected growth of international sales and challenges in the timing of certain international expansion plans, the domestic natural personal care category had not recovered in accordance with the Company's projections. Following the comprehensive reevaluation, the Company recognized a goodwill impairment charge of $258 million.

**Illustration 11–24**
Goodwill Impairment Disclosure—The Clorox Company

Real World Financials

---

# International Financial Reporting Standards

**Impairment of Value—Goodwill.** Highlighted below are some important differences in accounting for the impairment of goodwill between U.S. GAAP and *IAS No. 36*.

● LO11–10

| | U.S. GAAP | IFRS |
|---|-----------|------|
| **Level of Testing** | *Reporting unit*—a segment or a component of an operating segment for which discrete financial information is available. | *Cash-generating unit (CGU)*—the lowest level at which goodwill is monitored by management. A CGU can't be lower than a segment. |
| **Measurement** | *A two-step process:* 1. Compare the fair value of the reporting unit with its book value. A loss is indicated if fair value is less than book value. 2. The impairment loss is the excess of book value over implied fair value. | *A one-step:* Compare the recoverable amount of the CGU to book value. If the recoverable amount is less, reduce goodwill first, then other assets. The recoverable amount is the higher of fair value less costs to sell and value-in-use (present value of estimated future cash flows). |

*IAS No. 36* requires goodwill to be tested for impairment at least annually. U.S. GAAP allows a company to avoid annual testing by making qualitative evaluations of the likelihood of goodwill impairment to determine if step one is necessary. Both U.S. GAAP and *IAS No. 36* prohibit the reversal of goodwill impairment losses.

Let's look at an illustration highlighting these differences.

Canterbury LTD. has $38 million of goodwill in its balance sheet from the 2011 acquisition of Denton, Inc. At the end of 2013, Canterbury's management provided the following information for the year-end goodwill impairment test ($ in millions):

**IFRS ILLUSTRATION**

| | |
|---|---|
| Fair value of Denton (determined by appraisal) | $132 |
| Fair value of Denton's net assets (excluding goodwill) | 120 |
| Book value of Denton's net assets (including goodwill) | 150 |
| Present value of Denton's estimated future cash flows | 135 |

(continued)

(concluded)

Assume that Denton is considered a reporting unit under U.S. GAAP and a cash-generating unit under IFRS, and that its fair value approximates fair value less costs to sell. What is the amount of goodwill impairment loss that Canterbury should recognize, if any, under U.S. GAAP? Under IFRS?

| U.S. GAAP | Fair value of Denton | $132 |
| | Fair value of Denton's net assets (excluding goodwill) | 120 |
| | Implied value of goodwill | $ 12 |
| | | |
| | Book value of goodwill | $38 |
| | Implied value of goodwill | 12 |
| | Impairment loss | $ 26 |

| IFRS | The recoverable amount is $135 million, the higher of the $135 million value-in-use (present value of estimated future cash flows) and the $132 million fair value less costs to sell. | |
| | Denton's book value | $150 |
| | Recoverable amount | 135 |
| | Impairment loss | $ 15 |

Nestle SA, a Swiss company, is one of the largest food and nutrition companies in the world. The company prepares its financial statements according to IFRS. The following disclosures describe the company's goodwill impairment policy as well as a $105 million Swiss franc goodwill impairment loss related to its Sports Nutrition unit.

**Impairment of Goodwill (in part)**
Goodwill is tested for impairment at least annually and upon the occurrence of an indication of impairment.
The impairment tests are performed annually at the same time each year at the cash-generating unit (CGU) level. . . . The impairment tests are performed by comparing the carrying value of the amount of assets of these CGU with their recoverable amount, based on their future projected cash flows discounted at an appropriate pre-tax rate.

**Impairment charge during the period (in part)**
Goodwill related to the acquisition of PowerBar in 2000 has been allocated for the impairment test to the Cash-Generating Unit (CGU) Sports Nutrition Worldwide. . . . Competitive environment and economic conditions in the USA led to lower than anticipated sales demand, resulting in downward revision of projected cash flows since the last impairment test and the recoverable amount of the CGU is lower than its carrying amount. An impairment of goodwill amounting to CHF 105 million has been recognized.

# Assets to Be Sold

We have been discussing the recognition and measurement for the impairment of value of assets to be held and used. We also test for impairment of assets held for sale. These are assets management has actively committed to immediately sell in their present condition and for which sale is probable.

An asset or group of assets classified as held for sale is measured at the lower of its book value, or fair value less cost to sell. An impairment loss is recognized for any write-down to fair value less cost to sell.[21] Except for including the cost to sell, notice the similarity to

**For assets held for sale, if book value exceeds fair value less cost to sell, an impairment loss is recognized for the difference.**

---

[21]If the asset is unsold at the end of a subsequent reporting period, a gain is recognized for any increase in fair value less cost to sell, but not in excess of the loss previously recognized.

impairment of assets to be held and used. We don't depreciate or amortize these assets while classified as held for sale and we report them separately in the balance sheet. Recall from our discussion of discontinued operations in Chapter 4 that similar rules apply for a component of an entity that is classified as held for sale.

Illustration 11–25 summarizes the guidelines for the recognition and measurement of impairment losses.

| Type of Asset | When to Test for Impairment | Impairment Test |
|---|---|---|
| **To Be Held and Used** | | |
| Property, plant, and equipment and finite-life intangible assets | When events or circumstances indicate book value may not be recoverable. | Step 1—An impairment loss is required only when book value is not recoverable (undiscounted sum of estimated future cash flows less than book value). Step 2—The impairment loss is the excess of book value over fair value. |
| Indefinite-life intangible assets (other than goodwill) | At least annually, or more frequently if indicated. | If book value exceeds fair value, an impairment loss is recognized for the difference. |
| Goodwill | At least annually, or more frequently if indicated. Option to avoid annual testing by making qualitative evaluations of the likelihood of goodwill impairment to determine if step one is necessary. | Step 1—A loss is indicated when the fair value of the reporting unit is less than its book value. Step 2—An impairment loss is measured as the excess of book value over implied fair value. |
| **To Be Sold** | When considered held for sale | If book value exceeds fair value less cost to sell, an impairment loss is recognized for the difference. |

**Illustration 11–25**

Summary of Asset Impairment Guidelines

# Where We're Headed

As we discussed briefly in Chapter 10 on page 540, the FASB and IASB have developed a new joint standard update involving revenue recognition that allows sellers to capitalize, as an intangible asset, the incremental costs of obtaining and fulfilling a long-term (longer than one year) contract. Sales commissions is an example of a contract acquisition cost that could be capitalized, rather than expensed, under this new ASU. If capitalized, these intangible assets are amortized on a systematic basis consistent with the pattern of transfer of the goods or services to which the asset relates. An impairment loss would be recognized to the extent that the book value of the intangible asset exceeds its recoverable amount. The recoverable amount is the amount of consideration the company expects to receive from the sale of goods or services to which the asset relates less costs related directly to providing those goods or services.

● LO11–10

## Impairment Losses and Earnings Quality

What do losses from the write-down of inventory and restructuring costs have in common? The presence of these items in a corporate income statement presents a challenge to an analyst trying to determine a company's permanent earnings—those likely to continue in the future. We discussed these issues in prior chapters.

An analyst must decide whether to consider asset impairment losses as transitory in nature or as a part of permanent earnings.

We now can add asset impairment losses to the list of "big bath" accounting techniques some companies use to manipulate earnings. By writing off large amounts of assets, companies significantly reduce earnings in the year of the write-off but are able to increase future earnings by lowering future depreciation, depletion, or amortization. Here's how. We measure the impairment loss as the difference between an asset's book value and its fair value. However, in most cases, fair value must be estimated, and the estimation process usually involves a forecast of future net cash flows the company expects to generate from the asset's use. If a company underestimates future net cash flows, fair value is understated. This has two effects: (1) current year's income is unrealistically low due to the impairment loss being overstated and (2) future income is unrealistically high because depreciation, depletion, and amortization are based on understated asset values.

## Where We're Headed

● LO11–10

The FASB and IASB have identified impairment as a topic for longer-term convergence.

In their 2006 *Memorandum of Understanding*, the FASB and IASB included impairment as one of their short-term convergence projects. However, in 2008 the Boards agreed to defer work on impairment. Early in 2009, the Boards identified impairment as a topic for longer term convergence. When this text was published, no specific impairment project had been proposed.

## PART C — SUBSEQUENT EXPENDITURES

Now that we have acquired and measured assets, we can address accounting issues incurred subsequent to their acquisition. This part of the chapter deals with the treatment of expenditures made over the life of these assets to maintain and/or improve them.

### Expenditures Subsequent to Acquisition

● LO11–9

Many long-lived assets require expenditures to repair, maintain, or improve them. These expenditures can present accounting problems if they are material. In general, a choice must be made between capitalizing the expenditures by either increasing the asset's book value or creating a new asset, or expensing them in the period in which they are incurred. Conceptually, we can refer to the matching principle that requires the capitalization of expenditures that are expected to produce benefits beyond the current fiscal year. Expenditures that simply maintain a given level of benefits are expensed in the period they are incurred.

Expenditures related to assets can increase future benefits in the following ways:

1. An extension of the *useful life* of the asset.
2. An increase in the *operating efficiency* of the asset resulting in either an increase in the quantity of goods or services produced or a decrease in future operating costs.
3. An increase in the *quality* of the goods or services produced by the asset.

Theoretically, expenditures that cause any of these results should be capitalized initially and then expensed in future periods through depreciation, depletion, or amortization. This permits the matching of the expenditure with the future benefits. Of course, materiality is an important factor in the practical application of this approach.

Many companies do not capitalize any expenditure unless it exceeds a predetermined amount that is considered material.

For expediency, many companies set materiality thresholds for the capitalization of any expenditure. For example, a company might decide to expense all expenditures under $200 regardless of whether or not future benefits are increased. Judgment is required to determine the appropriate materiality threshold as well as the appropriate treatment of expenditures over $200. There often are practical problems in capitalizing these expenditures. For example, even if future benefits are increased by the expenditure, it may be difficult to determine how long the benefits will last. It's important for a company to establish a policy for treating these expenditures and apply it consistently.

We classify subsequent expenditures as (1) repairs and maintenance, (2) additions, (3) improvements, or (4) rearrangements.

## Repairs and Maintenance

These expenditures are made to *maintain* a given level of benefits provided by the asset and do not *increase* future benefits. For example, the cost of an engine tune-up or the repair of an engine part for a delivery truck allows the truck to continue its productive activity. If the maintenance is not performed, the truck will not provide the benefits originally anticipated. In that sense, future benefits are provided; without the repair, the truck will no longer operate. The key, though, is that future benefits are not provided *beyond those originally anticipated.* Expenditures for these activities should be expensed in the period incurred.

> Expenditures for *repairs and maintenance* generally are expensed when incurred.

# Additional Consideration

> If repairs and maintenance costs are seasonal, interim financial statements may be misstated. For example, suppose annual maintenance is performed on a company's fleet of delivery trucks. The annual income statement correctly includes one year's maintenance expense. However, for interim reporting purposes, if the entire expenditure is made in one quarter, should that quarter's income statement include as expense the entire cost of the annual maintenance? If these expenditures can be anticipated, they should be accrued evenly throughout the year by crediting an allowance account. The allowance account is then debited when the maintenance is performed.

## Additions

As the term implies, additions involve adding a new major component to an existing asset and should be capitalized because future benefits are increased. For example, adding a refrigeration unit to a delivery truck increases the capability of the truck, thus increasing its future benefits. Other examples include the construction of a new wing on a building and the addition of a security system to an existing building.

> The costs of *additions* usually are capitalized.

   The capitalized cost includes all necessary expenditures to bring the addition to a condition and location for use. For a building addition, this might include the costs of tearing down and removing a wall of the existing building. The capitalized cost of additions is depreciated over the remaining useful life of the original asset or its own useful life, whichever is shorter.

## Improvements

Expenditures classified as improvements involve the replacement of a major component of an asset. The replacement can be a new component with the same characteristics as the old component or a new component with enhanced operating capabilities. For example, an existing refrigeration unit in a delivery truck could be replaced with a new but similar unit or with a new and improved refrigeration unit. In either case, the cost of the improvement usually increases future benefits and should be capitalized by increasing the book value of the related asset (the delivery truck) and depreciated over the useful life of the improved asset. There are three methods used to record the cost of improvements.

> The costs of *improvements* usually are capitalized.

1. *Substitution.* The improvement can be recorded as both (1) a disposition of the old component and (2) the acquisition of the new component. This approach is conceptually appealing but it is practical only if the original cost and accumulated depreciation of the old component can be separately identified.

2. *Capitalization of new cost.* Another way to record an improvement is to include the cost of the improvement (net of any consideration received from the disposition of the old component) as a debit to the related asset account, without removing the original cost and accumulated depreciation of the original component. This approach is acceptable only

if the book value of the original component has been reduced to an immaterial amount through prior depreciation.

3. *Reduction of accumulated depreciation.* Another way to increase an asset's book value is to leave the asset account unaltered but decrease its related accumulated depreciation. The argument for this method is that many improvements extend the useful life of an asset and are equivalent to a partial recovery of previously recorded depreciation. This approach produces the same book value as the capitalization of cost to the asset account. However, cost and accumulated depreciation amounts will differ under the two methods.

The three methods are compared in Illustration 11–26.

## Illustration 11–26
Improvements

The Palmer Corporation replaced the air conditioning system in one of its office buildings that it leases to tenants. The cost of the old air conditioning system, $200,000, is included in the cost of the building. However, the company has separately depreciated the air conditioning system. Depreciation recorded up to the date of replacement totaled $160,000. The old system was removed and the new system installed at a cost of $230,000, which was paid in cash. Parts from the old system were sold for $12,000.
Accounting for the improvement differs depending on the alternative chosen.

**Substitution**
**(1) Disposition of old component.**

| | | |
|---|---|---|
| Cash ........................................................... | 12,000 | |
| Accumulated depreciation—buildings ........................... | 160,000 | |
| Loss on disposal (difference) ................................ | 28,000 | |
|    Buildings ............................................ | | 200,000 |

**(2) Acquisition of new component.**

| | | |
|---|---|---|
| Buildings .................................................... | 230,000 | |
|    Cash ................................................. | | 230,000 |

**Capitalization of new cost**

| | | |
|---|---|---|
| Buildings .................................................... | 218,000 | |
|    Cash ($230,000 − 12,000) ............................. | | 218,000 |

**Reduction of accumulated depreciation**

| | | |
|---|---|---|
| Accumulated depreciation—buildings ........................... | 218,000 | |
|    Cash ($230,000 − 12,000) ............................. | | 218,000 |

## Rearrangements

The costs of material *rearrangements* should be capitalized if they clearly increase future benefits.

Expenditures made to restructure an asset without addition, replacement, or improvement are termed **rearrangements**. The objective is to create a new capability for the asset and not necessarily to extend its useful life. Examples include the rearrangement of machinery on the production line to increase operational efficiency and the relocation of a company's operating plant or office building. If these expenditures are material and they clearly increase future benefits, they should be capitalized and expensed in the future periods benefited. If the expenditures are not material or if it's not certain that future benefits have increased, they should be expensed in the period incurred.

Illustration 11–27 provides a summary of the accounting treatment for the various types of expenditures related to property, plant, and equipment.

## Costs of Defending Intangible Rights

The costs incurred to *successfully* defend an intangible right should be capitalized.

Repairs, additions, improvements, and rearrangements generally relate to property, plant, and equipment. A possible significant expenditure incurred subsequent to the acquisition of intangible assets is the cost of defending the right that gives the asset its value. If an intangible right is *successfully* defended, the litigation costs should be capitalized and amortized over the remaining useful life of the related intangible. This is the appropriate treatment of these expenditures even if the intangible asset was originally developed internally rather than purchased.

The costs incurred to *unsuccessfully* defend an intangible right should be expensed.

If the defense of an intangible right is *unsuccessful,* then the litigation costs should be expensed as incurred because they provide no future benefit. In addition, the book value of any intangible asset should be reduced to realizable value. For example, if a company is unsuccessful in defending a patent infringement suit, the patent's value may be eliminated. The book value of the patent should be written off as a loss.

| Type of Expenditure | Definition | Usual Accounting Treatment |
|---|---|---|
| Repairs and maintenance | Expenditures to maintain a given level of benefits | Expense in the period incurred |
| Additions | The addition of a new major component to an existing asset | Capitalize and depreciate over the remaining useful life of the *original asset or its own useful life, whichever is shorter* |
| Improvements | The replacement of a major component | Capitalize and depreciate over the useful life of the improved asset |
| Rearrangements | Expenditures to restructure an asset without addition, replacement, or improvement | If expenditures are material and clearly increase future benefits, capitalize and depreciate over the future periods benefited |

**Illustration 11–27**

Expenditures Subsequent to Acquisition

# International Financial Reporting Standards

Costs of Defending Intangible Rights. Under U.S. GAAP, litigation costs to successfully defend an intangible right are capitalized and amortized over the remaining useful life of the related intangible. Under IFRS, these costs are expensed, except in rare situations when an expenditure increases future benefits.[22]

● LO11–10

## Financial Reporting Case Solution

1. *Is Penny correct? Do the terms depreciation, depletion, and amortization all mean the same thing? (p. 590)*    Penny is correct. Each of these terms refers to the cost allocation of assets over their service lives. The term *depreciation* is used for plant and equipment, *depletion* for natural resources, and *amortization* for intangibles.

2. **Weyerhaeuser determines depletion based on the "volume of timber estimated to be available." Explain this approach.** *(p. 594)*    Weyerhaeuser is using the units-of-production method to determine depletion. The units-of-production method is an activity-based method that computes a depletion (or depreciation or amortization) rate per measure of activity and then multiplies this rate by actual activity to determine periodic cost allocation. The method is used by Weyerhaeuser to measure depletion of the cost of timber harvested and the amortization of logging railroads and truck roads. The costs of logging are intangible assets because the company does not own the roads.

3. **Explain how asset impairment differs from depreciation, depletion, and amortization. How do companies measure impairment losses for property, plant, and equipment and intangible assets with finite useful lives?** *(p. 613)*    Depreciation, depletion, and amortization reflect a gradual consumption of the benefits inherent in a long-lived asset. An implicit assumption in allocating the cost of an asset over its useful life is that there has been no significant reduction in the anticipated total benefits or service potential of the asset. Situations can arise, however, that cause a significant decline or *impairment* of those benefits or service potentials. Determining whether to record an impairment loss for an asset and actually recording the loss is a two-step process. The first step is a recoverability test—an impairment loss is required only when the undiscounted sum of estimated future cash flows from an asset is less than the asset's book value. The measurement of impairment loss—step 2—is the difference between the asset's book value and its fair value. If an impairment loss is recognized, the written-down book value becomes the new cost base for future cost allocation. ●

---

[22]"Intangible Assets," *International Accounting Standard No. 38* (IASCF), par. 20, as amended effective January 1, 2011.

# The Bottom Line

- **LO11–1** The use of property, plant, and equipment and intangible assets represents a consumption of benefits, or service potentials, inherent in the assets. The matching principle requires that the cost of these inherent benefits or service potentials that were consumed be recognized as an expense. As there very seldom is a direct relationship between the use of assets and revenue production, accounting resorts to arbitrary allocation methods to achieve a matching of expenses with revenues. (p. 590)

- **LO11–2** The allocation process for plant and equipment is called *depreciation*. Time-based depreciation methods estimate service life in years and then allocate depreciable base, cost less estimated residual value, using either a straight-line or accelerated pattern. Activity-based depreciation methods allocate the depreciable base by estimating service life according to some measure of productivity. (p. 592)

- **LO11–3** The allocation process for natural resources is called *depletion*. The activity-based method called units-of-production usually is used to determine periodic depletion. (p. 602)

- **LO11–4** The allocation process for intangible assets is called *amortization*. For an intangible asset with a finite useful life, the capitalized cost less any estimated residual value must be allocated to periods in which the asset is expected to contribute to the company's revenue-generating activities. An intangible asset that is determined to have an indefinite useful life is not subject to periodic amortization. Goodwill is perhaps the most typical intangible asset with an indefinite useful life. (p. 603)

- **LO11–5** A change in either the service life or residual value of property, plant, and equipment and intangible assets should be reflected in the financial statements of the current period and future periods by recalculating periodic depreciation, depletion, or amortization. (p. 609)

- **LO11–6** A change in depreciation, depletion, or amortization method is considered a change in accounting estimate that is achieved by a change in accounting principle. We account for these changes prospectively, exactly as we would any other change in estimate. One difference is that most changes in estimate do not require a company to justify the change. However, this change in estimate is a result of changing an accounting principle and therefore requires a clear justification as to why the new method is preferable. (p. 610)

- **LO11–7** A material error in accounting for property, plant, and equipment and intangible assets that is discovered in a year subsequent to the year of the error requires that previous years' financial statements that were incorrect as a result of the error are retrospectively restated to reflect the correction. Any account balances that are incorrect as a result of the error are corrected by journal entry. If retained earnings is one of the incorrect accounts, the correction is reported as a prior period adjustment to the beginning balance in the statement of shareholders' equity. In addition, a disclosure note is needed to describe the nature of the error and the impact of its correction on income. (p. 611)

- **LO11–8** Conceptually, there is considerable merit for a policy requiring the write-down of an asset when there has been a *significant* decline in value below carrying value (book value). The write-down provides important information about the future cash flows to be generated from the use of the asset. However, in practice this policy is very subjective. GAAP [FASB ASC 360] establishes guidance for when to recognize and how to measure impairment losses of property, plant, and equipment and intangible assets that have finite useful lives. GAAP [FASB ASC 350] also provides guidance for the recognition and measurement of impairment for indefinite-life intangibles and goodwill. (p. 613)

- **LO11–9** Expenditures for repairs and maintenance generally are expensed when incurred. The costs of additions and improvements usually are capitalized. The costs of material rearrangements should be capitalized if they clearly increase future benefits. (p. 622)

- **LO11–10** Among the several differences between U.S. GAAP and IFRS with respect to the utilization and impairment of property, plant, and equipment and intangible assets pertains to reporting assets in the balance sheet. IFRS allows a company to value property, plant, and equipment (PP&E) and intangible assets subsequent to initial valuation at (1) cost less accumulated depreciation/amortization or (2) fair value (revaluation). U.S. GAAP prohibits revaluation. There also are significant differences in accounting for the impairment of property, plant, and equipment and intangible assets. (pp. 597, 600, 604, 606, 615, 617, 619, 621, 622, and 625) ●

# Comparison With Macrs (Tax Depreciation)

**APPENDIX 11A**

Depreciation for financial reporting purposes is an attempt to distribute the cost of the asset, less any anticipated residual value, over the estimated useful life in a systematic and rational manner that attempts to match revenues with the use of the asset. Depreciation for income tax purposes is influenced by the revenue needs of government as well as the desire to influence economic behavior. For example, accelerated depreciation schedules currently allowed are intended to provide incentive for companies to expand and modernize their facilities thus stimulating economic growth.

The federal income tax code allows taxpayers to compute depreciation for their tax returns on assets acquired after 1986 using the **modified accelerated cost recovery system (MACRS)**.[23] Key differences between the calculation of depreciation for financial reporting and the calculation using MACRS are:

1. Estimated useful lives and residual values are not used in MACRS.
2. Firms can't choose among various accelerated methods under MACRS.
3. A half-year convention is used in determining the MACRS depreciation amounts.

Under MACRS, each asset generally is placed within a recovery period category. The six categories for personal property are 3, 5, 7, 10, 15, and 20 years. For example, the 5-year category includes automobiles, light trucks, and computers.

Depending on the category, fixed percentage rates are applied to the original cost of the asset. The rates for the 5-year asset category are as follows:

| Year | Rate |
|------|------|
| 1 | 20.00% |
| 2 | 32.00 |
| 3 | 19.20 |
| 4 | 11.52 |
| 5 | 11.52 |
| 6 | 5.76 |
| Total | 100.00% |

These rates are equivalent to applying the double-declining-balance method with a switch to straight-line in the year straight-line yields an equal or higher deduction than DDB. In most cases, the half-year convention is used regardless of when the asset is placed in service.[24] The first-year rate of 20% for the five-year category is one-half of the DDB rate for an asset with a five-year life ($2 \times 20\%$). The sixth year rate of 5.76% is one-half of the straight-line rate established in year 4, the year straight-line depreciation exceeds DDB depreciation.

Companies have the option to use the straight-line method for the entire tax life of the asset, applying the half-year convention, rather than using MACRS depreciation schedules. Because of the differences discussed above, tax depreciation for a given year will likely be different from GAAP depreciation.

# Retirement And Replacement Methods Of Depreciation

**APPENDIX 11B**

**Retirement** and **replacement** depreciation methods occasionally are used to depreciate relatively low-valued assets with short service lives. Under either approach, an aggregate asset account that represents a group of similar assets is increased at the time the initial collection is acquired.

---

[23]For assets acquired between 1981 and 1986, tax depreciation is calculated using the accelerated cost recovery system (ACRS), which is similar to MACRS. For assets acquired before 1981, tax depreciation can be calculated using any of the depreciation methods discussed in the chapter. Residual values are used in the calculation of depreciation for pre-1981 assets.

[24]In certain situations, mid-quarter and mid-month conventions are used.

## Retirement Method

Using the retirement depreciation method, the asset account also is increased for the cost of subsequent expenditures. When an item is disposed of, the asset account is credited for its cost, and depreciation expense is recorded for the difference between cost and proceeds received, if any. No other entries are made for depreciation. As a consequence, one or more periods may pass without any expense recorded. For example, the following entry records the purchase of 100 handheld calculators at $50 acquisition cost each:

| | | |
|---|---|---|
| Calculators (100 × $50) ........................................................... | 5,000 | |
|    Cash ..................................................................................... | | 5,000 |
| *To record the acquisition of calculators.* | | |

If 20 new calculators are acquired at $45 each, the asset account is increased.

| | | |
|---|---|---|
| Calculators (20 × $45) ............................................................. | 900 | |
|    Cash ..................................................................................... | | 900 |
| *To record additional calculator acquisitions.* | | |

Thirty calculators are disposed of (retired) by selling them secondhand to a bookkeeping firm for $5 each. The following entry reflects the retirement method:

| | | |
|---|---|---|
| Cash (30 × $5) .......................................................................... | 150 | |
| Depreciation expense (difference) ...................................... | 1,350 | |
|    Calculators (30 × $50) ...................................................... | | 1,500 |
| *To record the sale/depreciation of calculators.* | | |

Notice that the retirement system assumes a FIFO cost flow approach in determining the cost of assets, $50 each, that were disposed.

## Replacement Method

By the replacement depreciation method, the initial acquisition of assets is recorded the same way as by the retirement method; that is, the aggregate cost is increased. However, depreciation expense is the amount paid for new or replacement assets. Any proceeds received from asset dispositions reduces depreciation expense. For our example, the acquisition of 20 new calculators at $45 each is recorded as depreciation as follows:

| | | |
|---|---|---|
| Depreciation expense (20 × $45) ...................................... | 900 | |
|    Cash ..................................................................................... | | 900 |
| *To record the replacement/depreciation of calculators.* | | |

The sale of the old calculators is recorded as a reduction of depreciation:

| | | |
|---|---|---|
| Cash (30 × $5) .......................................................................... | 150 | |
|    Depreciation expense ....................................................... | | 150 |
| *To record the sale of calculators.* | | |

The asset account balance remains the same throughout the life of the aggregate collection of assets.

Because these methods are likely to produce aggregate expense measurements that differ from individual calculations, retirement and replacement methods are acceptable only in situations where the distortion in depreciation expense does not have a material effect on income. These methods occasionally are encountered in regulated industries such as utilities. ●

# Questions For Review of Key Topics

Q 11–1    Explain the similarities in and differences among depreciation, depletion, and amortization.

Q 11–2    Depreciation is a process of cost allocation, not valuation. Explain this statement.

Q 11–3    Identify and define the three characteristics of an asset that must be established to determine periodic depreciation, depletion, or amortization.

Q 11–4    Discuss the factors that influence the estimation of service life for a depreciable asset.

Q 11–5    What is meant by depreciable base? How is it determined?

Q 11–6    Briefly differentiate between activity-based and time-based allocation methods.

Q 11–7    Briefly differentiate between the straight-line depreciation method and accelerated depreciation methods.

Q 11–8    Why are time-based depreciation methods used more frequently than activity-based methods?

Q 11–9    What are some factors that could explain the predominant use of the straight-line depreciation method?

Q 11–10   Briefly explain the differences and similarities between the group approach and composite approach to depreciating aggregate assets.

Q 11–11   Define depletion and compare it with depreciation.

Q 11–12   Compare and contrast amortization of intangible assets with depreciation and depletion.

Q 11–13   What are some of the simplifying conventions a company can use to calculate depreciation for partial years?

Q 11–14   Explain the accounting treatment required when a change is made to the estimated service life of a machine.

Q 11–15   Explain the accounting treatment and disclosures required when a change is made in depreciation method.

Q 11–16   Explain the steps required to correct an error in accounting for property, plant, and equipment and intangible assets that is discovered in a year subsequent to the year the error was made.

Q 11–17   Explain what is meant by the impairment of the value of property, plant, and equipment and intangible assets. How should these impairments be accounted for?

Q 11–18   Explain the differences in the accounting treatment of repairs and maintenance, additions, improvements, and rearrangements.

🌐 **IFRS**   Q 11–19   Identify any differences between U.S. GAAP and International Financial Reporting Standards in the subsequent valuation of property, plant, and equipment and intangible assets.

🌐 **IFRS**   Q 11–20   Briefly explain the difference between U.S. GAAP and IFRS in the *measurement* of an impairment loss for property, plant, and equipment and finite-life intangible assets.

🌐 **IFRS**   Q 11–21   Briefly explain the differences between U.S. GAAP and IFRS in the measurement of an impairment loss for goodwill.

🌐 **IFRS**   Q 11–22   Under U.S. GAAP, litigation costs to successfully defend an intangible right are capitalized and amortized over the remaining useful life of the related intangible. How are these costs typically accounted for under IFRS?

# Brief Exercises

**BE 11–1**
Cost allocation
● LO11–1

At the beginning of its fiscal year, Koeplin Corporation purchased a machine for $50,000. At the end of the year, the machine had a fair value of $32,000. Koeplin's controller recorded depreciation expense of $18,000 for the year, the decline in the machine's value. Why is this an incorrect approach to measuring periodic depreciation?

**BE 11–2**
Depreciation methods
● LO11–2

On January 1, 2013, Canseco Plumbing Fixtures purchased equipment for $30,000. Residual value at the end of an estimated four-year service life is expected to be $2,000. The company expects the machine to operate for 10,000 hours. Calculate depreciation expense for 2013 and 2014 using each of the following depreciation methods: (a) straight line, (b) sum-of-the-years'-digits, (c) double-declining balance, and (d) units-of-production using machine hours. The machine operated for 2,200 and 3,000 hours in 2013 and 2014, respectively.

**BE 11–3**
Depreciation methods; partial years
● LO11–2

Refer to the situation described in BE 11–2. Assume the machine was purchased on March 31, 2013, instead of January 1. Calculate depreciation expense for 2013 and 2014 using each of the following depreciation methods: (a) straight line, (b) sum-of-the-years'-digits, and (c) double-declining balance.

**BE 11–4**
Group depreciation
● LO11–2

Mondale Winery depreciates its equipment using the group method. The cost of equipment purchased in 2013 totaled $425,000. The estimated residual value of the equipment was $40,000 and the group depreciation rate was determined to be 18%. What is the annual depreciation for the group? If equipment that cost $42,000 is sold in 2014 for $35,000, what amount of gain or loss will the company recognize for the sale?

**BE 11–5**
Depletion
● **LO11–3**

Fitzgerald Oil and Gas incurred costs of $8.25 million for the acquisition and development of a natural gas deposit. The company expects to extract 3 million cubic feet of natural gas during a four-year period. Natural gas extracted during years 1 and 2 were 700,000 and 800,000 cubic feet, respectively. What was the depletion for year 1 and year 2?

**BE 11–6**
Amortization
● **LO11–4**

On June 28 Lexicon Corporation acquired 100% of the common stock of Gulf & Eastern. The purchase price allocation included the following items: $4 million, patent; $3 million, developed technology; $2 million, in-process research and development; $5 million, goodwill. Lexicon's policy is to amortize intangible assets using the straight-line method, no residual value, and a five-year useful life. What is the total amount of expenses (ignoring taxes) that would appear in Lexicon's income statement for the year ended December 31 related to these items?

**BE 11–7**
Change in estimate; useful life of equipment
● **LO11–5**

At the beginning of 2011, Robotics Inc. acquired a manufacturing facility for $12 million. $9 million of the purchase price was allocated to the building. Depreciation for 2011 and 2012 was calculated using the straight-line method, a 25-year useful life, and a $1 million residual value. In 2013, the estimates of useful life and residual value were changed to 20 years and $500,000, respectively. What is depreciation on the building for 2013?

**BE 11–8**
Change in principle; change in depreciation method
● **LO11–6**

Refer to the situation described in BE 11–7. Assume that instead of changing the useful life and residual value, in 2013 the company switched to the double-declining-balance depreciation method. How should Robotics account for the change? What is depreciation on the building for 2013?

**BE 11–9**
Error correction
● **LO11–7**

Refer to the situation described in BE 11–7. Assume that 2011 depreciation was incorrectly recorded as $32,000. This error was discovered in 2013. How should Robotics account for the error? What is depreciation on the building for 2013 assuming no change in estimate of useful life or residual value?

**BE 11–10**
Impairment; property, plant, and equipment
● **LO11–8**

Collison and Ryder Company (C&R) has been experiencing declining market conditions for its sportswear division. Management decided to test the assets of the division for possible impairment. The test revealed the following: book value of division's assets, $26.5 million; fair value of division's assets, $21 million; sum of estimated future cash flows generated from the division's assets, $28 million. What amount of impairment loss should C&R recognize?

**BE 11–11**
Impairment; property, plant, and equipment
● **LO11–8**

Refer to the situation described in BE 11–10. Assume that the sum of estimated future cash flows is $24 million instead of $28 million. What amount of impairment loss should C&R recognize?

**BE 11–12**
IFRS; impairment; property, plant, and equipment
● **LO11–8,**
**LO11–10**

🌐 **IFRS**

Refer to the situation described in BE 11–10. Assume that the present value of the estimated future cash flows generated from the division's assets is $22 million and that their fair value approximates fair value less costs to sell. What amount of impairment loss should C&R recognize if the company prepares its financial statements according to IFRS?

**BE 11–13**
Impairment; goodwill
● **LO11–8**

WebHelper Inc. acquired 100% of the outstanding stock of Silicon Chips Corporation (SCC) for $45 million, of which $15 million was allocated to goodwill. At the end of the current fiscal year, an impairment test revealed the following: fair value of SCC, $40 million; fair value of SCC's net assets (excluding goodwill), $31 million; book value of SCC's net assets (including goodwill), $42 million. What amount of impairment loss should Web-Helper recognize?

**BE 11–14**
Impairment; goodwill
● **LO11–8**

Refer to the situation described in BE 11–13. Assume that the fair value of SCC is $44 million instead of $40 million. What amount of impairment loss should WebHelper recognize?

**BE 11–15**
**IFRS; impairment;**
**goodwill**
● **LO11–10**

 **IFRS**

Refer to the situation described in BE 11–13. Assume that SCC's fair value of $40 million approximates fair value less costs to sell and that the present value of SCC's estimated future cash flows is $41 million. If Web-Helper prepares its financial statements according to IFRS and SCC is considered a cash-generating unit, what amount of impairment loss, if any, should WebHelper recognize?

**BE 11–16**
**Subsequent**
**expenditures**
● **LO11–9**

Demmert Manufacturing incurred the following expenditures during the current fiscal year: annual maintenance on its machinery, $5,400; remodeling of offices, $22,000; rearrangement of the shipping and receiving area resulting in an increase in productivity, $35,000; addition of a security system to the manufacturing facility, $25,000. How should Demmert account for each of these expenditures?

# Exercises

**An alternate exercise and problem set is available on the text website: www.mhhe.com/spiceland7e**

**E 11–1**
**Depreciation**
**methods**
● **LO11–2**

On January 1, 2013, the Excel Delivery Company purchased a delivery van for $33,000. At the end of its five-year service life, it is estimated that the van will be worth $3,000. During the five-year period, the company expects to drive the van 100,000 miles.

**Required:**
Calculate annual depreciation for the five-year life of the van using each of the following methods. Round all computations to the nearest dollar.
1. Straight line.
2. Sum-of-the-years' digits.
3. Double-declining balance.
4. Units of production using miles driven as a measure of output, and the following actual mileage:

| Year | Miles |
| --- | --- |
| 2013 | 22,000 |
| 2014 | 24,000 |
| 2015 | 15,000 |
| 2016 | 20,000 |
| 2017 | 21,000 |

**E 11–2**
**Depreciation**
**methods**
● **LO11–2**

On January 1, 2013, the Allegheny Corporation purchased machinery for $115,000. The estimated service life of the machinery is 10 years and the estimated residual value is $5,000. The machine is expected to produce 220,000 units during its life.

**Required:**
Calculate depreciation for 2013 and 2014 using each of the following methods. Round all computations to the nearest dollar.
1. Straight line.
2. Sum-of-the-years' digits.
3. Double-declining balance.
4. One hundred fifty percent declining balance.
5. Units of production (units produced in 2013, 30,000; units produced in 2014, 25,000).

**E 11–3**
**Depreciation**
**methods; partial**
**years**
● **LO11–2**

[This is a variation of Exercise 11–2 modified to focus on depreciation for partial years.]
On October 1, 2013, the Allegheny Corporation purchased machinery for $115,000. The estimated service life of the machinery is 10 years and the estimated residual value is $5,000. The machine is expected to produce 220,000 units during its life.

**Required:**
Calculate depreciation for 2013 and 2014 using each of the following methods. Partial-year depreciation is calculated based on the number of months the asset is in service. Round all computations to the nearest dollar.
1. Straight line.
2. Sum-of-the-years' digits.
3. Double-declining balance.
4. One hundred fifty percent declining balance.
5. Units of production (units produced in 2013, 10,000; units produced in 2014, 25,000).

**E 11–4**
**Depreciation methods; asset addition**
● LO11–2,
LO11–9

Funseth Company purchased a five-story office building on January 1, 2011, at a cost of $5,000,000. The building has a residual value of $200,000 and a 30-year life. The straight-line depreciation method is used. On June 30, 2013, construction of a sixth floor was completed at a cost of $1,650,000.

**Required:**
Calculate the depreciation on the building and building addition for 2013 and 2014 assuming that the addition did not change the life or residual value of the building.

**E 11–5**
**Depreciation methods; solving for unknowns**
● LO11–2

For each of the following depreciable assets, determine the missing amount (?). Abbreviations for depreciation methods are SL for straight line, SYD for sum-of-the-years' digits, and DDB for double-declining balance.

| Asset | Cost | Residual Value | Service Life (Years) | Depreciation Method | Depreciation (Year 2) |
|-------|------|----------------|----------------------|---------------------|-----------------------|
| A | ? | $ 20,000 | 5 | DDB | $ 24,000 |
| B | $ 40,000 | ? | 8 | SYD | 7,000 |
| C | 65,000 | 5,000 | ? | SL | 6,000 |
| D | 230,000 | 10,000 | 10 | ? | 22,000 |
| E | 200,000 | 20,000 | 8 | 150%DB | ? |

**E 11–6**
**Depreciation methods**
● LO11–2

On April 29, 2013, Quality Appliances purchased equipment for $260,000. The estimated service life of the equipment is six years and the estimated residual value is $20,000. Quality's fiscal year ends on December 31.

**Required:**
Calculate depreciation for 2013 and 2014 using each of the three methods listed. Quality calculates partial year depreciation based on the number of months the asset is in service. Round all computations to the nearest dollar.
1. Straight-line.
2. Sum-of-the-years' digits.
3. Double-declining balance.

**E 11–7**
**IFRS; depreciation**
● LO11–2,
LO11–10

 IFRS

On June 30, 2013, Rosetta Granite purchased a machine for $120,000. The estimated useful life of the machine is eight years and no residual value is anticipated. An important component of the machine is a specialized high-speed drill that will need to be replaced in four years. The $20,000 cost of the drill is included in the $120,000 cost of the machine. Rosetta uses the straight-line depreciation method for all machinery.

**Required:**
1. Calculate depreciation for 2013 and 2014 applying the typical U.S. GAAP treatment.
2. Repeat requirement 1 applying IFRS.

**E 11–8**
**IFRS; revaluation of machinery; depreciation**
● LO11–10

 IFRS

Dower Corporation prepares its financial statements according to IFRS. On March 31, 2013, the company purchased equipment for $240,000. The equipment is expected to have a six-year useful life with no residual value. Dower uses the straight-line depreciation method for all equipment. On December 31, 2013, the end of the company's fiscal year, Dower chooses to revalue the equipment to its fair value of $220,000.

**Required:**
1. Calculate depreciation for 2013.
2. Prepare the journal entry to record the revaluation of the equipment. Round calculations to the nearest thousand.
3. Calculate depreciation for 2014.
4. Repeat requirement 2 assuming that the fair value of the equipment at the end of 2013 is $195,000.

**E 11–9**
**Group depreciation**
● LO11–2

Highsmith Rental Company purchased an apartment building early in 2013. There are 20 apartments in the building and each is furnished with major kitchen appliances. The company has decided to use the group depreciation method for the appliances. The following data are available:

| Appliance | Cost | Residual Value | Service Life (in Years) |
|-----------|------|----------------|-------------------------|
| Stoves | $15,000 | $3,000 | 6 |
| Refrigerators | 10,000 | 1,000 | 5 |
| Dishwashers | 8,000 | 500 | 4 |

In 2016, three new refrigerators costing $2,700 were purchased for cash. The old refrigerators, which originally cost $1,500, were sold for $200.

**Required:**
1. Calculate the group depreciation rate, group life, and depreciation for 2013.
2. Prepare the journal entries to record the purchase of the new refrigerators and the sale of the old refrigerators.

**E 11–10**
**Double-declining-balance method; switch to straight line**
● **LO11–2,**
**LO11–6**

On January 2, 2013, the Jackson Company purchased equipment to be used in its manufacturing process. The equipment has an estimated life of eight years and an estimated residual value of $30,625. The expenditures made to acquire the asset were as follows:

|                       |           |
|-----------------------|-----------|
| Purchase price        | $154,000  |
| Freight charges       | 2,000     |
| Installation charges  | 4,000     |

Jackson's policy is to use the double-declining-balance (DDB) method of depreciation in the early years of the equipment's life and then switch to straight line halfway through the equipment's life.

**Required:**
1. Calculate depreciation for each year of the asset's eight-year life.
2. Discuss the accounting treatment of the depreciation on the equipment.

**E 11–11**
**Depletion**
● **LO11–3**

On April 17, 2013, the Loadstone Mining Company purchased the rights to a coal mine. The purchase price plus additional costs necessary to prepare the mine for extraction of the coal totaled $4,500,000. The company expects to extract 900,000 tons of coal during a four-year period. During 2013, 240,000 tons were extracted and sold immediately.

**Required:**
1. Calculate depletion for 2013.
2. Discuss the accounting treatment of the depletion calculated in requirement 1.

**E 11–12**
**Depreciation and depletion**
● **LO11–2,**
**LO11–3**

At the beginning of 2013, Terra Lumber Company purchased a timber tract from Boise Cantor for $3,200,000. After the timber is cleared, the land will have a residual value of $600,000. Roads to enable logging operations were constructed and completed on March 30, 2013. The cost of the roads, which have no residual value and no alternative use after the tract is cleared, was $240,000. During 2013, Terra logged 500,000 of the estimated five million board feet of timber.

**Required:**
Calculate the 2013 depletion of the timber tract and depreciation of the logging roads assuming the units-of-production method is used for both assets.

**E 11–13**
**Cost of a natural resource; depletion and depreciation; Chapters 10 and 11**
● **LO11–2,**
**LO11–3**

[This exercise is a continuation of Exercise 10–4 in Chapter 10 focusing on depletion and depreciation.]

Jackpot Mining Company operates a copper mine in central Montana. The company paid $1,000,000 in 2013 for the mining site and spent an additional $600,000 to prepare the mine for extraction of the copper. After the copper is extracted in approximately four years, the company is required to restore the land to its original condition, including repaving of roads and replacing a greenbelt. The company has provided the following three cash flow possibilities for the restoration costs:

|   | Cash Outflow | Probability |
|---|--------------|-------------|
| 1 | $300,000     | 25%         |
| 2 | 400,000      | 40%         |
| 3 | 600,000      | 35%         |

To aid extraction, Jackpot purchased some new equipment on July 1, 2013, for $120,000. After the copper is removed from this mine, the equipment will be sold for an estimated residual amount of $20,000. There will be no residual value for the copper mine. The credit-adjusted risk-free rate of interest is 10%.

The company expects to extract 10 million pounds of copper from the mine. Actual production was 1.6 million pounds in 2013 and 3 million pounds in 2014.

**Required:**
1. Compute depletion and depreciation on the mine and mining equipment for 2013 and 2014. The units-of-production method is used to calculate depreciation.
2. Discuss the accounting treatment of the depletion and depreciation on the mine and mining equipment.

**E 11–14**
**Amortization**
● **LO11–4,**
**LO11–5**

Janes Company provided the following information on intangible assets:
a. A patent was purchased from the Lou Company for $700,000 on January 1, 2011. Janes estimated the remaining useful life of the patent to be 10 years. The patent was carried on Lou's accounting records at a net book value of $350,000 when Lou sold it to Janes.

b. During 2013, a franchise was purchased from the Rink Company for $500,000. The contractual life of the franchise is 10 years and Janes records a full year of amortization in the year of purchase.

c. Janes incurred research and development costs in 2013 as follows:

| | |
|---|---:|
| Materials and supplies | $140,000 |
| Personnel | 180,000 |
| Indirect costs | 60,000 |
| Total | $380,000 |

d. Effective January 1, 2013, based on new events that have occurred, Janes estimates that the remaining life of the patent purchased from Lou is only five more years.

**Required:**

1. Prepare the entries necessary for years 2011 through 2013 to reflect the above information.

2. Prepare a schedule showing the intangible asset section of Janes's December 31, 2013, balance sheet.

**E 11–15**
Patent amortization; patent defense
● LO11–4,
LO11–9

On January 2, 2013, David Corporation purchased a patent for $500,000. The remaining legal life is 12 years, but the company estimated that the patent will be useful only for eight years. In January 2015, the company incurred legal fees of $45,000 in successfully defending a patent infringement suit. The successful defense did not change the company's estimate of useful life.

**Required:**
Prepare journal entries related to the patent for 2013, 2014, and 2015.

**E 11–16**
Change in estimate; useful life of patent
● LO11–4,
LO11–5

Van Frank Telecommunications has a patent on a cellular transmission process. The company has amortized the patent on a straight-line basis since 2009, when it was acquired at a cost of $9 million at the beginning of that year. Due to rapid technological advances in the industry, management decided that the patent would benefit the company over a total of six years rather than the nine-year life being used to amortize its cost. The decision was made at the end of 2013 (before adjusting and closing entries).

**Required:**
Prepare the appropriate adjusting entry for patent amortization in 2013 to reflect the revised estimate.

**E 11–17**
IFRS; revaluation of patent; amortization
● LO11–10

 **IFRS**

Saint John Corporation prepares its financial statements according to IFRS. On June 30, 2013, the company purchased a franchise for $1,200,000. The franchise is expected to have a 10-year useful life with no residual value. Saint John uses the straight-line amortization method for all intangible assets. On December 31, 2013, the end of the company's fiscal year, Saint John chooses to revalue the franchise. There is an active market for this particular franchise and its fair value on December 31, 2013, is $1,180,000.

**Required:**

1. Calculate amortization for 2013.

2. Prepare the journal entry to record the revaluation of the patent.

3. Calculate amortization for 2014.

**E 11–18**
Change in estimate; useful life and residual value of equipment
● LO11–2,
LO11–5

Wardell Company purchased a minicomputer on January 1, 2011, at a cost of $40,000. The computer was depreciated using the straight-line method over an estimated five-year life with an estimated residual value of $4,000. On January 1, 2013, the estimate of useful life was changed to a total of 10 years, and the estimate of residual value was changed to $900.

**Required:**

1. Prepare the appropriate adjusting entry for depreciation in 2013 to reflect the revised estimate.

2. Repeat requirement 1 assuming that the company uses the sum-of-the-years'-digits method instead of the straight-line method.

**E 11–19**
Change in principle; change in depreciation methods
● LO11–2, LO11–6

Alteran Corporation purchased a machine for $1.5 million in 2010. The machine is being depreciated over a 10-year life using the sum-of-the-years'-digits method. The residual value is expected to be $300,000. At the beginning of 2013, Alteran decided to change to the straight-line depreciation method for this machine.

**Required:**
Prepare the 2013 depreciation adjusting entry.

**E 11–20**
**Change in principle; change in depreciation methods**
● LO11–2, LO11–6

For financial reporting, Clinton Poultry Farms has used the declining-balance method of depreciation for conveyor equipment acquired at the beginning of 2010 for $2,560,000. Its useful life was estimated to be six years, with a $160,000 residual value. At the beginning of 2013, Clinton decides to change to the straight-line method. The effect of this change on depreciation for each year is as follows:

|  | ($ in 000s) | | |
|---|---|---|---|
| **Year** | **Straight Line** | **Declining Balance** | **Difference** |
| 2010 | $ 400 | $ 853 | $453 |
| 2011 | 400 | 569 | 169 |
| 2012 | 400 | 379 | (21) |
| | $1,200 | $1,801 | $601 |

**Required:**
1. Briefly describe the way Clinton should report this accounting change in the 2012–2013 comparative financial statements.
2. Prepare any 2013 journal entry related to the change.

**E 11–21**
**Error correction**
● LO11–2, LO11–7

In 2013, internal auditors discovered that PKE Displays, Inc., had debited an expense account for the $350,000 cost of a machine purchased on January 1, 2010. The machine's life was expected to be five years with no residual value. Straight-line depreciation is used by PKE.

**Required:**
1. Prepare the appropriate correcting entry assuming the error was discovered in 2013 before the adjusting and closing entries. (Ignore income taxes.)
2. Assume the error was discovered in 2015 after the 2014 financial statements are issued. Prepare the appropriate correcting entry.

**E 11–22**
**Impairment; property, plant, and equipment**
● LO11–8

Chadwick Enterprises, Inc., operates several restaurants throughout the Midwest. Three of its restaurants located in the center of a large urban area have experienced declining profits due to declining population. The company's management has decided to test the assets of the restaurants for possible impairment. The relevant information for these assets is presented below.

| | |
|---|---|
| Book value | $6.5 million |
| Estimated undiscounted sum of future cash flows | 4.0 million |
| Fair value | 3.5 million |

**Required:**
1. Determine the amount of the impairment loss, if any.
2. Repeat requirement 1 assuming that the estimated undiscounted sum of future cash flows is $6.8 million and fair value is $5 million.

**E 11–23**
**IFRS; impairment; property, plant, and equipment**
● LO11–10

🌐 **IFRS**

Refer to the situation described in Exercise 11–22.

**Required:**
How might your solution differ if Chadwick Enterprises, Inc., prepares its financial statements according to International Financial Reporting Standards? Assume that the fair value amount given in the exercise equals both (a) the fair value less costs to sell and (b) the present value of estimated future cash flows.

**E 11–24**
**IFRS; Impairment; property, plant, and equipment**
● LO11–8, LO11–10

🌐 **IFRS**

Collinsworth LTD., a U.K. company, prepares its financial statements according to International Financial Reporting Standards. Late in its 2013 fiscal year, a significant adverse change in business climate indicated to management that the assets of its appliance division may be impaired. The following data relate to the division's assets:

| | (£ in millions) |
|---|---|
| Book value | £220 |
| Undiscounted sum of estimated future cash flows | 210 |
| Present value of future cash flows | 150 |
| Fair value less cost to sell (determined by appraisal) | 145 |

**Required:**

1. What amount of impairment loss, if any, should Collinsworth recognize?

2. Assume that Collinsworth prepares its financial statements according to U.S. GAAP and that fair value less cost to sell approximates fair value. What amount of impairment loss, if any, should Collinsworth recognize?

**E 11–25**
**Impairment;**
**property, plant,**
**and equipment**
● **LO11–8**

General Optic Corporation operates a manufacturing plant in Arizona. Due to a significant decline in demand for the product manufactured at the Arizona site, an impairment test is deemed appropriate. Management has acquired the following information for the assets at the plant:

| | |
|---|---|
| Cost | $32,500,000 |
| Accumulated depreciation | 14,200,000 |
| General's estimate of the total cash flows to be generated by selling the products manufactured at its Arizona plant, not discounted to present value | 15,000,000 |

The fair value of the Arizona plant is estimated to be $11,000,000.

**Required:**

1. Determine the amount of impairment loss, if any.

2. If a loss is indicated, where would it appear in General Optic's multiple-step income statement?

3. If a loss is indicated, prepare the entry to record the loss.

4. Repeat requirement 1 assuming that the estimated undiscounted sum of future cash flows is $12,000,000 instead of $15,000,000.

5. Repeat requirement 1 assuming that the estimated undiscounted sum of future cash flows is $19,000,000 instead of $15,000,000

**E 11–26**
**Impairment;**
**goodwill**
● **LO11–8**

In 2011, Alliant Corporation acquired Centerpoint Inc. for $300 million, of which $50 million was allocated to goodwill. At the end of 2013, management has provided the following information for a required goodwill impairment test:

| | |
|---|---|
| Fair value of Centerpoint, Inc. | $220 million |
| Fair value of Centerpoint's net assets (excluding goodwill) | 200 million |
| Book value of Centerpoint's net assets (including goodwill) | 250 million |

**Required:**

1. Determine the amount of the impairment loss.

2. Repeat requirement 1 assuming that the fair value of Centerpoint is $270 million.

**E 11–27**
**IFRS; impairment;**
**goodwill**
● **LO11–10**

 **IFRS**

Refer to the situation described in Exercise 11–26, requirement 1. Alliant prepares its financial statements according to IFRS, and Centerpoint is considered a cash-generating unit. Assume that Centerpoint's fair value of $220 million approximates fair value less costs to sell and that the present value of Centerpoint's estimated future cash flows is $225 million.

**Required:**
Determine the amount of goodwill impairment loss Alliant should recognize.

**E 11–28**
**Goodwill**
**valuation and**
**impairment;**
**Chapters 10**
**and 11**
● **LO11–8**

On May 28, 2013, Pesky Corporation acquired all of the outstanding common stock of Harman, Inc., for $420 million. The fair value of Harman's identifiable tangible and intangible assets totaled $512 million, and the fair value of liabilities assumed by Pesky was $150 million.

Pesky performed a goodwill impairment test at the end of its fiscal year ended December 31, 2013. Management has provided the following information:

| | |
|---|---|
| Fair value of Harman, Inc. | $400 million |
| Fair value of Harman's net assets (excluding goodwill) | 370 million |
| Book value of Harman's net assets (including goodwill) | 410 million |

**Required:**

1. Determine the amount of goodwill that resulted from the Harman acquisition.

2. Determine the amount of goodwill impairment loss that Pesky should recognize at the end of 2013, if any.

3. If an impairment loss is required, prepare the journal entry to record the loss.

**E 11–29**
FASB codification research
● LO11–8

The *FASB Accounting Standards Codification* represents the single source of authoritative U.S. generally accepted accounting principles.

**Required:**
1. Obtain the relevant authoritative literature on the impairment or disposal of long-lived assets using the FASB's Codification Research System at the FASB website (www.fasb.org). Indicate the Codification topic number that provides guidance on accounting for the impairment of long-lived assets.
2. What is the specific citation that discusses the disclosures required in the notes to the financial statements for the impairment of long-lived assets classified as held and used?
3. Describe the disclosure requirements.

**E 11–30**
FASB codification research
● LO11–2,
   LO11–4,
   LO11–6,
   LO11–8

Access the FASB's Codification Research System at the FASB website (www.fasb.org). Determine the specific citation for each of the following items:
1. Depreciation involves a systematic and rational allocation of cost rather than a process of valuation.
2. The calculation of an impairment loss for property, plant, and equipment.
3. Accounting for a change in depreciation method.
4. Goodwill should not be amortized.

**E 11–31**
Subsequent expenditures
● LO11–9

Belltone Company made the following expenditures related to its 10-year-old manufacturing facility:
1. The heating system was replaced at a cost of $250,000. The cost of the old system was not known. The company accounts for improvements as reductions of accumulated depreciation.
2. A new wing was added at a cost of $750,000. The new wing substantially increases the productive capacity of the plant.
3. Annual building maintenance was performed at a cost of $14,000.
4. All of the machinery on the assembly line in the plant was rearranged at a cost of $50,000. The rearrangement clearly increases the productive capacity of the plant.

**Required:**
Prepare journal entries to record each of the above expenditures.

**E 11–32**
IFRS; amortization; cost to defend a patent
● LO11–4,
   LO11–9,
   LO11–10

 IFRS

On September 30, 2011, Leeds LTD. acquired a patent in conjunction with the purchase of another company. The patent, valued at $6 million, was estimated to have a 10-year life and no residual value. Leeds uses the straight-line method of amortization for intangible assets. At the beginning of January 2013, Leeds successfully defended its patent against infringement. Litigation costs totaled $500,000.

**Required:**
1. Calculate amortization of the patent for 2011 and 2012.
2. Prepare the journal entry to record the 2013 litigation costs.
3. Calculate amortization for 2013.
4. Repeat requirements 2 and 3 assuming that Leeds prepares its financial statements according to IFRS.

**E 11–33**
Depreciation methods; disposal; Chapters 10 and 11
● LO11–2

Howarth Manufacturing Company purchased a lathe on June 30, 2009, at a cost of $80,000. The residual value of the lathe was estimated to be $5,000 at the end of a five-year life. The lathe was sold on March 31, 2013, for $17,000. Howarth uses the straight-line depreciation method for all of its plant and equipment. Partial-year depreciation is calculated based on the number of months the asset is in service.

**Required:**
1. Prepare the journal entry to record the sale.
2. Assuming that Howarth had instead used the sum-of-the-years'-digits depreciation method, prepare the journal entry to record the sale.

**E 11–34**
Concepts; terminology
● LO11–1 through
   LO11–6, LO11–8

Listed below are several items and phrases associated with depreciation, depletion, and amortization. Pair each item from List A with the item from List B (by letter) that is most appropriately associated with it.

| List A | List B |
|---|---|
| ___ 1. Depreciation | a. Cost allocation for natural resource. |
| ___ 2. Service life | b. Accounted for prospectively. |
| ___ 3. Depreciable base | c. When there has been a significant decline in value. |
| ___ 4. Activity-based methods | d. The amount of use expected from an operational asset. |
| ___ 5. Time-based methods | e. Estimates service life in units of output. |
| ___ 6. Double-declining balance | f. Cost less residual value. |
| ___ 7. Group method | g. Cost allocation for plant and equipment. |
| ___ 8. Composite method | h. Does not subtract residual value from cost. |
| ___ 9. Depletion | i. Accounted for in the same way as a change in estimate. |
| ___ 10. Amortization | j. Aggregates assets that are similar. |
| ___ 11. Change in useful life | k. Aggregates assets that are physically unified. |
| ___ 12. Change in depreciation method | l. Cost allocation for an intangible asset. |
| ___ 13. Write-down of asset | m. Estimates service life in years. |

**E 11–35**
**Retirement and replacement depreciation**
● **Appendix B**

Cadillac Construction Company uses the retirement method to determine depreciation on its small tools. During 2011, the first year of the company's operations, tools were purchased at a cost of $8,000. In 2013, tools originally costing $2,000 were sold for $250 and replaced with new tools costing $2,500.

**Required:**
1. Prepare journal entries to record each of the above transactions.
2. Repeat requirement 1 assuming that the company uses the replacement depreciation method instead of the retirement method.

# CPA and CMA Review Questions

**CPA Exam Questions**

The following questions are adapted from a variety of sources including questions developed by the AICPA Board of Examiners and those used in the Kaplan CPA Review Course to study property, plant, and equipment and intangible assets while preparing for the CPA examination. Determine the response that best completes the statements or questions.

● **LO11–2**

1. Slovac Company purchased a machine that has an estimated useful life of eight years for $7,500. Its salvage value is estimated at $500. What is the depreciation for the second year of the asset's life, assuming Slovac uses the double-declining balance method of depreciation?
   a. $1,406
   b. $1,438
   c. $1,875
   d. $3,750

● **LO11–2**

2. Calculate depreciation for year 2 based on the following information:

   Historical cost $40,000
   Useful life 5 years
   Salvage value $3,000
   Year 1 depreciation $7,400

   a. $7,000
   b. $7,400
   c. $8,000
   d. $8,600

● **LO11–3**

3. A company pays $20,000 for the rights to a well with 5 million gallons of water. If the company extracts 250,000 gallons of water in the first year, what is the total depletion in year 1?
   a. $ 400
   b. $1,000
   c. $1,250
   d. $5,000

● **LO11–4**

4. Black, Inc., purchased another company for $5,000,000. The fair value of all identifiable tangible and intangible assets was $4,500,000. Black will amortize any goodwill over the maximum number of years allowed. What is the annual amortization of goodwill for this acquisition?
   a. $12,500
   b. $20,000

c.  $25,000

d.        0

● LO11–4    5.  On January 2, 2013, Rafa Company purchased a franchise with a useful life of 10 years for $50,000. An additional franchise fee of 3% of franchise operating revenues also must be paid each year to the franchisor. Revenues during 2013 totaled $400,000. In its December 31, 2013, balance sheet, what net amount should Rafa report as an intangible asset-franchise?

a.  $33,000

b.  $43,800

c.  $45,000

d.  $50,000

● LO11–5    6.  JME acquired a depreciable asset on January 1, 2011, for $60,000 cash. At that time JME estimated the asset would last 10 years and have no salvage value. During 2013, JME estimated the remaining life of the asset to be only three more years with a salvage value of $3,000. If JME uses straight-line depreciation, what is the depreciation for 2013?

a.  $ 6,000

b.  $12,000

c.  $15,000

d.  $16,000

● LO11–8    7.  The following information concerns Franklin Inc.'s stamping machine:

> Acquired: January 1, 2007
> Cost: $22 million
> Depreciation: straight-line method
> Estimated useful life: 12 years
> Salvage value: $4 million

As of December 31, 2013, the stamping machine is expected to generate $1,500,000 per year for five more years and will then be sold for $1,000,000. The stamping machine is

a.  Impaired because expected salvage value has declined.

b.  Not impaired because annual expected revenue exceeds annual depreciation.

c.  Not impaired because it continues to produce revenue.

d.  Impaired because its book value exceeds expected future cash flows.

● LO11–9    8.  During 2012, Yvo Corp. installed a production assembly line to manufacture furniture. In 2013, Yvo purchased a new machine and rearranged the assembly line to install this machine. The rearrangement did not increase the estimated useful life of the assembly line, but it did result in significantly more efficient production. The following expenditures were incurred in connection with this project:

| | |
|---|---|
| Machine | $75,000 |
| Labor to install machine | 14,000 |
| Parts added in rearranging the assembly line to provide future benefits | 40,000 |
| Labor and overhead to rearrange the assembly line | 18,000 |

What amount of the above expenditures should be capitalized in 2013?

a.  $ 75,000

b.  $ 89,000

c.  $107,000

d.  $147,000

Beginning in 2011, International Financial Reporting Standards are tested on the CPA exam along with U.S. GAAP. The following questions deal with the application of IFRS.

● LO11–10    9.  On January 1, 2013, D Company acquires for $100,000 a new machine with an estimated useful life of

 IFRS        10 years and no residual value. The machine has a drum that must be replaced every five years and costs $20,000 to replace. The company uses straight-line depreciation. Under IFRS, what is depreciation for 2013?

a.  $10,000.

b.  $10,800.

c.  $12,000.

d.  $13,200.

● LO11–10

IFRS

10. Under IFRS, when a company chooses the revaluation model as its accounting policy for measuring property, plant, and equipment, which of the following statements is correct?

   a. When an asset is revalued, the entire class of property, plant, and equipment to which the asset belongs must be revalued.

   b. When an asset is revalued, individual assets within a class of property, plant, and equipment to which that asset belongs can be revalued.

   c. Revaluations of property, plant, and equipment must be made every three years.

   d. An increase in an asset's carrying value as a result of the first revaluation must be recognized as a component of profit and loss.

● LO11–10

IFRS

11. Under IFRS, the initial revaluation of equipment when book value exceeds fair value results in

   a. An increase in net income.

   b. A decrease in net income.

   c. An increase in other comprehensive income.

   d. A decrease in other comprehensive income.

● LO11–10

IFRS

12. Under IFRS, a company that acquires an intangible asset may use the revaluation model for subsequent measurement only if

   a. The useful life of the intangible asset can be readily determined.

   b. An active market exists for the intangible asset.

   c. The cost of the intangible asset can be measured reliably.

   d. The intangible asset is a monetary asset.

● LO11–10

IFRS

13. The management of Clayton LTD. determined that the cost of one of its factories may be impaired. Below are data related to the assets of the factory ($ in millions):

| | |
|---|---:|
| Book value | $400 |
| Undiscounted sum of future estimated cash flows | 420 |
| Present value of future cash flows | 320 |
| Fair value less costs to sell (determined by appraisal) | 330 |

Under IFRS, what amount of impairment loss, if any, should Clayton recognize?

   a. $90 million.

   b. $80 million.

   c. $70 million.

   d. No impairment loss is required.

● LO11–10

IFRS

14. Blankbank Corporation has $150 million of goodwill on its books from the 2011 acquisition of Walsh Technology. Walsh is considered a cash-generating unit under IFRS. At the end of its 2013 fiscal year, management provided the following information for its annual goodwill impairment test ($ in millions):

| | |
|---|---:|
| Fair value of Walsh less costs to sell | $455 |
| Fair value of Walsh's net assets (excluding goodwill) | 400 |
| Book value of Walsh's net assets (including goodwill) | 500 |
| Present value of estimated future cash flows | 440 |

Under IFRS, what amount of goodwill impairment loss, if any, should Blankbank recognize?

   a. $100 million.

   b. $60 million.

   c. $50 million.

   d. $45 million.

**CMA Exam Questions**

The following questions dealing with property, plant, and equipment and intangible assets are adapted from questions that previously appeared on Certified Management Accountant (CMA) examinations. The CMA designation sponsored by the Institute of Management Accountants (www.imanet.org) provides members with an objective measure of knowledge and competence in the field of management accounting. Determine the response that best completes the statements or questions.

● LO11–3

1. WD Mining Company purchased a section of land for $600,000 in 2002 to develop a zinc mine. The mine began operating in 2004. At that time, management estimated that the mine would produce 200,000 tons of quality ore. A total of 100,000 tons of ore was mined and processed from 2004 through December 31, 2011. During January 2012, a very promising vein was discovered. The revised estimate of ore still to be mined was 250,000 tons. Estimated salvage value for the mine land was $100,000 in both 2004 and 2012. Assuming that 10,000 tons of ore was mined in 2012, the computation WD Mining Company should use to determine the amount of depletion to record in 2012 would be

   a. (($600,000 − $100,000)/450,000 tons) × 10,000 tons.

   b. (($600,000 − $100,000)/350,000 tons) × 10,000 tons.

   c. (($600,000 − $100,000 − $250,000)/350,000 tons) × 10,000 tons.

   d. (($600,000 − $100,000 − $250,000)/250,000 tons) × 10,000 tons.

● LO11–4

2. On September 1, year 1, for $4,000,000 cash and $2,000,000 notes payable, Norbend Corporation acquired the net assets of Crisholm Company, which had a fair value of $5,496,000 on that date. Norbend's management is of the opinion that the goodwill generated has an indefinite life. During the year-end audit for year 3 after all adjusting entries have been made, the goodwill is determined to be worthless. The amount of the write-off as of December 31, year 3 should be

  a. $504,000.

  b. $478,800.

  c. $466,200.

  d. $474,600.

● LO11–9

3. Costs that are capitalized with regard to a patent include

  a. Legal fees of obtaining the patent, incidental costs of obtaining the patent, and costs of successful patent infringement suits.

  b. Legal fees of obtaining the patent, incidental costs of obtaining the patent, and research and development costs incurred on the invention that is patented.

  c. Legal fees of obtaining the patent, costs of successful patent infringement suits, and research and development costs incurred on the invention that is patented.

  d. Incidental costs of obtaining the patent, costs of successful and unsuccessful patent infringement suits, and the value of any signed patent licensing agreement.

# Problems

An alternate exercise and problem set is available on the text website: www.mhhe.com/spiceland7e

**P 11–1**
Depreciation
methods; change
in methods
● LO11–2,
  LO11–6

The fact that generally accepted accounting principles allow companies flexibility in choosing between certain allocation methods can make it difficult for a financial analyst to compare periodic performance from firm to firm.

  Suppose you were a financial analyst trying to compare the performance of two companies. Company A uses the double-declining-balance depreciation method. Company B uses the straight-line method. You have the following information taken from the 12/31/13 year-end financial statements for Company B:

**Income Statement**

| | |
|---|---|
| Depreciation expense | $ 10,000 |

**Balance Sheet**

| | |
|---|---|
| Assets: | |
| Plant and equipment, at cost | $200,000 |
| Less: Accumulated depreciation | (40,000) |
| Net | $160,000 |

You also determine that all of the assets constituting the plant and equipment of Company B were acquired at the same time, and that all of the $200,000 represents depreciable assets. Also, all of the depreciable assets have the same useful life and residual values are zero.

**Required:**

1. In order to compare performance with Company A, estimate what B's depreciation expense would have been for 2013 if the double-declining-balance depreciation method had been used by Company B since acquisition of the depreciable assets.

2. If Company B decided to switch depreciation methods in 2013 from the straight line to the double-declining-balance method, prepare the 2013 adjusting journal entry to record depreciation for the year.

**P 11–2**
Comprehensive
problem;
Chapters 10 and 11
● LO11–2, LO11–4

At December 31, 2012, Cord Company's plant asset and accumulated depreciation and amortization accounts had balances as follows:

| Category | Plant Asset | Accumulated Depreciation and Amortization |
|---|---|---|
| Land | $ 175,000 | $ — |
| Buildings | 1,500,000 | 328,900 |
| Machinery and equipment | 1,125,000 | 317,500 |
| Automobiles and trucks | 172,000 | 100,325 |
| Leasehold improvements | 216,000 | 108,000 |
| Land improvements | — | — |

**Depreciation methods and useful lives:**
Buildings—150% declining balance; 25 years.
Machinery and equipment—Straight line; 10 years.
Automobiles and trucks—150% declining balance; 5 years, all acquired after 2009.
Leasehold improvements—Straight line.
Land improvements—Straight line.

Depreciation is computed to the nearest month and residual values are immaterial. Transactions during 2013 and other information:

a. On January 6, 2013, a plant facility consisting of land and building was acquired from King Corp. in exchange for 25,000 shares of Cord's common stock. On this date, Cord's stock had a fair value of $50 a share. Current assessed values of land and building for property tax purposes are $187,500 and $562,500, respectively.

b. On March 25, 2013, new parking lots, streets, and sidewalks at the acquired plant facility were completed at a total cost of $192,000. These expenditures had an estimated useful life of 12 years.

c. The leasehold improvements were completed on December 31, 2009, and had an estimated useful life of eight years. The related lease, which would terminate on December 31, 2015, was renewable for an additional four-year term. On April 29, 2013, Cord exercised the renewal option.

d. On July 1, 2013, machinery and equipment were purchased at a total invoice cost of $325,000. Additional costs of $10,000 for delivery and $50,000 for installation were incurred.

e. On August 30, 2013, Cord purchased a new automobile for $12,500.

f. On September 30, 2013, a truck with a cost of $24,000 and a carrying amount of $9,100 on date of sale was sold for $11,500. Depreciation for the nine months ended September 30, 2013, was $2,650.

g. On December 20, 2013, a machine with a cost of $17,000 and a book value of $2,975 at date of disposition was scrapped without cash recovery.

**Required:**

1. Prepare a schedule analyzing the changes in each of the plant asset accounts during 2013. This schedule should include columns for beginning balance, increase, decrease, and ending balance for each of the plant asset accounts. Do not analyze changes in accumulated depreciation and amortization.

2. For each asset category, prepare a schedule showing depreciation or amortization expense for the year ended December 31, 2013. Round computations to the nearest whole dollar.

*(AICPA adapted)*

**P 11–3**
Depreciation methods;
Chapters 10 and 11
● LO11–2

[This problem is a continuation of Problem 10–3 in Chapter 10 focusing on depreciation.]

**Required:**
For each asset classification, prepare a schedule showing depreciation expense for the year ended December 31, 2013, using the following depreciation methods and useful lives:

Land improvements—Straight line; 15 years.
Building—150% declining balance; 20 years.
Machinery and equipment—Straight line; 10 years.
Automobiles—150% declining balance; 3 years.

Depreciation is computed to the nearest month and no residual values are used.

*(AICPA adapted)*

**P 11–4**
Partial-year depreciation;
asset addition;
increase in useful life
● LO11–2,
 LO11–5,
 LO11–9

On April 1, 2011, the KB Toy Company purchased equipment to be used in its manufacturing process. The equipment cost $48,000, has an eight-year useful life, and has no residual value. The company uses the straight-line depreciation method for all manufacturing equipment.

On January 4, 2013, $12,350 was spent to repair the equipment and to add a feature that increased its operating efficiency. Of the total expenditure, $2,000 represented ordinary repairs and annual maintenance and $10,350 represented the cost of the new feature. In addition to increasing operating efficiency, the total useful life of the equipment was extended to 10 years.

**Required:**
Prepare journal entries for the following:

1. Depreciation for 2011 and 2012.

2. The 2013 expenditure.

3. Depreciation for 2013.

**P 11–5**
**Property,**
**plant, and**
**equipment and**
**intangible assets;**
**comprehensive**

● **LO11–2**

The Thompson Corporation, a manufacturer of steel products, began operations on October 1, 2011. The accounting department of Thompson has started the fixed-asset and depreciation schedule presented below. You have been asked to assist in completing this schedule. In addition to ascertaining that the data already on the schedule are correct, you have obtained the following information from the company's records and personnel:

a.  Depreciation is computed from the first of the month of acquisition to the first of the month of disposition.

b.  Land A and Building A were acquired from a predecessor corporation. Thompson paid $812,500 for the land and building together. At the time of acquisition, the land had a fair value of $72,000 and the building had a fair value of $828,000.

c.  Land B was acquired on October 2, 2011, in exchange for 3,000 newly issued shares of Thompson's common stock. At the date of acquisition, the stock had a par value of $5 per share and a fair value of $25 per share. During October 2011, Thompson paid $10,400 to demolish an existing building on this land so it could construct a new building.

d.  Construction of Building B on the newly acquired land began on October 1, 2012. By September 30, 2013, Thompson had paid $210,000 of the estimated total construction costs of $300,000. Estimated completion and occupancy are July 2014.

e.  Certain equipment was donated to the corporation by the city. An independent appraisal of the equipment when donated placed the fair value at $16,000 and the residual value at $2,000.

f.  Machine A's total cost of $110,000 includes installation charges of $550 and normal repairs and maintenance of $11,000. Residual value is estimated at $5,500. Machine A was sold on February 1, 2013.

g.  On October 1, 2012, Machine B was acquired with a down payment of $4,000 and the remaining payments to be made in 10 annual installments of $4,000 each beginning October 1, 2013. The prevailing interest rate was 8%.

**THOMPSON CORPORATION**
**Fixed Asset and Depreciation Schedule**
**For Fiscal Years Ended September 30, 2012, and September 30, 2013**

| Assets | Acquisition Date | Cost | Residual | Depreciation Method | Estimated Life in Years | Depreciation for Year Ended 9/30 2012 | 2013 |
|---|---|---|---|---|---|---|---|
| Land A | 10/1/11 | $(1) | N/A | N/A | N/A | N/A | N/A |
| Building A | 10/1/11 | (2) | $47,500 | SL | (3) | $14,000 | $(4) |
| Land B | 10/2/11 | (5) | N/A | N/A | N/A | N/A | N/A |
| Building B | Under construction | 210,000 to date | — | SL | 30 | — | (6) |
| Donated Equipment | 10/2/11 | (7) | 2,000 | 150% Declining balance | 10 | (8) | (9) |
| Machine A | 10/2/11 | (10) | 5,500 | Sum-of-the-years'-digits | 10 | (11) | (12) |
| Machine B | 10/1/12 | (13) | — | SL | 15 | — | (14) |

N/A = not applicable

**Required:**
Supply the correct amount for each numbered item on the schedule. Round each answer to the nearest dollar.

*(AICPA adapted)*

**P 11–6**
**Depreciation**
**methods;**
**partial-year**
**depreciation; sale**
**of assets**

● **LO11–2**

On March 31, 2013, the Herzog Company purchased a factory complete with machinery and equipment. The allocation of the total purchase price of $1,000,000 to the various types of assets along with estimated useful lives and residual values are as follows:

| Asset | Cost | Estimated Residual Value | Estimated Useful Life in Years |
|---|---|---|---|
| Land | $  100,000 | N/A | N/A |
| Building | 500,000 | none | 25 |
| Machinery | 240,000 | 10% of cost | 8 |
| Equipment | 160,000 | $13,000 | 6 |
| Total | $1,000,000 | | |

On June 29, 2014, machinery included in the March 31, 2013, purchase that cost $100,000 was sold for $80,000. Herzog uses the straight-line depreciation method for buildings and machinery and the sum-of-the-years'-digits method for equipment. Partial-year depreciation is calculated based on the number of months an asset is in service.

**Required:**

1. Compute depreciation expense on the building, machinery, and equipment for 2013.

2. Prepare the journal entries to record (1) depreciation on the machinery sold on June 29, 2014, and (2) the sale of machinery.

3. Compute depreciation expense on the building, remaining machinery, and equipment for 2014.

**P 11–7**
Depletion;
change in
estimate
● LO11–3,
  LO11–5

In 2013, the Marion Company purchased land containing a mineral mine for $1,600,000. Additional costs of $600,000 were incurred to develop the mine. Geologists estimated that 400,000 tons of ore would be extracted. After the ore is removed, the land will have a resale value of $100,000.

To aid in the extraction, Marion built various structures and small storage buildings on the site at a cost of $150,000. These structures have a useful life of 10 years. The structures cannot be moved after the ore has been removed and will be left at the site. In addition, new equipment costing $80,000 was purchased and installed at the site. Marion does not plan to move the equipment to another site, but estimates that it can be sold at auction for $4,000 after the mining project is completed.

In 2013, 50,000 tons of ore were extracted and sold. In 2014, the estimate of total tons of ore in the mine was revised from 400,000 to 487,500. During 2014, 80,000 tons were extracted, of which 60,000 tons were sold.

**Required:**

1. Compute depletion and depreciation of the mine and the mining facilities and equipment for 2013 and 2014. Marion uses the units-of-production method to determine depreciation on mining facilities and equipment.

2. Compute the book value of the mineral mine, structures, and equipment as of December 31, 2014.

3. Discuss the accounting treatment of the depletion and depreciation on the mine and mining facilities and equipment.

**P 11–8**
Amortization
● LO11–4

The following information concerns the intangible assets of Epstein Corporation:

a. On June 30, 2013, Epstein completed the acquisition of the Johnstone Corporation for $2,000,000 in cash. The fair value of the net identifiable assets of Johnstone was $1,700,000.

b. Included in the assets purchased from Johnstone was a patent that was valued at $80,000. The remaining legal life of the patent was 13 years, but Epstein believes that the patent will only be useful for another eight years.

c. Epstein acquired a franchise on October 1, 2013, by paying an initial franchise fee of $200,000. The contractual life of the franchise is 10 years.

**Required:**

1. Prepare year-end adjusting journal entries to record amortization expense on the intangibles at December 31, 2013.

2. Prepare the intangible asset section of the December 31, 2013, balance sheet.

**P 11–9**
Straight-line
depreciation;
change in useful
life and residual
value
● LO11–2,
  LO11–5

The property, plant, and equipment section of the Jasper Company's December 31, 2012, balance sheet contained the following:

| Property, plant, and equipment: | | |
|---|---:|---:|
| Land | | $120,000 |
| Building | $ 840,000 | |
| Less: Accumulated depreciation | (200,000) | 640,000 |
| Equipment | 180,000 | |
| Less: Accumulated depreciation | ? | ? |
| Total property, plant, and equipment | | ? |

The land and building were purchased at the beginning of 2008. Straight-line depreciation is used and a residual value of $40,000 for the building is anticipated.

The equipment is comprised of the following three machines:

| Machine | Cost | Date Acquired | Residual Value | Life in Years |
|---|---|---|---|---|
| 101 | $70,000 | 1/1/10 | $7,000 | 10 |
| 102 | 80,000 | 6/30/11 | 8,000 | 8 |
| 103 | 30,000 | 9/1/12 | 3,000 | 9 |

The straight-line method is used to determine depreciation on the equipment. On March 31, 2013, Machine 102 was sold for $52,500. Early in 2013, the useful life of machine 101 was revised to seven years in total, and the residual value was revised to zero.

**Required:**

1. Calculate the accumulated depreciation on the equipment at December 31, 2012.

2. Prepare the journal entry to record the sale of machine 102. Also prepare the journal entry to record 2013 depreciation on machine 102 up to the date of sale.

3. Prepare the 2013 year-end adjusting journal entries to record depreciation on the building and equipment.

**P 11–10**
**Accounting changes; three accounting situations**
● LO11–2,
LO11–5,
LO11–6

Described below are three independent and unrelated situations involving accounting changes. Each change occurs during 2013 before any adjusting entries or closing entries are prepared.

a.  On December 30, 2009, Rival Industries acquired its office building at a cost of $10,000,000. It has been depreciated on a straight-line basis assuming a useful life of 40 years and no residual value. Early in 2013, the estimate of useful life was revised to 28 years in total with no change in residual value.

b.  At the beginning of 2009, the Hoffman Group purchased office equipment at a cost of $330,000. Its useful life was estimated to be 10 years with no residual value. The equipment has been depreciated by the sum-of-the-years'-digits method. On January 1, 2013, the company changed to the straight-line method.

c.  At the beginning of 2013, Jantzen Specialties, which uses the sum-of-the-years'-digits method, changed to the straight-line method for newly acquired buildings and equipment. The change increased current year net income by $445,000.

**Required:**
For each situation:
1.  Identify the type of change.
2.  Prepare any journal entry necessary as a direct result of the change as well as any adjusting entry for 2013 related to the situation described. (Ignore income tax effects.)
3.  Briefly describe any other steps that should be taken to appropriately report the situation.

**P 11–11**
**Error correction; change in depreciation method**
● LO11–2,
LO11–6,
LO11–7

Collins Corporation purchased office equipment at the beginning of 2011 and capitalized a cost of $2,000,000. This cost figure included the following expenditures:

| | |
|---|---|
| Purchase price | $1,850,000 |
| Freight charges | 30,000 |
| Installation charges | 20,000 |
| Annual maintenance charge | 100,000 |
| Total | $2,000,000 |

The company estimated an eight-year useful life for the equipment. No residual value is anticipated. The double-declining-balance method was used to determine depreciation expense for 2011 and 2012.

In 2013, after the 2012 financial statements were issued, the company decided to switch to the straight-line depreciation method for this equipment. At that time, the company's controller discovered that the original cost of the equipment incorrectly included one year of annual maintenance charges for the equipment.

**Required:**
1.  Ignoring income taxes, prepare the appropriate correcting entry for the equipment capitalization error discovered in 2013.
2.  Ignoring income taxes, prepare any 2013 journal entry(s) related to the change in depreciation methods.

**P 11–12**
**Depreciation and amortization; impairment**
● LO11–2,
LO11–4,
LO11–8

At the beginning of 2011, Metatec Inc. acquired Ellison Technology Corporation for $600 million. In addition to cash, receivables, and inventory, the following assets and their fair values were also acquired:

| | |
|---|---|
| Plant and equipment (depreciable assets) | $150 million |
| Patent | 40 million |
| Goodwill | 100 million |

The plant and equipment are depreciated over a 10-year useful life on a straight-line basis. There is no estimated residual value. The patent is estimated to have a 5-year useful life, no residual value, and is amortized using the straight-line method.

At the end of 2013, a change in business climate indicated to management that the assets of Ellison might be impaired. The following amounts have been determined:

| | |
|---|---|
| Plant and equipment: | |
|     Undiscounted sum of future cash flows | $ 80 million |
|     Fair value | 60 million |
| Patent: | |
|     Undiscounted sum of future cash flows | $ 20 million |
|     Fair value | 13 million |
| Goodwill: | |
|     Fair value of Ellison Technology | $450 million |
|     Fair value of Ellison's net assets (excluding goodwill) | 390 million |
|     Book value of Ellison's net assets (including goodwill) | 470 million* |

*After first recording any impairment losses on plant and equipment and the patent.

**Required:**

1. Compute the book value of the plant and equipment and patent at the end of 2013.
2. When should the plant and equipment and the patent be tested for impairment?
3. When should goodwill be tested for impairment?
4. Determine the amount of any impairment loss to be recorded, if any, for the three assets.

**P 11–13**
Depreciation and depletion; change in useful life; asset retirement obligation; Chapters 10 and 11

● LO11–2,
LO11–3,
LO11–5

On May 1, 2013, Hecala Mining entered into an agreement with the state of New Mexico to obtain the rights to operate a mineral mine in New Mexico for $10 million. Additional costs and purchases included the following:

| | |
|---|---|
| Development costs in preparing the mine | $3,200,000 |
| Mining machinery | 140,000 |
| Construction of various structures on site | 68,000 |

After the minerals are removed from the mine, the machinery will be sold for an estimated residual value of $10,000. The structures will be torn down.

Geologists estimate that 800,000 tons of ore can be extracted from the mine. After the ore is removed the land will revert back to the state of New Mexico.

The contract with the state requires Hecala to restore the land to its original condition after mining operations are completed in approximately four years. Management has provided the following possible outflows for the restoration costs:

| Cash Outflow | Probability |
|---|---|
| $600,000 | 30% |
| 700,000 | 30% |
| 800,000 | 40% |

Hecala's credit-adjusted risk-free interest rate is 8%. During 2013, Hecala extracted 120,000 tons of ore from the mine. The company's fiscal year ends on December 31.

**Required:**

1. Determine the amount at which Hecala will record the mine.
2. Calculate the depletion of the mine and the depreciation of the mining facilities and equipment for 2013, assuming that Hecala uses the units-of-production method for both depreciation and depletion. Round depletion and depreciation rates to four decimals.
3. How much accretion expense will the company record in its income statement for the 2013 fiscal year?
4. Are depletion of the mine and depreciation of the mining facilities and equipment reported as separate expenses in the income statement? Discuss the accounting treatment of these items in the income statement and balance sheet.
5. During 2014, Hecala changed its estimate of the total amount of ore originally in the mine from 800,000 to 1,000,000 tons. Briefly describe the accounting treatment the company will employ to account for the change *and* calculate the depletion of the mine and depreciation of the mining facilities and equipment for 2014 assuming Hecala extracted 150,000 tons of ore in 2014.

## Broaden Your Perspective

**Apply your critical-thinking ability to the knowledge you've gained. These cases will provide you an opportunity to develop your research, analysis, judgment, and communication skills. You also will work with other students, integrate what you've learned, apply it in real world situations, and consider its global and ethical ramifications. This practice will broaden your knowledge and further develop your decision-making abilities.**

**Analysis Case 11–1**
Depreciation, depletion, and amortization

● LO11–1

The terms depreciation, depletion, and amortization all refer to the process of allocating the cost of an asset to the periods the asset is used.

**Required:**

Discuss the differences between depreciation, depletion, and amortization as the terms are used in accounting for property, plant, and equipment and intangible assets.

**Communication Case 11–2**
Depreciation

● LO11–1

At a recent luncheon, you were seated next to Mr. Hopkins, the president of a local company that manufactures bicycle parts. He heard that you were a CPA and made the following comments to you:

Why is it that I am forced to recognize depreciation expense in my company's income statement when I know that I could sell many of my assets for more than I paid for them? I thought that the purpose of the balance sheet was to reflect the value of my business and that the purpose of the income statement was to report the net change in value or wealth of a company. It just doesn't make sense to penalize my profits when there hasn't been any loss in value from using the assets.

At the conclusion of the luncheon, you promised to send him a short explanation of the rationale for current depreciation practices.

**Required:**

Prepare a letter to Mr. Hopkins. Explain the accounting concept of depreciation and include a brief example in your explanation showing that over the life of the asset the change in value approach to depreciation and the allocation of cost approach will result in the same total effect on income.

**Judgment Case 11–3**
Straight-line method; composite depreciation
● LO11–1, LO11–2

Portland Co. uses the straight-line depreciation method for depreciable assets. All assets are depreciated individually except manufacturing machinery, which is depreciated by the composite method.

**Required:**

1. What factors should have influenced Portland's selection of the straight-line depreciation method?
2. a. What benefits should derive from using the composite method rather than the individual basis for manufacturing machinery?
   b. How should Portland have calculated the manufacturing machinery's annual depreciation in its first year of operation?

*(AICPA adapted)*

**Judgment Case 11–4**
Depreciation
● LO11–1, LO11–2

At the beginning of the year, Patrick Company acquired a computer to be used in its operations. The computer was delivered by the supplier, installed by Patrick, and placed into operation. The estimated useful life of the computer is five years, and its estimated residual value is significant.

**Required:**

1. a. What costs should Patrick capitalize for the computer?
   b. What is the objective of depreciation accounting?
2. What is the rationale for using accelerated depreciation methods?

*(AICPA adapted)*

**Judgment Case 11–5**
Capitalize or expense; materiality
● LO11–9

Redline Publishers, Inc. produces various manuals ranging from computer software instructional booklets to manuals explaining the installation and use of large pieces of industrial equipment. At the end of 2013, the company's balance sheet reported total assets of $62 million and total liabilities of $40 million. The income statement for 2013 reported net income of $1.1 million, which represents an approximate 3% increase from the prior year. The company's effective income tax rate is 30%.

Near the end of 2013, a variety of expenditures were made to overhaul the company's manufacturing equipment. None of these expenditures exceeded $750, the materiality threshold the company has set for the capitalization of any such expenditure. Even though the overhauls extended the service life of the equipment, the expenditures were expensed, not capitalized.

John Henderson, the company's controller, is worried about the treatment of the overhaul expenditures. Even though no individual expenditure exceeded the $750 materiality threshold, total expenditures were $70,000.

**Required:**

Should the overhaul expenditures be capitalized or expensed?

**Communication Case 11–6**
Capitalize or expense; materiality
● LO11–9

The focus of the case is the situation described in Case 11–5. Your instructor will divide the class into two to six groups depending on the size of the class. The mission of your group is to determine the treatment of the overhaul expenditures.

**Required:**

1. Each group member should deliberate the situation independently and draft a tentative argument prior to the class session for which the case is assigned.
2. In class, each group will meet for 10 to 15 minutes in different areas of the classroom. During the meeting, group members will take turns sharing their suggestions for the purpose of arriving at a single group treatment.
3. After the allotted time, a spokesperson for each group (selected during the group meetings) will share the group's solution with the class. The goal of the class is to incorporate the views of each group into a consensus approach to the situation.

Whaley Distributors is a wholesale distributor of electronic components. Financial statements for the year ended December 31, 2013, reported the following amounts and subtotals ($ in millions):

| | Assets | Liabilities | Shareholders' Equity | Net Income | Expenses |
|---|---|---|---|---|---|
| 2012 | $640 | $330 | $310 | $210 | $150 |
| 2013 | $820 | $400 | $420 | $230 | $175 |

In 2014 the following situations occurred or came to light:

a. Internal auditors discovered that ending inventories reported in the financial statements the two previous years were misstated due to faulty internal controls. The errors were in the following amounts:

| | |
|---|---|
| 2012 inventory | Overstated by $12 million |
| 2013 inventory | Understated by $10 million |

b. A patent costing $18 million at the beginning of 2012, expected to benefit operations for a total of six years, has not been amortized since acquired.

c. Whaley's conveyer equipment has been depreciated by the sum-of-the-years'-digits (SYD) method since constructed at the beginning of 2012 at a cost of $30 million. It has an expected useful life of five years and no expected residual value. At the beginning of 2014, Whaley decided to switch to straight-line depreciation.

**Required:**

For each situation:

1. Prepare any journal entry necessary as a direct result of the change or error correction as well as any adjusting entry for 2014 related to the situation described. (Ignore tax effects.)

2. Determine the amounts to be reported for each of the items shown above from the 2012 and 2013 financial statements when those amounts are reported again in the 2014, 2013, and 2012 comparative financial statements.

There are various types of accounting changes, each of which is required to be reported differently.

**Required:**

1. What type of accounting change is a change from the sum-of-the-years'-digits method of depreciation to the straight-line method for previously recorded assets? Under what circumstances does this type of accounting change occur?

2. What type of accounting change is a change in the expected service life of an asset arising because of more experience with the asset? Under what circumstances does this type of accounting change occur?

*(AICPA adapted)*

The company controller, Barry Melrose, has asked for your help in interpreting the authoritative accounting literature that addresses the recognition and measurement of impairment losses for property, plant, and equipment and intangible assets. "We have a significant amount of goodwill on our books from last year's acquisition of Churchill Corporation. Also, I think we may have a problem with the assets of some of our factories out West. And one of our divisions is currently considering disposing of a large group of depreciable assets."

Your task as assistant controller is to research the issue.

**Required:**

1. Obtain the relevant authoritative literature on accounting for the impairment of property, plant, and equipment and intangible assets using the FASB's Codification Research System. You might gain access at the FASB website (www.fasb.org). Cite the reference locations regarding impairment of property, plant, and equipment and intangible assets.

2. When should property, plant, and equipment and intangible assets be tested for impairment?

3. Explain the process for measuring an impairment loss for property, plant, and equipment and intangible assets to be held and used.

4. What are the specific criteria that must be met for an asset or asset group to be classified as held-for-sale? What is the specific citation reference from the FASB's Codification Research System that contains these criteria?

5. Explain the process for measuring an impairment loss for property, plant, and equipment and intangible assets classified as held-for-sale.

**Ethics**
**Case 11–10**
Asset impairment
● LO11–8

At the beginning of 2011, the Healthy Life Food Company purchased equipment for $42 million to be used in the manufacture of a new line of gourmet frozen foods. The equipment was estimated to have a 10-year service life and no residual value. The straight-line depreciation method was used to measure depreciation for 2011 and 2012.

Late in 2013, it became apparent that sales of the new frozen food line were significantly below expectations. The company decided to continue production for two more years (2014 and 2015) and then discontinue the line. At that time, the equipment will be sold for minimal scrap values.

The controller, Heather Meyer, was asked by Harvey Dent, the company's chief executive officer (CEO), to determine the appropriate treatment of the change in service life of the equipment. Heather determined that there has been an impairment of value requiring an immediate write-down of the equipment of $12,900,000. The remaining book value would then be depreciated over the equipment's revised service life.

The CEO does not like Heather's conclusion because of the effect it would have on 2013 income. "Looks like a simple revision in service life from 10 years to 5 years to me," Dent concluded. "Let's go with it that way, Heather."

**Required:**

1. What is the difference in before-tax income between the CEO's and Heather's treatment of the situation?
2. Discuss Heather Meyer's ethical dilemma.

**Judgment**
**Case 11–11**
Earnings
management
and accounting
changes;
impairment
● LO11–5,
   LO11–6,
   LO11–8

Companies often are under pressure to meet or beat Wall Street earnings projections in order to increase stock prices and also to increase the value of stock options. Some resort to earnings management practices to artificially create desired results.

**Required:**

1. How can a company manage earnings by changing its depreciation method? Is this an effective technique to manage earnings?
2. How can a company manage earnings by changing the estimated useful lives of depreciable assets? Is this an effective technique to manage earnings?
3. Using a fictitious example and numbers you make up, describe in your own words how asset impairment losses could be used to manage earnings. How might that benefit the company?

**Judgment**
**Case 11–12**
Subsequent
expenditures
● LO11–9

The Cummings Company charged various expenditures made during 2013 to an account called repairs and maintenance expense. You have been asked by your supervisor in the company's internal audit department to review the expenditures to determine if they were appropriately recorded. The amount of each of the transactions included in the account is considered material.

1. Engine tune-up and oil change on the company's 12 delivery trucks—$1,300.
2. Rearrangement of machinery on the main production line—$5,500. It is not evident that the rearrangement will increase operational efficiency.
3. Installation of aluminum siding on the manufacturing plant—$32,000.
4. Replacement of the old air conditioning system in the manufacturing plant with a new system—$120,000.
5. Replacement of broken parts on three machines—$1,500.
6. Annual painting of the manufacturing plant—$11,000.
7. Purchase of new forklift to move finished product to the loading dock—$6,000.
8. Patching leaks in the roof of the manufacturing plant—$6,500. The repair work did not extend the useful life of the roof.

**Required:**

For each of the transactions listed above, indicate whether the expenditure is appropriately charged to the repair and maintenance expense account, and if not, indicate the proper account to be charged.

**Real World**
**Case 11–13**
Disposition and
depreciation;
Chapters 10
and 11; Caterpillar
● LO11–1

*Real World Financials*

Caterpillar Inc. (CAT) is a world leader in the manufacture of construction and mining equipment, diesel and natural gas engines, and industrial gas turbines. CAT reported the following in a disclosure note accompanying its 2010 financial statements:

| | 2010 | 2009 |
|---|---|---|
| ($ in millions) | | |
| Property, plant and equipment | $24,906 | $24,221 |
| Less: Accumulated depreciation | 12,367 | 11,835 |
| Property, plant and equipment - Net | $12,539 | $12,386 |

Also, Note 8 disclosed that the total cost of property, plant, and equipment included $682 and $639 (dollars in millions) in land at the end of 2010 and 2009, respectively. In addition, the statement of cash flows for the year ended December 31, 2010, reported the following as cash flows from investing activities:

| ($ in millions) | |
|---|---|
| Payments for property, plant and equipment | $(2,586) |
| Proceeds from disposition of property, plant and equipment | 1,469 |

The statement of cash flows also reported 2010 depreciation and amortization of $2,296 million (depreciation of $2,220 and amortization of $76).

**Required:**

1. Assume that all property, plant, and equipment acquired during 2010 were purchased for cash. Determine the amount of gain or loss from dispositions of property, plant, and equipment that Caterpillar recognized during 2010.

2. Assume that Caterpillar uses the straight-line method to depreciate plant and equipment. What is the approximate average service life of CAT's depreciable assets?

**Real World Case 11–14**
Depreciation and depletion method; asset impairment; subsequent expenditures; Chevron

● LO11–2, LO11–3, LO11–8, LO11–9

Real World Financials

EDGAR, the Electronic Data Gathering, Analysis, and Retrieval system, performs automated collection, validation, indexing, and forwarding of submissions by companies and others who are required by law to file forms with the U.S. Securities and Exchange Commission (SEC). All publicly traded domestic companies use EDGAR to make the majority of their filings. (Some foreign companies file voluntarily.) Form 10-K, which includes the annual report, is required to be filed on EDGAR. The SEC makes this information available on the Internet.

**Required:**

1. Access EDGAR on the Internet. The web address is **www.sec.gov**.

2. Search for **Chevron Corporation**. Access the 10-K filing for most recent fiscal year. Search or scroll to find the financial statements and related notes.

3. Answer the following questions related to the company's property, plant, and equipment and intangible assets:
   a. Describe the company's depreciation and depletion policies.
   b. Describe the company's policy for subsequent expenditures made for plant and equipment.

**IFRS Case 11–15**
Subsequent valuation of property, plant, and equipment; comparison of U.S. GAAP and IFRS; GlaxoSmithKline

● LO11–10

Real World Financials

**GlaxoSmithKline** is a global pharmaceutical and consumer health-related products company located in the United Kingdom. The company prepares its financial statements in accordance with International Financial Reporting Standards.

**Required:**

1. Use the Internet to locate GlaxoSmithKline's most recent annual report. The address is **www.gsk.com/investors**. Locate the significant accounting policies disclosure note.

2. How does the company value its property, plant, and equipment? Does the company have any other options under IFRS for valuing these assets? How do these options differ from U.S. GAAP?

3. What are the company's policies for possible reversals of impairment losses for goodwill and for other non-current assets? How do these policies differ from U.S. GAAP?

**Analysis Case 11–16**
Depreciation and amortization

● LO11–2, LO11–4

**DELL**

Refer to the financial statements and related disclosure notes of **Dell** in Appendix B located at the back of the text.

**Required:**

1. What amount of depreciation and amortization did the company report in the fiscal year ended January 30, 2011?

2. What depreciation method is used for financial reporting purposes and what are the service lives of depreciable assets?

# Air France—KLM Case

 **AIRFRANCE /**

● LO11–10

IFRS

Air France–KLM (AF), a French company, prepares its financial statements according to International Financial Reporting Standards. AF's annual report for the year ended March 31, 2011, which includes financial statements and disclosure notes, is provided with all new textbooks. This material also is included in AF's "Registration Document 2010–11," dated June 15, 2011 and is available at www.airfranceklm.com.

**Required:**

1. AF's property, plant, and equipment is reported at cost. The company has a policy of not revaluing property, plant, and equipment. Suppose AF decided to revalue its flight equipment on March 31, 2011, and that the fair value of the equipment on that date was €12,000 million. Prepare the journal entry to record the revaluation assuming that the journal entry to record annual depreciation had already been recorded. (*Hint:* you will need to locate the original cost and accumulated depreciation of the equipment at the end of the year in the appropriate disclosure note.)

2. Under U.S. GAAP, what alternatives do companies have to value their property, plant, and equipment?

3. AF calculates depreciation of plant and equipment on a straight-line basis, over the useful life of the asset. Describe any differences between IFRS and U.S. GAAP in the calculation of depreciation.

4. When does AF test for the possible impairment of fixed assets? How does this approach differ from U.S. GAAP?

5. Describe the approach AF uses to determine fixed asset impairment losses. (*Hint:* see Note 3.14) How does this approach differ from U.S. GAAP?

6. The following is included in AF's disclosure note 3.12: "Intangible assets are held at initial cost less accumulated amortization and any accumulated impairment losses." Assume that on March 31, 2011, AF decided to revalue its Other intangible assets (see Note 16) and that the fair value on that date was determined to be €360 million. Amortization expense for the year already has been recorded. Prepare the journal entry to record the revaluation.

# CPA Simulation 11–1

**Fukisan Inc.**
Depreciation;
change in estimate

 **KAPLAN**

**CPA Review**

Test your knowledge of the concepts discussed in this chapter, practice critical professional skills necessary for career success, and prepare for the computer-based CPA exam by accessing our CPA simulations at the text website: www.mhhe.com/spiceland7e.

The Fukisan Inc. simulation tests your knowledge of calculating depreciation using various methods and accounting for the change in the useful life of a depreciable asset.

# 12 Investments

In this chapter you will learn about various approaches used to account for investments that companies make in the debt and equity of other companies. An investing company always has the option to account for these investments at fair value, with changes in fair values reported on the income statement. However, depending on the nature of an investment, investors can use alternative accounting approaches that ignore most fair value changes (e.g., *held-to-maturity* investments) or that include fair value changes only in other comprehensive income (e.g., *available-for-sale* investments). And, when an equity investor can significantly influence an investee but does not control it, the investor can use the *equity method* of accounting, which ignores fair value changes but includes the investee's income when reporting the investor's income. In appendices to this chapter, you will learn about other types of investments, and also about how to deal with other-than-temporarily impairments. The chapter concludes with a Where We're Headed Supplement explaining in detail a proposed Accounting Standards Update (hereafter, "the proposed ASU") that the FASB plans to issue in 2012 that substantially changes how we account for investments.

## LEARNING OBJECTIVES

**After studying this chapter, you should be able to:**

- **LO12–1** Demonstrate how to identify and account for investments classified for reporting purposes as held-to-maturity. (*p. 656*)

- **LO12–2** Demonstrate how to identify and account for investments classified for reporting purposes as trading securities. (*p. 659*)

- **LO12–3** Demonstrate how to identify and account for investments classified for reporting purposes as available-for-sale securities. (*p. 663*)

- **LO12–4** Explain what constitutes significant influence by the investor over the operating and financial policies of the investee. (*p. 680*)

- **LO12–5** Demonstrate how to account for investments accounted for under the equity method. (*p. 680*)

- **LO12–6** Explain the adjustments made in the equity method when the fair value of the net assets underlying an investment exceeds their book value at acquisition. (*p. 682*)

- **LO12–7** Explain how electing the fair value option affects accounting for investments. (*pp. 672* and *688*)

- **LO12–8** Discuss the primary differences between U.S. GAAP and IFRS with respect to investments. (*pp. 672, 673, 674, 679, 688,* and *701*)

# FINANCIAL REPORTING CASE

## A Case of Coke

You are the lone accounting major in your five-member group in your Business Policy class. A part of the case your group is working on is the analysis of the financial statements of the **Coca-Cola Company**.

The marketing major in the group is confused by the following disclosure note from Coca-Cola's 2010 annual report:

### NOTE 3: INVESTMENTS (in part)
### Certain Debt and Marketable Equity Securities

Investments in debt and marketable securities, other than investments accounted for under the equity method, are classified as trading, available-for-sale or held-to-maturity. Our marketable equity investments are classified as either trading or available-for-sale with their cost basis determined by the specific identification method. Realized and unrealized gains and losses on trading securities and realized gains and losses on available-for-sale securities are included in net income. Unrealized gains and losses, net of deferred taxes, on available-for-sale securities are included in our consolidated balance sheets as a component of AOCI.

Our investments in debt securities are carried at either amortized cost or fair value. Investments in debt securities that the Company has the positive intent and ability to hold to maturity are carried at amortized cost and classified as held-to-maturity. Investments in debt securities that are not classified as held-to-maturity are carried at fair value and classified as either trading or available-for-sale.

"They say unrealized gains and losses on available-for-sale securities are reported as part of AOCI. What's that? I don't see these gains and losses on the income statement," he complained. "And held-to-maturity securities—why are they treated differently? And what about equity method investments? On the balance sheet they have almost $9 *billion* of investments accounted for under the equity method. They made over $1 billion on those investments in 2010! Is that cash they can use?"

---

By the time you finish this chapter, you should be able to respond appropriately to the questions posed in this case. Compare your response to the solution provided at the end of the chapter.

**QUESTIONS**

1. How should you respond? Why are held-to-maturity securities treated differently from other investment securities? (*p. 656*)

2. Why are unrealized gains and losses on trading securities reported in the income statement? (*p. 660*)

3. Why are unrealized gains and losses on available-for-sale securities not reported in the income statement, but instead are in other comprehensive income, and then shown in accumulated other comprehensive income (AOCI) in the balance sheet? (*p. 664*)

4. Explain why Coke accounts for some of its investments by the equity method and what that means. (*p. 681*)

To finance its operations, and often the expansion of those operations, a corporation raises funds by selling equity securities (common and preferred stock) and debt securities (bonds and notes). These securities, also called financial instruments, are purchased as investments by individual investors, mutual funds, and also by other corporations. In later chapters we discuss equity and debt securities from the perspective of the issuing company. Our focus in this chapter is on the corporations that invest in debt and equity securities issued by other corporations as well as debt securities issued by governmental units (bonds, Treasury bills, and Treasury bonds).

Most companies invest in financial instruments issued by other companies. For some investors, these investments represent ongoing affiliations with the companies whose securities are acquired. For instance, recent investments include **Pfizer**'s acquisition of **Wyeth** for $68 billion, creating the world's largest pharmaceutical company, and the Belgian company **InBev**'s acquisition of **Anheuser-Busch** for $52 billion, creating the global leader in beer. Some investments, though, are made not to obtain a favorable business relationship with another firm but simply to earn a return from the dividends or interest the securities pay or from increases in the market prices of the securities—the same reasons that might motivate you to buy stocks, bonds, or other investment securities.

With such diversity in investment objectives, it's not surprising that there is diversity in the approaches used to account for investments. As you'll discover when reading this chapter, investments are accounted for in five primary ways, depending on the nature of the investment relationship and the preferences of the investor. Before we discuss the approaches in detail, see the quick overview in Illustration 12–1.

In Part A of this chapter we discuss accounting for investments when the investor lacks significant influence over the operating and financial policies of the investee. In Part B we discuss accounting for "significant influence" investments. In both Parts A and B, we first discuss specific reporting methods and then discuss how the reporting changes if the investor elects the fair value option.

# PART A INVESTOR LACKS SIGNIFICANT INFLUENCE

The reporting approaches we use for investments differ according to how the approaches account for one or more of the four critical events that an investor experiences in the life of an investment:

1. Purchasing the investment.
2. Recognizing investment revenue (interest in the case of debt, dividends in the case of equity).
3. Holding the investment during periods in which the investment's fair value changes (and thus incurring *unrealized holding* gains and losses, since the security has not yet been sold).
4. Selling the investment (and thus incurring *realized* gains and losses, since the security has been sold and the gains or losses actually incurred).

As shown in Illustration 12–1, when the investor lacks significant influence over the investee, the investment is classified in one of three categories: held-to-maturity securities (HTM), trading securities (TS), and available-for-sale securities (AFS). Each type of investment has its own reporting method. However, regardless of the investment type, investors can elect the "fair value option" that we discuss later in the chapter and classify HTM and AFS securities as TS. The key difference among the reporting approaches is how we account for unrealized holding gains and losses (critical event number 3 above), as shown in Illustration 12–2.

**Illustration 12–1**
Reporting Categories for Investments

| Control Characteristics of the Investment | Reporting Method Used by the Investor |
|---|---|
| **The investor *lacks significant influence* over the operating and financial policies of the investee:** | |
| Investments in debt securities for which the investor has the "positive intent and ability" to hold to maturity | **Held-to-maturity ("HTM")**—investment reported at amortized cost* |
| Investments held in an active trading account | **Trading securities ("TS")**—investment reported at fair value (with unrealized holding gains and losses included in net income) |
| Other | **Securities available-for-sale ("AFS")**—investment reported at fair value (with unrealized holding gains and losses excluded from net income and reported in other comprehensive income)* |
| **The investor *has significant influence* over the operating and financial policies of the investee:** | |
| Typically the investor owns between 20% and 50% of the voting stock of the investee | **Equity method**—investment cost adjusted for subsequent earnings and dividends of the investee* |
| **The investor *controls* the investee:** | |
| The investor owns more than 50% of the investee | **Consolidation**—the financial statements of the investor and investee are combined as if they are a single company |

*If the investor elects the *fair value option,* this type of investment also can be accounted for using the same approach that's used for trading securities, with the investment reported at fair value and unrealized holding gains and losses included in net income.

**Illustration 12–2**
Accounting for Unrealized Holding Gains and Losses When Investor Lacks Significant Influence

| Reporting Approach | Treatment of Unrealized Holding Gains and Losses | Investment Reported in the Balance Sheet at |
|---|---|---|
| **Held-to-maturity** (HTM): used for debt that is planned to be held for its entire life | Not recognized | Amortized Cost |
| **Trading** (TS): used for debt or equity that is held in an active trading account for immediate resale. | Recognized in net income, and therefore in retained earnings as part of shareholders' equity | Fair Value |
| **Available-for-sale** (AFS): used for debt or equity that does not qualify as held-to-maturity or trading | Recognized in other comprehensive income, and therefore in accumulated other comprehensive income in shareholders' equity | Fair Value |

Illustration 12–3 provides a description from a recent annual report of how the **Bank of America** accounts for its debt investments in each of the three reporting categories.

**Illustration 12–3**
Disclosure about Investments—Bank of America

**Real World Financials**

**Note 1 (in part): Securities**

Debt securities which management has the intent and ability to hold to maturity are classified as held-to-maturity (HTM) and reported at amortized cost. Debt securities that are bought and held principally for the purpose of resale in the near term are classified as trading and are carried at fair value with unrealized gains and losses included in trading account profits (losses). Other debt securities are classified as AFS and carried at fair value with net unrealized gains and losses included in accumulated OCI on an aftertax basis.

Why treat unrealized gains and losses differently depending on the type of investment? As you know, the primary purpose of accounting is to provide information useful for making decisions. What's most relevant for that purpose is not necessarily the same for each investment a company might make. For example, a company might invest in corporate bonds to provide a steady return until the bonds mature, in which case day-to-day changes in market value may not be viewed as very relevant, so the held-to-maturity approach is preferable. On the other hand, a company might invest in the same bonds because it plans to sell them at a profit in the near future, in which case the day-to-day changes in market value could be viewed as very relevant, and the trading security or available-for-sale approach is preferable.

Let's examine the three reporting classifications, one by one.

# Securities to Be Held to Maturity

● LO12–1

Unlike a share of stock, a bond or other debt security has a specified date on which it matures. On its maturity date, the principal (also called the "face amount") is paid to investors. In the meantime, interest equal to a specified percentage of the principal is paid to investors on specified interest dates. Think of the principal and interest payments of the bond as a stream of cash flows that an investor will receive in exchange for purchasing the bond. The investor values that stream of cash flows using the prevailing market interest rate for debt of similar risk and maturity. If the interest rate paid by the bond (the "stated rate") is higher than the market rate, the bond can be sold for more than its maturity value (so it is "sold at a premium"). If the stated rate is lower than the market rate, the bond must be sold for less than its maturity value (so it is "sold at a discount"). For an example of valuing a bond, see Illustration 12–4.

**Illustration 12–4**

Bonds Purchased at a Discount

Because interest is paid semiannually, the present value calculations use:
a.  one-half the stated rate (6%),
b.  one-half the market rate (7%), and
c.  6 (= 3 × 2) semiannual periods.

On July 1, 2013, Masterwear Industries issued $700,000 of 12% bonds, dated July 1. Interest of $42,000 is payable semiannually on June 30 and December 31. The bonds mature in three years, on June 30, 2016. The market interest rate for bonds of similar risk and maturity is 14%. The entire bond issue was purchased by United Intergroup, Inc.*

**Calculation of the Price of the Bonds**

|  | | Present Values |
|---|---|---|
| Interest | $ 42,000 × 4.76654** = | $200,195 |
| Principal (face amount) | $700,000 × 0.66634† = | 466,438 |
| Present value (price) of the bonds | | $666,633 |

*The numbers in this illustration are the same as those in Illustration 14–3 in Chapter 14 (except for some differences in dates between the two chapters). This helps us to better appreciate in Chapter 14 how Masterwear's accounting for its bond liability to United compares to United's accounting for its investment in Masterwear bonds. You can find an explanation of why we calculate the bond price this way on page 801.
**Present value of an ordinary annuity of $1: n = 6, i = 7% (Table 4).
†Present value of $1: n = 6, i = 7% (Table 2).
Note: Present value tables are provided at the end of this textbook. If you need to review the concept of the time value of money, refer to the discussions in Chapter 6.

The market value of a fixed-rate investment moves in the opposite direction of market rates of interest.

The fair value of a bond changes when market interest rates change. If market rates of interest *rise* after a fixed-rate security is purchased, the value of the fixed-interest payments declines. So, the fair value of the investment falls. Conversely, if market rates of interest *fall* after a fixed-rate security is purchased, the fixed interest payments become relatively more attractive, so the fair value of the investment rises.

Increases and decreases in fair value between the day a debt security is acquired and the day it matures to a prearranged maturity value are less important if sale before maturity isn't an alternative. For this reason, if an investor has the "positive intent and ability" to hold the securities to maturity, investments in debt securities can be classified as **held-to-maturity (HTM)** and reported at their *amortized cost* in the balance sheet.[1] A debt security cannot be classified as held-to-maturity if the investor might sell it before maturity in response to changes in market prices or interest rates, to meet the investor's liquidity needs, or similar factors.

Changes in market value are less relevant to an investor who will hold a security to its maturity regardless of those changes.

Let's use the bond from Illustration 12–4 to see how we account for an investment in held-to-maturity debt securities.

## PURCHASE OF INVESTMENT.
The journal entry to record the *purchase* of the HTM investments is:

| July 1 | | |
|---|---|---|
| Investment in bonds (face amount) .................................................. | 700,000 | |
|     Discount on bond investment (difference) .................................... | | 33,367 |
|     Cash (price paid for the bonds) ..................................................... | | 666,633 |

All investment securities are initially recorded at cost.

Discount on bond investment is a contra-asset to the investment in bonds asset account that serves to reduce the carrying value of the bond asset to its cost at the date of purchase.

## RECOGNIZE INVESTMENT REVENUE.
The Masterwear bonds pay cash interest at a rate of 12%, but were issued at a time when the market rate of interest was 14%. As a result, the bonds were sold at a discount that was large enough to provide bond purchasers with the same effective rate of return on their investment (14%) that they could get elsewhere in the market. Think of it this way: a little piece of that initial discount serves each period to make up the difference between the relatively low rate of interest that the bond pays (12%) and the higher rate of interest that the market demands (14%). Recording interest each period as the *effective market rate of interest multiplied by the outstanding balance of the investment* is referred to as the effective interest method. This simply is an application of the accrual concept, consistent with accruing all revenues as they are earned, regardless of when cash is received.

The effective interest on debt is the market rate of interest multiplied by the outstanding balance of the debt.

Continuing our example, the initial investment is $666,633. Since the effective interest rate is 14%, interest recorded as revenue to the investor for the first six-month interest period is $46,664:

$$\underset{\text{Outstanding balance}}{\$666,633} \quad \times \quad \underset{\text{Effective rate}}{[14\% \div 2]} \quad = \quad \underset{\text{Effective interest}}{\$46,664}$$

However, the bond calls for semiannual interest payments of only $42,000—the *stated* rate (12% ÷ 2 = 6%) times the *face amount* ($700,000). As always, when only a portion of revenue is received, the remainder becomes an asset (a receivable). In this case we increase the investment by $4,664 by reducing the discount to $28,703 ($33,367 − 4,664). The journal entry to record the interest received for the first six months as investment revenue is:

| December 31 | | |
|---|---|---|
| Cash (stated rate × face amount) ...................................................... | 42,000 | |
| Discount on bond investment (difference) ......................................... | 4,664 | |
|     Investment revenue (market rate × outstanding balance) ............. | | 46,664 |

---

[1]FASB ASC 320–10–25–1: Investments–Debt and Equity Securities–Overall–Recognition (previously "Accounting for Certain Investments in Debt and Equity Securities," *Statement of Financial Accounting Standards No. 115* (Norwalk, Conn.: FASB, 1993)).

The amortized cost of the investment now is $700,000 − $28,703 = $671,297.

Illustration 12–5 demonstrates interest being recorded at the effective rate over the life of this investment. As you can see, the amortization of discount gradually increases the carrying value of the investment, until the investment reaches its face amount of $700,000 at the time when the debt matures.

We discuss accounting for discounts and premiums in much greater detail in Chapter 14.

## Illustration 12–5

Amortization Schedule—Discount

If a bond is purchased at a discount, less cash is received each period than the effective interest earned by the investor, so the unpaid difference increases the outstanding balance of the investment.

| Date | Cash Interest | Effective Interest | Increase in Balance | Outstanding Balance |
|---|---|---|---|---|
| | (6% × Face amount) | (7% × Outstanding balance) | (Discount reduction) | |
| 7/1/2013 | | | | 666,633 |
| 12/31/2013 | 42,000 | .07 (666,633) = 46,664 | 4,664 | 671,297 |
| 6/30/2014 | 42,000 | .07 (671,297) = 46,991 | 4,991 | 676,288 |
| 12/31/2014 | 42,000 | .07 (676,288) = 47,340 | 5,340 | 681,628 |
| 6/30/2015 | 42,000 | .07 (681,628) = 47,714 | 5,714 | 687,342 |
| 12/31/2015 | 42,000 | .07 (687,342) = 48,114 | 6,114 | 693,456 |
| 6/30/2016 | 42,000 | .07 (693,456) = 48,544* | 6,544 | 700,000 |
| | 252,000 | 285,367 | 33,367 | |

*Rounded.

**DO NOT RECOGNIZE UNREALIZED HOLDING GAINS AND LOSSES FOR HTM INVESTMENTS.** Suppose that, as of the end of the first reporting period, the market interest rate for similar securities has fallen to 11%. A market participant valuing the Masterwear bonds at that time would do so at the current market interest rate (11%) because that's the rate of return she or he could get from similar bonds. Calculating the present value of the bonds using a lower discount rate results in a higher present value. Let's say that checking market prices in *The Wall Street Journal* indicates that the fair value of the Masterwear bonds on that date is $714,943. How will United account for this increase in fair value? If United views the bonds as HTM investments, that change in fair value will be ignored so long as it is viewed as temporary.[2] The investment simply will be recorded

**Using Excel, enter:**
=PV(.055,5,42000,700000)
Output: 714,946

**Using a calculator:**
enter: [N] 5 [I] 5.5
[PMT] −42000
[FM] −700000
Output: = [PV] 714,946

# Additional Consideration

Suppose the bonds are not traded on an active exchange. How would you determine the fair value of the Masterwear bonds on December 31, 2013? Recall from Chapter 1 that GAAP identifies different ways that a firm can determine fair value. If the Masterwear bonds are publicly traded, United can find the fair value by looking up the current market price (this way of obtaining fair value is consistent with "level one" of the fair value hierarchy). On the other hand, if the bonds are not publicly traded, United can calculate the fair value by using the present value techniques shown in Illustration 12–1 (this way of obtaining fair value is consistent with "level two" of the fair value hierarchy). With five interest periods remaining, and a current market rate of 11% (5.5% semi-annually), the present value would be $714,943:

| | | | Present Values |
|---|---|---|---|
| Interest | $ 42,000 × 4.27028* | = | $179,352 |
| Principal | $700,000 × 0.76513† | = | 535,591 |
| | Present value of the bonds | | $714,943 |

*Present value of an ordinary annuity of $1: n = 5, i = 5.5%. (Table 4)
†Present value of $1: n = 5, i = 5.5%. (Table 2)

---

[2]If an unrealized loss from holding an HTM investment is not viewed as temporary, an "other-than-temporary impairment" (OTT impairment) may have to be recorded. We discuss OTT impairments in more detail in Appendix 12B.

at amortized cost (the amounts in the right-hand column of the amortization schedule in Illustration 12–5). United will *disclose* the fair value of its HTM investments in a footnote, but will not recognize any fair value changes in the income statement or balance sheet.[3]

**SELL HTM INVESTMENTS.**    Typically, held-to-maturity investments are—you guessed it—held to maturity. However, suppose that due to unforeseen circumstances the company decided to sell its debt investment for $725,000 on January 15, 2014.[4] United would record the sale as follows (for simplicity we ignore any interest earned during 2014):

| January 15, 2014 | | |
| --- | --- | --- |
| Cash ............................................................................... | 725,000 | |
| Discount on bond investment ................................................... | 28,703 | |
| Investment in Masterwear bonds .......................................... | | 700,000 |
| Gain on sale of investments (to balance) .............................. | | 53,703 |

In other words, United would record this sale just like any other asset sale, with a gain or loss determined by comparing the cash received with the carrying value (in this case, the amortized cost) of the asset given up.

We will revisit our discussion of investments in debt securities to be "held to maturity" in Chapter 14, "Bonds and Long-Term Notes." This way we can more readily see that accounting by the company that issues bonds and by the company that invests in those bonds is opposite but parallel; that is, each side of the transaction is the mirror image of the other.

Obviously, not all investments are intended to be held to maturity. When an investment is acquired to be held for an *unspecified period of time,* we classify the investment as either (a) "trading securities" or (b) "securities available-for-sale." These include investments in *debt* securities that are not classified as held-to-maturity and *equity* securities that have *readily determinable fair values.* You'll notice that, unlike held-to-maturity securities, we report investments in the other two categories at their fair values.

# Trading Securities

● LO12–2

Some companies—primarily financial institutions—actively and frequently buy and sell securities, expecting to earn profits on short-term differences in price. Investments in debt or equity securities acquired principally for the purpose of selling them in the near term are classified as **trading securities**. The holding period for trading securities generally is measured in hours and days rather than months or years. These investments typically are reported among the investor's current assets. Relatively few investments are classified this way, because usually only banks and other financial operations invest in securities in the manner and for the purpose necessary to be categorized as trading securities.

Just like other investments, trading securities initially are recorded at cost—that is, the total amount paid for the securities, including any brokerage fees. However, when a balance sheet is prepared in subsequent periods, this type of investment is written up or down to its fair value, or "marked to market."

Be sure to notice that fair value accounting is a departure from amortized cost, which is the way most assets are reported in balance sheets. Why the difference? For these investments, fair value information is more relevant than for other assets intended primarily to be used in company operations, like buildings, land and equipment, or for investments to be *held to maturity.*[5]

For instance, consider an investment in debt. As interest rates rise or fall, the fair value of the investment will decrease or increase. Movements in fair values are less relevant if the

*Trading securities are actively managed in a trading account for the purpose of profiting from short-term price changes.*

*Unrealized holding gains and losses for trading securities are included in net income in the period in which fair value changes.*

---

[3]If United had chosen the fair value option for this investment, it would classify the investment as a trading security rather than as an HTM security. We'll illustrate the fair value option when we discuss trading securities.

[4]GAAP [FASB ASC 320–10–25–6: Investments–Debt and Equity Securities–Overall–Recognition, previously *SFAS No. 115*] lists major unforeseen events that could justify sale of an HTM investment. Sale for other reasons could call into question whether the company actually had the intent and ability to hold the investment to maturity. In that case, the company's HTM classification is viewed as "tainted," and the company can be required to reclassify *all* of its HTM investments as AFS investments and avoid using the HTM classification for two years. Similar provisions exist under IFRS for public companies.

[5]Investments to be held to maturity, of course, include only debt securities.

investment is to be held to maturity; the investor receives the same contracted interest payments and principal at maturity, regardless of changes in fair value.

However, if the debt investment is held for active trading, changes in market values, and thus market returns, provide an indication of management's success in deciding when to acquire the investment, when to sell it, whether to invest in fixed-rate or variable-rate securities, and whether to invest in long-term or short-term securities. For that reason, it makes sense to report unrealized holding gains and losses on trading securities in net income during a period that fair values change, even though those gains and losses haven't yet been realized through the sale of the securities.

To see how we account for trading securities, let's modify the example we used for HTM securities. We'll assume that those debt investments are held in an active trading portfolio, with United intending to profit from short-term changes in price. In addition, let's add a couple of equity (stock) investments to highlight that, while the HTM approach applies only to debt securities, the TS approach applies to both debt and equity securities. The relevant facts are included in Illustration 12–6. Assuming all investments are classified as trading securities, the accounting would be as follows.

**FINANCIAL Reporting Case**

Q2, p. 653

**Illustration 12–6**
Accounting for Trading Securities and Securities Available-for-Sale

United Intergroup, Inc. buys and sells both debt and equity securities of other companies as investments. United's fiscal year-end is December 31. The following events during 2013 and 2014 pertain to the investment portfolio.

| | |
|---|---|
| **Purchase Investments** July 1, 2013 | • Purchased Masterwear Industries' 12%, 3-year bonds for $666,633 to yield an effective interest rate of 14%.<br>• Purchased $1,500,000 of Arjent, Inc., common stock.<br>• Purchased $1,000,000 of Bendac common stock. |
| **Receive Investment Revenue** December 31, 2013 | • Received a semi-annual cash interest payment of $42,000 from Masterwear.<br>• Received a cash dividend of $75,000 from Arjent. (Bendac does not pay dividends) |
| **Adjust Investments to Fair Value** December 31, 2013 | • Valued the Masterwear bonds at $714,943.<br>• Valued the Arjent stock at $1,450,000.<br>• Valued the Bendac stock at $990,000. |
| **Sell Investments** January 15, 2014 | • Sold the Masterwear bonds for $725,000.<br>• Sold the Arjent stock for $1,446,000. |
| **Adjust Remaining Investments to Fair Value** December 31, 2014 | • Valued the Bendac stock at $985,000. |

**PURCHASE INVESTMENTS.** The journal entry to record the purchase of the bond investment is the same as it is for HTM securities. The journal entries to record the equity investments are even simpler, just exchanging one asset (cash) for another (investment):

All investment securities are recorded initially at cost.

| July 1, 2013 | | |
|---|---|---|
| Investment in Masterwear bonds | 700,000 | |
| Discount on bond investment | | 33,367 |
| Cash | | 666,633 |
| Investment in Arjent stock | 1,500,000 | |
| Cash | | 1,500,000 |
| Investment in Bendac stock | 1,000,000 | |
| Cash | | 1,000,000 |

**RECOGNIZE INVESTMENT REVENUE.** The journal entry to record the receipt of bond interest is the same as it is for HTM securities, with the carrying value of the investment increasing due to amortization of $4,664 of discount. The journal entry to record the receipt of dividends related to the Arjent equity investment is straightforward. There is no entry for the Bendac equity investment, because Bendac doesn't pay dividends.

| December 31, 2013 | | |
|---|---|---|
| Cash (6% × $700,000)............................................................. | 42,000 | |
| Discount on bond investment (difference)..................................... | 4,664 | |
|     Investment revenue (interest: 7% × $666,633)........................ | | 46,664 |
| Cash........................................................................................... | 75,000 | |
|     Investment revenue (dividends) ............................................. | | 75,000 |

Dividend and interest income are included in net income.

## ADJUST TRADING SECURITY INVESTMENTS TO FAIR VALUE (2013).

Unlike HTM securities, trading securities are carried at fair value in the balance sheet, so their carrying value must be adjusted to fair value at the end of every reporting period. Rather than increasing or decreasing the investment account itself, we use a valuation allowance, *fair value adjustment,* to increase or decrease the carrying value of the investment. At the same time, we record an unrealized holding gain or loss that is included in net income in the period in which fair value changes (the gain or loss is *unrealized* because the securities haven't actually been sold). The next table summarizes the relevant facts for United's investments.

Trading securities are adjusted to their fair value at each reporting date.

### December 31, 2013

| Security | Amortized Cost | Fair Value | Fair Value Adjustment |
|---|---|---|---|
| Masterwear | $ 671,297 | $ 714,943 | $ 43,646 |
| Arjent | 1,500,000 | 1,450,000 | (50,000) |
| Bendac | 1,000,000 | 990,000 | (10,000) |
| Total | $3,171,297 | $3,154,943 | $(16,354) |
| Existing balance in fair value adjustment: | | | –0– |
| Increase (decrease) needed in fair value adjustment: | | | ($16,354) |

United has an unrealized loss of $16,354. Note that, to determine the amount of unrealized holding gain or loss on the Masterwear bonds, United first identifies the bonds' *amortized cost* and then determines the amount necessary to adjust them to fair value:

| | |
|---|---|
| Face amount of the bond | $700,000 |
| Less: Discount on bond investment | |
|     $33,367 initial discount | |
|       (4,664) accumulated amortization | |
|     $28,703 discount at 12/31/2013 | (28,703) |
| Amortized cost of the bonds | 671,297 |
| +/– Fair value adjustment (plug) | + 43,646 |
| Fair value of the bond at 12/31/2013 | $714,943 |

There is no discount to amortize for the equity investments, so for the Arjent and Bendac investments, their amortized cost is simply their initial cost. The journal entry to record the unrealized loss in United's fair value adjustment is:

| December 31, 2013[6] | | |
|---|---|---|
| Net unrealized holding gains and losses—I/S[7] .......................... | 16,354 | |
|     Fair value adjustment ................................................................ | | 16,354 |

For trading securities, *unrealized* gains or losses are included in net income.

---

[6]Sometimes companies don't bother with a separate fair value adjustment account and simply adjust the investment account to fair value. Also, sometimes companies set up separate fair value adjustment accounts for each investment.

[7]We title this account "Net unrealized holding gains and losses—I/S" to highlight that, for trading securities, unrealized holding gains and losses are included in the income statement (I/S) in the period in which they occur.

# Additional Consideration

**Don't Shoot the Messenger**

Or, as written in *The Economist,* "Messenger, Shot: Accounting rules are under attack. Standard-setters should defend them. Politicians and banks should back off."[8] Using fair values that are hard to estimate is controversial. For example, during the recent financial crisis many financial-services companies had to recognize huge unrealized losses associated with their investments. Some blamed their losses on GAAP for requiring estimates of fair value that were driven by depressed current market prices, argued that those losses worsened the financial crisis, and lobbied for a move away from fair-value accounting. Others countered that these companies were using GAAP's requirement for fair value accounting as a "scapegoat" for their bad investment decisions. "Fair value accounting . . . does not create losses but rather reflects a firm's present condition," says Georgene Palacky, director of the CFA's financial reporting group."[9]

**SELL TRADING SECURITY INVESTMENTS.** To record the gain or loss realized on the sale of the Masterwear and Arjent investments, United records the receipt of cash ($725,000 for Masterwear and $1,446,000 for Arjent), removes all balance sheet accounts that are directly associated with the investments, and calculates the difference to determine realized gain or loss.[10]

*Realized* gain or loss for the difference between carrying value and the cash received from selling a trading security is included in net income.

**January 15, 2014**

| | | |
|---|---|---|
| Cash (amount received) ............................................................. | 725,000 | |
| Discount on bond investment (account balance) ........................ | 28,703 | |
|     Investment in Masterwear bonds (account balance) .............. | | 700,000 |
|     Gain on sale of investments (to balance) ............................... | | 53,703 |
| Cash (amount received) ............................................................. | 1,446,000 | |
| Loss on sale of investments (to balance) .................................... | 54,000 | |
|     Investment in Arjent stock (account balance) ........................ | | 1,500,000 |

When trading securities are sold, *unrealized* gains or losses that were recorded previously are removed from the fair value adjustment and net income at the end of the accounting period.

For the Masterwear bonds, this journal entry is identical to what United used when recording the sale of held-to-maturity investments. However, United isn't done yet. Now that those investments are sold, United needs to remove the fair value adjustment from the balance sheet. Also, because United has recognized in this period's net income the entire gain or loss *realized* on sale of the investments, it must back out of this period's net income any *unrealized* gains and losses that were included in net income in prior periods. That way, this period's net income includes only the fair value changes arising since the last period, and United avoids double counting gains and losses (once when unrealized, and again when realized). United can accomplish all of this when it adjusts its investment portfolio to fair value at the end of the reporting period.

**ADJUST TRADING SECURITY INVESTMENTS TO FAIR VALUE (2014).** The following table summarizes the situation at the end of 2014:

**December 31, 2014**

| Security | Amortized Cost | Fair Value | Fair Value Adjustment |
|---|---|---|---|
| Masterwear | (sold) | –0– | –0– |
| Arjent | (sold) | –0– | –0– |
| Bendac | $1,000,000 | $985,000 | ($15,000) |
|     Total | $1,000,000 | $985,000 | ($15,000) |
| | | Existing balance in fair value adjustment: | ($16,354) |
| | | Increase (decrease) needed in fair value adjustment: | $ 1,354 |

[8]"Messenger, Shot," *The Economist,* April 8, 2009.

[9]Sarah Johnson, "The Fair Value Blame Game," CFO.com, March 19, 2008.

[10]For purposes of this example, we ignore any unpaid interest associated with the bonds. In practice, that amount would be added to the sales price of the bonds and included in investment revenue.

The journal entry necessary to show the appropriate balance in the fair value adjustment at the end of 2014 is

| December 31, 2014 | | |
|---|---|---|
| Fair value adjustment ................................................. | 1,354 | |
| Net unrealized holding gains and losses—I/S ...................... | | 1,354 |

This journal entry serves two purposes: it (a) accounts for changes in the fair value of investments that have not been sold (in this case, Bendac), and (b) removes from the fair value adjustment and net income any unrealized holding gains or losses that were recognized in prior periods and that are associated with investments that now have been sold (in this case, Masterwear and Arjent). We discuss those purposes in more detail when we show later in this chapter how these investments would be accounted for as available-for-sale securities.

**FINANCIAL STATEMENT PRESENTATION.**    We present trading securities in the financial statements as follows:

- **Income Statement and Statement of Comprehensive Income:** For trading securities, fair value changes are included in the income statement in the periods in which they occur, regardless of whether they are realized or unrealized. Investments in trading securities do not affect other comprehensive income.
- **Balance Sheet:** Investments in trading securities are reported at fair value, typically as current assets, and do not affect accumulated other comprehensive income in shareholders' equity.
- **Cash Flow Statement:** Cash flows from buying and selling trading securities typically are classified as operating activities, because the financial institutions that routinely hold trading securities consider them as part of their normal operations. However, as discussed in more detail later, it may be appropriate to classify cash flows from buying and selling some trading securities as investing activities if they are not held for sale in the near term (which is particularly likely when an investment is classified as a trading security as a result of electing the fair value option).[11]

United's 2013 and 2014 financial statements will include the amounts shown in Illustration 12–7 on the next page.

# Securities Available-for-Sale

● LO12–3

When you or I buy stock in a corporation, say Coca-Cola, we hope the market value will rise before we sell it. We also may look forward to the cash dividends Coca-Cola pays its shareholders every three months. We may even have planned when we will sell the stock, or we may intend to wait and see what happens to market prices. In either case, we aren't planning to trade the investment actively, but our investment is available to sell given the right combination of market factors and our own cash situation. These same considerations apply to companies that invest in the securities of other corporations or governmental entities. When a company acquires an investment, not for an active trading account (as a financial institution might) or to be held to maturity (which of course couldn't be stock because it has no maturity date), the company classifies its investment as securities available-for-sale (AFS). Like trading securities, we report investments in AFS securities in the balance sheet at fair value. Unlike trading securities, though, unrealized holding gains and losses on AFS securities are *not* included in net income. Instead, they are reported in the statement of comprehensive income as other comprehensive income (OCI).

Investments in available-for-sale securities typically are reported at their fair values.

---

[11]FASB ASC 320: Investments (previously "The Fair Value Option for Financial Assets and Financial Liabilities," *Statement of Financial Accounting Standards No. 159* (Norwalk, Conn.: FASB, 2007, par. A42)). The relevant paragraphs from the original standard are not codified in the FASB Research System as they primarily provide a basis for conclusions.

**Illustration 12–7**

Reporting Trading Securities

For trading securities, fair value changes affect net income in the period in which they occur.

Trading securities are reported at fair value in the balance sheet.

Cash flows from buying and selling trading securities are classified as operating activities.

| Income Statement | 2013 | 2014 |
|---|---|---|
| Revenues | $ ◆ | $ ◆ |
| Expenses | ◆ | ◆ |
| Other income (expense): | | |
|    Interest and dividend income | 121,664[a] | –0– |
|    Realized and unrealized gains and losses on investments | (16,354)[b] | $1,057[c] |
| Tax expense | ◆ | ◆ |
| Net income | ◆ | ◆ |
| **Balance Sheet** | | |
| Assets: | | |
|    Trading securities | 3,154,943 | 985,000 |
| **Statement of Cash Flows (direct method)** | | |
| Operating Activities: | | |
|    Cash from investment revenue | 117,000 | –0– |
|    Purchase of trading securities | (3,166,633) | –0– |
|    Sale of trading securities | –0– | 2,171,000 |

[a]$121,664 is the sum of $46,664 interest revenue from Masterwear and $75,000 dividends from Arjent.
[b]$16,354 is the net unrealized loss from the 2013 fair value adjustment.
[c]$1,057 is the $1,354 net unrealized gain from the 2014 fair value adjustment minus the $297 loss realized on sale of investments during 2014 (the $297 net realized loss results from the $54,000 loss realized on sale of the Arjent stock and the $53,703 gain realized on sale of the Masterwear bonds).

Comprehensive income includes not only net income, but also other changes in equity that don't arise from transactions with owners.

**COMPREHENSIVE INCOME.**  You may recall from Chapter 4 that comprehensive income is a more all-encompassing view of changes in shareholders' equity, including not only net income but also all other changes in equity that do not arise from transactions with owners.[12] Comprehensive income therefore includes net income and *other comprehensive income (OCI)*. Both net income and OCI accumulate in shareholders' equity in the balance sheet, but in different accounts. While net income accumulates in retained earnings, OCI accumulates in *accumulated other comprehensive income (AOCI)*.

**FINANCIAL Reporting Case**

Q3, p. 653

**RATIONALE FOR AFS TREATMENT OF UNREALIZED HOLDING GAINS AND LOSSES.**  Why use an approach for accounting for AFS securities that differs from that used for trading securities? The big concern is that including in net income unrealized holding gains and losses on AFS investments might make income appear more volatile than it really is. For example, many companies purchase AFS investments for the purpose of having the changes in fair value of those investments offset changes in the fair value of liabilities. This *hedging* insulates the company from risk and ensures that earnings are stable. However, if fair value changes for investments were to be recognized in income (as is the case with trading securities), but the offsetting fair value changes for liabilities were not recognized in income as well, we could end up with income appearing very volatile when in fact the underlying assets and liabilities are hedged effectively.[13]

More generally, because AFS securities are likely to be held for multiple reporting periods, one could argue that there is sufficient time for unrealized holding gains in some periods to balance out with unrealized holding losses in other periods, so including unrealized holding gains and losses in income would confuse investors by making income appear more volatile than it really is over the long run. Of course, one could counter-argue that these unrealized holding gains and losses still are relevant, given that each period an investor has discretion over whether or not to continue holding the security or sell that security to realize a gain or loss.

---

[12]Transactions with owners primarily include dividends and the sale or purchase of shares of the company's stock.

[13]The option to report in earnings changes in the fair value of liabilities was not permitted at the time the FASB wrote the initial standard (*SFAS No. 115*) that specified appropriate accounting for investments in debt and equity securities. As we will see in Chapter 14, that option now is allowed.

To consider accounting for AFS investments, refer to the facts shown in Illustration 12–6. Let's assume now that United classifies its investments as AFS rather than trading securities.

**PURCHASE INVESTMENTS.**  The journal entries to record the purchase of the investments are the same for AFS securities as they are for trading securities:

| July 1, 2013 | | |
|---|---|---|
| Investment in Masterwear bonds ............................................... | 700,000 | |
|    Discount on bond investment ................................................ | | 33,367 |
|    Cash ................................................................................... | | 666,633 |
| Investment in Arjent stock ....................................................... | 1,500,000 | |
|    Cash ................................................................................... | | 1,500,000 |
| Investment in Bendac stock ..................................................... | 1,000,000 | |
|    Cash ................................................................................... | | 1,000,000 |

*All investment securities are initially recorded at cost.*

**RECOGNIZE INVESTMENT REVENUE.**  The journal entries to record the receipt of investment revenue also are the same for AFS securities as they are for trading securities.

| December 31, 2013 | | |
|---|---|---|
| Cash (6% × $700,000) ............................................................. | 42,000 | |
| Discount on bond investment ................................................... | 4,664 | |
|    Investment revenue (interest: 7% × $666,633) ....................... | | 46,664 |
| Cash ........................................................................................ | 75,000 | |
|    Investment revenue (dividends received) ............................. | | 75,000 |

*Interest income and dividends on AFS investments are included in net income.*

**ADJUST AFS INVESTMENTS TO FAIR VALUE (2013).**  Let's first recall the facts:

### December 31, 2013

| Security | Amortized Cost | Fair Value | Fair Value Adjustment |
|---|---|---|---|
| Masterwear | $ 671,297 | $ 714,943 | $ 43,646 |
| Arjent | 1,500,000 | 1,450,000 | (50,000) |
| Bendac | 1,000,000 | 990,000 | (10,000) |
| Total | $3,171,297 | $3,154,943 | $(16,354) |
| | Existing balance in fair value adjustment: | | –0– |
| | Increase (decrease) needed in fair value adjustment: | | ($ 16,354) |

Like trading securities, AFS securities are adjusted to fair value at the end of each reporting period, which produces an unrealized holding gain or loss due to holding the securities while their fair values change. The journal entry to record United's unrealized holding loss is:

| December 31, 2013 | | |
|---|---|---|
| Net unrealized holding gains and losses—OCI[14] ....................... | 16,354 | |
|    Fair value adjustment..... ................................................... | | 16,354 |

*AFS securities are adjusted to their fair value at each reporting date.*

Notice that the amount of unrealized holding loss is the same as with trading securities. What differs is that the net unrealized holding loss of $16,354 is included in net income for trading securities and in OCI for AFS securities.[15] At the end of the reporting period the

*For AFS securities, unrealized holding gains and losses from fair value changes are not included in net income, but instead are recorded as OCI.*

---

[14]We title this account "Net unrealized holding gains and losses—OCI" to highlight that, for available-for-sale securities, unrealized holding gains and losses are included in other comprehensive income (OCI) in the period in which they occur.
[15]As with trading securities, we could have not used a separate valuation allowance and simply adjusted the AFS investment account itself to fair value, and we also could set up separate valuation allowances and record separate journal entries for each AFS investment.

net unrealized holding loss ends up being closed to a shareholders' equity account for both approaches. What differs is that it gets closed to retained earnings for trading securities and to AOCI for AFS securities.

### SELL AFS INVESTMENTS.

AFS investments require the same journal entry on the date of sale as is made to record the sale of trading securities. United simply records the receipt of cash, removes from the balance sheet any accounts that are directly associated with the investment, and calculates the difference to determine realized gain or loss.

*Realized* gain or loss for the difference between carrying value and the cash received from selling a trading security is included in net income.

**January 15, 2014**

| | | |
|---|---|---|
| Cash (amount received) | 725,000 | |
| Discount on bond investment (account balance) | 28,703 | |
|     Investment in Masterwear bonds (account balance) | | 700,000 |
|     Gain on sale of investments (to balance) | | 53,703 |
| | | |
| Cash (amount received) | 1,446,000 | |
| Loss on sale of investments (to balance) | 54,000 | |
|     Investment in Arjent stock (account balance) | | 1,500,000 |

When AFS securities are sold, *unrealized* gains or losses that were recorded previously are removed from the fair value adjustment and OCI.

United also needs to adjust the fair value adjustment account and AOCI to remove any unrealized gains or losses previously recorded that relate to the sold investments. That is typically done at the end of the accounting period as part of the journal entry that adjusts the AFS investment portfolio to fair value, as we see below.

### ADJUST AFS INVESTMENTS TO FAIR VALUE (2014).

The following table summarizes the situation at the end of 2014:

**December 31, 2014**

| Security | Amortized Cost | Fair Value | Fair Value Adjustment |
|---|---|---|---|
| Masterwear | (sold) | –0– | –0– |
| Arjent | (sold) | –0– | –0– |
| Bendac | $1,000,000 | $985,000 | ($15,000) |
|     Total | $1,000,000 | $985,000 | ($15,000) |
| | Existing balance in fair value adjustment: | | ($16,354) |
| | Increase (decrease) needed in fair value adjustment: | | $ 1,354 |

This analysis indicates that United needs to increase the fair value adjustment by $1,354 and record an unrealized gain of the same amount in OCI.

**December 31, 2014**

| | | |
|---|---|---|
| Fair value adjustment | 1,354 | |
|     Net unrealized holding gains and losses—OCI | | 1,354 |

This journal entry serves two purposes: it (a) accounts for new changes during 2014 in the fair value of investments that haven't been sold, and (b) removes amounts associated with investments that were sold during 2014.

| | |
|---|---|
| ($5,000) | to add 2014 unrealized loss associated with investments not sold |
| 6,354 | to remove 2013 net unrealized loss that's no longer unrealized |
| $1,354 | 2014 adjustment to OCI |

Let's consider the two purposes separately.

**New changes in the fair value of investments held.** The first purpose of the journal entry is to record in OCI any new unrealized gains or losses associated with investments that have not been sold. For United, that's the Bendac stock. The new unrealized gain or loss equals whatever amount is necessary to report the Bendac investment at fair value as of the end of 2014.

|  |  |
|---|---|
| $1,000,000 | initial cost of Bendac stock |
| (985,000) | fair value at the end of 2014 |
| $ 15,000 | balance needed at end of 2014 |
| (10,000) | balance at end of 2013 |
| $ 5,000 | new unrealized loss in 2014 |

If the 2014 journal entry had focused only on this first purpose, the journal entry would have been to recognize an unrealized holding loss of $5,000:

| | | |
|---|---|---|
| Net unrealized holding gains and losses—OCI ......................... | 5,000 | |
| Fair value adjustment ............................................................. | | 5,000 |

**Reclassification adjustment.**   The second purpose of the journal entry is to remove from OCI any amounts associated with *sold* investments. What amounts must United consider? Last year, in 2013, United recorded a net unrealized loss of $6,354 on the Arjent and Masterwear investments as part of the $16,354 fair value adjustment made at the end of that year.

|  |  |
|---|---|
| $50,000 | 2013 unrealized loss for the Arjent stock |
| 43,646 | 2013 unrealized gain for the Masterwear bonds |
| $ 6,354 | net unrealized loss in 2013 |

If the *2013* fair value adjustment had only included the net unrealized loss on the Arjent and Masterwear investments, it would have been:

| | | |
|---|---|---|
| Net unrealized holding gains and losses—OCI ......................... | 6,354 | |
| Fair value adjustment ............................................................. | | 6,354 |

> For AFS securities, *unrealized* gains and losses affect OCI and accumulate in AOCI until such time as the investment is sold.

Because those investments have now been sold, United must reverse this entry in 2014 to remove their effects from OCI and the fair value adjustment. If the 2014 journal entry had focused only on this second purpose, it would have been:

| | | |
|---|---|---|
| Fair value adjustment ............................................................. | 6,354 | |
| Net unrealized holding gains and losses—OCI ..................... | | 6,354 |

See how the two purposes combine to create the single journal entry we use?

| | | |
|---|---|---|
| Fair value adjustment ($6,354 – 5,000) ........................................ | 1,354 | |
| Net unrealized holding gains and losses—OCI ..................... | | 1,354 |

Now, why is this often referred to as a "reclassification adjustment"? Remember that United included a $6,354 unrealized loss in 2013 OCI (and therefore in AOCI). Then, in 2014, it backed out that amount from OCI (and AOCI) as part of the fair value adjustment entry, and included the realized gain or loss in net income (and therefore retained earnings) as part of the journal entry that recorded the sale of those investments. From the perspective of shareholders' equity, the amount was basically reclassified from AOCI to retained earnings in the period of sale.[16]

Note that we don't separately *record* this reclassification. That happens automatically as part of the fair value adjustment entry at the end of the period. What we do is *report* the reclassification in the statement of comprehensive income, as you will see in the next section.

---

[16]Reclassification also avoids double accounting with respect to comprehensive income and equity. If United didn't back out the 2013 unrealized loss from 2014 OCI, it would end up having included it in comprehensive income twice, once in OCI (2013) and once in net income (2014), thereby overstating total shareholders' equity.

**FINANCIAL STATEMENT PRESENTATION.** We present AFS securities in the financial statements as follows:

- **Income Statement and Statement of Comprehensive Income:** *Realized* gains and losses are shown in net income in the period in which securities are sold. *Unrealized* gains and losses are shown in OCI in the periods in which changes in fair value occur, and reclassified out of OCI in the periods in which securities are sold.
- **Balance Sheet:** Investments in AFS securities are reported at fair value. *Unrealized* gains and losses affect AOCI in shareholders' equity, and are reclassified out of AOCI in the periods in which securities are sold.
- **Cash Flow Statement:** Cash flows from buying and selling AFS securities typically are classified as investing activities.

United's 2013 and 2014 financial statements will include the amounts shown in Illustration 12–8.

**Illustration 12–8**

Reporting Available-for-Sale Securities

Only *realized* gains and losses are included in net income.

Other comprehensive income includes *unrealized* holding gains and losses *that occur during the reporting period*.

AFS securities are reported at fair value.

AOCI (in shareholders' equity) includes net unrealized holding gains or losses *accumulated over the current and prior periods*.

Cash flows from buying and selling AFS securities are classified as investing activities.

| | 2013 | | 2014 | |
|---|---|---|---|---|
| **Comprehensive Income Statement** | | | | |
| Revenues | $ | ◆ | $ | ◆ |
| Expenses | | ◆ | | ◆ |
| Other income (expense): | | | | |
| Interest and dividend income | 121,664[a] | | –0– | |
| Realized net loss on sale of investments | –0– | | (297)[c] | |
| Tax Expense | | ◆ | | ◆ |
| Net income | | ◆ | | ◆ |
| Other comprehensive income (loss) items (OCI):[17] | | | | |
| Unrealized holding gains (losses) on investments | (16,354)[b] | | (5,000)[d] | |
| Reclassification adjustment for net gains and losses included in net income | –0– | | 6,354[e] | |
| Total | (16,354) | | 1,354 | |
| Comprehensive income | | ◆ | | ◆ |
| **Balance Sheet** | | | | |
| Assets: | | | | |
| Available-for-sale securities | 3,154,943 | | 985,000 | |
| Stockholders' equity: | | | | |
| Accumulated other comprehensive income (AOCI) | (16,354) | | (15,000) | |
| **Statement of Cash Flows (direct method)** | | | | |
| Operating Activities: | | | | |
| Cash from investment revenue | 117,000 | | –0– | |
| Investing Activities: | | | | |
| Purchase of available-for-sale securities | (3,166,633) | | –0– | |
| Sale of available-for-sale securities | –0– | | 2,171,000 | |

[a]$121,664 is the sum of $46,664 interest revenue from Masterwear and $75,000 dividends from Arjent.
[b]$16,354 is the net unrealized loss from the 2013 fair value adjustment.
[c]$297 is the loss realized on sale of investments during 2014, resulting from the $54,000 loss realized on sale of the Arjent stock and the $53,703 gain realized on sale of the Masterwear bonds.
[d]$5,000 is the new net unrealized loss included in the 2014 fair value adjustment for Bendac.
[e]$6,354 is the reclassification adjustment included in the 2014 fair value adjustment to remove from AOCI amounts associated with investments that now have been sold.

---

[17]This illustration follows ASU 2011-05 (Comprehensive Income (Topic 220): *Presentation of Comprehensive Income* (Norwalk, Conn.: FASB 2011)), which requires that, for items reclassified from OCI to net income, reclassification adjustments be presented on the face of the financial statement where the components of net income and OCI are presented. Prior to ASU 2011-05, reclassification adjustments typically were only disclosed in the notes.

Individual securities available for sale are classified as either current or noncurrent assets, depending on how long they're likely to be held. An example from the 2011 annual report of **Cisco Systems** is shown in Illustration 12–9.

**Illustration 12–9**

Investments in Securities Available-for-Sale— Cisco Systems

Real World Financials

**Item 1A: Risk Factors (in part)**
We maintain an investment portfolio of various holdings, types, and maturities. These securities are generally classified as available-for-sale and, consequently, are recorded on our Consolidated Balance Sheets at fair value with unrealized gains or losses reported as a component of accumulated other comprehensive income, net of tax.

**Note 7: Investments (in part)**
The following tables summarize the Company's in available-for-sale investments (in millions):

| July 30, 2011 | Amortized Cost | Gross Unrealized Gains | Gross Unrealized Losses | Fair Value |
|---|---|---|---|---|
| Fixed income securities: | | | | |
| U.S. Government securities | $  19,087 | $  52 | $  — | $19,139 |
| U.S. Government agency securities | 8,742 | 35 | (1) | 8,776 |
| Non-U.S. Gov't agency securities | 3,119 | 14 | (1) | 3,132 |
| Corporate debt securities | 4,333 | 65 | (4) | 4,394 |
| Asset-backed securities | 120 | 5 | (4) | 121 |
| Total fixed income securities | 35,401 | 171 | (10) | 35,562 |
| Publicly traded equity securities | 734 | 639 | (12) | 1,361 |
| Total | $  36,135 | $  810 | $  (22) | $36,923 |

## Comparison of HTM, TS, and AFS Approaches

Illustration 12–10 compares accounting for the Masterwear bonds under the three different approaches used when an investor lacks significant influence.

**Illustration 12–10**  Comparison of HTM, TS, and AFS Approaches

| | Held-to-Maturity (Htm) | Trading (TS) | Available-for-Sale (AFS) |
|---|---|---|---|
| **Purchase bonds at a discount** | Investments  700,000<br>  Discount         33,367<br>  Cash              666,633 | Same as HTM | Same as HTM |
| **Receive investment revenue** | Cash       42,000<br>Discount    4,664<br>  Invest. income    46,664 | Same as HTM | Same as HTM |
| **Adjust to fair value** | No entry (unless impaired) | FV adjustment        43,646<br>  Net unrealized<br>    gain/loss—I/S              43,646 | FV adjustment        43,646<br>  Net unrealized<br>    gain/loss—OCI              43,646 |
| **Sell bonds for a realized gain** | Discount      28,703<br>Cash       725,000<br>  Investments        700,000<br>  Gain                 53,703 | Recognize gain or loss:<br>      Same as HTM<br>Reverse out previously recorded unrealized gain or loss that's no longer unrealized (automatically part of next adjustment to fair value):<br>Net unrealized<br>  gain/loss—I/S      43,646<br>  FV adjustment              43,646 | Recognize gain or loss:<br>      Same as HTM<br>Reverse out previously recorded unrealized gain or loss that's no longer unrealized (automatically part of next adjustment to fair value):<br>Net unrealized<br>  gain/loss—OCI   43,646*<br>  FV adjustment              43,646 |

*Reported as a reclassification adjustment in the statement of comprehensive income.

This side-by-side comparison highlights several aspects of these accounting approaches:

- To record the purchase of an investment and the receipt of investment revenue, we use identical entries in all three approaches.
- To record changes in fair value, the entries we use for TS and AFS securities have the same effect on the investment (via the fair value adjsiment valuation allowance) and the same eventual effect on shareholders' equity. What differs is whether the unrealized gain or loss is recognized in the income statement and then in retained earnings (TS) or recognized in OCI and then in AOCI (AFS).
- To record the sale of the security, we use identical entries in all three approaches. For TS and AFS securities, the fair value adjustment and unrealized holding gains and losses associated with sold securities are dealt with automatically as part of the next adjustment to fair value.
- Regardless of approach, the cash flows are the same, and the same total amount of gain or loss is recognized in the income statement (TS: $43,646 in 2013 + [$53,703 − $43, 646] in 2014 = $53,703 total; AFS and HTM: $53,703 in 2014). Thus, the question is not how much total net income is recognized, but *when* that net income is recognized.

# Additional Consideration

## Available-for-Sale Investments and Income Taxes

When comparing accounting for TS and AFS securities, we saw that total shareholders' equity ends up being the same amount, regardless of whether unrealized gains and losses are included in net income and closed to retained earnings in shareholders' equity (for TS) or included only in OCI and shown in AOCI in shareholders' equity (for AFS securities). But what about taxes? Tax expense affects net income, so retained earnings includes after-tax amounts. For AOCI to be equivalent to retained earnings, it also should include only after-tax amounts. Therefore, adjustments must be made to OCI and AOCI to account for tax effects. Typically these adjustments also give rise to deferred tax assets and liabilities, as unrealized holding gains and losses rarely affect the current period's taxes payable. The effect of taxes on each component of OCI must be disclosed in the notes to the financial statements or presented in the statement in which OCI is presented.

# International Financial Reporting Standards

**Accounting for Investments When Investor Lacks Significant Influence.** Until recently, *IAS No. 39*[18] was the standard that specified appropriate accounting for investments under IFRS. The primary categories in *IAS No. 39* are similar to those in U.S. GAAP, consisting of "Fair Value through Profit & Loss" ("FVTPL," similar to TS), HTM, and AFS.

*IFRS No. 9*,[19] issued November 12, 2009, will be required after January 1, 2015, and earlier adoption is allowed in some jurisdictions, so in the time period between 2010 and 2014 either *IAS No. 39* or *IFRS No. 9* might be in effect for a particular company. *IFRS No. 9* eliminates the HTM and AFS classifications, replaced by new classifications that are more restrictive. Specifically, under *IFRS No. 9*:

- Investments in debt securities are classified as either "Amortized Cost" or FVTPL. Like the HTM classification, debt in the amortized cost classification is accounted for at (you guessed it) amortized cost. However, to be included in the amortized cost category, a debt investment has to meet both (a) the "cash flow characteristics" test (which requires that the debt instrument consist of only principal and interest payments) and (b) the "business model test" (which requires that the objective of the company's business model is to hold the investment to collect the contractual cash flows rather than to sell

(continued)

---

[18]"Financial Instruments: Recognition and Measurement," *International Accounting Standard No. 39* (IASCF), as amended effective January 1, 2011.

[19]"Financial Instruments," *International Financial Reporting Standard No. 9* (IASCF), November 12, 2009, as amended effective January 1, 2011.

(concluded)

the investment at a gain). If debt isn't classified in "amortized cost," it is classified in FVTPL—there is no equivalent to AFS accounting for debt under *IFRS No. 9*.

- Investments in equity securities are classified as either "FVTPL" or "FVTOCI" ("Fair Value through Other Comprehensive Income"). If the equity is held for trading, it must be classified as FVTPL, but otherwise the company can irrevocably elect to classify it as FVTOCI. Like the previous AFS classification, equity in the FVTOCI category has *unrealized* gains and losses included in OCI. However, unlike AFS, *realized* gains and losses are not reclassified out of OCI and into net income when the investment is later sold. Rather, the accumulated gain or loss associated with a sold investment is just transferred from AOCI to retained earnings (both shareholders' equity accounts), without passing through the income statement.

One other difference between U.S. GAAP and IFRS is worth noting. U.S. GAAP allows specialized accounting (beyond the scope of this textbook) for particular industries like securities brokers/dealers, investment companies, and insurance companies. IFRS does not.

# Transfers between Reporting Categories

At acquisition, an investor assigns debt and equity securities to one of the three reporting classifications—held-to-maturity, available-for-sale, or trading. At each reporting date, the appropriateness of the classification is reassessed. For instance, if the investor no longer has the ability to hold certain securities to maturity and will now hold them for resale, those securities would be reclassified from HTM to AFS. When a security is reclassified between two reporting categories, the security is transferred at its fair value on the date of transfer. Any unrealized holding gain or loss at reclassification should be accounted for *in a manner consistent with the classification into which the security is being transferred.* A summary is provided in Illustration 12–11.

> A transfer of a security between reporting categories is accounted for at fair value and in accordance with *the new reporting classification.*

**Illustration 12–11**
Transfer between Investment Categories

| Transfer from: | To: | Unrealized Gain or Loss from Transfer at Fair Value |
|---|---|---|
| Either HTM or AFS | Trading | Include in current net income the total unrealized gain or loss, as if it all occurred in the current period. |
| Trading | Either HTM or AFS | Include in current net income any unrealized gain or loss that occurred in the current period prior to the transfer. (Unrealized gains and losses that occurred in prior periods already were included in net income in those periods.) |
| Held-to-maturity | Available-for-sale | No current income effect. Report total unrealized gain or loss as a separate component of shareholders' equity (in AOCI). |
| Available-for-sale | Held-to-maturity | No current income effect. Don't write off any existing unrealized holding gain or loss in AOCI, but amortize it to net income over the remaining life of the security (fair value amount becomes the security's amortized cost basis). |

Reclassifications are quite unusual, so when they occur, disclosure notes should describe the circumstances that resulted in the transfers. Other note disclosures are described in a later section.

# International Financial Reporting Standards

● LO12–8

**IFRS ILLUSTRATION**

Real World Financials

**Transfers Between Investment Categories.** Until recently, IFRS did not allow transfers out of the "Fair Value through P&L" (FVTPL) classification (which is roughly equivalent to the trading securities classification in U.S. GAAP). However, in October 2008 the IASB responded to the financial crisis underway at that time by amending *IAS No. 39* to allow transfers of debt investments out of the FVTPL category into AFS or HTM in "rare circumstances," and indicated that the financial crisis qualified as one of those circumstances.[20] The change was justified as increasing convergence to U.S. GAAP, which also allows transfers out of the trading security category, but in fact reclassifications in U.S. GAAP continue to be rarer events than occurred under IFRS with this change.

This change allowed banks in October 2008 to transfer investments out of the FVTPL category as of July 1, 2008, and thus avoid recognizing in earnings the losses they knew had already occurred during the third quarter of 2008. The effect on bank profits was substantial. A study by J. P. Morgan indicated that 32 of 43 West European banks it covered reclassified assets worth almost €620 billion, increasing pretax profits by almost €27 billion.[21]

**Lloyds Banking Group** of the United Kingdom wrote the following explanation:

#### Note 49 Financial Risk Management (in part)

Reclassification of Financial Assets
In accordance with the amendment to IAS 39 as disclosed in note 2, the Group reviewed the categorisation of its assets classified as held for trading and available-for-sale financial assets. On the basis that there was no longer an active market for some of those assets, which are therefore more appropriately managed as loans, the Group reclassified £2,993 million of assets classified as held for trading (measured at fair value through profit or loss immediately prior to reclassification) to loans and receivables with effect from 1 July 2008 . . . If the assets had not been transferred and had been kept as held for trading, a loss of £347 million would have been recognised in the income statement for the six months to 31 December 2008 within net trading income.

Under *IFRS No. 9* (discussed earlier in this chapter), transfers of debt investments between the FVTPL and the amortized cost categories can occur only if the company changes its business model with respect to the debt investment. No transfers of equity investments between the FVTPL and FVTOCI categories are allowed.

## Fair Value Option

● LO12–7

TS already are accounted for at fair value, so there is no need to choose the fair value option for them.

Choosing the fair value option for HTM and AFS investments just means reclassifying those investments as TS.

You may recall from Chapter 1 that GAAP allows a fair value option that permits companies to elect to account for most financial assets and liabilities at fair value. Under the fair value option, unrealized gains and losses are recognized in net income in the period in which they occur. That accounting approach should sound familiar—it's the same approach we use to account for trading securities.

Here's how the fair value option works for these investments. When a security that qualifies for HTM or AFS treatment is purchased, the investor makes an irrevocable decision about whether to elect the fair value option. The company can elect the fair value option for some securities and not for identical others—it's entirely up to the company, but the company has to explain in the notes why it made a partial election. If the fair value option is elected for a security that would normally be accounted for as HTM or AFS, the company just classifies that security as a trading security, and that's how it appears in the financial statements.[22] The only difference is that, unlike most trading securities, purchases and sale of investments accounted for under the fair value option are likely to be classified as investing activities in the statement of cash flows, because those investments are not held for sale

---

[20]"Reclassification of Financial Assets" *Amendments to IAS 39 Financial Instruments: Recognition and Measurement and IFRS 7 Financial Instruments: Disclosures,* IASB, October 2008.

[21]J.P. Morgan, *IAS 39 Reclassification: Impact on Banks' FY 08 Results and Equity,* May 11, 2009.

[22]FASB ASC 825–10–25: Financial Instruments–Overall–Recognition (previously "The Fair Value Option for Financial Assets and Financial Liabilities," *Statement of Financial Accounting Standards No. 159* (Norwalk, Conn.: FASB, 2007, par. 29)).

in the near term and therefore are not operational in nature. Also, note that electing the fair value option is irrevocable. If a company elects the fair value option and later believes that the fair value of an investment is likely to decline, it can't change the election and discontinue use of fair value accounting.

Why allow the fair value option? Recall that a primary reason for creating the AFS approach was to allow companies to avoid excess earnings volatility that would result from reporting in earnings the fair value changes of only part of a hedging arrangement. As described in Appendix A of the text, other accounting rules apply to hedging arrangements that involve derivatives, but those rules are very complex and don't cover all forms of hedging arrangements. The fair value option simplifies this process by allowing companies to choose whether to use fair value for most types of financial assets and liabilities. Thus, when a company enters into a hedging arrangement, it just has to make sure to elect the fair value option for each asset and liability in the hedging arrangement, and fair value changes of those assets and liabilities will be included in earnings.

# International Financial Reporting Standards

**Fair Value Option.** International accounting standards are more restrictive than U.S. standards for determining when firms are allowed to elect the fair value option. Under both *IAS No. 39* and *IFRS No. 9*, companies can elect the fair value option only in specific circumstances. For example, a firm could elect the fair value option for an asset or liability in order to avoid the "accounting mismatch" that occurs when some parts of a fair value risk-hedging arrangement are accounted for at fair value and others are not. Although U.S. GAAP indicates that the intent of the fair value option is to address these sorts of circumstances, it does not require that those circumstances exist.

● LO12–8

# Impairment of Investments

In this chapter we've seen that declines (as well as increases) in the fair value of some investments are reported in earnings. For instance, if the fair value of an investment in trading securities declines, we reduce the reported amount of that investment in the balance sheet and include the loss from the fair value decline in the income statement. Likewise, if the investor has elected the fair value option for HTM or AFS investments, those investments are accounted for as trading securities, so fair value changes always are recognized in earnings. Otherwise, fair value changes for HTM and AFS investment typically are not recognized in earnings.

However, there is an exception. If the fair value of an HTM or AFS investment declines below the amortized cost of the investment, and that decline is deemed to be *other-than-temporary (OTT)*, the company recognizes an OTT impairment loss in earnings. The specific process for determining whether an investment has an OTT impairment differs between equity and debt investments.[23] For equity investments, the question is whether the company has the intent and ability to hold the investment until fair value recovers. If it doesn't, the company recognizes an OTT impairment loss in earnings and reduces the carrying value of the investment in the balance sheet by that amount. For debt investments, the process is more complicated than for equity investments, both in determining whether an impairment is OTT and in determining the amount of the impairment to include in earnings. For both equity and debt investments, after an OTT impairment is recognized, the ordinary treatment of unrealized gains and losses is resumed; that is, further changes in fair value are reported in OCI for AFS investments and not recognized for HTM investments. An in-depth discussion of accounting for OTT impairments is provided in Appendix 12B.

An "other-than-temporary" impairment loss is recognized in net income even though the security hasn't been sold.

---

[23]FASB ASC 320–10–35: Investments–Overall–Subsequent Measurement (previously "Recognition and Presentation of Other-Than-Temporary Impairments," *FASB Staff Position No. 115-2 and 124-2* (Norwalk, Conn.: FASB April 9, 2009)).

# Additional Consideration

### What if the Fair Value Isn't "Readily Determinable"?

According to GAAP, the fair value of an equity security is considered readily determinable only if its selling price is currently available on particular securities exchanges or over-the-counter markets.[24] If the fair value of an equity security is *not* readily determinable, we use the *cost method* (except when the equity method described in Part B of this chapter is appropriate). The cost method is so named because the investment is carried in the balance sheet at cost, and temporary unrealized holding gains and losses are not recognized in either net income or other comprehensive income. Any dividends received are reported as investment revenue, and any gain or loss realized upon selling the investment is included in income. However, fair values still matter under the cost method, because the investment still is subject to testing for other-than-temporary impairments. Therefore, even if the fair value of an equity investment isn't viewed as readily determinable, companies have to determine it if there are indications that the investment has been impaired.

# International Financial Reporting Standards

● LO12–8

**Cost Method.** Under *IAS No. 39*, equity investments typically are measured at fair value, even if they are not listed on an exchange or over-the-counter market. The cost method is used only if fair value cannot be measured reliably, which occurs when the range of reasonable fair value estimates is significant and the probability of various estimates within the range cannot be reasonably estimated. *IFRS No. 9* does not allow the cost method, but may allow cost as an estimate of fair value in some circumstances. In general, use of the cost method is less prevalent under IFRS than under U.S. GAAP.

# Concept Review Exercise

**VARIOUS INVESTMENT SECURITIES**

Diversified Services, Inc., offers a variety of business services, including financial services through its escrow division. Diversified's fiscal year ends on December 31. The only securities held by Diversified at December 1 were 12 million common shares of Shelby Laminations, Inc., purchased in November for $50 million and classified as available-for-sale. Diversified entered into the following investment activities during the last month of 2013 and the first week of 2014:

**2013**

Dec. 1   Purchased $30 million of 12% bonds of Vince-Gill Amusement Corporation and $24 million of 10% bonds of Eastern Waste Disposal Corporation, both at face value and both to be held until they mature. Interest on each bond issue is payable semiannually on November 30 and May 31.

9   Sold one-half of the Shelby Laminations common shares for $26 million.

29   Received cash dividends of $1.5 million from the Shelby Laminations common shares.

30   Purchased U.S. Treasury bonds for $5.8 million as trading securities hoping to earn profits on short-term differences in prices.

31   Recorded the necessary adjusting entry(s) relating to the investments.

---

[24]FASB ASC 320–10–20: Investments–Overall–Glossary–Readily Determinable Fair Value (previously "Accounting for Certain Investments in Debt and Equity Securities (as amended)," *Statement of Financial Accounting Standards No. 115* (Norwalk, Conn.: FASB 2008), par. 3a).

The year-end market price of the Shelby Laminations common stock was $4.25 per share. The fair values of the bond investments were $32 million for Vince-Gill Amusement Corporation and $20 million for Eastern Waste Disposal Corporation. A sharp rise in short-term interest rates on the last day of the year caused the fair value of the Treasury bonds to fall to $5.7 million.

**2014**

Jan. 7    Sold the remaining Shelby Laminations common shares for $27 million.

**Required:**

Prepare the appropriate journal entry for each transaction or event and show the amounts that would be reported in the company's 2013 income statement relative to these investments. Determine the effects of the Shelby Laminations investment on net income, other comprehensive income, and comprehensive income for 2013, 2014, and combined over both years.

**2013**

Dec. 1    Purchased $30 million of 12% bonds of Vince-Gill Amusement Corporation and $24 million of 10% bonds of Eastern Waste Disposal Corporation, both at face value and both to be held until they mature. Interest on each bond issue is payable semiannually on November 30 and May 31.

| | | |
|---|---|---|
| Investment in Vince-Gill Amusement bonds ....................................... | 30 | |
| Investment in Eastern Waste Disposal bonds ..................................... | 24 | |
|    Cash .................................................................................... | | 54 |

Dec. 9    Sold one-half of the Shelby Laminations common shares for $26 million.

Sale of one-half of the Shelby Laminations shares results in a $1 million gain ($26 million sales price − [$50 million cost ÷ 2]).

| | | |
|---|---|---|
| Cash (selling price) ............................................................................. | 26 | |
|    Investment in Shelby Laminations common shares ($50 × ½) .......... | | 25 |
|    Gain on sale of investments (difference) ......................................... | | 1 |

Dec. 29    Received cash dividends of $1.5 million from the Shelby Laminations common shares.

| | | |
|---|---|---|
| Cash ................................................................................................... | 1.5 | |
|    Investment revenue .......................................................................... | | 1.5 |

Dec. 30    Purchased U.S. Treasury bonds for $5.8 million as trading securities, hoping to earn profits on short-term differences in prices.

| | | |
|---|---|---|
| Investment in U.S. Treasury bonds ...................................................... | 5.8 | |
|    Cash .................................................................................................. | | 5.8 |

Dec. 31    Recorded the necessary adjusting entry(s) relating to the investments.

**Accrued Interest (one month)**

| | | |
|---|---|---|
| Investment revenue receivable—Vince-Gill Amusement ($30 million × 12% × ¹⁄₁₂) ................................................... | 0.3 | |
| Investment revenue receivable—Eastern Waste Disposal ($24 million × 10% × ¹⁄₁₂) ...................................................... | 0.2 | |
|    Investment revenue ........................................................................ | | 0.5 |

**Fair Value Adjustments**

| | | |
|---|---|---|
| Net unrealized holding gains and losses—I/S ($5.7 − 5.8) | 0.1 | |
|    Fair value adjustment, TS investments | | 0.1 |
| Fair value adjustment, AFS investments ([12 million shares × ½ × $4.25] − [$50 million × ½]) ................................ | 0.5 | |
|    Net unrealized holding gains and losses—OCI ...................................... | | 0.5 |

Note: Securities held-to-maturity are not adjusted to fair value.

| Reported in the 2013 Income Statement: | ($ in millions) |
|---|---|
| Investment revenue ($1.5 dividends + 0.5 interest) | $2.0 |
| Gain on sale of investments (Shelby) | 1.0 |
| Unrealized holding loss on investments (trading securities) | (0.1) |

Note: The $0.5 million unrealized holding gain for the Shelby Laminations common shares is not included in income because it pertains to securities available-for-sale rather than trading securities, and so is reflected in OCI.

### 2014

Jan. 7     Sold the remaining Shelby Laminations common shares for $27 million.

The fair value of the Shelby shares at the time of sale is $27 million. Those shares were purchased for $25 million ($50 million × ½), so the gain realized on the sale is $2 million.

| | | |
|---|---|---|
| Cash (selling price) ...................................................................................... | 27 | |
|    Investment in Shelby Laminations common shares (cost: ½ × $50) ...... | | 25 |
|    Gain on sale of investments (difference) ............................................... | | 2 |

Given that the fair value adjustment for the Shelby shares has a $0.5 million balance (recorded on 12/31/2013), we need to remove that amount and eliminate the corresponding unrecognized gain from AOCI. This happens automatically when we next adjust the portfolio to fair value. If we were to make the adjustment separately, the entry would be:

| | | |
|---|---|---|
| Net unrealized holding gains and losses—OCI ...................................... | 0.5 | |
|    Fair value adjustment, AFS investments ................................................ | | 0.5 |

The Shelby investment's unrealized and realized gains and losses affected net income, other comprehensive income, and comprehensive income as follows ($ in millions):

**2013**

| | |
|---|---|
| $1.0 | realized gain on sale of investments (in net income) |
| 0.5 | unrealized gain on investments (in OCI) |
| $1.5 | total 2013 effect in comprehensive income |

**2014**

| | |
|---|---|
| $2.0 | realized gain on sale of investments (in net income) |
| (0.5) | reclassification out of OCI of previously recognized unrealized gain associated with sold investments |
| $1.5 | total 2014 effect in comprehensive income |
| | |
| $3.0 | grand total effect in comprehensive income ($1.5 + 1.5). |
| $3.0 | grand total effect in net income ($1.0 + 2.0). |
| $0.0 | grand total effect in other comprehensive income ($0.5 + (0.5)). |

Note that the $3.0 grand total effect of the Shelby shares on comprehensive income and net income reconciles with the difference between their purchase price ($50) and their sales price ($53, which is equal to the sum of $26 for the half sold in 2013 and $27 for the half sold in 2014). The only difference between comprehensive income and net income is timing.

# Financial Statement Presentation and Disclosure

Trading securities, held-to-maturity securities and available-for-sale securities are either current or noncurrent depending on when they are expected to mature or to be sold. However, it's not necessary that a company report individual amounts for the three categories of investments—held-to-maturity, available-for-sale, or trading—on the face of the balance sheet as long as that information is presented in the disclosure notes.[25]

On the statement of cash flows, inflows and outflows of cash from buying and selling trading securities typically are considered operating activities because, for companies that routinely transact in trading securities (financial institutions), trading in those securities constitutes an appropriate part of the companies' normal operations. But because held-to-maturity and available-for-sale securities are not purchased and held principally to be sold in the near term, cash flows from the purchase, sale, and maturity of these securities are considered investing activities. Also, if an investment that normally would be HTM or AFS is classified as a trading security because the company chose the fair value option, cash flows may be classified as investing, because they are viewed as nonoperating in nature.

Investors should disclose the following in the disclosure notes for each year presented:

- Aggregate fair value.
- Gross realized and unrealized holding gains.
- Gross realized and unrealized holding losses.
- Change in net unrealized holding gains and losses.
- Amortized cost basis by major security type.

The notes also include disclosures designed to help financial statement users understand the quality of the inputs companies use when determining fair values and to identify parts of the financial statements that are affected by those fair value estimates. For example, the notes should include the level of the fair value hierarchy (levels 1, 2, or 3) in which all fair value measurements fall. For fair value measurements that use unobservable inputs (level 3), the notes need to provide information about the effect of fair value measurements on earnings, including a reconciliation of beginning and ending balances of the investment that identifies:

**Extensive footnote disclosure is provided to help financial statement users assess the quality of fair value measurements and understand where they affect the financial statements.**

- Total gains or losses for the period (realized and unrealized), unrealized gains and losses associated with assets and liabilities still held at the reporting date, and where those amounts are included in earnings or shareholders' equity.
- Purchases, sales, issuances and settlements.
- Transfers in and out of level 3 of the fair value hierarchy (for example, because of changes in the observability of inputs used to determine fair values).
- For instruments accounted for under the fair value option, an estimate of the gains or losses included in earnings that are attributable to changes in instrument-specific credit risk.

For example, as shown in Illustration 12–12, note 2 of **Dell Inc.**'s 2011 annual report includes a discussion of fair values.

---

[25]FASB ASC 320–10–45–13: Investments–Debt and Equity Securities–Overall–Other Presentation Matters (previously *Statement of Financial Accounting Standards No. 115,* "Accounting for Certain Investments in Debt and Equity Securities," (Norwalk, Conn.: FASB, 1993), par. 18).

**Illustration 12–12**

Fair Value Disclosures of Investment Securities— Dell Inc.

Real World Financials

**Fair Value Measurements (partial)**

|  | January 28, 2011 | | | |
| --- | --- | --- | --- | --- |
|  | Level 1 | Level 2 | Level 3 | Total |
|  | Quoted Prices in Active Markets for Identical Assets | Significant Other Observable Inputs | Significant Unobservable Inputs | |
| Assets: | | | | |
| Cash equivalents: | | | | |
| Money market funds | $6,261 | $ — | $— | $ 6,261 |
| Commercial Paper | — | 2,945 | — | 2,945 |
| U.S. government and agencies | — | 1,699 | — | 1,699 |
| Debt Securities: | | | | |
| U.S. government and agencies | — | 79 | — | 79 |
| U.S. corporate | — | 464 | 32 | 496 |
| International corporate | — | 457 | — | 457 |
| State and municipal governments | — | — | — | — |
| Equity and other securities | — | 109 | — | 109 |
| Retained interest | — | — | — | — |
| Derivative instruments | — | 27 | — | 27 |
| Total assets | $6,261 | $5,780 | $32 | $12,073 |

|  | Fiscal Year Ended | | |
| --- | --- | --- | --- |
|  | January 28, 2011 | | |
|  | Retained Interest | U.S. Corporate | Total |
| Balance at beginning of period | $151 | $30 | $181 |
| Net unrealized gains included in earnings | — | 2 | 2 |
| Issuances and settlements | — | — | — |
| Transfers out of Level 3 | (151) | — | (151) |
| Balance at end of period | — | $32 | $ 32 |

We can see from these disclosures that Dell has relatively few level 3 investments (which are those with the most subjectively estimated fair values). That fact should give financial statement users more faith in the reliability of Dell's fair value estimates.

Recent changes in U.S. GAAP and IFRS have only increased the amount of disclosure that is required about fair values.[26] For example, for level 2 or 3 fair values, the notes to the financial statements must include a description of the valuation technique(s) and the inputs used in the fair value measurement process, and for level 3 fair values, the notes must indicate the significant inputs used in the fair value measurement, and the sensitivity of fair values to significant changes in those inputs. All of this disclosure is designed to provide financial statement users with information about those fair values that are most vulnerable to bias or error in the estimation process.

---

[26]FASB ASC 820–10–50: Fair Value Measurement–Overall–Disclosure (previously "Fair Value Measurement (Topic 820): Amendments to Achieve Common Fair Value Measurement and Disclosure Requirements in U.S. GAAP and IFRSs" *Accounting Standards Update No. 2011-04* (Norwalk, Conn.: FASB, May 2011)).

# Where We're Headed

● LO12–8

The FASB and the IASB are working together on a joint project that overhauls accounting for financial instruments. Under the proposed Accounting Standards Update, investments are classified in three categories that are similar to those used in U.S. GAAP: amortized cost (similar to HTM, but not requiring that investments be held to maturity), FV-NI (similar to TS), and FV-OCI (similar to AFS), but the criteria for classifying investments into those categories differ from current practice. In the supplement to this chapter we discuss these proposed changes in more detail.[27]

PART **B**

# INVESTOR HAS SIGNIFICANT INFLUENCE

When a company invests in the equity securities (primarily common stock) of another company, the investing company can benefit either (a) *directly* through dividends and/or market price appreciation or (b) *indirectly* through the creation of desirable operating relationships with the investee. The way we report a company's investment in the stock of another company depends on the nature of the relationship between the investor and the investee.

For reporting purposes, we classify the investment relationship in one of three ways, and account for the investment differently depending on the classification, as shown in Illustration 12–13.

| Relationship: How much does the investor influence the operating and financial policies of the investee? | Reporting Method |
|---|---|
| Lacks significant influence (usually < 20% equity ownership) | Varies by type of investment (see Part A of this chapter) |
| Has significant influence (usually 20%–50% equity ownership) | Equity method |
| Has control (usually > 50% equity ownership) | Consolidation |

**Illustration 12–13**
Reporting Classifications for Investment Relationships

We focused on situations in which the investor lacks significant influence in Part A of this chapter. In Part B of this chapter we focus on situations in which the investor has significant influence and discuss the **equity method** and **fair value option** that are used to account for those investments.

A detailed discussion of the third classification—consolidated financial statements—is beyond the scope of this book. That discussion often is a focus of the advanced accounting course or is taught as a separate consolidations course. In this chapter, we'll briefly overview consolidation only to provide perspective to aspects of the equity method that purposely mimic some effects of consolidation. Let's do that now, before addressing the specifics of the equity method.

The *equity method* can be used when an investor can't control, but can significantly influence, the investee.

# How the Equity Method Relates to Consolidated Financial Statements

If a company acquires more than 50% of the voting stock of another company, it's said to have a controlling interest, because by voting those shares, the investor actually can control the company acquired. The investor is referred to as the *parent;* the investee is termed the

---

[27]For the current status of both of these projects, see "Accounting for Financial Instruments" under "Projects" at www.fasb.org.

*subsidiary.* For reporting purposes (although not legally), the parent and subsidiary are considered to be a single reporting entity, and their financial statements are *consolidated.* Both companies continue to operate as separate legal entities and the subsidiary reports separate financial statements. However, because of the controlling interest, the parent company reports consolidated financial statements.

> *Consolidated financial statements* combine the individual elements of the parent and subsidiary statements.

**Consolidated financial statements** combine the separate financial statements of the parent and the subsidiary each period into a single aggregate set of financial statements as if there were only one company. This entails an item-by-item combination of the parent and subsidiary statements (after first eliminating any amounts that are shared by the separate financial statements).[28] For instance, if the parent has $8 million cash and the subsidiary has $3 million cash, the consolidated balance sheet would report $11 million cash.

> The acquired company's assets are included in consolidated financial statements at their fair values as of the date of the acquisition, and the difference between the acquisition price and the sum of the fair values of the acquired net assets is recorded as goodwill.

Two aspects of the consolidation process are of particular interest to us in understanding the equity method. First, in consolidated financial statements, the acquired company's assets are included in the financial statements at their fair values as of the date of the acquisition, rather than their book values on that date. Second, if the acquisition price is more than the sum of the separate fair values of the acquired net assets (assets less liabilities), that difference is recorded as an intangible asset—goodwill.[29] We'll return to the discussion of these two aspects when we reach the point in our discussion of the equity method where their influence is felt. As we'll see, the equity method is in many ways a partial consolidation.

We use the equity method when the investor can't control the investee but can exercise significant influence over the operating and financial policies of an investee.

## What Is Significant Influence?

● LO12–4

> Usually an investor can exercise significant influence over the investee when it owns between 20% and 50% of the investee's voting shares.

When effective control is absent, the investor still may be able to exercise significant influence over the operating and financial policies of the investee. This would be the case if the investor owns a large percentage of the outstanding shares relative to other shareholders. By voting those shares as a block, decisions often can be swayed in the direction the investor desires. When significant influence exists, the investment should be accounted for by the equity method. It should be presumed, in the absence of evidence to the contrary, that the investor has the ability to exercise **significant influence** over the investee when it owns between 20% and 50% of the investee's voting shares.[30]

## A Single Entity Concept

● LO12–5

> The investor's ownership interest in individual assets and liabilities of the investee is represented by a single investment account.

Much like consolidation, the equity method views the investor and investee collectively as a special type of single entity (as if the two companies were one company). However, using the equity method, the investor doesn't include separate financial statement items of the investee on an item-by-item basis as in consolidation. Instead, the investor reports its equity interest in the investee as a single investment account. For that reason, the equity method sometimes is referred to as a "one-line consolidation," because it essentially collapses the consolidation approach into single lines in the balance sheet and income statement, while having the same effect on total income and shareholders' equity.

Under the equity method, the investor recognizes investment income equal to its percentage share (based on stock ownership) of the net income earned by the investee rather than the portion of that net income received as cash dividends. The rationale for this approach is the presumption of the equity method that the fortunes of the investor and investee are

---

[28]This avoids double counting those amounts in the consolidated statements. For example, amounts owed by one company to the other are represented by accounts payable in one set of financial statements and accounts receivable in the other. These amounts are not included in the statements of the consolidated entity because a company can't "owe itself."

[29]This is the usual case because most companies are worth more than the sum of the values of individual components of the company due to reputation, longevity, managerial expertise, customer loyalty, or a host of other possibilities. Accounting for goodwill in acquisitions is discussed in Chapter 10.

[30]Shareholders are the owners of the corporation. By voting their shares, it is they who determine the makeup of the board of directors—who, in turn, appoint officers—who, in turn, manage the company. Common stock usually is the class of shares that has voting privileges. However, a corporation can create classes of preferred shares that also have voting rights. This is discussed at greater length in Chapter 18.

sufficiently intertwined that as the investee prospers, the investor prospers proportionately. Stated differently, as the investee earns additional net assets, the investor's share of those net assets increases.

Initially, the investment is recorded at cost. The carrying amount of this investment subsequently is:

- Increased by the investor's percentage share of the investee's net income (or decreased by its share of a loss).
- Decreased by dividends paid.

**FINANCIAL Reporting Case**

Q4, p. 653

# Additional Consideration

It's possible that a company owns more than 20% of the voting shares but still cannot exercise significant influence over the investee. If, for instance, another company or a small group of shareholders owns 51% or more of the shares, they control the investee regardless of how other investors vote their shares. GAAP provides this and other examples of indications that an investor may be unable to exercise significant influence:

- The investee challenges the investor's ability to exercise significant influence (through litigation or complaints to regulators).
- The investor surrenders significant shareholder rights in a signed agreement.
- The investor is unable to acquire sufficient information about the investee to apply the equity method.
- The investor tries and fails to obtain representation on the board of directors of the investee.[31]

In such cases, the equity method would not be appropriate, and the investment would likely be treated as AFS.

Conversely, it's also possible that a company owns less than 20% of the voting shares but is able to exercise significant influence over the investee. Ability to exercise significant influence with less than 20% ownership might be indicated, for example, by having an officer of the investor corporation on the board of directors of the investee corporation or by having, say, 18% of the voting shares while no other single investor owns more than 50%. In such cases the equity method would be appropriate.

To see how the equity method works, let's assume that United Intergroup purchased 30% of Arjent, Inc.'s, common stock for $1,500,000 cash. Illustration 12–14 highlights that buying 30% of Arjent can be viewed as buying 30% of all of Arjent's assets and liabilities. Those assets and liabilities likely have book values on Arjent's balance sheet that differ from their separate fair values. We can think of United as paying a price equal to 30% of the sum of the fair values of all of those assets and liabilities, plus an extra amount, goodwill, that captures 30% of the value of other attractive aspects of Arjent (e.g., loyal customers, well-trained workers) that GAAP doesn't capture as separate assets or liabilities. We will see that, under the equity method, all of those amounts are shown in a single investment account, but we still need to track their individual information to account for them correctly.

**PURCHASE OF INVESTMENT.**    Recording United's purchase of 30% of Arjent is straightforward. In fact, it requires the same entry used to record the purchase of the Arjent investment in Part A of this chapter.

*The cost principal governs the acquisition of assets.*

| | | |
|---|---|---|
| Investment in Arjent stock ........................................................ | 1,500,000 | |
| Cash ........................................................................................ | | 1,500,000 |

---

[31]FASB ASC 323–10–15–10: Investments–Equity Method and Joint Ventures–Overall–Scope and Scope Exceptions (previously "Criteria for Applying the Equity Method of Accounting for Investments in Common Stock," *FASB Interpretation No. 35* (Stamford, Conn.: FASB, 1981)).

**Illustration 12–14**
Equity Method

| Account | Book Value on Arjent's Financial Statements | Fair Value at Time of United's Investment |
|---|---|---|
| Buildings (10-year remaining useful life, no salvage value) | $1,000,000 | $ 2,000,000 |
| Land | 500,000 | 1,000,000 |
| Other net assets* | 600,000 | 600,000 |
| Net assets | 2,100,000 | 3,600,000 |
| Goodwill | | 1,400,000 (to balance) |
| | Total fair value of Arjent | $ 5,000,000 |
| | | × 30% purchased |
| | | $1,500,000 purchase price |

Other information:

| | |
|---|---|
| Arjent's 2013 net income: | $500,000 |
| Arjent's 2013 dividends: | $250,000 |

*Other net assets = other assets – liabilities

**RECORDING INVESTMENT REVENUE.**   Under the equity method, the investor includes in net income its proportionate share of the investee's net income. The reasoning is that, as the investee earns additional net assets, the investor's equity interest in those net assets also increases, so the investor increases its investment by the amount of income recognized. United's entry would be:

> *As the investee earns additional net assets, the investor's investment in those net assets increases.*

> *As the investee prospers, the investor prospers proportionately.*

| | | |
|---|---|---|
| Investment in Arjent stock .......................................................... | 150,000 | |
| Investment revenue (30% × $500,000) ...................................... | | 150,000 |

Of course, if Argent had recorded a net loss rather than net income, United would *reduce* its investment in Arjent and recognize a *loss* on investment for its share of the loss. Note that you won't always see these amounts called "investment revenue" or "investment loss." Rather, United might call this line "equity in earnings (losses) of affiliate" or some other title that suggests it is using the equity method.

**RECEIVING DIVIDENDS.**   Because investment revenue is recognized as it is earned by the investee, it would be inappropriate to recognize revenue again when earnings are distributed as dividends. That would be double counting. Instead, we view the dividend distribution as a reduction of the investee's net assets. The rationale is that the investee is returning assets to its investors in the form of a cash payment, so each investor's equity interest in the remaining net assets declines proportionately.

> *As the investee distributes net assets as dividends, the investor does not recognize revenue. Rather, the investor's investment in the investee's net assets is reduced.*

| | | |
|---|---|---|
| Cash .................................................................................................... | 75,000 | |
| Investment in Arjent stock (30% × $250,000) ................................. | | 75,000 |

# Further Adjustments

● LO12–6

When the investor's expenditure to acquire an investment exceeds the book value of the underlying net assets acquired, additional adjustments to both the investment account and investment revenue might be needed. The purpose is to approximate the effects of consolidation, without actually consolidating financial statements. More specifically, after the date of acquisition, both the investment account and investment revenue are adjusted for differences between net income reported by the investee and what that amount would have been if consolidation procedures had been followed. This process is often referred to as "amortizing the differential," because it mimics the process of expensing some of the difference between the price paid for the investment and the book value of the investment. Let's look closer at what that means.

As mentioned earlier, consolidated financial statements report (a) the acquired company's assets at their fair values on the date of acquisition rather than their book values, subsequently adjusted for amortization, and (b) goodwill for the excess of the acquisition price over the fair value of the identifiable net assets acquired.

The first of these two consequences of the consolidation process usually has an effect on income, and it's the income effect that we're interested in when applying the equity method. Increasing asset balances to their fair values usually will result in higher expenses in subsequent periods. For instance, if buildings, equipment, or other depreciable assets are written up to higher values, depreciation expense will be higher during their remaining useful lives. Likewise, if the recorded amount of inventory is increased, cost of goods sold will be higher when the inventory is sold. As a consequence of increasing these asset balances to fair value, expenses will rise and income will fall. It is this negative effect on income that the equity method seeks to imitate.

However, if it's land that's increased, there is no income effect because we don't depreciate land. Also, goodwill will not result in higher expenses. Goodwill is an intangible asset, but one whose cost usually is not charged to earnings.[32]

In our example, United needs to make adjustments for the fact that, at the time it purchased its investment in Arjent, the fair values of Arjent's assets and liabilities were higher than the book values of those assets and liabilities in Arjent's balance sheet. Illustration 12–15 highlights the portions of United's investment that may require adjustment:

Notice in Illustration 12–15 that United paid (in thousands) $1,500 for identifiable net assets that, sold separately, would be worth $1,080 and the $420 difference is attributable to goodwill. The identifiable net assets worth $1,080 have a book value of only $630, and we assumed the $450 difference is attributable to undervalued buildings ($300) and land ($150).

**Illustration 12–15**

Source of Differences between the Investment and the Book Value of Net Assets Acquired

| | Investee Net Assets ↓ | Net Assets Purchased ↓ | ($ in thousands)<br>Difference Attributed to: ↓ | |
|---|---|---|---|---|
| Cost | $5,000 × 30% = | $1,500 | Goodwill: | $420 |
| Fair value | $3,600 × 30% = | $1,080 | | |
| | | | Undervaluation of: | |
| | | | Buildings | $300 |
| | | | Land | $150 |
| Book value | $ 2,100 × 30% = | $630 | | |

## ADJUSTMENTS FOR ADDITIONAL DEPRECIATION.

When Arjent determines its net income, it bases depreciation expense on the book value of its buildings, but United needs to depreciate its share of the *fair value* of those buildings at the time it made its investment. Therefore, United must adjust its investment revenue for additional depreciation expense. Over the life of the buildings, United will need to recognize its 30% share of a total of $1,000,000 of additional depreciation expense ($2,000,000 fair value less $1,000,000 book value), or $300,000. Assuming a 10-year life of the buildings and straight-line depreciation, United must recognize $30,000 of additional depreciation each year. Had Arjent recorded that additional depreciation, United's portion of Arjent's net income would

*The investor adjusts its share of the investee's net income to reflect revenues and expenses associated with differences between the fair value and book value of the investee's assets and liabilities that existed at the time the investment was made.*

---

[32]Goodwill is not amortized periodically to expense. Only if the asset's value is subsequently judged to be impaired is all or a portion of the recorded amount charged against earnings. FASB ASC 350–20–35: Intangibles–Goodwill and Other–Goodwill–Subsequent Measurement (previously "Goodwill and Other Intangible Assets," *Statement of Financial Accounting Standards No. 141* (Norwalk, Conn.: FASB, 2001)). For review, see Chapter 11.

have been lower by $30,000 (ignoring taxes). To act as if Arjent had recorded the additional depreciation, United adjusts the accounts to reduce investment revenue and reduce its investment in Arjent stock by $30,000.

| | | |
|---|---|---|
| Investment revenue ......................................................................... | 30,000 | |
| Investment in Arjent stock (30% × [$2,000,000 − 1,000,000] ÷ 10 yrs.) ....... | | 30,000 |

### NO ADJUSTMENTS FOR LAND OR GOODWILL.

United makes no adjustments for land or goodwill. Land, unlike buildings, is not an asset that we depreciate. As a result, the difference between the fair value and book value of the land would not cause higher expenses, and we have no need to adjust investment revenue or the investment in Arjent stock for the land.

Recall from Chapter 11 that goodwill, unlike most other intangible assets, is not amortized. In that sense, goodwill resembles land. Thus, acquiring goodwill will not cause higher expenses, so we have no need to adjust investment revenue or the investment in Arjent stock for goodwill.

### ADJUSTMENTS FOR OTHER ASSETS AND LIABILITIES.

Also, because in our example there was no difference between the book value and fair value of the remaining net assets, we don't need an adjustment for them either. However, that often will not be the case.

> If the fair value of purchased inventory exceeds its book value, we usually assume the inventory is sold in the next year and reduce investment revenue in the next year by the entire difference.

For example, Arjent's inventory could have had a fair value that exceeded its book value at the time United purchased its Arjent investment. To recognize expense associated with that higher fair value, United would need to identify the period in which that inventory is sold (usually the next year) and, in that period, reduce its investment revenue and its investment in Arjent stock by its 30% share of the difference between the fair value and book value of the inventory. If, for instance, the $300,000 difference between fair value and book value had been attributable to inventory rather than buildings, and that inventory was sold by Arjent in the year following United's investment, United would reduce investment revenue by the entire $300,000 in the year following the investment. By so doing, United would be making an adjustment that yielded the same net investment revenue as if Arjent had carried the inventory on its books at fair value at the time the Arjent investment was made and therefore recorded higher cost of goods sold ($300,000) when it was sold in the next year. More generally, an equity method investor needs to make these sorts of adjustments whenever there are revenues or expenses associated with an asset or liability that had a difference between book value and fair value at the time the investment was made.

# Additional Consideration

> **Effect on Deferred Income Taxes**
>
> Investment revenue is recorded by the equity method when income is earned by the investee, but that revenue is not taxed until it's actually received as cash dividends. This creates a temporary difference between book income and taxable income. You will learn in Chapter 16 that the investor must report a deferred tax liability for the income tax that ultimately will be paid when the income eventually is received as dividends.

# Reporting the Investment

> The carrying amount of the investment is its initial cost plus the investor's equity in the undistributed earnings of the investee.

The fair value of the investment shares at the end of the reporting period is not reported when using the equity method. The investment account is reported at its original cost, increased by the investor's share of the investee's net income (adjusted for additional expenses like depreciation), and decreased by the portion of those earnings actually received as dividends. In other words, the investment account represents the investor's share of the investee's net assets initially acquired, adjusted for the investor's share of the subsequent increase in the investee's net assets (net assets earned and not yet distributed as dividends).

The balance of United's 30% investment in Arjent at December 31, 2013, would be calculated as follows:

**Investment in Arjent Stock**

| | | | |
|---|---|---|---|
| Cost | 1,500,000 | | |
| Share of income | 150,000 | | |
| | | 30,000 | Depreciation adjustment |
| | | 75,000 | Dividends |
| | 1,545,000 | | |

In the statement of cash flows, the purchase and sale of the investment are reported as outflows and inflows of cash in the investing section, and the receipt of dividends is reported as an inflow of cash in the operating section.[33]

**WHEN THE INVESTEE REPORTS A NET LOSS.** Our illustration assumed the investee earned net income. If the investee reports a *net loss* instead, the investment account would be *decreased* by the investor's share of the investee's net loss (adjusted for additional expenses).

# Additional Consideration

> It's possible that the investor's proportionate share of investee losses could exceed the carrying amount of the investment. If this happens, the investor should discontinue applying the equity method until the investor's share of subsequent investee earnings has equaled losses not recognized during the time the equity method was discontinued. This avoids reducing the investment account below zero.

**WHEN THE INVESTMENT IS ACQUIRED IN MID-YEAR.** Obviously, we've simplified the illustration by assuming the investment was acquired at the beginning of 2013, entailing a full year's income, dividends, and adjustments to account for the income effects of any differences between book value and fair value on the date the investment was acquired. In the more likely event that an investment is acquired sometime after the beginning of the year, the application of the equity method is easily modified to include the appropriate fraction of each of those amounts. For example, if United's purchase of 30% of Arjent had occurred on October 1 rather than January 2, we would simply record income, dividends, and adjustments for three months ($3/12$) of the year. This would result in the following entries to the investment account:

**Investment in Arjent Stock**

| | | | |
|---|---|---|---|
| Cost | 1,500,000 | | |
| Share of income | | | |
| ($3/12 \times \$150,000$) | 37,500 | | |
| | | | Depreciation adjustment |
| | | 7,500 | ($3/12 \times \$30,000$) |
| | | | Dividends |
| | | 18,750 | ($3/12 \times \$75,000$) |
| | 1,511,250 | | |

Changes in the investment account the first year are adjusted for the fraction of the year the investor has owned the investment.

---

[33]Some companies prepare a statement of cash flows using the indirect method of reporting operating activities. In that case, the operating section begins with net income and adjustments are made to back out the effects of accrual accounting and calculate cash from operations. For companies with equity method investments, net income will include investment revenue and gains or losses associated with sold investments, but cash from operations should include only cash dividends. As an example, because United's 2013 net income includes $120,000 of investment revenue from Arjent ($150,000 portion of income − $30,000 depreciation adjustment), but United received only $75,000 of dividends from Arjent, an indirect method statement of cash flows would include an adjustment, often titled "undistributed earnings of investee," that reduces net income by $45,000 ($75,000 − $120,000) when determining cash from operations.

AT&T reported its 2010 investments in affiliated companies for which it exercised significant influence using the equity method as shown in Illustration 12–16.

**Illustration 12–16**

Equity Method
Investments on the
Balance Sheet—AT&T

Real World Financials

|  | Dec 31, 2010 | Dec 31, 2009 |
|---|---|---|
| Total current assets | $ 19,951 | $ 25,187 |
| Property, plant, and equipment—Net | 103,196 | 99,519 |
| Goodwill | 73,601 | 72,782 |
| Licenses | 50,372 | 48,741 |
| Customer lists and relationships—Net | 4,708 | 7,393 |
| Other intangible assets—net | 5,440 | 5,494 |
| Investments in equity affiliates | 4,515 | 2,921 |
| Other assets | 6,705 | 6,275 |
| Total assets | $268,488 | $268,312 |

# What If Conditions Change?

Both the investment and retained earnings would be increased by the investor's share of the undistributed earnings in years prior to a change to the equity method.

## A CHANGE FROM THE EQUITY METHOD TO ANOTHER METHOD.

When the investor's level of influence changes, it may be necessary to change from the equity method to another method. For example, when Air-France–KLM's ownership interest in WAM (Amadeus) declined from 22% to 15% during the 2011 fiscal year, it changed from accounting for the investment under the equity method to accounting for the investment as AFS.

When this situation happens, *no adjustment* is made to the remaining carrying amount of the investment. Instead, the equity method is simply discontinued and the new method applied from then on. The balance in the investment account when the equity method is discontinued would serve as the new cost basis for writing the investment up or down to fair value on the next set of financial statements.

## A CHANGE FROM ANOTHER METHOD TO THE EQUITY METHOD.

Sometimes companies change from another method to the equity method. For example, in 2011 the Mitsubishi UFJ Financial Group converted its investment in the convertible preferred stock of Morgan Stanley into common stock, and as a result started accounting for that investment under the equity method. When a change *to* the equity method is appropriate, the investment account should be retroactively adjusted to the balance that would have existed if the equity method always had been used. As income also would have been different, retained earnings would be adjusted as well. For example, assume it's determined that an investor's share of investee net income, reduced by dividends, was $4 million during a period when the equity method was not used, but additional purchases of shares cause the equity method to be appropriate now. The following journal entry would record the change (ignoring taxes):

|  | ($ in millions) | |
|---|---|---|
| Investment in equity securities ............................................................... | 4 | |
| Retained earnings (investment revenue from the equity method) ......... | | 4 |

In addition to the adjustment of account balances, financial statements would be restated to the equity method for each year reported in the annual report for comparative purposes. Also, the income effect for years prior to those shown in the comparative statements is reported on the statement of retained earnings as an adjustment to beginning retained earnings of the earliest year reported. A disclosure note also should describe the change. Reporting accounting changes is described in more detail in Chapter 20.

## If an Equity Method Investment Is Sold

When an investment reported by the equity method is sold, a gain or loss is recognized if the selling price is more or less than the carrying amount (book value) of the investment. For example, let's continue our illustration and assume United sells its investment in Arjent on January 1, 2014, for $1,446,000. A journal entry would record a loss as follows:

> When an equity method investment is sold, a gain or loss is recognized for the difference between its selling price and its carrying amount.

| | | |
|---|---|---|
| Cash ................................................................... | 1,446,000 | |
| Loss on sale of investments (to balance) ................................. | 99,000 | |
| Investment in Arjent stock (account balance) | | 1,545,000 |

## Comparison of Fair Value and the Equity Method

Illustration 12–17 compares accounting for the Arjent investment at fair value (as trading securities or securities available for sale, discussed in Part A of this chapter) and under the equity method (covered in Part B of this chapter):

**Illustration 12–17**  Comparison of Fair Value and Equity Methods

| | Fair Value | | Equity Method | |
|---|---|---|---|---|
| Purchase equity investment | Investment in Arjent    1,500,000<br>    Cash                    1,500,000 | | Same as Fair Value Method | |
| Recognize proportionate share of investee's net income and any related adjustments | No entry | | Investment in Arjent 150,000<br>    Investment revenue        150,000<br>Investment revenue   30,000<br>    Investment in Arjent        30,000 | |
| Adjust investment to reflect changes in fair value from $1,500,000 to $1,450,000 | Net unrealized gain/loss*    50,000<br>    FV adjustment                50,000 | | No entry | |
| Receive dividend | Cash                    75,000<br>    Investment revenue        75,000 | | Cash                    75,000<br>    Investment in Arjent        75,000 | |
| Sell equity investment | Recognize gain or loss:<br>    Cash                1,446,000<br>    Loss (to balance)    54,000<br>        Investment in Arjent    1,500,000 | | Cash            1,446,000<br>Loss (to balance)    99,000<br>    Investment in Arjent    1,545,000 | |
| | Reverse out previously recorded unrealized gain or loss that's no longer unrealized (automatically part of next adjustment to fair value):<br><br>    FV adjustment            50,000<br>        Net unrealized gain/loss*    50,000 | | | |

*Net unrealized holding gains and losses are reported in net income for trading securities and in other comprehensive income for available-for-sale securities.

This side-by-side comparison highlights several aspects of these accounting approaches:

- To record the purchase of an investment, we use identical entries for both approaches.
- The two approaches differ in whether we record investment revenue when dividends are received and whether we recognize unrealized holding gains and losses associated with changes in the fair value of the investment.
- The differences in how the two approaches account for unrealized holding gains and losses result in different book values for the investment at the time the investment is sold, and therefore result in different realized gains or losses when the investment is sold.

- Regardless of approach, the same cash flows occur, and the same total amount of net income is recognized over the life of the investment. In the case of Arjent:
  - **Fair value method:** A total of $21,000 of net income is recognized over the life of the investment, equal to $75,000 of dividend revenue minus $54,000 realized loss on sale of investment.
  - **Equity method:** A total of $21,000 of net income is recognized over the life of the investment, equal to $150,000 of United's portion of Arjent's income minus $30,000 depreciation adjustment and minus $99,000 realized loss on sale of investment.
  - Thus, the question is not how much total net income is recognized, but *when* that net income is recognized.

## Fair Value Option

● LO12–7

We learned in Part A of this chapter that GAAP allows a fair value option with respect to investments that otherwise would be accounted for using the held-to-maturity or available-for-sale approaches. Electing the fair value option for those investments is simple—the investments are reclassified as trading securities and accounted for in that manner.

Companies also can choose the fair value option for "significant influence" investments that otherwise would be accounted for under the equity method. The company makes an irrevocable decision about whether to elect the fair value option, and can make that election for some investments and not for others. As shown for the fair value method in Illustration 12–17, the company carries the investment at fair value in the balance sheet and includes unrealized gains and losses in earnings.

However, investments that otherwise would be accounted for under the equity method but for which the fair value option has been elected are not reclassified as trading securities. Instead, these investments are shown on their own line in the balance sheet or are combined with equity method investments with the amount at fair value shown parenthetically. Still, they are reported at fair value with changes in fair value reported in earnings as if they were trading securities. Also, all of the disclosures that are required when reporting fair values as well as some of those that would be required under the equity method still must be provided.[34]

Exactly how a company does the bookkeeping necessary to comply with these broad requirements is up to the company. One alternative is to account for the investment using entries similar to those that would be used to account for trading securities. A second alternative is to record all of the accounting entries during the period under the equity method, and then record a fair value adjustment at the end of the period. Regardless of which alternative the company uses to account for the investment during the period, though, the same fair value is reported in the balance sheet at the end of the period, and the same total amount is shown on the income statement (the fair value adjustment amount plus the investment revenue recorded).

> If the fair value option is chosen for investments otherwise accounted for by the equity method, the amount that is reported at fair value is clearly indicated.

# International Financial Reporting Standards

● LO12–8

**Equity Method.** Like U.S. GAAP, international accounting standards require the equity method for use with significant influence investees (which they call "associates"), but there are a few important differences. First, *IAS No. 28* governs application of the equity method and requires that the accounting policies of investees be adjusted to correspond to those of the investor when applying the equity method.[35] U.S. GAAP has no such requirement.

Second, IFRS does not provide the fair value option for most investments that qualify for the equity method. U.S. GAAP provides the fair value option for all investments that qualify for the equity method.

(continued)

---

[34]FASB ASC 825–10–50–28: Financial Instruments–Overall–Disclosure–Fair Value Option (previously "The Fair Value Option for Financial Assets and Financial Liabilities," *Statement of Financial Accounting Standards No. 159* (Norwalk, Conn.: FASB, 2007), paragraph 18.f).

[35]"Investments in Associates," *International Accounting Standard 28* (London, UK: IASCF, 2003), as amended effective January 1, 2011.

(concluded)

Third, IFRS is in transition with respect to a particular type of investment, called a *joint venture*, in which two or more investors have joint control of another entity. Under *IAS No. 31* investors can account for a joint venture using either the equity method or a method called "proportionate consolidation," whereby the investor combines its proportionate share of the investee's accounts with its own accounts on an item-by-item basis.[36] U.S. GAAP requires that the equity method be used to account for joint ventures.

For a quick example of proportionate consolidation, return to Illustration 12–14 but assume that United spends $2,500,000 to invest in a joint venture called Arjent. With its investment, United owns 50% of Argent, another investor owns the other 50%, and the two investors must agree on decisions concerning Arjent's activities. Recall that the journal entry to record the investment under the equity method was:

| | | |
|---|---|---|
| Investment in Arjent stock ................................................... | 2,500,000 | |
| Cash............................................................................... | | 2,500,000 |

If United instead accounted for its investment under proportionate consolidation, the effect of the purchase would be disaggregated and assigned to the appropriate accounts in United's balance sheet:

| | | |
|---|---|---|
| Buildings (50% × $2,000,000 fair value ............................. | 1,000,000 | |
| Land (50% × $1,000,000 fair value) | 500,000 | |
| Other net assets (50% × $600,000) | 300,000 | |
| Goodwill (50% × $1,400,000) | 700,000 | |
| Cash............................................................................... | | 2,500,000 |

Note that the net effect under proportionate consolidation is the same as under the equity method, with United adding net assets of $2,500,000 in exchange for $2,500,000 of cash. However, under proportionate consolidation the effects are distributed across the balance sheet in the various asset and liability accounts, and in subsequent periods any income effects will appear on various lines in the income statement ("depreciation expense," for instance) rather than being aggregated and shown as part of investment revenue.

The IASB recently issued *IFRS No. 11*.[37] That standard clarifies the definition of a joint venture, and requires that only the equity method be used to account for joint ventures, thus doing away with proportionate consolidation. This change is a move towards convergence with U.S. GAAP, which likewise requires the equity method for these arrangements. Firms reporting under IFRS must comply with *IFRS No. 11* for fiscal years beginning after January 1, 2013, and earlier adoption is permitted.

## Concept Review Exercise

**THE EQUITY METHOD**

Delta Apparatus bought 40% of Clay Crating Corp.'s outstanding common shares on January 2, 2013, for $540 million. The carrying amount of Clay Crating's net assets (shareholders' equity) at the purchase date totaled $900 million. Book values and fair values were the same for all financial statement items except for inventory and buildings, for which fair values exceeded book values by $25 million and $225 million, respectively. All inventory on hand at the acquisition date was sold during 2013. The buildings have average remaining useful lives of 18 years. During 2013, Clay Crating reported net income of $220 million and paid an $80 million cash dividend.

---

[36]"Interests in Joint Ventures," *International Accounting Standard 31* (London, UK: IASCF, 2003), as amended effective January 1, 2011.
[37]"Joint Arrangements" *International Financial Reporting Standard No. 11* (London, UK: IASCF, 2011).

**Required:**

1. Prepare the appropriate journal entries during 2013 for the investment.
2. Determine the amounts relating to the investment that Delta Apparatus should report in the 2013 financial statements:
   a. As an investment in the balance sheet.
   b. As investment revenue in the income statement.
   c. As investing and/or operating activities in the statement of cash flows (direct method).

**Solution**

1. Prepare the appropriate journal entries during 2013 for the investment.

| | ($ in millions) | |
|---|---|---|
| **Purchase** | | |
| Investment in Clay Crating shares .................................................. | 540 | |
| Cash ................................................................................... | | 540 |
| **Net income** | | |
| Investment in Clay Crating shares (40% × $220 million) ................. | 88 | |
| Investment revenue ............................................................ | | 88 |
| **Dividends** | | |
| Cash (40% × $80 million) ......................................................... | 32 | |
| Investment in Clay Crating shares ........................................... | | 32 |
| **Inventory** | | |
| Investment revenue (as if 2013 cost of goods sold is higher because beginning inventory was adjusted to fair value) ................... | 10 | |
| Investment in Clay Crating shares (40% × $25 million) ............... | | 10 |
| **Buildings** | | |
| Investment revenue ([$225 million × 40%] ÷ 18 years) .................... | 5 | |
| Investment in Clay Crating shares ........................................... | | 5 |

| | Investee Net Assets ↓ | Net Assets Purchased ↓ | Difference Attributed to ↓ |
|---|---|---|---|
| Cost | | $540 ⎤ | |
| | | ⎬ | Goodwill: $80 [difference] |
| Fair value | $1,150† × 40% = | $460 ⎥ | Undervaluation of inventory $10 [$25 × 40%] |
| | | ⎬ | |
| Book value | $ 900 × 40% = | $360 ⎦ | Undervaluation of buildings $90 [$225 × 40%] |

†($900 + 25 + 225)

2. Determine the amounts that Delta Apparatus should report in the 2013 financial statements:
   a. As an investment in the balance sheet:

**Investment in Clay Crating Shares**

($ in millions)

| Cost | 540 | | |
|---|---|---|---|
| Share of income | 88 | | |
| | | 32 | Dividends |
| | | 10 | Cost of goods sold adjustment for inventory |
| | | 5 | Depreciation adjustment for buildings |
| **Balance** | **581** | | |

   b. As investment revenue in the income statement:

$$\$88 \text{ million} - [\$10 + 5] \text{ million} = \$73 \text{ million}$$
(share of income)        (adjustments)

c. In the statement of cash flows (direct method):

- Investing activities: $540 million cash outflow
- Operating activities: $32 million cash inflow

## Decision Makers' Perspective

The various approaches used to account for investments can have very different effects on an investor's income statement and balance sheet. Consequently, it's critical that both managers and external decision makers clearly understand those effects and make decisions accordingly.

To highlight key considerations, suppose that, on January 1, 2013, BigCo spent $5,000,000 to purchase 20% of TechStart, a small start-up company that is developing products that apply an exciting new technology. The purchase price included $500,000 for Big-Co's share of the difference between the fair value and book value of TechStart's inventory, all of which was then sold in 2013. TechStart paid a small dividend of $100,000 in 2013, so BigCo received 20% of it, or $20,000. TechStart incurs and expenses large amounts of research and development costs as it develops new technology, so it had a net loss in 2013 of $1,000,000. Yet, the future income-generating potential of the products that TechStart is developing has made TechStart a hot stock, and the fair value of BigCo's 20% investment increased to $5,500,000 by the end of 2013. Illustration 12–18 shows how BigCo's investment would be accounted for under three alternative approaches.

| | Trading Security | Available-for-Sale | Equity Method |
|---|---|---|---|
| Share of investee net income[a] | –0– | –0– | ($ 700,000) |
| Dividend income[b] | $ 20,000 | $ 20,000 | –0– |
| Increase in investee's fair value[c] | $ 500,000 | –0– | –0– |
| Total 2013 effect on net income | $ 520,000 | $ 20,000 | ($ 700,000) |
| 12/31/2013 investment book value[d] | $5,500,000 | $5,500,000 | $4,280,000 |

**Illustration 12–18**

Comparison of Methods Used to Account for Investments

[a]Not recognized for trading securities or available-for-sale securities. Under the equity method, investment revenue (loss) is 20% × ($1,000,000 loss) + ($500,000) additional expense for fair value inventory adjustment = ($700,000).
[b]Not recognized for equity method investments. Instead, dividends reduce book value of the investment.
[c]Recognized in net income for trading securities, in other comprehensive income for available-for-sale securities, and not recognized for equity method investments.
[d]Equals fair value for trading securities and available-for-sale securities. Equals initial cost plus income (or minus loss) and minus dividends for equity method.

The accounting method does not affect cash flows, but it has a big effect on net income in current and future periods. Also, because the accounting method affects the book value of the investment, it affects gain or loss on sale of that investment. In our example, if BigCo sold its TechStart investment at the beginning of 2014 for $5,000,000, it would recognize a $720,000 gain on sale if the investment was accounted for under the equity method, but a $500,000 loss if it was accounted for as a trading security or available-for-sale security. All of these income effects are predictable, but only if a user understands the relevant accounting methods and the fact that those methods all end up recognizing the same amount of total gain or loss over the life of an investment. Nevertheless, sometimes even experienced analysts get confused.[38]

*The way an investment is accounted for affects net income, investment book value, and the amount of gain or loss recognized in the future when the investment is sold.*

---

[38]For example, in 2000, analysts were accustomed to including **Intel**'s investment gains as ordinary income, because those amounts were not particularly large and could be viewed as part of Intel's business. However, in the 2nd quarter of 2000, Intel recorded a net $2.1 billion gain from selling securities in its available-for-sale portfolio. Analysts were surprised and confused, with some eliminating the gain from their earnings estimates but others including them ("Intel Says Net Jumped 79%; Analysts Upset," *The Wall Street Journal*, July 19, 2000, p. A3).

Managers may structure investments to include only the amount of equity that qualifies for their preferred accounting approach.

One strength of the equity method is that it prevents the income manipulation that would be possible if a company recognized income when it received dividends and could significantly influence an investee to pay dividends whenever the company needed an income boost. Remember, under the equity method dividends aren't income, but rather reduce the book value of the investment. Nevertheless, users still need to realize that managers may choose and apply methods in ways that make their company appear most attractive. For example, research suggests that investments sometimes are structured to avoid crossing the 20 to 25 percent threshold that typically requires using the equity method,[39] presumably to avoid the negative effect on earnings that comes from having to recognize the investor's share of investee losses and other income adjustments. Also, a company might smooth income by timing the sale of available-for-sale or equity method investments to realize gains in otherwise poor periods and realize losses in otherwise good periods. While consistent with GAAP, mixing these sorts of one-time gains and losses with operating income could encourage users to think that operating income is less volatile than it really is.

**If investments are not accounted for at fair value, their sale can be timed to recognize gains or losses in particular accounting periods.**

Of particular concern is the potential for inaccurate fair value estimates. Even if management is trying to provide the most accurate fair value estimate possible, there is much potential for error, particularly when making estimates at level 3 of the fair value hierarchy. Also, a company conceivably could use the discretion inherent in fair value estimation to manage earnings with respect to trading securities or other investments for which they have elected the fair value option. Given this potential for error and bias, it's not surprising that investors are nervous about the accuracy of fair value estimates. To address these sorts of concerns, the FASB has required extensive note disclosure about the quality of inputs associated with estimates of fair value, but financial statement users need to know to look for those disclosures and still must understand that they cannot assess fully the accuracy of fair value estimates. ●

**A concern with fair value accounting is that management has much discretion over fair values, and may not be able to estimate fair values accurately.**

# Financial Instruments and Investment Derivatives

A **financial instrument** is defined as:

- Cash,
- Evidence of an *ownership interest* in an entity,[40]
- A contract that (a) imposes on one entity an obligation to *deliver* cash (say accounts payable) or another financial instrument and (b) conveys to the second entity a right to *receive* cash (say accounts receivable) or another financial instrument, or
- A contract that (a) imposes on one entity an obligation to *exchange* financial instruments on potentially unfavorable terms (say the issuer of a stock option) and (b) conveys to a second entity a right to *exchange* other financial instruments on potentially favorable terms (say the holder of a stock option).[41]

*Derivatives* are financial instruments that "derive" their values from some other security or index.

A complex class of financial instruments exists in financial markets in response to the desire of firms to manage risks. In fact, these financial instruments would not exist in their own right, but have been created solely to hedge against risks created by other financial instruments or by transactions that have yet to occur but are anticipated. Financial futures, interest rate swaps, forward contracts, and options have become commonplace. These financial instruments often are called **derivatives** because they "derive" their values or contractually required cash flows from some other security or index. For instance, an option to buy an asset in the future at a preset price has a value that is dependent on, or derived from, the value of the underlying asset. Their rapid acceptance as indispensable components of the corporate capital structure has left the accounting profession scrambling to keep pace.

The urgency to establish accounting standards for financial instruments has been accelerated by headline stories in the financial press reporting multimillion-dollar losses on exotic

---

[39]E. E. Comiskey and C. W. Mulford, "Investment Decisions and the Equity Accounting Standard," *The Accounting Review* 61, no. 3 (July 1986), pp. 519–525.
[40]This category includes not just shares of stock, but also partnership agreements and stock options.
[41]FASB ASC Master Glossary: Financial Instrument (previously "Disclosure of Information about Financial Instruments with Off-Balance-Sheet Risk and Financial Instruments with Concentrations of Credit Risk," *Statement of Financial Accounting Standards No. 105* (Stamford, Conn.: FASB, 1990), par. 6).

derivatives by **Enron Corporation**, **Procter & Gamble**, **Orange County** (California), **Piper Jaffrey**, and **Gibson Greetings**, to mention a few. The headlines have tended to focus attention on the misuse of these financial instruments rather than their legitimate use in managing risk.

The FASB has been involved since 1986 in a project to provide a consistent framework for resolving financial instrument accounting issues, including those related to derivatives and other "off-balance-sheet" instruments. The financial instruments project has three separate but related parts: disclosure, recognition and measurement, and distinguishing between liabilities and equities. Unfortunately, issues to be resolved are extremely complex and will likely require several more years to resolve. To help fill the disclosure gap in the meantime, the FASB has offered a series of temporary, "patchwork" solutions. These are primarily in the form of additional disclosures for financial instruments. More recently, the FASB has tackled the issues of recognition and measurement. We discuss these requirements in Appendix A after we've spent some time with the measurement issues necessary to understand accounting for derivatives.

> The FASB's ongoing financial instruments project is expected to lead to a consistent framework for accounting for all financial instruments.

## Financial Reporting Case Solution

1. **How should you respond? Why are held-to-maturity securities treated differently from other investment securities?** *(p. 656)*  You should explain that if an investor has the positive intent and ability to hold the securities to maturity, investments in debt securities are classified as held-to-maturity and reported at amortized cost in the balance sheet. Increases and decreases in fair value are not reported in the financial statements. The reasoning is that the changes are not as relevant to an investor who will hold a security to its maturity regardless of those changes. Changes in the fair value between the time a debt security is acquired and the day it matures to a prearranged maturity value aren't as important if sale before maturity isn't an alternative.[42]

2. **Why are unrealized gains and losses on trading securities reported in the income statement?** *(p. 660)*  Trading securities are acquired for the purpose of profiting from short-term market price changes, so gains and losses from holding these securities while prices change are often viewed as relevant performance measures that should be included in net income.

3. **Why are unrealized gains and losses on available-for-sale securities not reported in the income statement, but instead are in other comprehensive income, and then shown in accumulated other comprehensive income (AOCI) on the balance sheet?** *(p. 669)*  Available-for-sale securities are not acquired for the purpose of profiting from short-term market price changes, so gains and losses from holding these securities while prices change are viewed as insufficiently relevant performance measures to be included in net income. Instead, those amounts are shown in other comprehensive income (OCI) and accumulated in an owners' equity account (AOCI). It's likely that holding gains in some periods will be offset by holding losses in other periods. When the investment is sold, the net amount of gain or loss is removed from AOCI and recognized in net income.

4. **Explain why Coke accounts for some of its investments by the equity method and what that means.** *(p. 681)*  When an investor does not have "control," but still is able to exercise *significant influence* over the operating and financial policies of the investee, the investment should be accounted for by the equity method. Apparently Coke owns between 20% and 50% of the voting shares of some of the companies it invests in. By the equity method, Coke recognizes investment income in an amount equal to its percentage share of the net income earned by those companies, instead of the amount of that net income it receives as cash dividends. The rationale is that as the investee earns additional net assets, Coke's share of those net assets increases. ●

---

[42]Interest rate futures were traded for the first time in 1975 on the Chicago Board of Trade. Interest rate swaps were invented in the early 1980s. They now comprise over 70% of derivatives in use.

# The Bottom Line

● **LO12–1** When an investor lacks significant influence over the operating and financial policies of the investee, its investment is classified for reporting purposes as held-to-maturity (HTM), available-for-sale (AFS), or trading securities (TS). If an investor has the positive intent and ability to hold the securities to maturity, investments in debt securities are classified as HTM and reported at amortized cost in the balance sheet. These investments are recorded at cost, and holding gains or losses from fair value changes are ignored. (*p. 656*)

● **LO12–2** Investments in debt or equity securities acquired principally for the purpose of selling them in the near term are classified as trading securities. They are reported at their fair values. Holding gains and losses for trading securities are included in earnings. (*p. 659*)

● **LO12–3** Investments in debt and equity securities that don't fit the definitions of the other reporting categories are classified as available-for-sale. They are reported at their fair values. Holding gains and losses from retaining securities during periods of price change are not included in the determination of income for the period; they are reported as a separate component of shareholders' equity. (*p. 663*)

● **LO12–4** When an investor is able to exercise significant influence over the operating and financial policies of the investee, the investment should be accounted for by the equity method. Usually an investor is presumed to have the ability to exercise significant influence when it owns between 20% and 50% of the investee's voting shares. (*p. 680*)

● **LO12–5** By the equity method, the investor recognizes investment income equal to its percentage share (based on share ownership) of the net income earned by the investee, rather than the portion of that net income received as cash dividends. The investment account is adjusted for the investor's percentage share of net income or loss reported by the investee. When the investor actually receives dividends, the investment account is reduced accordingly. (*p. 680*)

● **LO12–6** When the cost of an investment exceeds the book value of the underlying net assets acquired, both the investment account and investment revenue are adjusted for differences between net income reported by the investee and what that amount would have been if consolidation procedures had been followed. (*p. 682*)

● **LO12–7** The fair value option allows companies to account for most financial assets and liabilities in the same way they account for trading securities, with unrealized holding gains and losses included in net income and the investment carried at fair value in the balance sheet. For HTM and AFS investments, this simply requires reclassifying those investments as trading securities. For equity method investments, this requires clearly identifying the portion of those investments classified in the significant-influence category that is being accounted for at fair value. In all cases, additional disclosures are required that indicate the quality of inputs used to calculate fair values. (*pp. 672* and *688*)

● **LO12–8** U.S. GAAP and IFRS are similar in most respects concerning how they account for investments, but accounting in this area is being overhauled by both the IASB and the FASB, and IFRS companies may report under two different standards (either *IAS No. 39* or *IFRS No. 9*) for the 2009–2014 time period. IFRS allows proportionate consolidation as well as the equity method to account for joint ventures, although the option to use proportionate consolidation will be eliminated soon. IFRS is more restrictive in terms of the circumstances in which the fair-value option can be used. Finally, as discussed in Appendix 12B, IFRS recognizes different amounts of OTT impairment for HTM and AFS debt investments, and allows recovery of OTT impairments for debt investments (but not equity investments). (*pp. 672, 673, 674, 679, 688,* and *701*) ●

# APPENDIX 12A

## Other Investments (Special Purpose Funds, Investments in Life Insurance Policies)

### Special Purpose Funds

**Some special purpose funds—like petty cash—are current assets.**

It's often convenient for companies to set aside money to be used for specific purposes. You learned about one such special purpose fund in Chapter 7 when we discussed petty cash funds. Recall that a petty cash fund is money set aside to conveniently make small expenditures using currency rather than having to follow the time-consuming, formal procedures normally used to process checks. Similar funds sometimes are used to pay interest, payroll, or other short-term needs. Like petty cash, these short-term special purpose funds are reported as current assets.

Special purpose funds also are sometimes established to serve longer-term needs. It's common, for instance, to periodically set aside cash into a fund designated to repay bonds and other long-term debt. Such funds usually accumulate cash over the debt's term to maturity and are composed of the company's periodic contributions plus interest or dividends from investing the money in various return-generating investments. In fact, some debt contracts require the borrower to establish such a fund to repay the debt. In similar fashion, management might voluntarily choose to establish a fund to accumulate money to expand facilities, provide for unexpected losses, buy back shares of stock, or any other special purpose that might benefit from an accumulation of funds. Of course, funds that won't be used within the upcoming operating cycle are noncurrent assets. They typically are reported as part of investments. The same criteria for classifying securities into reporting categories that we discussed previously should be used to classify securities in which funds are invested. Any investment revenue from these funds is reported as such on the income statement.

> A special purpose fund can be established for *virtually any purpose.*

> Noncurrent special purpose funds are reported within the category *investments and funds.*

## Investments in Life Insurance Policies

Companies frequently buy life insurance policies on the lives of their key officers. Under normal circumstances, the company pays the premium for the policy and, as beneficiary, receives the proceeds when the officer dies. Of course, the objective is to compensate the company for the untimely loss of a valuable resource in the event the officer dies. However, some types of life insurance policies can be surrendered while the insured is still alive in exchange for a determinable amount of money, called the cash surrender value. In effect, a portion of each premium payment is not used by the insurance company to pay for life insurance coverage, but instead is invested on behalf of the insured company in a fixed-income investment. Accordingly, the cash surrender value increases each year by the portion of premiums invested plus interest on the previous amount invested. This is simply a characteristic of whole life insurance, unlike term insurance that has lower premiums and that provides death benefits only.

> Certain life insurance policies can be surrendered while the *insured is still alive in* exchange for its *cash surrender value.*

From an accounting standpoint, the periodic insurance premium should not be expensed in its entirety. Rather, part of each premium payment, the investment portion, is recorded as an asset. Illustration 12A–1 provides an example. ●

> Part of each insurance premium represents an increase in the cash surrender value.

---

> ## Illustration 12A–1
> Cash Surrender Value

Several years ago, American Capital acquired a $1 million insurance policy on the life of its chief executive officer, naming American Capital as beneficiary. Annual premiums are $18,000, payable at the beginning of each year. In 2013, the cash surrender value of the policy increased according to the contract from $5,000 to $7,000. The CEO died at the end of 2013.

| | | |
|---|---|---|
| Insurance expense (difference) .................................................. | 16,000 | |
| Cash surrender value of life insurance ($7,000 – 5,000) ............ | 2,000 | |
|    Cash (2013 premium) ............................................................ | | 18,000 |

*To record insurance expense and the increase in the investment.*

> Part of the annual premium represents a build-up in the cash surrender value.

The cash surrender value is considered to be a noncurrent investment and would be reported in the investments and funds section of the balance sheet. Of course when the insured officer dies, the corporation receives the death benefit of the insurance policy, and the cash surrender value ceases to exist because canceling the policy no longer is an option. The corporation recognizes a gain for the amount of the death benefit less the cash surrender value:

| | | |
|---|---|---|
| Cash (death benefit) ................................................................. | 1,000,000 | |
|    Cash surrender value of life insurance (balance) .................... | | 7,000 |
|    Gain on life insurance settlement (difference) ........................ | | 993,000 |

*To record the proceeds at death.*

> When the death benefit is paid, the cash surrender value becomes null and void.

# APPENDIX 12B

## Impairment of Investments

An "other-than-temporary" impairment loss is recognized in net income even though the security hasn't been sold.

We saw in Chapter 11 that intangible assets and property, plant, and equipment are subject to impairment losses that reduce earnings if a decline in fair value indicates that the assets' value has been impaired. The same is true for investments. As indicated in Chapter 12, if the fair value of an investment declines to a level below cost, and that decline is not viewed as temporary, companies typically have to recognize an other-than-temporary (OTT) impairment loss in earnings. We don't need to worry about OTT impairments for trading securities or other investments for which a company has chosen the fair value option, because all changes in the fair values of those investments (whether temporary or OTT) always are recognized in earnings. However, that is not the case for HTM and AFS investments. Declines in fair value typically are ignored for HTM investments and recorded in OCI for AFS investments. Therefore, companies need to evaluate HTM and AFS investments to determine whether an OTT impairment loss has occurred.

We use a three-step process to determine whether an OTT impairment loss must be recognized and how that loss is to be measured and recorded: (1) determine if the investment is impaired, (2) determine whether any impairment is OTT, (3) determine where to report the OTT impairment.[43] Illustration 12B–1 summarizes those steps. As you can see, the specifics of accounting for OTT impairments depend on whether the investment is in equity or debt, so we'll discuss each in turn.

**Illustration 12B–1**

Other-Than-Temporary Impairment of Equity Investments and Debt Investments Compared

|  | Equity Investment | Debt Investment |
|---|---|---|
| **Is the investment impaired?** | Yes, if the fair value is less than the investment's cost | Same (yes, if the fair value is less than the investment's amortized cost) |
| **Is any of the impairment *other-than-temporary* (OTT)?** | Yes, if the investor cannot assert that it has the intent and ability to hold the investment until fair value recovers | Yes, if the investor (a) intends to sell the investment, (b) believes it is "more likely than not" that the investor will be required to sell the investment prior to recovering the amortized cost of the investment, less any current-period credit loss, or (c) has incurred credit losses |
| **Where is the OTT impairment reported?** | In net income | In net income, if the investor intends to sell the security or is "more likely than not" to be required to sell it before recovery of its amortized cost. Otherwise: • Credit loss portion in net income. (Credit loss = amortized cost − PV of expected cash flows); • Noncredit loss portion in OCI (Noncredit loss portion = total impairment − credit loss) |

## Impairments of Equity Investments

Recall that OTT impairments don't apply to trading securities and that equity investments cannot be classified as held-to-maturity. Therefore, when we consider OTT impairments of equity investments, we are looking at available-for-sale investments. Here are the three steps:

1. ***Is the investment impaired?*** Impairment occurs when fair value has declined to a level below the investment's cost (which equals the investment's purchase price less previously recognized impairments and other adjustments).

---

[43]FASB ASC 320–10–35: Investments–Overall–Subsequent Measurement (originally "The Meaning of Other-Than-Temporary Impairment and Its Application to Certain Investments," *FASB Staff Position No. 115-1 and 124-1* (Norwalk, Conn.: FASB, November 3, 2005)).

2. ***Is any impairment other-than-temporary (OTT)?*** The impairment is temporary if the investing company can assert that it has the intent and ability to hold the investment until fair value recovers to a level that once again exceeds cost. That assertion is more difficult to defend if the expected recovery period is relatively long, the amount of impairment is large, or the financial condition of the investor or the issuer of the equity is weak.[44]

3. ***Where is the OTT impairment reported?*** A *temporary* impairment of an equity investment is simply accounted for as an unrealized loss in OCI, as demonstrated previously for fair value declines in AFS securities in Illustration 12–6. However, if the impairment is viewed as OTT, the investor recognizes the loss in the income statement, just as if the loss had been realized by selling the investment. Also, because the equity investment is classified as AFS, recognizing an OTT impairment likely will involve reclassifying amounts out of OCI that were recorded previously as unrealized gains or losses.

> Equity impairments are OTT if the investor cannot assert it has the intent and ability to hold the investment until fair value recovers.
>
> If an equity impairment is OTT:
> • Investment is written down to fair value
> • All of the OTT impairment loss is included in net income

Illustration 12B–2 provides a description of the OTT equity impairment process from **Bank of America**'s recent annual report.

---

**Note 1 (in part): Securities**

All AFS marketable equity securities are carried at fair value with net unrealized gains and losses included in accumulated OCI on an after-tax basis. If there is an other-than-temporary decline in the fair value of any individual AFS marketable equity security, the Corporation reclassifies the associated net unrealized loss out of accumulated OCI with a corresponding charge to equity investment income.

**Illustration 12B–2**

Disclosure about OTT Impairments of Equity Investments—Bank of America

**Real World Financials**

---

For an example of an OTT impairment of an equity investment, Illustration 12B–3 modifies a portion of Illustration 12–6:

---

United Intergroup, Inc., buys and sells both debt and equity securities of other companies as investments. United's fiscal year-end is December 31. The following events during 2013 and 2014 pertain to the investment portfolio.

**Illustration 12B–3**

Other-Than-Temporary (OTT) Impairment of an Equity Investment

**Purchase Investment**

| | |
|---|---|
| July 1, 2013 | Purchased $1,000,000 of Bendac common stock. |

**Adjust Investment to Fair Value**

| | |
|---|---|
| December 31, 2013 | Valued the Bendac stock at $990,000 and determined that the decline in FV should *not* be treated as an OTT impairment. |
| December 31, 2014 | Valued the Bendac stock at $985,000 and determined that the decline in FV should be treated as an OTT impairment. |

The journal entries to record the adjustments of the Bendac stock investment to fair value are:

**December 31, 2013**

| | | |
|---|---|---|
| Net unrealized holding gains and losses—OCI | 10,000 | |
|     Fair value adjustment | | 10,000 |

**December 31, 2014**

| | | |
|---|---|---|
| Other-than-temporary impairment loss—I/S | 15,000 | |
|     Investment in Bendac | | 15,000 |
| Fair value adjustment | 10,000 | |
|     Net unrealized holding gains and losses—OCI | | 10,000 |

---

The first 2014 journal entry in Illustration 12B–3 reduces the Bendac investment to reflect the OTT impairment and recognizes the entire $15,000 in 2014 earnings. United adjusts the Bendac investment directly rather than using a fair value adjustment account because the OTT impairment cannot be recovered. The second 2014 journal entry reclassifies any previously

---

[44]FASB ASC 320–10–S99: Investments–Overall–SEC Materials (previously "Other-Than-Temporary Impairment of Certain Investments in Equity Securities," *Staff Accounting Bulletin Topic 5.M*).

recognized unrealized losses associated with the investment, the same as if the investment had been sold. In 2013 United debited OCI and credited the fair value adjustment for $10,000 to reflect the decline in Bendac's fair value to $990,000, so the second 2014 journal entry reverses the 2013 entry to remove those amounts.

## Impairments of Debt Investments

As with equity investments, a three-step process is used to determine whether an impairment loss on debt investments must be recognized and how that loss is to be measured and recorded.[45] Debt investments can be classified either as HTM or AFS. We'll start with the assumption that the investment is AFS, and then indicate what is different if it is HTM.

**Debt impairments can be divided into credit losses and noncredit losses.**

***Credit losses*** **are due to anticipated reductions in cash flows from the debt investment; all others are** ***noncredit losses.***

1. ***Is the investment impaired?*** As with equity, impairment of a debt investment occurs when fair value has declined to a level below amortized cost. For debt investments, though, it also may be necessary to split the total amount of impairment into credit losses and noncredit losses. *Credit losses* reflect expected reductions in future cash flows from anticipated defaults on interest or principal payments. We calculate credit losses as the difference between the amortized cost of the debt and the *present value of the cash flows* expected to be collected, using a discount rate equal to the effective interest rate that existed at the date the investment was acquired. *Noncredit losses* capture other reductions in fair value such as those due to changes in general economic conditions.

**Debt impairments are OTT if the investor:**
**a. intends to sell the investment, or**
**b. believes it is more likely than not that they will sell the investment prior to fair value recovery, or**
**c. has suffered a credit loss.**

2. ***Is any impairment other-than-temporary (OTT)?*** We view a debt impairment as OTT if one of three conditions holds:

   a. The investor intends to sell the investment,
   b. The investor believes it is "more likely than not" that the investor will be required to sell the investment prior to recovering the amortized cost of the investment less any current-period credit losses, or
   c. The investor determines that a credit loss exists on the investment.

   The rationale for 2a and 2b is that an impairment is OTT if the investor is likely to sell the investment before fair value can recover. The rationale for 2c is that an impairment is OTT if the company believes the cash flows provided by the investment won't be enough to allow it to recover the amortized cost of the investment over the life of the investment.

**If a debt impairment is OTT:**
• **Investment is written down to fair value.**
• **If OTT because of (a) or (b), all of the OTT impairment loss is recognized in net income.**
• **If OTT because of (c), only the credit loss is recognized in net income; noncredit loss in OCI.**

3. ***Where is the OTT impairment reported?*** If the debt impairment is considered OTT, the investor always writes the investment down to fair value in the balance sheet, but the amount included in net income or other comprehensive income depends on the reason the impairment is considered OTT:

   a. If the impairment is considered OTT due to reasons 2a or 2b above, the entire impairment loss is included in net income, because it is likely that the company will incur a loss equal to the entire difference between fair value and amortized cost.
   b. If the impairment is considered OTT due to reason 2c above, *only the credit loss* component is included in net income, as that amount of amortized cost is unlikely to be recovered. Any noncredit loss component reduces OCI, similar to how we normally account for unrealized gains and losses on AFS investments.

   Also, if the debt investment is classified as AFS, recognizing an OTT impairment may involve reclassifying amounts out of OCI that were recorded previously as unrealized gains or losses.

   Illustration 12B–4 provides a description of the OTT debt impairment process from **Bank of America**'s recent annual report.

   For an example of an OTT impairment for a debt investment, we modify our Bendac example again in Illustration 12B–5. In both Cases 1 and 2 of Illustration 12B–5, the amortized cost of the investment is reduced by the amount of OTT impairment that is recognized in earnings. United achieves this by crediting a contra-asset, discount on bond investment,

---

[45]FASB ASC 320–10–35: Investments–Overall–Subsequent Measurement (previously "Recognition and Presentation of Other-Than-Temporary Impairments," *FASB Staff Position No. 115-2 and 124-2* (Norwalk, Conn.: FASB April 9, 2009)).

**Note 1 (in part): Securities**

The Corporation regularly evaluates each AFS and HTM debt security where the value has declined below amortized cost to assess whether the decline in fair value is other-than-temporary. In determining whether an impairment is other-than-temporary, the Corporation considers the severity and duration of the decline in fair value, the length of time expected for recovery, the financial condition of the issuer, and other qualitative factors, as well as whether the Corporation either plans to sell the security or it is more likely than not that it will be required to sell the security before recovery of its amortized cost. Beginning in 2009, under new accounting guidance for impairments of debt securities that are deemed to be other-than-temporary, the credit component of an other-than-temporary impairment (OTTI) loss is recognized in earnings and the non-credit component is recognized in accumulated OCI in situations where the Corporation does not intend to sell the security and it is not more-likely-than-not that the Corporation will be required to sell the security prior to recovery. If there is an OTTI on any individual security classified as HTM, the Corporation writes down the security to fair value with a corresponding charge to other income (loss).

which United amortizes over the remaining life of the debt the same way it would if it had initially purchased the debt at that discounted amount. In Case 2, the *noncredit loss* component of the impairment is recognized in OCI, the same way it would be if it were viewed as an unrealized loss under normal accounting for fair value declines of AFS investments. In both cases the carrying value of the debt becomes $950,000, reduced by the entire amount of the OTT impairment. In Case 1 this occurs via the $50,000 discount, and in Case 2 via the combination of the $30,000 discount and $20,000 fair value adjustment.

In both cases all of the OTT impairment is reflected in comprehensive income. The question is how much is reflected in net income as opposed to OCI. To clarify this distinction, GAAP requires that the entire OTT impairment be shown in the income statement, and then the portion attributed to noncredit losses backed out, such that only the credit loss portion reduces net income. That way, financial statement users are aware of the total amount as

United Intergroup, Inc., buys and sells both debt and equity securities of other companies as investments, and classifies these investments as AFS. United's fiscal year-end is December 31. The following events occurred during 2014.

**Purchase Investment**

| July 1, 2014 | Purchased $1,000,000 of Bendac bonds, maturing on December 31, 2019. |
|---|---|

**Adjust Investment to Fair Value**

| December 31, 2014 | Valued the Bendac bonds at $950,000. Of the $50,000 impairment, $30,000 is credit loss and $20,000 is noncredit loss. |
|---|---|

We'll consider two cases:

- Case 1: United either plans to sell the investment or believes it is more likely than not that it will have to sell the investment before fair value recovers (such that the impairment is viewed as OTT under 2a or 2b above).

- Case 2: United does *not* intend to sell the investment and does *not* believe it is more likely than not that it will have to sell the Bendac investment before fair value recovers, but estimates that $30,000 of credit losses have occurred (such that the impairment is viewed as OTT under 2c above).

|  | Case 1 | Case 2 |
|---|---|---|
| **December 31, 2014** | | |
| OTT impairment loss—I/S | 50,000 | 30,000 |
| Discount on bond investment | 50,000 | 30,000 |
| | | |
| OTT impairment loss—OCI | | 20,000 |
| Fair value adjustment—Noncredit loss | | 20,000 |

Note: if United had included unrealized gains or losses for this investment in OCI in a prior period, it also would have to make a reclassification entry, as demonstrated for an equity OTT impairment in Illustration 12B–3.

well as the amount included in net income. Continuing Illustration 12B–5, income statement presentation of the two cases would be as follows:

| Income Statement Presentation, December 31, 2014 | Case 1 | Case 2 |
|---|---|---|
| *OTT impairment of AFS investments:* | | |
| Total OTT impairment loss | $50,000 | $50,000 |
| Less: portion recognized in OCI | –0– | 20,000 |
| Net impairment loss recognized in net income | $50,000 | $30,000 |

# Additional Consideration

### A Little Credit Loss Goes a Long Way

Here's a twist: Consider Case 2 from Illustration 12B–5, in which United does *not* intend to sell its debt investment and does *not* consider it more likely than not that it will have to sell the investment prior to recovering fair value. According to GAAP, if the entire $50,000 impairment is due to noncredit loss, there is no credit loss, so the impairment is not viewed as OTT and does not show up on the income statement. On the other hand, if any of the impairment is due to credit loss, the impairment is viewed as OTT. Therefore, whether the impairment is OTT depends on whether it includes a credit loss, and a small amount of credit loss can matter a lot, as it makes the company show the entire impairment loss as OTT in the income statement and then back out the noncredit-loss portion to include in OCI.

What if a debt investment is classified as HTM rather than AFS? Most of the accounting is the same, but an important difference relates to the recognition of *noncredit* losses in OCI. HTM investments normally don't include unrealized gains and losses in OCI, so these won't routinely be adjusted up or down over time. Therefore, for HTM investments, GAAP requires that companies gradually reverse any amounts included in OCI over the remaining life of the investment, debiting the fair value adjustment and crediting OCI each period.

After an OTT impairment is recorded, the usual treatment of unrealized gains or losses is resumed. Changes in fair value are reported in OCI for AFS investments, and are ignored for HTM investments. Reversals of impairments of debt and equity securities are prohibited under U.S. GAAP (except, as indicated in Chapter 7, a debt investment is classified as a note or loan receivable). ●

# Additional Consideration

### OTT Impairments: An Ongoing Debate

Other-than-temporary impairments of debt instruments previously were accounted for the same as OTT impairments of equity instruments; that is, the entire impairment was shown in net income if it was viewed as OTT. Then the recent credit crisis hit, financial institutions started having to recognize huge OTT impairments for their investments, and impairment accounting was blamed by many for worsening the crisis. Critics argued that it is inappropriate to recognize impairment losses in earnings when all of the cash flows associated with an investment still are anticipated to be collected despite current fair value declines. Proponents argued that fair value declines still are relevant and that critics were simply looking for an accounting fix to reduce their losses. This disagreement came to a head in Spring of 2009, when the FASB responded to pressure from Congress by changing OTT impairment accounting to provide more latitude and avoid including noncredit losses in net income. Firms were allowed to use that approach for OTT impairments occurring in the first quarter of 2009. This had a large effect for some firms, for example, increasing the pretax earnings of twenty banks and other financial institutions by an estimated $4.9 billion in that quarter.[46]

---

[46]Credit Suisse, *Focusing on Fair Value: An Update,* June 4, 2009.

# International Financial Reporting Standards

**Accounting for OTT impairments.** Under *IAS No. 39*, companies recognize OTT impairments if there exists objective evidence of impairment. Objective evidence must relate to one or more events occurring after initial recognition of the asset that affect the future cash flows that are going to be generated by the asset. Examples of objective evidence include significant financial difficulty of the issuer and default on interest or principal payments. For an equity security, a significant or prolonged decline in fair value below cost is viewed as objective evidence.

● LO12–8

Calculation of the amount of impairment differs depending on the classification of an investment. For an HTM investment, the impairment is calculated as the difference between the amortized cost of the asset and the present value of expected future cash flows, estimated at the asset's original effective rate. So, the impairment is essentially equal to the amount that would be considered a credit loss in U.S. GAAP. For an AFS investment (debt or equity), the impairment is calculated as the difference between amortized cost and fair value. Thus, under IFRS, an OTT impairment for a debt investment is likely to be larger if it is classified as AFS than if it is classified as HTM, because it includes the entire decline in fair value if classified as AFS but only the credit loss if classified as HTM. Under IFRS, all OTT impairments are recognized in earnings (there is no equivalent to recognizing in OCI any non-credit losses on debt investments).

IFRS allows recoveries of impairments to be recognized in earnings for debt investments, but not for equity investments. This is a difference from U.S. GAAP, which does not allow recoveries of any OTT impairment of equity or debt (other than debt that is classified as a loan).

To illustrate, let's modify our Bendac debt example from Illustration 12B–2 to assume amortized cost of €1,000,000 and fair value of €950,000, with the €50,000 impairment consisting of €30,000 of credit losses and €20,000 of noncredit losses. If the investment was classified as AFS, IFRS would recognize a €50,000 OTT impairment:

| | | |
|---|---|---|
| Other-than-temporary impairment loss—I/S .......................... | 50,000 | |
|     Investment in Bendac ......................................................... | | 50,000 |

If Bendac had recognized any cumulative unrealized losses in AOCI associated with these investments, it would also need to reclassify those amounts out of AOCI and recognize them in the income statement by debiting the OTT impairment loss and crediting OCI.

If the investment had been classified as HTM rather than AFS, IFRS would recognize an OTT impairment of €30,000:

| | | |
|---|---|---|
| Other-than-temporary impairment loss—I/S ........................ | 30,000 | |
|     Investment in Bendac ......................................................... | | 30,000 |

If in a subsequent period the fair value of the debt investment improved by €15,000, IFRS would allow *reversal* of that amount of impairment charge:

| | | |
|---|---|---|
| Investment in Bendac ............................................................. | 15,000 | |
|     Reversal of other-than-temporary impairment loss—I/S .... | | 15,000 |

Recent events highlight the judgmental nature of OTT impairments. A financial crisis in Greece prompted OTT impairments of Greek government bonds by various European banks. In late 2011 the chairman of the IASB, Hans Hoogervorst, complained to the EU's market regulator about inconsistency in how banks were valuing the bonds. Some banks took only a 21% impairment, while others took an impairment of over 50% on the exact same bonds![47]

At the time this text was printed, the IASB had not yet finalized changes in impairment accounting with respect to *IFRS No. 9*. The IASB is considering impairments in collaboration with the FASB, as discussed further in the supplement to this chapter.

---

[47]Jones, A., and J. Thompson. "IASB Criticises Greek Debt Writedowns", *FT.com*, 8/30/2011.

# Questions For Review of Key Topics

**Q 12–1** All investments in *debt* securities and investments in *equity* securities for which the investor lacks significant influence over the operation and financial policies of the investee are classified for reporting purposes in one of three categories, and can be accounted for differently depending on the classification. What are these three categories?

**Q 12–2** When market rates of interest *rise* after a fixed-rate security is purchased, the value of the now-below-market, fixed-interest payments declines, so the market value of the investment falls. On the other hand, if market rates of interest *fall* after a fixed-rate security is purchased, the fixed-interest payments become relatively attractive, and the market value of the investment rises. Assuming these price changes are not viewed as giving rise to an other-than-temporary impairment, how are they reflected in the investment account for a security classified as held-to-maturity?

**Q 12–3** Does GAAP distinguish between fair values that are readily determinable from a securities exchange versus those needing to be calculated based on the company's own assumptions? Explain how a user will know about the reliability of the inputs used to determine fair value.

**Q 12–4** When an investment is acquired to be held for an unspecified period of time as opposed to being held to maturity, it is reported at the fair value of the investment securities on the reporting date. Why?

**Q 12–5** Reporting an investment at its fair value means adjusting its carrying amount for changes in fair value after its acquisition (or since the last reporting date if it was held at that time). Such changes are called unrealized holding gains and losses because they haven't yet been realized through the sale of the security. If the security is classified as available-for-sale, how are unrealized holding gains and losses reported if they are not viewed as giving rise to an other-than-temporary impairment?

**Q 12–6** What is "comprehensive income"? Its composition varies from company to company but may include which investment-related items that are not included in net income?

**Q 12–7** Why are holding gains and losses treated differently for trading securities and securities available-for-sale?

**Q 12–8** Western Die-Casting Company holds an investment in unsecured bonds of LGB Heating Equipment, Inc. When the investment was acquired, management's intention was to hold the bonds for resale. Now management has the positive intent and ability to hold the bonds to maturity. How should the reclassification of the investment be accounted for?

**Q 12–9** Is it necessary for an investor to report individual amounts for the three categories of investments—held-to-maturity, available-for-sale, or trading—in the financial statements? What information should be disclosed about these investments?

**IFRS** **Q 12–10** Under *IFRS No. 9*, which reporting categories are used to account for debt investments? What about for equity investments when the investor lacks the ability to significantly influence the operations of the investee?

**IFRS** **Q 12–11** Are there circumstances in which the cost method is required under U.S. GAAP but not under IFRS? Explain.

**Q 12–12** What is the effect of a company electing the fair value option with respect to a held-to-maturity investment or an available-for-sale investment?

**IFRS** **Q 12–13** Do U.S. GAAP and IFRS differ in the amount of flexibility that companies have in electing the fair value option? Explain.

**Q 12–14** Under what circumstances is the equity method used to account for an investment in stock?

**Q 12–15** The equity method has been referred to as a *one-line consolidation*. What might prompt this description?

**Q 12–16** In the application of the equity method, how should dividends from the investee be accounted for? Why?

**Q 12–17** The fair value of depreciable assets of Penner Packaging Company exceeds their book value by $12 million. The assets' average remaining useful life is 10 years. They are being depreciated by the straight-line method. Finest Foods Industries buys 40% of Penner's common shares. When adjusting investment revenue and the investment by the equity method, how will the situation described affect those two accounts?

**Q 12–18** Superior Company owns 40% of the outstanding stock of Bernard Company. During 2013, Bernard paid a $100,000 cash dividend on its common shares. What effect did this dividend have on Superior's 2013 financial statements?

**Q 12–19** Sometimes an investor's level of influence changes, making it necessary to change from the equity method to another method. How should the investor account for this change in accounting method?

**IFRS** **Q 12–20** How does IFRS differ from U.S. GAAP with respect to using the equity method?

**Q 12–21** What is the effect of a company electing the fair value option with respect to an investment that otherwise would be accounted for using the equity method?

**Q 12–22** Define a financial instrument. Provide three examples of current liabilities that represent financial instruments.

**Q 12–23** Some financial instruments are called derivatives. Why?

Q 12–24   (Based on Appendix 12A) Northwest Carburetor Company established a fund in 2010 to accumulate money for a new plant scheduled for construction in 2013. How should this special purpose fund be reported in Northwest's balance sheet?

Q 12–25   (Based on Appendix 12A) Whole-life insurance policies typically can be surrendered while the insured is still alive in exchange for a determinable amount of money called the *cash surrender value.* When a company buys a life insurance policy on the life of a key officer to protect the company against the untimely loss of a valuable resource in the event the officer dies, how should the company account for the cash surrender value?

Q 12–26   (Based on Appendix 12B) When market rates of interest *rise* after a fixed-rate security is purchased, the value of the now-below-market, fixed-interest payments declines, so the market value of the investment falls. If that drop in fair value is viewed as giving rise to an other-than-temporary impairment, how would it be reflected in the investment account for a security classified as held-to-maturity?

Q 12–27   (Based on Appendix 12B) Reporting an investment at its fair value requires adjusting its carrying amount for changes in fair value after its acquisition (or since the last reporting date if it was held at that time). Such changes are called unrealized holding gains and losses because they haven't yet been realized through the sale of the security. If a security is classified as available-for-sale, and an unrealized holding loss is viewed as giving rise to an other-than-temporary (OTT) impairment, how is it reported in the financial statements?

Q 12–28   (Based on Appendix 12B) The market value of Helig Forestry and Mining Corporation common stock dropped 6 ⅛ points when the federal government passed new legislation banning one of the company's primary techniques for extracting ore. Harris Corporation owns shares of Helig and classifies its investment as securities available-for-sale. How should the decline in market value be handled by Harris?

**IFRS**   Q 12–29   (Based on Appendix 12B) Do U.S. GAAP and IFRS differ in how they account for other-than-temporary impairments? Explain.

# Brief Exercises

**BE 12–1**
Securities held-to-maturity;
bond investment;
effective interest
● LO12–1

Lance Brothers Enterprises acquired $720,000 of 3% bonds, dated July 1, on July 1, 2013, as a long-term investment. Management has the positive intent and ability to hold the bonds until maturity. The market interest rate (yield) was 4% for bonds of similar risk and maturity. Lance Brothers paid $600,000 for the investment in bonds and will receive interest semiannually on June 30 and December 31. Prepare the journal entries (a) to record Lance Brothers' investment in the bonds on July 1, 2013, and (b) to record interest on December 31, 2013, at the effective (market) rate.

**BE 12–2**
Trading securities
● LO12–2

S&L Financial buys and sells securities expecting to earn profits on short-term differences in price. On December 27, 2013, S&L purchased **Coca-Cola** common shares for $875,000 and sold the shares on January 3, 2014, for $880,000. At December 31, the shares had a fair value of $873,000. What pretax amounts did S&L include in its 2013 and 2014 earnings as a result of this investment?

**BE 12–3**
Available-for-sale
securities
● LO12–3

S&L Financial buys and sells securities which it classifies as available-for-sale. On December 27, 2013, S&L purchased **Coca-Cola** common shares for $875,000 and sold the shares on January 3, 2014, for $880,000. At December 31, the shares had a fair value of $873,000, and S&L has the intent and ability to hold the investment until fair value recovers. What pretax amounts did S&L include in its 2013 and 2014 earnings as a result of this investment?

**BE 12–4**
Securities
available-for-sale;
adjusting entry
● LO12–3

For several years Fister Links Products has held shares of **Microsoft** common stock, considered by the company to be securities available-for-sale. The shares were acquired at a cost of $500,000. Their fair value last year was $610,000 and is $670,000 this year. At what amount will the investment be reported in this year's balance sheet? What adjusting entry is required to accomplish this objective?

**BE 12–5**
Classification
of securities;
reporting
● LO12–3

Adams Industries holds 40,000 shares of **FedEx** common stock. On December 31, 2012, and December 31, 2013, the market value of the stock is $95 and $100 per share, respectively. What is the appropriate reporting category for this investment and at what amount will it be reported in the 2013 balance sheet?

**BE 12–6**
Fair value option;
available-for-sale
securities
● LO12–7

S&L Financial buys and sells securities that it typically classifies as available-for-sale. On December 27, 2013, S&L purchased **Coca-Cola** common shares for $875,000 and sold the shares on January 3, 2014, for $880,000. At December 31, the shares had a fair value of $873,000. When it purchased the Coca-Cola shares, S&L Financial decided to elect the fair value option for this investment. What pretax amounts did S&L include in its 2013 and 2014 earnings as a result of this investment?

**BE 12–7**
Trading
securities,
securities
available-for-sale
and dividends
● **LO12–2,**
**LO12–3**

Turner Company owns 10% of the outstanding stock of ICA Company. During the current year, ICA paid a $5 million cash dividend on its common shares. What effect did this dividend have on Turner's 2013 financial statements? Explain the reasoning for this effect.

**BE 12–8**
Equity method
and dividends
● **LO12–5**

Turner Company owns 40% of the outstanding stock of ICA Company. During the current year, ICA paid a $5 million cash dividend on its common shares. What effect did this dividend have on Turner's 2013 financial statements? Explain the reasoning for this effect.

**BE 12–9**
Equity method
● **LO12–6**

The fair value of Wallis, Inc.'s depreciable assets exceeds their book value by $50 million. The assets have an average remaining useful life of 15 years and are being depreciated by the straight-line method. Park Industries buys 30% of Wallis's common shares. When Park adjusts its investment revenue and the investment by the equity method, how will the situation described affect those two accounts?

**BE 12–10**
Equity method
investments
● **LO12–6,**
**LO12–8**

 **IFRS**

Refer to the situation described in BE 12–9, but assume that Park Industries buys 50% of Wallis's common shares. Also assume that Park reports under International Financial Reporting Standards, and has elected the "proportionate consolidation" method to account for the Wallis investment. How would the situation described affect Park's depreciable asset accounts?

**BE 12–11**
Change in
principle; change
to the equity
method
● **LO12–5**

At the beginning of 2013, Pioneer Products' ownership interest in the common stock of LLB Co. increased to the point that it became appropriate to begin using the equity method of accounting for the investment. The balance in the investment account was $44 million at the time of the change but would have been $56 million if Pioneer had used the equity method and the account had been adjusted for investee net income and dividends. How should Pioneer report the change? Would your answer be the same if Pioneer is changing *from* the equity method rather than *to* the equity method?

**BE 12–12**
Fair value option;
equity method
investments
● **LO12–7**

Turner Company purchased 40% of the outstanding stock of ICA Company for $10,000,000 on January 2, 2013. Turner elects the fair value option to account for the investment. During 2013, ICA earns $750,000 of income and on December 30 pays a dividend of $500,000. On December 31, 2013, the fair value of Turner's investment has increased to $11,500,000. What journal entries would Turner make to account for this investment during 2013, assuming Turner will account for the investment similar to how it would account for a trading security?

**BE 12–13**
Available-for-
sale securities
and impairment
(Appendix 12B)
● **LO12–3**

LED Corporation owns 100,000 shares of Branch Pharmaceuticals common stock and classifies its investment as securities available-for-sale. The market price of LED's investment in Branch's stock fell more than 30%, by $4.50 per share, due to concerns about one of the company's principal drugs. The concerns were justified when the FDA banned the drug. $1.00 per share of that decline in value already had been included in OCI as a temporary unrealized loss in a prior period. What journal entries should LED record to account for the decline in market value in the current period? How should the decline affect net income and comprehensive income?

**BE 12–14**
Available-for-
sale securities
and impairment
(Appendix 12B)
● **LO12–3**

LED Corporation owns $1,000,000 of Branch Pharmaceuticals bonds and classifies its investment as securities available-for-sale. The market price of LED's investment in Branch's bonds fell by $450,000, due to concerns about one of the company's principal drugs. The concerns were justified when the FDA banned the drug. $100,000 of that decline in value already had been included in OCI as a temporary unrealized loss in a prior period. LED views $200,000 of the $450,000 loss as related to *credit* losses, and the other $250,000 as *noncredit* losses. LED thinks it is more likely than not that it will have to sell the investment before fair value recovers. What journal entries should LED record to account for the decline in market value in the current period? How should the decline affect net income and comprehensive income?

**BE 12–15**
Available-for-
sale securities
and impairment
(Appendix 12B)
● **LO12–3**

LED Corporation owns $1,000,000 of Branch Pharmaceuticals bonds and classifies its investment as securities available-for-sale. The market price of Branch's bonds fell by $450,000, due to concerns about one of the company's principal drugs. The concerns were justified when the FDA banned the drug. $100,000 of that decline in value already had been included in OCI as a temporary unrealized loss in a prior period. LED views $200,000 of the $450,000 loss as related to *credit* losses, and the other $250,000 as *noncredit* losses. LED does not plan to sell the investment and does not think it is more likely than not that it will have to sell the investment before fair value recovers. What journal entries should LED record to account for the decline in market value in the current period? How should the decline affect net income and comprehensive income?

**BE 12–16**
Recovery of
impairments
under IFRS
(Appendix 12B)
● **LO12–3,
LO12–8**

 **IFRS**

Wickum Corporation reports under IFRS, and recognized a $500,000 other-than-temporary impairment of an HTM debt investment in Right Corporation. Subsequently, the fair value of Wickum's investment in Right increased by $300,000. How would Wickum account for that increase in fair value?

# Exercises

**An alternate exercise and problem set is available on the text website: www.mhhe.com/spiceland7e**

**E 12–1**
Securities held-
to-maturity;
bond investment;
effective interest
● **LO12–1**

Tanner-UNF Corporation acquired as a long-term investment $240 million of 6% bonds, dated July 1, on July 1, 2013. Company management has the positive intent and ability to hold the bonds until maturity. The market interest rate (yield) was 8% for bonds of similar risk and maturity. Tanner-UNF paid $200 million for the bonds. The company will receive interest semiannually on June 30 and December 31. As a result of changing market conditions, the fair value of the bonds at December 31, 2013 was $210 million.

**Required:**
1. Prepare the journal entry to record Tanner-UNF's investment in the bonds on July 1, 2013.
2. Prepare the journal entry by Tanner-UNF to record interest on December 31, 2013, at the effective (market) rate.
3. At what amount will Tanner-UNF report its investment in the December 31, 2013, balance sheet? Why?
4. Suppose Moody's bond rating agency downgraded the risk rating of the bonds motivating Tanner-UNF to sell the investment on January 2, 2014, for $190 million. Prepare the journal entry to record the sale.

**E 12–2**
Securities
held-to-maturity
● **LO12–1**

FF&T Corporation is a confectionery wholesaler that frequently buys and sells securities to meet various investment objectives. The following selected transactions relate to FF&T's investment activities during the last two months of 2013. At November 1, FF&T held $48 million of 20-year, 10% bonds of Convenience, Inc., purchased May 1, 2013, at face value. Management has the positive intent and ability to hold the bonds until maturity. FF&T's fiscal year ends on December 31.

| | |
|---|---|
| Nov. 1 | Received semiannual interest of $2.4 million from the Convenience, Inc., bonds. |
| Dec. 1 | Purchased 12% bonds of Facsimile Enterprises at their $30 million face value, to be held until they mature in 2026. Semiannual interest is payable May 31 and November 30. |
| 31 | Purchased U.S. Treasury bills that mature in two months for $8.9 million. |
| 31 | Recorded any necessary adjusting entry(s) relating to the investments. |

The fair values of the investments at December 31 were:

| | |
|---|---|
| Convenience bonds | $44.7 million |
| Facsimile Enterprises bonds | 30.9 million |
| U.S. Treasury bills | 8.9 million |

**Required:**
Prepare the appropriate journal entry for each transaction or event.

**E 12–3**
FASB codification research
● LO12–1

The *FASB Accounting Standards Codification* represents the single source of authoritative U.S. generally accepted accounting principles.

**Required:**
1. Obtain the relevant authoritative literature on accounting for investments in held-to-maturity securities using the FASB's Codification Research System at the FASB website (**www.fasb.org**).
2. What is the specific citation that describes examples of circumstances under which an investment in debt is available to be sold and therefore should not be classified as held-to-maturity?
3. List the circumstances and conditions.

**E 12–4**
Purchase and sale of investment securities
● LO12–2, LO12–3

Shott Farm Supplies Corporation purchased 800 shares of General Motors stock at $50 per share and paid a brokerage fee of $1,200. Two months later, the shares were sold for $53 per share. The brokerage fee on the sale was $1,300.

**Required:**
Prepare entries for the purchase and the sale.

**E 12–5**
Various transactions relating to trading securities
● LO12–2

Rantzow-Lear Company buys and sells securities expecting to earn profits on short-term differences in price. The company's fiscal year ends on December 31. The following selected transactions relating to Rantzow-Lear's trading account occurred during December 2013 and the first week of 2014.

**2013**
Dec. 17    Purchased 100,000 Grocers' Supply Corporation preferred shares for $350,000.
28    Received cash dividends of $2,000 from the Grocers' Supply Corporation preferred shares.
31    Recorded any necessary adjusting entry relating to the Grocers' Supply Corporation preferred shares. The market price of the stock was $4 per share.

**2014**
Jan.  5    Sold the Grocers' Supply Corporation preferred shares for $395,000.

**Required:**
1. Prepare the appropriate journal entry for each transaction.
2. Indicate any amounts that Rantzow-Lear Company would report in its 2013 balance sheet and income statement as a result of this investment.

**E 12–6**
FASB codification research
● LO12–2, LO12–3, LO12–5

Access the *FASB's Codification Research System* at the FASB website (**www.fasb.org**).

**Required:**
Determine the specific citation for accounting for each of the following items:
1. Unrealized holding gains for trading securities should be included in earnings.
2. Under the equity method, the investor accounts for its share of the earnings or losses of the investee in the periods they are reported by the investee in its financial statements.
3. Transfers of securities between categories are accounted for at fair value.
4. Disclosures for available-for-sale securities should include total losses for securities that have net losses included in accumulated other comprehensive income.

**E 12–7**
Securities available-for-sale; adjusting entries
● LO12–3

Loreal-American Corporation purchased several marketable securities during 2013. At December 31, 2013, the company had the investments in common stock listed below. None was held at the last reporting date, December 31, 2012, and all are considered securities available-for-sale.

| | Cost | Fair Value | Unrealized Holding Gain (Loss) |
|---|---|---|---|
| Short term: | | | |
| Blair, Inc. | $ 480,000 | $ 405,000 | $(75,000) |
| ANC Corporation | 450,000 | 480,000 | 30,000 |
| Totals | $ 930,000 | $ 885,000 | $(45,000) |
| Long term: | | | |
| Drake Corporation | $ 480,000 | $ 560,000 | $ 80,000 |
| Aaron Industries | 720,000 | 660,000 | (60,000) |
| Totals | $1,200,000 | $1,220,000 | $ 20,000 |

**Required:**
1. Prepare the appropriate adjusting entry at December 31, 2013.
2. What amounts would be reported in the income statement at December 31, 2013, as a result of the adjusting entry?

**E 12–8**
Classification
of securities;
adjusting entries
● LO12–3

On February 18, 2013, Union Corporation purchased 10,000 shares of IBM common stock as a long-term investment at $60 per share. On December 31, 2013, and December 31, 2014, the market value of IBM stock is $58
and $61 per share, respectively.

**Required:**
1.  What is the appropriate reporting category for this investment? Why?
2.  Prepare the adjusting entry for December 31, 2013.
3.  Prepare the adjusting entry for December 31, 2014.

**E 12–9**
Various
transactions
related to
securities
available-for-sale
● LO12–3

Construction Forms Corporation buys securities to be available for sale when circumstances warrant, not to profit
from short-term differences in price and not necessarily to hold debt securities to maturity. The following selected
transactions relate to investment activities of Construction Forms whose fiscal year ends on December 31. No
investments were held by Construction Forms at the beginning of the year.

**2013**

| | |
|---|---|
| Mar.  2 | Purchased 1 million Platinum Gauges, Inc., common shares for $31 million, including brokerage fees and commissions. |
| Apr. 12 | Purchased $20 million of 10% bonds at face value from Zenith Wholesale Corporation. |
| July 18 | Received cash dividends of $2 million on the investment in Platinum Gauges, Inc., common shares. |
| Oct. 15 | Received semiannual interest of $1 million on the investment in Zenith bonds. |
| 16 | Sold the Zenith bonds for $21 million. |
| Nov.  1 | Purchased 500,000 LTD International preferred shares for $40 million, including brokerage fees and commissions. |
| Dec. 31 | Recorded the necessary adjusting entry(s) relating to the investments. The market prices of the investments are $32 per share for Platinum Gauges, Inc., and $74 per share for LTD International preferred shares. |

**2014**

| | |
|---|---|
| Jan. 23 | Sold half the Platinum Gauges, Inc., shares for $32 per share. |
| Mar.  1 | Sold the LTD International preferred shares for $76 per share. |

**Required:**
1.  Prepare the appropriate journal entry for each transaction or event.
2.  Show the amounts that would be reported in the company's 2013 combined statement of net income and other comprehensive income relative to these investments.

**E 12–10**
Securities
available-for-sale;
journal entries
● LO12–3

On January 2, 2013, Sanborn Tobacco Inc. bought 5% of Jackson Industry's capital stock for $90 million as a
temporary investment. Sanborn classified the securities acquired as available-for-sale. Jackson Industry's net
income for the year ended December 31, 2013, was $120 million. The fair value of the shares held by Sanborn
was $98 million at December 31, 2013. During 2013, Jackson declared a dividend of $60 million.

**Required:**
1.  Prepare all appropriate journal entries related to the investment during 2013.
2.  Indicate the effect of this investment on 2013 income before taxes.

**E 12–11**
Various
investment
securities
● LO12–1,
LO12–2,
LO12–3

At December 31, 2013, Hull-Meyers Corp. had the following investments that were purchased during 2013, its
first year of operations:

| | Cost | Fair Value |
|---|---|---|
| **Trading Securities:** | | |
| Security A | $  900,000 | $  910,000 |
| Security B | 105,000 | 100,000 |
| Totals | $1,005,000 | $1,010,000 |
| **Securities Available-for-Sale:** | | |
| Security C | $  700,000 | $  780,000 |
| Security D | 900,000 | 915,000 |
| Totals | $1,600,000 | $1,695,000 |
| **Securities to Be Held-to-Maturity:** | | |
| Security E | $  490,000 | $  500,000 |
| Security F | 615,000 | 610,000 |
| Totals | $1,105,000 | $1,110,000 |

No investments were sold during 2013. All securities except Security D and Security F are considered short-
term investments. None of the fair value changes is considered permanent.

**Required:**

Determine the following amounts at December 31, 2013.

1. Investments reported as current assets.

2. Investments reported as noncurrent assets.

3. Unrealized gain (or loss) component of income before taxes.

4. Unrealized gain (or loss) component of accumulated other comprehensive income in shareholders' equity.

**E 12–12**
Securities
available-for-sale;
adjusting entries
● LO12–3

The accounting records of Jamaican Importers Inc. at January 1, 2013, included the following:

| Assets: | |
|---|---|
| Investment in IBM common shares | $1,345,000 |
| Less: Fair value adjustment | (145,000) |
| | $1,200,000 |
| Shareholders' Equity: | |
| Accumulated unrealized holding gains and losses | $ 145,000 |

No changes occurred during 2013 in the investment portfolio.

**Required:**

Prepare appropriate adjusting entry(s) at December 31, 2013, assuming the fair value of the IBM common shares was:

1. $1,175,000

2. $1,275,000

3. $1,375,000

**E 12–13**
Securities
available-for-sale;
fair value
adjustment
● LO12–3

The investments of Harlon Enterprises included the following cost and fair value amounts:

| ($ in millions) | | Fair Value, Dec. 31 | |
|---|---|---|---|
| **Securities Available-for-Sale** | **Cost** | **2013** | **2014** |
| A Corporation shares | $ 20 | $14 | na |
| B Corporation bonds | 35 | 35 | $ 37 |
| C Corporation shares | 15 | na | 14 |
| D Industries shares | 45 | 46 | 50 |
| Totals | $115 | $95 | $101 |

Harlon Enterprises sold its holdings of A Corporation shares on June 1, 2014, for $15 million. On September 12, 2014, it purchased the C Corporation shares.

**Required:**

1. What is the effect of the sale of the A Corporation shares and the purchase of the C Corporation shares on Harlon's 2014 pretax earnings?

2. At what amount should Harlon's securities available-for-sale portfolio be reported in its 2014 balance sheet? What adjusting entry is needed to accomplish this? What is the effect of the adjustment on Harlon's 2014 pretax earnings?

**E 12–14**
Investment
securities and
equity method
investments
compared
● LO12–3,
   LO12–4,
   LO12–5

As a long-term investment, Painters' Equipment Company purchased 20% of AMC Supplies Inc.'s 400,000 shares for $480,000 at the beginning of the fiscal year of both companies. On the purchase date, the fair value and book value of AMC's net assets were equal. During the year, AMC earned net income of $250,000 and distributed cash dividends of 25 cents per share. At year-end, the fair value of the shares is $505,000.

**Required:**

1. Assume no significant influence was acquired. Prepare the appropriate journal entries from the purchase through the end of the year.

2. Assume significant influence was acquired. Prepare the appropriate journal entries from the purchase through the end of the year.

**E 12–15**
Equity method;
purchase;
investee
income;
dividends
● LO12–4,
   LO12–5

As a long-term investment at the beginning of the fiscal year, Florists International purchased 30% of Nursery Supplies Inc.'s 8 million shares for $56 million. The fair value and book value of the shares were the same at that time. During the year, Nursery Supplies earned net income of $40 million and distributed cash dividends of $1.25 per share. At the end of the year, the fair value of the shares is $52 million.

**Required:**

Prepare the appropriate journal entries from the purchase through the end of the year.

**E 12–16**
**Change in principle; change to the equity method**
● LO12–5

The Trump Companies Inc. has ownership interests in several public companies. At the beginning of 2013, the company's ownership interest in the common stock of Milken Properties increased to the point that it became appropriate to begin using the equity method of accounting for the investment. The balance in the investment account was $31 million at the time of the change. Accountants working with company records determined that the balance would have been $48 million if the account had been adjusted for investee net income and dividends as prescribed by the equity method.

**Required:**
1. Prepare the journal entry to record the change in principle.
2. Briefly describe other steps Trump should take to report the change.
3. Suppose Trump is changing *from* the equity method rather than *to* the equity method. How would your answers to requirements 1 and 2 differ?

**E 12–17**
**Error corrections; investment**
● LO12–1,
  LO12–2,
  LO12–3

On December 12, 2013, an investment costing $80,000 was sold for $100,000. The total of the sale proceeds was credited to the investment account.

**Required:**
1. Prepare the journal entry to correct the error assuming it is discovered before the books are adjusted or closed in 2013. (Ignore income taxes.)
2. Prepare the journal entry to correct the error assuming it is not discovered until early 2014. (Ignore income taxes.)

**E 12–18**
**Equity method; adjustment for depreciation**
● LO12–5,
  LO12–6

Fizer Pharmaceutical paid $68 million on January 2, 2013, for 4 million shares of Carne Cosmetics common stock. The investment represents a 25% interest in the net assets of Carne and gave Fizer the ability to exercise significant influence over Carne's operations. Fizer received dividends of $1 per share on December 21, 2013, and Carne reported net income of $40 million for the year ended December 31, 2013. The fair value of Carne's common stock at December 31, 2013, was $18.50 per share.
• The book value of Carne's net assets was $192 million.
• The fair value of Carne's depreciable assets exceeded their book value by $32 million. These assets had an average remaining useful life of eight years.
• The remainder of the excess of the cost of the investment over the book value of net assets purchased was attributable to goodwill.

**Required:**
Prepare all appropriate journal entries related to the investment during 2013.

**E 12–19**
**Equity method**
● LO12–5,
  LO12–6

On January 1, 2013, Cameron Inc. bought 20% of the outstanding common stock of Lake Construction Company for $300 million cash. At the date of acquisition of the stock, Lake's net assets had a fair value of $900 million. Their book value was $800 million. The difference was attributable to the fair value of Lake's buildings and its land exceeding book value, each accounting for one-half of the difference. Lake's net income for the year ended December 31, 2013, was $150 million. During 2013, Lake declared and paid cash dividends of $30 million. The buildings have a remaining life of 10 years.

**Required:**
1. Prepare all appropriate journal entries related to the investment during 2013, assuming Cameron accounts for this investment by the equity method.
2. Determine the amounts to be reported by Cameron:
   a. As an investment in Cameron's 2013 balance sheet.
   b. As investment revenue in the income statement.
   c. Among investing activities in the statement of cash flows.

**E 12–20**
**Proportionate consolidation of investments under IFRS**
● LO12–6,
  LO12–8

🌐 **IFRS**

[This is a variation of Exercise 12–19 focusing on using proportionate consolidation to account for joint ventures under IFRS.]
Refer to the situation described in Exercise 12–19, but assume that Cameron bought 50% of the outstanding stock of Lake for $750 million cash, that half of the book value and fair value of Lake's individual net assets is attributable to land and the other half to buildings, that Cameron reports under IFRS, and that Cameron has elected the proportionate consolidation method to account for its investment in Lake.

**Required:**
1. What would be the effect on January 1, 2013, of the Lake investment on the following accounts on Cameron's consolidated balance sheet?
   a. Buildings
   b. Land
   c. Goodwill
   d. Equity method investments

2. What would be the effect on December 31, 2013, of the Lake investment on the following accounts on Cameron's consolidated balance sheet?

   a. Buildings

   b. Land

   c. Goodwill

   d. Equity method investments

3. Would the effect on Cameron's December 31, 2013, retained earnings differ between an equity method and a proportionate consolidation treatment? Explain.

---

**E 12–21**

**Fair value option; held-to-maturity investments**

● **LO12–1,**
  **LO12–2,**
  **LO12–7**

[This is a variation of Exercise 12–1 focusing on the fair value option.]

Tanner-UNF Corporation acquired as a long-term investment $240 million of 6% bonds, dated July 1, on July 1, 2013. Company management has the positive intent and ability to hold the bonds until maturity, but when the bonds were acquired Tanner-UNF decided to elect the fair value option for accounting for its investment. The market interest rate (yield) was 8% for bonds of similar risk and maturity. Tanner-UNF paid $200 million for the bonds. The company will receive interest semiannually on June 30 and December 31. As a result of changing market conditions, the fair value of the bonds at December 31, 2013, was $210 million.

**Required:**

1. Would this investment be classified on Tanner-UNF's balance sheet as held-to-maturity securities, trading securities, available-for-sale securities, significant-influence investments, or other? Explain.

2. Prepare the journal entry to record Tanner-UNF's investment in the bonds on July 1, 2013.

3. Prepare the journal entry used by Tanner-UNF to record interest on December 31, 2013, at the effective (market) rate.

4. Prepare any journal entry necessary to recognize fair value changes as of December 31, 2013.

5. At what amount will Tanner-UNF report its investment in the December 31, 2013, balance sheet? Why?

6. Suppose Moody's bond rating agency downgraded the risk rating of the bonds motivating Tanner-UNF to sell the investment on January 2, 2014, for $190 million. Prepare the journal entry to record the sale.

---

**E 12–22**

**Fair value option; available-for-sale investments**

● **LO12–2,**
  **LO12–3,**
  **LO12–7**

[This is a variation of Exercise 12–10 focusing on the fair value option.]

On January 2, 2013, Sanborn Tobacco, Inc., bought 5% of Jackson Industry's capital stock for $90 million as a temporary investment. Sanborn realized that these securities normally would be classified as available-for-sale, but elected the fair value option to account for the investment. Jackson Industry's net income for the year ended December 31, 2013, was $120 million. The fair value of the shares held by Sanborn was $98 million at December 31, 2013. During 2013, Jackson declared a dividend of $60 million.

**Required:**

1. Would this investment be classified on Sanborn's balance sheet as held-to-maturity securities, trading securities, available-for-sale securities, significant-influence investments, or other? Explain.

2. Prepare all appropriate journal entries related to the investment during 2013.

3. Indicate the effect of this investment on 2013 income before taxes.

---

**E 12–23**

**Fair value option; equity method investments**

● **LO12–2,**
  **LO12–5,**
  **LO12–7**

[This is a variation of Exercise 12–15 focusing on the fair value option.]

As a long-term investment at the beginning of the fiscal year, Florists International purchased 30% of Nursery Supplies Inc.'s 8 million shares for $56 million. The fair value and book value of the shares were the same at that time. The company realizes that this investment typically would be accounted for under the equity method, but instead chooses the fair value option. During the year, Nursery Supplies earned net income of $40 million and distributed cash dividends of $1.25 per share. At the end of the year, the fair value of the shares is $52 million.

**Required:**

1. Would this investment be classified on Florists' balance sheet as held-to-maturity securities, trading securities, available-for-sale securities, significant-influence investments, or other? Explain.

2. Prepare all appropriate journal entries related to the investment during 2013.

3. Indicate the effect of this investment on 2013 income before taxes.

---

**E 12–24**

**Life insurance policy (Appendix 12A)**

Edible Chemicals Corporation owns a $4 million whole life insurance policy on the life of its CEO, naming Edible Chemicals as beneficiary. The annual premiums are $70,000 and are payable at the beginning of each year. The cash surrender value of the policy was $21,000 at the beginning of 2013.

**Required:**

1. Prepare the appropriate 2013 journal entry to record insurance expense and the increase in the investment assuming the cash surrender value of the policy increased according to the contract to $27,000.

2. The CEO died at the end of 2013. Prepare the appropriate journal entry.

**E 12–25**
Life insurance policy
(Appendix 12A)

Below are two unrelated situations relating to life insurance.

**Required:**
Prepare the appropriate journal entry for each situation.
1. Ford Corporation owns a whole life insurance policy on the life of its president. Ford Corporation is the beneficiary. The insurance premium is $25,000. The cash surrender value increased during the year from $2,500 to $4,600.
2. Petroleum Corporation received a $250,000 life insurance settlement when its CEO died. At that time, the cash surrender value was $16,000.

**E 12–26**
Held-to-maturity securities; impairments
(Appendix 12B)
● **LO12–1**

Bloom Corporation purchased $1,000,000 of Taylor Company 5% bonds at par with the intent and ability to hold the bonds until they matured in 2020, so Bloom classifies their investment as HTM. Unfortunately, a combination of problems at Taylor Company and in the debt market caused the fair value of the Taylor investment to decline to $600,000 during 2013.

**Required:**
For each of the following scenarios, prepare appropriate entry(s) at December 31, 2013, and indicate how the scenario will affect the 2013 income statement (ignoring income taxes).
1. Bloom now believes it is more likely than not that it will have to sell the Taylor bonds before the bonds have a chance to recover their fair value. Of the $400,000 decline in fair value, Bloom attributes $250,000 to credit losses, and $150,000 to noncredit losses.
2. Bloom does not plan to sell the Taylor bonds prior to maturity, and does not believe it is more likely than not that it will have to sell the Taylor bonds before the bonds have a chance to recover their fair value. Of the $400,000 decline in fair value, Bloom attributes $250,000 to credit losses, and $150,000 to noncredit losses.
3. Bloom does not plan to sell the Taylor bonds prior to maturity, and does not believe it is more likely than not that it will have to sell the Taylor bonds before the bonds have a chance to recover their fair value. Bloom attributes the entire $400,000 decline in fair value to noncredit losses.

**E 12–27**
Available-for-sale debt securities; impairments
(Appendix 12B)
● **LO12–3**

(Note: This exercise is a variation of Exercise 12–26, modified to categorize the investment as securities available-for-sale.)
Assume all of the same facts and scenarios as E12–26, except that Bloom Corporation classifies their Taylor investment as AFS.

**Required:**
1. For each of the scenarios shown in E12–26, prepare the appropriate entry(s) at December 31, 2013. Indicate how the scenario will affect the 2013 income statement, OCI, and comprehensive income.
2. Repeat requirement 1, but now assume that, at the end of 2012, Bloom had recorded a temporary unrealized loss (not an OTT impairment) of $100,000 on the Taylor investment.

**E 12–28**
Available-for-sale equity securities; impairments
(Appendix 12B)
● **LO12–3**

In early December of 2013, Kettle Corp purchased $50,000 of Icalc Company common stock, which constitutes less than 1% of Icalc's outstanding shares. By December 31, 2013, the value of Icalc's investment had fallen to $40,000, and Kettle recorded an unrealized loss. By December 31, 2014, the value of the Icalc investment had fallen to $25,000, and Kettle determined that it can no longer assert that it has both the intent and ability to hold the shares long enough for their fair value to recover, so Kettle recorded an OTT impairment. By December 31, 2015, fair value had recovered to $30,000.

**Required:**
Prepare appropriate entry(s) at December 31, 2013, 2014, and 2015, and for each year indicate how the scenario will affect net income, OCI, and comprehensive income.

**E 12–29**
Accounting for impairments under IFRS
(Appendix 12B)
● **LO12–1,
LO12–3,
LO12–8**

🌐 **IFRS**

(Note: This exercise is a variation of E12–26 modified to consider accounting under IFRS.)
Flower Corporation uses IFRS, and purchased €1,000,000 of James Company 5% bonds at face value during 2013. Unfortunately, a combination of problems at James Company and in the debt market caused the fair value of the James investment to decline to €600,000 by December 31, 2013. On December 31, 2013, Flower calculated the present value of the future cash flows expected to be collected from the James investment (using the interest rate effective when the investment was made) to equal €750,000. Flower recognized an OTT impairment. By December 31, 2014 the fair value of the investment increased to €875,000, and Flower calculated the present value of the future cash flows expected to be collected from the James investment (again using the interest rate effective when the investment was made) to equal €800,000.

**Required:**
1. Prepare appropriate entry(s) to account for the James investment at December 31, 2013, assuming Flower classifies its James investment as held to maturity.

2. Prepare appropriate entry(s) to account for the James investment at December 31, 2014, assuming Flower classifies its James investment as held to maturity.

3. Prepare appropriate entry(s) to account for the James investment at December 31, 2013, assuming Flower classifies its James investment as available for sale.

4. Prepare appropriate entry(s) to account for the James investment at December 31, 2014, assuming Flower classifies its James investment as available for sale.

5. How would your answer to requirement 4 change if the James investment was equity rather than debt?

# CPA and CMA Review Questions

**CPA Exam Questions**

The following questions are adapted from a variety of sources including questions developed by the AICPA Board of Examiners and those used in the Kaplan CPA Review Course to study investments while preparing for the CPA examination. Determine the response that best completes the statements or questions.

● LO12–2

1. During year 4, Wall Co. purchased 2,000 shares of Hemp Corp. common stock for $31,500 as a short-term investment. The investment was appropriately classified as a trading security. The market value of this investment was $29,500 at December 31, year 4. Wall sold all of the Hemp common stock for $14 per share on January 15, year 5, incurring $1,400 in brokerage commissions and taxes. On the sale, Wall should report a realized loss of:
   a. $1,500
   b. $2,900
   c. $3,500
   d. $4,900

● LO12–3

2. The following information pertains to Lark Corp.'s long-term marketable equity securities portfolio:

|  | December 31 | |
|---|---|---|
|  | 2013 | 2012 |
| Cost | $200,000 | $200,000 |
| Fair value | 240,000 | 180,000 |

Differences between cost and market values are considered to be temporary. The decline in market value was properly accounted for at December 31, 2012. At December 31, 2013, what is the net unrealized holding gain or loss to be reported as:

|  | Other Comprehensive Income | Accumulated Other Comprehensive Income |
|---|---|---|
| a. | $60,000 gain | $40,000 gain |
| b. | $40,000 gain | $60,000 gain |
| c. | $20,000 loss | $20,000 loss |
| d. | –0– | –0– |

● LO12–3

3. The following information was extracted from Gil Co.'s December 31, 2013, balance sheet:

| Noncurrent assets: | |
|---|---|
| Long-term investments in marketable equity securities (at fair value) | $96,450 |
| Stockholders' equity: | |
| Accumulated other comprehensive income** | (25,000) |

**Includes a net unrealized holding loss on long-term investments in marketable equity securities of $19,800.

The historical cost of the long-term investments in marketable equity securities was:
   a. $ 63,595
   b. $ 76,650
   c. $ 96,450
   d. $116,250

● LO12–3

4. On both December 31, 2012, and December 31, 2013, Kopp Co.'s only equity security investment had the same fair value, which was below its original cost. Kopp considered the decline in value to be temporary in 2012 but other-than-temporary in 2013. At the end of both years the security was classified as

a noncurrent asset. Kopp could not exercise significant influence over the investee. What should be the effects of the determination that the decline was other-than-temporary on Kopp's 2013 net noncurrent assets and net income?

a. Decrease in both net noncurrent assets and net income.
b. No effect on both net noncurrent assets and net income.
c. Decrease in net noncurrent assets and no effect on net income.
d. No effect on net noncurrent assets and decrease in net income.

● LO12–5      5. When the equity method is used to account for investments in common stock, which of the following affect(s) the investor's reported investment income?

|   | A Change in Fair Value of Investee's Common Stock | Cash Dividends from Investee |
|---|---|---|
| a. | Yes | Yes |
| b. | No | Yes |
| c. | Yes | No |
| d. | No | No |

● LO12–5      6. A corporation uses the equity method to account for its 40% ownership of another company. The investee earned $20,000 and paid $5,000 in dividends. The investor made the following entries:

| | | |
|---|---|---|
| Investment in affiliate ................................................................ | $8,000 | |
| Equity in earnings of affiliate ...................................................... | | $8,000 |
| Cash ......................................................................................... | 2,000 | |
| Dividend revenue ..................................................................... | | 2,000 |

What effect will these entries have on the investor's statement of financial position?
a. Investment in affiliate overstated, retained earnings understated.
b. Financial position will be fairly stated.
c. Investment in affiliate overstated, retained earnings overstated.
d. Investment in affiliate understated, retained earnings understated.

● LO12–6      7. Park Co. uses the equity method to account for its January 1, 2013, purchase of Tun Inc.'s common stock. On January 1, 2013, the fair values of Tun's FIFO inventory and land exceeded their carrying amounts. How do these excesses of fair values over carrying amounts affect Park's reported equity in Tun's 2013 earnings?

|   | Inventory Excess | Land Excess |
|---|---|---|
| a. | Decrease | Decrease |
| b. | Decrease | No effect |
| c. | Increase | No effect |
| d. | Increase | Increase |

● LO12–4      8. On January 2, 2013, Well Co. purchased 10% of Rea Inc.'s outstanding common shares for $400,000. Well is the largest single shareholder in Rea, and Well's officers are a majority on Rea's board of directors. Rea reported net income of $500,000 for 2013, and paid dividends of $150,000. In its December 31, 2013, balance sheet, what amount should Well report as investment in Rea?

a. $435,000
b. $450,000
c. $400,000
d. $385,000

Beginning in 2011, International Financial Reporting Standards are tested on the CPA exam along with U.S. GAAP. The following questions deal with the application of IFRS to accounting for investments.

● LO12–8      9. Under *IFRS No. 9,* which of the following is *not* a category into which a debt investment can be classified?

a. FVTPL ("fair value through profit and loss").
b. FVTOCI ("fair value through other comprehensive income").
c. Amortized cost.
d. Parts a–c are all classifications in which a debt investment might be classified under *IFRS No. 9.*

● LO12–8      10. Under *IFRS No. 9,* which of the following is *not* a category in which an equity investment can be classified?

a. FVTPL ("Fair Value through Profit and Loss").
b. FVTOCI ("Fair Value through Other Comprehensive Income").
c. Amortized cost.
d. Parts a–c are all classifications in which an equity investment is classified under *IFRS No. 9.*

● LO12–8

🌐 IFRS

11. Which of the following is *not* true about transfers between investment categories under IFRS?

    a. Under *IAS No. 39,* transfers of debt investments out of FVTPL into AFS or HTM is permitted under rare circumstances.

    b. Under *IFRS No. 9,* transfers of debt investments out of FVTPL to amortized cost are possible if the business model changes with respect to the debt investment.

    c. Under *IFRS No. 9,* transfers of equity investments out of FVTOCI to FVTPL are possible if the business model changes with respect to the equity investment.

    d. Parts a–c are all true about transfers between investment categories under IFRS.

● LO12–8

🌐 IFRS

12. Which of the following is true about use of the equity method under IFRS?

    a. IFRS allows use of the fair value option under essentially the same circumstances as does U.S. GAAP for investments that otherwise would be accounted for under the equity method.

    b. *IFRS No. 11* allows proportionate consolidation rather than the equity method for investments that qualify as joint ventures.

    c. FVTPL is preferred to the equity method when the investor can exercise significant influence over the operations of the investee.

    d. *IAS No. 28* requires that the accounting policies of investees be adjusted to correspond to those of the investor.

● LO12–8

🌐 IFRS

13. Which of the following is true about accounting for other-than-temporary impairments under IFRS?

    a. Recoveries of OTT impairments for debt investments can be recognized in earnings.

    b. Recoveries of OTT impairments for equity investments can be recognized in earnings.

    c. Under IFRS, the amount of OTT impairment calculated for a debt investment is the same regardless of whether the investment is classified as held-to-maturity or available-for-sale.

    d. Two of the three answers included in a-c are true.

**CMA Exam Questions**

The following questions dealing with investments are adapted from questions that previously appeared on Certified Management Accountant (CMA) examinations. The CMA designation sponsored by the Institute of Management Accountants (www.imanet.org) provides members with an objective measure of knowledge and competence in the field of management accounting. Determine the response that best completes the statements or questions.

● LO12–3

1. An investment in available-for-sale securities is valued on the balance sheet at

    a. The cost to acquire the asset.

    b. Accumulated income minus accumulated dividends since acquisition.

    c. Fair value.

    d. The par or stated value of the securities.

Questions 2 and 3 are based on the following information concerning Monahan Company's portfolio of debt securities at May 31, year 2 and May 31, year 3. All of the debt securities were purchased by Monahan during June, year 1. Prior to June, year 1, Monahan had no investments in debt or equity securities.

| As of May 31, Year 2 | Amortized Cost | Fair Value |
| --- | --- | --- |
| Cleary Company bonds | $164,526 | $168,300 |
| Beauchamp Industry bonds | 204,964 | 205,200 |
| Morrow Inc. bonds | 305,785 | 285,200 |
| Total | $675,275 | $658,700 |

| As of May 31, Year 3 | Amortized Cost | Fair Value |
| --- | --- | --- |
| Cleary Company bonds | $152,565 | $147,600 |
| Beauchamp Industry bonds | 193,800 | 204,500 |
| Morrow Inc. bonds | 289,130 | 291,400 |
| Total | $635,495 | $643,500 |

● LO12–3

2. Assuming that the above securities are properly classified as available-for-sale securities under U.S. GAAP, the unrealized holding gain or loss as of May 31, year 3 would be

    a. recognized as an $8,005 unrealized holding gain on the income statement.

    b. recognized in accumulated other comprehensive income by a year-end credit balance of $8,005.

    c. recognized in accumulated other comprehensive income by a year-end debit balance of $8,005.

    d. not recognized.

● LO12–1

3. Assuming that the above securities are properly classified as held-to-maturity securities under U.S. GAAP, the unrealized holding gain or loss as of May 31, year 3 would be

    a. recognized as an $8,005 unrealized holding gain on the income statement.

    b. recognized in accumulated other comprehensive income by a year-end credit balance of $8,005.

    c. recognized in accumulated other comprehensive income by a year-end debit balance of $8,005.

    d. not recognized.

# Problems

An alternate exercise and problem set is available on the text website: www.mhhe.com/spiceland7e

**P 12–1**
Securities held-to-maturity; bond investment; effective interest
● LO12–1

Fuzzy Monkey Technologies, Inc., purchased as a long-term investment $80 million of 8% bonds, dated January 1, on January 1, 2013. Management has the positive intent and ability to hold the bonds until maturity. For bonds of similar risk and maturity the market yield was 10%. The price paid for the bonds was $66 million. Interest is received semiannually on June 30 and December 31. Due to changing market conditions, the fair value of the bonds at December 31, 2013, was $70 million.

**Required:**
1. Prepare the journal entry to record Fuzzy Monkey's investment on January 1, 2013.
2. Prepare the journal entry by Fuzzy Monkey to record interest on June 30, 2013 (at the effective rate).
3. Prepare the journal entry by Fuzzy Monkey to record interest on December 31, 2013 (at the effective rate).
4. At what amount will Fuzzy Monkey report its investment in the December 31, 2013, balance sheet? Why?
5. How would Fuzzy Monkey's 2013 statement of cash flows be affected by this investment?

**P 12–2**
Trading securities; bond investment; effective interest
● LO12–2

[This problem is a variation of Problem 12–1, modified to categorize the investment as trading securities.]
  Fuzzy Monkey Technologies, Inc., purchased as a short-term investment $80 million of 8% bonds, dated January 1, on January 1, 2013. Management intends to include the investment in a short-term, active trading portfolio. For bonds of similar risk and maturity the market yield was 10%. The price paid for the bonds was $66 million. Interest is received semiannually on June 30 and December 31. Due to changing market conditions, the fair value of the bonds at December 31, 2013, was $70 million.

**Required:**
1. Prepare the journal entry to record Fuzzy Monkey's investment on January 1, 2013.
2. Prepare the journal entry by Fuzzy Monkey to record interest on June 30, 2013 (at the effective rate).
3. Prepare the journal entry by Fuzzy Monkey to record interest on December 31, 2013 (at the effective rate).
4. At what amount will Fuzzy Monkey report its investment in the December 31, 2013, balance sheet? Why? Prepare any entry necessary to achieve this reporting objective.
5. How would Fuzzy Monkey's 2013 statement of cash flows be affected by this investment?

**P 12–3**
Securities available-for-sale; bond investment; effective interest
● LO12–3

[This problem is a variation of Problem 12–1, modified to categorize the investment as securities available-for-sale.]
  Fuzzy Monkey Technologies, Inc., purchased as a long-term investment $80 million of 8% bonds, dated January 1, on January 1, 2013. Management intends to have the investment available for sale when circumstances warrant. For bonds of similar risk and maturity the market yield was 10%. The price paid for the bonds was $66 million. Interest is received semiannually on June 30 and December 31. Due to changing market conditions, the fair value of the bonds at December 31, 2013, was $70 million.

**Required:**
1. Prepare the journal entry to record Fuzzy Monkey's investment on January 1, 2013.
2. Prepare the journal entry by Fuzzy Monkey to record interest on June 30, 2013 (at the effective rate).
3. Prepare the journal entry by Fuzzy Monkey to record interest on December 31, 2013 (at the effective rate).
4. At what amount will Fuzzy Monkey report its investment in the December 31, 2013, balance sheet? Why? Prepare any entry necessary to achieve this reporting objective.
5. How would Fuzzy Monkey's 2013 statement of cash flows be affected by this investment?

**P 12–4**
Fair value option; bond investment; effective interest
● LO12–1,
  LO12–2,
  LO12–3,
  LO12–7

[This problem is a variation of Problem 12–3, modified to cause the investment to be accounted for under the fair value option.]
  Fuzzy Monkey Technologies, Inc., purchased as a long-term investment $80 million of 8% bonds, dated January 1, on January 1, 2013. Management intends to have the investment available for sale when circumstances warrant. When the company purchased the bonds, management elected to account for them under the fair value option. For bonds of similar risk and maturity the market yield was 10%. The price paid for the bonds was $66 million. Interest is received semiannually on June 30 and December 31. Due to changing market conditions, the fair value of the bonds at December 31, 2013, was $70 million.

**Required:**
1. Prepare the journal entry to record Fuzzy Monkey's investment on January 1, 2013.
2. Prepare the journal entry by Fuzzy Monkey to record interest on June 30, 2013 (at the effective rate).
3. Prepare the journal entries by Fuzzy Monkey to record interest on December 31, 2013 (at the effective rate).
4. At what amount will Fuzzy Monkey report its investment in the December 31, 2013, balance sheet? Why? Prepare any entry necessary to achieve this reporting objective.

5. How would Fuzzy Monkey's 2013 statement of cash flows be affected by this investment?

6. How would your answers to requirements 1–5 differ if management had the intent and ability to hold the investments until maturity?

**P 12–5**
**Various transactions related to securities available-for-sale**
● **LO12–3**

The following selected transactions relate to investment activities of Ornamental Insulation Corporation. The company buys securities, *not* intending to profit from short-term differences in price and *not* necessarily to hold debt securities to maturity, but to have them available for sale when circumstances warrant. Ornamental's fiscal year ends on December 31. No investments were held by Ornamental on December 31, 2012.

**2013**

| Feb. 21 | Acquired Distribution Transformers Corporation common shares costing $400,000. |
| Mar. 18 | Received cash dividends of $8,000 on the investment in Distribution Transformers common shares. |
| Sep. 1 | Acquired $900,000 of American Instruments' 10% bonds at face value. |
| Oct. 20 | Sold the Distribution Transformers shares for $425,000. |
| Nov. 1 | Purchased M&D Corporation common shares costing $1,400,000. |
| Dec. 31 | Recorded any necessary adjusting entry(s) relating to the investments. The market prices of the investments are: |

| | |
|---|---|
| American Instruments bonds | $ 850,000 |
| M&D Corporation shares | $1,460,000 |

(Hint: Interest must be accrued for the American Instruments' bonds.)

**2014**

| Jan. 20 | Sold the M&D Corporation shares for $1,485,000. |
| Mar. 1 | Received semiannual interest of $45,000 on the investment in American Instruments bonds. |
| Aug. 12 | Acquired Vast Communication common shares costing $650,000. |
| Sept. 1 | Received semiannual interest of $45,000 on the investment in American Instruments bonds. |
| Dec. 31 | Recorded any necessary adjusting entry(s) relating to the investments. The market prices of the investments are: |

| | |
|---|---|
| Vast Communication shares | $670,000 |
| American Instruments bonds | $830,000 |

**Required:**

1. Prepare the appropriate journal entry for each transaction or event during 2013.

2. Indicate any amounts that Ornamental Insulation would report in its 2013 balance sheet and income statement as a result of these investments.

3. Prepare the appropriate journal entry for each transaction or event during 2014.

4. Indicate any amounts that Ornamental Insulation would report in its 2014 balance sheet and income statement as a result of these investments.

**P 12–6**
**Various transactions relating to trading securities**
● **LO12–2**

American Surety and Fidelity buys and sells securities expecting to earn profits on short-term differences in price. For the first 11 months of 2013, gains from selling trading securities totaled $8 million, losses were $11 million, and the company had earned $5 million in investment revenue. The following selected transactions relate to American's trading account during December 2013, and the first week of 2014. The company's fiscal year ends on December 31. No trading securities were held by American on December 1, 2013.

**2013**

| Dec. 12 | Purchased FF&G Corporation bonds for $12 million. |
| 13 | Purchased 2 million Ferry Intercommunications common shares for $22 million. |
| 15 | Sold the FF&G Corporation bonds for $12.1 million. |
| 22 | Purchased U.S. Treasury bills for $56 million and Treasury bonds for $65 million. |
| 23 | Sold half the Ferry Intercommunications common shares for $10 million. |
| 26 | Sold the U.S. Treasury bills for $57 million. |
| 27 | Sold the Treasury bonds for $63 million. |
| 28 | Received cash dividends of $200,000 from the Ferry Intercommunications common shares. |
| 31 | Recorded any necessary adjusting entry(s) and closing entries relating to the investments. The market price of the Ferry Intercommunications stock was $10 per share. |

**2014**

| Jan. 2 | Sold the remaining Ferry Intercommunications common shares for $10.2 million. |
| 5 | Purchased Warehouse Designs Corporation bonds for $34 million. |

**Required:**

1. Prepare the appropriate journal entry for each transaction or event during 2013, including the closing entry to income summary for the year.
2. Indicate any amounts that American would report in its 2013 balance sheet and income statement as a result of these investments.
3. Prepare the appropriate journal entry for each transaction or event during 2014.

**P 12–7**
Securities held-to-maturity, securities available for sale, and trading securities
● LO12–1, LO12–2, LO12–3

Amalgamated General Corporation is a consulting firm that also offers financial services through its credit division. From time to time the company buys and sells securities intending to earn profits on short-term differences in price. The following selected transactions relate to Amalgamated's investment activities during the last quarter of 2013 and the first month of 2014. The only securities held by Amalgamated at October 1 were $30 million of 10% bonds of Kansas Abstractors, Inc., purchased on May 1 at face value. The company's fiscal year ends on December 31.

**2013**

| | |
|---|---|
| Oct. 18 | Purchased 2 million preferred shares of Millwork Ventures Company for $58 million as a speculative investment to be sold under suitable circumstances. |
| 31 | Received semiannual interest of $1.5 million from the Kansas Abstractors bonds. |
| Nov. 1 | Purchased 10% bonds of Holistic Entertainment Enterprises at their $18 million face value, to be held until they mature in 2018. Semiannual interest is payable April 30 and October 31. |
| 1 | Sold the Kansas Abstractors bonds for $28 million because rising interest rates are expected to cause their fair value to continue to fall. |
| Dec. 1 | Purchased 12% bonds of Household Plastics Corporation at their $60 million face value, to be held until they mature in 2028. Semiannual interest is payable May 31 and November 30. |
| 20 | Purchased U. S. Treasury bonds for $5.6 million as trading securities, hoping to earn profits on short-term differences in prices. |
| 21 | Purchased 4 million common shares of NXS Corporation for $44 million as trading securities, hoping to earn profits on short-term differences in prices. |
| 23 | Sold the Treasury bonds for $5.7 million. |
| 29 | Received cash dividends of $3 million from the Millwork Ventures Company preferred shares. |
| 31 | Recorded any necessary adjusting entry(s) and closing entries relating to the investments. The market price of the Millwork Ventures Company preferred stock was $27.50 per share and $11.50 per share for the NXS Corporation common. The fair values of the bond investments were $58.7 million for Household Plastics Corporation and $16.7 million for Holistic Entertainment Enterprises. |

**2014**

| | |
|---|---|
| Jan. 7 | Sold the NXS Corporation common shares for $43 million. |

**Required:**
Prepare the appropriate journal entry for each transaction or event.

**P 12–8**
Securities available-for-sale; fair value adjustment; reclassification adjustment
● LO12–3

At December 31, 2013, the investments in securities available-for-sale of Beale Developments were reported at $78 million:

| | | |
|---|---|---|
| Securities available-for-sale | $74 | |
| Plus: Fair value adjustment | 4 | $78 |

During 2014, Beale sold its investment in Schwab Pharmaceuticals, which had cost $25 million, for $28 million. Those shares had a fair value at December 31, 2013, of $27 million. No other investments were sold. At December 31, 2014, the investments in securities available-for-sale included the cost and fair value amounts shown below.

| ($ in millions) Securities Available-for-Sale | Cost | Fair Value | Unrealized Gain (Loss) |
|---|---|---|---|
| Daisy Theaters, Inc. shares | $40 | $42 | $2 |
| Orpheum Entertainment bonds | 9 | 12 | 3 |
| Totals | $49 | $54 | $5 |

**Required:**

1. At what amount should Beale report its securities available-for-sale in its December 31, 2014, balance sheet?
2. What journal entry is needed to enable the investment to be reported at this amount?
3. What is the amount of the reclassification adjustment to 2014 other comprehensive income? Show how the reclassification adjustment should be reported.

**P 12–9**

Investment securities and equity method investments compared

● **LO12–3, LO12–4, LO12–5, LO12–6**

On January 4, 2013, Runyan Bakery paid $324 million for 10 million shares of Lavery Labeling Company common stock. The investment represents a 30% interest in the net assets of Lavery and gave Runyan the ability to exercise significant influence over Lavery's operations. Runyan received dividends of $2.00 per share on December 15, 2013, and Lavery reported net income of $160 million for the year ended December 31, 2013. The market value of Lavery's common stock at December 31, 2013, was $31 per share. On the purchase date, the book value of Lavery's net assets was $800 million and:

a. The fair value of Lavery's depreciable assets, with an average remaining useful life of six years, exceeded their book value by $80 million.

b. The remainder of the excess of the cost of the investment over the book value of net assets purchased was attributable to goodwill.

**Required:**

1. Prepare all appropriate journal entries related to the investment during 2013, assuming Runyan accounts for this investment by the equity method.

2. Prepare the journal entries required by Runyan, assuming that the 10 million shares represent a 10% interest in the net assets of Lavery rather than a 30% interest.

**P 12–10**

Fair value option; equity method investments

● **LO12–2, LO12–4, LO12–7**

[This problem is a variation of Problem 12–9 focusing on the fair value option.]

On January 4, 2013, Runyan Bakery paid $324 million for 10 million shares of Lavery Labeling Company common stock. The investment represents a 30% interest in the net assets of Lavery and gave Runyan the ability to exercise significant influence over Lavery's operations. Runyan chose the fair value option to account for this investment. Runyan received dividends of $2.00 per share on December 15, 2013, and Lavery reported net income of $160 million for the year ended December 31, 2013. The market value of Lavery's common stock at December 31, 2013, was $31 per share. On the purchase date, the book value of Lavery's net assets was $800 million and:

a. The fair value of Lavery's depreciable assets, with an average remaining useful life of six years, exceeded their book value by $80 million.

b. The remainder of the excess of the cost of the investment over the book value of net assets purchased was attributable to goodwill.

**Required:**

1. Prepare all appropriate journal entries related to the investment during 2013, assuming Runyan accounts for this investment under the fair value option in a manner similar to what they would use for trading securities.

2. What would be the effect of this investment on Runyan's 2013 net income?

**P 12–11**

Fair value option; equity method investments

● **LO12–2, LO12–4, LO12–5, LO12–7**

[This problem is an expanded version of Problem 12–10 that considers alternative ways in which a firm might apply the fair value option to account for significant-influence investments that would normally be accounted for under the equity method.]

Companies can choose the fair value option for investments that otherwise would be accounted for under the equity method. If the fair value option is chosen, the investment is shown at fair value in the balance sheet, and unrealized holding gains and losses are recognized in the income statement. However, exactly how a company complies with those broad requirements is up to the company. This problem requires you to consider alternative ways in which a company might apply the fair value option for investments that otherwise would be accounted for under the equity method.

On January 4, 2013, Runyan Bakery paid $324 million for 10 million shares of Lavery Labeling Company common stock. The investment represents a 30% interest in the net assets of Lavery and gave Runyan the ability to exercise significant influence over Lavery's operations. Runyan chose the fair value option to account for this investment. Runyan received dividends of $2.00 per share on December 15, 2013, and Lavery reported net income of $160 million for the year ended December 31, 2013. The market value of Lavery's common stock at December 31, 2013, was $31 per share. On the purchase date, the book value of Lavery's net assets was $800 million and:

a. The fair value of Lavery's depreciable assets, with an average remaining useful life of six years, exceeded their book value by $80 million.

b. The remainder of the excess of the cost of the investment over the book value of net assets purchased was attributable to goodwill.

**Required:**

1. Prepare all appropriate journal entries related to the investment during 2013, assuming Runyan accounts for this investment under the fair value option, and simply accounts for the Lavery investment in a manner similar to what it would use for trading securities. Indicate the effect of these journal entries on 2013 net income, and show the amount at which the investment is carried in the December 31, 2013, balance sheet.

2. Prepare all appropriate journal entries related to the investment during 2013, assuming Runyan accounts for this investment under the fair value option, but uses equity method accounting to account for Lavery's income and dividends, and then records a fair value adjustment at the end of the year that allows it to comply with GAAP. Indicate the effect of these journal entries on 2013 net income, and show the amount at which the investment is carried in the December 31, 2013, balance sheet. (Note: You should end up with the same total 2013 income effect and same carrying value on the balance sheet for requirements 1 and 2.)

**P 12–12**
**Equity method**
● **LO12–5,**
   **LO12–6**

Northwest Paperboard Company, a paper and allied products manufacturer, was seeking to gain a foothold in Canada. Toward that end, the company bought 40% of the outstanding common shares of Vancouver Timber and Milling, Inc., on January 2, 2013, for $400 million.

At the date of purchase, the book value of Vancouver's net assets was $775 million. The book values and fair values for all balance sheet items were the same except for inventory and plant facilities. The fair value exceeded book value by $5 million for the inventory and by $20 million for the plant facilities.

The estimated useful life of the plant facilities is 16 years. All inventory acquired was sold during 2013.

Vancouver reported net income of $140 million for the year ended December 31, 2013. Vancouver paid a cash dividend of $30 million.

**Required:**
1. Prepare all appropriate journal entries related to the investment during 2013.
2. What amount should Northwest report as its income from its investment in Vancouver for the year ended December 31, 2013?
3. What amount should Northwest report in its balance sheet as its investment in Vancouver?
4. What should Northwest report in its statement of cash flows regarding its investment in Vancouver?

**P 12–13**
**Equity method**
● **LO12–5,**
   **LO12–6**

On January 2, 2013, Miller Properties paid $19 million for 1 million shares of Marlon Company's 6 million outstanding common shares. Miller's CEO became a member of Marlon's board of directors during the first quarter of 2013.

The carrying amount of Marlon's net assets was $66 million. Miller estimated the fair value of those net assets to be the same except for a patent valued at $24 million above cost. The remaining amortization period for the patent is 10 years.

Marlon reported earnings of $12 million and paid dividends of $6 million during 2013. On December 31, 2013, Marlon's common stock was trading on the NYSE at $18.50 per share.

**Required:**
1. When considering whether to account for its investment in Marlon under the equity method, what criteria should Miller's management apply?
2. Assume Miller accounts for its investment in Marlon using the equity method. Ignoring income taxes, determine the amounts related to the investment to be reported in its 2013:
   a. Income statement.
   b. Balance sheet.
   c. Statement of cash flows.

**P 12–14**
**Classifying investments**
● **LO12–1 through**
   **LO12–5**

Indicate (by letter) the way each of the investments listed below most likely should be accounted for based on the information provided.

| Item | Reporting Category |
|---|---|
| _____ 1. 35% of the nonvoting preferred stock of American Aircraft Company. | T. Trading securities |
| _____ 2. Treasury bills to be held to maturity. | M. Securities held-to-maturity |
| _____ 3. Two-year note receivable from affiliate. | A. Securities available-for-sale |
| _____ 4. Accounts receivable. | E. Equity method |
| _____ 5. Treasury bond maturing in one week. | C. Consolidation |
| _____ 6. Common stock held in trading account for immediate resale. | N. None of these |
| _____ 7. Bonds acquired to profit from short-term differences in price. | |
| _____ 8. 35% of the voting common stock of Computer Storage Devices Company. | |
| _____ 9. 90% of the voting common stock of Affiliated Peripherals, Inc. | |
| _____ 10. Corporate bonds of Primary Smelting Company to be sold if interest rates fall ½%. | |
| _____ 11. 25% of the voting common stock of Smith Foundries Corporation: 51% family-owned by Smith family; fair value determinable. | |
| _____ 12. 17% of the voting common stock of Shipping Barrels Corporation: Investor's CEO on the board of directors of Shipping Barrels Corporation. | |

**P 12–15**
Fair value option;
held-to-maturity
investments

● **LO12–1,**
  **LO12–7**

On January 1, 2013, Ithaca Corp. purchases Cortland Inc. bonds that have a face value of $150,000. The Cortland bonds have a stated interest rate of 6%. Interest is paid semiannually on June 30 and December 31, and the bonds mature in 10 years. For bonds of similar risk and maturity, the market yield on particular dates is as follows:

| | |
|---|---|
| January 1, 2013 | 7.0% |
| June 30, 2013 | 8.0% |
| December 31, 2013 | 9.0% |

**Required:**

1. Calculate the price Ithaca would have paid for the Cortland bonds on January 1, 2013 (ignoring brokerage fees), and prepare a journal entry to record the purchase.

2. Prepare all appropriate journal entries related to the bond investment during 2013, assuming Ithaca accounts for the bonds as a held-to-maturity investment. Ithaca calculates interest revenue at the effective interest rate as of the date it purchased the bonds.

3. Prepare all appropriate journal entries related to the bond investment during 2013, assuming that Ithaca chose the fair value option when the bonds were purchased, and that Ithaca determines fair value of the bonds semi-annually. Ithaca calculates interest revenue at the effective interest rate as of the date it purchased the bonds.

**P 12–16**
Accounting
for other-than-
temporary
impairments
(Appendix 12B)

● **LO12–1,**
  **LO12–2,**
  **LO12–3**

Stewart Enterprises has the following investments, all purchased prior to 2013:

1. Bee Company 5% bonds, purchased at face value, with an amortized cost of $4,000,000, and classified as held to maturity. At December 31, 2013, the Bee investment had a fair value of $3,500,000, and Stewart cal-culated that $240,000 of the fair value decline is a credit loss and $260,000 is a noncredit loss. At December 31, 2014, the Bee investment had a fair value of $3,700,000, and Stewart calculated that $140,000 of the dif-ference between fair value and amortized cost was a credit loss and $160,000 was a noncredit loss.

2. Oliver Corporation 4% bonds, purchased at face value, with an amortized cost of $2,500,000, classified as a trading security. Because of unrealized losses prior to 2013, the Oliver bonds have a fair value adjustment account with a credit balance of $200,000, such that the carrying value of the Oliver investment is $2,300,000 prior to making any adjusting entries in 2013. At December 31, 2013, the Oliver investment had a fair value of $2,200,000, and Stewart calculated that $120,000 of the difference between amortized cost and fair value is a credit loss and $180,000 is a noncredit loss. At December 31, 2014, the Oliver investment had a fair value of $2,700,000.

3. Jones Inc. 6% bonds, purchased at face value, with an amortized cost of $3,500,000, and classified as an available-for-sale investment. Because of unrealized losses prior to 2013, the Jones bonds have a fair value adjustment account with a credit balance of $400,000, such that the carrying value of the Jones investment is $3,100,000 prior to making any adjusting entries in 2013. At December 31, 2013, the Jones investment had a fair value of $2,700,000, and Stewart calculated that $225,000 of the difference between amortized cost and fair value is a credit loss and $575,000 is a noncredit loss. At December 31, 2014, the Jones investment had a fair value of $2,900,000, and Stewart calculated that $125,000 of the difference between amortized cost and fair value is a credit loss and $475,000 is a noncredit loss.

4. Helms Corp. equity, purchased for $1,000,000, classified as available for sale. Because of unrealized gains prior to 2013, the Helms shares have a fair value adjustment account with a debit balance of $120,000, such that the carrying value of the Helms investment is $1,120,000 prior to making any adjusting entries in 2013. At December 31, 2013 and 2014, the Helms investment had a fair value of $600,000 and $700,000, respectively.

Stewart does not intend to sell any of these investments and does not believe it is more likely than not that it will have to sell any of the bond investments before fair value recovers. However, Stewart cannot assert that it has the ability to hold the Helms equity investment before fair value recovers.

**Required:**
Prepare the appropriate adjusting journal entries to account for fair value changes during 2013 and 2014, assuming that each investment is viewed as qualifying as an other-than-temporary (OTT) impairment as of December 31, 2013, and then is accounted for normally during 2014 (with no additional OTT impairment in 2014).

**P 12–17**
Accounting
for other-than-
temporary
impairments
under IFRS
(Appendix 12B)

● **LO12–1, LO12–2,**
  **LO12–3, LO12–8**

**IFRS**

[This problem is a variation of Problem 12–16, modified to consider accounting for impairments under IFRS.]

**Required:**
Consider the facts presented in P12–16, and assume that Stewart accounts for its investments under IFRS. Pre-pare the appropriate adjusting journal entries to account for fair value changes during 2013 and 2014, assuming that Stewart views each investment as meeting any criteria necessary for recognizing an other-than-temporary (OTT) impairment as of December 31, 2013, and then is accounted for normally during 2014 (with no additional OTT impairment in 2014).

# Broaden Your Perspective

Apply your critical-thinking ability to the knowledge you've gained. These cases will provide you an opportunity to develop your research, analysis, judgment, and communication skills. You also will work with other students, integrate what you've learned, apply it in real world situations, and consider its global and ethical ramifications. This practice will broaden your knowledge and further develop your decision-making abilities.

**Real World Case 12–1**
Intel's investments
● LO12–3

The following disclosure note appeared in the July 2, 2011 quarterly financial statement of the **Intel Corporation**.

**Note 7: Available-for-Sale Investments (partial)**

**Table 1:** Available-for-sale investments as of July 2, 2011, and December 25, 2010, were as follows:

| (In millions) | July 2, 2011 | | | | December 25, 2010 | | | |
| --- | --- | --- | --- | --- | --- | --- | --- | --- |
| | Adjusted Cost | Gross Unrealized Gains | Gross Unrealized Losses | Fair Value | Adjusted Cost | Gross Unrealized Gains | Gross Unrealized Losses | Fair Value |
| Commercial paper | $ 3,777 | $ — | $ — | $ 3,777 | $ 5,312 | $ — | $ — | $ 5,312 |
| Government bonds | 1,392 | 1 | (1) | 1,392 | 10,075 | 9 | (5) | 10,079 |
| Corporate bonds | 1,332 | 13 | (3) | 1,342 | 2,250 | 9 | (4) | 2,255 |
| Bank deposits | 1,155 | — | (1) | 1,154 | 1,550 | 1 | — | 1,551 |
| Marketable equity securities | 334 | 568 | (10) | 892 | 380 | 629 | (1) | 1,008 |
| Asset-backed securities | 69 | — | (10) | 59 | 76 | — | (9) | 67 |
| Money market fund deposits | 550 | — | — | 550 | 34 | — | — | 34 |
| **Total available-for-sale investments** | **$ 8,609** | **$ 582** | **$ (25)** | **$ 9,166** | **$19,677** | **$ 648** | **$ (19)** | **$20,306** |

**Table 2:** The before-tax net unrealized holding gains (losses) on available-for-sale investments that have been included in accumulated other comprehensive income (loss) were as follows:

| (In millions) | Three Months Ended | | Six Months Ended | |
| --- | --- | --- | --- | --- |
| | July 2, 2011 | June 26, 2010 | July 2, 2011 | June 26, 2010 |
| Net unrealized holding gains (losses) included in other comprehensive income (loss) | $ (12) | $ (17) | $ 24 | $ 134 |
| Net gains (losses) reclassified from accumulated other comprehensive income (loss) into earnings | $ 44 | $ 7 | $ 88 | $ 74 |

**Required:**

1. Looking only at Table 1, draw a T-account that shows the change between the December 25, 2010, and July 2, 2011, balances for the fair value adjustment associated with Intel's AFS investments for the first half of 2011. By how much did the fair value change during the first half of 2011?

2. Now look at Table 2, and prepare a journal entry that recognizes for the first six months of 2011 any net unrealized holding gains and losses. Ignore income taxes.

3. Using your journal entry from requirement 2, adjust your T-account from requirement 1. Have you accounted for the entire change in the fair value adjustment that occurred during the first half of 2011? Reconsider Table 2, and speculate as to what could be causing the difference.

**Real World Case 12–2**
Reporting securities available-for-sale; obtain and critically evaluate an annual report
● LO12–3

Investments in common stocks potentially affect each of the various financial statements as well as the disclosure notes that accompany those statements.

**Required:**

1. Locate a recent annual report of a public company that includes a disclosure note that describes an investment in securities available-for-sale. You can use EDGAR at **www.sec.gov**.

2. Under what caption are the investments reported in the comparative balance sheets? Are they reported as current or noncurrent assets?

3. Are realized gains or losses reported in the comparative income statements?

4. Where are unrealized gains or losses reported in the comparative financial statements?

5. Under what caption are unrealized gains or losses listed in the comparative balance sheets? Why are unrealized gains or losses reported here rather than in the income statements?

6. Are cash flow effects of these investments reflected in the company's comparative statements of cash flows? If so, what information is provided by this disclosure?

7. Does the disclosure note provide information not available in the financial statements?

**International Case 12–3**
Comparison of equity method between IFRS and U.S. GAAP
● LO12–4, LO12–5, LO12–6, LO12–8

 IFRS

The following are excerpts from the 2010 financial statements of **Renault**, a large French automobile manufacturer.

---

**14–INVESTMENT IN NISSAN**

A–Nissan consolidation method
Following the operations described in "Significant events," Renault's investment in Nissan was down slightly, from 44.3% in 2009 to 43.4% in 2010. Renault and Nissan have chosen to develop a unique type of alliance between two distinct companies with common interests, uniting forces to achieve optimum performance. The Alliance is organized so as to preserve individual brand identities and respect each company's corporate culture.

Consequently:

- Renault does not hold the majority of Nissan voting rights.

- The terms of the Renault-Nissan agreements do not entitle Renault to appoint the majority of Nissan directors, nor to hold the majority of voting rights at meetings of Nissan's Board of Directors; at December 31, 2010 as in 2009, Renault supplied four of the total nine members of Nissan's Board of Directors.

- Renault Nissan BV, owned 50% by Renault and 50% by Nissan, is the Alliance's joint decision-making body for strategic issues concerning either group individually. Its decisions are applicable to both Renault and Nissan. This entity does not enable Renault to direct Nissan's financial and operating strategies, and cannot therefore be considered to represent contractual control by Renault over Nissan. The matters examined by Renault Nissan BV since it was formed have remained strictly within this contractual framework, and are not an indication that Renault exercises control over Nissan.

- Renault can neither use nor influence the use of Nissan's assets in the same way as its own assets.

- Renault provides no guarantees in respect of Nissan's debt.

In view of this situation, Renault is considered to exercise significant influence in Nissan, and therefore uses the equity method to include its investment in Nissan in the consolidation.

F–Nissan financial information under IFRS (partial)
(When accounting for its investment in Nissan, Renault makes restatements that) include adjustments for harmonisation of accounting standards and the adjustments to fair value of assets and liabilities applied by Renault at the time of acquisitions in 1999 and 2002.

---

**Required:**

1. Go to Deloitte's IAS Plus website and examine the summary of the IASB's *IAS No. 28* (at http://www.iasplus .com/standard/ias28.htm), which governs application of the equity method. Focus on two areas: Identification of Associates and Applying the Equity Method of Accounting.

2. Evaluate Renault's decision to use the equity method to account for its investment in Nissan. Does Renault have insignificant influence, significant influence, or control?

3. Evaluate the fact that, when accounting for its investment in Nissan under the equity method, Renault makes adjustments that take into account the fair value of assets and liabilities at the time Renault invested in Nissan.

Give an example of the sorts of adjustments that might be made. Are such adjustments consistent with IFRS? With U.S. GAAP? Explain.

4. Evaluate the fact that, when accounting for its investment in Nissan under the equity method, Renault makes adjustments for harmonization of accounting standards. Are such adjustments consistent with IFRS? With U.S. GAAP? Explain.

**International Case 12–4**
Comparison of equity method and proportionate consolidaton under IFRS
● LO12–5, LO12–8

 IFRS

Obtain the 2011 annual report of Vodafone (**www.vodafone.com**).

**Required:**

1. Contrast the accounting approaches used in Notes 13 for "investments in joint ventures" and 14 for "investments in associated undertakings." What are key similarities and differences? *Hint:* Note 2 is useful here as well.

2. Do you think it is likely that Vodafone's accounting for joint ventures will change after it implements *IFRS No. 11*? Explain.

**Research Case 12–5**
Researching the way investments are reported; retrieving information from the Internet
● LO12–1, LO12–2, LO12–3

All publicly traded domestic companies use EDGAR, the Electronic Data Gathering, Analysis, and Retrieval system, to make the majority of their filings with the SEC. You can access EDGAR at **www.sec.gov**.

**Required:**

1. Search for a public company with which you are familiar. Access its most recent 10-K filing. Search or scroll to find financial statements and related notes.

2. Answer the following questions. (If the chosen company does not report investments in the securities of other companies, choose another company.)

   a. What is the amount and classification of any investment securities reported in the balance sheet? Are unrealized gains or losses reported in the shareholders' equity section?

   b. Are any investments reported by the equity method?

   c. What amounts from these investments are reported in the comparative income statements? Has that income increased or decreased over the years reported?

   d. Are any acquisitions or disposals of investments reported in the statement of cash flows?

**Real World Case 12–6**
Merck's investments
● LO12–3, LO12–4, LO12–5

Corporations frequently invest in securities issued by other corporations. Some investments are acquired to secure a favorable business relationship with another company. On the other hand, others are intended only to earn an investment return from the dividends or interest the securities pay or from increases in the market prices of the securities—the same motivations that might cause you to invest in stocks, bonds, or other securities. This diversity in investment objectives means no single accounting method is adequate to report every investment.

**Merck & Co., Inc.**, invests in securities of other companies. Access Merck's 2010 10-K (which includes financial statements) using EDGAR at **www.sec.gov**.

**Required:**

1. What is the amount and classification of any investment securities reported on the balance sheet? In which current and noncurrent asset categories are investments reported by Merck? What criteria are used to determine the classifications?

2. How are unrealized gains or losses reported? Realized gains and losses?

3. Are any investments reported by the equity method?

4. What amounts from equity method investments are reported in the comparative income statements?

5. Are cash flow effects of these investments reflected in the company's comparative statements of cash flows? If so, what information is provided by this disclosure?

**Real World Case 12–7**
Comprehensive income— Microsoft
● LO12–3

As required by GAAP [FASB ASC 320, previously *SFAS No. 115*], **Microsoft Corporation** reports its investments available-for-sale at the *fair value* of the investment securities. The *net* unrealized holding gain is not reported in the income statement. Instead, it's reported as part of Other comprehensive income and added to Accumulated other comprehensive income in shareholders' equity.

Comprehensive income is a broader view of the change in shareholders' equity than traditional net income, encompassing all changes in equity from nonowner transactions. Microsoft chose to report its Other comprehensive income as a separate statement in a disclosure note in its 2011 annual report.

**NOTE 19 OTHER COMPREHENSIVE INCOME**
The activity in other comprehensive income and related income tax effects were as follows:

(in millions)

| Year Ended June 30 | 2011 | 2010 | 2009 |
|---|---|---|---|
| Net unrealized gains on derivatives: | | | |
| Unrealized gains, net of tax effect of $(340), $188, and $472 | $ (632) | $ 349 | $ 876 |
| Reclassification adjustment for gains included in net income, net of tax effect of $2, $(173), and $(309) | 5 | (322) | (574) |
| Net unrealized gains on derivative | (627) | 27 | 302 |
| Net unrealized gains (losses) on investments: | | | |
| Unrealized gains (losses), net of tax effect of $726, $263, and $(142) | 1,349 | 488 | (263) |
| Reclassification adjustment for losses (gains) included in net income, net of tax effect of $(159), $(120), and $16 | (295) | (223) | 30 |
| Net unrealized gains (losses) on investments | 1,054 | 265 | (233) |
| Translation adjustments and other, net of tax effects of $205, $(103), and $(133) | 381 | (206) | (240) |
| Other comprehensive income (loss) | $ 808 | $ 86 | $ (171) |

The components of accumulated other comprehensive income were as follows:

(in millions)

| Year Ended June 30 | 2011 | 2010 | 2009 |
|---|---|---|---|
| Net unrealized gains on derivatives | $ (163) | $ 464 | $ 437 |
| Net unrealized gains on investments | 1,821 | 767 | 502 |
| Translation adjustments and other | 205 | (176) | 30 |
| Accumulated other comprehensive income | $1,863 | $1,055 | $ 969 |

**Required:**

1. The note indicates Unrealized holding losses during 2011 in the amount of $1,349 million. Is this the balance of accumulated other comprehensive income that Microsoft would include as a separate component of shareholders' equity? Explain.

2. What does Microsoft mean by the term, "Reclassification adjustment for (losses) gains included in net income"?

**Trueblood Accounting Case 12–8**
Impairments
(Appendix 12B)
● LO12–3

The following Trueblood case is recommended for use with this chapter. The case provides an excellent opportunity for class discussion, group projects, and writing assignments. The case, along with Professor's Discussion Material, can be obtained from the Deloitte Foundation at its website: **www.deloitte.com/us/truebloodcases**.

*Case: 03–7: Impaired Abilities*
This case gives students an opportunity to discuss accounting for other-than-temporary impairments.

**Research Case 12–9**
Changes in accounting for other-than-temporary impairments
(Appendix 12B)
● LO12–1, LO12–3

In Appendix 12B you learned that accounting for other-than-temporary impairments has changed recently. You also learned that these changes were controversial. In fact, two of the five members of the FASB voted against the changes and provided an explanation for their position when the standard that defined the changes was issued. That information isn't included in the FASB's Accounting Standards Codification, but you can find it in the original standard, "Recognition and Presentation of Other-Than-Temporary Impairments," FASB Staff Position (FSP) No. 115-2 and 124-2 (Norwalk, Conn.: FASB April 9, 2009), which is available under the "Standards" link at **www.FASB.org**.

**Required:**

Access the FSP and turn to p. 17, and read why FASB members Linsmeier and Siegel dissented. What were their major concerns with the new approach for accounting for OTT impairments? Do you find those concerns compelling?

# Air France–KLM Case

● LO12–8

 IFRS

Air France–KLM (AF), a French company, prepares its financial statements according to International Financial Reporting Standards. AF's annual report for the year ended March 31, 2011, which includes financial statements and disclosure notes, is provided with all new textbooks. This material also is included in AF's "Registration Document 2010–11," dated June 15, 2011 and is available at **www.airfranceklm.com**.

**Required:**

1. Read Notes 3.10.2, 3.10.5, 22, 32.3 and 32.4. Focusing on investments accounted for at fair value through profit and loss (FVTPL):

   a. As of March 31, 2011, what is the balance of those investments in the balance sheet? Be specific regarding which line of the balance sheet includes the balance.

   b. How much of that balance is classified as current and how much as noncurrent?

   c. Is that balance stated at fair value? How do you know?

   d. How much of the fair value of those investments is accounted for using level 1, level 2, and level 3 inputs of the fair value hierarchy? Given that information, assess the reliability (representational faithfulness) of this fair value estimate.

2. Complete Requirement 1 again, but for investments accounted for as available for sale.

3. Read Notes 3.3.2, 10, and 20.

   a. When AF can exercise significant influence over an investee, what accounting approach do they use to account for the investment? How does AF determine if it can exercise significant influence?

   b. If AF exercises joint control over an investee by virtue of a contractual agreement, what accounting method does it use? Is there an alternative?

   c. Why did AF change how it accounts for its investment in WAM (Amadeus)? What was the initial approach that AF used, and what approach did it change to using for this investment?

   d. What is the carrying value of AF's equity-method investments in its March 31, 2011 balance sheet?

   e. How did AF's equity-method investments affect AF's 2011 net income from continuing operations?

# CPA Simulation 12–1

**Barbados Investments**
Investments

**KAPLAN**

**CPA Review**

Test your knowledge of the concepts discussed in this chapter, practice critical professional skills necessary for career success, and prepare for the computer-based CPA exam by accessing our CPA simulations at the text website: **www.mhhe.com/spiceland7e**.

The Barbados Investments simulation tests your knowledge of (a) the way we classify investment securities among the categories of trading securities, available-for-sale securities, and those held-to-maturity, (b) how we account for those investments, (c) the way accounting for investments affects comprehensive income, and (d) the appropriate use of the equity method.

As on the CPA exam itself, you will be asked to use tools including a spreadsheet, a calculator, and generally accepted accounting principles, to conduct research, derive solutions, and communicate conclusions related to these issues in a simulated environment.

Specific tasks in the simulation include:

● Analyzing various transactions involving investment securities and determining their appropriate balance sheet classification.

● Applying judgment in the application of the equity method.

● Determining the amount of interest revenue to be reported from a debt investment.

● Demonstrating an understanding of comprehensive income and how it is affected by investments in securities.

● Communicating the way we account for investments using the equity method.

● Researching the financial reporting ramifications of changing the classification of investment securities.

# Where We're Headed

**PREFACE** ──────● The FASB and the IASB are collaborating on several major new standards designed in part to move U.S. GAAP and IFRS closer together (convergence). This reading is based on the FASB's Exposure Draft of an Accounting Standards Update (ASU) that addresses accounting for financial instruments and "tentative decisions" of the Board after receiving feedback about the Exposure Draft as of the date this text went to press.[48]

Even after the proposed ASU is issued, previous GAAP will be relevant until the proposed ASU becomes effective, and students taking the CPA or CMA exams will be responsible for the previous GAAP until six months after that effective date. Conversely, prior to the effective date of the proposed ASU, it is useful for students to have an understanding of the new guidance on the horizon.

The FASB and the IASB have been working to revise accounting for financial instruments for several years. Although the two boards intend to develop a joint approach, their development of new guidance in this area has been somewhat separate. The FASB issued an exposure draft of a proposed ASU in 2010,[49] subsequently revised that ASU in important ways, and likely will re-expose major changes in the future. As discussed in the main chapter, the IASB issued *IFRS No. 9* in 2009, but is not requiring adoption until 2015, and as of the date this text was written the European Union had not yet endorsed *IFRS No. 9* for use by members of the EU.[50] Also, the IASB has indicated that it will request comments on the FASB's new proposed ASU as it considers in the future whether *IFRS No. 9* should be modified. So, it's fair to say that accounting in the area of financial instruments remains in a state of change.

In this chapter supplement we discuss the main points of the proposed ASU. We focus in particular on important changes from current GAAP, identified with a *GAAP Change* note in the margin of the supplement. We also use IFRS boxes to identify key differences between the proposed ASU and *IFRS No. 9*.

It's important to understand that much of the proposed ASU is very similar to current GAAP. As shown in Illustration 12–19, the proposed ASU uses the same five basic categories to account for investments that you learned about in the main chapter, but with different names and minor differences. The journal entries we use to account for the investments in each category are the same as they are under current GAAP.

> The five categories used in the proposed ASU to classify and account for investments are very similar to those used in current U.S. GAAP.

---

[48]Because the proposed ASU had not been finalized as of the date this text went to press, it is possible that some aspects of the proposed ASU are different from what we show in this supplement. Check the FASB Updates page (**http://lsb.scu.edu/jsepe/fasb-update-7e .htm**) to see if any changes have occurred.

[49]*Proposed Accounting Standards Update*, "Accounting for Financial Instruments and Revisions to the Accounting for Derivative Instruments and Hedging Activities (Topics 825 and 815)," (Norwalk, Conn.: FASB, May 26, 2010).

[50]"Financial Instruments," *International Financial Reporting Standard No. 9* (IASCF, November 12, 2009, as amended effective January 1, 2011).

| Reporting Category Used in | | Accounting Approach |
|---|---|---|
| **Current GAAP** | **Proposed ASU** | |
| **Held-to-maturity ("HTM")\*** | **Amortized Cost\*\*** | Investment reported at amortized cost. |
| **Trading securities ("TS")** | **Fair Value through Net Income ("FV-NI")** | Investment reported at fair value. Unrealized holding gains and losses included in net income. |
| **Securities available-for-sale ("AFS")\*** | **Fair Value through Other Comprehensive Income ("FV-OCI") \*\*** | Investment reported at fair value. Unrealized holding gains and losses excluded from net income and reported in OCI. Gains and losses reclassified from OCI and reported in net income when realized through the sale of the investment. |
| **Equity method\*** | **Equity method\*\*** | Investment reported at cost adjusted for subsequent earnings and dividends of the investee. |
| **Consolidation** | **Consolidation** | The financial statements of the investor and investee are combined as if they are a single company. |

\*If the investor elects the *fair value option*, this type of investment also can be accounted for using the same approach that's used for trading securities, with the investment reported at fair value and unrealized holding gains and losses included in net income.
\*\*The proposed ASU eliminates the fair value option for almost all investments. The only exception occurs when the investor manages a group of financial assets and liabilities according to their net exposure to market risks and reports information on that basis to management. In that case, the investor can irrevocably elect the fair value option when the investments are acquired.

The proposed ASU
differs from current
GAAP primarily in the
criteria used to classify
investments within the
first three categories.

The proposed ASU differs from current GAAP primarily in the criteria we use to classify an investment into one of the three categories when the investor lacks significant influence over the investee (under the proposed ASU, those categories are amortized cost, fair value through net income, and fair value through other comprehensive income). In addition, the proposed ASU eliminates the fair value option for almost all investments, and impairment rules differ between the proposed ASU and current GAAP.

We start by discussing criteria for determining how to account for *equity* investments. Then we discuss criteria for determining how to account for *debt* investments. We finish with discussions of accounting for impairments and the equity method.

## Accounting for Equity Investments

Determining how to account for equity investments (investments in stock) under the proposed ASU is easy. If the investor does not have "significant influence"[51] over the investee, the equity investment is accounted for as FV-NI.[52] If the investor has significant influence over the investee, but lacks *control*, the equity method is used. If the investor has *control*, the investment is consolidated.

Equity investments are
always accounted for as
FV-NI if the investor lacks
significant influence over
the investee.

---

[51]Remember from the main chapter that we assume an investor has significant influence over the investee when the investor owns between 20% and 50% of the investee's voting shares of stock. However, we also may conclude from additional evidence that an investor who owns less than 20% is able to exercise significant influence.
[52]The proposed ASU provides a "practicability exception" when investors that do not sell shares of stock to the public (those investors are called "nonpublic entities") hold equity that is not sold frequently (called "nonmarketable equity"). Nonpublic investors can measure nonmarketable equity investments at cost, adjusted for impairments and any changes in the price of the equity observed when sales of similar equity occur.

*GAAP Change*

Current GAAP requires the equity method or consolidation under the same circumstances as the proposed ASU requires, but differs in its treatment of investments when the investor lacks significant influence. Under current GAAP, the investor accounts for the equity investment as a trading security if the investment is held for trading purposes, or as an AFS security if it is held for a more long-term investment purpose. Under the proposed ASU, an equity investment *always* is treated as FV-NI (equivalent to being accounted for as a trading security). This difference means that we will see many more unrealized gains and losses on equity investments reported in net income under the proposed ASU, because there is no opportunity for the investments to be classified as AFS with unrealized gains and losses shown in OCI.

# International Financial Reporting Standards

**Accounting for Equity Investments When Investor Lacks Significant Influence.** Under *IFRS No. 9*, investments in equity securities typically are classified as "FVTPL" ("Fair Value through Profit and Loss," equivalent to "FV-NI"). However, if the equity is not held for trading, the investor has the option to irrevocably classify it as "FVTOCI" ("Fair Value through Other Comprehensive Income," equivalent to "FV-OCI"). Thus, *IFRS No. 9* offers two alternative treatments of equity investments, similar to the trading and AFS categories in current GAAP, and *IFRS No. 9* differs from the proposed ASU in the same way that current GAAP does. Equity investments may have unrealized gains and losses in OCI under *IFRS No. 9*, but not under the proposed ASU.

## Accounting for Debt Investments

Accounting for a debt investment depends on (1) the characteristics of the debt and (2) the business activity in which the debt is used.

Determining how to account for debt investments under the proposed ASU is more complicated than accounting for equity investments. Under the proposed ASU we base classification of debt investments on two criteria: (a) the characteristics of the debt instrument and (b) the business activity in which the instrument is used. We discuss each of the criteria in turn.

### CHARACTERISTICS OF THE DEBT INSTRUMENT

The first criterion we look at when classifying a debt instrument is to identify whether it is **simple** or **complex**.[53] As shown in Illustration 12–20, "simple" debt has characteristics that you would typically associate with debt.

**Illustration 12–20**

Characteristics of a Simple Debt Instrument Under the Proposed ASU

---

**Characteristics of a Simple Debt Instrument**

1. An amount is transferred to the borrower (debtor) when the debt instrument is issued that will be returned to the lender (creditor) when the debt matures or is settled. The amount is the principal or face amount of the debt adjusted for any discount or premium.
2. The debt cannot be prepaid or settled in such a way that the lender does not recover substantially all of its original investment, unless the lender chooses to allow it.
3. The debt instrument is not a derivative.[54]

---

*Simple* debt involves return of principal to the lender and can only be settled by the lender's choice.

In other words, simple debt is not a derivative, involves a lender providing an amount up front that eventually must be repaid, and doesn't permit the borrower to prepay or settle the debt unless the lender allows it. Accounts receivable and notes receivable would qualify as simple debt instruments, as would a bond.[55]

---

[53]The proposed ASU indicates two categories but does not use the terms *simple* and *complex* to describe them. We use those terms for clarity as we discuss the criteria for debt classification.
[54]We discuss derivatives in an appendix to this book.
[55]We discuss bonds in Chapter 14.

Debt that lacks one or more of the characteristics of simple debt is considered *complex*. Under the proposed ASU, debt that is complex always is classified as FV-NI. As discussed in the next section, the accounting approach used for debt that is simple depends on the business purpose of the debt.

If debt is not simple, it is *complex*. Complex debt always is accounted for as FV-NI.

## Business Purpose of a Debt Instrument

For simple debt, we next must consider the business activity that motivates the investor to hold the debt. The proposed ASU identifies three primary business activities: lending, long-term investing, or held for sale. Illustration 12–21 summarizes the three business purposes discussed in the proposed ASU and the accounting approach that's appropriate for each.

| Business Purpose | Accounting Approach |
|---|---|
| **Lending:** | |
| The debt holder's **purpose is lending or customer financing** with a focus on collecting cash flows (interest and principal). The debt holder must have the ability to renegotiate, sell or settle the debt to minimize losses due to a borrower's deteriorating credit.[56] | Amortized Cost |
| **Investing:** | |
| The debt holder may choose to hold on to the debt investment or sell it as a way of either (a) maximizing its **return on investment** or (b) **managing risk**. | FV-OCI |
| **Held for Sale:** | |
| The debt instrument is either (a) held for the **purpose of being sold** or (b) actively managed internally on a **fair value** basis but doesn't qualify for FV-OCI. | FV-NI |

**Illustration 12–21**

Business Purposes of Debt Investments Under the Proposed ASU

If simple debt is used for *lending* or customer financing, it is accounted for at amortized cost.

If simple debt is used for long-term *investing*, it is accounted for as FV-OCI.

If simple debt is *held for sale* when acquired, it is accounted for as FV-NI.

Although the requirements listed in Illustration 12–21 may seem complicated, the basic ideas are straightforward. If debt is held to facilitate lending or customer financing, the focus is on collecting all of the cash flows that are contractually specified in the debt. Therefore, fair values are not very relevant to current operations, and the debt investment is accounted for at amortized cost with interest revenue included in net income.

However, if debt instead is held as an investment, the focus is on maximizing investment returns or managing risk. For such long-term investments, unrealized gains or losses due to fair value changes are not that relevant to assessing current performance (because fair values likely will fluctuate over time), so those amounts are shown in OCI, and only *realized* gains or losses are reported in net income.

And if debt is acquired with the intention of selling it soon, unrealized gains and losses are very relevant to assessing current performance because managers could choose to realize them at any time. So, those gains and losses are reported in net income.

The proposed ASU focuses on the business activity the company uses to manage a portfolio of debt instruments. So, it's possible that identical debt instruments (say bonds issued by IBM) that are held for two different purposes could be accounted for in two different ways by the same company. Illustration 12–22 clarifies this distinction.

The proposed ASU does not allow transfers of debt from one category to another. After the debt is initially classified, reclassifications are not permitted.

The proposed ASU does not allow transfers between reporting categories.

The classification criteria for debt investments differ in important ways from current GAAP. First, there is no characteristics criterion (simple vs. complex) in current GAAP. Also, while current GAAP does base classification of debt investments on the intent of the investor, the specifics differ from the proposed ASU. Under current GAAP, an investor

*GAAP Change*

---

[56]Although this supplement focuses on investments, the amortized cost category also would apply to accounts receivable and notes receivable that are discussed in Chapter 7.

**Illustration 12–22**

Classifying Debt According to Business Activity

Gregg Associates purchased 100 IBM bonds. Gregg intends to use the bonds in the following activities:

- Twenty of the bonds will be held for immediate resale to another company that wants to invest in them.
- Eighty of the bonds will be held as a long-term investment. Gregg may sell the bonds if the price of the bonds increases sufficiently, or it may hold the bonds until the bonds mature.

Gregg also made a long-term loan to a customer to facilitate the customer's purchase of Gregg's products.

How would Gregg account for these investments?

- The twenty bonds held for immediate resale would be accounted for at **FV-NI**.
- The eighty bonds held as a long-term investment would be accounted for as **FV-OCI**.
- The long-term loan would be accounted for at **amortized cost**.

should only account for debt at amortized cost if the investor intends to hold the debt to maturity, and an investor that sells HTM debt prior to maturity may be disallowed from using the HTM classification in subsequent years. The proposed ASU does not require that debt classified as amortized cost be held to maturity. Current GAAP also is not as explicit as the proposed ASU regarding how to determine whether an investment should be classified as trading (FV-NI in the proposed ASU) or AFS (FV-OCI in the proposed ASU). And, current GAAP allows transfers between classifications. The proposed ASU does not.

One other difference relates to disclosure. The proposed ASU requires that the balance sheet parenthetically display fair value as well as amortized cost for investments reported at amortized cost. Current GAAP requires disclosure of the fair value of these investments in the notes to the financial statements, but not on the face of the balance sheet. Receivables due within one year would not be subject to this requirement.

# International Financial Reporting Standards

**Accounting for Debt Investments When the Investor Lacks Significant Influence.**
Under *IFRS No. 9*, investments in debt securities are classified either as amortized cost or as "FVTPL" ("Fair Value through Profit and Loss," equivalent to "FV-NI"). Similar to the proposed ASU, to be included in the amortized cost category a debt investment must meet both (a) the "cash flow characteristics" test (which requires that the debt instrument consist of only principal and interest payments) and (b) the "business model test" (which requires that the objective of the company's business model is to hold the investment to collect the contractual cash flows). If debt isn't classified in "amortized cost," it is classified in FVTPL—there is no equivalent to FV-OCI for debt under *IFRS No. 9*. Therefore, it's likely that more debt would be accounted for under FVTPL under *IFRS No. 9* than is accounted for under FV-NI under the proposed ASU. All else equal, this would lead to more volatile earnings under *IFRS No. 9*.

Another difference is that *IFRS No. 9* allows reclassification to a new category when the business model changes with respect to the debt. *IFRS No. 9* has been criticized for providing this flexibility and potential incomparability. The proposed ASU does not allow reclassification.

Illustration 12–23 summarizes the classification criteria for determining how to account for investments in debt and equity securities for which the investor does not exercise significant influence.

**Illustration 12–23**
Classifying Investments
Under the Proposed ASU

| Classification Criteria | Accounting Approach |
|---|---|
| **Debt investment** | |
| *Characteristics:* Simple Debt | |
| *Business Purpose:* | |
| • Lending or Customer Financing | **Amortized Cost** |
| • Investment Returns or Risk Management | **FV-OCI** |
| • Trading Gains from Sale | **FV-NI** |
| *Characteristics:* Complex Debt | **FV-NI** |
| **Equity investment** | **FV-NI** |

## Other Issues

### INITIAL MEASUREMENT

You have seen throughout this book that assets typically are initially recorded at the transaction price at which they are acquired. Under the proposed ASU, that is the case for investments reported at amortized cost or at FV-OCI. However, the proposed ASU requires that investments reported at FV-NI be recorded initially at fair value, which might differ from the transaction price in some unusual circumstances.[57]

### IMPAIRMENTS WHEN THE INVESTOR DOES NOT EXERCISE SIGNIFICANT INFLUENCE

Because equity investments are reported at FV-NI, no impairment guidance is necessary. The same is true for debt investments recorded at FV-NI. Declines in fair value always are reported in net income.

However, for debt investments reported at amortized cost or at FV-OCI, impairment losses are possible. As indicated in Appendix 12B, this is a controversial topic, and one that the FASB and IASB have struggled to come to terms with. At the date this textbook was written, the Boards were working on a "three-bucket" approach in which impairment losses would be recognized and an allowance for losses would be established to capture three phases of deterioration of credit quality. All investments would start in bucket 1 and then transfer to bucket 2 and then 3 as credit worthiness deteriorates:

**Bucket 1: Investments *not affected* by observed events.** This bucket contains portfolios of debt investments that are evaluated individually or collectively for impairment in light of general risks of future default.

**Bucket 2: Investments *affected* by observed events (but individual defaults have not been identified).** This bucket contains portfolios of debt investments that have been affected by events that indicate potential for future default, but specific investments have not been identified as suffering default.

**Bucket 3: Individual debt investments *suffering credit losses*.** This bucket contains specific investments for which default has occurred or is expected to occur.

For bucket 1, expected losses would be estimated for the near term (say, one or two years). For buckets 2 and 3, expected losses would be estimated for the life of the investment. Expected losses would include all expected losses of contractual cash flows (interest and principal), discounted for the time value of money.

This approach differs from current GAAP. As indicated in Appendix 12B, current GAAP focuses on the intent and ability to hold the investment until fair value recovers, and for

*GAAP Change*

---

[57]If fair value differs from the transaction price upon acquisition of a FV-NI investment, the investor may need to record a gain or loss immediately upon acquisition. That situation is beyond the scope of an intermediate accounting course.

some debt investments also accounts differently for credit losses (due to not being able to collect future cash flows) and noncredit losses (due to other fair-value changes).

## EQUITY METHOD

The criteria for applying the equity method are the same in the proposed ASU as in current GAAP. If a company is holding an investment for sale that normally would qualify for the equity method, the investment is accounted for as FV-NI. As with most other investments, the proposed ASU eliminates the fair value option for the equity method. If qualitative factors suggest that it is more likely than not that an equity method investment is impaired, the investor recognizes an amount of impairment equal to the excess of the investment's carrying value over its fair value. If fair value increases in future periods, impairments cannot be reversed.

*The proposed ASU applies the equity method very similarly to current GAAP.*

## Concept Review Exercise

**IDENTIFYING THE ACCOUNTING APPROACH USED FOR INVESTMENTS**

MelCo purchases residential mortgages from banks and either holds them or sells them to various investors. In January of 2013, MelCo purchased 20 mortgages. The mortgages do not allow early settlement by the homeowners unless MelCo chooses to permit it. MelCo's intentions with respect to the mortgages are as follows:

- Pool A consists of five mortgages that MelCo intends to sell within the next month to meet near-term cash flow needs.
- Pool B consists of seven mortgages that MelCo is holding for future business needs. It is possible that MelCo will sell the mortgages, particularly if the price it can receive for the mortgages is sufficiently high. Alternatively, MelCo may hold the mortgages until the mortgages mature.
- Pool C consists of eight mortgages that MelCo intends to hold until maturity. MelCo maintains those mortgages as part of a business model under which the payments from the mortgages will meet MelCo's obligations to provide interest payments to creditors.

MelCo also purchased a mortgage by which Welch Construction is permitted to prepay the mortgage at a substantial discount within two years. In the event Welch chooses prepayment, MelCo could suffer a loss on the mortgage. MelCo believes prepayment is unlikely, and MelCo's intention is to hold this mortgage until it matures.

MelCo also invested in the stock of two other banks during January.

- MelCo purchased 2% of the outstanding shares of BigBank. MelCo has no seat on BigBank's board of directors. Three other shareholders have 10–20% of outstanding shares and sit on BigBank's board of directors.
- MelCo purchased 30% of the outstanding shares of SmallBank. No other shareholder has more than a 10% ownership stake. MelCo's CEO and CFO were named to SmallBank's board of directors.

**Required:**

1. Classify each of MelCo's debt and equity investments according to the accounting approach that would be used for the investment under the proposed ASU.
2. Briefly summarize how each of the accounting approaches indicated in your answer to requirement 1 would have MelCo account for (a) unrealized gains and losses due to fair value changes and (b) realized gains and losses due to sales of the investment.

**Solution:**

1. Classify each of MelCo's debt and equity investments according to the accounting approach that would be used for the investment under the proposed ASU.

   The mortgages in Pools A–C all are "simple" debt, because they consist primarily of payments that include interest and return of principal, do not allow the debtor to choose prepayment that could provide a loss to MelCo unless MelCo allows it, and do not involve derivatives. Therefore, those mortgages are classified according to the business activity that motivates investing in them.

- **Pool A:** FV-NI, because the mortgages are held for sale.
- **Pool B:** FV-OCI, because the mortgages are held for investment.
- **Pool C:** amortized cost, because the mortgages are held to collect contractual cash flows.

**Welch mortgage:** FV-NI, because this is "complex" debt, including a prepayment option for Welch that could result in losses for MedCo.

**BigBank stock:** FV-NI, because this is an equity investment for which MelCo cannot exercise significant influence over the activities of the investee.

**SmallBank stock**: equity method, because this is an equity investment for which MelCo can exercise significant influence over the activities of the investee.

2. Briefly summarize how each of the accounting approaches indicated in your answer to requirement 1 would have MelCo account for (a) unrealized gains and losses due to fair value changes, and (b) realized gains and losses due to sales of the investment.

- **FV-NI:** include unrealized and realized gains and losses in net income.
- **FV-OCI:** include unrealized gains and losses in OCI. Reclassify unrealized gains and losses from OCI to NI when those gains and losses are realized due to sales of the investment.
- **Amortized cost:** do not include unrealized gains and losses in OCI or NI. Recognize only gains and losses realized through sale in NI.
- **Equity method:** do not include unrealized gains and losses in OCI or NI. Recognize only gains and losses realized through sale in NI.

Respond to the questions, brief exercises, exercises, and problems in this Supplement with the presumption that the guidance provided by the proposed Accounting Standards Update is being applied.

## Questions For Review of Key Topics

**Q 12–30**  What are the three reporting classifications by which investors can account for debt investments?

**Q 12–31**  What criteria indicate that a debt investment should be accounted for at amortized cost?

**Q 12–32**  What criteria indicate that a debt investment should be accounted for at FV-OCI?

**Q 12–33**  What criteria indicate that a debt investment should be accounted for at FV-NI?

**Q 12–34**  How is an equity investment accounted for when the investor lacks the ability to significantly influence the investee? Are there any exceptions?

## Brief Exercises

**BE 12–17**
Accounting for fair value changes in debt investments.

Lemp LLP purchases a bond for $1,000 with the intention of holding the bond for investment purposes. The bond promises to pay Lemp semiannual interest payments and to return to Lemp a principal of $1,000 after 10 years. During the first year of purchase, the bond's fair value declines to $900. How would Lemp report that change in its financial statements, if at all?

**BE 12–18**
Accounting for fair value changes in debt investments.

Fowler Inc. accepts a $75,000 note from an affiliate. Fowler's intention is to sell the note as quickly as possible to a third party. During the first year of the note, the fair value of the note increases to $80,000. How would Fowler report that change in its financial statements, if at all?

**BE 12–19**
Accounting
for fair value
changes in debt
investments.

Assume the same facts as in BE12–18, but that Fowler issued the note to provide customer financing and intends to hold the note until it is collected. How would Fowler report that change in its financial statements, if at all?

**BE 12–20**
Accounting
for fair value
changes in equity
investments.

Barrett Associates purchased $100,000 of equity in the Atkinson Group. Barrett does not have significant influence over Atkinson's operations. As of the end of the fiscal year, the fair value of Barrett's equity investment has declined to $80,000, but Barrett is confident the fair value will recover within the next month, well before Barrett intends to sell the investment. How would Barrett report that change in fair value in its financial statements, if at all?

# Exercises

**E 12–30**
Accounting for
debt investments

Watney Inc. purchased $10,000 of 6% Hamel bonds at par on July 1, 2013. The bonds pay interest semiannually. Watney intends to hold the Hamel bonds for the life of the bonds. During the second half of 2013, an increase in interest rates reduced the fair value of the bonds to $9,000.

**Required:**
1. Prepare a journal entry to record Watney's receipt of six months of interest revenue.
2. Prepare a journal entry (if any is required) to record any unrealized gains or losses on the Hamel bonds during 2013. (Only consider ordinary accounting for unrealized gains or losses. Do not consider whether an impairment should be recorded.)

**E 12–31**
Accounting for
debt investments

Assume the same facts as in E12–30, but that Watney intends to sell half of the Hamel bonds immediately and to hold the other half of the bonds to sell once the price of the bonds appreciates sufficiently.

**Required:**
1. Prepare a journal entry to record Watney's receipt of six months of interest revenue.
2. Prepare a journal entry (if any is required) to record any unrealized gains or losses on the Hamel bonds during 2013. (Only consider ordinary accounting for unrealized gains or losses. Do not consider whether an impairment should be recorded.)

# Problem

**P 12–18**
Accounting for
debt and equity
investments

Feherty, Inc., purchased the following investments during December 2013:

1. **50 of Donald Company's $1,000 bonds.** The bonds pay semiannual interest payments and return principal in eight years. Feherty plans to hold 10 of the bonds to collect contractual cash flows over the life of the investment, to hold 10 for investment purposes, possibly selling the bonds if their price appreciates sufficiently, and to sell 30 of the bonds within a few weeks following purchase. Subsequent to Feherty's purchase of the bonds, but prior to December 31, the fair value of the bonds increased to $1,040 per bond, and Feherty sold 15 of the 30 bonds it had held for sale. Feherty also sold 5 of the 10 bonds it had planned to hold to collect contractual cash flows over the life of the investment, and 5 of the bonds it had planned to hold for investment purposes. The fair value of the bonds remained at $1,040 as of December 31, 2013.

2. **$25,000 of Watson Company common stock.** Feherty does not have the ability to significantly influence the operations of Watson. Subsequent to Feherty's purchase of the equity, the fair value of the equity declined to $20,000, which was the fair value of the equity as of December 31, 2013. Ignore taxes.

**Required:**
1. Indicate how Feherty would account for its investments when it acquired the Donald bonds and Watson stock.
2. Calculate the effect of unrealized gains and losses associated with the Donald bonds and the Watson equity on Feherty's net income, other comprehensive income, and comprehensive income for the year ended December 31, 2013.

"... derivatives are financial weapons of mass destruction ..."

— Warren Buffett, Berkshire Hathaway CEO

"... the growing use of complex financial instruments known as derivatives does not pose a threat to the country's financial system ..."

— Alan Greenspan, Federal Reserve Chairman

"Total world derivatives are $1000 trillion or 19 times the total world GDP of $54 trillion."

— Chuck Burr, *Culture Change*

In today's global economy and evolving financial markets, businesses are increasingly exposed to a variety of risks, which, unmanaged, can have major impacts on earnings or even threaten a company's very existence. Risk management, then, has become critical. Derivative financial instruments have become the key tools of risk management.[1]

*Derivatives* are financial instruments that "derive" their values from some other security or *index*.

Derivatives are financial instruments that "derive" their values or contractually required cash flows from some other security or index. For instance, a contract allowing a company to buy a particular asset (say steel, gold, or flour) at a designated future date at a predetermined price is a financial instrument that derives its value from expected and actual changes in the price of the underlying asset. Financial futures, forward contracts, options, and interest rate swaps are the most frequently used derivatives. Derivatives are valued as tools to manage or hedge companies' increasing exposures to risk, including interest rate risk, price risk, and foreign exchange risk. The variety, complexity, and magnitude of derivatives have grown rapidly in recent years. Accounting standard-setters have scrambled to keep pace.

Derivatives serve as a form of "insurance" against risk.

A persistent stream of headline stories has alerted us to multimillion-dollar losses by many companies and the financial collapse of Bear Stearns and AIG. Focusing on these headlines, it would be tempting to conclude that derivatives are risky business indeed. Certainly they can be quite risky, if misused, but the fact is, these financial instruments exist to lessen, not increase, risk. Properly used, they serve as a form of "insurance" against risk. In fact, if a company is exposed to a substantial risk and does not hedge that risk, it is taking a gamble. On the other hand, if a derivative is used improperly, it can be a huge gamble itself. Total world derivatives are $1,000 trillion or 19 times the total world GDP of $54 trillion.

## Derivatives Used to Hedge Risk

*Hedging* means taking a risk position that is opposite to an actual position that is exposed to risk.

Hedging means taking an action that is expected to produce exposure to a particular type of risk that is precisely the *opposite* of an actual risk to which the company already is exposed. For instance, the volatility of interest rates creates exposure to interest-rate risk for companies that issue debt—which, of course, includes most companies. So, a company that frequently arranges short-term loans from its bank under a floating (variable) interest rate agreement is exposed to the risk that interest rates might increase and adversely affect borrowing costs. Similarly, a company that regularly reissues commercial paper as it matures faces the possibility that new rates will be higher and cut into forecasted income. When borrowings are large, the potential cost can be substantial. So, the firm might choose to hedge its position by entering into a transaction that would produce a *gain* of roughly the same amount as the potential loss if interest rates do, in fact, increase.

Hedging is used to deal with three areas of risk exposure: fair value risk, cash flow risk, and foreign currency risk. Let's look at some of the more common derivatives.

---

[1] Almost all financial institutions and over half of all nonfinancial companies use derivatives.

**FINANCIAL FUTURES** A futures contract is an agreement between a seller and a buyer that requires the seller to deliver a particular commodity (say corn, gold, or pork bellies) at a designated future date, at a *predetermined* price. These contracts are actively traded on regulated futures exchanges. When the "commodity" is a *financial instrument,* such as a Treasury bond, Treasury bill, commercial paper, or a certificate of deposit, the agreement is referred to as a *financial futures contract.*[2]

To appreciate the way these hedges work, you need to remember that when interest rates rise, the market price of interest-bearing securities goes down. For instance, if you have an investment in a 10% bond and market interest rates go up to, say, 12%, your 10% bond is less valuable relative to other bonds paying the higher rate. Conversely, when interest rates decline, the market price of interest-bearing securities goes up. This risk that the investment's value might change is referred to as *fair value risk.* The company that issued the securities is faced with fair value risk also. If interest rates decline, the fair value of that company's debt would rise, a risk the borrower may want to hedge against. Later in this section, we'll look at an illustration of how the borrower would account for and report such a hedge.

Now let's look at the effect on a contract to sell or buy securities (or any asset for that matter) at preset prices. One who is contracted to *sell* securities at a *preset* price after their market price has fallen benefits from the rise in interest rates. Consequently, the value of the *contract* that gives one the right to sell securities at a preset price goes up as the market price declines. The seller in a futures contract derives a gain (loss) when interest rates rise (decline).[3] Conversely, the one obligated to *buy* securities at a preset price experiences a loss. This risk of having to pay more cash or receive less cash is referred to as *cash flow risk.*

Another example of cash flow risk would be borrowing money by issuing a variable (floating) rate note. If market interest rates rise, the borrower would have to pay more interest. Similarly, the lender (investor) in the variable (floating) rate note transaction would face cash flow risk that interest rates would decline, resulting in lower cash interest receipts.

Let's look closer at how a futures contract can mitigate cash flow risk. Consider a company in April that will replace its $10 million of 8.5% bank notes when they mature in June. The company is exposed to the risk that interest rates in June will have risen, increasing borrowing costs. To counteract that possibility, the firm might enter a contract in April to deliver (sell) bonds in June at their *current* price. Since there are no corporate bond futures contracts, the company buys Treasury bond futures, which will accomplish essentially the same purpose. In essence, the firm agrees to sell Treasury bonds in June at a price established now (April). Let's say it's April 6 and the price of Treasury bond futures on the International Monetary Market of the Chicago Mercantile Exchange is quoted as 95.24.[4] Since the trading unit of Treasury bond futures is a 15-year, $100,000, 8% Treasury bond, the company might sell 105 Treasury bond futures to hedge the June issuance of debt. This would effectively provide a hedge of $105 \times \$100,000 \times 95.24\% = \$10,000,200$.[5]

Here's what happens then. If interest rates rise, borrowing costs will go up for our example company because it will have to sell debt securities at a higher interest cost (or lower price). But that loss will be offset (approximately) by the gain produced by being in the opposite position on Treasury bond futures. Take note, though, this works both ways. If interest rates go down causing debt security prices to rise, the potential benefit of being able to issue debt at that lower interest rate (higher price) will be offset by a loss on the futures position.

A very important point about futures contracts is that the seller does not need to have actual possession of the commodity (the Treasury bonds, in this case), nor is the purchaser of the contract required to take possession of the commodity. In fact, virtually all financial futures contracts are "netted out" before the actual transaction is to take place. This is

---

[2]Note that a financial futures contract meets the definition of a financial instrument because it entails the exchange of financial instruments (cash for Treasury bonds, for instance). But, a futures contract for the sale or purchase of a nonfinancial commodity like corn or gold does not meet the definition because one of the items to be exchanged is not a financial instrument.

[3]The seller of a futures contract is obligated to sell the bonds at a future date. The buyer of a futures contract is obligated to buy the bonds at a future date. The company in our example, then, is the seller of the futures contract.

[4]Price quotes are expressed as a percentage of par.

[5]This is a simplification of the more sophisticated way financial managers determine the optimal number of futures.

simply a matter of reversing the original position. A seller closes out his transaction with a purchase. Likewise, a purchaser would close out her transaction with a sale. After all, the objective is not to actually buy or sell Treasury bonds (or whatever the commodity might be), but to incur the financial impact of movements in interest rates as reflected in changes in Treasury bond prices. Specifically, it will buy at the lower price (to reverse the original seller position) at the same time it's selling its new bond issue at that same lower price. The financial futures market is an "artificial" exchange in that its reason for existing is to provide a mechanism to transfer risk from those exposed to it to those willing to accept the risk, not to actually buy and sell the underlying financial instruments.

If the impending debt issue being hedged is a short-term issue, the company may attain a more effective hedge by selling Treasury *bill* futures since Treasury bills are 90-day securities, or maybe certificate of deposit (CD) futures that also are traded in futures markets. The object is to get the closest association between the financial effects of interest rate movements on the actual transaction and the effects on the financial instrument used as a hedge.

**The effectiveness of a hedge is influenced by the closeness of the match between the item being hedged and the financial instrument chosen as a hedge.**

**FINANCIAL FORWARD CONTRACTS** A forward contract is similar to a futures contract but differs in three ways:

1. A forward contract calls for delivery on a specific date, whereas a futures contract permits the seller to decide later which specific day within the specified month will be the delivery date (if it gets as far as actual delivery before it is closed out).
2. Unlike a futures contract, a forward contract usually is not traded on a market exchange.
3. Unlike a futures contract, a forward contract does not call for a daily cash settlement for price changes in the underlying contract. Gains and losses on forward contracts are paid only when they are closed out.

**OPTIONS** Options frequently are purchased to hedge exposure to the effects of changing interest rates. Options serve the same purpose as futures in that respect but are fundamentally different. An option on a financial instrument—say a Treasury bill—gives its holder the right either to buy or to sell the Treasury bill at a specified price and within a given time period. Importantly, though, the option holder has no obligation to exercise the option. On the other hand, the holder of a futures contract must buy or sell within a specified period unless the contract is closed out before delivery comes due.

**FOREIGN CURRENCY FUTURES** Foreign loans frequently are denominated in the currency of the lender (Japanese yen, Swiss franc, Euro, and so on). When loans must be repaid in foreign currencies, a new element of risk is introduced. This is because if exchange rates change, the dollar equivalent of the foreign currency that must be repaid differs from the dollar equivalent of the foreign currency borrowed.

**Foreign exchange risk often is hedged in the same manner as interest rate risk.**

To hedge against "foreign exchange risk" exposure, some firms buy or sell foreign currency futures contracts. These are similar to financial futures except specific foreign currencies are specified in the futures contracts rather than specific debt instruments. They work the same way to protect against foreign exchange risk as financial futures protect against fair value or cash flow risk.

**INTEREST RATE SWAPS** Over 65% of derivatives are interest rate swaps. These contracts exchange fixed interest payments for floating rate payments, or vice versa, without exchanging the underlying principal amounts. For example, suppose you owe $100,000 on a 10% fixed rate home loan. You envy your neighbor who also is paying 10% on her $100,000 mortgage, but hers is a floating rate loan, so if market rates fall, so will her loan rate. To the contrary, she is envious of your fixed rate, fearful that rates will rise, increasing her payments. A solution would be for the two of you to effectively swap interest payments using an interest rate swap agreement. The way a swap works, you both would

**Interest rate swaps exchange fixed interest payments for floating rate payments, or vice versa, without exchanging the underlying notional amounts.**

continue to actually make your own interest payments, but would exchange the net cash difference between payments at specified intervals. So, in this case, if market rates (and thus floating payments) increase, you would pay your neighbor; if rates fall, she pays you. The net effect is to exchange the consequences of rate changes. In other words, you have effectively converted your fixed-rate debt to floating-rate debt; your neighbor has done the opposite.

Of course, this technique is not dependent on happening into such a fortuitous pairing of two borrowers with opposite philosophies on interest rate risk. Instead, banks or other intermediaries offer, for a fee, one-sided swap agreements to companies desiring to be either fixed-rate payers or variable-rate payers. Intermediaries usually strive to maintain a balanced portfolio of matched, offsetting swap agreements.

Theoretically, the two parties to such a transaction exchange principal amounts, say the $100,000 amount above, in addition to the interest on those amounts. It makes no practical sense, though, for the companies to send each other $100,000. So, instead, the principal amount is not actually exchanged, but serves merely as the computational base for interest calculations and is called the *notional amount*. Similarly, the fixed-rate payer doesn't usually send the entire fixed interest amount (say 10% × $100,000 = $10,000) and receive the entire variable interest amount (say 9% × $100,000 = $9,000). Generally, only the net amount ($1,000 in this case) is exchanged. This is illustrated in Illustration A–1.

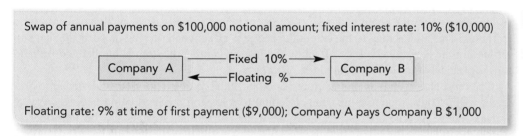

Swap of annual payments on $100,000 notional amount; fixed interest rate: 10% ($10,000)

Company A — Fixed 10% → Company B
← Floating % —

Floating rate: 9% at time of first payment ($9,000); Company A pays Company B $1,000

**Illustration A–1**
Interest Rate Swap—
Shortcut Method

From an accounting standpoint, the central issue is not the operational differences among various hedge instruments, but their similarities in functioning as hedges against risk.

## Accounting for Derivatives

A key to accounting for derivatives is knowing the purpose for which a company holds them and whether the company is effective in serving that purpose. Derivatives, for instance, may be held for risk management (hedging activities). The desired effect, and often the real effect, is a reduction in risk. On the other hand, derivatives sometimes are held for speculative position taking, hoping for large profits. The effect of this activity usually is to *increase* risk. Perhaps more important, derivatives acquired as hedges and intended to reduce risk may, in fact, unintentionally increase risk instead.

It's important to understand that, serving as investments rather than as hedges, derivatives are extremely speculative. This is due to the high leverage inherent in derivatives. Here's why. The investment outlay usually is negligible, but, the potential gain or loss on the investment usually is quite high. A small change in interest rates or another underlying event can trigger a large change in the fair value of the derivative. Because the initial investment was minimal, the change in value relative to the investment itself represents a huge percentage gain or loss. Their extraordinarily risky nature prompted Warren Buffett, one of the country's most celebrated financiers, to refer to derivatives as "financial weapons of mass destruction." Accounting for derivatives is designed to treat differently (a) derivatives designated as hedges and those not designated as hedges as well as (b) the effective portion and the ineffective portion of gains and losses from intended hedges.

The basic approach to accounting for derivatives is fairly straightforward, although implementation can be quite cumbersome. All derivatives, no exceptions, are carried on the

*Derivatives not serving as hedges are extremely speculative due to the high leverage inherent in such investments.*

balance sheet as either assets or liabilities at fair (or market) value.[6] The reasoning is that (a) derivatives create either rights or obligations that meet the definition of assets or liabilities, and (b) fair value is the most meaningful measurement.

Accounting for the gain or loss on a derivative depends on how it is used. Specifically, if the derivative is not designated as a hedging instrument, or doesn't qualify as one, any gain or loss from fair value changes is recognized immediately in earnings. On the other hand, if a derivative is used to hedge against exposure to risk, any gain or loss from fair value changes is either (a) recognized immediately in earnings along with an offsetting loss or gain on the item being hedged or (b) deferred in comprehensive income until it can be recognized in earnings at the same time as earnings are affected by a hedged transaction. Which way depends on whether the derivative is designated as a (a) fair value hedge, (b) cash flow hedge, or (c) foreign currency hedge. Let's look now at each of the three hedge designations.

> Each derivative contract has a "fair value," which is an amount that one side owes the other at a particular moment.

## FAIR VALUE HEDGES

A company can be adversely affected when a change in either prices or interest rates causes a change in the fair value of one of its assets, its liabilities, or a commitment to buy or sell assets or liabilities. If a derivative is used to hedge against the exposure to changes in the fair value of an asset or liability or a firm commitment, it can be designated as a fair value hedge. In that case, when the derivative is adjusted to reflect changes in fair value, the other side of the entry recognizes a gain or loss to be included *currently* in earnings. At the same time, though, the loss or gain from changes in the fair value (due to the risk being hedged)[7] of the item being hedged also is included currently in earnings. This means that, to the extent the hedge is effective in serving its purpose, the gain or loss on the derivative will be offset by the loss or gain on the item being hedged. In fact, this is precisely the concept behind the procedure.

> A gain or loss from a *fair value hedge* is recognized immediately in earnings along with the loss or gain from the item being hedged.

The reasoning is that as interest rates or other underlying events change, a hedge instrument will produce a gain approximately equal to a loss on the item being hedged (or vice versa). These income effects are interrelated and offsetting, so it would be improper to report the income effects in different periods. More critically, the intent and effect of having the hedge instrument is to *lessen* risk. And yet, recognizing gains in one period and counterbalancing losses in another period would tend to cause fluctuations in income that convey an *increase* in risk. However, to the extent that a hedge is ineffective and produces gains or losses different from the losses or gains being hedged, the ineffective portion is recognized in earnings immediately.

> The income effects of the hedge instrument and the income effects of the item being hedged should affect earnings at the same time.

Some of the more common fair value hedges use:

- An interest rate swap to synthetically convert fixed-rate debt (for which interest rate changes could change the fair value of the debt) into floating-rate debt.
- A futures contract to hedge changes in the fair value (due to price changes) of aluminum, sugar, or some other type of inventory.
- A futures contract to hedge the fair value (due to price changes) of a firm commitment to sell natural gas or some other asset.

## ILLUSTRATION

Because interest rate swaps comprise over 65% of derivatives in use, we will use swaps to illustrate accounting for derivatives. Let's look at the example in Illustration A–2 on the next page.

When the floating rate declined from 10% to 9%, the fair values of both the derivative (swap) and the note increased. This created an offsetting gain on the derivative and holding loss on the note. Both are recognized in earnings at the same time (at June 30, 2013).

---

[6]FASB ASC 815–10: Derivatives and Hedging–Overall (previously "Accounting for Derivative Instruments and Hedging Activities," *Statement of Financial Accounting Standards No. 133* (Norwalk, Conn.: FASB, 1998)).

[7]The fair value of a hedged item might also change for reasons other than from effects of the risk being hedged. For instance, the hedged risk may be that a change in interest rates will cause the fair value of a bond to change. The bond price might also change, though, if the market perceives that the bond's default risk has changed.

Wintel Semiconductors issued $1 million of 18-month, 10% bank notes on January 1, 2013. Wintel is exposed to the risk that general interest rates will decline, causing the fair value of its debt to rise. (If the fair value of Wintel's debt increases, its effective borrowing cost is higher relative to the market.) To hedge against this fair value risk, the firm entered into an 18-month interest rate swap agreement on January 1 and designated the swap as a hedge against changes in the fair value of the note. The swap calls for the company to *receive payment* based on a 10% fixed interest rate on a notional amount of $1 million and to *make payment* based on a floating interest rate tied to changes in general rates.[8] As the Illustration will show, this effectively converts Wintel's fixed-rate debt to floating-rate debt. Cash settlement of the net interest amount is made semiannually at June 30 and December 31 of each year with the net interest being the difference between the $50,000 fixed interest [$1 million × (10% × ½)] and the floating interest rate times $1 million at those dates.

Floating (market) settlement rates were 9% at June 30, 2013, 8% at December 31, 2013, and 9% at June 30, 2014. Net interest receipts can be calculated as shown below. Fair values of both the derivative and the note resulting from those market rate changes are assumed to be quotes obtained from securities dealers.

|  | 1/1/13 | 6/30/13 | 12/31/13 | 6/30/14 |
|---|---|---|---|---|
| Fixed rate | 10% | 10% | 10% | 10% |
| Floating rate | 10% | 9% | 8% | 9% |
| Fixed payments ($1 million × [10% × ½]) |  | $ 50,000 | $ 50,000 | $ 50,000 |
| Floating payments ($1 million × ½ floating rate) |  | 45,000 | 40,000 | 45,000 |
| Net interest receipts |  | $ 5,000 | $ 10,000 | $ 5,000 |
| Fair value of interest rate swap | 0 | $ 9,363 | $ 9,615 | 0 |
| Fair value of note payable | $1,000,000 | $1,009,363 | $1,009,615 | $1,000,000 |

**January 1, 2013**

| Cash | 1,000,000 | |
| Notes payable | | 1,000,000 |

To record the issuance of the note.

*The interest rate swap is designated as a fair value hedge on this note at issuance.*

**June 30, 2013**

| Interest expense (10% × ½ × $1 million) | 50,000 | |
| Cash | | 50,000 |

To record interest.

| Cash ($50,000 − [9% × ½ × $1 million]) | 5,000 | |
| Interest expense | | 5,000 |

To record the net cash settlement.

*The swap settlement is the difference between the fixed interest (5%) and variable interest (4.5%).*

| Interest rate swap[9] ($9,363 − 0) | 9,363 | |
| Holding gain—interest rate swap | | 9,363 |

To record change in fair value of the derivative.

*The fair value of derivatives is recognized in the balance sheet.*

| Holding loss—hedged note | 9,363 | |
| Note payable ($1,009,363 − 1,000,000) | | 9,363 |

To record change in fair value of the note due to interest rate changes.

*The hedged liability (or asset) is adjusted to fair value as well.*

The net interest settlement on June 30, 2013, is $5,000 because the fixed rate is 5% (half of the 10% annual rate) and the floating rate is 4.5% (half of the 9% annual rate).

---

[8] A common measure for benchmarking variable interest rates is LIBOR, the London Interbank Offered Rate, a base rate at which large international banks lend funds to each other.

[9] This would be a liability rather than an investment (asset) if the fair value had declined.

As with any debt, interest expense is the effective rate times the outstanding balance.

| December 31, 2013 | | |
|---|---|---|
| Interest expense ............................................................................ | 50,000 | |
|     Cash (10% × ½ × $1,000,000) ................................................. | | 50,000 |
| *To record interest.* | | |

The settlement is the difference between the fixed interest (5%) and variable interest (4%).

| Cash ($50,000 – [8% × ½ × $1 million]) ............................................ | 10,000 | |
|---|---|---|
|     Interest expense .................................................................... | | 10,000 |
| *To record the net cash settlement.* | | |

The derivative is increased by the change in fair value. The note is increased by the change in fair value.

| Interest rate swap ($9,615 – 9,363) .................................................. | 252 | |
|---|---|---|
|     Holding gain—interest rate swap ............................................ | | 252 |
| *To record the change in fair value of the derivative.* | | |
| Holding loss—hedged note ............................................................. | 252 | |
|     Note payable ($1,009,615 – 1,009,363) ................................... | | 252 |
| *To record the change in fair value of the note due to interest rate changes.* | | |

The fair value of the swap increased by $252 (from $9,363 to $9,615). Similarly, we adjust the note's carrying value by the amount necessary to increase it to fair value. This produces a holding loss on the note that exactly offsets the gain on the swap. This result is the hedging effect that motivated Wintel to enter the fair value hedging arrangement in the first place.

At June 30, 2014, Wintel repeats the process of adjusting to fair value both the derivative investment and the note being hedged.

The net interest received is the difference between the fixed interest (5%) and floating interest (4.5%).

| June 30, 2014 | | |
|---|---|---|
| Interest expense ............................................................................ | 50,000 | |
|     Cash (10% × ½ × $1,000,000) ................................................. | | 50,000 |
| *To record interest.* | | |
| Cash [$50,000 – (9% × ½ × $1 million)] ............................................ | 5,000 | |
|     Interest expense .................................................................... | | 5,000 |
| *To record the net cash settlement.* | | |

The swap's fair value now is zero.

| Holding loss—interest rate swap ..................................................... | 9,615 | |
|---|---|---|
|     Interest rate swap ($0 – 9,615) ............................................... | | 9,615 |
| *To record the change in fair value of the derivative.* | | |
| Note payable ($1,000,000 – 1,009,615) ............................................. | 9,615 | |
|     Holding gain—hedged note ..................................................... | | 9,615 |
| *To record the change in fair value of the note due to interest rate changes.* | | |
| Note payable ................................................................................... | 1,000,000 | |
|     Cash ....................................................................................... | | 1,000,000 |
| *To repay the loan.* | | |

The net interest received is the difference between the fixed rate (5%) and floating rate (4.5%) times $1 million. The fair value of the swap decreased by $9,615 (from $9,615 to zero).[10] That decline represents a holding *loss* that we recognize in earnings. Similarly, we record an offsetting holding *gain* on the note for the change in its fair value.

Now let's see how the carrying values changed for the swap account and the note:

| | Swap | | | Note | |
|---|---|---|---|---|---|
| Jan. 1, 2013 | | | | | 1,000,000 |
| June 30, 2013 | 9,363 | | | | 9,363 |
| Dec. 31, 2013 | 252 | | | | 252 |
| June 30, 2014 | | 9,615 | | 9,615 | |
| | | | | 1,000,000 | |
| | 0 | | | | 0 |

---

[10]Because there are no future cash receipts from the swap arrangement at this point, the fair value of the swap is zero.

The income statement is affected as follows:

**Income Statement + (−)**

| | | |
|---|---|---|
| *June 30, 2013* | (50,000) | Interest expense—fixed payment |
| | 5,000 | Interest expense—net cash settlement |
| | 9,363 | Holding gain—interest rate swap |
| | (9,363) | Holding loss—hedged note |
| | (45,000) | Net effect—same as floating interest payment |
| *Dec. 31, 2013* | (50,000) | Interest expense—fixed payment |
| | 10,000 | Interest expense—net cash settlement |
| | 252 | Holding gain—interest rate swap |
| | (252) | Holding loss—hedged note |
| | (40,000) | Net effect—same as floating interest payment |
| *June 30, 2014* | (50,000) | Interest expense—fixed payment |
| | 5,000 | Interest expense—net cash settlement |
| | 9,615 | Holding gain—interest rate swap |
| | (9,615) | Holding loss—hedged note |
| | (45,000) | Net effect—same as floating interest payment |

As this demonstrates, the swap effectively converts fixed-interest debt to floating-interest debt.

# Additional Consideration

### Fair Value of the Swap

The fair value of a derivative typically is based on a quote obtained from a derivatives dealer. That fair value will approximate the present value of the expected net interest settlement receipts for the remaining term of the swap. In fact, we can actually calculate the fair value of the swap that we accepted as given in our illustration.

Since the June 30, 2013, floating rate of 9% caused the cash settlement on that date to be $5,000, it's reasonable to look at 9% as the best estimate of future floating rates and therefore assume the remaining two cash settlements also will be $5,000 each. We can then calculate at June 30, 2013, the present value of those expected net interest settlement receipts for the remaining term of the swap:

| | | |
|---|---|---|
| Fixed interest | 10% × ½ × $1 million | $ 50,000 |
| Expected floating interest | 9% × ½ × $1 million | 45,000 |
| Expected cash receipts for both Dec. 31, 2013 and June 30, 2014 | | $ 5,000 |
| | | × 1.87267* |
| Present value | | $ 9,363 |

*Present value of an ordinary annuity of $1: $n = 2$, $i = 4.5\%$ (½ of 9%) (from Table 4)

### Fair Value of the Notes

The fair value of the note payable will be the present value of principal and remaining interest payments discounted at the *market rate*. The market rate will vary with the designated floating rate but might differ due to changes in default (credit) risk and the term structure of interest rates. Assuming it's 9% at June 30, 2013, we can calculate the fair value (present value) of the notes:

| | | |
|---|---|---|
| Interest | $50,000* × 1.87267[†] = | $ 93,633 |
| Principal | $1,000,000 × .91573[‡] = | 915,730 |
| | | $1,009,363 |

*½ of 10% × $1,000,000
[†]Present value of an ordinary annuity of $1: $n = 2$, $i = 4.5\%$ (from Table 4)
[‡]Present value of $1: $n = 2$, $i = 4.5\%$ (from Table 2)

(continued)

(concluded)

Note: Often the cash settlement rate is "reset" as of each cash settlement date (thus the floating rate actually used at the end of each period to determine the payment is the floating market rate as of the *beginning* of the same period). In our illustration, for instance, there would have been no cash settlement at June 30, 2013, since we would use the beginning floating rate of 10% to determine payment. Similarly, we would have used the 9% floating rate at June 30, 2013, to determine the cash settlement six months later at December 31. In effect, each cash settlement would be delayed six months. Had this arrangement been in effect in the current illustration, there would have been one fewer cash settlement payments (two rather than three), but would not have affected the fair value calculations above because, either way, our expectation would be cash receipts of $5,000 for both Dec. 31, 2013, and June 30, 2014.

**CASH FLOW HEDGES** The risk in some transactions or events is the risk of a change in cash flows, rather than a change in fair values. We noted earlier, for instance, that *fixed-rate* debt subjects a company to the risk that interest rate changes could change the fair value of the debt. On the other hand, if the obligation is *floating-rate* debt, the fair value of the debt will not change when interest rates do, but cash flows will. If a derivative is used to hedge against the exposure to changes in cash inflows or cash outflows of an asset or liability or a forecasted transaction (like a future purchase or sale), it can be designated as a cash flow hedge. In that case, when the derivative is adjusted to reflect changes in fair value, the other side of the entry is a gain or loss to be deferred as a component of other comprehensive income and included in earnings later, at the same time as earnings are affected by the hedged transaction. Once again, the effect is matching the earnings effect of the derivative with the earnings effect of the item being hedged, precisely the concept behind hedge accounting.

> A gain or loss from a *cash flow hedge* is deferred as other comprehensive income until it can be recognized in earnings along with the earnings effect of the item being hedged.

To understand the deferral of the gain or loss, we need to revisit the concept of comprehensive income. Comprehensive income, as you may recall from Chapters 4, 12, 17, and 18, is a more expansive view of the change in shareholders' equity than traditional net income. In fact, it encompasses all changes in equity other than from transactions with owners.[11] So, in addition to net income itself, comprehensive income includes up to four other changes in equity that don't (yet) belong in net income, namely, net holding gains (losses) on investments (Chapter 12), gains (losses) from and amendments to postretirement benefit plans (Chapter 17), gains (losses) from foreign currency translation, and deferred gains (losses) from derivatives designated as cash flow hedges.[12]

Some of the more commonly used cash flow hedges are:

- An interest rate swap to synthetically convert floating rate debt (for which interest rate changes could change the cash interest payments) into fixed rate debt.
- A futures contract to hedge a forecasted sale (for which price changes could change the cash receipts) of natural gas, crude oil, or some other asset.

**FOREIGN CURRENCY HEDGES** Today's economy is increasingly a global one. The majority of large "U.S." companies are, in truth, multinational companies that may receive only a fraction of their revenues from U.S. operations. Many operations of those companies are located abroad. Foreign operations often are denominated in the currency of the foreign country (the Euro, Japanese yen, Russian rubles, and so on). Even companies without foreign operations sometimes hold investments, issue debt, or conduct other transactions denominated in foreign currencies. As exchange rates change, the dollar equivalent of the

> The possibility that foreign currency exchange rates might change exposes many companies to foreign currency risk.

---

[11]Transactions with owners primarily include dividends and the sale or purchase of shares of the company's stock.
[12]FASB ASC 220–10–55–2: Comprehensive Income–Overall–Implementation Guidance and Illustrations (previously "Reporting Comprehensive Income," *Statement of Financial Accounting Standards No. 130* (Norwalk, Conn.: FASB, 1997)).

foreign currency changes. The possibility of currency rate changes exposes these companies to the risk that some transactions require settlement in a currency other than the entities' functional currency or that foreign operations will require translation adjustments to reported amounts.

A **foreign currency hedge** can be a hedge of foreign currency exposure of:

- A firm commitment—treated as a fair value hedge.
- An available-for-sale security—treated as a fair value hedge.
- A forecasted transaction—treated as a cash flow hedge.
- A company's net investment in a foreign operation—the gain or loss is reported in *other comprehensive income* as part of unrealized gains and losses from foreign currency translation.[13]

**HEDGE EFFECTIVENESS** When a company elects to apply hedge accounting, it must establish at the inception of the hedge the method it will use to assess the effectiveness of the hedging derivative as well as the measurement approach it will use to determine the ineffective portion of the hedge.[14] The key criterion for qualifying as a hedge is that the hedging relationship must be "highly effective" in achieving offsetting changes in fair values or cash flows based on the hedging company's specified risk management objective and strategy.

An assessment of this effectiveness must be made at least every three months and whenever financial statements are issued. There are no precise guidelines for assessing effectiveness, but it generally means a high correlation between changes in the fair value or cash flows of the derivative and of the item being hedged, not necessarily a specific reduction in risk. Hedge accounting must be terminated for hedging relationships that no longer are highly effective.

> To qualify as a hedge, the hedging relationship must be highly effective in achieving offsetting changes in fair values or cash flows.

**HEDGE INEFFECTIVENESS** In Illustration A–2, the loss on the hedged note exactly offset the gain on the swap. This is because the swap in this instance was highly effective in hedging the risk due to interest rate changes. However, the loss and gain would not have exactly offset each other if the hedging arrangement had been ineffective. For instance, suppose the swap's term had been different from that of the note (say a three-year swap term compared with the 18-month term of the note) or if the notional amount of the swap differed from that of the note (say $500,000 rather than $1 million). In that case, changes in the fair value of the swap and changes in the fair value of the note would not be the same. The result would be a greater (or lesser) amount recognized in earnings for the swap than for the note. Because there would not be an exact offset, earnings would be affected, an effect resulting from hedge ineffectiveness. That is a desired effect of hedge accounting; to the extent that a hedge is effective, the earnings effect of a derivative cancels out the earnings effect of the item being hedged. However, even if a hedge is highly effective, all ineffectiveness is recognized currently in earnings.

> Imperfect hedges result in part of the derivative gain or loss being included in current earnings.

**FAIR VALUE CHANGES UNRELATED TO THE RISK BEING HEDGED** In Illustration A–2, the fair value of the hedged note and the fair value of the swap changed by the same amounts each year because we assumed the fair values changed only due to interest rate changes. It's also possible, though, that the note's fair value would change by an amount different from that of the swap for reasons unrelated to interest rates. Remember from our earlier discussion that the market's perception of a company's creditworthiness, and thus its ability to pay interest and principal when due, also can affect the value of debt, whether interest rates change or not. In hedge accounting, we ignore those changes. We recognize

---

[13]This is the same treatment previously prescribed for these translation adjustments by *Statement of Financial Accounting Standards No. 52* [FASB ASC 830: Foreign Currency Matters].

[14]Remember, if a derivative is not designated as a hedge, any gains or losses from changes in its fair value are recognized immediately in earnings.

only the fair value changes in the hedged item that we can attribute to the risk being hedged (interest rate risk in this case). For example, if a changing perception of default risk had caused the note's fair value to increase by an additional, say $5,000, our journal entries in Illustration A–2 would have been unaffected. Notice, then, that although we always mark a *derivative* to fair value, the reported amount of the *item being hedged* may not be its fair value. We mark a hedged item to fair value only to the extent that its fair value changed due to the risk being hedged.

*Fair value changes unrelated to the risk being hedged are ignored.*

## Disclosure of Derivatives and Risk

To be adequately informed about the effectiveness of a company's risk management, investors and creditors need information about strategies for holding derivatives and specific hedging activities. Toward that end, extensive disclosure requirements provide information that includes:

- Objectives and strategies for holding and issuing derivatives.
- A description of the items for which risks are being hedged.
- For forecasted transactions: a description, time before the transaction is expected to occur, the gains and losses accumulated in other comprehensive income, and the events that will trigger their recognition in earnings.
- Beginning balance of, changes in, and ending balance of the derivative component of other comprehensive income.
- The net amount of gain or loss reported in earnings (representing aggregate hedge ineffectiveness).
- Qualitative and quantitative information about failed hedges: canceled commitments or previously hedged forecasted transactions no longer expected to occur.

The intent is to provide information about the company's success in reducing risks and consequently about risks not managed successfully. Remember, too, that when derivatives are employed ineffectively, risks can escalate. Ample disclosures about derivatives are essential to maintain awareness of potential opportunities and problems with risk management.

In addition, newly issued GAAP requires companies to provide enhanced disclosures indicating (a) how and why the company uses derivative instruments, (b) how the company accounts for derivative instruments and related hedged items, and (c) how derivative instruments and related hedged items affect the company's balance sheet, income statement, and cash flows.[15] The required disclosures includes two tables, one that highlights the location and fair values of derivative instruments in the balance sheet, and another that indicates the location and amounts of gains and losses on derivative instruments in the income statement. The two tables distinguish between derivative instruments that are designated as hedging instruments and those that are not. The tables also categorize derivative instruments by each major type—interest rate contracts, foreign exchange contracts, equity contracts, commodity contracts, credit contracts and other types of contracts.

Even for some traditional liabilities, the amounts reported on the face of the financial statements provide inadequate disclosure about the degree to which a company is exposed to risk of loss. To provide adequate disclosure about a company's exposure to risk, additional information must be provided about (a) concentrations of credit risk and (b) the fair value of all financial instruments.[16]

---

[15]FASB ASC 815: Derivatives and Hedging (previously "Disclosures about Derivative Instruments and Hedging Activities—an amendment of FASB Statement No. 133," *Statement of Financial Accounting Standards No. 161* (Stamford, Conn.: FASB, 2008)).

[16]FASB ASC 825–10–50–1: Financial Instruments–Overall–Disclosure (previously "Disclosures About Fair Values of Financial Instruments," *Statement of Financial Accounting Standards No. 107* (Norwalk, Conn.: FASB, 1991), as amended by *Statement of Financial Accounting Standards No. 133,* "Accounting for Derivative Instruments and Hedging Activities" (Norwalk, Conn.: FASB, 1998)).

## Extended Method for Interest Rate Swap Accounting

A shortcut method for accounting for an interest rate swap is permitted when a hedge meets certain criteria. In general, the criteria are designed to see if the hedge supports the assumption of "no ineffectiveness." Illustration A–2 of a fair value hedge met those criteria, in particular, (a) the swap's notional amount matches the note's principal amount, (b) the swap's expiration date matches the note's maturity date, (c) the fair value of the swap is zero at inception, and (d) the floating payment is at the market rate.[17] Because Wintel can conclude that the swap will be highly effective in offsetting changes in the fair value of the debt, it can use the changes in the fair value of the swap to measure the offsetting changes in the fair value of the debt. That's the essence of the shortcut method used in Illustration A–2. The extended method required when the criteria are *not* met for the short-cut method is described in this section (Illustration A–3). It produces the same effect on earnings and in the balance sheet as does the procedure shown in Illustration A–2.

Wintel Semiconductors issued $1 million of 18-month, 10% bank notes on January 1, 2013. Wintel is exposed to the risk that general interest rates will decline, causing the fair value of its debt to rise. (If the fair value of Wintel's debt increases, its effective borrowing cost is higher relative to the market.) To hedge against this fair value risk, the firm entered into an 18-month interest rate swap agreement on January 1 and designated the swap as a hedge against changes in the fair value of the note. The swap calls for the company to *receive payment* based on a 10% fixed interest rate on a notional amount of $1 million and to *make payment* based on a floating interest rate tied to changes in general rates. Cash settlement of the net interest amount is made semiannually at June 30 and December 31 of each year with the net interest being the difference between the $50,000 fixed interest [$1 million × (10% × ½)] and the floating interest rate times $1 million at those dates.

Floating (market) settlement rates were 9% at June 30, 2013, 8% at December 31, 2013, and 8% at June 30, 2014. Net interest receipts can be calculated as shown below. Fair values of both the derivative and the note resulting from those market rate changes are assumed to be quotes obtained from securities dealers.

| | 1/1/13 | 6/30/13 | 12/31/13 | 6/30/14 |
|---|---|---|---|---|
| Fixed rate | 10% | 10% | 10% | 10% |
| Floating rate | 10% | 9% | 8% | 9% |
| Fixed payments | | | | |
| [$1 million × (10% × ½)] | | $ 50,000 | $ 50,000 | $ 50,000 |
| Floating payments | | | | |
| ($1 million × ½ floating rate) | | 45,000 | 40,000 | 45,000 |
| Net interest receipts | | $ 5,000 | $ 10,000 | $ 5,000 |
| Fair value of interest rate swap | 0 | $ 9,363 | $ 9,615 | 0 |
| Fair value of note payable | $1,000,000 | $1,009,363 | $1,009,615 | $1,000,000 |

**Illustration A–3**

Interest Rate Swap—Extended Method

When the floating rate declined in Illustration A–3 from 10% to 9%, the fair values of both the derivative (swap) and the note increased. This created an offsetting gain on the derivative and holding loss on the note. Both are recognized in earnings the same period (June 30, 2013).

| **January 1, 2013** | | |
|---|---|---|
| Cash ................................................................................ | 1,000,000 | |
|    Notes payable ........................................................... | | 1,000,000 |
| *To record the issuance of the note.* | | |

The interest rate swap is designated as a fair value hedge on this note at issuance.

---

[17]There is no precise minimum interval, though it generally is three to six months or less. Other criteria are specified by previously FASB ASC 815–20–25–104: Derivatives and Hedging–Hedging–General–Recognition–Shortcut Method, *SFAS No. 133* (para. 68) in addition to the key conditions listed here.

The swap settlement is the difference between the fixed interest (5%) and variable interest (4.5%).

**June 30, 2013**

| | | |
|---|---|---|
| Interest expense (10% × ½ × $1 million) ............................................. | 50,000 | |
|    Cash ..................................................................................... | | 50,000 |
| *To record interest.* | | |

The fair value of derivatives is recognized in the balance sheet.

| | | |
|---|---|---|
| Cash ($50,000 – [9% × ½ × $1 million]) ............................................. | 5,000 | |
| Interest rate swap ($9,363 – 0) ......................................................... | 9,363 | |
|    Interest revenue (10% × ½ × $0) ................................................ | | 0 |
|    Holding gain—interest rate swap (to balance) ............................... | | 14,363 |
| *To record the net cash settlement, accrued interest on the swap,* | | |
| *and change in the fair value of the derivative.* | | |

The hedged liability (or asset) is adjusted to fair value as well.

| | | |
|---|---|---|
| Holding loss—hedged note ................................................................ | 9,363 | |
|    Notes payable ($1,009,363 – 1,000,000) ....................................... | | 9,363 |
| *To record change in fair value of the note due to interest rate changes.* | | |

The net interest settlement on June 30, 2013, is $5,000 because the fixed rate is 5% (half of the 10% annual rate) and the floating rate is 4.5% (half of the 9% annual rate). A holding gain ($14,363) is produced by holding the derivative security during a time when an interest rate decline caused an increase in the value of that asset. A portion ($5,000) of the gain was received in cash and another portion ($9,363) is reflected as an increase in the value of the asset.

We also have holding loss of the same amount. This is because we also held a liability during the same time period, and the interest rate change caused its fair value to increase as well.

As with any debt, interest expense is the effective rate times the outstanding balance.

**December 31, 2013**

| | | |
|---|---|---|
| Interest expense (9% × ½ × $1,009,363) ............................................. | 45,421 | |
| Notes payable (difference)* ............................................................... | 4,579 | |
|    Cash (10% × ½ × $1,000,000) ...................................................... | | 50,000 |
| *To record interest.* | | |

The cash settlement is the difference between the fixed interest (5%) and variable interest (4%).

Interest ($421) accrues on the asset.

| | | |
|---|---|---|
| Cash [$50,000 – (8% × ½ × $1 million)] ............................................. | 10,000 | |
| Interest rate swap ($9,615 – 9,363) ................................................... | 252 | |
|    Interest revenue (9% × ½ × $9,363) ............................................. | | 421 |
|    Holding gain—interest rate swap (to balance) ............................... | | 9,831 |
| *To record the net cash settlement, accrued interest on the swap,* | | |
| *and change in the fair value of the derivative.* | | |

The note is increased by the change in fair value.

| | | |
|---|---|---|
| Holding loss—hedged note ................................................................ | 4,831 | |
|    Notes payable ($1,009,615 – 1,009,363 + 4,579) ......................... | | 4,831 |
| *To record the change in fair value of the note due to interest rate changes.* | | |

*We could use a premium on the note to adjust its carrying amount.

We determine interest on the note the same way we do for any liability, as you learned earlier—at the effective rate (9% × ½) times the outstanding balance ($1,009,363). This results in reducing the note's carrying amount for the cash interest paid in excess of the interest expense.

The fair value of the swap increased due to the interest rate decline by $252 (from $9,363 to $9,615). The holding gain we recognize in earnings consists of that increase (a) plus the $10,000 cash settlement also created by the interest rate decline and (b) minus the $421 increase that results not from the interest rate decline, but from interest accruing on the asset.[18] Similarly, we adjust the note's carrying value by the amount necessary to increase it to fair value, allowing for the $4,579 reduction in the note in the earlier entry to record interest.

At June 30, 2014, Wintel repeats the process of adjusting to fair value both the derivative investment and the note being hedged.

---

[18]The investment in the interest rate swap represents the present value of expected future net interest receipts. As with other such assets, interest accrues at the effective rate times the outstanding balance. You also can think of the accrued interest mathematically as the increase in present value of the future cash flows as we get one period nearer to the dates when the cash will be received.

**June 30, 2014**

| | | |
|---|---:|---:|
| Interest expense (8% × ½ × $1,009,615) | 40,385 | |
| Notes payable (difference) | 9,615 | |
| Cash (10% × ½ × $1,000,000) | | 50,000 |

*To record interest.*

| | | |
|---|---:|---:|
| Cash [$50,000 − (9% × ½ × $1 million)] | 5,000 | |
| Holding loss—interest rate swap (to balance) | 5,000 | |
| Interest rate swap ($0 − $9,615) | | 9,615 |
| Interest revenue (8% × ½ × $9,615) | | 385 |

*To record the net cash settlement, accrued interest on the swap, and change in the fair value of the derivative.*

| | | |
|---|---:|---:|
| Notes payable ($1,000,000 − 1,009,615 + 9,615) | 0 | |
| Holding gain—hedged note | | 0 |

*To record the change in fair value of the note due to interest rate changes.*

| | | |
|---|---:|---:|
| Note payable | 1,000,000 | |
| Cash | | 1,000,000 |

*To repay the loan*

*Interest expense is the effective rate times the outstanding balance.*

*The net interest received is the difference between the fixed interest (5%) and floating interest (4.5%).*

*The swap's fair value now is zero.*

The net interest received is the difference between the fixed rate (5%) and floating rate (4.5%) times $1 million. The fair value of the swap decreased by $9,615 (from $9,615 to zero).[19] The holding loss we recognize in earnings consists of that decline (a) minus the $5,000 portion of the decline resulting from it being realized in cash settlement and (b) plus the $385 increase that results not from the interest rate change, but from interest accruing on the asset.

Now let's see how the carrying values changed for the swap account and the note:

| | Swap | | | | Note |
|---|---:|---:|---:|---:|---:|
| Jan. 1, 2013 | | | | | 1,000,000 |
| June 30, 2013 | 9,363 | | | | 9,363 |
| Dec. 31, 2013 | 252 | | | 4,579 | 4,831 |
| June 30, 2014 | | 9,615 | | 9,615 | |
| | | | | 1,000,000 | |
| | 0 | | | | 0 |

The income statement is affected as follows:

| Income Statement + (−) | | |
|---|---:|---|
| June 30, 2013 | (50,000) | Interest expense |
| | 0 | Interest revenue (no time has passed) |
| | 14,363 | Holding gain interest rate swap |
| | (9,363) | Holding loss—hedged note |
| | (45,000) | Net effect—same as floating interest payment |
| Dec. 31, 2013 | (45,421) | Interest expense |
| | 421 | Interest revenue |
| | 9,831 | Holding gain—interest rate swap |
| | (4,831) | Holding loss—hedged note |
| | (40,000) | Net effect—same as floating interest payment |
| June 30, 2014 | (40,385) | Interest expense |
| | 385 | Interest revenue |
| | (5,000) | Holding gain—interest rate swap |
| | 0 | Holding loss—hedged note |
| | (45,000) | Net effect—same as floating interest payment |

[19]Because there are no future cash receipts or payments from the swap arrangement at this point, the fair value of the swap is zero.

As this demonstrates, the swap effectively converts Wintel's fixed-interest debt to floating-interest debt.

# International Financial Reporting Standards

**Accounting for Derivatives.**

*"With IAS 39, if you understand it, you haven't read it properly,"* said International Accounting Standards Board Chairman, Sir David Tweedie.[20]

As with U.S. GAAP, accounting for derivatives under IFRS is quite complex. In fact, *IAS No. 39* provides an example of international accounting that defies the usual characterization of IFRS as being "principles-based accounting" in comparison with "rules-based" U.S. GAAP. Like U.S. GAAP, all freestanding derivatives are recognized in the balance sheet and measured at fair value under IFRS. And, unless they qualify as hedging instruments in a cash flow hedge or net investment in a foreign operation, all changes in fair value are recognized immediately in net income, as under U.S. GAAP. Although the hedging models under U.S. GAAP and IFRS are similar, several differences exist. Here are a few significant ones:

- The short-cut method for interest rate swaps described in this Appendix is not permitted under IFRS.
- The key criterion for qualifying as a hedge is that the hedging relationship must be "highly effective" in achieving offsetting changes in fair values or cash flows, which under U.S. GAAP generally means a high correlation between changes in the fair value or cash flows of the derivative and the item being hedged. Highly effective is more precisely defined under IFRS: the hedge must be within the range of 80–120 percent effective.
- U.S. GAAP does not permit a single hedging instrument to hedge more than one risk in two or more hedged items. However, IFRS allows a single hedging instrument to be designated as a hedge of more than one type of risk if the risks being hedged can be clearly identified, the hedge effectiveness can be demonstrated, and specific designation to different risk positions can be ensured.

# Where We're Headed

The Financial Accounting Standards Board and the International Accounting Standards Board, after working jointly on new guidance for when companies would be allowed to offset financial assets and financial liabilities in the balance sheet, a practice also known as "netting," issued an Exposure Draft of a new Accounting Standards Update in January 2011. The new ASU would have drawn U.S. GAAP closer to IFRS with regard to presenting a single net amount in the balance sheet only when it (a) has an unconditional and legally enforceable right to set off the financial asset and liability and (b) intends to settle on a net basis (or to realize the financial asset and liability simultaneously). And, because master netting agreements usually include only a conditional right of offset, many more derivatives would have been reported gross (rather than net) in the balance sheet.

In June 2011, the FASB, under pressure from constituents, had a change of mind. The U.S. Board decided to support an approach for derivatives very close to what is permitted currently under U.S. GAAP. Financial institutions in particular lobbied the FASB to continue to allow companies to net derivatives that are subject to master netting agreements, a practice critical to leverage and other key measures that affect debt covenants and other contractual agreements.

The following month, the IASB decided that although they would not be issuing a joint ASU, the two boards agreed to at least fill the gap with additional disclosure requirements to enable users to sort out the differences.

---

[20]Michael Cohn, "Tweedie Says FASB Will Always Play a Role," WebCPA, December 11, 2008.

## The Bottom Line

● **LOA–1**   All derivatives are reported in the balance sheet at fair value.

● **LOA–2**   *Hedging* means taking a risk position that is opposite to an actual position that is exposed to risk. For a derivative used to hedge against exposure to risk, treatment of any gain or loss from fair value changes depends on whether the derivative is designated as (a) a fair value hedge, (b) a cash flow hedge, or (c) a foreign currency hedge.

● **LOA–3**   We recognize a gain or loss from a *fair value hedge* immediately in earnings along with the loss or gain from the item being hedged. This is so the income effects of the hedge instrument and the income effects of the item being hedged will affect earnings at the same time.

● **LOA–4**   We defer a gain or loss from a *cash flow hedge* as part of other comprehensive income until it can be recognized in earnings along with the earnings effect of the item being hedged.

● **LOA–5**   Imperfect hedges result in part of the derivative gain or loss being included in current earnings. We ignore market value changes unrelated to the risk being hedged.

● **LOA–6**   Extensive disclosure requirements about derivatives are designed to provide investors and creditors information about the adequacy of a company's risk management and the company's success in reducing risks, including risks not managed successfully.  ●

## Questions For Review of Key Topics

Q A–1   Some financial instruments are called derivatives. Why?

Q A–2   Should gains and losses on a fair value hedge be recorded as they occur, or should they be recorded to coincide with losses and gains on the item being hedged?

Q A–3   Hines Moving Company held a fixed-rate debt of $2 million. The company wanted to hedge its fair value exposure with an interest rate swap. However, the only notional available at the time, on the type of swap it desired, was $2.5 million. What will be the effect of any gain or loss on the $500,000 notional difference?

Q A–4   What is a futures contract?

Q A–5   What is the effect on interest of an interest rate swap?

Q A–6   How are derivatives reported on the balance sheet? Why?

Q A–7   When is a gain or a loss from a cash flow hedge reported in earnings?

## Exercises

**E A–1**
Derivatives-hedge classification

Indicate (by abbreviation) the type of hedge each activity described below would represent.

**Hedge Type**

FV    Fair value hedge
CF    Cash flow hedge
FC    Foreign currency hedge
N     Would not qualify as a hedge

Activity

_____ 1. An options contract to hedge possible future price changes of inventory.

_____ 2. A futures contract to hedge exposure to interest rate changes prior to replacing bank notes when they mature.

_____ 3. An interest rate swap to synthetically convert floating rate debt into fixed rate debt.

_____ 4. An interest rate swap to synthetically convert fixed rate debt into floating rate debt.

_____ 5. A futures contract to hedge possible future price changes of timber covered by a firm commitment to sell.

_____ 6. A futures contract to hedge possible future price changes of a forecasted sale of tin.

_____ 7. ExxonMobil's net investment in a Kuwait oil field.

_____ 8. An interest rate swap to synthetically convert floating rate interest on a stock investment into fixed rate interest.

_____ 9. An interest rate swap to synthetically convert fixed rate interest on a held-to-maturity debt investment into floating rate interest.

_____ 10. An interest rate swap to synthetically convert floating rate interest on a held-to-maturity debt investment into fixed rate interest.

_____ 11. An interest rate swap to synthetically convert fixed rate interest on a stock investment into floating rate interest.

**E A–2**
Derivatives;
interest rate
swap; fixed rate
debt

On January 1, 2013, LLB Industries borrowed $200,000 from Trust Bank by issuing a two-year, 10% note, with interest payable quarterly. LLB entered into a two-year interest rate swap agreement on January 1, 2013, and designated the swap as a fair value hedge. Its intent was to hedge the risk that general interest rates will decline, causing the fair value of its debt to increase. The agreement called for the company to receive payment based on a 10% fixed interest rate on a notional amount of $200,000 and to pay interest based on a floating interest rate. The contract called for cash settlement of the net interest amount quarterly.

Floating (LIBOR) settlement rates were 10% at January 1, 8% at March 31, and 6% June 30, 2013. The fair values of the swap are quotes obtained from a derivatives dealer. Those quotes and the fair values of the note are as indicated below.

|  | January 1 | March 31 | June 30 |
|---|---|---|---|
| Fair value of interest rate swap | 0 | $ 6,472 | $ 11,394 |
| Fair value of note payable | $200,000 | $206,472 | $211,394 |

**Required:**

1. Calculate the net cash settlement at March 31 and June 30, 2013.

2. Prepare the journal entries through June 30, 2013, to record the issuance of the note, interest, and necessary adjustments for changes in fair value.

**E A–3**
Derivatives;
interest rate
swap; fixed rate
investment

(This is a variation of Exercise A–2, modified to consider an investment in debt securities.)

On January 1, 2013, S&S Corporation invested in LLB Industries' negotiable two-year, 10% notes, with interest receivable quarterly. The company classified the investment as available-for-sale. S&S entered into a two-year interest rate swap agreement on January 1, 2013, and designated the swap as a fair value hedge. Its intent was to hedge the risk that general interest rates will decline, causing the fair value of its investment to increase. The agreement called for the company to make payment based on a 10% fixed interest rate on a notional amount of $200,000 and to receive interest based on a floating interest rate. The contract called for cash settlement of the net interest amount quarterly.

Floating (LIBOR) settlement rates were 10% at January 1, 8% at March 31, and 6% June 30, 2013. The fair values of the swap are quotes obtained from a derivatives dealer. Those quotes and the fair values of the investment in notes are as follows:

|  | January 1 | March 31 | June 30 |
|---|---|---|---|
| Fair value of interest rate swap | 0 | $ 6,472 | $ 11,394 |
| Fair value of the investment in notes | $200,000 | $206,472 | $211,394 |

**Required:**

1. Calculate the net cash settlement at March 31 and June 30, 2013.

2. Prepare the journal entries through June 30, 2013, to record the investment in notes, interest, and necessary adjustments for changes in fair value.

**E A–4**
Derivatives;
interest rate
swap; fixed rate
debt; fair value
change unrelated
to hedged risk

(This is a variation of Exercise A–2, modified to consider fair value change unrelated to hedged risk.)

LLB Industries borrowed $200,000 from Trust Bank by issuing a two-year, 10% note, with interest payable quarterly. LLB entered into a two-year interest rate swap agreement on January 1, 2013 and designated the swap as a fair value hedge. Its intent was to hedge the risk that general interest rates will decline, causing the fair value of its debt to increase. The agreement called for the company to receive payment based on a 10% fixed interest rate on a notional amount of $200,000 and to pay interest based on a floating interest rate.

Floating (LIBOR) settlement rates were 10% at January 1, 8% at March 31, and 6% at June 30, 2013. The fair values of the swap are quotes obtained from a derivatives dealer. Those quotes and the fair values of the note are as indicated below. The additional rise in the fair value of the note (higher than that of the swap) on June 30 was due to investors' perceptions that the creditworthiness of LLB was improving.

|  | January 1 | March 31 | June 30 |
|---|---|---|---|
| Fair value of interest rate swap | 0 | $ 6,472 | $ 11,394 |
| Fair value of note payable | $200,000 | $206,472 | $220,000 |

**Required:**

1. Calculate the net cash settlement at June 30, 2013.

2. Prepare the journal entries on June 30, 2013, to record the interest and necessary adjustments for changes in fair value.

**E A–5**
Derivatives;
interest rate swap;
fixed rate debt;
extended method

(This is a variation of Exercise A–2, modified to consider the extended method.)

On January 1, 2013, LLB Industries borrowed $200,000 from Trust Bank by issuing a two-year, 10% note, with interest payable quarterly. LLB entered into a two-year interest rate swap agreement on January 1, 2013, and designated the swap as a fair value hedge. Its intent was to hedge the risk that general interest rates will decline, causing the fair value of its debt to increase. The agreement called for the company to receive payment based on a 10% fixed interest rate on a notional amount of $200,000 and to pay interest based on a floating interest rate. The contract called for cash settlement of the net interest amount quarterly.

Floating (LIBOR) settlement rates were 10% at January 1, 8% at March 31, and 6% at June 30, 2013. The fair values of the swap are quotes obtained from a derivatives dealer. Those quotes and the fair values of the note are as follows:

|  | January 1 | March 31 | June 30 |
|---|---|---|---|
| Fair value of interest rate swap | 0 | $ 6,472 | $ 11,394 |
| Fair value of note payable | $200,000 | $206,472 | $211,394 |

**Required:**

Prepare the journal entries through June 30, 2013, to record the issuance of the note, interest, and necessary adjustments for changes in fair value. Use the extended method demonstrated in Illustration A–3.

**E A–6**
**Derivatives;**
**interest rate**
**swap; fixed-rate**
**debt; fair value**
**change unrelated**
**to hedged**
**risk; extended**
**method**

(Note: This is a variation of Exercise A–5, modified to consider fair value change unrelated to hedged risk.) On January 1, 2013, LLB Industries borrowed $200,000 from trust Bank by issuing a two-year, 10% note, with interest payable quarterly. LLB entered into a two-year interest rate swap agreement on January 1, 2013, and designated the swap as a fair value hedge. Its intent was to hedge the risk that general interest rates will decline, causing the fair value of its debt to increase. The agreement called for the company to receive payment based on a 10% fixed interest rate on a notional amount of $200,000 and to pay interest based on a floating interest rate. The contract called for cash settlement of the net interest amount quarterly.

Floating (LIBOR) settlement rates were 10% at January 1, 8% at March 31, and 6% June 30, 2013. The fair values of the swap are quotes obtained from a derivatives dealer. Those quotes and the fair values of the note are as indicated below. The additional rise in the fair value of the note (higher than that of the swap) on June 30 was due to investors' perceptions that the creditworthiness of LLB was improving.

|  | January 1 | March 31 | June 30 |
|---|---|---|---|
| Fair value of interest rate swap | 0 | $ 6,472 | $ 11,394 |
| Fair value of note payable | $200,000 | 206,472 | 220,000 |

**Required:**

1. Calculate the net cash settlement at June 30, 2013.
2. Prepare the journal entries on June 30, 2013, to record the interest and necessary adjustments for changes in fair value. Use the extended method demonstrated in Illustration A–3.

## Problems

**P A–1**
**Derivatives—**
**interest rate swap**

On January 1, 2013, Labtech Circuits borrowed $100,000 from First Bank by issuing a three-year, 8% note, payable on December 31, 2015. Labtech wanted to hedge the risk that general interest rates will decline, causing the fair value of its debt to increase. Therefore, Labtech entered into a three-year interest rate swap agreement on January 1, 2013, and designated the swap as a fair value hedge. The agreement called for the company to receive payment based on an 8% fixed interest rate on a notional amount of $100,000 and to pay interest based on a floating interest rate tied to LIBOR. The contract called for cash settlement of the net interest amount on December 31 of each year.

Floating (LIBOR) settlement rates were 8% at inception and 9%, 7%, and 7% at the end of 2013, 2014, and 2015, respectively. The fair values of the swap are quotes obtained from a derivatives dealer. These quotes and the fair values of the note are as follows:

|  | January 1 | December 31 |  |  |
|---|---|---|---|---|
|  | 2013 | 2013 | 2014 | 2015 |
| Fair value of interest rate swap | 0 | $ (1,759) | $ 935 | 0 |
| Fair value of note payable | $100,000 | $98,241 | $100,935 | $100,000 |

**Required:**

1. Calculate the net cash settlement at the end of 2013, 2014, and 2015.
2. Prepare the journal entries during 2013 to record the issuance of the note, interest, and necessary adjustments for changes in fair value.
3. Prepare the journal entries during 2014 to record interest, net cash interest settlement for the interest rate swap, and necessary adjustments for changes in fair value.

4. Prepare the journal entries during 2015 to record interest, net cash interest settlement for the interest rate swap, necessary adjustments for changes in fair value, and repayment of the debt.
5. Calculate the carrying values of both the swap account and the note in each of the three years.
6. Calculate the net effect on earnings of the hedging arrangement in each of the three years. (Ignore income taxes.)
7. Suppose the fair value of the note at December 31, 2013, had been $97,000 rather than $98,241 with the additional decline in fair value due to investors' perceptions that the creditworthiness of Labtech was worsening. How would that affect your entries to record changes in the fair values?

**P A–2**
**Derivatives;**
**interest**
**rate swap;**
**comprehensive**

CMOS Chips is hedging a 20-year, $10 million, 7% bond payable with a 20-year interest rate swap and has designated the swap as a fair value hedge. The agreement called for CMOS to receive payment based on a 7% fixed interest rate on a notional amount of $10 million and to pay interest based on a floating interest rate tied to LIBOR. The contract calls for cash settlement of the net interest amount on December 31 of each year.
　At December 31, 2013, the fair value of the derivative and of the hedged bonds has increased by $100,000 because interest rates declined during the reporting period.

**Required:**
1. Does CMOS have an unrealized gain or loss on the derivative for the period? On the bonds? Will earnings increase or decrease due to the hedging arrangement? Why?
2. Suppose interest rates increased, rather than decreased, causing the fair value of both the derivative and of the hedged bonds to decrease by $100,000. Would CMOS have an unrealized gain or loss on the derivative for the period? On the bonds? Would earnings increase or decrease due to the hedging arrangement? Why?
3. Suppose the fair value of the bonds at December 31, 2013, had increased by $110,000 rather than $100,000, with the additional increase in fair value due to investors' perceptions that the creditworthiness of CMOS was improving. Would CMOS have an unrealized gain or loss on the derivative for the period? On the bonds? Would earnings increase or decrease due to the hedging arrangement? Why?
4. Suppose the notional amount of the swap had been $12 million, rather than the $10 million principal amount of the bonds. As a result, at December 31, 2013, the swap's fair value had increased by $120,000 rather than $100,000. Would CMOS have an unrealized gain or loss on the derivative for the period? On the bonds? Would earnings increase or decrease due to the hedging arrangement? Why?
5. Suppose BIOS Corporation is an investor having purchased all $10 million of the bonds issued by CMOS as described in the original situation above. BIOS is hedging its investment, classified as available-for-sale, with a 20-year interest rate swap and has designated the swap as a fair value hedge. The agreement called for BIOS to make *payment* based on a 7% fixed interest rate on a notional amount of $10 million and to *receive* interest based on a floating interest rate tied to LIBOR. Would BIOS have an unrealized gain or loss on the derivative for the period due to interest rates having declined? On the bonds? Would earnings increase or decrease due to the hedging arrangement? Why?

**P A–3**
**Derivatives;**
**interest rate**
**swap; fixed rate**
**debt; extended**
**method**

(Note: This is a variation of Problem A–1, modified to consider the extended method demonstrated in Illustration A–3.)
On January 1, 2013, Labtech Circuits borrowed $100,000 from First Bank by issuing a three-year, 8% note, payable on December 31, 2015. Labtech wanted to hedge the risk that general interest rates will decline, causing the fair value of its debt to increase. Therefore, Labtech entered into a three-year interest rate swap agreement on January 1, 2013, and designated the swap as a fair value hedge. The agreement called for the company to receive payment based on an 8% fixed interest rate on a notional amount of $100,000 and to pay interest based on a floating interest rate tied to LIBOR. The contract called for cash settlement of the net interest amount on December 31 of each year.
　Floating (LIBOR) settlement rates were 8% at inception and 9%, 7%, and 7% at the end of 2013, 2014, and 2015, respectively. The fair values of the swap are quotes obtained from a derivatives dealer. Those quotes and the fair values of the note are as follows:

|  | January 1 | December 31 | | |
|---|---|---|---|---|
|  | **2013** | **2013** | **2014** | **2015** |
| Fair value of interest rate swap | 0 | $ (1,759) | $    935 | 0 |
| Fair value of note payable | $100,000 | $ 98,241 | 100,935 | $100,000 |

**Required:**
Use the extended method demonstrated in Illustration A–3.
1. Calculate the net cash settlement at the end of 2013, 2014, and 2015.
2. Prepare the journal entries during 2013 to record the issuance of the note, interest, and necessary adjustments for changes in fair value.

3. Prepare the journal entries during 2014 to record interest, net cash interest settlement for the interest rate swap, and necessary adjustments for changes in fair value.

4. Prepare the journal entries during 2015 to record interest, net cash interest settlement for the interest rate swap, necessary adjustments for changes in fair value, and repayment of the debt.

5. Calculate the carrying values of both the swap account and the note in each of the three years.

6. Calculate the net effect on earnings of the hedging arrangement in each of the three years. (Ignore income taxes.)

7. Suppose the fair value of the note at December 31, 2013, had been $97,000 rather than $98,241 with the additional decline in fair value due to investors' perceptions that the creditworthiness of Labtech was worsening. How would that affect your entries to record changes in the fair values?

# Broaden Your Perspective

**Apply your critical-thinking ability to the knowledge you've gained. These cases will provide you an opportunity to develop your research, analysis, judgment, and communication skills. You also will work with other students, integrate what you've learned, apply it in real world situations, and consider its global and ethical ramifications. This practice will broaden your knowledge and further develop your decision-making abilities.**

**Real World Case A–1**
Derivative losses; recognition in earnings

The following is an excerpt from a disclosure note of Johnson & Johnson:

### 15. Financial Instruments (in part)

As of December 28, 2008, the balance of deferred net gains on derivatives included in accumulated other comprehensive income was $121 million after-tax. The Company expects that substantially all of this amount will be reclassified into earnings over the next 12 months as a result of transactions that are expected to occur over that period.

**Required:**

1. Johnson & Johnson indicates that it expects that substantially all of the balance of deferred net gains on derivatives will be reclassified into earnings over the next 12 months as a result of transactions that are expected to occur over that period. What is meant by "reclassified into earnings"?

2. What type(s) of hedging transaction might be accounted for in this way?

**Communication Case A–2**
Derivatives; hedge accounting

A conceptual question in accounting for derivatives is: Should gains and losses on a hedge instrument be recorded as they occur, or should they be recorded to coincide (match) with income effects of the item being hedged?

ABI Wholesalers plans to issue long-term notes in May that will replace its $20 million of 9.5% bonds when they mature in July. ABI is exposed to the risk that interest rates in July will have risen, increasing borrowing costs (reducing the selling price of its notes). To hedge that possibility, ABI entered a (Treasury bond) futures contract in May to deliver (sell) bonds in July at their *current* price.

As a result, if interest rates rise, borrowing costs will go up for ABI because it will sell notes at a higher interest cost (or lower price). But that loss will be offset (approximately) by the gain produced by being in the opposite position on Treasury bond futures.

Two opposing viewpoints are:

**View 1:** Gains and losses on instruments designed to hedge anticipated transactions should be recorded as they occur.

**View 2:** Gains and losses on instruments designed to hedge anticipated transactions should be recorded to coincide (match) with income effects of the item being hedged.

In considering this question, focus on conceptual issues regarding the practicable and theoretically appropriate treatment, unconstrained by GAAP. Your instructor will divide the class into two to six groups depending on the size of the class. The mission of your group is to reach consensus on the appropriate accounting for the gains and losses on instruments designed to hedge anticipated transactions.

**Required:**

1. Each group member should deliberate the situation independently and draft a tentative argument prior to the class session for which the case is assigned.

2. In class, each group will meet for 10 to 15 minutes in different areas of the classroom. During that meeting, group members will take turns sharing their suggestions for the purpose of arriving at a single group treatment.

3. After the allotted time, a spokesperson for each group (selected during the group meetings) will share the group's solution with the class. The goal of the class is to incorporate the views of each group into a consensus approach to the situation.

**Real World Case A–3**
Researching the way interest rate futures prices are quoted on the Chicago Mercantile Exchange; retrieving information from the Internet

The **Chicago Mercantile Exchange**, or Merc, at 30 S. Wacker Drive in Chicago, is the world's largest financial exchange, an international marketplace enabling institutions and businesses to trade futures and options contracts including currencies, interest rates, stock indices, and agricultural commodities.

**Required:**

1. Access the Merc on the Internet. The web address is **www.cme.com**.

2. Access the daily settlement prices within the site. Scroll to find "Interest products" and, within that, the 13-week Treasury bill futures.

3. What are the settlement prices for September futures contracts?

**Research Case A–4**
Issue related to the derivatives standard; research an article

In an effort to keep up with the rapidly changing global financial markets, the FASB issued standards on accounting for and disclosure of derivative financial instruments. A *Journal of Accountancy* article that discusses this standard is "The Decision on Derivatives," by Arlette C. Wilson, Gary Waters, and Barry J. Bryan, November 1998.

**Required:**

On the Internet, go to the AICPA site at **www.aicpa.org** and find the article mentioned.

1. What are the primary problems or issues the FASB attempts to address regarding accounting for derivative financial instruments?

2. In considering the issues, the FASB made four fundamental decisions that became the cornerstones of the statement issued in 1998. What are those fundamental decisions? Which do you think is most critical to fair financial reporting?

# Dell Annual Report (selected pages)

UNITED STATES
SECURITIES AND EXCHANGE COMMISSION
Washington, D.C. 20549

## Form 10-K

(Mark One)

☒   **ANNUAL REPORT PURSUANT TO SECTION
13 OR 15(d) OF THE SECURITIES
EXCHANGE ACT OF 1934**

**For the fiscal year ended January 28, 2011**

or

☐   **TRANSITION REPORT PURSUANT TO
SECTION 13 OR 15(d) OF THE SECURITIES
EXCHANGE ACT OF 1934**

**For the transition period from _____ to _____**

**Commission file number: 0-17017**

## Dell Inc.

(Exact name of registrant as specified in its charter)

| **Delaware** | **74-2487834** |
|---|---|
| (State or other jurisdiction of   incorporation or organization) | (I.R.S. Employer   Identification No.) |

**One Dell Way, Round Rock, Texas 78682**
(Address of principal executive offices) (Zip Code)
Registrant's telephone number, including area code: **1-800-BUY-DELL**

**Securities registered pursuant to Section 12(b) of the Act:**

| Title of each class | Name of each exchange on which registered |
|---|---|
| **Common Stock, par value $.01 per share** | **The NASDAQ Stock Market LLC** |
| | **(NASDAQ Global Select Market)** |

Securities Registered Pursuant to Section 12(g) of the Act: None

Indicate by check mark if the registrant is a well-known seasoned issuer, as defined in Rule 405 of the Securities Act. Yes ☐ No ☑

Indicate by check mark if the registrant is not required to file reports pursuant to Section 13 or Section 15(d) of the Act. Yes ☐ No ☑

Indicate by check mark whether the registrant (1) has filed all reports required to be filed by Section 13 or 15(d) of the Securities Exchange Act of 1934 during the preceding 12 months (or for such shorter period that the registrant was required to file such reports), and (2) has been subject to such filing requirements for the past 90 days. Yes ☑ No ☐

Indicate by check mark whether the registrant has submitted electronically and posted on its corporate Web site, if any, every Interactive Data File required to be submitted and posted pursuant to Rule 405 of Regulation S-T during the preceding 12 months (or for such shorter period that the registrant was required to submit and post such files). Yes ☑ No ☐

Indicate by check mark if disclosure of delinquent filers pursuant to Item 405 of Regulation S-K is not contained herein, and will not be contained, to the best of registrant's knowledge, in definitive proxy or information statements incorporated by reference in Part III of this Form 10-K or any amendment to this Form 10-K. ☑

Indicate by check mark whether the registrant is a large accelerated filer, an accelerated filer, a non-accelerated filer, or a smaller reporting company. See the definitions of "large accelerated filer," "accelerated filer," and "smaller reporting company" in Rule 12b-2 of the Exchange Act.

| | |
|---|---|
| Large accelerated filer ☑ | Accelerated filer ☐ |
| Non-accelerated filer ☐   (Do not check if a smaller reporting company) | Smaller reporting company ☐ |

Indicate by check mark whether the registrant is a shell company (as defined in Rule 12b-2 of the Act). Yes ☐ No ☑

Approximate aggregate market value of the registrant's common stock held by non-affiliates as of July 30, 2010, based upon the last sale price reported for such date on the NASDAQ Global Select Market     $22.3 billion
Number of shares of common stock outstanding as of March 4, 2011     1,906,749,664

**Report of Independent Registered Public Accounting Firm**

To the Board of Directors and
Shareholders of Dell Inc.:

In our opinion, the consolidated financial statements listed in the accompanying index present fairly, in all material respects, the financial position of Dell Inc. and its subsidiaries (the "Company") at January 28, 2011 and January 29, 2010, and the results of their operations and their cash flows for each of the three years in the period ended January 28, 2011 in conformity with accounting principles generally accepted in the United States of America. Also, in our opinion, the Company maintained, in all material respects, effective internal control over financial reporting as of January 28, 2011, based on criteria established in *Internal Control — Integrated Framework* issued by the Committee of Sponsoring Organizations of the Treadway Commission (COSO). The Company's management is responsible for these financial statements, for maintaining effective internal control over financial reporting and for its assessment of the effectiveness of internal control over financial reporting, included in Management's Report on Internal Control Over Financial Reporting appearing under Item 9A. Our responsibility is to express opinions on these financial statements, and on the Company's internal control over financial reporting based on our integrated audits. We conducted our audits in accordance with the standards of the Public Company Accounting Oversight Board (United States). Those standards require that we plan and perform the audits to obtain reasonable assurance about whether the financial statements are free of material misstatement and whether effective internal control over financial reporting was maintained in all material respects. Our audits of the financial statements included examining, on a test basis, evidence supporting the amounts and disclosures in the financial statements, assessing the accounting principles used and significant estimates made by management, and evaluating the overall financial statement presentation. Our audit of internal control over financial reporting included obtaining an understanding of internal control over financial reporting, assessing the risk that a material weakness exists, and testing and evaluating the design and operating effectiveness of internal control based on the assessed risk. Our audits also included performing such other procedures as we considered necessary in the circumstances. We believe that our audits provide a reasonable basis for our opinions.

As described in Note 1, in Fiscal 2011, the Company changed the manner in which it accounts for variable interest entities and transfers of financial assets and extinguishments of liabilities; and, in Fiscal 2010, the Company changed the manner in which it accounts for business combinations.

A company's internal control over financial reporting is a process designed to provide reasonable assurance regarding the reliability of financial reporting and the preparation of financial statements for external purposes in accordance with generally accepted accounting principles. A company's internal control over financial reporting includes those policies and procedures that (i) pertain to the maintenance of records that, in reasonable detail, accurately and fairly reflect the transactions and dispositions of the assets of the company; (ii) provide reasonable assurance that transactions are recorded as necessary to permit preparation of financial statements in accordance with generally accepted accounting principles, and that receipts and expenditures of the company are being made only in accordance with authorizations of management and directors of the company; and (iii) provide reasonable assurance regarding prevention or timely detection of unauthorized acquisition, use, or disposition of the company's assets that could have a material effect on the financial statements.

Because of its inherent limitations, internal control over financial reporting may not prevent or detect misstatements. Also, projections of any evaluation of effectiveness to future periods are subject to the risk that controls may become inadequate because of changes in conditions, or that the degree of compliance with the policies or procedures may deteriorate.

/s/ PRICEWATERHOUSECOOPERS LLP

Austin, Texas
March 15, 2011

**DELL INC.**

**CONSOLIDATED STATEMENTS OF FINANCIAL POSITION**

(in millions)

| | January 28, 2011 | January 29, 2010 |
|---|---|---|
| **ASSETS** | | |
| Current assets: | | |
| Cash and cash equivalents | $ 13,913 | $ 10,635 |
| Short-term investments | 452 | 373 |
| Accounts receivable, net | 6,493 | 5,837 |
| Financing receivables, net | 3,643 | 2,706 |
| Inventories, net | 1,301 | 1,051 |
| Other current assets | 3,219 | 3,643 |
| Total current assets | 29,021 | 24,245 |
| Property, plant, and equipment, net | 1,953 | 2,181 |
| Investments | 704 | 781 |
| Long-term financing receivables, net | 799 | 332 |
| Goodwill | 4,365 | 4,074 |
| Purchased intangible assets, net | 1,495 | 1,694 |
| Other non-current assets | 262 | 345 |
| Total assets | $ 38,599 | $ 33,652 |
| **LIABILITIES AND STOCKHOLDERS' EQUITY** | | |
| Current liabilities: | | |
| Short-term debt | $ 851 | $ 663 |
| Accounts payable | 11,293 | 11,373 |
| Accrued and other | 4,181 | 3,884 |
| Short-term deferred services revenue | 3,158 | 3,040 |
| Total current liabilities | 19,483 | 18,960 |
| Long-term debt | 5,146 | 3,417 |
| Long-term deferred services revenue | 3,518 | 3,029 |
| Other non-current liabilities | 2,686 | 2,605 |
| Total liabilities | 30,833 | 28,011 |
| Commitments and contingencies (Note 11) | | |
| Stockholders' equity: | | |
| Common stock and capital in excess of $.01 par value; shares authorized: 7,000; shares issued: 3,369 and 3,351, respectively; shares outstanding: 1,918 and 1,957, respectively | 11,797 | 11,472 |
| Treasury stock at cost: 976 and 919 shares, respectively | (28,704) | (27,904) |
| Retained earnings | 24,744 | 22,110 |
| Accumulated other comprehensive loss | (71) | (37) |
| Total stockholders' equity | 7,766 | 5,641 |
| Total liabilities and stockholders' equity | $ 38,599 | $ 33,652 |

The accompanying notes are an integral part of these consolidated financial statements.

**DELL INC.**

**CONSOLIDATED STATEMENTS OF INCOME**
(in millions, except per share amounts)

| | Fiscal Year Ended | | |
| --- | --- | --- | --- |
| | January 28, 2011 | January 29, 2010 | January 30, 2009 |
| *Net revenue:* | | | |
| Products | $ 50,002 | $ 43,697 | $ 52,337 |
| Services, including software related | 11,492 | 9,205 | 8,764 |
| Total net revenue | 61,494 | 52,902 | 61,101 |
| *Cost of net revenue:* | | | |
| Products | 42,068 | 37,534 | 44,670 |
| Services, including software related | 8,030 | 6,107 | 5,474 |
| Total cost of net revenue | 50,098 | 43,641 | 50,144 |
| Gross margin | 11,396 | 9,261 | 10,957 |
| *Operating expenses:* | | | |
| Selling, general, and administrative | 7,302 | 6,465 | 7,102 |
| Research, development, and engineering | 661 | 624 | 665 |
| Total operating expenses | 7,963 | 7,089 | 7,767 |
| Operating income | 3,433 | 2,172 | 3,190 |
| Interest and other, net | (83) | (148) | 134 |
| Income before income taxes | 3,350 | 2,024 | 3,324 |
| Income tax provision | 715 | 591 | 846 |
| Net income | $ 2,635 | $ 1,433 | $ 2,478 |
| Earnings per share: | | | |
| Basic | $ 1.36 | $ 0.73 | $ 1.25 |
| Diluted | $ 1.35 | $ 0.73 | $ 1.25 |
| Weighted-average shares outstanding: | | | |
| Basic | 1,944 | 1,954 | 1,980 |
| Diluted | 1,955 | 1,962 | 1,986 |

The accompanying notes are an integral part of these consolidated financial statements.

## DELL INC.

### CONSOLIDATED STATEMENTS OF CASH FLOWS
(in millions)

| | Fiscal Year Ended | | |
|---|---|---|---|
| | January 28, 2011 | January 29, 2010 | January 30, 2009 |
| Cash flows from operating activities: | | | |
| Net income | $ 2,635 | $ 1,433 | $ 2,478 |
| Adjustments to reconcile net income to net cash provided by operating activities: | | | |
| Depreciation and amortization | 970 | 852 | 769 |
| Stock-based compensation | 332 | 312 | 418 |
| Effects of exchange rate changes on monetary assets and liabilities denominated in foreign currencies | (4) | 59 | (115) |
| Deferred income taxes | (45) | (52) | 86 |
| Provision for doubtful accounts — including financing receivables | 382 | 429 | 310 |
| Other | 26 | 102 | 34 |
| Changes in assets and liabilities, net of effects from acquisitions: | | | |
| Accounts receivable | (707) | (660) | 480 |
| Financing receivables | (709) | (1,085) | (302) |
| Inventories | (248) | (183) | 309 |
| Other assets | 516 | (225) | (106) |
| Accounts payable | (151) | 2,833 | (3,117) |
| Deferred services revenue | 551 | 135 | 663 |
| Accrued and other liabilities | 421 | (44) | (13) |
| Change in cash from operating activities | 3,969 | 3,906 | 1,894 |
| Cash flows from investing activities: | | | |
| Investments: | | | |
| Purchases | (1,360) | (1,383) | (1,584) |
| Maturities and sales | 1,358 | 1,538 | 2,333 |
| Capital expenditures | (444) | (367) | (440) |
| Proceeds from sale of facility and land | 18 | 16 | 44 |
| Purchase of financing receivables | (430) | - | - |
| Collections on purchased financing receivables | 69 | | |
| Acquisition of business, net of cash received | (376) | (3,613) | (176) |
| Change in cash from investing activities | (1,165) | (3,809) | 177 |
| Cash flows from financing activities: | | | |
| Repurchase of common stock | (800) | - | (2,867) |
| Issuance of common stock under employee plans | 12 | 2 | 79 |
| Issuance (repayment) of commercial paper (maturity 90 days or less), net | (176) | 76 | 100 |
| Proceeds from debt | 3,069 | 2,058 | 1,519 |
| Repayments of debt | (1,630) | (122) | (237) |
| Other | 2 | (2) | - |
| Change in cash from financing activities | 477 | 2,012 | (1,406) |
| Effect of exchange rate changes on cash and cash equivalents | (3) | 174 | (77) |
| Change in cash and cash equivalents | 3,278 | 2,283 | 588 |
| Cash and cash equivalents at beginning of the period | 10,635 | 8,352 | 7,764 |
| Cash and cash equivalents at end of the period | $ 13,913 | $ 10,635 | $ 8,352 |
| | | | |
| Income tax paid | $ 435 | $ 434 | $ 800 |
| Interest paid | $ 188 | $ 151 | $ 74 |

The accompanying notes are an integral part of these consolidated financial statements.

## DELL INC.

### CONSOLIDATED STATEMENTS OF STOCKHOLDERS' EQUITY
(in millions)

| | Common Stock and Capital in Excess of Par Value | | Treasury Stock | | Retained Earnings | Accumulated Other Comprehensive Income/(Loss) | Total |
|---|---|---|---|---|---|---|---|
| | Issued Shares | Amount | Shares | Amount | | | |
| **Balances at February 1, 2008** | 3,320 | $ 10,589 | 785 | $ (25,037) | $ 18,199 | $ (16) | $ 3,735 |
| Net income | - | - | - | - | 2,478 | - | 2,478 |
| Change in net unrealized gain or loss on investments, net of taxes | - | - | - | - | - | (29) | (29) |
| Foreign currency translation adjustments | - | - | - | - | - | 5 | 5 |
| Change in net unrealized gain or loss on derivative instruments, net of taxes | - | - | - | - | - | 349 | 349 |
| *Total comprehensive income* | - | - | - | - | - | - | 2,803 |
| Stock issuances under employee plans and other[a] | 18 | 173 | - | - | - | - | 173 |
| Repurchases of common stock | - | - | 134 | (2,867) | - | - | (2,867) |
| Stock-based compensation expense | - | 419 | - | - | - | - | 419 |
| Net tax benefit from employee stock plans | - | 8 | - | - | - | - | 8 |
| **Balances at January 30, 2009** | 3,338 | 11,189 | 919 | (27,904) | 20,677 | 309 | 4,271 |
| Net income | - | - | - | - | 1,433 | - | 1,433 |
| Change in net unrealized gain or loss on investments, net of taxes | - | - | - | - | - | 6 | 6 |
| Foreign currency translation adjustments | - | - | - | - | - | (29) | (29) |
| Change in net unrealized gain or loss on derivative instruments, net of taxes | - | - | - | - | - | (323) | (323) |
| *Total comprehensive income* | - | - | - | - | - | - | 1,087 |
| Stock issuances under employee plans and other[a] | 13 | 3 | - | - | - | - | 3 |
| Stock-based compensation expense | - | 312 | - | - | - | - | 312 |
| Net tax shortfall from employee stock plans | - | (32) | - | - | - | - | (32) |
| **Balances at January 29, 2010** | 3,351 | 11,472 | 919 | (27,904) | 22,110 | (37) | 5,641 |
| Net income | - | - | - | - | 2,635 | - | 2,635 |
| Adjustment to consolidate variable interest entities | - | - | - | - | (1) | - | (1) |
| Change in net unrealized gain or loss on investments, net of taxes | - | - | - | - | - | (1) | (1) |
| Foreign currency translation adjustments | - | - | - | - | - | 79 | 79 |
| Change in net unrealized gain or loss on derivative instruments, net of taxes | - | - | - | - | - | (112) | (112) |
| *Total comprehensive income* | - | - | - | - | - | - | 2,600 |
| Stock issuances under employee plans and other[a] | 18 | 7 | - | - | - | - | 7 |
| Repurchases of common stock | - | - | 57 | (800) | - | - | (800) |
| Stock-based compensation expense | - | 332 | - | - | - | - | 332 |
| Net tax shortfall from employee stock plans | - | (14) | - | - | - | - | (14) |
| **Balances at January 28, 2011** | 3,369 | $ 11,797 | 976 | $ (28,704) | $ 24,744 | $ (71) | $ 7,766 |

(a) Stock issuance under employee plans is net of shares held for employee taxes.

The accompanying notes are an integral part of these consolidated financial statements.

## DELL INC.

## NOTES TO CONSOLIDATED FINANCIAL STATEMENTS

### NOTE 1 — DESCRIPTION OF BUSINESS AND SUMMARY OF SIGNIFICANT ACCOUNTING POLICIES

*Description of Business* — Dell Inc., a Delaware corporation (both individually and together with its consolidated subsidiaries, "Dell"), offers a broad range of technology product categories, including mobility products, desktop PCs, software and peripherals, servers and networking products, storage, and services. Dell sells its products and services directly to customers through dedicated sales representatives, telephone-based sales, and online at www.dell.com, and through a variety of indirect sales channels. Dell's business segments are Large Enterprise, Public, Small and Medium Business and Consumer. References to Commercial business refer to Large Enterprise, Public, and Small and Medium Business.

*Fiscal Year* — Dell's fiscal year is the 52 or 53 week period ending on the Friday nearest January 31. The fiscal years ended January 28, 2011, January 29, 2010, and January 30, 2009, included 52 weeks.

*Principles of Consolidation* — The accompanying consolidated financial statements include the accounts of Dell Inc. and its wholly-owned subsidiaries and have been prepared in accordance with accounting principles generally accepted in the United States of America ("GAAP"). All significant intercompany transactions and balances have been eliminated.

*Use of Estimates* — The preparation of financial statements in accordance with GAAP requires the use of management's estimates. These estimates are subjective in nature and involve judgments that affect the reported amounts of assets and liabilities, the disclosure of contingent assets and liabilities at fiscal year-end, and the reported amounts of revenues and expenses during the fiscal year. Actual results could differ from those estimates.

*Cash and Cash Equivalents* — All highly liquid investments, including credit card receivables due from banks, with original maturities of three months or less at date of purchase, are reported at fair value and are considered to be cash equivalents. All other investments not considered to be cash equivalents are separately categorized as investments.

*Investments* — Dell's investments are primarily in debt securities, which are classified as available-for-sale and are reported at fair value (based primarily on quoted prices and market observable inputs) using the specific identification method. Unrealized gains and losses, net of taxes, are reported as a component of stockholders' equity. Realized gains and losses on investments are included in interest and other, net. An impairment loss will be recognized and will reduce an investment's carrying amount to its fair market value when a decline in the fair market value of an individual security below its cost or carrying value is determined to be other than temporary.

Dell reviews its investment portfolio quarterly to determine if any investment is other than temporarily impaired. Dell determines an impairment is other than temporary when there is intent to sell the security, it is more likely than not that the security will be required to be sold before recovery in value or it is not expected to recover its entire amortized cost basis ("credit related loss"). However, if Dell does not expect to sell a debt security, it still evaluates expected cash flows to be received and determines if a credit-related loss exists. In the event of a credit-related loss, only the amount of impairment associated with the credit-related loss is recognized in earnings. Amounts relating to factors other than credit-related losses are recorded in other comprehensive income. See Note 3 of Notes to the Consolidated Financial Statements for additional information.

*Financing Receivables* — Financing receivables consist of customer receivables, residual interest and retained interest in securitized receivables. Customer receivables include revolving loans and fixed-term leases and loans resulting from the sale of Dell products and services. Based on how Dell assesses risk and determines the appropriate allowance levels, Dell has two portfolio segments, (1) fixed-term leases and loans and (2) revolving loans. Portfolio segments are further segregated into classes based on operating segment and whether the receivable was owned by Dell since its inception or was purchased subsequent to its inception. Financing receivables are presented net of the allowance for losses. See Note 4 of Notes to Consolidated Financial Statements for additional information.

*Asset Securitization* — Dell enters into securitization transactions to transfer certain financing receivables for fixed-term leases and loans to special purpose entities. During Fiscal 2011, Dell adopted the new accounting guidance that removes the concept of a qualifying special purpose entity and removes the exception from applying variable interest entity accounting. Adoption of the new guidance requires an entity to perform an ongoing analysis to determine whether the entity's variable interest or interests give it a controlling financial interest in a variable interest entity. The adoption of the new guidance resulted in Dell's consolidation of its two qualifying special purpose entities with asset securitizations now being accounted for as secured borrowings. See Note 4 of Notes to Consolidated Financial Statements for additional information on the impact of the consolidation.

Prior to Fiscal 2011, these receivables were removed from the Consolidated Statement of Financial Position at the time they were sold. Receivables were considered sold when the receivables were transferred beyond the reach of Dell's creditors, the transferee had the right to pledge or exchange the assets, and Dell had surrendered control over the rights and obligations of the receivables. Gains and losses from the sale of fixed-term leases and loans were recognized in the period the sale occurred, based upon the relative fair value of the assets sold and the remaining retained interest. Retained interest was recognized at fair value with any changes in fair value recorded in earnings. In estimating the value of retained interest, Dell made a variety of financial assumptions, including pool credit losses, payment rates, and discount rates. These assumptions were supported by both Dell's historical experience and anticipated trends relative to the particular receivable pool.

*Allowance for Doubtful Accounts* — Dell recognizes an allowance for losses on accounts receivable in an amount equal to the estimated probable losses net of recoveries. The allowance is based on an analysis of historical bad debt experience, current receivables aging, and expected future write-offs, as well as an assessment of specific identifiable customer accounts considered at risk or uncollectible. The expense associated with the allowance for doubtful accounts is recognized as selling, general, and administrative expense.

*Allowance for Financing Receivables Losses* — Dell recognizes an allowance for losses on financing receivables in an amount equal to the probable losses net of recoveries. The allowance for losses is generally determined at the aggregate portfolio level based on a variety of factors, including historical and anticipated experience, past due receivables, receivable type, and customer risk profile. Customer account principal and interest are charged to the allowance for losses when an account is deemed to be uncollectible or when the account is 180 days delinquent. While Dell does not place financing receivables on non-accrual status during the delinquency period, accrued interest is included in the allowance for loss calculation and Dell is therefore adequately reserved in the event of charge off. Recoveries on receivables previously charged off as uncollectible are recorded to the allowance for financing receivables losses. The expense associated with the allowance for financing receivables losses is recognized as cost of net revenue. Both fixed and revolving receivable loss rates are affected by macro-economic conditions including the level of GDP growth, unemployment rates, the level of commercial capital equipment investment, and the credit quality of the borrower. See Note 4 of Notes to Consolidated Financial Statements for additional information.

*Inventories* — Inventories are stated at the lower of cost or market with cost being determined on a first-in, first-out basis.

## DELL INC.

## NOTES TO CONSOLIDATED FINANCIAL
## STATEMENTS (Continued)

*Property, Plant, and Equipment* — Property, plant, and equipment are carried at depreciated cost. Depreciation is provided using the straight-line method over the estimated economic lives of the assets, which range from ten to thirty years for buildings and two to five years for all other assets. Leasehold improvements are amortized over the shorter of five years or the lease term. Gains or losses related to retirements or disposition of fixed assets are recognized in the period incurred. Dell capitalizes eligible internal-use software development costs incurred subsequent to the completion of the preliminary project stage. Development costs are amortized over the shorter of the expected useful life of the software or five years.

*Impairment of Long-Lived Assets* — Dell reviews long-lived assets for impairment when circumstances indicate the carrying amount of an asset may not be recoverable based on the undiscounted future cash flows of the asset. If the carrying amount of the asset is determined not to be recoverable, a write-down to fair value is recorded. Fair values are determined based on quoted market values, discounted cash flows, or external appraisals, as applicable. Dell reviews long-lived assets for impairment at the individual asset or the asset group level for which the lowest level of independent cash flows can be identified.

*Business Combinations and Intangible Assets Including Goodwill* — During Fiscal 2010, Dell adopted the new guidance from the Financial Accounting Standards Board ("FASB") on business combinations and non-controlling interests. Dell accounts for business combinations using the acquisition method of accounting and accordingly, the assets and liabilities of the acquired business are recorded at their fair values at the date of acquisition. The excess of the purchase price over the estimated fair values is recorded as goodwill. Any changes in the estimated fair values of the net assets recorded for acquisitions prior to the finalization of more detailed analysis, but not to exceed one year from the date of acquisition, will change the amount of the purchase prices allocable to goodwill. All acquisition costs are expensed as incurred and in-process research and development costs are recorded at fair value as an indefinite-lived intangible asset and assessed for impairment thereafter until completion, at which point the asset is amortized over its expected useful life. Any restructuring charges associated with a business combination are expensed subsequent to the acquisition date. The results of operations of acquired businesses are included in the Consolidated Financial Statements from the acquisition date.

Identifiable intangible assets with finite lives are amortized over their estimated useful lives. They are generally amortized on a non-straight line approach based on the associated projected cash flows in order to match the amortization pattern to the pattern in which the economic benefits of the assets are expected to be consumed. Intangible assets are reviewed for impairment if indicators of potential impairment exist. Goodwill and indefinite-lived intangible assets are tested for impairment on an annual basis in the second fiscal quarter, or sooner if an indicator of impairment occurs.

*Foreign Currency Translation* — The majority of Dell's international sales are made by international subsidiaries, most of which have the U.S. dollar as their functional currency. Dell's subsidiaries that do not have the U.S. dollar as their functional currency translate assets and liabilities at current rates of exchange in effect at the balance sheet date. Revenue and expenses from these international subsidiaries are translated using the monthly average exchange rates in effect for the period in which the items occur.

Local currency transactions of international subsidiaries that have the U.S. dollar as the functional currency are remeasured into U.S. dollars using current rates of exchange for monetary assets and liabilities and historical rates of exchange for non-monetary assets and liabilities. Gains and losses from remeasurement of monetary assets and liabilities are included in interest and other, net. See Note 6 of Notes to Consolidated Financial Statements for additional information.

*Hedging Instruments* — Dell uses derivative financial instruments, primarily forwards, options, and swaps, to hedge certain foreign currency and interest rate exposures. The relationships between hedging instruments and hedged items are formally documented, as well as the risk management objectives and strategies for undertaking hedge transactions. Dell does not use derivatives for speculative purposes.

All derivative instruments are recognized as either assets or liabilities on the Consolidated Statements of Financial Position and are measured at fair value. Hedge accounting is applied based upon the criteria established by accounting guidance for derivative instruments and hedging activities. Derivatives are assessed for hedge effectiveness both at the onset of the hedge and at regular intervals throughout the life of the derivative. Any hedge ineffectiveness is recognized currently in earnings as a component of interest and other, net. Dell's hedge portfolio includes derivatives designated as both cash flow and fair value hedges.

For derivative instruments that are designated as cash flow hedges, hedge ineffectiveness is measured by comparing the cumulative change in the fair value of the hedge contract with the cumulative change in the fair value of the hedged item, both of which are based on forward rates. Dell records the effective portion of the gain or loss on the derivative instrument in accumulated other comprehensive income (loss) ("OCI"), as a separate component of stockholders' equity and reclassifies the gain or loss into earnings in the period during which the hedged transaction is recognized in earnings.

For derivatives that are designated as fair value hedges, hedge ineffectiveness is measured by calculating the periodic change in the fair value of the hedge contract and the periodic change in the fair value of the hedged item. To the extent that these fair value changes do not fully offset each other, the difference is recorded as ineffectiveness in earnings as a component of interest and other, net.

For derivatives that are not designated as hedges or do not qualify for hedge accounting treatment, Dell recognizes the change in the instrument's fair value currently in earnings as a component of interest and other, net.

Cash flows from derivative instruments are presented in the same category on the Consolidated Statements of Cash Flows as the cash flows from the underlying hedged items. See Note 6 of Notes to Consolidated Financial Statements for a full description of Dell's derivative financial instrument activities.

*Treasury Stock* — Dell accounts for treasury stock under the cost method and includes treasury stock as a component of stockholders' equity.

*Revenue Recognition* — Net revenues include sales of hardware, software and peripherals, and services. Dell recognizes revenue for these products when it is realized or realizable and earned. Revenue is considered realized and earned when persuasive evidence of an arrangement exists; delivery has occurred or services have been rendered; Dell's fee to its customer is fixed and determinable; and collection of the resulting receivable is reasonably assured. Dell classifies revenue and cost of revenue related to standalone software sold with Post Contract Support ("PCS") in the same line item as services on the Consolidated Statements of Income. Services revenue and cost of services revenue captions on the Consolidated Statements of Income include Dell's services and software from Dell's software and peripherals product category. This software revenue and related costs include software license fees and related PCS that is sold separately from computer systems through Dell's software and peripherals product category.

**DELL INC.**

**NOTES TO CONSOLIDATED FINANCIAL
STATEMENTS (Continued)**

Products

Revenue from the sale of products is recognized when title and risk of loss passes to the customer. Delivery is considered complete when products have been shipped to Dell's customer, title and risk of loss has transferred to the customer, and customer acceptance has been satisfied. Customer acceptance is satisfied through obtaining acceptance from the customer, the acceptance provision lapses, or Dell has evidence that the acceptance provisions have been satisfied.

Dell records reductions to revenue for estimated customer sales returns, rebates, and certain other customer incentive programs. These reductions to revenue are made based upon reasonable and reliable estimates that are determined by historical experience, contractual terms, and current conditions. The primary factors affecting Dell's accrual for estimated customer returns include estimated return rates as well as the number of units shipped that have a right of return that has not expired as of the balance sheet date. If returns cannot be reliably estimated, revenue is not recognized until a reliable estimate can be made or the return right lapses.

Dell sells its products directly to customers as well as through indirect channels, including retailers. Sales through Dell's indirect channels are primarily made under agreements allowing for limited rights of return, price protection, rebates, and marketing development funds. Dell has generally limited the return rights through contractual caps. Dell's policy for sales through indirect channels is to defer the full amount of revenue relative to sales for which the rights of return apply unless there is sufficient historical data to establish reasonable and reliable estimates of returns. To the extent price protection or return rights are not limited and a reliable estimate cannot be made, all of the revenue and related costs are deferred until the product has been sold to the end-user or the rights expire. Dell records estimated reductions to revenue or an expense for indirect channel programs at the later of the offer or the time revenue is recognized.

Dell defers the cost of shipped products awaiting revenue recognition until revenue is recognized.

Services

Services include transactional, outsourcing and project-based offerings. Revenue is recognized for services contracts as earned, which is generally on a straight line basis over the term of the contract or on a proportional performance basis as the services are rendered and Dell's obligations are fulfilled. Revenue from time and materials or cost-plus contracts is recognized as the services are performed. Revenue from fixed price contracts is recognized on a straight line basis, unless revenues is earned and obligations are fulfilled in a different pattern. These service contracts may include provisions for cancellation, termination, refunds, or service level adjustments. These contract provisions would not have a significant impact on recognized revenue as Dell generally recognizes revenue for these contracts as the services are performed.

For sales of extended warranties with a separate contract price, Dell defers revenue equal to the separately stated price. Revenue associated with undelivered elements is deferred and recorded when delivery occurs or services are provided. Revenue from extended warranty and service contracts, for which Dell is obligated to perform, is recorded as deferred revenue and subsequently recognized over the term of the contract on a straight-line basis.

Revenue from sales of third-party extended warranty and service contracts or software PCS, for which Dell is not obligated to perform, and for which Dell does not meet the criteria for gross revenue recognition under the guidance of the FASB , is recognized on a net basis. All other revenue is recognized on a gross basis.

Software

The Company recognizes revenue in accordance with industry specific software accounting guidance for all software and PCS that are not essential to the functionality of the hardware. Accounting for software that is essential to the functionality of the hardware is accounted for as specified below in "Multiple Deliverables". Dell has established vendor specific objective evidence ("VSOE") on a limited basis for certain software offerings. When Dell has not established VSOE to support a separation of the software license and PCS elements, the revenue and related costs are generally recognized over the term of the agreement.

As more fully explained in *Recently Issued and Adopted Accounting Pronouncements* below, effective with the first quarter of Fiscal 2011, certain Dell storage products are no longer included in the scope of the software revenue recognition guidance. Prior to the new guidance, Dell established fair value for PCS for these products based on VSOE and used the residual method to allocate revenue to the delivered elements. Under the new guidance, the revenue for what was previously deemed PCS is now considered part of a multiple deliverable arrangement. As such, any discount is allocated to all elements based on the relative selling price of both delivered and undelivered elements. The impact of applying this new guidance was not material to Dell's Consolidated Financial Statements for Fiscal 2011 or 2010.

Multiple Deliverables

Dell's multiple deliverable arrangements generally include hardware products that are sold with essential software or services such as extended warranty, installation, maintenance, and other services contracts. The nature and terms of these multiple deliverable arrangements will vary based on the customized needs of Dell's customers. Each of these deliverables in an arrangement typically represents a separate unit of accounting. Dell's service contracts may include a combination of services arrangements including deployment, asset recovery, recycling, IT outsourcing, consulting, applications development, applications maintenance, and business process services. As more fully explained in *Recently Issued and Adopted Accounting Pronouncements* below, effective with the first quarter of Fiscal 2011, Dell allocated revenue to all deliverables based on their relative selling prices. The new guidance permits a company to make its best estimate of the selling price of deliverables when more objective evidence of selling price is not available. The hierarchy to be used to determine the selling price to be used for allocating revenue to deliverables is: (1) VSOE, (2) third-party evidence of selling price ("TPE"), and (3) best estimate of the selling price ("ESP"). A majority of Dell product and service offerings are sold on a standalone basis. Because selling price is generally available based on standalone sales, Dell has limited application of TPE, as determined by comparison of pricing for products and services to the pricing of similar products and services as offered by Dell or its competitors in standalone sales to similarly situated customers. As new products are introduced in future periods, Dell may be required to use TPE or ESP, depending on the specific facts at the time.

**DELL INC.**

**NOTES TO CONSOLIDATED FINANCIAL
STATEMENTS (Continued)**

For Fiscal 2010 and Fiscal 2009, pursuant to the previous guidance for *Revenue Arrangements with Multiple Deliverables,* Dell allocated revenue from multiple element arrangements to the elements based on the relative fair value of each element, which was generally based on the relative sales price of each element when sold separately. The adoption of the new guidance in the first quarter of Fiscal 2011 did not change the manner in which Dell accounts for its multiple deliverable arrangements as Dell did not use the residual method for the majority of its offerings and its services offerings are generally sold on a standalone basis where evidence of selling price is available.

Other

Dell records revenue from the sale of equipment under sales-type leases as product revenue at the inception of the lease. Sales-type leases also produce financing income, which is included in net revenue in the Consolidated Statement of Income and is recognized at consistent rates of return over the lease term. Customer revolving loan financing income is also included in net revenue and recognized on an accrual basis.

Dell reports revenue net of any revenue-based taxes assessed by governmental authorities that are imposed on and concurrent with specific revenue-producing transactions.

*Warranty Liabilitie*s — Dell records warranty liabilities for its standard limited warranty at the time of sale for the estimated costs that may be incurred under its limited warranty. The specific warranty terms and conditions vary depending upon the product sold and the country in which Dell does business, but generally includes technical support, parts, and labor over a period ranging from one to three years. Factors that affect Dell's warranty liability include the number of installed units currently under warranty, historical and anticipated rates of warranty claims on those units, and cost per claim to satisfy Dell's warranty obligation. The anticipated rate of warranty claims is the primary factor impacting the estimated warranty obligation. The other factors are less significant due to the fact that the average remaining aggregate warranty period of the covered installed base is approximately 15 months, repair parts are generally already in stock or available at pre-determined prices, and labor rates are generally arranged at pre-established amounts with service providers. Warranty claims are relatively predictable based on historical experience of failure rates. If actual results differ from the estimates, Dell revises its estimated warranty liability. Each quarter, Dell reevaluates its estimates to assess the adequacy of its recorded warranty liabilities and adjusts the amounts as necessary.

*Vendor Rebates* — Dell may receive consideration from vendors in the normal course of business. Certain of these funds are rebates of purchase price paid and others are related to reimbursement of costs incurred by Dell to sell the vendor's products. Dell recognizes a reduction of cost of goods sold and inventory if the funds are a reduction of the price of the vendor's products. If the consideration is a reimbursement of costs incurred by Dell to sell or develop the vendor's products, then the consideration is classified as a reduction of that cost in the Consolidated Statements of Income, most often operating expenses. In order to be recognized as a reduction of operating expenses, the reimbursement must be for a specific, incremental, identifiable cost incurred by Dell in selling the vendor's products or services.

*Loss Contingencies* — Dell is subject to the possibility of various losses arising in the ordinary course of business. Dell considers the likelihood of loss or impairment of an asset or the incurrence of a liability, as well as Dell's ability to reasonably estimate the amount of loss, in determining loss contingencies. An estimated loss contingency is accrued when it is probable that an asset has been impaired or a liability has been incurred and the amount of loss can be reasonably estimated. Dell regularly evaluates current information available to determine whether such accruals should be adjusted and whether new accruals are required.

*Shipping Costs* — Dell's shipping and handling costs are included in cost of sales in the Consolidated Statements of Income.

*Selling, General, and Administrative* — Selling expenses include items such as sales salaries and commissions, marketing and advertising costs, and contractor services. Dell expenses advertising costs as incurred. General and administrative expenses include items for Dell's administrative functions, such as Finance, Legal, Human Resources, and Information Technology support. These functions include costs for items such as salaries, maintenance and supplies, insurance, depreciation expense, and allowance for doubtful accounts.

*Research, Development, and Engineering Costs* — Research, development, and engineering costs are expensed as incurred. Research, development, and engineering expenses primarily include payroll and headcount related costs, contractor fees, infrastructure costs, and administrative expenses directly related to research and development support.

*Website Development Costs* — Dell expenses, as incurred, the costs of maintenance and minor enhancements to the features and functionality of its websites.

*Income Taxes* — Deferred tax assets and liabilities are recorded based on the difference between the financial statement and tax basis of assets and liabilities using enacted tax rates in effect for the year in which the differences are expected to reverse. Dell calculates a provision for income taxes using the asset and liability method, under which deferred tax assets and liabilities are recognized by identifying the temporary differences arising from the different treatment of items for tax and accounting purposes. In determining the future tax consequences of events that have been recognized in the financial statements or tax returns, judgment and interpretation of statutes are required. Additionally, Dell uses tax planning strategies as a part of its global tax compliance program. Judgments and interpretation of statutes are inherent in this process.

The accounting guidance for uncertainties in income tax prescribes a comprehensive model for the financial statement recognition, measurement, presentation, and disclosure of uncertain tax positions taken or expected to be taken in income tax returns. Dell recognizes a tax benefit from an uncertain tax position in the financial statements only when it is more likely than not that the position will be sustained upon examination, including resolution of any related appeals or litigation processes, based on the technical merits and a consideration of the relevant taxing authority's administrative practices and precedents.

*Comprehensive Income* — Dell's comprehensive income is comprised of net income, unrealized gains and losses on marketable securities classified as available-for-sale, foreign currency translation adjustments, and unrealized gains and losses on derivative financial instruments related to foreign currency hedging.

*Earnings Per Share* — Basic earnings per share is based on the weighted-average effect of all common shares issued and outstanding, and is calculated by dividing net income by the weighted-average shares outstanding during the period. Diluted earnings per share is calculated by dividing net income by the weighted-average number of common shares used in the basic earnings per share calculation plus the number of common shares that would be issued assuming exercise or conversion of all potentially dilutive common shares outstanding. Dell excludes equity instruments from the calculation of diluted earnings per share if the effect of including such instruments is anti-dilutive. See Note 13 of Notes to Consolidated Financial Statements for further information on earnings per share.

## DELL INC.

## NOTES TO CONSOLIDATED FINANCIAL
## STATEMENTS (Continued)

*Stock-Based Compensation* — Dell measures stock-based compensation expense for all share-based awards granted based on the estimated fair value of those awards at grant-date. The cost of restricted stock units and performance-based restricted stock units are determined using the fair market value of Dell's common stock on the date of grant. Dell also has a limited number of performance-based units that include a market-based condition. The fair value of the market-condition and performance-condition portion of the award is estimated using the Monte Carlo simulation valuation model. The expense recognized for these market-condition and performance-condition based awards were not material for Fiscal 2011. The fair values of stock option awards are estimated using a Black-Scholes valuation model. The compensation costs of stock options, restricted stock units, and awards with a cliff vesting feature are recognized net of any estimated forfeitures on a straight-line basis over the employee requisite service period. Compensation cost for performance based awards is recognized on a graded accelerated basis net of estimated forfeitures over the requisite service period. Forfeiture rates are estimated at grant date based on historical experience and adjusted in subsequent periods for differences in actual forfeitures from those estimates. See Note 15 of Notes to Consolidated Financial Statements included for further discussion of stock-based compensation.

### *Recently Issued and Adopted Accounting Pronouncements*

*Revenue Arrangements with Multiple Elements and Revenue Arrangements with Software Elements* — In September 2009, the Emerging Issues Task Force of the FASB reached a consensus on two issues which affects the timing of revenue recognition. The first consensus changes the level of evidence of standalone selling price required to separate deliverables in a multiple deliverable revenue arrangement by allowing a company to make its best estimate of the selling price of deliverables when more objective evidence of selling price is not available and eliminates the residual method. The consensus applies to multiple deliverable revenue arrangements that are not accounted for under other accounting pronouncements and retains the use of VSOE if available and third-party evidence of selling price when VSOE is unavailable. The second consensus excludes sales of tangible products that contain essential software elements, that is, software enabled devices, from the scope of revenue recognition requirements for software arrangements. Dell elected to early adopt this accounting guidance at the beginning of the first quarter of Fiscal 2011 on a prospective basis for applicable transactions originating or materially modified after January 29, 2010. The adoption of this guidance did not have a material impact to Dell's consolidated financial statements.

*Variable Interest Entities and Transfers of Financial Assets and Extinguishments of Liabilities* — In June 2009, the FASB issued a new pronouncement on transfers of financial assets and extinguishments of liabilities which removes the concept of a qualifying special purpose entity and removes the exception from applying variable interest entity accounting to qualifying special purpose entities. See "Asset Securitization" above for more information.

*Credit Quality of Financing Receivables and the Allowance for Credit Losses* — In July 2010, FASB issued a new pronouncement that requires enhanced disclosures regarding the nature of credit risk inherent in an entity's portfolio of financing receivables, how that risk is analyzed, and the changes and reasons for those changes in the allowance for credit losses. The new disclosures require information for both the financing receivables and the related allowance for credit losses at more disaggregated levels. Disclosures related to information as of the end of a reporting period became effective for Dell in Fiscal 2011. Specific disclosures regarding activities that occur during a reporting period will be required for Dell beginning in the first quarter of Fiscal 2012. As these changes relate only to disclosures, they will not have an impact on Dell's consolidated financial results.

*Notes 2, 3, 4, 5, and 6 are not included in Appendix B, but are available in the 2011 Dell Annual Report at* www.dell.com.

## NOTE 7 — ACQUISITIONS

### Fiscal 2011 Acquisitions

Dell completed five acquisitions during Fiscal 2011, Kace Networks, Inc. ("KACE"), Ocarina Networks Inc. ("Ocarina"), Scalent Systems Inc. ("Scalent"), Boomi, Inc. ("Boomi"), and InSite One, Inc., ("InSite"), for a total purchase consideration of approximately $413 million. KACE is a systems management appliance company with solutions tailored to the requirements of mid-sized businesses. KACE is being integrated primarily into Dell's Small and Medium Business and Public segments. Ocarina is a provider of de-duplication solutions and content-aware compression across storage product lines. Scalent is a provider of scalable and efficient data center infrastructure software. Boomi is a provider of on-demand integration technology. Ocarina, Scalent, and Boomi will be integrated into all of Dell's Commercial segments. InSite provides cloud-based medical data archiving, storage, and disaster-recovery solutions to the health care industry. InSite will be integrated into Dell's Public segment.

Dell has recorded these acquisitions using the acquisition method of accounting and recorded their respective assets and liabilities at fair value at the date of acquisition. The excess of the purchase prices over the estimated fair values were recorded as goodwill. Any changes in the estimated fair values of the net assets recorded for these acquisitions prior to the finalization of more detailed analyses, but not to exceed one year from the date of acquisition, will change the amount of the purchase prices allocable to goodwill. Any subsequent changes to the purchase price allocations that are material to Dell's consolidated financial results will be adjusted retroactively. Dell recorded approximately $284 million in goodwill and $141 million in intangible assets related to these acquisitions. The goodwill related to these acquisitions is not deductible for tax purposes. In conjunction with these acquisitions, Dell will incur $56 million in compensation-related expenses that will be expensed over a period of one to three years. There was no contingent consideration related to these acquisitions.

Dell has not presented pro forma results of operations for the Fiscal 2011 acquisitions because these acquisitions are not material to Dell's consolidated results of operations, financial position, or cash flows on either an individual or an aggregate basis.

### Fiscal 2010 Acquisitions

On November 3, 2009, Dell completed its acquisition of all the outstanding shares of the Class A common stock of Perot Systems, a worldwide provider of information technology and business solutions, for $3.9 billion in cash. This acquisition is expected to provide customers a broader range of IT services and solutions and better position Dell for its own immediate and long-term growth and efficiency. Perot Systems was primarily integrated into the Large Enterprise and Public segments for reporting purposes. Perot Systems' results of operations were included in Dell's results beginning November 3, 2009.

## DELL INC.

### NOTES TO CONSOLIDATED FINANCIAL STATEMENTS (Continued)

The following table summarizes the consideration paid for Perot Systems and the amounts of assets acquired and liabilities assumed recognized at the acquisition date:

|  | Total |
|---|---|
|  | (in millions) |
| Cash and cash equivalents | $ 266 |
| Accounts receivable, net | 410 |
| Other assets | 58 |
| Property, plant, and equipment | 323 |
| Identifiable intangible assets | 1,174 |
| Deferred tax liability, net[(a)] | (424) |
| Other liabilities | (256) |
| Total identifiable net assets | 1,551 |
| Goodwill | 2,327 |
| Total purchase price | $ 3,878 |

(a) The deferred tax liability, net primarily relates to purchased identifiable intangible assets and property, plant, and equipment and is shown net of associated deferred tax assets.

The goodwill of $2.3 billion represents the value from combining Perot Systems with Dell to provide customers with a broader range of IT services and solutions as well as optimizing how these solutions are delivered. The acquisition has enabled Dell to supply even more Perot Systems customers with Dell products and extended the reach of Perot Systems' capabilities to Dell customers around the world. Goodwill of $679 million, $1,613 million, and $35 million was assigned to the Large Enterprise, Public, and SMB segments, respectively.

Identifiable intangible assets included customer relationships, internally developed software, non-compete agreements, and trade names and other assets. These intangible assets are being amortized over their estimated useful lives based on the pattern of expected future economic benefit, which is generally on a non-straight-line basis based upon their expected future cash flows.

The following table summarizes the cost of amortizable intangible assets related to the acquisition of Perot Systems:

|  | Estimated Cost | Weighted-Average Useful Life |
|---|---|---|
|  | (in millions) | (years) |
| Customer relationships | $ 1,081 | 11.0 |
| Technology | 44 | 3.0 |
| Non-compete agreements | 39 | 5.2 |
| Tradenames | 10 | 1.5 |
| Total amortizable intangible assets | $ 1,174 | 10.4 |

Accounts receivable was comprised primarily of customer trade receivables. As such, the fair value of accounts receivable approximates its carrying value of $410 million. The gross amount due is $423 million, of which $13 million was expected to be uncollectible.

In conjunction with the acquisition, Dell incurred $93 million in cash compensation payments made to former Perot Systems employees who accepted positions with Dell related to the acceleration of Perot Systems unvested stock options and other cash compensation payments. These cash compensation payments were expensed as incurred and are recorded in selling, general, and administrative expenses in the Consolidated Statements of Income for Fiscal 2010. During Fiscal 2010, Dell incurred $116 million in acquisition-related costs for Perot Systems, including the payments above, and an additional $23 million in other acquisition-related costs such as bankers' fees, consulting fees, other employee-related charges, and integration costs.

There was no contingent consideration related to the acquisition.

The following table provides unaudited pro forma results of operations for the fiscal years ended January 29, 2010, and January 30, 2009, as if Perot Systems had been acquired at the beginning of the fiscal year ended January 30, 2009. Due to the different fiscal period ends, the pro forma results for the fiscal years ended January 29, 2010, and January 30, 2009, are combined with the results of Perot Systems for the twelve months ended January 29, 2010, and December 31, 2008, respectively. The pro forma results are adjusted for intercompany charges, but do not include any anticipated cost synergies or other effects of the planned integration of Perot Systems. Accordingly, such pro forma results are not necessarily indicative of the results that actually would have occurred had the acquisition been completed on the dates indicated, nor are they indicative of the future operating results of the combined company.

|  | Fiscal Year Ended | |
|---|---|---|
|  | January 29, 2010 | January 30, 2009 |
|  | (in millions, except per share data, unaudited) | |
| Pro forma net sales | $ 54,739 | $ 63,835 |
| Pro forma net income | $ 1,422 | $ 2,398 |
| Pro forma earnings per share — diluted | $ 0.72 | $ 1.21 |

### Fiscal 2009 Acquisitions

Dell completed three acquisitions in Fiscal 2009, including The Networked Storage Company, MessageOne, Inc. ("MessageOne"), and Allin Corporation ("Allin"), for approximately $197 million in cash. Dell recorded approximately $136 million of goodwill and approximately $64 million of purchased intangible assets related to these acquisitions. Dell also expensed approximately $2 million of in-process research and development ("IPR&D") related to these acquisitions in Fiscal 2009. The largest of these transactions was the purchase of MessageOne for approximately $164 million in cash plus an additional $10 million to be used for management retention. MessageOne, Allin, and The Networked Storage Company have been integrated into Dell's Commercial segments.

**DELL INC.**

**NOTES TO CONSOLIDATED FINANCIAL
STATEMENTS (Continued)**

The acquisition of MessageOne was identified and acknowledged by Dell's Board of Directors as a related party transaction because Michael Dell and his family held indirect ownership interests in MessageOne. Consequently, Dell's Board of Directors directed management to implement a series of measures designed to ensure that the transaction was considered, analyzed, negotiated, and approved objectively and independent of any control or influence from the related parties.

Dell has not presented pro forma results of operations for the Fiscal 2009 acquisitions because these acquisitions were not material to Dell's consolidated results of operations, financial position, or cash flows on either an individual or an aggregate basis.

**NOTE 8 — GOODWILL AND INTANGIBLE ASSETS**

*Goodwill*

Goodwill allocated to Dell's business segments as of January 28, 2011, and January 29, 2010, and changes in the carrying amount of goodwill for the respective periods, were as follows:

| | Fiscal Year Ended | | | | | January 29, 2010 |
|---|---|---|---|---|---|---|
| | January 28, 2011 | | | | | |
| | Large Enterprise | Public | Small and Medium Business | Consumer | Total | Total |
| | (in millions) | | | | | |
| Balance at beginning of period | $ 1,361 | $ 2,026 | $ 389 | $ 298 | $ 4,074 | $ 1,737 |
| Goodwill acquired during the period | 62 | 135 | 87 | - | 284 | 2,327 |
| Adjustments | 1 | 3 | - | 3 | 7 | 10 |
| Balance at end of period | $ 1,424 | $ 2,164 | $ 476 | $ 301 | $ 4,365 | $ 4,074 |

Goodwill is tested annually during the second fiscal quarter and whenever events or circumstances indicate an impairment may have occurred. If the carrying amount of goodwill exceeds its fair value, estimated based on discounted cash flow analyses, an impairment charge would be recorded. Based on the results of the annual impairment tests, no impairment of goodwill existed at July 30, 2010. Further, no triggering events have transpired since July 30, 2010, that would indicate a potential impairment of goodwill as of January 28, 2011. Dell does not have any accumulated goodwill impairment charges as of January 28, 2011. The goodwill adjustments are primarily the result of contingent purchase price considerations related to prior period acquisitions and the effects of foreign currency fluctuations.

*Intangible Assets*

Dell's intangible assets associated with completed acquisitions at January 28, 2011 and January 29, 2010, are as follows:

| | January 28, 2011 | | | January 29, 2010 | | |
|---|---|---|---|---|---|---|
| | Gross | Accumulated Amortization | Net | Gross | Accumulated Amortization | Net |
| | (in millions) | | | | | |
| Customer relationships | $ 1,363 | $ (309) | $ 1,054 | $ 1,324 | $ (117) | $ 1,207 |
| Technology | 647 | (322) | 325 | 568 | (196) | 372 |
| Non-compete agreements | 68 | (26) | 42 | 64 | (8) | 56 |
| Tradenames | 54 | (31) | 23 | 51 | (17) | 34 |
| Amortizable intangible assets | 2,132 | (688) | 1,444 | 2,007 | (338) | 1,669 |
| In-process research and development | 26 | - | 26 | - | - | - |
| Indefinite lived intangible assets | 25 | - | 25 | 25 | - | 25 |
| Total intangible assets | $ 2,183 | $ (688) | $ 1,495 | $ 2,032 | $ (338) | $ 1,694 |

During Fiscal 2011, Dell recorded additions to intangible assets and in-process research and development of $126 million and $26 million, respectively, which were primarily related to Dell's Fiscal 2011 business acquisitions. During Fiscal 2010, Dell recorded additions to intangible assets of $1.2 billion, which were related to Dell's acquisition of Perot Systems.

Amortization expense related to finite-lived intangible assets was approximately $350 million and $205 million in Fiscal 2011 and Fiscal 2010, respectively. During the fiscal years ended January 28, 2011, and January 29, 2010, Dell did not record any impairment charges as a result of its analysis of its intangible assets.

Estimated future annual pre-tax amortization expense of finite-lived intangible assets as of January 28, 2011, over the next five fiscal years and thereafter is as follows:

| Fiscal Years | (in millions) |
|---|---|
| 2012 | $ 313 |
| 2013 | 279 |
| 2014 | 240 |
| 2015 | 147 |
| 2016 | 117 |
| Thereafter | 348 |
| Total | $ 1,444 |

**DELL INC.**

**NOTES TO CONSOLIDATED FINANCIAL
STATEMENTS (Continued)**

## NOTE 9 — WARRANTY AND DEFERRED EXTENDED WARRANTY REVENUE

Dell records liabilities for its standard limited warranties at the time of sale for the estimated costs that may be incurred. The liability for standard warranties is included in accrued and other current and other non-current liabilities on the Consolidated Statements of Financial Position. Revenue from the sale of extended warranties is recognized over the term of the contract or when the service is completed, and the costs associated with these contracts are recognized as incurred. Deferred extended warranty revenue is included in deferred services revenue on the Consolidated Statements of Financial Position. Changes in Dell's liabilities for standard limited warranties and deferred services revenue related to extended warranties are presented in the following tables:

|  | Fiscal Year Ended | | |
|---|---|---|---|
|  | January 28, 2011 | January 29, 2010 | January 30, 2009 |
|  | (in millions) | | |
| *Warranty liability:* | | | |
| Warranty liability at beginning of period | $ 912 | $ 1,035 | $ 929 |
| Costs accrued for new warranty contracts and changes in estimates for pre-existing warranties[a][b] | 1,046 | 987 | 1,180 |
| Service obligations honored | (1,063) | (1,110) | (1,074) |
| Warranty liability at end of period | $ 895 | $ 912 | $ 1,035 |
| Current portion | $ 575 | $ 593 | $ 721 |
| Non-current portion | 320 | 319 | 314 |
| Warranty liability at end of period | $ 895 | $ 912 | $ 1,035 |

|  | Fiscal Year Ended | | |
|---|---|---|---|
|  | January 28, 2011 | January 29, 2010 | January 30, 2009 |
|  | (in millions) | | |
| *Deferred extended warranty revenue:* | | | |
| Deferred extended warranty revenue at beginning of period | $ 5,910 | $ 5,587 | $ 5,233 |
| Revenue deferred for new extended warranties[b] | 3,877 | 3,481 | 3,470 |
| Revenue recognized | (3,371) | (3,158) | (3,116) |
| Deferred extended warranty revenue at end of period | $ 6,416 | $ 5,910 | $ 5,587 |
| Current portion | $ 2,959 | $ 2,906 | $ 2,601 |
| Non-current portion | 3,457 | 3,004 | 2,986 |
| Deferred extended warranty revenue at end of period | $ 6,416 | $ 5,910 | $ 5,587 |

(a)  Changes in cost estimates related to pre-existing warranties are aggregated with accruals for new standard warranty contracts. Dell's warranty liability process does not differentiate between estimates made for pre-existing warranties and new warranty obligations.

(b)  Includes the impact of foreign currency exchange rate fluctuations.

*Note 10 is not included in Appendix B, but is available in the 2011 Dell Annual Report at* www.dell.com.

## NOTE 11 — COMMITMENTS AND CONTINGENCIES

<u>Lease Commitments</u> — Dell leases property and equipment, manufacturing facilities, and office space under non-cancelable leases. Certain of these leases obligate Dell to pay taxes, maintenance, and repair costs. At January 28, 2011, future minimum lease payments under these non-cancelable leases are as follows: $106 million in Fiscal 2012; $71 million in Fiscal 2013; $53 million in Fiscal 2014; $44 million in Fiscal 2015; $33 million in Fiscal 2016; and $68 million thereafter.

Rent expense under all leases totaled $87 million, $93 million, and $116 million for Fiscal 2011, Fiscal 2010, and Fiscal 2009, respectively.

<u>Purchase Obligations</u> — Dell has contractual obligations to purchase goods or services, which specify significant terms, including fixed or minimum quantities to be purchased; fixed, minimum, or variable price provisions; and the approximate timing of the transaction. As of January 28, 2011, Dell has $293 million, $43 million, and $29 million in purchase obligations for Fiscal 2012, Fiscal 2013, and Fiscal 2014 and thereafter, respectively.

<u>Restricted Cash</u> — As of January 28, 2011, and January 29, 2010, Dell had restricted cash in the amounts of $25 million and $147 million, respectively, included in other current assets on the Consolidated Statements of Financial Position. The balance at January 29, 2010, was primarily related to an agreement between DFS and CIT, which required Dell to maintain an escrow cash account that was held as recourse reserves for credit losses, performance fee deposits related to Dell's private label credit card, as well as amounts maintained in escrow accounts related to Dell's acquisitions. In the third quarter of Fiscal 2011, the agreement between DFS and CIT was terminated and the restricted cash that was held on deposit was returned to CIT. The balance at January 28, 2011, primarily relates to various escrow accounts in connection with Dell's acquisitions.

<u>Legal Matters</u> — Dell is involved in various claims, suits, assessments, investigations, and legal proceedings that arise from time-to-time in the ordinary course of its business, including those identified below, consisting of matters involving consumer, antitrust, tax, intellectual property, and other issues on a global basis.

## DELL INC.

## NOTES TO CONSOLIDATED FINANCIAL
## STATEMENTS (Continued)

The following is a discussion of Dell's significant on-going legal matters and other proceedings:

*SEC Investigation and Related Settlements* — In August 2005, the SEC initiated an inquiry into certain of Dell's accounting and financial reporting matters and requested that Dell provide certain documents. The SEC expanded that inquiry in June 2006 and entered a formal order of investigation in October 2006. In August 2006, because of potential issues identified in the course of responding to the SEC's requests for information, Dell's Audit Committee, on the recommendation of management and in consultation with PricewaterhouseCoopers LLP, Dell's independent registered public accounting firm, initiated an independent investigation into certain accounting and financial reporting matters, which was completed in the third quarter of Fiscal 2008. Dell subsequently restated its annual and interim financial statements for Fiscal 2003, Fiscal 2004, Fiscal 2005, Fiscal 2006, and the first quarter of Fiscal 2007.

On July 22, 2010, Dell reached a settlement with the SEC resolving the SEC's investigation into Dell's disclosures and alleged omissions prior to Fiscal 2008 regarding certain aspects of its commercial relationship with Intel Corporation ("Intel") and into separate accounting and financial reporting matters. The SEC agreed to settlements with both the company and Michael Dell, who serves as the company's Chairman and Chief Executive Officer. The company and Mr. Dell entered into the settlements without admitting or denying the allegations in the SEC's complaint, as is consistent with common SEC practice.

Under its settlement, the company consented to a permanent injunction against future violations of antifraud provisions, non-scienter (negligence) based fraud provisions and other non-fraud based provisions related to reporting, the maintenance of accurate books and records, and internal accounting controls under Section 17(a) of the Securities Act of 1933 (the "Securities Act"), Sections 10(b), 13(a), 13(b)(2)(A) and 13(b)(2)(B) of the Securities Exchange Act of 1934 (the "Exchange Act") and Rules 10b-5, 12b-20, 13a-1 and 13a-13 under the Exchange Act. The company also agreed to perform, and has initiated, certain undertakings, including retaining and working with an independent consultant, to enhance its disclosure processes, practices and controls. Pursuant to the settlement terms, the company expects to have completed or implemented these undertakings within 36 months after court approval of the settlement on October 13, 2010. In addition, the company paid into an escrow account a civil monetary penalty of $100 million and discharged the liability during the second quarter of Fiscal 2011.

The SEC's allegations with respect to Mr. Dell and his settlement were limited to the alleged failure to provide adequate disclosures with respect to the company's commercial relationship with Intel prior to Fiscal 2008. Mr. Dell's settlement did not involve any of the separate accounting fraud charges that were settled by the company. Moreover, Mr. Dell's settlement was limited to claims in which only negligence, and not fraudulent intent, is required to establish liability, as well as secondary liability claims for other non-fraud charges. Under his settlement, Mr. Dell consented to a permanent injunction against future violations of these negligence-based provisions and other non-fraud based provisions related to periodic reporting. Specifically, Mr. Dell consented to be enjoined from violating Sections 17(a)(2) and (3) of the Securities Act and Rule 13a-14 under the Exchange Act and from aiding and abetting violations of Section 13(a) of the Exchange Act and Rules 12b-20, 13a-1 and 13a-13 under the Exchange Act. In addition, Mr. Dell agreed to a civil monetary penalty of $4 million. The settlement does not include any restrictions on Mr. Dell's continued service as an officer or director of the company.

The independent directors of the Board of Directors unanimously determined that it is in the best interests of Dell and its stockholders that Mr. Dell continue to serve as the Chairman and Chief Executive Officer of the company.

The settlements with the company and Mr. Dell were approved by the U.S. District Court for the District of Columbia on October 13, 2010.

*Securities Litigation* — Four putative securities class actions filed between September 13, 2006, and January 31, 2007, in the U.S. District Court for the Western District of Texas, Austin Division, against Dell and certain of its current and former directors and officers were consolidated as In re Dell Securities Litigation, and a lead plaintiff was appointed by the court. The lead plaintiff asserted claims under Sections 10(b), 20(a), and 20A of the Exchange Act based on alleged false and misleading disclosures or omissions regarding Dell's financial statements, governmental investigations, internal controls, known battery problems and business model, and based on insiders' sales of Dell securities. This action also included Dell's independent registered public accounting firm, PricewaterhouseCoopers LLP, as a defendant. On October 6, 2008, the court dismissed all of the plaintiffs claims with prejudice and without leave to amend. On November 3, 2008, the plaintiff appealed the dismissal of Dell and the officer defendants to the Fifth Circuit Court of Appeals. The appeal was fully briefed, and oral argument on the appeal was heard by the Fifth Circuit Court of Appeals on September 1, 2009. On November 20, 2009, the parties to the appeal entered into a written settlement agreement whereby Dell would pay $40 million to the proposed class and the plaintiff would dismiss the pending litigation. The settlement was preliminarily approved by the District Court on December 21, 2009. The settlement was subject to certain conditions, including opt-outs from the proposed class not exceeding a specified percentage and final approval by the District Court. During the first quarter of Fiscal 2011, the original opt-out period in the notice approved by the District Court expired without the specified percentage being exceeded. The District Court subsequently granted final approval for the settlement and entered a final judgment on July 20, 2010. Dell paid $40 million into an escrow account to satisfy this settlement and discharged the liability during the second quarter of Fiscal 2011. Certain objectors to the settlement have filed notices of appeal to the Fifth Circuit Court of Appeals with regard to approval of the settlement. While there can be no assurances with respect to litigation, we believe it is unlikely that the settlement will be overturned on appeal.

*Copyright Levies* — In many European Union ("EU") member countries, there are requirements to collect and remit levies to collecting societies based on sales of certain devices. These levies apply to Dell and others in the industry. The amount of levies is generally based upon the number of products sold and the per-product amounts of the levies. Levies are intended to compensate copyright holders for "fair use" copying of copyrighted materials. The collecting societies then distribute the levies to copyright holders. Some EU member countries that do not yet have levies on digital devices are expected to implement similar legislation to enable them to extend existing levy schemes, while some other EU member countries are expected to limit the scope of levy schemes and their applicability in the digital hardware environment. Dell, other companies and various industry associations have opposed the extension of levies to the digital environment and have advocated alternative models of compensation to rights holders. As described below, there are multiple proceedings involving Dell or its competitors in certain EU member countries, where plaintiffs are seeking to impose or modify levies upon equipment (such as multifunction devices, phones, personal computers ("PCs") and printers), alleging that these devices enable copying of copyrighted materials. Even if Dell is not a party to all these proceedings, however, the decisions could impact Dell's business and the amount of copyright levies Dell may be required to collect. These various proceeding also challenge whether the levy schemes in those countries comply with EU law.

## DELL INC.

### NOTES TO CONSOLIDATED FINANCIAL
### STATEMENTS (Continued)

There are multiple proceedings in Germany that could impact Dell's obligation to collect and remit levies in Germany. In July 2004, VG Wort, a German collecting society, filed a lawsuit against Hewlett-Packard Company ("HP") in the Stuttgart Civil Court seeking copyright levies on printers. On December 22, 2004, the court held that HP was liable for payments regarding all printers using ASCII code sold in Germany. HP appealed the decision and after an intermediary ruling upholding the trial court's decision, the German Federal Supreme Court ("GFSC") in December 2007 issued a judgment that printers are not subject to levies under the German copyright law that was in effect until December 31, 2007. Based upon the GFSC's ruling, Dell concluded there was no obligation for Dell to collect or accrue levies for printers sold by it prior to December 31, 2007. VG Wort filed a claim with the German Constitutional Court ("GCC") challenging the GFSC's ruling that printers are not subject to levies. On September 21, 2010, the GCC revoked the GFSC decision and referred the case back to the GFSC to determine if the ruling gave due credit to the copyright owner's property rights under the German Constitution and whether the GFSC should have referred the case to the European Court of Justice ("ECJ"). The GFSC has set a hearing date of March 24, 2011. Dell believes that the GFSC can decide to refer the case to the ECJ, confirm its prior decision, or conclude that printers are subject to levies under German law. Dell has not accrued any liability in this matter, as Dell does not believe there is a probable and estimable claim.

In a separate matter, on December 29, 2005, Zentralstelle Für private Überspielungrechte ("ZPÜ"), a joint association of various German collecting societies, instituted arbitration proceedings against Dell's German subsidiary before the Board of Arbitration at the German Patent and Trademark Office ("Arbitration Body") in Munich. ZPÜ claimed an audio-video levy of €18.42 for each PC sold by Dell in Germany from January 1, 2002, through December 31, 2005. On July 31, 2007, the Arbitration Body recommended a levy of €15 on each PC sold by Dell during that period for audio and visual copying capabilities. Dell and ZPÜ rejected the recommendation, and on February 21, 2008, ZPÜ filed a lawsuit in the German Regional Court in Munich with respect to levies to be paid through the end of calendar year 2007. On December 23, 2009, ZPÜ and the German industry association, BCH, reached a settlement regarding audio-video copyright levy litigation. The settlement provided for payment of levies in the amount of €3.15 for calendar years 2002 and 2003, €6.30 for calendar years 2004 through 2007, and €12.15 (for units excluding a burner) and €13.65 (for units including a burner) for calendar years 2008 through 2010. Dell joined this settlement on February 23, 2010 and has paid the amounts due thereunder. Because the settlement agreement expired on December 31, 2010, the amount of levies payable after calendar year 2010, as well as Dell's ability to recover such amounts through increased prices, remains uncertain.

Additionally, there are proceedings in Spain to which Dell is not a party, but that could impact Dell's obligation to collect and remit levies across the EU. In March 2006, Sociedad General de Autores y Editores de Espana ("SGAE"), a Spanish collecting society, sued Padawan SL, a company unaffiliated with Dell, in the Commercial Court number four of Barcelona in Spain claiming that Padawan owed levies on the CD-Rs, CD-RWs, DVD-Rs, and MP3 players sold by Padawan. In June 2007, the trial court upheld SGAE's claim and ordered Padawan to pay specified levies. Padawan appealed the decision to the Audiencia Provincial de Barcelona, which stayed the proceedings in order to refer the case to the ECJ. The ECJ considered the interpretation of the term "fair compensation" under the European Copyright Directive ("Directive"). On October 21, 2010, the ECJ issued its decision and outlined how fair compensation should be considered under the Directive by the EU member states. The ECJ stated that fair compensation must be calculated based on the harm caused to the authors of protected works by private copying. The ECJ also stated that the indiscriminate application of the private copying levy to devices not made available to private users and clearly reserved for uses other than private copying is incompatible with the Directive. The matter has been referred back to the Spanish court to determine whether the Spanish copyright levy scheme is compatible with the Directive based on the guidance provided by the ECJ. It is unclear at this time what the effect of this decision will be on copyright levies in Spain and the other EU member states. Dell continues to collect and remit levies in Spain and other EU countries where it has determined that based on local law it is probable that Dell has an obligation.

The ultimate resolution of these matters and the associated financial impact to Dell, if any, including the number of units potentially affected, the amount of levies imposed, and the ability of Dell to recover such amounts remains uncertain at this time. Should the courts determine there is liability for previous units shipped beyond what Dell has collected or accrued, Dell would be liable for such incremental amounts. Recovery would only be possible on future collections related to future shipments.

*Sharp Corporation v Dell Inc.* — Sharp Corporation ("Sharp") filed a suit against Dell in October 2008 for trademark infringement, unfair competition and dilution in the U.S. District Court in the State of New Jersey. Sharp alleges that it is the owner of the "SHARP" mark and that this mark and related marks are used in connection with Sharp's sale of a wide variety of electrical and consumer electronic products. Sharp alleges that Dell has infringed the "SHARP" mark by using the "UltraSharp" and "Dell UltraSharp" marks to promote, advertise and sell computer monitors and notebook computers, from 2002 to the present. Sharp alleges that Dell's use of "UltraSharp" has and will continue to cause actual consumer confusion regarding the source of "UltraSharp". In addition, Sharp has asserted a claim for dilution of its SHARP marks on the alleged ground that Dell's use of DELL UltraSharp and UltraSharp has weakened the distinctive value of its marks. Sharp seeks damages measured by Dell's profits made from the sale of DELL UltraSharp products, treble damages, punitive damages, costs and attorneys' fees. Sharp also seeks a permanent injunction precluding the use of Dell's allegedly infringing "UltraSharp" mark. Dell disputes the claims and is vigorously defending the case. Trial in this matter is currently scheduled for June 2011. The ultimate resolution of this matter and the associated financial impact to Dell, if any, remains uncertain at this time.

*Chad Brazil and Steven Seick v Dell Inc.* — Chad Brazil and Steven Seick filed a class action suit against Dell in March 2007 in the U.S. District Court for the Northern District of California. The plaintiffs allege that Dell advertised discounts on its products from false "regular" prices, in violation of California law. The plaintiffs seek compensatory damages, disgorgement of profits from the alleged false advertising, injunctive relief, punitive damages and attorneys' fees. In December 2010, the District Court certified a class consisting of all California residents who had purchased certain products advertised with a former sales price on the consumer segment of Dell's website during an approximately four year period between March 2003 and June 2007. The Court of Appeals is currently considering Dell's request for an interlocutory appeal of the certification order. Dell disputes the claims and is vigorously defending the case. The ultimate resolution of this matter and the associated financial impact to Dell, if any, remain uncertain at this time.

*Other Litigation* — The various legal proceedings in which Dell is involved include commercial litigation and a variety of patent suits. In some of these cases, Dell is the sole defendant. More often, particularly in the patent suits, Dell is one of a number of defendants in the electronics and technology industries. Dell is actively defending a number of patent infringement suits, and several pending claims are in various stages of evaluations. While the number of patent cases has grown over time, Dell does not currently anticipate that any of these matters will have a material impact on Dell's financial condition , results of operations, or cash flows.

*Other Matters* — In the second quarter of Fiscal 2011, Dell became aware of instances in which certain peripheral product sales made to U.S. federal government customers under Dell's General Services Administration ("GSA") Schedule 70 Contract were not compliant with contract requirements implementing the Trade Agreements Act. Dell self-reported the discovery to the GSA's Office of the Inspector General and has presented a report of its findings which conclude that less than $1 million of non-compliant products may have been sold. Dell continues to work with the GSA's Office of the Inspector General to reach final resolution of this matter with that office .

## DELL INC.

## NOTES TO CONSOLIDATED FINANCIAL STATEMENTS (Continued)

While Dell does not expect that the ultimate outcomes in these proceedings or matters, individually or collectively, will have a material adverse effect on its business, financial position, results of operations, or cash flows, the results and timing of the ultimate resolutions of these various proceedings and matters are inherently unpredictable. Whether the outcome of any claim, suit, assessment, investigation, or legal proceeding, individually or collectively, could have a material effect on Dell's business, financial condition, results of operations, or cash flows will depend on a number of variables, including the nature, timing, and amount of any associated expenses, amounts paid in settlement, damages or other remedies or consequences. Dell accrues a liability when it believes that it is both probable that a liability has been incurred and that it can reasonably estimate the amount of the loss. Dell reviews these accruals at least quarterly and adjusts them to reflect ongoing negotiations, settlements, rulings, advice of legal counsel, and other relevant information. To the extent new information is obtained and Dell's views on the probable outcomes of claims, suits, assessments, investigations, or legal proceedings change, changes in Dell's accrued liabilities would be recorded in the period in which such determination is made.

*Certain Concentrations* — Dell's counterparties to its financial instruments consist of a number of major financial institutions with credit ratings of AA and A by major credit rating agencies. In addition to limiting the amount of agreements and contracts it enters into with any one party, Dell monitors its positions with, and the credit quality of the counterparties to, these financial instruments. Dell does not anticipate nonperformance by any of the counterparties.

Dell's investments in debt securities are in high quality financial institutions and companies. As part of its cash and risk management processes, Dell performs periodic evaluations of the credit standing of the institutions in accordance with its investment policy. Dell's investments in debt securities have effective maturities of less than five years. Management believes that no significant concentration of credit risk for investments exists for Dell. As of January 28, 2011, Dell does not have significant concentrations of cash and cash equivalent deposits with its financial institutions.

Dell markets and sells its products and services to large corporate clients, governments, health care and education accounts, as well as small and medium-sized businesses and individuals. No single customer accounted for more than 10% of Dell's consolidated net revenue during Fiscal 2011, Fiscal 2010, or Fiscal 2009.

Dell purchases a number of components from single or limited sources. In some cases, alternative sources of supply are not available. In other cases, Dell may establish a working relationship with a single source or a limited number of sources if Dell believes it is advantageous to do so based on performance, quality, support, delivery, capacity, or price considerations.

Dell also sells components to certain contract manufacturers who assemble final products for Dell. Dell does not recognize the sale of these components in net sales and does not recognize the related profits until the final products are sold by Dell to end users. Profits from the sale of these parts are recognized as a reduction of cost of sales at the time of sale. Dell has net settlement agreements with the majority of these contract manufacturers that allow Dell to offset the accounts payable to the contract manufacturers from the amounts receivable from them. The net balances that are receivables for Dell are included in other current assets or accounts payable if Dell is in a net payable position. Non-trade receivables from four of these contract manufacturers accounted for the majority of gross non-trade receivables of $2.7 billion and $2.5 billion as of January 28, 2011 and January 29, 2010, respectively. As of January 28, 2011, and January 29, 2010, these four contract manufacturers were in net payable positions.

*Notes 12, 13, and 14 are not included in Appendix B, but are available in the 2011 Dell Annual Report at* www.dell.com.

## NOTE 15 — STOCK-BASED COMPENSATION AND BENEFIT PLANS

### Stock-based Compensation

*Description of the Plans*

*Employee Stock Plans* — Dell is currently issuing stock grants under the Dell Amended and Restated 2002 Long-Term Incentive Plan (the "2002 Incentive Plan"), which was approved by shareholders on December 4, 2007. There are previous plans that have been terminated, except for options previously granted under those plans which remain outstanding. The 2002 Incentive Plan and the previous plans are all collectively referred to as the "Stock Plans."

The 2002 Incentive Plan provides for the granting of stock-based incentive awards to Dell's employees and non-employee directors. Awards may be incentive stock options within the meaning of Section 422 of the Internal Revenue Code, non-qualified stock options, restricted stock, or restricted stock units. There were approximately 344 million, 320 million, and 313 million shares of Dell's common stock available for future grants under the Stock Plans at January 28, 2011, January 29, 2010, and January 30, 2009, respectively. To satisfy stock option exercises and vested restricted stock awards, Dell has a policy of issuing new shares as opposed to repurchasing shares on the open market.

*Stock Option Agreements* — The right to purchase shares pursuant to existing stock option agreements typically vests pro-rata at each option anniversary date over a three- to five-year period. The options, which are granted with option exercise prices equal to the fair market value of Dell's common stock on the date of grant, generally expire within ten to twelve years from the date of grant. Compensation expense for stock options is recognized on a straight-line basis over the requisite services period.

*Restricted Stock Awards* — Awards of restricted stock may be either grants of restricted stock, restricted stock units, or performance-based stock units that are issued at no cost to the recipient. For restricted stock grants, at the date of grant, the recipient has all rights of a stockholder, subject to certain restrictions on transferability and a risk of forfeiture. Restricted stock grants typically vest over a three- to seven-year period beginning on the date of the grant. For restricted stock units, legal ownership of the shares is not transferred to the employee until the unit vests, which is generally over a three- to five-year period. Dell also grants performance-based restricted stock units as a long-term incentive in which an award recipient receives shares contingent upon Dell achieving performance objectives and the employee's continuing employment through the vesting period, which is generally over a three- to five-year period. Compensation costs recorded in connection with these performance-based restricted stock units are based on Dell's best estimate of the number of shares that will eventually be issued upon achievement of the specified performance criteria and when it becomes probable that certain performance goals will be achieved. The cost of these awards is determined using the fair market value of Dell's common stock on the date of the grant.

Compensation costs for restricted stock awards with a service condition is recognized on a straight-line basis over the requisite service period. Compensation costs for performance-based restricted stock awards is recognized on an accelerated multiple-award approach based on the most probable outcome of the performance condition.

## DELL INC.

### NOTES TO CONSOLIDATED FINANCIAL STATEMENTS (Continued)

*Acceleration of Vesting of Options* — On January 23, 2009, Dell's Board of Directors approved the acceleration of the vesting of unvested "out-of-the-money" stock options (options that have an exercise price greater than the current market stock price) with exercise prices equal to or greater than $10.14 per share for approximately 2,800 employees holding options to purchase approximately 21 million shares of common stock. Dell concluded the modification to the stated vesting provisions was substantive after Dell considered the volatility of its share price and the exercise price of the amended options in relation to recent share values. Because the modification was considered substantive, the remaining unearned compensation expense of $104 million was recorded as an expense in Fiscal 2009. The weighted-average exercise price of the options that were accelerated was $21.90.

*Stock Option Activity*

The following table summarizes stock option activity for the Stock Plans during Fiscal 2011:

| | Number of Options | | Weighted-Average Exercise Price | Weighted-Average Remaining Contractual Term | Aggregate Intrinsic Value |
|---|---|---|---|---|---|
| | (in millions) | | (per share) | (in years) | (in millions) |
| Options outstanding — January 29, 2010 | 205 | $ | 30.00 | | |
| Granted | 17 | | 14.82 | | |
| Exercised | (1) | | 9.18 | | |
| Forfeited | (2) | | 13.85 | | |
| Cancelled/expired | (58) | | 36.44 | | |
| Options outstanding — January 28, 2011 | 161 | $ | 26.49 | | |
| Vested and expected to vest (net of estimated forfeitures) — January 28, 2011[a] | 158 | $ | 26.73 | 3.7 | $ 33 |
| Exercisable — January 28, 2011[a] | 139 | $ | 28.61 | 3.0 | $ 10 |

(a) For options vested and expected to vest and options exercisable, the aggregate intrinsic value in the table above represents the total pre-tax intrinsic value (the difference between Dell's closing stock price on January 28, 2011, and the exercise price multiplied by the number of in-the-money options) that would have been received by the option holders had the holders exercised their options on January 28, 2011. The intrinsic value changes based on changes in the fair market value of Dell's common stock.

The following table summarizes stock option activity for the Stock Plans during Fiscal 2010:

| | Number of Options | | Weighted-Average Exercise Price | Weighted-Average Remaining Contractual Term | Aggregate Intrinsic Value |
|---|---|---|---|---|---|
| | (in millions) | | (per share) | (in years) | (in millions) |
| Options outstanding — January 30, 2009 | 230 | $ | 31.85 | | |
| Granted | 11 | | 9.83 | | |
| Exercised | - | | 12.05 | | |
| Forfeited | - | | 14.73 | | |
| Cancelled/expired | (36) | | 35.59 | | |
| Options outstanding — January 29, 2010 | 205 | $ | 30.00 | | |
| Vested and expected to vest (net of estimated forfeitures) — January 29, 2010[a] | 204 | $ | 30.15 | 3.5 | $ 35 |
| Exercisable — January 29, 2010[a] | 194 | $ | 31.16 | 3.1 | $ 1 |

(a) For options vested and expected to vest and options exercisable, the aggregate intrinsic value in the table above represents the total pre-tax intrinsic value (the difference between Dell's closing stock price on January 29, 2010, and the exercise price multiplied by the number of in-the-money options) that would have been received by the option holders had the holders exercised their options on January 29, 2010. The intrinsic value changes based on changes in the fair market value of Dell's common stock.

The following table summarizes stock option activity for the Stock Plans during Fiscal 2009:

| | Number of Options | | Weighted-Average Exercise Price | Weighted-Average Remaining Contractual Term | Aggregate Intrinsic Value |
|---|---|---|---|---|---|
| | (in millions) | | (per share) | (in years) | (in millions) |
| Options outstanding — February 1, 2008 | 264 | $ | 32.30 | | |
| Granted | 13 | | 19.71 | | |
| Exercised | (4) | | 19.08 | | |
| Forfeited | (4) | | 23.97 | | |
| Cancelled/expired | (39) | | 33.14 | | |
| Options outstanding — January 30, 2009 | 230 | $ | 31.85 | | |
| Vested and expected to vest (net of estimated forfeitures) — January 30, 2009[a][b] | 230 | $ | 31.86 | 3.9 | $ - |
| Exercisable — January 30, 2009[a][b] | 230 | $ | 31.86 | 3.9 | $ - |

(a) For options vested and expected to vest and options exercisable, the aggregate intrinsic value in the table above represents the total pre-tax intrinsic value (the difference between Dell's closing stock price on January 30, 2009, and the exercise price multiplied by the number of in-the-money options) that would have been received by the option holders had the holders exercised their options on January 30, 2009. The intrinsic value changes based on changes in the fair market value of Dell's common stock.

(b) No options were in-the-money at January 30, 2009.

## DELL INC.

## NOTES TO CONSOLIDATED FINANCIAL
## STATEMENTS (Continued)

Other information pertaining to stock options for the Stock Plans is as follows:

| | Fiscal Year Ended | | |
| --- | --- | --- | --- |
| | January 28, 2011 | January 29, 2010 | January 30, 2009 |
| | (in millions, except per option data) | | |
| Weighted-average grant date fair value of stock options    granted per option | $ 5.01 | $ 3.71 | $ 5.87 |
| Total fair value of options vested[a] | $ 13 | $ - | $ 187 |
| Total intrinsic value of options exercised[b] | $ 7 | $ - | $ 15 |

(a) Includes the $104 million of charges for accelerated options in Fiscal 2009.

(b) The total intrinsic value of options exercised represents the total pre-tax intrinsic value (the difference between the stock price at exercise and the exercise price multiplied by the number of options exercised) that was received by the option holders who exercised their options during the fiscal year.

At January 28, 2011, January 29, 2010, and January 30, 2009, there was $65 million, $28 million, and $1 million of total unrecognized stock-based compensation expense related to stock options expected to be recognized over a weighted-average period of 2.0 years, 2.2 years, and 2.3 years, respectively.

### *Valuation of Stock Options*

Dell uses the Black-Scholes option pricing model to estimate the fair value of stock options at grant date. The estimated fair values incorporate various assumptions, including volatility, expected term, and risk-free interest rates. Expected volatility is based on a blend of implied and historical volatility of Dell's common stock over the most recent period commensurate with the estimated expected term of Dell's stock options. Dell uses this blend of implied and historical volatility, as well as other economic data, because management believes such volatility is more representative of prospective trends. The expected term of an award is based on historical experience and on the terms and conditions of the stock awards granted to employees. The dividend yield of zero is based on the fact that Dell has never paid cash dividends and has no present intention to pay cash dividends.

The weighted-average fair value of stock options was determined based on the Black-Scholes option pricing model weighted for all grants utilizing the assumptions in the following table:

| | Fiscal Year Ended | | |
| --- | --- | --- | --- |
| | January 28, 2011 | January 29, 2010 | January 30, 2009 |
| Expected term (in years) | 4.5 | 4.5 | 3.6 |
| Risk-free interest rate (U.S. Government Treasury Note) | 2.2% | 1.8% | 2.3% |
| Volatility | 37% | 44% | 37% |
| Dividends | -% | -% | -% |

### *Restricted Stock Awards*

Non-vested restricted stock awards and activities were as follows:

| | Fiscal 2011 | | Fiscal 2010 | | Fiscal 2009 | |
| --- | --- | --- | --- | --- | --- | --- |
| | Number of Shares | Weighted-Average Grant Date Fair Value | Number of Shares | Weighted-Average Grant Date Fair Value | Number of Shares | Weighted-Average Grant Date Fair Value |
| | (in millions) | (per share) | (in millions) | (per share) | (in millions) | (per share) |
| *Non-vested restricted stock:* | | | | | | |
| Beginning balance | 40 | $ 16.84 | 36 | $ 22.45 | 36 | $ 24.90 |
| Granted | 26 | 14.53 | 22 | 11.39 | 18 | 19.11 |
| Vested[a] | (17) | 19.10 | (13) | 22.78 | (10) | 24.64 |
| Forfeited | (7) | 15.21 | (5) | 18.23 | (8) | 23.15 |
| Non-vested restricted stock ending balance | 42 | $ 14.71 | 40 | $ 16.84 | 36 | $ 22.45 |

(a) Upon vesting, restricted stock units are generally sold to cover the required withholding taxes. However, select participants may choose the net shares settlement method to cover withholding tax requirements. Total shares withheld were approximately 354,000, 157,000, and 48,000 for Fiscal 2011, Fiscal 2010, and Fiscal 2009, respectively. Total payments for the employee's tax obligations to the taxing authorities were $5 million, $2 million, and $1 million in Fiscal 2011, Fiscal 2010, and Fiscal 2009, respectively, and are reflected as a financing activity within the Consolidated Statements of Cash Flows.

For the Fiscal 2011, Fiscal 2010, and Fiscal 2009, total estimated vest date fair value of restricted stock awards was $250 million, $134 million, and $197 million.

At January 28, 2011, January 29, 2010, and January 30, 2009, there was $341 million, $393 million, and $507 million, respectively, of unrecognized stock-based compensation expense, net of estimated forfeitures, related to non-vested restricted stock awards. These awards are expected to be recognized over a weighted-average period of approximately 1.9, 1.8, and 2.0 years, respectively.

**DELL INC.**

**NOTES TO CONSOLIDATED FINANCIAL
STATEMENTS (Continued)**

*Stock-based Compensation Expense*

Stock-based compensation expense was allocated as follows:

| | Fiscal Year Ended | | |
|---|---|---|---|
| | January 28, 2011 | January 29, 2010 | January 30, 2009 |
| | (in millions) | | |
| *Stock-based compensation expense:* | | | |
| Cost of net revenue | $ 57 | $ 47 | $ 62 |
| Operating expenses | 275 | 265 | 356 |
| Stock-based compensation expense before taxes | 332 | 312 | 418 |
| Income tax benefit | (97) | (91) | (131) |
| Stock-based compensation expense, net of income taxes | $ 235 | $ 221 | $ 287 |

Stock-based compensation in the table above includes $104 million of expense for accelerated options and a reduction of $1 million for the release of the accrual for expired stock options in Fiscal 2009, as previously discussed.

**Employee Benefit Plans**

*401(k) Plan* — Dell has a defined contribution retirement plan (the "401(k) Plan") that complies with Section 401(k) of the Internal Revenue Code. Substantially all employees in the U.S. are eligible to participate in the 401(k) Plan. Effective January 1, 2008, Dell matches 100% of each participant's voluntary contributions, subject to a maximum contribution of 5% of the participant's compensation, and participants vest immediately in all Dell contributions to the 401(k) Plan. Dell's contributions during Fiscal 2011, Fiscal 2010, and Fiscal 2009 were $132 million, $91 million, and $93 million, respectively. Dell's contributions are invested according to each participant's elections in the investment options provided under the Plan. Investment options include Dell common stock, but neither participant nor Dell contributions are required to be invested in Dell common stock. During Fiscal 2010, Dell also contributed $4.2 million to Perot Systems' 401(k) Plan (the "Perot Plan") after the acquisition of the company on November 3, 2009. The Perot Plan was merged into the 401(k) Plan during Fiscal 2011.

*Deferred Compensation Plan* — Dell has a non-qualified deferred compensation plan (the "Deferred Compensation Plan") for the benefit of certain management employees and non-employee directors. The Deferred Compensation Plan permits the deferral of base salary and annual incentive bonus. The deferrals are held in a separate trust, which has been established by Dell to administer the Plan. The assets of the trust are subject to the claims of Dell's creditors in the event that Dell becomes insolvent. Consequently, the trust qualifies as a grantor trust for income tax purposes (known as a "Rabbi Trust"). In accordance with the accounting provisions for deferred compensation arrangements where amounts earned are held in a Rabbi Trust and invested, the assets and liabilities of the Deferred Compensation Plan are presented in long-term investments and accrued and other liabilities in the Consolidated Statements of Financial Position, respectively. The assets held by the trust are classified as trading securities with changes recorded to interest and other, net. These assets were valued at $99 million at January 28, 2011, and are disclosed in Note 3 of Notes to Consolidated Financial Statements. Changes in the deferred compensation liability are recorded to compensation expense.

**NOTE 16 — SEGMENT INFORMATION**

Dell's four global business segments are Large Enterprise, Public, Small and Medium Business ("SMB"), and Consumer. Large Enterprise includes sales of IT infrastructure and service solutions to large global and national corporate customers. Public includes sales to educational institutions, governments, health care organizations, and law enforcement agencies, among others. SMB includes sales of complete IT solutions to small and medium-sized businesses. Consumer includes sales to individual consumers and retailers around the world.

The business segments disclosed in the accompanying Consolidated Financial Statements are based on this organizational structure and information reviewed by Dell's management to evaluate the business segment results. Dell's measure of segment operating income for management reporting purposes excludes severance and facility closure expenses, broad based long-term incentives, acquisition-related charges, and amortization of intangibles.

**DELL INC.**

**NOTES TO CONSOLIDATED FINANCIAL STATEMENTS (Continued)**

The following table presents net revenue by Dell's reportable global segments as well as a reconciliation of consolidated segment operating income to Dell's consolidated operating income:

| | Fiscal Year Ended | | |
| --- | --- | --- | --- |
| | January 28, 2011 | January 29, 2010 | January 30, 2009 |
| | (in millions) | | |
| *Net revenue:* | | | |
| Large Enterprise | $ 17,813 | $ 14,285 | $ 18,011 |
| Public | 16,851 | 14,484 | 15,338 |
| Small and Medium Business | 14,473 | 12,079 | 14,892 |
| Consumer | 12,357 | 12,054 | 12,860 |
| Total | $ 61,494 | $ 52,902 | $ 61,101 |
| *Consolidated operating income:* | | | |
| Large Enterprise | $ 1,473 | $ 819 | $ 1,158 |
| Public | 1,484 | 1,361 | 1,258 |
| Small and Medium Business | 1,477 | 1,040 | 1,273 |
| Consumer | 65 | 107 | 306 |
| Consolidated segment operating income | 4,499 | 3,327 | 3,995 |
| Severance and facility actions | (129) | (481) | (282) |
| Broad based long-term incentives[(a)] | (350) | (353) | (418) |
| In-process research and development | - | - | (2) |
| Amortization of intangible assets | (349) | (205) | (103) |
| Acquisition-related costs[(a)(b)] | (98) | (116) | - |
| Other[(c)] | (140) | - | - |
| Total | $ 3,433 | $ 2,172 | $ 3,190 |

(a) Broad based long-term incentives includes stock-based compensation, but excludes stock-based compensation related to acquisitions, which are included in acquisition-related costs. Stock-based expense for Fiscal 2009 also includes $104 million of expense for accelerated options. See Note 15 of Notes to Consolidated Financial Statements for additional information.

(b) Acquisition-related costs consist primarily of retention payments, integration costs, and consulting fees.

(c) Other includes the $100 million settlement for the SEC investigation and a $40 million settlement for a securities litigation lawsuit that were both incurred in the first quarter of Fiscal 2011.

The following table presents assets by Dell's reportable global segments. Segment assets primarily consist of accounts receivable and inventories.

| | January 28, 2011 | January 29, 2010 |
| --- | --- | --- |
| | (in millions) | |
| *Total assets:* | | |
| Corporate | $ 30,264 | $ 26,240 |
| Large Enterprise | 2,934 | 2,604 |
| Public | 2,545 | 2,464 |
| Small and Medium Business | 1,398 | 1,051 |
| Consumer | 1,458 | 1,293 |
| Total | $ 38,599 | $ 33,652 |

The following table presents depreciation expense by Dell's reportable business segments:

| | Fiscal Year Ended | | |
| --- | --- | --- | --- |
| | January 28, 2011 | January 29, 2010 | January 30, 2009 |
| | (in millions) | | |
| *Depreciation expense:* | | | |
| Large Enterprise | $ 180 | $ 175 | $ 180 |
| Public | 170 | 177 | 174 |
| Small and Medium Business | 146 | 148 | 151 |
| Consumer | 125 | 147 | 161 |
| Total | $ 621 | $ 647 | $ 666 |

**DELL INC.**

**NOTES TO CONSOLIDATED FINANCIAL
STATEMENTS (Continued)**

The following tables present net revenue and long-lived asset information allocated between the U.S. and foreign countries:

| | Fiscal Year Ended | | | | | |
|---|---|---|---|---|---|---|
| | January 28, 2011 | | January 29, 2010 | | January 30, 2009 | |
| | (in millions) | | | | | |
| *Net revenue:* | | | | | | |
| United States | $ | 31,912 | $ | 28,053 | $ | 31,569 |
| Foreign countries | | 29,582 | | 24,849 | | 29,532 |
| Total | $ | 61,494 | $ | 52,902 | $ | 61,101 |

| | January 28, 2011 | | January 29, 2010 | |
|---|---|---|---|---|
| | (in millions) | | | |
| *Long-lived assets:* | | | | |
| United States | $ | 1,419 | $ | 1,536 |
| Foreign countries | | 534 | | 645 |
| Total | $ | 1,953 | $ | 2,181 |

The allocation between domestic and foreign net revenue is based on the location of the customers. Net revenue and long-lived assets from any single foreign country did not constitute more than 10% of Dell's consolidated net revenues or long-lived assets during Fiscal 2011, Fiscal 2010, or Fiscal 2009. No single customer accounted for more than 10% of Dell's consolidated net revenue during Fiscal 2011, Fiscal 2010, or Fiscal 2009.

The following table presents net revenue by product and services categories:

| | Fiscal Year Ended | | | | | |
|---|---|---|---|---|---|---|
| | January 28, 2011 | | January 29, 2010 | | January 30, 2009 | |
| | (in millions) | | | | | |
| *Net revenue:* | | | | | | |
| Enterprise Solutions and Services: | | | | | | |
| Enterprise Solutions: | | | | | | |
| Servers and networking | $ | 7,609 | $ | 6,032 | $ | 6,512 |
| Storage | | 2,295 | | 2,192 | | 2,667 |
| Services | | 7,673 | | 5,622 | | 5,351 |
| Software and peripherals | | 10,261 | | 9,499 | | 10,603 |
| Client: | | | | | | |
| Mobility | | 18,971 | | 16,610 | | 18,604 |
| Desktop PCs | | 14,685 | | 12,947 | | 17,364 |
| Net revenue | $ | 61,494 | $ | 52,902 | $ | 61,101 |

## NOTE 17 — SUPPLEMENTAL CONSOLIDATED FINANCIAL INFORMATION

### Supplemental Consolidated Statements of Financial Position Information

The following table provides information on amounts included in accounts receivable, net, and inventories, net , property, plant, and equipment, net , accrued and other liabilities, and other non-current liabilities, as well as prepaid expenses as of January 28, 2011 and January 29, 2010.

| | January 28, 2011 | | January 29, 2010 | |
|---|---|---|---|---|
| | (in millions) | | | |
| *Accounts receivable, net:* | | | | |
| Gross accounts receivable | $ | 6,589 | $ | 5,952 |
| Allowance for doubtful accounts | | (96) | | (115) |
| Total | $ | 6,493 | $ | 5,837 |
| *Inventories, net:* | | | | |
| Production materials | $ | 593 | $ | 487 |
| Work-in-process | | 232 | | 168 |
| Finished goods | | 476 | | 396 |
| Total | $ | 1,301 | $ | 1,051 |
| Prepaid expenses[a] | $ | 374 | $ | 539 |
| *Property, plant, and equipment, net:* | | | | |
| Computer equipment | $ | 2,275 | $ | 2,118 |
| Land and buildings | | 1,674 | | 1,686 |
| Machinery and other equipment | | 780 | | 848 |
| Total property, plant, and equipment | | 4,729 | | 4,652 |
| Accumulated depreciation and amortization | | (2,776) | | (2,471) |
| Total | $ | 1,953 | $ | 2,181 |

(a)  Prepaid expenses are included in other current assets in the Consolidated Statements of Financial Position.

**DELL INC.**

**NOTES TO CONSOLIDATED FINANCIAL
STATEMENTS (Continued)**

**Supplemental Consolidated Statements of Financial Position Information (cont.)**

| | January 28, 2011 | January 29, 2010 |
|---|---|---|
| | (in millions) | |
| *Accrued and other current liabilities:* | | |
| Compensation | $ 1,550 | $ 1,112 |
| Warranty liability | 575 | 593 |
| Income and other taxes | 529 | 426 |
| Other | 1,527 | 1,753 |
| Total | $ 4,181 | $ 3,884 |
| | | |
| *Other non-current liabilities:* | | |
| Warranty liability | $ 320 | $ 319 |
| Income and other taxes | 2,293 | 2,085 |
| Other | 73 | 201 |
| Total | $ 2,686 | $ 2,605 |

**Supplemental Consolidated Statements of Income**

The table below provides advertising costs for Fiscal 2011, Fiscal 2010, and Fiscal 2009. Advertising costs are included in selling, general, and administrative in the Consolidated Statements of Income.

| | Fiscal Year Ended | | |
|---|---|---|---|
| | January 28, 2011 | January 29, 2010 | January 30, 2009 |
| | (in millions) | | |
| Advertising costs | $ 730 | $ 619 | $ 811 |

The table below provides details of interest and other, net for Fiscal 2011, Fiscal 2010, and Fiscal 2009:

| | Fiscal Year Ended | | |
|---|---|---|---|
| | January 28, 2011 | January 29, 2010 | January 30, 2009 |
| | (in millions) | | |
| *Interest and other, net:* | | | |
| Investment income, primarily interest | $ 47 | $ 57 | $ 180 |
| Gains (losses) on investments, net | 6 | 2 | (10) |
| Interest expense | (199) | (160) | (93) |
| Foreign exchange | 4 | (59) | 115 |
| Other | 59 | 12 | (58) |
| Interest and other, net | $ (83) | $ (148) | $ 134 |

**Supplemental Statement of Stockholders' Equity**

The table below provides the cumulative balance for foreign currency translation adjustments as of January 28, 2011, January 29, 2010, and January 30, 2009. Cumulative foreign currency translation adjustments are included as a component of accumulated other comprehensive income (loss) in stockholders' equity.

| | January 28, 2011 | January 29, 2010 | January 30, 2009 |
|---|---|---|---|
| | (in millions) | | |
| Cumulative income (loss) for foreign currency translation adjustments | $ 39 | $ (40) | $ (11) |

## DELL INC.

### NOTES TO CONSOLIDATED FINANCIAL
### STATEMENTS (Continued)

**Valuation and Qualifying Accounts**

| Fiscal Year | Description | Balance at Beginning of Period | Charged to Income Statement | Charged to Allowance | Balance at End of Period |
|---|---|---|---|---|---|
| **Trade Receivables:** | | | | | |
| 2011 | Allowance for doubtful accounts | $ 115 | $ 124 | $ 143 | $ 96 |
| 2010 | Allowance for doubtful accounts | $ 112 | $ 185 | $ 182 | $ 115 |
| 2009 | Allowance for doubtful accounts | $ 103 | $ 151 | $ 142 | $ 112 |
| **Customer Financing Receivables[a]:** | | | | | |
| 2011 | Allowance for doubtful accounts | $ 237 | $ 258 | $ 254 | $ 241 |
| 2010 | Allowance for doubtful accounts | $ 149 | $ 244 | $ 156 | $ 237 |
| 2009 | Allowance for doubtful accounts | $ 96 | $ 159 | $ 106 | $ 149 |
| **Trade Receivables:** | | | | | |
| 2011 | Allowance for customer returns | $ 79 | $ 581 | $ 558 | $ 102 |
| 2010 | Allowance for customer returns | $ 69 | $ 541 | $ 531 | $ 79 |
| 2009 | Allowance for customer returns | $ 91 | $ 401 | $ 423 | $ 69 |

(a)  Charge-offs to the allowance for financing receivable losses for customer financing receivables includes principal and interest.

## NOTE 18 — UNAUDITED QUARTERLY RESULTS

The following tables present selected unaudited Consolidated Statements of Income for each quarter of Fiscal 2011 and Fiscal 2010:

| | Fiscal Year 2011 | | | |
|---|---|---|---|---|
| | First Quarter | Second Quarter | Third Quarter | Fourth Quarter |
| | (in millions, except per share data) | | | |
| Net revenue | $ 14,874 | $ 15,534 | $ 15,394 | $ 15,692 |
| Gross margin | $ 2,516 | $ 2,586 | $ 3,003 | $ 3,291 |
| Net income | $ 341 | $ 545 | $ 822 | $ 927 |
| Earnings per share: | | | | |
| Basic | $ 0.17 | $ 0.28 | $ 0.42 | $ 0.48 |
| Diluted | $ 0.17 | $ 0.28 | $ 0.42 | $ 0.48 |
| Weighted-average shares outstanding: | | | | |
| Basic | 1,961 | 1,952 | 1,939 | 1,924 |
| Diluted | 1,973 | 1,960 | 1,949 | 1,938 |

| | Fiscal Year 2010 | | | |
|---|---|---|---|---|
| | First Quarter | Second Quarter | Third Quarter | Fourth Quarter |
| | (in millions, except per share data) | | | |
| Net revenue | $ 12,342 | $ 12,764 | $ 12,896 | $ 14,900 |
| Gross margin | $ 2,168 | $ 2,391 | $ 2,233 | $ 2,469 |
| Net income | $ 290 | $ 472 | $ 337 | $ 334 |
| Earnings per share: | | | | |
| Basic | $ 0.15 | $ 0.24 | $ 0.17 | $ 0.17 |
| Diluted | $ 0.15 | $ 0.24 | $ 0.17 | $ 0.17 |
| Weighted-average shares outstanding: | | | | |
| Basic | 1,949 | 1,955 | 1,956 | 1,957 |
| Diluted | 1,952 | 1,960 | 1,966 | 1,971 |

## NOTE 19 — SUBSEQUENT EVENTS

In February, 2011, Dell completed its acquisitions of Compellent Technologies, Inc. ("Compellent"), a provider of virtual storage solutions for enterprise and cloud computing environments, and SecureWorks Inc. ("SecureWorks"), a global provider of information security service, for approximately $938 million and $612 million, respectively. Both Compellent and SecureWorks will be integrated into Dell's Commercial segments. Because the acquisitions have recently closed, Dell has not completed the purchase accounting and initial purchase price allocation for these acquisitions. Dell expects to complete the purchase accounting and initial purchase price allocations in the first quarter of Fiscal 2012.

# IFRS Comprehensive Case

Air France–KLM (AF), a French company, prepares its financial statements according to International Financial Reporting Standards. AF's annual report for the year ended March 31, 2011, which includes financial statements and disclosure notes, is provided with all new textbooks. This material also is included in AF's "Registration Document 2010-11," dated June 15, 2011 and is available at **www.airfranceklm.com**. This case addresses a variety of characteristics of financial statements prepared using IFRS often comparing and contrasting those attributes of statements prepared under U.S. GAAP. Questions are grouped in parts according to various sections of the textbook.

**AIRFRANCE /**

## Part A: Financial Statements, Income Measurement, and Current Assets

A1. What amounts did AF report for the following items for the 2011 fiscal year ended March 31, 2011?
   a.  Total revenues
   b.  Income from current operations
   c.  Net income (AF equity holders)
   d.  Total assets
   e.  Total equity

A2. What was AF's basic earnings per share for the 2011 fiscal year?

A3. Examine Note 3.1.1 of AF's annual report. What accounting principles were used to prepare AF's financial statements? Under those accounting principles, could AF's financial information differ from that of a company that exactly followed IFRS as published by the IASB? Explain.

A4. Describe the apparent differences in the order of presentation of the components of the balance sheet between IFRS as applied by Air France–KLM (AF) and a typical balance sheet prepared in accordance with U.S. GAAP.

A5. How does AF classify operating expenses in its income statement? How are these expenses typically classified in a U.S. company income statement?

A6. How does AF classify interest paid, interest received, and dividends received in its statement of cash flows? What other alternatives, if any, does the company have for the classification of these items? How are these items classified under U.S. GAAP?

A7. In note 3.6, AF indicates that "Upon issuance, both passenger and cargo tickets are recorded as "Deferred revenue on ticket sales" and that "Sales related to air transportation are recognized when the transportation service is provided."
   a.  Examine AF's balance sheet. What is the total amount of deferred revenue on ticket sales as of March 31, 2011?
   b.  When transportation services are provided with respect to the deferred revenue on ticket sales, what journal entry would AF make to reduce deferred revenue?
   c.  Does AF's treatment of deferred revenue under IFRS appear consistent with how these transactions would be handled under U.S. GAAP? Explain.

A8. AF has a frequent flyer program, "Flying Blue," which allows members to acquire "miles" as they fly on Air France or partner airlines that are redeemable for free flights or other benefits.

a. How does AF account for these miles?

b. Does AF report any liability associated with these miles as of March 31, 2011?

c. Is AF's accounting approach under IFRS consistent with how U.S. GAAP accounts for multiple deliverable contracts? Explain.

A9. In note 3.10.1, AF describes how it values trade receivables. How does the approach used by AF compare to U.S. GAAP?

A10. In note 24, AF reconciles the beginning and ending balances of its valuation allowance for trade accounts receivable. Prepare a T-account for the valuation allowance and include entries for the beginning and ending balances and any reconciling items that affected the account during 2011.

A11. Examine note 26. Does AF have any bank overdrafts? If so, are the overdrafts shown in the balance sheet the same way they would be shown under U.S. GAAP?

A12. What method does the company use to value its inventory? What other alternatives are available under IFRS? Under U.S. GAAP?

A13. AF's inventories are valued at the lower of cost and net realizable value. How does this approach differ from U.S. GAAP?

## Part B: Property, Plant, and Equipment and Intangible Assets

B1. What method does AF use to amortize the cost of computer software development costs? How does this approach differ from U.S. GAAP?

B2. AF does not report any research and development expenditures. If it did, its approach to accounting for research and development would be significantly different from U.S. GAAP. Describe the differences between IFRS and U.S. GAAP in accounting for research and development expenditures.

B3. AF does not report the receipt of any governments grants. If it did, its approach to accounting for government grants would be significantly different from U.S. GAAP. Describe the differences between IFRS and U.S. GAAP in accounting for government grants. If AF received a grant for the purchase of assets, what alternative accounting treatments are available under IFRS?

B4. AF's property, plant, and equipment is reported at cost. The company has a policy of not revaluing property, plant, and equipment. Suppose AF decided to revalue its flight equipment on March 31, 2011, and that the fair value of the equipment on that date was €12,000 million. Prepare the journal entry to record the revaluation assuming that the journal entry to record annual depreciation had already been recorded. (Hint: you will need to locate the original cost and accumulated depreciation of the equipment at the end of the year in the appropriate disclosure note.)

B5. Under U.S. GAAP, what alternatives do companies have to value their property, plant, and equipment?

B6. AF calculates depreciation of plant and equipment on a straight-line basis, over the useful life of the asset. Describe any differences between IFRS and U.S. GAAP in the calculation of depreciation.

B7. When does AF test for the possible impairment of fixed assets? How does this approach differ from U.S. GAAP?

B8. Describe the approach AF uses to determine fixed asset impairment losses. (Hint: see Note 3.14) How does this approach differ from U.S. GAAP?

B9. The following is included in AF's disclosure note 3.12: "Intangible assets are held at initial cost less accumulated amortization and any accumulated impairment losses." Assume that on March 31, 2011, AF decided to revalue its Other intangible assets (see Note 16) and that the fair value on that date was determined to be €360 million. Amortization expense for the year already has been recorded. Prepare the journal entry to record the revaluation.

## Part C: Investments

C1. Read Notes 3.10.2, 3.10.5, 22, 32.3 and 32.4. Focusing on investments accounted for at fair value through profit and loss (FVTPL):

a. As of March 31, 2011, what is the balance of those investments in the balance sheet? Be specific regarding which line of the balance sheet includes the balance.

b. How much of that balance is classified as current and how much as noncurrent?

c. Is that balance stated at fair value? How do you know?

d. How much of the fair value of those investments is accounted for using level 1, level 2, and level 3 inputs of the fair value hierarchy? Given that information, assess the reliability (representational faithfulness) of this fair value estimate.

C2. Complete Requirement 1 again, but for investments accounted for as available for sale.

C3. Read Notes 3.3.2, 10, and 20.

a. When AF can exercise significant influence over an investee, what accounting approach do they use to account for the investment? How does AF determine if it can exercise significant influence?

b. If AF exercises joint control over an investee by virtue of a contractual agreement, what accounting method does it use? Is there an alternative?

c. Why did AF change how it accounts for its investment in WAM (Amadeus)? What was the initial approach that AF used, and what approach did it change to using for this investment?

d. What is the carrying value of AF's equity-method investments in its March 31, 2011 balance sheet?

e. How did AF's equity-method investments affect AF's 2011 net income from continuing operations?

## Part D: Liabilities

D1. Read Notes 3.6 and 31. What do you think gave rise to total deferred income of €121 as of the end of fiscal 2011? Would transactions of this type be handled similarly under U.S. GAAP?

D2. Is the threshold for recognizing a provision under IFRS different than it is under U.S. GAAP? Explain.

D3. Note 29 lists "provisions and retirement benefits."

a. Do the beginning and ending balances of total provisions and retirement benefits shown in Note 29 for fiscal 2011 tie to the balance sheet? By how much has the total amount of the AF's "provisions and retirement benefits" increased or decreased during fiscal 2011?

b. Write journal entries for the following changes in the litigation provision that occurred during fiscal 2011, assuming any amounts recorded on the income statement are recorded as "provision expense", and any use of provisions is paid for in cash. In each case, provide a brief explanation of the event your journal entry is capturing.

   i. New provision.

   ii. Use of provision.

   iii. Reversal of unnecessary provisions.

c. Is AF's treatment of litigation provision under IFRS similar to how it would be treated under U.S. GAAP?

D4. Note 29.3 lists a number of contingent liabilities. Are amounts for those items recognized as a liability on AF's balance sheet? Explain.

D5. **Sealy Corporation** reported the following line items in its statement of cash flows for the nine months ended February 27, 2011:

| | |
|---|---:|
| Amortization of discount on secured notes.................................... | 382,000 |
| Amortization of debt issuance costs and other.............................. | 1,175,000 |

In AF's financial statements, Note 30: "Financial Debt" describes the company's long-term debt. Neither of the two items above is reported in the financial statements of Air France, and neither is likely to appear there in the future. Why?

D6. Examine the long-term borrowings in AF's balance sheet and the related note. Note that AF has convertible bonds outstanding that it issued in 2005. Prepare the journal entry AF would use to record the issue of convertible bonds. Prepare the journal entry AF would use to record the issue of the convertible bonds if AF used U.S. GAAP.

D7. AF does not elect the fair value option (FVO) to report its financial liabilities. Examine Note 32.3. "Market value of financial instruments." If the company had elected the FVO for all of its debt measured at amortized cost, what would be the balance at March 31, 2011, in the fair value adjustment account?

D8. Is IFRS or U.S. GAAP more restrictive for determining when firms are allowed to elect the fair value option for financial assets and liabilities? Explain.

## Part E: Leases, Income Taxes, and Pensions

E1. In Note 3: Summary of accounting policies, part 3.13.4: Leases, AF states that "leases are classified as finance leases when the lease arrangement transfers substantially all the risks and rewards of ownership to the lessee." Is this the policy companies using U.S. GAAP follow in accounting for capital leases? Explain.

E2. Look at AF's Note 30: Financial debt and Note 33: Lease commitments. Does AF obtain use of its aircraft more using operating leases or finance leases? Do lessees report operating and finance lease commitments the same way? Explain.

E3. Where in its March 31, 2011, balance sheet does AF report deferred taxes? How does this approach differ from the way deferred taxes are reported using U.S. GAAP? Using the Internet, determine how deferred taxes would be reported using IFRS at the time of your research. Explain why that approach might differ from the way AF reported deferred taxes at March 31, 2011.

E4. Here's an excerpt from one of AF's notes to its financial statements:

> **Deferred taxes (in part)**
>
> The Group records deferred taxes using the balance sheet liability method, providing for any temporary differences between the carrying amounts of assets and liabilities for financial reporting purposes and the amounts used for taxation purposes. The tax rates used are those enacted or substantively enacted at the balance sheet date.

Is this policy consistent with U.S. GAAP? Explain.

E5. Here's an excerpt from one AF's notes to its financial statements:

> **Deferred taxes (in part)**
>
> Deferred tax assets related to temporary differences and carry forwards are recognized only to the extent it is probable that a future taxable profit will be available against which the asset can be utilized at the tax entity level.

Is this policy consistent with U.S. GAAP? Explain.

E6. Air France did not report past service cost (called prior service cost under U.S. GAAP). If AF revised its pension plan and incurred past service cost, how would the company report that amount if it used the new IFRS guidance described in this chapter, how would the company report a change in one of these assumptions? Is that reporting method the same or different from the way we report prior service cost under U.S. GAAP?

E7. Look at note 29.1, "Retirement Benefits." AF incorporates estimates regarding staff turnover, life expectancy, salary increase, retirement age and discount rates. If AF used the new IFRS guidance described in this chapter, how would the company report a change in one of these assumptions? Is that reporting method the same or different from the way we report changes under U.S. GAAP?

E8. In its income statement and notes to the statements, AF does not report a single amount that represents net pension cost. If AF used the new IFRS guidance described in Chapter 17, would the company report a single amount that represents net pension cost? Is that reporting method the same or different from the way we report pension expense under U.S. GAAP?

## Part F: Shareholders' Equity and Additional Financial Reporting Issues

F1.  Air France-KLM lists four items in the shareholders' equity section of its balance sheet. If AF used U.S. GAAP, what would be the likely account titles for the first and fourth of those components?

F2.  Locate Note 27.4 in AF's financial statements. What items comprise "Reserves and retained earnings" as reported in the balance sheet? If Air France-KLM used U.S. GAAP, what would be different for the reporting of these items?

F3.  Describe the apparent differences in the order of presentation of the components of liabilities and shareholders' equity between IFRS as applied by AF and a typical balance sheet prepared in accordance with U.S. GAAP.

F4.  What is the amount that AF reports in its income statement for its stock options for the year ended March 31, 2011? [*Hint:* See Note 28: "Share-Based Compensation."] Are AF's share options cliff vesting or graded vesting? How does accounting differ between U.S. GAAP and IFRS for graded-vesting plans?

F5.  What amount(s) of earnings per share did AF report in its income statement for the year ended March 31, 2011? If AF used U.S. GAAP would it have reported EPS using the same classification?

F6.  What are the primary classifications into which AF's cash inflows and cash outflows are separated? Is this classification the same as or different from cash flow statements prepared in accordance with U.S. GAAP?

F7.  How are cash inflows from dividends and interest and cash outflows for dividends and interest classified in AF's cash flow statements? Is this classification the same as or different from cash flow statements prepared in accordance with U.S. GAAP?

# Glossary

**Accounting equation** the process used to capture the effect of economic events; Assets = Liabilities + Owner's Equity.

**Accounting Principles Board (APB)** the second private sector body delegated the task of setting accounting standards.

**Accounts** storage areas to keep track of the increases and decreases in financial position elements.

**Accounts payable** obligations to suppliers of merchandise or of services purchased on open account.

**Accounts receivable** receivables resulting from the sale of goods or services on account.

**Accounts receivable aging schedule** applying different percentages to accounts receivable balances depending on the length of time outstanding.

**Accretion** increase in the carrying value of an asset or liability.

**Accretion expense** the increase in an asset retirement obligation that accrues as an operating expense.

**Accretion revenue** the increase in a lessor's residual asset that accrues as revenue.

**Accruals** when the cash flow comes after either expense or revenue recognition.

**Accrual accounting** measurement of the entity's accomplishments and resource sacrifices during the period, regardless of when cash is received or paid.

**Accrued interest** interest that has accrued since the last interest date.

**Accrued liabilities** expenses already incurred but not yet paid (accrued expenses).

**Accrued receivables** the recognition of revenue earned before cash is received.

**Accumulated benefit obligation (ABO)** the discounted present value of estimated retirement benefits earned so far by employees, applying the plan's pension formula using existing compensation levels.

**Accumulated other comprehensive income** amount of other comprehensive income (nonowner changes in equity other than net income) accumulated over the current and prior periods.

**Accumulated postretirement benefit obligation (APBO)** portion of the EPBO attributed to employee service up to a particular date.

**Acid-test ratio** current assets, excluding inventories and prepaid items, divided by current liabilities.

**Acquisition costs** the amounts paid to acquire the rights to explore for undiscovered natural resources or to extract proven natural resources.

**Activity-based method** allocation of an asset's cost base using a measure of the asset's input or output.

**Actuary** a professional trained in a particular branch of statistics and mathematics to assess the various uncertainties and to estimate the company's obligation to employees in connection with its pension plan.

**Additions** the adding of a new major component to an existing asset.

**Adjusted trial balance** trial balance after adjusting entries have been recorded.

**Adjusting entries** internal transactions recorded at the end of any period when financial statements are prepared.

**Allocation base** the value of the usefulness that is expected to be consumed.

**Allocation method** the pattern in which the usefulness is expected to be consumed.

**Allowance method** recording bad debt expense and reducing accounts receivable indirectly by crediting a contra account (allowance for uncollectible accounts) to accounts receivable for an estimate of the amount that eventually will prove uncollectible.

**American Institute of Accountants (AIA)/American Institute of Certified Public Accountants (AICPA)** national organization of professional public accountants.

**Amortization** cost allocation for intangibles.

**Amortization schedule** schedule that reflects the changes in the debt over its term to maturity.

**Annuity** cash flows received or paid in the same amount each period.

**Annuity due** cash flows occurring at the beginning of each period.

**Antidilutive securities** the effect of the conversion or exercise of potential common shares would be to increase rather than decrease, EPS.

**Articles of incorporation** statement of the nature of the firm's business activities, the shares to be issued, and the composition of the initial board of directors.

**Asset retirement obligations (AROs)** obligations associated with the disposition of an operational asset.

**Assets** probable future economic benefits obtained or controlled by a particular entity as a result of past transactions or events.

**Asset turnover ratio** measure of a company's efficiency in using assets to generate revenue.

**Assigning** using receivables as collateral for loans; nonpayment of a debt will require the proceeds from collecting the assigned receivables to go directly toward repayment of the debt.

**Attribution** process of assigning the cost of benefits to the years during which those benefits are assumed to be earned by employees.

**Auditors** independent intermediaries who help ensure that management has appropriately applied GAAP in preparing the company's financial statements.

**Auditor's report** report issued by CPAs who audit the financial statements that informs users of the audit findings.

**Average collection period** indication of the average age of accounts receivable.

**Average cost method** assumes cost of goods sold and ending inventory consist of a mixture of all the goods available for sale.

**Average days in inventory** indicates the average number of days it normally takes to sell inventory.

**Bad debt expense** an operating expense incurred to boost sales; inherent cost of granting credit.

**Balance sheet** a position statement that presents an organized list of assets, liabilities, and equity at a particular point in time.

**Balance sheet approach** determination of bad debt expense by estimating the net realizable value of accounts receivable to be reported in the balance sheet.

**Bank reconciliation** comparison of the bank balance with the balance in the company's own records.

**Bargain purchase option (BPO)** provision in the lease contract that gives the lessee the option of purchasing the leased property at a bargain price.

**Bargain renewal option** gives the lessee the option to renew the lease at a bargain rate.

**Basic EPS** computed by dividing income available to common stockholders (net income less any preferred stock dividends) by the weighted-average number of common shares outstanding for the period.

**Billings of construction contract** contra account to the asset construction in progress; subtracted from construction in progress to determine balance sheet presentation.

**Board of directors** establishes corporate policies and appoints officers who manage the corporation.

**Bond indenture** document that describes specific promises made to bondholders.

**Bonds** A form of debt consisting of separable units (bonds) that obligates the issuing corporation to repay a stated amount at a specified maturity date and to pay interest to bondholders between the issue date and maturity.

**Book value** assets minus liabilities as shown in the balance sheet.

**Callable** allows the issuing company to buy back, or call, outstanding bonds from the bondholders before their scheduled maturity date.

**Capital budgeting** The process of evaluating the purchase of operational assets.

**Capital leases** installment purchases/sales that are formulated outwardly as leases.

**Capital markets** mechanisms that foster the allocation of resources efficiently.

**Cash** currency and coins, balances in checking accounts, and items acceptable for deposit in these accounts, such as checks and money orders received from customers.

**Cash basis accounting/net operating cash flow** difference between cash receipts and cash disbursements during a reporting period from transactions related to providing goods and services to customers.

**Cash disbursements journal** record of cash disbursements.

**Cash discounts** sales discounts; represent reductions not in the selling price of a good or service but in the amount to be paid by a credit customer if paid within a specific period of time.

**Cash equivalents** certain negotiable items such as commercial paper, money market funds, and U.S. Treasury bills that are highly liquid investments quickly convertible to cash.

**Cash equivalents** short-term, highly liquid investments that can be readily converted to cash with little risk of loss.

**Cash flow hedge** a derivative used to hedge against the exposure to changes in cash inflows or cash outflows of an asset or liability or a forecasted transaction (like a future purchase or sale).

**Cash flows from financing activities** both inflows and outflows of cash resulting from the external financing of a business.

**Cash flows from investing activities** both outflows and inflows of cash caused by the acquisition and disposition of assets.

**Cash flows from operating activities** both inflows and outflows of cash that result from activities reported on the income statement.

**Cash receipts journal** record of cash receipts.

**Certified Public Accountants (CPAs)** licensed individuals who can represent that the financial statements have been audited in accordance with generally accepted auditing standards.

**Change in accounting estimate** a change in an estimate when new information comes to light.

**Change in accounting principle** switch by a company from one accounting method to another.

**Change in reporting entity** presentation of consolidated financial statements in place of statements of individual companies, or a change in the specific companies that constitute the group for which consolidated or combined statements are prepared.

**Closing process** the temporary accounts are reduced to zero balances, and these temporary account balances are closed (transferred) to retained earnings to reflect the changes that have occurred in that account during the period.

**Commercial paper** unsecured notes sold in minimum denominations of $25,000 with maturities ranging from 30 to 270 days.

**Committee on Accounting Procedure (CAP)** the first private sector body that was delegated the task of setting accounting standards.

**Comparability** the ability to help users see similarities and differences among events and conditions.

**Comparative financial statements** corresponding financial statements from the previous years accompanying the issued financial statements.

**Compensating balance** a specified balance (usually some percentage of the committee amount) a borrower of a loan is asked to maintain in a low-interest or noninterest-bearing account at the bank.

**Completed contract method** recognition of revenue for a long-term contract when the project is complete.

**Complex capital structure** potential common shares are outstanding.

**Complex debt** debt that lacks one or more of the characteristics of simple debt.

**Composite depreciation method** physically dissimilar assets are aggregated to gain the convenience of group depreciation.

**Compound interest** interest computed not only on the initial investment but also on the accumulated interest in previous periods.

**Comprehensive income** traditional net income plus other nonowner changes in equity.

**Conceptual framework** deals with theoretical and conceptual issues and provides an underlying structure for current and future accounting and reporting standards.

**Conservatism** practice followed in an attempt to ensure that uncertainties and risks inherent in business situations are adequately considered.

**Consignment** the consignor physically transfers the goods to the other company (the consignee), but the consignor retains legal title.

**Consistency** permits valid comparisons between different periods.

**Consolidated financial statements** combination of the separate financial statements of the parent and subsidiary each period into a single aggregate set of financial statements as if there were only one company.

**Construction in progress** asset account equivalent to the asset work-in-progress inventory in a manufacturing company.

**Contingently issuable shares** additional shares of common stock to be issued, contingent on the occurrence of some future circumstance.

**Conventional retail method** applying the retail inventory method in such a way that LCM is approximated.

**Convertible bonds** bonds for which bondholders have the option to convert the bonds into shares of stock.

**Copyright** exclusive right of protection given to a creator of a published work, such as a song, painting, photograph, or book.

**Corporation** the dominant form of business organization that acquires capital from investors in exchange for ownership interest and from creditors by borrowing.

**Correction of an error** an adjustment a company makes due to an error made.

**Cost effectiveness** the perceived benefit of increased decision usefulness exceeds the anticipated cost of providing that information.

**Cost of goods sold** cost of the inventory sold during the period.

**Cost recovery method** deferral of all gross profit recognition until the cost of the item sold has been recovered.

**Cost-to-cost ratio** ratio found by calculating the percentage of estimated total cost that has been incurred to date.

**Cost-to-retail percentage** ratio found by dividing goods available for sale at cost by goods available for sale at retail.

**Coupons bonds** name of the owner was not registered; the holder actually clipped an attached coupon and redeemed it in accordance with instructions on the indenture.

**Credits** represent the right side of the account.

**Cumulative** if the specified dividend is not paid in a given year, the unpaid dividends accumulate and must be made up in a later dividend year before any dividends are paid on common shares.

**Current assets** includes assets that are cash, will be converted into cash, or will be used up within one year or the operating cycle, whichever is longer.

**Current liabilities** expected to require current assets and usually are payable within one year.

**Current maturities of long-term debt** the current installment due on long-term debt, reported as a current liability.

**Current ratio** current assets divided by current liabilities.

**Date of record** specific date stated as to when the determination will be made of the recipient of the dividend.

**Debenture bond** secured only by the "full faith and credit" of the issuing corporation.

**Debits** represent the left side of the account.

**Debt issue cost** with either publicly or privately sold debt, the issuing company will incur costs in connection with issuing bonds or notes, such as legal and accounting fees and printing costs, in addition to registration and underwriting fees.

**Debt to equity ratio** compares resources provided by creditors with resources provided by owners.

**Decision usefulness** the quality of being useful to decision making.

**Default risk** a company's ability to pay its obligations when they come due.

**Deferred annuity** the first cash flow occurs more than the one period after the date the agreement begins.

**Deferred tax asset** taxes to be saved in the future when future deductible amounts reduce taxable income (when the temporary differences reverse).

**Deferred tax liability** taxes to be paid in the future when future taxable amounts become taxable (when the temporary differences reverse).

**Deficit** debit balance in retained earnings.

**Defined benefit pension plans** fixed retirement benefits defined by a designated formula, based on employees' years of service and annual compensation.

**Defined contribution pension plans** fixed annual contributions to a pension fund; employees choose where funds are invested—usually stocks or fixed-income securities.

**Depletion** allocation of the cost of natural resources.

**Depreciation** cost allocation for plant and equipment.

**Derivatives** financial instruments usually created to hedge against risks created by other financial instruments or by transactions that have yet to occur but are anticipated and that "derive" their values or contractually required cash flows from some other security or index.

**Detachable stock purchase warrants** the investor has the option to purchase a stated number of shares of common stock at a specified option price, within a given period of time.

**Development costs** for natural resources, costs incurred after the resource has been discovered but before production begins.

**Diluted EPS** incorporates the dilutive effect of all potential common shares.

**Direct financing lease** lease in which the lessor finances the asset for the lessee and earns interest revenue over the lease term.

**Direct method** the cash effect of each operating activity (i.e., income statement item) is reported directly on the statement of cash flows.

**Direct write-off method** an allowance for uncollectible accounts is not used; instead bad debts that do arise are written off as bad debt expense.

**Disclosure notes** additional insights about company operations, accounting principles, contractual agreements, and pending litigation.

**Discontinued operations** the discontinuance of a component of an entity whose operations and cash flows can be clearly distinguished from the rest of the entity.

**Discount** arises when bonds are sold for less than face amount.

**Discounting** the transfer of a note receivable to a financial institution.

**Distributions to owners** decreases in equity resulting from transfers to owners.

**Dividend** distribution to shareholders of a portion of assets earned.

**Dollar-value LIFO (DVL)** Inventory is viewed as a quantity of value instead of a physical quantity of goods. Instead of layers of units from different purchases, the DVL inventory pool is viewed as comprising layers of dollar value from different years.

**Dollar-value LIFO retail method** LIFO retail method combined with dollar-value LIFO.

**Double-declining-balance (DDB) method** 200% of the straight-line rate is multiplied by book value.

**Double-entry system** dual effect that each transaction has on the accounting equation when recorded.

**DuPont framework** depict return on equity as determined by profit margin (representing profitability), asset turnover (representing efficiency), and the equity multiplier (representing leverage).

**Early extinguishment of debt** debt is retired prior to its scheduled maturity date.

**Earnings per share (EPS)** the amount of income earned by a company expressed on a per share basis.

**Earnings quality** refers to the ability of reported earnings (income) to predict a company's future earnings.

**Economic events** any event that directly affects the financial position of the company.

**Effective interest method** recording interest each period as the effective rate of interest multiplied by the outstanding balance of the debt.

**Effective rate** the actual rate at which money grows per year.

**Emerging Issues Task Force (EITF)** responsible for providing more timely responses to emerging financial reporting issues.

**Employee share purchase plans** permit all employees to buy shares directly from their company, often at favorable terms.

**Equity method** used when an investor can't control, but can significantly influence, the investee.

**Equity multiplier** depicts leverage as total assets divided by total equity.

**Equity/net assets** called shareholders' equity or stockholders' equity for a corporation; the residual interest in the assets of an entity that remains after deducting liabilities.

**Estimates** prediction of future events.

**Ethics** a code or moral system that provides criteria for evaluating right and wrong.

**Ex-dividend date** date usually two business days before the date of the record and is the first day the stock trades without the right to receive the declared dividend.

**Executory costs** maintenance, insurance, taxes, and any other costs usually associated with ownership.

**Expected cash flow approach** adjusts the cash flows, not the discount rate, for the uncertainty or risk of those cash flows.

**Expected economic life** useful life of an asset.

**Expected postretirement benefit obligation (EPBO)** discounted present value of the total net cost to the employer of postretirement benefits.

**Expected return on plan assets** estimated long-term return on invested assets.

**Expenses** outflows or other using up of assets or incurrences of liabilities during a period from delivering or producing good, rendering services, or other activities that constitute the entity's ongoing major, or central, operations.

**Exploration costs** for natural resources, expenditures such as drilling a well, or excavating a mine, or any other costs of searching for natural resources.

**Extended warranties** an additional, extended service that covers new problems arising after the buyer takes control of the product.

**External events** exchange between the company and a separate economic entity.

**Extraordinary items** material events and transactions that are both unusual in nature and infrequent in occurrence.

**F.O.B. (free on board) shipping point** legal title to the goods changes hands at the point of shipment when the seller delivers the goods to the common carrier, and the purchaser is responsible for shipping costs and transit insurance.

**F.O.B. destination** the seller is responsible for shipping and the legal title does not pass until the goods arrive at their destination.

**Factor** financial institution that buys receivables for cash, handles the billing and collection of the receivables, and charges a fee for this service.

**Fair value hedge** a derivative is used to hedge against the exposure to changes in the fair value of an asset or liability or a firm commitment.

**Fair value hierarchy** prioritizes the inputs companies should use when determinig fair value.

**Fair value option** allows companies to report their financial assets and liabilities at fair value.

**Faithful representation** exists when there is agreement between a measure or description and the phenomenon it purports to represent.

**Financial accounting** provides relevant financial information to various external users.

**Financial Accounting Foundation (FAF)** responsible for selecting the members of the FASB and its Advisory Council, ensuring adequate funding of FASB activities, and exercising general oversight of the FASB's activities.

**Financial Accounting Standards Board (FASB)** the current private sector body that has been delegated the task of setting accounting standards.

**Financial activities** cash inflows and outflows from transactions with creditors and owners.

**Financial instrument** cash; evidence of an ownership interest in an entity; a contract that imposes on one entity an obligation to deliver cash or another financial instrument, and conveys to the second entity a right to receive cash or another financial instrument; and a contract that imposes on one entity an obligation to exchange financial instruments on potentially unfavorable terms and conveys to a second entity a right to exchange other financial instruments on potentially favorable terms.

**Financial leverage** by earning a return on borrowed funds that exceeds the cost of borrowing the funds, a company can provide its shareholders with a total return higher than it could achieve by employing equity funds alone.

**Financial reporting** process of providing financial statement information to external users.

**Financial statements** primary means of communicating financial information to external parties.

**Finished goods** costs that have accumulated in work-in-process are transferred to finished goods once the manufacturing process is completed.

**First-in, first-out (FIFO) method** assumes that items sold are those that were acquired first.

**Fiscal year** the annual time period used to report to external users.

**Fixed-asset turnover ratio** used to measure how effectively managers used PP&E.

$$\text{Fixed-asset turnover ratio} = \frac{\text{Net sales}}{\text{Average-fixed assets}}$$

**Foreign currency futures contract** agreement that requires the seller to deliver a specific foreign currency at a designated future date at a specific price.

**Foreign currency hedge** if a derivative is used to hedge the risk that some transactions require settlement in a currency other than the entities' functional currency or that foreign operations will require translation adjustments to reported amounts.

**Forward contract** calls for delivery on a specific date; is not traded on a market exchange; does not call for a daily cash settlement for price changes in the underlying contract.

**Fractional shares** a stock dividend or stock split results in some shareholders being entitled to fractions of whole shares.

**Franchise** contractual arrangement under which the franchisor grants the franchisee the exclusive right to use the franchisor's trademark or tradename within a geographical area, usually for specified period of time.

**Franchisee** individual or corporation given the right to sell the franchisor's products and use its name for a specified period of time.

**Franchisor** grants to the franchisee the right to sell the franchisor's products and use its name for a specific period of time.

**Freight-in** transportation-in; in a periodic system, freight costs generally are added to this temporary account, which is added to purchases in determining net purchases.

**Full-cost method** allows costs incurred in searching for oil and gas within a large geographical area to be capitalized as assets and expensed in the future as oil and gas from the successful wells are removed from that area.

**Full-disclosure principle** the financial reports should include any information that could affect the decisions made by external users.

**Funded status** difference between the employer's obligation (PBO) and the resources available to satisfy that obligation (plan assets).

**Future deductible amounts** the future tax consequence of a temporary difference will be to decrease taxable income relative to accounting income.

**Futures contract** agreement that requires the seller to deliver a particular commodity at a designated future date at a specified price.

**Future taxable amounts** the future tax consequence of temporary difference will be to increase taxable income relative to accounting income.

**Future value** amount of money that a dollar will grow to at some point in the future.

**Gain or loss on the PBO** the decrease or increase in the PBO when one or more estimates used in determining the PBO require revision.

**Gains** increases in equity from peripheral, or incidental, transactions of an entity.

**General journal** used to record any type of transaction.

**General ledger** collection of accounts.

**Generally Accepted Accounting Principles (GAAP)** set of both broad and specific guidelines that companies should follow when measuring and reporting the information in their financial statements and related notes.

**Going concern assumption** in the absence of information to the contrary, it is anticipated that a business entity will continue to operate indefinitely.

**Goodwill** unique intangible asset in that its cost can't be directly associated with any specifically identifiable right and it is not separable from the company itself.

**Government Accounting Standards Board (GASB)** responsible for developing accounting standards for governmental units such as states and cities.

**Gross investment in the lease** total of periodic rental payments and residual value.

**Gross method** For the buyer, views a discount not taken as part of the cost of inventory. For the seller, views a discount not taken by the customer as part of sales of revenue.

**Gross profit method (gross margin method)** estimates cost of goods sold which is then subtracted from cost of goods available for sale to estimate ending inventory.

**Gross profit/ratio** highlights the important relationship between net sales revenue and cost of goods sold.

$$\text{Gross profit ratio} = \frac{\text{Gross profit}}{\text{Net sales}}$$

**Group depreciation method** collection of assets defined as depreciable assets that share similar service lives and other attributes.

**Half-year convention** record one-half of a full year's depreciation in the year of acquisition and another half year in the year of disposal.

**Hedging** taking an action that is expected to produce exposure to a particular type of risk that is precisely the opposite of an actual risk to which the company already is exposed.

**Historical costs** original transaction value.

**Horizontal analysis** comparison by expressing each item as a percentage of that same item in the financial statements of another year (base amount) in order to more easily see year-to-year changes.

**Illegal acts** violations of the law, such as bribes, kickbacks, and illegal contributions to political candidates.

**Impairment of value** operational assets should be written down if there has been a significant impairment (fair value less than book value) of value.

**Implicit rate of interest** rate implicit in the agreement.

**Improvements** replacement of a major component of an operational asset.

**Income from continuing operations** revenues, expenses (including income taxes), gain, and losses, excluding those related to discontinued operations and extraordinary items.

**Income statement** statement of operations or statement of earnings is used to summarize the profit-generating activities that occurred during a particular reporting period.

**Income statement approach** estimating bad debt expense as a percentage of each period's net credit sales; usually determined by reviewing the company's recent history of the relationship between credit sales and actual bad debts.

**Income summary** account that is a bookkeeping convenience used in the closing process that provides a check that all temporary accounts have been properly closed.

**Income tax expense** provision for income taxes; reported as a separate expense in corporate income statements.

**Indirect method** the net cash increase or decrease from operating activities is derived indirectly by starting with reported net income and working backwards to convert that amount to a cash basis.

**Initial direct costs** costs incurred by the lessor that are associated directly with originating a lease and are essential to acquire the lease.

**Initial market transactions** provide for new cash by the issuance of stocks and bonds by the corporation.

**In-process research and development** the amount of the purchase price in a business acquisition that is allocated to projects that have not yet reached technological feasibility.

**Installment notes** notes payable for which equal installment payments include both an amount that represents interest and an amount that represents a reduction of the outstanding balance so that at maturity the note is completely paid.

**Installment sales method** recognizes revenue and costs only when cash payments are received.

**Institute of Internal Auditors** national organization of accountants providing internal auditing services for their own organizations.

**Institute of Management Accountants (IMA)** primary national organization of accountants working in industry and government.

**Intangible assets** operational assets that lack physical substance; examples include patents, copyrights, franchises, and goodwill.

**Interest** "rent" paid for the use of money for some period of time.

**Interest cost** interest accrued on the projected benefit obligation calculated as the discount rate multiplied by the projected benefit obligation at the beginning of the year.

**Interest rate swap** agreement to exchange fixed interest payments for floating rate payments, or vice versa, without exchanging the underlying principal amounts.

**Internal control** a company's plan to encourage adherence to company policies and procedures, promote operational efficiency, minimize errors and theft, and enhance the reliability and accuracy of accounting data.

**Internal events** events that directly affect the financial position of the company but don't involve an exchange transaction with another entity.

**International Accounting Standards Board (IASB)** objectives are to develop a single set of high-quality, understandable global accounting standards, to promote the use of those standards, and to bring about the convergence of national accounting standards and International Accounting Standards.

**International Accounting Standards Committee (IASC)** umbrella organization formed to develop global accounting standards.

**International Financial Reporting Standards (IFRS)** developed by the IASB and used by more than 100 countries.

**Intraperiod tax allocation** associates (allocates) income tax expense (or income tax gross profit net sales benefit if there is a loss) with each major component of income that causes it.

**Intrinsic value** the difference between the market price of the shares and the option price at which they can be acquired.

**Inventories** goods awaiting sale (finished goods), goods in the course of production (work in process), and goods to be consumed directly or indirectly in production (raw materials).

**Inventory** goods acquired, manufactured, or in the process of being manufactured for sale.

**Inventory turnover ratio** measures a company's efficiency in managing its investment in inventory.

**Investing activities** involve the acquisition and sale of long-term assets used in the business and non-operating investment assets.

**Investments by owners** increases in equity resulting from transfers of resources (usually cash) to a company in exchange for ownership interest.

**Irregularities** intentional distortions of financial statements.

**Journal** a chronological record of all economic events affecting financial position.

**Journal entry** captures the effect of a transaction on financial position in debit/credit form.

**Just-in-time (JIT) system** a system used by a manufacturer to coordinate production with suppliers so that raw materials or components arrive just as they are needed in the production process.

**Land improvements** the cost of parking lots, driveways, and private roads and the costs of fences and lawn and garden sprinkler systems.

**Last-in, first-out (LIFO) method** assumes units sold are the most recent units purchased.

**Leasehold improvements** account title when a lessee makes improvements to leased property that reverts back to the lessor at the end of the lease.

**Lessee** user of a leased asset.

**Lessor** owner of a leased asset.

**Leveraged lease** a third-party, long-term creditor provides nonrecourse financing for a lease agreement between a lessor and a lessee.

**Liabilities** probable future sacrifices of economic benefits arising from present obligations of a particular entity to transfer assets or provide services to other entities in the future as a result of past transactions or events.

**LIFO conformity rule** if a company uses LIFO to measure taxable income, the company also must use LIFO for external financial reporting.

**LIFO inventory pools** simplifies recordkeeping and reduces the risk of LIFO liquidation by grouping inventory units into pools based on physical similarities of the individual units.

**LIFO liquidation** the decline in inventory quantity during the period.

**LIFO reserve** contra account to inventory used to record the difference between the internal method and LIFO.

**Limited liability company** owners are not liable for the debts of the business, except to the extent of their investment; all members can be involved with managing the business without losing liability protection; no limitations on the number of owners.

**Limited liability partnership** similar to a limited liability company, except it doesn't offer all the liability protection available in the limited liability company structure.

**Line of credit** allows a company to borrow cash without having to follow formal loan procedures and paperwork.

**Liquidating dividend** when a dividend exceeds the balance in retained earnings.

**Liquidity** period of time before an asset is converted to cash or until a liability is paid.

**Long-term solvency** the riskiness of a company with regard to the amount of liabilities in its capital structure.

**Loss contingency** existing, uncertain situation involving potential loss depending on whether some future event occurs.

**Losses** decreases in equity arising from peripheral, or incidental, transactions of the entity.

**Lower-of-cost-or-market (LCM)** recognizes losses in the period that the value of inventory declines below its cost.

**Management discussion and analysis (MDA)** provides a biased but informed perspective of a company's operations, liquidity, and capital resources.

**Managerial accounting** deals with the concepts and methods used to provide information to an organization's internal users (i.e., its managers).

**Matching principle** expenses are recognized in the same period as the related revenues.

**Materiality** if a more costly way of providing information is not expected to have a material effect on decisions made by those using the information, the less costly method may be acceptable.

**Measurement** process of associating numerical amounts to the elements.

**Minimum lease payments** payments the lessee is required to make in connection with the lease.

**Minimum pension liability** an employer must report a pension liability at least equal to the amount by which its ABO exceeds its plan assets.

**Model Business Corporation Act** designed to serve as a guide to states in the development of their corporation statutes.

**Modified accelerated cost recovery system (MACRS)** The federal income tax code allows taxpayers to compute depreciation for their tax returns using this method.

**Monetary assets** money and claims to receive money, the amount of which is fixed or determinable.

**Monetary liabilities** obligations to pay amounts of cash, the amount of which is fixed or determinable.

**Mortgage bond** backed by a lien on specified real estate owned by the issuer.

**Multiple-deliverable arrangements** require allocation of revenue to multiple elements that qualify for separate revenue recognition.

**Multiple-step** income statement format that includes a number of intermediate subtotals before arriving at income from continuing operations.

**Natural resources** oil and gas deposits, timber tracts, and mineral deposits.

**Net income/net loss revenue + gains − (expenses and losses for a period)** income statement bottom line.

**Net interest cost/income** interest rate times the net difference between the defined benefit obligation (DBO) and plan assets using IFRS.

**Net markdown** net effect of the change in selling price (increase, decrease, increase).

**Net markup** net effect of the change in selling price (increase, increase, decrease).

**Net method** For the buyer, considers the cost of inventory to include the net, after-discount amount, and any discounts not taken are reported as interest expense. For the seller, considers sales revenue to be the net amount, after discount, and any discounts not taken by the customer as interest revenue.

**Net operating loss** negative taxable income because tax-deductible expenses exceed taxable revenues.

**Net realizable less a normal profit margin (NRV − NP)** lower limit of market.

**Net realizable value** the amount of cash the company expects to actually collect from customers.

**Net realizable value (NRV)** upper limit of market.

**Neutrality** neutral with respect to parties potentially affected.

**Noncash investing and financing activities** transactions that do not increase or decrease cash but that result in significant investing and financing activities.

**Noninterest-bearing note** notes that bear interest, but the interest is deducted (or discounted) from the face amount to determine the cash proceeds made available to the borrower at the outset.

**Nonoperating income** includes gains and losses and revenues and expenses related to peripheral or incidental activities of the company.

**Note payable** promissory note (essentially an IOU) that obligates the issuing corporation to repay a stated amount at or by a specified maturity date and to pay interest to the lender between the issue date and maturity.

**Notes receivable** receivables supported by a formal agreement or note that specifies payment terms.

**Objectives-oriented/principles-based accounting standards** approach to standard setting stresses professional judgment, as opposed to following a list of rules.

**Onerous performance obligation** The proposed ASU on revenue recognition may require the seller to recognize a liability and expense for an unprofitable performance obligation satisfied over a period of time greater than one year.

**Operating activities** inflows and outflows of cash related to transactions entering into the determination of net income.

**Operating cycle** period of time necessary to convert cash to raw materials, raw materials to finished product, the finished product to receivables, and then finally receivables back to cash.

**Operating income** includes revenues and expenses directly related to the principal revenue-generating activities of the company.

**Operating leases** fundamental rights and responsibilities of ownership are retained by the lessor and that the lessee merely is using the asset temporarily.

**Operating loss carryback** reduction of prior (up to two) years' taxable income by a current net operating loss.

**Operating loss forward** reduction of future (up to 20) years' taxable income by a current net operating loss.

**Operating segment** a component of an enterprise that engages in business activities from which it may earn revenues and incur expenses (including revenues and expenses relating to transactions with other companies of the same enterprise); whose operating results are regularly reviewed by the enterprise's chief operating decision maker to make decisions about resources to be allocated to the segment and assess its performance; for which discrete financial information is available.

**Operational assets** property, plant, and equipment, along with intangible assets.

**Operational risk** how adept a company is at withstanding various events and circumstances that might impair its ability to earn profits.

**Option** gives the holder the right either to buy or sell a financial instrument at a specified price.

**Option pricing models** statistical models that incorporate information about a company's stock and the terms of the stock option to estimate the option's fair value.

**Ordinary annuity** cash flows occur at the end of each period.

**Other comprehensive income** certain gains and losses that are excluded from the calculation of net income, but included in the calculation of comprehensive income.

**Paid-in capital** invested capital consisting primarily of amounts invested by shareholders when they purchase shares of stock from the corporation.

**Parenthetical comments/modifying comments** supplemental information disclosed on the face of financial statements.

**Participating** preferred shareholders are allowed to receive additional dividends beyond the stated amount.

**Patent** exclusive right to manufacture a product or to use a process.

**Pension plan assets** employer contributions and accumulated earnings on the investment of those contributions to be used to pay retirement benefits to retired employees.

**Percentage-of-completion method** allocation of a share of a project's revenues and expenses to each reporting period during the contract period.

**Performance obligations** promises to transfer goods and services to buyer.

**Periodic inventory system** the merchandise inventory account balance is not adjusted as purchases and sales are made but only periodically at the end of a reporting period when a physical count of the period's ending inventory is made and costs are assigned to the quantities determined.

**Periodicity assumption** allows the life of a company to be divided into artificial time periods to provide timely information.

**Permanent accounts** represent assets, liabilities, and shareholders' equity at a point in time.

**Permanent difference** difference between pretax accounting income and taxable income and, consequently, between the reported amount of an asset or liability in the financial statements and its tax basis that will not "reverse" resulting from transactions and events that under existing tax law will never affect taxable income or taxes payable.

**Perpetual inventory system** account inventory is continually adjusted for each change in inventory, whether it's caused by a purchase, a sale, or a return of merchandise by the company to its supplier.

**Pledging** trade receivables in general rather than specific receivables are pledged as collateral; the responsibility for collection of the receivables remains solely with the company.

**Point-of-sale** the goods or services sold to the buyer are delivered (the title is transferred).

**Post-closing trial balance** verifies that the closing entries were prepared and posted correctly and that the accounts are now ready for next year's transactions.

**Posting** transferring debits and credits recorded in individual journal entries to the specific accounts affected.

**Postretirement benefits** all types of retiree benefits; may include medical coverage, dental coverage, life insurance, group legal services, and other benefits.

**Potential common shares** Securities that, while not being common stock may become common stock through their exercise, conversion, or issuance and therefore dilute (reduce) earnings per share.

**Predictive value/confirmatory value** confirmation of investor expectations about future cash-generating ability.

**Preferred stock** typically has a preference (a) to a specified amount of dividends (stated dollar amount per share or percentage of par value per share) and (b) to distribution of assets in the event the corporation is dissolved.

**Premium** arises when bonds are sold for more than face amount.

**Prepaid expense** represents an asset recorded when an expense is paid in advance, creating benefits beyond the current period.

**Prepayments/deferrals** the cash flow precedes either expense or revenue recognition.

**Present value** today's equivalent to a particular amount in the future.

**Prior period adjustment** addition to or reduction in the beginning retained earnings balance in a statement of shareholders' equity due to a correction of an error.

**Prior service cost** the cost of credit given for an amendment to a pension plan to employee service rendered in prior years.

**Product costs** costs associated with products and expensed as cost of goods sold only when the related products are sold.

**Profit margin on sales** net income divided by net sales; measures the amount of net income achieved per sales dollar.

**Pro forma earnings** actual (GAAP) earnings reduced by any expenses the reporting company feels are unusual and should be excluded.

**Projected benefit obligation (PBO)** the discounted present value of estimated retirement benefits earned so far by employees, applying the plan's pension formula using projected future compensation levels.

**Property dividend** when a noncash asset is distributed.

**Property, plant, and equipment** land, buildings, equipment, machinery, autos, and trucks.

**Prospective approach** the accounting change is implemented in the present, and its effects are reflected in the financial statements of the current and future years only.

**Proxy statement** contains disclosures on compensation to directors and executives; sent to all shareholders each year.

**Purchase commitments** contracts that obligate a company to purchase a specified amount of merchandise or raw materials at specified prices on or before specified dates.

**Purchase discounts** reductions in the amount to be paid if remittance is made within a designated period of time.

**Purchase option** a provision of some lease contracts that gives the lessee the option of purchasing the leased property during, or at the end of, the lease term at a specified price.

**Purchase return** a reduction in both inventory and accounts payable (if the account has not yet been paid) at the time of the return.

**Purchases journal** records the purchase of merchandise on account.

**Quality assurance warranty** obligation by the seller to make repairs or replace products that are later demonstrated to be defective for some period of time after the sale.

**Quasi reorganization** a firm undergoing financial difficulties, but with favorable future prospects, may use a quasi reorganization to write down inflated asset values and eliminate an accumulated deficit.

**Rate of return on stock investment**

$$\frac{\text{Dividends} + \text{Share price appreciation}}{\text{Initial investment}}$$

**Ratio analysis** comparison of accounting numbers to evaluate the performance and risk of a firm.

**Raw materials** cost of components purchased from other manufacturers that will become part of the finished product.

**Real estate lease** involves land—exclusively or in part.

**Realization principle** requires that the earnings process is judged to be complete or virtually complete, and there is reasonable certainty as to the collectibility of the asset to be received (usually cash) before revenue can be recognized.

**Rearrangements** expenditures made to restructure an asset without addition, replacement, or improvement.

**Reasonably assured to be entitled** seller's experience indicates that it will be entitled to receive an amount of uncertain consideration.

**Receivables** a company's claims to the future collection of cash, other assets, or services.

**Receivables turnover ratio** indicates how quickly a company is able to collect its accounts receivable.

**Recognition** process of admitting information into the basic financial statements.

**Redemption privilege** might allow preferred shareholders the option, under specified conditions, to return their shares for a predetermined redemption price.

**Related-party transactions** transactions with owners, management, families of owners or management, affiliated companies, and other parties that can significantly influence or be influenced by the company.

**Relevance** one of the primary decision-specific qualities that make accounting information useful; made up of predictive value and/or feedback value, and timeliness.

**Reliability** the extent to which information is verifiable, representationally faithful, and neutral.

**Remeasurement gains** gains from changes in pension assumptions or actual return on plan assets exceeding the interest rate.

**Remeasurement losses** losses from changes in pension assumptions or actual return on plan assets being less than the interest rate.

**Rent abatement** lease agreements may call for uneven rent payments during the term of the lease, e.g., when the initial payment (or maybe several payments) is waived.

**Replacement cost (RC)** the cost to replace the item by purchase or manufacture.

**Replacement depreciation method** depreciation is recorded when assets are replaced.

**Representational faithfulness** agreement between a measure or description and the phenomenon it purports to represent.

**Residual asset** the carrying amount of a leased asset not transferred to the lessee.

**Residual value** or salvage value, the amount the company expects to receive for the asset at the end of its service life less any anticipated disposal costs.

**Restoration costs** costs to restore land or other property to its original condition after extraction of the natural resource ends.

**Restricted stock** shares subject to forfeiture by the employee if employment is terminated within some specified number of years from the date of grant.

**Retail inventory method** relies on the relationship between cost and selling price to estimate ending inventory and cost of goods sold; provides a more accurate estimate than the gross profit method.

**Retained earnings** amounts earned by the corporation on behalf of its shareholders and not (yet) distributed to them as dividends.

**Retired stock** shares repurchased and not designated as treasury stock.

**Retirement depreciation method** records depreciation when assets are disposed of and measures depreciation as the difference between the proceeds received and cost.

**Retrospective approach** financial statements issued in previous years are revised to reflect the impact of an accounting change whenever those statements are presented again for comparative purpose.

**Return on assets (ROA)** indicates a company's overall profitability.

**Return on shareholders' equity (ROE)** amount of profit management can generate from the assets that owners provide.

**Revenues** inflows or other enhancements of assets or settlements of liabilities from delivering or producing goods, rendering services, or other activities that constitute the entity's ongoing major, or central, operations.

**Reverse stock split** when a company decreases, rather than increases, its outstanding shares.

**Reversing entries** optional entries that remove the effects of some of the adjusting entries made at the end of the previous reporting period for the sole purpose of simplifying journal entries made during the new period.

**Right of conversion** shareholders' right to exchange shares of preferred stock for common stock at specified conversion ratio.

**Right of return** customers' right to return merchandise to retailers if they are not satisfied.

**Right-of-use asset** the right to use an asset for a specified period of time.

**Rules-based accounting standards** a list of rules for choosing the appropriate accounting treatment for a transaction.

**S corporation** characteristics of both regular corporations and partnerships.

**SAB No. 101** *Staff Accounting Bulletin 101* summarizes the SEC's views on revenue recognition.

**Sale-leaseback transaction** the owner of an asset sells it and immediately leases it back from the new owner.

**Sales journal** records credit sales.

**Sales return** the return of merchandise for a refund or for credit to be applied to other purchases.

**Sales-type lease** in addition to interest revenue earned over the lease term, the lessor receives a manufacturer's or dealer's profit on the sale of the asset.

**Sarbanes-Oxley Act** law provides for the regulation of the key players in the financial reporting process.

**Secondary market transactions** provide for the transfer of stocks and bonds among individuals and institutions.

**Securities and Exchange Commission (SEC)** responsible for setting accounting and reporting standards for companies whose securities are publicly traded.

**Securities available-for-sale** equity or debt securities the investor acquires, not for an active trading account or to be held to maturity.

**Securities to be held-to-maturity** debt securities for which the investor has the "positive intent and ability" to hold the securities to maturity.

**Securitization** the company creates a special purpose entity (SPE), usually a trust or a subsidiary; the SPE buys a pool of trade receivables, credit card receivables, or loans from the company and then sells related securities.

**Separation of duties** an internal control technique in which various functions are distributed amongst employees to provide cross-checking that encourages accuracy and discourages fraud.

**Serial bonds** more structured (and less popular) way to retire bonds on a piecemeal basis.

**Service cost** increase in the projected benefit obligation attributable to employee service performed during the period.

**Service life (useful life)** the estimated use that the company expects to receive from the asset.

**Service method** allocation approach that reflects the declining service pattern of the prior service cost.

**Share purchase contract** shares ordinarily are sold in exchange for a promissory note from the subscriber—in essence, shares are sold on credit.

**Short-term investments** investments not classified as cash equivalents that will be liquidated in the coming year or operating cycle, whichever is longer.

**Significant influence** effective control is absent but the investor is able to exercise significant influence over the operating and financial policies of the investee (usually between 20% and 50% of the investee's voting shares are held).

**Simple capital structure** a firm that has no potential common shares (outstanding securities that could potentially dilute earnings per share).

**Simple debt** (1) involves a lender providing an amount up front that eventually must be repaid, (2) doesn't permit the borrower to prepay or settle the debt unless the lender allows it, and (3) is not a derivative.

**Simple interest** computed by multiplying an initial investment times both the applicable interest rate and the period of time for which the money is used.

**Single-step** income statement format that groups all revenues and gains together and all expenses and losses together.

**Sinking fund debentures** bonds that must be redeemed on a prespecified year-by-year basis; administered by a trustee who repurchases bonds in the open market.

**Source documents** relay essential information about each transaction to the accountant, e.g., sales invoices, bills from suppliers, cash register tapes.

**Special journal** record of a repetitive type of transaction, e.g., a sales journal.

**Specific identification method** each unit sold during the period or each unit on hand at the end of the period to be matched with its actual cost.

**Specific interest method** for interest capitalization, rates from specific construction loans to the extent of specific borrowings are used before using the average rate of other debt.

**Start-up costs** whenever a company introduces a new product or service, or commences business in a new territory or with a new customer, it incurs one-time costs that are expensed in the period incurred.

**Statement of cash flows** change statement summarizing the transactions that caused cash to change during the period.

**Statement of shareholders' equity** statement disclosing the source of changes in the shareholders' equity accounts.

**Stock appreciation rights (SARs)** awards that enable an employee to benefit by the amount that the market price of the company's stock rises above a specified amount without having to buy shares.

**Stock dividend** distribution of additional shares of stock to current shareholders of the corporation.

**Stock options** employees aren't actually awarded shares, but rather are given the option to buy shares at a specified exercise price within some specified number of years from the date of grant.

**Stock split** stock distribution of 25% or higher, sometimes called a *large* stock dividend.

**Straight line** an equal amount of depreciable base is allocated to each year of the asset's service life.

**Straight-line method** recording interest each period at the same dollar amount.

**Subordinated debenture** the holder is not entitled to receive any liquidation payments until the claims of other specified debt issues are satisfied.

**Subsequent event** a significant development that takes place after the company's fiscal year-end but before the financial statements are issued.

**Subsidiary ledger** record of a group of subsidiary accounts associated with a particular general ledger control account.

**Successful efforts method** requires that exploration costs that are known not to have resulted in the discovery of oil or gas be included as expense in the period the expenditures are made.

**Sum-of-the-years'-digits (SYD) method** systematic acceleration of depreciation by multiplying the depreciable base by a fraction that declines each year.

**Supplemental financial statements** reports containing more detailed information than is shown in the primary financial statements.

**T-account** account with space at the top for the account title and two sides for recording increases and decreases.

**Taxable income** comprises revenues, expenses, gains, and losses as measured according to the regulations of the appropriate taxing authority.

**Technological feasibility** established when the enterprise has completed all planning, designing, coding, and testing activities that are necessary to establish that the product can be produced to meet its design specifications including functions, features, and technical performance requirements.

**Temporary accounts** represent changes in the retained earnings component of shareholders' equity for a corporation caused by revenue, expense, gain, and loss transactions.

**Temporary difference** difference between pretax accounting income and taxable income and, consequently, between the reported amount of an asset or liability in the financial statements and its tax basis which will "reverse" in later years.

**Time-based methods** allocates the cost base according to the passage of time.

**Timeliness** information that is available to users early enough to allow its use in the decision process.

**Times interest earned ratio** a way to gauge the ability of a company to satisfy its fixed debt obligations by comparing interest charges with the income available to pay those charges.

**Time value of money** money can be invested today to earn interest and grow to a larger dollar amount in the future.

**Trade discounts** percentage reduction from the list price.

**Trademark (tradename)** exclusive right to display a word, a slogan, a symbol, or an emblem that distinctively identifies a company, a product, or a service.

**Trade notes payable** formally recognized by a written promissory note.

**Trading securities** equity or debt securities the investor (usually a financial institution) acquires principally for the purpose of selling in the near term.

**Transaction analysis** process of reviewing the source documents to determine the dual effect on the accounting equation and the specific elements involved.

**Transaction obligation** the unfunded accumulated postretirement benefit obligation existing when *SFAS 106* was adopted.

**Transaction price** the amount the seller expects to be entitled to receive from the buyer in exchange for providing goods and services.

**Transactions** economic events.

**Treasury stock** shares repurchased and not retired.

**Troubled debt restructuring** the original terms of a debt agreement are changed as a result of financial difficulties experienced by the debtor (borrower).

**Trustee** person who accepts employer contributions, invests the contributions, accumulates the earnings on the investments, and pays benefits from the plan assets to retired employees or their beneficiaries.

**Unadjusted trial balance** a list of the general ledger accounts and their balances at a particular date.

**Understandability** users must understand the information within the context of the decision being made.

**Unearned revenues** cash received from a customer in one period for goods or services that are to be provided in a future period.

**Units-of-production method** computes a depreciation rate per measure of activity and then multiplies this rate by actual activity to determine periodic depreciation.

**Unqualified opinion** auditors are satisfied that the financial statements present fairly the company's financial position, results of operations, and cash flows and are in conformity with generally accepted accounting principles.

**Variable consideration** transaction price is uncertain because some of the price is to be paid to the seller depending on future events.

**Valuation allowance** indirect reduction (contra account) in a deferred tax asset when it is more likely than not that some portion or all of the deferred tax asset will not be realized.

**Verifiability** implies a consensus among different measurers.

**Vertical analysis** expression of each item in the financial statements as a percentage of an appropriate corresponding total, or base amount, but within the same year.

**Vested benefits** benefits that employees have the right to receive even if their employment were to cease today.

**Weighted-average interest method** for interest capitalization, weighted-average rate on all interest-bearing debt, including all construction loans, is used.

**Without recourse** the buyer assumes the risk of bad debts.

**With recourse** the seller retains the risk of uncollectibility.

**Working capital** differences between current assets and current liabilities.

**Work-in-process inventory** products that are not yet complete.

**Worksheet** used to organize the accounting information needed to prepare adjusting and closing entries and the financial statements.

# Photo Credits

# Subject Index

Notes: Page numbers followed by *n* indicate material in footnotes. General information about standards and standard-setting organizations may be found in this index. Specific standards and pronouncements are listed in the Accounting Standards Index.

trading securities, 660, 1266*n*
lump-sum purchases, 540–541, 563
recording, 59, 65, 91
Purchase commitments, 505–506
contract beyond fiscal year, 506
contract within fiscal year, 505, 505*n*
Purchase discounts, 428*n,* 428–429, 491
Purchase discounts lost account, 428*n*
Purchased R&D, 562, 562*n*
Purchase method, 14, 14*n*
Purchase obligations, B-14
Purchase returns, 424, 428, 491
Purchases journal, 91
PXG Canada, 187

## Q

QSPEs (qualifying SPEs), 385*n,* 385–386, 387
Qualified opinion, 131
Qualified pension plans, 1011
Qualifying SPEs (QSPEs), 385*n,* 385–386, 387
Qualitative characteristics of financial
    information. *See* Financial information
Quasi reorganizations, 1113–1114
"Quick assets," 135, 363
Quick ratio. *See* Acid-test ratio
Quick (acid-test) ratio, 135, 363, 737

## R

Raiborn, Cecily, 189*n*
Rajan, M. V., 746*n*
Rate of return, 6
Rate of return on assets ratio, 817, 817*n*
Ratio analysis, 133, 140
    acid-test ratio, 135, 363, 767
    activity ratios, 263–264, 270
        asset turnover, 263, 267
        average collection period, 268, 389
        average days in inventory, 264, 267,
            268, 451
        in evaluating asset management,
            545–546, 564
        fixed asset turnover, 546, 546*n,* 564
        inventory turnover, 264, 264*n,* 268,
            445, 451
        receivables turnover, 263*n,* 263–264,
            268, 389
    asset turnover ratio, 263, 267
    average collection period, 268, 389
    average days in inventory ratio, 264, 267,
        268, 451
    cash flow ratios, 1298–1299, 1299*n*
    "cost-to-cost ratio," 249
    current ratio, 134, 135, 363, 748–749, 766–767
    debt-to-equity ratio (*See* Debt-to-equity ratio)
    dividend payout ratio, 1173–1174
    financing ratios, 135–138
        debt-to-equity ratio (*See* Debt-to-equity
            ratio)
        times interest earned ratio, 138, 138*n,*
            816, 1036
    fixed asset turnover ratio, 546, 546*n,* 564
    gross profit ratio, 444–445, 451, 485–486
    industry context and, 363–364
    inventory turnover ratio, 264, 264*n,* 268, 445
    liquidity ratios, 134–135
        acid-test ratio, 135, 363, 767
        current ratio, 134, 135, 363, 748–749,
            766–767

decision makers' perspective, 363–364
price-earnings ratio, 1108, 1173
profitability ratios, 264–266, 270
    decision makers' perspective, 363–364
    pension information and, 1036
    profit margin on sales, 264–265
    return on assets, 264, 265, 267, 891, 1036
    return on shareholders' equity (ROE)
        ratio, 137, 137*n,* 264, 265*n,* 265–266,
        268, 1108, 1109
profit margin on sales ratio, 264–265
quick (acid-test) ratio, 135, 363, 737
rate of return on assets ratio, 817, 817*n*
receivables turnover ratio, 263*n,* 263–264,
    268, 389
return on assets ratio, 264, 265, 267,
    891, 1036
return on shareholders' equity (ROE) ratio,
    137, 137*n,* 264, 265*n,* 265–266, 268,
    1108, 1109
summary of ratios, 266
times interest earned ratio, 138, 138*n,*
    816, 1036
Raw materials inventory, 118, 422
Raytheon Company, 245, 380
RC (replacement cost), 477
Reacquired shares, 1108, 1155–1156
Reader's Digest Association, Inc., 1088
Real estate leases, 897–898, 898*n*
Real estate sales, 239
Realistic interest rates, 811–812
Realization principle
    adjusting entries required for, 67
    criteria for revenue recognition, 234
    LCM rule in violation of, 478–479
    leases, 864
    in revenue recognition, 27–28, 232, 232*n,*
        233, 233*n,* 238
Realized holding gains (losses), 654, 662, 666,
    668, 677
Rearrangements, 624, 625, 626
Receipts (petty cash), 394
Receivables
    accounts receivable (*See* Accounts receivable)
    accrued, 71, 72
    assignment of, 379–380, 388
    current (*See* Current receivables)
    efficiency in collecting, 263
    factoring, 743, 743*n*
    financial reporting case, 359, 391
    impairment of, 395*n,* 395–396
    installment receivables, 241
    investment revenue, 1275
    leases receivable, 887
    long-term receivables, 867
    nontrade receivables, 118, 364, 1266
    notes receivable (*See* Notes receivable)
    sale of, 379, 380–382, 381*n,* 392
        deciding on sale approach, 383–385,
            384*n,* 387
        with recourse, 382
        without recourse, 381, 382, 382*n*
    trade receivables as operating assets, 1266*n*
    in troubled debt restructuring, 397
    used as collateral, 379, 381, 382
Receivables management, 388–390, 392
Receivables turnover ratio, 263*n,* 263–264,
    268, 389

Reclassification adjustment, 667, 667*n,*
    668*n,* 669*n*
Recognition
    of asset retirement obligations, 535
    of gross profit (loss)
        comparison of methods, 251–256
        general approach, 247–248
        percentage-of-completion method,
            248–250, 249*n,* 250*n,* 269
    income recognition, 251, 251*n*
    of revenues (*See* Revenue recognition)
Recognition concept, 20, 27–29, 33, 36
    convergence efforts, 34
    expense recognition: matching, 28*n,* 28–29
    general criteria, 27, 27*n*
    revenue recognition: realization, 27–28
Reconstructed journal entries, 1269, 1271, 1304
Recording transactions
    accrued interest on debt, 871, 872
    adjusting entries, 69–70, 91, 91*n*
    components of net pension cost, 1038–1039
    donated assets, 544, 544*n*
    funding of pension plan assets, 1032, 1033
    gross method (*See* Gross method)
    indirect, of retained earnings, 55
    investment purchases, 670
        AFS securities, 665
        HTM securities, 657
        trading securities, 659, 660
    in journals, 56, 91
    net method (*See* Net method)
    periodic inventory system, 60, 65
    perpetual inventory system, 59
    postretirement benefit expense, 1044
    purchase of investment, equity method, 681
    recording bonds at issuance, 799*n,* 799–801
Recourse obligation, 382
Recoverability test, 614, 614*n,* 616
Redemption privilege, 1089
Refinancing obligations, 749*n,* 749–750, 895
Refundable deposits, 746, 747
Registered bonds, 799
Reinvestment ratio, 1298
Related-party transactions, 127, 127*n*
Relative market values, 824
Relevance, 21, 22, 22*n,* 27, 177
Reliability, 27
Remeasurement cost, 1038, 1039
"Remeasurement" gains and losses, 1030,
    1030*n,* 1050
Renegotiation of debt, 397
Renewal of lease term, 863, 863*n,* 868*n*
Rent
    prepaid rent, 68, 74
    unearned rent revenue, 60–61, 69
Rent abatement, 867
Rent expense, 866
Rent holiday, 867
Rent revenue, 866
Repairs, 623, 625, 626
Replacement cost (RC), 477–478
Replacement depreciation method, 627, 628
Reporting entity
    change in, 1219, 1219*n,* 1220
    convergence efforts, 34
    goodwill inseparable from, 617
Reporting segment information. *See* Operating
    segments

# Accounting Standards Index

Notes: Page numbers followed by *n* indicate material in footnotes. Specific standards and pronouncements are found in this index; general information about standards and standard-setting organizations is found in the Subject Index. Unless otherwise noted, standards will be found under the name of the issuing organization.

# Present and Future Value Tables

This table shows the future value of $1 at various interest rates ($i$) and time periods ($n$). It is used to calculate the future value of any single amount.

**TABLE 1**    Future Value of $1

$$FV = \$1\,(1 + i)^n$$

| n/i | 1.0% | 1.5% | 2.0% | 2.5% | 3.0% | 3.5% | 4.0% | 4.5% | 5.0% | 5.5% | 6.0% | 7.0% | 8.0% | 9.0% | 10.0% | 11.0% | 12.0% | 20.0% |
|---|---|---|---|---|---|---|---|---|---|---|---|---|---|---|---|---|---|---|
| 1 | 1.01000 | 1.01500 | 1.02000 | 1.02500 | 1.03000 | 1.03500 | 1.04000 | 1.04500 | 1.05000 | 1.05500 | 1.06000 | 1.07000 | 1.08000 | 1.09000 | 1.10000 | 1.11000 | 1.12000 | 1.20000 |
| 2 | 1.02010 | 1.03022 | 1.04040 | 1.05063 | 1.06090 | 1.07123 | 1.08160 | 1.09203 | 1.10250 | 1.11303 | 1.12360 | 1.14490 | 1.16640 | 1.18810 | 1.21000 | 1.23210 | 1.25440 | 1.44000 |
| 3 | 1.03030 | 1.04568 | 1.06121 | 1.07689 | 1.09273 | 1.10872 | 1.12486 | 1.14117 | 1.15763 | 1.17424 | 1.19102 | 1.22504 | 1.25971 | 1.29503 | 1.33100 | 1.36763 | 1.40493 | 1.72800 |
| 4 | 1.04060 | 1.06136 | 1.08243 | 1.10381 | 1.12551 | 1.14752 | 1.16986 | 1.19252 | 1.21551 | 1.23882 | 1.26248 | 1.31080 | 1.36049 | 1.41158 | 1.46410 | 1.51807 | 1.57352 | 2.07360 |
| 5 | 1.05101 | 1.07728 | 1.10408 | 1.13141 | 1.15927 | 1.18769 | 1.21665 | 1.24618 | 1.27628 | 1.30696 | 1.33823 | 1.40255 | 1.46933 | 1.53862 | 1.61051 | 1.68506 | 1.76234 | 2.48832 |
| 6 | 1.06152 | 1.09344 | 1.12616 | 1.15969 | 1.19405 | 1.22926 | 1.26532 | 1.30226 | 1.34010 | 1.37884 | 1.41852 | 1.50073 | 1.58687 | 1.67710 | 1.77156 | 1.87041 | 1.97382 | 2.98598 |
| 7 | 1.07214 | 1.10984 | 1.14869 | 1.18869 | 1.22987 | 1.27228 | 1.31593 | 1.36086 | 1.40710 | 1.45468 | 1.50363 | 1.60578 | 1.71382 | 1.82804 | 1.94872 | 2.07616 | 2.21068 | 3.58318 |
| 8 | 1.08286 | 1.12649 | 1.17166 | 1.21840 | 1.26677 | 1.31681 | 1.36857 | 1.42210 | 1.47746 | 1.53469 | 1.59385 | 1.71819 | 1.85093 | 1.99256 | 2.14359 | 2.30454 | 2.47596 | 4.29982 |
| 9 | 1.09369 | 1.14339 | 1.19509 | 1.24886 | 1.30477 | 1.36290 | 1.42331 | 1.48610 | 1.55133 | 1.61909 | 1.68948 | 1.83846 | 1.99900 | 2.17189 | 2.35795 | 2.55804 | 2.77308 | 5.15978 |
| 10 | 1.10462 | 1.16054 | 1.21899 | 1.28008 | 1.34392 | 1.41060 | 1.48024 | 1.55297 | 1.62889 | 1.70814 | 1.79085 | 1.96715 | 2.15892 | 2.36736 | 2.59374 | 2.83942 | 3.10585 | 6.19174 |
| 11 | 1.11567 | 1.17795 | 1.24337 | 1.31209 | 1.38423 | 1.45997 | 1.53945 | 1.62285 | 1.71034 | 1.80209 | 1.89830 | 2.10485 | 2.33164 | 2.58043 | 2.85312 | 3.15176 | 3.47855 | 7.43008 |
| 12 | 1.12683 | 1.19562 | 1.26824 | 1.34489 | 1.42576 | 1.51107 | 1.60103 | 1.69588 | 1.79586 | 1.90121 | 2.01220 | 2.25219 | 2.51817 | 2.81266 | 3.13843 | 3.49845 | 3.89598 | 8.91610 |
| 13 | 1.13809 | 1.21355 | 1.29361 | 1.37851 | 1.46853 | 1.56396 | 1.66507 | 1.77220 | 1.88565 | 2.00577 | 2.13293 | 2.40985 | 2.71962 | 3.06580 | 3.45227 | 3.88328 | 4.36349 | 10.69932 |
| 14 | 1.14947 | 1.23176 | 1.31948 | 1.41297 | 1.51259 | 1.61869 | 1.73168 | 1.85194 | 1.97993 | 2.11609 | 2.26090 | 2.57853 | 2.93719 | 3.34173 | 3.79750 | 4.31044 | 4.88711 | 12.83918 |
| 15 | 1.16097 | 1.25023 | 1.34587 | 1.44830 | 1.55797 | 1.67535 | 1.80094 | 1.93528 | 2.07893 | 2.23248 | 2.39656 | 2.75903 | 3.17217 | 3.64248 | 4.17725 | 4.78459 | 5.47357 | 15.40702 |
| 16 | 1.17258 | 1.26899 | 1.37279 | 1.48451 | 1.60471 | 1.73399 | 1.87298 | 2.02237 | 2.18287 | 2.35526 | 2.54035 | 2.95216 | 3.42594 | 3.97031 | 4.59497 | 5.31089 | 6.13039 | 18.48843 |
| 17 | 1.18430 | 1.28802 | 1.40024 | 1.52162 | 1.65285 | 1.79468 | 1.94790 | 2.11338 | 2.29202 | 2.48480 | 2.69277 | 3.15882 | 3.70002 | 4.32763 | 5.05447 | 5.89509 | 6.86604 | 22.18611 |
| 18 | 1.19615 | 1.30734 | 1.42825 | 1.55966 | 1.70243 | 1.85749 | 2.02582 | 2.20848 | 2.40662 | 2.62147 | 2.85434 | 3.37993 | 3.99602 | 4.71712 | 5.55992 | 6.54355 | 7.68997 | 26.62333 |
| 19 | 1.20811 | 1.32695 | 1.45681 | 1.59865 | 1.75351 | 1.92250 | 2.10685 | 2.30786 | 2.52695 | 2.76565 | 3.02560 | 3.61653 | 4.31570 | 5.14166 | 6.11591 | 7.26334 | 8.61276 | 31.94800 |
| 20 | 1.22019 | 1.34686 | 1.48595 | 1.63862 | 1.80611 | 1.98979 | 2.19112 | 2.41171 | 2.65330 | 2.91776 | 3.20714 | 3.86968 | 4.66096 | 5.60441 | 6.72750 | 8.06231 | 9.64629 | 38.33760 |
| 21 | 1.23239 | 1.36706 | 1.51567 | 1.67958 | 1.86029 | 2.05943 | 2.27877 | 2.52024 | 2.78596 | 3.07823 | 3.39956 | 4.14056 | 5.03383 | 6.10881 | 7.40025 | 8.94917 | 10.80385 | 46.00512 |
| 25 | 1.28243 | 1.45095 | 1.64061 | 1.85394 | 2.09378 | 2.36324 | 2.66584 | 3.00543 | 3.38635 | 3.81339 | 4.29187 | 5.42743 | 6.84848 | 8.62308 | 10.83471 | 13.58546 | 17.00006 | 95.39622 |
| 30 | 1.34785 | 1.56308 | 1.81136 | 2.09757 | 2.42726 | 2.80679 | 3.24340 | 3.74532 | 4.32194 | 4.98395 | 5.74349 | 7.61226 | 10.06266 | 13.26768 | 17.44940 | 22.89230 | 29.95992 | 237.37631 |
| 40 | 1.48886 | 1.81402 | 2.20804 | 2.68506 | 3.26204 | 3.95926 | 4.80102 | 5.81636 | 7.03999 | 8.51331 | 10.28572 | 14.97446 | 21.72452 | 31.40942 | 45.25926 | 65.00087 | 93.05097 | 1469.77160 |

This table shows the present value of $1 at various interest rates (*i*) and time periods (*n*). It is used to calculate the present value of any single amount.

**TABLE 2** Present Value of $1

$$PV = \frac{\$1}{(1+i)^n}$$

| n/i | 1.0% | 1.5% | 2.0% | 2.5% | 3.0% | 3.5% | 4.0% | 4.5% | 5.0% | 5.5% | 6.0% | 7.0% | 8.0% | 9.0% | 10.0% | 11.0% | 12.0% | 20.0% |
|---|---|---|---|---|---|---|---|---|---|---|---|---|---|---|---|---|---|---|
| 1 | 0.99010 | 0.98522 | 0.98039 | 0.97561 | 0.97087 | 0.96618 | 0.96154 | 0.95694 | 0.95238 | 0.94787 | 0.94340 | 0.93458 | 0.92593 | 0.91743 | 0.90909 | 0.90090 | 0.89286 | 0.83333 |
| 2 | 0.98030 | 0.97066 | 0.96117 | 0.95181 | 0.94260 | 0.93351 | 0.92456 | 0.91573 | 0.90703 | 0.89845 | 0.89000 | 0.87344 | 0.85734 | 0.84168 | 0.82645 | 0.81162 | 0.79719 | 0.69444 |
| 3 | 0.97059 | 0.95632 | 0.94232 | 0.92860 | 0.91514 | 0.90194 | 0.88900 | 0.87630 | 0.86384 | 0.85161 | 0.83962 | 0.81630 | 0.79383 | 0.77218 | 0.75131 | 0.73119 | 0.71178 | 0.57870 |
| 4 | 0.96098 | 0.94218 | 0.92385 | 0.90595 | 0.88849 | 0.87144 | 0.85480 | 0.83856 | 0.82270 | 0.80722 | 0.79209 | 0.76290 | 0.73503 | 0.70843 | 0.68301 | 0.65873 | 0.63552 | 0.48225 |
| 5 | 0.95147 | 0.92826 | 0.90573 | 0.88385 | 0.86261 | 0.84197 | 0.82193 | 0.80245 | 0.78353 | 0.76513 | 0.74726 | 0.71299 | 0.68058 | 0.64993 | 0.62092 | 0.59345 | 0.56743 | 0.40188 |
| 6 | 0.94205 | 0.91454 | 0.88797 | 0.86230 | 0.83748 | 0.81350 | 0.79031 | 0.76790 | 0.74622 | 0.72525 | 0.70496 | 0.66634 | 0.63017 | 0.59627 | 0.56447 | 0.53464 | 0.50663 | 0.33490 |
| 7 | 0.93272 | 0.90103 | 0.87056 | 0.84127 | 0.81309 | 0.78599 | 0.75992 | 0.73483 | 0.71068 | 0.68744 | 0.66506 | 0.62275 | 0.58349 | 0.54703 | 0.51316 | 0.48166 | 0.45235 | 0.27908 |
| 8 | 0.92348 | 0.88771 | 0.85349 | 0.82075 | 0.78941 | 0.75941 | 0.73069 | 0.70319 | 0.67684 | 0.65160 | 0.62741 | 0.58201 | 0.54027 | 0.50187 | 0.46651 | 0.43393 | 0.40388 | 0.23257 |
| 9 | 0.91434 | 0.87459 | 0.83676 | 0.80073 | 0.76642 | 0.73373 | 0.70259 | 0.67290 | 0.64461 | 0.61763 | 0.59190 | 0.54393 | 0.50025 | 0.46043 | 0.42410 | 0.39092 | 0.36061 | 0.19381 |
| 10 | 0.90529 | 0.86167 | 0.82035 | 0.78120 | 0.74409 | 0.70892 | 0.67556 | 0.64393 | 0.61391 | 0.58543 | 0.55839 | 0.50835 | 0.46319 | 0.42241 | 0.38554 | 0.35218 | 0.32197 | 0.16151 |
| 11 | 0.89632 | 0.84893 | 0.80426 | 0.76214 | 0.72242 | 0.68495 | 0.64958 | 0.61620 | 0.58468 | 0.55491 | 0.52679 | 0.47509 | 0.42888 | 0.38753 | 0.35049 | 0.31728 | 0.28748 | 0.13459 |
| 12 | 0.88745 | 0.83639 | 0.78849 | 0.74356 | 0.70138 | 0.66178 | 0.62440 | 0.58966 | 0.55684 | 0.52598 | 0.49697 | 0.44401 | 0.39711 | 0.35553 | 0.31863 | 0.28584 | 0.25668 | 0.11216 |
| 13 | 0.87866 | 0.82403 | 0.77303 | 0.72542 | 0.68095 | 0.63940 | 0.60057 | 0.56427 | 0.53032 | 0.49856 | 0.46884 | 0.41496 | 0.36770 | 0.32618 | 0.28966 | 0.25751 | 0.22917 | 0.09346 |
| 14 | 0.86996 | 0.81185 | 0.75788 | 0.70773 | 0.66112 | 0.61778 | 0.57748 | 0.53997 | 0.50507 | 0.47257 | 0.44230 | 0.38782 | 0.34046 | 0.29925 | 0.26333 | 0.23199 | 0.20462 | 0.07789 |
| 15 | 0.86135 | 0.79985 | 0.74301 | 0.69047 | 0.64186 | 0.59689 | 0.55526 | 0.51672 | 0.48102 | 0.44793 | 0.41727 | 0.36245 | 0.31524 | 0.27454 | 0.23939 | 0.20900 | 0.18270 | 0.06491 |
| 16 | 0.85282 | 0.78803 | 0.72845 | 0.67362 | 0.62317 | 0.57671 | 0.53391 | 0.49447 | 0.45811 | 0.42458 | 0.39365 | 0.33873 | 0.29189 | 0.25187 | 0.21763 | 0.18829 | 0.16312 | 0.05409 |
| 17 | 0.84438 | 0.77639 | 0.71416 | 0.65720 | 0.60502 | 0.55720 | 0.51337 | 0.47318 | 0.43630 | 0.40245 | 0.37136 | 0.31657 | 0.27027 | 0.23107 | 0.19784 | 0.16963 | 0.14564 | 0.04507 |
| 18 | 0.83602 | 0.76491 | 0.70016 | 0.64117 | 0.58739 | 0.53836 | 0.49363 | 0.45280 | 0.41552 | 0.38147 | 0.35034 | 0.29586 | 0.25025 | 0.21199 | 0.17986 | 0.15282 | 0.13004 | 0.03756 |
| 19 | 0.82774 | 0.75361 | 0.68643 | 0.62553 | 0.57029 | 0.52016 | 0.47464 | 0.43330 | 0.39573 | 0.36158 | 0.33051 | 0.27651 | 0.23171 | 0.19449 | 0.16351 | 0.13768 | 0.11611 | 0.03130 |
| 20 | 0.81954 | 0.74247 | 0.67297 | 0.61027 | 0.55368 | 0.50257 | 0.45639 | 0.41464 | 0.37689 | 0.34273 | 0.31180 | 0.25842 | 0.21455 | 0.17843 | 0.14864 | 0.12403 | 0.10367 | 0.02608 |
| 21 | 0.81143 | 0.73150 | 0.65978 | 0.59539 | 0.53755 | 0.48557 | 0.43883 | 0.39679 | 0.35894 | 0.32486 | 0.29416 | 0.24151 | 0.19866 | 0.16370 | 0.13513 | 0.11174 | 0.09256 | 0.02174 |
| 24 | 0.78757 | 0.69954 | 0.62172 | 0.55288 | 0.49193 | 0.43796 | 0.39012 | 0.34770 | 0.31007 | 0.27666 | 0.24698 | 0.19715 | 0.15770 | 0.12640 | 0.10153 | 0.08170 | 0.06588 | 0.01258 |
| 25 | 0.77977 | 0.68921 | 0.60953 | 0.53939 | 0.47761 | 0.42315 | 0.37512 | 0.33273 | 0.29530 | 0.26223 | 0.23300 | 0.18425 | 0.14602 | 0.11597 | 0.09230 | 0.07361 | 0.05882 | 0.01048 |
| 28 | 0.75684 | 0.65910 | 0.57437 | 0.50088 | 0.43708 | 0.38165 | 0.33348 | 0.29157 | 0.25509 | 0.22332 | 0.19563 | 0.15040 | 0.11591 | 0.08955 | 0.06934 | 0.05382 | 0.04187 | 0.00607 |
| 29 | 0.74934 | 0.64936 | 0.56311 | 0.48866 | 0.42435 | 0.36875 | 0.32065 | 0.27902 | 0.24295 | 0.21168 | 0.18456 | 0.14056 | 0.10733 | 0.08215 | 0.06304 | 0.04849 | 0.03738 | 0.00506 |
| 30 | 0.74192 | 0.63976 | 0.55207 | 0.47674 | 0.41199 | 0.35628 | 0.30832 | 0.26700 | 0.23138 | 0.20064 | 0.17411 | 0.13137 | 0.09938 | 0.07537 | 0.05731 | 0.04368 | 0.03338 | 0.00421 |
| 31 | 0.73458 | 0.63031 | 0.54125 | 0.46511 | 0.39999 | 0.34423 | 0.29646 | 0.25550 | 0.22036 | 0.19018 | 0.16425 | 0.12277 | 0.09202 | 0.06915 | 0.05210 | 0.03935 | 0.02980 | 0.00351 |
| 40 | 0.67165 | 0.55126 | 0.45289 | 0.37243 | 0.30656 | 0.25257 | 0.20829 | 0.17193 | 0.14205 | 0.11746 | 0.09722 | 0.06678 | 0.04603 | 0.03184 | 0.02209 | 0.01538 | 0.01075 | 0.00068 |

This table shows the future value of an ordinary annuity of $1 at various interest rates ($i$) and time periods ($n$). It is used to calculate the future value of any series of equal payments made at the *end* of each compounding period.

**TABLE 3**  Future Value of an Ordinary Annuity of $1

$$FVA = \frac{(1+i)^n - 1}{i}$$

| n/i | 1.0% | 1.5% | 2.0% | 2.5% | 3.0% | 3.5% | 4.0% | 4.5% | 5.0% | 5.5% | 6.0% | 7.0% | 8.0% | 9.0% | 10.0% | 11.0% | 12.0% | 20.0% |
|---|---|---|---|---|---|---|---|---|---|---|---|---|---|---|---|---|---|---|
| 1 | 1.0000 | 1.0000 | 1.0000 | 1.0000 | 1.0000 | 1.0000 | 1.0000 | 1.0000 | 1.0000 | 1.0000 | 1.0000 | 1.0000 | 1.0000 | 1.0000 | 1.0000 | 1.0000 | 1.0000 | 1.0000 |
| 2 | 2.0100 | 2.0150 | 2.0200 | 2.0250 | 2.0300 | 2.0350 | 2.0400 | 2.0450 | 2.0500 | 2.0550 | 2.0600 | 2.0700 | 2.0800 | 2.0900 | 2.1000 | 2.1100 | 2.1200 | 2.2000 |
| 3 | 3.0301 | 3.0452 | 3.0604 | 3.0756 | 3.0909 | 3.1062 | 3.1216 | 3.1370 | 3.1525 | 3.1680 | 3.1836 | 3.2149 | 3.2464 | 3.2781 | 3.3100 | 3.3421 | 3.3744 | 3.6400 |
| 4 | 4.0604 | 4.0909 | 4.1216 | 4.1525 | 4.1836 | 4.2149 | 4.2465 | 4.2782 | 4.3101 | 4.3423 | 4.3746 | 4.4399 | 4.5061 | 4.5731 | 4.6410 | 4.7097 | 4.7793 | 5.3680 |
| 5 | 5.1010 | 5.1523 | 5.2040 | 5.2563 | 5.3091 | 5.3625 | 5.4163 | 5.4707 | 5.5256 | 5.5811 | 5.6371 | 5.7507 | 5.8666 | 5.9847 | 6.1051 | 6.2278 | 6.3528 | 7.4416 |
| 6 | 6.1520 | 6.2296 | 6.3081 | 6.3877 | 6.4684 | 6.5502 | 6.6330 | 6.7169 | 6.8019 | 6.8881 | 6.9753 | 7.1533 | 7.3359 | 7.5233 | 7.7156 | 7.9129 | 8.1152 | 9.9299 |
| 7 | 7.2135 | 7.3230 | 7.4343 | 7.5474 | 7.6625 | 7.7794 | 7.8983 | 8.0192 | 8.1420 | 8.2669 | 8.3938 | 8.6540 | 8.9228 | 9.2004 | 9.4872 | 9.7833 | 10.0890 | 12.9159 |
| 8 | 8.2857 | 8.4328 | 8.5830 | 8.7361 | 8.8923 | 9.0517 | 9.2142 | 9.3800 | 9.5491 | 9.7216 | 9.8975 | 10.2598 | 10.6366 | 11.0285 | 11.4359 | 11.8594 | 12.2997 | 16.4991 |
| 9 | 9.3685 | 9.5593 | 9.7546 | 9.9545 | 10.1591 | 10.3685 | 10.5828 | 10.8021 | 11.0266 | 11.2563 | 11.4913 | 11.9780 | 12.4876 | 13.0210 | 13.5795 | 14.1640 | 14.7757 | 20.7989 |
| 10 | 10.4622 | 10.7027 | 10.9497 | 11.2034 | 11.4639 | 11.7314 | 12.0061 | 12.2882 | 12.5779 | 12.8754 | 13.1808 | 13.8164 | 14.4866 | 15.1929 | 15.9374 | 16.7220 | 17.5487 | 25.9587 |
| 11 | 11.5668 | 11.8633 | 12.1687 | 12.4835 | 12.8078 | 13.1420 | 13.4864 | 13.8412 | 14.2068 | 14.5835 | 14.9716 | 15.7836 | 16.6455 | 17.5603 | 18.5312 | 19.5614 | 20.6546 | 32.1504 |
| 12 | 12.6825 | 13.0412 | 13.4121 | 13.7956 | 14.1920 | 14.6020 | 15.0258 | 15.4640 | 15.9171 | 16.3856 | 16.8699 | 17.8885 | 18.9771 | 20.1407 | 21.3843 | 22.7132 | 24.1331 | 39.5805 |
| 13 | 13.8093 | 14.2368 | 14.6803 | 15.1404 | 15.6178 | 16.1130 | 16.6268 | 17.1599 | 17.7130 | 18.2868 | 18.8821 | 20.1406 | 21.4953 | 22.9534 | 24.5227 | 26.2116 | 28.0291 | 48.4966 |
| 14 | 14.9474 | 15.4504 | 15.9739 | 16.5190 | 17.0863 | 17.6770 | 18.2919 | 18.9321 | 19.5986 | 20.2926 | 21.0151 | 22.5505 | 24.2149 | 26.0192 | 27.9750 | 30.0949 | 32.3926 | 59.1959 |
| 15 | 16.0969 | 16.6821 | 17.2934 | 17.9319 | 18.5989 | 19.2957 | 20.0236 | 20.7841 | 21.5786 | 22.4087 | 23.2760 | 25.1290 | 27.1521 | 29.3609 | 31.7725 | 34.4054 | 37.2797 | 72.0351 |
| 16 | 17.2579 | 17.9324 | 18.6393 | 19.3802 | 20.1569 | 20.9710 | 21.8245 | 22.7193 | 23.6575 | 24.6411 | 25.6725 | 27.8881 | 30.3243 | 33.0034 | 35.9497 | 39.1899 | 42.7533 | 87.4421 |
| 17 | 18.4304 | 19.2014 | 20.0121 | 20.8647 | 21.7616 | 22.7050 | 23.6975 | 24.7417 | 25.8404 | 26.9964 | 28.2129 | 30.8402 | 33.7502 | 36.9737 | 40.5447 | 44.5008 | 48.8837 | 105.9306 |
| 18 | 19.6147 | 20.4894 | 21.4123 | 22.3863 | 23.4144 | 24.4997 | 25.6454 | 26.8551 | 28.1324 | 29.4812 | 30.9057 | 33.9990 | 37.4502 | 41.3013 | 45.5992 | 50.3959 | 55.7497 | 128.1167 |
| 19 | 20.8109 | 21.7967 | 22.8406 | 23.9460 | 25.1169 | 26.3572 | 27.6712 | 29.0636 | 30.5390 | 32.1027 | 33.7600 | 37.3790 | 41.4463 | 46.0185 | 51.1591 | 56.9395 | 63.4397 | 154.7400 |
| 20 | 22.0190 | 23.1237 | 24.2974 | 25.5447 | 26.8704 | 28.2797 | 29.7781 | 31.3714 | 33.0660 | 34.8683 | 36.7856 | 40.9955 | 45.7620 | 51.1601 | 57.2750 | 64.2028 | 72.0524 | 186.6880 |
| 21 | 23.2392 | 24.4705 | 25.7833 | 27.1833 | 28.6765 | 30.2695 | 31.9692 | 33.7831 | 35.7193 | 37.7861 | 39.9927 | 44.8652 | 50.4229 | 56.7645 | 64.0025 | 72.2651 | 81.6987 | 225.0256 |
| 30 | 34.7849 | 37.5387 | 40.5681 | 43.9027 | 47.5754 | 51.6227 | 56.0849 | 61.0071 | 66.4388 | 72.4355 | 79.0582 | 94.4608 | 113.2832 | 136.3075 | 164.4940 | 199.0209 | 241.3327 | 1181.8816 |
| 40 | 48.8864 | 54.2679 | 60.4020 | 67.4026 | 75.4013 | 84.5503 | 95.0255 | 107.0303 | 120.7998 | 136.6056 | 154.7620 | 199.6351 | 259.0565 | 337.8824 | 442.5926 | 581.8261 | 767.0914 | 7343.8578 |

This table shows the present value of an ordinary annuity of $1 at various interest rates (*i*) and time periods (*n*). It is used to calculate the present value of any series of equal payments made at the *end* of each compounding period.

**TABLE 4**  Present Value of an Ordinary Annuity of $1

$$PVA = \frac{1 - \frac{1}{(1+i)^n}}{i}$$

| n/i | 1.0% | 1.5% | 2.0% | 2.5% | 3.0% | 3.5% | 4.0% | 4.5% | 5.0% | 5.5% | 6.0% | 7.0% | 8.0% | 9.0% | 10.0% | 11.0% | 12.0% | 20.0% |
|---|---|---|---|---|---|---|---|---|---|---|---|---|---|---|---|---|---|---|
| 1 | 0.99010 | 0.98522 | 0.98039 | 0.97561 | 0.97087 | 0.96618 | 0.96154 | 0.95694 | 0.95238 | 0.94787 | 0.94340 | 0.93458 | 0.92593 | 0.91743 | 0.90909 | 0.90090 | 0.89286 | 0.83333 |
| 2 | 1.97040 | 1.95588 | 1.94156 | 1.92742 | 1.91347 | 1.89969 | 1.88609 | 1.87267 | 1.85941 | 1.84632 | 1.83339 | 1.80802 | 1.78326 | 1.75911 | 1.73554 | 1.71252 | 1.69005 | 1.52778 |
| 3 | 2.94099 | 2.91220 | 2.88388 | 2.85602 | 2.82861 | 2.80164 | 2.77509 | 2.74896 | 2.72325 | 2.69793 | 2.67301 | 2.62432 | 2.57710 | 2.53129 | 2.48685 | 2.44371 | 2.40183 | 2.10648 |
| 4 | 3.90197 | 3.85438 | 3.80773 | 3.76197 | 3.71710 | 3.67308 | 3.62990 | 3.58753 | 3.54595 | 3.50515 | 3.46511 | 3.38721 | 3.31213 | 3.23972 | 3.16987 | 3.10245 | 3.03735 | 2.58873 |
| 5 | 4.85343 | 4.78264 | 4.71346 | 4.64583 | 4.57971 | 4.51505 | 4.45182 | 4.38998 | 4.32948 | 4.27028 | 4.21236 | 4.10020 | 3.99271 | 3.88965 | 3.79079 | 3.69590 | 3.60478 | 2.99061 |
| 6 | 5.79548 | 5.69719 | 5.60143 | 5.50813 | 5.41719 | 5.32855 | 5.24214 | 5.15787 | 5.07569 | 4.99553 | 4.91732 | 4.76654 | 4.62288 | 4.48592 | 4.35526 | 4.23054 | 4.11141 | 3.32551 |
| 7 | 6.72819 | 6.59821 | 6.47199 | 6.34939 | 6.23028 | 6.11454 | 6.00205 | 5.89270 | 5.78637 | 5.68297 | 5.58238 | 5.38929 | 5.20637 | 5.03295 | 4.86842 | 4.71220 | 4.56376 | 3.60459 |
| 8 | 7.65168 | 7.48593 | 7.32548 | 7.17014 | 7.01969 | 6.87396 | 6.73274 | 6.59589 | 6.46321 | 6.33457 | 6.20979 | 5.97130 | 5.74664 | 5.53482 | 5.33493 | 5.14612 | 4.96764 | 3.83716 |
| 9 | 8.56602 | 8.36052 | 8.16224 | 7.97087 | 7.78611 | 7.60769 | 7.43533 | 7.26879 | 7.10782 | 6.95220 | 6.80169 | 6.51523 | 6.24689 | 5.99525 | 5.75902 | 5.53705 | 5.32825 | 4.03097 |
| 10 | 9.47130 | 9.22218 | 8.98259 | 8.75206 | 8.53020 | 8.31661 | 8.11090 | 7.91272 | 7.72173 | 7.53763 | 7.36009 | 7.02358 | 6.71008 | 6.41766 | 6.14457 | 5.88923 | 5.65022 | 4.19247 |
| 11 | 10.36763 | 10.07112 | 9.78685 | 9.51421 | 9.25262 | 9.00155 | 8.76048 | 8.52892 | 8.30641 | 8.09254 | 7.88687 | 7.49867 | 7.13896 | 6.80519 | 6.49506 | 6.20652 | 5.93770 | 4.32706 |
| 12 | 11.25508 | 10.90751 | 10.57534 | 10.25776 | 9.95400 | 9.66333 | 9.38507 | 9.11858 | 8.86325 | 8.61852 | 8.38384 | 7.94269 | 7.53608 | 7.16073 | 6.81369 | 6.49236 | 6.19437 | 4.43922 |
| 13 | 12.13374 | 11.73153 | 11.34837 | 10.98319 | 10.63496 | 10.30274 | 9.98565 | 9.68285 | 9.39357 | 9.11708 | 8.85268 | 8.35765 | 7.90378 | 7.48690 | 7.10336 | 6.74987 | 6.42355 | 4.53268 |
| 14 | 13.00370 | 12.54338 | 12.10625 | 11.69091 | 11.29607 | 10.92052 | 10.56312 | 10.22283 | 9.89864 | 9.58965 | 9.29498 | 8.74547 | 8.24424 | 7.78615 | 7.36669 | 6.98187 | 6.62817 | 4.61057 |
| 15 | 13.86505 | 13.34323 | 12.84926 | 12.38138 | 11.93794 | 11.51741 | 11.11839 | 10.73955 | 10.37966 | 10.03758 | 9.71225 | 9.10791 | 8.55948 | 8.06069 | 7.60608 | 7.19087 | 6.81086 | 4.67547 |
| 16 | 14.71787 | 14.13126 | 13.57771 | 13.05500 | 12.56110 | 12.09412 | 11.65230 | 11.23402 | 10.83777 | 10.46216 | 10.10590 | 9.44665 | 8.85137 | 8.31256 | 7.82371 | 7.37916 | 6.97399 | 4.72956 |
| 17 | 15.56225 | 14.90765 | 14.29187 | 13.71220 | 13.16612 | 12.65132 | 12.16567 | 11.70719 | 11.27407 | 10.86461 | 10.47726 | 9.76322 | 9.12164 | 8.54363 | 8.02155 | 7.54879 | 7.11963 | 4.77463 |
| 18 | 16.39827 | 15.67256 | 14.99203 | 14.35336 | 13.75351 | 13.18968 | 12.65930 | 12.15999 | 11.68959 | 11.24607 | 10.82760 | 10.05909 | 9.37189 | 8.75563 | 8.20141 | 7.70162 | 7.24967 | 4.81219 |
| 19 | 17.22601 | 16.42617 | 15.67846 | 14.97889 | 14.32380 | 13.70984 | 13.13394 | 12.59329 | 12.08532 | 11.60765 | 11.15812 | 10.33560 | 9.60360 | 8.95011 | 8.36492 | 7.83929 | 7.36578 | 4.84350 |
| 20 | 18.04555 | 17.16864 | 16.35143 | 15.58916 | 14.87747 | 14.21240 | 13.59033 | 13.00794 | 12.46221 | 11.95038 | 11.46992 | 10.59401 | 9.81815 | 9.12855 | 8.51356 | 7.96333 | 7.46944 | 4.86958 |
| 21 | 18.85698 | 17.90014 | 17.01121 | 16.18455 | 15.41502 | 14.69797 | 14.02916 | 13.40472 | 12.82115 | 12.27524 | 11.76408 | 10.83553 | 10.01680 | 9.29224 | 8.64869 | 8.07507 | 7.56200 | 4.89132 |
| 25 | 22.02316 | 20.71961 | 19.52346 | 18.42438 | 17.41315 | 16.48151 | 15.62208 | 14.82821 | 14.09394 | 13.41393 | 12.78336 | 11.65358 | 10.67478 | 9.82258 | 9.07704 | 8.42174 | 7.84314 | 4.94759 |
| 30 | 25.80771 | 24.01584 | 22.39646 | 20.93029 | 19.60044 | 18.39205 | 17.29203 | 16.28889 | 15.37245 | 14.53375 | 13.76483 | 12.40904 | 11.25778 | 10.27365 | 9.42691 | 8.69379 | 8.05518 | 4.97894 |
| 40 | 32.83469 | 29.91585 | 27.35548 | 25.10278 | 23.11477 | 21.35507 | 19.79277 | 18.40158 | 17.15909 | 16.04612 | 15.04630 | 13.33171 | 11.92461 | 10.75736 | 9.77905 | 8.95105 | 8.24378 | 4.99660 |

This table shows the future value of an annuity due of $1 at various interest rates ($i$) and time periods ($n$). It is used to calculate the future value of any series of equal payments made at the *beginning* of each compounding period.

**TABLE 5** Future Value of an Annuity Due of $1

$$FVAD = \left[\frac{(1+i)^n - 1}{i}\right] \times (1+i)$$

| n/i | 1.0% | 1.5% | 2.0% | 2.5% | 3.0% | 3.5% | 4.0% | 4.5% | 5.0% | 5.5% | 6.0% | 7.0% | 8.0% | 9.0% | 10.0% | 11.0% | 12.0% | 20.0% |
|---|---|---|---|---|---|---|---|---|---|---|---|---|---|---|---|---|---|---|
| 1 | 1.0100 | 1.0150 | 1.0200 | 1.0250 | 1.0300 | 1.0350 | 1.0400 | 1.0450 | 1.0500 | 1.0550 | 1.0600 | 1.0700 | 1.0800 | 1.0900 | 1.1000 | 1.1100 | 1.1200 | 1.2000 |
| 2 | 2.0301 | 2.0452 | 2.0604 | 2.0756 | 2.0909 | 2.1062 | 2.1216 | 2.1370 | 2.1525 | 2.1680 | 2.1836 | 2.2149 | 2.2464 | 2.2781 | 2.3100 | 2.3421 | 2.3744 | 2.6400 |
| 3 | 3.0604 | 3.0909 | 3.1216 | 3.1525 | 3.1836 | 3.2149 | 3.2465 | 3.2782 | 3.3101 | 3.3423 | 3.3746 | 3.4399 | 3.5061 | 3.5731 | 3.6410 | 3.7097 | 3.7793 | 4.3680 |
| 4 | 4.1010 | 4.1523 | 4.2040 | 4.2563 | 4.3091 | 4.3625 | 4.4163 | 4.4707 | 4.5256 | 4.5811 | 4.6371 | 4.7507 | 4.8666 | 4.9847 | 5.1051 | 5.2278 | 5.3528 | 6.4416 |
| 5 | 5.1520 | 5.2296 | 5.3081 | 5.3877 | 5.4684 | 5.5502 | 5.6330 | 5.7169 | 5.8019 | 5.8881 | 5.9753 | 6.1533 | 6.3359 | 6.5233 | 6.7156 | 6.9129 | 7.1152 | 8.9299 |
| 6 | 6.2135 | 6.3230 | 6.4343 | 6.5474 | 6.6625 | 6.7794 | 6.8983 | 7.0192 | 7.1420 | 7.2669 | 7.3938 | 7.6540 | 7.9228 | 8.2004 | 8.4872 | 8.7833 | 9.0890 | 11.9159 |
| 7 | 7.2857 | 7.4328 | 7.5830 | 7.7361 | 7.8923 | 8.0517 | 8.2142 | 8.3800 | 8.5491 | 8.7216 | 8.8975 | 9.2598 | 9.6366 | 10.0285 | 10.4359 | 10.8594 | 11.2997 | 15.4991 |
| 8 | 8.3685 | 8.5593 | 8.7546 | 8.9545 | 9.1591 | 9.3685 | 9.5828 | 9.8021 | 10.0266 | 10.2563 | 10.4913 | 10.9780 | 11.4876 | 12.0210 | 12.5795 | 13.1640 | 13.7757 | 19.7989 |
| 9 | 9.4622 | 9.7027 | 9.9497 | 10.2034 | 10.4639 | 10.7314 | 11.0061 | 11.2882 | 11.5779 | 11.8754 | 12.1808 | 12.8164 | 13.4866 | 14.1929 | 14.9374 | 15.7220 | 16.5487 | 24.9587 |
| 10 | 10.5668 | 10.8633 | 11.1687 | 11.4835 | 11.8078 | 12.1420 | 12.4864 | 12.8412 | 13.2068 | 13.5835 | 13.9716 | 14.7836 | 15.6455 | 16.5603 | 17.5312 | 18.5614 | 19.6546 | 31.1504 |
| 11 | 11.6825 | 12.0412 | 12.4121 | 12.7956 | 13.1920 | 13.6020 | 14.0258 | 14.4640 | 14.9171 | 15.3856 | 15.8699 | 16.8885 | 17.9771 | 19.1407 | 20.3843 | 21.7132 | 23.1331 | 38.5805 |
| 12 | 12.8093 | 13.2368 | 13.6803 | 14.1404 | 14.6178 | 15.1130 | 15.6268 | 16.1599 | 16.7130 | 17.2868 | 17.8821 | 19.1406 | 20.4953 | 21.9534 | 23.5227 | 25.2116 | 27.0291 | 47.4966 |
| 13 | 13.9474 | 14.4504 | 14.9739 | 15.5190 | 16.0863 | 16.6770 | 17.2919 | 17.9321 | 18.5986 | 19.2926 | 20.0151 | 21.5505 | 23.2149 | 25.0192 | 26.9750 | 29.0949 | 31.3926 | 58.1959 |
| 14 | 15.0969 | 15.6821 | 16.2934 | 16.9319 | 17.5989 | 18.2957 | 19.0236 | 19.7841 | 20.5786 | 21.4087 | 22.2760 | 24.1290 | 26.1521 | 28.3609 | 30.7725 | 33.4054 | 36.2797 | 71.0351 |
| 15 | 16.2579 | 16.9324 | 17.6393 | 18.3802 | 19.1569 | 19.9710 | 20.8245 | 21.7193 | 22.6575 | 23.6411 | 24.6725 | 26.8881 | 29.3243 | 32.0034 | 34.9497 | 38.1899 | 41.7533 | 86.4421 |
| 16 | 17.4304 | 18.2014 | 19.0121 | 19.8647 | 20.7616 | 21.7050 | 22.6975 | 23.7417 | 24.8404 | 25.9964 | 27.2129 | 29.8402 | 32.7502 | 35.9737 | 39.5447 | 43.5008 | 47.8837 | 104.9306 |
| 17 | 18.6147 | 19.4894 | 20.4123 | 21.3863 | 22.4144 | 23.4997 | 24.6454 | 25.8551 | 27.1324 | 28.4812 | 29.9057 | 32.9990 | 36.4502 | 40.3013 | 44.5992 | 49.3959 | 54.7497 | 127.1167 |
| 18 | 19.8109 | 20.7967 | 21.8406 | 22.9460 | 24.1169 | 25.3572 | 26.6712 | 28.0636 | 29.5390 | 31.1027 | 32.7600 | 36.3790 | 40.4463 | 45.0185 | 50.1591 | 55.9395 | 62.4397 | 153.7400 |
| 19 | 21.0190 | 22.1237 | 23.2974 | 24.5447 | 25.8704 | 27.2797 | 28.7781 | 30.3714 | 32.0660 | 33.8683 | 35.7856 | 39.9955 | 44.7620 | 50.1601 | 56.2750 | 63.2028 | 71.0524 | 185.6880 |
| 20 | 22.2392 | 23.4705 | 24.7833 | 26.1833 | 27.6765 | 29.2695 | 30.9692 | 32.7831 | 34.7193 | 36.7861 | 38.9927 | 43.8652 | 49.4229 | 55.7645 | 63.0025 | 71.2651 | 80.6987 | 224.0256 |
| 21 | 23.4716 | 24.8376 | 26.2990 | 27.8629 | 29.5368 | 31.3289 | 33.2480 | 35.3034 | 37.5052 | 39.8643 | 42.3923 | 48.0057 | 54.4568 | 61.8733 | 70.4027 | 80.2143 | 91.5026 | 270.0307 |
| 25 | 28.5256 | 30.5140 | 32.6709 | 35.0117 | 37.5530 | 40.3131 | 43.3117 | 46.5706 | 50.1135 | 53.9660 | 58.1564 | 67.6765 | 78.9544 | 92.3240 | 108.1818 | 126.9988 | 149.3339 | 566.3773 |
| 30 | 35.1327 | 38.1018 | 41.3794 | 45.0003 | 49.0027 | 53.4295 | 58.3283 | 63.7524 | 69.7608 | 76.4194 | 83.8017 | 101.0730 | 122.3459 | 148.5752 | 180.9434 | 220.9132 | 270.2926 | 1418.2579 |
| 40 | 49.3752 | 55.0819 | 61.6100 | 69.0876 | 77.6633 | 87.5095 | 98.8265 | 111.8467 | 126.8398 | 144.1189 | 164.0477 | 213.6096 | 279.7810 | 368.2919 | 486.8518 | 645.8269 | 859.1424 | 8812.6294 |

This table shows the present value of an annuity due of $1 at various interest rates (*i*) and time periods (*n*). It is used to calculate the present value of any series of equal payments made at the *beginning* of each compounding period.

**TABLE 6** Present Value of an Annuity Due of $1

$$PVAD = \left[\frac{1 - \frac{1}{(1+i)^n}}{i}\right] \times (1 + i)$$

| n/i | 1.0% | 1.5% | 2.0% | 2.5% | 3.0% | 3.5% | 4.0% | 4.5% | 5.0% | 5.5% | 6.0% | 7.0% | 8.0% | 9.0% | 10.0% | 11.0% | 12.0% | 20.0% |
|---|---|---|---|---|---|---|---|---|---|---|---|---|---|---|---|---|---|---|
| 1 | 1.00000 | 1.00000 | 1.00000 | 1.00000 | 1.00000 | 1.00000 | 1.00000 | 1.00000 | 1.00000 | 1.00000 | 1.00000 | 1.00000 | 1.00000 | 1.00000 | 1.00000 | 1.00000 | 1.00000 | 1.00000 |
| 2 | 1.99010 | 1.98522 | 1.98039 | 1.97561 | 1.97087 | 1.96618 | 1.96154 | 1.95694 | 1.95238 | 1.94787 | 1.94340 | 1.93458 | 1.92593 | 1.91743 | 1.90909 | 1.90090 | 1.89286 | 1.83333 |
| 3 | 2.97040 | 2.95588 | 2.94156 | 2.92742 | 2.91347 | 2.89969 | 2.88609 | 2.87267 | 2.85941 | 2.84632 | 2.83339 | 2.80802 | 2.78326 | 2.75911 | 2.73554 | 2.71252 | 2.69005 | 2.52778 |
| 4 | 3.94099 | 3.91220 | 3.88388 | 3.85602 | 3.82861 | 3.80164 | 3.77509 | 3.74896 | 3.72325 | 3.69793 | 3.67301 | 3.62432 | 3.57710 | 3.53129 | 3.48685 | 3.44371 | 3.40183 | 3.10648 |
| 5 | 4.90197 | 4.85438 | 4.80773 | 4.76197 | 4.71710 | 4.67308 | 4.62990 | 4.58753 | 4.54595 | 4.50515 | 4.46511 | 4.38721 | 4.31213 | 4.23972 | 4.16987 | 4.10245 | 4.03735 | 3.58873 |
| 6 | 5.85343 | 5.78264 | 5.71346 | 5.64583 | 5.57971 | 5.51505 | 5.45182 | 5.38998 | 5.32948 | 5.27028 | 5.21236 | 5.10020 | 4.99271 | 4.88965 | 4.79079 | 4.69590 | 4.60478 | 3.99061 |
| 7 | 6.79548 | 6.69719 | 6.60143 | 6.50813 | 6.41719 | 6.32855 | 6.24214 | 6.15787 | 6.07569 | 5.99553 | 5.91732 | 5.76654 | 5.62288 | 5.48592 | 5.35526 | 5.23054 | 5.11141 | 4.32551 |
| 8 | 7.72819 | 7.59821 | 7.47199 | 7.34939 | 7.23028 | 7.11454 | 7.00205 | 6.89270 | 6.78637 | 6.68297 | 6.58238 | 6.38929 | 6.20637 | 6.03295 | 5.86842 | 5.71220 | 5.56376 | 4.60459 |
| 9 | 8.65168 | 8.48593 | 8.32548 | 8.17014 | 8.01969 | 7.87396 | 7.73274 | 7.59589 | 7.46321 | 7.33457 | 7.20979 | 6.97130 | 6.74664 | 6.53482 | 6.33493 | 6.14612 | 5.96764 | 4.83716 |
| 10 | 9.56602 | 9.36052 | 9.16224 | 8.97087 | 8.78611 | 8.60769 | 8.43533 | 8.26879 | 8.10782 | 7.95220 | 7.80169 | 7.51523 | 7.24689 | 6.99525 | 6.75902 | 6.53705 | 6.32825 | 5.03097 |
| 11 | 10.47130 | 10.22218 | 9.98259 | 9.75206 | 9.53020 | 9.31661 | 9.11090 | 8.91272 | 8.72173 | 8.53763 | 8.36009 | 8.02358 | 7.71008 | 7.41766 | 7.14457 | 6.88923 | 6.65022 | 5.19247 |
| 12 | 11.36763 | 11.07112 | 10.78685 | 10.51421 | 10.25262 | 10.00155 | 9.76048 | 9.52892 | 9.30641 | 9.09254 | 8.88687 | 8.49867 | 8.13896 | 7.80519 | 7.49506 | 7.20652 | 6.93770 | 5.32706 |
| 13 | 12.25508 | 11.90751 | 11.57534 | 11.25776 | 10.95400 | 10.66333 | 10.38507 | 10.11858 | 9.86325 | 9.61852 | 9.38384 | 8.94269 | 8.53608 | 8.16073 | 7.81369 | 7.49236 | 7.19437 | 5.43922 |
| 14 | 13.13374 | 12.73153 | 12.34837 | 11.98318 | 11.63496 | 11.30274 | 10.98565 | 10.68285 | 10.39357 | 10.11708 | 9.85268 | 9.35765 | 8.90378 | 8.48690 | 8.10336 | 7.74987 | 7.42355 | 5.53268 |
| 15 | 14.00370 | 13.54338 | 13.10625 | 12.69091 | 12.29607 | 11.92052 | 11.56312 | 11.22283 | 10.89864 | 10.58965 | 10.29498 | 9.74547 | 9.24424 | 8.78615 | 8.36669 | 7.98187 | 7.62817 | 5.61057 |
| 16 | 14.86505 | 14.34323 | 13.84926 | 13.38138 | 12.93794 | 12.51741 | 12.11839 | 11.73955 | 11.37966 | 11.03758 | 10.71225 | 10.10791 | 9.55948 | 9.06069 | 8.60608 | 8.19087 | 7.81086 | 5.67547 |
| 17 | 15.71787 | 15.13126 | 14.57771 | 14.05500 | 13.56110 | 13.09412 | 12.65230 | 12.23402 | 11.83777 | 11.46216 | 11.10590 | 10.44665 | 9.85137 | 9.31256 | 8.82371 | 8.37916 | 7.97399 | 5.72956 |
| 18 | 16.56225 | 15.90765 | 15.29187 | 14.71220 | 14.16612 | 13.65132 | 13.16567 | 12.70719 | 12.27407 | 11.86461 | 11.47726 | 10.76322 | 10.12164 | 9.54363 | 9.02155 | 8.54879 | 8.11963 | 5.77463 |
| 19 | 17.39827 | 16.67256 | 15.99203 | 15.35336 | 14.75351 | 14.18968 | 13.65930 | 13.15999 | 12.68959 | 12.24607 | 11.82760 | 11.05909 | 10.37189 | 9.75563 | 9.20141 | 8.70162 | 8.24967 | 5.81219 |
| 20 | 18.22601 | 17.42617 | 16.67846 | 15.97889 | 15.32380 | 14.70984 | 14.13394 | 13.59329 | 13.08532 | 12.60765 | 12.15812 | 11.33560 | 10.60360 | 9.95011 | 9.36492 | 8.83929 | 8.36578 | 5.84350 |
| 21 | 19.04555 | 18.16864 | 17.35143 | 16.58916 | 15.87747 | 15.21240 | 14.59033 | 14.00794 | 13.46221 | 12.95038 | 12.46992 | 11.59401 | 10.81815 | 10.12855 | 9.51356 | 8.96333 | 8.46944 | 5.86958 |
| 25 | 22.24339 | 21.03041 | 19.91393 | 18.88499 | 17.93554 | 17.05837 | 16.24696 | 15.49548 | 14.79864 | 14.15170 | 13.55036 | 12.46933 | 11.52876 | 10.70661 | 9.98474 | 9.34814 | 8.78432 | 5.93710 |
| 30 | 26.06579 | 24.37608 | 22.84438 | 21.45355 | 20.18845 | 19.03577 | 17.98371 | 17.02189 | 16.14107 | 15.33310 | 14.59072 | 13.27767 | 12.15841 | 11.19828 | 10.36961 | 9.65011 | 9.02181 | 5.97472 |
| 40 | 33.16303 | 30.36458 | 27.90259 | 25.73034 | 23.80822 | 22.10250 | 20.58448 | 19.22966 | 18.01704 | 16.92866 | 15.94907 | 14.26493 | 12.87858 | 11.72552 | 10.75696 | 9.93567 | 9.23303 | 5.99592 |